The Official History of t Secretaries

This book is the official history of British Cabinet Secretaries, the most senior civil servants in UK government, from the post-war period up to 2002.

In December 1916 Maurice Hankey sat at the Cabinet table to take the first official record of Cabinet decisions. Prior to this there had been no formal Cabinet agenda and no record of Cabinet decisions. Using authoritative government papers, some of which have not yet been released for public scrutiny, this book tells the story of Hankey's post-war successors as they advised British Prime Ministers and recorded Cabinet's crucial decisions as the country struggled through the exhaustion that followed World War II, grappled with a weak economy that could not support its world ambitions, saw the end of the post-war economic and social consensus and faced the 9/11 attack on the Twin Towers symbol of Western dominance. It looks at events through the eyes of politically neutral senior civil servants, the mandarins of Britain. It shows how the dramatic foreshortening of timescales and global news have complicated the working lives of those who daily face the deluge of potentially destabilising events – the skills required to see dangers and opportunities around corners, when to calm things down and when to accelerate action; why secrecy is endemic when government comes close to losing control or when political ambition threatens self-destruction.

This book will be of great interest to students of British politics, British history and British government.

Ian Beesley served in the Cabinet Office, H.M. Treasury and 10 Downing Street, where he was Head of the Efficiency Unit under Margaret Thatcher, and he has a PhD in History from Queen Mary University of London.

Whitehall Histories: Government Official History Series

ISSN: 1474-8398

The Government Official History series began in 1919 with wartime histories, and the peacetime series was inaugurated in 1966 by Harold Wilson. The aim of the series is to produce major histories in their own right, compiled by historians eminent in the field, who are afforded free access to all relevant material in the official archives. The Histories also provide a trusted secondary source for other historians and researchers while the official records are not in the public domain. The main criteria for selection of topics are that the histories should record important episodes or themes of British history while the official records can still be supplemented by the recollections of key players; and that they should be of general interest, and, preferably, involve the records of more than one government department.

Churchill's Mystery Man
Desmond Morton and the World of Intelligence
Gill Bennett

The Official History of Privatisation
Vol. I: The Formative Years 1970–1987
Vol. II: Popular Capitalism 1987–1997
David Parker

Secrecy and the Media
The Official History of the D-Notice System
Nicholas Wilkinson

The Official History of the Civil Service
Reforming the Civil Service
Vol. I: The Fulton Years, 1966–1981
Rodney Lowe

The Official History of North Sea Oil and Gas
Vol. I: The Growing Dominance of the State
Vol. II: Moderating the State's Role
Alex Kemp

The Official History of Britain and the European Community
Vol. II: From Rejection to Referendum, 1963–1975
Stephen Wall

The Official History of the Joint Intelligence Committee
Volume I: From the Approach of the Second World War to the Suez Crisis
Michael S. Goodman

The Official History of the Cabinet Secretaries
Ian Beesley

The Official History of the Cabinet Secretaries

Ian Beesley

Routledge
Taylor & Francis Group
LONDON AND NEW YORK

First published 2017
by Routledge
2 Park Square, Milton Park, Abingdon, Oxon OX14 4RN

and by Routledge
711 Third Avenue, New York, NY 10017

First issued in paperback 2017

Routledge is an imprint of the Taylor & Francis Group, an informa business

British Library Cataloguing in Publication Data
A catalogue record for this book is available from the British Library

Library of Congress Cataloging in Publication Data
A catalog record for this book has been requested

ISBN 13: 978-1-138-49348-3 (pbk)
ISBN 13: 978-1-138-18861-7 (hbk)

Typeset in Times New Roman
by Wearset Ltd, Boldon, Tyne and Wear

Ian Beesley has had unprecedented access to the files of half-a-dozen of Whitehall's ultimate men of secrets, the Cabinet Secretaries – the powerful yet elusive figures at the elbows of successive Prime Ministers. His pages brim with knowledge of who they were and how they did their job, all set in the wider political context of their time in office. Anyone interested in how British government works will learn heaps from this book.

Peter Hennessy, *Attlee Professor of Contemporary British History at Queen Mary, University of London*

In preparing the authorised biography of Margaret Thatcher, I have been struck by how much modern Prime Ministers owe to the Cabinet Secretary of the day. Yet the public know very little about these people, what they do, and how much good government depends upon their wisdom and cool judgment. Now, thanks to this book, with its full use of official records, we all have the chance to find out.

Charles Moore, *author of Margaret Thatcher: The Authorised Biography*

In the 100-year existence of the Cabinet Office there have been just eleven Cabinet Secretaries and little is known about their role, styles and influence. That gap has now been filled by this detailed account of the post-war years to 2002.

Gus O'Donnell, *Cabinet Secretary, 2005–2011*

Contents

List of Illustrations

Acknowledgements

Dedicated to the memory of DA Stott, Headmaster of Limeside County Primary School, Oldham, who first saw potential in me and without whose encouragement none of this would have happened.

This Official History has been nine years in the making. It looks at the conduct of government unashamedly from the point of view of senior officials, whose integrity and devotion to the well-being of the United Kingdom as a whole is often unsung but never unnecessary. The original idea arose out of conversations with the contemporary historian Peter Hennessy (now Lord Hennessy) but the task would not have been possible without the vision of Sir Gus O'Donnell (now Lord O'Donnell) and the earlier Cabinet Secretaries who were alive in 2007 (Lord Hunt, Lord Armstrong, Lord Butler, Lord Wilson, Lord Turnbull). As Prime Minister, Tony Blair approved the project and announced it to Parliament on 26 April 2007. David Cameron continued the support, as has Sir Jeremy Heywood, the current Cabinet Secretary.

I have been guided by a steering group comprising Tessa Stirling of the Official History programme, Sir Paul Britton, Deputy Cabinet Secretary and Head of the Domestic Secretariat in the Cabinet Office (2001–09) Sir John Chilcot, Rodney Lowe the Official Historian of the Civil Service, Patrick Salmon the head of Histories in the Foreign and Commonwealth Office and the former Cabinet Secretary Lord Wilson of Dinton. Their knowledge of the inner workings of collective government is unrivalled. They have stimulated, pointed up important issues that perhaps I would have underestimated and given a sense of context that has made the content of the official files come alive. Nowhere, however, have they sought to influence my judgements or my choice of what evidence to deploy.

I have interviewed many people and read a great number of official files, some put at my disposal by the National Archives, some not yet officially released. My text has been vetted against the interests of national security and international relations. The redactions sought have been few and do not distort the overall picture. Academic historians are right to worry about this aspect of official histories and those who take on the task have a special duty to maintain high standards of intellectual integrity and honesty. They must not be afraid to do battle if they feel that important information is being withheld on grounds outside protecting the national interest. I believe that I have trodden this line with due care and have no hesitation in declaring that in my opinion the text gives a fair account of the Cabinet Secretaries' contribution to good government in the period covered.

I am especially indebted to the former Cabinet Secretaries who have given generously of their time; to Sir David Omand whose insights into security and intelligence in particular have been inspirational and to the late Sir Brian Cubbon who never let me off the intellectual hook. My colleagues as official historians, especially Professor Michael Goodman of King's College, Professor Matthew Jones of the LSE and Sir Stephen Wall, created a stimulating and supportive small community behind the solid steel door of the Cabinet Office room cleared for top secret documents. Nor can I stop without thanking Sue Gray, Roger Smethurst and Sally Falk of the Cabinet Office for their support and Deborah Neal and David Richardson for their patience in guiding me through the jungle of official files. I have borrowed insights from many but I have made my own mistakes.

Ian Beesley
London

The author and publishers are grateful to the following for permission to reproduce copyright photographs:

Photograph 1 from the Churchill Archive Centre of Churchill College, Cambridge. Photograph 2 from Cunard and the Churchill Archive Centre of Churchill College, Cambridge. Photograph 3 from the National Portrait Gallery. Photograph 4 from Martin J Hunt. Photograph 5 from the National Archives. Photograph 6 from the artist Daphne Todd, the photography Hugh Gilbert and Lord Armstrong. Photograph 7 from Lord Butler. Photograph 8 from the photographer Mark de Rond and Lord Wilson. Photograph 9 from Lord Wilson.

Principal Abbreviations

ACARD	Advisory Committee for Applied Research and Development, replaced by ACOST in 1987
AC(H)	Official Committee on Communism at Home
ACOST	Advisory Committee on Science and Technology
ADP	Automatic data processing
AEA	Atomic Energy Authority
AG	Attorney General
AGR	Advanced gas-cooled reactor for nuclear power generation
AHGG	Ad hoc Ministerial Group on the Gulf 1990–91
AIOC	Anglo-Iranian Oil Company
BBC	British Broadcasting Corporation
BOAC	British Overseas Airways Corporation (long-haul)
BTC	British Transport Corporation (Clement Attlee)
C	Chief of SIS (MI6)
CCU	Civil Contingencies Unit
CDS	Chief of the Defence Staff
CEO	Chief Executive
CESG	Communications-Electronics Security Group at GCHQ
CHOGM	Commonwealth Heads of Government Meeting
CIA	Central Intelligence Agency (USA)
COBR	Cabinet Office Briefing Room
COCOM	Coordinating Committee for Multilateral Export Controls
CPRS	Central Policy Review Staff
CSCE	Commission on Security and Cooperation in Europe
CSR	Comprehensive Spending Review (Tony Blair)
DE	Department of Employment
DES	Department of Education & Science
DfEE	Department for Education and Employment
DG	Director General, Security Service (MI5)
DHSS	Department of Health and Social Security
DIS	Defence Intelligence Service
DO	Defence and Overseas Committee
DOE	Department of the Environment

DRA	Defence Research Agency, later Defence Evaluation and Research Agency, later QinetiQ
DSS	Department of Social Security
DTI	Department of Trade and Industry
EA(LG)	Sub-committee of the Economic Strategy Cabinet Committee dealing with local authority matters
ECSC	European Coal and Steel Community (forerunner of the European Union)
ED(L)	Committee on disposal of government assets (Margaret Thatcher)
EDP	Cabinet Committee on Economic and Domestic Policy
EDS	Economic and Domestic Secretariat (Cabinet Office)
EDX	The Star Chamber for settling the most intractable public expenditure budget issues
EEC	European Economic Community (forerunner of the European Union)
EOKA	Paramilitary organisation aiming for the union of Cyprus with Greece
EU	European Unit (Cabinet Office)
EY	Committee on economic strategy (Harold Wilson)
FCO	Foreign and Commonwealth Office
FDA	First Division Association (representing the most senior grades in the Civil Service)
FOI	Freedom of Information Act
FPS	Future Policy Study (Harold Macmillan)
FSB	Civil Service Final Selection Board
GCHQ	Government Communications Head Quarters
GCSF	Government Communications Staff Federation
GEC	General Electric Company Ltd
GEN	Ad hoc Cabinet Committee (designation alternating with MISC)
GOC	Government Organisation Committee (Clement Attlee)
HM C&E	Her Majesty's Customs & Excise
HMG	Her Majesty's Government (of the UK)
HO	Home Office
IAG	Industrial Assessment Group (Edward Heath)
ICJ	International Court of Justice (judicial organ of the United Nations)
ILO	International Labour Organisation (a United Nations body)
IMF	International Monetary Fund
IPMCS	Institute of Civil Service Professionals, Managers and Specialists
IRA	Irish Republican Army
IRD	Information Research Department (FCO)
IS	Ministerial Intelligence Committee
ISC	Intelligence and Security Committee of Parliamentarians
JASP	Joint Approach to Social Policy (Harold Wilson)
JIC(A)	Joint Intelligence Committee (defence and overseas)

JIC(B)	Joint Intelligence Committee (economic)
MAFF	Ministry of Agriculture, Fisheries and Food
MISC	Ad hoc Cabinet Committee (designation alternating with GEN)
MOD	Ministry of Defence
MTTA	Machine Tools Trades Association
NAO	National Audit Office
NEW	National Economy in War Committee (Clement Attlee)
NHS	National Health Service
OAL	Office of Arts and Libraries
OD	Cabinet Oversea and Defence Committee under Thatcher 1979–90
OD(DIS)	Sub-Committee of OD dealing with memoirs
OEEC	Organisation for European Economic Co-operation
OPD	Cabinet Oversea and Defence Committee
OPD(G)	Sub-committee of OPD dealing with the 1st Gulf War 1991
OPD(G)(O)	Official Committee at PUS level supporting OPD(G)
OPSS	Office of Public Service and Science
OSIP	Official Committee on Defence, Intelligence and Security Information Policy
P&O	Penninsular & Orient Steamship Company Ltd
PAC	Public Accounts Committee
PCA	Parliamentary Commissioner for Administration (Ombudsman)
PEP	Political and Economic Planning Group (a research body)
PES	Public Expenditure Survey
PII	Public Interest Immunity
PIRA	Provisional Irish Republican Army
PMDU	Prime Minister's Delivery Unit (Tony Blair)
PSIS	Permanent Secretary-level committee overseeing the expenditure of the intelligence agencies
PSX	Committee on Public Services and Public Expenditure (Tony Blair)
PUS	Permanent Under-Secretary (the top departmental position for civil servants)
QPM	Questions of Procedure for Ministers (later The Ministerial Code)
RTZ	Rio Tinto Zinc
SACEUR	Supreme Allied Commander Europe
SASC	SENIOR Appointments Selection Committee
SCI	Standing Committee on the Interception of Communications
SCS	Senior Civil Service
Sherpa	Prime Minister's personal representative preparing Summit meetings
S(H)	Home Security Committee
SIGINT	Signals Intelligence
SIS	Secret Intelligence Service (MI6)
SIV	Single Intelligence Vote

SPAD	Special Adviser to a Minister
SPL	Committee on Subversion in Public Life
SSAB	Senior Salaries Advisory Body
SSRB	Senior Salaries Review Board
TCSSC	Parliamentary Treasury and Civil Service Select Committee
TSRB	Top Salaries Review Board
TUC	Trades Union Congress
UKREP	UK Permanent Representative to the European Union and its predecessors
UNPROFOR	United Nations Protection Force during the Bosnian War
UNSC	United Nations Security Council

1 To Make Ministers Appear More Competent Than They Could Possibly Be

Shortly before taking up office as head of the British Government's Central Policy Review Staff Victor Rothschild told a friend, 'Until this week I never realised the country was run by two men whom I'd never heard of.'[1] One was Sir Burke Trend, the Cabinet Secretary, of whom Henry Kissinger wrote: 'he made the Cabinet ministers he served appear more competent than they could possibly be.'[2] Trend himself was more prosaic: 'Your concern is to see that issues are processed up properly and that they finally reach Cabinet – when they've got to go to Cabinet – in a sufficiently compact, intelligible, clear form for the Cabinet to know what it is they've got to decide; what are the pros and cons.[3] This echoes Niccolò Machiavelli, in Sixteenth Century Florence who gave the governors of Florence 'the information necessary to make appropriate and timely decisions'.[4]

This account examines how six modern Cabinet Secretaries, who held office between 1947 and 2002, lived up to the challenge implied by Kissinger's acclaim and pulls back a curtain of secrecy surrounding their activities. It is published as the office reaches its centenary. During that time there have been just 11 incumbents. The first, Maurice Hankey, held the position for 22 years, between 1916 and 1938. He was succeeded by Edward Bridges, the son of the Poet Laureate, who carried the position through the Second World War. Neither is discussed in detail in this volume. The former because there are already two significant studies;[5] the latter because the requirements under Churchill during total war were exceptional. Nor are the three office holders after 2002 considered in detail, but for different reasons – notably the difficulty of achieving historical perspective at so short a distance.

Cabinet itself pre-dates the office of Cabinet Secretary. When George I came to the throne in 1714[6] it was a tradition that the Sovereign presided over a small selection of Privy Councillors assembled to give advice orally in his 'cabinet.' To protect the secrecy of that advice no unnecessary record of the discussions was made. However, King George did not speak English and ceased to attend the meetings, so that by the second half of the eighteenth and early nineteenth centuries a record of the discussions was taken and reported confidentially to the Sovereign.[7] Yet in May 1839 minute taking fell into disrepair.[8] Cabinet became an informal conversation between political allies, with no formal agenda and no record other than a private report from the Prime Minister to the Sovereign, of which there were only two copies. Cabinet Ministers raised issues orally, sometimes without warning, giving their colleagues scant opportunity to consult officials about the implications for departmental work. This had advantages – discussion was political not administrative and members of Cabinet were unlikely to have been captured by Departmental self-interest. On the other hand, Ministers sometimes left Cabinet meetings with differing views of what they believed had been agreed.[9]

The First World War

The First World War changed all that. It brought the mobilisation of national resources on a scale hitherto unknown and a new tautness in the administration of a five-man War Cabinet. In December 1916 David Lloyd-George,[10] the newly chosen Prime Minister, brought in Colonel Maurice Hankey, who was the pre-war Secretary of the Committee of Imperial Defence, to a new office as Secretary to the Cabinet. At 11.30 am on Saturday, 9 December 1916 the 39 year-old Hankey, accompanied by Lieutenant Colonel Dally Jones, sat down alongside the Prime Minister at the Cabinet table to record the decisions of the new Administration's first War Cabinet.[11] Lloyd George's intention was that the record of War Cabinet decisions should be clear, so that the Departments knew what was expected of them. It was not his intention to give a verbatim account of the discussions and this has remained the case.[12] Members of the Cabinet Office Secretariat record the logic of discussion, mainly without attribution, leading to an unambiguous agreement on action to follow, based on the Prime Minister's summing up of the sense of the meeting. Formal votes are unusual and sometimes the Cabinet Secretariat (acting under the authority of the Cabinet Secretary) must extrapolate the decision that the Prime Minister would have recorded in a summing up – *had there been one*. Minute taking of this type is a skill of a high order. As Lord Radcliffe[13] put it in a judgement about official secrecy, 'Government is not to be conducted in the interests of history.'[14]

After the end of wartime conditions and the fall of Lloyd George in 1922 the arrangement barely survived an attempt by Bonar Law[15] and Warren Fisher[16] to incorporate the secretarial duties into the Treasury.[17] The separate Cabinet Office Vote ceased; from 1923/4 provision for the 'Offices of the Cabinet' was carried on the Treasury Vote and by March 1923 staff numbers had been reduced from 123 a year earlier to 39. But Bonar Law fell ill and resigned on 20 May 1923 and that was as far as retrenchment went. His successor, Stanley Baldwin,[18] did not have a secure political position and may well have been glad of the support of the Cabinet Office rump; and Ramsay MacDonald's[19] Administration of January 1924 had only four members with previous experience of office, so that they were more dependent on officials for the conduct of business than their predecessors. By the middle of the 1920s criticisms of the Cabinet Office had largely died away and procedures had been established that lasted up to the outbreak of the Second World War.

The Second World War

On 31 July 1938 Hankey retired, to be replaced by Edward Bridges from the Treasury who served until 1947 when he transferred back as Treasury Permanent Secretary[20] – then the more senior of the two posts. His successor, Norman Brook, summarised Bridges' contribution as, 'Most people nowadays take the Cabinet Secretariat for granted – or, if they think about it at all, assume that it just sprang fully armed from the head of Hankey. In fact what Hankey created was the machinery – and very good machinery too, which has stood the test of time – but it was Bridges who breathed life into it and gave it flexibility and capacity for growth.'[21]

On the fall of Chamberlain on 10 May 1940 Churchill formed a War Cabinet of five members (later to become eight). He was both Prime Minister and Minister of Defence, with undefined powers that allowed him a personal, direct, ubiquitous and continuous control.[22] This War Cabinet initially met every day at 11.30 am and sometimes also later during the day and evening – in all meeting 1226 times during the war in Europe.[23] The process was far from smooth, however, with Ministers sometimes being kept waiting outside the Cabinet room for long periods or, if discussion took an unexpected turn, not being in attendance when issues of direct relevance to them were decided. So much time was spent in Cabinet that Churchill decreed that no ministerial boxes of papers requiring attention were to be sent to Ministers when they were in Cabinet except when unavoidable.[24]

On the home front the Lord President's Committee, created in June 1940 under Sir John Anderson,[25] progressively emerged as the principal organ dealing with social and economic matters. Thus, Bridges separated domestic policy from military issues, leaving the main task of liaison with the Chiefs of Staff to Hastings 'Pug' Ismay,[26] (though Bridges was present at almost all meetings of the War Cabinet), and making good use on the civil side of things of his deputy Rupert Howorth,[27] and later Norman Brook.[28] SS Wilson's history of the Cabinet Office records that '… in effect [Bridges] became Churchill's chief civilian staff officer.'[29]

With Bridges' support Churchill endeavoured to avoid large attendance at Cabinet Committees (when many of those present would not be directly involved) and by insisting that papers and the minutes of meetings should not be over elaborate.[30] The minutes ceased to be circulated in draft – under wartime conditions, there was no time for the Prime Minister to review them and in any case he gave them scant importance, commenting to Bridges that, 'I cannot allow Cabinet minutes to be sent out of the country, or made any use of. They are nothing more than your jottings down of lengthy conversations. No one who is really busily engaged in the war has time to read them, still less to correct them. I have repeatedly told you that your records are far too lengthy. In their present condition they are a most imperfect and misleading record.'[31]

Nevertheless, government largely remained a written culture until towards the end of the twentieth century and in this Churchill was no different. He complained that, 'To do our work, we all have to read a mass of papers. Nearly all of them are far too long. This wastes time, while energy has to be spent in looking for the essential points.'[32] Yet on 19 July 1940 he also sent Bridges and Ismay an instruction: 'Let it be very clearly understood that all directives emanating from me are made in writing, or should be immediately afterwards confirmed in writing, and that I do not accept any responsibility for matters relating to national defence on which I am alleged to have given decisions unless they are recorded in writing.'[33]

We Won the War, How Do We Win the Peace?

At the end of 1944 Bridges described the functions of the Cabinet Secretariat prosaically as:

(a) Normal Secretarial duties – including follow-up action to make sure that decisions are carried out.
(b) The preparation of material affecting several Departments.
(c) Official correspondence with overseas authorities that is not the responsibility of any single Minister.
(d) Other – (1) urgent issues where the primary responsibility is not clear; (2) the organisation of Cabinet Committees; (3) as a temporary home for organisations not easily attached to some other Department; (4) certain international conferences and security issues – best treated as a personal arrangement for the Prime Minister.

Later, in evidence to the 1966 Fulton Committee inquiry into the civil service, he acknowledged that 'my concern was not with policy, but to see that the general business of the War Cabinet ran smoothly.'[34] His valedictory advice to Brook was: (1) That the Office continued to retain civil and military officers working alongside one another; (2) that administrative staff should be kept small in number; (3) that the Cabinet Secretariat should mainly be staffed by secondments of 2–4 years from Departments (to provide expertise and to emphasise that the Cabinet Office operated on behalf of the whole of government); (4) that the main duties of the Cabinet Office were seen as normal secretarial duties.[35]

Bridges and Brook faced the daunting task of switching the government machine from wartime to peace and supporting the Attlee Administration in the mobilisation of an exhausted nation. It was perhaps not surprising that for the 1946 examination of the machinery of government required for peacetime, they largely ignored the stimulus that might have come from outsiders. Bridges' guidance to Permanent Secretaries at the start of the work was that, 'things would return to normal'. Nevertheless, Brook successfully enhanced the Cabinet Committee system to enable the creation of the Big State envisaged by the Attlee government, even though, as his briefing for successive Cabinets shows, he was personally not persuaded by all of the socialisation of industry. He helped take the first steps to detach the military from its privileged wartime position at the centre of government. He standardised Cabinet Office briefing for Ministers with form following function, comprising a succinct summary of the key issues to be decided, guidance on the conduct of the meeting, the likely attitudes of participants, and suggestions as to how the chairman might sum up the discussion.

Brook was not close to Attlee – but then who was? Yet Attlee entrusted him with sensitive tasks requiring the ability to cut a path through a jungle of emotion, such as his 1948 tour of the Dominions to assess attitudes to India and Pakistan's potential Commonwealth membership on an equal footing. It was after the Conservatives returned to power in 1951 that his influence expanded to a point where he became a central confidante to three Prime Ministers with Harold Macmillan referring to him as 'one of the greatest public servants of all time'. Lord Franks[36] wrote to Brook, 'But you are, whatever Ministers may think of themselves, one of the chief architects of post-war Great Britain as a going concern and it so easily might not have gone at all, or at least, slowly and badly.'[37] The bonds of trust forged during wartime, together with his longevity in office, brought the potential for great influence that he was not afraid to exercise and the need for an apparatus to handle the emerging threat from the Soviet Union provided a canvas on which to design the architecture of the Cold War. Thanks to re-establishment in 1947 of the distinction between the Cabinet Secretary and the Head of the Home Civil Service he was able to concentrate on being the Prime Minister's principal adviser. In evidence to the Fulton Committee Bridges and Brook both argued against combining the Cabinet Secretary and Civil Service roles as the former 'is too much at the Prime Minister's bid and call to devote much time to the needs of the Service.'[38]

The Dog Years

With Burke Trend, who succeeded Brook at the start of 1963, an administrative system based on calm deliberation and rationality reached a peak. The words that come to mind from those who worked under Trend at that time are about style: thorough, discreet, unobtrusive, punctiliously politically neutral (he is said never to have voted), austere yet often kind – a witness to well-mannered national decline. Trend himself described Cabinet Secretaries as craftsmen (dedicated to the machine) or artists (revelling in the detail of action).[39] He would have put himself in the latter category, with a hint of superiority, arguing most issues from first principles and adopting a Socratic approach to briefing for Cabinet: on the lines of 'Ministers might ask themselves ... ;' yet as Freddie Bishop, Macmillan's Principal Private Secretary, had complained in July 1961, 'Almost every piece of paper put to the Prime Minster ought to include or to be accompanied by a procedural recommendation.'[40] Henry Kissinger's tribute to his friend is well judged; the Prime Minister could rely on sound, comprehensive advice that covered all the angles and always protected his back; but it was not driven by results, as briefing during the long-drawn-out saga of the Rhodesian illegal declaration of independence indicates. By the time Trend left for the academic haven of Lincoln College, Oxford, Whitehall self-confidence had been severely damaged under the pressures of economic failure, devaluation, the declining importance of the Commonwealth and withdrawal from East of Suez.

Trend was succeeded by John Hunt who began a transformation of the Cabinet Office from 'normal secretarial duties' to a government Department in its own right, led by a managerial Permanent Secretary. He introduced more rigorous planning of Cabinet business through a formal forward-look exercise carried out three times a year, and showed toughness in dealing with 'that endless upward surge of business, driving it downward as much as he can'.[41] Whilst not as intellectual as the don manqué, Trend, nor as sinuous as his successor, Armstrong, Hunt was pivotal in steadying nerves during the IMF crisis of 1975. He largely built the central structure for handling civil emergencies and established British influence at the centre of preparatory work for the increasingly important Summit meetings of the leaders of the West. He drove changes in structure and attitude in the Whitehall committee system after accession to the European Economic Community; he negotiated a concordat with Bernard Donoughue for the creation of the Prime Minister's Policy Unit that smoothed the entry for Special Advisers into the civil service in the face of Permanent Secretaries' hostility. He was the first Cabinet Secretary to appear publicly in a court of law (and therefore in the media) as he fought unsuccessfully to prevent publication of the posthumous diaries of the former Cabinet Minister Richard Crossman. It was a task for which he was almost wholly unprepared and marked a seismic shift in public expectations of openness in government business.

Conviction Leadership

With Robert Armstrong the scene shifted. Brook, Trend and Hunt had each served four Prime Ministers and each had operated under Conservative and Labour administrations. In eight years of office as Cabinet Secretary Armstrong served one Prime Minister (Margaret Thatcher) though he had been Principal Private Secretary to Harold Wilson between 1974 and 1975. Also, unlike Brook, Trend and Hunt, after 1981 he combined being Cabinet Secretary with being Head of the Home Civil Service and this set a pattern of dual responsibilities that lasted until a failed return to separation in 2010. His tenure saw a development in the political class in which Ministers were more inclined than in the past to back their own judgement irrespective of official advice and were more dependent on staying in office for their livelihoods.[42] After the mid-80s few had had a career outside government and few had served an apprenticeship as a junior minister. Close media scrutiny of the government exposed scandals, with the Cabinet Secretary increasingly required to protect the Prime Minister's back. He had to pick up the pieces from the Westland affair as well as deal with allegations of treachery in the Security Service and other intelligence failures.

Temperamentally a backroom operator of great skill (with a touch of pugnacity) he enjoyed the exercise of power. His successes were private, a failure was public as he was shown to be ill adjusted to the media glare in the cut and thrust of court advocacy during the Spycatcher trial. When dealing with politicians and senior officials in private, however, he was incomparable, as the negotiations with the Irish Government over the Anglo-Irish Agreement of 1985 show. During his tenure little was deducted from the tasks performed by the Cabinet Secretary but some things were added – notably further exposure to public view, not just over the Spycatcher affair but also in the worsening industrial relations with the civil service. These included the 1981 civil service strike and the banning of trades unions at the Government Communications Headquarters (GCHQ). His re-assertion of traditional civil service standards in the face of modernising and streamlining pressures coming from the government and Parliament contributed to a sense that the Service was on the defensive and his occasional visible discomfort on the public stage contributed to a further decline in civil service self-esteem.

Robin Butler made it a priority to rebuild civil service morale, adopting a conscious stance of talking continuity but practising transformation, notably in his commitment in the face of Treasury opposition to the restructuring into Executive Agencies of many of the governmental operations. Butler's open nature and strong competitive spirit brought a new sense of momentum that offered the hope of rediscovered self-belief for civil servants. After the defenestration of Thatcher he forged a strong relationship with Major, especially as events moved against the government and the personal position of the Prime Minister weakened. During the Exchange Rate Mechanism crisis of Black Wednesday, the backbench revolt over the Maastricht Bill and the marriage break-up of Prince Charles and Princess Diana, Butler steadied the ship. Nevertheless, he also found himself the subject of media criticism, accused of gullibility over who had paid a bill for a stay at the Paris Ritz by the then Minister for Defence Procurement and again over his handling of the cash-for-questions scandal. During the Scott enquiry into the Customs and Excise prosecutions over arms for Iraq he was criticised for a remark that whilst ministers must always tell the truth, the public interest could mean not revealing the whole truth. His strong support for open competition in civil service appointments offered the prospect of new talent but also created uncertainty and reinforced caution in the minds of existing personnel who could no longer rely on advancement in a benign environment.

In his eleventh year in the post Butler oversaw the arrival of Tony Blair and a new generation of politicians for whom he seemed to represent the past and a block on reform. Leading the civil service took a much greater share of available time and emotional energy than for any of his predecessors; in time of crisis Ministers still turned to their officials to lead them out of the minefields but the number of Special Advisers reached critical mass with the result that the Cabinet Secretary could no longer claim a privileged position with the Prime Minister. Under Blair, Cabinet was no longer a decision-taking body, having reverted to something akin to the eighteenth century informal conversation between political colleagues.

To follow, Butler Blair chose Richard Wilson, who had made his name as someone who turned political initiatives into workable policies, especially during the later Thatcher years. Wilson strove to keep the eternal verities of collective government and a politically neutral civil service alive in the closely-knit world of New Labour where informality was the preferred style and where the competition between the Prime Minister and the Chancellor of the Exchequer hampered collective processes. Initially, his responsibilities as Head of the Home Civil Service dominated the agenda and his attempts to assert a sense of unity in the government machine stuttered, drawing him into dangerous waters in seeking to implement Blair's intentions to reshuffle Ministers. His attempts to advise the Prime Minister on reform of the civil service came up against the obstacle that, although often speaking of the reform agenda, Blair was personally uninterested in the mechanics of government. When crisis struck, however, such as the fuel protests of 2000, the foot and mouth epidemic of 2001 and the Al Qaeda attack on the Twin Towers, also in 2001, the role of the Cabinet Secretary as a calming influence but at the same time driving the government response and securing effective action came back into focus.

In 18 weeks at the end of 2001, during intense military activity with air strikes in Afghanistan, there were 46 formal ministerial meetings with Wilson in the traditional role of Cabinet Secretary. The underpinning of collective discussion provided by the Cabinet Office Secretariat was preserved and sprang into renewed life during the last stage of Blair's leadership and that of Gordon Brown. Wilson's tenure saw an improvement in the co-ordination of policies across departments, in the transparency of government and in civil service opportunities for the disabled and the disadvantaged; yet his support from the Permanent Secretaries was hindered by the Blair/Brown split and he was caught between the reforming zeal of Downing Street and the conservatism of the senior bureaucracy. Crucially, he opposed merging the Downing Street staff and that of the Cabinet Office, including the offer of leading the new organisation, putting the interests of constitutional correctness above self-interest in the best traditions that the giants of the Northcote-Trevelyan reforms and the twentieth century politically neutral civil service would have applauded.

What Does All This Tell Us About Changes in the Face of Government and the Civil Service?

Despite a number of attempts to start a knowledgeable discussion about what the country needs from its civil service there has been no equivalent of the 1918 Haldane Report: 'To enquire into the responsibilities of the various Departments of the central executive Government, and to advise in what manner the exercise and distribution of the Government of its functions should be improved.'[43] There is a feeling that central government has drifted into changes propelled by the prevailing winds of fashion. In the past 100 years Britain has changed beyond recognition and Cabinet Secretaries, like the politicians they served, have had to operate in the context of their time. The twin responsibilities of the Cabinet Secretary, to ensure the smooth running of a complex government machine and to ensure the smooth transition of power after a General Election, remain at the heart of the job. But the task has become more difficult as timescales have shortened, with media operating on a continuous 24-hour basis and technology encouraging expectations of real-time responses. Wilson has commented on how greatly this development complicates the ability to structure considered decision taking. It fuelled the exchanges he had with Alastair Campbell during the first Blair Administration when Campbell wanted to make a government statement on emerging issues within hours whereas Wilson considered that sometimes the response required collective discussion because it engaged collective responsibility.[44] The loss of Empire and the transfer of certain decision-taking powers to Brussels and to the devolved administrations in Scotland, Wales and Northern Ireland have left Ministers more focused on executive action (known as 'delivery') than hitherto. Further, the growth of direct interaction between world leaders, most of whom have large White House/Elysée/Chancellory staff, has reaffirmed the need to develop the Cabinet Office as a department in its own right. Thus, the context in which the Cabinet Secretary must operate has changed – and it will change again. The idea of a fixed and crystalline constitutional arrangement independent of political circumstances defies experience and evidence.

On the other hand in such a fluid situation there can be confusion when individual civil servants are being held more publicly accountable for their actions (but so far not for the advice they give, which remains closed). In the absence of an all-party agreement on the range, scope and limitations of this accountability the situation is unstable. What is the civil servant to do if pressed by a Select Committee as to why a policy has not been successful if she had advised against its practicality in the first place? If Ministers prefer to take advice from special advisers of a like mind and ignore official advice, what is the escalation procedure open to the official? Conversely, is the notion prevalent during John Hunt's tenure that political neutrality means withholding the last few percentage of commitment still relevant? As Richard Wilson found, action by the Cabinet Secretary to assert the authority of the Prime Minister over a fellow Minister can easily stray over a constitutional red line. It may be that seeking the facts on behalf of the Prime Minister is acceptable but acting on them (including delivering a message) is for the Prime Minister alone. Even then, as Robin Butler found, establishing the facts can be difficult in the absence of forensic skills.

Nevertheless, there are some pointers to the qualities a Cabinet Secretary requires for success from the experience of the years covered in this account. I have identified six:

The ability to cope with the disordered way in which events intrude – they compete for attention and must be prioritised and brought under control; with a strong sense of timing, as the most difficult issues often require Cabinet's attention many times before a collective resolution is possible.

The ability to distinguish the important from the urgent – for example, Brook's repeated inclusion of immigration on the agenda for Eden's Cabinet; Trend's attempts to get a better discussion of public expenditure and economic strategy; Hunt's separation of the day-to-day European issues from the strategic direction of policy; Wilson's struggles to get advance warning of what ministers would raise orally in Blair's Cabinet.

To know when to be a calming influence and when to drive things along – on the one hand there are times when important decisions are made in an atmosphere of high emotion. For example, the Thatcher Cabinet decision to go ahead with a Green Paper on the Poll Tax[45] was taken at the same Cabinet meeting from which Michael Heseltine stormed out to resign over the Westland affair. On the other hand, as Gordon Brown[46] is reported to have said during the September 2000 crisis over fuel prices, 'the Government could always recover from short-term unpopularity, but once they lost their reputation for strength, they would look forever weak.'[47] Cumulative short-term risk avoidance may eventually bring a much more significant risk.

The stamina to handle the gruelling toll of the workload through the highs and lows of office – a high will inevitably be followed by low points in a world of instant news and suspicion of those in authority. Gone is the time when senior civil servants could remain in the shadows behind Ministers. Political 'spin' has become expected and discounted by a sceptical public, making it difficult for the Cabinet Secretary to command authority and public respect, yet at the same time protagonists sometimes appeal to the office as a kind of national referee in the court of public opinion and sometimes it is necessary to act as a public shield for the Prime Minister, as Armstrong found in an Australian court.

To have an eye for continuity – the stability of the country has benefited during periods of potential constitutional crisis or emergency because the Cabinet Secretaries have implicitly accepted a duty to build strong foundations on which the political processes can operate and have been prepared, as was Wilson, to take decisive action during the 9/11 emergency. These are perhaps their finest hours.

The ability to command trust – the Cabinet Secretary must tread a delicate path to keep the trust of the Prime Minister <u>and</u> other Cabinet Ministers. In this they have been generally successful, but their power with senior colleagues to provide the continuity, aggregation and integration that collective government needs will wax and wane with the standing of the Prime Minister in the country and the extent to which they are seen to be part of the most trusted group around the Prime Minister. Wilson found that we may want our senior officials to be politically neutral and to speak truth unto power but that has a cost.

Increasingly too there is a question of public confidence in the office in the face of cynicism about the behaviour of political and economic elites, and that lies at the heart of preparing for the future. Armstrong and Butler both suffered from appearing to be 'too clever by half.' The 11 incumbents have all been men, mostly educated at public schools (three were state grammar school boys) and all barring Hankey at some stage attended an Oxbridge College. The profile is largely homogeneous. So one important challenge is to recognise that the route to the Cabinet Secretary post requires active talent management by the leaders of the civil service to generate a wider field of talented men and women candidates when the time comes to choose an incumbent. The position is too important to risk a failed appointment, but the route to credibility as a candidate can be thought as Private Office experience with a senior minister, at least one senior position in a large department under stress, a spell in the Treasury and, ideally press secretary experience also with a senior Minister. That is a daunting career path and it neglects the personal pressures of a skewed work-life balance. Burke Trend told the widowed John Hunt that he needed the support of a wife in order to survive in the role. By which he meant a support hinterland that in the twenty-first century can be more diverse.

My aim in what follows is to examine how six exemplary public servants fared as Cabinet Secretary in good times and bad. The story shows how the Cabinet Office has matured into a crucial driver of government policy, to explain what was happening behind the closed doors of the Cabinet Secretary's room and to contribute to the department's corporate memory. For the general reader it provides a unique insight into how what was being done in their name came to be. The judgements and the mistakes are my own; the credit belongs to the self-less service of senior central government officials, at the pinnacle of which sits the Cabinet Secretary.

Notes

1 Hennessy, *The Times*, 08.03.76
2 Henry Kissinger, *White House Years*, Little Brown, 1979, p. 93
3 BBC Radio 3 *How Cabinet Government Works*, 12.03.76
4 Maurizio Viroli, introduction to *The Prince*, Oxford Classics, 2008, p. x
5 Stephen Roskill, *Hankey Man of Secrets*, Collins 1970; John F Naylor, *A Man & An Institution*, CUP 1984
6 George I, King of Great Britain and Ireland, 1714–27
7 *The Times*, 23.12.31 reporting an address by Sir John Simon at King's College London
8 Hankey *Diplomacy By Conference*, Ernest Benn Ltd, 1946, p. 51
9 Hankey, op. cit, pp. 54–56
10 Prime Minister 1916–22
11 CAB 23/1/1, 09.12.16
12 Roskill, op. cit, pp. 337–8
13 Appeal judge and prominent member of the 'Great and the Good' called upon to lead inquiries into government matters
14 Heward, *The Great and the Good*, Barry Rose, 1994, p. 219
15 Prime Minister 1922–23
16 Head of the Home Civil Service 1919–39
17 SS Wilson *The Cabinet Office to 1945*, Public Record Office 1975, chapter 5
18 Prime Minister 1923–24, 1924–29 and 1935–39
19 Prime Minister 1924 and 1929–35
20 From 1945 to 1947 Bridges combined the roles of Cabinet Secretary (jointly with Brook) and Permanent Secretary at the Treasury
21 Bodleian, MS. Eng. lett.c273, 11.01.63
22 Ismay, *Memoirs*, Heinemann 1960, p. 159
23 Ibid
24 CAB 21/1324, 21.11.41
25 Lord Privy Seal 1938–39; Home Secretary 1939–40; Lord President of the Council 1940–43, Chancellor of the Exchequer 1943–45
26 Deputy Secretary (military) to the War Cabinet 1940–45
27 Deputy Cabinet Secretary 1930–42

28 Brook replaced Howorth on 17.03.42 and continued until appointed Permanent Secretary of the new Ministry for Reconstruction
29 Wilson, op. cit, chapter 9
30 Ibid
31 CAB 21/2865, 29.04.41
32 CAB 21/2809, 09.08.40
33 Churchill, *Their Finest Hour*, p. 17
34 Wheeler-Bennett (ed.), *Action This Day*, p. 226
35 CAB 21/2797, 04.09.44, *Functions of the Cabinet Secretariat*
36 Bodleian, MS. Eng. lett.c273, 11.01.63
37 Bridges, *Portrait of a Profession*, Rede Lecture, CUP 1950
38 BA 1/8, Evidence to Fulton Committee
39 Lee, Jones & Burnham, *At the Centre of Whitehall*, p. 141
40 Cabinet Office archive, 31.07.61
41 Herman, *Up From the Country*, p. 167
42 Barberis, *The Elite of the Elite*, p. 219
43 Ministry of Reconstruction, Report of the Machinery of Government Committee, Cm 9230, 1918
44 Correspondence with Lord Wilson of Dinton, 30.10.15
45 Ill-fated reform of local government finance based on a per capita charge on residents, abandoned after civil unrest
46 Chancellor of the Exchequer 1997–2007 and Prime Minister 2007–2010
47 Andrew Rawnsley, *Servants of the People*, p. 413

2 The Craftsman

Sir Norman Brook
Cabinet Secretary
1947–62

Brook in fur hat: Norman Brook in Moscow 1959

Source: Churchill Archive Centre of Churchill College, Cambridge

Norman Brook was the third person to occupy the office of Cabinet Secretary, after Maurice Hankey (1916–1938) and Edward Bridges (1938–1947). During World War II he was deputy to Bridges after 1942, except for a spell of 18 months from November 1943 when he was made the Permanent Secretary of the new Ministry of Reconstruction. He returned to the Cabinet Office in 1945 as joint Cabinet Secretary with Bridges and succeeded him in 1947 on Bridges' appointment as Permanent Secretary of the Treasury. A grammar school boy who had won a scholarship to Wadham College, Oxford, he had been ranked second in the 1925 Civil Service Administrative Class examinations, had been assigned to the Home Office and had risen slowly, as was normal between the wars, to the rank of Assistant Secretary where he was responsible for planning

Brook dancing: An enveloping style of dancing

Source: Churchill Archive Centre of Churchill College, Cambridge

for civil emergencies, the 'War Book' and defence regulations.[1] At the time of his application to the civil service (aged 23) his academic referee, J Wells of Wadham College, Oxford, and Vice Chancellor of the University, wrote:

'Mr Norman Craven Brook was elected to our Senior Scholarship at the end of 1920 and is just completing his fourth year of residence. He obtained an exceedingly good First Class in Classical Moderations, and I have every reason to believe that he will obtain a First Class also in his Final School (Litterae Humaniores).[2] I have seen a certain amount of his work and this confirms the report of his tutors that he is an exceptionally able man. I cannot speak too highly of him in every respect. He has been a great force in the College and his influence has always been on the side of all that was best. He rowed in the College Eight and almost obtained his Trials cap from the University; he plays in our rugby team; and he is exceedingly musical having a very fine voice. With all these good gifts he is one of the most modest of men, most pleasant to work with and a man who would be universally liked. I cannot too strongly commend him for an administrative post, for he has ability, character and tact.'[3]

Sixty years later, Jock Coville[4] summed up the challenge of assessing Brook's contribution to public life as: 'There are people who were widely known in their own generation, who sparkled when they talked, who were concerned with the important events of their day but whose names, because they left nothing behind in writing, are destined to be mere footnotes in the memoirs and histories of their times. Brendan Bracken was one, Lady Desborough another, Lord Normanbrook a third.'[5] Assiduous trawling through over 700 files in The National Archives reveals a mass of writing by Brook on many of the most important issues of the day and demonstrates a political neutrality in officials that still characterises the British way. There are also numerous comments (usually tributes) to him in the writing of others; but no diaries or memoirs by Brook himself, which is hardly surprising given his defence of the confidentiality of the relationship between Ministers and officials and his total opposition to officials keeping diaries about their working life.

The most frequent comments from those who worked with Brook refer to his calmness when others were at risk of losing their heads and his delight and skill in finding the next procedural step that would keep things moving when it looked as if they had entered a cul-de-sac. A plea by Harold Macmillan's Principal Private Secretary, Freddie Bishop, in July 1961 for all submissions to the Prime Minister to have a procedural recommendation points to the importance of this hidden skill. Brook excelled in it, both where he was closely involved (such as over the future of the independent nuclear deterrent) and where he left the briefing largely to others (such as the approach to European integration). His calming influence is evident in matters large (e.g., the calls for restrictions on personal freedom during the Korean War) or small (e.g. when Macmillan scribbled, 'Can nothing be done to suppress or get rid of Mr Chapman Pincher?').[6] The overwhelming impression is of a man with strict personal control and an ever 'open door' for Ministers or senior officials to confide and seek solace. His own confidences, such as they are, are to be found in authors that he would never have thought would reveal them – notably the memoirs of George Mallaby (for some years Brook's deputy) and the diaries of Winston Churchill's personal physician, Lord Moran. Mallaby describes Brook as a master of order and precision who felt that, even when he was personally unsympathetic to the policies, 'he must exercise [his] power in such a way as to bring about the most orderly and rapid transaction of Government business.'[7] 'From Brook I have learned the strength and power of a truly calm, objective and unhurried judgement.'[8] He also wrote, 'When Winston was excited about something Norman Brook was always there as a steadying influence, and Winston came to rely on him enormously ... he was quite sure he could get Norman Brook's wise judgement on any issue entirely untinged by personal considerations.'[9] Moran adds to this that '[Brook] has an honest mind, and is on the whole more approachable than Bridges: it is easy to understand how the whole Cabinet trust him and rely on his judgement.'[10] At the time of Macmillan's 'Night of the Long Knives' a former Secretary of State for Scotland wrote: 'You display colossal patience through all these crises: I can't think how you control yourself!'[11] The nearest we can get to Brook's own ideal is, perhaps, an assessment he made of David Maxwell-Fyfe (Home Secretary 1951–54, and later Lord Chancellor): 'David was very conscientious. What I like about him is that if you have a problem he will at once offer to help and take any amount of trouble to find a solution. He has good judgement, and when his report is ready every aspect is considered. Nothing is left out. It is pretty dull stuff, but when David has done the Cabinet doesn't want to discuss it further, but is ready to pass on to the next item on the agenda.'[12]

During the research for this book another 'grammar school' Permanent Secretary, who served under Brook (also originally at the Home Office) offered an opinion that Brook's fabled control was a defence mechanism against the innate 'public school' snobbery of the then ruling mandarins. Brook could simply not afford to relax his guard. It was Maurice Bowra at Wadham College, Oxford, who said of him 'Very quick, Brook. Learned the tricks, learned the tricks. Came up with a front pocket stuffed full of pens. Soon disappeared inside. Learned the tricks.'[13] Harold Macmillan also could be snobbish, commenting to Moran that Brook 'had no background.'[14] However, Brook induced fear in other civil servants. To most except the closest colleagues (and to some of them too) he appeared cold, conventional and uninterested in his fellow men and women – whereas from his successor, Burke Trend, onwards there are notable examples of successful women at the top of the Cabinet Office whereas there appears to be none during Brook's tenure. The wife of a later Cabinet Secretary kept a cutting from *The Daily Mail* from 28 November 1961 for over 45 years before passing it on to the author. It began. 'There is a golden rule for every ambitious Civil Servant: "Don't cross Norman Brook." Some people say it is a golden rule for every ambitious politician too.' Harold Kent, the former Treasury Solicitor says, 'Brook had a powerful mind, strength of character, which included an ability to lose his temper on rare occasions ...'[15] He was, also according to Kent, 'The cool, professional, executive type – tall and physically impressive and dressed well in a quiet way – handwriting was neat and firm – sense of humour quiet and restrained – jealous of his time and you could only see him by appointment, for which you had to make a good case – he generally managed to get home for dinner. Most civil servants who knew them both well seemed fonder of Bridges. It was otherwise with Ministers: 'Bridges had an intellectual fastidiousness and moral rectitude which could make him forbidding ... Brook was personally more ambitious, and he enjoyed the political game, and Ministers were more at home with him'.[16]

Whilst Brook delighted in the exercise of power he was careful to keep key officials on side, notably Sir Patrick Dean at the Foreign Office, Sir Roger Makins at the Treasury and Sir Frank Newsam at the Home Office. His relationship with Bridges was more complex, not the least over Suez where Eden excluded Bridges from those allowed to see the invasion papers.[17] The official boundary between the Head of the Treasury, then the more senior of the two posts, and the Cabinet Secretary was sometimes unclear; thus, for example, whilst Brook conducted the first quick investigation into the Commander Crabb fiasco it was Bridges who conducted the full inquiry. In public they praised each other: Brook said, 'Hankey created the machinery ... but it was Bridges who breathed life into it and gave it flexibility and capacity for growth.'[18] In an undated note Bridges wrote to Brook, 'But I'm sure that, since there has been a Cab[inet] Office, nobody in it has ever done as good job as you have done on Palestine. And nobody has ever given a more perfect demonstration ... of how much "the official" can do for Ministers.'[19] But the files show a certain formality in their dealings that goes wider than was required by the conventions of the time and does not show the free flow of ideas that characterised, for example, Brook's dealings with Patrick Dean.

Throughout his tenure 'money was the root of all evil' – Britain had been left effectively bankrupt after the war and the struggle both to return its economy to a peacetime footing and to pay for the country's fading status as a world power and the social reforms presaged by the Beveridge Report dominated. The Official Historian of the post-war financial settlement, L S Pressnell, describes four massive external economic problems: (1) the end of US Mutual Aid/Lend-Lease; (2) financial liabilities of £3,355 million (equivalent to two and a half years of exports at the 1938 volume) with lower gold and dollar reserves (a ratio of reserves to debt of 1:7 compared to 1¼:1 in 1939); (3) the challenge of financing the inevitable balance of payments deficit during the transition to peace and, in particular, in the light of a severe dollar shortage; (4) Article VII of the 1942 Lend-Lease agreement that had committed Britain to less restrictive world trading arrangements than hitherto.[20] Furthermore, the fear of Russia and a Communist threat was ever present in Ministerial minds and those of their senior officials.

Some of the key policies of the Attlee years, including much of the socialisation programme, were personally unwelcome to Brook – he was no advocate of the big state; in 1954 he referred to 'six years of Socialist rule during which we certainly had too much "government"'[21] – yet he drove the central machinery effectively to deliver Ministerial agreements, setting the tone for the higher civil service into the twenty-first century. (Delivery by the outer mass of the civil service or other public sector workers was evidently not his worry – even when he became Head of the Home Civil Service.) However, he was not a policy innovator and unlike, say, Frank Newsam at the Home Office, would have been uncomfortable leading a policy department. His defence of civil liberties when they came under threat during the Korean War was both brave and principled. His handling of Aneurin Bevan's resignation was a beacon of calmness in a sea of emotion. His guidance as government moved to a peacetime footing was an unsung success; but he failed to compensate for Attlee's lack of interest and knowledge of economics and underestimated the weakness of the economy. He was not close to Attlee but few were. Mallaby observed that Attlee was 'like a schoolmaster who kept order very well but did not teach you very much' – his dealings with officials were equally impersonal.[22]

There is no doubt that Brook found Churchill a more sympathetic character and was more on a wavelength with him, politically and personally. It was during Churchill's 1952 administration that the Conservative and Labour parties started to move apart, with Labour's National Executive document *Challenge to Britain* advocating greater state control of industry, health services and education, including the abolition of independent schools.' Meanwhile, the Conservative journal *The Spectator* judged that 'If there is one thing we have learnt … it is that the argument over who shall own certain large industries is to a great extent irrelevant to the efficiency of those industries'; and *The Tablet* offered the view that 'The underlying idea that runs through the new Labour Party Programme … is not a challenge but a threat to bring back the claustrophobia of a closely regulated national-Socialist economy.'[23]

Moreover, Churchill's working style suited that of Brook. He preferred paper. 'That meant he did not have to make up his mind forthwith. He had time to think it over.'[24] He was not an administrator; Brook was. (Bridges was also a skilled administrator, but Brook was generally seen to be more approachable. '[Bridges] does not exactly radiate geniality' recorded Moran[25]). There was also something complementary to Churchill in Brook's passion for accuracy (Churchill could be indifferent to the facts when seized with an idea) and in Brook's 'craving almost, for order and neatness and balance.'[26] That Brook had a closeness to Churchill's set is evidenced by his attendance at Lord Camrose's Savoy election party in 1952 and his membership of Churchill's Other Club – not an honour offered to Bridges – though perhaps questionable for a politically neutral Cabinet Secretary. Along with Bridges he was a pallbearer at Churchill's funeral and he was very protective of Churchill's reputation. When Alanbrooke's diaries were thought likely to be critical of Churchill as a military strategist Brook rallied. 'The P.M. prevented any quarrelling between the three Services and coordinated their work. Winston's courage in 1940 will, I am sure, survive any criticism of his conduct of the war. He had two valuable qualities: he never frittered away his time attending social functions, public dinners and the like (he must have gone to only a fraction of those Attlee attended), and he was ruthless during the war in selecting the two or three subjects which he decided to master.'[27]

Did Brook go too far and cross the line between political neutrality and partisanship? His admission in May 1955 that he had done all he could to get Churchill involved in the General Election campaign but had failed suggests that he might have done so.[28] However, it seems likely that this intervention stemmed not from party political motives so much as from deep affection for Churchill, which was offended by the evident pain exclusion from the campaign was causing. Towards the end of 1959 Brook spoke revealingly to Moran: '... if it had not been for Winston, anything might have happened after Dunkirk. While he was there, bargaining with Hitler was out of the question, a separate peace unthinkable.'[29] The extensive help Brook gave Churchill with his history of The Second World War, and the permission he facilitated for Churchill to quote official documents, prompted David Reynolds to conclude that Churchill's war memoirs were likely a readable surrogate for an official history. Not that Brook and Churchill were always at one. He was wise enough to recognise the difference between organisation for war and organisation under peace when he joined Bridges in opposing Churchill's experiment to recreate Ministerial Overlords in peacetime.

With Anthony Eden, too, there is evidence of strong rapport. After Eden's retirement they met quite often and Brook stayed with the former Prime Minister and his wife. A manuscript note sent by Brook to Eden under seal on the disposition of Cabinet over Suez, with a scarcely disguised 'between the lines' message of support for the military occupation of the Suez Canal is remarkable. So too is his offer of help with Eden's rapid defence of the failed initiative in the memoir *Full Circle*; and his now well documented destruction of the British copy of the Sèvres memorandum of understanding between Britain, France and Israel is still controversial. Asked if he would have obeyed Eden's instruction, one later Cabinet Secretary said he would – but only after having made a photocopy. To Eden he appeared a Suez supporter; to the head of the Foreign Office Middle

East Department, Evelyn Shuckburgh,[30] he appeared an opponent. 'I was sad that I had to stop,' Eden wrote to Brook, 'but you, above all others, gave me the strength to carry on;' and in 1967 Brook wrote to Freddie Bishop that 'The news from the Middle East really is most extraordinary and I expect [Eden] will have a good deal to say about it. I think things have turned out well from his point of view ...'[31] Yet Shuckburgh records in his diary for 5 December 1956 that Brook thought the invasion to be 'folly.'[32] Assuming the diary entry is correct, this would suggest that Brook avoided controversy at all costs, including going along with the perceived wisdom of the day, at least in public.

By the time Macmillan became Prime Minister Brook's technical and procedural skills were consummate and his longevity as Cabinet Secretary put him in an enviable position. It was to Brook that Macmillan usually turned to to have ideas tested and it was of Brook's Cabinet minutes that Macmillan said, 'Historians reading this 50 or 100 years hence will get a totally false picture ... that Cabinet were so intellectually disciplined that they argued each issue methodically and logically through to a set of neat and precise conclusions.'[33] However, Macmillan's search for a grand strategy through the 1959 Future Policy Study marked a point where Brook's great skill as a mechanic of compromise fell short of what the Prime Minister needed and where his long involvement at the top of government had become a prison; his steering of the studies was essentially through the rear view mirror and he was constrained by the conservatism of the Permanent Secretaries. One of Macmillan's biographers, D R Thorpe, considered that as Prime Minister he catered for a national mood of self-deception[34] – and Brook is not immune to a similar charge. Understandably, the years when Britain had stood in the vanguard against Nazi tyranny were the reference point for exhausted men and women who had endured superhuman effort during the war years. Brook and many of his contemporaries continued to work with something like the same intensity as during the war – it is astonishing to see how full the official files are with their output of papers and briefs. The extraordinary amount of effort Brook put into securing amendments to Arthur Bryant's history of the war, based on the diaries of Alanbrooke, in order to strike a balance between the achievements of Churchill and of Alanbrooke bear witness to the intensity of residual feeling long after the end of hostilities.[35]

Perhaps Macmillan sensed some limitations when he refused a study on Britain's economic future using the mechanism of the Future Policy Study. Perhaps it would have been better if he had replaced Brook in 1957 or 1958 when it must have been clear that the burden of adding the responsibilities of Head of the Home Civil Service to those of the Cabinet Secretary was inhuman. But it would be churlish not to recognise the warmth Macmillan felt for the support Brook had given him. In response to Brook's message of support when he resigned as Prime Minister, Macmillan wrote, 'I do not think I have ever received a letter which has given me more pleasure ... During all those creative years I depended very much on you and you know how I have tried to make you feel that.'[36]

An indication of the regard in which Brook was held by four very different Prime Ministers can be deduced from the extent to which he accompanied them on important overseas travels:

1945	Attlee	Potsdam Conference
1948	Attlee	Canada, Australia, New Zealand
1950	Attlee	Ceylon, India, Pakistan
1951	Attlee	Paris
1951/52	Attlee	Washington, New York, Ottawa
1953	Churchill	Bermuda Conference
1955	Eden	Geneva Summit
1957	Macmillan	Bermuda Conference
1957	Macmillan	Washington, Ottawa
1957	Macmillan	Paris (NATO)
1958	Macmillan	Commonwealth tour
1958	Macmillan	Washington, Ottawa
1959	Macmillan	Moscow
1959	Macmillan	Washington, Ottawa
1960	Macmillan	Africa tour
1961	Macmillan	New York, Jamaica, Washington
1961	Macmillan	Bermuda
1962	Macmillan	New York, Washington, Toronto, Ottawa

He had the misfortune to be Cabinet Secretary as it became clear, in the cruel words of *Time* magazine, when Britain had become 'a butterfly content to flutter pathetically on the periphery of the world.'[37] However, Brook is open to criticism for being too comfortable with a Conservative government that worked in step with public opinion and did not seek to lead it; and for a general failure to take initiatives or introduce reforms when Head of the Home Civil Service. At the end of 1964 he turned down Edward Heath's invitation to join a confidential committee 'to assess whether control of the administration through the Cabinet system is effective' preferring to offer 'advice informally outside [the committee].'[38] Historians may also pause over Colville's reference to Brook wanting to suggest changes in the government to Churchill, including moving Eden from the Foreign Office[39] and Macmillan's diary entry that Brook agreed that Selwyn Lloyd must go.[40] It is further noticeable that in debate about how to consult the Commonwealth about the British application to join the EEC Brook was insistent that there should be a meeting of Commonwealth Heads of Government 'confined to the Common Market issue,' and that, unusually, the Colonies should be properly represented even though not formally members of the Commonwealth.[41]

Nevertheless, let the last words rest with Lord Franks, who said of Brook, 'But you are, whatever Ministers may think of themselves, one of the chief architects of post-war Great Britain as a going concern and it so easily might not have gone at all, or at least, slowly and badly.'[42] Brook's greatness was in maintaining for so long the scaffolding that held up the edifice of government – he was the ultimate 'safe pair of hands'; his sins were sins of omission.

Early Career

At the Home Office Brook's promise was spotted by Sir John Anderson, then Permanent Secretary and later Minister. In 1938 Anderson became Lord Privy

Seal and appointed Brook his Principal Private Secretary, keeping him in the same post in October 1940 when made Lord President of the Council,[43] and from early in 1941 'de facto' Minister for the Home Front, thus freeing up Churchill as the war leader. In 1942 Brook was seconded to the Cabinet Office, serving as secretary to the Lord President's Committee from March to November 1943.[44] It was during this spell that he came into regular contact with Winston Churchill as his duties included keeping the Prime Minister in the picture about the home front.[45] He established a reputation for keeping business moving, adept at finding the compromise or procedural device that would allow officials from different departments, with different interests, to co-operate in preparing issues for ministerial discussion.[46] They were skills recognised by Bridges who made Brook his deputy in 1942, with a focus on civil issues, alongside General Hastings 'Pug' Ismay who handled military matters.[47] In 1945, when Sir Richard Hopkins[48] retired as Permanent Secretary at the Treasury, Bridges took over his role without formally relinquishing the post of Cabinet Secretary – a device thought appropriate because of officials' sensitivity to the closeness between Churchill and Ismay, which was thought to preclude Ismay reporting to Brook as they had been of equal status during wartime.

The government machine had been stripped down of historical procedures that were judged unsuitable for the conditions of total war. Some Cabinet conventions had been lifted – e.g. the requirement for five days between the circulation of a Cabinet paper and its discussion was reduced to two; the convention that Ministers did not have access to the papers of earlier administrations was lifted temporarily and the requirement for the Prime Minister to authorise circulation of Cabinet conclusions was abandoned. Others had been added – e.g. compiling a schedule of War Cabinet decisions and lists of outstanding actions.[49] Shortly after his arrival as Prime Minister in May 1940 Churchill let it be known that he wanted the record of the War Cabinet discussions to be less prolix than had been the case with the Cabinet in the inter-war years. War Cabinet conclusions should: 'avoid, so far as practicable, reference to opinions expressed by particular Ministers. Such was the pressure of total war that, "The record in respect of each item will be limited to the Conclusion of the War Cabinet thereon, together with a brief explanatory summary." '[50] Further, on 30 May 1940 following a second complaint by Churchill that meetings of the War Cabinet lasted too long Bridges put forward proposals to shorten them by cutting out the recital of war news from the past 24 hours in favour of a written daily summary.[51] A few weeks later, as the Battle of Britain began in earnest, Bridges went further in urging Churchill to issue a directive for a stripped down decision-taking process in which, 'Departments and Committees should be told to produce Reports, not in carefully polished officialese, but in short, snappy sentences. Whenever possible, instead of circulating a full-dress Report, the practice should be adopted of circulating (or handing round at the Meeting) an aide-memoire, consisting of headings only, which could be expanded orally when necessary,' adding, 'If active operations were going on in or around this country, we should have to use simpler machinery. Would it not be a good plan to start the process now so that the transition, if it comes, will not be too difficult?' Additionally, Churchill castigated Bridges;

> 'I cannot allow the Cabinet minutes to be sent out of the country, or made any use of. They are nothing more than your jottings down of lengthy conversations. No one who is really busy engaged in the war has time to read them, still less to correct them. I have repeatedly told you that your records are far too lengthy. In their present condition they are a most imperfect and misleading.'[52]

By March 1941 Churchill was calling for a cull of 25% in the number of Government committees – thought to be around 800 though only 751 could be identified. Bridges happily reported in May that 32% had been killed off – though acknowledging that many of those stopped had really been defunct.

Ministers complained of time wasted waiting in the Cabinet anteroom because of the difficulty in estimating the time needed for agenda items.[53] For those locked in Cabinet it was hard to keep up with Departmental business and the practice developed of Ministerial boxes being taken into the Cabinet room during sessions, until Churchill objected to the interruptions.[54] A radical suggestion that the War Cabinet should comprise Ministers without Portfolio was firmly rejected.[55] Meanwhile, in a note to the Cabinet Office Secretariat Bridges mused: '... it will also probably be desirable that I should send a note to the P.M. explaining any special point on the [Cabinet] agenda, e.g. that it is essential that decisions should be reached on a particular Paper by a certain date.'[56]

The existential struggle also meant that the manner in which decisions were taken was not always ideal and some complaints preceded Churchill as Prime Minister. Thus, in October 1939 Bridges reported the Lord President's dissatisfaction that decisions seemed to be orchestrated before the issue came to his committee. At the end of the same month Sir Samuel Hoare (Lord Privy Seal) complained to Horace Wilson (Head of the Home Civil Service) that he was 'very much disturbed by the way in which important decisions were virtually settled before they came before the Home Policy Committee.'[57] Eight months later Hugh Dalton (then Minister for Economic Warfare), complained that the justification of a Cabinet decision to seize Italian cargoes of war materials as they approached Gibraltar and Aden had been unilaterally altered on the advice of Foreign Office lawyers: 'During the short period that I have held this Office this is not the first occasion (I am thinking of Narvik)[58] on which decisions having a strong flavour of Economic Warfare have been taken behind my back and without any consultation with me.'[59] Bridges appealed to the exigencies of total war.[60] Later, in a lecture on *Cabinet Government*, given to Home Office officials on 26 June 1959, Brook spent one third of the time describing the workings of Cabinet government during war when, 'the system must be such that it can ensure that all aspects of the national life and all the national resources are subordinated to a single strategic aim.'[61] His emphasis was on taking decisions when they were needed – on the basis of honest facts[62] and balanced arguments with all relevant people (especially the Permanent Secretaries) consulted before an issue went to Ministers. And Brook followed in that tradition. Burke Trend (Brook's successor) later described him as 'essentially regulatory, rather than innovative, in character' pursuing 'the reconciliation of multiple and differing views rather than the pursuit of a single undivided purpose,' with a natural disposition to be a co-ordinator, a smoother of paths and oiler of wheels.[63]

If one beneficial legacy of the wartime exertions was a modest streamlining of Cabinet procedure, a less suitable inheritance was a civil service whose upper echelons looked to procedural arrangements for problem solving rather than individual effort; of people who knew how to turn policy into action on conventional lines rather than through innovation. Thus, Bridges set the scene for the 1946 internal inquiry into the structure of the peacetime civil service with an assumption that things would return to normal after the wartime disruptions. But there were undoubted further positive attributes – a tradition of selfless integrity (the bible of ethics, *Notes of Guidance for Ministers*, was first issued in 1946);[64] a self-belief amongst top officials that encouraged them to formulate what was the national interest, and a relationship with Ministers, born of wartime, which tolerated officials speaking truth unto power. Also part of the inheritance, however, was an addiction to secrecy and a widespread assumption that central control was a pre-requisite of economic progress and social cohesion. With the departure of the 'Whitehall irregulars,' as Peter Hennessy has christened the wartime influx to the civil service of academics and business people, officialdom largely returned to complacency as exemplified by official attitudes to public irritation over restrictions, rationing and their evasion.

This was all the more disappointing because planning for peace had started as early as November 1940 when the Committee on War Aims, under Clement Attlee's chairmanship, obtained permission to create a small secretariat under Sir George Chrystal, lately retired as Secretary of the Ministry of Health, to support a Committee of Ministers 'for the study of Reconstruction Problems under the Chairmanship of the Minister without Portfolio' (Arthur Greenwood).[65] The ministerial Committee was promulgated on 24 February 1941 following a draft work programme sent by Greenwood to Churchill on 6 January and diverted by the Prime Minister to the Lord President's Committee.[66] Churchill was at pains to focus Greenwood's committee on practical steps of reconstruction rather than a 'high level Ministerial Committee with a balance of the political Parties … [which would] relieve Cabinet of its responsibility for giving guidance on the main questions of principle, as Greenwood wanted.[67] And on 21 October 1943 Cabinet approved Churchill's directive for planning for transition from war to peace,[68] drafted in characteristically terse and confident style:

> 'It is the duty of His Majesty's Government to prepare for the tasks which will fall upon us at the end of the war. The urgent needs are:
>
> (a) A sound scheme of demobilisation, having regard to the undoubted need of keeping considerable garrisons in enemy-occupied territory.

(b) The provision of food for our island on a scale better than the wartime rations.
(c) The resumption of the export trade and the restoration of our Mercantile Marine.
(d) The general turnover of industry from war to peace.

And above all:

(e) The provision during a transition period of employment for all able-bodied persons seeking it and especially for the ex-Servicemen.'[69]

On 11 November Lord Woolton, the newly designated Minister of Reconstruction inherited the group and requested Brook as his Permanent Secretary. In fact, Brook was already playing an important role in planning the post-war reconstruction, initially over the government response to the Beveridge Report, arguing that, 'It is for the government to make now the best forecast it can of the financial and economic position of the country after the war and on that basis to take a major decision as to the items which it is prepared to carry through into law before the end of the war.'[70] At 41 he was the youngest official of Permanent Secretary rank 'recognised as one of the best of the younger generation in the Civil Service.' He was not replaced directly as Deputy Secretary (Civil) to the War Cabinet; Bridges proposed two equal, but lower-ranked, officers dealing respectively with overseas and foreign affairs and the domestic side of collective government.[71] This arrangement lasted until Bridges was additionally made Secretary to the Treasury in March 1945 and Brook returned to the Cabinet Office as Additional Secretary to the Cabinet, at Permanent Secretary rank, responsible for all the effective work of arranging and recording the Cabinet's business, leaving Bridges freer to concentrate on Treasury matters (which at that time included responsibility for the Civil Service). This cumbersome arrangement was made in preference to a straight posting of Bridges to the Treasury alone and Brook to be Cabinet Secretary because Churchill did not want Ismay (the Military Secretary to the War Cabinet) to be subordinate to someone who had been his equal in the War Cabinet organisation. Brook only became Cabinet Secretary in his own right, so to speak, once again at the recommendation of Bridges, when Ismay retired at the end of 1946. He was supported by W. S. Murrie on the civil side and Major-General Sir Leslie Hollis on the military side.[72]

The Attlee Government (July 1945–October 1951)

With the arrival of peace and the July 1945 landslide electoral victory of Attlee's Labour Party the stage was set for implementation of the radical economic and social reforms anticipated in Churchill's broadcast to the nation of 21 March 1943. In that broadcast the Conservative wartime Prime Minister and leader of the National Government proposed a four-year plan for 'the transition and reconstruction which will follow the downfall of Hitler.'[73] Chief among the ideas were compulsory national insurance to provide, 'the magic of averages to the rescue of the millions,' cradle-to-grave social welfare, improved health for the population, better education, and equal opportunities for all so that, 'the path to the higher functions throughout our society and Empire is really open to the children of every family … tested by fair competition.' The peace was to be 'Not like last time [when] bickering and confusion … mocked and squandered the hard-won victory which we gained a quarter of a century ago.' Expectations of a New Jerusalem had been raised high; Churchill may have spoken the prologue but the electorate thought a Labour government would be best placed for the acts to follow.

Cabinet

An important issue was whether the organs of government were suited to a shift in tempo set by an interventionist government intent on planning the post-war society. As Michael Young has argued, Brook and his colleagues responded well to those initiatives, such as the social welfare reforms, that had been part of the wartime coalition consensus and for which they had, therefore, planned. But less well to the radical policies such as nationalisation of industry (known at the time as socialisation) that were not part of that understanding and for which they had not planned. Important wartime innovations in Cabinet procedure were confirmed at the start of December 1945.[74] Notably that papers should be circulated two working days in advance; they should be brief, as should Ministerial interventions in discussion, and that the minutes should record only points relevant to the conclusion – and then usually anonymously, an exception being when matters were especially contentious (such as might lead to Ministerial resignation).[75] The former requirement for the Prime Minister to approve Cabinet minutes before circulation was not resuscitated[76] but participants had a three-day window in which to argue (usually unsuccessfully) for amendments. Cabinet was, perforce, becoming more executive and less a talking shop between political allies.

In April 1943 the Machinery of Government Committee[77] had recommended four Standing Cabinet Committees: Defence; Social Services; Legislation; National Development, Overseas Economic Relations and Foreign Policy.[78] That same month Brook drafted '*Notes for Secretaries*' as the bible for Cabinet Secretariat members;[79] to be followed in May 1946 by *Questions of Procedure for Ministers.*[80] A requirement that Cabinet papers should include the costs of proposals in men and money was agreed in November 1948.[81] Brook successfully lobbied for a document to be issued in Attlee's name about efficiency in committee proceedings; it included a statement that 'The Cabinet *Committee system* [emphasis added] has a valuable part to play in the central machinery of government.' But the geography of committees and their scope was still confusing to many Ministers and committee behaviour also left something to be desired. Attlee felt it necessary to issue a further Cabinet paper[82] explaining that four Ministers, in addition to himself 'are free to exercise coordinating functions: 'The Lord President,' (Herbert Morrison), 'as my deputy and Leader of the House of Commons' covered legislation, Parliamentary business and all domestic matters other than the economy; Sir Stafford Cripps, Minister for Economic Affairs, coordinated home and overseas economic policy through development of an economic plan; the Minister of Defence (A.V. Alexander); and the Lord Privy Seal (Viscount Addison) who led the House of Lords and also dealt with Commonwealth matters. The same paper repeated requests for brevity, business-like discussion, adding punctuality, secrecy, not anticipating decisions in speeches and, wherever possible, personal contact instead of correspondence. At about the same time Attlee also called for a review of interdepartmental committees at official level.[83] Brook defended the list robustly pointing out that many official committees lightened what would otherwise be the load on Ministers, suggesting that only 7 of 46 official committees serviced by the Cabinet Office could be abolished leaving:

Number of Official committees serviced by the Cabinet Office, October 1947

Defence committees	5
Imperial and foreign affairs	7
Economic affairs	13
Home affairs	5
Scientific subjects	4
Miscellaneous	5

Brook then had to admit to Bridges that he had 'overlooked the fact that since 1943 the Treasury have assumed central responsibility for these reviews of official Committee business;'[84] Bridges responded that central statistical returns were not the answer; better results would come from encouraging Departments to cut out duplicate attendance at committee meetings, amalgamating overlapping committees and putting the onus on parent committees to limit the lives of their sub-committees.[85]

The introduction of Cabinet Committees was praised in the press: 'A method has been discovered for dividing up the work that would otherwise fall upon the Cabinet and yet of maintaining the essential harmony of policy among the government as a whole.'[86] Brook was less confident, challenging their efficiency,[87] worrying about piecemeal decisions that had no reference to strategy and about the frequent failure to bring out the consequences of proposed actions.[88] Thus, in April 1950 he proposed that two Cabinet sessions a year should be devoted to the future course of public expenditure: 'It is remarkable,' he wrote, 'that the present Government have never reflected upon the great increase in public expenditure, and the substantial change in its pattern which has come about during the past five years in consequence of their policies in the field of the social services.'[89]

The exigencies of war had resulted in Ministers sometimes challenging the Cabinet record and complaining about decisions that affecting them being taken in their absence.[90] The same could not be said when Aneurin Bevan complained, in October 1947, that the Cabinet minutes fell between the stools of a full record of the discussion or a summary record of the decisions taken.[91] It was not easy to meet the general requirement of short minutes and the wish of individual Ministers to have their interventions recorded – particularly when they had argued against the eventual decision. Bevan had form in these matters. In September he had objected to the minutes of Cabinet from 1 August which read: 'THE MINISTER OF HEALTH said that, while he recognised that there must be some reduction in housing, he hoped that any cuts would be selective.' Bevan sought a change to: 'THE MINISTER OF HEALTH said that, while he recognised that the housing programmes in mining and agricultural areas could only be increased at the expense of a reduction in other areas, he hoped that the total housing programme would not be reduced.'[92] Attlee's recollection supported the issued minutes and defended the Cabinet Office note takers. 'Minute taking is a very difficult task,' he wrote to Bevan, 'but in my experience and that of the Cabinet Secretaries complaints are very infrequent ... The Minutes must, in my view, include some summary of the reasons for the Cabinet conclusions and, on occasion, an indication of the course of the discussion which led to the conclusion.'[93]

Bevan returned to the issue more forcefully in August 1950 over increased defence expenditure. He argued that a request that his opposition to the planned increases should be recorded in the minutes had not been honoured. Brook countered that Bevan had used the word 'doubts' and not 'opposed'; furthermore on a matter as important as this a Minister who remained opposed to a decision of his colleagues could not remain a member of the government since that meant that he or she was not prepared to take his or her share of Cabinet collective responsibility. Bevan, however, thought that there would be no breach of collective responsibility if the minutes made clear that the opposition had been voiced before the decision was taken and provided that the Minister concerned did not then reveal their opposition publicly. The disagreement was left unresolved, but festering, as in October Bevan once again sought unsuccessfully to have his dissent over the agreement to nationalise British Sugar recorded in the Cabinet minutes. All of which led to officials compiling a dossier in November about Bevan's attitude to collective responsibility and led Brook to remind Bevan when it became clear that he was about to resign from the government over the introduction of NHS prescription charges that the obligation of collective responsibility would not be lifted either for an exchange of resignation letters or for the customary subsequent resignation speech to Parliament.[94]

Secrecy

Government attachment to secrecy is demonstrated by two Cabinet documents from 1946. In May Cabinet approved guidance on *The Publication of Information from Cabinet Documents*[95] that acknowledged that memoirs about the war period were bound to emerge, irrespective of how stringent restrictions were laid down. They ought, therefore, to be treated *sui generis* and restrictions of a military or security nature might be lifted when the considerations that kept the information secret no longer applied. Further, Ministers should be entitled to defend their stewardship in memoirs and the like, subject to keeping secret information whose disclosure would be injurious to the United Kingdom in relation to other nations; or would be destructive of the confidential relationships between Ministers and between Ministers and their advisers, outside bodies or private persons. Bridges called a meeting of Permanent Secretaries for 18 June to consider the implications of these principles for the Crown Services. Brook was unable to attend but sent written comments that demonstrated a more nuanced approach than the blanket restrictions proposed. He argued that senior members of the Armed Forces and some Ambassadors were in a comparable position to Ministers, in being held to account for their actions, and so should not be as restricted as the individual civil servant who 'should be able, and usually is able, to shelter under the tradition of anonymity.' Additionally, in the general case of civil servants, with the passage of time 'I would have said that we have little to lose and perhaps much to gain by adopting a rather less restrictive policy in this matter. It is a common complaint that the Civil Service is misunderstood and misrepresented by the public. The best way of combatting this, surely, is to see that the public get a better idea of what the Civil Servant is and does.'[96]

The result was a paper to Cabinet on 22 July that distinguished between current Civil Servants, retired Civil Servants, senior officers in the Armed Services and Diplomats along the lines suggested by Brook.[97] However, retired officials would not be permitted to use unpublished information and should not deal with matters on which they had been involved, lest this threaten the civil service reputation for political impartiality. Brook let it be generally known that he expressly forbade diary keeping by officials.[98] Herbert Morrison, the Lord President, announced the policy in the House of Commons on 15 August.[99] It was soon tested when Churchill wrote to Attlee in September, 'I should like to know, without necessarily accepting the view as final, whether in principle there would be any objection to the publication of the kind of memoranda which are attached to this note.' (These were papers written by Churchill himself, his Minutes of instruction or inquiry, personal correspondence with Roosevelt and others.) Cabinet granted Churchill's wish on 10 October against an undertaking that his text would be submitted for final revision on behalf of the government in the light of the circumstances of the time. (The likely principal opponent, the Foreign Secretary, was not present that day.) A similar permission was granted to Lord Beaverbrook over correspondence with Harry Hopkins from Roosevelt's staff.[100]

Bridges tried to get Brook to take over responsibility for the relatively burdensome task of vetting cases involving the use of official information in all private publications.[101] Brook was having none of it, restricting the Cabinet Office interest to memoirs by ex-Ministers and ex-officials.[102] This was demanding enough. Hankey had set a precedent in 1926 when he scrutinised Churchill's volume, *World Crisis*. Now Brook became heavily involved with Churchill over the latter's history of World War II, seeking to enforce the standards agreed in 1946 including persuading a reluctant Churchill not to reveal the secret of the Bletchley Park Ultra code-breaking successes. But his contribution to Churchill's volumes went well beyond protecting confidentiality, to include tasks usually associated with copy editing and substantive guidance on the treatment of the North African and Mediterranean campaign, the importance of the victory at El Alamein, and explanations of the strategic bombing of German cities and the Arnhem debacle. Not all were accepted, though several resulted in memorable additions, including 'Before Alamein we never had a victory. After Alamein we never had a defeat;' and leading to speculation that Brook had effectively coined the title *The Hinge of Fate* when he referred to the Middle Eastern theatre as 'the hinge on which our ultimate victory turned.' There is also clear evidence that he ghosted some sensitive passages concerning the Battle of the River Plate and a major disagreement between Churchill and Sir Stafford Cripps in 1942. So much so that Churchill intended to include Brook's name in the acknowledgements for *The Hinge of Fate*. However, Brook had kept the scope of his involvement out of Attlee's sight and so declined to be included: 'I should have been very proud if my name could have been included in the Acknowledgements [but] after reflecting very carefully on this I have come to the conclusion that, in view of my official relations with members of the existing Government, it would be better that you should not make this public acknowledgement of my help.'[103]

The Civil Service

A pamphlet of July 1941 from the Political and Economic Planning Group (PEP) had spoken (mistakenly as later evidence showed) of the United Kingdom's crippling inferiority to the Nazis in organisation and the machinery of government.[104] The pamphlet argued for a new concept of government 'as the nation's instrument for planning and acting in order to safeguard and develop the collective inheritance and the social and economic welfare of the country,' under which 'the principle of complete ministerial and therefore departmental autonomy in matters of administration must give way to the insistence of war and the social needs of post war reconstruction.' Though an official file[105] contains a copy of the pamphlet it is silent on the extent to which officials were influenced. The effect of the pamphlet externally was to stimulate criticism. In October 1945, for example, an editorial in *The Observer* looked forward to the challenges arising from the programme of the Attlee Government and was noticeably critical of the civil service.[106] The influence of PEP's thinking on Bridges and Brook appears to have been negligible as they appeared confident in the ability of the old ways to respond to the challenges of economic exhaustion and reconstruction. Thus, when the Labour MP for Middlesbrough West, Geoffrey Cooper, suggested that a Select Committee enquiry should look at the civil service[107] Bridges advanced a contention that things would return to normal: 'I have been disposed to think of the change-over from war to peace, as it affects the civil service, largely in terms of what happened at the end of the last war. In that war, too, large numbers of business men, industrialists and others came into the civil service, and at the end of it, when the war problems came to an end, they packed up and went back to their businesses.'[108] The Permanent Secretaries met under his chairmanship on 2 March to discuss the post-war civil service; colleagues, including Brook, at that Saturday morning meeting did not demur.[109] Brook later went on record that Cooper was, 'seen as mad and a nuisance by most Ministers.'[110]

The meeting quickly decided that the special circumstances of the civil service required an internal study. Five working groups were set up including Efficiency in Government; this Working Group, chaired by Sir Alan Barlow of the Treasury, had Brook as a member along with seven other Permanent Secretaries.[111] The Group took limited evidence from outsiders, notably Colonel Urwick of Urwick Orr and Sir Henry Benson of Price Waterhouse. They submitted substantial papers and were invited to present to the Group on respectively 23 July and 13 August. However, in each case they were asked to withdraw before discussion of their ideas. Benson had suggested that the government reliance on cash accounting brought distortions that hindered long-term efficiency and proposed accountancy-trained financial controllers. The discussion of his evidence decided that the form of Government Accounts was outside their remit but went so far as to suggest a further investigation of the merits of moving to commercial (i.e. accruals) accounting, probably by a Royal Commission. Terms of Reference were agreed but the inquiry never happened because of problems in finding a private sector chairman who could give enough time to the task. An identical proposal had been made at the end of the First World War and had found traction with Departments but had rubbed the Treasury up the wrong way. In that case an inquiry under, ironically, the then Senior Partner of Price Waterhouse had comprehensively dismissed the idea. It was not until November 1993 that it was announced that accruals accounting (known as Resource Accounting) would be introduced across central government.

However, in November 1946, on Brook's recommendation, Attlee reconstituted a Machinery of Government Committee, 'To keep under review the executive machinery of Government and to deal with such machinery of Government questions as require consideration by Ministers.' It was a precautionary measure. Brook advised 'We do not expect any rush of work for this Committee'.[112] Also in November, Attlee agreed to a committee to fix manpower ceilings for each department and made a series of challenging observations – was there enough delegation? How many obsolete restrictive practices still applied? Were efficiency advances outside the civil service sufficiently emulated? Were the civil service unions too powerful?[113] To a significant extent the questions fell on stony ground as far as the Efficiency Working Party was concerned. On 17 July 1947 it met to agree a draft report. This was presented to the Machinery of Government Committee, with Sir Stafford Cripps (the Chancellor of the Exchequer), in the chair on 6 January 1948.[114] The Committee met only twice in that year and petered out after 1949. Moreover, at the change of government in 1951 Brook did not include the committee in his list of suggested Cabinet Committees for the incoming Churchill and it was declared dead in November 1953.[115]

The 1948 document contained much about the higher organisation of departments and financial management but also pithy recommendations on the conduct of official business in the broadest sense. The latter were reprinted and widely circulated throughout the civil service.[116] In many ways this document was ahead of its time, beautifully written in highly accessible language, free of management jargon. 'Efficiency,' it argued, 'must be assessed, not in the abstract, but in relation to a particular function,' finding that, 'there is in every Department, especially at the middle levels, a pervading atmosphere of caution and a stifling of initiative ... the price paid to avoid mistakes was too high.' Ministers must accept the risk of mistakes in the interests of speed of administration and must be prepared to defend that attitude by using the argument that 'a man who never makes a mistake never makes anything.' Long hours, 'usually mean a slow pace,' and 'work which is stale and uninspired.' '... for the most part official documents can be written in straightforward English prose, viz., in language which is clear, direct, simple and concise. That they should be so written is desirable, not merely for elegance, but for efficiency – so that they may convey their meaning clearly and quickly.' Unfortunately the only step towards implementation lay in the support expressed by Bridges in the foreword as, 'I hope that everybody who reads it will find, as I have done, much that is stimulating, and much of that practical wisdom without which none of us can do our jobs to the utmost of our capacity.' The ministerial Machinery of Government Committee merely 'took note' of the full report. And that was it; so much effort and insight to so little effect.

With Bridges at the Treasury and Head of the Home Civil Service, Brook was entitled to feel that the machinery of government was, at best, a shared endeavour. Relations between the two were not perhaps as close as would have been ideal. National manpower shortages led Bridges to announce a freeze on civil service (non-industrial) numbers: (722,294 as at 1 January 1947).[117] A target was set for 1 January 1948 at 686,000. Yet when Bridges launched an enquiry by the Government Organisation Committee (GOC) into Whitehall organisation for 'economic issues' it met only twice over 16 months, leaving a Working Group to identify and grapple with the issues, relatively unguided by the Permanent Secretaries. Brook queried why Harold Wilson's 1948 'bonfire of controls' at the Board of Trade had not produced manpower savings in the civil service[118] and briefed for Cabinet that, 'I am sure there is quite a substantial amount of money to be saved through staff economy.'[119] Wilson had told the House of Commons that he had eliminated the issue of approximately 200,000 licences or permits by the Board of Trade (which in turn had brought to an end the rationing of clothing and textiles) yet manpower savings accounted for only 943 posts (with relaxation of the unpopular building controls[120] accounting for only 169 staff.)[121]

The GOC (chaired by Bridges) was particularly ineffective at handling big issues, partly hamstrung by only being able to focus on interdepartmental issues, but timid and prone to reject innovative ideas. In February 1950, for example, a review of regional organisation provoked Johnston of the Cabinet Secretariat to tell Brook that proposals to roll up regions were 'calculated to lose the advantages of regionalisation while retaining all the disadvantages. If the town of Berwick-on-Tweed is to be administered from Leeds, it is futile to speak about close personal contact. I should have thought that the local authority in such a case would much prefer to deal with Whitehall than with a remote regional Headquarters. The Committee ... seem even to contemplate with equanimity Departments rolling up regions differently ... Under these circumstances, regional administration would become one big muddle.'[122]

The Committee produced an interim report on the Whitehall organisation of economic matters, for discussion on 27 February 1951. Brook severely criticised the lack of guidance given to its Working Group. He warned Bridges that 'I believe that the only way of getting this work done is to make the senior people take a view first, and then get others to work out its implications under direction.' He made five detailed points – the report reflected a doctrine that the official in Whitehall knew best; it ducked the issue of relations with the socialised industries; it made no attempt to measure costs; little was said about the proper function of trade associations; too much was remitted for later study. His commentary also included a fierce attack on Whitehall:

> 'There is an alarming amount of paper floating round Whitehall these days – and what is even more alarming is the number of officials who are willing, nay eager, to read it. It was recently stated, with truth, that there are a lot of people in Whitehall who, when they have read a paper and understood it, feel that by that alone they have in some way contributed to the public good. This dangerous tendency may well be encouraged by the conception of a production authority brooding over the affairs of an industry in respect of which it has no direct administrative or executive function. I myself would prefer that studies of the contacts between Government Departments and industry should start from the specific duties which Departments have to perform.'[123]

In time-honoured fashion, the Steering Group responded by charging Brook (in conjunction with Lee of the Treasury and Emmerson of the Ministry of Works) to identify what those specific issues should be; but, perhaps understandably, his heart was not in the task and after the General Election of 25 October 1951 in which the Conservatives returned to power he was reluctant to continue the work. Bridges hit back: 'If those of us who have lived all our working lives in Whitehall and have studied the Whitehall organisation, give up as hopeless all attempt to reform it from inside, then what hope is there of any reform in our time?'[124]

The Socialisation of Industry

An important element of the 1945 Labour Party manifesto, *Let Us Face the Future*, was economic reform, 'in order that the ruin of our wealth may be rapidly repaired, in order that employment and production shall be at a high level, and that goods and services shall be interchanged between man and man and between one nation and another under the best conditions and on the largest scale.'[125] Although opinion polls of the time indicated that only 6% of the population put the ownership of industry as a priority (compared, for instance to 41% that put housing at the top of their list)[126] the Attlee Government set about taking what it saw as the commanding heights of the economy (coal, electricity, gas, rail, road and air transport, iron and steel) into public ownership under the umbrella term 'socialisation.' At the start of 1946 a full-blown Ministerial Socialisation Committee was appointed 'To consider questions of policy which arise in the working out of schemes, to give effect to approved projects for socialising industries and to ensure a desirable measure of consistency in the preparation of those schemes.'[127] Brook dutifully helped guide the legislative process to achieve this but showed little positive enthusiasm for the measures leaving the detailed briefing to a more junior official, Alex Johnston, who was appointed the lead secretary for the Socialisation Committee (badged SI(M), standing for the Socialisation of Industry (Ministerial) Committee). Johnston strongly supported the aims of socialisation, arguing, for instance, that 'Transport belongs to the public utilities, where monopoly is necessary for efficiency;[128] and suggesting to a reluctant Brook that the SI(M) terms of reference should be enlarged to cover the running of the socialised industries.[129]

By the spring of 1947 Brook was increasingly sensitive to the costs of socialisation both in financial terms (where, for example, he briefed against more than token compensation on the nationalisation of the electricity and gas industries)[130] and in the opportunity cost to the legislative programme (especially in arguing for postponement of the nationalisation of iron and steel from the 1947/48 Session of Parliament). In May he went further, suggesting that Cabinet ought to re-examine the case for iron and steel nationalisation, recognised as the most complex of the nationalisations, driven by political considerations and much delayed – it was not enacted until 1951.[131] A year later, in the run-up to a special meeting of Cabinet on 7 June 1948 Edwin Plowden, Head of the Central Economic Planning Staff, argued that to introduce iron and steel nationalisation would be an act of economic irresponsibility;[132] Robert Hall, the Chief Economic Adviser, queried whether the risks of the Bill were understood,[133] and Brook argued that for an industry about which the Minister of Supply (George Strauss) admitted 'there is no question in this industry of inefficiency, or of disinclination or inability to carry through essential modernisation'[134] the justification that a basic industry should not be left in private hands 'may not seem to be a sufficiently convincing reason for going forward with this scheme.' He challenged whether, 'earlier experiments in socialisation achieved such success, in increased efficiency and lower cost, to justify the nationalisation; whether the claim by some trades unions that socialisation had not been successful because they made insufficient provision for workers' control might prove embarrassing and claimed that socialisation removed incentives to efficiency because it removed the profit motive and put nothing in its place.[135]

Brook was also only too aware that socialisation did not bring economic harmony. In a telling commentary on proposals from the National Union of Mineworkers on how to increase coal production he noted that the NUM: 'ask for further concessions but do not tie them to better output from the existing workforce.'[136] At the beginning of the following year, acknowledging that 'The inflationary situation revealed in C.P. (48) 27 must give cause for serious alarm, particularly for its effect on the export drive,' he continued with, 'the Government will certainly be open to criticism if it can be shown that socialised industries are leading the way in a wages movement which threatens to get out of hand ... the Socialisation of Industries Committee might be asked to consider the point.'[137]

Political criticism of socialisation at the time centred on the appointment of the Board, the pay of directors and the absence of worker representatives at Board level.[138] Despite having opposed extension of the SI(M) terms of reference to cover the running of the industries, Brook's unflinching eye continued to monitor this aspect. In late November 1949 he was strongly critical of the British Transport Commission for taking too narrow a view, failing to give a strategic lead on transport integration, and hindering the shift from road freight to rail by hiking rail freight rates by 16⅔% to threaten much needed exports.[139] Tellingly, he briefed, 'This is the dreariest piece of official jargon I have seen for some time ... no one can have confidence in the judgement of a person who can write this sort of stuff.'[140] But he also protected the right of the managers to manage and resisted interference by Ministers, arguing in October 1949 that proposals for the nationalisation of Dorman Long should allow the Company to hive off its structural engineering and chemical interests (employing 11,000 of the Company's total workforce of 27,000) despite political considerations.[141] And in March 1951 arguing that should Ministers exercise a veto on proposed BTC transport charges they would open up a clash with the authority charged with running transport;[142] thus putting his finger on the problem (but not the solution) of how to give Parliament control over nationalised industries when Ministers did not interfere in day-to-day discussions.[143]

In July, after the Attlee Government majority was slashed in the General Election of February 1950, Brook questioned whether the problems of water supply were so great that the proposed nationalisation under direct Ministry of Health administration (removing it from local authority control) as suggested by the Minister of Health, Aneurin Bevan, was justified. In an acerbic but telling comment Brook questioned whether matters would be improved; 'Ministers may think it fair to ask whether such progress has now been made in overcoming the difficulties of the Health Service and the housing programme that the Ministry of Health can take in hand another major, complicated and controversial project.'[144] He followed this with doubts about whether socialisation of the sugar industry would improve existing tight government controls[145] and in December doubted if state owned auction houses for fruit and vegetables would be a financial success.[146] So he continued, expressing the view that the water proposals were too complex and would increase costs[147] and opposing proposals for the railways to be able to defer call-up for military service – they should not look to a solution of their recruitment difficulties in this way.[148]

There was a drawn-out Cabinet debate about how to encourage greater efficiency in the nationalised industries lasting about a year. In April 1950 Cabinet had a general discussion of the administration of socialised industries against a contention from the Lord President that their Boards were too complacent and standoffish. It fell to Johnston to prepared the brief on how to secure a greater measure of accountability without undue interference in management's business, rather than Brook, who sent it forward without comment.[149] Little thought seems to have been given to how performance should be assessed, so that when the Conservative Opposition suggested in the spring of 1951 that a Select Committee should be set up to consider how the House of Commons might be better informed about the affairs of nationalised industries and exercise effective measures of control, Brook commented that, 'The subject of Parliamentary control over nationalised industries raises very difficult issues.' The SI(M) committee had concluded that 'it is not practicable to go beyond annual debates and periodical enquiries (say at intervals of five years),' and Brook pointed out that to have one or more Select Committees sitting in permanent session on each industry 'would no doubt make it very difficult for these industries to do their work efficiently.'[150] The insularity of senior officials and Ministers (and perhaps political aversion to the private sector) seemingly precluded contact with leading industrialists to explore options for improvement and Brook took no initiative other than to propose (unsuccessfully) in March 1951 that the Chancellor of the Exchequer should become Chairman of the Socialisation of Industries Committee 'because of the necessity of ensuring that sufficient emphasis was placed on making the socialised industries pay their way.'[151]

Subsequently, some economists, including Alec Cairncross the former Chief Economic Adviser at the Treasury, have argued that it took the post-war governments a long time to realise that the commanding heights of the economy were not the socialised industries but the balance of payments and energy supplies that determined the power to manage the economy. Despite Ministers recognising the difficulties of improving output from the coal mines (which supplied over 90% of energy), the acute dollar shortage and the problems of the post-war financial settlement, including the devaluation in 1949, Brook admirably supported political priorities about which he had doubts but, as far as the official records show, did not stand back to provide a wider economic perspective.

The Economy

Switching the economy from a wartime footing to peace was extremely difficult, compounded by the ravages conflict had visited on the industrial base, the cancellation of Lend-Lease by the United States only six days after the surrender of Japan and the continuing dependence of the UK on American dollar aid (estimated by Keynes, the UK chief negotiator at the start of the talks with the USA at $5 billion).[152] The potential volatility of sterling balances held by overseas governments, a chronic weakness in the balance of payments position and the simultaneous commitment to build a new welfare state added to the stresses on an exhausted country. Competing claims for economic resources was one of the strong arguments used to justify central planning. The official files are peppered with illustrations of a struggle between planning and control on the one hand and releasing the energies of the citizenry on the other. Private consumption and investment by private sector businesses often came low in the queue and shortages of basic commodities persisted. To make matters worse, January 1947 saw

Britain in the grip of the most extreme and protracted winter of the century, which brought great privations and damaged national morale.[153] It made matters worse that shortages were, on occasion, worse than in wartime.

Brook's interventions generally represented a counterweight to the enthusiasms of the economic planners, rather than a coherent programme, and they often contained a reminder that Sir Hartley Shawcross's[154] infamous words 'We are the masters at the moment – and not only for the moment, but for a very long time to come,'[155] generally did not stimulate enterprise and innovation, and was hard to align with individual aspiration in the broader population. Thus, on 1 October and again on 1 December 1945 Brook argued against universal labour control as unenforceable and undermining morale. Production departments and industry should look to provide their own manpower and not rely on the Ministry of Labour.[156] Then, at the end of 1947 when potatoes were put on ration, he protested at the absurdities of applying rationing to a commodity whose consumption varied greatly between persons and which was widely cultivated in private gardens and allotments.[157] Again, in January 1948, as Cabinet discussed whether to end the ban on foreign travel and what to do about petrol rationing, his brief quoted the damage the travel ban was having on the Foreign Secretary's European policy and said of the latter: 'The question for the Cabinet's decision is whether, in the atmosphere of prejudice which has already been created (one law for the rich etc.) the voice of reason can be made to be heard.'[158] He returned to this theme when the idea was floated, in March, to restrict private motoring to 90 miles a month. His brief pointed to the complication of administration which would inevitably give rise to extraordinary anomalies, would increase middle class dissatisfaction with the restrictions imposed by the government and encourage recourse to the black market with the courts unwilling to enforce the available penalties. 'The fact is that in peacetime it is almost impossible to administer petrol rationing efficiently, with a basic ration, unless a fairly generous basic ration can be given.'[159]

Scepticism about the sheer detail of central economic control and the difficulty of steering individual freedom of choice also came through in wider economic and trade briefing. At first, for example, Brook supported intervention in commercial aircraft specification and purchase. 'There is clearly a danger that, without some co-ordinating body, the three [Airways] Corporations will demand different basic designs without real justification.'[160] But in the light of a report by the Hanbury-Williams committee of business men that came down strongly on putting the operator and the manufacturer into direct touch over the ordering of civil aircraft he tempered this advice. 'I venture to suggest … that the findings of this Committee cannot lightly be rejected.' But there should be a transitional period, because the committee argued that B.O.A.C. would not want to buy the Brabazon aircraft (which had been already developed as part of the Ministry of Supply long-term programme) since its commercial success was doubtful.[161] Three months earlier he had supported abolition of the Petroleum Board and a return to commercial competition in oil products.[162] At the end of the year the Cabinet Office briefed Attlee that relaxation of day-to-day control in Germany was the only basis on which an effective and responsible system of democratic government could be established.[163] In June 1949 Brook continued in the same vein, opposing a 'thoroughly bad Bill' to restrict entry to hairdressing.[164] Then in March 1950 he argued that a proposed relaxation of private house building licences was probably political sleight of hand with no real extra freedom as it all depended on how the scheme was administered.[165]

UK dependence on American help, notably as a recipient of Marshall Aid,[166] was a further complication. Shortly after the General Election *The Spectator* summed up the British predicament as 'Without America's military aid we could not have survived the war: Without her financial aid we could not have survived the peace.'[167] Brook was tough and realistic. Initially he manoeuvred to secure Cabinet Office influence over obtaining and using Marshall Aid. The British organisation was complex, comprising the British Supply Organisation in Washington, a delegation to the Continuing Organisation in Brussels (later Paris), and the London Committee, which handled the programme interdepartmentally in the UK).[168] Bevin made clear that he wanted to establish a clear personal control over at least the Washington end of the machinery, Brook secured Cabinet Office dominance over the London Committee.[169] But by May 1948 the London Committee was struggling to cope with a remit that covered both policy and programmes – Brook lamented the large attendance at its meetings (sometimes as many as 37 people).[170] And it was reorganised to separate the two aspects.[171] Even so, by 1949 the Cabinet Office burden amounted to 100 meetings a month and Brook moved to confine its input further, to the main London Committee (now handling only policy), the Overseas Negotiations Committee, the Programmes Committee and the Exports Committee – thereby saving the need to service 30 meetings a month.[172]

Attlee, meanwhile, thought that the focus on Marshall Aid made too much of the Government's agenda subordinate to the Marshall Aid programme.[173] Brook agreed; in April he had commented to Attlee that 'we are paying a high price in general inconvenience to strengthen our claim for Marshall Aid'[174] and he briefed, for instance, in favour of arms sales to Latin America, contrary to American lobbying.[175] However, the economy was still seriously weak and the summer of 1949 saw a further crisis when, shortly after a drain on dollar holdings, sterling collapsed. The Chancellor and Chief Economic Adviser (Robert Hall) got short shrift in Brook's brief for the Cabinet discussion over their explanation of the dollar shortage without suggested actions to follow. In Brook's view this left a consequent acute risk that Cabinet would not face up to the issues because there would be no proposed actions on which to focus.[176] Hall continued to highlight a fundamental divergence in economic goals between Britain and America. The UK put economic stability before growth but the US wanted the opposite and, he argued, until the UK reached dollar equilibrium the country would have to adjust accordingly.[177] So, despite £100 million of emergency cuts in imports in July, Cabinet agreed a devaluation of sterling against the Dollar to \$2.8 = £1 to be announced on 18 September. Devaluation was followed by public expenditure cuts and, a wages freeze intended to free resources to be mobilised in support of a better balance of payments position. (Interestingly, at the key Cabinet meeting on 19 August at which the decision to devalue was taken, it was Bridges who acted as secretary, not Brook.)[178] Also in November, as Cabinet discussed public expenditure control, on the basis of papers from the Chancellor of the Exchequer that proposed six-monthly monitoring, Brook wanted to go further and set limits 'prescribing provisional ceilings beyond which the various groups cannot be allowed to rise ... [which] would largely solve the problem of securing economies in policy ... without derogating from the responsibility of the Departmental Minister.'[179]

By early 1950 the devaluation was having an effect. Robert Hall argued, however, that, though devaluation had helped bring the UK nearer to economic independence from the US than it had been for many years, relations between the two countries would profoundly affect the whole of the UK's economic and political situation to such an extent that it was essential to seek an understanding with the United States on basic economic policies. Only as the trading position and that of the currency reserves improved should the UK be prepared to take more of the risks associated with freer trade.[180] Brook, meanwhile sought modest but symbolically important relaxation of central control: on the hotel industry to allow building resources to be used for hotel provision in London and for the abolition of food points rationing, an irritation to the housewife and a source of much unnecessary administrative work in the Ministry of Food and in the food trades.[181]

A big political issue after the General Election of 23 February 1950 (which saw Labour's overall majority reduced from 146 to just five seats) was how far the government should make powers to control the economy permanent. The Lord President (Herbert Morrison) wanted to do this quickly before the wartime powers expired on 10 December. Brook disagreed, pointing to a political vulnerability: 'The critics will be able to say that, for purposes of economic planning in peace-time, the Government are seeking to retain permanently all the war-time emergency powers (except the power to direct labour) which were conceded in the atmosphere of 1940'; and argued that this was not consistent with its stance as a caretaker administration.[182]

By the close of the year discussions had started with the United States on the American proposal to announce the ending of Marshall Aid to the UK. The UK claim had always been presented in the form of a dollar deficiency. This deficiency disappeared at the beginning of 1950 – by November Robert Hall reported that the dollar reserves were growing very quickly.[183] The Economic Policy Committee emphasised two considerations (1) not to jeopardise $112 million of outstanding payments from the 1950/51 Marshall Aid allocation of $287 million; (2) not to link this request for the outstanding $112 million with defence requirements since the UK had established a position as a partner in a combined programme and not a supplicant. The Committee concluded that 'The ending of Marshall Aid would be welcome in that we should no longer be so strictly bound to fall in with United States economic requirements.'[184] (Memories of the disastrous and short-lived move in 1947, under American pressure, to make sterling convertible were still raw.) Announcement of the withdrawal of

Marshall Aid was made on 13 December 1950.[185] However the euphoria associated with improvements in the dollar reserves was short-lived. The strains of austerity coupled with a requirement for rearmament against possible Soviet aggression, taking advantage of the Korean crisis, led to a split in Cabinet, resulting in the resignation of Aneurin Bevan over a proposal to introduce charges for aspects of the National Health Service.

If emergency controls and macro-economic policies were two legs of the economic stool, the third was handling persistent problems over industrial output. On Brook's suggestion Attlee revived the pre-war Supply and Transport Committee in the shape of the Industrial Emergencies Committee:

> 'To keep under review on behalf of the Cabinet questions of wages policy and other questions of policy arising from industrial disputes; and to authorise such emergency action as may be necessary, by reason of industrial disputes, to maintain supplies and services essential to the life of the community.'

The Chancellor of the Exchequer (Hugh Dalton) was nominated as Chairman, members were the President of the Board of Trade, the Home Secretary, and the Ministers of Labour and National Service, War Transport, and Food.[186] When a dispute started in the road haulage industry in January 1947, however, Attlee and the Chancellor had to be reminded by Brook of the Committee's existence.[187] It had never met and Dalton asked to be relieved of the Chairmanship, which passed to the Home Secretary. Two meetings in the third week of January also pointed to the first part of its terms of reference already being handled by the Lord President's Committee so these were amended to focus on the maintenance of supplies and services in an emergency.[188]

By April 1947 the circumstances were also propitious for removing restrictions, imposed in March the preceding year on the repeal of the Trades Disputes Act, that planning for maintaining essential supplies and services in an industrial emergency could only be undertaken by senior Whitehall officials lest government was thought to be establishing the means of strike breaking. Henceforth, regional organisations could be involved and, with memories of the 1947 appalling weather emergencies fresh in the public mind, Brook suggested that the precautions could be made more palatable by relating them to all emergencies, not just those of an industrial kind.[189] By contrast, in June 1949 he argued that it would be wrong to impose special conditions on Post Office workers to undertake wider related duties during an industrial dispute – this had not been done in the 1926 General Strike and in any case there were other more essential tasks:[190] unofficial dock strikes, for instance, were particularly troublesome despite the National Dock Labour Scheme that, from July 1947, had ended casual labour in the docks, proffered a guaranteed wage but also continued the wartime Order 1305 that limited the right to strike and required compulsory arbitration before withdrawal of labour. There were high-profile strikes centred on London and Liverpool docks in 1947, 1948 and 1949; out of the 14.3 million working days lost to strikes in all industries between 1945 and 1951 over 20% were due to the dock workers even though they accounted for only 4% of the workforce.[191] Brook's advice was clearly focused on the wider public good and needs of the economy, but also mindful of what was proper. During the 1949 London Dock strike he encouraged the government to bring in troops to unload food and to declare a state of emergency as an instrument for ending the strike rather than for maintaining essential supplies.[192] Yet a meeting of senior officials held under his chairmanship on 7 July concluded decisively that the government information services could not properly play any further part (as had been requested by the Lord President) in an attempt to convince the strikers that Communists were misleading them. This was a matter for political speeches. But a quarry of such information as was available could be prepared for political speeches.[193] On 30 August Brook met Sir Thomas Gardiner (acting chairman of the National Dock Labour Board) who told him that liaison between the Ministry of Labour and the Emergency Committee set up to take charge of operations in the Port of London (the Maxwell Committee) had been patchy; and those with the Ministry of Transport (which had set up the Committee) had been distant. However, something like the Maxwell Group would be needed in future, in part because the Port of London Authority Emergency Committee had only had the interests of the employers at heart and because the Ministry of Transport carried insufficient clout to mobilise Whitehall. In October he briefed in favour of measures to remind employees of their obligation to abide by the conditions of their employment contracts[194] and in July 1951 he supported continuation of that part of the 1940 Order 1305 that had enforced compulsory arbitration in industrial disputes.[195] Significantly, however, he did nothing to encourage the fears of Ministers that the dock strikes were a Communist plot even though the unofficial strike in the London docks that lasted from May to July 1949 had started in support of the Communist-led Canadian Seamen's Union strike against Canadian ship owners and that a subsequent Transport and General Workers' Union inquiry into the dispute disciplined six out of the seven unofficial strike leaders (all Communists).

Nor could low productivity be laid wholly at the door of poor industrial relations. In July 1948, for example, the Government Organisation Committee (now chaired by Bridges) considered a report by James (Jim) Silberman, Chief of Productivity and Technology Development at the Anglo-American Council on Productivity (which had been set up by Sir Stafford Cripps and Paul G Hoffman, the CEO of Studebaker Motors, the American Administrator of the Marshall Plan). After visiting 35 British factories from May to July 1948, covering half a dozen industries, Silberman confirmed estimates already made by the British economic statistician, Laszlo Rostas,[196] that UK productivity was less than half that of comparable industries in the USA.[197] Poor capital equipment after wartime starvation of investment, complacent management, and a legacy of industrial strife between workers and management that had not been removed by socialisation, all contributed to a weak international competitive performance. However, Silberman also concluded that 'basic scientific research and technology are at least as far advanced in Europe as in the United States', it was 'the application of technology to industrial methods [that] has not progressed so far. In short, America has more "know how".'[198]

Social Policy

A 1943 broadcast by Churchill in response to the Beveridge Report had included reference to improving the health of the general population and a great deal of planning followed, including the publication of a White Paper, *The National Health Service*, in 1944.[199] On the wider front Attlee reconstituted the Domestic Affairs Committee immediately after the 1945 General Election. It operated until October 1947 with wide terms of reference:

(a) To consider questions of internal economic policy and to keep under review the general trend of our economic development; and
(b) To deal as required, with other questions of domestic policy not specifically assigned to other Committees.

And in October 1947 economic issues were taken referred to a new Production Committee, leaving the Lord President 'To deal with questions of domestic policy outside the economic field which are not specifically assigned to other Committees.'[200]

The National Health Service (NHS)

Quite soon after the launch of the NHS in July 1948 costs began to run away:[201]

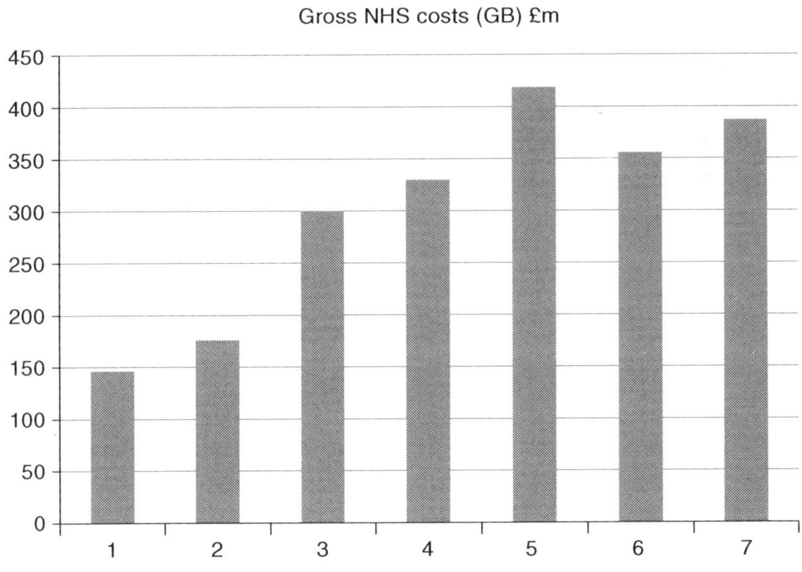

1. Financial memorandum in NHS Bill; 2. 1948/49 estimates (full year equivalent – the NHS came into being on 5 July); 3. revised 1948/49 estimates December 1948; 4. 1949/50 estimates; 5. 1949/50 estimates plus supplementary estimate; 6. 1950/51 reported in E.P.C. (49)76; 7. 1951/52 estimates reported in E.P.C. (49)76. Pre-NHS spending was estimated to have been £225 million p.a.

At the start of March 1950 Cabinet asked Bevan for a memorandum explaining the modifications needed to the financial basis of the NHS to be able to exercise closer control over expenditure.[202] That memorandum came to Cabinet on 13 March[203] but discussion was pre-empted by planning for the House of Commons debate of the following day on the NHS Supplementary Estimate. The plan was to resume discussion of the wider financial issue at a later date, but this conclusion was questioned by Bevan at the succeeding Cabinet (16 March) and Cabinet backed down by agreeing to discuss the possibility of imposing charges for some NHS facilities, should that become necessary to stay within the original 1950/51 NHS Estimates, in the run-up to the 1950 Budget.[204]

Johnston of the Cabinet Secretariat told Brook on 20 March 1950 that the Foreign Secretary (Bevin), a political rival to Nye Bevan the Minister of Health, had twice queried whether Ministers had had the opportunity of discussing the mounting costs of the NHS.[205] Johnston put the blame for failure to handle the escalating costs down to delays on the part of Cripps, the Chancellor, who 'on various grounds has postponed discussion of this matter and, as far as can be seen, did nothing to implement decisions which the Cabinet reached in May 1949 [to examine the adequacy of the existing methods of controlling the expenditure of public funds by Regional Hospital Boards]'.[206]

On 29 March 1950 Brook sent a dossier, compiled by Johnston, to Attlee and Bridges which showed how costs had run away, but he remained neutral as between the arguments of Bevin and Bevan. Bevan had not sought to conceal escalating costs but nor had he attempted to deal with them. Further, no substantial financial points had been raised at the Legislation Committee, which approved the NHS Bill in March 1946, nor during passage of the Bill in Parliament. At the end of 1948 Bevan had reported to colleagues, five months into the new NHS, revealing an increase in costs from £176 million for a full year to £300 million.[207] Bevan's memorandum had said 'That, then, is the cost of this social innovation. The justification of the cost will depend upon how far we get full value for our money; and that, in turn, will depend upon how successfully my Department administers the service generally, eradicates abuses – whether by professional people or by the public – and is able to control the inevitable tendency to expand in price, which is inherent in so comprehensive and ambitious a scheme as this.'[208] Cripps, meanwhile, had avoided a request from Attlee to report on the working of the NHS from the point of view of the Treasury, and had argued against discussion of Bevan's paper prior to the 1949 Budget. Cabinet, at a discussion delayed until 23 May, had decided: (1) there should be no cutting down of essential hospital services; (2) the recent Supplementary Estimate (so soon after the Budget Estimates) could not be accepted in principle; all possible endeavours should be made to live within the Budget Estimate; (3) the adequacy of existing methods of controlling expenditure should be examined by the Health Ministers in consultation with the Chancellor of the Exchequer.[209]

It was this last conclusion that Johnston reported had never been implemented. Nor had a decision, taken at the time of the 19 September 1949 devaluation of sterling, to reduce the costs of the NHS by £10 million through imposing a one shilling charge for prescriptions been implemented as instructed. Such was the strength of personal and political feelings about the NHS, however, that officials from the Departments involved were precluded from discussing how to implement the statement made by Cripps (with Cabinet authority) that the 1950/51 estimates were a ceiling not be exceeded. Hence in the run into the 1950 Budget Cabinet could only discuss the principle of imposing charges and Brook's brief for Attlee simply posed the question whether it was 'politically possible for the Government to abandon the principle of a free and universal Health Service.' On the other hand, he argued, the decision to impose a one shilling charge for prescriptions already breached the principle of a free service and to go no further would mean that the government would have all the administrative difficulty of charging, all the odium of abandoning free provision, and all for the sake of a mere £6 million. Further, the Cabinet as a whole was entitled to some sort of guarantee that expenditure would be controlled, especially as the Health Ministers and the Chancellor assumed that there would be future demands for extensions and developments of the NHS, which it would be politically impossible to resist. The financial credit of the government was at risk. General assurances of economies through tightening of administration were of no comfort to those facing the hard necessities of balancing a Budget. 'And, given the history of this Service, I should have thought that the Chancellor of the Exchequer would be justified in demanding some more reliable guarantee ...'[210]

Cabinet was still bitterly divided and levels of trust between Ministers were low. The Lord President (Morrison) recalled that when he had defended the government's economic record in a House of Commons debate the preceding October he had said, with the full authority of Cabinet, that 'Anyone who imagines that the present list [of expenditure reductions] represents the end of the government's efforts to achieve economies is going to be undeceived before long.'[211] There was 'some disposition' on the part of Cripps and Bevan to challenge Morrison's assertion that he had spoken with full Cabinet approval. Morrison then made it a condition of his accepting Attlee's invitation to be a member of a committee to keep the costs of the NHS under review that '... all policies behind expenditure and of new developments involving expenditure, are first submitted to the Committee by the Health Ministers after discussion with the Treasury, and before any action is taken' and that '... the Committee will include the fixing of a ceiling figure for the national resources to be available to the National Health Service, and for taking from time to time whatever action may be necessary to ensure that expenditure is in future kept within this limit.'[212] Attlee's reply was deadpan.[213] Brook had to admit that 'I have a pretty clear recollection that the Lord President did in fact say something to this effect, either in the Cabinet or in the Economic Policy Committee. I can, however, find nothing to support my recollection in the formal records of these meetings ... It is perhaps rather more surprising that I can find no trace of any such remark [that the Lord President had made it a condition of speaking in the October 1949 debate that the Government would continue their search for further economies] in my manuscript notes of the meetings.'[214]

The onset of the Korean war put even more focus on economies to fund a massive expansion of the defence effort and as the Ministerial debate on NHS charges continued into 1951, with Hugh Gaitskell now in the Chancellor's seat, Brook's briefing for Cabinet became more direct, emphasising the importance of solidarity between Prime Minister and Chancellor. The latter proposed NHS economies amounting to £30 million for 1951/52:

Dental charges	£7 million
Spectacles charges	£4.5 million
Prescription charges	£8 million
General NHS economies	£10.3 million
Economies in TB treatment	£1.1 million

Brook advised that for dental and optician charges 'There is likely to be wide public support for these charges, partly because many people who needed these benefits have already secured them, but mainly because it has been widely recognised that there has been a good deal of abuse of this part of the Service. The average member of the public does not want to see others getting something for nothing; and he is shocked by the unnecessary waste of public money ... [but] The charge on prescription forms is more difficult. It will be regarded as a retrograde step.'[215] Bevan's position was that he could not agree to any of these economies until he knew what the Chancellor proposed to do about taxation in the 1951 Budget. Brook was at pains to prevent this erosion of the Chancellor's freedom of action. 'You will decline to allow the Chancellor to be "put into commission" in this way and will insist that there can be no Cabinet discussion of the Budget as a whole until the evening before it is to be opened to the House. You will also wish to support the Chancellor's insistence on reductions in public expenditure, and to refer to the political difficulties which would arise if he were forced to the conclusion that his Budget would not command the full support of his Cabinet colleagues.' If Bevan would agree to the charges for dental work and for spectacles then Gaitskell might be persuaded to drop prescription charges.[216] The record of the relevant Cabinet discussions (C.M.(51) 25th–29th) were not circulated at the time – for one thing, the convention was that the Cabinet discussion of the Chancellor's Budget proposals was not minuted, and also because, in Brook's words, 'I excluded [the discussions on the National Health Service Bill] because it was not clear at the time whether these two Ministers [Bevan and Wilson] would resign. I did, however, make confidential records.'[217] Bevan resigned the following month. Delay in implementing the charges, Brook would later point out, meant that £13 million of the economies melted away as consumers took precautionary action in anticipation of their imposition.[218]

Capital Punishment

Prominent amongst other controversial social issues was the future of capital punishment. In late 1947 Sydney Silverman (Labour Member for Nelson and

Colne) tabled an amendment to a Criminal Justice Bill to abolish the death penalty for murder. Cabinet decided that on such an issue of conscience backbenchers should have a free vote but was itself split, with an important minority favouring abolition. However, as Brook pointed out in a brief for a Cabinet discussion on whether this concession should be extended to members of the government, 'Parliament is entitled to hear from the government what, in their view, are the risks to law and order.' The issue combined both a moral and an administrative dimension. The most relevant precedent he could find was the issue of Sunday opening discussed in 1931–32 when Ministers had been given a free vote and the Foreign Secretary (Arthur Henderson) had voted against the government. Subsequent committee stage discussions, however, had been slow and had not been completed at the change of government in the autumn of 1931. The moral Brook drew was 'that wide ranging measures left to a free vote made no progress and the government were forced in the end to take responsibility for framing a practical measure which would command the greatest possible measure of support, and passing it with the support of the government Whip.' Meanwhile, he suggested, Ministers who could not support the Government in opposing the Silverman amendment might like to absent themselves from the debate to avoid the government going into different lobbies.[219]

In a muddled compromise the Cabinet decided that the Home Secretary would argue against the amendment on behalf of the government but that all members of the government would have a free vote. Meanwhile, the Prime Minister should summon them to explain the reasons behind the government position (and no doubt put pressure on them to toe the line). In the event the Bill sent to the House of Lords included abolition proposals (though not for all classes of murder). The Lords rejected the Bill and the attempt to differentiate between classes of murder was torn to shreds. So once again Brook found himself summarising a complicated position for Attlee. On 21 July 1949, in a lengthy brief, he argued that there was not enough public support for abolition to justify overruling the Lords using the Parliament Act and that Ministers should resist a temptation to say they would legislate on capital punishment at a later date, because of the practical difficulties of framing legislation other than complete abolition, for which he was sure there was not a majority in public opinion.

The government contemplated setting up a Royal Commission as a way of deferring a difficult decision and buying off the abolitionists. Brook was politely scathing, advising Attlee:

> '... may not the appointment of a Royal Commission be a waste of time and effort ... What is required is a judgement – not on the moral issue, but on the question whether a majority of people in this country wish to see a change in the law. Is it not arguable that that is the responsibility of Government and Parliament? And if neither Government nor the Parliament is able at the present time to pass a final judgment, is it not reasonable to draw the conclusion that the existing law must be left unchanged for the time?'

Further, he argued, the Home Secretary's administrative discretion to decide in each case whether the death sentence for murder should be carried out is exercised by interpretation of the state of public opinion. 'It is, after all, the change in public opinion which has caused the progressive "humanisation" of those principles over the last fifty years or so; and that development can continue, and can be accelerated.' Nevertheless, after a defeat in the House of Commons and facing the prospect of conflict with the House of Lords the long grass of a Royal Commission was appealing and so on 20 January 1949 Attlee announced that Sir Ernest Gowers would be the chairman. The Lord President later named eleven members.[220] Long grass it was; the issue was buried for 4½ years until a 503-page report with 89 recommendations surfaced; by which time Winston Churchill had been the Conservative Prime Minister for almost two years.

Security

So soon after the end of World War II it was inevitable that government was alive to signs of possible re-emergence of Fascism; and with the Communist Party of Great Britain having secured two elected MPs in 1945[221] there were also concerns about the threat from Soviet-inspired action. Realistically, the Fascists posed no great threat. In April 1946 the Ministerial Committee looking at the re-emergence of Fascism concluded that they were divided into a number of factions, most of which were at loggerheads with each other. Brook recommended no specific action against the Fascists to supplement the existing laws of sedition.[222] Early in the following year, however, Ministers agreed to set up a secret committee on subversion 'To keep under consideration the activities of subversive movements, at home and abroad, and to make recommendations from time to time on any counter measures that appear to be desirable.' It reported to the Cabinet Defence Committee but was so secret that, highly unusually, there was no entry in the Cabinet Office Committee Book, the register of committee activities serviced by the Cabinet Secretary and his secretariat staff.[223] The Minister of Defence (AV Alexander) chaired the Ministerial Committee and Brook its official shadow.

It was not long before both Committees received worrying information. A Canadian Royal Commission set up to investigate a recent spy ring revealed by the Soviet defector Igor Gouzenko threw disquieting light on the methods used by the Russians to recruit agents and to obtain information from Canadian Government servants.[224] In addition to those who had been recruited as spies, a further 20 government servants admitted that they had been approached by the Russians, but although they had rebuffed the approach 'none of them had ever contemplated reporting to the Canadian authorities what they could not have failed to know was a criminal request.' The Communist Movement was the principal base within which the espionage network was recruited. The British concluded that 'We see nothing to suggest that the social and economic structure in Canada particularly favoured the growth of the Russian espionage organisation ... we cannot escape the conclusion that what was done in Canada might be attempted with comparable if not equal success in any other democratic country, including this one.' What was to be done, especially as the Communist Party of Great Britain was a legal organisation with two members in the House of Commons? The response was decisive, if uncomfortable. '... we are forced to the conclusion that the only safe course is to declare that a member of the [Communist] Party is ineligible for employment on work where he may have access to secret information.'[225] In addition a blanket ban should apply to nine departments: the three Service Departments, the Cabinet Office, the Foreign Office, the Control Office, the Home Office, the Department of Scientific and Industrial Research and the Ministry of Defence. A wider ban could not be justified, especially as the working party could not guarantee that the existence of the rule would stay secret and it might not be easy to justify publicly the denial of opportunity of employment in the State Service or in a wide range of branches within it; though the wide publicity given to the Nunn May[226] espionage case could go some way to blunting the edge of public criticism. The response by senior officials and ministers alike was humane. In an undated brief for Attlee Brook reported that the Official Committee was in general agreement with the conclusions of the Working Party but thought their remedies too draconian – particularly in the range of grades to be vetted for Communist sympathies and in the blanket ban proposed for the three Service Departments. This was partly a judgement on risk but mainly on the burdens that would be imposed on the Security Service (between them the Service Departments employed one in seven civil servants). The Ministerial Committee's judgement also included political reasons for a less comprehensive restriction and recommended that the ban on known or undercover members of parties countenancing subversive activities should not cover whole departments. It should be restricted to areas where there was access to really secret information and should not be applied to 'young people who happen to have joined a Political Club at the Universities.'[227] Attlee replied on 21 December 'We cannot afford to take risks here, and the general public will support us. Fellow travellers may protest, but we should face up to this.' At an ad hoc ministerial meeting on 2 March 1948 it was decided that individual Departments should decide whether to segregate secret work into particular branches in which Communists and Fascists would not be posted. Attlee announced the policy on 15 March, assuring MPs that this action was being taken on grounds of risk management since experience showed that the loyalty of such individuals to the State could not be relied upon.[228] Detailed processes for implementation were agreed at Cabinet on 25 March.[229]

The government was tying itself in knots trying to be fair to legitimate political parties; the Communist Party had received 102,780 votes (0.4% of the total) at the 1945 General Election, slightly less than the left-wing Common Wealth Party (110,634 votes). The Fascists were far less important politically but conjured up more vivid images of oppression. Hence, also in March 1948, the government found itself in an illogical position where Cabinet decreed that political censorship should not be imposed on the Fascist newspaper *Action* but was not prepared to allocate scarce newsprint to it. So the Board of Trade, having no authority to grant or to refuse a licence for newsprint, had left all applications and letters unanswered. Brook pointed out that this was akin to a refusal: 'If the state controls paper, there is no difference in principle between refusing a licence and deliberately refraining from granting a licence.'

Cabinet accepted that a review of Communist and Fascist influences in the United Kingdom must be undertaken as part of the measures to counter the 'Soviet threat to western Europe.'[230] A week after Attlee's announcement of the 'purge' of Fascists and Communists Brook told Drew of the Cabinet Office Secretariat that the Prime Minister had approved his suggestion that the Home Office should now institute such a review. The first meeting of an interdepartmental group was held on 5 April.[231] Tempting fate, the Home Office chairman opened the discussion with a bald statement that 'the measures already taken were adequate to prevent any dangerous penetration of the civil service and the Armed Forces by members of subversive organisations or those associated with them; there was no great risk, as there was in some European countries, of a subversive leaven corrupting the whole of the public services.'[232] Within two years Britain had been rocked by the conviction of the refugee from Nazism, the atomic scientist Klaus Fuchs, for supplying atomic secrets to the Russians. Worms were already in the apple. The first year of the 'purge' procedure, meanwhile resulted in 19 suspensions, 14 individuals transferred to less sensitive work and three resignations.[233] Meanwhile, an enquiry under Sir Christopher Masterman recommended loosening the political restrictions on 275,000 civil servants in minor grades and 400,000 in the industrial grades leaving 450,000 unable to undertake political activities.[234] And a compromise was reached on a JIC proposal to restrict the flow of publicly available economic and industrial information – there would be no change in the publication of general economic statistics but there would be a limit on publication of data about key commodities.[235] Brook steered a delicate course, calming fears and opposing precipitate action but seeking to strengthen cultural defences against subversion. For instance, he advised positively on a suggestion from SC Leslie of the Treasury that Ministers should be helped to put across that 'Communists were trying for their own purposes to sabotage the country's efforts to increase industrial production.'[236] He thought that Leslie should be given the opportunity to present his ideas to GEN 231, though the timing was delicate since 'it would be unfortunate if this idea were aired prematurely at a Ministerial meeting e.g. in connection with the current dock strike.'

On the other hand when Communist North Korea invaded the South on 25 June 1950 there was a heightened possibility of subversion by pro-Communist sympathisers in the United Kingdom. This was especially so when the Attlee Government agreed, against the advice of the Chiefs of Staff and Brook, that, in addition to the Royal Navy in the Far East which had been placed under US/UN control on 28 June, it would send British land troops to Korea as part of the United Nations forces.[237] (Brook briefed Attlee for Cabinet on 25 July in favour of increased Royal Navy presence in the Far East but urged caution on the deployment of ground troops. This ran counter to the advice of HM Ambassador in Washington (Oliver Franks) and Lord Tedder (Chairman of the British Joint Services Mission in Washington DC) who were lobbying for a small force on the grounds that it would improve UK/USA relations).[238]

In September Cabinet agreed that 'a British subject who consorted with the North Koreans might lay himself open to a charge of treason.'[239] A month later the Attorney-General confirmed that the UK was technically at war with North Korea according to UK law and that, in consequence, 'the law of treason would apply to any who lend aid and comfort to the North Koreans, and that the Foreign Enlistment Act would make it an offence for a British subject to engage in the forces of the North Koreans.[240] It was not long before the advice became relevant. On 3 November *The Daily Worker* correspondent in Korea, Alan Winnington, published a pamphlet, *I Saw the Truth in Korea*, alleging atrocities by South Korean and American troops. The case was discussed at Cabinet shortly afterwards when it decided that, for mainly political reasons, prosecution for treason should not be started. Brook briefed that the pamphlet was clearly treason – but as the only punishment for treason was a death sentence that would be seen to be so extreme in this case that a jury would probably refuse to return a verdict of guilty. He suggested asking the Attorney General to consider the lesser crime of sedition, which carried a maximum penalty of two years' imprisonment.[241] The Attorney did not think the suggestion worth pursuing and it was not discussed further.[242] But some six months later, in June 1951, Cabinet agreed to look at introducing other punishments for treason following a decision not to prosecute Mrs Monica Felton who had visited North Korea whilst hostilities were still under way.[243]

The *Daily Worker* pamphlet seemed to be the only known case that would be affected by a proposed Security of Forces Bill, leaving the government open to criticism for using the proposed powers not against interference with military operations but against someone who expressed an inconvenient point of view. However, following a serious explosion on 14 July in an ammunition lighter in Portsmouth harbour, that was thought to have been possible sabotage.[244] Cabinet agreed to prepare legislation making it an offence to try to interfere with supplies destined for UK military forces on active operations.[245] Brook was critical of what he saw as rushed legislative proposals. He queried how the law would be enforced against dockworkers who refused to handle military supplies for Korea.[246] He also argued that if the Portsmouth explosions were shown to be sabotage existing legislation would cover the offence.[247] Aspects of the Bill were highly controversial (e.g. hindrance of supplies for US forces even when the UK was not involved, or application of the proposed law to propaganda). Parliamentary approval would be needed before the powers could be brought into play on any particular occasion.[248] Further, argued Brook, there was no evidence of subversive acts against supplies for UK forces fighting in Korea[249] and the Prime Minister's statement about the explosions did not lead to pubic agitation about possible subversion. Brook thought that unless public opinion was overwhelmingly behind the proposals the Bill would be likely to be so watered down during the House of Commons committee stage that it was not worth having;[250] why do this when doing nothing to increase powers against a general Communist conspiracy against essential services in the home country?[251] In November Cabinet agreed not to go ahead.[252]

Between March 1948 and mid-1982 50 British civil servants resigned and 88 were transferred from sensitive work because of their political sympathies (all but one were Communist sympathisers). In the United States Senator McCarthy's un-American activities committee started a witch hunt for Communist sympathisers. After 1945 American security purges led to 9,500 federal sackings and 15,000 resignations during investigation for suspected communist affiliations. In the USA all those investigated were named. In the UK the aim was not to make any martyrs.[253] By 1950 around 2,500 people a week were being vetted by the Security Service with only around one per cent of cases producing a substantial adverse record.[254] Between March 1948 and April 1950 the Security Service notified departments of over 600 people with a Communist record who were employed in branches classified secret. The Cabinet Committee on Subversive Activities (GEN 183) discussed the situation on 5 April 1950 with Attlee in the chair and Brook present.[255] The aim was to lighten the burden of routine cases on the Security Service and to allow it to concentrate more searching enquiries on a narrower field. As sometimes happens, however, the conclusion pointed to an increased load on the Service, 'while vetting as at present conducted should be maintained for the generality of cases, further thought should be given to the possibility of defining a limited class of case in which more positive enquiries should be made.'[256] The conviction of Klaus Fuchs at the beginning of March was fresh in the minds of those present.[257] The hope was that something like 200 posts would qualify for more intensive investigation.

A Treasury-led committee under John Winnifrith conducted the further study recommended by GEN 183, reporting via Brook to Attlee at the end of October. Brook's initial covering note to Attlee was neutral tending to scepticism. Winnifrith's group had concluded that 'positive vetting' was feasible, the numbers to be covered had grown five-fold to 1,000 but few adverse findings were likely. These numbers were manageable but there was a distinct danger that the procedure might become public knowledge.[258] Later, however, in more formal briefing when the Winnifrith report was discussed at GEN 183 his briefing was more positive '... administratively I think this is right ... the recommended change of attitude on the part of establishment authorities, and the consequent enquiries and additional check of records, can do nothing but good.'[259] But, he asked, were Ministers prepared politically to defend more stringent security measures against concern for the traditional liberties of the subject? Winnifrith recommended that a department 'having first made sure that the Security Service had no adverse record of the candidate, should itself make a conscious effort to confirm his reliability using – in a minority of cases – specific enquiries undertaken by the Security Service ... The total number of posts [subject to this check] is unlikely to exceed 1,000 [and] ... will lead to only some 75 to 100 special enquiries to be made each year.'[260] This was a serious underestimate. It ignored the fact that vetting could not be a one-off occurrence as personal circumstances change so that with refresher vetting, by the time the Security Service passed responsibility for the positive vetting enquiries back to departments in June 1998 the burden on the Service had become prohibitive.

Prompted by concern about the effectiveness of security in France for handling military information a tripartite Security Working Group comprising representatives of France, the UK and the USA was set up. It met in Washington and in London with Brook delivering a low-key and self-satisfied description of the Inter-Departmental Committee on Security.[261] 'Speak slowly' he scribbled at the top of the text. Nemesis struck, however, when on 15 August Brook found himself in the unenviable position of having to advise Attlee that the UK was non-compliant with one of the Working Group's recommendations concerning vetting. 'If, therefore, we accept [the recommendation] without modifying our existing practice, there is a risk that the Americans may be able to tax us in future with having acted disingenuously.'[262] More than pride was at stake since the United States was in the throes of McCarthyism, which Brook found repugnant:

> 'I myself believe that before very long we shall have to make a general stand against the recurrent American criticisms of our security practices and tell them bluntly that some of their practices would be quite repugnant to public opinion in this country and that, in dealing with our own people, we must be allowed to judge where we shall draw the line in reconciling the inevitable conflict between the demands of the security experts and the principle of personal liberty.'

The Committee on Positive Vetting was charged with establishing what changes in UK practice were necessary to claim compliance with best practice as identified by the tripartite group. It reported in January 1952 having identified two loopholes in vetting – the enquiries about temporary civilian staff were often less comprehensive than for permanent staff and, alarmingly, a large number of staff appointed to secret departments before 1948 had not been cleared by the Security Service. Reliance on the Security Service monitoring of Communists 'should, however, make it treasonable to assume the reliability of these staffs.' Subject to mentioning these points to the Americans the Committee concluded that 'we can reasonably confirm that the United Kingdom Security procedure complies with the spirit of the recommendations of the Tripartite Security Conference.'[263] It was not until three years later, in January 1955, that PV clearance was extended beyond civil servants, employees of the Atomic Energy Authority (AEA) and members of the Armed Forces to a limited number of key contractors' senior personnel working on secret government contracts. The Cabinet Security Committee noting that 'some of [these contactors] were in a much better position to obtain knowledge of Government secrets than many civil servants or employees of the AEA. Such persons constituted a greater potential threat to security than civil servants because so much less was known about them.'[264] It was also significant that Brook had warned the Home Secretary a week earlier that 'there is reason to fear that we shall not be able to get a satisfactory agreement with the Americans on atomic energy co-operation, unless we are in a position to say that we are prepared in principle to extend positive vetting to a limited number of contractors' employees.'[265]

Ministers met on 6 February 1951. Brook had assured Attlee that the officials who were now making the proposals for a ministerial committee to combat the spread of Communism in the UK fully recognised the legitimacy of the Communist Party as a political movement in the country. But, he pointed out, their recommendations were also based on the fact that Communism was a worldwide force directed from the centre in the interests of Russian imperialism and that in consequence it was not possible to separate the two. There was evidence of attempts to infiltrate, amongst others, the Armed Forces and higher education and the recent decision to accelerate the defence programmes in the UK had already been a target for attack by Communists. Brook then successfully recommended creating appropriate machinery at Ministerial level and in mid February the Lord President sought the approval of the Committee for (a) interdepartmental monitoring of attempts at subversion in the UK and (b) assembling 'briefing on the economic impacts objects and purposes and progress of rearmament programmes.' The Ministerial group would be assisted by an official committee to be chaired by Brook.[266]

The Treasury was anxious about public reactions to anti-Communist activity. It felt that legitimate concerns about liberty might rebound on the case for rearmament and foreign policy more widely.[267] Brook raised these worries with Sir Pierson Dixon of the Foreign Office who he found fully on board with the need for Ministers to tackle education of the home public about the case for rearmament. Meanwhile, the Official Committee was constituted on 7 June, comprising Brook (as chairman), CFA Warner (FO), Winnifrith (HMT), SJ Baker (HO), Sir Maurice Dean (Defence), Sir Robert Gould (Labour and National Service) and Dick White (Security Service). Dixon made a further point that some of the covert anti-Communist activities of the Information Research Department in the Foreign Office might not be suitable for airing in the ministerial group and the two men agreed that these matters would be brought to the Official Committee. Nor, they agreed, should the formal chain of responsibility of the anti-Communist briefing group to the Prime Minister be used; rather hold ad hoc meetings normally comprising the Foreign Secretary, the Chancellor, the Minister of Defence and the Secretary of State for Commonwealth Relations.

The Official Committee started in a flurry of activity with five meetings between mid June and the start of October, circulating 12 papers, mainly from the Foreign Office.

Brook gave little overt lead, acting as a neutral chairman, as in March 1951 when he briefed Attlee that a Foreign Office paper for Cabinet concerning the possible screening in the UK of a film of the recent Berlin Youth Rally was unsatisfactory because it did not come to a conclusion on whether to ban the film because it made Communism look attractive, or to allow it because it exposed Communism's Nazi-like characteristics.[268] Then, after the defection to Moscow

AC(H): The first dozen papers

Ref	*Title*	*Date*
1	Constitution and terms of reference (Cabinet Office)	7 June
2	Countering Communism (Foreign Office)	7 June
3	Sociological study of the Soviet Union (Foreign Office)	7 June
4	Future of the Bureau of Current Affairs (Foreign Office)	8 June
5	TASS Agency radio monitoring (Ministry of Defence)	7 June
6	Communism in the schools and universities (Committee Secretaries)	27 June
7	Indoctrination of the Armed Forces against Communism (Ministry of Defence)	5 July
8	Proposals for a National Security Board (Sir Ralph Glyn MP)	6 July
9	Communist teachers in the UK (Foreign Office)	13 July
10	Future business of the Committee (Foreign Office)	13 July
11	Control of the import of Communist propaganda into the UK (Foreign Office)	16 July
12	Communist propaganda in the African colonies (Foreign Office)	28 September

of the British diplomats Guy Burgess and Donald Maclean at the end of May[269] Brook was appointed a member of the internal inquiry led by Cadogan into Foreign Office regulations and practices.[270] He also advised on the membership of a Cabinet ad hoc committee under the Lord Chancellor to examine 'whether, consistently with the preservation of the personal freedoms which in this country we regard as indispensable, changes to the existing law [relating to subversive activities] should be made.[271] And in a late July briefing he supported imposing the need for special permission for citizens wishing to travel to Communist countries, quoting the case of Guy Burgess in support.[272]

An Atlantic or a European Alliance?

Following the end of World War II as the Soviet Union extended its control over a large part of Eastern Europe the non-Communist Western powers began to challenge the growth of Soviet influence.[273] In the United States, on 12 March 1947, President Truman stated that the USA would intervene in support of any nation threatened by a takeover by an armed minority; and in June General George Marshall (US Secretary of State) trailed the process that lead to the European Recovery Programme (the Marshall Plan).[274] American foreign policy was directed to using Marshall Aid as leverage on the European states to move towards economic union. The USA specified in July 1948 'that the annual aid requests should be coordinated into one common long-term economic recovery plan for Europe.'[275] Meanwhile in Britain the Foreign Secretary, Bevin, became convinced that only the USA could guarantee the future security of Western Europe and British involvement with the rest of Western became a means to greater influence over, and more benefit from, Marshall Aid. The tug of Commonwealth trade continued to be strong.[276] Gorell-Barnes (a former official at the Colonial Office and personal assistant to Attlee) meanwhile argued that, far from seeking to escape from under the restrictions of Marshall Aid, just as the United Kingdom had benefited from the scrutiny of British use of Lend-Lease funds, it could similarly do so under the Marshall Aid programme. Scrutiny could ensure that the aid was used for a real effort of recovery and not merely to postpone a drop in living standards. He told Attlee that the proper role of the United Kingdom was: 'to lead the fight for tolerable conditions [for the receipt of Marshall Aid] both for ourselves and for other recipients of aid.'[277] He was, however, strongly opposed to European proposals for a customs union, describing them as: 'a project which will almost certainly come to nothing and which, if it were to come to anything, would almost certainly be to our disadvantage.'[278] Whilst in no way subordinate to Brook, or likely to be under his influence, these views would seem to coincide, perhaps in a more colourful expression, with those of Brook and his colleagues.

Brook's attitude to Europe indicates a dawning recognition of its economic importance to Britain but no support for the political ambitions of closer union. In British eyes the main threat was the military threat from the Soviet Government and there was some recognition that a more unified Europe would be a more difficult mouthful for the Soviets to swallow. But initially, official opinion saw discussions aimed at closer economic co-operation in Europe as a sideshow. The Cabinet Economic Section, headed by Robert Hall and supported by Brook, argued that a study of the implications for Britain of greater European integration, as proposed by Bevin, would take up too much time and resource.[279] The Colonies, the Dominions and the United States were thought to be: 'very much more important for us, as markets, as sources of supply and as trade rivals. Strategically, too, we might hesitate to become economically too dependent on an area which we might not possess the ability to defend in time of war.'[280] At the same time, however, Attlee was being briefed against continued assisted emigration to the Dominions because of domestic manpower shortages.[281]

A three-way tug of war was developing between the military need to stay close to the Americans, the cultural undertow of 'kith and kin' in the Dominions and slow recognition that the economic strength required to finance Britain's aspirations as an, albeit second rank, world power was increasingly dependent on European links. The Soviet response to the Truman doctrine was a visible readjustment of foreign policy by which collaboration with non-Communist bodies (including the Marshall Plan) was terminated. Discussions at the Council of Foreign Ministers on the future of Germany collapsed in December 1947 and subsequent talks between Bevin and Marshall and Bevin and Bidault of France started a process that led to the Brussels Treaty of March 1948 whereby Britain, France and the Benelux countries promised mutual assistance in the case of attack by foreign powers. Convoluted negotiations followed with the Americans to secure a United States commitment to the defence of Western Europe, culminating eventually in the North Atlantic Treaty (NATO) of April 1949 signed by the five Brussels Treaty powers, the United States, Canada, Denmark, Iceland, Italy, Norway and Portugal.

In the months prior to the Brussels Treaty Bevin proposed to Cabinet in January 1948 that in the light of the developing hostility of the Soviet Government Britain should use overseas publicity to expose: 'the true aims of Soviet foreign policy' and explode: 'the myth of the "workers' paradise" in the Soviet Union;' that this publicity should extol the advantages of British Social Democracy; 'that the United Kingdom should make a positive bid for the "spiritual and moral" leadership of western Europe;' and 'that it should be our aim to create some form of political union of western Europe.'[282]

Brook's brief for Attlee was severely critical of the Foreign Secretary's intention to advocate features of the British system, 'which belong peculiarly to the Labour Party.' This, he argued, risked losing the spirit of unity in people of all shades of political opinion who were in support of the government's foreign policy and would alienate public feeling in the United States. (He was married to a successful American literary agent.) Bevin had written: 'we should attack the principles and practice of Communism, and also the inefficiency, social injustice and moral weakness of unrestrained capitalism.'[283] Would it not be better, argued Brook, to lay the main emphasis on civil liberties, human rights and social and political justice and to position the United Kingdom mid-way between Europe and the USA? The UK was undeniably economically dependent on the US 'with whom the economic power now rests,' but 'it is certainly true that [the UK] has a political contribution to make, especially in view of the political and administrative immaturity of the United States. We have already shown, in the discussions on Marshall Aid in Paris and Washington, that we can assume the leadership among the European claimants to Marshall Aid ... can we not exploit still further this position as an intermediary – by ranging ourselves by the side of the United States as her primary assistant in organising the economic recovery of Europe?' A subservient economic position to the United States was no more than recognition of the economic facts and might allow the United Kingdom to, 'bring our greater political sagacity more effectively to bear in adjusting American policies and thereby achieve the political and spiritual leadership of Europe at which the Foreign Secretary aims?'[284] It was a position that foreshadowed Churchill's attempts to recreate the wartime intimacy with the USA and advance a positioning of Britain as the link in interlocking circles of foreign policy between the USA, the Commonwealth and Europe.

Later in 1948 an interdepartmental study group created by Cabinet[285] reported that a Commonwealth Customs Union (first suggested by Bevin in a speech at the TUC Conference in Southport on 3 September 1947) was politically impracticable, as other Commonwealth countries would regard it as an attempt to keep them in permanent economic subordination.[286] The group also concluded that, whilst moves towards a European Customs Union would probably end in full economic union and that would further complicate the British position, the United Kingdom should continue to participate in study of the possibility. Brook expressed concern that Cabinet could be drifting into a European union because of a lack of clarity about ends and means, combined with the practice of taking decisions piecemeal. On 11 and 20 February 1948 he pointed out that discussions with France and Benelux countries towards a defence pact implied movement to western union and required a publicity and propaganda effort in the country.[287] It was not until October 1950 that the British delegation to the group studying a European Customs Union was given a firm instruction that the UK saw no prospect of participation in the foreseeable future.[288]

It was not the case, however, that the British and the Americans saw eye to eye over the strategic future of Europe as a buffer against possible Soviet expansion. In December 1948 American plans for development of the Anglo-American zone in Berlin were submitted unilaterally to the OEEC (which had been founded in April to co-ordinate activities under the Marshall Plan) without consultation with the British, who judged that the plans were both unrealistic and against British interests.[289] The French too were reportedly alarmed at the scope of US plans for the economic viability of Germany.[290] However, Brook warned that deep differences of opinion in Cabinet over what should be the British negotiating position were irreconcilable and would weaken the British position.[291] There was a wide divergence of view between the Cabinet Committee charged with examining proposals for closer European union and the Foreign Office. The Committee interpreted the general feeling in Europe as in favour of a European Assembly chosen by the various domestic legislative chambers, free to set its own agenda. Bevin and the Foreign Office were prepared to block such a development, in favour of members nominated by governments, with discussion limited to matters placed before it by the Committee of Ministers of the Council of Europe.

The following month Brook briefed against American proposals to permit 167 out of 381 German industrial plants, scheduled as part of reparations, to be retained in Germany because, 'The retention ... would materially increase the war potential of a united Germany or a power occupying Western Germany ... which may jeopardise our future security.'[292] Later in the year the three Western Occupying Powers (France, the UK and the USA) agreed to a merger of the zones they controlled to form the independent Federal Republic of Germany on 23 May 1949. The Russians retaliated by creating the satellite German Democratic Republic (GDR) in October.

The question of how far Britain should participate in European ambitions came to a head in May 1950 when Robert Schuman came to London to argue for Britain to join the plans for a European Coal and Steel Community (ECSC). The Attlee Government supported putting control of heavy German industry into the Schuman plan but gave no indication of the longer-term implications of that move[293] and formally rejected UK participation in the ECSC in June, six months before the end of Marshall Aid receipts. Shortly before, there were two days of Ministerial debate in preparation for 'Fundamental Discussions with the United States.' Brook offered handling advice in the light of disagreements between Sir Stafford Cripps and his colleagues during the opening discussions.[294] Cripps had said that 'we should aim at freeing ourselves from the political and economic hegemony of the United States, and look forward to the day when we could lead a "Third Force" which would stand mid-way between American capitalism and

Russian Communism.' Brook thought this inconsistent with Cripps' acceptance, also during the day, of a close partnership with the United States in economic matters and reminded Attlee that the Economic Policy Committee had discussed and discarded the 'Third Force' concept in favour of an 'Atlantic Community' on 7 July the preceding year.[295] Attlee barely needed a reminder. In his memoirs he wrote that Europe was a collection of disunited elements trying to create some form of federation but: 'Without Britain such a grouping would not be strong enough to hold its own. On the other hand Britain has never regarded itself as just a European power. Her interests are worldwide. She is the heart of a great Commonwealth and tends to look outwards from Europe, though maintaining a close interest in all that goes on in that Continent.'[296] Additionally, as Brook pointed out, Cripps feared that plans to create a standing body of 'Deputies' under NATO would transfer economic power away from Britain (i.e. the Treasury) and that rumours that, when Marshall Aid ended, the continuing work of the OEEC might transfer to NATO could mean the Foreign Office intended to try to take over the international economic work of the Treasury.

Brook argued that 'Now that NATO is established under General Eisenhower and the Americans play a direct role in European councils we should use the opportunity of European Defence Integration to recapture the leadership of Europe in the period 1947–50, won during Marshall Aid but lost with its ending and with the emergence of 'Schumania' which we opposed.'[297]

The Commonwealth

Known as a staunch supporter of the Commonwealth, it is appropriate to ask whether Brook thought that the Commonwealth was a viable alternative to closer economic association with Europe. It seems likely that there was a conflict between his head and his heart. Thus, he offered no comment when Edwin Plowden reported in May 1948 on the prospects for colonial development[298] though a month later, in the light of the EPC conclusion that the prospect of a Commonwealth Customs Union was likely to upset Canada, the United States and the colonies, he offered the view that, ultimately, Britain would not join the European movement because of Commonwealth interests.[299] In mid July, in preparation for a Ministerial discussion of consultation procedures with the Commonwealth, he reported that steps to make the Commonwealth a more effective world force were failing. No progress had been made on the co-ordination of defence policy. Whilst the mechanisms were in place for technical cooperation, there was no continuity in political discussion of defence aims. By contrast, he pointed out, the Foreign Office and the State Department were in daily communication. Contacts with Commonwealth governments were both more remote and more intermittent; information flowed from the mother country but consultation was far more limited – dealing in the main with questions of special interest to Commonwealth countries rather than with forging unity of purpose – which 'can only be built up on constant contact and exchange of views on the daily developments in international affairs.' So he advocated standing arrangements for the exchange of views on long-term economic planning, defence and foreign policy. But only the Minister of Defence (Alexander) supported the idea; the Foreign Secretary and the Commonwealth Relations Secretary were strongly opposed on the grounds that the suggestion was 'impracticable.' Attlee summed up against him: the proposal for standing arrangements covering defence and foreign affairs (i.e. the heart of the matter if the Commonwealth was to be a political force in the United Nations) should not be accepted, but closer consultations on long-term economic planning might be pursued.[300]

A year later Brook had to report that a scheme conceived during the war to use land in Tanganyika to produce groundnuts had been a terrible mistake. In January 1948 he had submitted a mainly factual brief on the scheme with just a hint of likely trouble to come,[301] but by November the following year the scheme was clearly a disaster. Following a long series of misjudgements by those working on the project and serious mishaps, costs had risen from £24 million to £48 million, there had been a reduction in scope from 3,210,000 acres to just 600,000 and a lengthening of the time before harvesting from 1952–53 to 1953–54.[302] There was no satisfactory alternative, he advised, to coming clean and admitting to failure. Whilst by no means representative of the Commonwealth as a whole, the episode seemed to illustrate the naivety of hoping to drive an economic miracle from the mother country.

In all of this it seems most likely that Brook was primarily interested in the political and social development of Commonwealth countries and in their political relationship with the mother country. 'I want to be involved in any talks to consider constitutional changes in Commonwealth countries,' he told Attlee in July 1948,[303] relishing challenges such as devising a constitution for an independent Gold Coast that satisfied the nationalists yet left ultimate power in British hands.[304] He rejected a suggestion that the Foreign Office should take over from the Commonwealth Relations Office on the grounds that 'Such a development would not be acceptable to public opinion in this country, which is insistent that the Cabinet should include a senior Minister who can voice the interests of the Commonwealth. Nor would it be consistent with the special nature of the relationship between the self-governing members of the Commonwealth.'

Shortly after the ad hoc Ministerial meeting on greater Commonwealth cohesion of July 1948 Brook left for a tour of Canada, Australia and New Zealand to gauge their views on how the Commonwealth should accommodate the independence of India and Pakistan. (The intention was to put forward informal proposals at an October meeting of Commonwealth Heads of Government.) The thrust of his report was a more formal recognition of two-tier Commonwealth membership – deriving from unease about the advent of new members whose outlook was so different from that of the old members and determination that nothing should weaken the ties between the older members. The solution was to develop new methods of consultation between individual Commonwealth countries or between three or four of them and to place less emphasis on meetings of representatives of all Commonwealth countries where the modern view was that 'all countries of the Commonwealth are on an equality'. As a minimum, membership should require recognition of the Crown in respect of external affairs. There was an opportunity, he briefed, to legislate to allow India to remain in the Commonwealth by changing 'colony' to 'overseas territory' and by defining 'Dominion' and 'British subjects' better – but there was no great enthusiasm amongst British officials to do so.[305] The following year Brook opposed proposals to allow the deportation of non-British Commonwealth citizens because, he argued, the right of entry and abode in the mother country is 'the one solid benefit attaching to the possession of British Nationality ... we have not by any means excluded the possibility that, as time goes on, "Commonwealth citizenship" will emerge but in the meantime Cabinet should not tie the hands of the Home Secretary on naturalisation policy.'[306] Meanwhile he supported the development of native-born administrators through the Colonial Civil Service.[307]

Then at the end of January 1950 there was more political trouble. The South African Government advised London not to appoint Seretse Khama as chief of the Bamengwato Tribe in Bechuanaland. Brook did not want to accept this advice, on the grounds that a judicial enquiry had said, '[Seretse Khama] is admittedly the lawful and legitimate heir and, save for his unfortunate marriage [to a white woman], would be in our opinion, a fit and proper person to assume the chieftainship.' But Cabinet decided to postpone the decision for a number of years and then struggled as the Secretary of State for Commonwealth Relations (Patrick Gordon-Walker) wavered over whether, during this period, Seretse Khama would be excluded from the Bamengwato tribal Reserve or the whole Protectorate. Brook first argued that whatever decision was taken the less said about it the better, adding, 'It is most unfair to some successive Government to pile up a lot of troubles and make no effort to think through the probable course of future events.'[308] Later, however, whilst maintaining this position, he stressed that in view of the likely public criticism of the Government's decision, 'If the Cabinet now take any account of South African views they must, I suggest, be prepared to admit in public discussion that they have allowed these considerations to influence their decision.'[309]

Defence

A Defence White Paper of 1946 made clear that, in continuance of the arrangements from Churchill's wartime coalition, 'The Prime Minister will retain the supreme responsibility for Defence.'[310] However, policy – defined as the 'business of preparing the nation for war' – would be the responsibility of the eight-strong Cabinet Defence Committee (DO)[311] chaired by the Prime Minister with terms of reference:

> 'To discuss defence questions and to keep the Defence situation as a whole constantly under review so as to ensure that defence preparations and plans, and the expenditure thereupon, are co-ordinated and framed to meet policy,

> and that full information as to the changing naval, military and air situation is always available.'[312]

Members of DO were the Minister of Defence, the Lord President, the Foreign Secretary, the Chancellor of the Exchequer, the Minister of Labour and National Service, and the three Service Ministers. The Chiefs of Staff, the professional leaders of the three armed services, were not members but attended meetings and retained their right of direct access to the Prime Minister. Typically the Committee met twice a month, sometimes with Brook as secretary and sometimes with Cabinet Office Secretariat staff in that role (notably Lt. General Sir Leslie Hollis and W S Murrie, Brook's deputy). The planning and intelligence staffs that supported the Chiefs were transferred from the Cabinet Office (where they had resided during the war) to the Ministry. The Minister of Defence had no departmental responsibility for the three armed services, whose Ministers (as Secretaries of State) outranked him but, unlike him, were not members of Cabinet. It was an unstable muddle deriving from practice during the Second World War.

At the outset of the Attlee Government Brook was unhappy about the organisation of the Ministry of Defence. He proposed that Attlee should centralize ministerial responsibility, change the title of the War Office and remove the status of Secretary of State from the Service Ministers.[313] The 1946 White Paper was a significant step towards centralization leaving the Minister of Defence, in Brook's description, responsible for the: allocation of resources between the three Services; encouraging convergence in policies between the Services and for running inter-service organisations such as medicine, chaplaincy, education, and welfare. He did not think that a further extension of central executive power was required.[314] However, not all Defence officials were so taken with the reorganization. Sir Maurice Dean (a Deputy Secretary in the Ministry) wrote to Brook complaining that, 'Before the war there were three Ministries dealing with defence. Now there are five. This is an unwelcome (and I personally think unnecessary) complication.'[315]

Successive discussions with the senior defence personnel proved inconclusive. It was common ground that the Service Ministers should look to the Minister of Defence for leadership and should ensure co-operation with him. There was also general agreement that after the General Election, due in 1950, the Prime Minister ought to fill the respective Ministerial defence posts with individuals who would sign up to the new arrangements. But in other respects there was no common ground. Sir Henry Tizard (chairman of the Defence Research Policy Committee) wanted the demarcation spelt out forcefully – others thought it impracticable at this time. Brook and Dean tried to paper over the cracks by making it a long-term goal for the Minister of Defence to be supreme in all respects. But this was opposed by Air Marshal Elliot (Chief Staff Officer to the Chiefs of Staff) and by Sir Harold Parker (the Permanent Secretary of the Ministry and Dean's superior).[316] As a result, the brief for the incoming Prime Minister (once again Attlee) fudged the recommendation: 'The Minister [of Defence] could exercise more high-level supervision and authority, while leaving the execution of policy to the Service Ministers ... All that is needed is to emphasise rather more, in the new Administration, the position of leadership which you wish the Minister of Defence to assume in relation to the Service Ministers – who should be ready to work together as a team, recognising the Minister of Defence as the captain of the team and accepting his leadership.'[317]

During the first Attlee Cabinet, with AV Alexander as Minister of Defence, it was the Prime Minister himself who exercised a dominant influence over defence policy. He attended most meetings of the Defence Committee. He consulted freely with the Chiefs of Staff (COS), frequently chairing what were described as 'staff conferences' but were, in fact, COS meetings and played a leading part during defence debates in the House of Commons. After the 1950 General Election the new Minister was Emanuel Shinwell, whose relationship with Attlee was never easy, and the resignation of Hugh Dalton in 1947 combined with the deaths of Bevin and Cripps left only Attlee and Herbert Morrison, of the 'Big Five' who had dominated the Labour government in its earlier years. Shinwell was now a formidable Minister – in personality, experience and Parliamentary ability. Then the resignations from Cabinet of Bevan and Harold Wilson early in 1951 made Shinwell's support even more important to Attlee.

Brook's distinctive contribution was on organisational issues. In keeping with this, as an interlocutor for the government as a whole, in June 1950 he was appointed chairman of the Atlantic (Official) Committee charged with framing instructions for the Foreign Secretary to send to the UK member of the North Atlantic Council.[318] When called upon to brief for Cabinet or DO his tendency was to dismiss idealism, demolishing arguments for the international control of atomic weapons[319] or promoting the deterrent effects of Mutually Assured Destruction (MAD).[320] But when Dalton and Cripps challenged the cost of atomic weapons in October 1946[321] there is no record of him intervening.

His vision was that the Ministry was a staff organisation serving a group of Cabinet committees, similar to 'interdepartmental committees assisted by a relatively small central staff organised as a Secretariat.'[322] But the various relationships were far from smooth. At the time of the 1951 Defence White Paper Parker described defence policy as conducted in a state 'nearer to war and further from peace' than had been hoped in 1946.[323] Although interdepartmental committees, including a new Defence (Transition) Committee (chaired by Brook) had been created to ensure action by those involved in preparing the nation for war, there was a fundamental problem. Brook identified it in a memorandum to Parker: committees could not take administrative action, that fell to the Service Departments whose Ministers were directly responsible to Parliament for those actions. He returned to this issue in February 1951 when he pointed out that though a relatively junior Cabinet Minister could exercise a coordinating influence (for example over 'progressing' the defence production programme, which touched a number of departments), the same was not true of the Permanent Secretaries. Brook's proposal, therefore, was to appoint W R Vernon-Smith, Assistant Managing Director of the Bristol Aeroplane Co Ltd (then aged 38), who was already a member of the Government Economic Planning Board, as full-time chairman of the Joint War Production Committee. Committees did, however, take decisions of policy and these were the collective responsibility of the government as a whole, for which the interdepartmental committee chairman (even if the Minister of Defence) had no individual constitutional responsibility. Thus, a structure intended for peacetime and for preventing war by preparing for it, might not work well when there was a limited conflict such as in Korea, or diplomatic and military tension such as in Berlin in 1948.

Halting the Spread of Communism

In parallel to worries about penetration on the home front, the spread of Communism internationally was a worry to senior Whitehall figures. Having attended the Potsdam Conference in 1945 Brook was well aware of Russian ambitions and tactics. North Korea and Czechoslovakia went Communist in 1948 and not long after Britain's 1947 decision to suspend military and economic aid to Greece and Turkey,[324] President Truman in the United States proclaimed a policy of containment '[to] support free people who are resisting subjugation by armed minorities or outside pressures ... primarily through economic and financial aid.' In Britain Brook supported the collection of material 'to project in the most effective manner our treatment of Colonial peoples';[325] but when Marshal of the Royal Air Force Sir John Slessor, Commandant of the Imperial Defence College, used an early despatch to call for more effective machinery to combat Communism abroad[326] Brook supported the Foreign Secretary, Bevin, who preferred to remit the issue to a group of 'wise men.' Brook told the Foreign Office Permanent Under-Secretary (the newly appointed Strang) about an ad hoc committee, GEN 231, set up by Attlee to promote counter-Communist propaganda.[327] But Brook was not persuaded of the need to match the American eagerness to oppose the Eastern bloc. In December 1948 he had intervened in a dispute between Bevin and Cripps about economic policy towards Eastern Europe, arguing '... we cannot afford to neglect any opportunity to deploy our trade on reasonable terms with the great food and raw material producing areas of Eastern Europe [since] the achievement of economic recovery must continue to be the principal concern of Western Europe for some years to come [and] the overriding need is to develop sources of supply outside the Western Hemisphere.' 'The threat of war is not yet sufficiently imminent to justify the adoption of a policy which might prejudice that development.'[328]

The 'wise men' were assembled under Gladwyn Jebb of the Foreign Office in late May 1949. Jebb had been severely critical of the Truman doctrine, which he believed threatened the prospects for disarmament and international co-operation on economic aid.[329] Brook received the first report from the group (a description of Communist penetration in the world) in August, followed by recommendations in early November.[330] Bridges (now PUS at the Treasury) saw them as 'rather difficult.'[331] 'The Home Office, the natural lead department for any anti-Communist activities, refused to be part of the domestic campaign as they felt that they, and the Police, must continue to show a strict impartiality as between

Communists and members of other political Parties. Bridges concluded that 'A house so divided against itself would not, I think, stand long.' Ministers would not feel that the time was right to set up an organisation to combat Communism at home. Brook agreed that it would be inexpedient to make changes in domestic policy before the General Election (due by July 1950) but thought that such reticence need not apply overseas: restrictions on subversive propaganda to Communist-controlled countries and on seeking to provoke others into such actions should be removed and an official committee set up to co-ordinate anti-Communist activities overseas.[332] On 19 December GEN 231 was converted to the Ministerial Committee on Communism, chaired by the Prime Minister and shadowed by an official committee, which Jebb chaired. The Ministerial committee reported to the Cabinet Defence Committee and the existence of both was kept secret. A similar proposal for action on the home front was, as recommended by Brook and Bridges, rejected, though in 1950 positive vetting was successfully introduced for civil servants in the most sensitive posts.

Shortly after the second report from the Jebb group the Communist rebels, led by Mao Zedong, took power in China on 1 October 1949 and the Nationalist leader General Chiang Kai-shek retreated to the island of Formosa. By May 1950 British residents were advised to leave Shanghai with Brook reporting that it was no longer possible to evacuate British residents by ship. He advised Attlee not to go along with the Chiefs of Staff recommendation that the UK should make an immediate declaration that Britain would hold on to Hong Kong in all circumstances. Commonwealth moral support for the UK position (and particularly support from India) would be essential 'All that we need, and can, say at present is that we intend to hold Hong Kong while conditions on the mainland continue to be unsettled.'[333] Later, whilst agreeing that it was inopportune to discuss the future of Hong Kong with the Chinese authorities Brook was equally keen to avoid giving a hostage to fortune by saying that the UK would never hand the colony over to a Communist regime – as was proposed by the Foreign and Colonial Secretaries (Bevin & Griffiths).[334]

The outbreak of the Korean War on 25 June 1950 when the Communist North Korea invaded the non-Communist South brought the position of Hong Kong more into contention; especially when, on 24 November 1950, some 250,000 Chinese troops crossed the Yalu river in support of North Korea, forcing General MacArthur's troops back south of the 38th Parallel (the original boundary between North and South Korea). Brook had briefed Attlee for a meeting of the Cabinet Defence Committee (DO) on the implications of the war for wider British interests in the Far East, arguing that intelligence that China would attack Formosa & Hong Kong should be 'treated with great reserve.'[335] His speaking note for Attlee for Cabinet on 17 July stressed the importance of localising the Korean conflict and avoiding a Chinese attack on Formosa,[336] though the British privately assumed that Formosa would revert to China in due course.[337] He also argued, however, that 'It is one thing to say … that if Communist China had been admitted to the United Nations [as Britain had wanted] and taken her place on the Security Council, she might have been more likely to act responsibly in relation to Korea … It is not, however, the same thing to say now that we ought to press for China's admission to the United Nations, despite her intervention in Korea.' The policy should be held in abeyance.[338]

Meanwhile, the Cabinet Office Defence Secretariat voiced concerns that a lack of consistency in American policy and their unwillingness to consult other powers had led to blunders and suspicion.[339] (A contention borne out in November when the United States bombed power stations close to the Yalu River border between North Korea and China without consultation with its allies, thereby, in British eyes at least, seriously increasing the risks in the conflict.) Furthermore, the risks seemed to worsen: at the end of the month a statement by President Truman, at a press conference, was widely interpreted as a readiness to use the atomic bomb. In much of British public opinion and on both sides of the House of Commons there was consternation. 100 Labour MPs signed a letter to Attlee critical of the presidential statement and early in December the Prime Minister went to Washington for talks aimed at a number of improvements to collaboration between the United States and Britain, notably to resurrect the wartime agreement for British participation in any American decision to use nuclear weapons. Brook was not part of the Attlee team travelling to Washington, which was military and diplomatic; the resulting communiqué did not mention an undertaking to consult but the British believed that one had been given, contrary to the Americans who argued that the initial statement by Truman that the British were quoting had been rescinded. Professor Margaret Gowing's official history *Independence and Deterrence* concluded 'Once more the atomic promise of a President of the United States to a Prime Minister was being broken …'[340] The US National Security Archive confirms this with a memorandum for the record by Special Assistant to the Secretary of State R Gordon Arneson which says 'Arneson's description of the [Truman-Attlee] meeting and the enclosures record Truman's personal commitment to Atlee (sic), the process by which Truman and his advisers tried to withdraw it, and the British refusal to accept a change in the meeting record.'[341] It is unlikely that even the administrative skills of Brook could have found a way forward through this thicket.

In a terse opening paragraph the communiqué following the Attlee/Truman talks said that 'The military capabilities of the United States and the United Kingdom should be increased as rapidly as possible.' *The Times* summed up the position as 'The years 1950–51 will go down to history as the years in which a Labour Government … concluded that Britain could not enjoy social security without national security.'[342] The burdens on Britain grew. The defence budget tripled; increased by £100 million for 1951/52. In September 1950 conscription for adult males was increased to 24 months. Two months later the government, under US pressure, agreed to contribute up to £12 million of economic aid to Korea – 15% of the total with the US contributing 65% and the rest of the UN 20%.[343] Brook prepared the speaking note for Attlee to announce to Cabinet that the UK was accelerating the pace of defence preparations. On 18 December Cabinet agreed to 'increase and accelerate our defence preparations still further,' inviting the Chiefs of Staff to consider what form the increase should take.[344]

As 1951 started, the North Koreans pushed the UN forces 100 miles below the 38th Parallel. The Americans were pressing for a United Nations Resolution to condemn Chinese aggression. The British opposed this move since they believed that the dispute must eventually be settled through negotiation with the Chinese. But at the same time the military situation had to be stabilised as a precursor to negotiation, so Cabinet agreeing to seek Commonwealth support for a position advocating no general withdrawal of UN forces from Korea and no branding of China as an aggressor nation. Cabinet discussed the position three times, with a majority in favour of voting against the US Resolution to show what the United Kingdom really thought and to demonstrate an independence that would make the US more likely to listen to British views in future.[345] Nevertheless, at the third discussion, on 29 January, it was agreed that the UK delegation at the UN should support a revised and watered down text from the Americans. Also at this third meeting there were further complaints about General MacArthur, on account of a reference to 'freeing Asia,' and Brook's minutes of the Cabinet Defence Committee on 9 May went further: 'It was pointed out in discussion that at least some of the directives which governed General MacArthur's actions had never been seen by HMG. A situation was now arising in which British Forces were being commanded by a General in whom we had no confidence and who appeared to be trying to involve us in a war with China, contrary to our accepted policy.'[346]

As for rearmament, the newly appointed Minister of Labour (Aneurin Bevan who had been moved from the Ministry of Health) was disposed to question the intelligence agencies' estimates of Soviet military strength, arguing that weaknesses in Soviet steel production precluded their conduct of a long war. All that was needed was sufficient Western rearmament to prevent being knocked out in the first round of conflict. Whilst Brook accepted the argument that current Soviet capability could not sustain a prolonged war he pointed out that if the Soviets could overrun the Federal Republic of Germany they would acquire the productive potential of the Ruhr and Western readiness for opposition to a potential first strike was far from complete, leaving the Western powers dangerously exposed. In Brook's view, the intelligence estimates were based on a wide range of sources and had been subjected to careful comparison and cross-checking. He encouraged Attlee to cross examine the chairman of the JIC (Patrick Reilly of the Foreign Office) and of the Joint Intelligence Bureau (Major General K.W.D. Strong) so that he could tell Cabinet that he had satisfied himself that the proposals were based on a serious appreciation of the position.[347] And in an extensive handling brief Brook advised first concentrating on the proposed scale of the defence and civil defence proposals from the Chiefs of Staff, suggesting a general discussion that would allow the Minister of Labour to raise his objections and the Chancellor (Gaitskell) to discuss their affordability. Unusually, he suggested that the Prime Minister should set a time limit (11.00 am) for that aspect of the discussion and then turn to the detail, which he further suggested would not be affected even if Ministers had concluded that the burdens of extra spending would be too large. (The Treasury had already voiced concerns in the autumn of 1950 about the damaging effect on the economy of proceeding with the full defence programme without, or with little, aid from America.)[348] The conclusion to be sought, he recommended, was for Cabinet to have the authority to use direct methods of economic control to whatever extent became necessary as general financial assistance from the USA was both unlikely and would be too restraining on the United Kingdom's political independence: 'We have certainly been in a better position to assert our political independence, and to bring some influence to bear on United States policies, since we ceased to receive Marshall Aid.' The supply of specific equipment from the USA was, however, a different matter and should be sought on the basis of repayment in kind rather than in scarce dollars.[349]

But there had been no declaration of war. The Foreign Office recommended that the Korean War should be a new class of military activity, 'collective police action.'[350] Brook was far from convinced. The idea of UN military action as 'collective police actions' rather than war was fraught with unresolved questions: (1) it might need UK legislation to put into the black and white of domestic law the theoretical conceptions of the international lawyers; (2) a vast body of rights and obligations had been built up in conditions of war – in collective police action against a country with which the UK had commercial and other links there could be a good deal of confusion about public and private rights and duties; (3) would there be one UN force or a force of allies acting under one supreme commander?[351]

A further consequence of the necessary focus on Korea was that the actions of the official committee on Communism were cautious: by the end of the first year of operation proposals for propaganda behind the iron curtain (to be carried out in full co-operation with the Americans) were limited in scope and seen to be in the nature of an experiment; and proposals to prevent BBC broadcasts to Eastern Europe being jammed were held up in discussion with the Treasury.[352] After agreeing the case for a briefing quarry on rearmament in February 1951 the Ministerial Committee did not meet again during the Attlee Government and was not recreated under Churchill. Its official shadow survived but struggled to command attention.[353]

Preparing for the Worst

Since 1947 Brook had been engaged in a labour that lasted throughout his tenure. Two and a half years after the end of the war, and with deterioration in relations with the Soviet Union, France raised the question of the extent of military support on which they could count in the event of hostilities in Western Europe should the Four-Power Conference of Foreign Ministers on German disarmament break down. The possibility of a treaty that excluded the Soviets was put to Cabinet,[354] and Brook sought permission to overhaul the British machinery for transition to war, casting this in non-threatening terms: 'merely as a matter of official routine ... to make sure the lessons of 1939 are placed on record while the individuals who handled these matters at first-hand are still available.'[355] He proposed a standing official committee of 14 Departments under his own chairmanship, '... which could play a more active role in concerting inter-departmental preparations for war, under the aegis of the [Cabinet] Defence Committee, if the international situation should deteriorate.'

In the first phase of activity (which lasted until April 1951) much of the work was undertaken through the GEN 317 Committee (later the Official Committee on the National Economy in War (N.E.W.)) also chaired by Brook, who drove its agenda. On 21 March 1950 a number of studies were commissioned.[356] In advance Brook had circulated a paper proposing the areas for which planning assumptions would be needed:[357]

Strategic assumptions	Enemies/allies; theatres of operations; dates of peak risk of war; the nature of the attack expected; state of the Armed Forces; the UK as an advanced base of operations or an arsenal of war production; best/worst/most realistic case; what warning will be given?
Essential needs of the civilian population	Percentage of productive capacity to be devoted to non-warlike activities, including Civil Defence
External finance	How to pay for the essential imports of food and raw materials
Import programme	Tonnage of dry cargo and tanker shipping required; need for strategic stocks and import agreements; port and inland transport needs
Industry	The size of the export trade; munitions production; what contraction of civil industrial production and where geographically
Man-power	The distribution of man-power in the first year of war
Internal finance	Taxable capacity; checking inflation
General	To what date should the answers relate?

The studies appeared to have assumed that war with the Soviet Union was inevitable, whereas defence policy increasingly took the prevention of war as its first priority. However, only five years since V-E day it appeared obvious that the lessons of the inter-war years for military preparedness must be learned and planning was to be undertaken on the basis of an arbitrary total of 22 atomic bombs dropped on British ports and cities.[358] A report on the effects of the assumed air attacks was circulated on 6 November 1950 and discussed two weeks later.[359] There was some progress in assessing the effects of an attack on specimen target areas in Britain and on manpower planning. But talks with the Americans on the international supply organisation that would be required and on financing a future war had been inconclusive. It was clear that dry cargo shipping would be inadequate for the required level of imports and work was needed to estimate the industrial disruption required to build up stocks of war-like material until wastage (a euphemism for destruction) could be met from current production. Despite a dissenting voice from Sir Frank Lee of the Ministry of Food who queried whether the studies encouraged over-insurance, two further new studies were commissioned from the Treasury Economic Section and the Central Statistical Office: these covered the essential needs of the civilian population and estimates of internal finance (the reserve of taxable capacity; how to check inflation, and what assumptions could be made about the nature of wages policy during a future war). It was confirmed that plans should continue to be based on war in 1957 and on a general air attack rather than an attempt to second-guess Soviet targeting systems.

The Joint Intelligence Committee (JIC), meanwhile, had concluded that there were serious flaws in the estimates it had prepared on the vulnerability of the UK to a knock-out blow by the Soviet Union and withdrew its assessment (as many as 100 copies of documents based on the JIC report were thought to be in circulation). The JIC re-tasked the assessment staff in the Joint Intelligence Organisation to report on the 'scale and nature of strategic air attack on the United Kingdom and the target systems most likely to be selected, for the years 1951 and 1954.'[360] Brook resisted attempts to ask the Chiefs of Staff to give a single authoritative estimate of the scale and direction of air attack, arguing that 'We have always agreed in the N.E.W. Committee that we must proceed by trial and error … [including] If these reports from Departments show that it is impossible for the life of the country to continue effectively under the estimated scale of attack, then – odd as it may seem – we shall have to look again at the assumption about the scale of attack.'[361] But by January 1951 some sectors, such as fuel and power, were struggling to handle general assumptions about the nature of an attack and started examination of the damage likely to be sustained from a more precise (though still assumed) pattern of attack.[362]

In April 1951, as the policy emphasis shifted towards the need for conventional rearmament in the face of the localised Korean War, the N.E.W. Committee was subsumed partly into a re-energised Defence (Transition) Sub-Committee and partly into the Economic Steering Committee. The focus shifted to preparations for war. But 16 months later N.E.W. was revived, to focus on civil defence. Brook summarised progress as at April 1951 and this serves as a good checkpoint at the end of the Attlee administration. There had been no progress in relation to financial negotiations with the United States even though 'It is clear … that unless we got very substantial financial help, or some pooling arrangement in a future war, our war effort would quickly run down simply because we would be unable to pay for our imports.'[363] Preliminary soundings in Washington by Robert Hall had indicated that it would be unwise to try for more than informal technical discussions of these issues with the Americans and that there was a tricky balance to be struck in disclosing British assumptions about the likely manner of attack without the Americans concluding that it was unsound to put many assets in the UK because of the risk of early elimination during a future conflict.[364] Not only that, the deficiency between the manpower needed to meet NATO commitments and to produce the weapons etc. needed by the armed forces was so large 'as to make a nonsense of any attempts to plan the civil economy.' In short, in the event of war the United Kingdom would not be a going concern.

Furthermore, as Brook had advised Attlee in July 1951, there was no guarantee that the enemy might not open the next war with a clandestine atomic attack on London on the model of the Japanese attack on Pearl Harbour. It would be practicable for the Russians to do so and there were no certain methods of preventing this – but it was legitimate to ask why the Russians would bother to adopt elaborate clandestine methods when a simple military aircraft attack might do the job more effectively. Hence, he argued, 'I am very doubtful whether the increased security which might be obtained by adopting any of these [preventative measures which the Chiefs of Staff wanted examined] could outweigh the very serious disadvantages, political and economic, which would be entailed.' Attlee agreed to discuss the issue further with the Foreign Secretary and Minister of Defence but this could not be arranged before the election at which the Labour government was defeated.[365] At about the same time a Cabinet document had to be withdrawn because it revealed that work on the London South Bank Site was, 'an extension of providing heavily protected accommodation for the nucleus of Government in time of war'.[366]

What this planning exercise did not attempt to address, however, was anything short of total atomic war with the Soviet Union. The international situation was deteriorating in a different but also a dangerous way. Between 8 April 1948 when the Russians imposed restrictions on travel by the land corridor between the Federal republic of Germany and Berlin, and 12 May 1949 when the blockade was lifted defence preparations were exposed by a Russian blockade of transport communications between West Germany and the four-power enclave of Berlin, situated well inside the then Russian zone of Germany (later to become East Germany). The blockade was lifted by a massive airlift of supplies by the Western Powers. The British flew 175,000 sorties during the airlift and transported 542,000 tons of supplies (42% of the total)[367] in an operation codenamed PLAINFARE. The Chiefs of Staff were at pains throughout to ensure that Attlee and the political leadership were aware of the acute limitations on British military capability. Brook played a very limited part in the discussions, confined to setting up an ad hoc group on the crisis (GEN 241), in effect, a sub-committee of the Cabinet Defence Committee.[368] Although the Prime Minister chaired both the GEN group and the Defence Committee, Brook effectively left the main secretarial position to W. S. Murrie, who was on secondment from the Home Office to the Cabinet Secretariat. Further, in August and September 1948 Brook was absent when Cabinet discussed the emergency because he was travelling to the Commonwealth Dominions to gauge their reactions to Indian independence. It was during this crisis that the question arose of basing American B29 bombers in Britain – the British Ambassador in Washington conveyed approval for this on 1 July 1948, despite being warned of potential political difficulties and Attlee insisted that the issue came to the Defence Committee before Parliament reassembled in the autumn of 1948.[369]

Towards the end of the Berlin crisis attention turned back to the aftermath of World War II because of a difference in interpretation of a Cabinet discussion about how to handle four German Generals accused of war crimes. Unlike the former Cabinet Secretary, Hankey, who opposed the war trials, Brook cut through the debate, arguing that a proposal from the Secretary of State for War that as two of the Generals (Feldmarshal Gerd von Runstedt and Generaloberst Adolf Strauss) were unfit to stand trial it would be unreliable to try a third (Feldmarshal Erich von Manstein) because von Runstedt would appear for the defence and would claim full responsibility for the crimes committed.[370] Brook argued that the Attorney General should be asked whether an English civil court would judge the two unfit, commenting that, 'In this country accused persons have to be in a very serious physical state before they are relieved from the necessity of standing their trial, particularly in the graver type of offence.' However, his advice did not prevail, the unanimous view of the Lord Chancellor, the Attorney General and Sir Henry Cohen, Director of the Displaced Persons Camp in the American sector of Germany, was that on the medical evidence the officers were unfit to stand trial.

Review of Intelligence

In the spring of 1950 Attlee told Brook that he wanted the intelligence agencies reviewed with special reference to the co-ordination of effort between MI5, MI6 and GCHQ, the distribution of funds between them and ministerial responsibility.[371] Initially Attlee had General 'Pug' Ismay in mind as the reviewer but was persuaded by Bevin (who presumably feared too strong a Defence bias with Ismay) that Brook would be a better choice and that he should be asked to carry out a general review rather than work under tight terms of reference.[372] Unusually, Brook undertook the field work himself, largely based on interviews with senior officers in each agency and with members of the Joint Intelligence Committee (JIC) though C.A.L. Cliffe, an Assistant Secretary in the Cabinet Office Secretariat, acted as secretary to the inquiry. Brook told potential interviewees: 'I am trying to devote Friday of each week to this enquiry'. In an age of deference to hierarchy it was unlikely that he would be told much that contradicted the official view as formulated by the Agency Head but, even so, it was limiting that he felt obliged to say, for instance, to Percy Sillitoe (Head of the Security Service) 'I wonder whether it would be a good idea if I began by meeting your heads of sections, with you, and hearing from each of them an account of their operations,' (emphasis added).

The conclusion of Brook's N.E.W. Committee was that without financial help the UK would not be able to fight another total war and the position in peacetime was not much better. On 20 October 1950 Attlee met with Bevin and Alexander to discuss a putative bid for extra resources for the Secret Intelligence Service (SIS). Its chief (known as 'C' after the first incumbent, Sir Mansfield Cumming), had it in mind to bid for £1.5 million over two years to be ready for total war by 1952. Much of the extra funding would be spent on stores for the Middle East in case of shipping difficulties. There had been discussions between SIS and the Chiefs of Staff on the matter but neither the Foreign Secretary (politically responsible for SIS) nor HM Treasury had been consulted. Brook was already conducting an enquiry into the secret intelligence organisations and warned Attlee that to agree the proposals even in principle would make scrutiny of the detailed spend nigh on impossible and, furthermore, he challenged the whole basis of the bid as 'quite out of scale with our other preparations,' which took 1954 as the target date and were based strategically on the deterrent effects of being prepared for war rather than taking it as inevitable that there would be war. C's service, which by definition was covert, had no deterrent value.[373]

At about the same time, five months into the review of the Agencies, Brook gave Attlee an outline of tentative findings.[374] He felt that it was impracticable to put the Agencies under one individual; better to house MI5 and MI6 together so they could better share information of common interest; but not to separate GCHQ and SIS from responsibility to the Foreign Secretary. He was minded to recommend putting MI5 under the Home Secretary and creating a committee of Permanent Secretaries to review budgets and the allocation of authority to spend. However, no junior Minister should be tasked taking an interest in secret intelligence, since it was convenient for Ministers in peacetime to know as little about covert activities as possible, so that government could disclaim knowledge of them if necessary. Brook continued that to compare the Agencies' performance against wartime operations was unfair. Russia was probably the most difficult target that had ever been set for an intelligence or counter-espionage service. His impression was that, given all the difficulties, a fairly creditable amount of intelligence was being collected but he professed himself less confident that the best use was being made of what was available. GCHQ's budget should be increased, but SIS needed more time rather than more money, as sought by 'C' (Sir Stuart Menzies).

Attlee, Bevin and Alexander discussed the SIS bid for an extra £1.5 million on 20 October, remitting it for further study to a group under a Reilly of the Foreign Office and with Brook, Sir Maurice Dean of the MoD, and Burke Trend who was then at the Treasury. Bevin forwarded its conclusions to Attlee on 16 December. The group had taken oral evidence from 'C'. The original estimate had been shaved by a third and 'C' had persuaded them that an extra £1 million spent over two years would help improve UK-USA intelligence liaison under the new head of the CIA, General Bedell Smith.[375]

Brook's interim conclusions were deepened rather than amended during the remaining four months of investigation.[376] In a report with 27 recommendations, the most important conclusion was that though the JIC was 'seriously concerned about the inadequacy of intelligence on the countries within the Soviet orbit and in particular on Soviet intentions and preparedness for war,' the organisation of intelligence was broadly satisfactory and the budget broadly appropriate.[377] Russia was very difficult to penetrate from scratch – the Foreign Office had ordered SIS to limit operations against Russia whilst she was a wartime ally – 'no spectacular results would be secured by spending substantially more money on the gathering of intelligence ... But, as between the established collection agencies, [GCHQ] seems to be providing a greater volume of valuable information than SIS.' He confirmed a conclusion that there should be no change in Ministerial responsibility for SIS or GCHQ (the latter via SIS where 'C' would retain ultimate responsibility to the Foreign Secretary for both organisations). Were the head of SIS not responsible for GCHQ, he thought, it would be more likely that 'C' would 'allow his people to compromise the sources of [GCHQ's] information,' whereas 'there were occasions during the last war when the head of SIS thought it right to expose his own agents to grave risk of capture rather than protect them by means which might have compromised [GCHQ's] sources.' By contrast, Brook felt that the conclusion of a 1945 review by Sir Findlater Stewart that the Security Service was part of the defence machinery of the country and 'should be responsible to the Prime Minister pending the appointment of a separate Minister of Defence' was simply wrong. The Service had more in common with the Home Office, which had the ultimate constitutional responsibility for 'defending the Realm.' Hence, the Head of MI5 (known as DG) should report on a day-to-day basis to the Home Secretary (from whom, in any case, the Service had to obtain Warrants for 'special measures; – usually the planting of microphones and opening of mail). Finally, to keep the budget allocations in check he repeated the interim finding that there should be a standing committee of Permanent Secretaries under Treasury chairmanship, to scrutinise the annual Estimates in the light of JIC priorities.

Unsurprisingly, the two heads of agencies objected to the tone of the argument (SIS) and the organisational recommendations (MI5). 'C' took great exception to Brook's conclusion that SIS carried a disproportionately heavy administrative overhead where '*officers*' were primarily engaged in organising the collection of intelligence rather than in agent-running and, in particular, to the opinion that 'SIS may be in some danger of becoming too respectable and losing, in the process, some of its former vigour, initiative and enterprise – in short its buccaneering spirit.'[378] In nine pages of comments, DG (Percy Sillitoe) fought against being subject, on a day-to-day basis, to the Home Secretary.[379]

Attlee summoned an ad hoc group of Ministers to give first consideration to the report; this comprised Attlee, Morrison (Foreign Secretary), Shinwell (Defence), Gordon-Walker (Commonwealth) and Chuter Ede (Home Secretary). They met in the Prime Minister's room at the House of Commons at 5.30 pm on 5 June with Brook present to defend his proposals. The main casualty was the suggestion that DG should report to the Home Secretary, abandoned in the light of Sillitoe's opposition and Chuter Ede's lack of appetite for the change. After a brief further discussion all other recommendations were remitted to the Committee of Permanent Secretaries recommended by Brook to supervise the Estimates.[380] This group was formed under Bridges' chairmanship, meeting for the first time on 11 July as GEN 374 and three further times during the year.[381] Other members were Strang (FO), Newsam (HO), Parker (Defence). It endorsed Brook's findings (including the comments about SIS that had provoked Menzies' anger) and devised a subtle work – around whereby DG was to be advised that 'it would be advantageous if Sir Percy Sillitoe acquired the habit of visiting and consulting Sir Frank Newsam more frequently.'[382] In due course, after the

Conservatives under Winston Churchill defeated the Attlee Government at the October 1951 General Election, the original Brook recommendation for DG to report to the Home Secretary was reinstated and formalised as part of the 1952 Maxwell-Fyfe Directive on DG's powers and responsibilities (which updated an earlier Directive of April 1946).[383]

Palestine

The Middle East was an urgent concern, notably the UN mandate to Britain in Palestine. Brook was pragmatic, unsentimental about the Jews, realistic about the Americans and aware of growing Arab nationalism. Cabinet discussed the issue on 15 January 1946 with Brook's brief pointing up 'the strategic importance to the Commonwealth of retaining [the UK's] present position in the Middle East,' politically as a World Power, commercially to safeguard oil supplies. (Consumption of fuel oil, for example, was estimated to grow from one million tons p.a. in early 1947 to six million tons p.a. by the early summer of 1948 as the conversion of industrial plant and railway locomotives to diesel fuel was completed and a similar conversion of the power stations contemplated.) His brief continued: 'we should maintain military forces in Palestine and so that the forces can be used to full advantage we must retain the friendship of the neighbouring Arab peoples.' He judged that it was inevitable that the matter should revert to the United Nations where 'we need to prevent a position where the Soviet Government are supporting the Arab states against us.'

The options, according to Brook, were to establish an independent unitary Palestine in which the Arabs exercised the dominant interest with safeguards provided for the Jewish minority; or establish a provisional plan for an autonomous state, acceptable to the Arabs perhaps 'by including practical assurance of rapid progress towards self-government and independence in a bi-national state comprising Jewish and Arab Provinces and a central government in which Jews and Arabs might come to collaborate.'[384] Ministers favoured a third option – partition – a course which Brook was hesitant to endorse without further study: 'I may give the impression of assuming a "pro-Arab" attitude … but I think it is right that the Cabinet should consider [the] implications [of Partition] before they finally invite the Foreign Secretary to … [seek] a solution on the lines of Partition,' and, ' no-one rates very high the prospects of persuading the Americans.'[385] Meanwhile, noted Brook, Jewish terrorism and illegal Jewish immigration into Palestine were having a punishing effect on the protectorate's finances.[386]

As Britain moved slowly through 1947 towards withdrawal from Palestine and abandonment of the UN mandate (completed at midnight on 14 May 1948 after the UN General Assembly had agreed on 29 November 1947 to partition between Arabs and Jews) Brook continued to analyse the financial repercussions, including advocating openness that Palestine would be excluded from the sterling area so as to protect the international value of the Pound,[387] and pointing up the difficulty of protecting the oil pipelines after withdrawal from the area.[388]

The state of Israel was born as Britain left. The first military conflict between Arabs and Israelis started the following day. Cabinet vetoed sending extra police to help stem the bloodshed and in the minds of would-be political leaders in colonial countries 'Palestine was a declaration. The British would no longer fight to the finish.'[389]

A Further Taste of Things to Come

On 20 March 1951, somewhat unexpectedly, the new Iranian Government of Dr Mossadegh announced that it would nationalise the oil refineries of the British owned Anglo-Iranian Oil Co (AIOC), whose 40-year lease on exploration and refining (at the world's largest oil refinery at Abadan), contributed about £100 million p.a. to the UK balance of payments.[390] This was widely seen in Britain as expropriation of British property. Herbert Morrison had just taken over at the Foreign Office following the death of Bevin and along with the Minister of Defence (Shinwell) was inclined to a show of force. Meanwhile, Cabinet confirmed the strategic importance of the refinery. The minutes of a discussion on 10 May record 'Our strategic decisions in the Middle East were dependent on our ability to maintain our position in Persia.'[391] Throughout the crisis Brook supported Attlee in urging restraint. Thus, in June he warned that it might be necessary to activate Operation MIDGET to evacuate the 4,500 British employees of the Company;[392] and after the UK took its case to the International Court of Justice (ICJ) in The Hague he helped prevent precipitate action, providing a way out for those Ministers who doubted the wisdom of Morrison's attitude by recommending an analysis of the pros and cons of military action, arguing that the risks were political as well as military: the likely Persian Government reactions; the significant risk of an adverse response from the USA, the Commonwealth and domestic Labour voters. Would the Soviets retaliate from the North, he asked. A call-up of reservists would be necessary but would it be understood domestically in the UK when there were already British troops in the Middle East?[393] The Board of Trade warned against imposing economic sanctions on Persia and Ministers considered whether further concessions could be made to keep negotiations going against a background of impending failure. Brook asked (1) should all British AIOC employees be asked to move to Abadan? (2) When should operation MIDGET (now retitled BUCCANEER) to rescue British personnel be activated? (3) How far should economic pressure be brought to bear on Persia? (4) Should Persian holdings of sterling be frozen? (5) Should there be a general statement of the government's intentions?

All but a handful of staff were evacuated from Abadan by 4 October. Dean Acheson would later make a withering assessment of the AIOC Board in a parody of Churchill's famous tribute to the Royal Air Force: 'Never had so few lost so much so stupidly and so fast.'[394] At the time of the 1951 General Election the ICJ case was still outstanding, but in its first year of office the Conservative government of Churchill was confronted with a judgement that the Court had no jurisdiction in the matter.

The End Is Nigh

On 25 October 1951, at a General Election, Labour obtained 48.8% of the vote as against a Conservative share of 48% (but only 295 Labour seats against 321 Conservative). In the words of Christopher Booker, the Labour experiment begun in July 1945 had 'petered out in a grim slog through years of austerity and rationing' It left behind a legacy of regulation and control which were increasingly resented by the private sector and private citizens – complaints that had been recognised by many Ministers but which had been dismissed because the government was too busy to stop and reconsider.

The words that come to mind in considering Brook's relationship with the Attlee Government are diligent, dutiful, controlled, ordered and authoritative. They convey a sense of respectful distance between the civil servants and their masters and that is undoubtedly an important part of the story. But it is not the whole story. It is the contrast with the warmth of Brook's relationship to Churchill, Eden and Macmillan that points up a thoroughly professional and proper relationship to Attlee and his Ministers, but not one to fire a shared passion for reform. Brook's hesitancy over the socialisation of industry, his confidence in interpreting public feeling over capital punishment and his defence of civil liberties at the time of the Korean War all suggest that he wanted to apply the brake to radical policies. His opposition to Bevin's proposed bid for the cultural and spiritual leadership of Europe, which he condemned as politically partisan and likely to alienate a significant proportion of the population, is a further indication of standing apart.

Attlee's Administration was a government for austere times which contained some austere personalities and there is also a tinge of austerity in the stripped-down form of administrative process that Brook pioneered. There is a sense, too, that the personal control that had enabled the grammar school boy to shine in the company of public school colleagues suited his relationship with Ministers. Where there is a sense of affinity with Attlee is in Brook's calmness under pressure, his practical contribution to resisting the spread of Communism and his sense of moral purpose with leadership of the Commonwealth. For Attlee he brought attention to detail, a forensic skill that could disentangle the most complex of administrative knots, and total reliability. For himself, he invested many hours in developing national preparedness for an uncertain nuclear age, adopting this substantive area as one in which he could make his own mark and escape, for a time, into a largely non-partisan therapeutic world.

Churchill Victorious

'*Britain Strong and Free*' was the title of the 1951 Conservative Party election manifesto yet the following three and a half years of Conservative rule under Churchill did not set out to change many of the policies implemented by the preceding Labour administration. The Conservative electoral victory was narrow (a 17-seat overall majority) described by the *News Chronicle* as '[the country] has got rid of a party it does not want in favour of one it does not trust'. In the words of the political historian Vernon Bogdanor, 'The greatest problem faced by the Conservatives was to show that they could govern without putting the clock back, that the Conservative government would not lead to mass unemployment and poor social conditions.'[395] At home Identity Cards were abolished in February 1952, Building Licences went in 1954 but only two nationalisations were reversed (road haulage and iron and steel), austerity rationing continued well into the electoral term (Food Ration Books were withdrawn in 1954) the withdrawal of food subsidies was hotly debated in Cabinet as part of measures to help control civil public expenditure in 1954 and the social housing programme was greatly accelerated at a long-term cost to the economic potential of the country that was largely unrecognised. In defence and foreign affairs there continued to be overseas emergencies whilst government had to adjust to the dramatic increase in the destructive potential from atomic and thermo-nuclear weapons. At the start of the period Britain's world standing was high but built on economic sand and a romantic belief in American generosity to its old ally of the war. Norman Brook's influence grew as Churchill's vigour was sapped (he had recovered from the exhaustion at the end of the war but was 77 years old when he became Prime Minister). A closeness developed which could be construed as occasionally crossing the boundary of political neutrality but Brook's input was mostly organisational rather than substantive policy innovation.[396] The historian of the Conservative Party, John Ramsden, summed up the period after the 1951 electoral victory as: 'What emerged was strikingly unoriginal in terms of pure policy but very successful as party strategy ... a major piece of cosmetic surgery.'[397]

The initial economic situation was bleak. The end of 1951 saw Britain suffering the worst balance of payments deficit since the war with the gold and dollar reserves draining away at the rate of $300 million a month.[398] Inflation associated with the effects of the Korean War on commodity prices (or United Nations police action as the Korean conflict was now designated) had significantly eroded the trade advantage from the 1949 30% sterling devaluation. (Britain's terms of trade were 33% worse in 1951 than they had been in 1938 though the following year this movement was reversed as commodity prices collapsed after the Korean armistice). Industrial relations and productivity were still poor, between 1948 and 1953 British industrial productivity rose by 14% compared to 20% in the USA and in Sweden and 27% in France and the Netherlands.[399] Shortages of coal and steel were holding back industrial production. Basic food was still rationed and for the most part remained so until the mid-1950s. Housing starts had run at an annual average of 200,000 under Labour but the housing programme had not yet made inroads into war damage.

Brook and Bridges presented the Treasury's assessment of the economic predicament to Churchill at his home in Hyde Park Gate the day after the General Election.[400] 'RAB' Butler, as Chancellor of the Exchequer, was given the same bleak message over lunch at the Athenaeum: Britain 'was heading for early bankruptcy unless immediate remedies were employed'[401] and the Chancellor's opening assessment to his colleagues stressed that internationally Britain was exposed.[402] Domestically the light at the end of the tunnel was flickering and threatened to go out, yet by June 1954, and largely due to external good fortune that largely masked the failure to deal with fundamental supply-side problems, *The Economist* verdict on the Churchill years was 'The miracle has happened: full employment without inflation.'

Internationally there was great political sensitivity about the role the Federal Republic of Germany should play in the defence of Western Europe – Brook, for instance, opposed putting a government pamphlet about its rearmament into Post Offices and Ministry of Labour Exchanges[403] – and Cabinet vacillated over the type of German rearmament to be approved. The dominating threat, however, was fear of Soviet expansion across Europe and Communist influence across the world. Speaking in 1946 Churchill had claimed, 'From Stettin in the Baltic to Trieste in the Adriatic, an iron curtain has descended across the continent;' by 1951 a communist insurrection threatened Malaya;[404] the Korean war rested in stalemate; ten days before the British General Election Egypt had renounced the defence treaty that gave Britain a strategic base in the Middle East.

Yet, as Colville recorded, Churchill alone of the world's political leaders was placed by millions of people on a pedestal wearing a halo. His return to power seemed to many to presage the recovery of hopes tarnished by the dismal aftermath of the war.'[405] And though the world had moved on from 1945 he began by trying to recreate the situation as he had left it at the end of the war. One symbol of this nostalgia was the short-lived decision to combine the Premiership with the office of Minister of Defence, (an arrangement that lasted only until the end of February 1952 with the appointment of Field Marshal Lord Alexander as Minister of Defence). A second was the flirtation with 'overlord' ministers to co-ordinate related departments (see below). However, by the end of his life Churchill confided to his Private Secretary 'I could have defended the British Empire against anyone except the [indifference of] the British people;' and to Lord Boothby 'Historians are apt to judge war ministers less by the victories achieved under their direction than by the political results which flowed from them … Judged by that standard, I am not sure that I shall be held to have done very well.' Eighteen months after Churchill's retirement the Suez fiasco brought into new focus a pattern of decline under which, far from being able to defend Britain's world status, the country had become a second ranking power unable to act in the face of American opposition.

Brook had spent the evening of 25 October 1951 at an election night party at the Savoy[406] as the guest of Lord Camrose, newspaper owner and financial benefactor to Churchill.[407] The briefing prepared under Brook's guidance, 'on the assumption that a Conservative government would be formed after the General Election of October 1951'[408] comprised a dozen topics of which Brook took responsibility for three (size and composition of Cabinet; Cabinet Committees; Supervising Ministers). George Mallaby, Brook's civil deputy, defined the then role of the Cabinet Secretary as 'responsible for very complex and very important articulating machinery.'[409] To this Brook added, 'responsibility for ensuring that action is taken on all war plans and preparations not coming within the responsibility of the Minister of Defence or the Home Secretary' and advising the Prime Minister if there were gaps or inconsistencies in war planning as a whole.

Lord Moran, Churchill's doctor, recorded 'The Tories are full of doubts. On all sides they are saying that Winston is too old and will never take advice.'[410] Churchill himself volunteered 'We are not going to have just the old gang as you call them.'[411] In wartime Churchill had been something of a law unto himself. Now Brook reminded Churchill that 'The composition of your Cabinet must be influenced by personal and political considerations ... The advantages of a relatively small Cabinet are obvious ... The ideal size, in peace, is probably somewhere between 12 and 16.'[412] However, it is unclear whether Brook was involved in advising on the formation of Cabinet – though 'All the important people came to Downing Street, but Brook was sent forth to sound out the smaller fry and bring back reports .... I am sure that Brook entered into the spirit of the thing and got a natural kick out of playing a part in these stirring events.'[413] – and it was the King's Private Secretary Sir Alan Lascelles who asked that the designation of Sir Anthony Eden as Deputy Prime Minister should be withdrawn, as constitutionally this was a non-existent post and potentially a fetter on the Royal Prerogative.[414] Colville records, however, that on 20 June 1952 Brook was party to a discussion at Chartwell to persuade Churchill to move Anthony Eden from the Foreign Office; and in August 1953 at Chequers he participated in a discussion about the impending reshuffle.[415]

Nevertheless Brook was already a trusted confidant of the Prime Minister, as is shown when Macmillan was made minister responsible for housing. Churchill said of the target of 300,000 homes a year (adopted at the Conservative Party Conference of autumn 1950), 'It is a gamble – [which] will make or mar your political career. But every humble home will bless you if you succeed,'[416] and, as recorded in Macmillan's diaries when asked what was the present housing set-up, responded that he did not know, 'But the boys would know. So the boys (Sir Edward Bridges, Head of the Home Civil Service and Sir Norman Brook, Cabinet Secretary) were sent for – also some whisky'.[417]

Cabinet

The first Churchill Cabinet was on 30 October. Brook immediately sought the Prime Minister's approval of the style of recording of the discussion: 'I trust that you will approve the general form of these minutes of yesterday's Cabinet. I have tried to keep them as short as possible, as we did during the war, and to avoid all unnecessary attribution of views to particular Ministers.'[418] Churchill approved. Furthermore, the Prime Minister liked to have familiar faces around him and countermanded a planned move for Brook. It had already been announced that Thomas Padmore of the Treasury would succeed Brook as Cabinet Secretary (he was described as Cabinet Secretary designate on the attendance page of committee minutes). Brook would transfer to the Treasury as Head of the Central Economic Planning Staff in succession to Plowden and also

Bridges' deputy, positioned to take over as Head of the Department (and Head of the Home Civil Service) when Bridges retired in five years' time. The Cabinet Secretary post was then junior to the Head of the Treasury, and there is no doubt that, with mixed feelings, Brook was expecting to move.[419] (He had opposed a Machinery of Government Working Group suggestion to look at the organisation of HM Treasury because of his planned move.[420]) No respecter of bureaucratic niceties, however, Churchill vetoed Padmore (whom he wickedly nicknamed 'Potsdam'[421]) and also insisted that Jock Colville who had worked with him during the war should be appointed joint Principal Private Secretary alongside the incumbent appointed a month previously (David Pitblado of the Treasury). Paradoxically this may have been a decisive moment in the ascendancy of the Cabinet Secretary's influence and power, as to the extent that Churchill's decision thwarted any ambition to lead the civil service, it kept Brook in a position to which he was better suited than would have been the case with the Central Economic Planning Staff.

Early in November Brook made a second suggestion about Cabinet; he set out the potential benefits from including 'Parliamentary Business' as a standing agenda item for the mid-week Cabinet.[422] This would bring order into the arrangements for deciding which Ministers should speak in forthcoming debates, which was especially important because these early days were potentially politically difficult for the government since their Parliamentary position was far from secure. Hence, on 12 November, as Churchill prepared for a broadcast to the nation on the need for continuing austerity he was anxious not to revive an atmosphere of electioneering and Brook asked Pitblado, the Principal Private Secretary inherited from the outgoing Attlee regime, to remind the Prime Minister that his would be a political broadcast to which the Opposition would have the right of reply.[423] The structure of Cabinet was one area where Opposition attacks could be expected. Churchill planned to have four coordinating 'overlord' Ministers, all from the House of Lords. Only three of those approached accepted the appointment (Lords Cherwell, Leathers and Woolton; Lord Anderson declined).[424]

Brook supplied Churchill with defensive arguments, including that there was nothing new in the arrangements since Attlee had created a statutory post of Minister of Defence in the Cabinet yet excluded the Service Ministers, which had never been done before in time of peace.[425] The parallel was not strong, however, since the coordinating Ministers would not have significant staffs of their own – they were more akin to chairmen of committees – the individual Ministers whose policies were to be coordinated would remain accountable to Parliament. Brook had, in fact, argued against the idea of 'overlords' in the briefing prepared for an incoming Conservative government (brief 3 of which had brought out the constitutional difficulties involved).[426] He made six points, concluding that the difficulties would not apply if the system of standing committees was used instead:

Brook's Arguments Against 'Overlord' Ministers

1. Difficulty in reconciling the appointments with the doctrine of Ministerial responsibility;
2. Inconsistency with the principle that policies should be formulated by those who would have to implement them;
3. Policy could not be divorced from administration;
4. Likely friction between Cabinet Ministers who would be subordinate to other Cabinet Ministers;
5. Difficulties if 'overlord' staff tried to dictate to departmental staff who would generally be more knowledgeable;
6. The 'overlord' would inevitably be drawn into details and the benefits of detachment thus lost.

This was not the first time that the suggestion of a de facto Cabinet hierarchy had arisen – in 1918 the Haldane Committee[427] had recommended super ministries and super ministers and it had been Churchill's wartime practice. But as *The Economist* expressed it in October 1948, under Attlee '[a] method has been discovered for dividing up the work that would otherwise fall upon the Cabinet and yet of maintaining the essential harmony of policy among the Government as a whole … [by] the device of the standing Committee, empowered to take decisions in the name of the Cabinet.'[428] This, *The Economist* further argued, enabled the splitting up of a number of elephantine offices such as the Board of Trade, Ministry of Health, Commonwealth Relations Office, and the Ministry of Fuel & Power, in the interests of effective Ministerial control. However, Churchill was not a convert to Cabinet Committees (he preferred interdepartmental co-ordination to be through Cabinet itself and told Moran in April 1953 that, 'I am a great believer in bringing things before Cabinet. If a Minister has got anything in his mind and he has the sense to get it argued by the Cabinet he will have the machine behind him')[429] and particularly resented official committees that shadowed Ministerial counterparts as he felt that they usurped Ministerial discussion.[430] He instructed Brook to reduce committee numbers;[431] and carried on with the appointment of three 'overlords'.

Brook showed a remarkable ability to develop defensive arguments against his former advice. Thus, on 2 May he sent Churchill a three-page memo that argued the coordinating ministers were a modern development in an increasingly complex world, to help a Minister exercise his personal responsibility in the context of his collective responsibility and represented no more than an extension of the role typically carried by the chairmen of Cabinet Committees such as the Lord President of the Council and the Lord Privy Seal. The coordinators had no powers to issue orders, 'No Departmental Minister can be required to remain in government and carry out, in administration for which he is personally accountable to Parliament, policies imposed upon him by a coordinating Minister against his better judgement;' there was no diminution of Parliamentary control.[432] The brief formed the basis for the Prime Minister's statement on 6

May against the background of pretty hostile press commentary. A leader in *The Manchester Guardian*, for example, said, 'If Mr Churchill runs his Cabinet as a group of personal friends whom Parliament cannot get at because they are only "coordinators" we are seeing a new kind of constitutional practice.'[433] The Prime Minister's statement partially mollified the critics and appeared to sort things out on the technical level, but not on the broader political plane where *The Manchester Guardian* retorted that, 'On the whole the old system, though it had less showy window-dressing, was preferable.' *The Times* agreed, 'After the Prime Minister's statement yesterday the impression must persist that there has been some considerable lessening of the departmental Minister's responsibility for the formation of policy.'[434] Opposition attacks continued. In March 1953 the Prime Minister was again forced to defend the concept of supervising ministers.[435] But after a Cabinet reshuffle in September, in the November Debate on the Queen's Speech, he brought the experiment to an end, passing off its demise as the difference between wartime and peacetime requirements.[436] Brook's description of how to achieve interdepartmental co-ordination without coordinating ministers came in handy but in truth was misleading.[437] The future Head of the Home Civil Service, William Armstrong, in an interview with Anthony Seldon commented that all the Conservative governments of the period 1951 to 1964 were troubled by stovepipe thinking.[438]

Amongst the most important Cabinet meetings of 1952 were three sessions over 28 and 29 February when the ROBOT scheme to float sterling within certain limits was discussed. It has been argued by some commentators, in hindsight, that by not going ahead with the scheme fundamental industrial reform was delayed by 30 years;[439] but looked at through the eyes of the time it appeared that the likely (possibly inevitable) short-term drop in the sterling exchange rate would push up import prices, hence wage demands and hence unemployment. Retaliation by holders of blocked sterling deposits and by the United States because of the threat to the Bretton Woods currency agreements were forecast. Those, at least, were the political calculations the opponents of ROBOT deployed, perhaps knowing that Churchill would appreciate the political risks but not the potential stimulus to reform of the creaking industrial economy and that reappraisal of Britain's role in the world that would have been necessary. Brook made little contribution to the initial debates except, jointly with Bridges, to urge the Prime Minister first to have a private meeting with the Foreign Secretary (fixed for 11.30 on 28th and then to 'take the Cabinet into your confidence on ROBOT' with special Cabinet meetings spread over the next day and a half.)[440] He produced very full 'no circulation' minutes, however, against the possibility that 'If this or some similar scheme should subsequently be approved by the Cabinet, I will include this record in the printed version of the Cabinet Minutes.'[441] Meanwhile, he told the Chancellor, 'Only two copies of this record are in existence. The other is held by me.'[442] Those minutes record that the leading opponent of the scheme was the Paymaster General (Lord Cherwell) who argued that there were no sufficient grounds for the violent reversal of policy proposed by the Chancellor. Churchill played little part in the discussion, perhaps because economic problems were quite beyond his ken even though he had served as Chancellor of the Exchequer in the 1920s.[443] He summed up at the second meeting that, 'Many Ministers, with every desire to help the Chancellor in his difficult task, remained unconvinced that the advantages which might be gained from adoption of this plan, if all went well, outweighed its manifest disadvantages and dangers. So long as there was so large a division of opinion within the Cabinet on the merits of the plan, it would be hazardous for the Chancellor to proceed with it. His own conclusion was that, at the present time, there was not within Cabinet a sufficient body of support for this plan to enable the Chancellor to launch it with the confidence that he had behind him the conviction, as well as the loyalty, of his colleagues.' The final decision was a desire to let sterling find its market level – but not just yet! Hence the more dramatic of the Chancellor's alternative actions to deal with the balance of payments problems should be 'framed as to conform as far as practicable with the government's ultimate objectives.'[444]

Four months later Brook was advising against a prompt decision on an alternative plan for sterling in advance of a planned discussion at a forthcoming Commonwealth Economic Conference in November: 'a proposal of this far-reaching importance should not be presented as one requiring immediate decision, unless the economic facts themselves make an immediate decision necessary ... this plan would make a far deeper impression if it were announced in the context of a concerted Commonwealth policy.'[445] A Confidential Annex to the Cabinet minutes for 8 July record the Prime Minister as saying, 'there was unlikely to be any large body of opinion in the Cabinet in favour of undertaking at the present time the hazardous operation of setting sterling free at a floating rate of exchange.'[446]

During the Churchill administration overt advice from the Cabinet Secretary other than on procedural or structural matters was rare; departments were acknowledged as knowing more about their business than the Cabinet Office ever could, and Churchill was both hard to shift when he had made up his mind and yet averse to thinking things out, preferring to wait for situations to develop and then to adapt himself to them.[447] But there were subtle ways of influencing him. Moran thought that 'Winston's mind is only alert when England's security is at stake.'[448] Contemporaries such as Leslie Rowan, Head of the Overseas Finance Division of the Treasury and co-sponsor, along with George Bolton of the Bank of England and Otto Clarke, his deputy, of the ROBOT scheme said at the time that the Prime Minister had lost his tenacity; 'he no longer pushed a thing through. He has lost, too, his power of fitting in all the problems one to another.'[449] All of which give credence to Mallaby's assertion that Brook's power lay in 'The arrangements for preliminary consultation and discussion, whether in this Committee or in that, the decision to submit them to the Cabinet itself and the manner in which they should be submitted – all these are questions on which the advice of the Secretary of the Cabinet and his staff is indispensable.'[450] It is not surprising, therefore, that the files in The National Archive contain examples of Brook convening informal meetings of Permanent Secretaries at which the discussion appears to be procedural and where the crucial decision on who would carry work forward had been taken in advance by Brook in consultation with the relevant Permanent Secretary.

On a weekly basis he submitted draft Cabinet agenda to the Prime Minister covering a Tuesday and a Thursday Cabinet. In 1952, for example, there were 108 meetings of the full Cabinet with 455 papers. This was a high point during the Administration but on average, for the three full years 1952–54, there were 94 meetings a year with 406 papers and the incidence never fell below 81 meetings (366 papers). The suggested agenda was rarely altered but sometimes extra items would be added at the Prime Minister's request, often stimulated by short-term issues arising from press reports. Most of the items at a normal Cabinet were short-term, the more strategically important issues were usually discussed at special Cabinets such as a programme of meetings to discuss the Chancellor's plans for import cuts, restrictions on investment to free resources for export and to extend the period of the defence programme, to be announced as a package on the 21st.[451] Occasionally the same agenda would veer between the macro (e.g. discussion of the Schuman Plan) and the micro (detailed decisions on whether to allow the construction of a new hotel in Portman Square, London).[452] The burden on departmental ministers was heavy, leading Brook to announce the Prime Minister's agreement that, save for special Cabinet meetings, questions should only be put to Cabinet when the point to be settled had been narrowed to a defined issue; and the Treasury should be consulted in advance on any public expenditure, general financial or economic policy implications.[453]

Churchill's Stroke

There had been signs of a weakening of the Prime Minister's mental capacity in a difficulty in getting through Defence Committee papers and indeed in keeping him sufficiently interested to chair the Committee's meetings.[454] And on the evening of 23 June 1953 during the closing stages of a dinner at 10 Downing Street for the Italian Prime Minister, Christian Democrat Alcide de Gasperi, Churchill had a further stroke. He was not expected to live beyond the weekend.[455] Amazingly he presided over Cabinet the following day, members merely noticing that the Prime Minister was more silent than usual.[456] Subsequent Cabinets were held under the chairmanship of Butler as Eden was still convalescing from a serious remedial biliary tract operation, undergone in America in April. Cabinet was simply told, on 29 June, that 'the Prime Minister was suffering from severe over-strain and was in need of a complete rest. His doctors had advised him to abandon his proposed journey to Bermuda and to lighten his duties for at least a month ... During his absence the Prime Minister would continue to receive the more important official papers, and decisions on major questions of policy would be referred to him.'[457]

For the following seven weeks Jock Colville, his Principal Private Secretary, Christopher Soames, his son-in-law and Parliamentary Private Secretary, and Brook effectively dealt with these papers. The Press Lobby was told that Cabinet had been postponed from 25 to 28 June and that 'The Prime Minister is going to Chartwell for lunch and will stay there until Monday so that he can get clear from the heavy pressure of other work and concentrate on the preparations for the [Bermuda] Conference.'[458] The first public admission of the seriousness of the medical position was not made until March 1955 in the heat of a House of Commons debate on defence when Churchill responded to criticisms from Bevan: 'I was struck down by a very sudden illness which paralysed me completely, physically.'[459] Colville observed that 'A second factor of great help to us was the wisdom and coolness of the Secretary of the Cabinet, Sir Norman Brook, whom I consulted as soon as the crisis occurred ... Discussion of how best to handle [decisions] whether by postponement, by consultation with the Minister or Under Secretary responsible or, in some cases, by direct reply on the Prime Minister's behalf were the subject of daily discussion with the Secretary of the Cabinet.'[460]

One of those topics was the introduction of a Regency Bill to meet HM The Queen's wish that the Duke of Edinburgh should become Regent if she was incapacitated and her heir had not attained adulthood (18 years of age). Colville recorded on 26 June that he had put to the Prime Minister the proposals about the Regency Bill and his views were to press ahead with full speed though adding that Churchill's message acknowledged that he would not himself be able to take part in progressing the Bill.[461] When the *Daily Express* broke a story on 7 July that a planned amendment to the Regency Act would switch the Regency away from Princess Margaret, Churchill was well enough to initial a personal minute to 'RAB' Butler, in inimitable Churchillian language, to the effect that the government should do what it conceived to be its duty and should not be swayed by the press. 'The world does not come to an end because there is a caterwaul for two or three days,' it said. 'Statements affecting Cabinet proceedings and policy should not be made in relation to reports in particular newspapers ... The proper course, however, is to await a Question in Parliament.'[462]

By 19 July the Prime Minister was sufficiently recovered to do some light work on political papers. He returned to chair Cabinet on 18 August though confessing that he was very tired and did not want to do anything; 'Tired but happy,' as Brook put it. Brook also told Moran that he did not think that anyone noticed anything different except that 'Winston let other people talk more than usual perhaps – he certainly talked less himself... He has dipped his foot in water, and it wasn't cold; he wants to go on. This isn't the moment to make decisions about retiring.'[463] Eden was still convalescing and a week later Brook added, 'I think now [Churchill] ought to go on for a while; it would probably be best for the country. As for the Prime Minister's personal happiness, I have no doubt about the choice. He talked to me one day before his illness, saying he could not bear to see things mishandled and might feel angry and frustrated. Besides all this, I am astonished at the speed of his recovery after what happened. In some ways he seems better than before his stroke.'[464]

Nevertheless, by the end of the year Brook was contrasting Churchill's current powers of concentration unfavourably with those during the war, 'During the war the Prime Minister had a gift for picking out two or three things and getting them up in detail – that was his strength. He made no attempt in those days to keep up with a lot of things. Now, of course, he is a lazy Prime Minister; he reads novels after breakfast. But it is much better from the Country's point of view that he should stay on.'[465] It was not until April 1954 that he came round to the view that Churchill should retire: 'They are thinking of a General election in the autumn of 1955 ... They want younger men, full of energy and drive.' Asked how Churchill would cope with retirement he continued that he hoped the novel-reading habit would grow, 'Though, of course, zip may go out of it when it is no longer forbidden fruit.'[466]

Churchill did not retire until a year later, hanging on in the hope of pulling off one last coup in the form of an understanding on peaceful co-existence between the West and Russia after the death of Stalin on 6 March 1953 and in the face of the potential for nuclear destruction. He was still dominant in Cabinet. Moran wrote that grown men stood in awe of his personality and that he frightened them, 'Even to rouse him from his mid-afternoon sleep was something of an adventure.'[467] During the war his obsession with absolute victory whatever it might cost was the essential core of this dominance. Brook's view was that 'If it had not been for Winston, anything might have happened after [the defeat and evacuation of the British Expeditionary Force from] Dunkirk. While he was there bargaining with Hitler was out of the question, a separate peace unthinkable.'[468] Churchill remained apart from others but as he became aware of declining mental powers he bolstered his dominance with resistance to change, 'It made him angry, he could see no sense in this restless search for new methods. It was not so much that change in itself was undesirable; in Churchill's eyes it was decidedly improper.'[469] Thus, when Macmillan (already chairman of the Liaison Committee between the party and Government set up by Churchill in 1951) suggested in February 1954 that one of the two weekly Cabinet Meetings might start with a political discussion which would have neither a formal agenda nor minutes, Brook countered that the Prime Minister was quite content that he could say whatever he wanted at the start of Cabinet meetings – but other Ministers could not.[470]

Atomic Weapons & Summitry

The remainder of 1954 saw the highs and the lows of Churchill's Cabinet. Almost immediately after taking up the reins in 1951 Churchill had been briefed on the development of atomic weapons and had been shocked to find that Attlee had neither involved his full Cabinet nor kept Parliament wholly informed. 'The Labour government spent a hundred millions on atomic research without telling anyone,' he complained to Lord Moran, his personal physician, 'without any Parliamentary sanction whatever. Their Party knew nothing about it ... they just divided the money between seven or eight departments.'[471] So, in line with his belief that Ministers should expose their most important decisions to a full Cabinet, after discussions in the ad hoc Cabinet Committee on atomic energy development (GEN 464) had reached agreement that Britain should make its own hydrogen bomb and the Cabinet Defence Committee had endorsed the decision, Churchill took the issue to full Cabinet on 7 July. He argued 'that we could not expect to maintain our influence as a World Power unless we possessed the most up-to-date nuclear weapons ... He had no doubt that the best hope of preserving world peace was to make it clear to potential aggressors that they had no hope of shielding themselves from a crushing retaliatory use of atomic power.'[472] Not all those present were immediately convinced. Harry Crookshank (Lord Privy Seal) argued that those Ministers who were not members of GEN 464 or the Defence Committee had had no notice of such a momentous decision and needed time to consider it. There were two further discussions, including detailed discussion of the cost, international implications and morality of nuclear weapons, the last question at the behest of the Prime Minister and following a resolution of the London Methodist Conference. Finally on 26 July agreement was recorded and in February the following year Macmillan (Minister of Defence) told the House of Commons.

A low point occurred in July when, returning by sea from defence discussions with President Eisenhower in Washington, Churchill's enthusiasm for a US/UK/Russia summit meeting to promote world peace led him to telegraph an offer of talks to the Russian leadership from aboard the *Queen Elizabeth*, without informing Cabinet of his intentions. Brook was not a member of the travelling party and his legendary calm and judgement on procedural matters were missed. Eden made the case for a discussion in Cabinet before taking an initiative but was fobbed off by a reference to wartime precedents when Churchill had sent telegrams to the President without any censorship. [473] There was uproar at two acrimonious Cabinet meetings on the Prime Minister's return with threats of resignation and a split in the Conservative Party, especially on 23 July.[474] Churchill was unrepentant, quoting the wartime precedents and the need to seize the moment,[475] but the split did not widen as Malenkov came forward on 24 July with a proposed conference of all European governments.

As hopes for a last spectacular success on the world stage receded, the Prime Minister set a date to retire early in April 1955. This almost became a false dawn for the Prime Minister in waiting, Anthony Eden, when Churchill heard that Eisenhower was contemplating a trip to Europe to celebrate the 10th anniversary of V-E Day at the start of May. Colville records that Brook warned Eden that Churchill was likely to renege on the planned retirement date.[476] Discreetly a message was conveyed to the US Ambassador, Aldrich, that because of the likelihood of a General Election it would be preferable for Eisenhower to delay his planned visit but in the event, at Cabinet on 15 March, Churchill yielded to his colleagues' arguments and confirmed he would retire. He tendered his resignation to HM The Queen at 5.30 pm on 5 April, Brook tactfully asking him to draw to the attention of all Ministers that his resignation meant that they had resigned too. As a last act as Churchill's Cabinet Secretary Brook then helped draft Eden's House of Commons tribute to the great man.

Overlap with Bridges

I have discussed Brook's contribution to Cabinet government at some length because that is where his mastery of the government machine is most evident in this period. From 1947 to 1956 when Brook took on both roles, his predecessor as Cabinet Secretary, Bridges, was the Head of the Home Civil Service. The roles of the two were not always as distinct as might have been wished, nor the unity of the two men complete. Thus, whilst Brook is remembered primarily for administrative skills in support of collective discussion and responsibility he was not much interested in reform of government as a whole. He opposed Bridges in 1952 when he sought to resurrect the Government Organisation Committee causing Bridges to send him an anguished message. Bridges argued that the new government showed no signs of changing tack and the balance of payment problems would require continued central direction and control: 'If those of us who have lived all our working lives in Whitehall and have studied the Whitehall organisation give up as hopeless all attempts to reform it from inside, then what hope is there of any reform in our time?'[477] Over the next two months Brook, assisted by Frank Lee, Harold Emmerson and Alexander Johnston, produced a shopping list of areas of economic organisation requiring improvement. They reported in June 1952[478] with suggestions that included looking at the coordinating role of the Treasury; the organisation of overseas economic issues; the demarcation between the Ministries of Supply and Materials; departmental responsibility for the promotion of industrial productivity and for the distribution of industry; arguing that it would be dangerous to consult external bodies such as the Federation of British Industries, the National Union of Mine Workers or the Trades Union Congress until government had reached provisional conclusions on its own account. By November 1953, however, Brook pronounced the Ministerial Machinery of Government Committee defunct: since April 1951 there had been a reduction of 25,460 in the number of civil servants (about 2½%).[479]

Hence, when in February 1954 Lord Woolton circulated a draft paper on the machinery of government appropriate to a Conservative government it was perhaps inevitable that Brook would duck the wider issue it raised, hiding behind a specific decision to abolish the Ministry of Materials.[480] But Woolton wrote of discussions when in Opposition that 'looked forward to a freer society which relied less on either direction or support from Government departments,' and referred back to committee discussions under Sir John Anderson towards the end of the wartime coalition, when there had been deep political divisions: The Socialists wanted large and powerful Ministries and kept them; with the exceptions I have mentioned [merging Pensions and Insurance and Civil Aviation and Transport] we are doing the same, and since we came into office the Cabinet has never discussed this question, which is not one of economy but one of principle.

Churchill was little interested in the mechanics of government and both Bridges and Brook seemed to take it as read that the Conservative government showed no real appetite for changes in policy and assumed that the perennial balance of payments problems pointed to the need for 'continuance of the kind of measures of direction and control which we have had to endure since 1945.' Hence, Brook was unwilling to run with Woolton's suggestion for a Cabinet Committee 'to find out what sort of machinery of government is best suited to the issues and the personnel of government in the next decade,' dismissing the paper 'which has become somewhat academic.'[481]

Crichel Down

One issue that Brook could not ignore was the public outcry against abuse of power caused by the Crichel Down case in 1954. In brief, the facts were that when some land in Dorset, purchased compulsorily by the Air Ministry for wartime use, was transferred to the Ministry of Agriculture in 1949 and by them to the Agricultural Land Commission for development as a single food producing farm it was not offered to the original owners. Following on from a celebrated tragedy when a property owner (Mr Pilgrim) committed suicide when faced with a compulsory purchase order, political pressure built up for a public enquiry and there were allegations of corrupt officials. Brook warned the Prime Minister, who showed little interest except to say, 'Better wash dirty linen in public than let it grow verminous.'[482] Sir Andrew Clark QC was appointed amidst massive hostile press reaction to administrative decisions that disregarded the interests of citizens and reported in May 1954[483] that whilst there was no evidence of corruption there had been maladministration; named officials were censured. The main response fell to Bridges as Head of the Home Civil Service. Brook advised him that it would be riskier to the reputation of the civil service to dispute the findings than to express regret.[484] He feared that the discussions 'may broaden out into a general attack on officialdom. Sir Andrew Clark's report has, I think, released a pent-up feeling of irritation against bureaucracy which has accumulated over the six years of war and another six years of Socialist rule during which we certainly had too much "government".'[485] At the end of July Bridges called a meeting of Permanent Secretaries to consider the wider implications of the case – Brook did not attend.[486] As a result Bridges asked each Permanent Secretary to circulate in their departments a note warning against high-handedness in dealings with the public, 'Some civil servants' it said, 'are not sufficiently conscious of their duty to treat the public as persons to whom they owe prompt and considerate attention … the citizen has a right to expect that his personal feelings, no less than his rights as an individual, will be sympathetically and fairly considered.'[486] Brook felt that this message was not relevant to the Cabinet Office, which had no dealings with the public as clients.[487] No doubt he was strictly correct but key Cabinet Office senior staff were usually on secondment from other departments where the message was entirely relevant.

A Fading World Power

Two months after his 1951 election victory Churchill sailed aboard the *Queen Mary* for meetings with President Truman in Washington. He was looking to rekindle the old wartime feeling of closeness and to keep Britain in the front rank of world powers despite the loss of India, Burma and Ceylon from the Empire, the visible decline in authority demonstrated by the Persian seizure of the Abadan oil refinery, the abandonment of the Palestine mandate, withdrawal from Greece and the dire economic position. But the Prime Minister was only too aware of a loss of status, 'When I have come to America before it has been as an equal,' he told Moran, adding 'They have become so great and we are now so small.'[488] Nevertheless, being back in the business of statesmanship was rejuvenating. Brook, who travelled as a member of the Churchill party, commented that the Prime Minister was so glad to be back in Washington that he'd be happy even if they threw bricks at him.[489] Advance press reports from Washington suggested that the Truman administration might do just that.

Brook had suggested that the talks should cover six broad areas: the Cold War, policy in the Far East, the Middle East, NATO and supreme political direction in peace and in war, US support for the British defence effort, and atomic weapons.[490] The proposals were sent to Washington over Christmas, *The Times* reporting from Washington that 'Those "official sources" who provide advance information on the Government's attitude have spent the last two weeks telling the United States how uncompromising they intend to be in saying "no" on a variety of matters and how many difficult questions they are ready to ask.'[491] On the Atlantic Command, on policy towards China and on standardisation of weapons the best that could be agreed was to defer decisions; but complete accord was recorded on the aims of Middle Eastern policy and, crucially for the British, the final communiqué said that 'Under arrangements made for the common defence, the United States has the use of certain bases in the United Kingdom. We reaffirm the understanding that the use of these bases in an emergency would be a matter for joint decision by His Majesty's Government and the United States Government in the light of the circumstances prevailing at the time.'[492]

The British were still smarting over the 1946 MacMahon Act that prevented the United States from sharing atomic secrets with other countries and the explicit abandonment by the Americans in 1948 of the 1943 Quebec Agreement for shared joint control of the use of atomic weapons, wherever in the world they were deployed. Churchill argued vigorously that Britain ought to be consulted before an atomic bomb was sent off from airfields in East Anglia. Some of the President's advisers countered that a considerable proportion of US bombing personnel were in Britain and that they would, in that case, be subject to a British veto; threatening that if the veto were maintained it might be wise to withdraw the troops.[493] Brook later confirmed that though the British had sought joint control of atomic weapons wherever they were deployed in the world, they had had to be satisfied with a weaker statement confined to deployment in the British Isles and modified in June that same year by the addition of the escape clause 'if time permitted.'

In a letter to Padmore, standing in for Brook back in London, Mallaby described Brook and himself as 'Both tired and cross, but on the whole [the visit] has been fairly successful.'[494] Brook was less positive; in another letter to

Padmore he wrote that 'Until the P.M. left for New York we had hardly a moment for anything but the immediate affairs of the Conference,' adding that the journey out had been fraught because 'the P.M. found himself without newspapers or telephones [and] at once convinced himself that all activity in Whitehall had stopped. He would not be persuaded otherwise ... We are feeling jaded ... During the period of the talks I was never in bed before 2.30.'[495] A week later Churchill addressed Congress, during which he floated a suggestion that the US might put in a token force alongside the British in the Suez Canal Zone. The speech had a muted reception in the British camp – 'all right but not in highest class' in Mallaby's judgement.[496]

British attempts to revive the 1950 private understanding between Truman and Attlee that the President regarded the two countries as 'partners in this matter' and that he would not use the atomic bomb without consulting London unless the United States was under attack,[497] were once again rejected after the November 1952 Presidential election that brought Eisenhower to power. Nowadays it is the convention that the British Cabinet Secretary seeks reaffirmations of the US/UK agreements on nuclear and intelligence matters whenever leadership changes occur in London or Washington.[498] Early in 1953 reassurance on the agreement over atomic weapons was sought by the Foreign Secretary, Anthony Eden, from the US Secretary of State, Foster Dulles. Dulles refused to go back to the Truman/Attlee understanding and was backed in this by Eisenhower. Limitations on the 'freedom of action' to wage war were impermissible – besides, Eisenhower and Dulles argued that nuclear weapons were just another kind of ammunition.[499] It had become clear not just to the Prime Minister but to members of his government and to the Opposition that Britain's world standing had declined. Harold Macmillan confided to his diary that: 'Perhaps the most noticeable, and painful, difference between our position now and when we were last in office is our relationship to the US. Then we were on an equal footing – a respected ally. Then it was the Churchill–Roosevelt combination (or its aftermath). Now we are treated by the Americans with a mixture of patronising pity and contempt ...'[500] Hugh Dalton's diary says: '... we, in our mismanaged mixed-economy, over-populated little island, shall become a second-rate power, with no influence and continuing "crises."'[501]

Then on 4 March 1953 news started to come through that Josef Stalin had suffered a stroke and was not expected to live (he died a day later). The Foreign Office were already working on future policy toward Soviet Russia and had sent two sensitive papers to Brook about likely Soviet reactions to possible Western actions in Soviet 'sore spots' – Scandinavia, Germany, Austria, Yugoslavia, Albania, Turkey, Persia and the Far East – which concluded on an optimistic note that post-Stalin the West had greater freedom of action without incurring an unacceptable risk of major war.[502] A tri-partite Conference on foreign policy and defence (US/UK/France) in Bermuda had been postponed because of Churchill's stroke and was now rescheduled for December. The objectives were defined as 'unity amongst the 3 Western Powers in order to counteract centrifugal tendencies in the Western Alliance'[503] or, as the press put it, 'whether the western leaders should meet the new Russian rulers in conference.'[504] A steering brief on the approach to be taken was circulated to Cabinet.[505] Brook and Colville (of the No 10 Private Office) kept an informal record of the sessions (which were not minuted) and which formed the basis for the Prime Minister's report on the Conference for HM The Queen. No decisions had been sought but the informal record noted that 'it seems likely that the American Delegation were impressed by the dangers of the course which they had been proposing to follow' to adopt a more vigorous military offensive using atomic weapons against military objectives north of the Yalu river on the border of Korea and China should the armistice be broken and hostilities resumed.[506] In a separate session the French warned that the European Defence Community proposals were unlikely to be ratified in the Assemblée Nationale.

In a curious episode Brook noted that at the opening session of the Conference the sole American official present made no notes. As this was the session where the British urged the Americans to think twice before changing their military stance in Korea Brook thought that it was 'desirable that some record of this very important discussion should be available in Washington,' and proposed giving the Americans a copy of the British record of the meeting.[507] To his surprise, however, it later emerged that they had a full record. 'I was astonished to find that [the Americans] had been able to produce something which is virtually a verbatim report of the whole meeting. I have checked it, in part, against my own manuscript notes – and it is more full and detailed than they are.'[508] Charitably Brook ascribed this tour de force to the conscientiousness of the American interpreter who, 'took full notes, for the purposes of interpretation, of pretty nearly everything that was said.'[509]

Brook led on the logistical arrangements. The provisional budget for the British delegation over the four days of the Conference was put at £42,500 (equivalent to about £3.75 million at 2014 prices) – a very large sum for the times, which is put into perspective by detailed examination of the administrative arrangements. Single rooms for the 43-strong UK party were only allowed for those of Under-Secretary rank or above, and only the following items could be taken out of the country – 'a wedding ring, engagement ring, watch, cigarette case, fur coat (unless of exceptional value) together with a cash sum not exceeding £5 in notes and £2 in silver'. 'For evening wear, both during the voyage and in Bermuda, a dinner gown should be taken by ladies and a dinner jacket by the men. Those men who possess white jackets should take them. Unless advised later to the contrary, it will not be necessary for men to take full evening dress.'[510]

Back home the results of the conference were judged to be underwhelming. Attlee described Churchill on his return as 'a Father Christmas without any presents.'[511] Nevertheless, Brook thought the Opposition open to a 'rather more responsible line' on disarmament and foreign policy. Indeed, he suggested to the Prime Minister that if their call for 'an immediate initiative by us [towards the Russians] ... had asked instead that we should take advantage of the earliest promising opportunity for a meeting, it would have been in line with your own earlier statements.' But, he suggested, the line to take was that, 'The Opposition now, as always, are clinging to the hope that peace can be ensured by throwing away the means of self-protection ... There are in fact no short cuts to disarmament or to world peace ... we shall never achieve security if our policy is dominated by fear of our own strength.'[512] There then followed an exhaustive trawl through the official records, which established that the Churchill/Roosevelt Quebec agreement of 19 August 1943 on the development and use of atomic weapons had not been disclosed to the War Cabinet, nor the 1948 modus vivendi, which abrogated it, revealed by the Labour government. The search also revealed that the United States had lost its signed copy of the 1944 Hyde Park aide memoire between Churchill and Roosevelt that 'Full collaboration between the United States and the British Government in developing Tube Alloys [atomic energy] for military and commercial purposes should continue after the defeat of Japan unless terminated by joint agreement.'[513]

Churchill raised two queries with Brook: what efforts had the British made to prevent the passing of the 1946 McMahon Act, and why had the government not published the Quebec Agreement as part of those efforts? Brook replied on 21 May[514] that Attlee had protested to Truman about the McMahon Act on 6 June 1946, though the Act was then a relatively minor issue in the major Anglo-American row over the interpretation of agreements over the sharing of atomic materials. The President had not replied since he had already told Attlee on 20 April that it was never contemplated that the US would help the UK build an atomic pile. Further, as the British Embassy in Washington pointed out, 'The Bill was drafted not by the United States Administration, but by the Senate Committee and we do not see how they could have taken account of arrangements of which they had no official knowledge and perhaps no knowledge at all.' Attention had then shifted to the drafting of the 1948 modus vivendi, which took the McMahon Act as its starting point.

As to publication of the Quebec Agreement, Attlee had concluded, in the light of Britain's urgent need for American economic aid, that as the Agreement had not been put before Congress and remained secret, it did not have the force of a treaty and it was not for him to intervene if the US Government chose to conceal its existence from Congress. 'Relations with members of the Labour Government at that time were neither close nor cordial,' Brook added; however, 'As against this we have the statement (made to you by Mr McMahon) that, if the Senate had known the terms of the Quebec Agreement the McMahon Act would never have been passed.' Churchill was cross, annotating Brook's explanation with 'There is no excuse for the British Ministers not having forced the publication of the document. We should have got fair play from the Americans.' But, he added, 'I do not think they would have fulfilled the agreement in the difficult circumstances prevailing after the war.'

It was during these years that Churchill sought to revive his dream of one last grand Summit involving the new Soviet leadership to secure peaceful co-existence. He telegrammed Molotov in the Kremlin on 4 July 1954 in warm terms; 'I should be very glad if you let me know if they like the idea of a friendly meeting, with no agenda and no object but to find a reasonable way of living side by side in growing confidence, easement and prosperity.'[515] Anthony Eden, the Foreign Secretary, thought it unwise to meet the Russians on these terms and was shocked by the aggressive posture of the Americans at the Bermuda Conference.[516] In Cabinet on 12 and 13 March 1952 he destroyed a suggestion from Macmillan that Britain might join a European confederation similar to the Commonwealth. Receiving an honorary degree from the University of Columbia in January of that year he firmly rejected a closer relationship with Europe as 'something which we know, in our bones, we cannot do,' stressing that Britain's interests lay far beyond the continent of Europe without which 'we should be no more than some millions of people living on an island off the coast of Europe, in which nobody wants to take any particular interest.'[517] Eden's preference was 'to cultivate the idea of an Atlantic Community based on the three pillars of the United States, United Kingdom (including the Commonwealth) and Continental Europe.'[518] Macmillan and Maxwell Fyfe, who had supported his idea in Cabinet, backed off, recognising that Eden was supreme in the kingdom of foreign policy, notwithstanding Churchill's interference. Brook wisely stayed out of the arguments, ever the consummate organiser, trusted by all sides, adept at finding and keeping things moving forward, however slowly that might be, and prepared to smooth the path to the Prime Minister. This last contribution was most evident during Churchill's incapacity in 1953 with Brook; for instance, drafting a memo for the Chancellor to put to the Prime Minister about a difference in Cabinet over how far to go in holding on to the Falkland Islands and how far to go in exploratory talks with the Argentinians and the Chileans about the basis for a possible agreement over the islands and dependencies.[519]

The Commonwealth

Britain Strong and Free contained four proposals about Commonwealth co-operation and Brook convened a meeting of officials from the Treasury, Colonial Office, Defence and Commonwealth Relations Office shortly before the General Election to consider how they should be handled in the briefing for incoming Ministers should the Conservatives win a majority. The results were predictable: the suggestion of an Empire Economic Conference was dismissed as irrelevant to the problems of the Sterling Area; that of permanent civil liaison staff was thought to be unrealistic given that subject expertise was required for most of the issues likely to arise; defence co-ordination through an advisory council, a combined staff and standardisation of equipment, organisation and training was similarly judged to be at odds with the known defence postures of India, Pakistan and even Canada. Only the call for a greater share of the Colonies in responsibility for defence had any traction and even here the Colonial Office said that it was by no means certain that the manpower concerned might be better used to strengthen colonial industrial and agricultural sectors.[520]

Meetings of Heads of Commonwealth Governments were still held in the London Cabinet room. The United Kingdom assumed a natural leadership as befitted the mother country, though two years after the 1953 meeting following the Coronation of Queen Elizabeth II the more powerful Dominions would challenge that pattern. There was also a growing irritation caused on the one hand by London acting on behalf of the whole Commonwealth in relations with the United States,[521] particularly as India, in particular, had very different foreign policy views from those of the United Kingdom. On the other hand Churchill was disinclined to carry a mandate from the Commonwealth with all that might entail for his freedom of action and in the run-up to the UK/US Bermuda Conference at the end of the year neither Churchill nor Brook favoured a suggestion from the New Zealand Prime Minister that the Americans be told in advance, in writing, that the British would be speaking for the whole of the Commonwealth. In the United Kingdom at large, however, there was much indifference to Commonwealth issues.[522]

Brook acted, in effect, as Secretary General, organising the conferences, proposing their agenda and corralling the principal advisers to delegates. In 1953 many were already in London for the Coronation, which was to be followed by an immediate Commonwealth Conference, and Brook's influence is perhaps illustrated by his issuing an invitation to drinks at his home in Chelsea 'to a few old friends … with whom we shall be dealing during the next ten days' at 24 hours' notice. Only three Whitehall officials were included (Liesching of the Commonwealth Relations Office, Dixon of the Foreign Office and Lee of the Board of Trade) and, again, it is perhaps illustrative of their relationship with Brook that his letter of invitation clearly implied that they had not been to his home before.[523]

The Conference lasted from 3–10 June with a heavy emphasis on foreign policy and defence. It aimed at convergence through the exchange of information and explanation of position with Brook steering the Prime Minister's briefing. The brief on the Middle East is a good example of a concise and incisive analysis of where things stood, setting up a discussion by arguing that the importance of Middle East oil to the Commonwealth in general, and local suspicion of military or commercial means of securing stability in the region, called for new methods. It would not be enough to withdraw and leave a power vacuum. But on what new methods should be considered the brief was silent. At the preparation of the Conference communiqué Brook once again strode onto the stage assuring Churchill that a coded message about the importance to all concerned of the Suez military base was as far as Mr Nehru could be persuaded to go and that it would be necessary to recognise that the Indian foreign policy was based on holding aloof from 'power blocs' 'I believe they will be unwilling to go on record as welcoming any international defence organisation: they will not publicly endorse either the European Defence Community or the North Atlantic Treaty Organisation.'[524]

There were the two big Commonwealth issues: the march to independence of former colonies and the issue of what a Commonwealth comprising a disparate group of countries could represent. Way back in 1942 Churchill had said that he had not become the King's First Minister to preside over the liquidation of the

Empire but of course, Indian independence in August 1947 closely followed by that of Burma and Ceylon had been only the start of a progressive dismembering of Empire. Already in 1948 'RAB' Butler, then in the Opposition, had advanced an argument that the link to the Crown was the defining structural criterion for Commonwealth membership. He was reported as postulating a two-tiered structure under which, 'We might well find ourselves moving towards a state of things in which there was a solid core of the Commonwealth which recognised the King and was united by that link, together with associated States outside.'[525] Brook had earlier heard similar sentiments during a secret trip he made to Canada, Australia, and New Zealand in September that same year to gauge Dominion attitudes to the consequences of Indian independence. But he also recognised that Commonwealth membership was not something for the United Kingdom alone, 'it is clearly [a question] on which all the Commonwealth Governments must, if possible, reach a common view.' That common view was that India, Pakistan and Ceylon should remain Commonwealth members even though they did not meet a test of a link to the Crown in external relations.

Two impending grants of independence raised the issue of Commonwealth membership once again. The Sudan was not a British Colonial territory and so could be treated as a special case in advance of further discussion of the general issue, which was remitted to an ad hoc ministerial group under Lord Swinton.[526] Swinton was attracted by the idea of a two-tier system and asked the committee to consider how best to achieve this, how it would work in practice and how it could be made acceptable.[527] But discussion in the UK about the constitutional arrangements for the Gold Coast – and in particular drawing distinctions between 'self-government,' 'full self-government in the Commonwealth' and 'full and independent membership of the Commonwealth' appeared to Brook to raise questions about a two-tier arrangement before it had been worked out in detail.[528] Swinton backed him completely, 'We cannot breathe a word of this in public until we have cleared our own minds and have a definite plan and have discussed that secretly (and I think separately) with the old Dominions.'[529] His committee received the product of the discussions at official level led by Brook at the end of November. The rapid growth of nationalism and the consequent pace of political development in the Central African federation, the Gold Coast, Nigeria, a West Indian Federation and a Malayan Federation were all identified as presenting an immediate challenge to the flexibility of the Commonwealth connection. The advantages to the UK in keeping these countries together in the political association of the Commonwealth were assessed as strengthening the influence it could exercise throughout the world as primus inter pares in a group of independent Commonwealth countries; adding political cohesion to the Sterling Area; strengthening defence potential and, more broadly, deploying the British traditions and outlook on life to work for peace. Immodestly, the report identified the key Commonwealth members as including at least one country of outstanding importance and influence in each continent of the world and people of all the main religions of the world. The essential link was not blood, nor allegiance to the Crown but that through their once being part of the British Empire they inherit 'by birth or by upbringing, British traditions, methods of Government and Parliamentary institutions. Their common past makes it likely that there will be a broad similarity in their approach to major international problems ... To preserve, strengthen and develop it should be a prime object of Commonwealth policy.' Not that the Commonwealth could be presented as a politically articulated group; the bonds were much more subtle and flexible as was demonstrated when Britain introduced a licensing system for shipping to control trade with China and Korea. It soon discovered that it could not prosecute colonial ships that broke the conditions of licence or traded without a licence altogether.[530]

Swinton's report rejected the idea of a two-tier Commonwealth as impracticable, potentially requiring Ceylon, Pakistan and the Central African Federation to withdraw from the inner circle to which they had grown accustomed; and wrong in principle if the object was to strengthen a common outlook, potentially driving those in the second tier of membership under a foreign sphere of influence. It struck an immediate chord with the Foreign Secretary, Anthony Eden, who commented: 'An excellent paper. I agree with every word of it. An encouraging and important feature is that Commonwealth countries are beginning to talk to each other much more than they did even a few years ago. We must encourage, though it is apt to irritate the Americans sometimes.'[531] Swinton put a report (accompanied by the officials' report) to Cabinet in December with a recommendation that there was no alternative to automatic Commonwealth membership when Colonial territories obtained full self-government. Brook offered a gloss that if it was well known that a colony would, on attaining full self-government, go Communist it must be open to the United Kingdom to argue that such a move was inconsistent with Commonwealth ideals and, therefore, membership. [532] Not all of the 'Old Commonwealth' agreed. In particular, Liesching reported to Brook a conversation in Cape Town with a senior South African official who had worked closely with General Smuts that like him, 'he had been opposed to India's admission [to the Commonwealth] as a republic and still remained of that view ... he was a good deal taken aback at the possibility of having a new African member of the Commonwealth [the Gold Coast]' but he understood the possibility of disruption if some former colonies were banished to second-class membership.[533] Liesching and Brook were agreed that the drive behind African nationalism was not going to be stemmed by economic devices. Brook wrote 'Even in our own evolution the conception of economic freedom for the individual did not emerge until political freedom had been established for some time.'[534] The question was put on the agenda for the 1955 Commonwealth Prime Ministers' Conference at which Churchill presided over all sessions.

The Defence Budget

Churchill started the new administration as his own Minister of Defence. Brook's brief, presented a week after the 1951 election victory, described how the central organisation of defence had moved on from an Office of the Minister of Defence (essentially the military wing of the Cabinet Secretariat) to a full-blown Ministry. Whilst he thought that Churchill would want to assume direct responsibility for the formulation of the strategic plan for the employment of the Armed Forces and their size and shape, he thought that it would probably not be the Prime Minister's wish to undertake all the duties involved in rearmament and defence production, research and development and common administrative issues. A junior minister in the Ministry of Defence would be needed. However, as Brook soon found out, Churchill doubted the need for a Defence Headquarters of the size inherited from Labour. 'Pray let me have the Treasury view on the reductions which should be made in the Ministry of Defence Headquarters. You have called for reductions in all departments and I should like to set an example,' he wrote to the Chancellor of the Exchequer.[535]

Provided that the Prime Minister and Chancellor were united, the defence budget could be led by affordability.[536] A struggle between the financial and the politico-military interests characterised the Churchill years. 'RAB' Butler, the incoming Chancellor, soon determined that the rearmament programme was at risk of breaking the financial limits previously agreed and overburdening the engineering sector at the expense of much needed exports. Meanwhile, the Foreign Secretary, Anthony Eden, listed the fundamentals of British foreign policy as world responsibilities, an economic dependence on external trade and a continuing external threat from Communism. He concluded that if a review of the scope for reducing external obligations showed that the demands were beyond the existing economic capacity of the country 'a choice of the utmost difficulty lies before the British people, for they must either give up, for a time, some of the advantages which a high standard of living confers upon them, or, by relaxing their grip in the outside world, see their country sink to the level of a second-class power, with injury to their essential interests and way of life of which they can have little conception,' concluding that once the prestige of a country had started to slide there was no knowing where it would stop. [537]

Debate between the Treasury and the Defence Ministry continued through the second half of 1952, culminating on 7 November when Cabinet accepted a compromise budget for 1953/54, provided that 'a radical review of the future pattern of our defence effort was set in hand immediately paying due regard to financial and economic factors as well as to strategic needs and foreign commitments.[538] Mallaby advised Brook that 'the only real way to do this is for Ministers themselves to undertake an examination, to hear a great deal of evidence and make up their own plan ... they would, of course, require some general advice on the sort of questions which they ought to put and some basic papers ... these are functions which you yourself could fulfil without giving offence in Whitehall, and without having to do violence to departmental briefs, since you enjoy freedom from departmental instructions.'[539]

Though there was a precedent from 1933 for a civilian official to chair a committee on which the Chiefs of Staff sat as members, Brook was reluctant to push himself onto the Chiefs and refused to recommend in writing that he should be the chairman. It seems likely, however, that, on Mallaby's advice, he did so orally as Churchill put Brook and the Cabinet Office in the lead[540] with a target to report by mid February 1953. Ministers needed an answer to, 'What is the best plan that can be devised upon the assumption that a rising curve of defence expenditure must be avoided?' Overseas commitments should not be excluded, 'We must review our overseas commitments and find ways of filling them at lower cost.'

The Brook committee (comprising officials from the Treasury, Foreign Office, Home Office, Ministry of Defence and the Chiefs of Staff) struggled to get at base costings. The Chiefs were familiar with estimates of dead and wounded and the loss of kit in war but had not had significant experience of financial costing during peacetime. They tended to misunderstand the base figures in Churchill's minute and preached dire warnings that prompted Ian Bancroft (from Butler's private office), amongst others in the Treasury, to dismiss their arguments as hysterical.[541] The Chancellor himself was still looking for a reduction in expenditure, whereas the Churchill assumptions had been a flat line of expenditure. He told his officials that 'I will *not* approve [the Brook report] until I get an assurance that the Brook Committee realises the position broadly with which the Exchequer is faced ... The Government *can't go on* as we are going ...' accusing the Brook committee of failing to tie down the issue of costs.[542] In this, the Chancellor's frustration with the Service Ministers and the Chiefs maligned Brook who had been charged 'to assemble data for ministerial review and to identify the decisions to be made and the risks involved.'[543]

At the Brook committee the Chiefs of Staff took their bat home, going no further than to state that 'no reductions in defence expenditure can be achieved, unless our overseas commitments are reduced; indeed if the defence expenditure is held to the same level as [1953/54], it will not be possible to proceed with the planned re-equipment of our forces,'[544] 'In our view, either Her Majesty's Government must change [defence] policy or they must provide the military resources required to carry it out.'[545] This fell short of what might have been expected of the government's professional military advisers and left the field to the Treasury, whose representative told the Committee that on the Chiefs' own strategy, adopted by Cabinet, 'we are paying an insurance policy in the hope of avoiding war, not of winning a war.'[546] Mallaby advised that he was 'not quite sure that the figures bear out [the Chiefs'] general conclusion, except in the case of the Army.'[547] Later, on 26 March, in response to estimates of the costs of training[548] he expostulated, 'It seems to me to be the sort of working paper which we should at all costs not show to the Prime Minister [who tended to believe that overheads in the military were much too high]. I have no doubt that there are good explanations for all the figures, but at first sight it does seem rather extraordinary, for example, that roughly speaking – in the Army and the Air Force it takes one man to train one man.'[549] It must have been no surprise, therefore, that Brook's Committee had great difficulty in coming to an agreed report. Brook himself displayed a breathtaking mastery of presentation and language in a complete redraft of the opening section. The files contain his handwritten text which sets the rearmament programme in context, explains the effects of spreading the spend over six years and the significance of the new strategic assumption of an extended cold war.[550] It is an outstanding example of the succinctness and clarity admired by Churchill and, later, Macmillan and speaks for itself, as the following extract shows:

> 'In 1947, when the phase of demobilisation was over, the Government decided that annual expenditure on the Armed Forces should be kept within a fixed limit of £780 millions. While that limit was applied the Forces were almost as strong in numbers as they are today, but they were required to live on the stores and equipment that had accumulated during the war. No provision was made for re-equipment, and the effective power of the Forces declined progressively.'
>
> 'The programme of rearmament launched in 1951 was designed to remedy this. But it had also an important political purpose. It was our contribution to the aim of giving some military substance to the conception of the North Atlantic Alliance; it was to help in persuading the Americans to commit themselves to keep substantial Forces in Europe and in encouraging our European Allies to increase their defence effort.'
>
> 'This was launched as a three-year programme. It was envisaged as an intensive phase of re-equipment, at the end of which our Forces and those of our Allies in the North Atlantic treaty would have reached a state of preparedness sufficient to deter aggression in Western Europe. It was thought that after that point our defence expenditure would level out or even decline. On that basis it was thought that the burden on the national economy would not be too great.'
>
> 'In the event that assumption was falsified – by the intensification of the cold war, in Korea and elsewhere, by rising costs and by enlargement of the re-equipment programmes. We have thus been compelled to seek economies – and we have found them not by reducing the planned scale of our defence effort but, in the main, by postponing the production programmes. This device of "rolling the programme forward," which has now been adopted on three occasions, inevitably has the effect of storing up heavy expenditure for future years. As a result, the re-equipment originally envisaged in 1951 as a three year process has not yet reached its peak: we are now in 1953 presented with programmes involving a level of expenditure which continues to rise over another three years until 1955 – an even then, under present policies, the process of re-equipment will not be complete.'
>
> 'Meanwhile, there has been a significant change in the strategic appreciation. Originally we planned to raise the Forces to a state of preparedness that might deter aggression in Europe in 1954 – after which it was assumed, the tension might relax. It is now thought that the danger of actual war in Europe has receded, and plans are now to be related to the hypothesis that a "cold-war period" of tension will continue for a considerable number of years. This new conception may not make a substantial difference to the general pattern of our defence effort. But it certainly affects its scale. The national economy might have been able under the first hypothesis, to sustain the burden of a three-year programme of re-equipment that ended either in war or in a diplomatic détente. It certainly cannot sustain that level of expenditure as a peacetime commitment extending over an indefinite period of years … [The committee] is asked to consider how defence expenditure could in the years ahead be kept within the limits fixed for 1953.'

The problem was that no amount of felicitous drafting could disguise the underlying split between the Chiefs, who wanted overseas commitments reduced, the Foreign Office, who thought that: 'We must contrive to maintain our overseas positions. If we surrender any one of them ... we abdicate from our position as a Great Power. This is obviously unacceptable,'[551] and the Treasury, who had both to raise the money and to solve the perennial balance of payments problems. Brook tried to hand off the Foreign Office by inserting text to the effect that 'Present plans make no assumption about changes in our overseas commitments. [But it is] wrong to assume that e.g. the scale of operations in Korea or Malaya or the size of our garrison in the Canal Zone will continue indefinitely – though admittedly it is difficult to predict on what specific date it will end. We have tried to formulate a picture of our overseas commitments as they might stand, on a reasonably moderate view, as at 1st April 1955, and to gauge the effect on defence expenditure of starting now to plan on the basis that those favourable assumptions will be realised.'[552] Successive redrafting sought to sugar the pill but could not avoid a conclusion that 'The only sound solution is to reduce the size of the forces ... This can only be done if diplomatic action brings about some relaxation of tension in the cold war, or if Ministers are prepared to take certain risks with our defensive preparations.'[553] Still the Chiefs stuck to their argument that commitments must give. From the Treasury Bridges concluded that 'the Chiefs of Staff are themselves quite incompetent to produce any alternative [pattern of expenditure].'[554] Mallaby recognised that there was a great gap in the report in that 'the problem of American aid runs through the past, present and future and I rather doubt if we could deal with it all.'[555] On behalf of the Chiefs, Air Chief Marshal Sir William Dickson, wrote in terms, 'My Dear Brook' (so often a bad sign) on notepaper amended to draw up to his full height as GCB, KBE, DSO, AFC demonstrating over four and a half pages how little movement there had been: 'Your committee was not asked, and we agreed it was not an appropriate task for us, to work out a revised strategic concept. But until that is done it would be most dangerous to start drawing conclusions about major alterations in the size and shape of the forces, or in the research and development programme,' adding that 'we should not give money figures of possible savings except for the savings which would follow directly from certain hypothetical developments in the Cold War.'[556] As Brook told the First Sea Lord, Sir Rhoderick McGrigor, 'by trying to behave like a continental land animal, we are doing something which we have never before attempted in our history.'[557]

Eventually Brook reported to the Ministerial Committee (comprising the Prime Minister, Home Secretary, Chancellor of the Exchequer, Minister of Defence, Commonwealth Secretary, three Service ministers, Minister of Supply, and Paymaster-General) in May.[558] Advised by the Paymaster General (his longtime friend Lord Cherwell) Churchill directed that the figures in the Brook report for 1955/56 should be cut by £308 million to meet the Chancellor's wishes.[559] Further, the six areas the committee had identified for reducing costs (commitments outside NATO, overseas bases and establishments, conventional weapons, research and development, atomic energy, administration) should be sublimated to two strategic imperatives – survival in the first six months of war and maintaining a minimum of garrisons to retain the UK position as a world power. Both reflected the influence of the Prime Minister who had been strongly influenced by reports of the American test of a hydrogen bomb at Eniwetok in the South Pacific (though a decision in favour of heavy protection of a South Bank site in London as the nucleus of government during war pre-dated this discussion)[560] and, after the death of Stalin, was starting to see his crowning achievement as securing a summit agreement for peaceful coexistence involving the USA and Russia. The whole episode had raised questions, however, whether the then Service Chiefs yet had the wherewithal to translate their strategic analysis into military reality in the new atomic, and soon to be nuclear, age. In the event external circumstances intervened, for once benignly. The Korean Armistice held, the Malayan emergency came under control, though it lasted until 1960, and the last British soldiers left the garrison in the Canal Zone on 13 June 1956. The outturn on the defence budget for 1953/54 was £1,364.5 million rising to £1,435.9 million in 1954/55 and falling back to £1,404.9 million in 1955/56.

Churchill's interest in and attendance at the Defence Committee was spasmodic. There were a few signs of the old leader's enthusiasm for technical developments such as when Lord Cherwell told him that it would be possible to detect and home in on 'snorting' U-boats (sic) by smell.[561] In the early years of the Administration the Committee considered papers such as the future of the German financial contribution to the costs of maintaining British forces there, the extent to which Germany should be brought into European defence and allowed to manufacture tactical atomic weapons, and what should be the response if the Chinese Government were to move against Hong Kong or elsewhere in South East Asia. But Churchill was not present at the discussion on South East Asia in April 1952, requiring the Minister of Defence, who was in the chair, to sum up that whilst the Committee agreed the proposals put forward by the Chiefs of Staff it would be necessary for him to obtain the Prime Minister's endorsement before any instructions were sent to embassies etc.[562]

By early in February 1953 a discussion on the production of atomic weapons had to be deferred and a week later Brook was somewhat plaintively identifying for the Prime Minister topics for discussion at a further meeting on 9 February – the defence of Malaya; the likelihood of general war with the Soviet Union up to the end of 1955; a forthcoming White Paper on Defence – ending his brief: 'I hope therefore that you will be willing to preside over this meeting.'[563] On 29 April discussion covered only one scheduled topic, Communism in the UK, leaving items on Egypt, Israel and the Middle East, and on chemical warfare to be rescheduled. Meetings on 11 and 28 May went ahead, without Churchill, discussing a Five-Power Conference on South East Asia, the readiness of transition to war planning, and a number of defence export issues. Discussion of concessions to married servicemen overseas, chemical warfare, security forces for Korea and Defence R&D were postponed because of Churchill's stroke in June. And by spring 1954 Mallaby reported to Brook and General Brownjohn (the joint secretary of the Committee) that 'I am very much concerned about our inability to get meetings of the Defence Committee.' There had been four meetings before mid February followed by a lull during the Radical review with only two papers circulated (on retaliation in Korea) but between mid March and 5 April the secretaries had made three submissions to the Prime Minister asking for the Committee to meet – all to no avail. This prompted Brook to write to Churchill that, 'I am becoming concerned about the difficulty of arranging meetings of the Defence Committee ... there is an accumulation of business ... but what concerns me even more is the danger that the Defence Committee may lose its importance if it meets irregularly and at long intervals.'[564] During the rest of 1954 there were three further meetings. The following year, with the appointment of a Chief of Staff to the Minister of Defence who was the permanent chairman of the Service Chiefs Committee, Brook moved to break the last vestige of the wartime link between the Cabinet secretariat and the military side of the Ministry of Defence.[565] Henceforth support for the Defence Committee would be a Cabinet Office task.

Civil Defence and Preparations for War

On the home front, in May 1952 the Home Secretary revealed to the Defence Committee that expenditure on civil defence was set to rise dramatically and would account for £316 million over the period 1951–55.[566] Though Churchill was the chairman of this Committee he nevertheless instructed that the expenditure should be discussed at Cabinet.[567] The truth was that he believed that to spend this amount of money was ill judged. Though politically necessary to create an impression of activity in civil defence Churchill's view was that the civil defence programme should not be allowed to spend resources that could be better used to prevent war, or that would be more valuable in the early stages of war. Hence, as Brook set out in his brief for the Defence Committee, expenditure on civil defence need not move in hand with that on active defence preparations; it was unrealistic to assume these increases in spending without setting them in the context of Cabinet discussion of the defence programme more widely.[568] And the following year when the House of Commons Estimates Committee was critical of the civil defence effort,[569] Brook described their report as misconceived. Government policy was to spend to prevent war not to prepare for it '... neither this Government nor the last have ever intended to do more than build a façade of civil defence.'[570] This prompted Churchill to forward the brief to the Home Secretary: 'Home Secretary: You should see this. I think it is too much anyway for what is after all only a façade.'[571] A façade maybe, but when Coventry City Council and some newspapers suggested that civil defence was irrelevant in the age of the hydrogen bomb Cabinet decided that there should be a definitive statement that though the role of the civil defence services might be altered by the advent of the H-bomb the need for them remained. While no structural precautions could provide protection against a direct hit by a hydrogen bomb, large numbers of people trained in fire fighting, rescue and welfare would still be important at the periphery of such an explosion.[572]

Indeed, on 6 August 1952 an ad hoc meeting under Brook's chairmanship involving Treasury, Defence, Home Office and Cabinet Office officials to discuss revising civil defence projects and other war preparations of civil departments in the light of a new strategic appreciation by the Chiefs of Staff[573] had concluded that the disbanded National Economy in War Committee should be revived. Whilst Britain was a participant in the Korean emergency that had started in mid 1950, the focus of the N.E.W. work was on an attack on the United Kingdom itself. In preparation for the revival Mallaby drafted a report on the state the various N.E.W. studies had reached at the time of the Committee's abolition. Brook annexed Mallaby's report to a paper for the revived committee. It described a desperately over-stretched economy. First, Britain would be unable to put up much of a fight without extensive external financial and material help: 'unless we get very substantial financial help, or some pooling arrangement in a future war, our war effort would quickly run down simply because we would be unable to pay for our imports.' The United States was the obvious potential source of such help but soundings of the Truman regime in Washington in 1950 had been dispiriting. '... during Mr Attlee's visit we were advised that American internal political conditions made the time unsuitable for discussion of financial relations, and we have been waiting ever since for the time to be suitable.' And in September 1951 the Americans presented Britain with a bill (denominated in dollars) for stores, equipment, transport and medical services provided to the two British brigades fighting alongside them in Korea. The Treasury concluded that 'since we reached no prior agreement with them under which they would undertake to waive charges, it is entirely within their discretion to do so or not as they choose.'[574] Second, '... there is a very wide gap between the manpower required to meet U.K. obligations to N.A.T.O. and to produce the equipment needed by the armed forces we are committed to find, and the manpower which will actually be available ... the deficiency is so large as to make nonsense of any attempts to plan the civil economy.'[575]

Brook went on, seven weeks later, to set out questions for discussion at the first meeting of the Committee:

a) What should be assumed for the relationship between industrial manpower and the armed forces which it must equip?
b) How far should the gap be closed by scaling down the armed forces and how far by assuming additional supplies of equipment?
c) Is it safe to assume that our needs for finished equipment and payment for essential imports will be met without discussion with the United States and Canada? What might that mean for the standardisation of equipment? If it is not safe to make such assumptions how can we make progress with North Atlantic discussions?
d) Should discussions be linked to possible joint economic control or organisation in war?[576]

The Committee met in the afternoon of 17 October. Underlying the discussion was a dilemma arising from the most recently approved defence policy and global strategy which 'appreciated that a future war would consist of an intense initial phase lasting a few weeks, during which the United Kingdom would be subjected to very heavy atomic attack, and a subsequent long-drawn-out phase during which sporadic action would take place while the opposing forces attempted to build up their strength for renewed offensive.'

On this scenario the only useful planning would be about the situation on the outbreak of war. On the other hand, in case war took a more conventional form it would be a mistake not to prepare the best plans possible to cater for such a situation. Brook summed up the discussion with 'our plans should be based on the assumption that war did not take the drastic form forecast in the strategic hypothesis and that it proceeded on more conventional lines. Robert Hall of the Cabinet Office Economic Section would lead the technical work on manpower and imports of materials. Sir Leslie Rowan of the Treasury would ponder on the difficult issue of war finance. It was unsafe to assume American (and other) help over import payments yet maintenance of military commitments implied that 'If we became dependent on external assistance for a substantial part of our effort, then we should have lost a great deal of our liberty of action from the outset, apart from the effect on our post-war economy.'[577]

There was no great hurry over the war planning schemes and the N.E.W. Committee met only once a year. However, Ministers in the Conservative government would have known nothing of the Attlee/Truman discussions of 1950. So, in July 1953 Brook agreed with Rowan that a start should be made with making them aware of the potentially crippling financial issues that had been identified; he suggested that Rowan should start with his own Ministers in the Treasury, without prejudice to the timing of any approach to the Americans.[578] Rowan put up a short summary of the state of play on 31 July and the Chancellor subsequently wrote that 'work can certainly proceed on [the basis of Rowan's July submission].'[579] In general officials, led by Brook, continued to be shy of approaching the Americans on war finance, preferring to concentrate on more pressing issues, but putting down a marker that the UK would want to discuss questions of international finance in any future 'total' war when the Americans were ready to do so. Sir Eric Bowyer of the Ministry of Supply, for example, argued that if the UK indicated that it thought a large part of its industry would be knocked out in the first few weeks of war this would result in an end to American purchases of British equipment. Hall was in favour of a direct approach from the Prime Minister to the President to secure authority for informal exchanges on the likely British dependence on America.[580] Optimistically Brook thought it best to let the financial issues emerge naturally from discussions of supply, annotating a submission on war finance from Mallaby with the pessimistic observation that 'I am beginning to wonder whether we should be wise in any event to begin with the question of finance – on which in effect we offer nothing and ask for everything.'[581] The year closed with the Chancellor (Butler) agreeing to suggest an ad hoc meeting of ministers (Chancellor, Defence, Commonwealth, Colonial, Board of Trade, Supply, Minister of State Foreign Office, Economic Secretary) based on a document from Brook advocating a gradualist approach.[582]

Other issues crowded out Ministerial discussion such that by spring 1954 the military assumptions on which it was based were out of date.[583] On 11 May the N.E.W. Committee decided to suspend seeking Ministerial approval until the financial implications of the new strategic hypothesis had been assessed.[584] This hypothesis completely changed the assumptions. Freddy Bishop, the Secretary of the N.E.W. Committee, minuted that 'If the policy conclusions contained in the Chiefs of Staff's strategic re-assessment are accepted (namely, that there will not be a major war within four or five years; and that meanwhile our defence policy should be based on the primary aim of maintaining our position and influence as a world power, and discharging our Commonwealth and Colonial responsibilities, and secondly of making an effective contribution to the task of containing Communism), the need for detailed economic war-time planning becomes less urgent.'[585] He followed up with another warning in August: 'the studies which have so far been made of economic conditions in a future war have been overtaken by the hydrogen bomb and have become out of date if we assume that a future war will be waged with hydrogen bombs ... our economic thinking will have to be entirely different, and will have to be directed to cover the need, in a hydrogen bomb attack, to ensure mere survival, rather than the continuation of any industrial or military production.'[586] John Grieve Smith of the Treasury agreed; 'We seem, though, to be reaching (or have reached) the point where certain economic problems no longer arise because we could have little or no industrial production left ... the field for study is limited to the distribution of relief to the survivors in the U.K. from any allies better placed outside. The question of reviving the U.K. as an industrial economy is rapidly fading out of the picture.'[587] In these circumstances Bishop felt that the role of the Committee was becoming increasingly obscure.[588] Nevertheless the Committee survived until 1960.

Despite infrequent meetings and a significant hiatus in activity in the first year of the Churchill administration the planning had been a significant call on the time of the few officials involved (knowledge of its existence and work were kept to a small circle). It mostly operated below ministerial radar but it left those involved with a clear picture of the fragility of the United Kingdom's world aspirations. Under the supportive but questioning gaze of Brook the War Plans Secretariat operated under the day-to-day leadership of William Strath. Its achievements included a comprehensive specification of the machinery of government in war, plans for the continuity of the state with government operating from underground bunkers in the case of nuclear attack and elaborate War Book exercises to test the machinery. Ministers would shortly come face to face with the awful facts of nuclear conflict with the Strath report of March 1955 on the effects of a nuclear attack on the U.K.,[589] and would experience the limitations of British power during the Suez crisis.

Domestic Policy

The inheritance from Attlee of the nationalised industries was problematic. Public ownership had not yet achieved the hoped-for improvements in performance.

There were problems over the industries' structure, the relationship with Ministers and with Parliament, financial targets, the customer voice in markets where the customer had no choice, and how to deal with non-commercial activities.[590] The manifesto had been relatively silent on how the Conservatives would control the industries saying merely that 'All industries remaining nationalised will come within the purview of the Monopolies Commission.' Jock Colville records that the Prime Minister was exercised by how to denationalise road transport without making the railways insolvent.[591] The Economic Policy Committee (chaired by the Chancellor of the Exchequer) met 31 times (and considered 152 papers) in 1952. Most of the briefing fell to Mallaby in the Cabinet Office.[592] It was much concerned with restrictions on East-West trade championed by the United States, which the British wished to oppose but felt constrained by their dependence on American economic aid.[593]

Later in 1953 it set up a group to look at how to maintain production in light of a downturn in the American economy for which Brook proposed the Chancellor as chairman, with the Chancellor of the Duchy of Lancaster, Commonwealth Secretary, Minister of Labour, Minister of Housing, President of the Board of Trade and Postmaster General as members.[594] Control of public expenditure (then referred to as Supply Expenditure) was also a pressing issue with Brook's position somewhat harder on civil departments than on defence. He advocated charges for education (June 1953), opposed MAFF plans for government controlled meat marketing in favour of a free market (October), instructed that civil departments' spending on war preparations should be identified and collected together (April 1954), helped Lord Swinton (the Commonwealth Secretary) set up a committee to find options to save £100 million in 1955/56.[595] Yet when the Swinton Committee reported in July with proposals for £113 million of savings he was at pains to point up the political downside of some of the suggestions (mainly concerned with food prices and the National Health Service, totalling £36 million) – wouldn't Ministers have recognised these points for themselves anyway? – riding both horses by suggesting deferral of decisions on these items and that 'it would be helpful if they could approve in principle as many of the Committee's recommendations as possible.'[596]

It was in February 1954 that *The Economist* coined the phrase 'Butskellism' to describe the similarity in the economic policies of the Conservative and Labour parties during the Churchill administration. The following month, however, Brook warned the Prime Minister that punitive taxation was a disincentive to hard work and encouraged tax evasion – for which he was criticised in 1997 by the former Labour Party Deputy Leader, Roy Hattersley, for being overtly political and undermining of the Chancellor – thereby illustrating how the tolerance of 'truth unto power' had declined over the decades since 1954.[597] Hattersley quoted the ending of Brook's memorandum: 'If, therefore, ministers concluded – as Mr Butler does – that we have to go on for years and years in a long slow grind with income tax at 9s 6d in the pound [47½%] surtax at its present levels [up to 97½%], they will, in fact, be deciding that a Conservative government must perpetuate, or is at least powerless to alter, the pattern of society which the Socialists set out deliberately to create. It may be that this is inevitable. But ministers should look at this prospect squarely in the face before deciding that this is so.'

Also indicative of how behaviour changes over time there is a curious note from the Chancellor, RAB Butler, on 29 July 1954, responding to a suggestion of savings to be made by the use of contract labour for government cleaning. He wrote: 'We are honour bound by the National Whitley Agreement of 1938. This was to the effect that an experiment in cleaning by contract labour ... would not be extended without a prior opportunity for the expression of Staff Side views, and further that direct employment would be the[598] normal practice where the volume of cleaning would necessitate the employment of one or more cleaners.'

Brook had a comparable code of honour. In the face of a possible railway strike at the end of 1953 the Postmaster General sought confirmation from colleagues that Post Office van drivers should not be asked to carry by road mails which would ordinarily go by rail. Brook reported to the Home Secretary that the relevant official committee accepted the decision as it had been taken by the Postmaster General himself, but he felt that there was an important point of principle at stake and welcomed a review of the decision by Ministers. 'On expediency, the course proposed by the Post Office may be the wiser,' he wrote. 'But the case on the other side is that these mail-van drivers are Civil Servants and that it is the duty of all Civil Servants in an emergency to do whatever is needed to keep running the essential public services committed to their care.' He informed Maxwell-Fyfe, 'for your own information' that this very point had been considered by the Labour government in 1949 and had concluded that 'Civil Servants could be asked to undertake work different from, though analogous to, that on which they were ordinarily employed where this was necessary for the maintenance of essential services.' And in a second, more sensitive briefing explained that discussion at the Official Committee had been misinformed about the Labour government's intentions during a 1949 dock strike. 'It is not, as you know, my duty to disclose decisions of earlier Governments and I am sure you will not make public use of what I have written below,' he warned, 'But I thought it was dangerous to leave you under any impression that Labour Ministers had been ready to call for civilian volunteers to maintain essential services in a strike.'[599]

Analysis of Brook's 1953 Cabinet briefings points to over half addressing domestic issues (27% economic policy, 16% social policy, 14% the Coronation and other Royal Family matters). He could be brutally direct advising, for instance, on proposals to relieve unemployment in Northern Ireland: 'Northern Ireland's economic difficulties are due fundamentally to the fact that the trade unions have forced wages up to a point where her industries are no longer competitive. Should not the Minister of Labour be asked to see that this fact is brought home to the trade unions responsible?'[600] On another occasion he offered the opinion that 'The uneconomic level of rents is the most important outstanding relic of the fools' paradise in which the country was allowed to rest in the years immediately following the end of the war,'[601] and commenting on a proposal to remove controls on feeding stuffs and cereals:[602] 'If some people prefer white bread and indigestion is it still a duty of Government in 1953 to see that "the significant nutrients (so far as these can at present be identified) are added." '[603] Similarly, he was adamant that the government's aim should be to avoid getting left with any responsibility for dealing with a Sunday Observance Bill.[604] 'I had first-hand experience of it in 1931/32, when I was helping Oliver Stanley [Conservative MP for Bristol West, then Parliamentary Under-Secretary in the Home Office] with the Sunday Entertainment Bills; and I am sure that if he had still been alive he would have advised the Government at all costs to avoid getting embroiled again in Government legislation on this question. A free vote has to be allowed – and a Government Bill with a free vote nearly always ends in political embarrassment for the Government: strong passions are aroused on either side, and the "sides" do not at all correspond with normal Party divisions. Oliver Stanley certainly got very tired of being supported in the Division Lobbies by people who were normally his political opponents and finding himself constantly voting against his political friends.'[605]

But Brook also recognised the innate elitism of the ruling class, and the conservatism on social issues of the general public. The first is demonstrated particularly clearly in the debate over additional television channels to compete with the BBC. In June 1953 Brook briefed that the government should reverse an earlier policy decision in favour of sponsored television on the grounds that the House of Lords would reject the idea and the House of Commons might well also oppose it. 'In the country I would guess that there is a substantial body of opinion against sponsored television which would welcome the change of policy. In the long-run, when the storm has blown over, I believe that the Government would get credit for having decided not to risk a dangerous experiment.'[606] A week later Cabinet decided on a holding statement in the hope that opposition to sponsored television would grow and it would be possible to allow a free vote in the autumn, at the same time rejecting a suggestion that the opening of Parliament might be televised. '... as the Queen's speech ... is a political statement, the occasion is not a suitable one for television.'[607] And in the autumn the ministerial committee set up to look into the possibilities for a new channel reported that the least worst case was to make the transmission network a public corporation which would sell time to independent producers and finance itself by advertisements.[608]

Brook's recognition of the conservatism of the general public shines through when the Report of the Royal Commission on Capital Punishment landed with a thud in the government's in-tray during September 1953, two months after Churchill's emergence from convalescence. With a cruel irony the high priest of plain English and clear drafting, Sir Ernest Gowers whose *Plain Words* (first published in 1948) became the style bible for generations of civil servants, had presided over an opaque set of recommendations (89 in total). With some malice Brook reported on 30 July 1954 that 'Cabinet had no hesitation yesterday in rejecting the main recommendations of the Royal Commission on Capital Punishment ... The work of this Royal Commission occupied four and a half years and cost £23,000. I thought you might be interested in these figures, especially as you have been active lately in preventing the appointment of further Royal Commissions. This one, at least, seems to have been a lamentable waste of public time and money.'[609] It was left to Eden to see matters to a close. He informed Parliament on 24 November 1955 that the government was ready to provide time for a debate at the first reasonable opportunity.[610] Backbenchers would be afforded a free vote but Ministers would be expected to support the government line, which was a more extensive use of the Prerogative of Mercy, described by Brook as 'more in line with public opinion generally' than complete abolition. And it was Brook who wrote to Ministers on 15 February and 8 March to instruct them accordingly – but his private secretary, John Hunt refused to allow him to do so for the Committee Stage of the Bill proposing amendment of the law relating to murder (as recommended by the Royal Commission) as no specific government policy had been laid down on the amendments and in debate the Home Secretary might not give a sufficient lead on each one.[611]

Security

In *Defence of the Realm: the authorised history of MI5*, Christopher Andrew's judgement is that '[MI5] benefited from the confidence of the immensely influential Sir Norman Brook', who, as reported in the preceding section, was asked by Attlee in 1950 to conduct an inquiry into the Security Service.[612] Andrew describes how Brook was at first inclined to the view that counter-subversion was the Cinderella to counter-espionage and in Andrew's view, though persuaded away from that conclusion, Brook had been correct. Both aspects would be present in Brook's work during the Churchill administration, as was improvement in ministerial control of the intelligence agencies. Brook advocated that day to day the Security Service should be accountable to the Home Secretary though the Prime Minister would retain overall responsibility.[613] Attlee had rejected the idea, but in 1952 Churchill approved it and a revised Directive was issued by the Home Secretary (David Maxwell-Fyfe) to the Director General (DG) of the Service (Percy Sillitoe) which defined the role as, 'The Security Service is part of the Defence Forces of the country. Its task is the Defence of the Realm as a whole, from external and internal dangers arising from attempts of espionage and sabotage, or from actions of persons and organisations whether directed from within or without the country, which may be judged to be subversive of the state.'[614] Definition of actions 'which may be judged to be subversive of the state' was left to the DG so that the Service was largely self-tasking; hence Brook implemented his earlier recommendation for a committee of Permanent Secretaries (PSIS) to oversee its management, notably its staffing and budget[615] and continued to be a driving force for the Ministerial and Official Committees on Communism, as Secretary of the former and Chairman of the latter. Individual operations by the Security Service in the United Kingdom required authorisation by the Home Secretary, including, after 1953, those conducted on British soil on behalf of the Secret Intelligence Service (MI6).[616]

The Cadogan inquiry, set up into Foreign Service Regulations and practice in July 1951 in the wake of defections to Russia by the diplomats Burgess and Maclean, reported in mid 1952 recommending strengthening arrangements for assessing and reporting on the personal reliability of staff by those best placed to know. 'We therefore recommend that special steps should be taken to bring it home to all heads of sections in the Foreign Office that, despite the existence of the Security and Personnel Departments, it remains an important part of their responsibility to concern themselves with the security of the work of their section and the reliability of their staff' and should put themselves in a position where they are likely to be aware of any conduct or weakness of character which might carry a risk to security.[617] Brook had been one of three members and had been involved, together with Bridges, in concurrent action to secure the Prime Minister's support for continuation of the drive to purge the civil service of Communists and Fascists started by Attlee. Churchill suggested that candidates for especially sensitive posts should swear on oath whether they were, or had been, associated with the Communist party. Further consideration in a committee led by the Home Secretary found the idea to be impracticable since anyone who was discovered to have lied on oath was liable to prosecution for perjury and proof of association with the Communist party would mean the authorities disclosing their sources, many of which would be covert. Brook reported this to Churchill, at the same time reminding him that his formal approval for a policy of continuing to exclude Communists from access to secret government work was outstanding. Churchill's annotation to the note read 'Yes pro tem,' presumably referring to not pressing the suggestion of answering under oath.[618] In the face of Staff Side objections, however, he insisted that Cabinet ratify the vetting policy.[619]

The chief focus for preventative security was the official Committee on Communism at home (AC(H)) and some of the ideas generated could be innovative, or even bizarre. In December 1951 SIS suggested using satire to ridicule Communism in the minds of the population at large: 'Listening last night to *Take it From Here* on the BBC, which I hope you find as funny as I do, I heard some extraordinarily amusing and really quite subtle anti-Communist gags. It struck me that this show – and Jimmy Edwards in particular – offered excellent opportunities for a new activity on the home front.' Another possible broadcaster who might be used was Wilfred Pickles whose radio show, *Have a Go*, reached a home audience of over 20 million.[620] There followed an exchange between Cabinet Office officials that questioned whether good-humoured comedians were quite right for satire – 'A humorous attack ... must be based on satire which will really hurt and not on too easy-going English type of humour which tends to make out the opponents as not such bad fellows after all.' Brook responded by musing whether Noel Coward was 'the sort of person I should be more inclined to favour,' adding, 'though I can believe that from other points of view he might not be a safe bet. Perhaps people of a satirical turn of mind are not apt to be "reliable": but you may be able to think of one who is.'[621]

This suggestion apart, the agenda Brook put forward for AC(H) was mostly designed to ensure that the Security Service, and the government more generally, focused sufficient attention on Communist penetration of areas of British life with influence on the population. These included academics, teachers, the BBC, and the higher civil service; *plus* Communist-controlled front organisations and Communist-inspired conferences. Members of the Committee approached a number of universities to discuss infiltration – Brook, for instance, spoke to Cambridge about the extent of Communist influence in the Economics Faculty. The Committee did not accept the Ministry of Education view that 'nothing could be done to deal with Communists or fellow-travellers among the school teachers.' In its view it would be best to lay the emphasis on countering Soviet propaganda, especially in the Teacher Training Schools; scientists and economists were thought especially susceptible to Communist doctrine. Steps were also taken to monitor the Soviet-controlled network in the United Kingdom, to resist the setting up in the UK of Communist-controlled bodies such as the International Association of Democratic Lawyers, to monitor a Science for Peace Conference in 1952, to restrict the number of foreign delegates attending a Conference of the Communist Party of Great Britain and to limit access to foreign exchange for people travelling to Communist functions abroad.[622] On the other hand the Committee found no reason to take action to strengthen legislation on subversive activities, treason or trading with the enemy.[623] Meanwhile, in a handover briefing for an incoming secretary of the official committee, outstanding actions included regularising allies' intelligence activities in Britain to prevent expenditure from secret funds other than through the agency of SIS; to rule out the use of the UK as a base for agent recruitment, except as an exceptional measure and only with the prior approval of SIS and the Security Service.'[624]

Positive vetting of civil servants for sensitive posts continued, with Brook seeking to remove the distinction between vetting for atomic posts (which required field enquiries) and other vetting (which left the decision to the discretion of Departments). In January 1955 the Personnel Security Committee agreed that 'it was unwise to employ Communists in senior civil service posts, particularly at the rank of Under-Secretary and above; but to exclude them from such posts when the nature of the work was not vital to the security of the State was not in accordance with existing Government policy.'[625] By the autumn of 1954 the number of posts falling within the ambit of positive vetting had risen from 2,000 as recommended by Bridges in March 1950 to 10,000.[626] At Higher Executive Officer and above the number of actions arising from personnel deemed to be a security risk were:[627]

Year	*Dismissed*	*Transferred*	*Resigned*
1951	Nil	4	Nil
1952	Nil	Nil	1
1953	Nil	Nil	Nil
1954	Nil	2	Nil
1955	Nil	1	Nil

Meanwhile, discussions with the US authorities on the security of atomic energy were continuing with a tripartite meeting (US/UK/France) scheduled for late January 1955. The primary British objective was to satisfy the United States that its atomic energy security standards were sufficiently rigorous to ensure Congressional agreement to bilateral co-operation.[628] After an informal (but minuted) discussion with Edwin Plowden (of the Atomic Energy Authority) Patrick Dean (FO) and Dick White (MI5) a draft negotiating brief for the Authority to use in informal discussions was submitted to the Official Committee on Security (S(O)) and agreed on 17 January.[629] The British had been hoping to use the sessions to negotiate agreement on collaboration despite 'the present unsatisfactory basis of our positive vetting policy in the field of atomic energy.'[630] But the S(O) Committee settled for the American preference for fact-finding informal discussions to be led by the Atomic Energy Authority and Security Service to smoke out the American requirements with a view to formal negotiations later.

Offensive action against the spread of Communism was of more interest to Ministers than preventative measures but less well articulated and open to ridicule – the Home Secretary banned four Soviet women from attending a conference in London in March 1952, described by the *Daily Express* as 'a congress of cranks that every sane Briton will laugh at ... Let them see what life is like in a free country.'[631] Churchill proposed to President Truman an idiosyncratic idea for Western military pilots to drop propaganda leaflets over the USSR, arguing that 'the brave young men of the Air Forces of the West would surely be ready to risk their lives "in carrying truth rather than death" to the people of the Soviet Union and its satellites' to spell out what life was like under Communism. But as Brook pointed out, the inhabitants already knew what it was like, pilots' lives would be put at risk to no real purpose.[632] And as the SIS representative on the Committee argued in July, key government policies towards the Soviet Union were opaque. 'At the moment no one knew whether HMG was in favour of the liberation of the satellite peoples or not ...'[633] Similarly when, on 17 August, a *Sunday Express* report implied that an atomic bomb test would take place in Australia in November the Prime Minister had to be reminded by Brook that four months earlier he had approved a deception operation aimed at the Russians about the nature and date of the test (codename operation HURRICANE).[634] Brook added, however, 'It is certainly arguable whether an organisation for practising deception, as evolved during the war, should be maintained in time of peace.'

All of which bore out Brook's sense of disappointment with the performance of the Committees on Communism at home and overseas. He had said as much in May when preparing for discussions with the Australian intelligence agencies.[635] Now, as the Chiefs of Staff joined the fray, soliciting the views of AC(H) members on how to combat Communism – but putting forward none of their own.[636] Brook feared 'that we should get nothing out of them if we asked what they had in mind ... but they will expect some response.' On the overseas side the Chiefs would be told that intensification of work in Commonwealth countries and in the Far East was under consideration and that a move had been made in NATO to stimulate further action from other Western countries against their Communist problem. On the home front he mused that the Committee should be asked to 'consider whether we would think it right to do any more than the little we have done up to date,' adding 'I have no suggestions to make myself; but I think we ought to get the other members of the Committee to think a little about this.'[637] A report on the achievements of the AC(H) Committee was circulated the following January. In 1951 there had been five meetings of AC(H) with 12 papers; in 1952 four meetings with 21 papers but few decisions had led to firm action and Brook's own leadership had been cautious.

His response was to reorganise. At the beginning of the Churchill administration the Prime Minister had not questioned continuation of the two official committees on anti-Communist activities at home (AC(H)) and overseas (AC(O)) but was not thought to be aware of the scope of their work.[638] The Ministerial Committee (AC(M)) was to all intents and purposes defunct – it had not met since July 1951. First the terms of reference of the Ministerial committee on vetting were widened to cover any security issue.[639] Then an official Anti-Communism at home Committee was set up, chaired by Brook with its members drawn from the Foreign Office, Home Office, Treasury, Defence, Supply, Admiralty, War Office, Air Ministry, and MI5.[640] But problems persisted, with the Chiefs of Staff frustrated at the opportunities in the AC(O) committee to air their views on anti-Communist propaganda overseas (in particular concerning South East Asia) and the chairman (Ward of the FO) conscious that the Foreign Secretary (Anthony Eden) was protective of what he saw as his preserve, and hence finding himself required to act as a brake on the Committee's ideas. Yet Brook was powerless to solve this problem. A Ministerial Committee on overseas activity was unthinkable without the Foreign Secretary; he could not be a neutral chairman who could rule on differences between the Chiefs and his own Department; the Prime Minister would have to chair the discussions and at the start of 1955 Brook was clear that 'there was no prospect of his doing so.' The best Brook could offer was that if Ministerial decisions were required 'we should suggest a meeting between the Foreign Secretary and the Minister of Defence.'[641] The hope had to be that the Prime Minister's impending retirement would remove the problem.

Memoirs

Dr Tom Jones was Deputy Cabinet Secretary from 1916 to 1930 and in 1938 had delivered the first Welsh National Lecture.[642] It was a romp through the skills and reputations of Prime Ministers ranging from Peel ('[whose] smile was compared to the silver plate on a coffin lid') through Gladstone ('Oxford on the surface, and Liverpool beneath') to Lloyd-George ('[who] concentrated his entire attention upon you; you were the one person he wished to see. Whatever your experience he was prepared to learn from it.'). Jones had kept a diary during his time in the Cabinet Office and in 1947 Bridges got wind that he was planning to publish a memoir based, in part, on the diaries.[643] The draft text arrived on Bridges' desk in 1953 and he crawled through it, conscious that Maurice Hankey had also planned to publish a memoir of his time in office but was still refused permission to do so. Indeed, Attlee's last word on Hankey's book had been, 'Lord Hankey must also cut out detailed records about his day to day relations with Ministers and the relations between Ministers.'[644] Nevertheless, Bridges thought that the two cases were very different. Jones was writing simply about the people he met and the interesting things they said – with suitable excisions 'the mere fact that the book was based on a diary was no reason why it should be wholly banned.' He concluded that permission should be granted 'provided that passages are excised from the book which impinge on the confidential relationship [between Ministers and civil servants].' But, he added, 'the odds are that we shall have further trouble with Hankey.' On 28 May Brook advised the Prime Minister of Jones' text and sought Ministerial guidance on what should and should not be allowed to pass.

At first Churchill was sympathetic to publication. 'Even the Soviet cannot prevent a man keeping a secret diary. I hope some have. No hard and fast rule can be laid down. Time passes its sponge across the significance of all records ... Show me, as examples, the dozen passages of Dr Jones' book which you consider the most questionable.'[645] Having read some of the extracts, however, including one critical of the accuracy of Churchill's own account of his appointment to the Admiralty, the Prime Minister did a volte face and instructed that 'every lawful or proper method [be] used to prevent their publication.'[646] Thus, Bridges made contact with Jones on the basis of a draft letter prepared by Brook, which explained in general terms the nature of the objections to the then text. In words that come oddly from a Wolverhampton grammar school boy, Brook wrote 'It may be that no man is a hero to his valet; but a man who relaxes his self-control in his valet's presence usually assumes that his valet will not write memoirs.'[647] Jones, shortly to be 83 years old, replied that revision would be difficult so he had decided not to publish this first volume in his own lifetime but to press on with volume two covering 1931–50 (by which time he had left the civil service and become secretary of the Pilgrim Trust).[648]

Brook and Bridges thought this sinuous since it would leave the text unchanged, no doubt in the hope that Jones' son or executor would be able to publish it soon after he died.[649] Volume two was published in the autumn of 1954 and in mid June the following year Bridges heard that volume one was being printed privately in Switzerland.[650] Churchill had of course retired and Eden was now Prime Minister. Four months later Jones died, prompting Brook to draft for Bridges to acquaint Jones' son with the position; there was no official veto but if certain changes were to be made to the text the official objections previously raised to its publication might well be withdrawn.[651] However, Bridges was reluctant to write so soon after Jones' death to a son he had never met and proposed instead to exercise a behind-the-scenes influence at the proposed publisher (the OUP). They appeared uncertain about proceeding with publication of volume one and so Bridges decided to let things rumble on.[652] In the event the political memoirs were published under the title *Whitehall Diary* between 1969 and 1971; but the battle with Hankey continued into the premiership of Macmillan.

Churchill Retires

After Churchill's stroke in 1953 it would have been natural for a 79 year old to lay down the burdens of office. In December Brook told Lord Moran during the Bermuda Conference that Churchill had become lazy, but that 'it is much better from the country's point of view that he should stay on.'[653] Nevertheless, at the beginning of April the following year he reported to Moran that there was a feeling that younger men who were full of energy and drive were needed in the government and that there would be a row if Churchill did not step down by the end of July.[654] Close though Brook was to the Prime Minister, understandably he was reluctant to give this message to Churchill directly,[655] though at about the same time Churchill confided in Butler that 'I feel like an aeroplane at the end of its flight, in the dusk, with the petrol running out, in search of a safe landing.'[656] As it became apparent that the hopes for a major power summit that would defuse tension and set the scene for peaceful co-existence would not be realised Lord Woolton records that Churchill announced on 15 December 1954 that he was planning to retire the following July.[657] Eden argued that this would not allow sufficient time to be ready for a General Election and by February Churchill had decided for himself that he should go somewhat earlier, fixing the date as 5 April.[658] In the middle of March, however, he received news that Eisenhower wanted a great celebration on 8 May to mark the tenth anniversary of V-E Day, followed by a four-power meeting aimed at securing peaceful co-existence between the West and the Soviets. Brook warned Eden of potential backsliding by Churchill. However, no retirement discussion at Cabinet is minuted, nor do Brook's Cabinet Secretary notebooks indicate a discussion.[659] Lord Woolton's papers appear to suggest one, nevertheless. Eisenhower's visit was put off and Churchill did step down on 5 April as he intended. As twist of fate, a strike in the newspaper industry meant that the retirement was not reported at the time. The partnership between Churchill and Brook had been particularly close and contrasts markedly with Brook's relationship to Attlee. The acerbic language in which Brook described some of the Attlee administration's domestic policies points to where his sympathies lay. The question now was whether the accession of Anthony Eden would break the spell.

Succession

Having been Churchill's heir apparent since 1940 and a Cabinet Minister for the whole of that time Anthony Eden's appointment as Prime Minister was warmly greeted by the press and the Conservative party. He was 57 years of age – young in relation to Churchill but seasoned and experienced at the highest levels of government. As John Ramsden, the historian of the Conservative party, put it, the press credited Eden with all sorts of outstanding abilities, a personal skill for the maintenance of Anglo-American relations, a particular understanding of his party, and a special qualification to head the Cabinet itself because of his knowledge and understanding of Cabinet methods and processes.[660] Allied with Brook's talent for the orderly conduct of business and coolness under pressure the combination should have been made in Heaven. But Eden was a politician of narrow experience and narrow interests.[661] On foreign affairs, during the war, he was the main voice arguing for closeness with the Russians, but otherwise appears to have 'played next to no part in the day-to-day creation of a grand strategy.'[662] And on all domestic matters Butler, the inherited Chancellor, consciously set out to 'manage him from behind'.[663] Within two years of replacing Churchill, Eden's administration was brought low by procrastination over domestic policies and by a major failure in foreign policy.

It all started so well. Eden called an early General Election[664] and was returned on 26 May 1955 with an increased Conservative share of the vote (up from 48.0% in 1951 to 49.7%) and a comfortable overall majority of 58.[665] But there were early signs of trouble. As early as 5 May (i.e. at the start of the election campaign) Eden complained that the Cabinet Conclusions of the Meeting on Tuesday 3 May were too full – with special mention of an item alleging that the Labour MP Richard Crossman had incited violence when in Cyprus in March. Brook apologised for the specific reference (admitting that perhaps he had been mistaken in recording the exchange – the conclusion had simply been that the incident should not be mentioned by government spokesmen in a debate scheduled for 5 May at the instigation of the Opposition) but argued strongly that Eden was wrong to claim that 'Cabinet minutes are distributed far and wide.' They were not; furthermore, as Brook pointed out, to curtail the circulation would interfere with 'the principle of collective responsibility and the efficient conduct of Government business.'[666] After the election victory there was no reshuffling of Ministers to stamp Eden's mark on the new Cabinet and on 10 April Eden solicited information from his colleagues about issues requiring early attention, presaging a questioning and intrusive style that would infuriate many.[667] Brook had instituted a weekly Cabinet forward look for Churchill that would have been the basis for a more-than-adequate draft list and would have set the new Prime Minister firmly in the leadership seat, even on those domestic matters Butler thought he could engineer from beneath. But as Brook later commented to William Clark, Eden's press secretary, 'Our Prime Minister is very difficult. He wants to be Foreign Secretary, Minister of Defence and Chancellor.'[668]

Cabinet

An unwelcome inheritance was that Cabinet had grown used, under Churchill, to discursive sessions that sometimes failed to reach even early agenda items. In the words of John Ramsden again, under Churchill: 'Often the whole time allocated for the meeting was taken up with general discussion of political problems, none of which were on the agenda or prepared for by the Secretariat and the ministers present.'[669] Cabinet had not been the incisive or decisive body that informed commentators expected, and there were early signs that Eden-led Cabinet discussions would not wholly reverse that tendency. On 28 April Brook pointed up the need to press ahead with the Clean Air Bill and he warned again on 27 June of the risks of delay, even if the price of progress was that local authorities should make a bigger contribution to costs.[670] On 6 June he advised delaying a decision on whether to change the 50-year rule for access to government documents.[671] On 26 July Macmillan's diary records: 'The last item on the agenda was an FO [Foreign Office] item – the vast and complicated problem of Arab/Israel relations – the Anglo-American plan on which we had long been working (known as ALPHA) ... However, the item before was the suggested road changes at Hyde Park Corner. So we never got as far as Egypt or Palestine.'[672]

Eden too was showing signs of frustration at delays in developing firm policies.[673] In April he told the Home Secretary (Gwyllam Lloyd George) he wanted the issue of Jamaican immigrants discussed at Cabinet[674] yet by November Brook was pointing out that Cabinet had already discussed colonial immigration 15 times without reaching a decision between those who wanted legislation to 'guard against the long-term threat to the racial character of the British people' and those who thought that 'colonial immigration was not yet a matter of general public concern.'[675] Cabinet had previously decided that Conservative candidates in the May General Election should be advised to say no more on the subject than that colonial immigration, 'might be a suitable subject for some form of public enquiry.'[676] The British Nationality Act 1948 had granted the subjects of the British Empire the right to live and work in the UK; Commonwealth citizens were not, therefore, subject to immigration control and a subsequent Home Office estimate is that the net intake of immigrants from all origins from January 1955 to June 1962 was around 472,000, i.e. about 63,000 p.a.[677] A major component was Irish immigration but that from the colonies was accelerating (from 3,000 in 1953 to 10,000 in 1954 and 35,000 in 1955).[678] In a classic manoeuvre designed to keep the proposal in play until a more propitious moment, Brook suggested a re-examination of how legislation to control immigration might work yet not restrict entry for 'kith and kin' from the colonies. The ploy was, and is, well practised; it can prevent a damaging split in Cabinet, allow the Prime Minister to stack an ad hoc committee with supporters and, often, since the result is advice that is very close to the prevailing position (in this case a draft Bill commissioned in December 1954 and discussed on 7 July)[679] it removes the stigma associated with proposals for controversial change – people have become more used to the proposals, have discussed them before, grown familiar with the language of change and perhaps no longer regard what is proposed as quite so novel or contentious. Still Cabinet remained reluctant to move openly, a committee under the Lord Chancellor (the former Home Secretary Viscount Kilmuir) concluding that it was inevitable that restrictions would be put on immigration but not yet.[680]

The initial Eden Cabinet was, however, relatively united around an intention to tackle Trades Union power, though the Minister, Walter Monckton, was not in favour of such a course and Brook showed little urgency; for example, over a report on industrial relations from the British Employers' Federation which discussed whether compulsory arbitration should be a permanent feature of industrial disputes.[681] The Cabinet Industrial Relations Committee, chaired by the Chancellor (Butler) twice deferred a decision on whether to commission an independent inquiry which would have addressed the vexed issue of secret ballots for union elections and before official strike action, believed by many influential industrialists to be of crucial importance, (including Lord Nuffield who lobbied the Prime Minister in July about the importance of secret ballots, particularly in union elections where there was great concern about growing Communist influence). At Brook's recommendation, the Committee was wound up as ineffective in April 1956.[682] Brook's lack of drive in this area is significant because by April the following year the anti-subversion committee (AC(H) of which he was the chairman) identified that the Communist Party of Great Britain put gaining influence and control at union executive committees as a higher priority than influence over individual strikes.[683]

After Butler's expansionist spring Budget in 1955 and an election pledge for an industrial boom, inflation was creeping up, imports soared and sterling was under pressure. Though the Prime Minister specifically asked Brook to keep him in touch with economic matters,[684] for the most part he left advice on economic matters to Bridges and Treasury officials. But when Butler, spurred on by Eden and Macmillan, started to talk about the potential contribution a reimposition of building controls might make towards curbing inflation his grasp of the practicalities of turning policy into practice compelled Brook to intervene forcefully. On 25 July he wrote to Eden, 'The real difficulties about building control arise, however, not from doctrinaire objections but from severely practical considerations ... In peace-time, building control is a thing which no sensible administrator would care to attempt ... It involves creating ... a whole series of dreary offences for actions which are not morally reprehensible ... It involves a risk of corruption ... [and] as we found under the Labour Government, it is far more difficult to apply in peace-time criteria related to the improvement of the national economy. And it is certainly true that we have never yet attempted to use building control for the purpose of contracting the total quantity of building activity ... and there would certainly be an uproar if we started to do so.'[685] By February he was convinced that government action to curb demand was motivationally wrong and could be represented as repressive. 'The root cause of inflation is, surely, that people are not working hard enough for what they earn ... . Should we not make it clear that there is nothing wrong with a high level of consumption, so long as it is earned; and that investment is also positively desirable when we have earned the money to pay for it? The right message to the workers now is that they should work harder or longer to earn their television sets and washing machines, and should also save in order to help to finance the investment which will ultimately bring them an even higher standard of living.'[686] Eden's manuscript annotations indicate agreement, but also caution as '[the] Treasury have never liked the theme [of deferred consumption] and have been slow about savings schemes.' In hindsight Brook's advice seems curiously puritanical after the tribulations of post-war austerity suffered by the victorious population and out of touch with electoral reality.

On social policy Brook, meanwhile, warned in mid October 1955 that the recommendations of the Royal Commission on capital punishment would be peripheral to the main question, which was possible abolition – and that was outside the Commission's remit.[687] Cabinet endorsed the Prime Minister's view that 'although any announcement would doubtless give fresh impetus to the demand that the death penalty should be abolished, nothing in his view had occurred to warrant any modification of the view which the Cabinet had previously taken. An announcement of the Government's decisions on the matter should therefore be made at the first suitable opportunity.'[688] But the abolitionists seized the initiative with a Private Member's Bill sponsored by Sydney Silverman[689] and Eden's Parliamentary Private Secretary (Robert Carr) reported that the mood in the House of Commons was swinging in favour of abolition but the House of Lords remained opposed[690] such that when the issue again came before Cabinet in February 1956 Brook foresaw great difficulties if the government announced that it would be guided by a free vote in the Commons, as had been promised.[691] He argued that when the Commons had carried a clause in 1948 in favour of an experiment of abolition the Lords had rejected it 'and appeared to be a better judge of public opinion than the Commons.' Would it be asking too much, he speculated, to ask the Commons to wait until the Lords had made their view known and then for the government to decide on the course to follow? His view was supported in this by a letter from Oliver Poole (Chairman of the Conservative Party) to the effect that most Conservatives did not want abolition and were angry that the government had allowed the present situation to arise.[692] Ministers were told that they would not be free to vote as their consciences dictated on the Second Reading of the Bill to abolish the death penalty.[693]

The real Parliamentary objective, according to Brook, was to produce a feeling that it was not worthwhile to change the existing law; hence, the government was under no obligation to make the abolitionists' Private Members Bill a workmanlike measure. On the other hand, by September he had swung round in favour of a Government Bill, which would retain capital punishment. In Brook's view this would 'accord with the majority of opinion throughout the country [and] the Government's authority and reputation would be strengthened … A Government which leaves an issue to a free vote in Parliament, because it cannot make up its own mind about it, does not enhance its reputation and usually gets into political difficulties. And on this issue, which directly affects the preservation of law and order, the Government has a duty to take a line and stick to it.' Furthermore, 'with Suez and the economic situation, let alone rent restriction, we cannot expect a period of friendly co-operation between the parties … Parliament … would be better occupied, surely, in discussing this than in passing legislation on slaughterhouses, land drainage, Geneva conventions or other projects in the legislative programme ... It would be a topsy-turvy world in which the Government were unable to put through major measures which would hold public attention and enhance their reputation ... because the legislative programme was so full of dreary Departmental Bills that no Parliamentary time was available for major measures of reform.'[694]

The Constitution

At about the same time Princess Margaret wrote to the Prime Minister in August 1955 about whether she would seek the permission of Her Majesty The Queen to marry the divorcee, Group Captain Peter Townsend, as would be required by the Royal Marriages Act, 1772. In a manuscript letter she indicated that she was uncertain whether her feelings for Group Captain Townsend were sufficiently strong to go down this route: 'At the end of October or early November I very much hope to be in a position to tell you and the other Commonwealth Prime Ministers what I intend to do.'[695] Also in manuscript, Brook advised Eden that 'I am quite clear that this is not a matter for the Prime Minister alone. The advice given must be the advice of the Government.'[696] However, a day later Eden and Brook agreed that delay '[sic] do the monarchy no good if the decision were held up much longer.'[697] Conscious that the public mood (which had been sympathetic to the princess's situation) 'could change to one containing some elements of boredom and exasperation'[698] Brook worked energetically with Sir Michael Adeane of the Palace staff to clarify the procedure to be followed if the princess were to decide to marry Townsend (including the approval of Commonwealth Governments).[699] By October his researches into the conditions surrounding a marriage by the princess pointed to a possible complication over £6,000 a year she received from the Civil List. That emolument was subject to conditions laid down by the Sovereign and, since it was first paid during the reign of King George VI, 'it is possible that the late King might have made some condition relevant to the situation which we have been discussing.'[700] In the event, Princess Margaret issued a statement on 31 October 1955, which said: 'Mindful of the Church's teachings that Christian marriage is indissoluble, and conscious of my duty to the Commonwealth, I have resolved to put these considerations before others.'

Death of Optimism

Meanwhile, such was the inherited weakness in Cabinet discipline that in mid December Brook approved a circular reminding Ministers that they must consult Cabinet (or one of its committees) on small but controversial issues that might bring criticism of the government as well as on questions of major policy.[701] Brook's private papers[702] contain many glowing tributes from ministers referring to his unending willingness to help and guide them both procedurally through Cabinet and as a rock during political storms. But in the autumn of 1955 his health showed signs of weakening[703] and he missed Cabinet, leaving much of the briefing from the middle of October to Hooper (head of the Civil Committee Secretariat in the Cabinet Office). A Cabinet reshuffle on 20 December did little to improve perceptions of the government – Eden's official biographer concludes that 'Anthony never built a Cabinet in his own mould. He inherited one, and then tinkered with it,' – the replacement of Walter Monckton by Iain Macleod as Minister for Labour and National Service, for instance, was unlikely to be welcomed by the right wing of the party and unlikely to press urgency in trades union reform.[704] Monckton went to be Minister of Defence, with awkward consequences during the early stages of the Suez crisis and was replaced by Anthony Head in October 1956.

By early 1956 the initial optimism of the press had been rapidly eroded. On 2 January *The Times* complained of a flabby government supported by a flabby civil service; and on 3 March the normally loyal *Daily Telegraph* referred to a lack of firm government. The polls pointed to the Prime Minister's personal approval rating having fallen from 70% in the autumn of 1955 to 40% by the spring of 1956.[705] For Brook, however, there was an unsolicited expression of admiration from the new Chancellor (Macmillan) who wrote 'Last night I read your record of Tuesday's two Cabinet meetings. I should like to congratulate you and your assistants on your quite extraordinary efficiency and accuracy. I freely confess that, having read them, I am much clearer than before exactly where I stand now on my "packet" of measures.'[706] But mastery of the machinery was not enough to end the charge of drift. Reform of the House of Lords was another case in point. In May Brook identified the key outstanding questions and pressed the case for reform; he did so again in July but little progress had been made by September when he concluded that the crisis over nationalisation of the Suez Canal would inevitably mean further postponement and by the end of the year it was doubtful if the government could command a majority in the Commons for a reform package.[707]

On most of these social and economic issues Brook played an essentially reactive role responding to the proposals of others. An exception was reform of the House of Lords where he consistently encouraged Eden to have the courage to press ahead with proposals for Life Peers and for restrictions on the numbers of hereditary peers in the House. In a typical brief from mid 1956 he would argue that it would be greatly to the government's credit to have made the attempt at reform even if it were to fail and if it could pull off reform the credit with the public would be overriding.[708] But the Suez crisis intervened and by September Brook was advocating a 12-month delay.[709] Meanwhile, behind the scenes, Brook was a lead adviser to the Prime Minister on defence strategy and organisation, the security of the state and certain aspects of Britain's place in the world, notably the Commonwealth, the legacy of empire and what should be Britain's relationship with a renascent Europe.

Streamlining Defence

The aftermath of vastly increased defence spending in response to the Korean War of 1950–53 was still being felt when Eden replaced Churchill. As Foreign Secretary, he had supported the Chiefs of Staff during the 1952 radical review of defence spending; but on assuming the premiership he soon moved his position to that of support for Treasury attempts to rein in the defence budget which accounted for £1.4 billion (7.1% of GDP) in 1955/56.[710] Against GNP the position was even starker at 9%, twice the level of other NATO countries and it had never been below 8% since 1945.[711] Conscious, perhaps, that he did not command Churchill's authority in defence matters (nor share the old man's passion for it) Eden needed a strong ministerial ally within the defence ambit to control the ambitions of the Chiefs of Staff and the Service Ministers. Expenditure battles with the Treasury tended to be fought out through evaluation of rival weapons systems – unknown territory for the new Prime Minister where he relied on the guidance of Brook and Bishop (his Principal Private Secretary) on how to challenge the competing Service claims. Further, a higher defence structure, which had four ministers, three chiefs of staff, four permanent secretaries and a separate Ministry of Supply, also with a minister and permanent secretary, suggested bureaucratic duplication and waste on a large scale.

Thus, Brook found it necessary to immerse himself in both the detail of individual projects and programmes and in the grand strategy for defence of the West including the mechanics of decision-making. At the detailed level he made a case for stopping the development of chemical weapons (which he judged unimportant to the main objective of defence policy – the prevention of global war);[712] he challenged the Royal Air Force view of the urgency to settle the number of fighter and bomber aircraft;[713] and, at a more reflective level, argued that 'Ministers really cannot accept a position in which they settle only the cash and the commitments and leave the whole business of policy and programmes to the Services or the Service Departments … The proper way to proceed is to form provisional views on these various aspects of the problem, as we go along, and bring the whole thing together at the end when we make a final judgement on the size and shape of our defence effort.'[714]

At the same time he guided Eden in how to orchestrate a long-term review of commitments, in May pointing towards a change of emphasis in Europe, the Middle East and South East Asia away from total reliance on military presence to economic and propaganda initiatives.[715] In support of this he gathered a small group of senior officials from the Foreign Office, Ministry of Defence and Treasury to prepare a paper on the essential objects of British policy in political, military and economic terms. Informed by the Bulganin and Khrushchev talks in London in April, this led to the Prime Minister circulating as three basic assumptions for a Ministerial discussion: (1) the main threat to the United Kingdom now was political and economic rather than military; (2) the period of foreign aid to the United Kingdom was over and it must, therefore, cut its coat according to its cloth; (3) in defence too much was being done to guard against the least likely (though potentially catastrophic) risk – major war. He then set out, in early June, proposals for a network of committees to work up details on economic objectives; political and military objectives; the structure and sourcing of the deterrent; adjusting the shape and size of NATO forces to the new political situation; the defence of the homeland in the light of an assumption that war involving an attack on the United Kingdom was unlikely; putting the civil side of home defence on a care and maintenance basis; economies in the cost of military presence in the Middle East, Eastern Asia, Africa and other small out-of-area territories.[716] The Policy Review Committee under Eden's chairmanship authorised specific action on most of them at a meeting on 7 June, leaving aside action on economic issues and Commonwealth consultation. In the space of ten weeks or so all of this would be put on hold as the Suez crisis gripped the attention of the Prime Minister.

Internationally Brook sought to switch the emphasis in disarmament discussions 'to look rather more as though we were trying to find a way out of these difficulties – and spend rather less time in scoring points off the Russians … Would it not be preferable to place the emphasis on defending our own proposals, rather than criticising the Soviet position?'[717] Yet when, in July 1956 – two weeks before the Egyptians nationalised the Suez Canal, the Chiefs of Staff sought guidance on the specifics of should they plan for the possibility that the UK might alone, without Allies, be involved in a war against Egypt he advised that 'the contingency is so remote that we could take the risk of telling [the Chiefs] that they need not take account of it in their plans.'[718] And in the same brief he gave a startling answer to the Chiefs' question: Should they plan on the assumption that the question whether nuclear weapons would be used in a limited war would be a political decision to be taken at the time by the government of the day? He wrote, 'This must, of course, remain a political decision … There have been other signs recently that some, at least, of the Chiefs of Staff are beginning to think on the lines that nuclear weapons may not in the event be used and they must therefore be ready to fight an old-fashioned, "gentleman's war;" and continued, "I believe that nuclear weapons will be used tactically in the field – indeed in a few years' time, they will be the standard equipment of United States forces, which will not be able to go into action without them."' In fairness it must be added, however, that his brief concluded with sound advice that 'the factor which will determine the exercise of that discretion [to use tactical nuclear weapons], on both sides, will be the desire to avoid enlarging the area of conflict and thus precipitating a major war.'

Public pressure, meanwhile, was building for structural reform in the central organisation of defence and attempts were made to bring more power under the hands of the Minister of Defence at the expense of the Service Ministers and the Chiefs. In October 1955 Eden appointed the outgoing Chief of the Air Staff, Sir William Dickson, to a new position as permanent chairman of the Chiefs' Committee, which would help improve the discussion of defence policy within the Department and hence strengthen the position of the Minister. By the time Brook was first asked to look into the possibility of bringing the Ministry of Supply (whose main task was to manage the weapons research and development programmes) into the Ministry of Defence the Suez crisis had broken and circumstances were not propitious for major reorganisation;[719] but in December the Minister of Supply (Reginald Maudling) raised the issue once again and Brook set about consulting the relevant Permanent Secretaries. The result, once again, was stalemate.[720] However, views widely expressed in a House of Lords debate of November 1955 increased the pressure for internal reform in the Ministry of Defence itself. Brook was concerned that the government would be rushed into ill-prepared action – notably because not all the parties were yet ready to agree the way forward. He wrote to Sir Harold Parker, the Permanent Secretary at the Ministry of Defence) that it would be a mistake on constitutional and practical grounds to strengthen the powers of the Minister of Defence at the expense of the Service Secretaries of State since he believed that the real problem was that Monckton was not sufficiently assertive over the Service Ministers.[721] He set out for Monckton a formal statement of the maximum of his powers and invited him to consider if he wanted to suggest an extension.[722] The implication was, of course, that Brook could not see what was the obstacle to the Minister so behaving and after Monckton resigned over Suez in October the new Minister, Anthony Head confirmed this view, by ignoring the offer of extra powers leading Freddie Bishop to tell Eden that 'it follows that any trouble in this respect so far has really been due to a lack of resolution.'[723]

Homeland Security

Two strands dominate domestic security issues between 1955 and 1957. The most dramatic is the aftermath of the defection to Russia of Burgess and Maclean in May 1951, including the exoneration of Kim Philby by Harold Macmillan in the House of Commons in October 1955 against rumours (later confirmed to be true) that he was the 'third man' who had tipped off Burgess and Maclean prior to their flight; but more lasting effects came from the continuing drive to prevent Communists and their sympathisers having access to the West's secrets.

Towards the end of September the government published the report of the Cadogan inquiry into the disappearance of Burgess and Maclean.[724] Eden spoke to Brook about preparation for the subsequent House of Commons debate and asked him for sight of an earlier report by officials which considered whether powers should be taken to prevent a person suspected of espionage from leaving the United Kingdom. The report had come down against such action and Brook now said, 'I have read it again, and I still think it makes a convincing case against legislation of this kind … In a debate about Maclean, the thing to stress on this point is, as I see it, that up to the moment of his departure we had no proof of his guilt. We were still trying to obtain evidence on which he could have been brought before the courts. We had not at that time enough evidence on which to apply for a warrant for his arrest. What people now forget is that it was the fact of his bolting that proved the case against him.'[725] The following month Brook became even more determined in his opposition to the idea, with a defence of the historic freedoms, rights and liberties in the United Kingdom for which an occasional Maclean was not too high a price to pay.[726] Initially he was also opposed to Macmillan's conclusion that the government should lance the espionage boil by an inquiry into the efficacy of vetting but later came around to an ad hoc 'conference' of Privy Counsellors on the efficacy of security procedures, which was conceded during the House of Commons debate on Burgess and Maclean early in November. Details of the membership (Lord Privy Seal, Lord Chancellor, Home Secretary from the government side, Lord Jowitt; Herbert Morrison, George Strauss from the Opposition and, in Brook's absence with the Head of the Home Civil Service, Edward Bridges, as Secretary.)[727] At a meeting of officials under Bridges' chairmanship on 18 November particular problems to be drawn to the attention of the conference were listed as (a) when suspicions were aroused about an individual but proof of Communist sympathies was lacking; (b) how far Communist sympathies should be tolerated at Under-Secretary rank and above; (c) people with Communist friends or family; (d) the position of contractors' employees; (e) the possibility of House Unions in secret organisations; (f) character defects, under which heading homosexuals were described as 'a particular problem in the Foreign Office ... [but] there had been more defections to the Russians as a result of misconduct with women than from homosexual relationships'; (g) how far to involve the police in tracing character defects.

The Conference reported at the end of January; its conclusions were generally supportive of the vetting process and no great changes were suggested, though the Privy Counsellors were concerned about variations in the vetting standards between Departments and in paragraph 36 of the report said, 'We recommend that at least all posts held by officer of the rank of Under-Secretary and above should henceforth automatically be denied to Communists.'[728] An edited version went to Cabinet and formed the basis for a White Paper.[729] The Official Committee on Security met twice during July under Brook's chairmanship. It went into severe contortions to protect an individual's right to associate with, for example, a spouse or a sibling who was a Communist without damaging their own eligibility for appointment to an Under-Secretary post which did not regularly handle secret material (on the assumption that they were not a Communist sympathiser).[730]

Beyond the civil service there were persistent concerns about Communist influence in the trades unions. The Official Committee on Communism (Home), which Brook chaired, discussed the role of the Communist Party in industrial unrest 1953–55 in April 1956.[731] The Security Service reported that 'On first sight it might seem curious that while strikes were often instigated and maintained by individual Communists, the Party, as a Party, played little, if any part in them.'[732] Its aim was long-term control of union executives. Brook concluded that as this conclusion ran counter to popular (and Ministerial) perceptions, and as the government could not take direct action to prevent further penetration of the trades union movement (which was a matter for the unions themselves) they might alert Ministers and also coach anti-Communist union leaders, particularly over how to stop the political apathy of the non-Communist rank and file. He was opposed over this latter suggestion by Maston of the Ministry of Labour who argued that 'nothing should be done to jeapordise the Ministry of Labour's reputation for impartiality in helping to settle industrial disputes.' Brook duly advised Eden about the Communist Party of Great Britain's strategy[733] and followed this up with a note about a new initiative by union leaders through an organisation called Industrial Research and Information Service (IRIS) which would help counter Communist influence in the unions by exposing the records of Communists running for office.[734] The Committee returned to the issue three months later after Iain Macleod (the Minister of Labour) had raised the extent of Communist penetration with TUC leaders. Brook had, meanwhile, savaged Ministry of Labour officials in a further note to Eden in which he described them as 'most reluctant to advise their Minister to touch anything of this [IRIS] sort. They are, as you know, imbued with a laissez-faire philosophy and are in particular, frightened to death of doing anything which might be thought to impair the impartiality of their Minister as a "conciliator" in industrial disputes.'[735]

The Crabb Affair

In December 1962, in a speech at the US Military Academy at West Point, Dean Acheson, the former United States Secretary of State, succinctly put his finger on the British foreign policy problem of the latter half of the twentieth century. 'Great Britain has lost an Empire and has not yet found a role.'[736] At the time many in Britain were outraged by the comments but the challenge contained in his remarks was a recurring feature of Britain's post-war strategic foreign policy discussions. In April 1956, however, Eden seemed to have pulled off a propaganda coup when the Soviet leaders post-Stalin, Marshal Nikolai Bulganin and Nikita Khrushchev, paid an official visit to Britain from 18 to 27 April – seen in London as an important symbol of Britain's continuing world importance. Less than a month before the visit Brook was warning that the impression given by the Foreign Office options for conduct of the discussions was 'that we have very few positive or constructive things to say ... before we go further ... we ought to consider in a general way what we want to get out of this meeting, and how the discussions are to be handled.' Ministers should give a lead.[737] But the military and intelligence community knew what it wanted – Russian warships were rarely within range of British intelligence services and the visit presented a good opportunity to acquire information about the attributes of the Soviet cruiser the Ordzhonikidze with the Soviet leaders on board. But such was the political importance of the visit (the first by the Soviet leaders to the west) that Eden forbade British intelligence operations against the Russians whilst they were in Britain. In particular, in September 1955 he blocked proposals to test the thickness of the Russian ships' armour and their magnetic signal and in April 1956 when the Admiralty informed him of a plan (covered by Eden's standing approval for operations of this kind) to gather intelligence about their electronic equipment as the ships entered British waters (further described by the Admiralty as involving 'no risk of detection') Eden demurred: 'I am sorry but we cannot do anything of this kind on this occasion.'[738] In the former case he wrote, 'These ships are our guests and however we may think others would behave to us there are limits to what we should do to them. I therefore consider that we should take no action which involves the remotest risk of detection.'[739]

These instructions were known to the Director of Naval Intelligence and to the Foreign Office but by a series of misjudgements were not passed on to MI6 who mounted what should have been a relatively low-risk operation to obtain information about the Russian warships using a former naval frogman, Commander Crabb, who was an expert in shallow-water diving. Unfortunately, on 19 April the operation went badly wrong and Commander Crabb never surfaced from the dive – his partly decomposed headless body, minus hands, was found in Chichester harbour 14 months later. When Crabb failed to return to work the story began to break and the British press made hay of its colourful characteristics and the fact that the operation had not been constructed so as to be deniable by MI6. Brook carried out an immediate short investigation of the main facts, reporting on 8 May (24 hours before the Prime Minister was due to make a statement in the House of Commons) recommending a fuller inquiry before disciplinary actions were contemplated – to be conducted by the Head of the Home Civil Service, Edward Bridges.[740] Bridges' report was submitted ten days later.[741] Despite this failure, at an official level the Russian visit passed off without obvious discomfort – almost certainly the Russians had expected hostile intelligence activity; they had themselves gone to extraordinary lengths to ascertain intelligence about British naval ships during a visit by the Royal Navy to Leningrad in October 1955.[742]

The day after the Russian ships sailed from Portsmouth Brook gave Eden a list of what to do as a result of the talks: (1) the major issue of foreign policy now follows from the fact that 'we seem to have established the position that the Soviet Government do not want war, but may intend to pursue their objectives by other means'; (2) perhaps we should tone down the propaganda efforts of the Foreign Office Information Research Department (IRD)[743] to put across the British way of life; (3) look for improved trade opportunities with the Soviet Union that fall outside the NATO strategic controls; (4) shake up the British disarmament teams – 'My personal belief is that some of those who have been working on this problem for so long now are unable to see the wood for the trees'; (5) in the Middle East consider if we would lose much by an arrangement under the aegis of the United Nations for controlling arms supplies to areas of special tension and shift the emphasis of the Bagdad Pact from its military to its economic purposes.[744] The Prime Minister wrote to the Foreign Secretary in identical terms two days later.[745]

Fallout from the Crabb affair raised questions about the role of the Joint Intelligence Committee (JIC) in setting priorities for the Foreign Office intelligence agencies, MI6 and GCHQ. At that time it was the child of the Chiefs of Staff who were 'disqualified from doing the job in the round … there was no real way of looking on the intelligence problems from a broad policy point of view.'[746] As the author of the enquiry into the Crabb affair, it was natural for Bridges to lead on these issues concerning priorities, including procedures for clearing "special intelligence operations." The solution brokered with Brook was that the JIC should be transferred to the Cabinet Office.

Europe

On the burgeoning European moves towards integration Eden's known coolness had damaged his reputation with some important Conservatives, including Kilmuir (Lord Chancellor), Macmillan (who Eden appointed as his successor as Foreign Secretary), Eccles (Education), Sandys (Housing and Local Government), Heathcoat-Amory (MAFF), and Boothby (active in the Council of Europe). Brook showed little positive interest in the initiatives, leaving the overall assessment of the pros and cons to Treasury officials. Thus, when the Economic Section of the Treasury reported in June 1955 that the safest strategy in economic terms was for Britain to join the Messina Conference discussions[747] it was Burke Trend who was commissioned to investigate.[748] In September Bridges told the Chancellor that Britain's interests did not lie in the direction of a European customs union[749] and when the Trend group reported the following month it came as no surprise that the conclusion was that there would be little benefit to Britain but a difficult transition to membership.[750] Instead the British government concentrated its attention on an alternative option (named Plan G) for a European free-trade area. The crucial difference being that a customs union implied a common external tariff with all that that meant for the imperial preference Britain offered the Commonwealth, whereas the free-trade area did not (though the potential inclusion of agriculture implied significant repercussions on the Commonwealth). Brook had so far stayed out of the argument. At one level the issues were being discussed interdepartmentally and so there was no reason for him to intervene. But at another, as the official historian Alan Milward concluded, 'The decision not to join a European Customs Union was almost undebated but the result was very influential; the decision to adopt plan G, the free-trade area proposal, was part of a long and serious debate over the future of the nation. It led nowhere.'[751] However, not all Treasury officials agreed with Trend. In a dramatic step Frank Lee, then at the Board of Trade, made a personal statement at a meeting of the Economic Steering Committee in November which put him at odds with the views of his Minister, the President of the Board of Trade (Sir Peter Thorneycroft), arguing that on economic grounds the balance of advantage lay in entering the Customs Union and distancing himself from the Trend Committee's report.[752] The Economic Policy Committee chaired by the Chancellor, rejected joining in the development of what would become the European Economic Community at a meeting on 11 November.[753]

Nevertheless, there were those in Europe who still campaigned for British involvement, notably Paul Henri Spaak, the chairman of the Messina Conference preparatory committee, who saw Britain as a counter to German dominance;[754] and in September the following year the French Prime Minister, Guy Mollet, in

London for consultations about the developing Suez crisis, raised the possibility of reactivating Churchill's offer of June 1940 for an Anglo-French union. Meanwhile Eden asked Brook, to get involved.[755] Cabinet tended towards a view that Britain's future lay closer to Europe in the choice between the Commonwealth and Europe, when it resumed discussion of commercial policy on 18 November but was not yet ready to come to a definite conclusion.[756] Meanwhile Ministerial discussions of the Mollet initiative took place in GEN 551 under RAB Butler, the Chancellor. The Foreign Office argued strongly that an Anglo-French union was inappropriate in the post-war world and would upset the United States, the Commonwealth, Germany and the Northern Europeans. Britain would gain influence in weak and ineffective France but would inherit French unpopularity in the Middle and Far East and strengthened anti-Colonial prejudices. Union would not be natural, nor popular in either country.[757] The Treasury were similarly scathing about the French economy, 'a sluggishness and an unresponsiveness to change, to technical progress, and to the needs of large-scale organisation, leading to low productivity and great waste of manpower ... [and] a chronic tendency to inflation.'[758] Both Departments thought, in the words of the Foreign Office, 'An alternative line of response which might appeal to M. Mollet, since he is such a convinced European, would be that Franco-British union is too limited and antiquated a concept and that we should move instead towards wider European unity.' It was no surprise, therefore, when GEN 551 met on 24 September that the concept of union with France was dismissed, as were most of the other means of collaboration with France identified in the Foreign Office and Treasury papers[759] nor, two days later, that Cabinet endorsed the conclusions of GEN 551.[760] However, when Eden met Mollet at the Hotel Matignon on 27 September the French Prime Minister persisted in arguing for a closer political association and Brook was asked to look at the scope for French membership of the Commonwealth. He concluded that there was no formal reason why France (in common with other Republics) should not recognise the Queen as Head of the Commonwealth (itself a subtle shift away from owing allegiance to the Crown which had been made to accommodate continuing Indian membership of the Commonwealth after independence). But culturally there were any number of reasons why the proposition would not work in that the 'essence of the Commonwealth is that its members, though they are independent sovereign States with a developing system of separate citizenships, do not regard themselves as "foreign" to one another.'[761] Hence, the introduction of France could lead to its break-up, led by the Asian members in protest to French colonial policy. "I hope that my paper on Commonwealth membership will not seem to you to be merely obstructive,' he told Eden, 'But these are real difficulties, which must be taken into account.'

The Prime Minister himself took the chair for meetings of GEN 551 on 1 and 2 October, as a result of which Brook was instructed to set up a committee of officials, 'To consider urgently what form of political association with France, Belgium, the Netherlands and Norway could be devised which would be consistent with Plan G; to consider also what long term advantages for the United

Kingdom and the Commonwealth as a whole could be expected to flow from such an association, and the extent to which Commonwealth countries could be expected to see advantage in it; and to examine the constitutional, political and other problems to which proposals for such an association might give rise, and to report to the [GEN 551] Committee.'[762] This group became known as GEN 553 and in addition to Brook comprised two officials from each of the Treasury (Clarke and Rickett), Foreign Office (Kirkpatrick and Viscount Hood), CRO (Laithwaite and Maclennan) and Colonial Office (Macpherson and Poynton) plus Frank Lee from the Board of Trade. It met just once before the Suez crisis displaced further discussion,[763] preparing a draft interim report that suggested the 'most practicable gesture which we could make towards closer political co-operation with Europe would be to sponsor a merger of OEEC with the Council of Europe' even though the membership was not identical and to be clear that 'to give any substance to closer political association with Europe must involve a surrender of sovereignty.'[764] Discussion resumed in the spring after Macmillan had replaced Eden in January 1957 but by then the possibility of closer political association with France was discredited by the Suez fiasco and the rumours of collusion between the two countries. The spotlight returned to Plan G.

The Commonwealth

In the tug between the Commonwealth and Europe during this period it is clear that Brook felt that the obligations to the Commonwealth (and particularly the Dominions – Australia, Canada, New Zealand, South Africa) carried the day. He remained the principal organiser of the London meetings of Commonwealth Heads of Government, developed personal friendships with many of his counterparts that went wider than the Dominions, and his briefings contain evidence of a strong sense of loyalty to the Commonwealth as a post-imperial concept, with mutual obligations to all its members, combined with a practical realism when it came to dealing with individual countries. Thus, when Robert Menzies, the Prime Minister of Australia, renewed criticism that meetings had become dominated by set speeches at the expense of discussion across the table and that sessions were scheduled too close together to permit reflection and informal consultation.[765] Menzies, said Brook, was hankering after the leisurely pace of Imperial Conferences.[766] He defended the interests of those who would currently be disadvantaged by the dominance of the Prime Ministers of the UK, Australia and India: 'It would be unwise to allow this to develop to such a point that other Prime Ministers (some of whom find it easier to make prepared speeches) felt that they had not had a fair opportunity to express the views of their Governments,' he advised; adding, 'In my experience discussion at these Meetings tends to take the form desired by Mr Menzies when the Prime Ministers are considering some particular topic of current importance on which their Governments will or may have to take a definite line.'[767] Hence, future agendas might be more business-like, focused on current issues and an exchange of views that might lead to common approaches. The agenda for the 1956 meeting then reflected such a shift comprising (1) Relations with Soviet Russia; (2) Arab-Israeli tension and connected problems; (3) European security; (4) Future relations with China; (5) the economic position of the Sterling Area; (6) Nuclear energy for peaceful purposes.[768]

On the other hand, when it came to meeting the aspirations of Malta for full self-government within the Commonwealth and Ministers floated the idea of Maltese members of the House of Commons in London Brook was hardheaded. In July 1955 Macmillan (then Foreign Secretary) argued that although the idea was 'novel' and possibly 'eccentric,' 'I feel that at this moment in our history the voluntary and patriotic desire of Malta to join us is something we ought not to repel.'[769] Brook held out against the precise idea in favour of a general proposition of closer association between Malta and the UK.[770] What he meant by this was that, as Malta was then generally thought by UK political leaders and their officials to be unsustainable as a viable economy, the UK would provide funds sufficient to enable Malta to achieve the same result. Otherwise, he claimed, there were 20 other small Colonies in the same position, including Gibraltar, Cyprus, Bermuda, Bahamas and Mauritius. Westminster would become a Parliamentary Assembly of 'the United Kingdom and Colonies.'[771] The unwritten implication was that the colonial tail might wag the mother country dog. Nevertheless, Ministers overrode opposition from officials (including also the Treasury) and set up a constitutional conference for Malta under the former Lord Chancellor and Home Secretary, Viscount Kilmuir, which reported in December that, 'we believe that the people of Malta are entitled to a special road to political equality, and that, if they so choose, that road should be representation at Westminster.'[772] And so the people of Malta did, in a referendum on 11 and 12 February, despite opposition from the dominant Roman Catholic Church. On 17 February the results were declared – 75% voting for 'complete equality of status between the two peoples [of Malta and the UK],' including representation at Westminster in a 59% turnout which was far lower than in the Maltese General Elections of 1951 (75%), 1953 (80%), and 1955 (81%).[773] In the light of growing opposition from the Conservative Party and the Church of England (concerned about the Maltese marriage laws) the Colonial Policy Committee started to look for wriggle room around the referendum result, largely through a concession on financial aid[774] and the constitutional change fell away as Mintoff lost patience with London over Royal Navy plans affecting the Malta Dockyard. Brook had been shown to be on the right lines, though Malta went on to gain full independence in 1964.

The nationalist movements in the Colonies would come to dominate the Commonwealth during the Macmillan administration and Brook would be at the centre of the retreat from Empire. By 1955 Ministers had started to engage with emerging post-colonial issues but discussion was complicated by the tension between Departmental responsibility and collective responsibility. Brook picked up hints that Ministers were starting to complain that the Colonial Office failed to let them know in due time of developments it knew or suspected to be taking place. This prompted him to propose a Colonial Policy Committee comprising the Prime Minister, Foreign Secretary, Commonwealth Secretary, Colonial Secretary and Minister of Defence. Over the next twelve months, he argued, the Gold Coast, West Indies and Nigeria would advance to self-government and it would be preferable to have a standing committee to take a longer view on colonial policy as a whole.[775] As we shall see during the Macmillan years, the Committee was not wholly successful, but prompted by the Malta issue Brook raised wider questions when Cabinet discussed the future of the smaller colonies in October. The test for full Commonwealth status, he argued, should be 'the capacity to stand on your own feet and cut some ice in international affairs,' but maybe the way to get this accepted by the Colonies was to get it endorsed by the existing full members of the Commonwealth, adding, 'A difficulty is, of course, that the full members have a common interest in international affairs: the common interest of the "emergent" Territories is less obvious.' Meanwhile 'it would be helpful if, at some stage in this process, we could drop the words "Colony" and "Colonial."'[776]

The Propaganda War in the Colonies

Following his success in Malaya against the Communist-inspired insurrection, General Sir Gerald Templer addressed a nagging concern in a report on Colonial security in April 1955.[777] His policy in Malaya had been to win the hearts and minds of the people, combined with intelligence-led military operations. As a result, the British Security Service (MI5) trained an average of 250 colonial police each month during the following three years and as colonies moved towards independence their security services were organised in the British fashion, with intelligence and policing kept organisationally separate. Britain gave active security support for the newly independent governments.[778]

Meanwhile, partly conscious of the forthcoming visit to the United Kingdom by the new Soviet leaders, Brook floated an idea to call off hostile propaganda against the Soviet Union for a period to test whether there would be any response from the Russians.[779] On the other side of the argument the Chiefs of Staff wanted to ratchet up the propaganda effort, presenting a paper to the Official Committee on Communism (Overseas) for subversive aggression and strategic counter-planning.[780] They argued that: 'Communist subversion is not confined to one spot or territory. It is all part of one war and the defence interest is the residuary legatee of any failure to cope with it. There is a requirement for centralised direction of our counter-subversion effort ... [which] must also include subversion deriving from sources which au fond are not Communist such as racialism, nationalism, and so on, because the Communists have realised that penetration and/or exploitation of such movements is one of the most effective ways of damaging Western nations.' Moreover, prevention made good economic sense, as the Templer report had pointed out: 'For example, troops had to be sent to British Guiana because of the unreliability of the police. The cost of improving the conditions of the police might be measured in tens of thousands of pounds at the outside. The cost of maintaining the troops now exceeds £3 million.' It is clear from Brook's pencilled marginalia on a revised version of the Chiefs' document, circulated a week later, that he remained dove-like in approach, querying the potential cost and commenting 'shall we ever end [the] Cold War if we take an offensive role?'

On 19 October the Foreign Secretary joined the argument with a long note to Anthony Eden supporting the Chiefs in a forthright manner and suggesting a focus in the British Colonial territories. The newly formed Colonial Policy Committee should give a Ministerial lead and 'the sooner we get to work in some of these foreign territories and British colonies the easier our task will be and the cheaper to us in terms of manpower and money.'[781] Brook was furious, recognising in the Foreign Secretary's paper strong echoes of the Chiefs' message. 'You should know that the Chiefs of Staff have recently submitted to the Minister of Defence a rather feverish and muddled report,' he told Eden. Whilst agreeing that the priority should be counter-subversion in the Colonies and that the Colonial policy Committee should be in charge, he dismissed the role of the Anti-Communist (Overseas) Committee of officials (led by the Foreign Office) as 'compartmental' in view, inclined to forget that propaganda and covert operations are the servants of policy: 'I fear that Ministerial responsibility is being weakened by allowing the clandestine activities in the field to be "stimulated" by an interdepartmental committee of officials including a representative of the Chiefs of Staff ... Now that the risk of "hot war" has become more remote, the Chiefs of Staff have again become restive about the conduct of the "cold war."' He suggested dismantling the AC(O) Committee '... and, to put it crudely, to tell the Chiefs of Staff to mind their own business.'[782] A small senior group from the Foreign Office, the Commonwealth Relations Office, the Colonial Office, MI5 and MI6 should replace it – ideally chaired by Patrick Dean of the Foreign Office (a trusted confidante and friend of Brook) or, failing that, the Cabinet Secretary himself. And the term 'cold war' should be dropped: 'It has been responsible for a lot of muddled thinking – or, worse still, lack of thinking. It has certainly led the Chiefs of Staff to suppose that they are in some way responsible for matters which are essentially the business of the Foreign Secretary.'

Eden's comment was 'This is all excellent,' and he ordered Brook's minute to be recast as a Cabinet paper.[783] The term 'cold war' survived – defined by the Chiefs of Staff in November as 'the continuing world-wide struggle between Communism and the Free World waged by all means short of international armed conflict'[784] but the AC(O) committee was disbanded in March 1956 and Brook took over chairmanship of a new committee of officials reporting to the Ministerial Colonial Policy Committee.[785] By early March the composition of the new body (to be known as GEN 520) was agreed, Brook plus six members ('C,' Sir Dick White, Carstairs of the Colonial Office, Bishop of Commonwealth Relations, Patrick Dean, Major General Stirling representing the Chiefs of Staff). Its existence was to be kept secret. From the outset the Colonial Office dragged its feet over covert action.[786] Reports reached Brook that the recommendations of the Templer Report were being insufficiently supported.[787] His private secretary, John Hunt (later to become Cabinet Secretary himself) repeatedly clashed with the Colonial Office over the tardiness of their papers and often over the content when they did arrive. He described a Colonial Office paper on the Gold Coast as 'unduly complacent and contains no useful recommendations for your Committee. [the Gold Coast is one of the most crucial Colonial territories at the present time ... [with] a considerable amount of Communist literature passing through the Post Office. Who is it going to if there are only a handful of Communists?' as the Colonial Office asserts.'[788] Papers on British Guiana and on Communist penetration of student bodies in the United Kingdom were similarly condemned as complacent; progress with a pro-Western newspaper to counter a subversive campaign directed at British troops in Malaya was painfully judged slow and impractical;[789] Patrick Dean reported considerable concern in the US State Department and the CIA about the possibilities of trouble in Africa, culminating in a written complaint from Dean about the difficulties the IRD in the Foreign Office were having obtaining Colonial Office help. Brook took up the troubles over intelligence matters with Sir John Macpherson, the new Permanent Secretary at the Colonial Office who had replaced Sir Thomas Lloyd in September, reporting back to Dean that Macpherson had been 'very responsive;' 'I think on these subjects we shall find a better response in future.'[790]

GEN 520 was quite active, including papers on the Gold Coast, the Caribbean, the Central African Federation, Asian students in the UK, Malaya, India, Nigeria, policy across Africa as a whole, a general review of the Colonial Empire, Trinidad, Communist trading and technological agencies operating in Africa, Communist penetration of Ibadan University. But the results of all this work are unclear. There were two specific outcomes that bear mention. The first was the response to a commission from the Economic Steering Committee to rank Colonial and Commonwealth countries into three categories: (1) where Communist encroachment would vitally affect British interests; (2) where British interests would be involved but not vitally; (3) where Britain should not be particularly concerned.[791] The results were incorporated into a report by the Overseas Planning Committee (the vehicle for considering counter-subversion in foreign countries) so as to preserve the secret identity of GEN 520.[792] The second specific result went wider in the form of a review by Brook (drafted by John Hunt and submitted under a cover note that said 'I submit them tentatively under the heading of bricks without straw') of the situation across Africa which may well have helped establish an interest and an expertise in African affairs that would come to the fore in 1960 during Harold Macmillan's Africa tour in which he gave the important direction setting 'Winds of Change' speech in South Africa. However, there was much anguish to be borne before that breakthrough.

A Defining Moment: Nationalisation of the Suez Canal

If the leitmotiv of the first 15 months of the Eden administration was postponement and missed opportunity, events after 26 July 1956 changed all that irrevocably when the smack of firm government rebounded calamitously. On that day Colonel Nasser, the Egyptian President of just over a month,[793] declared that rather than wait until 1968 when the Suez Canal was due to pass into Egyptian hands the Canal would be nationalised forthwith under Egyptian control. This presented the British and French governments, the shareholders in the Suez Canal Company that operated the canal, with an open challenge. As recently as 1951, on taking office and in the knowledge that Egypt refused to allow Israel passage through the waterway, Churchill had declared that 'policy should now be based on the principle that it was the duty of the United Kingdom government to keep the Suez Canal open to shipping of the world, using such force as might be necessary for that purpose.'[794] Eden had agreed with the principle but warned against precipitate action since, technically, Egypt had a strong case since the Arab war with Israel of 1948 had not been formally terminated.[795] No action was taken by Britain or France to enforce Israeli access to the canal. Meanwhile resentment built up in British government circles about the behaviour of the American Government. Brook reminded Churchill in early 1954 that since the war Britain had tried to interest the United States in the Middle East (including Churchill's suggestion to Congress that the Americans might send a token contribution of troops to the Canal Zone) but now that they were interested the government got quite cross about the way they did it. It would be best to reach agreement with the American administration on common aims and the policies best pursued to achieve them.[796] He even went further in proposing to Eden (as Foreign Secretary), shortly before Churchill retired, that he might approach the Americans to propose joint maintenance of the Canal Zone.[797] As events in 1956 would prove this was both sound advice and hard to achieve given the fragmentation of American machinery of government.

Meanwhile Eden concluded an agreement with Egypt for British troops to withdraw from the Canal Zone, the final detachment leaving on 13 June 1956, and discussions started between the British Foreign Office and the American State Department on how to secure the fall of Nasser.[798] Earlier discussions in 1955 were unsuccessful, however, in persuading Egypt (or for that matter the USA) to join the defensive Bagdad Pact formed by the United Kingdom, Pakistan, Iraq, Iran and Turkey. Brook and other officials were calming influences. In April 1956, after King Hussein of Jordan had summarily dismissed the British commander of the Arab Legion (Glubb Pasha) and students in Bahrain had thrown stones and jeered at a car carrying the Foreign Secretary (Selwyn Lloyd) – both incidents widely sensationalised in the popular British press – Brook somewhat pointedly reminded Eden that 'you said in 1953 that our policy must be to harness nationalist movements rather than to struggle against them,' quoting a Cabinet document by Eden (C (53)65 of 16 February 1953) which included the judgement that 'it would be a delusion to suppose that, in Egypt or elsewhere in the Middle East, local opinion would tolerate occupation by American or French forces any more readily than the Egyptians tolerate the British garrison on the canal.' He went on to speculate 'These are the principles which should, I believe, guide our policy in the Middle East. I wonder whether, even now, we have discovered how to apply them in practice … we run the risk that, by the time [the nationalists] gain control, we shall, by our support of the existing authorities, have driven them into anti-British courses.'[799]

Freddie Bishop (the newly appointed Principal Private Secretary to Eden) replied 'I wish I could say that the PM received your view with delight or even appreciation … but he did not feel that the general principle you suggested could be easily or safely applied in Bahrain.'[800] Shortly afterwards, worried by Egyptian suggestions that they might procure arms from the Soviets and in the face of hostile public opinion at home, the United States Secretary of State (Foster Dulles) decided not to contribute to funding the construction of a major dam on the Nile at Aswan that would create a 300-mile lake and transform two million acres of potential agricultural land.[801] Britain followed suit. The reason given was a conclusion that the Egyptian economy was not up to the job. At the time only the French Ambassador in Washington (Couve de Murville) foresaw that the Egyptians would be honour bound to react. 'They will do something about Suez. That is the only way they can touch the Western countries.'[802] Ironically, at the beginning of July a committee under a junior Foreign Office Minister (Douglas Dodds-Parker) started work on non-military ways to influence the Middle East[803] and the day before Nasser's announcement of the planned nationalisation of the Suez Canal Brook was charged by the Policy Review Committee to set up a group to pull together recommendations for reallocating military money to support the Dodds-Parker proposals.[804]

News of the nationalisation was received in London on 26 July. Michael Goodman has analysed the progress of the Joint Intelligence Committee assessment of Nasser's actions through the various drafts prepared by the Assessment staff, including a passage not included in the final report that 'Hitherto [Nasser] has had the skill to deny the West a *casus belli*; but by interference with shipping [such as by blocking the Canal] he might well provide the occasion for Western occupation of the Canal; Zone and ensurance of transit rights by force.'[805] At Cabinet on the 27th it was agreed that any action by Britain should be based on the importance of the Canal to the West rather than the threat to British property. But objectives were mixed. On the one hand the aim was for the Canal to be run by an international commission in the interests of the shipping nations. (Brook would later remind Eden that 'from the outset we decided to use Nasser's actions to establish a lasting international regime for the Canal which would displace the original provision by which the Canal was to revert in 1968 to Egypt.')[806] But Cabinet also decided that if necessary, Britain should be prepared to take military action alone when 'our object would be the elimination of the present regime in Egypt.'[807] The Chiefs of Staff were instructed to submit a military plan in four days' time and a special Ministerial Committee (the Egypt Committee) was created. The same day Eden saw the Commonwealth High Commissioners to explain the position and at 6.05 pm he sent a message to President Eisenhower (in part drafted by Brook) stressing the importance of good management of the Canal and Britain's willingness to use force to have the Canal declared an international zone.[808]

From now on Brook was party to all decisions towards that end, though the arrangements for co-ordination across Government were a little confusing.

Cabinet discussed Suez on 49 occasions (24 before the ceasefire, 25 after it). Beneath the Cabinet sat the Egypt Committee comprising at that time the Prime Minister, Lord President (Salisbury), Foreign Secretary (Selwyn Lloyd), Chancellor (Macmillan), Minister of Defence (Monckton) and Commonwealth Secretary (Earl of Home) with Brook as one of its secretaries. Anthony Head, the Secretary of State for War, usually attended too, to the irritation of the Secretary of State for Air (Nigel Birch) and the First Lord of the Admiralty (at first Viscount Cilcennin and from September Viscount Hailsham) who were subsequently co-opted at Brook's suggestion in mid September.[809] It combined the roles of an inner Cabinet handling political issues and of military planning which would normally have fallen to the Cabinet Defence Committee (on which all three Service Ministers sat). It met 46 times between 27 July and 21 November 1956. In support of the Egypt Committee there was an official committee chaired by Brook which met nine times, whose papers are hidden under the title the Darracott papers, and whose main focus was on civil affairs in occupied Egypt, together with formulating a Political Directive for the Commanding Officer of the invading troops (prepared but never issued because of difficulties of defining the authority to undertake operations in countries such as Syria, to which Nasser was expected to send his air force).[810] Its terms of reference were never promulgated. In addition, the Defence Transition Committee (also chaired by Brook and attended by Permanent Secretary Heads of Department) was the main vehicle for ensuring all of government set appropriate planning in hand. This committee met 28 times between 27 July and 16 November, including daily between 30 October and 12 November.[811] A Foreign Office-chaired official committee on the Middle East (which Brook did not attend) prepared the material for two London Conferences of shipping nations aimed at support for an international authority to ensure the efficient operation of the Canal to be secured by peaceful means. (After the first Conference the Australian Prime Minister, Robert Menzies, sought to broker such a deal with Nasser but failed.)

Preventing the strands of policy from becoming entangled was complex. First, there was the London Conference and the subsequent negotiation with Nasser;[812] then the relationship with Britain's Suez Canal partner the French Government ('ready to go all the way with us');[813] then the hoped-for recruitment of the Americans to support Britain and France (Dulles saying that he saw no basis for military action and Eisenhower telling Eden of 'my personal conviction … as to the unwisdom even of contemplating the use of military force at this moment');[814] then the prospect of wider international support via the United Nations Security Council and General Assembly, including how the Commonwealth would react;[815] then military action likely to be vetoed by the Russians in the Security Council (described by Dulles' senior legal adviser as 'like a quicksand: once one gets into it one can never be sure how deep it is or whether one will get out');[816] then the worst case prospect of military action, including its legality (the Law Officers complained in November that they had not been consulted before the troops went in and could not support military action on legal grounds), preparations for the possible evacuation of British personnel from the

Middle East, and the logistics of supplies for an occupying force such as food stockpiles to feed the inhabitants of the Canal Zone;[817] then the domestic preparations as a consequence of military action (requisition of transport, call-up of reserves, fuel rationing, possible direction of labour, whether further emergency powers were needed, possible censorship, etc.);[818] then the handling of the House of Commons where the Conservatives and not just the Cabinet were likely to be split into hawks and doves and the Labour Opposition (so Gaitskell had told Eden privately) would only accept force if Nasser 'took further aggressive action'.[819]

Brook pulled the strands together for the Egypt Committee for the first time on 14 August in a document (EC (56)19) that was handed round during the meeting and collected up again at the end of the meeting;[820] but he also started to worry about events developing their own momentum. On 9 August, the day before the Chiefs of Staff produced their delayed first invasion plan for an attack through Alexandria (code name MUSKETEER), he told Eden's press secretary, William Clark, that, the idea of force is becoming increasingly unpopular, 'bluff is all very well until the armada sails, then you are committed because it could neither turn back nor sit offshore.[821] At about the same time Iain Mcleod (Minister of Labour and National Service) reported to Eden that the forthcoming TUC Conference was likely to back Gaitskell's line that force could not be justified unless Nasser did something more that was aggressive.[822] Cabinet Office officials started to quote the practical difficulties that would arise for any occupying forces in clearing the Canal and collecting dues.[823] In briefs for the Egypt Committee Brook counselled patience, not to decide on a date for military action until the London Conference was over (it finished 1 week later); and he started to push Eden towards greater recognition of just what would be involved in committing troops. Whilst the Government needed no additional emergency powers at home our political objective, he wrote, is to get out of Egypt as soon as possible after Nasser falls, so we must not plan for too long a military government; but it is exceedingly difficult to escape from a military commitment. You should consider whether any details of our military plans should be given to the USA and you must recognise that we have no powers to intern Egyptians in the UK unless we find ourselves in a state of war (though he added that he did not expect serious trouble from that quarter).[824]

On 24 August things came to a head when Macmillan seemed to suggest at the Egypt Committee that military action was a foregone conclusion (on 3 August Macmillan had written to Eden, 'can't [Israel] be encouraged to attack Egypt or at least make demonstrations to keep the Egyptian army on the east of the Canal?').[825] The Minister of Defence (Monckton) exploded and spelled out the moral implications and the practical obstacles of a military course to the embarrassment of his colleagues and, probably, of Brook who had not anticipated so dramatic a split. It would appear that Eden was badly shaken because the outburst prompted several of those present (including Brook) to send him handwritten personal messages of support.[826] Lennox Boyd (Colonial Secretary) wrote, 'I remain firmly convinced that if Nasser wins, or even appears to win, we might as well as a government (and indeed as a Country) go out of business.' Salisbury (Lord President) described the outburst as 'both painful and rather disturbing' and continued 'as the case for force will clearly need to be closely and cogently argued by those of us who agree with it, I need not say that I am absolutely at one with you ... ' Lord Home (Commonwealth Secretary) wrote, 'I thought that I had better warn you that I see a definite weakening in the attitude of some of our colleagues towards the use of force ... I had expected a cleavage of opinion in the [House of Commons] and possibly a few of our supporters dissenting but this I think represents something more serious ... I need not say more but I am convinced that we are finished if the Middle East goes and Russia and India and China rule from Africa to the Pacific.' Brook's letter is especially significant because it is longer and more cogently argued than the others and because it was sent wholly privately (hence handwritten and in an envelope sealed with wax). It shows him, at this stage, (which is, of course, before he was indoctrinated into the collusion with France and Israel)[827] at one with the importance of facing down Nasser and using force if necessary as a last resort. It is worth reproducing in full:[828]

Personal & Confidential

WHITEHALL 5422 *25th August '56*

I don't think that W[alter] M[onckton]'s statement, at Friday's meeting, need be taken too seriously. I think that he realises that it was ill judged and ill timed. He was provoked into it by H[arold] M[acmillan]'s speaking as though we were deciding then and there on the date of the operation. And, as Lord S[alisbury] said later, reference to the Security Council would be seen to be a hollow sham if we had already started, before it was made, to launch the operation.

As I see it, the position is this. All the members of the Cabinet, without exception, are solidly in agreement with you that we cannot afford to let Nasser get away with this – for, if he succeeds, we lose our oil and, with it, our standard of life in this country, not to mention our position in the Middle East and our influence as a world Power. The Cabinet are therefore agreed that we must stop this at all costs and that, in the last resort, if all other methods fail, we must be ready to use force. To this they have all assented – including W.M.; and I do not think that even he would try to withdraw from it. But some, in varying degrees, think that, before we resort to force, we must be able to show that we have made an honest effort to reach a settlement by peaceful means and have exhausted all the 'other methods.' For this purpose the first need was to mobilise a good measure of international support. We have had the conference, and we now have a plan for making at least a bow to the U.N. On that side of the affair the Cabinet will now be satisfied. But there may still be a feeling in some quarters that, even so, there should be some further provocative act by Nasser before we take the final step. Hence the support for your own idea of a concerted plan to stop payment of transit dues in Egypt. We have not yet found a specific place for this in the time-table which we were discussing on Friday. I believe that some Ministers will want to see this included, as well as the reference to the Security Council – as a means of bringing the issue finally to a head.

There is also the fact that we do not yet know with certainty that Nasser will reject our proposals outright.[829] If he were clever, he would send a reply somewhere between acceptance and rejection – and offer to negotiate a new Treaty. Until we know what his reply is, we shan't know what kind of a 'posture' he will have in the view of world opinion – and opinion here. And on this latter point I believe that there may be some uncertainty in the Cabinet. Some Ministers are less certain than others about the extent to which 'middle' opinion in this country would support forceful action at this stage i.e. before there had been some clearer occasion for the use of force.

All this leads me to the view that it would be a mistake to put the Cabinet at the final fence too soon. At least until we have Nasser's reply. I would not ask them to take the final decision. They are committed to using force 'in the last resort': the final question is whether they agree that the time has come to use it: I doubt whether that stage has yet been reached.

I can't end this letter without an attempt to guess who will be included among those who will want to postpone the use of force until all else has been tried, or until Nasser provides us with a good occasion, whichever happens earlier. My guess (and it is only a guess, for I haven't discussed this with any of them) is that, in varying degrees, this view may be held by the following

> W[alter].M[onckton], R.A.B., Selkirk, Chief Whip [Edward Heath] (qua H/Commons), Kilmuir (?), Macleod, Amery (?)

The unknown quantity might be J[ohn] S[tuart], B[uchanan]-H[epburn] and D[avid] E[ccles] The rest I would expect to be pretty solid.

Since I started this letter we have spoken on the telephone and I have said much of it in our conversation. But you may like to have it all the same.

I do hope you are having some rest.

Yours ever,

Norman Brook

The letter is especially significant because it hints at Brook's own view at this stage. It was extremely rare in the 1950s (possibly even unheard of) for a civil servant to write privately to a Minister about a policy decision. Brook did not have to send the letter since he had already spoken to Eden – almost certainly about the Cabinet disposition – he included a statement about the consequences for the United Kingdom of Nasser's actions which is only slightly disguised from identification as his own, and he went to the lengths of using sealing wax on the envelope to make sure that the private office would not open the letter. Hence, I conclude that he supported the use of force against Nasser if all else failed but also wished to emphasise that timing was all. This interpretation is further supported by evidence that in September 1968 Brook visited Eden at his home and volunteered that 'it was a calamity that we had to adapt our views over the Suez business to allay the qualms of the weaker brethren of whom RAB mattered most.'[830]

Writing to update Churchill in the South of France Brook elaborated further that 'Ministers' moods swing about' with Eden recognising the importance of taking the initiative to put the issue before the United Nations Security Council rather than to be arraigned subsequently if military action were to be needed.[831] Despite American reluctance to go down the UNSC route, however, the UK did refer Nasser's actions to the Council shortly afterwards.[832] Meanwhile, military preparations were confused. At a Staff Conference on 24 September the proposed landings of British troops were switched from Alexandria to Port Said, partly to minimise civilian casualties, and the commanding General (Keighley) complained that he was being pressured to land his troops too soon (a view that was later censored from Keighley's post-conflict dispatches).[833] Brook's concerns about the timing of a final Cabinet decision on military action must have been reinforced by these developments and also as he became aware of wilder plans being worked up to divert the waters of the White Nile at Owen Falls in the British colony of Uganda – later judged to be impracticable except as a piece of black propaganda to scare the less knowledgeable population of Egypt into a view that Nasser was putting the Nile at risk.[834] He was also aware that though a timetable had been put together for the evacuation of Britons from Egypt[835] Ministers decided three weeks later that the plan was impracticable.[836] He wrote openly to Churchill about the stressed relationship with Foster Dulles and about French irritation at the delays over military action.[837]

A ray of hope shone through when Patrick Dean, the Foreign Office chairman of the Joint Intelligence Committee, returned from talks with State Department officials and the CIA that indicated American support for bringing down Nasser, if necessary by engineering the occasion. Brook wanted Dean's report circulated to the Egypt Committee to strengthen the resolve of the 'weaker brethren'; Eden had not had time to study Dean's report in depth but was sceptical that much would result from the agreement and was proved correct when Foster Dulles insisted that the agreement be watered down to omit reference to bringing down Nasser.[838] Shortly afterwards Eden and Selwyn Lloyd met their French equivalents (Mollet and Pineau) and intensive secret discussions took place between the two countries, culminating in the infamous Sèvres protocol of agreed actions by the Israeli, French and British governments to bring down Nasser.[839] Brook certainly knew of the collusion; he was present at the Chequers meeting that dispatched the Foreign Secretary accompanied by Donald Logan, his assistant private secretary, to the first Sèvres meeting on 22 October and it was he who alerted Patrick Dean that Eden wished to see him early in the morning of 24 October, whence Dean was sent, against his will and accompanied by Logan, to the second meeting later that day as Eden's representative to ensure that 'it must now be made absolutely clear before final decisions were taken that British forces would not move unless the Israelis had advanced beyond their frontiers against Egypt and there was a clear military threat to the Canal.'[840] It was at that meeting that Dean initialled the pages of the protocol and signed the document ad referendum to Ministers.[841] Brook was also present at Cabinet on 23 and 24 October when Eden offered the half-truth that after secret talks with France and

Israel the choice was between early military action and prolonged negotiation, with a strong steer towards speedy action.[842]

When Dean reported back to Eden on the events at Sèvres on 24 October the Prime Minister was sufficiently worried that there was documentary proof of collusion between Britain, France and Israel that he instructed Dean and Logan to return to Sèvres and secure the destruction of all three signed copies of the protocol. After being kept locked in a room for several hours without food or water they were told that the Israelis had left and that the French were unwilling to surrender their copy.[843] Israel invaded four days later and British and French troops went in to fulfil the terms of the secret deal on 5 November. At about this time it appears that Brook started to feel estranged from his master's view. His warnings on timing had been ignored and rendered irrelevant by the secret deal with France and Israel. In the midst of all this, as if Brook was not burdened enough, at the end of October 1956 Bridges retired and Brook added the management role in HMT as Head of the Home Civil Service to his role with no lightening of the load.[844] William Clark further claims that Brook attended a party on the same evening as the troops went in, commenting that, 'no intelligent man could support the policy,' by which, given his earlier acquiescence of the use of force as a last resort, he must have meant the deceit.[845] If Clark's memory is true the behaviour and the words are so far out of line with Brook's usual reticence to suggest that he was near to breakdown.

Not surprisingly, Suez dominated the political agenda in the United Kingdom in the last quarter of 1956 to the relative neglect of other events of world importance, notably the demonstrations by 100,000 people in Budapest on 24 October, mostly students and young people, 'seeking a speedier movement of democratisation and a genuinely Hungarian road to Socialism.'[846] Public sympathy was strong in the United Kingdom for the right of the Hungarians to control their own political future, including letters to the *Daily Worker* from avowed British Communists. The paper itself claimed that the uprising was the result of 'counter revolutionary reactionaries' but also published opposing letters from its readers. Both were monitored by the Official Committee on Communism (Home) through extracts circulated for information.[847] The Joint Intelligence Committee noted on 4 November that 'operations to crush Hungarians' had started and that Khrushchev had stated that 'the Soviet Union will apply whatever force is needed to extinguish it [the Hungarian uprising]';[848] whilst in the United Kingdom the Lord Privy Seal (RAB Butler) told the House of Commons that 'Her Majesty's Government have in no way the intention of exploiting events in Eastern Europe to undermine the security of the Union of Soviet Socialist Republics.' Nevertheless, public sympathy was channelled into privately organised subscriptions to help refugees. By mid December the UK collection stood at £1.793 million and 11,000 refugees had reached the UK.[849] Officially, however, little was done to help financially; the Chancellor, for example, was not keen on using official channels to distribute the Lord Mayor of London's collection.[850]

On 14 November Eden sidestepped concerns about the legality of the military action with the result that Brook found himself in the uncomfortable position of recording that, as the Prime Minister had said that the Suez decision was a matter of policy not legality, the Law Officers appeared to accept Eden's declaration as providing cover for them to stay in the government, but would not defend the Suez action on legal grounds – hence, Ministers should cease to use the oft-repeated claim that the government was legally justified in what it did. Rumours of the Suez collusion soon emerged. Less than two weeks after the cessation of hostilities David Astor, the editor of the *Observer*, who had penned the phrase 'We had not realised that our government was capable of such folly and such crookedness,' wrote to Iain Macleod (Minister of Labour and National Service) to say that 'I believe that the "collusion" charge is going to be proved,' claiming that *The Economist* and *The Times* were both onto it. Brook was present when Macleod shared the letter with Freddie Bishop. They concluded that Eden ought to alert three or four of his Ministers and advised accordingly, adding, 'That Astor is using these tactics makes us feel quite sick, but it shows that he and others, are pressing this point [of opposition to the Suez venture] very hard.' Eden, however, did not feel a meeting of Ministers was necessary, departing for rest in Jamaica.[851] Yet it got worse. Eden having told the House of Commons that he had no foreknowledge of Israel's invasion, Brook met Edward Heath on leaving the Cabinet Room and said, 'He's told me to destroy all the relevant documents. I must go and get it done.'[852] Brook was clearly torn between his duty to the Prime Minister and his duty to preserve important state papers since (as subsequently discovered by Robert Armstrong) he recorded the fact of their destruction and that he had done so on the explicit instructions of the Prime Minister in a file kept locked in the Cabinet Secretary's safe.[853] Brook later confirmed his actions to Sir Robert Lusty in a conversation shortly before his death in 1967[854] and also told Sir Hugh Greene that 'Damned good care has been taken to see that the whole truth never does emerge.'[855] Yet, significantly, when Lord Kennet drew attention to the allegation of destruction from Professor Richard Neustadt in 1970[856] the then Cabinet Secretary (Burke Trend) neither sought to check it with Lord Avon nor, it would appear, to have the files searched. In particular his Private Secretary records that 'Sir Burke Trend does not, however, consider that it would be wise to suggest to Lord Kennett (sic) that he might ask the Professor what evidence he has for his allegation.'[857] Kennet was simply to be told that 'I am informed that there is no evidence in No. 10 that any files relating to the Suez Crisis have been burned and it would appear that Professor Neustadt's comment is based solely on surmise'[858] – the file referred to by Lord Armstrong was, of course, in the Cabinet Office not 10 Downing Street.

Despite any qualms he may have had about destroying state papers, Brook remained loyal to Eden, querying, for example, whether the words 'complete rest' were too revealing of the Prime Minister's state of mind as he left on 23 November for a three-week recuperative stay at Ian Fleming's house 'Goldeneye' in Jamaica;[859] keeping him sufficiently informed of developments at home to make him feel in touch but not sufficiently detailed to invite him to intervene from afar, proposing a new remit for the Ministerial Committee on the Middle East to produce an integrated policy for the area post-Suez,[860] partly in response to Eden's own insightful post mortem that pointed to smaller, more flexible and higher-quality armed forces, greater investment in non-military science and technology to improve the country's economic position and, most surprising given his earlier attitudes, turning to other European nations, such was his disillusion with the United States.[861] (In a lecture to the Royal Institute of International Affairs in 1982 Henry Kissinger, American Secretary of State 1973–77, conceded that whilst the British-French expedition against the Suez Canal was clearly misconceived, 'the fact remains that Eden had got hold of what was intellectually the right problem ... a dangerous precedent was being set ... Had Nasser's course been shown a failure a quite different pattern of international relations would have developed.'[862] As it was, Kissinger's lecture concluded that 'the humiliation of Britain and France over Suez was a shattering blow to these countries' role as world powers.'

Eden Resigns

Shortly after Eden returned home on 14 December, perhaps mindful of the confusion around Churchill's retirement plans, Brook advised him not to carry on as Prime Minister in the interests of his health.[863] Eden had hoped that he would be sufficiently restored to continue; but at 5 pm on 9 January he told Cabinet (using notes prepared by Brook) that his medical condition precluded him continuing in office and on 18 January he sailed to New Zealand for recuperation. He wrote to Brook, 'I was sad that I had to stop, but you, above all others, gave me the strength to carry on.'[864] The involvement with Eden did not end there, however. Brook would subsequently advise against agreeing to Eden's wish to see the correspondence with Bulganin at the time of Suez published (eventually Macmillan, the new Prime Minister gave in to Eden's persistence).[865] In 1959, at Macmillan's request to help finally settle the arguments, Brook drafted a statement of the events around Suez for the Prime Minister to use in Parliament that made no mention of the Sèvres protocol.[866] Throughout that year he conducted a lengthy and friendly correspondence with Eden over the manuscript of the former Prime Minister's memoirs (which made no mention of Sèvres or collusion); so much so that it has been alleged that the facilities granted to Eden so soon after the event, and the attention paid to helping with his manuscript, implied government support as a quasi-official history.[867] Close attention to the correspondence and the briefing when the memoir was published, however, indicate that the Macmillan Government was unhappy with Eden's work. In his memoirs the former Foreign Secretary, Selwyn Lloyd, complained (with some justification) that Eden was embittered by the failure of the United States to swing behind Britain after the cease-fire;[868] repeated attempts were made to get Eden to tone down his comments about Foster Dulles, to no avail, and in November Brook recorded that the UK would speak informally to the United States to say that it regretted Eden's harsh words.[869] From then on Brook sought to tighten up the rules of engagement for Ministerial memoirs and biographies telling Macmillan that new rules were needed – 'the Cabinet Secretary puts in a lot of work [vetting manuscripts] to little purpose,' and that following memoirs of the war years there had been too much latitude in allowing the use of material before its release under the 50-year rule.[870] Some other British ministers continued to deny the collusion in later memoirs – the former Lord Chancellor, Viscount Kilmuir, for instance, wrote in 1964 that the 'claims of collusion have no foundation in fact';[871] in the same year Eden acknowledged collusion for the first time when discussing Anthony Nutting's draft memoir *No End of a Lesson* with the then Leader of the Opposition, Harold Wilson.[872] More publicly, the French Prime Minister and Foreign Minister at the time of Suez, Guy Mollet and Christian Pineau, confirmed the fact when interviewed by Herman Finer.[873] Brook wrote to Eden on 11 June 1964 with the view that 'Finer's book ... seems to me to be pretty fair in its recognition of the shortcomings in United States policy and action in 1956.'[874] Three years later Brook told Freddie Bishop that 'The news from the Middle East really is most extraordinary and I expect [Eden] will have a good deal to say about it. I think things have turned out well from his point of view and certainly Nutting has not gained any advantages.'[875]

In many ways Brook appears as close to Eden as he was to Churchill. His loyalty went further than that expected of civil servant to master. Some of this was due, perhaps, to sympathy for Eden's predicament in coming to the top office so late and after the series of medical mishaps. An element, however, goes beyond the support for an incumbent or retired Prime Minister. Neither Hankey nor Bridges had been in a position of protecting, or attempting to rescue, a Prime Minister's reputation; and although with both Churchill and Eden a mutual respect and admiration is observable this does not wholly explain Brook's determined defence of the one and assistance to the other in putting across his story after leaving office. The Eden period is still so overshadowed by Suez that a judgement on how well Brook served Eden is inextricable bound up with that episode. As it unfolded there is evidence that Brook supported the intended outcome of continued strong British influence in the Middle East, even if he was ambivalent about the means. It is in the help Brook gave with the Eden memoir *Full Circle*, however, that a clue lies. Just as he had been at pains to assert the contribution of Churchill to the war victory against the claims of Alanbrooke, so Brook helped Eden in the defence of his actions over Suez at a time when recrimination was rife. In both cases the actions are consistent with a deeper motive than personal reputation, the competence of the State, as embodied in its Prime Minister. With the appointment of Harold Macmillan to succeed Eden, Brook once again served a larger-than-life politician who recognised the importance of the appearance of calm unflappability.

On 10 January 1957 Harold Macmillan became Prime Minister, preferred over the indecisive 'RAB' Butler. Eden felt that Butler had performed well whilst he (Eden) was in Jamaica and that his own debt to Butler, whilst Prime Minister, was very real. However, the Party turned to Macmillan, whose about-turn during Suez had established him as decisive, even if it gave rise to Harold Wilson's jibe, 'First in, first out.'[876] Over the next ten days Macmillan put together a ministerial team that was, in the words of his official biographer

Alistair Horne, 'an inspired concoction of balances and blends measured out with the finesse of an apothecary.'[877] Rebuilding structures and confidence after Eden's humiliation at the hands of President Eisenhower and Foster Dulles were the priority.[878] Five appointees out of a Cabinet of 18 had been in Churchill's 1951 Cabinet. If Butler's reluctant acceptance of appointment as Home Secretary signalled experience (he had wanted the Foreign Office), Selwyn Lloyd remaining as Foreign Secretary, indicated Macmillan's intentions both to take a leading role in foreign policy and not to be apologetic about Suez. The result was more a reshuffle than a reshaping.

The government faced a mountain of immediate problems, domestically notably the challenge of turning around public disenchantment after Suez, with a General Election due within two years. In one sense, however, this made Macmillan's position as Prime Minister unassailable; but it also gave him clear goals: improve the economy, repair the damage to the British international reputation (especially to repair fences with the United States) and win a third term victory. Over the next three years Macmillan achieved all three goals and a reputation as unflappable. Such was the recovery that in March 1960 the Downing Street Press Secretary, Harold Evans,[879] mused with Brook that, as Eden had been ruined by failure, would Macmillan be ruined by success?[880] His command over Cabinet was strong; he had an efficient and direct way of conducting business, dominating colleagues by intellectual mastery[881] and calling for brevity in interventions and delegation of business within departments.[882] Downing Street also showed signs of the Macmillan business inheritance, with efficient discharge of paper and a celebrated message 'Quiet calm deliberation disentangles every knot' affixed to the Cabinet door.[883] Macmillan's Private Office staff started to attend Cabinet meetings as observers[884] – a long cry from the problems Hankey had had when some claimed that only Privy Councillors should be in the room. Even so, follow-up to Cabinet decisions was still based on a belief that it was no business of officials to report on ministerial compliance. Thus, when Brook suggested in October that there might be a regular post mortem on Cabinet decisions; his deputy, Burke Trend countered that to do so would cause too much argument and consume scarce ministerial time to little purpose. Best let things go until a programme of peacetime official histories covered them.[885]

Also that month Viscount Attlee submitted the results of a five-month inquiry into the burden of work falling on Ministers.[886] The initiative had been announced publicly but the report mostly lacked new ideas, calling for greater delegation to junior ministers, brevity and a further number of procedural suggestions that Burke Trend advised Brook were questions of judgement and practice. As a result, 'Publication of the report is not particularly desirable. Parliament will expect some imaginative response. The results of the Government's consideration of the Report will not however be impressive let alone startling.'[887] In fact there were two tendentious suggestions: (a) that 'decisions on lesser questions of policy should rest with the subordinate Minister not the Permanent Secretary;' (b) that the Speaker should be encouraged to be stricter in what was allowed during Parliamentary Questions. Brook and Trend were nervous about opening the Pandora's box of relations between junior ministers and Permanent Secretaries – Brook going so far as to ask 'will it be necessary to pronounce on this if the Report is not going to the Cabinet?'[888] Trend thought that much of Parliamentary business was dull and that a more rigid policy towards Question time would deprive Members of interest and entertainment. And when a small group of senior ministers discussed the report at the end of October they found little to commend either suggestion.[889] Efficiency should not be allowed to impinge on respect for Parliament. Brook was called upon to explain the origins and rationale for the convention that prohibits Ministers from seeing the papers of a previous administration of a different political persuasion.[890] Two years later Macmillan rejected Brook's suggestion that Parliamentary Answers should be shortened.[891]

One of the government's leading Parliamentary opponents, Harold Wilson,[892] admired Macmillan's panache: 'The man's a genius. He's holding up the banner of Suez for the party to follow, and he's leading the party away from Suez.'[893] His colleague Selwyn Lloyd recorded a verdict on Macmillan's style, 'He believed in the Presidential form of Government. He modelled himself on an American President, with subordinates, not colleagues ... most of his ministers he would talk about as though they were junior officers in a unit he commanded ... Very rarely did he fail to get his own way ...'[894] These same judgements could have been made in an end of term report on Brook and may explain why Macmillan rated Brook so highly. The key to electoral success would be to re-establish a sense of personal and national security after the trauma of Suez, primarily economic security but also reassurance that Britain still counted in the world. Brook, who had taken on the role of Head of the Home Civil Service on Bridges' retirement, largely left policy issues in the former category to his co-Permanent Secretary at the Treasury, Roger Makins – a diplomat brought back from Washington in 1956 at Macmillan's insistence. This fateful decision prevented Peter Thorneycroft from appointing Frank Lee Head of the Treasury when he was made Chancellor of the Exchequer by Macmillan in 1957 – Lee who was arguably the most qualified official for the task and then the pro-European Permanent Secretary at the Board of Trade.

Repairing Fences

From the outset Brook was pivotal in repairing the damage done to Britain's relationship with the United States Government by Suez. Here the British had a stroke of luck. Macmillan and President Eisenhower shared a wartime bond from Macmillan's days as Minister Resident at the allied headquarters in the Mediterranean. After successfully securing re-election, President Eisenhower took the initiative to welcome Macmillan's appointment, thus allowing the Prime Minister to be the pursued rather than the suitor. The initial exchanges between Eisenhower and Macmillan read like declarations of true regard after both parties had said things in the heat of argument that they later regretted. Eisenhower wrote on the day Macmillan took over (though it was not received until six days later), 'This morning, upon learning of your designation by Her Majesty as the new Prime Minister, I sent you a formal message of congratulations, the kind that is approved even by State Departments. The purpose of this note is to welcome you to your new headaches ... Of course you have had your share in the past, but I assure you that the new ones will be to the old like a broken leg is to a scratched finger ... I predict that your journey will be a great one. But you must remember the old adage, "Now abideth faith, hope and charity – and greater than these is a sense of humour."' Macmillan replied immediately, 'I have no illusions about the headaches in store for me, but thirty-three years of parliamentary life have left me pretty tough, without, I hope, atrophying my sense of humour.'[895] A week later the American Ambassador relayed a message to Macmillan that Eisenhower was keen for an early meeting with him to review all the problems between the two countries.[896] Macmillan consulted Brook with a first approximation to the issues to be discussed and preparations began to assemble a practicable agenda, including the question of how much departmental briefing Macmillan should carry into the discussions. Brook worried that the emerging list was unmanageable; he added that the Prime Minister should bear in mind that the word in Washington was that Eisenhower was 'ageing and tends increasingly to deal in generalities.' It would be necessary for the Prime Minister to pin the President down to specific agreements.[897] (Eisenhower was, in fact, only three years and four months older than Macmillan.)

Brook (who was to be part of the Prime Minister's delegation) was also critical of the draft opening statement for Macmillan submitted by the Foreign Office on the grounds that it was too long and lacked a theme,[898] which Brook thought should raise the future of the United Kingdom commitments abroad.[899] Macmillan's briefing also included a suggestion that he should try to steer Eisenhower away from a discerned increasing tendency for the United States to look to the United Nations General Assembly for moral authority and to join in general criticisms of colonialism.[900] For his part, Eisenhower let it be known that he was personally affronted by continuing criticisms in the British press. That and differences over the British contribution to NATO and over the treatment of Colonel Nasser contributed to a tense start on 23 February. By the close, however, the sessions were seen as a triumph for Macmillan. Relations with Ike had been repaired so quickly, at least on the surface, that Eisenhower said the Bermuda discussions 'had re-established complete confidence between himself and the Head of the British Government. This was his firmest purpose.'[901] The record of discussions, however, show that whilst the Middle East, Western European Defence (including closer military association between Britain and the rest of Europe including nuclear weapons) and relations with the Soviet bloc (including disarmament) were covered, the question of British overstretch was not.[902]

It was not long before Eisenhower's warm words sounded hollow. In the summer of 1957 there was a rebellion against the rule of the Sultan of Muscat and Oman. The British went to his aid by deploying RAF troops but the Americans declared that the 'Eisenhower doctrine' formulated that year, which promised to come to the aid of any Middle Eastern country threatened by a nation 'controlled by international terrorism,' did not apply to internal difficulties.[903] '[Eisenhower] answers agreeably enough,' Macmillan recorded, 'but does nothing.'[904] However, a combination of a threatened Communist takeover in Syria and the success of the first (Russian) satellite launch shook American confidence with the result that Eisenhower agreed to Macmillan's suggestion for a second meeting in Washington in October to build on the foundations laid at Bermuda. In a report to Commonwealth governments Macmillan said that the discussions would 'inspire the free world with the vitality to outlast Soviet Communism.'[905]

During the visit, from 23–25 October, Brook once again in attendance, Macmillan successfully challenged the McMahon Act of 1946 that forbade the sharing of American atomic technology with any foreign nation. Its provisions began to be circumvented by an Eisenhower regime whose President thought the Act 'one of the most deplorable incidents in American history.'[906] Shortly afterwards, however, Macmillan received the report of an investigation, led by Sir William Penney,[907] into a fire at the Windscale nuclear power station at Seascale in Cumberland on 10 October. The fire had not only posed a serious risk to the health of residents and the ecology of an area of 200 square miles but revealed inadequate instrumentation, poor risk management procedures and organisation at the plant that could have seriously jeapordised Macmillan's recent breakthrough in US–UK nuclear collaboration. To suppress the report totally would almost certainly have led to a charge of 'a new Sèvres-style cover up.' However, the language in the report was hugely technical, dealing with the design and operation of a defence installation, and this gave Brook the justification for suggesting that Macmillan's Parliamentary statement on the accident, should withhold publication some parts of the report in the national interest – hardly be intelligible to most people, though perhaps a bit too intelligible to some.'[908]

The Search for a Grand Design

Between 1957 and 1961 there were three attempts to define Britain's role in the world and Brook was involved in all of them. The first was a study led by the Colonial Office following Macmillan's request for advice on 'the probable course of constitutional development in the Colonies over the years ahead.'[909] It should indicate which territories were likely to become ripe for independence, the likely date by which they would be ready, those that would qualify for full membership of the Commonwealth and the likely constitutional future for those that could not so aspire. It would also include 'something like a "profit and loss account" for each territory showing whether the United Kingdom would benefit or suffer from the financial and economic point of view as the territory left colonial status.[910] Macmillan added, 'This would need, of course, to be weighed against the political and strategic considerations involved in each case.' The study reported in September 1957 with the overall conclusion that 'profit and loss' would be roughly in balance provided that moves to independence were controlled and measured.[911] Dates were estimated by which colonies would either be ready for independence or internal self-government. One of Brook's contributions was to deploy his supreme drafting skills to balance the competing claims for gradualism in the hope that nationalist movements would not force the pace to independence and decisive action at the risk of some post-independence turbulence but avoiding the drain on the balance of payments of the policing required by a gradualist approach. In the event in both categories the report severely underestimated the rush to independence that followed the 1959 Conservative election victory and the replacement of the gradualist Lennox-Boyd as Colonial Secretary with the radical Iain Macleod.[912] The Indian Prime Minister, Nehru, had warned Butler as such earlier in the year at a private lunch during the Commonwealth Conference, arguing that Britain underestimated the 'seething aspirations and ideals of the East.'[913] And British speculation over how the Commonwealth might be made more cohesive without increasing the drain on sterling had come to naught.[914] But even then, Brook failed to understand the nationalist tide, commenting at the time of the formation of the short-lived Malayan Federation that 'We had always hoped that Malaya might federate with the other British territories in the area. For the smaller ones, the only hope of constitutional advance lies in federation with Malaya.'[915] (One of the so-called smaller territories, Singapore, joined the Federation of Malaysia in 1963 and left it in August 1965 and prospered as an independent state.)

The second report, also commissioned in 1957, reported in June 1958 into the future of Britain in world affairs. On 25 November 1957 Brook suggested that it was time to revisit 'the authority which we hope to continue to exert in world affairs and the means at our disposal for this purpose.'[916] Macmillan agreed only reluctantly, 'if you think it can be done without putting too heavy a burden on overworked officials.'[917] Brook's opening guidance on the manner in which the work should be done is significant in revealing the tension between the diplomats (Foreign Office, Commonwealth Relations Office, Colonial Office) and the Treasury. Brook started with a request for a memorandum to show how Britain's military strength would be deployed in, say, 1962; this would be followed by papers defining the country's essential interests and how they were affected or jeapordised by the military picture. Then the group would look at how non-military means, primarily economic measures, could supplement foreign and Commonwealth policy. It was left to the former diplomat, Roger Makins, now of the Treasury to point out that the priorities in the United Kingdom put consumption first (67% of GDP compared to 54% in the Federal Republic of Germany). Defence came third. The diplomats thought that expenditure on the welfare state was too high and curtailed the scope for supporting, 'the only truly successful Empire in history [which] we must somehow ensure that we were strong enough to maintain.'[918]

However, when the study reported, the diagnosis was crisp, summed up in an introduction that warned, 'We can no longer operate from the position of overwhelming strength – military, political and economic – which we enjoyed in the heyday of our Imperial power. But … we can still exercise a substantial influence in world affairs – partly in our own right and because of our position in

Europe, and partly as a leader of the independent Commonwealth ... in support of the superior material strength of the United States, in the world struggle between the forces of freedom and those of tyranny.'[919] Neutrality like Sweden or Switzerland would not do. Britain's political and economic aims must be based on the maximum Anglo-American co-operation and a Commonwealth association that was equally vital to the country's position of influence. 'Commonwealth cohesion and Anglo-American solidarity were therefore major aims in themselves. At this stage the arguments around whether to throw in Britain's lot with the emerging European Economic Community seemed not to be compelling.[920] Even so, after the French veto of the British plan to link the Six of the European Economic Community with a wider free-trade area, Macmillan told Konrad Adenauer that he did not see how you could have a united Europe militarily but a divided Europe economically.[921] And by 1963 the mood music had soured further with the Chancellor (Reginald Maudling), one week after the collapse of the negotiations for British entry into the EEC,[922] referring to UK defence spending through which 'in many parts of the world we were now carrying, in effect, the burden of defending the economic interests of our European Competitors.'[923]

Brook later admitted to Macmillan, when seeking approval, in February 1959, for the third major study of Britain's role (known as the Future Policy Study), that the work had not led to any radical reappraisal of external policy as a whole perhaps because, he said, it had not been good enough – though quite what he meant by this is not clear.[924] Comparing the Future Policy Study and the Future Role study suggests that he may have had in mind the failure of the earlier work to go beyond what was to be desired to how it could be brought about and a private doubt that the report raised problems without solutions. Thus, the mandarins had concluded that a balance of payments surplus of £350–400 million on current account was needed, adding grandly that, 'A high level of exports will be vital.' But even the best performance of the economy had never been that good.

Balance of payments on current account (£ million)

1946	*1947*	*1948*	*1949*	*1950*	*1951*	*1952*	*1953*	*1954*	*1955*	*1956*	*1957*
–153	–311	83	35	338	–330	229	204	160	–108	251	278

Source: UK Balance of Payments (The Pink Book) HMSO 2001

The group considered six possible ways of reducing overseas commitments: withdrawal of the British Army of the Rhine; abandonment of the nuclear deterrent; curtailment of defence R&D; reduction or withdrawal of garrisons in Cyprus, Hong Kong or Singapore; asking Australia and New Zealand to contribute more to the costs of the military presence in the Far East; realignment of foreign broadcasting. But they were imprisoned by the past and could not break out from the, as they saw it, interwoven strands of greatness: 'Our trading position is inextricably bound up with, and sustained by, our roles in Europe and in the Commonwealth and as the centre of the sterling area; none of which can be abandoned or modified in isolation. The question is however one of degree. We are already running down our oversea commitments as fast as circumstances allow us to do so with safety. But to do this wholesale would undermine the position of sterling and could break up the sterling area. We could not recommend such a policy as a fair risk.'[925] Nor could they see any scope for reducing defence expenditure. The burden of adjustment must fall on the home population: 'We suggest that it is in these wider fields [civil expenditure and taxation] that an answer to our world position is to be found rather than in abruptly seeking to reduce our oversea and defence expenditure below their present level.'[926]

It is small wonder that Macmillan, facing a General Election within two years, did nothing with the two reports. With the clarity of an outsider, the often angular Field Marshal, Lord Montgomery, had commented to him in May that, 'There is no surer way to disaster than to take what has been done in the past and do the same in the future – the problems have become different.'[927] And on 7 June 1959 Macmillan launched another attempt to get to grips with the imbalance between appetite and means with The Future Policy Study, once again with Brook as chairman of a Steering Group and with Patrick Dean of the Foreign Office as leader of the working group of officials. This time Brook made it abundantly clear from the start that 'the fundamental questions which we ought now to be asking go beyond the area which is the proper concern of the Chiefs of Staff' but could not be done without their active participation. The United Kingdom could never get a sensible weapons policy until 'some of the great unresolved questions affecting our "global strategy"' had been examined.[928] Further, the opening discussion at Chequers at which the Prime Minister would launch the work should avoid becoming bogged down with questions of whether democracy on the Westminster model was the most suitable form of constitution for Colonial territories achieving independence. More emphasis should be given to the economic aspects of oversea policy.[929] The focus was to be on the best interests of the mother country, not the demands of the Commonwealth and colonies, still less the European competitor countries.

Brook postulated that the purpose of the study was to peer into the future and try to see what the world situation would be in 10 years' time and what part the United Kingdom would be able to play in it. He went on to suggest that the work should assess how the direction of the United Kingdom's own policies might be adjusted in response to trends that were prejudicial to its national interests and to make sure that ambition was kept in line with resources, suggesting, for example, that the need for a British nuclear deterrent should be challenged; would it be safe to assume that nuclear parity between the USA and the USSR would 'give us a chance to reach some modus vivendi with the Russians in Europe?' Was the United Kingdom devoting so much of its resources to the defence of mainland Europe that it could not prevent its position elsewhere from being eroded? When Laithwaite of the Commonwealth Relations Office complained at being left out, Brook admitted that whilst he had configured questions for the study so that the Chiefs of Staff 'could not take the bone away into a corner and gnaw it by themselves,' he would not want the task widened to include the question of democracy in Commonwealth countries.[930]

The Steering Group met seven times during the second half of 1959, and four times in January 1960, approving a draft report that was circulated to Cabinet on 24 February.[931] Part I documented the likely developments in geopolitical affairs, drawing five large conclusions: (a) the struggle between the free world and the Communist *bloc* would intensify, especially in the underdeveloped world, and 'it is clear that the United Kingdom will need to make a substantial contribution; (b) the West would face increasing pressure to close the gap between the developed and the developing world in Asia and Africa; (c) The main challenge for the United Kingdom was likely to be how to defend its interests by combining with friends and allies; (d) the centre of gravity of the United Kingdom's international relationships might have to shift; (e) the greatest problems lay in the relationships with the USA, the Commonwealth and Western Europe. Part II discussed the resources available to the country, concluding that 'we cannot expect to reduce the 8½% of GNP devoted to defence, aid and other overseas activities.' Hence, 'This will call for restraint on the part of the public [and] the policies of HMG will need to be presented in such a way as to command the widest measure of understanding and support.'

The analysis did not even command universal support amongst Ministers, however. Lord Hailsham (Minister for Science and Technology since October 1959) found the report 'disappointing and depressing.' He argued that the predictions would only be true if 'we lack the will to do what we ought' and did not give enough credence to technological change. 'I should have thought it was beyond question that progress in science and technology was accelerating throughout the last ten years; and that this would have proportionately greater effects on industrial output ... [in] a gradually accelerating process.'[932] The Chancellor responded that issues of scale would inhibit the kind of growth Hailsham had in mind, prompting a characteristically robust reply that, 'At the moment it is an unpleasant fact that in this field civil industry is being dragged forward, as it were by its hair, by our research expenditure on our defence Budget. I look forward to the day when much larger sums of public money are spent on developing technologies which have a primary or directly civil interest.'[933]

Macmillan held a first inconclusive session with a small group of senior Ministers on 23 March.[934] He seemed to be too preoccupied with an impending visit to Eisenhower in Washington to give a strong lead.[935] Butler, Home and Watkinson thought, for a variety of reasons, that the survey of world trends was too pessimistic; Selwyn Lloyd and Heathcoat Amory disagreed, the latter stressing that he did not see how the United Kingdom could continue with its present commitments overseas even with help from friends and allies. Nor could it be comfortably assumed that the country could maintain a proportion of GNP of 8½% for overseas expenditure if the declared policy of the government to reduce taxes was to be held. Ministers were able to agree, however, that there was little room for manoeuvre on civil expenditure at home. Hailsham, who was not at the meeting, continued to show close interest in the debate, challenging the accepted views on the importance of the Commonwealth, the solidarity of Russia and China and the need for the United Kingdom always to be seen to be closely aligned with the Americans. Brook annotated the report of these views as 'V. interesting.'[936]

There were some, notably the former Foreign Office Minister Anthony Nutting, who argued that economic developments in Europe would leave Britain behind unless the government moved swiftly to avoid political exclusion from Europe.[937] On 6 November 1958 France had vetoed the first British approach (known as Plan G) to associate a wider free-trade area with the Common Market of the Six. Brook and Lee pressed Macmillan not to withhold the brutal truth from the leaders of Canada, Australia and New Zealand that they were not doing enough to help the UK.[938] Bishop and Zulueta in the Downing Street Private Office sought to focus the Prime Minister on a proposition for Europe involving an offer to share nuclear weapons with the French in return for economic concessions.[939] Macmillan called a meeting for 1 January 1960 'to make sure that the senior officials mainly concerned [with the European negotiations] are fully aware of the possibility of a "political understanding" with France, and that they will accordingly be ready to recommend what economic arrangements would be in our best interests.'[940] Brook was not amongst the attendees and his contribution when Lee produced a seminal report *The Six and the Seven* in April 1960 was to stress a close connection between the way of approaching the Americans over nuclear matters and the French over European economic issues.[941] Meanwhile, Bishop and de Zulueta feared that with a new administration imminent in Washington 'it is surely likely that in time the Americans will come to do independent deals [on nuclear weapons] first with the French and then with the Germans … and because the United States would take the decision to "give Europe the bomb" too late, they would probably also give it too generously.' Attitudes in the last few months of office of the Eisenhower Presidency were 'petrified' and risked throwing the Russians (who had a genuine fear of the revival of German militarism) into the arms of the Chinese. In Zulueta's words, 'our most important task now is to settle our relations with Europe and the pattern of the Western Alliance.'[942] Whilst Macmillan agreed that during the course of the summer the UK should try to think out a policy towards the incoming Kennedy Administration he confessed that, 'Quite frankly I feel almost too tired to do much in July.'[943]

It seems likely that the Future Policy Study Report must have influenced the way of thinking of those officials who had been involved (and there had been many who participated in the working groups) but formal follow-up dissolved, notwithstanding what had been said about the difficulties of finding savings in the defence budget, into a grinding pursuit of economies in weapons development and procurement. The Study had been conducted against a background of the EOKA crisis in Cyprus,[944] the stationing of American Thor nuclear missiles on British soil at Swaffham in Norfolk in March 1957, a successful UK test of a hybrid nuclear bomb in May of the same year and a Mutual Defence

Agreement had been signed with the United States in 1958 giving substance to the lifting of the McMahon Act ban on sharing atomic secrets with its allies. Over the same period, however, significant elements of British public opinion turned against nuclear weapons and January 1958 saw the birth of the Campaign for Nuclear Disarmament.

One green shoot was the 1958 agreement in Cyprus for two British Sovereign Base Areas paving the way for the granting of independence. But otherwise it was not until the Labour government of 1964 that the issues of defence commitments 'East of Suez' was faced up to. Brook reported progress on another round of studies at the beginning of 1961, clustered into three groups; (1) the United Kingdom's economic and financial problems (import controls, capital movement controls, external monetary policy, export assistance); (2) world economic and financial problems (international imbalance of payments, world liquidity, expanding world trade, organisation of the economic power of the free world); (3) European problems (the Six and the Seven, Tripartitism, the future of the independent nuclear deterrent)[945] – no hint here of opportunities and leveraging strengths, nor that under the existing Bretton Woods economic order of fixed exchange rates world trade would forge ahead.[946] Instead Brook found himself heavily engaged during the rest of 1961 with issues of expenditure savings, especially on weapons. In March he sought approval for extending the Future Policy Study's horizon from 1970 to 1975 in view of a perceived need to replace the fleet aircraft carriers and to update the deterrent capability.[947] At the same time the Chancellor was keen to make progress on reducing defence commitments in the Far East, Middle East and Mediterranean (Cyprus) with Lee suggesting another go at short-term emergency economies using the Future Policy Study (FPS) structure.[948] Macmillan was not keen; he half-heartedly agreed to extending the FPS timescale to 1975 'But perhaps we could have a word about the scale of all this;' and he flatly rejected another FPS emergency study in withering terms. 'If I may be quite frank I do not feel that the group of officials studying future policy, even restricted to the short term will give us what we need. The problems that confront us are questions of policy which can only be decided by Ministers. These questions are very difficult but they cannot be evaded.' And he instructed Brook to put together the facts of where money was being spent overseas,[949] which is perhaps indicative of the level of abstraction at which the FPS had been put to Ministers. On the basis of the facts now assembled by the Treasury Brook left the search for options to reduce overseas expenditure to Treasury officials and the MOD.

Defence Budget

Over the summer there were further signs of frustration between Macmillan and Brook. The Prime Minister rather pointedly commented that the Chancellor's work would 'raise important issues, but at any rate they will be for action instead of for talk.' Brook responded with a message that the aid budget could not be reduced, provoking in turn Macmillan to say, 'Pledges and agreements cannot be honoured if the dough is not there.' 'I don't think this calls for a reply,' scribbled Brook calling upon Ministers to give a lead on the possibilities for reducing overseas military expenditure that merited further consideration.[950] A meeting of Ministers was scheduled for 5 July at which the Minister of Defence suggested a general reshaping of defence policy towards a seaborne and airborne strategy at the expense of static troops and overseas bases. With no visible analysis to justify his claim, Brook argued in a brief for the Prime Minister that whilst overseas expenditure would be reduced the overall cost to the Exchequer would be increased and such a change could not be effected for many years.[951] Instead he pointed to Hong Kong and Far East Asia, which accounted for £56 million out of a total overseas spend of £229 million (i.e. 24%) as the most likely areas for reduction. No final decisions were taken. Further work was commissioned on savings for which Brook obtained Macmillan's agreement that, he should take the lead in examining possible savings from Hong Kong, Cyprus, Malta and Libya with an assumption of no overseas bases other than in Australia and Aden. Once again he voiced unease at leaving the MOD in the lead on political aspects of the issue.[952]

Whilst the FPS examination led by Brook was under way the Minister (Watkinson) sought a discussion with Macmillan on restructuring defence policy in the longer term, for which Brook (who would be away at the time) provided an outline of possible findings by the FPS group. The Ministry was charged to find £35 million of net annual savings outside Germany. The FPS study was considering a total annual spend of about £133 million and were looking at gross savings of about £35 million in the Mediterranean and Middle East with the possibility of more to come from the Far East if a seaborne strategy could be made to work. But, warned Brook, these were economies that would affect British prestige in the world and ought, therefore, to be considered in the context of foreign policy in total.[953] Macmillan met Watkinson on 13 September and again eight days later. The Minister argued that to force through the kind of radical restructuring envisaged would require him to have greater central powers. The Prime Minister recalled that such a move had been defeated at the time of the 1959 election and he did not think that it could be resurrected before the next election. Initially it appeared that in the event the Minister's fears were not realised, the Chiefs 'are all in agreement that a fundamental recasting of organisation and strategy ought to be tackled;'[954] but when the Joint Planning Staff produced their report on savings and air and sea mobility (JP(61)91) it had been mauled by the Chiefs with the result that the FPS assumption that it would be able to conduct its study of the Far East in the light of the seaborne and airborne strategy was invalid. Further, in the light of Watkinson's pressure for reorganisation in the Ministry Macmillan decided to drive decisions. He circulated a long paper (prepared in Brook's absence somewhat shamefacedly by Bishop) to a small group of the most concerned Ministers and to the Chiefs addressing the commitments to be maintained over the next decade and how the available resources would best be deployed.[955]

On return from leave Brook briefed for the Ministerial discussions on 10 October that versatile overseas military bases suitable for any purpose were

Gibraltar, Malta, Aden, Seychelles, and Ghana whilst those suitable only in total war or for small operations where local opinion might be defied were Libya, Cyprus, Kenya, and Singapore. He further suggested that in the light of increasing dependence on United States weapons an important justification of the nuclear deterrent (influence on US policy) would be so diminished and the independence of the British deterrent so compromised that Ministers should consider its future.[956] On the 17th of the month, in the light of the Ministerial discussion, he then drafted two political directives to be issued by the Prime Minister (the short term and the medium/longer term) to be used as the basis of planning by the Chiefs, suggesting clearance only with the Foreign Secretary and the Minister of Defence, to be issued to the Cabinet Defence Committee only for information. The £35 million annual savings were to be secured as soon as possible without radical changes in policy except for run-down of bases in Malta, Cyprus, Hong Kong and Kenya. Commonwealth countries would be pressed to take a greater share of the worldwide defence burden. It was issued on the 23rd by Macmillan with three changes: Bahrain had been added to the list of most valuable bases, the strategic nuclear deterrent would be reviewed when the future of the SKYBOLT missile was known and the vague hope for a détente with Russia after resolution of the current Berlin crisis had been altered to 'some détente'.

The Chiefs' study of short-term savings was ready in early December; the longer-term study had proved difficult to agree and had been through several iterations. The short-term measures amounted to £18 million of savings against a target of £35 million (but Germany, the Middle East and Malaysia/Singapore had been excluded from consideration on the instruction of the Prime Minister).[957] A proposed run-down in Malta accounted for by far the largest immediate opportunity (£7 million) with a reduction in East Africa when Kenya achieved independence worth £6 million). The problem was that the Maltese economy and political life would be devastated by an immediate adjustment of this scale; hence, it was decided to phase in the reductions over a number of years. A similar issue arose when the Chiefs finally presented their strategy for a gradual movement in the 1960s away from fixed bases to a combination of seaborne and airborne flexible forces with Brook now somewhat unhelpfully asking if the switch was worthwhile: 'The strategy proposed will lead to the development of airborne and seaborne forces operating from bases in the United Kingdom, in Australia and somewhere in the Middle East, many hundreds of miles from the territories in which they may be required to operate ... large logistic expenditure will be involved in terms of aircraft, ships, supply chains, stockpiles and so forth. Some Ministers may want to know whether it is worthwhile to spend these large sums of money in order to bring this small force into action.'[958] Which was all very well in reporting a possible objection to which the proponents ought to have an answer, but could hardly be raised as a valid objection at this late stage in what had been a very lengthy process; illustrating perhaps a weakness of the Cabinet Secretary's 'episodic involvement' with issues to which a less self-assured individual might have had regard.

Summitry & the Fear of Communism

No less than Churchill and Eden, Macmillan believed in the power of face-to-face talks between Heads of Government – particularly the four great powers (US, UK, France, USSR). As the Minister Resident in the Middle East during the Second World War Macmillan (born in 1894) already knew two of his fellow leaders who were contemporaries: Eisenhower (born in 1890) and de Gaulle (born in 1890). Similarly, in Brook (born in 1902) Macmillan was served by the last of the Churchill close confidantes. The emergence of Khrushchev (born in 1894) as the supreme Soviet leader in 1958 after the years of turmoil following Stalin's death offered at least a hope of coexistence but his was not a true generational shift – though to the Western leaders he was a relatively unknown and enigmatic quantity. It was not until the end of 1960 and the election of President John F Kennedy in the USA (born in 1917) that a generational shift started amongst the world's leaders. In that sense, at least, Brook brings to an end an era and it is one of Macmillan's remarkable achievements that the two men were able to establish a close and warm relationship with the first of a new generation of Western leaders.

Brook travelled extensively overseas with Macmillan, particularly concerning the relationship with the American Presidents Eisenhower and Kennedy, the Commonwealth and Summit preparations, much less so where relations with the European Economic Community was at issue:

1957	20–27 March	Bermuda Conference with President Eisenhower
	23–26 October	Washington and Ottawa
	13–21 December	Paris (NATO)
1958	7 Jan–14 Feb	Commonwealth tour (India, Pakistan, Ceylon, Singapore, New Zealand, Australia); 35,000 miles with 34 different stop-overs
	7–13 June	Washington and Ottawa
1959	21 Feb–3 March	Russia and Ukraine
	18–24 March	Washington and Ottawa
1960	5 Jan–15 Feb	Africa tour (Ghana, Nigeria, Central African Federation, Bechuanaland, South Africa – where Macmillan delivered the famous 'Wind of Change' speech)
1961	29 Mar–12 April	New York, Jamaica, Washington and Ottawa
	20–22 December	Bermuda Conference with President Kennedy
1962	25 Apr–2 May	New York, Washington, Ottawa, Toronto

Source: Bodleian Library, MS. Eng. lett.c273 box 490

Often Brook's role was to seem as insignificant as possible whilst exercising central direction and control of the proceedings in line with what the Prime

Minister was aiming to achieve. Often he shared Macmillan's private thoughts. At the start of November 1959 Macmillan wrote to him that 'Africa ... seems to be the biggest problem looming for us here at home. We just succeeded at the General Election in "getting by" on this ... young people of all Parties are uneasy about our moral basis. Something must be done to lift Africa on to a more national plane, as a problem to the solution of which we must all contribute, not out of spite ... but by some really imaginative effort ...'[959] At the end of the year he also wrote 'Africans are not the problem in Africa, it is the Europeans.'[960] The imaginative action was to undertake a gruelling Africa tour lasting from 5 January 1960 to 15 February. Anthony Sampson, who was a journalist accompanying the Prime Minister's party, described Brook as 'looking like a casual tourist who just happened to be following ... The local officials took little notice of him, and few of them realised that he was the central cog in the British Government machine.'[961] Harold Evans described 'Brook's dancing style is "enveloping", causing difficulties for the girls and they can hardly avoid implanting lipstick on the lapels of his white dinner jacket about which he then complains.'[962] In Nigeria Brook outlined how the British Government worked to the Council (the equivalent of Cabinet), leaving them in no doubt as to the centrality of his own role.[963] On return from the Africa tour he wrote to Macmillan in glowing terms: 'When you first mooted the idea of your Africa journey, I said that it was a tremendous risk but offered a great prize. You took the risk and you have won the prize. You steered a most skilful course, through very great difficulties, and you came through triumphantly.'[964] Photographs from these overseas trips show Brook as a tall, cravat-wearing individual with high-waisted trousers, as was the fashion, often standing discreetly at the side of his master in a pose that subtly mimicked the Prime Minister.[965] On touching down in a frozen Moscow on 21 February 1959 as part of the Prime Minister's entourage, wearing fur hats and long fur-collared coats, he commented to Harold Evans, 'we must look either very silly or very sinister. Probably both.'[966]

But as Anthony Sampson indicated, Brook's backroom contribution could be central in shaping the programme and the approach to negotiations. Thus, in July 1956 he had drafted the opening statement for Anthony Eden at the Commonwealth Conference about the world threat of Russia and Communism. In March 1958 a group he led considered whether it was possible to help the Indian Government fight the spread of Communism in trades unions – reluctantly concluding that only local propaganda was likely to be successful.[967] He is credited with co-authorship of Macmillan's seminal 'Wind of Change' speech given to the South African Parliament at 10.30 a.m. on 3 February 1960 when the British Prime Minister spoke of the awakening of national consciousness throughout the world, continuing, 'Today the same thing is happening in Africa, and the most striking of all the impressions I have formed since I left London a month ago is of the strength of this African national consciousness ... the wind of change is blowing through this continent, and, whether we like it or not, this growth of national consciousness is a political fact. We must accept it as a fact, and our national policies must take account of it.'[968] Subsequently, at the end of March

1961 when South Africa decided to leave the Commonwealth, Dr Verwoerd, the South African Prime Minister, spoke using a statement prepared in the UK by a team including Brook. Unlike, say, India in 1947, the decision to become a Republic had triggered a vote at the Commonwealth Conference of 8 March 1961 that failed to reelect South Africa as a member.

It is in the developing close relationship between Macmillan and Presidents Eisenhower and Kennedy that Brook's influence is at its most clear. After the euphoria of the Bermuda meeting a follow-up discussion was fixed for Washington in June 1958. Brook suggested a focus on (1) summit preparations; (2) disarmament; (3) nuclear reprisal; (4) South East Asia; (5) Interdependence and in mid June he wrote the report used by Macmillan in informing Cabinet of the results of the talks. The most important were that US/UK interdependence would be recognised by reform of the McMahon Act and that private consultation between the two countries would continue on all matters of common concern. On the other hand, the U.S. Government doubted the value of a Four-Power Summit because of doubts about Russian sincerity.[969] At about this time, however, Macmillan was becoming increasingly irritated by the imbalance between the Anglo-Saxons' acceptance of obligations to protect Western Europe militarily and the reluctance of European allies to help the British economy, in particular, on to its feet. He raged in a note to the Foreign Secretary that it is hard to imagine was more than an explosion for therapeutic effect, '... if Little Europe is formed without a parallel development of a Free Trade Area ... we should not allow ourselves to be destroyed little by little. We would fight back with every weapon in our armoury. We would take our troops out of Europe. We would withdraw from NATO. We would adopt a policy of isolationism. We would surround ourselves with rockets and we would say to the Germans, the French and all the rest of them: "Look after yourselves with your own forces. Look after yourselves when the Russians overrun your countries." '[970] In fact, Brook had warned Macmillan that the American THOR missiles were not sufficiently efficient to be an effective deterrent when deployed in Britain and that the American authorities had still not agreed to give the British Government an equivalent notification of nuclear carrying over-flights as they required of flights over American territory.[971] And on 10 November the risk of war became horribly real. Khrushchev announced that he had given the Western powers a deadline of 27 May 1959 that unless they withdrew their troops from West Berlin Russia would sign a peace treaty with East Germany that would end Allied rights in Berlin. It was against this background that Macmillan, accompanied amongst others, by Brook left for Moscow on 21 February for a week of talks with the Russian leadership. Brook drafted a statement for Macmillan to use at Cabinet which said '... this is no more than a reconnaissance. We shall be more concerned to find out what is in the minds of the Russian leaders than to disclose to them what is in ours. I do not feel therefore that we need any special Cabinet authority for what we shall be trying to do.'[972] Topics to be explored with the Russians were (i) Berlin and the related question of Germany's future and European security; (ii) Disarmament – especially nuclear tests and surprise attack; (iii) expanding Anglo-Soviet trade; (iv) cultural contacts. In delightfully euphemistic phrasing Brook explained that the Prime Minister would not be able to be kept au courant with government business at home 'owing to the security situation in Moscow.' He added two further warnings in manuscript, 'The colleagues must not talk about our "devices" in the Moscow embassy, since we do not want the Russians to know about the extent of our counter-measures;' and 'It is also important that Ministers should not give the impression that we sympathise a little with Russian view [sic] on Germany, and intend to try to move U.S. Govt. in that direction.'[973]

The Eisenhower Administration were not at all keen on Macmillan's decision to activate the invitation that had been given to Eden during the 1956 visit by the Russian leaders and a further manuscript note from Brook offers Macmillan the advice that 'I don't believe U.S. will listen to anyone but you. And For. Secy., if he went, couldn't confine himself merely to reporting. Best hope is to say now when you are going and urge the President, in effect, to suspend judgement until you arrive [in Washington on 18 March].'[974] Though not without rocky moments, the Moscow trip was a great domestic publicity coup for Macmillan some seven months before a General Election (held on 8 October). Internationally it established him as the go-between with Khrushchev and gave him the platform on which to pursue the patient handling of an otherwise dangerously explosive situation. Macmillan's biographer, Thorpe, describes the visit as giving Macmillan an insight into the impetuous and attention seeking Khrushchev that proved invaluable in the 1962 Cuban Missile Crisis and, paradoxically, established Macmillan in Khrushchev's mind as something of an enigma who had not been cowed by his crude behaviour.[975] The visit led to acrimonious exchanges between Macmillan and de Gaulle and Adenauer over the desirability of a Summit, thus weakening the British negotiating position for entry into the EEC.[976]

This coherence in the Western Alliance was further tested when Khrushchev wrote to Macmillan encouraging the idea of a Summit meeting and proposing a bilateral treaty of non-aggression. Macmillan replied robustly, using material proposed by Brook. He encouraged the idea of a Summit provided that it did not meet in an atmosphere of crisis. (There was no mention of the tension over East Germany and Berlin though it must have been in the minds of both men and at an informal meeting of British Ministers and officials on 14 June progress towards an agreement on Berlin was made a condition of proceeding with a Summit.)[977] However, he rejected a bilateral non-aggression pact arguing that progress had to be multinational. He stressed the integrity of the U.S. leaders that would prevent any notions of their promoting a war that would be fought on territories outside America but a passage by Brook that built on recently revised nuclear release procedures agreed with the USA and said, 'I must remind you that the United States bases in the United Kingdom cannot be used against the Soviet Union or against any other country without the permission of the United Kingdom Government. That is an inherent condition of our allowing them to be maintained upon our soil,' did not survive in the final reply.[978]

Privately, Brook expostulated to Macmillan: 'Fundamentally, our difficulty is that we do not think that the Western case, as it has been developed at [the Foreign Ministers' talks] at Geneva, offers a reasonable hope of a settlement [of the Berlin issue]. The n****rs (sic) in the woodpile are the French and the Germans. You had some success, at Camp David, in bringing the President to take a more realistic view of the situation; but we lost ground again as soon as the French and Germans were brought into the discussions ... it would be very awkward for the Western Powers to meet Mr. Khrushchev at a Summit without having first thrashed out their differences among themselves and tried to find some new position on the basis of which a negotiated settlement might be reached with the Russians.'[979] When de Zulueta advised the Prime Minister that 'the Foreign Office are at present prepared to admit we have already conceded that we have no legal right to insist on freedom of access [to Berlin] for civilians and civilian supplies ... [but] recognition of East Germany would show the East Germans themselves that even the Western Powers had accepted that their fate was in the Russian Hands ... [and] the peoples of Eastern Europe generally would see the last ray of hope for them extinguished;' Brook retaliated with *realpolitik*: arguing for a de facto recognition of East Germany. '... All we want is to be able to do our duty by the West Berliners and to prevent them from being engulfed in East Germany ... Germany must in practice remain divided for many years to come ... it is in our interests ... that it should remain divided.' He continued that 'liberation' of the people in East Germany did not accord with the existing facts and there was no hope of achieving it.[980]

Reelection

The October 1959 General Election was a triumph for Macmillan – he had been selected in 1957 as the leader of the Conservatives most likely to win and he did. The Conservatives took 49.4% of the vote (a sliver down on the 1955 performance of 49.7%) with an overall majority of 100 seats. By the end of the year he could also claim (in a note to the Foreign Secretary) that foreign policy prospects were good. Preparations for a consistent Western approach to a Four-Power Summit were in hand; a test-ban treaty looked feasible; there was hope that talks between the EEC and EFTA would resume positively. He had negotiated a deal with Eisenhower under which the British would acquire the American SKYBOLT missile to replace the cancelled outdated British BLUE STREAK missile and in return the United States would acquire a submarine base at Holy Loch in the West of Scotland.[981] Additionally, he claimed that 'I think we have certainly ... brought the French back to thinking of us as her main ally, and of Germany as a country that must be looked after for the general benefit. We have persuaded them that we are not opposed to the political work of the Six, and indeed like to see a strong France in Central Europe. I think we also made some progress in persuading them that our fears of the economic Six are well founded and must be removed.'[982] In a separate note about France he added, 'Now I come to the vital point. My purpose now must be to support de Gaulle on the political front and his desire to join the ranks of the Great Powers ... In return he must give to me the greatest practical accommodation that he can on the economic front. The future of British trade in Europe is far more important than whether a few French fighters are or are not to be put under the command of SACEUR.'[983]

Macmillan's luck then seemed to desert him when in May 1961 the Paris Four-Power Summit collapsed following Russian recriminations when an American U2 spy plane conducting covert surveillance over the Soviet Union was shot down over Sverdlovsk on 1 May. Macmillan himself saw this collapse of superpower negotiation as the most tragic moment of his life.[984] His diary entry for 30 June records, 'We are only now beginning to realise, as the weeks go by, the full extent of the Summit disaster in Paris. For me it is the collapse of the work of two or three years. For Eisenhower, it means an ignominious end to his Presidency. For Khrushchev, a set back to his conciliatory and sensible ideas. For the world, a step nearer to ultimate disaster.'

A New President – a New Beginning?

Six months after the collapse of the Paris Summit the world woke to the election of a forty-year-old Democratic Roman Catholic Senator, John F Kennedy, as successor to the seventy-year-old Republican Dwight D Eisenhower. In anticipation of the Presidential Election Philip de Zulueta suggested to the Prime Minister that he might contemplate 'an imaginative and comprehensive approach to a new Democratic Administration' with a plan for a united Atlantic area covering political, military, trade and international currency arrangements.[985] Zulueta's first draft of how an approach might look was passed to Brook by Freddie Bishop on 7 November. Brook then minuted Macmillan on the 10th to suggest that the Future Policy Study mechanism should be resurrected to look at the strategy of the West for containing Sino-Soviet encroachment.[986] 'He posed three questions: (1) Do we all agree that there is no military solution of East/West struggle? (2) If so, what is the minimum strength of nuclear deterrent required to maintain the stalemate? (3) The Communists will continue to pursue their aim (mainly outside Europe) by economic penetration and political subversion. Is the West adequately organised to counter this?' 'After all,' he continued, 'much of the American strategy ... was formulated when the West had overwhelming nuclear superiority: it does not follow that the same strategy will suit a situation of nuclear stalemate,' adding '... you ought to base yourself in this, not on the Foreign Office alone, but on a rather wider segment of the Whitehall machine.' Such a review would 'put into the right political perspective' studies into NATO and weapons systems currently under way in the Ministry of Defence.'

In outline Brook's text (based on interdepartmental discussions) summarised the United Kingdom attitude to the East/West confrontation. It was long on what should be the aim of the West but short on how to bring that about or new ideas. In a forceful comment Freddie Bishop did not think the draft fitted the bill at all. For example, where Brook had written 'Thirdly there is the special problem of

Europe,' Bishop's annotation reads, 'The US don't look at it this way. Wouldn't it be best "to lose this problem" in expansion of trade?' More generally he annotated, Kennedy will get letters from everybody about the need for unity etc etc ... [we should] recognise [the] lead must come from US [and] UK wd not claim to be in "special position".' 'I do not think that ... general views ... would be sufficiently novel or forceful to arrest Mr Kennedy's attention ... The essence of the different approach which I had in mind would be the inclusion of some particular proposals which would give the approach as a whole the character of an offer by the United Kingdom to do something.' The key, according to Bishop, was to square the French (i.e. de Gaulle) with a political agreement that involved nuclear power status. 'Our independent strategic nuclear capability is (as I suppose everybody would agree) a wasting asset. But at the moment it is an asset of great international political value.'[987]

The strength of Brook's position was that his draft commanded the support of the Departments, as he emphasised to Macmillan when he put it forward on 24 November. But that support also hemmed him in and earlier ideas of a World Economic Conference and of putting the British V-bomber force in trust for NATO, controlled jointly by the United Kingdom and France, had had to be dropped. Further, he reported that 'The Departments are very doubtful whether it would be wise for you to send any document of this kind to Washington until informal soundings have been taken about the reception which it is likely to meet.' Had the draft message resonated with Macmillan he would have brushed aside such bureaucratic niceties and asserted political direction. As it was, he felt that the text was 'neither quite one thing nor the other' and asked Brook to make it more of a personal letter. Let us wait, advised Brook, until we have reports from the British Ambassador (Caccia) from a first encounter with Kennedy and from the long-standing British family friend of the Kennedys, David Ormsby-Gore.[988] And it was Zulueta who finally offered a text that satisfied Macmillan and the Foreign Secretary (since July the Earl of Home) combining a call for a Western rethink on economic, military and political stances with putting Kennedy centre stage in the Western world and adroitly promoting the position of the United Kingdom with 'Although the U.K.'s power in the world is relatively so much less than yours, I believe that our special ties with every continent and the new relationships which we have built up since the war in transforming the old Empire into the new Commonwealth, give us the opportunity of being of real and important service to the cause of freedom.'[989] Neither Bishop nor Brook thought the text quite right – too detailed and insufficiently positive – but as Brook annotated, 'I have ascertained that the Foreign Secretary and the Chancellor like this draft, and the P.M. is specially anxious himself to write in this vein. I do not therefore propose to offer any comments.'[990]

Shortly before Macmillan wrote, Caccia reported from Washington that Kennedy had in mind a meeting with Macmillan for the spring of 1961[991] and lively exchanges continued in Whitehall over the next three months with Brook, Bishop, de Zulueta and the Foreign Office competing for Macmillan's ear. Over the Christmas/New Year period Macmillan himself penned a 32-page memorandum, primarily to clear his own thinking but shown in confidence to Selwyn Lloyd and Frank Lee at the Treasury, which started with a stark warning that 'The Free World cannot, on a realistic assessment, enter on 1961 with any great degree of satisfaction. In the struggle against Communism, there have been few successes and some losses over the past decade,' militarily, economically and politically. There is a consistent theme running through this period in which the leaders of the West repeatedly refer to Communist progress in catching up the Capitalist World because of the former's central direction and the latter's fragmentation. Brook had devoted no less than one third of a lecture to Home Office Officials on Cabinet government in June 1959 to the organisation of Cabinet in wartime.[992] TURNSTILE, the secret Cotswold evacuation complex for the government during nuclear war was completed in the same month. Macmillan now spelt out how and why the USA, Britain and Europe (sic) must organise in a coherent effort to withstand the Communist tide all over the world – 'We are all now ready to sup with Mr. Khrushchev. We may have varying views as to the length of the spoon required. But still, we are prepared to sup.'[993]

In particular Brook disagreed with Bishop over the state of the 'special relationship' between the UK and USA. In a secret note Bishop contested Caccia's view from the end of November that 'a working relationship of unparalleled intimacy has been established,' arguing that the appropriate test of the strength of the relationship was '... not whether officials have frequent contacts with their opposite number, but whether United States policy decisions pay attention to our interests and our representations,' and listed seven important instances where it was arguable that they did not (Laos, NATO medium range ballistic missiles, discussion of nuclear strategy, the conditions applying to the POLARIS bases in Scotland, UN resolutions on colonialism, EFTA/EEC relations, and failings in intelligence sharing – notably over the U2 debacle.) Brook interpreted the mood music from the US differently. 'I'm afraid I dissent from much of this,' he wrote to Bishop and after receipt of Kennedy's letter suggesting a spring meeting, 'P.M. need not fear that the days of a special relationship are over.'[994]

In a sense both were right and the difference between them was one of emphasis. Bishop concluded his note with the advice that 'I agree with the view, expressed by Sir Winston Churchill, that the fortunes of the United Kingdom are indissolubly linked to those of the United States ... I would not myself shrink from a closer political union between the two countries. But we must be realistic ... They will only continue [the "special relationship"], such as it is, if we make sure that it is of value to them and to our joint interests.' Meanwhile, Brook was totally hardheaded when it came to the value of the UK nuclear deterrent to the United States. By 1962, he assessed that the UK V-bomber force would have sufficient capacity to inflict an 'unacceptable' blow to the Russians (50% destruction of 44 major Russian cities) and would give the UK Government a better chance of persuading the United States Government to be resolute in a period of tension.[995] Further, the UK's economic accommodation sought with the Six in Europe would not be possible without American goodwill. 'This might be won on political grounds, but it will be as a result of subordination of their economic interests to their political interests. An accommodation between the Six and the Seven must necessarily lead to increased discrimination against American exports, and this will be particularly disturbing to them at a time when they are worried about their balance of payments.'[996]

In preparation for the planned Washington meeting with Kennedy, and after discussion of his Christmas/New Year paper with the Foreign Secretary and Chancellor, Macmillan asked Brook to pursue a number of studies on which he had reported to the Prime Minister on 10 January.[997] Almost all concerned economic policy (including import controls, control of capital movements, external monetary policy, assistance to exports, the international imbalance of payments, increasing world liquidity, expanding world trade, organisation of the economic power of the Free World, a settlement between the Six and the Seven). Brook had ten days before Macmillan would hold a weekend Chequers meeting to discuss all of this.

The report was submitted on 18 January followed by a detailed handling brief.[998] This restated the problem – on Europe the balance of economic and political advantages lay in favour of drawing closer to mainland Europe but were Ministers prepared to advocate the sacrifices that would be involved (by the Commonwealth and by domestic agriculture) and was it right to think that the key was a political arrangement with France? For NATO could the French be persuaded to co-operate properly and could the development of independent nuclear capabilities in the Alliance (France again) be prevented? Should there be investment to update the UK deterrent before its value depreciated any further because of the growing need to develop missile delivery systems? The brief then identified the main choice as between putting the UK deterrent under the control of NATO or trying to help France 'rise up to the level of our own special position.' Brook pointed to the second as more palatable to UK public opinion and less of a threat to the UK's world standing but added, 'I would like to emphasise two particular points: (a) ... weapons which are strategic for us are regarded by the United States as tactical ... [though] I suspect that they are far too large to be used, sensibly, against tactical targets' ... Nevertheless this, apparently, is what SACEUR intends ... (b) It cannot yet be taken for granted that it will be possible to devise a system of NATO control which will preserve the "credibility" of the deterrent.' Brook concluded with prescient insight that 'If it is his aim that France should continue to play the leading part in Europe, on what terms could he afford to have us there?' Later, in December 1962 when de Gaulle concluded, following a visit to Rambouillet by Macmillan, that Britain was not yet ready for membership of the EEC the same point was made (but more colourfully) by the French Agriculture Minister – with the Six there were five hens and one cock; if Britain joined, there would be two cocks.[999]

Throughout February debates continued over the arguments to be deployed by Macmillan with the President. Officialdom was struggling to meet the challenge of a new beginning. Bishop found himself feeling 'some embarrassment at appearing so often to criticise the attitude of a number of Departments to the preparation of material for the Prime Minister's discussions with President

Kennedy.'[1000] He railed that 'This sort of general attitude [on the East-West struggle] needs to be buttressed by specific policy ideas. A certain number have been put forward, but the Departments have been more concerned to destroy these than to improve them, or to find substitutes.'[1001] A similar point arose on a Foreign Office brief on the 'Wider Aspects of Colonialism'[1002] – where the British often felt that the anti-colonial stance of the United States, particularly in the forum of the United Nations, was simplistic and damaging to the process of converting Empire into Commonwealth.[1003] (Their own General Twining, for example, had identified military bases in some of the British dependent territories as particularly important and the Foreign Office paper also referred to the undesirability of rushing withdrawal from Empire in the light of developments in the Congo).[1004] Brook was dissatisfied with proposals (developed under his leadership) for managing international aid to counter Communist encroachment – which he described as 'lame'.[1005] He rejected drafting suggestions from Shuckburgh at the Foreign Office that emphasised existing mechanisms of consultation Brook considered too rigid for dealing with the Communist threat in particular areas with the countries directly concerned.[1006] The theme for Macmillan to develop was clear – what can Britain and America do to reverse the propaganda gains of the Communist bloc at the expense of the West? The challenge was that the new Administration in Washington would expect the British to have concrete ideas and hard proposals.[1007]

Somewhat surprisingly after the Chequers discussions of 21–22 February, the Foreign Office came forward in the second half of March with a proposal to offer to put the UK deterrent into a collective NATO nuclear pool in the hope that this would contain French ambitions to develop an independent nuclear weapons capacity. Brook dismissed the idea with the withering rhetorical question to Macmillan, 'Do we really think that France will be deterred from developing an independent nuclear capacity by proposals of ours which do not satisfy in any way her aspirations to be treated as a great Power? ... I am also doubtful whether we should even tell the Americans ... They might well think it is a sensible division of effort that we should leave them to provide the strategic nuclear deterrent and concentrate on maintaining stronger conventional forces in the bases which are available to us around the world.' He advised Macmillan to probe Kennedy on his willingness to make nuclear concessions to France and on how to cure the malaise in NATO caused by France's refusal to co-operate fully in the alliance; but to go no further.[1008]

In the event, Brook's positive interpretation of how matters stood with the United States was vindicated when on 24 March Kennedy appealed to Macmillan to make a 3,600 mile round trip[1009] to Key West in Florida the following day to exchange views face to face on the crisis in Laos. Macmillan counselled the President to show restraint, conscious that there would be no appetite in the post-Suez UK for another expeditionary force. In the words of his biographer Macmillan established himself in the President's mind as a father figure.[1010] Macmillan later wrote of that first encounter that, 'Although we have never met and belonged to such different generations, he was just forty and I was nearly seventy, we seemed immediately to talk as friends'.[1011] This initial rapport was further strengthened ten days later when the Washington meeting took place over four days from 5–8 April. The official joint communiqué spoke of the two men talking as partners but recognising the rights and interests of other nations. It did not refer to the agreed joint follow-up action on 14 points ranging from an urgent study of international liquidity to contingency planning in respect of the Berlin crisis to reforms in the United Nations.[1012] These agreed actions reflected part of the British briefing but by no means all. But in preparation for Kennedy visiting de Gaulle in Paris later in April Brook resurrected the Grand Plan for a more coherent Western Powers' response to Communist economic and political initiatives in the Middle East, Africa, Asia and South America in a memorandum that pointed to signs of cleavage between the 'Europeans' led by France and the 'Anglo-Saxons' over the Congo, Laos, Disarmament and NATO co-operation.[1013] He suggested that the dangers these developments brought could be averted if the UK were to join the Six; if France could be persuaded to forego its independent nuclear ambitions and if, in consequence, France were to be accepted as a nuclear partner alongside the US and the UK. Macmillan drew substantially on the submission when he briefed Kennedy at the end of the month. However, following the meeting with de Gaulle Kennedy told Macmillan that the United States could not share nuclear know-how with France;[1014] and in July the following year Macmillan asked Brook to examine the practical possibilities of Anglo-French nuclear co-operation. By the time the report was ready in December ill health and hospitalisation prevented Brook from submitting it. His successor, Burke Trend, did so on 6 December with the advice that there were no fruitful possibilities of Anglo-French co-operation in any of these fields.[1015]

Weak Economic Foundations

Treasury studies pointed to closer ties with the Six on economic grounds and Macmillan was quite aware of the fragile domestic base on which the world role of the United Kingdom rested. In April 1957 he commissioned a report from the Minister of Labour on how far the country could be protected from the effects of strikes in basic industries.[1016] In the much-quoted Bedford speech of 20 July 1957 he not only said, 'Let us be frank about it, most of our people have never had it so good,' but went on to add, 'What is beginning to worry some of us, is it too good to be true, or perhaps I should say, is it too good to last?' Brook was now joint PUS at the Treasury but left most of the economic issues to his partner PUS, after Bridges' retirement first Sir Roger Makins and from 1960 Sir Frank Lee. Burke Trend, a Treasury official on secondment to the Cabinet Office, took on most of the Cabinet and committee briefing on economic issues. For his part, Sir Robert Hall, Chief Economic Adviser in the Treasury thought that the Cabinet minutes did not always show a proper understanding of the effects of wage increases[1017] but it is unclear whether Makins passed on the message to Brook. Where Brook was active was in setting the course for work undertaken by others. Thus, for example, on 9 May he chaired a discussion of senior officials on how to conduct the study the Prime Minister had commissioned on the effects of industrial stoppages on the economy.[1018] After a discussion in which it was argued that not all strikes were more damaging than further wage increases and that it was a misconception that the conciliation functions of government implied an obligation to avert all strikes if possible, Otto Clarke was put in charge of the detailed work (tagged GEN 596) and Brook summed up. The study 'should show the extent and limitations of the government's power to maintain essential services, assess the economic consequences of the type of strikes which Ministers had in mind, and indicate those other sectors of the economy where least damage would be done by allowing a dispute to be settled by strike action.'[1019] Two months later the report was ready.

The GEN 596 group argued that whilst strikes, in general, caused a loss of production the effects of excessive wage increases were likely to be worse and there was no way of knowing in advance what would be the outcome of a specific prolonged strike that was keenly contested. The industries with the most power to disrupt were power generation, coal mining, railways, engineering, and the docks. Brook summarised these findings and translated them into policy terms – notably that it was a mistake to assume that the conciliation duties of the Ministry of Labour must always prevent strikes at any cost and added that the government Emergency Organisation cannot be used for the purpose of mitigating the economic effects of a strike. It could be invoked only for the purposes of preserving order and maintaining 'supplies essential to the life of the community' and could not be used at all in a strike that did not imperil the supply of essentials to the general public.[1020] The commissioning group of Permanent Secretaries met on 24 July to consider the report, by which time Brook had already put his interpretation of the findings to the Prime Minister. He directed that there should be no minute prepared of the meeting – the most likely explanation being that conclusions were politically inflammatory at a time shortly after a London bus drivers' strike had petered out.

By contrast, it looks unlikely that Brook played a significant part in the discussions on Public expenditure at the end of 1957 that led to the resignation of the Chancellor (Peter Thorneycroft) and his entire ministerial team (Nigel Birch and Enoch Powell) over a £50 million gap in what he was prepared to sanction for government expenditure in 1958/59 and what the Prime Minister and Cabinet would accept, though the gap was less than 1% of the total of £4,000 million of government spending. Macmillan's proposed departure date for the tour of the Commonwealth (7 January) had curtailed the time available to mediate but Makins later indicated to Alistair Horne that the Treasury Ministerial team did not have the backing in this of their senior officials.[1021]

Changing Social Behaviour

Beyond the boundaries of Whitehall and Westminster pressure was building for social change. To many the Macmillan Administration came to symbolise an out-of-touch governing elite. Macmillan confided to Nigel Nicholson that, 'The masses now took prosperity for granted ... The country simply did not realise that we were living beyond our income, and would have to pay for it sooner or later.'[1022] Notable developments included the Wolfenden Report, recommending that 'homosexual behaviour between consenting adults in private should no longer be a criminal offence,' published in September 1957.[1023] There were serious race riots in Nottingham and in Notting Hill, London in August 1958. The Crowther Report *15 to 18* recommended the expansion of comprehensive schools, raising the school leaving age from 15 to 16, the introduction of what became the GCSE examination, and drew attention to the wastage to society from pupils who 'dropped out' of education.[1024] In a celebrated 1960 court case Penguin Books were found not guilty of obscenity for publishing DH Lawrence's 1928 novel *Lady Chatterley's Lover*. During the trial the prosecuting counsel, Mervyn Griffith-Jones, seemed to personify outdated attitudes when he asked 'Is it a book that you would even wish your wife or your servants to read?'[1025] In October 1961 an appeal led by the editor of the *Architectural Review* to preserve the Doric Arch at Euston station fell on deaf Prime Ministerial ears and demolition began before the end of the year. Dr Beeching, the technical director of Imperial Chemical Industries, was appointed to head British Rail with a remit to make the railways pay. The result was the loss of one third of the 18,000 miles of track and a severe cull of rural branch lines that fed mainline train services.[1026] The Robbins report, also of 1963, recommended a dramatic enlargement of the university system. It was followed by the Newsom report *Half Our Future* on secondary modern schooling and the Buchanan Report *Traffic in Towns* of November the same year. There was a sense that the ice was breaking up and that the winds of change were about to blow not just in Africa but much, much closer, to home. Brook was not immune from these forces but struggled to contain them.

The central contention of this history is that the first duty of the Cabinet Secretary is to make Ministers look in control of events, farsighted and wise, governing in the interests of the nation as a whole. As a subsidiary element of this, the processes of government must appear rational and smooth no matter what is going on beneath the surface. The more these processes can be kept secret the better the chances of success. Macmillan understood this instinctively. Soon after ascending to the premiership he wrote, 'I can only say that, if I thought that the present holder of this office was keeping a private diary, my official relations with him would be very different to what they are now.'[1027] Brook was entirely at one with him in this although he backed the recommendation of the Grigg Report on Departmental Records that Cabinet papers should be open to the public after 50 years.[1028] Back in May 1956 he had taken the first steps in an unsuccessful attempt to bring the diplomats and armed forces into line with the restrictions on home officials.[1029] Although he and Trend argued that by 1958 the time had come to rein in the discretion that had prevailed in the immediate aftermath of the war Macmillan recognised the political danger inherent in seeming to tighten censorship generally and no matter how much he might oppose extending the latitude to home civil servants Macmillan did not judge it expedient to try to re-corral horses that had long since bolted.[1030]

Brook invested vast amounts of time in scrutinising and negotiating amendments to memoirs and histories by those who had been ministers or held senior rank in the military or diplomatic service. His comments and drafting suggestions on Arthur Bryant's war histories, *Triumph in the West* and *The Turn of the Tide* in 1956 and 1959 ran to 16 foolscap pages and went far wider than issues of national security. Bryant's text was based on the war diaries of Field Marshal Alanbrooke, which revealed details of many disagreements with Churchill over military strategy and the conduct of the war. Neither Macmillan nor Brook thought that Alanbrooke should have allowed access to the diaries (they were not published in their own right in the UK until 2002) and Brook worked hard to correct, as he saw it, a bias against Churchill. So extensive were his suggestions that Bryant wanted to credit his help in the acknowledgements section of the volumes – which Brook declined, citing that he had been commenting in the line of his official duties.[1031]

During the Macmillan period, other books Brook vetted included *Full Circle* (Anthony Eden, published 1960). Eden started to submit the text in May 1958 – 16 months after he had left office, which at the time was the first highly current political memoir and Brook's vetting reflected the topicality of Eden's views, especially over Suez – Moran's diary offers the opinion that the question invariably asked by the Cabinet Secretary was not 'Is this damaging to national security?' but 'Is this likely to offend the Americans?'[1032] Brook was particularly sensitive to Eden's criticisms of Foster Dulles, deleting comments such as, 'Two of the more backward countries in the Middle East and in Africa, South Africa and Liberia are where American interests play a conspicuously large part.'[1033] He confessed that, 'Our difficulty arises from the fact that the control we can exercise over anyone in Sir Anthony's position cannot be more than persuasion,'[1034] but he nevertheless convinced Eden to defer publication until after the 1959 General Election. Such was his energy and influence that Eden invited him to be a trustee of his literary trust (an offer once again declined with an offer of whatever help he could give).[1035] Which caused Moran to speculate whether *Full Circle* was an official history in all but name.[1036]

Brook also offered comments on *The Story of Peter Townsend*, (Norman Barrymaine, published 1958);[1037] *The Prof in Two Worlds* (Lord Birkenhead, published 1961);[1038] and *Neville Chamberlain* (Iain Macleod, published 1962).[1039] But the most troublesome issue, by far, concerned the memoirs of the first Cabinet Secretary, Maurice Hankey, based on diaries he had kept whilst serving. Permission to publish had first been refused in 1944 by Bridges, confirmed by Attlee in 1946, reconfirmed by Churchill in 1953, and by Macmillan in 1957 and many times from then on until *The Times* announced serialisation of *The Supreme Command 1914–18* on 11 December 1960.[1040] Hankey simply refused to give up and there were extensive detailed exchanges directly and indirectly with Brook during 1957–60. Macmillan, Brook and Trend objected to publication on principle. 'The Cabinet Secretary ought not to keep a diary,' argued Macmillan;[1041] Hankey's work was objectionable on the grounds that it was based on a diary and that it was an exercise in self-promotion that would invite retaliation from others, argued Brook.[1042] He dismissed Hankey's arguments that precedents had been set by military and diplomatic memoirs – arguing that a Cabinet Secretary was not in a public position and therefore had no claim to justify his actions, still less his confidential advice to Ministers.[1043] But in the same advice he conceded that it would not be expedient to prosecute Hankey were he to go ahead against the Prime Minister's advice. There was only a small chance of getting across to a judge the subtle distinction in this regard between the Cabinet Secretary and a diplomat or a military man (*pace* Alanbrooke and also General Ismay who was believed to be close to publishing a memoir) and no chance at all of doing so to the public at large. In the event Hankey published with Macmillan annotating Brook's notification of this intention with a double underlined 'NO LEGAL ACTION.' Small wonder that Brook put in a plea to the Prime Minister for a public statement that the rules would be tightened – 'We put in a lot of work on these books, to little purpose.'[1044] Some years later when George Mallaby published his memoirs Macmillan wrote to Brook, 'What is George Mallaby up to? Have you seen his stuff? Hankey was improper, but happily unreadable, I fear this may be more amusing.'[1045]

The second illustration of Brook's austere attitudes concerns the future of broadcasting. In 1957 the government had to decide who should succeed Sir Kenneth Clark as chairman of the Independent Television Authority – created in 1954 to supervise the creation of the first commercial television network in the United Kingdom. On 1 July Brook minuted the Prime Minister in characteristic form. '*The Times* has been good enough,' he wrote, 'to set out the qualities required for this job – without however indicating how we are to get a paragon of this kind to devote the whole of his time to this job, while still in his fifties, for £3,000 a year ... I am beginning to doubt whether there would be a good reception for the appointment of someone who was nothing more than a "tough business-man" ... I believe that informed public opinion would like to see someone in this position who has, if not a cultural background, at least some interest in broadening the outlook of the younger generation.'[1046] Then in 1959 when the government finally thought that the time might be ripe for an independent enquiry into the future of broadcasting, the BBC complained privately to Brook about inadequate consultation on whether to have an enquiry at all, in effect asserting its position as 'the main instrument for broadcasting in the United Kingdom' laid out in a 1953 White Paper (Cmnd 9005) before the creation of the Independent Television Authority. Brook showed something of a hidebound nature in an emollient reply to its Director General, Sir Ian Jacob;[1047] as he did to the Royal Commission on Broadcasting when Cabinet was minded to allow an experiment in subscription television 18 months before the Commission had reported. 'If the experiment were successful,' he advised, 'either in the sense of revealing a popular demand or turning out profitable to its promoters (which amounts to the same thing), I cannot help thinking that – especially with the strong reinforcing argument of the export market – the Government would feel bound to allow subscription television on a more general basis, whatever the Pilkington Committee might have said.'[1048]

Intelligence, Security and Spies

Almost immediately after the election triumph of 1959 there was no shortage of crises. The fear of Communist gains at the expense of the West became consuming. In May 1958 Brook had successfully taken control through the Permanent Secretaries Intelligence Committee (PSIS) of the programme of Special Political Actions (though not of individual actions) because of fears of Communist subversion in the colonies.[1049] By early 1960 Macmillan was beginning to interfere in his colleagues' conduct of business and 'the Paris summit in May 1960 marked the moment when his luck began to run out.'[1050] At the end of 1960 the Joint Intelligence Committee had been in the Cabinet Office for over three years and had successfully diversified its reports to include political as well as military topics. One of the main reasons for the move out of the Ministry of Defence had been to make it easier for Ministers to commission reports from the Committee – in November 1957, for example, Brook had suggested a study of the strength of the nationalist movements in Arab countries.[1051] However, the JIC failed to predict the erection of the Berlin Wall in 1961 though it correctly perceived its lack of strategic significance and the JIC advocacy of a diplomatic rather than military response tallied with Macmillan's views.[1052]

Until 1961 the work of the secret committee Brook chaired on combatting Communism at home was still quite gentle.[1053] Its agenda focused on assessments of Communism in the trades unions, Communist front organisations operating in Britain, the attitude of the Communist Party of Great Britain to unilateral disarmament, the growth of Communist radio broadcasting etc.[1054] The Berlin crisis and events at home in 1961 changed all that. Ministers and the civil service were shaken by a series of spy scandals. Both Macmillan and RAB Butler the Home Secretary had little grasp of the work of the Security Service and Macmillan in particular, burned by the experience of having to clear Kim Philby in 1955 in the House of Commons because of the lack of proof that he was a Soviet spy, hated spy scandals. 'It was, in his view, "dangerous and bad for our general national interest" – as well as embarrassing for the government – for such matters to be discussed in public.' In March 1961, following a lead from a Polish intelligence officer, Harry Houghton and Ethel 'Bunty' Gee of the British Underwater Detection Establishment were convicted of spying for the Russians and Security Service surveillance of the pair led to the identification of a Soviet illegal intelligence officer in Britain using the bogus name and nationality of Gordon Lonsdale and two further members of what became known as the Portland spy ring, Peter and Helen Kroger (aka Morris and Lona Cohen, veteran KGB illegals in America). As if this were not enough, just as the trial of the Portland spy ring was coming to an end a defector told the CIA that the KGB had an agent in MI6 who was later identified as George Blake, convicted and sentenced to 42 years in prison.[1055] Then in September 1962 an Admiralty clerk with an extravagant lifestyle (John Vassall, who despite a modest salary as a clerk, lived in an exclusive block in Dolphin Square, London) confessed to spying for the Soviets since 1955.[1056]

Partly because of these revelations and partly because of the ongoing crisis over Berlin, Brook injected a sense of urgency into precautionary measures. On 18 April he had been the one to tell a disbelieving Macmillan about yet another spy in the camp in Vassall[1057] and it fell to him as the Head of the Home Civil Service to implement the recommendations of the external review, under Lord Radcliffe, of protective security. The number of posts to be subject to positive Vetting (PV) rose from 13,500 at the end of 1957 to well over 50,000 (including all posts at Under-Secretary and above) by May 1962. The backlog of people awaiting clearance stood at nearly 5,000 in May 1962.[1058] The Brook committee also edited the Radcliffe Report for publication, removing the chapters on Communism in the civil service and Communists in the Civil Service Staff Associations and Trades Unions together with all references to normal vetting procedures (NV); the former to avoid rousing public interest before a comprehensive plan of action was ready, the latter to avoid an unmanageable number of appeals.[1059] Publication of the two redacted chapters would have been political dynamite and thrown a shadow over the reputation of the civil service for competence. Permanent Secretaries were called to an emergency meeting on 13 April at which Brook gave details of the extent of Communist penetration in the civil service – described in the Radcliffe Report as having 'achieved a higher degree of penetration in the Civil Service Staff Associations than in almost any other sector of the trade union movement and that this was dangerous to security however one defined it.'[1060] The penetration was thought to be as high as 25%. True to form, Brook was not panicked into draconian action – he argued successfully at the committee that the only Departments from which there should be complete exclusion were those which were *thought of by the public* as being predominantly engaged in secret work [emphasis added]. Subsequently Brook admitted in regard to the number of unresolved cases of suspected Communist association that the steps in hand would not meet the expectations of the Radcliffe Committee but 'we must be realistic' about the resources available to do so.[1061]

Meanwhile, the government contemplated taking emergency powers because of the Berlin crisis[1062] and Brook suggested to Macmillan that he should appoint a ministerial committee to supervise the military and non-military preparations 'in the event that we cannot reach a negotiated settlement over Berlin.'[1063] Macmillan demurred, arguing that since any war would soon become a nuclear war all that was needed was to conform 'with a reasonable posture at the cheapest possible cost on our own or foreign currency.'[1064] But shortly afterwards, overnight on 12/13 August, Berliners awoke to the border between East and West Berlin having been closed and work started to erect a 140 kilometre barrier along the border that eventually rose 3.6 metres in height, known in the West as the Berlin Wall. On 25 August Brook wrote to Lee, his joint Permanent Secretary at the Treasury, warning that 'we face a period of fluctuating political tension over Berlin.' If the crisis started to dominate other business Whitehall should move on to a precautionary state with 24-hour working in key departments (10 Downing Street, the Cabinet Office Secretariat, JIC, Foreign Office, Home Office, Defence, Commonwealth Relations and the secret departments; arrangements for the speedy distribution of material between control points; daily JIC meetings reporting to daily ministerial meetings; and if serious military action threatened government should move to War Book operations.[1065] Macmillan continued to argue to President Kennedy that so long as Khrushchev could be kept talking he could be deflected from carrying out the worst threats – even when American and Soviet tanks stood muzzle to muzzle across the Berlin border on 10 October and eventually a series of conciliatory suggestions to Khrushchev (the so-called 'battle of notes') defused the situation[1066] to the extent that the city remained divided and the Wall remained intact until the collapse of the DDR and the Wall in November 1989.

Macmillan's confidence was shaken by the succession of spy scandals. The unmasking of the Portland spy ring, the convictions of George Blake and of John Vassall, and the defection of Kim Philby to Moscow took their toll on the Prime Minister. In October 1955, as Foreign Secretary, Macmillan had exonerated Philby: 'I have no reason to conclude that Mr. Philby has at any time betrayed the interests of his country, or to identify him with the so-called "Third Man", if indeed there was one.' Now he knew that there had been a 'Third Man' and that he had, in good faith and unknowingly, misled the House of Commons about Philby. Then a story broke about an affair between John Profumo (Secretary of State for War) and a model and show girl, Christine Keeler, who was simultaneously intimately involved with a Russian intelligence officer, Yevgeny Ivanov. Suspicions of espionage were inevitable, though never confirmed. Allegations were made that Ivanov used his friendship with Keeler and her associate Stephen Ward to try to obtain information about the stationing of nuclear weapons in Germany. But what called Macmillan's judgement into question was his seeming gullibility in March in accepting Profumo's denials of sexual misconduct, at first repeated in the House of Commons and then retracted in shame and disgrace. In 2010 *The Spectator* assessed this to be the most important political scandal of the post-war years: 'Before Profumo the public were in the dark about the private lives of members of the establishment. Most assumed that great men occupied the moral high ground with the same ease with which they occupied high society ... Profumo paved the way for every political scandal since. After his trial in 1963, the press would never be so discreet again, nor the public so naïve.'[1067]

Undoubtedly one component in Macmillan's handling of Profumo was a belief that a Minister would behave honourably when challenged by his peers. In the report of the enquiry into the Profumo affair under the chairmanship of Lord Denning, Master of the Rolls, Denning said, 'I am sure that the Prime Minister and all the Ministers were satisfied of the truth of [Profumo's] statement [in the House of Commons]. They could not conceive that any of their colleagues would have the effrontery to make a false statement to the House. The business of the country could not be carried on if a member of the Government could not accept the word of another implicitly.'[1068]

Brook may have inadvertently contributed to Macmillan's lack of rigour in tackling Profumo because he had never reported to the Prime Minister that, in

August 1961, on the advice of the Security Service, he had warned Profumo off too close an association with Ward and Ivanov because of the risk that Ivanov would seek to exploit a friendship for espionage.[1069] Denning exonerated Brook from criticism but had Macmillan known of the warning he may have taken a tougher line with Profumo over his association with Keeler (which, to be fair, neither the Security Service nor Brook had known about in August 1961).[1070] What Denning did not address, however, was at what stage Brook heard of the rumour about Profumo and Keeler. At the end of January 1963, one month after Brook retired, Christine Keeler told her story to the *News of the World* and the *Sunday Pictorial*. That was when the Security Service got to know of it.[1071] On the assumption that Brook would have seen the same newspaper story, it is reasonable to ask if he should have contacted the Prime Minister or the new Cabinet Secretary, Burke Trend. Brook's decision not to tell the Prime Minister about the warning of August 1961 was then compounded by the correct decision by the Head of MI5, Sir Roger Hollis, in February 1963 that since there was no threat to the state the matter was outside the Security Service's lawful remit.[1072]

In hindsight it was a rare mistake on Brook's part not to alert the Prime Minister about Profumo and Ward/Ivanov – a Russian intelligence officer with connections to the Secretary of State for War ought to have set alarm bells ringing given the escalating tensions around Berlin and East Germany, which Brook certainly knew about. His mistakes were so rare that it is worth a brief mention of another, from 1958, because they point to sins of omission rather than sins of commission. On 16 July 1958 King Hussein of Jordan appealed to Britain for support to resist a threat from Syria. Cabinet decided to send two battalions of paratroopers by air from Cyprus and they left that same night. This required the planes to fly over Israel but in the haste to act nobody had obtained Israeli consent. Macmillan recorded in his diary for 17 July, 'Some machines (with about 200 men) had gone into Amman. Then the order was given to stop and other machines had to go back ... poor Norman Brook spent three hours trying to get through [by telephone to Tel Aviv] ... Brook (who thought it was his fault) was almost in tears.'[1073]

In other circumstances selective omission of some facts was an essential part in presenting Britain in a favourable light. On 18 March *The Daily Mail*, for instance, wrote to the War Office to validate allegations of ill-treatment of German prisoners of war between 1945 and 1947 made by two private soldiers who were among the guards at one of the nine locations around Britain run by the Prisoner of War Interrogation Section of the Directorate of Military Intelligence – the 'London Cage' in Kensington Palace Gardens.[1074] The prisoners were all alleged War Criminals (SS Colonel General Brochart, SS Colonel Erich Zacharias, and Generals Von Manstein, Von Mackenson and Fritz Knoechlein). The alleged mistreatment ranged from sleep deprivation for four days without a break and without food to assault and, in the case of Knoechlein, being taken into a room where a rope hung from the ceiling and told he would be hanged, sooner or later (as indeed he was later). The Secretary of State for War had ascertained that, 'It appears that there may be some substance in these allegations, though at this late stage there is little chance of getting the full facts,' and had suggested an approach to Lord Rothermere to try to persuade him not to publish. Macmillan sent for Brook who suggested, in a carefully worded note, that the line to be taken with Rothermere was that 'These allegations refer to events in 1945–7. It is not the first time that allegations of this kind have been made. It does not follow that any are true. After this long lapse of time it would probably be impossible to establish the facts with certainty,' and went on to refer to a refutation of the claims by the chief interrogator at the London Cage (rescinded in 1954) and a denial of knowledge of any such happenings by its Commandant. Rothermere was duly telephoned by the PUS at the War Office (Wray) and nothing more was heard from the newspaper but in 2005 the story surfaced again in *The Guardian* and further revelations were made in 2012 in *The Daily Mail.*[1075]

Punching Above its Weight – Political Control of the Military

Under Churchill, Macmillan had been made Minister for Defence in 1954 and held that office until Eden made him Foreign Secretary in 1955. This was a brief but unhappy spell. Though the Minister was a Cabinet member, he was not wholly in charge of the Ministry, which still had Service Ministers ranked as Secretaries of State (i.e. senior to the Minister in protocol terms) and Chiefs of Staff who had independent access to the Prime Minister. In Churchill there was also a Prime Minister who would not hesitate to interfere in defence matters. Macmillan confided to his diary: 'This new Ministry of mine is a queer kind of affair. I have no power and I am responsible for everything – especially if it goes wrong.'[1076] Hence, an important ingredient of the mix for Macmillan's own administration was the central organisation of defence policy and who to appoint as Minister for Defence so soon after Suez. Also, in the light of Soviet atomic weapons, the nature of the military threat had changed at a time when the United Kingdom faced straitened economic times.

Eden had started a reappraisal with a Cabinet Policy Review Committee 'to consider ... what adjustments should be made in government policy in view of changes to the methods, if not the objectives, of the Soviet Union. This review, which will take account of our own economic and financial circumstances, will cover changes in domestic and overseas policy and adjustments in our defence programmes.'[1077] The aim was to complete as many as possible of the studies by mid July 1956 but its work was not completed when the Suez crisis occurred. As Chancellor, Macmillan sat on the steering group for the review.[1078] Now, as Prime Minister, he wanted retrenchment in defence spending and reform in its higher organisation.[1079]

Against the advice of Brook who thought that 'the rows would be too great,'[1080] Macmillan chose as Minister of Defence the hardworking and ruthless Duncan Sandys, a man who often showed brutal disregard for the feelings of others and who might, therefore, be a good choice for the internal battles ahead. Sandys had been strongly influenced by American academics who argued that the threat of thermo-nuclear war required a new way of thinking for which conventional civilian and military education was a hindrance.[1081] The influence of this factor was an important component of the attitudes of Macmillan and Sandys. Meanwhile, senior military professionals watched the emergence of left-wing factions in the British Labour Party with genuine ideological commitment to pacifism. The Chiefs of Staff foresaw the possibility, no matter how remote, of a government of the Left which would oppose existing defence policy and might appoint a Minister of Defence to dismantle rather than strengthen Britain's defences. Further, after the mixed reception received by the Soviet leaders Bulganin and Khrushchev in the United Kingdom in 1956, relations with Russia were hard to predict and contributed to a sense of insecurity. So the scene was set for internal conflict in the preparation of the 1958 White Paper *Central Organisation for Defence.*[1082]

The debate started with a draft directive from Macmillan, four days into the new administration, which said, 'The Chairman of the Chiefs of Staff Committee will be the Chief Staff Officer of the Minister of Defence, to whom in that capacity he will be solely responsible.'[1083] As a military officer, however, the Chairman of the Chiefs of Staff faced a difficult balancing act as a bridge between advising (in which he would be alongside the civilian Permanent Secretary) and being responsible for executing it (in which he would be alongside the individual Chiefs of Staff (COS)). And there was a third element in this marriage, the individual Service Ministers, political champions of their respective armed forces and politically responsible for their administration. The boundaries were ill-defined. Everyone was unhappy.[1084]

Increasingly contentious arguments between Sandys and his PUS (Powell) on the one hand and the Chiefs of Staff on the other, culminated in the First Sea Lord (Mountbatten) preparing to canvass support from US admirals against cuts in the Navy budget[1085] and the Controller of Munitions in the War Office (Lieutenant General Sir John Cowley) openly criticising the policy of relying on nuclear deterrence.[1086] Brook was called in to conduct an investigation of the possibility of integrating the Service headquarters organisations into a single Department organised functionally into Personnel, Administration, and Procurement.[1087] He recognised that the idea was 'bristling with difficulties.'[1088] But later added: 'This is essentially a "machinery of government problem", and I cannot escape the conclusion that it is my business to assume responsibility for supervising the enquiry.'[1089] J G Owen, a Treasury Assistant Secretary, was appointed to help and undertook much of the slog and initial thinking. At this stage Brook was mainly the public face of the enquiry towards the Permanent Secretaries and Service Ministers – alerting them privately on 5 June about how Macmillan would outline the reforms to Sandys and the Service Ministers. Although Macmillan would reject a move to amalgamate the three Fighting Services, Brook would examine the feasibility of a unified department combining headquarters administration and policy control, to be organised functionally.[1090]

Brook let Owen have his head from May to mid July to see if a practicable structure could be devised. There is no record of him expressing a view until late July when he somewhat ambiguously annotated Owen's draft report:

'I have always thought that this question (the degree of "responsibility" of the "Deputy Ministers") was crucial. After all the genesis of our enquiry is that the Minister of Defence wants *power* to decide (not merely *authority*) over the whole field: and the big question is whether he can have it without the full responsibility (in the constitutional sense) which may make it impossible to exercise powers effectively …'.

The crucial issue was how to avoid overloading the Minister. By mid August Owen had concluded that the practical difficulties of an integrated Ministry on functional lines were too great. Brook's annotated his text: 'A very useful note.'[1091] By now only Sandys and Powell favoured an integrated Ministry. In Sandys' view the Minister was often confronted by three shopping lists (one for each Service) with no powers to investigate and likely to be accused of interference if he tried to probe. As to the Chiefs, they were not fully effective either as Commanders-in-Chief or as Chiefs of Staff. Owen and Brook disagreed.[1092] They prepared to contradict Sandys:

'Our lack of a clear defence policy and the general dissatisfaction with the central organisation are largely due to the fact that over the last few years the original concept of the Ministry of Defence as a purely policy-making Department has been gradually transformed into the concept of a Department which should concern itself with detailed Service administration as well.'[1093]

These comments appear not to recognise the force of the Chiefs of Staffs' argument that to divorce policy formulation and implementation was dangerous. They hint at why Brook was regarded by at least some of his peers as essentially a Chef de Cabinet, without insights into how policies would be delivered.[1094]

It took another four months to finalise a report (i.e. longer than the investigation itself) and Macmillan began to grow impatient: 'There are three $64,000 questions for which we are wanting answers. On the reply to these questions depends whether we should proceed now with the re-organisation of Whitehall. All this hangs together, but we ought to reach decisions this month.'[1095] The final document came down unequivocally against an integrated Ministry on a functional basis. It reasserted the authority of the Cabinet and the Defence Committee over policy; with the Ministry in support using committees with political, civil and military members; the Service Ministers would be responsible for policy delivery. The post of Chairman of the Chiefs of Staff Committee would be abolished.

There followed seven months of in-fighting. Sandys reacted violently to the report, dismissing the proposals as 'purely destructive'[1096] and came back with a renewed demand for integration. Macmillan also found Brook's recommendations unconvincing: 'Not quite what Parliament and the nation are expecting.'[1097] Instead he asked Brook and Powell to work together to find a way forward. Powell produced a draft proposal on the last day of 1957.[1098] The main battle was then between Powell and the Chiefs over the proposed abolition of the Chief of Staffs' Committee and the creation of a new post, Chief of the Defence Staff, responsible to the Minister of Defence as his principal military adviser and to whom the three Service Chiefs would serve as deputies though, as the professional heads of their respective services, they would retain a right of access to the Prime Minister.

In the face of continued opposition from Sandys, Brook was once again asked to recast the proposals. He suggested modifications to bolster the importance of the Cabinet Defence Committee and to limit the Chiefs' access to the Prime Minister. But the most important result was that Brook took the opportunity when he accompanied Macmillan on a five and a half week tour of Commonwealth Governments[1099] to persuade the Prime Minister that to abolish the Chief of Staffs Committee would be politically unwise, '... as the scope of the [COS committee] is narrowly limited to military operations and strategy, the title is not important from the Minister's point of view. It is however of great importance from the point of view of getting the whole organisation accepted by military opinion – both existing and past Chiefs of Staff.'[1100] Trend, then in the Cabinet Secretariat, added that, 'for political reasons it would be undesirable that the Chiefs of Staff should no longer be available to tender collective military advice to the Government as a whole.'

Meanwhile, Sir William Dickson, the chairman of the COS, wrote that co-operation from the individual Service chiefs was reluctant to the point of non-existence: 'For the first time in my career, I am filling a post in which there is no clear definition of its rank, no delegation of responsibility, and one in which I cannot give my best service.'[1101] A month later the Chiefs fired a broadside, 'We still believe that advice without responsibility is dangerous' and ended their message with, 'We believe that we are the constitutional military advisers to the Government. If it has been decided to give up asking for our advice, it could only be because of a lack of confidence in us, or because it is thought that we are neither so constituted nor organised as to give sound advice.'

Macmillan circulated a further draft directive that included a Defence Council, ('for the purpose of ensuring that the Service Ministers and the Minister of Supply are kept in touch with developments in defence policy which affect their responsibility for administration'); a Defence Executive (to assist the Minister of Defence in the performance of his functions); and a Defence Secretariat combining military and civilian staff under the Permanent Secretary); plus a new post of Chief of the Defence Staff (CDS) to have overall responsibility for 'inter-Service planning' and for seeing that 'all appropriate business' was handled on an inter-Service basis. The Chiefs ridiculed the idea of a Defence Executive with no executive powers; and a CDS with responsibility but little power. They argued that the CDS should only be *primus inter pares* and passed a message to Brook about their worries over the increasing influence of the Permanent Secretary. Brook left them in no doubt that, 'the Minister and the Permanent Secretary are anxious to do everything they can to obtain a more complete authority over the Chief of the Defence Staff.'[1102]

Macmillan, assisted by Brook, undertook further redrafting during the rest of April and May 1958. Brook advised that he was, 'Increasingly doubtful whether it will be possible to secure a sufficient measure of support in the Cabinet for the sort of changes the Minister of Defence wants to make' and, 'for the first time in my experience since 1940 – and I am sorry to have to say this – there has developed something like a rift between the civil and the military elements in our central defence organisation.'[1103] Two days later he returned to the central issue of principle in a note to Macmillan, namely, to whom the joint Defence Secretariat should report – to the Chiefs of Staff Committee or to the CDS.[1104] Macmillan confided to his diary on 29 June that, 'the row about Defence organisation gets worse and worse.'[1105] Indeed it did. Cabinet discussed the draft Directive with the Chiefs present on successive days (10 and 11 July 1958). A combination of the participants having argued themselves to a standstill and public expectations built up by leaks and the anxious comments of military elder statesmen led to a feeling that the most politically damaging thing of all would be to do nothing.

A White Paper was introduced on 15 July[1106] with (a) a Cabinet Defence Committee of eleven, including the Service Ministers, under the Prime Minister's chairmanship. The Chiefs would attend and receive all papers except the most sensitive confidential annexes; and it was left open that they might, on occasion, also attend the full Cabinet; (b) a Defence Board to assist the Minister and to resolve inter-Service problems; (c) a new appointment of Chief of the Defence Staff as the Minister's principal military adviser and chairman of the Chief of Staffs Committee, which would be 'collectively responsible to the government for professional advice on strategy and military operations and on the military implications of defence problems generally;' and, of course, for the conduct of military operations.

But twelve months into the new structure renewed talk of reform began to surface. Sir Maurice Dean, the Permanent Secretary at the Air Ministry wrote to Brook: 'The new organisation has worked badly,' because of duplication of effort between the civilian and military staffs and because the civilian staff increasingly act like a second Treasury, contributing to inertia, and with matters of Service administration pulled up into a Defence Board some of whose members know literally nothing about the subject.[1107] It is open to interpretation whether this latter development was a ploy by the Service Chiefs to swamp the Defence Board with detail. Meanwhile, Macmillan was discussing possible further changes with Sandys, Powell and the CDS, Lord Mountbatten, who had suggested making the Service Ministers subordinate to the Minister of Defence (and in the process strengthening his own hand). The problem was timing, Macmillan had in mind to make changes in the summer of 1960 after a General Election whereas Powell wanted quicker action to prevent further inertia.

In the event the Macmillan Government went to the country on 8 October 1959. On the eve of the poll Brook reported to Macmillan that Mountbatten now felt that he already had the powers he needed and that further formalisation might impede him.[1108] Where Brook disagreed with Mountbatten, however, was in the latter's call for the Minister of Defence to assume the portfolios of the three Service Ministers and the Ministry of Supply, which he thought would bring Parliamentary difficulties and friction with the Permanent Secretaries of the three Service Departments. Macmillan was keen that 'something was being done to bring into the uniformed staff of the Services a sense of being members of one Service,' and spoke of the need for a Bill to remove from the three Service Ministers the rank of Secretary of State.[1109] Yet after the General Election Macmillan moved Sandys to a new portfolio and replaced him with Harold Watkinson who reported, two months later, that no further organisational changes were required.[1110]

Time produced a healing of wounds. In October 1960 a new Permanent Secretary at Defence (Sir Edward Playfair) reported that with the exception of CDS the view of officials was to leave well alone. Neither the individual Chiefs nor the Service Ministers had shown an inclination to challenge the decisions of the more emollient Watkinson and a new generation of military officers was coming to the top who were accustomed to inter-Service co-operation. At approximately the same time, Brook reported that there was no support for the amalgamation of the Service Departments or for the CDS' proposal to reduce Service Ministers to the status of assistants to the Minister.[1111] Attention switched to the case for a unified command structure overseas, particularly in the Far East, which produced a great deal of debate with Brook arguing that to create a unified command structure would be seen as another milestone on the way to closer Service integration in the United Kingdom.[1112] His last shot in this battle, fired in May 1962, was to advise Macmillan, 'You may find it necessary to remind the Secretary [of Defence] that in the last resort the organisation locally is of less importance than the proper consideration of policy in London.'[1113] He might well have questioned whether all the effort had been worthwhile; by the end of 1962 the die was still not cast and Macmillan, writing to a hospitalised Brook about the challenges ahead could only ponder, 'On the administrative side, has the time come to grasp the defence nettle?'[1114] Meanwhile despite repeated attempts to get to grips with an imbalance between what the country could afford and the role it sought to play on the world stage, defence budget issues remained unsolved.

Defence Budget

In late 1958 Brook proposed an independent committee to consider the best means of delivery for the nuclear deterrent when the V-bomber force became obsolete in the second half of the 1960s.[1115] Initially the idea was opposed by the Minister of Defence[1116] but Brook continued to maintain that economies likely to satisfy the Chancellor of the Exchequer in the longer term should be based on strategic considerations not just financial constraints. It was the classic dilemma of defence budgeting – what can the economy sustain *versus* what is needed to safeguard against an existential threat. And early in January 1959 Powell told him that 'he had come to the conclusion that a formal enquiry was needed to consider the future of the independent British deterrent;' but as Powell was doubtful if his Minister would welcome such a move, the initiative would need to come from the Prime Minister.[1117]

Brook and Trend came to the conclusion that, in view of the Future Policy Study, such a move would have to wait and by early the following year, when Macmillan called a Ministerial discussion on defence policy coincident with the findings of the Future Policy Study, Brook came out in favour of maintaining a viable nuclear force, arguing that: '... the material strength of the United Kingdom will decline over the next ten years, relative to the "giants" ... But our ability to maintain our position in the world will depend increasingly on the way in which the national effort in defence and economic aid is fitted in with those of our friends to further common objective [and] ... to retain our status in the Alliance, we must make a significant effort in the field of the strategic nuclear deterrent.' In a long brief for the Prime Minister for an extended discussion on 20 February 1960 he went on to advocate abandoning the development of a British missile to replace the V-bombers (Blue Streak) in favour of acquiring an American one, suggesting that, 'The Americans are anxious for a base for their Polaris submarines in the Gairloch. Cannot more use be made of this as the basis for a firm understanding about the early supply to us of Polaris and of two or three of their submarines?'[1118] At that meeting and a follow-up on 23 February (both of which Brook attended) Ministers accepted proposals substantially based on Brook's briefing, commissioning work to draw up a practical programme for developing a mobile weapon for delivering the nuclear deterrent and for tapering off effort on Blue Streak if it could not be used for scientific and technological research.[1119]

Health Problems, Retirement and Legacy to Burke Trend

In the autumn of 1962, much to his chagrin, Brook was *hors de combat*, hospitalised with 'an obscure skin condition, accompanied by swollen joints; and the skin man from St Thomas's (Dr Wallace), who came to see me yesterday, says that I must remain in bed for another two or three weeks. I am very sorry to desert you at this moment, and it is a confounded bore from every point of view. But I am advised that complete rest is essential, and I must do as I am told.'[1120] He had told Harold Evans 'he didn't feel that he would be able to carry on for more than another couple of years without having a physical and mental breakdown – he was doing the rounds of Harley Street.'[1121] He never resumed duties as Cabinet Secretary. Initially his deputy, Sir Michael Cary, stepped up (including during the Cuba Missile crisis of late October) until Burke Trend arrived as Cabinet Secretary at the beginning of 1963.[1122] Macmillan did not have anything like as close a relationship with Cary, who had been Deputy Cabinet Secretary only since 1961, as with Brook. So whilst history records that the Cabinet was about to go to the 'Precautionary Stage' according to Nuclear Retaliation Procedures[1123] when Khrushchev backed down on Sunday 28th. It is interesting (and chilling) to speculate whether, if Brook had been around during the critical hours, he would have argued differently. His track record during the Korean War and during both Berlin crises suggests he would not.

A week after the crisis Macmillan found the time to write to him in hospital, 'Although I have not bothered you with letters I have been very glad to hear about you almost daily ... We have struggled on through one thing and another. You know what it is – the usual descent from the sublime to the ridiculous. This week's crisis was exhausting but fascinating. We have certainly learnt a great deal. What stood up so well was Anglo-American co-operation and confidence in each other. I was very pleased about this,' adding, 'We are having a lot of the usual worries – security, etc., but the next big questions are going to be: on the economic side, is the economy slipping and should it be pushed up a bit, as we did two or three years ago?'[1124] Brook replied, 'I am particularly sorry that I have not been there to help you over this Vassall business – for which I cannot help but feeling a special personal responsibility. I hate to think that the Civil Service has involved you and other Ministers in so much embarrassment – and it irks me to think that I was not there to do what little I could to mitigate it. It is a maddening irony that, the more efficient the Security Service are in detecting espionage, the more we lay ourselves open to the criticism that our security standards throughout the Civil Service are inadequate. I also find it ironic that it is through traitors from the Soviet side that we unmask traitors on our own – and that no thought of this should occur to our critics. But I suppose it would be too much to expect the public to take such an objective view of the intelligence underworld.'

Cabinet was told of Brook's illness on 23 October[1125] and given the news that he was progressing favourably on 11 November.[1126] But he did not return to office, retiring formally at the end of the year. Oliver Franks wrote: 'I have been so sorry that you could not finish at your desk as I think you would have wished but instead were laid low, sent to hospital and so to speak counted out from there.'[1127] It was the end of an epoch that had taken Britain from victory in the Second World War through a peace of shortage and penury to an insecure position at the world's 'top table' but where the country's destiny was never seriously questioned by those in power and Whitehall still retained a strong sense of self-confidence. Cabinet presented him with a gift of silver on 3 February; at a retirement party in the Cabinet Office on 5 February 1963 he was presented with a bowl inscribed with Commonwealth theme decorations and with a Latin message.[1128] His Private Office gave him a set of carpentry tools. On 12 February Ministers feted him at a bi-partisan farewell party.

Notes

1 There were, typically at this time, six administrative class ranks and Assistant Secretary lay mid-way up the ladder, responsible for a discrete area of policy
2 In the event Brook was awarded 2nd Class Honours in his finals
3 CSC 11/30
4 Sir John (Jock) Colville was Assistant Private Secretary to three Prime Ministers, Neville Chamberlain, 1939–40, Winston Churchill, 1940–41 and 1943–45, and Clement Attlee, 1945. He is best remembered for his diaries, published as *The Fringes of Power: Downing Street Diaries 1939–1955*, and other memoirs
5 Colville, *Footprints in Time*
6 PREM 11/2800, 04.05.59

7 Mallaby, *From My Level*, p. 53
8 Op. cit, p. 139
9 Mallaby, quoted in Seldon, *Churchill's Indian Summer* p. 189
10 Moran, *Churchill, the Struggle for Survival 1940–65*, pp. 675–8
11 J Stuart, Bodleian, MS. Eng. lett.c.273
12 Moran op. cit, p. 678
13 Hennessy, *Whitehall* pp. 145–6
14 Moran, op. cit, diary entry for 03.08.59, pp. 795–6
15 Kent, *In on the Act*, pp. 29–30
16 Kent, op. cit, pp. 231–2
17 Hennessy, op. cit, p. 145
18 Bodleian, MS. Eng. lett.c.489
19 Bodleian, MS. Eng. lett.c 273
20 LS Pressnell, *The Post-War Financial Settlement*, pp. 1–14
21 CAB 21/2865, 29.06.54
22 Mallaby, *From My Level*, p. 58
23 *The Spectator* 02.10.53; *The Tablet* 20.06.53; JB Figgins in *The Labour Monthly*, August 1953
24 Moran, op. cit, p. 701
25 Moran, op. cit, pp. 221–2
26 Mallaby, op. cit, p. 51
27 Moran, op. cit, p. 677
28 Moran, op. cit, p. 654
29 Moran, op. cit, pp. 765 & 781
30 Evelyn Shuckburgh, Principal Private Secretary to the Foreign Secretary, Anthony Eden, 1951–54 and from 1954 to 1956 Assistant Under-Secretary at the Foreign Office in charge of Middle East affairs
31 Bodleian, MS. Eng. lett.c.274, 12.06.67
32 Shuckburgh, *Descent to Suez*, p. 366
33 Mallaby. *From My Level*, p. 17
34 D R Thorpe, *Supermac*, p. 614
35 CAB 21/4312 and 4313, 18.09.56 and 21.04.59
36 Bodleian, MS. Eng. lett.c273, 17.10.63
37 *Time* magazine 02.02.70
38 Bodleian, MS. Eng. lett.c.273, 22.12.64 and 15.01.65
39 Colville, op. cit, diary entry for 20.06.52
40 Macmillan, *Diaries*, 08.07.62
41 CAB 21/4614, 02.03.62
42 Bodleian, MS. Eng. lett.c273, 11.01.63
43 CAB 21/1998
44 CAB 4/63/2, A brief history of the Lord President's Committee is given in a memorandum, *Functions of the Cabinet Secretariat*, circulated by Bridges on 14.09.44
45 CAB 21/1586
46 *Dictionary of National Biography*
47 Bridges was Cabinet Secretary from 01.08.38 until 31.12.46 when he was succeeded by Brook
48 Permanent Secretary HM Treasury and Head of the Home Civil Service 1942–45
49 CAB 21/1324, War Cabinet paper W.P.(G)(39)143 by the Prime Minister (Chamberlain) 12.12.39, Bridges: Heeney (Clerk of the Privy Council Office, Ottawa) 18.03.42
50 Ibid, note by Bridges, 27.06.40
51 CAB 21/1324, Bridges to Churchill, 30.05.40
52 CAB 21/2865
53 CAB 21/1324, 10.11.41

54 Ibid, 21.11.41
55 HoC Hansard 29.04.41 cols 345–6
56 CAB 21/1324, 28.04.42
57 Ibid, 30.10.39
58 Ibid, a reference to the decision to withdraw from Narvik following the failed attempt to invade which had led to the fall of Neville Chamberlain, the minutes of which were regarded as a military secret to be confided to the smallest number of people, 05.06.40
59 Ibid, 04.06.40
60 Ibid, 04 and 05.06.40
61 CAB 21/4959
62 The Central Statistical Office was founded in January 1941, mainly to avoid disputes at Cabinet over the facts
63 *Dictionary of National Biography*
64 CAB 21/2809, C.P.(46)199, 22.05.46
65 CAB 21/1584, 22.11.40
66 Ibid
67 CAB 21/1583, 04.01.41
68 W.M.(43)144th Conclusions, Minute 1
69 W.P.(43)467, 19.10.43
70 CAB 21/1588, 16.07.43
71 Cabinet Office paper, 05.01.44
72 10 Downing Street Press Notice 16.12.46
73 CAB 21/1588, the broadcast was reprinted by the Army Bureau of Current Affairs, 05.06.43
74 T 199/139
75 CAB 21/1324, *Notes on War Cabinet procedure*, 26.03.42
76 Ibid, 28.04.42
77 Chaired by the Sir John Anderson, Lord President of the Council
78 CAB 21/1998, M.G.(43)2 (Second Revise), April 1943
79 CAB 21/2809 11.04.43
80 Ibid, C.P.(46)199
81 Ibid, C.P.(48)2a82
82 Ibid, C.P.(47) 288
83 CAB 21/393, 13.09.47 and 10.10.47
84 Ibid, 19.11.47
85 Ibid, 27.10.47
86 *The Economist*, 'More Ministries' 02.10.48
87 CAB 21/1701–1703
88 CAB 21/2243, brief on C.P. (48)56 21.02.48
89 CAB 21/1626, 21.04.50
90 CAB 21/1324
91 CAB 21/2809
92 PREM 8/432
93 PREM 8/432
94 For the exchanges between Bevan and Brook see CAB 21/4324
95 CAB 129/9, C.P.(46)188, 10.05.46
96 CAB 21/3741, 18.06.46
97 C.P.(46)273
98 CAB 21/3741, quoted in a letter to Sir Robert Armstrong from Sir Edmund Compton
99 HoC *Hansard*, 15.08.46 col 1213
100 C.M.(46)85th
101 Ibid, 13.07.49

102 Ibid, 18.07.49
103 For a full treatment of Brook's involvement with Churchill in this matter see David Reynolds, *Official History: how Churchill and the Cabinet Office wrote the Second World War*, Historical Research, vol 78, no 201, August 2005
104 *Planning*, PEP broadsheet No 173, 15.07.41
105 CAB 21/1588
106 *The Observer*, 07.10.45
107 T 273/9, February 1946
108 Ibid, 26.02.46
109 Saturday was the half-day at the end of a normal 5½ day peacetime working week, relatively free from duties towards Ministers, when the formal dress code was relaxed in favour of sports jacket and flannels for senior officials – most of whom in 1946 were male
110 CAB 21/2250, July 1951
111 T 162/881 and T 162/944
112 CAB 21/1743, 06.11.46
113 CAB 21/2277
114 CAB 134/505, MG(48)2
115 CAB 21/3343
116 The Conduct of Business in Government Departments
117 CAB 21/2243, Treasury Circular 7/47, 03.03.47
118 CAB 21/3334, 05.11.48
119 CAB 21/2245, brief on C.P.(49) 216, 221, & 228, 09.11.49
120 CAB 21/3334, In 1948 the GOC listed six hurdles for the industrialist who wanted to invest in a new building: (1) Sponsoring Department support; (2) Investment Committee approval for schemes over £500,000; (3) Distribution of Industry Committee approval for location; (4) Ministry of Works licence for exemption from the ban on industrial building; (5) Regional Building Committee agreement of a starting date for work over £500; (6) The Material Allocation Committee's agreement to adequate steel and timber allocations
121 Ibid, brief for the GOC meeting 02.02.49
122 Ibid, brief on GOC(50)3, 23.02.50
123 CAB 21/3342, 26.02.51
124 Ibid, 28.03.52
125 *Let Us Face the Future*, Labour Party Manifesto 1945
126 Hennessy, *Never Again* p. 80
127 PREM 8/293
128 CAB 21/2341, brief on SI(M)(46)11, 28.03.46
129 CAB 21/2482, 04.12.47
130 CAB 21/2243
131 Ibid, 05.05.47
132 Ibid, 24.05.48
133 CAB 21/2243, 25.05.48
134 CAB 129/27, brief on C.P. (48) 123, 20.05.48
135 CAB 21/2243, 29.05.48
136 Ibid, 15.04.47
137 Ibid, 26.01.48
138 CAB 21/2311, note by the secretary of SI(M), 28.03.51
139 CAB 21/2250
140 CAB 21/2245, brief on C.P.(49)239, 23.11.49
141 CAB 21/2246, brief on C.P.(49)195, 11.10.49
142 CAB 21/2249, 17.03.51
143 Ibid, brief on C.P.(51)121, 02.05.51
144 CAB 21/2248 brief on C.P.(50)145, 07.07.50

145 Ibid, 18.10.50
146 Ibid, 06.12.50
147 CAB 21/2249, brief of 14.02.51
148 CAB 21/2250, 25.07.51
149 CAB 21/2247, brief on C.P.(50)60, 18.04.50
150 PREM 8/1576, 02.05.51
151 CAB 21/2948, 08.03.51
152 Morgan *Labour in Power 1945–51*, pp. 144–45, see also LS Pressnell, *The Post-War Financial Settlement*, pp. 1–14 for a description of the precarious economic position Britain faced in 1945
153 See David Kynaston, *Austerity Britain* pp. 189–200 for an account of what the winter meant for ordinary Britons
154 Lead prosecutor at the Nuremburg trials and Attorney General 1945–51
155 HC Deb, 02/04/46 col 1213
156 PREM 8/81
157 CAB 21/2243, 22.10.47
158 Ibid
159 Ibid, 20/03/48
160 Ibid, brief on C.P.(48)21, 17.01.48
161 Ibid, 28/07/48
162 Ibid, 17.04.48
163 Ibid, 14.12.48
164 CAB 21/2245, 22.06.49
165 CAB 21/2247, brief on C.P.(50)30, 08.03.50
166 Inaugurated on 5 June 1947; Britain received $2.7 billion in aid
167 *The Spectator*, 26.10.51, p. 525
168 CAB 21/3008, 23.03.48
169 Ibid, 07.01.48
170 Ibid, 12.05.48
171 CP (48)137, 02.06.48
172 CAB 21/3008, 24.05.49
173 Ibid, 28.05.48
174 CAB 21/2243, 12.02.48
175 Ibid, 08.04.48
176 CAB 21/2245, brief on C.P.(49)72, 30.06.49
177 Ibid, Hall brief on E.P.C.(49)73, 05.07.49
178 CAB 128/21, 19.08.49
179 CAB 21/2245, 09.11.49
180 CAB 21/2247, Hall brief on E.P.C.(50)44, 03.05.50
181 Ibid, brief on C.P.(50)111, 17.05.50
182 Ibid, brief on C.P.(50)49, 29.03.50
183 PREM 8/1412, brief on E.P.C.(50)115
184 Ibid, P.C.(50)27th meeting, 10.11.50
185 HoC *Hansard* 13.12.50, col 1168
186 CAB 21/2511, I.E.C.(45)1, 26.10.45
187 Ibid, 13.01.47
188 Ibid, 23.01.47
189 CAB 21/2243, 16.04.47
190 CAB 21/2245, brief on C.P.(49)143
191 J Phillips, The Post-war Political Consensus and Industrial Unrest in the Docks 1945–55, *Twentieth Century British History*, 6/3 (1995) p. 304
192 CAB 21/2245, 06.07.49
193 CAB 21/3626, 07.07.49
194 CAB 21/2245, 17.10.49

195 CAB 21/2250, 25.07.51
196 British economist and statistician, Board of Trade 1946–51, Cambridge University 1951–54
197 CAB 21/2243
198 E Clague, *TNA Productivity, Employment and Living Standards*, Conference on TNA Productivity, Milwaukee, Wisconsin p. 7; quoted in SF Wasser and ML Dolfman, *BLS and the Marshall Plan: the forgotten story*, Monthly Labor review June 2005, pp. 44–52
199 Cmd 6502
200 CAB 21/1709
201 Sources: 1 Financial memorandum in NHS Bill; 2 1948/49 Estimates (full year equivalent – the NHS came into being on 5 July); 3 Revised 1948/49 Estimates December 1948; 4 1949/50 Estimates; 5 1949/50 Estimates plus Supplementary Estimate; 6 1950/51 reported in E.P.C (49)76; 7 1951/52 Estimates reported in E.P.C.(49)76. Pre-NHS spending was estimated to have been £225 million p.a.
202 C.M.(50)9th Conclusions, Minute 1
203 C.P.(50)31
204 C.M.(50)11th Conclusions, Minute 1
205 CAB 21/1733
206 C.M.(49)37th, 23.05.49
207 C.P.(48) 302
208 Ibid
209 C.M.(49)37th, 23.05.49
210 CAB 21/2247, brief on C.P.(50) 53, 56 and 57, 01.04.50
211 HoC *Hansard*, 27.10.49 cols 1554–5
212 CAB 21/1733, 17.04.50
213 Ibid, 19.04.50
214 Ibid, 04.04.50
215 CAB 21/2249, undated
216 Ibid, 17.03.51
217 PREM 8/1480
218 Ibid, brief on C.P.(51)116, 25/26.04.51
219 For Brook's successive briefing see PREM 8/739
220 HoC *Hansard*, 28.04.49, Col 355
221 Willie Gallacher (first elected for West Fife in 1935) and Phil Piratin (elected for Mile End in 1945)
222 PREM 8/1410, 06.04.46
223 CAB 21/24, the Committee was badged GEN 183 under the Prime Minister's chairmanship C.M.(48)4th, 15.01.48
224 CAB 21/2496, report on the Employment of Civil Servants etc. Exposed to Communist Influence
225 Ibid
226 The first of the 'atom spies' to be unmasked, Andrew, *The Defence of the Realm* pp. 342–348
227 CAB 21/4010, 20.12.47
228 House of Commons *Hansard*, 15.03.48, cols 1703–1708
229 CM(48)25th Item 1
230 CAB 21/2243, brief on C.P. (48) 86, 20/03/48
231 CAB 21/4018, 05.04.48
232 Ibid
233 House of Commons *Hansard*, 27.06.49 col 66
234 CM(48)4th 15.01.48; Cmd 7718 June 1949
235 CAB 21/2245, brief on C.P.(49)138, 20.07.49
236 CAB 21/4040, 19.07.49

237 CAB 21/2248, 05.07.50
238 Ibid, 22.07.50
239 CM(50)60th 18/09/50
240 CAB 195/8, C.P.(50)207, 16.10.50
241 CAB 21/2248, brief on C.P.(50)259 & 260, 03.11.50
242 Cabinet Conclusions 06.11.50, item 4, TNA CAB 128/18
243 PREM 8/1525, 21.06.51
244 HC Debates 19.07.50 Vol 477 Cols 2266–68
245 CM(50)48th minute 2
246 CAB 21/2248, brief on C.P.(50)174, 19.07.50
247 Ibid, brief on C.P.(50)174,19.07.50
248 Ibid, brief on C.P.(50)183, 24.07.50
249 PREM 8/1525, 15.10.50
250 CAB 21/2248, brief on C.P.(50)206, 15.09.50
251 Ibid, brief on C.P.(50)269, 15.11.50
252 CM (50)76th minute 7
253 Hennessy, Britain's Cold War Security Purge: The Origins of Positive Vetting, *The Historical Journal*, 25,4 (1982) pp. 965–973
254 CAB 21/4014, Security Service note on vetting procedures, April 1950
255 Others present were Chuter Ede (Home Secretary), Shinwell (Minister of Defence), Strachey (Secretary of State for War), Henderson (Secretary of State for Air), Edwards (Civil Lord of the Admiralty), and Sillitoe (Director General of the Security Service)
256 CAB 21/4014, GEN 183/5th, 05.04.50
257 Ibid, 29.03.50
258 Ibid, 31.10.50
259 Ibid, 10.11.50
260 CAB 21/2248, brief on GEN 183/8, 10.11.50
261 CAB 21/3247, 03.05.51
262 Ibid, 15.08.51
263 Ibid, P.V.(52)1, 08.01.52
264 CAB 21/4024, S.C.(M)(55) 1st, 09.01.55
265 Ibid, 11.01.55
266 CAB 21/5003, AC(M)(51), 2,02.51
267 Ibid, 25.05.51
268 CAB 21/2249, 28.03.51
269 HoC *Hansard* 11.06.51 col 1677
270 PREM 8/1524
271 CAB 21/2249
272 CAB 21/4040, 24.07.51
273 Documents on British Policy Overseas, Series 1, Volume X pp. ix–xxix
274 Ibid, p ix
275 Milward, *The Rise & Fall of a National Strategy*, p. 37
276 CAB 21/2245, brief on C.P.(49)203, 26.10.49
277 CAB 21/2243, brief on C.P.(47)279, 08.10.47
278 Ibid, brief on E.P.C.(47)11, 06.11.47
279 Ibid, brief on C.P.(47)35, 27.01.47
280 Ibid, extract from Economic Section comments on C.P.(47)35
281 Ibid, 25.02.47 and 05.03.47
282 CAB 129/23, C.P.(48) 6, 7 and 8, 04 and 05.01.48
283 Ibid, C.P.(48) 8
284 PREM 8/1431, 07.01.48
285 CAB 129/23, C.M.(47)77th
286 CO 537/281, E.P.C.(48) 34 & 37

287 CAB 21/2243, briefs for Attlee on C.P.(48)11, and C.P.(48)46, 20.02.48.
288 PREM 8/1146, E.P.C.(50)24th, 19.10.50
289 CAB 21/2243, brief on C.P.(48)101, 106 & 109
290 Ibid, 21.12.48
291 CAB 21/2245, brief on C.P.(49)3, 11.01.49
292 Ibid, brief on C.P.(49)23, 07.02.49
293 CAB 21/2249, 04.06.51
294 CAB 21/1761, 05.05.50
295 E.P.C.(49)27th
296 Attlee, *As it Happened*, pp. 172–3
297 CAB 21/2250, brief on C.P.(51)230, 27.07.51
298 CAB 21/2243, 05.05.48
299 PREM 8/1146, 14.06.48
300 Ad hoc meeting of Ministers on the arrangements for consultation with Commonwealth countries, 28.07.48, Cabinet Office paper
301 CAB 21/2243, brief on C.P.(48)18, 17.01.48
302 CAB 21/2245, brief on C.P.(49)231 & 232, 12.11.49
303 CAB 21/2243, 27/07/48
304 CAB 21/2245, 12.10.49
305 Ibid, brief on C.P.(49)77,13.05.49
306 CAB 21/2247, 17.01.50
307 CAB 21/2248, 19.07.50
308 CAB 21/2247, brief on C.P.(50)13, 30.01.50, and C.P.(50)27, 06.03.50
309 Ibid, brief on C.P.(50)138, 28.06.50
310 Cmd 6743
311 In discussing the central organisation of defence here and in later periods I have drawn on unfinished research by Professor Donald Cameron Watt for the Cabinet Office
312 PREM 8/151, D.O.(47)148
313 CAB 21/2277, 22.11.46
314 CAB 21/3361, 17.05.49
315 Papers of Sir Henry Tizard, Def/17, 16.12.49
316 CAB 21/3361, manuscript note, 31.05.49 and note for the record, 22.12.49
317 Ibid, 24.02.50
318 PREM 8/1435
319 PREM 8/911, 07.01.47
320 CAB 130/16
321 PREM 13/2, 25.10.46
322 CAB 21/2950 undated memorandum Brook forwarded to Parker on 08.05.51
323 Ibid, 12.05.51
324 CM (47)14, 30.01.47
325 CAB 21/2243, 21.07.48
326 CAB 21/2504, 20.07.48
327 Ibid, 01.04.49 and 20.04.49
328 CAB 21/2243, brief on E.P.C.(48) 104, 108, 114 & 115, 13.12.48
329 FO 371/67582, 19.03.47
330 The second report was later circulated to Cabinet as C(49)16
331 CAB 21/4040, 12.12.49
332 Ibid, 16.12.49
333 CAB 21/2247, brief for meeting with the Commissioner General for South East Asia and the Commanders in Chief, 19.05.50
334 CAB 21/2248, 25.08.50
335 CAB 21/2102, brief on DO(50) 51, 07.07.50
336 CAB 21/2248, 14.07.50

337 Ibid, 01.09.50; CAB 128/18/15, Cabinet conclusions, 04.09.50
338 Ibid, brief on C.P.(50)267, 10.11.50
339 CAB 21/2247, 01.09.50
340 Quoted in Harris, *Attlee*, p. 465
341 National Security Archive Electronic Briefing Book No 159 document 1, 01.07.2005
342 *The Times* 19.10.51
343 CAB 21/1989
344 CAB 21/2248, 17.12.50
345 CAB 21/2102, CM(51)1st· 02.01.51, CM(51)5th· 22.01.51 and CM(51)8th 24.01.51
346 CAB 21/2103, DO(51) 8th, 09.05.51
347 CAB 21/2249, brief on the Minister of Labour's questioning of the scale of defence augmentation, JIC(51)6 Final, 24.01.51
348 CAB 21/2776, 05.09.50
349 CAB 21/2249, 24.01.51
350 CAB 21/1991, C.P.(50)307, 11.12.50
351 CAB 21/2248, brief on C.P.(50)307, 30.12.50
352 CAB 21/5003, 20.12.50
353 Ibid
354 CAB 129/22, C.P.(47) 326, 10.12.47
355 CAB 21/2243, 31.12.47
356 CAB 134/517, N.E.W. (50)
357 T230/257, 13.03.50
358 CAB 21/3195, GEN 317 conclusions, 21.06.50
359 Ibid, N.E.W.(50)5 discussed on 21.11.50
360 Ibid, JIC(50) 132nd meeting, 06.12.50
361 Ibid, 11.12.50
362 Ibid, 09.01.51
363 Ibid, 14.08.52
364 CAB 21/3197, 30.05.51
365 PREM 8/1547, 12.07.51
366 CAB 21/2250, brief on C.P.(51)260, 05.10.51
367 www.raf.mod.uk/history/BerlinAirlift.cfm
368 CAB 21/1885–1892, created on 25.06.48 comprising the Prime Minister, Lord President of the Council, Foreign Secretary, Minister of Defence and the Chiefs of Staff; W Murrie was its lead secretary.
369 CAB 21/1888
370 CAB 21/2245, brief on C.P.(49)73, 30.03.49; brief on C.P.(49)90, 27.04.49; brief on C.P.(49)97, undated
371 CAB 301/18, 20.04 50
372 Ibid, 20.05.50
373 PREM 8/1527
374 Ibid, 25.10.50
375 Ibid
376 CAB 301/18 and 17
377 Ibid, JIC criticisms were voiced in paper JIC(50)81, which Brook judged to do 'rather less than justice to the results achieved'
378 Brook report para 17
379 The comments by 'C' and DGSS are on CAB 301/18, 16.04.51 and 05.04.51
380 Ibid, 05.06.51
381 CAB 301/23
382 Ibid, GEN 374 1st meeting
383 CAB 301/20, 20.02.52; CAB 301/30, 17.04.46

384 CAB 21/2243, 14.01.47
385 Ibid, 21.01.47
386 Ibid,19.05.47
387 Ibid
388 PREM 8/1252, 26.01.48
389 Morris, *Farewell the Trumpets*, pp. 511–12
390 Kinzer, *All the Shah's Men: An American Coup and the Roots of Middle East Terror*, p. 90
391 CM(51) 35
392 CAB 21/2249, 22.06.51
393 CAB 21/2250, 04.07.51 & 09.07.51
394 Acheson, *Present at the Creation* p. 503
395 Bogdanor, *Britain in the 20th Century – The Conservative Reaction 1951–65*
396 Moran's diary has numerous examples of a closer friendship between Brook and Churchill than might have been expected of a politician and civil servant, even allowing for their having been through the war together. Ismay's private papers contain correspondence that show that Brook read some sections of Churchill's war memoirs in draft; quoted in Seldon p. 547
397 Ramsden, *Winston Churchill and the Conservative Party* in *The Conservatives*, ed Lord Butler (1977) p. 417
398 T 236/32430 and T 236/3070, 15.12.51
399 Barnett *The Verdict of Peace* p. 269
400 Lord Moran, *Winston Churchill: The Struggle for Survival 1940–65* pp. 1–2
401 Macmillan p. 378
402 CAB 134/856, EA(E)(51)1, 30.11.51
403 CAB 21/3864, 22.08.52
404 The emergency lasted from February 1951 to June 1957
405 Colville, *The Fringes of Power*, p. 633
406 Colville ascribes the offer of Principal Private Secretary to Churchill to Brook having been a co-guest at this party. op. cit, p. 631
407 It was Camrose who helped organise the purchase of Chartwell as a gift to the National Trust, on condition that Churchill should be able to live there for his lifetime, Colville, op. cit, p. 735
408 The official title of the file, now CAB 21/2654
409 Mallaby, *Each in His Office* p. 52
410 Moran, op. cit, p. 343
411 Ibid, p. 344
412 CAB 21/2654, undated
413 Kent, *In on the Act*, Macmillan 1979 p. 232
414 CAB 21/2773, 28.10.51
415 Colville, op. cit, p. 652
416 Harold Macmillan, *Tides of Fortune*, p. 364
417 Quoted in *Events, Dear Boy, Events*, ed R Winstone p. 204
418 CAB 21/2776, 31.10.51
419 Seldon quotes interviews with Sir Robert Marshall (Brook's Private Secretary, 1950–53) and Sir Alexander Johnston (Deputy Cabinet Secretary 1948–51) to this effect p. 513
420 CAB 21/3342
421 Colville, op. cit, p. 635; paradoxically at the start of 1952 when Churchill and Brook were absent in Washington Padmore took the minutes of Cabinet, CC(52)1st Conclusions
422 CAB 21/2250, 08.11.51
423 Ibid, 12.11.51
424 Cherwell for scientific R&D, atomic research and production plus the Prime

Minister's Statistical Branch; Leathers for Transport, Fuel and Power, Woolton for Agriculture, Fisheries and Food. Lord Anderson was intended to co-ordinate economic Ministries.

425 CAB 21/2250. 20.11.51
426 CAB 21/2654, 17.10.51 and PREM 5/225
427 *Report of the Machinery of Government Committee*, Ministry of Reconstruction, 14.12.1918, Cd 9230
428 *The Economist*, 02.10.48
429 Moran, op. cit, p. 404
430 Daalder, *Cabinet Reform in Britain 1914–63*, p. 225
431 CAB 21/3931, 12.11.51
432 CAB 21/2804, 02.05.52
433 *The Manchester Guardian*, 03.05.52
434 Respective leader articles, 07.05.52
435 *HoC Hansard*, 24.03.53, cols 649–652
436 *HoC Hansard* 03.11.53, col 20
437 CAB 21/2804, undated
438 Seldon, *Churchill's Indian Summer*, p. 426
439 Barnett, op. cit, pp. 152–76
440 CAB 21/3864, 27.02.52
441 Note to the Chancellor of the Exchequer, Cabinet Office paper, 21.03.52
442 Ibid
443 Moran op. cit, entry for 30.12.51, p. 351
444 No circulation record of Cabinet discussions, Cabinet Office paper, 28 & 29.02.52
445 Note to Prime Minister, Cabinet Office paper, 30.06.52
446 CAB 128/40/1, 28 & 29.02.52 and 08.07.52
447 Moran op. cit, pp. 180 & 223
448 Moran, op. cit, p. 371
449 Moran op. cit, p. 354
450 Mallaby, op. cit, p. 52
451 CAB 21/3864, 03.07.52
452 Ibid, 16.07.52
453 CAB 21/2776, 28.12.52
454 CAB 21/2971, 09.02.52 & 29.04.52
455 Moran records several previous serious medical problems: a mild heart attack in Washington in 1952, a stroke in Monte Carlo in 1949, a disturbance of cerebral circulation in February 1950 and a stroke in July 1952
456 Colville, op. cit, p. 668
457 CAB 128/26, CC(53)37th
458 CAB 21/3073, 25.06.53
459 HoC *Hansard*, 02.03.55, col 2116
460 Colville, op. cit, p. 669
461 CAB 21/3712, 26.06.53
462 CAB 21/3712, 09.07.53
463 Moran, op. cit, p. 455
464 Moran, op. cit, p. 461
465 Moran, op. cit, p. 507
466 Moran, op. cit, p. 532
467 Moran, op. cit, p. 773
468 Moran, op. cit, p. 781
469 Moran, op. cit, p. 772
470 CAB 21/2776, 02.02.54;
471 Moran, op. cit, p. 352
472 CAB 128/27, CC(54)48 item 2

473 Moran, op. cit, p. 573
474 CAB 128/27/52
475 PREM 11/669
476 Colville, op. cit, 13.03.55
477 CAB 21/3342, 28.03.52
478 CAB 21/3342, GOC(SC)(52)2, 06.06.52,
479 *HoC Hansard* 10.11.53
480 CAB 21/2243
481 CAB 21/3343, 13.05.54
482 CAB 21/2996, 15.04.54
483 HMSO Cmnd 9176, May 1954
484 CAB 21/2996, 01.06.54
485 CAB 21/2865, 29.06.54
486 T 215/265, 30.07.54
487 CAB 21/2875, 15.04.55
488 Moran, op. cit, p. 353
489 Moran, op. cit, p. 356
490 CAB 21/3057, 13.11.51
491 *The Times*, 29.12.51
492 Extract from joint communiqué, CAB 21/3057, 10.01.52
493 Moran, op. cit, p. 361
494 CAB 21/3057, 09.01.52
495 CAB 21/3057, 10.01.52
496 Ibid, 17.01.52
497 National Security Archive, electronic briefing No 159, 01.07.2005
498 Ibid
499 Ibid
500 *The Macmillan Diaries: The Cabinet Years, 1950–57*, entry for 27.09.52
501 *The Political Diaries of Hugh Dalton 1945–60*, entry for 30.06.52
502 CAB 21/3217, 01.02.52 and 08.09.52.
503 CAB 21/3074, 19.11.53
504 *The Times*, 23.06.53
505 CAB 21/3074, C(53) 330, discussed on 26.11.53
506 Ibid, 11.12.53
507 Ibid, 14.12.53
508 Ibid, 22.04.54
509 Ibid
510 Ibid, 25.06.53
511 *HoC Hansard*, 17.12.53 col 586
512 CAB 21/4059, 02.04.54
513 Ibid, manuscript note by Peck, 02.04.54
514 Ibid
515 Cabinet Office paper
516 Rhodes James, *Anthony Eden*, p. 374
517 Eden, *Full Circle*, p. 36
518 CC(52) 29th and 30th
519 CAB 21/3286, 16.07.53 (file to be open from 01.01.16)
520 CAB 21/2776, 15.10.51
521 Acheson to Ismay during Churchill's 1952 Washington visit, quoted in Seldon p. 343
522 *The Economist* 29.11.52
523 CAB 21/3061, 27.05.53
524 CAB 21/3061. 09.06.53
525 CAB 21/3126, address to the Allied Circle, 08.11.48

526 Ibid, & 3865, 10.11.52 & 13.04.53
527 Ibid, May 1953
528 Ibid, brief on C(53)244, 09.09.53
529 Ibid, 11.09.53
530 CAB 21/3865, 07.07.53
531 CAB 21/3126, 07.04.54
532 Ibid, 27.10.54
533 Ibid, 12.02.54
534 Ibid, 04.04.54
535 CAB 101/244/5, Prime Minister's Personal Minute M.66(c)/51, 17.11.51
536 *Notes on Government Organisation: No 9 – Central Organisation for Defence*, June 1950
537 DEFE 5/40, D(52)26
538 CC(52)94th Conclusions
539 CAB 21/3504, 10.11.52
540 Prime Minister's Minute 588/52, 31.12.52
541 DM 263/378/02, 03.11.52
542 Ibid, 18.02.53
543 DP(O)(53)1st meeting, 16.01.53
544 CAB 21/3504, 02.03.53
545 DEFE 5/41, COS(52)514
546 DM 263/378/02, 16.03.53
547 CAB 21/3504, 13.03.53
548 DPO(O)(53)21
549 CAB 21/3504, 26.03.53
550 Ibid, 31.03.53
551 Ibid, 30.04.53
552 Ibid, manuscript annotation to draft report, undated
553 Ibid, undated
554 Ibid, 20.03.53
555 Ibid, 24.04.52
556 Ibid, 24.04.53
557 Ibid, 11.05.53
558 CAB 134/809, DP(M)(53)2
559 Ibid, DP(M)(53)1st Meeting, 18.05.53
560 CAB 21/2250, 05.10.51
561 CAB 21/2971, 14.07.53
562 Ibid, record of discussion of D(52) 13, 30.04.52
563 Ibid, 02 and 0–9.02.53
564 Ibid, 09.04.54
565 CAB 21/3361, 20.10.55
566 PREM 11/606, D(52)18, 06.05.52
567 Ibid, 11.05.52
568 Ibid, 14.05.52
569 First Report of the Estimates Committee session 1953–54, *Civil Defence*
570 PREM 11/606, 23.12.53
571 Ibid, 24.12.53
572 C(54)149, 13.04.54 and CC(54)29th, 15.04.54
573 CAB 21/4235, 06.08.52
574 CAB 134/492, MAC(51)141, 21.09.51
575 CAB 21/3195, 14.08.52
576 Ibid, N.E.W.(52)3 09.10.52
577 CAB 134/1056, N.E.W.(52)1st meeting
578 CAB 21/3196, 27.07.53

579 Ibid, 31.07.53
580 T 230/259, 20.10.53
581 CAB 21/3196, 21.10.53
582 Ibid, 20.11.53
583 Ibid, and T 230/259, 29.04.54 and 04.05.54
584 CAB 134/1056, 11.05.54
585 CAB 21/3196, 16.06.54
586 Ibid, 18.08.54
587 T 230/259, 28.06.54 and 17.08.54
588 CAB 21/3196, 13.05.55 and undated draft
589 CAB 134/940, HDC(55)3, 08,03,55
590 Chester, *The Nationalisation of British Industry 1945–51* pp. 1058–59
591 *The Fringes of Power*, entry for 19.04.52, p. 645
592 George Mallaby, former schoolmaster recruited to the Military Secretariat of the War Cabinet and Under-Secretary in the Cabinet office 1950–54. Later High Commissioner, New Zealand.
593 CAB 21/3865, Jan-Mar 1953 and 09–16.11.53
594 Ibid, 20.05.53
595 CAB 21/3865 and 3192
596 CAB 21/3193, 19.07.54
597 R Hattersley, *Fifty Years On – A Prejudiced History of Britain Since the War* p. 77
598 CAB 21/3193
599 CAB 21/4460, 16.12.53
600 CAB 21/3865, 27.04.53
601 Ibid, commenting on papers C(53)23–26 and 33, 04.02.53
602 C(53)12,
603 CAB 21/3865, 13.01.53
604 C(53)29,
605 CAB 21/3865, 26.01.53
606 Ibid, 23.06.53
607 Ibid, 01.07.53
608 Ibid, 05.10.53
609 CAB 21/3131, 30.07.54
610 Ibid, brief on C.P.(55)202, 02.01.56
611 Ibid, note for the record, 23.04.56
612 *Defence of the Realm* p. 324
613 CAB 301/20
614 *Defence of the Realm* p. 325
615 CAB 21/3247, 29.07.53
616 Cabinet Office paper, 29.07.53
617 CAB 21/3878, Extract from Cadogan Report, sent to Heads of Mission 20.06.52
618 CAB 21/4011, 01.02.52
619 CAB 21/4014, 17.02.52
620 CAB 21/4040, 14.12.51
621 Ibid, 21.12.51
622 Ibid, various dates in 1952
623 Ibid, minutes of AC(H) meetings 1–3, March – July 1952
624 Ibid, AC(O)(52)22, draft agreement, 23.07.52
625 CAB 21/4011, Personnel Security Committee 1st Meeting, 06.01.55
626 House of Commons *Hansard*, cols 136–9, 21.10.54
627 House of Commons *Hansard*, col 94, 20.03.56
628 CAB 21/4028, 05.01.55
629 Ibid, S(O)(55)1
630 Ibid

631 *Daily Express* leader, 07.03.52
632 CAB 21/4042, 21.03..52
633 Ibid, 25.07.52
634 Ibid, 18.07.52
635 CAB 21/4040, 21.05.52
636 Ibid, 08.10.52
637 Ibid
638 Ibid, December 1951
639 CAB 21/5330, 23.10.53
640 Ibid, 08.12.53
641 CAB 21/5003, 28.02.55
642 Broadcast by the BBC on 6 October 1938, reprinted in *The Listener*, 13.10.38
643 CAB 21/3743, 22.01.47
644 Ibid, quoted by Bridges, 24.04.53
645 Ibid, 02.07.53
646 Ibid, 04.08.53
647 Ibid, 31.08.53
648 Ibid, 05.09.53
649 Ibid, 09.10.53
650 A copy is held in the National Library of Wales
651 CAB 21/3743, 24.10.55
652 Ibid, 19 & 21.12.55
653 Moran p. 535, 06.12.53
654 Moran p. 560 17.04.58
655 Moran p. 17.04.58
656 Quoted in Pelling, *Winston Churchill* (1974) p. 612
657 Moran p. 616, 30.07.54
658 Moran, diary entries for 03.02.55 and 26.02.55
659 CAB 195/13, 15.12.54, 15/03/55
660 Ramsden, *The Conservatives from Churchill to Heath*, Allen & Unwin 1977, p. 435
661 Boyd-Carpenter J, *Way of Life*, Sidgwick & Jackson, 1980 p. 123
662 Roberts, *Masters and Commanders*, Allen Lane, 2008 p. 82
663 Hennessy *Having It So Good* p. 359
664 During the election campaign such was Brook's affection for Churchill that he lobbied the Conservatives to make more use of the grand old man
665 Butler D, *British Political Facts* (2011) p. 267
666 CAB 21/3867, 05.05.55 and 12.05.55
667 PREM 11/948, 10.04.55
668 Clark, *In Three Worlds*, p. 172, diary entry for 9 August 1956
669 Ramsden, op. cit, p. 431
670 CAB 21/3867, 28.04.55, 27.06.55, 11.07.55
671 CAB 21/3867
672 Quoted in Winstone, op. cit, p. 245
673 For example, on immigration and on House of Lords reform, CAB 21/3721, 01.11.55
674 PREM 11/824, 22.04.55
675 CAB 21/3867, 10.11.55
676 CAB 128/29, CM(55) 9th conclusion 5, 03.05.55
677 Home Office *Control of Immigration, statistics UK 1999*, table 6.6 footnote 1
678 CAB 129/81, 22.06.56
679 CAB 128/30
680 CAB 21/3868, brief on C(56)145, 04.07.56
681 CAB 21/4459

682 CAB 134/1273, 17.04.56
683 AC(H)(56)1st meeting, CAB 21/4019, 13.04.56
684 PREM 11/414
685 Brief on CP(56) 166 & 187, 25.07.56
686 PREM 11/1320, 26.02.56
687 PREM 11/1241, brief on CP(55)148, 17.10.55
688 CAB 128/29, CM(55)35th conclusion 4, 18.10.55
689 Sydney Silverman MP, left-wing Labour member for Nelson & Colne 1935–68
690 PREM11/1241, 23.11.55
691 Ibid, brief on CP(56) 43, 21.02.56
692 Ibid, 22.02.56
693 CAB 21/3131, 08.03.56
694 CAB 21/3868, 25.09.56
695 PREM 11/ 1565, 15.08.55
696 Ibid, 22.08.55
697 Ibid, 23.08.55
698 Ibid, undated, unsigned manuscript note probably by Eden
699 Ibid, 17.10.55
700 Ibid, 10.10.55
701 CAB 21/3867, 15.12.55
702 Bodleian, MS. Eng. lett.c.273 and 274
703 CAB 21/3878, 29.11.55
704 In 2013 Douglas Hurd described Macleod's approach as: 'Doucement, doucement, and we'll solve the dispute.'
705 Ramsden op. cit, p. 439
706 CAB 21/3868, 26.01.56
707 Ibid, 17.07.56, 25.07.56, 25.09.56 and 19.12.56
708 PREM 11/2029, 16.05.56 and 25.07.56
709 Ibid, 25.09.56
710 House of Commons Library, SN/SG/113, 16.10.09
711 Barnett, *Verdict of Peace* p. 484
712 The 1956 Defence White Paper Cmd 9691 set the top political and military objective as avoiding global war; see CAB 21/3868 for Brook's brief on DC(56)13 Revise, 09.07.56
713 PREM 11/1191, briefs on DC(55)7, 30.04.55; PR(56)22 & 23, 19.07.56
714 Ibid, 19.07.56
715 CAB 21/3508, 01.05.56
716 CAB 21/3508, 02.06.56
717 PREM 11/1191, brief on CP(56)117, 14.05.56
718 CAB 21/4019, brief on DC(56)18, 09.07.56
719 PREM 11/1864, 15.08.56
720 Ibid, 10.01.57
721 PREM 11/2352, 15.12.55
722 PRO CAB 21/3361, 16.02.56
723 PREM 11/2352, 17.10.56
724 Cmd 9577, HMSO, 23.09.55
725 PREM 11/1578, 30.09.55
726 Ibid, CAB 21/3878, 19.10.55
727 CAB 21/4042, 18.11.55
728 PREM 11/1578, 26 01.56, CAB 5330, 15.06.56
729 HMSO, Cmnd 9715, 08.03.56
730 CAB 21/4011, 27.07.56
731 CAB 134/740, AC(H)(56)1st, 13.04.56
732 CAB 134/740, AC(H)(56)4

733 PREM 11/1238, 28.04.56
734 PREM 11/1238, 02.05.56
735 PREM 11/1238, 30.05.5 6
736 Acheson, *Vital Speeches*, p. 163
737 CAB 21/3221, 22.03.56
738 PREM 11/1268, 12.04.56
739 Ibid, 25.09.55
740 CAB 301/120, 08.05.56
741 CAB 21/301/120, 18.05.56. For a fuller examination of the Crabb affair see Goodman, *The Tentacles of Failure: British Intelligence, Whitehall and the Buster Crabb affair*
742 PREM 11/1268, 05.05.56
743 This was a secret and deliberately misleadingly named department for countering Communist propaganda of all kinds; it operated from 1948 to 1977 when the then Foreign Secretary (David Owen) closed it down
744 CAB 21/3221, 28.04.56
745 Cab 21/3217, 30.04.56
746 Cabinet Office paper, talk between Bridges, Dean.(FO) and Dick White (MI6), 19.09.56
747 FO 371/115999
748 CAB 134/1029, 14.07.55
749 T 232/433, 20.09.55
750 CAB 134/1044, 14.10.55
751 Milward, *The Rise and Fall of a National Strategy 1945–63,* p. 251
752 CAB 134/887, ES(55) 8th meeting, 01.11.55, quoted in Milward p. 178
753 CAB 134/1226, EP(55)11th meeting
754 PREM 11/1337, 28.02.56
755 PREM 11/1236, 17.09.56
756 CAB 128/30, CM(56) 66th Conclusions, Minute 2, 18.09.56
757 PREM 11/1352, GEN 551/2, 22.09.56
758 Ibid, GEN 551/1, 22.09.56
759 Ibid, GEN 551/1st Meeting, 24.09.56
760 CAB 128/30, CM(56)67th Conclusions, Minute 6, 26.09.56
761 PREM 11/1352, GEN 551/4, 29.09.56
762 Ibid, GEN 551/3rd meeting, minute 2, 02.10.56
763 PREM 11/1352, GEN 553/1st Meeting, 04.10.56
764 CAB 21/3323, undated
765 CAB 21/3081, comments made at the 1955 Conference
766 Ibid, 12.10.55
767 Ibid, 12.11.55
768 CAB 21/3085, undated
769 PREM 11/1432, 02.07.55
770 Ibid, brief on CP(55)59, 04.07.55
771 Ibid, 04.07.55
772 Ibid, 09.12.55
773 The full referendum proposals were circulated to the Cabinet as CP(56)16 on 17.01.56
774 PREM 11/1432, CA(56)9th meeting, minute 1, 17.02.56
775 PREM 11/2617, 26.08.55
776 CAB 21/2931, 05.10.55
777 GEN 485/14, April 1955
778 PREM 11/34; CAB 21/2925
779 CAB 21/4019, 28.07.55
780 CAB 21/4019, AC(O)(55)50, 21.09.55
781 CAB 21/4019, 19.10.55

782 Ibid, 21.10.55 and 28.10.55
783 CAB 21/6006, S 50/96/4, 14.12.55
784 CAB 21/4042,
785 CAB 21/4019, S.50/96/4/1st Meeting, 24.02.56; CAB 21/2992, 09.03.56
786 Ibid, 15.03.56; CAB 21/2972, 16.03.56
787 CAB 21/2931, 16.12.55
788 CAB 21/4019, 16.04.56
789 Ibid, 15.05.56, 17.05.56, 28.06.56
790 Ibid, 24.09.56
791 Ibid, 17.04.56
792 CAB 21/4019, 17.05.56
793 Nasser was elected President unopposed on 23 June 1956
794 CAB 128/23, CC(51)1, 20.10.51
795 Kyle, *Suez* p. 38
796 Cabinet Office paper, 18.02.54
797 Cabinet Office paper, 15.03.54
798 PREM 11/2287, 28.11.55
799 PREM 11/1457, 14.04.56
800 Ibid, 14–15.04.56
801 Foster Dulles, the US Secretary of State, told the Egyptian ambassador of the decision on 19.06.56; President Eisenhower was convalescing from a heart attack at the time and out of the loop
802 Maurice Couve de Murville, JF Dulles Oral History Project, Seeley, G, Mudd Manuscript Library, Princeton University
803 CAB 21/4207, 05.07.56
804 CAB 21/3306, 25.07.56
805 Goodman, M, *Official History of the JIC*, Routledge 2014, p. 384
806 CAB 21/4113, 11. 09.56
807 CAB 128/30, CM(56)54th, 27.07.56
808 PREM 11/1098, 27.07.56
809 CAB 21/4113, 13.09.56
810 CAB 21/3094 and 4114
811 CAB 21/4114
812 CAB 21/4113, 09.09.56
813 PREM 11/1098, 30.07.56
814 PREM 11/1098, 30 and 31.07.56
815 CAB 21/4113, 14 and 15.08.56
816 CAB 21/3314
817 PREM 11/1129, 07 and 13.11.56; Cab 21/3094, 22.08.56
818 CAB 21/ 3306, CAB 21/3542, CAB 21/3783, CAB 21/4113, CAB 134/815
819 CAB 21/4113, 03.08.56
820 Ibid, and CAB 134/1217
821 Clark, *In Three Worlds*, pp. 171–2
822 CAB 21/3092, 14.08.56
823 CAB 21/3094, 15.08.56
824 PREM 11/1100; CAB 21/4113
825 CAB 21/4113, 03.08.56
826 PREM 11/1152
827 Though Brook was not present when Britain, France and the USA met on 29 July and agreed that force was a last resort it can be assumed that he knew of the outcome of the meeting. PREM 11/1098
828 PREM 11/1152, 25.08.56
829 In August Eden had vetoed proposed intelligence actions against Egyptian targets, PREM 11/1166

830 Thorpe, *Eden*, p. 563
831 CAB 21/4113 and CAB 21/3314, 21.09.56
832 CAB 21/4113, 23.09.56
833 CAB 134/1217, 24.09.56
834 CAB 21/4113, 25.09.56
835 CAB 21/4114, 01.10.56
836 Ibid, and CAB 21/3542, 19.10.56
837 CAB 21/4114, 04.10.56
838 Ibid, 08.10.56 and 02.11.56
839 CAB 21/5596, FO 800/725, FCO 73/205
840 CAB 164/1359, Logan's account of the Sèvres meetings, 27.10.86
841 CAB 164/1359, 27.10.86, Dean's account of what had transpired at the Sèvres meetings
842 CAB 128/30/296 and 297, 23 and 24.10.56
843 FCO 73/205, 25.10.56
844 The diplomat Roger Makins, then Ambassador Washington, was brought back as a reluctant head of the economic side of the Treasury
845 Clark, *In Three Worlds* p. 210
846 DAILY WORKER, 24.10.56
847 CAB 134/740, AC(H)(56)15, 15.11.56
848 Goodman, *Official History of the Joint Intelligence Committee*, pp. 269–71
849 House of Commons Hansard, 12.12.56, col 40
850 CAB 21/3705, 07.12.56
851 PREM 11/1127, 14.11.56
852 Heath, *Course of My Life* pp. 177–8
853 E-mail from Lord Armstrong, 14.08.14
854 Lusty, *Bound to be Read*, Cape, 1975
855 Greene, letter to TIMES, 27.06.78
856 Neustadt, *Alliance Politics* p xi
857 PREM 15/719, 02.06.71
858 Ibid, 11.06.71
859 CAB 21/1548, 18.11.56
860 PREM 11/1732, 14.12.56
861 PREM 11/1138, undated
862 Kissinger, *Reflections on a Partnership*, 1982
863 CAB 21/2773, 08.01.57
864 Bodleian, MS. Eng. lett.c273, 16.01.57
865 CAB 21/3314 07–23.05.57
866 CAB 21/5077, PREM 11/2653 16.01.57 and 05.03.57
867 Moran, *Classified*, pp. 216–37
868 Kyle *Suez*, p. 468
869 CAB 21/4477, 03.11.59
870 Ibid, 24.11.59 and 07.03.60
871 Kilmuir, *Political Adventure*, p. 278
872 PREM 13/1556, 12.04.64
873 Finer, *Dulles Over Suez*, 1964 and *Dossier secret: il y a 10 ans: Suez*, 1967
874 Bodleian, MS. Eng. lett.c273, 11.06.64
875 Bodleian, MS. Eng. lett.c273, 12.06.67
876 Alistair Horne, *Macmillan, Volume II, 1957–86*, p. 441
877 Horne, op. cit, p. *6*
878 Ramsden et al., op. cit, p. 445
879 Public relations adviser to the Prime Minister 1957–64
880 Evans, *Downing Street Diary* p. 111
881 Ramsden et al., op. cit, p. 447
882 PREM 11/1734, 11.03.57

883 Thorpe, *Supermac* p. 376
884 Lee, Jones & Burnham *At the Centre of Whitehall*, p. 67
885 CAB 21/4728, 08.10.57 and 17.10.57
886 CAB 21/3342, 11.10.57
887 Ibid, 15.10.57
888 Ibid, annotation to Trend's note of 11.10.57
889 Ibid, 31.10.57, Macmillan, Butler, Kilmuir, Selwyn Lloyd, Thorneycroft, Home, Heath
890 CAB 21/4337, 03.07.57
891 PREM 11/2771, 05.11.59
892 Shadow Chancellor of the Exchequer, 1955–61, later Leader of the Labour Party
893 Ramsden et al., op. cit, p. 447
894 Churchill College, Cambridge, Selwyn Lloyd papers, SELO 314(2)
895 PREM 11/2199 10.01.57 and 16.01.57
896 PREM 11/1835, 22.01.57
897 PREM 11/1835, 06.02.57
898 PREM 11/1835, 14.02.57
899 PREM 11/1835, 21.02.57
900 CAB 21/3096, 25.02.57
901 Cabinet Office paper, 23.03.57
902 Cabinet Office paper
903 The doctrine underestimated the reaction of Arab nationalism to outside interference and did not survive the death of US Secretary of State Foster Dulles, who had crafted it, in May 1959
904 Macmillan diary entries for 16 and 20 August 1957, PREM 11/2329, 11.10.57
905 PREM 11/1725, 08.11.57
906 Thorpe, *Supermac* p. 394
907 Macmillan's chief adviser on nuclear policy and 'father' of the British Atomic and Hydrogen bombs
908 Cabinet Office paper, Notes for Supplementaries for statement on 08.11.57
909 CAB 134/1555, 28.01.57
910 Ibid
911 PREM 11/2617, 06.09.57
912 See Hennessy *Having it so Good*, pp. 480–81 for a comparison of the report's conclusions and the actual dates of independence for territories
913 PREM 11/1726, 04.07.57
914 Ibid, 22.07.57
915 Prime Minister's personal note M.214/60, 27.06.60 and 06.07.60
916 PREM 11/2321, 25.11.57
917 Ibid, 28.11.57
918 CO/1032/166, Informal note of discussions to launch the study, 09.12.57
919 PREM 11/2321, forwarded to Macmillan on 05.06.58
920 Ibid, and CAB 134/1555, 05.06.58
921 PREM 11/2328, 09.12.58
922 Evans, *Downing Street Diary*, p. 250
923 CAB 131/28, D(63)3rd meeting, 09.02.63
924 CAB 21/3840, 20.02.59
925 PREM 11/2321
926 Ibid
927 CAB 21/3360, 08.05.58
928 CAB 21/3840, 20.02.59
929 Ibid, 25.05.59
930 Ibid, 25.06.59
931 Minutes of the Steering Group meetings are on CAB 134/1930–1931 and the final report on CAB 21/3841 and CAB 134/1929

932 PREM 11/3432, 19.02.60
933 CAB 21/3841, 28.02.60
934 In addition to Macmillan attendees were Butler (Home Secretary), Selwyn Lloyd (Foreign Secretary). Heathcote Amory (Chancellor), Lord Home (Commonwealth Relations and Lord President of the Council), Watkinson (Defence); Brook, Dean and CIGS were also present
935 CAB 21/4492, observation by Orme, secretary at the meeting, 22.04.60
936 CAB 21/3841, 29.03.60
937 Anthony Nutting, *Europe Will Not Wait*, Hollis & Carter, 1960
938 CAB 21/4492, 04.05.60
939 PREM 11/3432, 02 and 03.06.60
940 CAB 21/3325, 30.12.59
941 PREM 11/3133, 20.05.60
942 Ibid, 03.06.60
943 Ibid, 09.07.60
944 EOKA was a nationalist guerrilla movement in Cyprus wanting unification with Greece, active from 1955 to 1959
945 CAB 21/5552, 10.01.61
946 Andrew Terborgh, *The Post-War Rise in World Trade*, LSE, 2003, estimates that joint participation in the Bretton Woods System increased trade between countries by about 20%
947 CAB 21/4492, 13.03.61
948 Ibid, 02.05.61
949 Ibid, 08.05.61
950 Ibid, 24, 27, 29.06.61
951 Ibid, 05.07.61
952 Ibid, 12, 21 and 24.07.61
953 Ibid, 11.09.61
954 Ibid, Watkinson, 21.09.61
955 Ibid, 02.10.61
956 Ibid, 09.10.61
957 CAB 21/5901, brief by Cary, Brook's deputy, 05.12.61
958 Ibid, C(62)24, 9 and 13.03.62
959 Macmillan Archive, quoted by Horne, *Macmillan 1957–86* pp. 183–5
960 Ibid, p. 188, 28.12.59
961 *Anatomy of Britain*, p. 244
962 *Downing Street Diary*, p. 106
963 *Supermac*, p. 454
964 *Macmillan 1957–86*, pp. 197–8
965 A selection of photographs from the tours is contained in Bodleian Library, MS. Eng. lett.c273 box 490
966 *Downing Street Diary* p. 75
967 CAB 21/4042, report of GEN 639, 19.03.58
968 DO 35/10570, 03.02.60
969 PREM 11/2330, 16.05.58, 16.06.58
970 PREM 11/2315, 24.06.58
971 PREM 11/2324, 09.06.58
972 PREM 11/2690, 18.02.59
973 Ibid, undated manuscript notes
974 Ibid
975 *Supermac*, p. 428
976 FO 371/145616, 10.03.59, PREM 11/2717, 13.03.59, CAB 21/3300, 25 and 30.04.59
977 PREM 11/2685, 14.06.59. Attendees were Macmillan, Selwyn Lloyd, Brook, Hoyer Millar (FO), Adeane (HM the Queen's Private Secretary)

978 CAB 21/3300, 14 and 29.04.59, undated draft reply to Khrushchev
979 CAB 21/4103, 17.06.59
980 CAB 21/4103, 19.06.59
981 Announced in the Queen's Speech, *HC Hansard*, 01.11.60
982 PREM 11/2990, 22.12.59
983 PREM 11/2991, 22.12.59. France had withdrawn its forces from the NATO command at this time
984 BBC interview 06.06.72 quoted in *Thorne, Supermac* p. 473
985 Ibid, 10.10.60
986 CAB 21/4411, 28.10.60
987 Ibid, 22.10.60
988 Then Minister of State at the Foreign Office, from 1961–65, Caccia's successor as British Ambassador in Washington
989 CAB 21/4411, 19.12.60
990 Ibid, 19.12.60
991 Ibid, 16.12.60, confirmed by a letter from Kennedy, 31.12.60
992 CAB 21/4959
993 CAB 21/4411, 11.01.61
994 Ibid, 07 and 09.01.61
995 CAB 21/4413, amendments to a Ministry of Defence paper on the British independent contribution to the Western strategic nuclear deterrent, 06.01.61
996 Ibid, 12.01.61
997 CAB 21/4411, 11.01.61
998 Ibid, 18 and 20.01.61
999 *Supermac*, p. 537
1000 CAB 21/4413, 22.02.61
1001 Ibid, 23.02.61
1002 Ibid, 23.02.61
1003 CAB 21/4412, 27.02.61
1004 The Congo degenerated into civil war shortly after a rushed independence from Belgium
1005 CAB 21/4413, 22.02.61
1006 Ibid, 28.02.61
1007 CAB 21/4411, 28.02.61
1008 CAB 21/4112, 22.03.61
1009 Macmillan was in Trinidad on 24 March on the first stage of a West Indies tour when he was asked to meet the President the following day
1010 *Supermac*, pp. 492–3
1011 *Pointing the Way*, 1959–61 p. 336
1012 CAB 21/4112, Washington telegrams Nos 867 and 886
1013 Cabinet Office paper, 15.04.61
1014 Cabinet Office paper, 08.05.61
1015 Cabinet Office paper, 06.12.62
1016 CAB 21/4460, 08.04.57
1017 Ibid, 28.03.57
1018 Those present were Brook, Trend, Clarke (HMT), Newsam (HO), Neden (Labour), Maud (Power), Stedman (Transport), Andrews (Trade)
1019 CAB 21/4460, 13.05.57
1020 Ibid, 22.07.57; However the threat of an unofficial dock strike in December 1960 did lead to Brook agreeing that Trend could take the chair at the Official Committee on Emergencies in the absence of the normal chairman, Sir Charles Cunningham of the Home Office
1021 *Macmillan 1957–86* p. 75
1022 Nigel Nicholson, *Letters and Diaries 1945–62*, 26.06.57

1023 Report of the Departmental Committee on Homosexual Offences and Prostitution, 04.09.57 Cmnd 267
1024 *15 to 18*, 24.07.59
1025 *Supermac*, p. 489
1026 27.03.63
1027 CAB 21/4479, 23.05.57
1028 *Report of the Committee on Departmental Records* (Cmd 9163) July 1954, paras 145–7
1029 CAB 21/3741, 04.05.56
1030 CAB 21/4548, 14.05.58 and CAB 21/3742, 18.04.59
1031 CAB 21/4312 and 4313, 18.09.56, 15.12.56, 21.04.59
1032 *Churchill: The Struggle for Survival*, p. 218
1033 PREM 11/4234
1034 CAB 164/1297
1035 CAB 21/3750, 25.09.57 and 02.10.57
1036 Moran op. cit, p. 225
1037 PREM 11/2482, September 1958
1038 PREM 11/3227, May–June 1961
1039 PREM 11/3228, July–October 1961
1040 CAB 21/4479
1041 Ibid, 06.10.57
1042 Ibid, 25.06.57
1043 Ibid, 20.11.57
1044 CAB 21/3742, 24.11.59
1045 Bodleian, MS. Eng. lett.c273, 22.02.65
1046 CAB 21/4725, 01.07.57
1047 CAB 21/4725, 27.05.59 and 10.06.59
1048 Ibid, 09.01.61; the Pilkington Committee was published on 05.06.62 (Cmnd 1753)
1049 Cabinet Office paper
1050 *Supermac*, p. 463
1051 CAB 21/4739, 22.11.57
1052 For a fuller analysis of the JIC post 1957 see Goodman, *Official History of the JIC*, Volume 2
1053 Other members of the Committee (badged AC(H)) were the Permanent Secretaries of the Foreign Office, Treasury, Home Office, Ministry of Defence, Ministry of Labour and the Director General of the Security Service
1054 CAB 134/1342–5
1055 For a full description of the Macmillan spy scandals see Andrew, *The Defence of the Realm*, especially pp. 483–91
1056 Hollis reported the arrest of Vassall to the JIC on 13.09.62
1057 PREM 11/4463, undated draft affidavit to the Radcliffe Committee
1058 CAB 21/2496, 4016, 4017, CAB 134/740
1059 Ibid, SC(O)(62) 2nd meeting, 22.01.62
1060 Ibid, meeting on 13.04.62
1061 Ibid, 14.06.62
1062 CAB 21/4959, 13.07.61
1063 PREM 11/3815, 28.07.61
1064 Ibid, 29.07.61
1065 Ibid, 25.08.61
1066 *Macmillan 1957–86* p. 314
1067 *The Spectator's* Guide to the Top 50 Political Scandals, July 2009
1068 Lord Denning's Report (Cmnd 2152) September 1963, paragraph 185
1069 Denning, paragraphs 33–35
1070 Lord Radcliffe interviewed on the BBC television programme *Panorama*, 05.08.63

1071 Denning, paragraphs 68–69 and 259
1072 Denning paragraph 264–8
1073 *Macmillan 1957–1986* pp. 94–6
1074 CAB 21/3184
1075 *The Guardian*, 12.11.05; *The Daily Mail*, 26.10.12
1076 Diary entry for 1 November 1954 quoted in H Macmillan *Tides of Fortune* 1945–55, p. 560
1077 CAB 21/4280, PR(56)1, 04.06.56
1078 Eden chaired the steering group; other members were the Lord President (Salisbury), the Chancellor (Macmillan), the Foreign Secretary (Selwyn Lloyd) and the Minister of Defence (Monckton)
1079 Horne, op. cit, p. 8
1080 Ibid, p. 48
1081 For example, H Kissinger, *Nuclear Weapons and Foreign Policy*, Harper & Brothers, 1957
1082 Cmnd 476, 1958
1083 Mountbatten papers, N. 99, Sir William Dickson reminiscences, University of Southampton
1084 DEFE 13/152, note by Sir Richard Powell, Permanent Secretary, quoted in Sandys to Macmillan, 17.03.58
1085 Horne, op. cit, p. 49
1086 Future Trends in Warfare, *Journal of the Royal United Services Institution* 105, February 1960 pp. 6–10
1087 PREM 11/1779, Prime Minister's Personal Minute M 191/57, 16.05.57
1088 Ibid, 14.05.57
1089 Ibid, 23.05.57
1090 CAB 21/3359
1091 Manuscript annotation on Owen: Brook, 16.08.57, CAB 21/1779
1092 Owen: Brook and annotations, 23.08.57, Ibid
1093 Draft minute by Brook annexed to the draft report, 28.08.57, Ibid
1094 Lowe, *Official History of the British Civil Service*, p. 107
1095 CAB 21/3359, Macmillan: Brook, 05.11.57
1096 DEFE 13/152, annotation, 23.11.57
1097 CAB 21/3359, Prime Minister's Personal Minute M629(57), 27.12.57
1098 Ibid, Powell: Brook 31.12.57
1099 The tour lasted from 7 January to 14 February 1958
1100 PREM 11/2352, Brook, Bishop and Macmillan notes, 04.03.58
1101 DEFE 13/152 WFD/M/265, 02.01.58
1102 CAB 21/3360, notes of 16 & 17.04.58
1103 PREM 11/2352, 19.04.58
1104 CAB 21/3360
1105 Quoted in Horne, p. 51
1106 *Central Organisation for Defence*, Cmnd 476
1107 CAB 21/4874
1108 Ibid
1109 Ibid
1110 Ibid
1111 PREM 11/3717
1112 Ibid, 10.01.61
1113 PREM 11/3717
1114 Bodleian MS. Eng. lett.c273, 05.11.62
1115 CAB 21/4072, 03.12.58
1116 Ibid, 10.12.58
1117 Ibid, 05.01.59

1118 Ibid, 19.02.60
1119 Ibid, minutes of a meeting on deterrent policy, 23.02.60
1120 Bodleian, MS. Eng. lett.c.273, 14.10.62
1121 *Downing Street Diary*, p129
1122 Trend's appointment had been foreshadowed in *The Daily Telegraph* on 29.07.62
1123 DEFE 25/49, 23.01.62
1124 Bodleian, MS. Eng. lett.c273, 05.11.62
1125 CAB 21/4959
1126 *Downing Street Diary*, p. 229
1127 Bodleian, MS. Eng. lett.c273, 11.01.63
1128 CAB 21/4959

3 The Mandarins' Mandarin

Sir Burke Trend
Cabinet Secretary
1963–73

Trend in robes: Burke Trend academic manqué

Source: © National Portrait Gallery

As he prepared to go on leave at the beginning of August 1962, knowing that he was the chosen successor, Burke Trend wrote in generous terms to Norman Brook:

> 'The luggage is packed and the cat is beginning to make panting noises at the front door. But I didn't want to leave London without thanking you, better than I have been able to [do] so far, for the last ten days. I look

> forward to my future responsibilities with misgiving and an acute sense of inadequacy; but even if I had no other example to follow than the combination of firmness and humanity with which you have dealt with a difficult situation, I should be encouraged. In fact, I owe you other lessons, as we both know – a good many of them in one way and another. And I shall try not to forget them.'
>
> 'I am sorry that it should all have been so difficult for you. I've admired you and the way you've coped, more than I can say: and I hope that you can now have a rest and a splendid holiday.'[1]

Having taken a double first in Greats from Merton College, Oxford, Trend took the civil service exam in 1936. He was assigned to the Ministry of Education (his first choice of departments on the civil service application forms). One of his referees, the philosopher Geoffrey Mure of Merton, wrote:

> 'Mr Trend is the best pupil I have ever had ... I have little doubt of Mr Trend's cutting to the top in any career which he adopts ... He has a force of character and intellect combined which will soon make him a "leader" in practical life ...'[2]

After only one year at Education he was moved to the Treasury, working initially on control of defence spending. But towards the end of 1939 he was given a significant accolade by being moved to the Chancellor's private office as Assistant Private Secretary where he served Sir John Simon and Sir Kingsley Wood.[3] As a man famous for his drafting skills – Douglas Hurd would later refer to Trend and Sir Denis Greenhill,[4] as 'The two great mandarins of Britain ... rediscovering the skills and pleasures of their desk-bound youth'[5] – his first submission to Simon was returned torn into four pieces.[6] He continued in the Treasury for a further 16 years (including a spell of four years as Principal Private Secretary to Chancellors Hugh Dalton and Stafford Cripps).[7] There followed a year with the Lord Privy Seal[8] and three years as deputy to Norman Brook in the Cabinet Office (1956–59), where he drafted much of the Cabinet briefing for Brook though his own style was more formal and, in particular he was less intimate with Macmillan. If leanings towards political parties had been declared, Brook would have gone towards the Conservatives and, despite his demonstrative political neutrality (which included never voting after he became Cabinet Secretary) Trend would have inclined towards Labour.

He returned to the Treasury as Third (later Second) Secretary and succeeded Brook at the start of 1963, though he did not combine the post with Head of the Home Civil Service which, on the advice of Lord Plowden, was separated from the Cabinet Secretary and went to Lawrence Helsby.[9] Mure's reference from 1936 said: 'I suppose he must be called a student rather than a "leader of mens ... "'[10] The civil service role would not have played to his strengths as his austere message to the Fulton Committee and his rather formal condolences to Hankey's widow indicate.[11]

In an astute move, he brought with him as Cabinet Secretary responsibility for oversight of the intelligence agencies' finances (the Secret Vote which covered spending by the Security Service (MI5), the Secret Intelligence Service (SIS also known as MI6) and the Government Communications Headquarters (GCHQ). He served four Prime Ministers. His years as Cabinet Secretary were dominated by anxieties: worsening trouble in Northern Ireland, a weak economy, a declining 'special relationship' with the United States, two failed attempts to join the European Communities, fears of widespread penetration of the higher reaches of British government by Soviet agents and the divisive Rhodesian rebellion. Ministers geo-political ambitions were unmatched by domestic economic success, hampered by poor industrial management, inadequate capital investment and deteriorating industrial relations. The period ended with the low of the three-day working week due to power shortages during the 1974 miners' industrial action and the false dawn of a reborn United Kingdom on accession to the European Community.

Harold Wilson described him as 'The best Civil Servant I have ever known.'[12] Richard Crossman's verdict was 'He's a strange character – a nanny-like, very able, very sweet, very shy man. He strengthens Harold in all his most establishment tentativeness, making him on the whole less abrasive and less radical,' and a member of Wilson's inner circle.[13] William Waldegrave described him as 'the embodiment of the old ways'.[14] Noble Frankland, who was one of the Official Military Historians at the Cabinet Office between 1951 and 1958 described Trend as '... an excellent classical scholar and, as such, expected to find order and symmetry in history. As I was later to learn, he also thought that it should be tailored to suit the convenience and the politics of the time in which it was written.' Ben Pimlott, Harold Wilson's biographer, refers to Trend as 'So unobtrusive and reassuring that no one quarrelled with him,' and a don manqué.[15] But the final word from contemporaries must go to Henry Kissinger who wrote of Trend 'He skilfully made the Cabinet ministers he served appear more competent than they could possibly be.'[16] My analysis supports a view that he defines the gold standard for the Cabinet Secretary working in the old ways when government was more closed, more remote and less hurried than subsequently proved to be the case. His analysis left nothing out and dealt with threats perceptively but it was less well suited to identifying opportunities, which he would have seen as in he territory for politicians. He was the last of a generation insulated from challenge by Select Committee or hostile media. Whilst it is true that the report of the Fulton Committee on the Civil Service (published in 1968)[17] came six years into Trend's ten-year tenure, it hardly troubled him. He had little understanding of public relations, risk-averse and focused on the downside – e.g. when, in 1971, the Home Office operation FOOT led to the removal of 105 Soviet spies from diplomatic and trade positions in London he counselled omitting from public statements the proposed references to the spies' role in plotting sabotage should the Soviet Union invade Britain, – on the grounds that such explanations could lead to 'hysterical spy mania which it might be difficult to contain.'[18]

It has often been said that Trend was emotionally attached to the Commonwealth and the Anglo-American relationship with little instinctive sympathy for the European ideal. Contemporaries felt that he felt the decline of the United Kingdom personally.[19] Yet I have found that he gave no less good handling advice in favour of Heath's European policies, in particular, than to other aspects of foreign policy. And whilst he lacked the sensitivity and flexibility to reflect Heath's managerial instincts for streamlining Cabinet business, it was into his Cabinet Office that the Central Policy Review Staff (CPRS), Civil Contingencies Unit (CCU) and European Unit were launched. His successor John Hunt was the driving force in the last two instances but there is no feeling from the official files that Trend sought to limit Hunt's effectiveness. (Though there is evidence that he felt that the CPRS presented a threat to the Cabinet Secretariat.) He identified two gaps in Cabinet co-ordination: the absence of buy-in to the Budget as part of economic strategy (historically the exclusive preserve of the Chancellor of the Exchequer) and the poor government handling of issues concerning science and space. However, he solved neither. By contrast, when the Labour government of 1964 came in with plans to change the machinery of government radically the creation of the Department of Economic Affairs, the Ministry of Technology, the Welsh Office and the Ministry for Land and Natural Resources were accomplished smoothly as later was the birth of mammoth departments such as the Department of Health and Social Security and the Department of Employment and Productivity.

His was a working environment where each individual was expected to, and was allowed to, give of their best consistent with anonymity, political neutrality and incorruptibility. As a young inexperienced chairman of the Staff Side of the Cabinet Office Whitley Council[20] I was conscious of that Trend set a tone for the Department that was at once personally kind but professionally demanding. And as Michael Herman of the Joint Intelligence Committee observed, 'The Cabinet Secretary has to deal with that endless upward surge of business, driving down as much as he can' – hence Trend's defence of the committee system and his description on Radio 3 in 1976 that the job of the Cabinet Secretary was to see that Cabinet worked smoothly, knew what it had to decide and to set out the pros and cons of what Ministers were proposing.[21] Looking back over three predecessors and forward over his successor he liked to categorise Cabinet Secretaries as craftsmen or artists[22] putting himself firmly in the artist camp. That said, a Cabinet Secretary must bend to the style of the Prime Minister under whom they serve. Alec Douglas-Home was more available than Harold Macmillan and less interfering than Brook had found Anthony Eden – Home's chief concern was the weakening of Christian morality as a basis for personal action and the breakdown of imperial connections as a focus for patriotism;[23] he was Trend's favourite Prime Minister. Harold Wilson was 'almost wholly a political operator and manager [with] no personal views on what actually to use that power to achieve'[24] – for whom Trend's well developed sense of positioning in the Cabinet dispositions was indispensible. Heath stated policies not strategies and so was inflexible with the economy at the centre of concerns[25] – neither aspect suited Trend's strengths. John Hunt summed up the relationship as 'productive and always correct [but] there was no great personal warmth or rapport and Trend's retirement was not unwelcome on either side.'[26] He could be dismissive of the private sector – his attitude to Ronald Prain's views on Rhodesia, reactions to the effects of sanctions on business and to the likelihood that firms would be put out of business by the imposition of import surcharges are all significant indications. Also, though in the United States softer management styles deriving from Maslow's hierarchy of needs started to spread,[27] and Alfred Chandler argued that organisational form should follow strategy and function[28] there is no indication that Trend (or indeed others at the top of Whitehall) were aware of these developments, nor of the prospect of transformation in working practices when IBM introduced the System/360 modular mainframe computer. After retirement, as Rector of Lincoln College, he was popular with undergraduates, less so with the fellows, who thought him unworldly.[29]

Constitutionally Trend served during a transitional period. The Douglas-Home conventions allowing limited contact between Opposition front bench spokesmen and senior officials in the run-up to a General Election eased the transition from opposition to government. The arrangements protecting the inviolability of a previous administration's papers were confirmed, as were *Questions of Procedure for Ministers*. A Parliamentary Ombudsman was proposed and the introduction of Government Green Papers allowed ideas to be considered widely in the country before government policy had to be firmed up in White Papers. A Royal Commission on Devolution reported with radical proposals after 4½ years of deliberation.[30] But there was no doubting a requirement that the workings of government should be kept secret. Trend told the Franks Enquiry into the working of the Official Secrets Act, '... you are conscious that at the back of everything you say and do all day long there is a tremendous sanction.'[31] 'Once you embark on the business of striptease of a government – where do you stop?'[32] Nevertheless, he was opposed to prosecution under the Act,[33] preferring the deterrent effect of always knowing that to leak information was both morally and legally wrong.

In the Cabinet Office Trend left behind a system tuned to perform superbly under normal conditions – i.e. in the benevolent light of the post-war consensus. The secretariat managed the flow of Cabinet business, wrote the Cabinet Conclusions; it was the general custodian of Cabinet procedure and commanded Ministerial and interdepartmental respect. The Cabinet Secretary was well established as the principal adviser to the Prime Minister on security and intelligence; he was the caretaker of the secret state and carried out sensitive international missions on behalf of the Prime Minister but was still slightly junior to the Head of H.M. Treasury and Head of the Diplomatic Service (at least in their eyes).[34] The civil service was still self-confident and of high integrity, with a bias to analysis rather than to action and lacking the knowledge or skills to renew the apparatus of the state. Whilst it was relatively protected from public scrutiny signs were beginning to emerge of growing public cynicism and distrust of authority, with associated clamour for more openness in government.

Scandal

Almost as soon as Trend could get his feet under the Cabinet table the Macmillan Government was hit by a Parliamentary scandal when John Profumo, Secretary for War, was forced to resign, having misled Parliament over an extra-marital affair with Christine Keeler which, because Keeler was also involved sexually with a Russian Intelligence Officer (Yevgeny Ivanov) stationed in London, raised important security questions. Trend's involvement illustrates the tedious procedural complexity that can be at the heart of colourful events. Profumo was a Privy Counsellor and there were few modern precedents to follow. Fourteen Privy Counsellors had been stuck off in the seventeenth century, eight in the eighteenth century and two in the nineteenth. But only one had been struck off in the twentieth (Sir Edgar Speyer, removed when his British naturalisation was withdrawn in 1921).[35] Whilst Trend concluded that a simple resignation would be preferable (and would conform to the likely inclination of the Queen) the eventual decision was that this would not be enough, an Order in Council would be required since 'it is not really possible to resign an honour granted one by The Queen,'[36] and such an Order was enacted on 26 June.

With the Profumo scandal following closely on from the 1962 scandal over the Admiralty clerk John Vassal, who was convicted of passing secrets to the Russians after being compromised in a homosexual honeypot trap, the 1961 exposure of the MI6 officer George Blake as a Soviet spy and the defection in 1963 of another Soviet spy, Kim Philby of the Foreign Office, the accumulated impact seemed to indicate that good fortune had deserted the Macmillan administration and that the Prime Minister was increasingly out of touch with the modern world. Macmillan's diaries for 15 March 1963 record 'A silly story [about Vassall] excited the House of Commons last night ... After this episode I was forced to spend a great deal of today over a silly scrape (women this time, thank God, not boys) into which one of the ministers [Profumo] had got himself.' Macmillan's official biographer, Alistair Horne, records that Macmillan's view was that the information passed to the Soviets was less damaging than the demoralisation caused by *the fact* of treachery. 'Therefore, the less said about spies and traitors in public the better.' It was a view to which Trend would have subscribed.

For the Vassall case Trend resisted Macmillan's *volt face* to convert a planned internal inquiry into an inquiry under the 1921 Tribunals Act, which would put witnesses under oath. He told the Prime Minister that it would set a burdensome precedent, especially as there were four or five similar cases in the pipeline.[37] His advice was not accepted, but his ideas led to the creation of the Security Commission and were endorsed by the Vassall Tribunal under Lord Radcliffe[38] when it reported in April.[39] Initially Trend had thought that the public should be warned about the reality of the espionage threat: 'The Security Service have an uphill and thankless task,' he argued and lurid press reporting should be curbed.[40] A possible statement about the threat and the methods used by the Soviets was drafted,[41] which the Foreign Office opposed as likely to damage Anglo-Soviet relations. When Radcliffe reported, however, the findings were more positive than expected. Trend advised that 'the great thing is to remain calm over all this because Radcliffe has worked out pretty well from our point of view'[42] and whilst emphasising the need for constant vigilance, Macmillan wrote to William Armstrong (in his capacity of Head of the Home Civil Service) that 'Radcliffe and the debate in the House of Commons have broadly vindicated the standard of security in the public service ... Many of the shortcomings had been reduced after the Portland and Blake cases ...' Privately, however, Trend agonised over how to do justice to the rights and duties of the Press and yet protect security and the reputation of the government.[43] But concern in the 1964 Wilson and 1970 Heath Administrations switched to worries about subversion in public life and there Trend would be much involved.

Meanwhile, concern was growing about the operation of the D Notice system in the wake of the trial of Gordon Blake for espionage, when politically damaging reports had appeared in the foreign press about the real nature of Blake's activities. The D Notice system had been created in 1912, one year after the Official Secrets Act, and in Trend's words, 'It performs the necessary function of giving guidance to the Press about what they may print without infringing the Official Secrets Acts and of enabling government Departments to restrain the Press in a friendly way from publishing material detrimental to the national interest.'[44] Government representatives on the freestanding Services Press and Broadcasting Committee that administered the system through its secretary (in 1961 a retired Admiral) were representatives of the Service departments in the Ministry of Defence. Trend (commenting from the Treasury) put much of the success of the system down to this fact, with the Press being willing to co-operate in support of national security in a military sense. But he felt that 'this Committee should be brought into closer contact with the central machinery of Government,' and 'The Government side of the Committee must be capable of providing Ministers with urgent advice and of responding to Ministers' instructions without delay.' With some hesitation he supported Norman Brook's contention that the Committee should be brought under the aegis of the Ministry of Defence with its Permanent Secretary as chairman.[45] The Ministry itself thought that though the logic pointed that way, the timing was not propitious and the Press would see the suggestion as an attempt to subjugate them to the MOD. A compromise was reached, to strengthen the D Notice Committee Secretary's liaison with Whitehall through a secret link to the Secretary of the Joint Intelligence Committee – secret because 'there would be no question of his being contacted direct by journalists.'[46] Meanwhile, as the serving D Notice Secretary was over 70 years old, steps should be put in hand to find a successor acceptable to the press side of the Committee.

These proposals were overtaken, however, by a failed attempt in early July 1961 to persuade the Press to accept a D Notice covering British troop movements to Kuwait and a challenge from the Deputy Leader of the Opposition (George Brown) that a D Notice of 27 July about weapons and equipment went beyond what was essential in the interests of security. Under pressure from

Brown Macmillan conceded that the Radcliffe Committee investigating security in the public sector in the light of the Vassall case should be asked to review the D Notice system.[47] Part III of the 1963 Radcliffe report proposed that the PUS at the MOD be added to the Committee and that a successor to Admiral Thompson, as Secretary, should not be a journalist but should be familiar with the ways of the Press. By mid June the only follow-up action had been to appoint the PUS at MOD as a member of the Committee; Thompson had been ill for some time and Colonel Lohan, Deputy Press Officer at the MOD, had acted in his absence without a formal link to the central government machine. A meeting under Trend's chairmanship on 28 June agreed to offer the post of Secretary to Colonel Lohan who 'had given wide satisfaction in Whitehall' and who 'was known to and liked by the Press.' No representatives of the Press appear to have been consulted at this stage.

When Macmillan saw Sir William Hayley, Editor of The Times, on 29 July to hear the latter's complaint about a private and confidential message sent to editors on 11 July asking them not to report the defection of the Russian Anatoli Dolnytsin, Hayley said that 'so long as Admiral Thompson had been Secretary of the D Notice Committee the system worked. But once he had given up, it did not work ... Unless there was a good Secretary there was always likely to be some breakdown in the system.'[48] Intriguingly, in drawing this comment to the attention Sir Richard Way of the MOD and chairman of the D Notice Committee, Trend wrote, 'You will recall that I asked you to defer action of Phillip Allen's letter of 15th July, conveying Treasury authority for the terms of Lohan's appointment as Secretary to the Committee. I suppose that, in the light of Hayley's remarks – but without prejudice to the question whether we accept or endorse them – we had better reconsider Lohan's position?' In the event after Way had contacted available press members of the Committee and only one had voiced doubts, Colonel Lohan was confirmed in the position.[49] It turned out to be a colourful and controversial appointment which the Official Historian of the D Notice system sums up: 'There were many who within a few years came to regret the triumph of inertia over judgement.'[50]

Cabinet

As with Brook, Cabinet continued to be the fulcrum around which Whitehall pivoted and for the most part decisions were taken on the basis of papers circulated at least 48 hours before the discussion. In 1976, he described this aspect of the role thus:

> 'Your concern is to see that the issues are processed up properly and that they finally reach Cabinet, when they've got to go to Cabinet, in a sufficiently compact, intelligible, clear form for the Cabinet to know what it is they've got to decide, what are the pro's and con's.'[51]

In Trend's first year as Cabinet Secretary there were 73 Cabinet meetings and 220 circulated papers. Like Brook he summarised every paper for the Prime

Minister and gave handling advice on all agenda items, including those to be raised orally. This in itself was a Herculean labour, especially as most issues rising to the Cabinet table would be evenly balanced between options and quite often required more than one discussion before a decision was taken. These briefs for the Prime Minister were a meal in themselves and even now, with benefit of hindsight, provide a succinct guide to how decisions could be reached through rational analysis. In 2–3 pages he would summarise the issues and the arguments, give handling advice, identify the questions to be settled and usually set out the steps required for implementation or for further study. The Prime Minister would not need to read the documents themselves. Both Brook and Trend were vigilant over the logic of the papers circulated and were not afraid to challenge Ministerial proposals if they felt that the arguments put forward in the papers were weak or misleading. Such advice was almost always confidential to the Prime Minister and they almost never revealed their hand to Permanent Secretary colleagues except by virtue of preparatory work carried out in the official committees supporting Cabinet committees. In one respect, however, Trend departed from the immediate precedents. Whereas Brook, would sometimes make a direct recommendation to the Prime Minister, Trend nearly always cloaked his recommendations in the form of 'Cabinet may wish to assure itself that …' or, if he thought the way forward was straightforward, 'Cabinet may wish to agree that …' His advice was elliptical, in the form of Socratic questioning. Not that the Cabinet discussion always followed his logical route, but he gave the Prime Minister a route map which could be used to steer a discussion. Nor did it follow that Trend would omit political points. Like all the Cabinet Secretaries in this study he never made Party political points and never took the minutes of Party political discussions, demonstrably putting down his pen at such moments. But he would comment on the likely reception of a policy proposal in the country at large, by leading non-government participants such as the employers or the trades unions, or by other countries likely to be affected.[52]

He was in a special position to study the handling of Cabinet. He commented to Macmillan's biographer Alistair Horne, '[Macmillan] ran the Cabinet very gracefully – no sign of great effort. Sometimes he would show signs of impatience, but just enough to get things done … just as animals don't get angry, Macmillan seldom did; when he did he turned and he really swiped. But it was all over quickly …'[53] When Macmillan resigned in October 1963 after a prostate health scare Trend quite properly instructed that all material intended for the Prime Minister should be sent to 'RAB' Butler.[54] But the then obscure processes of the Conservative Party propelled Alec Douglas Home into the premiership. During the 362 days that Home was Prime Minister his handling skills greatly impressed Trend who said that he 'much admired Home's methods of working, finding him decisive, clear-minded and a good controller of the Cabinet agenda; he thought Home the best Chairman of Cabinet.[55] It was thought necessary for Lord Home (as he then was) to give up his hereditary peerage so as to be eligible for election to the House of Commons, thus providing an unlikely ally for Viscount Stansgate, who already sat in the Commons but was faced with having to resign when he inherited the title from his father, and was leading a campaign to allow him forfeit the title for his lifetime. Trend weighed in in support, advising that a hereditary peer should be free to renounce the title irrevocably during his own lifetime (but could receive a life peerage). Such a decision should not, however, be binding on the peer's successors who could reverse it.[56]

On taking office, Home told all ministers 'I have tried to take the first step [to getting the necessary decisions] by sending minutes to individual ministers on the topics which seem to need special attention or added effort; and I hope that during the next few weeks these questions will be brought forward, through the normal committee machines, and will be dealt with as promptly as possible.'[57] On the basis of the submissions received, Trend concluded that there were few areas where significant progress was easy before 1964, when a General Election was due.[58] On the advice of the former Chancellor, Selwyn Lloyd,[59] Home then planned to call for firmness of economic and financial purpose, and to challenge progress on a wide range of policies inherited from the Macmillan administration.[60] Trend thought the posture too negative; preferring an exhortation to Cabinet for decisiveness and financial responsibility. A month later, in mid December, he was already chasing Departments for progress reports on the priorities identified by Home at the end of November.[61] Brook's handover guidance had identified a lack of follow-up by the Cabinet Office on the implementation of Cabinet decisions[62] but it is unlikely that Trend's action derived from this as throughout his tenure he put great store by the independent responsibility of Cabinet Ministers to implement their collective decisions without central monitoring. Indeed, so strong was Trend's belief that it was for individual Ministers to do so that in September 1964 he fought to have a passage removed from David Irving's book 'The Mare's Nest' because it revealed that during the closing stages of the Blitz Duncan Sandys had ignored a Cabinet decision against using deception to divert German targeting of V1 and V2 rockets away from central London to south of the Thames.[63]

It was also the case that, at the end of his tenure, Brook had been reluctant to enlarge the Cabinet Office to provide a central policy staff but had been prevented from pressing this view on Macmillan because of the serious illness that had hospitalised him at the time of the Cuba crisis. Ironically, Michael Cary, who was his deputy and stood in as Cabinet Secretary during that crisis had argued the contrary, that it was inevitable that the Cabinet Office would become more the Prime Minister's servant.[64] Machinery of government changes continued to be in the air during the whole of 1963 and 1964 with Macmillan wanting smaller Cabinet agendas and deeper discussions[65] and Trend being both in favour of keeping on the EEC co-ordinating committees despite de Gaulle's veto of the British application to join[66] and of taking a general look at the demarcation of economic issues between departments.[67] Though in all this he was constitutionally conservative, offering little that was new on civil service skills, policy integration or links to Party politics, stressing the risks involved in separating policy formulation from policy execution.[68]

Britain's Place in the World

Adjustment to Britain's reduced importance in world affairs continued to bring pain. On 14 January 1963, General de Gaulle vetoed the British application to join the European Economic Community (EEC), declaring: 'l'Angleterre, ce n'est plus grand chose.' The immediate reaction from officials was that Britain should support a free trade agenda vigorously, look to improve the supply side of industry, rethink agricultural support and concert with the United States to stop EEC policies making the eventual accession of Britain more difficult.[69] Britain should not, Trend argued, make a grand gesture of intent to join the EEC but should continue to press its case for membership with the other five member states, leaving confrontation with France to the NATO arena, in which he queried how far British policy should be subordinated to American leadership.[70] In an additional attempt to regroup and avoid a crippling loss of morale, Trend also followed up the work by officials by suggesting that the President of the Board of Trade should be asked how ongoing negotiations with the European Free Trade Area (EFTA), the Commonwealth and under the United Nations General Agreement on Tariffs and Trade (GATT) hung together.[71]

Meanwhile, dismantling and transforming the British Empire into a Commonwealth of independent nations was well under way. In addition to the United Kingdom there were 15 Commonwealth members, including many powerful nations.[72] By the time Trend retired in the late summer of 1973 a further 18 (mainly smaller countries) had been added, though Pakistan had left in the first of many seesaw manoeuvres. Throughout Trend's time (and well beyond) two Commonwealth questions loomed large in foreign policy. First, at a time when the economic and political future of Britain was undergoing reappraisal, what was the Commonwealth for? The second, how to reconcile the aspirations of white settlers and indigenous populations in African member states – particularly in regard to South Africa and Southern Rhodesia which both discriminated electorally against non-whites.

Immediately, however, Commonwealth issues centred on Asia as China attacked India in October 1962 and in January 1963 President Sukarno of Indonesia condemned plans to form Malaysia as an amalgamation of the Federation of Malaya, Singapore and the Crown Colony/British protectorates of North Borneo and Sarawak. He committed Indonesia to an undeclared low-level war with the new state (which was formed in September 1963) along a 1,000 mile common border. The British embassy in Jakarta was burned down and, at its peak, 17,000 British troops were deployed to defend Malaysia together with eighty naval vessels and jet fighters. What concerned Trend was the implications for defence spending.[73] The China-India fighting looked like a proxy trial of strength associated with the Sino-Soviet split, with Pakistan loosely favouring China and India drawn towards the Russians. With a population of 100 million it was important that Sukarno was not driven into the arms of the Indonesian Communist Party (PKI), hence the British response needed to be carefully calibrated but also needed to be firm. This requirement led to a Whitehall innovation which

Trend thought could be relevant more widely (for example, in Cyprus), and that was to create a Foreign Office/Commonwealth Relations Office task force with executive authority, foreshadowing the merger of the two Departments,[74] which Trend had advocated (albeit by taking one step at a time) as early as July 1963.[75] Meanwhile, could Australia and New Zealand help more with the burden and did the commitment to Malaysia have to be indefinite, Trend queried.[76] He argued that the two Dominions underestimated the Indonesian threat[77] and that in the longer term Britain should retreat from its Singapore military base. Foreign Office planners agreed, fearing that attempts to retain a military presence in the face of rising Asian nationalism could drive local populations towards the Communist bloc.

In April 1965 Singapore was expelled from Malaysia, (by which time Labour had replaced the Conservatives as the government of the United Kingdom) Britain did decide to withdraw despite opposition from the United States, Australia and New Zealand in the light of American escalation in the Vietnam War.[78] Defence aid from Britain continued to both Malaysia and Singapore, however, and British patience paid off as Communist elements in the Indonesian army attempted a coup but were defeated in a bloody internal struggle during which the British held back on escalating the Confrontation so as to allow the Indonesian army to deal with the PKI. By March 1966 Sukarno's rule was all but over and an imaginative offer of £1 million in aid to Indonesia, together with a visit to Jakarta by the British Foreign Secretary, paved the way to an agreement in August 1966 by which the Confrontation was ended.[79]

Britain had largely exported its own system of democracy and the rule of law to its colonies. But by the early 1960s an association of states united by a colonial legacy was not enough and one of the unresolved questions Brook bequeathed to Trend was how to enhance the benefits of belonging to the Commonwealth, particularly for newly independent states that did not operate a Westminster-style democracy. Officials recognised that at the early stages of independence single party political systems could provide strong leadership and impose relative unity. In March 1960 the report of an inquiry into Commonwealth development was completed under Sir Gerald Templer, renowned for a successful 'hearts and minds' campaign during the Malayan Communist-led insurgency.[80] Amongst the Committee's recommendations was the creation of a Commonwealth Youth Trust to invest in the development of young people in Commonwealth countries and to give them a sense of belonging to an important voluntary association of democratic states with common values. Brook suggested that although the Commonwealth Relations Office was not keen on the idea Trend might like to consider promoting it within government.[81] For now Trend passed the ball to the Commonwealth Secretary via the Prime Minister, with rather vague suggestions about what might be done. As to the value of the Commonwealth more generally, the Conservative Chancellor of the Exchequer warned the D Committee that much of Britain's overseas spending seemed to defend the interests of European competitors.[82] Trend and his Private Secretary, William Reid, were inclined to agree. Whilst the potential of the Commonwealth for the defence and the communications industries was not given enough prominence in the Defence Committee, they recorded pessimistic views on the complacency of British exporters as inclined to stick with existing markets and be unenthusiastic about developing new ones.[83] In Trend and Reid's view investment in cultural diplomacy through the British Council was the best bet for cohesion between Commonwealth countries – whilst political issues might dominate in Southern Africa, in the rest of the Commonwealth cultural links were more important.[84] Further, investment in an existing organisation rather than in a specific new initiative such as the idea of a Commonwealth Youth Trust reduced the risk of looking like a rebound from the EEC veto.[85] When Sir Saville Garner badgered Home not to let the Commonwealth Secretary off the hook on producing ideas for Commonwealth development, Reid pointed out that what little had been forthcoming would need extra money and was directed at the new Commonwealth, which was inherently less attractive to Conservative Ministers than the old Commonwealth.[86] Trend responded that Britain needed to hang in until 'the Africans settle down and grow up' when the Commonwealth would become a stronger force in the world.[87] Meanwhile, events in South East Asia were likely to exacerbate the defence burden on the domestic economy.[88]

In Southern Africa the issues centred on political matters, notably the lack of political representation of the majority black populations.[89] This was especially true of the apartheid system of South Africa and of the less aggressive discrimination in favour of white settlers in Southern Rhodesia, the dominant partner in the Central African Federation of Southern Rhodesia, Northern Rhodesia and Nyasaland (CAF). The Federation had been created by Britain in 1953 as semi-independent of the United Kingdom with the intention of becoming a Dominion within the Commonwealth. In 1960 Southern Rhodesia had only 37% of the total population of the Federation but it had 72% of the white settlers and was characterised by relatively paternalistic white rule, in contrast to the more brutal South African apartheid system. By the early years of the decade, however, rising African political aspirations were challenging white minority rule based on franchise qualifications of property, education and income, led by Hastings Banda in Nyasaland and Kenneth Kaunda in Northern Rhodesia. A new Federation constitution was negotiated in 1961, after a review by the Monckton Commission, that reduced Britain's powers and in the same year South Africa left the Commonwealth. Further, after Monckton it was agreed that Nyasaland would be allowed to secede from the Federation in 1962. A year later Northern Rhodesia also left, effectively ending the 1953 structure. Both were granted independence in 1964 as Zambia and Malawi. Paradoxically, this left Southern Rhodesia which had been the most self-governing of the three at the start of the Federation now the laggard.

The point was not lost on Trend. In early December 1963 he told Home that even though the Prime Minister had told the Rhodesian Prime Minister in October that should the country declare independence, 'she would sacrifice a great deal,' there would be renewed pressure for an early grant of independence. The Commonwealth Secretary[90] was considering inviting Australia, Canada,

Tanganyika and Nigeria to meet Britain and Southern Rhodesia to 'work out a formula for to allow this to happen.'[91] Trend stressed that the intention to consult representatives of the Commonwealth was hard to reconcile with assurances given previously by 'RAB' Butler that 'Her Majesty's Government accept in principle that Southern Rhodesia, like other territories, will proceed through the normal processes to independence.'[92] The circle could only be squared if independence and Commonwealth membership were linked. Should the Southern Rhodesian Prime Minister (Winston Field) agree to attend the proposed constitutional meeting this would help avoid the United Kingdom having to take a position on a new initiative by the Secretary-General of the United Nations to involve the Organisation of African Unity as intermediary between Field and the Rhodesian African leaders. It would also bring home to the white settlers that if independence was to be attained within the Commonwealth then the terms of independence must be acceptable to the rest of the Commonwealth.

Should Field decide not to participate, the conference could go ahead anyway to show that 'we have done all we could to pursue our role as honest broker ... and should not be left to carry the whole of the moral responsibility for any disaster that might ensue.' On the other hand, by involving Commonwealth members in the way proposed by the Commonwealth Secretary, Trend added, 'we have virtually surrendered to (some members of) the rest of the Commonwealth the decision on the terms of Southern Rhodesia's independence but are left carrying the whole of the responsibility for dealing with the situation which may develop if those terms are unacceptable to Southern Rhodesian sentiment.' Perhaps, he mused prophetically, 'If we allow [Southern Rhodesia] to reach the point of frustration at which she declares her own independence unilaterally, our standing with the rest of the Commonwealth may emerge tolerably unimpaired.'[93]

When putting the proposal for a meeting to Field, the Colonial Secretary, Duncan Sandys, emphasised that though the normal processes for granting independence would be followed, he was endeavouring to bring the rest of the Commonwealth along with a solution acceptable to both Britain and Southern Rhodesia. Field objected to Commonwealth interference 'without precedent [that] would be widely construed as a breach of the principle of exclusive British responsibility' that the UK had always defended at the United Nations. Wider Commonwealth involvement would be dominated by doctrinaire considerations or national interests, which would have little bearing on the best interests of the people of Southern Rhodesia. Furthermore, the Rhodesian politicians firmly believed that they had been promised independence at the time of the break-up of the Federation.[94] They were not ready to amend the Land Apportionment Act, 1930, which allocated the best land and 50% of the total area of the country to white settlers.[95] Again Trend saw the dangers whilst being unable to avoid them: 'we must be careful that, in our anxiety to please everybody, we do not end up by pleasing nobody and finding ourselves left to deal, single-handed, with a mess.'[96]

In January 1964 Home, told Field that there were four conditions before independence could be granted: Majority Rule; no regressive amendments to the

Constitution; better African rights; and the agreement of the African majority population to the terms of independence.'[97] Briefing for Cabinet in February, Trend went on to explore further the consequences of a unilateral declaration of independence (UDI). In part this focused on constitutional matters (the relationship with the Crown and Rhodesia's international status) but it also addressed possible steps to win the public relations battle – a last attempt to dissuade Field from precipitate action, a public statement of the UK position aimed at rallying the substantial body of European opinion which was believed to oppose unconstitutional action and, significantly, 'How far could we make use of the fact that the armed forces of Southern Rhodesia have presumably taken the normal oath of personal loyalty to the Queen?'[98] The last question was particularly relevant because, earlier in the month, the British Chiefs of Staff had concluded that 'It cannot be contemplated that a situation should be allowed to develop in which HMG found itself in a position of being required to use military force to coerce a recalcitrant regime in Southern Rhodesia. There should be no question of using British forces against the white population of that country.'[99]

Trend had also given Home a private note in which he said, 'we do not see any way in which the [Rhodesian Army's] oath of allegiance could be turned to account by a direct appeal to the armed forces.' In Trend's subtle mind he would have distinguished between the actual use of force and the possible effects of threatening to use force. At this stage, however, Cabinet discussion did not progress beyond the constitutional questions and a desire to play the issues long.[100] Financial sanctions, he warned, would have little effect unless Northern Rhodesia (soon the become Zambia) and Nyasaland joined in, which would invite Southern Rhodesian retaliation, especially on the Kariba Dam, railways and air traffic. Perhaps, he speculated, Britain should pass legislation to remove Rhodesia from the Queen's Dominions as a low-key way of accepting the fact of independence and avoiding acrimony.[101]

Meanwhile, events in Southern Rhodesia turned against the UK. In April 1964 Ian Smith, the Deputy Prime Minister, ousted Winston Field after a vote of no confidence in Field's perceived weakness in dealing with the UK. Smith and his backers were hard-liners, dubbed by Joshua Nkomo the leader of the Soviet sympathising Zimbabwe African People's Union (ZAPU), 'a suicide squad ... interested not in the welfare of all the people but only their own.' In London, William Reid, Trend's private secretary, offered the opinion, having heard Smith speak at a Party Congress, that 'It is tragic to think that such a good people as the Southern Rhodesians might be placed in the hands of these characters. They really don't deserve it.'[102] Sir Roy Welensky, the former Prime Minister of the Federation advised Home that whilst Smith was 'a bad thing for Southern Rhodesia' the UK must avoid making him a martyr; a better tactic would be to formulate a way forward that would enable opposition to Smith to crystallise.[103] The approach looked promising, especially as Sir Saville Garner, Permanent Secretary at the Commonwealth Relations Office, offered the opinion that Smith was not likely to last long and put forward a draft public statement of the UK's policy to encourage opposition to Smith to break cover.[104] This statement contained the phrase 'conditions that are generally acceptable' when referring to the requirements before independence could be granted. Trend leapt upon the loose drafting like a lion hunting down a weak antelope. 'What is this meant to mean?' he scrawled to Reid. 'What he means is, "generally acceptable to the population, white and black, of Southern Rhodesia" (not generally acceptable to the Commonwealth'), was the response from Reid.[105] That was all very well, but Trend recognised a need to keep the rest of the Commonwealth involved at the same time as going slowly in the hope that Smith would fall.[106]

At this early stage in the putative rebellion it might have been sufficient to threaten military action to bring Southern Rhodesia to heel, particularly if a statement of policy offered educational assistance for would-be African voters as Trend had mooted back in March.[107] Sir Arthur Snelling, the Permanent Secretary at the Commonwealth Relations Office, commissioned military contingency plans if the governor of Southern Rhodesia were to ask for help to support loyal regular army units or if British subjects in surrounding African countries were threatened. But officials recognised that other coercive action would be largely ineffective and the possibility of military intervention was a crucial omission from their report on possible actions should Southern Rhodesia unilaterally declare independence.[108] Venturing into difficult waters, since the Secretary of State for Defence, Peter Thorneycroft, had given a direct instruction in late July,[109] Trend's three-page brief bluntly pointed out that economic sanctions would 'be largely ineffective [and] very difficult to administer'. He went on to claim that the 'signs are that the Governor and at least some of the Southern Rhodesia military and police forces would remain loyal after a unilateral declaration of independence. The Governor might call upon the British Government to send troops in their support.' This left the Committee to draw its own conclusions that the threat of military action might have a good chance of success.[110] The result was that Home decided that maintaining modest arms supplies to the Rhodesia armed forces would help keep the troops loyal to the Crown.[111]

Meanwhile, on the basis of experience in South Africa, London was pessimistic about the effects of isolation on the Rhodesian economy. A June briefing for Home contained the unwelcome assessment that, 'The hard fact is that since South Africa left the Commonwealth the white population is united as never before, the economy is booming, and Dr Verwoerd's Government is applying the policy of "separate development", with all the cruelty and discrimination it involves, with ever greater severity.'[112] Also, at an early evening meeting on 30 June between Home, Sandys and Trend, notwithstanding the desirability of making a public statement of policy to strengthen support for the anti-unilateralists in Southern Rhodesia, a decision was taken that the risk of provoking Smith into precipitate action, combined with a reluctance to expose too much surface to other Commonwealth Prime Ministers, meant that the UK should remain officially silent for the time being. Sandys opposed any initiative from the UK; Trend was less doctrinaire and set in hand work to investigate how Africanisation could be speeded up under the current Rhodesian constitution.[113] In this he was partly influenced by a briefing from the progressive businessman Sir

Ronald Prain, chairman of the copper mining company Rhodesian Selection Trust in the former Northern Rhodesia, now Zambia, in which he described Smith as surrounded by hard-liners and likely to go for UDI.[114]

As 1964 Commonwealth Prime Ministers were not prepared to see Smith present in London either officially or in the wings at their July Conference, face-to-face talks were deferred until 7–10 September. The resulting communiqué referred to granting independence when it could be shown to be 'acceptable to the people of the Territory as a whole.' Smith appeared to be confident that he could demonstrate this and on the eve of polling in the October British General Election he launched a traditional consultation with chiefs and headmen to gather support for independence under limited franchise well short of majority (African) rule. One of the last acts of the outgoing Conservative government was to disassociate itself from this exercise and to reject a claim made by Smith after the September talks that, at the time of the 1961 revision of the CAF constitution, Britain had promised Southern Rhodesia independence should the Federation fail.[115] The ball now passed to the inexperienced Wilson administration, striving to govern with a narrow majority in the House of Commons where compromise with Smith would be a hard policy to sell.

Defence

Trend continued Brook's practice of briefing for the Defence Committee (badged as D). This was no small matter. Brook had been selective about when to include substantive analysis in addition to handling advice. Trend, by contrast, set out from the outset to be the Prime Minister's principal advisor in substantive terms as well as in terms of process and presentation. An early sign of his insight and input came in February 1963 as he challenged the basic assumptions for a Chequers discussion of defence strategy designed to keep spending within 7% of GNP, particularly the geographical importance of a British defence presence and, thus, the role of the long-range Navy.[116] Michael Cary, head of the Defence secretariat, inclined to a view that the British presence in Aden was too high a price to pay as insurance against a theoretical loss of oil and would be useless as a staging post for action in Africa. Over time the British contribution to the South East Asia Treaty Organisation (SEATO) might be reduced and allow strengthening of the British NATO contingent in Europe in support of a strategy of deterrents at all levels (a conventional attack with conventional forces, tactical nuclears with tactical nuclears and strategic nuclears with strategic nuclears). 'Is it any longer credible in political and human terms,' he asked, 'that we should react to conventional attack on Berlin by committing suicide?' Trend disagreed. Dissecting NATO strategy in preparation for a visit by Robert McNamara[117] in March 1963 he wrote, 'We do not see wholly eye to eye with the Americans … Their current approach is … that a commander must have at his disposal a range of options extending from modest conventional warfare to the full nuclear exchange at the other.' The Europeans, and especially the Germans, however, 'do not believe in making Europe "safe for conventional war"; they believe that safety lies in compelling the Russians to calculate that in any case of sustained conventional aggression the West will be forced to use nuclear weapons in its own defence.'[118] Thus, in the European view 'conventional forces must not be so large that they could defeat or indefinitely hold a major Soviet attack by themselves.'[119]

The size of conventional forces on the mainland of Europe had important consequences for the UK Defence Budget. If there was no chance of reducing the commitment to 55,000 British troops in the British Army of the Rhine (BAOR) it seemed that Britain must look to the Middle East and Far East for steps to hold the defence budget below 7% of GNP as had been agreed by Ministers at Chequers in February.[120] This, Trend argued, 'will be a curiously illogical conclusion; for our longer term studies are likely to show that it is in the Middle and Far East (where the Americans can give us least help) that we can least afford to reduce our commitments, while it is in Europe that the risk of war is at its lowest.'[121] However Trend took the analysis no further; and it is arguable that the probability of European war might have been low but the impact on the United Kingdom would have been extreme whereas the probability of conflict in the Middle East and Far East was high but the likely impact on the United Kingdom was much lower.

In an attempt to move closer to an informed decision which would improve the match between Britain's commitments and what could be afforded Trend then successfully sought Macmillan's permission to launch studies to challenge conventional assumptions about the country's vital interests in having a military presence in the Middle East, the Far East and Western Europe; but failed to get authority to challenge the case for a UK nuclear deterrent.[122] It was, as Trend confided to Harold Caccia at the Foreign Office,[123] an exercise to ask Ministers for the least worse option to keep defence spending within the target limit.[124] The Chiefs of Staff were already worried about a possible rushed decision to withdraw from the Far East[125] and their general disposition towards the government was further challenged by an independent report from Hastings 'Pug' Ismay[126] and Ian Jacob[127] on the long-running issue of how the central defence organisation should be structured. Trend had strongly supported the setting up of an inquiry[128] and now vigorously supported their recommendations to give the Minister of Defence powers over the individual Service Ministers and the Chiefs:

> 'The general malaise which the Ismay-Jacob report is directed to curing is not something accidental or transitory. Nor is it the result of personal jealousies or inter-service rivalries. It results from the fact that the present organisation is kicking against the pricks in the sense of exposing itself to the way in which the machinery for planning the long-term decisions of Government policy is naturally and inevitably evolving. This is confirmed by, among other things, the fact that defence expenditure is growing and will continue to grow, while the commitments which it is designed to honour are inelastic ... Unless something is done to rationalise the central

> organisation for formulating policy and executing decisions, our defence policy will be at the mercy of a series of 'stop and go' decisions, which is neither efficient nor economic.'[129]

The result of the reorganisation (which was implemented at 1 April 1964) was to remove the burden of co-ordination of the three armed services from the Defence Committee and to put it on the Minister of Defence's shoulders. Further, this freedom allowed the committee to morph into the Oversea Policy and Defence Committee (OPD) bringing foreign and defence policy considerations into a single place. The foreign policy equivalent of the D Committee, the Overseas Co-ordinating Committee, was thought in the Cabinet Office to be only moderately successful because the Foreign Office 'found it difficult to accept that overseas policy could no longer be regarded as a thing in itself, but as a compound, and usually a compromise between a number of conflicting pressures, military factors, financial factors, and domestic political factors.'[130] Trend himself gave evidence to a committee of inquiry, once again under Lord Plowden, 'to review the purpose, structure and operation of the services responsible for representing the interests of the United Kingdom Government overseas, both in the Commonwealth and in foreign countries.'[131] He argued for a Cabinet Office-based planning staff to support the foreign policy co-ordinating committees similar to the assessment staff support for the Joint Intelligence Committee.[132] When the Plowden committee reported he briefed in favour of its recommendation of a single diplomatic service with policy planning geared in with Whitehall as a whole, adding prophetically, 'the greatest and the most obvious weakness in the Whitehall administrative structure is simply the fact that, nowadays, Departments are kept so busy by day-to-day routine work that they have no time to "think ahead" i.e. to foresee the contingencies of the future and to advise Ministers how best to try to anticipate them.'[133] As Home prepared for a visit to Washington and Ottawa, accompanied by Trend who had organised the briefing, Trend speculated whether American policy planning arrangements based on 'treaties' between the various Agencies were better than those negotiated in the British committee system under OPD(O) oversight.[134]

The Domestic Economy

An important element in the discussions about foreign policy and defence and also one of the chief arguments for Britain joining the EEC was a weak economy that struggled to pay its way internationally, as a reserve currency was vulnerable to balance of payments crises and in which domestic workers tended take in pay more than they were able to produce. As someone who had spent most of his career in the Treasury Trend was, unlike any of his predecessors, well placed to understand economic issues but also likely, for the same reasons, to be open to allegations that he favoured the Chancellor in debates about economic strategy and about public expenditure. It is greatly to his credit that this appears to have been no more than a theoretical concern, especially during the five years of experiment in the Wilson Governments when economic policy was split between the Treasury and thc Department of Economic Affairs. It was during the ill-fated policies of the second half of the 1960s that his input to economic issues was most active and when there is the strongest sense that he was sympathetic to the rational analysis of economic planning and the associated central imposition of pay and price restraint.

Before then his involvement in economic and commercial polices during 1963 and 1964 was limited. There were, however, hints of a fundamental sympathy for the efficacy of public expenditure in reducing wealth disparities in his briefing of Home for Cabinet in January 1964:

(a) An increase in public expenditure – and therefore in tax – is not necessarily a bad thing, in so far as it provides better social benefits for the less fortunate members of the community and eliminates the grosser disparities of wealth.
(b) 'By any reliable criterion of value for money, it is not always public expenditure that needs to be reduced. The private sector, [particularly consumption, may be the villain of the piece.'[135]

On 14 February he advised that Ministers would oppose a check on public expenditure, which was growing at about 6.5% p.a., on the grounds that 'it should be a question not of cutting the coat according to the cloth but of getting more cloth to make a bigger coat' and the keys to that were a voluntary incomes policy, some form of institution for examining price rises and steps to intensify competition. Hence, he briefed in favour of the immediate abolition of Resale Price Maintenance.[136] But he also challenged some of the accompanying proposals such as powers to break up mergers (on the grounds that the criteria were insufficiently robust), and the proposed role of the government in challenging restrictive practices (on the grounds whether it was wise to bequeath such powers to your political opponents).[137] Elsewhere he generally took a stance in favour of free trade, repeatedly supporting the approval of an Export Credit Guarantee Department (ECGD) line of credit for 450 buses to be sold to Cuba in the face of American anger, which he attributed more to pique at having been ousted as a monopoly supplier than to foreign relations concerns.[138] (The Prime Minister, Lord Home, subsequently said that 'There is no question of dictation by the US Government to this country over commercial relations with Cuba.'[139]) He also opposed the imposition of a 'Buy British' policy on the Air Ministry over the purchase of computers.

It was an independence of spirit shown early in Trend's tenure of office. In March 1963 the first of two reports by the Chairman of the British Railways Board, Dr Richard Beeching, into the future of the railway system were delivered.[140] The brief had been to create a railway of a size and pattern suited to modern conditions and prospects. In particular, a system to meet current needs, with the premise that the railways should be run as a profitable business. The report recommended the closure of a third of the network and over half the railway stations. In a number of critical briefings for Harold Macmillan Trend argued that the Ministry of Transport were looking at the issue too narrowly. First, road transport had to be planned if the rail closures were to be implemented; what was needed was a national transport plan and the population would, therefore, consider the report to be the concern of government not just the Railways Board. Second, that in this and in consideration of the Buchanan Report on 'Traffic in Towns' concerning urban and road planning the Ministry was also taking too narrow a view. In neither case were his interventions wholly successful. Macmillan did reject the Minister of Transport's first response to the Beeching report but most of the suggested closures were implemented without a national transport plan as a framework and the, admittedly, strong influence of the Buchanan report was due to its inspiration of local planners.[141]

Where industrial relations were concerned, however, he trod cautiously. When ideas were floated early in 1963 for making workers in essential industries obey management instructions he argued for more study of the large legal and practical issues involved before taking a decision. Not that he was entirely content with the status quo. 'It is discreditable that 18 years after the end of the war we face electricity cuts in a normal winter,' he told Macmillan in July 1963. But he consistently argued that the government case in public sector disputes and the possibility of resorting to emergency measures must be kept separate, arguing that because the government was the ultimate employer in the public sector did not give it the authority to impose emergency measures unless they would have been justified in a wholly private sector dispute.

The 1964 General Election

As the October 1964 deadline for calling a General Election approached Trend advised Home that an Election Business Committee should be set up in conformity with common practice since 1923. Its purpose was to advise government candidates factually about government policies.[142] At the same time, in view of the length of time that the Labour Party had been out of office and the known interest of the Opposition in changes to the machinery of government, informal contact was being made by the Opposition front bench with senior civil servants. (It was also rumoured that they were in touch with Lord Normanbrook who was still less than two years into retirement.) Tim Bligh (Home's Principal Private Secretary) put forward the suggestion that contact on machinery of government issues might help smooth the creation of a new Administration should the Conservatives lose.[143] In a significant gesture that would set a precedent that endures Home stressed that whilst he could agree to limited contact with the most senior civil servants about machinery of government issues he ought not to know anything further about the discussions. The upshot was a new convention that, 'by authority of the Prime Minister, in the last six months of a Parliament or when a general election has been called, Opposition parties may arrange, with the authority of their party leaders and through the head of the civil service, contacts with senior civil servants. These arrangements are designed to allow briefing on factual questions on departmental organisational changes which Opposition parties have in mind or which may result from Opposition party policies. The exchanges were to be confidential.'[144]

The whole of Home's Administration was in the shadow of an impending General Election after 13 years of Conservative rule. Along with the secretive manner in which Home had been chosen to succeed Macmillan that fact would make things electorally difficult for the Prime Minister. Hence Trend was unhappy with the draft memoirs of Viscount Kilmiur when they arrived for clearance in late 1963. He told Home that they contained three areas of concern: references to the handling of the Suez crisis, references to Churchill's advice to The Queen at the time of Eden's resignation and a damning judgement on, amongst others, 'RAB' Butler's 'fatal habit of publicly hedging his political bets.' Home asked Kilmuir to look again 'as a man of extreme fair-mindedness' at references to Butler, Dr Nkrumah, Churchill and Selwyn Lloyd. Trend followed this up with detailed comments, mainly about not revealing the details of Cabinet Committees and about the implications of what Kilmuir was saying about colleagues. Kilmuir replied that 'I shall, of course, do my utmost to see that they come out right in the final form.' Meanwhile, Trend proffered new rules to govern Ministerial memoirs and those by officials (except for the Armed Forces and the diplomats, which he considered too difficult for the time being.[145] Home was even more reluctant, ruling that the whole initiative was not politically practicable and should not be put before Cabinet.[146] Trend and his deputy Cary had to concede defeat, unable to see a constructive way forward.[147]

The General Election took place on 15 October 1964. The Conservatives had 43.4% of the vote (Labour 44.1%); 304 MPs compared to Labour's 317; the Liberals 11.2% of the vote but only nine seats, which gave Harold Wilson a four seat overall majority.

As a former official, Harold Wilson understood how to get the best out of civil servants and worked well with most of them, especially with the academic and calm Trend. At the start of the election year Wilson had been interviewed for the BBC's 'The Corridors of Power'; his views on senior civil servants were highly conservative – 'decent chaps – damned clever but whose isolation in Whitehall and general tendency to inbreeding left their antennae somewhat dulled.'[148] In his biography of Wilson, Ben Pimlott writes that Trend, 'became the Prime Minister's most valued Whitehall adviser. In the many crises of the late 1960s, Wilson relied increasingly on Trend, who … provided him with briefs on everything, advised him on security matters, and was consulted on Cabinet changes, much as Sir Edward Bridges had been by Attlee.' (Though Bridges had been Head of the Home Civil Service whereas Trend was not and the evidence on file bears out the extent of his briefing but, not surprisingly, contains little about the last point.) The election manifesto had painted a future that promised, 'mobilising the resources of technology under a national plan; harnessing our natural wealth in brains, our genius for scientific invention and medical discovery.' Back on 1st October 1963 Wilson had introduced the notion of the white heat of a technological revolution and proclaimed that, 'In the

Cabinet room and the boardroom alike, those charged with the control of our affairs must be ready to think and to speak in the language of our scientific age.'[149] At about the same time, a Committee of Enquiry into the Organisation of Civil Science had reported.[150] Its chairman was Trend and it spoke of the need for action to deal with the ramshackle nature of the then arrangements. Though the Committee argued that the financing of most scientific research in the universities should continue to be shared between the University Grants Committee and the Research Councils, it recommended a shake-up of the latter into five groups (Agriculture and Medical as already existed plus Science (pure and applied), Natural Resources and Industrial development). Thus, it subscribed to the so-called Haldane principle of a buffer between the government and the organisations conducting research.[151] This was opposed by the Secretary of State for Industry and the Lord President who wanted a closer link between those who undertook research and those who used its results. They argued that to separate the two was out of accord with the needs of a progressive economy where knowledge and its practical application should be diffused through government Departments and should inform policy making.[152]

The Wilson Government sought to square the circle, adopting the Trend recommendations for the arms-length funding of research and yet, creating a Ministry of Technology intended to support key industries such as computers, other electronics industries and machine tools and to secure the nation's research base, linking industry with applied research. But if the idea was exciting its execution was weak, notably in the appointment of two politically inexperienced Ministers, Frank Cousins, general secretary of the Transport and General Workers' Union, and C.P. Snow, a novelist whose main claim to fame were his writings about the science-arts divide. Neither lasted. By the end of 1966 they had gone, Cousins being replaced by the dynamic Anthony Wedgwood Benn as Secretary of State. Continuity was provided by the Permanent Secretary, Sir Maurice Dean, originally a mathematician and with experience in a range of customer departments for applied science. Trend's focus had moved on after the delivery of the report. As early as March 1964 when the report was dubbed the Trend report during an investigation into the emigration scientists and engineers he had commented that, 'I suppose it inevitable that my name should be tagged onto the Report to some extent. But it's not something that I like very much,' – civil servants should shun the public eye.[153]

First Impressions and Survival on a Slim Majority

Early indications of Wilson's pre-election assessment of the likely general situation he would face came from the Downing Street Private Office. For economic policy the most important need would be to reduce government dependency on the Treasury by establishing a triumvirate of economic departments comprising the Treasury, an economic planning department (the Department of Economic Affairs) and a trade department (the Board of Trade, Wilson's old fiefdom). Wilson also thought that the Treasury had lost control of public expenditure. The

Cabinet Office should give more expert technical briefing to the Prime Minister. On foreign policy Wilson was reported as sceptical whether the United States would keep to the Nassau bargain after the death of Kennedy. He gave the impression of wanting an independent defence policy but rejected the argument that possession of nuclear weapons was the key to a seat at the top table; he was opposed to the idea of a Multilateral Force and to aligning foreign policy with the EEC. A Commonwealth trading partnership could be a viable option for Britain but the home industrial base must be expanded. The report concluded that it was hard to tell what was political expediency and what Wilson believed was right; the strength of his convictions was obscured by the strength of his self-belief.[154]

On arrival in 10 Downing Street, problems from every continent poured onto the Prime Minister's desk. In Wilson's own words:

> 'The Chinese had, the previous day, exploded their first nuclear weapon ... There was a telegram appraising the situation in the Soviet Union following the overthrow, less than twenty-four hours earlier, of Mr Khrushchev ... There was a telephone call from President Johnson ... And, grimmest of all, there was the economic news.'[155]

But Trend knew that the urgent tasks were to agree the text of The Queen's Speech outlining priorities for the new Parliament and to settle on a programme of Bills for the Parliamentary session. He made submissions on each on 16 and 21 October respectively.[156] In addition, the Cabinet agenda for 22 October had items on the situation in Russia, the Chinese nuclear test, relations with Indonesia and with Spain, Northern and Southern Rhodesia and on a whether to resurrect the nationalisation of the iron and steel industry. Contrary to the expectations of some Ministers, the civil service had moved swiftly to support the Labour government and Wilson was particularly impressed, writing to Helsby to thank the Service for its response to the change of government: 'Never in the days of Bridges, John Henry Woods and the rest have I seen anything so impressive as all you have done in the past few days.'[157]

Scarcely less urgent was what to do about the dire economic forecasts. On the first evening in office the prime minister and economic ministers learned that the predicted balance of payments deficit for 1964, at £800 million, was twice what they had been expecting. Officials put forward three options (a) devaluation; (b) import quotas; (c) an import surcharge. The last of the three was chosen, on a temporary basis given the United Kingdom's dependency on world trade and the risk of retaliation. Trend's role at this stage, in what was to be a long-running debate over the future of sterling, seems to have been mainly confined to the practicalities of how to implement the chosen policy of imports deposits and its public presentation.[158] Thus he helped prepare Wilson's statement of 26 October on the economic situation[159] and attended a special ministerial meeting on the economic crisis on Tuesday 1 December where he picked up a remit to improve economic statistics that reported in July 1965 and led to the great expansion of statistical data under Claus Moser in the late 1960s and the 1970s.[160] He appears to have played no part in the decision to include the £800 million figure in the Economic White Paper that, in the words of Lord Croham, 'set a trail of a lack of confidence going.'[161] In the early part of 1965, however, Trend's briefing became more assertive, on 27 January heavily criticising as unrealistic the optimism of a Treasury paper for Cabinet on setting public expenditure priorities and on 17 February damning a proposed statement on government spending for 1965/66 as doing nothing to assuage the foreign markets on which the strength of sterling depended.[162] (With this latter point he cut across Harold Wilson who 'believed in doing everything by administrative techniques, not by market techniques.'[163]) Also, in both cases Trend's cautionary words clashed with the optimism of the new government. Cabinet approved the Chancellor's paper; public expenditure was to rise at 4.25% p.a. in real terms, anticipating accelerated growth in gross domestic product to 4% p.a. that did not happen and was later condemned as both unrealistic and too rigid: 'the essence of good planning is re-planning.'[164] The only concession to the Cabinet Secretary's warning was that in summing up the discussion, Harold Wilson said that: 'In assessing the programmes as submitted by Departments the Cabinet would also have to bear in mind the effect of their decisions in relation to public and overseas expenditure on the confidence of other countries in our ability to improve and strengthen the United Kingdom economy.'[165]

Wilson needed the support of the United States for the import deposit scheme to be seen to be appropriate. He travelled to Washington in December with Trend a member of his party. During this visit, despite the vulnerability of the United Kingdom to American pressure to send at least a token contingent of troops to fight in Vietnam, President Johnson's request was turned down by the Prime Minister.[166] A subsequent planned visit by Wilson and George Brown for April 1965 was blocked by the American administration and in July Trend was dispatched for talks with McGeorge Bundy[167] and Dean Rusk[168] that ranged wide over foreign policy and support for sterling, prior to a further visit by Wilson at the end of the year.[169]

Trend was also active in carrying forward Wilson's desire to see public expenditure better controlled through a forerunner of the 'Star Chamber' of the 1980s. He agreed with Otto Clarke of the Treasury the creation of a Ministerial Committee of non-departmental ministers attending in a personal capacity (badged MISC 64). ('Tommy' Balogh,[170] the Prime Minister's special adviser on economic policy was not a member and was also excluded from receiving relevant papers.) This reported to Cabinet in July 1965 emphasising that the government's attachment to a housing programme of 500,000 units p.a. together with linking some social welfare benefits to earnings would mean postponing the launch of the University of the Air (The Open University) and other adjustments. Trend pressed in vain for not taking the base programme as given: 'A "firm basis for future planning" is important but so is flexibility.'[171]

During the first Wilson Administration Cabinet met 106 times with 318 circulated papers – it was a decision taking-body. Already 24 hours after the general election, Trend submitted a draft of the Queen's Speech to open Parliament on 3 November; together with a possible legislative programme drawn out of the Labour election manifesto.[172] He warned that the capacity to introduce major programme Bills would be limited by the condition of the economy, the time required to reach collective agreement on policy decisions and the likely bottleneck of drafting by Parliamentary Counsel. Twelve days later, after intensive efforts by Ministers and officials, he could report that The Queen's Speech was substantially agreed and only a few queries remained on the legislative programme. This was the Rolls-Royce Cabinet system in high gear. Wilson later described the draft speech and legislative programme 'with all our major policy commitments and we felt it right to endorse them.'[173] Weekly meetings between Wilson and Trend looked ahead to future Cabinet agenda items;[174] with Wilson coming to depend heavily upon Trend, recognising his value from their early contact when Trend advised subtly on the formation of the 1964 Cabinet and laid out the parameters of *Questions of Procedure for Ministers* as they had been applied by Attlee.[175]

As an inexperienced Cabinet there were teething troubles over collective responsibility with Wilson backing Trend's unyielding application of precedent. Frank Cousins, probably the Cabinet Minister with least relevant experience, disassociated himself in the Committee on Economic Development (ED(PI)) from a pay offer to the staff at the Atomic Energy Authority, recording dissent in the minutes of that Committee but did not refer the matter to Cabinet as required by the Ministerial Precedent Book (of which he had probably no knowledge); hence he both had to accept collective responsibility for a decision against which he had fought without conceding defeat and was the person who then had to tell the Chairman of the Authority (Sir William Penney) of the decision.[176] On another occasion the two most important economic Ministers (Callaghan as Chancellor and Brown as First Secretary of State) disassociated themselves from a decision to publish a White Paper on the aid programme but were subjugated by an abrupt response from Wilson: 'The points made in your minute were fully deployed to the Cabinet and the decision taken was a formal collective one. I assume that there is no question of your wishing to dissociate yourself from it.' Trend, meanwhile, advised that with the development of the Cabinet Committee system the coverage of the term 'collective responsibility' 'might now be regarded as being rather wider than formerly.'[177] Similarly, when Richard Crossman, (Minister for Housing and Local Government 1964–66) challenged Trend's Cabinet minutes over the recording of a discussion of nuclear proliferation Trend is reported as using the immortal response '... we never do give verbatim what people say. We précis the sense and give the substance of what they say.' Nevertheless, in that instance Trend offered a compromise wording which Crossman accepted.[178]

It was this sovereignty over the administrative machine that enabled the Cabinet Office under Trend to coexist with the political Cabinets of Wilson's first Administration. It fell to Helsby, as Head if the Home Civil Service, to advise on machinery of government questions, including, of course, the creation of five new Departments: the Department of Economic Affairs, the Ministry of Technology, the Ministry of Land and Natural Resources, the Ministry of Overseas Development and the Welsh Office. But on matters affecting interdepartmental working Trend held the floor and did not readily welcome intruders. In May 1965 Peter Jay, then at the Treasury, started a study of the optimal arrangement of Departments 'to look systematically for evidence of constrictions in the flow of Government business in the past.'[179] His first report proposed a six-part classification of Departments in a 3×2 matrix (collective responsibility, co-ordination, policy formation × necessary under any circumstances, necessary under federated machinery of government). It did not please Trend who wrote: I have always found myself at rather a loss to express what I really feel' and then proceeded to demolish the Jay thesis as 'a highly theoretical exercise ... [which] assumes that the problems in question are problems of Departmental machinery – whereas, as we all know, they are at least as much problems of personal relationships. This country is governed by Ministers, not by Departments, i.e. by men not by machinery.'[180] The demolition continued:

> 'We have tried before in our history; and they have never worked particularly well – mainly, in my view, because what matters most to a Prime Minister in a moment of crisis is to have around him at the Cabinet table a sufficiently representative body of colleagues to make him feel confident that he has the support of his Party in whatever it is he wishes to do. I do not know how many men (sic) are required for this purpose; but I would not put it much below, say, sixteen or eighteen – unless a Prime Minister is prepared to take the very considerable political risk of operating in detachment from his Party political base in the House of Commons.'

It concluded with, 'I would certainly not endorse any approach to these questions, which implied that the Cabinet Office did not have a proper function to play in helping Departments to evolve a common policy. This is not at all the same thing as "itself forming a policy in competition with Departments"; and I do not think that it should be so regarded.'[181] (Though Wilson may not have entirely agreed since he hankered after a strengthened Cabinet Office to manage crises in a more direct way than Trend had shown he found comfortable.)[182] All three points were subsequently put by Philip Rogers to Jay's sponsor in the Treasury, Peter Baldwin. A similar intensity in defence of the Cabinet Office position in government emerged when the Labour government was about to introduce an Ombudsman, partly on the Scandinavian model, to investigate claims of maladministration. Trend argued that the Ombudsman should not have access to policy decisions or discretionary decisions by Ministers. Hence, the Ombudsman did not need access to Cabinet papers (or Cabinet Office papers) and it should be sufficient that Trend and his successors, as Cabinet Secretary, should be the authority to certify that a particular document related to Cabinet or one of its Committees and was, therefore, excluded.[183] In passing, it is interesting to note that such claim to impartial integrity sat alongside a comment that Trend was 'at a loss to understand' why some of the institutions proposed for exclusion should be so as 'many of them are both financed in part from public funds and capable of maladministration. But perhaps that is not our business!'[184] [Emphasis added]. His brief for the Cabinet discussion was that unlike in Sweden or New Zealand complainants should not be able to go direct to the Ombudsman as this would compete with the role of the constituency Member of Parliament whereas the concept was one of helping the MPs better discharge their constituency responsibilities. Finally, he added in a magnificent understatement, a scheme that will give the public access to the Ombudsman (by now called the Parliamentary Commissioner) only through Parliament may well be more acceptable to Parliament than to the public at large; and it would therefore be advisable that it should be endorsed by Parliament before any substantial public criticism had time to build up.[185] Later he added that the restriction to central government (necessary since local government was independent of Parliament) would not be widely supported either.[186]

A Ticking Time Bomb

Labour inherited the potentially explosive issue of Commonwealth immigration into the United Kingdom. Four years before Enoch Powell[187] made his infamous 'Rivers of Blood' speech warning against racial unrest, the outgoing Conservative government of 1964 had been grappling with the issue. In July the Home Secretary (Henry Brooke)[188] told his colleagues that he wanted to cut the net intake from the then 50–60,000 p.a. to 25–35,000 p.a.[189] Public justification for reducing the number of people admitted from India and Pakistan, in particular, would rest on the absorptive capacity of the economy rather than on social tensions.[190] One of the early decisions of the Labour Cabinet was then to commit to a review of the working of the Commonwealth Immigration Act with discussions with the overseas governments concerned.[191] Throughout 1965 the government struggled to find a public voice for its policy that would meet the concerns of British public opinion without incurring the wrath of Commonwealth governments.[192] Trend strove for the middle ground, arguing variously that permissions were biased in favour of dependants of those already in the United Kingdom, that special restrictions on immigration by East African Asians as they came under threat in newly independent former colonies would be racist, and that health checks should be switched from arrival in the United Kingdom prior to departure in the country of origin. Overall, his judgement seemed to be summed up in a brief for Cabinet in early July 1965 that the proposed tightening up on evasion of the immigration controls were practicable and modest in cost.[193] All this was, of course, before the storms that would hit the country in the late 1960s and 1970s as East African Asians were forced out of Kenya and Uganda.

A Small Nuclear Explosion

At the start of September 1965 Norman Brook (now Lord Normanbrook and Chairman of the BBC) contacted McIndoe in the Cabinet Office with a sensitive request. The Corporation had commissioned a television play about the likely effects of a nuclear attack on Britain, directed by Peter Watkins. Normanbrook was concerned about the effects that a showing of the programme might have on national morale and the likely demands for more expenditure on civil defence that it might trigger. Conscious of the stoutly defended independence of the BBC from political control he asked for a government view on whether the programme should be transmitted, adding that if officials were to advise against transmission the BBC would announce that it had taken a decision not to go ahead as 'it would not be in the public interest to show the film.'[194] At 4.30 pm on 24 September officials, including Trend, duly watched the film at the BBC Wood Lane site and on 6 October, after further discussion amongst the officials present, Trend reported their reactions to the Lord President and Leader of the House of Commons (Herbert Bowden).[195] The officials' verdict was that this was not a horror film, but that it grossly exaggerated the speed of escalation to nuclear war and was, thus, likely to cause unnecessary and undue alarm. The film was unfair in its portrayal of British Civil Defence (which was, in any case, already under review) but in reality the effects of nuclear attack could be much worse. It would be unwise to agree to a transmission of the programme but Ministers should see the film before giving Normanbrook an opinion, as the difficulty would be to find a convincing reason that did not look like government pressure on the BBC.[196] Harold Wilson then ruled that the government should not express a view on the showing of the film but that officials should give their views to Normanbrook privately.[197] By coincidence this happened on 5 November (the 360th anniversary of the Gunpowder Plot to blow up Parliament). Normanbrook said that it was his personal view that the film should not be shown and he would now consult further within the BBC, leaving Trend anxious lest the Corporation said that it took a decision 'after consultation with the Government'.[198] In the event, the BBC did not transmit the programme (though it was given private showings, including to Members of Parliament) and the Corporation's press notice said, 'This is the BBC's own decision. It has been taken after a good deal of thought and discussion, but not as a result of outside pressure of any kind ... the effect of the film has been judged by the BBC to be too horrifying for the medium of broadcasting.'[199]

Not long afterwards the government turned its attention to the future of broadcasting, in particular the prospect of a fourth television channel, possible extension of broadcast hours, the promise of colour television broadcasting and what to do about the future of light entertainment on radio. The papers on file point to Trend as conservative and patrician – opposed to a fourth television channel, preferring an extension of broadcasting hours to be used by the University of the Air; opposed to colour television, 'do we really want to increase consumer spending by as much as up to £100 million in the period up to 1970?' opposed to financing a music radio station to replace the BBC Light Programme by advertisements and concerned about the effects of television on newspaper advertising revenue.

The Election Won with a Sound Labour Working Majority

After 18 months of government, at the end of February, Harold Wilson moved to strengthen Labour's position by calling a General Election. Alec Douglas Home had resigned as leader of the Conservatives in July 1965 to be replaced by Edward Heath. The central theme of the campaign was, 'the Labour Government had done what it promised, and now needed the means to finish the job.'[200] At the start Wilson's personal standing, according to Gallup, was 20% ahead of Edward Heath; at the end it was a 24% lead.[201] The result was largely as expected, an overall majority of 97 seats. Throughout Wilson had stressed that Labour had shown that it could manage the economy better than the Conservatives. 'There is a great deal we have got to do, especially to make the country sound economically,' he claimed.[202] Trend agreed. Towards the end of April he identified no fewer than 10 priorities – four were about the economy (basic economic strategy, individual economic issues, prices and incomes, the role of the Department of Economic Affairs (DEA).[203] At this stage, six months before the unilateral declaration of independence by the Rhodesian Government, the split with Ian Smith[204] and his Cabinet which would take up so much of Wilson's time and political energy seemed to be containable, ranking last in Trend's list. In Trend's view, the focus of the Cabinet Office was the secretariat at the hub of the inter-departmental system to find workable compromises when Departments disagreed:

> 'Your concern is to see that the issues are processed up properly and that they finally reach Cabinet, when they've got to go to Cabinet, in a sufficiently compact, intelligible, clear form for the Cabinet to know what it is they've got to decide, what are the pro's and con's.'[205]

With the experience of how the DEA fared on the Whitehall battleground, despite having able and widely respected ex-Treasury officials such as Eric Roll, Douglas Allen, and Anne Mueller,[206] gaps in the machinery for co-ordinating economic policy had become more visible, notably where the traditional freedom of action of the Chancellor of the Exchequer was concerned. Early suggestions emerged that the Treasury should be split. On election day Balogh penned a recommendation that there should be a Bureau of the Budget and a Ministry of Industry.[207] He later also argued for centralising economic intelligence and forecasting.[208] Trend wanted the economic and scientific advisers (which included Balogh) more closely involved in interdepartmental work – probably partly in an attempt to lock them into the Whitehall process and to curtail maverick independent advice that might cut across it; and proposed better follow-up on committee decisions. '[The Cabinet Office] has carried a pretty heavy load since the last election [in 1964], which can perhaps be best illustrated – without, I think, any breach of proprieties! – by the simple statistical fact that, in 1963 (the last complete year of one-Party Government) we circulated 1,184 memoranda and serviced 387 meetings while in 1965 (the next complete year of one-Party Government) we circulated 1,591 memoranda and serviced 546 meetings.'[209] Wilson gave him 'carte blanche as far as I'm concerned. And don't stint yourself,' to increase staff. 'I should like to see the Cabinet Office machinery used more systematically to follow up decisions and to ensure that action is taken promptly and effectively. Centralised progress chasing is a technique which has to be employed with discretion if it is not to undermine the sense of Departmental responsibility. But there is room for rather more of it than we have recently had time to do.'[210]

Other adjustments to interdepartmental co-ordination included the requirement for all policy proposals put to committees to contain not just financial implications but also the implications for public sector manpower;[211] and an attempt was made to reduce the need for full Cabinet to discuss so much. 'The Cabinet Secretary has to deal with that endless upward surge of business, driving it downward as much as he can.'[212] The full Cabinet would meet less often and more business was to be settled in Cabinet Committee; following a successful political Cabinet at the Grand Hotel in Brighton (the first time that Cabinet had met outside London since the time George IV) when the Cabinet Office secretariat were excluded from the discussion,[213] the concept of 'political Cabinets' took hold. Then in April 1969 the Prime Minister announced in a personal minute to Ministers that they were expected to give priority to attending Cabinet Committees and that, in future, a Minister dissenting from a decision in a Cabinet Committee would not be able to escalate the issue to the full Cabinet unless the relevant Committee chairman recommends discussion at Cabinet.[214] A decision later modified informally at the request of the Chancellor (Callaghan) in relation to the Chief Secretary's position regarding the control of public expenditure.[215]

These were signs that a sizeable Parliamentary majority can be a mixed blessing. Whereas the small majority following the 1964 General Election had been a force to preserve at least the appearance of unity in the government, after the victory of 1966 the risk of leaks and dissention rose as Wilson strove to maintain a balance between the wings of the Labour Party and to protect his position against George Brown (appointed Foreign Secretary in August) and Jim Callaghan (who continued as Chancellor of the Exchequer). Trend advised Wilson repeatedly throughout the 1966 Administration about the damage caused by leaks. The first time was two months after the General Election, quoting three examples: British policy towards the European Launcher Development Organisation (ELDO) created in 1961 to develop a satellite launch vehicle; prices and incomes policy; and the report of the Court of Enquiry into the 1966 seamen's strike, and speculating whether Ministers should be subject to the same investigation procedures as applied to officials.[216] Then again eight months later when the Lord Chancellor (Lord Gardiner) drew attention to the risk of inadvertently giving journalists small amounts of information that could be pieced together. Trend responded that the proposals (which included severely restricting the flow of information) would threaten the smooth functioning of government but their intention was good.[217] In April he warned that 'although the leak procedure has hardly ever succeeded in tracing even one [leak] to a definite source, it has suggested from time to time that particular disclosures have their origin in unwise gossip by Ministers. The moral is that there is no substitute for absolute discretion and for great caution in dealing with the Press.'[218] But by October the same year he was warning Permanent Secretaries to tighten procedures around the protection of information by officials. In March 1968 he asked Wilson to restrict junior Ministers' access to Cabinet papers to be restricted to issues for which they were responsible. By the end of the year the position had become so bad that the Prime Minister told Cabinet that briefing of the press in ways which were likely to destroy confidence in the government had reached epidemic proportions over the past few days, '... if it continued he would have no alternative without further warning or further discussion to reconstruct the Cabinet';[219] and still leaks continued, with Trend finally giving vent to his frustration with a proposal to restrict junior Ministers' access to information to a 'need-to-know' basis, never to include Parliamentary Private Secretaries. Impracticably, he argued that attendance at committees by junior Ministers on behalf of Secretaries of State should be exceptional, limited to the relevant item(s) on the agenda and accompanied by a written submission from the Secretary of State giving his views on the issue to be debated.[220] Ministers who objected to a Cabinet decision as a matter of conscience, such as those against the National Lottery Bill in March 1968, should abstain from voting in the House of Commons or should be prepared to resign.[221] And where special permission was granted for a Minister to vote against a Bill as a matter of conscience (such as George Thomas, Secretary of State for Wales, on the Sunday Trading Bill) it was then illogical to insist that they stayed silent during the debate.[222]

In an early brief for Cabinet Trend drew the conclusion that the new Parliament would be less docile than that of 1964–66. Cabinet should be aware that pressure for more direct influence on the formulation of Government policy would not be satisfied unless Select Committees were organised to look at the whole of a Minister's departmental activities, which he thought 'doubtfully wise under our own system [of government].'[223] By November the Government were well on the way to an experiment on these lines, however, and Trend restricted his briefing to a series of questions about how the process would work, making no recommendation as to whether the Prime Minister should lead the discussion to one conclusion or another.[224] As preparations for the experiment proceeded he drafted guidelines for Ministers who might be asked to appear before a Select Committee. They could not be compelled to attend, but should accept reasonable requests to do so, confining their evidence to issues of policy not, for example, being drawn into comment about the implementation of policy by civil servants which properly should be addressed by the Select Committees to officials.[225] Similarly, in another early brief Trend identified that radical reform of the House of Lords was on the cards. The government should open up a debate on all-Party lines to decide the purposes the reformed Lords should serve.[226] The government committee looking at reform toyed with a two-tier system for the Lords, whereby only those who could commit to regular attendance would have the right to speak and vote. There was no logic in that proposal Trend argued – it would simply be a transitional measure to a House wholly comprised of nominated members. It would be better to accept at the outset that all the government required was a scheme that would give it a majority over the two Opposition parties.[227] A two-tier House with members who could speak but could not vote would undermine the credibility of the reformed House.[228] It was not the case, however, that Trend opposed all constitutional change. On one important issue – electoral reform – as the student protests of May 1968 escalated in France Trend argued that reducing the voting age from 21 to 18 could channel political energy into legitimate political avenues in place of demonstrations. He acknowledged that there was a risk that extremists would exploit the political naivety of teenagers, particularly perhaps through radicalisation attempts by some teachers and appeared to have a slight change of heart when the issue came up for decision at Cabinet, stressing that Cabinet should be satisfied that a reduction in the voting age really would combat tendencies to join extremist groups, otherwise it would be better to maintain parity with the age of consent (then still 21 years of age).[229] He also reversed opposition in May to Party labels appearing on ballot papers on the grounds that they would weaken the vitality of the link between constituent and MP when the issue reappeared in December.[230]

Domestic Policy – Economy

The second Wilson Administration started with Trend heavily involved with economic strategy, continued with struggles to manage public expenditure, prices and incomes policy and a proposal to reform industrial relations, ending with frequent and detailed involvement in rescue packages for failing British companies. The big question after the March 1966 election victory was, once again, whether to devalue sterling. International confidence in the currency was rocked by a six-week strike by the National Union of Seamen over a pay claim above the government recommended norm of 3.5% that led to a state of emergency after the first week of strike action. The BBC reported on 23 May 1966 that:

> 'The British government has declared a state of emergency a week after the nation's seamen went on strike. The new emergency powers will allow the government to cap food prices, allow the Royal Navy to take control and clear the ports and lift restrictions on driving vehicles to allow for the free movement of goods. Ports and docks around the country are becoming increasingly congested as ships are brought to a standstill by protesting members of the National Union of Seamen.'[231]

Wilson saw defeating the union challenge as crucial to the survival of the main plank of macro-economic strategy, control of prices and incomes. Unexpectedly, rather than strengthening sterling by demonstrating a determination to get the economy under control, international confidence was weakened.[232] Unwisely, Wilson declared on 20 June that the strike was the work of 'a tightly knit group of politically motivated men who, as the last General Election showed, utterly failed to secure acceptance of their views by the British electorate' and were now threatening the stability of the nation.[233] In hindsight it has been argued that the evidence for such a claim was anecdotal and weak. He has been severely criticised for making it.[234] Trend, despite close links with the Security Service, appears to have played no part in advising the Prime Minister to speak in this vein; his advice during the strike was essentially tactical and pragmatic – the possibilities of preventing price speculation as the effects of the strike began to bite;[235] caution over activating the Ports Emergency Committees to deal with congestion at the ports by prioritising the unloading of vessels.[236]

The strike ended on 1 July and the same day Wilson, Callaghan and Brown met to review longer-term economic strategy. Trend had already heeded a statement by Wilson during the election campaign; 'I hope no one is going to bring Sterling into this election ... Sterling should be above politics.'[237] Shortly after the election victory he advised putting the devaluation skeleton back in the cupboard in favour of either an import surcharge or an export subsidy, with a tax disincentive to employment in service industries provided by the proposed Selective Employment Tax.[238] Some former senior officials now argue that devaluation in 1966 might have worked;[239] but it remains unlikely that British industry had the capacity to expand exports to the degree necessary without draconian restrictions on domestic demand.[240] Other commentators have argued that the government's three main economic propositions were incompatible: the political necessity of going for a 4% p.a. growth target for Gross Domestic Product (GDP), maintaining the exchange rate and achieving GDP growth of even 3% p.a.[241] Deflationary measures in July 1966 effectively killed off the hope of 4% p.a. growth and with it indicative economic planning. Its sponsor, the Department of Economic Affairs, was then further weakened in August by transferring George Brown to the Foreign Office and replacing him with Michael Stewart, who Lord Croham and Jim Callaghan later described as having no rapport with industry or the unions.[242] He survived for only just over 12 months.

In June 1966 Trend submitted a long discourse on the case for a shock standstill on pay and prices to be followed by gradual adjustment to what employers and employees were prepared to accept[243] and the following month he again briefed that the economic situation had not changed, the reserves were still hemorrhaging, higher productivity was crucial and until the all-important improvements in productivity could be secured claims on goods and services had to be constrained. The only question was how quickly and how painfully.[244] So on the underlying question of devaluation, deflation or both, Trend sat firmly in the Wilson camp of using administrative techniques to improve the economic situation rather than turning to market mechanisms. After August, Trend's briefing on economic strategy veered between reassurance that the government was on the right path but needed to intensify the measures[245] and a growing realisation that domestic political pressures were mounting for reflation.[246] Underlying these swings was a feeling that, 'Until we know the causes, we cannot be sure of finding the right remedies and there is a danger that too much concentration at this stage on possible devices will lead to decisions that give the strategy a rather "hit and miss" air.'[247] (The devices concerned included allowing firms to offset 80% of the costs of industrial investment against Corporation Tax;[248] help for the motor industry, import savings in chemicals,[249] a regional employment premium to spread the burden of unemployment.)[250] By mid March 1967, though exports were picking up Trend warned that investment was still lagging and argued for a cautious approach to reflation.[251] This message was repeated in April,[252] again in May,[253] in June[254] and again in July[255] as Ministers started to turn their minds once again to devaluation – recommended by Trend in mid January.[256] On 26 June a highly secret discussion took place at the Economic Strategy Committee (SEP) on whether devaluation would accommodate higher growth. The only record of the discussion was circulated to Sir William Armstrong at the Treasury.[257] One fear was that without a surge in exports the only effect of devaluation would be to put up prices, particularly because of the importance of imported oil, and Trend pressed for a study to identify ways of reducing the dependency on oil rather than a plan to put it on ration.[258] Even now, however, he was reluctant to abandon the economic strategy, counselling waiting for more monthly economic figures before discussing a possible change in strategy, pinning hopes on a promising improvement in world trade yet aware that investment in machine tools (a precursor to increased production) was disappointing.[259]

On 13 November Trend advised that the external support needed to avoid devaluation could not be obtained from the International Monetary Fund (IMF) without politically unacceptable terms. Operation PATRIARCH (the code name for devaluation) should be put into a state of readiness with a deflationary package of £500 million that included abandoning raising the school leaving age.[260] Devaluation was eventually agreed. A 14% reduction in the value of sterling against the dollar (from £1=$2.80 to £1=$2.40) was announced on Saturday, 18 November 1967. During the previous week Trend kept a diary as events unfolded. He described the process of consultation with the American Government as 'the way in which diplomatic business of this sort should not be done.'[261] The Prime Minister had had a 'rush of blood to the head in the form of the projected flying visit to Washington' partly resulting from a hostile meeting of the Parliamentary Labour Party which left him 'doubtful if he could now hold the Party of Vietnam; nor … even hold the Cabinet any longer'; and partly from Cabinet having 'a clear desire to discuss devaluation' with 'hardly any support for a renewed effort to hold the existing parity.'[262] Trend continued, 'On both Vietnam and sterling the majority of his colleagues would now, I think, be disposed to opt for policies which, sooner or later, would carry us further away from the Americans rather than nearer to them … At the moment he has (I think!) got both his Foreign Secretary and his Chancellor of the Exchequer with him. But I am not certain that he could count on many other members of the Cabinet; and it remains to be seen whether the three of them, if they remain united, can outface all the others. (The "if" is, of course, a very big factor in the equation!) Trend had not heard of the proposed visit to Washington until around midnight by which time 'things had already got pretty far … And there was no point in trying, in the small hours of the morning, to mobilise any other support in an effort to stop the enterprise.'[263]

Finally, on 16 November Trend faced the inevitability of an exchange rate change, briefing Wilson that `[Cabinet] may come to the conclusion that more damage will be done by not devaluing than by taking the inevitable step.'[264] First reactions were muted. Trend reported that devaluation had been a technical success but had had no effect of French attitudes to Britain joining the EEC and the accompanying measures of deflation were only barely sufficient to satisfy the IMF whose support for Britain's economic strategy was shaky. Hence, the government should revisit its strategy for benefiting from the devaluation in the longer term.[265]

The PATRIARCH war book contains a draft of the Prime Minister's infamous broadcast of reassurance: '[Devaluation] does not mean that the value of the pound in the hands of the British consumer, the British housewife at her shopping, is cut correspondingly. It does not mean that the money in our pockets is worth [14%] less to us now than it was this morning.'[266]

In all this there is a contrast between sure footed comments on internal handling issues and vacillating advice on the central issue of devaluation at the centre of economic strategy. A further intriguing question is whether Trend knew of the public line Wilson was proposing to take to the British public - did he agree or did he seek to change the misleading reassurances it offered?

Edmund Dell recalled a conversation between Peter Shore (Secretary of State for Economic Affairs 1967–69) and Michael Clapham (President of the Confederation of British Industries 1972–74) when Shore asked why exports had not increased after devaluation. 'Because we don't have the capacity,' said Clapham. Why not? 'If you had given us two years' notice of devaluation we would have had the capacity.'[267] The government's economic advisers argued that technically there should be a stronger deflationary package so as to free resources for exports.[268] Trend suggested circulating their paper to SEP but as the Bank of England reported heavy losses of reserves (occasioned by speculation against the US dollar because of the costs of the Vietnam war) Wilson blocked circulation.[269] These losses continued throughout the first half of March and on the 14th the United States authorities asked Britain to close the London Gold Pool. Wilson, Jenkins (now Chancellor of the Exchequer) and O'Brien (Governor of the Bank of England) decided also to close the foreign exchange markets for 24 hours to try to defend the parity of sterling. The Foreign Secretary, George Brown, ought to have been involved too, but for disputed reasons was not found in time. This led to a furious reaction and a final resignation by Brown from the government. (He had threatened to resign many times before between April 1965 and November 1967 and may have calculated that so soon after devaluation Wilson could not risk losing him.)[270] Trend certainly thought so, telling Wilson that he thought Brown should stay in the government.[271] Wilson's own diary notes confirm this: 'Trend seemed slightly disturbed and thought I ought to put out a peace-feeler because he felt that some Ministers were anxious about the lack of consultation the night before.'[272] But Wilson had grown tired of Brown's brinkmanship and saw an opportunity to rid himself of the volatile colleague without opening up a policy wound in the Party.

More serious for the government was that the new fixed exchange rate might prove untenable. Floating sterling was likely to presage a plummeting pound.[273] Instead, contingency planning for the draconian step of blocking sterling balances and banning inessential imports, codenamed BRUTUS, were set in hand. Trend described the project as a response to a severe attack on sterling and the Dollar that involved accepting a major catastrophe to avoid chaos. It would mean a return to bilateral trade 'from which we might not emerge for a period of years,' but 'we cannot go on borrowing indefinitely.'[274] More deflation 'might not only entail a setback in production and employment but also lead financial opinion here and abroad to the conclusion that things are getting out of control again and so worsen the payments position, at any rate in the short term.' Contingency planning should be updated for import quotas and/or an import deposit scheme even though they would take many months to work through into the import figures.

The May import figures were worse than expected. Import quotas/deposits and BRUTUS were scheduled to be ready by mid June and a further project, code named BOOTSTRAP (to mobilise privately owned overseas portfolios) was set in hand. Conscious of the momentous step that BRUTUS and BOOTSTRAP would be (the proposal involved closing the banks for four days and prohibiting foreign holiday travel). Trend stressed that they should not be introduced if there was a fair prospect of borrowing abroad to ride out the crisis and there should be no automatic trigger point that would launch them.[275] Meanwhile, security should be tightened around the preparations – BRUTUS, for example, was renamed CRANMER in case it had been compromised. 9 July was set as the day on which the decision on CRANMER and BOOTSRAP would be taken. Showing ice-cool detachment verging on remoteness, Trend the economic administrator wrote, 'If we want the import deposit scheme to bite on the imports which we can forego with least damage, it will necessarily create serious difficulties for many businessmen; but this is the price which we must be prepared to pay.'[276] It must be doubtful if many in the government could have seen things in quite that way. In the event, 9 July came and went without a decision to implement CRANMER and the budget strategy of deflation started to show lower imports and consumer spending[277] though it had been and remained a close-run thing. Ministers recognised that action on imports could well provoke retaliation by overseas countries and Trend recognised that 'in the absence of some early collective action to recreate exchange stability we face a grim prospect ... we had better keep our contingency plans up to date ... in the immediate future, i.e. 1969, and over the next five or six years, we have no reasonable hope of paying our debts when they fall due.'[278] Further measures were kept in reserve – notably HECUBA which contemplated the exchange control and import restrictions necessary in the short term were a decision to be taken to float the pound.[279] If we introduce HECUBA, advised Trend, we should block all sterling payments to 'at least ensure that the horse stayed in the stable while we decided what to do about the door.' Work was needed on the posture to be adopted domestically and in politico-military terms.[280] As regards a possible IMF loan, the Fund's Letter of Intent would rule out import restrictions so there should be no mention in public of that possibility, even hypothetically. It would be better to prepare a stiff import deposit scheme even though experience indicated that it would not reduce imports, but at least it would improve the balance of payments by enforced loans from foreign suppliers.[281]

Short-Term Economic Management

Whilst at the DEA, George Brown had been noticeably successful in securing trades union and employer agreement to a voluntary national prices and incomes policy and a long-drawn-out battle to contain both wages and prices persisted through the second Labour Administration (paralleled in a struggle to control public expenditure). As early as 20 June 1966 Trend rehearsed the case for administering a shock to the prices and incomes policy through a standstill on both, to be followed by a gradual move to what employers and employees were prepared to accept.[282] Perhaps aware of the failed approach to the seamen's strike he advocated pragmatism in responding to the independent review bodies dealing with police, firemen, doctors, dentists and nurses and opposed lowering the burden of proof required for approval of price increases and of managerial salary increases.[283] As the election year came to a close his briefs on public expenditure became based on the judgement that 'As a nation, do we not have to start to earn our right to higher standards in public expenditure [and] to higher standards of personal living?'[284] Meanwhile, there were technical arguments to be settled about the treatment of transfer payments in the control of public expenditure[285] which 'must be looked at not only as a straight money outlay (as in the traditional Public Expenditure Survey Committee exercise) and in terms of its implications for taxation and the balance of payments ... but also in relation to its contribution to productive potential. (Public Expenditure now accounts for some 40% of GNP. It should clearly not be considered in isolation from the general examination of economic strategy.'[286] However, price stability should be the top priority of domestic economic policy, implying prior notification and evaluation of proposed increases by relevant Departments.) The French, he asserted, were finding that control of prices alone was sufficient without a corresponding control of wages – and this would avoid the risk of creating martyrs – 'we must push and prod the CBI and TUC into effective control of their members,[287] and the challenge is "to balance the desirability of achieving greater social equality against the danger of eroding incentives and holding back economic growth." '[288] If statutory powers were taken to reverse price and wage increases beyond the government norm they should be allowed to lie dormant because of the risk of showing the law to be unenforceable – it was vital to avoid bringing the law into disrepute.[289] 'Your own approach,' he told Wilson, 'envisaged that discussions with the Trades Union Council (TUC) on [prices and incomes policy] should be developed on rather gradualist lines, extending over a fairly lengthy period.'[290] In particular when he opposed taking powers to prevent wage and price increases retrospectively, he noted that Orders to prevent wage increases were more common than those to prevent price increases.[291] In the case of the gas, rail and postal prices, moreover, a proposal from George Brown that increases should be deferred pending an investigation of the potential for increased productivity, he argued that such action would damage management morale![292] Then, after devaluation, the whole policy should be reevaluated to see if a better voluntary system could be brought about – perhaps through the TUC suggestion of annual tripartite discussions of the pay norm (Government-Unions-Employers).

By March 1968 the government was beginning to get to grips with public expenditure control. Trend suggested to Wilson and William Armstrong the production of a monthly report for the Strategic Economic Policy Committee: 'The solution of the problem of effectively controlling public expenditure has eluded every Government since the end of the war; and the colossal effort which was required of the Cabinet in January is an indication of the obstinacy of this problem once it has got out of hand.'[293] Additionally, Wilson wanted to widen Ministerial consultation prior to the Budget, declaring that it was his view that the closed hand of the Treasury took over too soon in the process; suggesting that, 'This might be partly due to the former Chancellor's feelings about D.E.A., particularly just after the election when he nearly made it a resigning issue.'[294] With Callaghan's move to Home Secretary the opportunity arose to take another look at the arrangements around the run-in to the Budget. Trend speculated that if it were possible to disregard personalities a compact and coherent organisation for economic strategy would have one Department (DEA) managing the economy as a whole (finance and real resources) with no executive responsibilities but forecasting and prescribing action (e.g. disinflationary or reflationary) implemented by other Departments in an ancillary capacity:

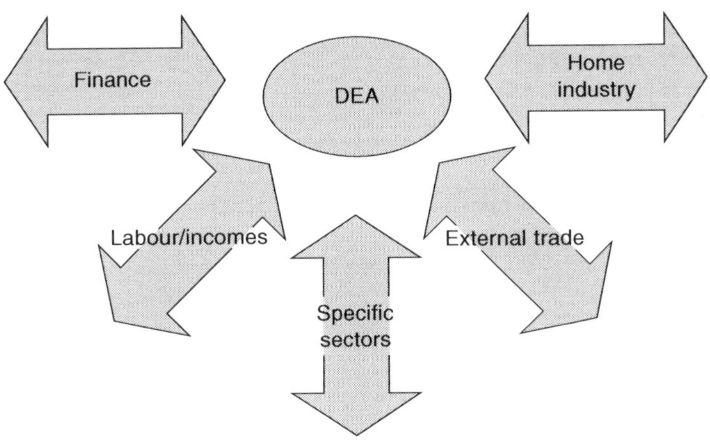

Hence, the Official Steering Committee on Economic Policy (SEP(O)) which oversaw the whole range of the government's economic responsibilities but had never discussed general questions of external finance, public expenditure or short-term management of the economy – 'for reasons which derive to some extent from personal factors' – might be made more effective.[295]

The first report on public expenditure was presented to the Ministerial SEP Committee on 6 May 1968 and made uncomfortable reading. Expenditure was running seriously ahead of plan and Roy Jenkins (the Chancellor of the Exchequer) wanted to curtail spending drastically for the rest of the year. Trend suggested that as 'It is regrettable that … projects should still be being pressed which, however desirable they may be in themselves, simply cannot be accommodated without corresponding cuts elsewhere'; to make offsetting savings in the same Vote did not make sense, the solution was to divide expenditure into blocks (Defence, Social Services, Assistance to Industry, R&D etc.) within which offsetting savings should be sought.[296] The planning of public expenditure was already done in this way; the next step was to apply the same approach to its control and might be introduced at the same time as any machinery of government changes following the Fulton Report into the civil service.[297] Meanwhile, the criteria for evaluating bids should be (a) the effect on the balance of payments, (b) avoiding increases in tax or charges, (c) reversing a serious imbalance of growth in public sector manpower (400,000 people largely working on ancillary tasks) and the manpower required for economic growth.[298] Even so, there were still issues outstanding on the 1968/69 totals in July (three months into the year);[299] discussion occupied nine Cabinet meetings. The next year, despite Trend and William Armstrong planning the disbandment of the DEA, was no better with seven Cabinet discussions and issues still being debated at the end of July.[300]

Structural Economic Change

From the middle of 1967 Trend's concern and involvement with the state of British industry began to grow. There were ominous signs that British companies would not be ready for increased exports. Machine tool manufacturers were not manufacturing for stock whereas importers were preparing for an upturn in demand by stocking foreign machine tools. The newly formed Industrial Reorganisation Corporation[301] proposed a machine tool hire-purchase scheme which Trend supported.[302] Nor did devaluation prevent the decline of traditional heavy industries such as shipbuilding, with increasingly frequent calls for government support to slow down the collapse of the Upper Clyde Shipbuilders (UCS) and others. In May 1969, despite the struggle to contain public expenditure, the SEP Committee agreed £3 million of support for UCS against the voice of Trend who argued that it was difficult to see how support could be justified on economic or commercial grounds.[303] UCS could not be seen as other than in decline and the initial £3 million of support was not enough to save it. A month later he supported the Chief Secretary of the Treasury in opposing another subvention, 'Can we seriously believe,' he wrote,' that another £5 million will do more than allow UCS to struggle on?' But he also suggested that whist 'No competent businessman would contemplate providing further financial assistance to UCS the Government cannot be guided by commercial criteria alone.' And he continued to doubt giving money to UCS: 'If liquidation comes, it will be as a result of a decision by the UCS Board not to accept a reasonable offer [of purchase] and a decision by the Boiler-makers not to give adequate assurances on pay and productivity.'[304] Further social payments to UCS cannot be justified 'as the company has been in serious difficulties through a boom time for shipbuilding and [ship] owners have lost confidence in it.'[305] 'As soon as the Government intervenes in the role of fairy-godmother, everyone else will sit back.'[306]

Yet, that one comment apart, it is difficult to detect a consistent economic or commercial approach in this and other industrial briefing other than to somehow consider each case on its merits (often acting as Devil's advocate) and on the basis of the quality of the submission put to the Committee. Thus, he advocated abandoning plans to take over the Beagle Aircraft Company when it became clear that its prospects had been grossly exaggerated and inadequate due diligence checks made on an agreement it had with the French Sud Aviation.[307] In January 1970 he dismissed Ministry of Technology proposals with, 'There is an air of rather forced argument and special pleading about the whole of the Minister's case'[308] (Tony Wedgwood Benn).[309] In February 'This is not the first time that the affairs of UCS have come before the Committee in some disorder; and I hope that you [the Prime Minister] may feel it possible to rule that it is not to happen again.'[310] A proposal from the Minister for Technology to award a contract for a police computer to the British firm International Computers Ltd (ICL) against foreign competition should not be risked because there was no guarantee that it would meet the performance specified.[311] Government policy to require foreign competitors to show a 25% margin in costs over ICL (and to deliver at least 12 months earlier) could not be justified publicly – and would undoubtedly leak.[312] For that reason it should not be revealed to a Select Committee unless a guarantee of secrecy was forthcoming.[313] British Leyland should not be protected against competition for supplying Army trucks from Volvo because of the high UK content of Volvo components.[314] Anthony Crosland's[315] idea of slowing the closure of gasworks because of a shortage of smokeless fuel was too expensive and too late.[316] To allow too much industry to fall under American ownership would harm British chances of EEC membership.[317] But it was also harmful to allow Continental firms to buy up British counterparts.[318] By contrast social assistance to the coal industry should be supported unless it was shown that allegations that coal workers would not accept jobs in other industries was proven.[319]

There are, nevertheless, a small number of examples of Trend acting to encourage new commercial ventures. In 1966 he favoured a government subsidy to British shipbuilders to enable them to compete for container ships on order from the consortium Ocean Containers Ltd (a forerunner of Maersk shipping and at one time, as P&O Ltd, the largest container operator in Europe.)[320] He briefly considered imaginative ideas for a third London airport on the grounds that 'The chances of avoiding a fourth airport would surely be a good deal better if we chose an estuarial site capable of extensive development,'[321] but nothing came of it. Inland Stansted was chosen as the site for the third airport instead. On the other hand, his encouragement of a merger of the airlines BEA and BOAC did see the light of day as British Airways, as did the development of regional airlines and support for the Civil Aviation Authority to be moved outside central government.[322] The Thames Barrier was another example of support for a good investment of public money.[323] Despite cost overruns and technical difficulties the Airbus consortium should be put on life support for four months to allow time for industry to sort out the problems since to withdraw from the project would be to abandon hope of a European aircraft industry. But Trend failed to recognise the potential for using the purchasing power of government as an instrument to improve efficiency in supplying firms – by the 1980s Marks & Spencer were well established as sovereign examples of what could be achieved in this way, but in 1967 Trend's view was that it was difficult to be inspiring over such an initiative.[324]

As the end of the Parliament neared, he reflected on the troubled experience of the past six years, that there was a need for three improvements: (1) a standard system for monitoring companies to which government assistance had been given; (2) a way of considering potential long-term liabilities, including the possible need for the government to honour debts – and whether the company was worth saving; (3) an awareness of how far the need for ongoing information would entail involvement in management of the enterprise.[325]

Industrial Relations

Faced with individual cases of industrial unrest Trend's natural caution came to the fore, urging that Cabinet should not take precautionary measures such as preparing to use troops in the docks whilst talks between employers and unions were continuing.[326] It was not necessary to declare a state of emergency in order to deploy them but the government should heed the risk of exacerbating the situation and must also be aware that the practicality of deployment could be limited because of the numbers of personnel required.[327] But he was also alive to improving labour relations – keen to end casual labour in the docks even before all restrictive practices were lifted and an advocate of worker representatives as members of the Regional Ports Authorities after nationalisation.[328]

When it came to reform of labour law, however, his view was that the First Secretary of State (Barbara Castle)[329] rushed things. The unions were not ready to accept secret ballots for union office and a 28-day cooling-off period for unofficial strikes in his view; and there would be pressure to use such provisions in unsuitable circumstances, leading to civil or even criminal proceedings.[330] He had already formed that view of Barbara Castle when the government contemplated an initiative on equal pay for women. Trend stressed the technical difficulties (how to define equal pay) and the likely economic consequences for incomes policy and for the balance of payments: 'to remove discrimination in pay on grounds of sex' as the draft policy proposed was vague and difficult to establish objectively.[331] By October 1969 he was warning that there was Ministerial unrest at extending union powers at a time when industrial unrest was rife and when the public found it hard to understand why the social welfare system subsidised strikes. Powers to require proper financial audit of unions were long overdue but any legislation on secondary (sympathetic) strikes would be best left vague.[332] As the 1970 Employment Law White Paper *In Place of Strife* began to take shape he returned to the theme of rushed preparations: The proposed Industrial Relations Bill was 'a courageous attempt to get a move on! But the Bill is likely to consist of at least 100 clauses; a good deal of it has still not been drafted ... it may need extensive Government amendment at the Committee stage. This is by way of a private warning. But while commending the First Secretary's zeal you may think it wise to warn her against too much of it.'[333] The following month he briefed against tightening union immunity from Tort and against penalties for failing to provide information on the grounds that there would be a strong reaction against the proposals from the Trades Union Congress. It was a far cry from the vigour with which he had greeted a rigorous incomes policy in March 1968 when he had argued 'If one has to be hanged for a lamb [one may as well be hanged for a sheep].'[334]

The Rhodesian Crisis

After the 1965 meeting of Commonwealth Prime Ministers there were hopes of a new relationship between the United Kingdom and other Commonwealth members; one that would move beyond the break-up of empire and acute sensitivity shown by former colonies. In mid July Trend forwarded to Sir Saville Garner[335] a proposal from Philip Rogers for a study to examine the scope for a new Commonwealth of equals that recognised that whilst Commonwealth members had no cohesive common interest, they shared certain cultural and professional values, including the importance of the English language.[336] Though constructive and far-sighted the idea all but disappeared in the face of the troubles in Southern Africa that convulsed Commonwealth leaders for almost 15 years. Labour had inherited a difficult relationship with Southern Rhodesia. The Labour Party offered a different stance from the outgoing Conservatives. It was more strongly antiapartheid and set greater store by the Commonwealth and the United Nations; it was hostile to European integration. It opposed the use of trade embargos for political purposes. But in Harold Wilson it had a leader who revelled in international diplomacy and believed that he had a unique personal relationship with international leaders.[337]

Wilson first met Ian Smith, the Prime Minister of Southern Rhodesia, at the funeral of Sir Winston Churchill in January 1965, forming the conclusion that Smith was intransigent and likely to go for a unilateral declaration of Rhodesian independence; hence British contingency planning should be started in earnest.[338] By early September things were looking bleak. 'Rhodesia is looking very ugly at the moment,' he told the United States Ambassador.[339] 'At any moment ... a situation could arise which would make the Congo look like a tea party. We might have to face the invasion of Portuguese territory by Tanzania, the problem of a Government in exile, the immediate activation of the United Nations and perhaps the destruction of Zambia before Smith went under.'[340] However, he ruled out the use of military force – an ad hoc Ministerial Committee (MISC 84) concluded that the only applicability of force would be to protect the power supply to Zambia from the Kariba Dam or to prevent civil unrest should the Smith regime collapse.[341] As long as the Rhodesian Government held Salisbury airport and Rhodesian troops were loyal to it rather than the Crown there was little chance of successful direct military action.[342] Trend reported that the United States Chiefs of Staff had come to the same conclusion.[343] Cabinet ruled out the use of force on 7 October, the day that Smith arrived in London for talks with Wilson. Those talks lasted five days. Trend's briefing was concerned with the aftermath of a possible unilateral declaration of Rhodesian independence (UDI, which he often referred to as IDI – illegal declaration of independence) – arguing that Britain should take direct rule of the rebel colony, even if that was more a matter of form than substance. He advocated financial help for judges and civil servants who refused to serve the rebel government, (ignored by Wilson who, fearing anarchy, advised them to carry on working); and expressed worries about being driven to use force. But he also challenged the Foreign Office view that the government should argue at the United Nations that this was a matter for the UK alone – '... we should not, certainly at the outset, abdicate our primary responsibility for dealing with the rebel government ... at the same time it is very much in our interest that any measures against Southern Rhodesia in the event of a u.d.i. should be, and be seen to be, a concerted move by the United Nations and not simply action by the United Kingdom to which the United Nations lends some support.'[344]

The talks of October 1965 ground to a halt with Smith saying that Rhodesians had no option but to take their independence. Subsequent evidence suggests that the threat of force may have caused Smith to back down but it seems clear that neither Wilson nor Trend had much inkling of this. On return from a last-ditch visit to Smith in Salisbury at the end of the month, Wilson broadcast to the world that 'If there are those in this country who are thinking in terms of a thunderbolt, hurtling through the sky and destroying their enemy, a thunderbolt in the shape of the Royal Air Force, let me say that this thunderbolt will not be coming.' Right up to the actual declaration of independence on 11 November 1965 Wilson saw Smith as a reasonable man, like himself groping for a compromise and willing to continue on with minority rule under the nominal control of Britain. Trend, who travelled to Salisbury with Wilson, did not contradict this. Possibly both parties doubted the willingness of their armed forces to fight 'kith and kin' in a surrogate civil war[345] and the British Chiefs of Staff were also concerned about the long supply lines through Zambia that would be needed. Furthermore, Wilson had concerns about the effect the use of force would have in the UK – the comparatively recent precedent of Suez was not good – the effect on a weak sterling could be dramatic, and he firmly believed there was an alternative to force – the efficacy and speed of economic sanctions.[346]

It was clear by 29 October that Wilson's personal mission to Salisbury had failed. Trend wrote to the British High Commissioner that, '... since the occasion may prove to be the final confrontation between the parties and the record may be published in due course, it seemed to be important that it should set out the course of the discussion *in extenso* and should indicate, so far as possible, what individual speakers had said.' He expressed the hope that history would adjudge the meeting to have been worthwhile but it is clear that he doubted that was so and felt that events were running away from the British. 'In the interests of saving time I am sending this [record of the meeting] by the hand of the B.O.A.C. pilot. I hope it isn't an undue risk in the circumstances'; he added, continuing, 'We had a pretty good trip home with very interesting discussions with Kaunda, Abubakar and Nkrumah, and an absolutely splendid time in Gibraltar, where all the local population turned out to line the streets and cheer!'[347]

Once home, preparations in the expectation of a declaration by the Rhodesians continued apace. Trend briefed on a proposal to compile a blacklist of Rhodesians disloyal to London (including a suggestion that United Kingdom citizens living in the United Kingdom who supported the rebel regime might lay themselves open to charges of treason), arguing that blacklisting was 'not the sort of area where it is fair, to anybody, that the decision should be left to administrative discretion'; the avoidance of ambiguity was vital. Other briefs concerned the possibility that UDI would be announced to come into effect at a later date, financial help for loyal civil servants fleeing Rhodesia and amendment of the Fugitive Offenders Act to prevent exploitation of asylum by conventional criminals.[348]

Rhodesian UDI was declared on 11 November 1965, triggering economic sanctions by the United Kingdom under which Rhodesia was expelled from the Sterling Area, removed Commonwealth preference and imposed a number of bans on Rhodesian exports (principally tobacco), financial assets and, ultimately, oil imports via the Mozambique port of Beira. At this early stage of sanctions, however, on 16 November in a brief for the OPD Committee, Trend argued against an oil embargo as too difficult to administer.[349] Wilson's belief that sanctions would be effective quickly was encouraged by a JIC assessment that certain sectors of the Rhodesian economy would be hit hard by January 1966 and that the effect on internal Rhodesian confidence would be evident by February/March.[350] Philip Rogers[351] and Trend accordingly presented Wilson with a proposal on Christmas Eve 1965 for a small Ministerial group (to comprise the Commonwealth, Foreign and Defence Secretaries) to work on a contingency plan to stimulate an alternative government to Smith. The proposals should be designed to make the maximum appeal to Europeans, consistent with what was wearable from the point of view of international, and especially African, political opinion. They should include how to find an emissary to send to South African, to whom Dr Verwoerd[352] would listen when asked to tell Smith that there was no future in the rebellion and that it would be better to quit now before irreparable damage was done to the Rhodesian economy.[353] Barbara Castle's diaries record Wilson's belief in the efficacy of sanctions.[354] At the Commonwealth Prime Ministers' Conference in Lagos on 11 January 1966 he went further and announced that, on the expert advice he had received, 'the cumulative effects of the economic and financial sanctions might well bring the rebellion to an end within a matter of weeks rather than months.'[355]

That was wishful thinking; particularly as the UK Sanctions Order only covered companies registered in Britain and did not apply to their foreign subsidiaries. Thus, South African and Portuguese subsidiary companies could supply oil to Rhodesia quite legally. This error was further compounded by over-optimistic economic projections from the Economic Planning Staff in the Department of Economic Affairs. Economic and political intelligence was thin on the ground and Trend tasked the JIC to improve its flow, using a covert action group working to a political directive which set the objective of policy as: '... to bring about the downfall of the Smith regime and a return to constitutional government and the rule of law in Rhodesia, with a view to the resumption of progress towards majority rule as quickly as possible.'[356] There were eight rules of political engagement: (1) a clear distinction was to be maintained between the rebel regime and the constitutional elements in Rhodesia; (2) it was not the British policy, and would be contrary to its interests, to stimulate black/white racial conflict; (3) the principal target for British action was the white community in Rhodesia; (4) at the same time African opinion outside Rhodesia must be convinced that British actions would be effective; (5) half measures would not be enough; (6) the public posture must be of complete confidence in the success of British policy; (7) the morale of the constitutional elements in Rhodesia should be bolstered; (8) actions that might precipitate war between Rhodesia and Zambia must be avoided. A Ministerial Group (MISC100/A) was set up to manage sanctions, for the first week meeting daily.[357] During the second phase, which lasted until April 1966, the hope was that sanctions would bring down the Smith regime; thereafter sanctions were seen as an adjunct to diplomatic efforts to find a solution.[358] British policy settled in for the long haul.[359] In February and March it was accepted by the British Government that hardship was inevitable for UK citizens in Rhodesia as a consequence of sanctions against sales of the Rhodesian Tobacco crop and the JIC reported that, though the Rhodesian economy was likely to be seriously affected by April, this should not be assumed to lead to a weakening of resolve.[360] With an election pending in the United Kingdom as Wilson sought to consolidate his position in the House of Commons, Trend briefed that at the immediate level sanctions were reasonably effective despite leakages in the embargo on oil supplies, but the government was losing the psychological battle. One difficulty, as Trend reported, was that Zambia was unwilling to close its border with Rhodesia for fear of the effect on its copper industry[361] and another that oil supplies from South Africa could easily make up the Rhodesian shortfall – 'if a pirate oil tanker reached [the Mozambique port of] Beira our oil embargo would be burst right open.' The best course, he thought, was a gradual progression towards the United Nations taking over the problem even though its involvement 'would be ineffectual and inflammatory,'[362] and even though a month earlier he had argued against such a course of action as a mark of failure.[363] Wilson was not persuaded, however, since the trap to be avoided was the imposition of UN sanctions on South Africa where British economic interests outranked the whole of the rest of Africa combined.[364] Meanwhile, whilst in principle Trend supported aid to Zambia to allow a 90% reduction in its trade with Rhodesia, when it came to sanctioning the expenditure he briefed only reluctantly in its favour.[365]

Handing over the Rhodesia problem to the United Nations was again considered prior to another round of talks between Wilson and Smith, aboard the veteran light cruiser HMS TIGER. A choppy Mediterranean sea seemed somehow symbolic of the situation. Once again Trend counselled that, 'there is no sudden and dramatic move which would enable us to transfer ourselves from the centre of the stage to the back row of the UN chorus.' Britain would remain morally responsible in the eyes of the world.[366] The talks ended in acrimony such that during 1967 a pessimistic Oversea and Defence Committee considered a number of further actions against the Smith regime, unable to decide whether a fundamental break was due or whether the hope was still for compromise.[367] The reports made to Ministers were not encouraging, but the Committee felt that the only course was to sit tight for the long haul as economic sanctions would only work if other nations were supportive in practice as well as in oratory – and Portugal argued, anyway, that most of the oil reaching Rhodesia came from subsidiaries of British companies.[368] Six months later it was indeed confirmed that British Petroleum and Shell were breaking the oil embargo.[369] Meanwhile, during 1967 and 1968 the central unit set up the preceding May as the Directorate of Economic Intelligence in the Ministry of Defence,[370] to collect information about sanctions-busting, reported widespread evasion from Japanese cars to American investment in nickel, from Italian aircraft to the activities of a German merchant bank.[371] It looked, at the end of 1967, that a long-term policy of disengagement, seeking to put the blame on the Smith regime, was the best option,[372] but then a Rhodesian decision to execute three black 'terrorists' (despite much lobbying from world opinion) put a stop to any idea that a deal between Britain and Smith might be possible.[373] Following a secret mission to Salisbury on behalf of Wilson by his solicitor friend Lord Goodman in August a further round of talks between the two Prime Ministers took place aboard the marine support ship HMS FEARLESS between 9 and 13 October 1968. Once again the talks failed and from this point onwards Harold Wilson lost interest in the Rhodesia issue. Smith introduced a new Constitution in February 1969 that further set back the advent of black equality and declared Rhodesia a republic in March 1970. The contest over the first five years of UDI was over for Wilson, though not for Trend, who carried it through to the Heath Government and until his retirement in 1973.

Disengagement and the NATO Alliance

Rhodesia was not the only part of the world where inhabitants had been encouraged to look to Britain as protector and many had defence treaties with the United Kingdom in return for agreements permitting British military bases on their territory. But the weak British economy dictated that resources were overstretched and had to be marshalled more selectively. Overseas defence commitments were where the financial shoe pinched most tightly and where the bulk of savings had to be found but all did not run smoothly. The War Book was updated to handle a fast-moving crisis (such as the Cuba crisis) as well as the slower build-up in Europe envisaged in the 1950s. Reform of the central organisation of defence had enabled the creation of a real Defence and Overseas Committee (OPD) where, in principle, foreign and defence policy could be unified and Trend battled hard to bring this about. As the Defence Review got under way in 1966 he argued that decisions on equipment should be taken on the basis of efficacy in supporting the military aspects of foreign policy and not on the basis of finance alone,[374] Those decisions would fix the shape of defence for years to come.[375] Arguments put forward by the Royal Air Force for the purchase of American F111A fighters put the cart before the horse,[376] and the draft 1966 Defence White Paper was a missed opportunity to show the interdependence of policies.[377] In contrast, the prospect of the end of confrontation with Indonesia over Malaysia would remove a major obstacle to the reduction of Far Eastern defence spending.[378] Rash statements should not be made that British forces would only remain in Germany if the full foreign exchange costs were met in full by the Germans and any withdrawal of troops should be minimal.[379] There should be no capitulation to Spain over Gibraltar;[380] nor was the time right to withdraw from the Persian Gulf;[381] and the Royal Navy could stay in Singapore if the Singaporeans met the costs of the naval base.[382] But, inevitably, much of his briefing concerned the orderly withdrawal of forces from overseas bases (from Simonstown in South Africa, from Aden, Malta, Swaziland, Cyprus, Libya, Brunei). The role of RAF aircraft was insufficiently clear in NATO strategy for a sensible procurement decision to be made;[383] the draft 1967 Defence White Paper did not bring out clearly enough the fundamental shift in policy to being only a European power.[384] And although the Cabinet Secretariat briefed against the need for a change of strategy after the Russian invasion of Czechoslovakia in August 1968 to put down the 'Prague Spring' rising,[385] Trend himself supported an increased British contribution to NATO in response.[386] In February, on return from a visit to Moscow, Trend had summed up the Russian leadership to Palliser as Brezhnev showing signs of affluence, Kosygin less ideologically bound and more pragmatic than the other leaders, Gromyko a born deputy but never a first-rank commander.[387] Nevertheless, the following year, at the time of the 20th Anniversary of the NATO alliance, he put forward thoughts on how to keep American commitment to and presence in Europe.[388]

It appears clear from the large number of briefs Trend submitted for the OPD Committee that he kept the goal of retrenchment in sight but was well aware of potential damage to the reputation of Britain as a reliable ally and determined foe. Thus, he supported as realistic a suggestion that the withdrawal of troops from Southern Arabia would be smoothed by giving Aden a guarantee of help against external aggression for six months after withdrawal; but he warned that the military plans to back up a pledge were undigested – particularly as permission would be needed to use the Masirah air base in Oman and no approach had been made to the Sultan.[389] He challenged the realism of obligations to the Falkland Islanders, suggesting that the United Kingdom should offer Argentina the opportunity of convincing them to become Argentinian,[390] arguing that the islands were impossible to defend against likely independent action by the Argentinian Government.[391] Communist provocation was becoming more dangerous but, wondered Trend, despite the help being given to the United States over Vietnam, could its assistance be relied upon should the going get really rough in Hong Kong?[392] An evacuation plan was needed.[393] Realism also dictated that there was a compelling need to stay out of internal conflict in Cyprus.[394] Throughout there is a strong streak of realism in the briefs, whether it be the almost certain difficulties at the United Nations if arms sales are made to South Africa[395] or arguing against basing POLARIS boats in the Far East (because of Australian opposition to having nuclear weapons in its territory),[396] or offering India military guarantees in the interests on non-proliferation,[397] or agreeing with George Wigg[398] that the UK was slipping into disarmament without thinking about the price to be extracted from potential opponents.[399]

Foreign Policy

By February 1968 the Foreign Secretary, George Brown, could advise Cabinet that the withdrawal from East of Suez completed the process of Imperial contraction leaving the UK with many commercial interests outside Europe that it would be unable to protect. The best hope was membership of the EEC and acting in harmony with the USA. Neither the Commonwealth nor a North American Free Trade Area was a viable alternative.[400] Inside the Cabinet Office Trend presided over a lively debate with members of the OD secretariat arguing that the strategy for 1969 and 1970 should be to keep the application to join the EEC open and meanwhile demonstrate a European outlook to show the Americans that the UK was essential to a stable Western Europe and to show Germany that the UK would be a reliable partner on European security and eventual German reunification.[401] There could be no foreign policy without facing up to the economic facts; the UK must rid itself of past attitudes to Germany.[402] Trend, himself, briefed in July in support of the Duncan Committee recommendations on the future of the diplomatic service that pointed to distinguishing between an 'area of concentration' (Europe and North America) and the rest of the world, adding that entry into the EEC would blur the distinction between home administration and diplomacy. The diplomats, he claimed, should be compensated handsomely for what they would lose.[403]

In his heart of hearts, however, Trend retained an emotional attachment to the Commonwealth. Back in September 1966 Cabinet had once again raised the question: what was the Commonwealth for? The percentage of UK exports going to Commonwealth countries was falling sharply, from over 40% in the 1950s to less than 30% in 1966,[404] with the economic future focused around joining the EEC. Savile Gardner took up the cudgels, to protest to George Brown about denigration of the Commonwealth in Cabinet discussions, referring to the monstrous way in which the Afro-Asian group in the Commonwealth had twisted the Prime Ministers' meetings into a pressure group on the United Kingdom.[405] Brown and other Labour Ministers were precluded from seeing earlier work in this area because of the conventions surrounding access to the documents of a previous (Conservative) administration. As the results of the new study started to emerge it was clear that although officials could think of a number of ways to strengthen Commonwealth bonds the crucial question had not been answered any better than it had under Norman Brook. Thus, the OPD Committee recommended, to enthusiastic support from Trend, greater Commonwealth collaboration in Law, Youth issues and the teaching of English, together with continuation of the favourable treatment given to Commonwealth citizens for migration to the United Kingdom and for acquiring British citizenship.[406] A year later he added the idea of Commonwealth citizenship.[407] This was not quite as abstract as it might appear. Back in February 1968 Trend had been warned by Harrison of the Defence and Oversea Secretariat that Kenya was discriminating against non-Kenyan passport holders over work permits. As a result, an emergency was likely as the 200,000 descendants of Asians brought to Kenya by the British in the nineteenth century as manual labourers were forced to leave. An Asian exodus from Kenya had accelerated with between 1,200 and 1,500 leaving for Britain.[408] In March, Trend briefed that the end of decolonisation was nigh and the government should not 'bend to sloganising,' but whilst 'we can no longer plan to give protection to Asians who are technically United Kingdom citizens in the same way as we can to those who have a real, as opposed to a primarily legal, connection with the United Kingdom ... it is virtually certain that Asians will be at least as subject to attack as Europeans, and perhaps even more so. In that event, would it be humanly possible for our forces to ignore the Asians [as was proposed by the Foreign Secretary] in attempting to save lives; and, even if it were, could we afford the political repercussions of doing so? Although we cannot offer full protection to all who have a legal right to be United Kingdom citizens we cannot discriminate on colour.'[409]

But establishing newly independent Commonwealth countries was troublesome, such as in Aden where planned independence at the start of 1968 and the vulnerability of the new state to external aggression pulled in opposite directions to the policy of disengagement East of Suez[410] the United Kingdom should resist pressures to extend the presence of troops on the ground in Southern Arabia despite the risks of a Communist insurgency; this would jeapordise the chances of stable government after the British left but was financially unavoidable.[411] Well established independent countries also brought headaches in the shape of a coup in Ghana in 1966 and the Nigerian civil war (1967–70) over the attempted secession of Biafra from the federation, neither of which was predicted by the government horizon scanning by the Joint Intelligence Committee.[412] On humanitarian grounds Trend opposed a blockade of the Biafran rebels even though the economic interests of Britain pointed to supporting the federal government to end the rebellion and restart the flow of Nigerian oil; and when the Secretary of the Commonwealth, the Canadian Arnold Smith, requested a British contribution to a peace-keeping force in February 1968 Trend was concerned that 'the force should be a genuinely Commonwealth force, not merely a British force which would entail our accepting sole responsibility for whatever it does.'[413] Remaining colonies, too, brought problems – e.g. the quarrel with Spain over Gibraltar and the future of the Falkland Islands. In both cases the wishes of the inhabitants sat like a roadblock across the track to decolonisation. In the former case, Trend saw no alternative to a referendum of the inhabitants over the future of the colony without any consultation with the Spanish Government[414] and at first supported planning a 'ladder of escalation' in retaliation for Spanish intimidation;[415] though he later changed tack in the light of doubts about where the money to aid the Gibraltarians would come from.[416] In the latter case, in the belief that the islands were indefensible[417] he favoured giving the Argentine Government the opportunity to convince the islanders to become its citizens.[418]

Relations with the USA

After the closeness of Macmillan to President Kennedy relations with President Johnson had cooled. Douglas-Home had stood beside the USA in foreign policy but had stood his ground in support of British economic interests. Many in the US were suspicious of a 'left-wing British politician' with Wilson's record on foreign affairs and disarmament. Nevertheless, Wilson's biographer describes, a symbiotic relationship existed with President Johnson. The President needed Wilson's support for American actions in South East Asia, for Britain to maintain a peacekeeping role East of Suez and to exert a calming influence on Commonwealth governments. Wilson urgently needed financial help to maintain market confidence in sterling and support in dealing with Southern Rhodesia.[419] In March 1967, before devaluation of the pound, Trend reported to Wilson that there were unofficial approaches from the Americans for a stabilisation loan to the UK of \$4–4½ billion.[420] The issue was far from clear-cut and 'although its origin, status and scope are obscure and it cannot by any means be described as declared Unites States policy, we must take it seriously.' The dilemma was that the more Britain took on debt, the stronger would be the American pressure to retain a British military presence East of Suez, ('designed to persuade us, once again, to live beyond our means,' as Trend put it) and the bigger the risk that the French would see it as another example of Britain's dependence on the United States, justifying their veto of British membership of the EEC. 'There is a great deal of self-interest in this [American] thinking – in the sense that the Americans are concerned for their own sakes that they should not be left alone in the world, particularly East of Suez. But the motive is not the less respectable for that.' If Britain were to reject the American advances, however, 'as the Americans have put it – "If Britain says 'No', with great regret we shall attend at your funeral."' The UK should continue to show interest in the suggestion but it would probably be a mistake to promote any kind of high-level discussion about it, though in early 1968 President Johnson protested at the withdrawal plans East of Suez (and the cancellation of orders for F 1–11 planes).[421] Shortly afterwards Trend sent Wilson a paper from the American economist Robert Roosa[422] which speculated about a possible North Atlantic trading association.[423]

The Vietnam War was another sore point. Trend had been in Wilson's party to Washington in December 1964, during which Wilson had skilfully avoided President Johnson's request to send token UK troops to the conflict despite his need for American financial support for sterling.[424] The following year, further visits by Wilson (and Brown) were blocked because of American sensitivity over Vietnam[425] but Trend was received in July for talks with McGeorge Bundy, Dean Rusk and Henry Fowler (Secretary of the U.S. Treasury).[426] The talks were wide ranging. Those on foreign policy covered Vietnam (the Prime Minster was still thinking about the President's request) and South East Asia (the confrontation with Indonesia was Britain's contribution to stability); the Middle East (how far was a military presence required to ensure the supply of oil at affordable prices and were the English-speaking countries carrying too much of the burden compared to the French-speaking countries?) and Indian subcontinent (there were too many non-aligned countries in the Commonwealth to use it as a lever against Indian nuclear ambitions; Pakistan was acting in such a way to make it hard to justify continued aid); Africa (where it was agreed that, with the exception of humanitarian action, too much attention had been focused on troubles where there was likely to be disorder and unrest for some years to come); Germany and Europe (it was 'important to get the Germans properly on board' i.e. aligned with US and UK interests); arms sales by Britain to the United States (where the only satisfactory course would be for the British to deal directly with Robert McNamara on a case-by-case basis); nuclear non-proliferation (an agreement with the Russians was unlikely in the short term); Britain's role in the world (where the Americans argued that reducing commitments East of Suez would not make sterling secure and that Britain's position in the world depended on her playing a full and active part. Trend countered that strengthening of the British economy did not depend simply on financial relief to the balance of payments; it was also a question of redeploying real resources more effectively); and the special difficulties of dealing with France under de Gaulle; (where the French should be given reasonable opportunities to join in, but if they chose not to do so Britain and the U.S. should, with the other western countries, proceed together). The talks on economic affairs dealt with support for sterling (Trend argued that 'the longer-term economic situation should not be elbowed aside too far by the purely psychological need to reassure international holders of sterling in the immediate future' and agreed that 'the Incomes Policy was taking time to show results, but stressed the increasing irritation of H.M. Ministers with labour attitudes.' Continuing talks with the U.S. authorities should take place 'in the wider interest of future politico-military policies.') He ended the report to the Prime Minister with three 'very clear impressions': (i) the Americans sympathise very much with our efforts to reorganise the British economy ... and provided that we do not take any drastic action which leaves them in the lurch will do all they can to help us; (ii) but they are alarmed that speculation against sterling may get out of hand; (iii) they believe that wages and prices must be brought under greater control such as by a freeze. A further visit took place in December, this time concerned with the

Rhodesian situation, Germany, and to explain the likely outcome of the British defence review.[427] There was no point in Britain as a world policeman without a truncheon.[428] Meanwhile, other Whitehall briefing continued to recommend that Britain should identify with the American cause in Vietnam. Michael Palliser thought that the Chinese behaviour in the Cultural Revolution was strengthening popular support for the Americans in Vietnam.[429] An October paper by the Foreign Office was so pro the United States stance that Trend thought that it might provoke 'anti-US sentiment at a time when we will soon need practical US financial help.'[430] Briefing for Cabinet two weeks later he spelt out the risks more clearly. 'To come out more strongly on the American side would be politically unacceptable "yet 'to turn against the Americans publicly would have disastrous effects.'" There was no option but 'committed detachment.' The arguments against this position would be moral arguments and 'There is little doubt that the United States' failure to match the Communist propaganda ... is a as serious in its effects, both at home and abroad, as their inability to achieve quick military victory in South Vietnam.'[431]

The irony was that the United Kingdom needed American support to maintain the value of sterling but the quid pro quo sought was maintaining a military presence East of Suez and to do that would simply exacerbate the balance of payments problem. Further, the British wanted part of the American support to be in the form of purchases of British military equipment but, as Trend was advised during the talks with Bundy and Rusk, the Pentagon was highly resistant to using other than home-grown military equipment such that the only course likely to bring success was to lobby directly at the Secretary of State for Defense (Robert McNamara).[432] As Wilson's biographer concludes, Britain had become a client of the United States, no longer a partner.[433]

Europe

It has been written of Harold Wilson that, 'Wilson's personal preference was for a new emphasis on the Commonwealth, and an expansion of Commonwealth trade. The Prime Minister had an attachment to the old dominions.'[434] The same could have been said of Trend who saw the Commonwealth as a potentially benevolent influence in the world, shaped by Britain and the Dominions. But the splits over Rhodesia and South Africa put an end to that notion and the period 1965–67 saw important aspects of Trend's briefing dancing to a European tune. The British relationship with France is a case in point. In March 1965 his advice was to play for time with de Gaulle, building functional links with the Six EEC countries without rushing to an association with them.[435] There should be no declaration of intent to reapply for EEC membership.[436] So when, early in 1966, de Gaulle announced that France would no longer assign its armed forces to NATO and would withdraw from the integrated NATO command structure in favour of full independence (the French Navy had been withdrawn from the Atlantic command in the summer of 1963) and allied military forces and headquarters should leave the country by 1 April 1967, Trend's first thoughts were that the

UK must show a determination to increase the cohesiveness of the remaining NATO forces and should also try to get US and Canadian bases relocated to Britain though he thought that it would be difficult to relocate the SHAPE Headquarters to London.[437] As an expression of solidarity with NATO he further advised Wilson that the extent of joint participation with France in military hardware projects and normal staff talks should be frozen.[438]

Meanwhile, a Chequers Cabinet discussion on 22 May had answered Trend's Socratic question, 'Do we need a European partner?'[439] with a majority decision that Wilson and George Brown (Foreign Secretary) should tour the capitals of the Six to see if the conditions were ripe for a possible new negotiation to enter the EEC. What alternative course to re-applying to join the EEC is open to us?' he reflected; decisions were needed on the mechanics of negotiation, the reassurances to be sought and an understanding of how far it would be possible to overrule the European Commission in the last resort.[440] The two Ministers should keep at the forefront of their minds the distinction between exploration and negotiation.[441] France was key to the process. Before the Prime Minister and Foreign Secretary set out Trend briefed that 'We have reached the point of no return on [the supersonic passenger aircraft project] Concord' (without the French 'e' at this stage); that it would cost as much to withdraw as to continue so, unless the French wanted to back out, the best plan was to look for ways of spreading or further limiting costs.[442] Similarly, at the end of 1966 he opposed a proposed American takeover of the Rootes motor vehicle company as too much industry was falling under US control and harming the chances of EEC entry;[443] and in March 1967 he maintained that the European Airbus project was important in retaining a degree of independence for a European, and therefore British, aircraft industry by keeping the ability to produce subsonic medium-range passenger aircraft.[444] For someone who was not personally enthusiastic about the EEC this was wholehearted compliance with the constitutional relationship between ministers and civil servants and illustrates the best traditions of the Northcote-Trevelyan concept.

Wilson, in particular, returned from the discussions with the Six optimistic, though Trend thought that, 'There is, of course, no prospect of [a guarantee of entry],'[445] noting that 'the Six went beyond the letter of the law and told us what they are getting away with (e.g. on regional policy).'[446] Trend's assessment was that 'we will have to face an extra strain on the balance of payments in the short term but our main impression is that the answer is not to be considered in economic terms alone.' He continued, 'It was your exposition of the larger role which an enlarged Community might play in the world, as the only European unit with sufficient political, economic and technological strength to achieve real independence and equality with the super powers, which gave the Six a new light on both our intentions and on our potentialities as a member of the Community.'[447] In reporting to Cabinet on the talks it would, however, be important to insist that Ministers were realistic in setting negotiating parameters and to keep in mind that it would be sensible to wait and see what the Commonwealth wanted out of the negotiations without jumping to conclusions. As to the

Common Agricultural Policy, which had become something of a bête noire in the public mind, the superiority of the British agricultural support system had been oversold.[448] The Prime Minister should be aware, however, that Continental doctrine and practice in legal and constitutional matters often differed, with the doctrine representing aspiration rather than reality; the former being prepared internally in government with no outside input.[449]

By the second half of April Cabinet discussions on the EEC were becoming fraught, with clear water between those who thought 'never,' those whose position was 'not yet' and those who argued for 'now.' An Atlantic Free Trade Area was not yet a runner and was unlikely unless there was a major disaster in relations between the USA and the EEC. The government economic advisers were against EEC entry, the permanent secretaries in favour. Trend was severely critical of the former – the decision was political not technical. His political judgement was that there was no reason why the Commonwealth should be a barrier to entry. Nor was immigration likely to be a problem. There would be a progressive limitation on national sovereignty, though the Law Officers advised that where there was a conflict the courts would back UK legislation and if it ever came to a question of leaving the EEC, whilst technically a member could not withdraw under international law, the courts would almost certainly back a decision of Parliament: '... there is in theory a risk of conflict between Parliament and the community in that there is no constitutional means of ensuring that no future Parliament would in fact legislate in conflict with community law (though, if it did, the Law Officers think that the courts would apply that legislation. They take the view, however, that this is purely a theoretical possibility which could only arise in practice in circumstances in which the United Kingdom had in any case decided to break with the Community.'[450] Nevertheless, was it wise for the Prime Minister to go so far in saying that 'our minimum conditions [for entry] should be negotiable and, indeed, should make it very difficult for the Six as a whole to reject our application?'[451]

He continued to brief in favour of co-operation with France – for example, on the development of a variable-geometry military aircraft despite reservations about cost control and on the joint development of military helicopters, where the case was much stronger because the British needed French know-how.[452] (Ironically France withdrew from the former project on cost grounds in July 1967, whilst the British struggled to establish firm cost estimates and faced inescapable increases in the costs of the helicopter project in November 1969.)[453] In vain; de Gaulle again blocked the British with a humiliating statement that entry to the EEC would be be earned: '[when] this great people, so magnificently gifted with ability and courage, should on their own behalf and for themselves achieve a profound economic and political transformation which could allow them to join the Six Continentals.'[454] De Gaulle delivered the formal French veto at a large press conference in late November 1967. Shortly before, partly on legal grounds, Trend had again advised that, 'we should now be ready to declare our support for the [Concord] project and to discount rumours of its impending cancellation' despite the then unresolved technical challenges of sonic boom, engine noise, weight growth and runway loading; and what he called 'far from rosy' economic prospects.[455] As to NATO, a French decision to leave the Alliance altogether was expected in 1969 so Trend argued that no British initiative about the Alliance should be taken before a meeting of the EEC Council of Ministers scheduled for 18/19 December 1967. Thereafter, Britain would have to choose between trying to maintain the American involvement in Europe (i.e. the Atlantic character of NATO) and trying to evolve a more specifically European system of European defence.[456] Britain should stress to the Germans that it would not accept a half-way house; it was all or nothing on the EEC.[457] The strategy should be to let the Five deal with the French intransigence and to play things long.[458] Even though the European space organisation was wasteful and technologically unsound, to withdraw would damage the UK's European credentials[459] and, in any case, defence practice was becoming more European as Britain withdrew East of Suez and in the light of events in Czechoslovakia.[460] There was a momentary hiccup in June 1969 when de Gaulle announced his retirement and Trend feared that Anthony Crosland would use the opportunity to reopen the EEC debate ('neither practicable nor desirable')[461] but the danger passed and the patient strategy eventually paid off, though by then Wilson had gone and the Conservative Party leader Edward Heath had become Prime Minister.

Secrecy and Privacy

At home pressures for greater openness in government affairs started to build; in July 1967 the government reduced the 50-year rule for access to official papers to 30 years[462] but political memoirs continued to be a thorn in its side and the leaking of information continued. The operation of the D-notice system to protect national security came under challenge. Trend was, at best, a reluctant party to greater openness, of the view that 'Contemporary history is all very well – but not at the price of undermining contemporary government,'[463] and he avoided contact with the press wherever possible. In June 1965 he opposed a suggestion from the Central Statistical Office (CSO) that it should publish commentaries on recent economic statistics in what became the CSO publication *Economic Trends* – on the grounds that to do so would threaten the public perception of the civil service as politically neutral. (The CSO technically came under him as an, albeit slightly detached, part of the Cabinet Office).[464] And when *The Sunday Times* made the innovative appointment of Anthony Howard as the first Whitehall correspondent (outside the Lobby system which provided journalists with official briefings) with a remit to seek out what really happened in government, neither Wilson nor Trend viewed the initiative positively. In February, the Prime Minister banned contact with Howard: Ministers should refuse him any facilities for fulfilment of his task.[465] Howard was forced to abandon the role, leaving Wilson to boast that he had 'seen off the animal' with 'his tail between his legs.'[466] Wilson's subsequent written warning to Ministers not to see the press unless accompanied by a Government Public Relations Officer was, however, against Trend's advice.[467]

He continued to be deployed to vet publications by ex-Ministers, with little success. In September 1966 he sought to exclude direct quotations from the former Labour Defence Minister's book, *Britain's Role Tomorrow*.[468] Mayhew simply asked for an official letter with the request and said that he would release it to the press.[469] Then, at the end of the year, he heard that the family of Maurice Hankey had commissioned an official biography of the former Cabinet Secretary and Minister, to be written by the naval historian Captain Stephen Roskill.[470] This, he thought, was technically compliant with the rules on disclosure since the 30-year rule would be in force by the time of publication; but he had discussed the prospect with Lord Normanbrook and both 'regard the prospect with a certain instinctive distaste' because it may revive controversies and 'cast doubt on the integrity and impartiality of the Secretariat which serves Ministers collectively and in a confidential capacity.[471] What was missing was a clear set of rules for what was permissible. 'An individual, who has carried in his own person, public responsibility for the management of public affairs ... is entitled to defend his record' but not at the expense of those currently carrying that responsibility.[472] Perhaps, wondered Wilson, Minsters should be required to sign something to say that they were aware of existing conventions and would comply with them.[473]

The next challenge came from the former Foreign Office Minister, Anthony Nutting, who had resigned in opposition to the Suez policy in 1956 and had now written an account of the events that led him to sacrifice his political career. 'Either I had to tell the whole story as I saw it, or say nothing at all,' he wrote. 'And as long as any of the chief protagonists of the Suez war still held high office in Britain it would clearly have been a grave disservice to the nation, which they still led and represented in the councils of the world, to have told the whole story.' Trend persistently opposed reopening the wounds. Six years later he opposed the commissioning of an official history of the Suez campaign as likely to open a floodgate of damaging revelations.[474] For now, his submission to Wilson on Nutting's book confessed that, 'I have found it extremely difficult to write and I have done my best throughout this affair to concentrate on what I believe to be my official duty without any regard to party political advantage or disadvantage, either way,' and went on to advise that the text offended against collective responsibility and threatened foreign (i.e. US) relations.[475] In a five-page reply, two days later, the Prime Minister said, 'I have now read ... the greater part of the book. I agree entirely with the line taken in your minute ... I take it that we have no sanction, apart from the brittle deterrent of the Official Secrets Act ... My anxieties both on international repercussions and on the position of Civil Servants relate more to the precedent that will be set by someone even more unscrupulous, and more speedy with his pen, than Nutting.'[476] Trend then asked Nutting not just to amend some of the text, but also to delete complete passages.[477] Nutting refused saying, 'This is as far as I am prepared to go,'[478] leaving Trend and the Prime Minister to decide whether to seek an injunction to prevent publication on the grounds of the national interest. Wisely they came down against,[479] which allowed *The Times* to serialise the book. Its editor,

William Rees-Mogg saying that we published because 'the constitutional duty not to deceive Parliament supersedes any other constitutional convention. A Prime Minister who plans to deceive Parliament cannot therefore claim the benefit of the secrecy of his colleagues.'[480] Trend refused to issue any form of counter statement,[481] telling a sceptical Wilson who thought that Rees-Mogg had a point[482] that, 'I cannot think that the Government will acquire anything but credit from upholding [the proprieties].'[483] If pressed, Trend conceded, the government would deny that Nutting had been given permission to publish.[484] There was no agreement whether the amendments sought by a Cabinet Secretary must be accepted by authors; 'Ministers' goodwill rather than written undertakings, must be the main safeguard.[485] They must accept or reject any changes that the Cabinet Secretary requested at their own risk.[486]

Concurrent with the trouble over Nutting's book, Trend was caught up in a more damaging episode. On 15 February 1967, an article in the *Daily Express*, written by Chapman Pincher, alleged that in 1961 the Labour leadership had tried to use MI5 to track down crypto-Communist Members of Parliament.[487] Wilson, now Prime Minister, asked if there was enough evidence to justify surveillance of Lohan, to be told by Roy Jenkins, the Home Secretary, that there was not.[488] By coincidence, the following day another Pincher article for the *Daily Express* claimed, 'thousands of private cables and telegrams sent out of Britain from the Post Office or from commercial cable companies are regularly being made available to the security authorities for scrutiny.' Pincher had a good relationship with Colonel 'Sammy' Lohan, the secretary of the D notice committee – a voluntary arrangement between the Ministry of Defence (MOD) and the Press whereby the latter agreed not to publish information identified by the Ministry as damaging to national security. A D notice was the mechanism through which the Ministry sought suppression of information. The government suspected that Lohan – who had a reputation for hard drinking – had tipped off, or inadvertently revealed this information to Pincher. Eighteen months earlier Trend had expressed doubts about the suitability of Lohan for his post.[489] He had disclosed to Wray, the MOD chairman of the Committee, in March 1966 that he had 'a feeling of residual dissatisfaction' because 'the balance of advantage probably inclines in favour of leaving [Lohan] where he is.' Somehow the letter was given to Lohan, either by mistake or by Wray.[490] Not surprisingly, it rattled Lohan, who then wrote to Wray, 'I must say that Burke Trend's letter was not the most joyful thing to start a Monday morning on … It really is disheartening to think he still dislikes me enough to wish to get rid of me. I wonder where the acid comes from.' Wray replied the same day, 'Don't take Burke's apparent hostility seriously at this stage. In fact he himself is not hostile and is now content.'[491] So much by way of background.

Three days after the cable vetting story broke, under acute Parliamentary pressure from the House of Commons, Wilson appointed a committee of inquiry under Lord Radcliffe 'to examine the circumstances surrounding the publication of an article in the *Daily Express* of 21 February entitled "Cable Vetting Sensation" in relation to the "D" notice system; and to consider what improvements, if any, are required in that system in order to maintain it as a voluntary system based on mutual trust and confidence between the Government and Press in the interests alike of the freedom of the Press and the security of the State.'[492] Whilst the committee was still at work, *The Spectator* published further references to the cable-vetting story, arguing that it was not covered by a D notice because it was 'a known method carried out in secrecy' not a secret method.[493]

Radcliffe reported late in May and was ready for publication by 12 June. To Wilson's dismay the committee had cleared Pincher of wrongdoing and he was loath to accept this judgement.[494] Nevertheless, in his and other Ministers' views the report would be seen as a cover-up if its findings were to be published without the evidence leading to them, as Trend wished.[495] At this point Trend told Wilson that he'd been unhappy with Lohan since 1965 but had not found a way to remove him.[496] Now he was not happy with the criticism of Lohan implied by the planned government to the report and he advised playing down the whole business.[497] Wilson, however, believed that Lohan had been part of a right-wing Conservative plot to remove him and hinted at this in the House of Commons. Events moved swiftly. On the 15th, at a Downing Street meeting it was decided that Lohan's handling of the cable-vetting story with the press and television had broken the rules of behaviour expected of a civil servant and he was sent on immediate paid 'gardening leave' pending a disciplinary hearing.[498] The following day Dunnett (PUS at the MOD) reported that Lohan would resign. Once again Wray seemed to feel that Lohan was being made the scapegoat for the government's political embarrassment. He wrote to Wilson's Principal Private Secretary (Michael Halls) to say that there had been no evidence from Positive Vetting (PV) that Lohan had leaked to Pincher. How solid this evidence was might be questioned, however, because, the D notice post did not require PV clearance and the process was not taken to its final stage when a recommendation would be made.[499]

To clear the air after further criticism, this time from the Opposition leader, Edward Heath, Wilson announced that, 'I am setting in motion an appropriate impartial procedure to enable Colonel Lohan, if he so wishes, to deal with government statements which he considers unfair.' Sir Lawrence Helsby, Head of the Home Civil Service, took the chair, accompanied by "Ned" Dunnett of the MOD and Harvey Druit, the Treasury Solicitor, as an independent member.[500] In carefully chosen words, on 8 August they reported that Lohan had been neither careless nor incompetent in his handling of the story, but had shown a lack of a proper sense of what was required of a responsible civil servant. In evidence to Radcliffe Lohan had said of Pincher 'I go as far as to say that I consider him to be one of my very great personal friends, apart from work.'[501] The civil service disciplinary finding was that his association with Chapman Pincher had 'affected his ability to discharge in the cable vetting incident the exceptional weight of responsibility that fell on him.' In other words, he had lost the confidence of Ministers, which was vital for the secretary of the D notice committee, as he had of the Cabinet Secretary. There remains a whiff that, dangerous as his drinking and lifestyle were by Whitehall standards, he was hung out to dry, in the words of the official historian of *Secrecy and the Press*, 'he was unfairly made the scapegoat for the collective shortcomings of a great many others.'[502]

To Trend it all made for a less-controlled and less-controllable media environment. To Wilson it was more evidence against the Foreign Office and he asked Trend to review the location of the UK desk of the anti-communist propaganda department, the Information Research Department.[503] Trend had a brief history of the Department compiled but otherwise made no proposals for change. 'The Security Service, as an advisory rather than executive organisation, concerned with obtaining intelligence not with acting on it, was inappropriate ... I have reviewed these arrangements with the Permanent Secretaries concerned and with the Director General of the Security Service; and we recommend they should continue unchanged.'[504]

In Trend's view, the main development was that as a result of the Radcliffe report 'There is a more cavalier attitude on the part of the press and authors writing about sensitive subjects.'[505] The following year, when word reached him that *The Times* was planning to reveal the Philby story, he repeated, 'The incident is merely another illustration of the way in which public interest and sensational journalism are gradually eroding the safeguards by which we have hitherto managed to protect our covert agencies.'[506] Lohan had operated in a shadowy world, much disapproved by Trend. Trend's 1968 evidence to the Fulton Committee investigating the performance of the civil service identified three indispensible characteristics – political impartiality, incorruptibility and anonymity. Secrecy was essential to two of them; in his view there was no half-way house between secrecy and openness – the Official Secrets Act had had a stabilising effect not unlike 'the cane in the best type of orthodox school.'[507] If the Civil Servant became known to the public this risked them fighting their own corner rather than identify with their Minister. Later, under the Heath Administration, Trend argued that Policy Analysis Review reports should not be published because doing so could reveal how decisions were taken;[508] and that to reveal the structure of Cabinet Committees would be the thin edge of a dangerous wedge, whetting the appetite of the media to expose divisions in the government:[509] 'When was [an issue] first examined? By what Committee or Committees? Was their advice unanimous; or was there a disagreement among their members? Was their recommendation to the Cabinet? Did the Cabinet endorse it? If not, why not?'

Recognising that the tide could not be turned, in the spring of 1969 Trend proposed a multi-volume history of intelligence in World War II as a counterbalance to sensationalism.[510] As discussion ground to a halt without a decision, he pressed for a history focused on the use of intelligence without reference to its collection;[511] and as a further concession, after Heath had defeated Wilson in the 1970 General Election, proposed that a decision whether or not to publish the work could be postponed.[512] Heath withdrew his objections but by the time the work was finished (in May 1978) Margaret Thatcher had replaced Heath as leader of the Conservative Party and opposed publication, only to be overruled by the Prime Minister, Jim Callaghan – advised by Trend's successor John

Hunt.[513] The result was the multi-volume *Official History of British Intelligence in the Second World War.*[514]

Trend's belief in secrecy for the official world was close to absolute; his attitude can be illustrated in his reaction when Sir Denis Greenhill (PUS at the Foreign Office) wanted Dick White's successor as the Head of SIS ('C') to be named and interviewed. He was concerned that this would loosen Ministerial control and that the press would not stop there: 'All experience shows that ... the appetite grows with eating.'[515] His support for protecting privacy in the private world was, however, limited by practicality. By the end of 1966 the 'Wilson doctrine,' by which the interception of Members of Parliaments' correspondence was forbidden, was in place in response to a number of telephone tapping scares. Wilson said, 'I reviewed the practice when we came to office and decided on balance – and the arguments were very fine – that the balance should be tipped the other way and that I should give this instruction that there was to be no tapping of the telephones of Members of Parliament.' There was an important gloss: 'But if there was any development of a kind which required a change in the general policy, I would, at such moment as seemed compatible with the security of the country, on my own initiative make a statement to the House about it'; i.e. it could be suspended by a Prime Minister but that fact not revealed until it was judged safe to do so.[516]

The following year there was concern in government that MPs would support a Select Committee inquiry into privacy and that the government would lose control of the situation.[517] Wilson was sympathetic to a government inquiry but it proved difficult to formulate appropriate terms of reference. The Prime Minister wanted the terms of reference to be about protecting citizens against 'unauthorised intrusions into privacy by private persons.'[518] Other Ministers thought that this was too restrictive. The Lord President (Richard Crossman) argued that such terms of reference were emasculated; the Lord Chancellor (Lord Gardiner) agreed, 'private persons' was too limiting, the BBC and ITV must be covered, as must commercial espionage. (One difficulty was that neither Minister had been indoctrinated into the work of the Security Service and GCHQ and it was thought unwise to do so.) Working with Sir Philip Allen (PUS Home Office) Trend proposed adding 'or organisations' to Wilson's draft; but he also pointed out that 'nobody was [currently] showing any particular interest in this question ... we should perhaps let sleeping dogs lie'[519] – which they did for nine months. A contemporary Home Office internal working party on unauthorised eavesdropping, for example, concluded that 'such unofficial eavesdropping (as distinct from telephone interception) as takes place constitutes only a very limited mischief. But the problem causes considerable public concern, and it may grow to more serious proportions if unchecked.'[520]

In November 1969 Brian Walden, (Labour member for Birmingham Parliamentary constituencies 1964–77) proposed to introduce a Private Member's Bill in the House of Commons to guarantee the protection of privacy. (The Bill would be drafted by the pressure group JUSTICE based on a new tort – infringement of privacy.) Trend went back to the idea of a committee of inquiry: '[It is] increasingly difficult to ignore the rising public interest and concern ... can we evade the issue any longer or must we now yield to the political pressure lest even worse befall us and we find ourselves in an uncontrollable situation in e.g. dealing with Mr. Walden's Bill?' It would be best to set up a committee with wide terms of reference (thereby reducing the risk of revolt by Labour back-benchers) and 'to rely on the discretion of the Chairman (who would have to be very carefully selected for more reasons than one) to keep it under control and within manageable scope. We should also have to insist from the outset that the terms of reference excluded the activities of the State.'[521] Wilson ordered an immediate stop to technical work by government statisticians on a population register and means of effecting data linkage.[522] By December Trend reluctantly accepted the Home Secretary's view that it would probably be impossible to get the Bill into an acceptable shape so as to give it government support;[523] and at a Downing Street meeting on 2 December 'It was agreed that the wisest course was for the Government to announce their intention to hold a departmental enquiry.' Here the subtlety of Trend's mind kicked in. Membership of the enquiry should not be drawn exclusively from Privy Counsellors lest this 'draw attention to the very aspects of privacy which we are anxious to protect from intrusion!'[524] On the other hand, the Prime Minster should not announce 'a searching and comprehensive inquiry.'[525]

Sir Kenneth Younger[526] was the trusted appointee to chair the review and after much redrafting terms of reference were set as 'To consider whether legislation is needed to give further protection to the individual citizen and to commercial and industrial interests against intrusions into privacy by private persons or organisations, or by companies, and to make recommendations.'[527] Brian Walden commented: 'the right to be left alone may not sound a very exciting freedom but it is the one about which the British people care the most.'[528]

Intelligence and Security

Military retreat East of Suez changed the requirements for intelligence. The Cold War was still very much in evidence and the requirements placed on SIS and the Security Service became more Euro-centric; though less so for GCHQ because of its close relationship with the National Security Agency in the United States. Wilson was fascinated by this secret world and harboured concerns, verging on paranoia, that members of that twilight world were conspiring to unseat him. In Trend he had a reliable conduit to the agencies of long standing; this he supplemented with politically and personally focused intelligence, sometimes obtained from gossip, from the Paymaster General, George Wigg.[529] He confirmed the special arrangements that dated back to 1952 that the Director General of the Security Service (DG) could have direct access to him, if necessary, though report on a day to day basis to the Home Secretary, and that, as Prime Minister, he might summon the DG also without notifying the Home Secretary.[530] During the seamen's strike in 1966 Wilson also asked for limited regular security and intelligence briefings on British industry, causing the Security Service to point out that its Charter only allowed for it to act when there was a threat to the State or evidence of a plot to unseat the government by undemocratic means.[531]

By mid 1967 there was open comment on the organisation of intelligence collection and handling. In June *The Economist* called for British intelligence to be reorganised on the American model, criticising the Foreign Secretary's control of SIS.[532] Pat Dean, the Ambassador in Washington,[533] offered a stout defence of Foreign Office control in a personal letter to his close friend Trend; '... it seems to me that the Foreign Office must take something very close to the primacy in a Governmental intelligence organisation, if only for the reason that in times of peace at any rate, it is by far the largest producer, assessor and user of intelligence of all sorts.' He continued, '... the idea that we should have something like the United States CIA is a gross error ... If one could get a Director of Central Intelligence, without the CIA and with only a very small staff ... and make him the Chairman of a sort of super JIC, which would meet less frequently and with fewer members than the present JIC, I believe that real progress might be made ... though it would seem sensible to me that the responsibility of the Director of Central Intelligence should be through the Secretary to the Cabinet direct to the Prime Minister.'[534]

Trend was in complete agreement: 'the CIA model – i.e. a body of "professional" intelligence assessors completely divorced from the maker's policy – is not for us; and our almost instinctive preference for some arrangement which gears the policy maker right into the business of assessment is preferable, both from the constitutional point of view and as a means of ensuring that our intelligence assessments are as realistic as possible ... as our military position overseas wanes it is increasingly accepted that our intelligence must henceforward be mainly a matter for the political and economic Departments.'[535] The directness of this private letter to Dean contrasts, however, with the official minutes of a meeting of Permanent Secretaries under Trend's chairmanship (MISC 155) that met on 29 June to discuss the interdepartmental committee structure for intelligence. Trend is recorded as summing up in an oblique but prescient fashion:

> 'THE CHAIRMAN, summing up, said that their primary concern should be to improve the machinery for the assessment of the information from covert, and difficultly available, sources. There appeared also to be some need for centralisation of resources for assessing overtly available information, but it would be as well to work gradually towards such an arrangement, making sure that any changes were a reflection of genuine needs. It seemed clear that there was room for improved co-ordination in the means by which intelligence requirements were made known to the collecting agencies, particularly in the economic sphere. It seemed also to be generally accepted that the Assessment Staff should be reinforced and improved in quality as a means to making its output more authoritative and of greater impact within Whitehall ... the balance of advantage lay in the Chairmanship ... being exercised on a part-time basis by departmental representatives and that this would act as a guarantee against the assessment machinery being divorced from reality.'[536]

After discussion with Wilson at the end of July the structure of the United Kingdom's intelligence collection effort remained unchanged, but it was agreed that Dick White (DG of the Security Service 1953–1956 and currently Head of the SIS) should become the first Intelligence Coordinator, located in the Cabinet Office.[537] His remit would include clearing out dead wood and rebalancing the intelligence-gathering effort in the light of the failures to foresee the fall of Khrushchev in October 1964, the Chinese nuclear test two days later, and the 1966 coups d'état in Nigeria and Ghana.[538] Then, in March 1968 Trend acknowledged that he felt the time now was ripe to voice doubts about the Joint Intelligence Committee (JIC) arrangements in the new world of shrunken military reach. His proposal was to revamp the Committee into a political intelligence committee (JIC(A)) and an economic intelligence committee (JIC(B)) jointly supported by a strengthened Assessments Staff reporting through the Intelligence Coordinator.[539] Trend contrasted these proposals with the American model: a Central Intelligence Agency (CIA) which was, 'a very large collection of "experts" on almost every subject under the sun, who will produce at a moment's notice an intelligence appreciation ... which is "technically" impeccable but may be politically irrelevant or misleading ... this rather arbitrary divorce between intelligence and policy-making is not only inefficient but, if it extends into the field of covert action as distinct from mere intelligence, can also be disastrous, as was evidenced by the Bay of Pigs episode.'[540] Subsequent experience was less kind, particularly about JIC(B). Anthony Verrier describes the JIC geography as 'The JIC "A" Committee ... deals ... with major issues. The "B" Committee handles the minor variety.'[541] Trend would himself later describe JIC(B) as a persistent sickly child.

In the period between July 1967 and March 1968 the Cabinet Office files also contain details of a strange incident one evening in the JIC offices – a restricted area on the second floor of 70 Whitehall out of bounds to staff other than the indoctrinated. Brooks Richards, then Head of the Assessment Staff advised David Heaton (the Cabinet Office Establishment Officer) that a Duty Clerk, Mr. Moon, 'a sensible and level headed person who would be unlikely to invent this story as a practical joke and who would be unlikely to report this incident unless he genuinely believed it to have occurred,' had reported supernatural goings-on in the JIC suite of offices:

> 'On Tuesday, 17th October 1967 at about 8.00 p.m., I was alone in the JIC suite of rooms. I had locked all the windows and presses and had put the box of keys in a combination lock press in Room 224. I turned the combination and ensured that the press was in fact locked. I then left the suite to wash my hands, locking the door to Room 221 (which until then was the only remaining unlocked door to the suite). When I returned I remained in Room 221 to check that all was secure. While doing this I saw the door to the corridor open until it reached an angle of approximately forty-five degrees. It then swung closed. The door is spring loaded and will only open under strong pressure. I could see into the corridor and as far as I could

ascertain there was no one pushing it. I then returned to Room 224 and saw the box of keys on the desk. Presuming that I had omitted to put them away I unlocked the combination press, put the box away, and relocked the press. I then went into Room 222 where I checked the windows and put out the lights. I returned again to Room 224 to find the box of keys once more upon the desk ... I said, "Very funny; do it again." The box then appeared to rise in the air to a height of approximately one foot above the desk. After a small pause it dropped and crashed down upon the desk. I remained motionless for a period of about two or three minutes. I saw no other strange happenings during that period.'[542]

The restructuring worked patchily. It allowed Trend occasionally to commission reports directly. Thus, in May 1968 as the student unrest in France and beyond gathered pace he asked for a report on its importance, origins and implications for the United Kingdom[543] and by January 1970 Trend could report that in the UK there existed an uneasy calm.[544] But intelligence gathering behind the Iron Curtain was a difficult business and the Committee was no more successful in interpreting the outcome of the military movements on the Czechoslovakian border that presaged the end of the Prague Spring, than had been the case of Ghana and Nigeria. Later analysts have concluded that the JIC was aware of the military build-up but had concluded that the pressure of world opinion would prevent invasion[545] – a mistake that has been attributed to a failure to integrate all relevant inputs[546] but to which it might also be relevant to ask, as the Butler enquiry into the evidence of Iraqi Weapons of Mass Destruction of 2004[547] did, to what extent a belief that others think in the same way as the British think contributed to the misinterpretation.

The 1970 General Election

The General Election of 18 June 1970 delivered a surprise result. The Conservatives, under Edward Heath, won 46.4% of the vote and returned 330 Members to the House of Commons, a comfortable overall majority of 30. The opinion polls had given Labour a 12 point lead up to the election date and the late swing in voting intentions has been variously assessed as working-class voter support for Enoch Powell's warnings about immigration, bad economic figures during election week and even to the effects of England's poor performance defending the soccer World Cup that the team had won in 1966. In public, Harold Wilson ascribed the loss to Labour complacency encouraged by the opinion polls.

Heath had become leader of the Conservatives in July 1965 in the wake of the party's narrow electoral defeat under Alec Douglas-Home's leadership. The Conservatives' process for choosing a leader had been revised after the opaque 'soundings' that had brought Douglas-Home to the fore in 1963 and in a ballot of House of Commons Conservative members Heath had run out victorious on the first round, defeating Enoch Powell and Reginald Maudling (the former Chancellor of the Exchequer). The choice of Heath signalled a generation shift in Conservative leadership, mirroring the change that had brought Harold Wilson the leadership of the Labour Party on the sudden death of Hugh Gaitskell in January 1963. Heath was a new departure for the Conservatives, a grammar school boy from a modest background, 'an abrasive and aggressive leader who might seek to divide the country rather than uniting it ... who would accept the need for change, would indeed embrace it with open arms.'[548] He fought an election campaign based on aggressive pro-growth economic policies and promised to pay no heed to continuity or to what should be preserved.[549] In the words of the journalist William Rees-Mogg, 'The document ... lacks ... the romantic idealism which has recurred in Tory history ... At the moment the real national and international situation of Britain is one which needs attention by men of detail rather than by men of dreams.'[550]

Heath's notes for his first Cabinet meetings as Prime Minister reveal a no-smoking rule and an immediate focus on the Queen's Speech, a strategy for the approach to Europe by the end of June, the sectarian situation in Northern Ireland, the state of the National Health Service, Britain's commitments East of Suez, the inherited stand-off with Rhodesia and its implications for Africa policy, industrial relations (particularly in the docks, and controlling public expenditure.[551] Trend made extensive comments on the speech – it indicated that Ministers would be overloaded; he doubted if everything in it was practicable and he questioned whether it was a balanced programme. Further, at 1050 words it was 50 words too long![552] The contents presaged the difficult time ahead during which, in particular, the economic strategy formulated in preparation for government was abandoned. Immediately, however, Trend faced the challenge of introducing Ministers to the disciplines of government after almost six years in opposition. Heath wanted to streamline the interdepartmental decision-taking processes; Trend had to somehow respond without jeopardising the Prime Minister's control – at the end of the first week, for example, he rapped the knuckles of the Ministry of Defence for not copying the Prime Minister into sensitive interdepartmental correspondence – but he faced Heath complaining that more issues should be settled at official level, citing public expenditure decisions, agreeing a text for the Public Expenditure White Paper, agreeing the text of the Defence White Paper, decisions on steel prices.[553] Trend explained that some of these issues had come to Cabinet due to shortage of time and took the opportunity to reiterate the rules for Cabinet papers – text should be agreed between Departments wherever possible, issues should not usually be escalated until all possible consultation had been exhausted, the financial implications of proposals must be discussed in advance with the Treasury and those for manpower with the Civil Service Department, all papers should be circulated to Cabinet 48 hours in advance of the meeting. Heath agreed: 'It is only in this way that we shall protect Ministers from the dangers of hasty and premature decisions and avoid cluttering the Cabinet with proposals which have not been completely coordinated.'[554]

Whitehall Reform – the Central Policy Review Staff

Much work had been done by the new government when in opposition to flesh out proposals to reform the Whitehall machinery. Heath had invited Norman Brook to join the discussions as a member of the party committee. Characteristically, Brook had declined to be seen to be advising openly, proposing instead informal contact with the leading proponents of reform. It is also likely that Heath had discussions with Trend about the central machinery of government as, in late March 1970 and again in late May, Trend wrote to William Armstrong (the Head of the Home Civil Service) with concerns about Treasury dominance of economic policy and ideas that later blossomed into the Central Policy Review Staff (CPRS), though not in the precise form in which Trend envisaged.[555] These discussions would have taken place under the so-called Douglas-Home rules promulgated before the 1964 General Election:

> 'In the run-up to an election, and if the Parliament runs its full course in the last six months of the Parliament, it is understood that the Leader of the Opposition may seek the Prime Minister's agreement, that he or members of his Shadow Cabinet may talk to Permanent Secretaries, particularly on questions of organisation, so as to be able to discuss questions of organisation that might arise in the event of a change of government but the initiative for that would come ... from the politician and not from the civil servants, and each contact would have to have been cleared with the Leader of the Opposition and, no doubt, with the Prime Minister of the day ... the purpose of the contacts would not be to clarify policies but would instead be related to questions of organisation. These conversations would be regarded as confidential with the member of the Shadow Cabinet concerned.'[556]

Officials were also reflecting on how the machinery for determining policy might be improved. Commenting in March on the Labour government's draft White Paper, *Planning in Government Departments*, Trend argued that, 'We are setting our sights too low for inter-departmental planning in areas other than the economy and external relations ... Our interdepartmental committees need staffs for research,' adding, 'A new Prime Minister would say, "We must do better than this. Devise for me a machine that will really bring together and synthesise the thinking in Whitehall about the basic problems – political, social and economic – which transcend Departmental boundaries, in such a way that my colleagues and I can see where we ought to be heading, where the greatest problems lie, what limitations on our freedom of action are likely to be, and what decisions we are going to have to take. And this please over the whole field of Government."'[557]

He followed this up a month before the election with a wide-ranging paper sent to William Armstrong which argued that 'at the end of the day one is left with a feeling that we are perhaps at some risk of asking ourselves what pattern of Departments or functions would suit us best in terms of tidy administrative working and forgetting to ask the even more basic question whether the resultant organisation would contribute to the efficient working of our particular system of Parliamentary democracy, which is, after all, what the whole thing is for.'[558] In a wide-ranging eleven-page paper Trend argued the case for collective ministerial responsibility facilitated by interdepartmental committees, chaired by non-departmental ministers:

> 'Sooner or later all Governments run into trouble. It may, or may not, be their fault. But it normally means that they have to face an uneasy, critical, even hostile, House of Commons, itself reflecting the same doubts and divisions in public opinion. At that juncture nothing is so important to a Government as its own internal cohesion.'

The interdepartmental machinery for government was key and could be improved significantly by:

> 'the assistance which could be provided by a staff capable of giving continuing attention to a Committee's work; of establishing the basic facts about a problem (which are often surprisingly elusive); of evaluating objectively the Departmental arguments for and against a particular solution; of relating separate problems to a single context of priorities and resource allocation; and of promoting the type of longer-term research over a whole area of policy which is becoming increasingly important in the formulation of a modern Government's policies.'

From the outset Heath asked Trend to formulate proposals for a central capability to:

> 'seek to reconcile differences in the analysis of interdepartmental problems; to clarify points of significant disagreement between departments; to identify the real issues for decision and the considerations which should be taken into account in deciding them; to set the issues in the context of the Government's strategy and priorities; and to report to Ministers collectively on an objective and non-departmental basis.'[559]

Lord Jellicoe, the Lord Privy Seal proposed a central capability 'to assist in identifying issues for collective Ministerial decision, to improve the presentation of policy issues and to strengthen the strategic framework within which collective Ministerial decisions can be taken.'[560]

The resulting Cabinet paper argued for a central review capability.[561] David Howell, Parliamentary Secretary at the Civil Service Department, who had been one of the main shapers of Conservative thinking in this area, expressed a hope that the review staff would support 'what is in a sense the most crucial function of all – namely, the presentation to the Prime Minister and his colleagues annually of the overall strategic picture and general direction of government policy.'[562] Some thought that a politician should head the unit (notably the special adviser Mark Schreiber, formerly of the Conservative Research Department) but at a meeting on 4 September Heath ruled out a political head. Otherwise the discussion of possible candidates (which did not include the eventual choice, Victor Rothschild) was inconclusive.[563] Heath inclined towards Kit McMahon of the Bank of England[564] or the economist Dick Ross who was subsequently appointed deputy head.[565] The main significance of the discussion, however, was that it was Trend who was charged with putting forward proposals for the structure and organisation of the Central Capability, for which he turned to a conventional Cabinet Office secondee from the Ministry of Defence, John Mayne.[566] It was Mayne who suggested the title 'Policy Review Staff,' later amended to Central Policy Review Staff and it was Mayne who carried out a first broad analysis of the 1970 Conservative Manifesto to link strategy to policies.[567] Subsequently, William Nield (Permanent Secretary, Cabinet Office under Trend) elaborated a link between the Departmental priorities shown in the Public Expenditure Survey (PES) and the Manifesto commitments, identifying seven main strategies and 71 derived policies which involved more than one department.[568] Meanwhile, the Prime Minister addressed the assembled Permanent Secretaries at their autumn Sunningdale Conference.[569] He told them that he wanted 'less government and better government, by fewer people ... with a skilful analysis within Government of all the possible options, and a presentation of the options for public consideration.' The government would bring within single large Departments a very much larger sweep of policy issues and responsibilities, thus reducing the need for interdepartmental discussion. Additionally, the government would have a central capability for identifying the range of options available to the Cabinet in an objective non-departmental way and placing them in a framework of British priorities as a whole.

On 14 October Cabinet approved a Programme Analysis and Review approach (PAR) to challenge existing public expenditure programmes and 'put brain behind the crude brawn of the Public Expenditure Survey Committee (PESC).'[570] Cabinet also approved a Central Policy Review Staff 'to assist Ministers collectively to work out the implications for their basic strategy in terms of policies in specific areas, to establish relative priorities ... and to identify the areas of policy in which new choices could be exercised.'[571] Trend was determined that the new capability should serve Ministers collectively – his preference was for experts to be placed in the various Cabinet Office secretariats. The following month he told his Private Secretary, Brian Norbury, that he had successfully headed off the involvement of CSD Ministers in its structure and staffing.[572] Preparations lasted three and a half months with Victor Rothschild appointed its head after almost a chance encounter with Trend, who scarcely knew him. 'I don't think I'd known him very well or very closely. But what I knew of him made me think that this was the right sort of man,' Trend said on BBC Radio 3.[573] It is not known exactly what he meant by that. But given Rothschild's reputation as a scientist, the emerging energy problems for the United Kingdom and Trend's own interest and concern about how government dealt with scientific issues and those concerning space it is possible to see why Rothschild might have appealed to him.[574]

The CPRS opened its doors for business at the start of February 1971 and Trend circulated a note to Permanent Secretaries with the terms of reference approved by Cabinet, that its work needed to go with the departmental grain and that there would be a need for rules of engagement – such as that Rothschild could say the CPRS were taking an interest in a subject but must not say that it had prepared a report.[575]

A first review by the CPRS of the government's progress was presented on 19 April at a meeting Heath held with William Armstrong, Trend and Rothschild.[576] The Prime Minister started by saying that he had been impressed by the difficulty of getting the country set on a clear course and seeing that course through. He then put three topics on the table: Rhodesia, Northern Ireland and the economy (especially wage demands). On Rhodesia it was agreed that almost any settlement would be better for the international reputation of the United Kingdom than to walk away from responsibility and that this would be a 'matter of finding some formula, the effect of which would be to say that we were trusting Mr. Ian Smith.' On Northern Ireland a discussion on options ranged from abandoning the Province, to probable civil war, and to continuing on much the same course as the Wilson Government produced the conclusion that talks with the Taoiseach should be aimed at co-operation over security supplemented by a review of the tactics of the security forces and the scope for improving counter-intelligence. In other words, dig in for a long campaign. On the economy Heath argued that a pessimistic assessment by Armstrong neglected the psychological effect of determined policies, though it was for consideration whether more should be done to get 'the balance of power in industry right,' for example by curbing Supplementary Benefit for strikers' families and forcing the unions to pay strike pay during official disputes.

Next month Rothschild suggested that the CPRS should prepare an analysis to warn of likely trouble ahead.[577] His team found it difficult to get departments to speculate in this way and the Treasury refused to participate in the exercise.[578] The handling of what would be inevitably a pessimistic document also caused worries.[579] Trend wanted to locate the work in the Cabinet Committee system, harking back to his earlier preference for experts placed in the various secretariats.[580] Heath thought of restricting access only to central ministers and not the full Cabinet.[581] As it was, reports were circulated, for information only, classified secret.[582] The whole exercise was a barely concealed failure. After less than seventeen months Rothschild suggested turning off life support, using the excuse that the main foreseeable problems would be covered in the reviews of progress against strategy.[583] The Prime Minister agreed.[584] And when Rothschild looked as if he might be wanting to reopen the issue[585] Heath's Principal Private Secretary, Robert Armstrong, responded that the 'PM's decision was fully considered and he would not take kindly to a proposal that it should be re-opened.'[586]

Another CPRS presentation on strategy was scheduled for mid May 1972 with preliminary suggestions of focusing on the relationship between inflation and unemployment and on the environment.[587] At which point Trend stepped in once again. The issues around inflation and unemployment were clear to those involved in the normal co-ordinating machinery and did not need further definition. By contrast, there were many other issues which were less well defined in areas such as the relationship with Europe, the exercise of military power, the role of government itself, the environment and social policy. The CPRS might formulate the key questions for each of them.[588] To Trend's mind, if the original proposals went ahead they would be supplanting the existing machinery not extending it. According to Rothschild, at a meeting of Permanent Secretaries on 16 May, though Trend stayed studiously neutral in the debate, participants 'put the boot in/put the shoe in' on the unit.[589] In fact the CPRS did make presentations on the economy, in May and again in September, that covered wages and price control that probably influenced the Conservative u-turn on economic policy of that autumn, but were not the only influences at work.[590]

Organisational questions about the centre of Whitehall stayed relatively quiet for about four months until William Armstrong responded to Heath's request that consideration be given to the subject once more. The Prime Minister discussed matters with Armstrong and Trend at Chequers on 13 September. The problem, as he saw it, was that there was no overall management of the economy. The Chancellor was too involved with the management of taxation and public expenditure at present. With Trend due to become Rector of Lincoln College, Oxford, in the autumn of 1973 the way, might be open for 'an arrangement whereby the Secretary of the Cabinet would be freer of the problems of day to day management of the business of Cabinet and Cabinet Committees, but would be in overall charge of a Cabinet Secretariat on the one hand, and of the Central Policy Review Staff on the other, each with its own head at or near Permanent Secretary level.'[591] Media speculation was already rife that William Armstrong would head such a reformed unit, in effect a Prime Minister's Department.[592] The indications are that Trend was reluctant to countenance such a move; he had already said that he was 'not quite sure what the assignment is and William [Armstrong] does not seem too clear either' – but otherwise it is not known how he might have advised Armstrong, with whom he had a close relationship, about the dangers to civil service political neutrality.[593]

Whitehall Reform – Cabinet Procedure

Trend may have thought that he had dealt with Heath's early complaints about unnecessary referrals to Cabinet but they came back in January 1971 and continued up until his retirement in late September 1973. On the suggestion of Robert Armstrong, Heath asked for Cabinet papers to be restricted to one page in length (plus annexes). 'We are adding unnecessarily to our burden of work by the length and prolixity of the memoranda circulated to Cabinet and Cabinet Committees,' Armstrong suggested he wrote. 'Try it on,' said Heath.[594] From discussion of this with Trend came a long-standing requirement that Cabinet papers should be no more than two pages. But when Rothschild tried to enter the fray, offering to look at how matters were presented to Cabinet, Armstrong reported to Heath that 'in informal discussion Sir Burke Trend has shown some signs of alarm at the implications of having the CPRS operating in this sort of area.'[595]

The questioning also covered the extensive complex of Cabinet Committees. The reforming zeal of the Heath administration might have largely run into the sands by the end of 1972 but at the start of the year there were still echoes of *The Re-organisation of Central Government* White Paper[596] in the Prime Minister's continued complaints to Trend about the inefficiency of Cabinet Committees:

> 'I am greatly concerned about two aspects of the machinery of Government – (a) the immense amount of time needed to get any decision taken in Whitehall; (b) the immense amount of time needed to implement a decision when taken. I believe this goes to the root of a good many of our troubles. I would like advice on how to deal with these two points. It seems to me that our machinery for decision-making has become so over-elaborate that it is now defeating its own purpose. We seem to lack almost completely any means of ensuring that decisions are speedily taken and then rapidly implemented; both are left to bumble along on their own. Our first task in 1972 as far as the machinery of government is concerned must be to deal with these two problems.'[597]

Heath was returning to a charge he had made in March the preceding year, when he had argued that there were too many committees, that issues tended to go through a chain of committees, being constantly refined and revised, but without decisions being taken and that individual committees were too large, diffuse and time-consuming.[598] Trend had replied with an eight-page apologia for the existing system. Now he appeared not to appreciate Heath's impatience and frustration with the interdepartmental grind.[599] In a fundamental misjudgement he once again responded with a defence of the existing system, arguing that Cabinet cohesion and collective responsibility was the strongest bulwark protecting the Prime Minister and this required something akin to the existing system. Greater use of task forces might relieve some of the burden on Ministers but would be liable to breed distrust and suspicion.[600] This written exchange continued into May, giving a new interpretation of what happens when an irresistible force meets an immovable object. In an eleven-page document that month Trend proposed 'certain changes which are directed to two main purposes – first, a reduction in the number of Committees and a simplification of the Committee structure as a whole; second an easing, as far as possible, of the Committee burden on Ministers, particularly those who have to take the chair.'[601] Robert Armstrong was better attuned to what Heath wanted. He pointed to deficiencies in Trend's response; notably that the arguments came from too much going back to first principles and too little attention being paid to the views of others. But in this Trend would never change. It would be better to turn a challenge to the committee system over to John Hunt who had arrived as Deputy Cabinet Secretary a couple of months earlier.[602] However, Heath waited until May 1973 by which time Hunt had been announced as Trend's successor. He then informed Hunt that he had four months to read himself in and to prepare a report on the organisation of government business.[603] Meanwhile, William Armstrong responded belatedly to an outstanding request of some duration for advice on how to improve the presentational style of government documents.[604] Substance mattered most in policy presentation but there was a need to bring in the Prime Minister at an earlier stage of discussion. 'Which is what I am always asking for,' scrawled Heath in the margins.[605]

It's the Economy, Stupid!

Bernard Donoughue, the Head of the Downing Street Policy unit for Harold Wilson and James Callaghan summed up the dominant domestic theme of the 1970s as: 'a long power struggle between the unions and central government, which ... would involve major abuses of unaccountable power by the trade union movement, and was progressively to break the post war truce between capital and labour.'[606] The difficulties had begun before the Heath Government but were exacerbated during it. New technology was putting the emphasis on efficiency in industry and there was a fear of job losses without the opportunity for the individual worker to adapt and a fear of a shift in union power away from national and regional officials towards shop stewards in individual industrial plants. Between 1969 and 1973 industrial stoppages rose by 87%; with the number of workers involved up by 22%; during this period the days lost to industrial action rose by 244% compared to 1960–68.[607] On 23 October 1969 Barbara Castle, the Labour First Secretary of State, had told Cabinet that an unofficial strike at Standard-Triumph's Liverpool factory did not arise from any failure on the management's part to operate procedures speedily; and that it was not due primarily to the militancy of trades union shop stewards. The indications were that it simply reflected a mood of near-anarchy on the shop floor.[608]

The main plank in the incoming Conservatives' strategy for combatting the ill discipline illustrated by Barbara Castle's comments was to introduce an Industrial Relations Bill which would remove many of the trades unions' legal immunities, make ballots compulsory before strikes and abolish the closed shop – whereby a worker could not be employed in a particular factory or production line unless a member of the relevant union. It was closely associated with demarcation disputes between unions which severely hampered workforce flexibility and pushed up costs. An Industrial Relations Court would judge cases where unions were alleged to have broken an agreement. In 2007 the BBC News Magazine sought eyewitness accounts of what life was like in 1970s Britain. Among memories of the power cuts and three-day working week one respondent described a prevailing anarchy: 'As a trainee engineer in 1976, I remember changing a toilet roll when on secondment to our Sheffield factory and being seriously worried that someone might find out and accuse me of doing somebody else's job. My predecessor had almost caused a strike by helping to sweep up some rubbish.'[609] Unsurprisingly, the Industrial Relations Bill (later the 1972 Act) was challenged by the unions, who saw it as a restriction on their freedom to negotiate.[610] Trend had advised Heath that: 'we are probably in for a long hard winter on the industrial front, plant bargaining has destroyed central union control, industrial peace – even relative and partial – can only be bought at the price of further industrial conflict.'[611] Heath's jottings in the margins indicate an anxiety over government contingency planning: 'I am not at all satisfied that officials have worked out for Ministers both strategy and tactics as well as the mobilisation of resources to deal with this situation.'[612] How right he was. The Home Office was where responsibility for preparations for civil emergencies lay, but its Permanent Secretary, Philip Allen, reflected a passive departmental attitude out of step with the Prime Minister's thinking. He believed that it was not possible to foresee disruption with enough precision to make meaningful plans to deal with it.[613] The weight of action fell, accordingly, on the industrial relations legislation with Trend questioning the wisdom of some of the proposed measures. Towards the end of the year he queried that whilst the government may as well be hung for a sheep as a lamb, was recovery of welfare payments to strikers sufficiently important in the fight against inflation to justify the recovery of Supplementary Benefit? Similarly, deferring payment of income tax refunds could not easily be justified unless a wider reform of the tax system made the refunds payable at the end of the financial year – and then Supplementary Benefit would have to be paid meanwhile. The Home Office continued to be unperturbed, probably because its intellectual energies were focused on the growing trouble in Northern Ireland. On 3 December Reginald Maudling, the Home Secretary, reported to Cabinet that unofficial strikes and demonstrations were likely on 8 December in protest at the Bill with consequent loss of production and inconvenience to the public. In London there was to be a mass march of 20,000 people or more from Tower Hill to Speakers' Corner in Hyde Park. But, he added, support for the protest appeared to be less strong than the organisers had hoped.[614] The conflict in attitudes with those of the Prime Minister would come to a head after the successful miners' strike of January/February 1972 which reinforced arguments in favour of a formal incomes policy.[615]

A second strand in the economic strategy in these early years of the Administration was to pin hopes of economic peace and productivity growth on a continuation of a voluntary consensus on pay between the government, employers and unions. In December, Brian Reading, the resident economic adviser in 10 Downing Street, proposed, for example, strengthening the National Economic Development Council (NEDC)[616] to make it akin to the Washington Council of Economic Advisers.[617] Hopes of wage restraint from national discussions between the three parties to the NEDC were soon damaged. On 20 January 1971 postal workers went on strike in support of a 15–20% pay rise. It lasted seven weeks, ending in defeat for the union when it ran out of strike funds and had to accept a complex offer lower than the 8% originally on offer. The moral was clear; do not organise a strike unless you mean it and can organise and mobilise to win. Trend's interpretation was twofold: the probability of success with influencing wage demands through talks at NEDC was low; and industrial subversion must be countered. Thus, in May 1971 he suggested contingency planning for a possible voluntary incomes policy;[618] and twelve months later, after the award of a 30% increase in wages for the miners by the Wilberforce Court of Enquiry[619] he continued to gamble on a voluntary package as Rothschild and the CPRS gave crucial advice in favour of wage/salary-dividend/price control.[620] The Economic Strategy Committee 'should try to take stock of the position and to ask themselves whether we are in fact doing enough to contain cost inflation ... or should we, in our own interests, be beginning to think in terms of something which could be called an incomes policy in a more specific sense? ... [and] create some kind of independent council to consider both general and specific pay questions.'[621] In such circumstances the approach to the unions would need to be both fair yet realistic.[622] During this time William Armstrong became dominant as the chief adviser to the Prime Minister on economic policy, acquiring a controversial reputation as 'the real Deputy Prime Minister.' Subsequent judgements accused Armstrong of crossing the divide between political neutrality and partisanship, particularly when, after confusion over the role, he was openly involved in the launch of a statutory incomes policy In November 1972. He continued to concentrate on process as a voluntary incomes policy gave way to a statutory policy.[623]

The same reticence is not visible on the political issues around industrial subversion. Back in March Trend favoured exposing the people behind attempts to wreck British industry (e.g. members of the then Ford Convenors' Committee). 'The Industrial Relations legislation will take time to bite; and in the interim there remains the problem of deliberate subversion within the union movement ... We met it, for example, in the case of the [Electricians' Trade Union] ballot-rigging; and we met it again in the [National Union of Seamen] strike ... And in each case we adopted the same means of meeting the challenge – i.e. public exposure and condemnation [for which] the essential work of mobilising public opinion must be done for it by "outside" spokesmen ... supported discreetly by continuous and affective staff service from within the Government itself.'[624] Heath agreed and added, 'They must get on with it. Look our ASLEF.'[625] Trend then proposed a study of subversion in industry – defined as 'contemplating the overthrow of the Government by unlawful means' and offered advice on discrediting the wreckers.[626] Victor Rothschild started an Early Warning System intended to help the government get prepared for industrial trouble.[627] This initiative struggled to establish itself against Treasury opposition and departmental reluctance to commit to a definite view of likely trouble spots and lasted less than eighteen months. The study of subversion, paradoxically, became a calming influence despite an inflammatory suggestion that there should be informal soundings of industry leaders to find those willing to fire bullets crafted by a camouflaged government – which, in the event, was not taken up.[628] Much of the credit for calming things down must go to the Security Service. In February 1972 Trend commissioned a report from the Service about the alleged conspirators, their relationships one with another, and the degree to which they had been penetrating important organisations. He planned a meeting with Heath and selected ministers where they could quiz the authors of the report.[629] These actions upset some prominent Conservative supporters with Geoffrey Tucker the political lobbyist complaining to Heath's Political Secretary (Douglas Hurd) that Trend was a barrier to effective action against industrial subversion.[630] This was very unfair, as Heath's Press Secretary, Donald Maitland, pointed out: 'I could not recall a time when so many people in different organisations had been expressing their anxiety about the activities of the New Left,' and emphasised that Trend was all in favour of taking remedial action.[631]

When it came in mid March, the Security Service report pointed to fragmentation and rivalry between factions on the extreme Left of politics. It dismissed the view that the efforts of subversive elements had been decisive in the miners' strike, industrial troubles at Upper Clyde Shipbuilders or in opposition to the Industrial Relations Act. It assessed that the 1971 'Little Red Schoolbook' aimed at leading children to question the education system, the authority of teachers and adults had been largely abortive. It put the number of committed supporters of subversive organisations at 40,000 ('a hell of a lot' Heath scrawled in the margins) and argued that the Communist Party of Great Britain (CPGB) did not want to wreck society – they wanted to take it over. The CPGB had a working majority on the Executive of the National Union of Seamen but no control over the Trades Union Congress or a significant union. However, the report did identify that Trotskyists were becoming more skilled at 'identifying local disputes (for example Pilkingtons, Fine Tubes and Fisher Bendix) in which their influence can play a significant part and attract publicity.' It counselled against media exposure, which might backfire and give publicity to subversive groups.[632]

Heath thought the report 'naïve' in dismissing Communist influence, especially in television broadcasting. At first Trend thought that '[The report] does not take us very far, we should know more and do more; perhaps MI5 stick too rigidly to the Charter but better they err on that side.[633] 'Ministers should give firm direction and take responsibility for all aspects of industrial policy (including covert anti-subversion action) through the Economic Strategy Committee. There should be restrictions on secondary picketing and on the payment of welfare benefits to strikers.[634] But the following month he supported the Security Service contention that there was no conscious and organised threat to society – the issue was 'a pervasive climate of opinion' which should be changed by 'activity which is as pervasive, oblique and "unattributable" as the influences which it is seeking to combat.' This should be organised through an interdepartmental team to be led by Sir Leslie Glass (the retired head of IRD).[635] However, Glass was too ill to take on the task, which then fell to the retired Patrick Dean, acting in an unpaid capacity. Its terms of reference, formulated by Trend, safeguarded the Security Service Charter: 'Under the direction of the Lord President to develop methods, including appropriate publicity and exposure, by which certain types of subversive activity can be countered; to implement, subject to Ministerial approval, specific projects for this purpose; and to make periodical reports to the Ministerial Group' (GEN 92).[636] The Department of Employment, meanwhile, argued for positive rather than negative messages. Sir Denis Barnes, the PUS, described the problem as subversion of the proper function of the unions, which should be combatted by building up a 'group of people within the unions who would argue the moderate case from inside.'[637]

At the end of July Trend told the Deputy Director General of the Security Service that Heath wanted more to be done to expose the hidden hand of Communists in industrial subversion and unrest. At the same time, Trend and Robert Armstrong suggested a JIC-like body, a working group on subversion, which was launched in September and known as the committee on Subversion in Public Life (SPL), which conducted long-term studies into industrial relations participants (e.g. into the National Union of Miners; the Amalgamated Union of Engineering Workers (AUEW); the Ford plants in the UK, the railway industry, and the New Left in politics). 'Jimmy' Waddell of the Home Office was appointed the chairman, working to terms of reference 'To supervise and direct the collection of threats to the internal security of Great Britain arising from subversive activities, particularly in industry; and to make regular reports to the Ministers concerned.' Other members came from the Department of Employment, the Security Service, the Scottish Office, the FCO(IRD), the Cabinet Office and the Head of the Metropolitan Police Special Branch. Michael Herman (Cabinet Office) and David Hilary (Home Office) were the joint secretaries.[638] Trend told the group that 'The Prime Minister attaches particular importance to Ministers receiving comprehensive reviews of the position at regular intervals and not merely when some critical situation has already developed.'[639] No record of meetings was taken but its first report, *The impact of subversive groups on Trades Union activity* (SPL(72)1), was completed on 13 October 1972.[640] A second report, on potential disputes in public sector (Local authority manual workers; electricity workers), SPL(72)4(Final), came at the end of the month.[641] Other reports included Claimants Unions, the NUM, and labour relations at the Ford Motor Company and at British Rail. The Significance of the Ultra Left in the UK and the Communist Party of Great Britain.[642] SPL was supplemented by a weekly intelligence report on emergencies (The Intelligence Assessment Group – IAG) but most of those documents were accidentally destroyed through confusion over where responsibility for their preservation lay. Robert Armstrong pressed Heath to widen the Security Service terms of reference to allow operations against people aiming for the subversion of social order.[643] But Trend dissuaded him.[644] At the end of the year he told Heath that the new Director General of the Security Service (Hanley) was more sympathetic than the outgoing man (Furnivall Jones) to operating in the grey areas of the Service's Charter where militancy might be construed as having a political motive against the State.[645] The CPRS pondered whether Whitehall, all about compromise not confrontation, was fit for the job in hand.[646] (Back in June 1970 Trend had described the Cabinet Office secretariat function as sitting at the hub of a compromise-making system.)[647]

Initially, Trend stayed calm, briefing that enforcement of existing law on picketing and secondary industrial action would bring a marked improvement in the conduct of industrial disputes.[648] He updated Heath on the state of play on four industrial disputes at the end of November. The most important messages were that though the AUEW was refusing to obey the National Industrial Relations Court the situation was unlikely to deteriorate further and that although ancillary workers in the National Health Service were unlikely to strike the Civil Contingencies Unit was looking for volunteers to man hospital laundries if necessary.[649] But then the mood deteriorated. After the 1972 Christmas holiday Michael Herman came back to an update on events around the New Year which began: 'Burke electrified us all by calling a meeting on Friday 29 December at very short notice to discuss handling of current intelligence by the Waddell Group.'[650] A month later Trend concluded that 'industrial unrest, merging at some point into political disaffection, must now be regarded as a more or less permanent feature of life.'[651] Robert Armstrong later recalled that 'Those last months in the autumn of 1973 onwards were as difficult a time as any period faced by any government. There was so much going on it was difficult to keep pace with it all.'[652]

Reorientation Towards Europe

The most significant foreign policy achievement of the Heath administration was to complete the overtures to the EEC Six first attempted by Macmillan and subsequently by Wilson. It was a continuation of a fundamental shift for Britain from world power to European power and it was a key policy of the new Administration for Britain to be accepted as a new member of the European Community. This it achieved by January 1972 when Heath signed the Treaty of Accession.[653] During the prior eighteen months briefing for the Ministerial Committee on the approach to Europe (AE) mostly fell to Bill Nield and Peter Thornton in the Cabinet Office. Trend took responsibility for the overall organisation of the approach, advising Heath in July 1970, for instance, that establishing the factual position with the EEC negotiators (covering the Common Agriculture Policy (CAP), the common external trade tariff, the Coal and Steel Community (ECSC), The European Atomic Energy Community (Euratom) and legal translations of Community documents etc.) was well in hand in the Committee; but there was no question of revealing the United Kingdom's negotiating position before October.[654] At home, the Treasury was anxious to promote optimism about the effects of entry on the balance of payments so as to avoid any threat of devaluation.[655] In briefing for a Cabinet discussion on the Community budget, however, Trend took a different view, advising of the need to avoid charges that the government was misleading the population by ignoring the wider balance of payments costs of entry.[656]

By the end of this period of negotiation with the Six Heath and Trend were increasingly divergent: the Prime Minister elevating the European connection above the 'special relationship' with the United States; the Cabinet Secretary an Atlanticist and a Commonwealth man. Both were firm believers in the power of the intellect to solve the most intractable problems; but the one was direct and managerial, the other took a Socratic approach. It was rumoured that during the early years of his administration, as he sought to streamline government decision-making, Heath harboured thoughts of early retirement for Trend[657] to be replaced by someone more in tune with his own style.[658] However, Trend's pension was not due to be paid until early 1974 (at age 60) and could only be activated earlier if he were to be retired compulsorily. That ran the risk that the outside world would infer a damaging loss of confidence between the Prime Minister and the Cabinet Secretary which, together with the likely accompanying appointment of William Armstrong as 'Chief of Staff',[659] could have been seen as a significant step towards a presidential style of government, especially as it was widely understood in the media that Armstrong and Trend worked in tandem to run the show.[660]

Nevertheless, as a man with high professional integrity, Trend approached the organisational challenge of reorientation with undisguised relish. Early in May 1971 he speculated on how departments could build up expertise in community ways of working 'We ourselves have never favoured [the idea of a Minister for Europe] if only because our relations with the Communities would be liable to concern practically every Department in Whitehall and the creation of a co-ordinating or general "European" Department could only lead to confusion and complication ...' There would inevitably be a sizeable demand for extra staff during the period 1972–74 – perhaps amounting to 750–1,000 new posts.[661] In June in concert with William Armstrong and Denis Greenhill he further elaborated the proposals to Heath.[662] In July he drafted a note from the Prime Minister to tell Whitehall departments that they needed to adjust their attitude to policy making – 'we must not only learn to "think European" but also develop a clear and hard headed concept of the real scope and nature of our interests as a member of the EEC and of the action which it will be open to us to take to promote those interests'.[663] Ministers were also concerned about the changes in attitude and process that would be needed. As the date of entry to the Community approached David Howell, Parliamentary Secretary at the Civil Service Department, raised the question of how conformance with an overall strategy for membership of the Community would be enforced. Heath responded with a message to Robert Armstrong: 'I must get a grip on this at once.'[664] He followed this up with detailed ideas in a telex from Chequers. The manner in which the Cabinet Secretariat worked was: 'just not good enough in the modern world.' Heath wanted a new unit:

> 'It must be central, ultimately responsible to me, though in its day today working it can be responsible to another central minister. It must be fully equipped to think ahead, plan ahead, and take all necessary initiatives. In all its work it must realise that we are no longer thinking in terms of compromise in Whitehall. What we are concerned with is to establish the necessary bargaining positions to achieve our objectives in Brussels ... the old system of internal haggling has gone forever. Ministers must be presented with all the options stark and clear, instead of the customary messy compromise. The unit must also be capable of working out the negotiating ploys and tactics to secure

> our objectives ... in conjunction with [others] ... But it must all be directed from the centre in Whitehall. This is what I mean by saying that we must have a new unit for the creation and the control of our European Strategy. There is not a moment to be wasted.'[665]

Trend responded in May with proposals that became known as the European Interdepartmental Unit, with John Hunt leading it, working to the chairman of the Ministerial Committee on Europe (EUM), the Foreign Secretary, Sir Alec Douglas-Home.[666] All this was consistent with the long-standing Cabinet Committee system inherited from Norman Brook. However, by November, when John Davies MP[667] transferred to the Cabinet Office as Minister for Europe, after an unhappy spell as Secretary of State for Trade and Industry, a new pattern started. Hunt's brief for the incoming Davies described the evolving situation thus: 'It is worth noting that a good deal of Parliamentary and quasi-legal work will be handled centrally in the Cabinet Office in future ... and you will be answerable to Parliament for this ... To do this work we have a staff in the Cabinet office whose work goes beyond the normal servicing of Committees.'[668] Through the European Unit, the *individual* responsibility of a Minister to Parliament and not just the *collective* responsibility of the government would involve the Cabinet Office which was set on a new path to executive responsibility. The boundary between the responsibility of the Foreign Secretary and that of Davies was particularly sensitive because an earlier decision had rejected both the creation of a Ministry for Europe and putting the Foreign and Commonwealth Office (FCO) in the driving seat for Whitehall co-ordination.[669] The former because of the need to get all departments to think European; the latter to reflect the Prime Minister's personal interest in Europe, reinforced by the Cabinet Office's perceived neutrality between departments. A subsequent fine-tuning of the arrangements saw the separation of a ministerial committee concerned with strategy and a larger ministerial group to handle day-to-day issues.[670]

In April 1973, assessing the first one hundred days of membership Hunt told Heath that the balance came down clearly on the credit side, but there was room for improvement – especially on the presentation of Community matters at home and on the contribution from the FCO. The FCO European Integration Department (EID) had a tendency to probe home departments' policies – which was the role of the European Unit.[671] The FCO role was to advise on the negotiability and impact of proposed policies and assist in delivering them through greater use, rather than less, of traditional diplomacy. Despite FCO attempts to reverse their perceived loss of influence the interdepartmental neutrality of the Cabinet Office had prevailed.[672] What this report could not address, however, was the effect that Community membership was having on the 'special relationship' with the United States.

USA

As negotiations for entry to the EEC progressed it was Trend, rather than Heath, who nurtured the 'special relationship' with the USA. The government vision was that a Europe with Britain at its heart would be an equal partner with the United States in a Europe-USA 'special relationship' born out of the Anglo-American one.[673] But as Heath's biographer concluded: 'The most radical aspect of Heath's foreign policy – differentiating his Government sharply from every previous post-war administration, Conservative or Labour, ... was his decision not to have a special relationship with the United States. On the contrary he was determined to assert Britain's European identity ... [and] to show Pompidou[674] that Britain was not an American Trojan Horse. He, therefore, quite deliberately made no early visit to Washington and made very little use of the transatlantic telephone.'[675] In these circumstances it was natural that Trend, who had a close friendship with Henry Kissinger,[676] would act as an intermediary at the highest levels between the two governments.

Heath knew of, and commented on, the exchanges. It is known that some of the most significant of these occurred during 1973 in response to Kissinger's 'Year of Europe' initiative, but there were earlier, equally important, talks on the British nuclear deterrent and on the exchange of intelligence material. By June 1971 Trend was already warning that Kissinger seemed depressed by Pentagon leaks about the war in Vietnam and was 'maybe a little scared.'[677] Six months later John Hunt assessed the state of Anglo-American relations as one of US neglect and warned that 'the pages of history are strewn with examples of world leaders who have got what they didn't want, because they weren't prepared to pay enough to prevent it happening'.[678] 'We have done our best to reassure the US intelligence community that our accession to the EEC need not, and will not, involve any weakening of the intelligence link between London and Washington, the value of which it is impossible to exaggerate. Mutterings of doubt, however, continue to reach us from time to time; and I am considering with the FCO what further reassurance we can give our friends,' Trend advised. Heath scrawled 'very important' in the margins of this note and asked to be kept informed of progress.[679] By the middle of 1972 Trend could say that 'The last report from Washington which I had indicated whatever fears they may have originally entertained have now been allayed; and, provided that we continue to take pains to keep close to them, I doubt whether we need worry any more on this point.'[680] However, at a more general level the Foreign Office view was that 'US/European relations have suffered in recent years from lack of attention by the White House' – because of American concentration on its triangular relationship with Moscow and Peking. Hence, the British Ambassador, Lord Cromer,[681] expressed the hope that a visit by Trend to Washington, planned for July 1972, was an opportunity to ensure that Kissinger knew the British position on a number of issues that were likely to put European-American relations under further strain (monetary reform, international trade, regulation of multinational corporations, American troop levels in Europe etc.). Downing Street was in doubt, though, that the prime reason for the visit was nuclear policy.

The talks between Trend and Kissinger took place over 27–29 July and included half an hour with President Nixon. Trend reported that Kissinger 'was in top form and is clearly riding high ... I have little doubt that he is speaking sincerely and in earnest when he assures us – as he assured me several times – that, so far as the President and he himself are concerned, there is the maximum of basic goodwill towards the United Kingdom within the necessary limits imposed by Unites States interests and the realities of domestic politics.' The topics ranged from nuclear policy (where he was assured that the continuing effectiveness of the British nuclear deterrent was the Administration's policy and that provision of the Poseidon replacement for Polaris would be examined) to Kissinger's modern take on the global balance of power, to worries about the state of India–Pakistan relations. They included a request from the US side for British views on a possible US–USSR Nuclear Non-Aggression Treaty (subsequently known in the UK as project HULLABALOO).[682] Sir Thomas Brimelow[683] (FCO) and Pat Nairne of the Ministry of Defence were despatched to clarify the US intentions. By mid August the outline of what HULLABALOO might mean was beginning to emerge, to the disquiet of the British, who saw no chance of moving Kissinger away from the idea. Trend was convinced that 'so far as [HULLABALOO] goes, it confirms our initial impression that there is no deliberate intention on the part of the United States to relax the pressure on the Soviet Union in Europe or to jeapordise the interests of the Alliance. But that is not to say that it would not have this effect in practice.' Heath found the texts too imprecise to be other than 'a danger to international peace and open to ridicule if published.'[684] The Foreign Secretary (Alec Douglas-Home) thought 'it would be better if the White House were not to follow up the Soviet proposal [for a Nuclear Non-Aggression agreement] … If Dr Kissinger is to be dissuaded from a course which evidently appeals to him, we shall have to demonstrate that the consequences … would be overwhelmingly adverse; and this, in my opinion, we cannot do.' Hence, suggestions for redrafting would be sent to Washington.[685] Trend, Brimelow and Nairne were in Washington again on 19 April when, together with Lord Cromer and Richard Sykes of the British Embassy had discussions with Kissinger and some of his associates for nearly four hours. Kissinger appeared not to have read the British proposed amendments and 'continues to be obsessed by the problem of coming to grips with a Europe which will not speak with one voice on any subject and appears incapable of understanding that all the various subjects of current concern are as organically interrelated as K's [i.e. Kissinger's] own conceptual approach requires them to be … there is no doubt that, as regards Europe, he is now a man in a hurry. There was a new urgency and an additional impatience in his approach … from his increasing realisation that time is beginning to run against him … and that the Watergate affair,[686] if it develops into the really major scandal which it seems likely to become, could pre-empt … the President's moral authority.'[687] As Matthew Jones has revealed using American sources, however, Kissinger had been advised that Brimelow's draft was 'gloomy,' his brief criticised the paper for its 'mild fatalism' and attitude that transatlantic negotiations were 'doomed from the start.'[688] That said, the British had been severely hampered by the risk of embarrassment with other members of the European Community so soon after Accession and by a reluctance to expose their own position in any detail. The result pleased no one.

This reluctance was all the more depressing from the American point of view because, when Heath had visited the President in January, Kissinger had asked Trend how membership of the European Community would affect Anglo-American relations, especially the old basis of easy informality and mutual trust. Trend had given a seemingly optimistic reply in characteristically guarded, not to say opaque, terms. There was no reason why this should not continue 'provided that the Americans for their part made the mental adjustment which is required by the fact that we are now a member of the EEC and that all we say and do henceforward cannot be unaffected by that fact.'[689] Heath himself had been told by the long-standing Republican Senator Javits[690] that: 'All of us who are concerned with the future of US-EEC relations in the context of maintaining the present cordial ties between the United States and Great Britain are very hopeful that your two day visit to Washington will begin to lay the foundation for a renewed and invigorated Atlantic partnership.'[691] Meanwhile, the Head of the Assessments Staff supporting the JIC (Percy Cradock) had offered the view that 'the EEC may seem preoccupied with internal assimilation of new members and inert in foreign policy.'[692]

Then, on 23 April 1973, in a speech to the Associated Press annual lunch in the Waldorf-Astoria Hotel, New York, Kissinger launched 'The Year of Europe' intended to put pride back into public perceptions of the Atlantic Alliance: 'In short, we deal with each other regionally and even competitively on an integrated basis in defence, and as nation States in diplomacy ... after a generation of evolution and with the new weight and strength of our allies, the various parts of the construction are not always in harmony and sometimes obstruct each other.' The initiative would 'lay the basis for a new era of creativity in the West.'[693] In assessing the importance of the initiative for Britain, the Atlanticist Trend warned that 'it may be inviting us, in effect, to subordinate the economic interests of Europe to the political exigencies of Washington.' On the other hand once made it could not be rebuffed. Nevertheless, Britain should not leap to lead the European response, nor gather other European reactions to the proposals.[694] As Matthew Jones puts it, for Kissinger here was an opportunity for Britain to seize the lead in the European Community; for Britain on the other hand here was a distraction that threatened its European credentials in the eyes of its partners.[695] On 10 May, during a visit to London, Kissinger regretted that the United Kingdom 'had at times appeared to lack understanding of American intentions, and to complicate with inappropriate procedural debates the issues confronting the Alliance's proposals.' In his memoirs Kissinger said he left London frustrated at a lacklustre British response in which 'The various ministers and officials, in their skilfully insinuating manner, steered the talks towards procedure, elegantly avoiding any discussions of the substance of our proposal.'[696]

Discussions between Trend and Kissinger continued through the year with Kissinger showing growing signs of frustration and the British both anxious to avoid upsetting European colleagues and increasingly seeing Nixon as a lame duck president. Kissinger records, for example, that when Trend arrived in Washington on 29 May 'the wise and gentle' Trend 'had nothing to talk about

... We both realized ... that we were at a turning point in Atlantic relations.' Trend showed his distress as closely as 'the code of discipline of the British Civil Service' would permit.[697] Heath asked Lord Cromer for an assessment of the impact of the Watergate scandal on Nixon's ability to carry policies through Congress;[698] and Trend advised that any response to the Year of Europe principles should be co-ordinated with the rest of the European Community before further consultation with the United States.[699] At the start of July Sir Denis Greenhill, PUS at the FCO, told Trend that the proposed draft principles for Atlantic co-operation caused major problems of substance, procedure, tactics and timing;[700] and that the American redrafts of the text showed substantial concessions to American views without equally substantial concessions to Europe.[701] Not that it was easy to say what were the European views. Trend admitted that he was struggling to get a Community response to Kissinger – France was proving intransigent in opposing bilateral meetings between Community members.[702] Kissinger for his part asked if the White House could at least see a British draft of the declaration of the new Atlantic principles before it was circulated to European partners. No, replied Brimelow. To find the British discussing matters with their European partners before discussing it with them was a traumatic shock. 'Such a procedure,' maintained Kissinger, 'was incompatible with the sort of relationship the US had with Britain in the past as well as insulting ... If old friends treated the US Government like that, the US would deal with them as they did with Luxembourg. If an adversary relationship was to develop then Europe must accept the consequences, and they would be very painful ... the Year of Europe was over.'[703]

The pain started soon afterwards. Despite Heath agreeing promptly to an American request to enhance the military base on the British island of Diego Garcia[704] Kissinger moved to punish Britain, with the agreement of the President. Four days later a telegram from the British Embassy in Washington reported that the new Director of Central Intelligence (DCI), William Colby, had suspended the supply of Latin America and Europe intelligence material.[705] On appointment as DCI Colby had instituted a review of intelligence exchange and on Kissinger's instructions had stopped the UK receipt of some material (though not all, and arguably not the most important from the point of view of NATO). Messages from the CIA to the British confirmed that the US action was political and symbolic[706] and shortly afterwards the supply was reinstated.

Throughout, Trend showed a clear appreciation of the new obligations that membership of the European Community brought and, despite a long-standing sympathy for and understanding of the Anglo-American relationship, he was clear minded about the risks that Kissinger's 'Year of Europe' entailed for the UK. Moreover, perhaps because of his good friendship with Kissinger, he was robust in arguing the British case with the Americans.[707] But as Matthew Jones has concluded, what started as an effort to foster Atlantic unity turned into a device to organise all the democracies against the United States.[708]

Emergencies

Nowhere did Heath's managerial tendencies show more clearly than with regard to civil emergencies. He epitomised that when the building is on fire you do not consult, you instruct. As early as December 1970 after industrial disputes in local government, in the state-run electricity supply industry and in the docks Robert Armstrong reported that Heath believed that 'There is a case for considering whether we should have in the field of civil emergencies the same sort of arrangement that the Foreign Office have for international crises: standing plans to set up an emergency operations centre in Whitehall with good communications and contacts, from which a civil emergency could be centrally managed,' and that Heath questioned why it was the Home Office that took the lead in civil emergencies when these were as likely to be a logistical challenge as a challenge to public order (perhaps more so).[709] The Home Office defence of the position did nothing to persuade him of the arrangements either – 'Useless' he scrawled on their response.[710] Ever emollient, Trend suggested that, 'although the machinery had creaked and groaned a bit, it had stood up to the electricity emergency pretty well,' but we need an operations centre to handle matters during an emergency. Heath agreed. 'Every major emergency so far I have had to take over myself; that certainly means that a central project team could organise effectively.'[711] However, to bring executive action to the centre – even in an emergency – seemed to Trend to contradict the constitutional position of departments.[712] Rather, he supported a proposal from Philip Allen at the Home Office that there should be a review of organisation for civil emergencies and persuaded Heath to go along with this idea. An Assistant Secretary in the Home Office called Weiler led the work, deciding early on that a central operations room outside the Home office was not desirable. Philip Allen put this emerging conclusion to Reginald Maudling the Home Secretary in February.[713]

During the remainder of the month Trend havered, reluctant to contradict Allen but aware that in the Prime Minister's Office Robert Armstrong was complaining that Heath wanted a more positive and executive role for the Cabinet Office. Finally, on Trend's advice, Heath conceded the argument to the Home Secretary and matters stayed as they were – for the time being. A message in May from the Home Office that everything was in hand to improve what was now being referred to as a communications room rather than an operational capability did little to assuage Heath, or Trend for that matter, who hankered after an operations room. But it was agreed to give the revised Home Office arrangements a try and to keep an eye on performance.[714] This was followed by the final report from Weiler on 11 June – in which he proposed minor technical improvements to the Home Office capability, no more. In a PhD thesis in 2012 Rosaleen Hughes concluded that Edward Heath's vision of a central system for managing emergencies had been defeated by Trend's bureaucratic conservatism and the determination of the Home Office to defend its turf.[715] In August Maudling reported that the state of preparedness for Thames flooding, possible winter conditions, likely industrial disputes, emergency regulations and the operation of communications and duty rooms was good, 'the importance which we have attached to the need for proper contingency planning is beginning to pay dividends.'

Then on 9 January 1972 the coal miners went on strike, the first time since the General Strike of 1926. Their grievance was the erosion of pay differentials. By 1960, miners' wages had risen to 7.4% above the average pay of workers in manufacturing industries; but this premium had not lasted and by 1970 miners were earning 3.1% less than the average worker in manufacturing. The strike lasted seven weeks with a state of emergency being declared on 9 February. At the same time the government faced a clutch of deteriorating situations – in Northern Ireland (where Bloody Sunday occurred over the weekend of 29–30 January); that same weekend there was a cold snap and the Central Electricity Generating Board warned publicly of power cuts; there were continuing difficulties with the EEC negotiations, unemployment was rising and worries that the 1971 collapse of Rolls-Royce presaged further failing industries. In mid January, Trend reported optimistically that despite the coal strike stocks were holding up. It was true that the government had concentrated on coal stocks but it had neglected how to get those stocks out to the power stations[716] and two days after Trend's reassurance the Department of Trade and Industry warned that power cuts were likely within days.[717] Over 7/8 February Ministers in the Economic Strategy Committee were divided over whether to declare a state of emergency; Trend had advised against doing so two weeks earlier since it could lead the miners to conclude that they were winning the battle.[718] When it was finally decided to declare a state of emergency (on the 9th) a ministerial group (GEN 78) was created to manage the accumulating industrial emergencies.[719] The priority was to end the picketing of coal stocks (made notably effective by the introduction of flying pickets to swamp sites) and to get the miners back to work. A settlement was agreed on 19 February and the miners returned to work on the 25th.

Heath commissioned Trend to conduct a post-mortem on the emergency. Robert Armstrong told him that: 'The Prime Minister finds it hard to believe that the way in which the miners' dispute developed was unplanned and he has asked for the preparation of an analysis to show who was responsible for the organisation of this episode ... [and] an urgent analysis of how the dispute had been managed by the Ministerial Committee on emergencies and on Pay.'[720] After consultations with the Permanent Secretaries Trend reported that the emergencies organisation had not performed well; there should have been more perceptive forward planning and more effective executive handling during the emergency; information had been too slow to reach those at the top and decisions took too long. But Trend still argued that it would be constitutionally improper to give responsibility to a central unit, as well as being a perceived humiliation for the Home Secretary. He suggested a new clearing unit for Ministers (which Allen naturally wanted in the Home Office and Barnes thought should be in the Ministry of Labour). Emergencies should be rehearsed like war games. As to the handling of the pay negotiations, Trend's report concluded that in focusing on preserving incomes policy the government had been slow to recognise the case for an inquiry. It had underestimated the challenge to authority that the miners had been able to mount by mobilising picketing more effectively than hitherto and by the strength of their solidarity that had kept the strike going longer than the government had expected.[721] Heath's immediate reaction was that 'These conclusions seem right and should be implemented.' However, it is also fair to describe the main message as much had gone wrong; but no one is to blame. 'The report combined clarity of analysis with evasion of responsibility – identifying several points of serious failure while exonerating those who took the decisions.'[722] Allen, meanwhile, sent Heath a Security Service analysis of those involved in the strike, which concluded that there was no evidence that it had been organised by the Communist Party organisation.[723] Heath scrawled, 'I don't find this very convincing. What are Sir Denis Barnes' comments on this? We must discuss.'[724]

At the end of April the Prime Minister returned to the charge. He instructed Robert Armstrong to chivvy Trend on the establishment of one command post for the whole of Whitehall dealing with the strategy for emergencies, not just immediate instances. 'Even if the present threats do not all materialise, we mat well be threatened with a more serious situation from next autumn onwards.'[725] And after a fiasco for the government over a cooling-off order and a compulsory strike ballot applied to a railway dispute that started the same month and lasted two months, he set up two ad hoc committees to deal with the dispute – GEN 94, a ministerial group concerned with strategy and GEN 96 a small official group chaired by the Lord Privy Seal (Earl Jellicoe) and with John Hunt (then Second Permanent Secretary in the Cabinet Office) his deputy.[726] GEN 96 was a step nearer the command post Heath so desired. It met daily during the railways dispute, around noon, and by the end of the month Hunt could tell Jellicoe that GEN 96 'has brought home to most Departments (if not to all Ministers) the desirability both of putting the Cabinet Office in the lead and of our organising ourselves to do the work properly. We now want to strike while the iron is hot and to establish more satisfactory standing arrangements.'[727] These arrangements would be a new official committee for strategic planning comprising those responsible in departments for contingency planning against civil emergencies, supported by a small unit in the Cabinet Office based in a new Situation Centre.[728] Heath approved Hunt's proposals within 24 hours but delayed telling Cabinet until August. Meanwhile, Trend proposed tidying up the Cabinet Committee structure dealing with civil emergencies to 'eliminate some of the miscellaneous bodies which we have had to create during the last few months and to produce a simpler and more streamlined system of Committee working.'[729] His suggestion was for a ministerial committee on Industrial Relations Policy (IRPC), chaired by the Prime Minister and carrying the final responsibility, short of the Cabinet itself, for dealing with all major questions of industrial relations and associated emergencies or natural disasters; a ministerial committee on Pay Negotiations (CPN), chaired by the Chancellor of the Exchequer; and

Hunt's suggested official committee for strategic planning on Civil Contingencies, chaired by the Lord Privy Seal (Earl Jellicoe) with John Hunt as Deputy Chairman. Thus was born the Civil Contingencies Unit (CCU) in the Cabinet Office, with terms of reference:

> 'To co-ordinate the preparation of plans for ensuring in an emergency the supplies and services essential to the life of the community; to keep the plans under regular review; to supervise their prompt and effective implementation in specific emergencies; and to report as appropriate to the IRPC'.[730]

Jellicoe commissioned an urgent Cabinet Office study of preparedness for future emergencies. Its conclusions included that the stockpiling of animal feed outside the ports was more urgent than the stockpiling of food itself. Alternative ports to Liverpool and Tilbury should be sought for bringing in grain; the use of unregistered ports prepared, there should be greater cross-Channel sourcing of electricity and an urgent look at the demands placed on the police by the control of picketing.[731] In mid December the CCU contemplated commissioning a review of the ability to withstand a triple alliance strike (railways, mines, docks).[732] One of its proposals was opposed: that there should be training in driving articulated lorries for soldiers in the Regular Army. The Chiefs of Staff were nervous about possible charges of strike breaking. Hunt (supported by Barnes) was having none of it. He wrote to 'Ned' Dunnett at the MOD: 'We ought not to get the matter out of proportion [but] ... Ministers have always taken the view that they must be able to use the Armed Forces in times of civil emergencies ... the statutory basis for this is the Defence (Armed Forces) Regulations 1938 which were made permanent by the Emergency Powers Act, 1964.' A decision to deploy troops would be made by Ministers collectively, who would be free, as a last resort and only when they judged the national interest so demanded, to enlist the help of the Services in a civil emergency.[733] Its first test was a dock strike called in August. Trend's advice was to 'play it cool and low' to avoid public alarm over possible shortages[734] and the CCU acquitted itself well.[735]

By June 1973, when Jim Prior succeeded Jellicoe on the latter's resignation following a sex scandal,[736] there had been 50 meetings of the CCU. After the end of each particular emergency, the CCU considered the immediate lessons for contingency planning. A more reflective study was then undertaken by Cabinet Office staff working to Hunt and approved by the IRPC in January 1973.[737] Indeed, so great was the pressure on emergency co-ordination that at the end of 1972 Hunt had had to establish rules of priority for the use of the Situation Room (which later became known as the Cabinet Office Briefing Room A – COBRA). Transition to War had first call, then terrorist incidents, and then civil emergencies.[738] When the Joint Intelligence Committee made enquiries about using the room for its meetings, the priority it could command was so low that the Committee abandoned all such thoughts.[739]

Whilst Hunt was taking the idea of a central Whitehall command post much further than Trend had contemplated, in the Industrial Relations Policy Committee Trend was calming things down. Amongst other actions, he supported increasing preparedness against strikes in the energy sector, railways and docks and once again rejected establishing a volunteer strike breaker force, but did contemplate the use of troops to drive trucks.[740] He briefed against amending the law on picketing and against reducing Supplementary Benefits paid to strikers through promulgating a 'deemed' strike pay (which he thought would be open to allegations of strike breaking) and advised that retrospective recovery of benefit paid was impracticable.[741] He supported preparing a booklet explaining the laws on picketing and precautionary work to have emergency restrictions on coach journeys ready if needed.[742]

Civil emergencies deriving from industrial action were not the only problem. At the beginning of August 1972 President Idi Amin of Uganda ordered that people of Indian origin who were not Ugandan citizens should be expelled from the country within 90 days. Around 50,000 left, of whom 60% came to Britain.[743] Towards the end of the month Heath became concerned that the British authorities were not in control of the situation as it affected the United Kingdom. 'I am extremely worried still about the apparent lack of grip on the presentation of the [Ugandan] Asians problem. Please speak to John Hunt about this and ask which Minister is in fact in overall control.'[744] Some Right-Wing Conservatives wanted to deny those who held British passports (about 50,000) the right to enter Britain. Government lawyers told Heath that this would be illegal. A domestic law to that effect (if enacted) could not override Britain's' international obligations.[745] Trend briefed on 6 September that 'we are now dealing with a man [Amin] who is in a highly suspicious frame of mind and may attack our "belongers" without warning … the evacuation of British subjects in the face of Ugandan resistance is therefore a real situation and, possibly, an imminent one.'[746] Despite the risk of a leak that would inflame the situation even more, preparations should be made to put troops on a 72-hour notice of mobilisation and 'to let it be quietly known that people who have no reason to stay in Uganda should leave as unobtrusively as possible.'[747] Shortly afterwards he asked for an investigation whether evacuation could be speeded up by detaching the 1st Parachute Regiment from its deployment in Northern Ireland and routing the exodus from Uganda through Nairobi in place of the intended route through the Seychelles.[748] At heart his position was not humanitarian; it was concerned with the reputation of the United Kingdom in the world. Thus, he advised against taking Uganda to the International Court of Justice on the substantive grounds of illegal expulsion, which could cause embarrassment over the continuing impasse on Rhodesia and over British immigration laws. It would be better to go to the court, he argued, on the grounds that people were being expelled without compensation, adding 'A favourable verdict would not, of course, secure compensation for the Asians; but it would satisfy public opinion that we had pursued the rights of our citizens vigorously.'[749]

Notes

1 Bodleian, MS. Eng. lett.c.273
2 CSC 11–257
3 Trend was Assistant Private Secretary 1939–41
4 PUS Foreign and Commonwealth Office 1969–73
5 Hurd, *Memoirs*, p. 195
6 Colville, *The Fringes of Power*, p. 35
7 Principal Private Secretary 1945–49
8 1955–56 with 'RAB' Butler
9 Plowden had made the recommendation in June 1961. Helsby served as Head of the Home Civil Service from 1963 to 1968
10 CSC 11–257
11 CAB 21/5256, 28.01.63
12 Barbara Castle, *The Castle Diaries 1964–70*, Weidenfeld & Nicolson, 1984, p. 115
13 Richard Crossman, *Diaries of a Cabinet Minister* Vol 1, Cape, 1975
14 Waldegrave, *A Different Kind of Weather: a memoir*, Constable 2015, p. 110
15 B Pimlott, *Harold Wilson*, HarperCollins 1992, pp. 347 & 622
16 Henry Kissinger, *White House Years*, Little Brown, 1979, p. 93
17 Fulton, *Report of An Inquiry into the Civil Service*, HMSO, 1968
18 PREM 15/1935, 20.09.71 quoted in Andrew, op. cit, pp. 565–87
19 Hennessy, *Whitehall*, Secker & Warburg, 1989, p. 215
20 Responsible for labour relations in the Department
21 Hennessy, op. cit, p. 388
22 Lee, Jones & Burnham, *At the Centre of Whitehall*, Macmillan, 1998 p. 141
23 Ramsden, *The Conservatives*, p. 464
24 Donoughue *Downing Street Diary Vol 1*, p. 13
25 Ramsden, op. cit, p. 470
26 Ball and Seldon, *The Heath Government 1970–74: A Reappraisal*, Longman 1996, p. 65
27 Maslow, *A Theory of Human Motivation*, Psychological review, 1943
28 Chandler, *Strategy and Structure: Chapters in the History of the Industrial Enterprise* Massachusetts Institute of Technology, 1962
29 Private information
30 *Royal Commission on the Constitution 1969–1973* (Cmnd 5460)
31 *Departmental Committee on Section 2 of the Official Secrets Act* Vol III p. 320
32 Ibid, pp. 324–5; the report was published on 29.09.72 it branded the Act a mess and called for its repeal
33 CAB 164/1295, 13.05.75
34 Interviews with Sir Douglas Wass and Sir Michael Palliser, 2007
35 CAB 21/5481, 11.06.63
36 Ibid, 25.06.63
37 PREM 11/3975, 11.11.62. It is not known to what Trend was referring but it seems likely that Kim Philby, who had defected at the start of the year and Anthony Blunt, who had confessed to the Security Service in return for indemnity against prosecution though he was not publicly identified as a Soviet recruiter until November 1979, would have been in his mind.
38 Lord of Appeal in Ordinary
39 Cmnd 2009, 25.04.63
40 CAB 21/4455 and 6076, 05.04.63
41 CAB 21/4455, 26.04.63
42 CAB 21/6076, 28.04.63
43 Ibid, 06.05.63
44 CAB 21/5163, draft paper for Cabinet, June 1961
45 Ibid, 27.06.61

46 Ibid, 10.07.61
47 Ibid, 04.08.61
48 Ibid, 29.07.63
49 CAB 21/6077, August 1963
50 Wilkinson, *Secrecy and the Media*, p. 275
51 *How Cabinet Government Works*, BBC Radio 3, 12.03.76
52 A small example illustrates the point. On 16.03.64 his brief on a proposal to transfer jurisdiction over divorce to the County Courts (C(64)72) identified that opposition from the Archbishop of Canterbury and from the Bar might mean the proposals would become an election issue. CAB 21/5932
53 Horne, 'Macmillan: The Official Biography' p. 159
54 PREM 11/4410, 18.10.63
55 Thorpe, 'Alec Douglas-Home,' p. 326
56 CAB 21/5796, brief on C(63)7, 08.05.63
57 CAB 128/38/1, and CAB 129/115, 22.10.63
58 CAB 21/5133, 01.11.63
59 Sacked by Macmillan in 1962 on the 'Night of the Long Knives' and resurrected by Home as Lord Privy Seal
60 CAB 21/5133, 15.11.63
61 Ibid, 19.12.63
62 CAB 21/4983, 06.02.63
63 CAB 21/5856, 18.09.64
64 CAB 21/5081, 29 and 30.08.62
65 Ibid, 11.01.63 and 21.02.63
66 PREM 11/4272, 12.02.63
67 CAB 21/5081, 29.04.63
68 Ibid, 17.01.64
69 CAB 21/5600, 06.02.63
70 Ibid, 01.03.63
71 CAB 21/5932, 22.05.63
72 Australia, Canada, Cyprus, Ghana, India, Jamaica, Malaysia, New Zealand, Nigeria, Pakistan, Sierra Leone, Sri Lanka, Tanzania, Trinidad & Tobago, Uganda
73 PREM 11/4189, 02.04.63; PREM 11/4347, 23.04.63; PREM 11/4905, 18.12.63; PREM 13/429, 04.02.65
74 CAB 21/5608, 02.10.64
75 CAB 21/5620, 19.07.63
76 PREM 11/4347, 23.04.63
77 PREM 11/4905, 18.12.63
78 CAB 148/18, OPD(65)37th, 31.08.65; box 281, Lyndon Baines Johnson Library
79 For a discussion of the Wilson Government's foreign policy in South East Asia see John Young, *The Labour Governments 1964–70*, volume 2 pp. 62–88
80 Between June 1948 and July 1960 Commonwealth troops (latterly when Templer was Governor General) fought (and eventually defeated) a guerrilla insurgency led by the military arm of the Malayan Communist Party. A campaign to win the support of rural tribes people was critical in denying support for the guerrillas
81 CAB 21/5060, 29.08.62
82 CAB 131/28, 09.02.63
83 CAB 21/5060, 12.11.63
84 Ibid, 28.10.63
85 CAB 21/5060, 15.03.63
86 Ibid, 01.11.63
87 CAB 131/28, 09.02.63; CAB 21/5060, 28.10.63, 05.11,63 and 12.11.63; CAB 21/5133, 02.01.64; CAB 21/ 5275, 29.06.64 and 20.07.64
88 PREM 11/4189, 02.04.63

89 Ibid, 28.10.63
90 From 1962–64 Duncan Sandys was both Commonwealth Secretary and Colonial Secretary
91 CAB 21/5063, 03.12.63
92 CAB 130/190, 04.04.63, 09.04.63, 23.04.63
93 CAB 21/5063, and 03.12.63
94 Coggins, *Wilson and Rhodesia: UDI and British Policy Towards Africa.* p. 364
95 Ibid
96 CAB 21/5063, 18.12.63
97 Quoted in Thorpe, *Alec Home*, p. 351
98 Ibid, briefing on CP(64)47, 18.02.64
99 Ibid, Annex to COS.1356/13/2/64, 13.02.64
100 CAB 128/38, 25.02.64
101 CAB 148/14 24.02.64 and 27.02.64
102 CAB 21/5063, manuscript note to Trend, 13.04.64
103 Ibid, 25.05.64
104 Ibid, 26.05.64 and 27.05.64
105 Ibid, 28.05.64
106 CAB 21/5064, 01.06.64
107 CAB 21/5063, 26.03.64
108 DO(64)47
109 CAB 21/5064, 26.06.64
110 Ibid, brief on DO(64)67, 21.07.64 and 31.07.64
111 Ibid, 07.08.64
112 CAB 133/201, 12.06.64
113 CAB 21/5064, 14.08.64
114 PREM 11/5026, 13.08.64
115 Ibid, 16.10.64
116 CAB 21/4782 and 5125, 08.02.63
117 US Secretary of Defense 1961–68
118 CAB 21/4783, brief on D(63)11 and 12, 29.03.63
119 Ibid
120 CAB 21/4872, 08.02.63
121 CAB 21/4783, 29.03.63
122 CAB 21/4782, 30.04.63 and 05.05.63
123 Permanent Secretary 1961–65
124 CAB 21/5901, 07.06.63
125 Ibid, 25.03.63
126 Churchill's chief military adviser during World War II and later the first Secretary General of NATO, 1952–57
127 Military Assistant Secretary to Churchill during World War II and later Director General of the BBC, 1952–59
128 PREM 11/4274, 30.11.62 and 28.12.62
129 Ibid, 23.02.63
130 CAB 21/5620, comments from Michael Cary, Deputy Cabinet Secretary, 26.09.63
131 The report was published as Cmnd 2276, working papers are on DO 193/91 at the National Archives
132 CAB 21/5620, 07.10.63
133 Ibid, brief on CP(64) 33 and 34, 05.02.64
134 CAB 21/5594, 03.0–6.64
135 PREM 11/4778 and 4779, 21 and 22.01.64
136 Whereby manufacturers were able, with legal backing, to specify a base price below which their goods could not be sold; the lifeline of many small shopkeepers, the

abolition of which may have contributed to the Conservatives losing the 1964 General election
137 CAB 21/5256, brief on CP(64)11 and 13, 10.01.64
138 CAB 21/5581, 24.09.63, 26.02.64 and 23.03.64
139 FO 371/174260, 24.09.63
140 *The Reshaping of British Railways* (1963) and *The Development of the Major Railway Trunk Routes* (1965) by Dr Richard Beeching
141 CAB 21/4956 29.03.63 to 31.05.63
142 PREM 11/4653, 15.09.64
143 PREM 11/4834, 22.04.64
144 HoC Hansard, 6th series, Vol 199, cols 527–8, 27.11.91
145 CAB 21/5809, 27.11.63
146 Ibid, 17.01.64
147 Ibid, 12.02.64
148 CAB 21/5081, 02.01.64
149 Quoted in Sandbrook, *White Heat: The History of Britain in the Swinging Sixties*, preface
150 Cmnd 2171, October 1963
151 The principle derived from the Haldane Committee report of 1918 on the Machinery of Government
152 CAB 21/6061, 06.01.64
153 Ibid, 06.03.64
154 PREM 11/4332, note by Philip de Zulueta, 24.11.63
155 Wilson, *The Labour Government 1964–70*, p. 23
156 PREM 13/077, 16 and 21.10.64
157 PREM 13/014, 21.10.64
158 CAB 21/5913, the briefing task was undertaken by Robert Armstrong, then serving in the Cabinet Office economic secretariat; though Trend did support a proposal to study how far the United States would be likely to support sterling for its own monetary policy purposes – CAB 21/5553, 29.12.65
159 CAB 21/5886
160 Ibid, 26.10.64 and 01.12.64
161 Contemporary British History, 11:2, pp. 129, Clifford & McMillan, *The Department of Economic Affairs*: witness seminar, 05.06.96
162 CAB 21/5541, 27.01.65 and 17.02.65
163 Alec Cairncross, Head of the Government Economic Service, 1964–69, at *The Department of Economic Affairs*: witness seminar, 05.06.96
164 Ibid, p. 139
165 CAB 128/39/21, CC(65)5, 28.01.65
166 CAB 21/5561, 6–10.12.64
167 United States National Security Adviser 1961–66
168 United States Secretary of State 1961–69
169 A full record of Trend's discussions with the Americans is on CAB 21/5552
170 Fellow of Balliol College Oxford and University Reader in economics, economic adviser to the Cabinet 1964–67
171 CAB 21/5541, 14.07.65
172 PREM 13/077, 16.10.64
173 Wilson *The Labour Government 1964–70* p. 45
174 CAB 21/5256, 02.11.64
175 PREM 13/0618.10.64
176 CAB 21/5197, 31.05.641 and 01.06.64
177 Ibid, manuscript note, 09.09.65
178 Crossman *Diaries of a Cabinet Minister* Vol I pp. 103–44, 15.12.64
179 CAB 21/5617, 02.04.65–13.10.65

180 Ibid, 11.08.66
181 Ibid
182 Cabinet Office paper, 24.12.65
183 CAB 21/5803, 18.01.66
184 Marginalia on CAB 21/5802, 08.02.65
185 CAB 21/5803, 05.04.65
186 Ibid, 21.07.65
187 Conservative Member of Parliament for Wolverhampton South-West 1950–74; Ulster Unionist Member for South Down, 1974–87
188 Conservative Member of Parliament for Lewisham West 1938–45 and for Hampstead 1950–66
189 CAB 21/5289, 29.07.64
190 Ibid, 09.09.64
191 CAB 128/39/6, CC(64)6th item 3, 05.11.64
192 CAB 21/5290, 26.01.65
193 CAB 21/5290, 30.01.65 to 26.07.65
194 CAB 21/5808, 07 and 09.09.65
195 Labour MP for Leicester South (later South West) 1945–67
196 CAB 21/5808, 06.10.65
197 Ibid, 12.10.65
198 Ibid, 22.11.65
199 Ibid, 24.11.65
200 Pimlott, *Harold Wilson*, p. 397
201 Butler and Butler, *Britiish Political Facts*, p. 259
202 *The Times*, 01.03.66
203 PREM 13/1546, 20.04.66
204 Leader of the Rhodesia Front and Prime Minister of Southern Rhodesia (after independence renamed Zimbabwe) 1964–79
205 Lord Trend for BBC Radio 3, *How Cabinet Government Works*, 12.03.76
206 Ten of the DEA officials would achieve Permanent Secretary rank, a remarkable track record for a small department
207 PREM 13/1546, 31.03.66
208 Ibid, 12.12.66
209 Ibid, 01.04.66
210 Ibid
211 CAB 171/1, 13.02.67
212 Herman, *Up from the Country*, p. 167
213 CAB 165/85, 04.10.66
214 CAB 164/426, 08.04.66
215 PREM 13/3072, 02 and 25.02.67
216 Ibid, 08.06.66
217 CAB 165/83, 13.02.67
218 Ibid, 10.04.67
219 PREM 13/3072, 10.12.68
220 Ibid, 17.02.70
221 CAB 165/256, 06.03.67
222 Ibid, 13.03.68
223 CAB 165/14, brief on CC(66)59, 19.04.66
224 CAB 165/23, brief on CC(66)163, 15.11.66
225 CAB 165/83, brief on CC(66)47, 10.04.67
226 CAB 165/14, brief on CC(66)87, 27.06.66
227 CAB 165/84, brief on CC(66)157, 10.10.67
228 CAB 165/256, brief on CC(68)26, 31.01.68
229 PREM 13/2076, 08.05.68 and CAB 165/256, brief on CC(68)74 & 76, 29.05.68

230 PREM 13/2076 and 2074, 08.05.68 and 11.12.68
231 News.bbc.co.uk/onthisday, 23.05.66
232 Pimlott, *Harold Wilson*, pp. 405–408
233 Wilson, *Labour Government*, p. 307
234 Pimlott, *Harold Wilson,* p. 407
235 CAB 165/14, 18.05.66
236 Ibid, 08.06.66
237 Stewart (ed.) *The Penguin Dictionary of Political Quotations*, p. 173
238 PREM 13/352, 25.04.66; the Selective Employment Tax was a payroll tax that subsidised manufacturing at the expense of service industries, introduced in 1966 and replaced by Value Added Tax in 1973
239 For example, Lord Croham, in Clifford & McMillan, *The department of economic affairs*, Contemporary British History, 11:2 p. 129
240 Ibid, Edmund Dell, p. 135
241 Ibid, Peter Jay, p. 132
242 Clifford & McMillan, op. cit, p. 128
243 CAB 165/14, brief on C(66)80–82, 20.06.66
244 Ibid, brief on C(66)99–103, 11.07.66
245 CAB 165/167, 21.10.66; 25.11.66
246 CAB 165/14, first acknowledged on 09.08.66; repeated in CAB 165/83, 28.11.66
247 CAB 165/167, 25.11.66
248 CAB 165/83, 28.11.66
249 CAB 165/167, briefs on SEP(66)11 and 14–16, 03.03.66
250 CAB 165/178, 12.01.67; CAB 165/167, briefs on SEP(67)23 & 28–29, 21.04.67, SEP(67)38–39, 22.05.67; CAB 165/83, brief on SEP(67)83, 24.05.67
251 Ibid, brief on SEP(67)13–14, 19–21, 17.03.67
252 Ibid, brief on SEP(67)24–26, 21.04.67
253 Ibid, brief on SEP(67)33–35, 22.05.67
254 Ibid, brief on SEP(67)41, 23.06.67
255 Ibid, brief on SEP(67)51 & 54, 21.07.67
256 Ibid, 12.01.67
257 Cabinet Office paper, 26.06.67
258 CAB 165/167, brief on SEP(67)50, 21.07.67
259 CAB 165/167, briefs on SEP(67)81 & 83–84, 13.10.67 and 07.11.67
260 Ibid
261 Cabinet Office paper 13.11.67
262 Ibid, 12.12.67
263 Ibid
264 CAB 164/84, 16.11.67 and CAB 164/86, 27.11.67
265 CAB 165/84, 16.11.67
266 Cabinet Office paper, 13.11.67
267 Retold in Clifford & McMillan op. cit, p. 139
268 Cabinet Office paper, 27.02.68,
269 Ibid, 28.02.68 and 05.03.68
270 The history of George Brown's resignations can be seen on PREM 5/483; Trend was often present during the reconciliations between Wilson and Brown
271 *Crossman Diaries*, 15.03.68 p. 712
272 Wilson Family Papers quoted in Pimlott, op. cit, p. 501
273 Cabinet Office paper, 31.05.68
274 PREM 13/2052, brief for MISC 205, 20.05.68
275 Ibid, 12 and 24.06.68
276 Ibid, 04.07.68
277 CAB 165/283, brief on SEP(68)84, 19.07.68
278 Cabinet Office papers 12.11.68 to 02.12.68

279 Cabinet Office paper, 03.02.69
280 Ibid
281 Ibid, 19.05.69
282 CAB 165/14, 20.06.66
283 PREM 13/1437, 14.11.66
284 CAB 165/23, 14.11.66
285 CAB 165/167, 28.20.66
286 CAB 165/84, 20.06.67
287 PREM 13/1437, 01.02.67
288 Ibid, 08.02.67
289 PREM 13/1437, 13 and 22.02.67
290 Ibid, 15.02.67
291 Ibid, 10.04.67
292 CAB 165/84, 26.07.67
293 Cabinet Office paper, 30.01.68 and 01.03.68
294 PREM 13/1540, 04.12.67
295 PREM 13/2135, 27.03.68
296 CAB 165/283, brief on SEP(68)31, 06.05.68
297 Ibid, brief on SEP(68)61, 26.06.68; for a full analysis of the Fulton Report see Lowe, *The Official History of the British Civil Service*, Routledge, 2011, pp. 114–129
298 Ibid, brief on SEP(68)63, 26.06.68
299 Ibid, brief on SEP(68)69 and 70, 05.07.68
300 CAB 165/345 and 165/844, 27.06.69 and 23.07.69
301 HMSO, *The Industrial Reorganisation Corporation* (Cmnd 2889), 1966
302 CAB 165/167, brief on SEP(67)42, 19.06.67
303 CAB 165/589, 05.05.69
304 CAB 165/589, 16.06.69
305 Ibid, 21.11.69
306 Ibid, 27.04.70 in relation to support for Cammell Laird shipbuilders
307 CAB 165/83, 07.12.66
308 CAB 165/589, 09.01.70
309 Minister of Technology 1966–70
310 CAB 165/589, 10.02.70
311 Ibid, 16.01.70
312 Ibid, 06.03.70
313 Ibid, 20.04.70
314 Ibid, 25.03.70
315 Secretary of State for Local Government and Regional Planning 1969–70
316 CAB 165/589, 07.04.70
317 Comments when opposing a Chrysler takeover of the British vehicle maker Rootes Ltd, CAB 165/83, 19.12.66
318 As when the electrical manufacturers Thorn and Philips were battling to acquire Pye, Ibid, 11.01.67
319 CAB 165/589, 21.11.69
320 CAB 165/83, 21.11.66
321 CAB 165/84, 08.11.67
322 CAB 165/589, 29.10.69
323 Ibid, 27.04.70
324 CAB 165/83, 06.06.67
325 CAB 165/469, 29.04.70
326 CAB 21/5737, 18 and 23.11.64
327 CAB 21/5736, 21.05.65
328 CAB 165/14, 31.05.67

329 Labour MP for Blackburn,1945–79, First Secretary of State and Secretary of State for Employment 1968–70
330 CAB 165/256, brief for MISC 230(68)1, 16.12.68
331 CAB 165/345, 24.09.67
332 Ibid, 29.10.69
333 CAB 165/844, 03.03.70
334 CAB165/256, 05.03.68
335 Permanent Secretary of the Commonwealth Relations Office & Commonwealth Affairs Office, 1962–68
336 CAB 21/5488, 01.07.65
337 Young, *The Labour Governments 1964–70* vol 2 pp. 1–4
338 CC(65)6, 30.01.65
339 David Bruce, US Ambassador to the United Kingdom, 1961–69
340 CAB 21/5552, 09.09.65
341 CAB 130/144, the Committee comprised officials, headed by Snelling of the CRO, and met 23 times between 4 October and the end of the year
342 CAB 130/206, 28.10.64; CAB 148/18, 22.09.65
343 PREM 13/1117, 09.03.66
344 CAB 130/144, 06.10.65
345 Baroness Williams – talk to the Mile End Group 28.02.13 and evidence from Pimlott, op. cit, pp. 369–71
346 PREM 13/86, 27.10.65
347 The record of discussions can be found on TNS CAB 21/5515; details of the extensive 'what if' briefing is on CAB 21/5514
348 Ibid
349 PREM 13/564, 16.11.65
350 CAB 21/5517, J.I.C./1053/65, 20.12.65
351 Deputy Secretary, Cabinet Office 1964–67
352 Hendrik Verwoerd, Prime Minister of South Africa 1958–66
353 CAB 21/5517
354 *Castle Diaries* 03.01.66, p. 90
355 Cmnd 2890, 12.01.6, 10.02.66
356 CAB 21/5516, 15.11.65
357 MISC 100/A documents can be found on CAB 165/37
358 PREM 13/356, PREM 13/1114, PREM 13/1116, 17.11.65, 05.01.66, 10.02.66
359 PREM 13/1738 and PREM 13/1739
360 CAB 165/122, 02.02.66 and CAB 159/61, 02.03.66
361 PREM 13/1117, 09.03.66
362 CAB 165/37, 07.03.66; CAB 165/122, 16.03.66; PREM 13/1117, 02.04.66 and CAB 148/25, 06.04.66
363 PREM 13/1117, 09.03.66
364 CAB 165/37, 16.04.66
365 CAB 165/564, 13.06.66 and 22.07.66
366 PREM 13/113, 18.11.66
367 CAB 165/122, CAB 165/124, CAB 165/175, CAB 165/564
368 Ibid, brief on OPD(67) 73 & 75, 17.10.67
369 PREM 13/3437, 22.04.68
370 CAB 164/898, 23.05.66
371 Trend's attempts to close loopholes in sanctions and to act against evasion are detailed in CAB 164/898
372 CAB 165/122, 07.12.67
373 Ibid, 07.03.68
374 Ibid, 18.01.66
375 Ibid, 23.06.67

376 Ibid, 08.02.66
377 CAB 165/14, 12.02.66
378 CAB 165/122, 16.03.66
379 Ibid, 11.08.66 and 09.02.67
380 Ibid, 27.10.66
381 Ibid, 04.01.67
382 Ibid, 31.10.66
383 Ibid, 27.07.68
384 Ibid, 01.07.67
385 Ibid, 24.09.68
386 Ibid, 30.10.68
387 CAB 148/83, 28.02.68
388 CAB 165/122, 25.03.69
389 Ibid, briefs on OPD(67) 18,19, 43–45, 09.03.67 and 09.06.67
390 Ibid, brief on OPD(67)20, 14.03.67
391 Ibid, briefs on OPD(69)51 and OPD(70)4, 23.10.69 and 26.02.70
392 Ibid, brief on OPD(67)39, 24.05.67
393 Ibid, brief on OPD(67)61, 27.07.67
394 Ibid,, brief on OPD(67)65, 27.07.67
395 Ibid, 20.03.68
396 Ibid, 21.01.66
397 Ibid, 25.07.66
398 Paymaster-General 1964–67 and unofficial adviser to Harold Wilson on defence and intelligence matters
399 Cabinet Office paper, 27.03.67
400 CAB 129/136/5
401 Cabinet Office paper, 03.02.69
402 Ibid
403 CAB 165/345, 09.07.69
404 J Young, *The Labour Governments 1964–70, Volume 2 International Policy*, Manchester University Press 2003, p. 11
405 Cabinet Office paper, 04.05.67
406 CAB 165/526, 25.07.67
407 CAB 165/122, 25.07.68
408 BBC News 04.02.67
409 CAB 165/122, 06.03.67
410 Ibid, brief on OPD(67) 18 & 19, 09.02.67
411 CAB 165/83, brief on C(67)78, 10.05.67
412 Young, op. cit, p. 14
413 CAB 165/273, 13.02.68
414 CAB 165/122, 24.05.67
415 Ibid, 14.07.67
416 Ibid, 30.10.69
417 Ibid, 23.10.69
418 Ibid, 14.03.67
419 Pimlott, *Harold Wilson* pp. 365–6
420 Cabinet Office paper, 18.03.67
421 T 23/68, 15.01.68
422 Former Treasury Under-Secretary under Presidents Kennedy and Johnson, Director of the Council for Foreign Relations 1966–81
423 Cabinet Office paper, 04.03.68
424 CAB 21/5561, 6–10.12.64
425 Ibid, 11.03.65
426 CAB 21/5552, 30–31.07.65

427 Ibid, 15–20.12.65
428 HMSO, *Statement on the Defence Estimates 1966*, Cmnd 2901
429 CAB 165/125, 25.08.67
430 CAB 165/86, 31.10.67
431 CAB/165/84, brief on C(67)180, 15.11.67
432 CAB 21/5552, 05.08.65
433 Pimlott, op. cit, p. 384
434 Pimlott, op. cit, p. 433
435 CAB 21/5600, 24.03.65
436 CAB 164/10, 06.12.65
437 CAB 165/122, briefing on OPD(66) 39 and 44, 09.03.66 and 04.04.66
438 Ibid, briefing on OPD(66) 52 and 99, 03.05.66 and 18.10.66
439 CAB 165/161, 21.05.66
440 CAB 165/83, 28.05.66
441 Ibid, 08.11.66
442 CAB 165/14, 29.06.66
443 CAB 165/83, 19.12.66
444 Ibid, 15.03.67
445 CAB 165/83, brief on C(67)12, 30.01.67
446 Ibid, 18.03.67
447 Ibid, 18.03.67
448 Ibid, 05.04.67
449 Ibid, 12.04.67 and 17.04.67
450 Ibid, brief on C(67)62, 26.04.67
451 Ibid, 19.04.67 and CAB 165/86, 22.04.67
452 CAB 165/122, briefing on OPD(67)2 and 35, 10.01.67 and 11.05.67.
453 Ibid, briefing on OPD(67)51 and 53, 04.07.67 on OPD(68)68, 06.11.68 and on OPD(69)62, 18.11.69
454 Pimlott, op. cit, p. 440
455 CAB 165/122, briefing on OPD(67)79, 02.11.67
456 Ibid, brief on OPD(67)87, 28.11.67
457 CAB 165/256, 17.01.68
458 Ibid, 26.02.68
459 Ibid, 10.04.68
460 Ibid, 11.11.68
461 CAB 165/345, 10.04.69
462 PREM 13/742 & 13/1957
463 PREM 13/2237, 25.01.67
464 CAB 21/5807, 15.06.65
465 PREM 13/501, 25.02.66
466 Moran op. cit, p. 141
467 PREM 13/3072, 08.06.66
468 Christopher Mayhew, Parliamentary Undersecretary of State for Defence 1964–66
469 CAB 164/23, 14.09.66
470 *Maurice Hankey: Man of Secrets*, Vols 1–3, Collins 1970–74
471 PREM 13/1554, 22.12.66
472 PREM 13/2237, 25.01.67
473 Ibid, 24.04.67
474 FCO 12/155, 03.04.73
475 CAB 164/65, 08.04.67
476 Ibid, 10.04.67
477 FCO 12/30, 20.04.67
478 Ibid, 25.04.67
479 PREM 13/1556, 26.04.67

480 CAB 164/65, 02.05.67
481 FCO 12/30, 02.05.67
482 CAB 164/65, 10.05.67
483 PREM 13/1556, 09.05.67
484 PREM 13/1556, 27.06.67
485 CAB 165/24 20.09.67 and PREM 13/2237, 21.10.67
486 PREM 13/2237, 24.10.67
487 *Daily Express* 15.02.67
488 PREM 13/1814, 20.02.67
489 Cabinet Office paper, 22.09.65
490 PREM 13/1814, 24.03.66
491 Ibid, 05.04.66
492 House of Commons Hansard, 28.02.67, cols 274–278
493 N Wilkinson, *Secrecy and the Media*, Routledge, 2009 p. 300
494 Andrew, op. cit, p. 532
495 PREM 13/1818 and 1819, 28 & 29.05.67
496 Cabinet Office paper 30.05.67
497 PREM 13/1818, 29 & 30.05.67, 13.06.67
498 PREM 13/1814, 15.06.67
499 Ibid, 29.06.67
500 Ibid, 05.07.67
501 Wilkinson, op. cit, p. 341
502 Ibid, p. 342
503 Cabinet Office paper, 19.03.68
504 Ibid, 26.07.68
505 Meeting in Burke Trend's room 03.11.67 quoted in Moran, op. cit, p. 164
506 Moran, op. cit, p. 168
507 CAB 164/640, 21.05.68
508 PREM 15/419, 31.03.71
509 BA 17/595, 15.04.72
510 DEFE 13/615, 25.03.69
511 Ibid, 24.07.69
512 DEFE 23/107, 01.03.71
513 DEFE 13/1304, 28.07.78
514 HMSO 1979–88 *British intelligence in the Second World War. Vols.1–3 Its influence on strategy and operations*, F.H. Hinsley … [et al.]
515 Cabinet Office paper, 03.11.67
516 HMSO, *Hansard* HoC 17.11.66, cols 634–641
517 PREM 13/1342, 09.10.67
518 Ibid, 09.11.67
519 PREM 13/1342, 31.01.68
520 Ibid, 01.01.69
521 Ibid, 17.11.69
522 Ibid, 23.11.69
523 Ibid, 01.12.69
524 Ibid
525 Ibid, 03.12.69
526 Labour MP for Grimsby, 1945–59, from 1959 Director of the Royal Institute of International Affairs
527 PREM 13/1342, 21.01.70
528 HMSO HoC Hansard 23.01.70
529 Paymaster General 1964–67
530 PREM 13/3471, 24.12.65
531 Cabinet Office paper, 14.10.66. The Security Service involvement in Wilson's

statement that the Seamen's strike is discussed more fully in Andrew, op. cit, pp. 527–531

532 *Sleuths and Diplomats*, The Economist, 24.06.67
533 Sir Patrick Dean, British Ambassador, Washington, 1965–69
534 Cabinet Office paper 30.06.67
535 Ibid, 10.07.67
536 Ibid, MISC 155(67)1st Meeting
537 PREM 13/2688 31.07.67
538 CAB 159/42, 12.09.67
539 Trend recommended that Dick White be once again moved, into the new slot as Intelligence Co-ordinator in view of his security and intelligence experience at the highest levels, a post he took up in April 1968
540 PREM 13/2688, 13.03.68
541 Verrier, *Through the Looking Glass*, pp. 9–10
542 Cabinet Office paper 24.10.67
543 Ibid, 21.05.68
544 Ibid, 19.01.70
545 Andrew, *Secret Service*, p. 498; Bower, *The Perfect English Spy* pp. 362–3
546 Dorril, *MI6: Fifty Years of Special Operations*, pp. 727–8
547 HC 898, 14.07.04
548 *The Conservatives*, p. 473
549 *Putting Britain Right Ahead*, the Conservative Party, July 1965
550 *Sunday Times*, 10.10.65
551 CAB 164/802 19.06.70 and PREM 15/007, 23.06.70
552 PREM 15/147, 24.06,70 and 25.06.70
553 PREM 15/076, 19.10.70
554 Ibid, 24.10.70 and 27.10.70
555 CAB 184/3, 26.03.70 and 21.05.70
556 HC 27 1993/94, Vol. 2, pp. 29–30, Contacts between senior civil servants and Opposition Parties in Treasury and Civil Service Committee, *The role of the civil service*, evidence by Sir Robert Armstrong, 27.11.85
557 CAB 184/3, 26.03.70
558 CAB 184/3, 21.05.70
559 CAB 184/1, 31.07.70
560 PREM 15/406, 28.07.70
561 CAB 129/151, 17.08.70
562 BA 17/1294, 20.08.70
563 BA 17/1294, 04.09.70 attended by Heath, Earl Jellicoe, David Howell, William Armstrong, Burke Trend and Robert Armstrong
564 PREM 15/406, 04.09.70; Armstrong reported on 17.09.70 that McMahon had ruled himself out
565 Conversation with Lord Butler of Brockwell, 04.06.15
566 CAB 184/1, Mayne was appointed on 23.07.70
567 BA 17/1294, 09.09.70 and 14.09.70
568 BA 17/1294, 14.10.70
569 CAB 184/3, 03.10.70
570 Hennessy, op. cit, p. 222
571 CAB 128/47, CM(70)29th Meeting Conclusions, 14.10.70
572 CAB 184/1, 11.11.70
573 BBC Radio 3, *Routine Punctuated by Orgies*, 07.11.83
574 See T11/4106 for Trend and science issues
575 PREM 15/406, 02.03.71
576 PREM 15/611, 19.04.71
577 PREM 15/1602, 26.05.71

578 Ibid, 23.07.71
579 Ibid, 03.06.72
580 Ibid, 20.09.71
581 Ibid, 17.07.72
582 Ibid, 24.07.72
583 Ibid, 05.09.72
584 Ibid, 07.09.72
585 Ibid, 21.09.72
586 Ibid, 29.09.72
587 PREM 15/926, 25.01.72
588 Ibid, 07.02.72
589 PREM 15/926, 16.05.72
590 Ibid, 27.05.72
591 PREM 15/1603, 13.09.72
592 *Financial Times* 23.08.72; *The Times* 24.08.72
593 PREM 15/1602, 18.07.72
594 PREM 15/762, 29.01.71
595 PREM 15/762, 27.06.71 and 01.07.71
596 Cmnd 4506, HMSO, 1970
597 PREM 15/940, 04.01.72
598 Ibid, 14.03.71
599 Ibid, 28.03.72
600 Ibid, 28.01.72
601 Ibid
602 Ibid, 10.05.72, Hunt arrived on 24 March
603 PREM 15/2014, 10.05.73, and 05.11.73
604 PREM 15/936, 23.11.70
605 Ibid, 17.05.72
606 Donoughue, *Downing Street Diary Vol 1*, p. 5
607 Rosaleen Hughes, *Governing in Hard Times*, unpublished PhD thesis 2012, University of London
608 CAB 128/44, Cabinet Conclusion 23.10.69
609 BBC News Channel, 07.07.07
610 CAB 165/475, 16.11.70, brief on paper C(70)103
611 Cabinet Office paper, 12.10.70
612 Ibid, 14.10.70
613 Ibid, 24.10.70
614 CAB 128/47, 03.12.70
615 PREM 15/19, 21.02.72
616 A corporatist body of employers, unions and government, modeled on the French Economic and Social Council, set up in 1962 by the Conservative Chancellor Selwyn Lloyd. It was influential until Margaret Thatcher became Prime Minister and was abolished by her successor, John Major, in 1992
617 PREM 15/084, 04.12.70
618 PREM 15/819, 26.05.71
619 HMSO Cmnd 4903, February 1972
620 PREM 15/926, 02.05.72 and PREM 15/819, 20.06.72
621 PREM 15/819,26.05.71
622 PREM 15/926, 07.07.72
623 CAB 165/974, 11.12.72
624 PREM 15/819, 26.05.71
625 PREM 15/983, 26.03.71
626 PREM 15/819, 26.05.71
627 PREM 15/1902, 14.06.71

628 PREM 15/983, 02.07.71
629 Ibid, 29.02.72
630 Ibid, 08.03.72
631 PREM 15/1902, 10.03.72
632 PREM 15/983, 17.03.72
633 On 27 January 1971 the Director General of the Security Service, Furnivall-Jones had sent Maudling a memo on the role of the Service in Industrial Action, which had firmly restated the traditional limits of the Charter. Andrew, op. cit, pp. 590–91
634 CAB 164/1158, 30.03.72
635 PREM 15/983, 18.04.72
636 Ibid, 12.05.72
637 Ibid, 20.04.72
638 CAB 163/269, 01.09.72
639 Andrew, op. cit, p. 597
640 PREM 15/983, 13.10.72
641 CAB 163/269, 31.10.72
642 Andrew, op. cit, p. 597
643 PREM 15/1679, 17.11.72
644 Add ref Andrew fn 53
645 Ibid, 20.12.72
646 Ibid, 07.11.72
647 PREM 13/3241, 10.06.70
648 CAB 165/974, 06.10.72, brief on IRP(72)
649 PREM 15/977, 22.11.72
650 CAB 163/269, 03.01.73
651 PREM15/1679.01.02.73
652 Hughes, op. cit, p. 189
653 PREM 15/062, 22.01.72
654 CAB 165/932, 15.07.70
655 PREM 15/062, 06.11.70
656 Ibid, 11.12.70 brief on CP(70)118
657 Private information
658 PREM 15/940, after two unsuccessful attempts to get Trend to axe Ministerial committees Heath switched the responsibility to John Hunt, 28.03.73
659 *Financial Times*, 23.08.72; Lord Croham confirmed on 09.09.08, that Edward Heath was pushing for this appointment
660 Trewin (ed.) *The Hugo Young Papers*, Allen Lane, 2008, p. 83
661 PREM 15/351, 05.05.71
662 PREM 15/418, 11.06.71
663 PREM 15/380, 21.07.71
664 PREM 15/940, 26.04.72
665 Ibid, 30.04.72
666 CAB 193/49, 09.05.72, and 12.05.72
667 MP for Knutsford, former oil company executive and Director General of the CBI
668 PREM 15/940, 06.11.72
669 Ibid, 09.05.72
670 PREM 15/1514, 19.12.72, the strategy group comprised the Prime Minister, Foreign Secretary, Chancellor of the Exchequer, Lord President, Secretary of State for Trade and Industry, Chancellor of the Duchy. Minister of Agriculture and Secretary of State for Defence; the larger group concerned with day to day matters comprised the Chancellor of the Duchy as Chairman, the Secretaries of State for Northen Ireland, the Environment, Scotland, Wales, Employment, Agriculture, Trade and Industry, the Lord Privy Seal, the Treasury Chief Secretary, the Minister of State Foreign Office and Sir William Armstrong

671 PREM 15/152912.04.73
672 Ibid, 14.04.73 and 04.06.73
673 See Niklas H Rossbach, *Heath, Nixon and the Rebirth of the Special Relationship*, Palgrave Macmillan 2009
674 Georges Pompidou, President of France, 1969–74
675 John Campbell, *Edward Heath: a biography*, Pimlico 1994, pp. 341–42
676 US National Security Adviser 1969–75; US Secretary of State 1973–77
677 PREM 15/1272, PREM 15/1380, 28.06.71
678 PREM 15/1362, 10.12.71
679 PREM 15/2203, 28.01.72
680 Ibid, 09.05.72
681 Governor of the Bank of England 1961–66; British Ambassador in Washington, 1971–74
682 PREM 15/1362
683 Soviet expert in the FCO and its PUS 1973–75
684 PREM 15/1362, 11.08.72
685 Ibid, 14.08.72
686 On 17 June 1972 burglars entered the Democratic Party National Committee Headquarters in Washington. Subsequent investigation implicated people connected to the Committee for the Re-election of the President and tapes from the President's Office pointed to a cover-up after the break-in. Faced with the risk of impeachment, President Nixon resigned on 9 August 1974
687 Ibid, 24.04.7 quoted in M Jones, *A Man in a Hurry*, Diplomacy and Statecraft 24:1, pp. 77–99, 25.02.13
688 Nixon Library, NSC files, Kissinger Office files, Country files-Europe, box 62, 18.04.73
689 PREM 15/1976, 17.01.73
690 Republican Senator in Washington 1957–81
691 PREM 15/1977, 01.02.73
692 PREM 15/1976, 23.01.73
693 The full text of Kissinger's speech is on PREM 15/1541
694 PREM 15/1541, 02.05.73
695 Jones, op. cit, p. 82
696 Kissinger, *Years of Upheaval*, pp. 162–63 and PREM 15/1380, 1543, 1541, 10.05.73
697 See Horne, *Kissinger's Year: 1973*, Weidenfeld and Nicolson, 2009, p. 118
698 PREM 15/1542, 10.06.73
699 Ibid; CAB 164/1234, 19.06.73
700 PREM 15/1542, 04.07.73
701 Ibid, 06.07.73
702 Ibid, 11.07.73
703 CAB 164/1235, PREM 15/1543, 30.07.73 and Kissinger, *Years of Upheaval* pp. 191–92
704 PREM 15.2034, the American request was received on 19.07.73 and approved by Heath on 26.07.73
705 Ibid, 13.08.73
706 Ibid, 20.08.73; Kissinger's action was reported in The Times and The Guardian on 05.02.74
707 See, for example, FCO: DBP O3, iv, no 179
708 Jones, op. cit, p. 77
709 PREM 15/1600, 15.12.70
710 Ibid, 18.12.70
711 PREM 15/1600, 23.12.70 and 30.12.70
712 Ibid, 05.01.71
713 Ibid, 10.02.71

714 Ibid, 12–13.05.71
715 Rosaleen Hughes, unpublished PhD thesis *Governing in Hard Times: the Heath Government and Civil Emergencies*, Queen Mary, University of London, 2012 p. 66
716 Hughes, op. cit, p. 101
717 PREM 15/984, 19 and 21.01.72
718 Ibid
719 CAB 130/559, 09.02.72
720 PREM 15/986, 21.02.72
721 PREM 15/1600, CAB 164/1139, 23.02.72
722 Hughes, op. cit, p. 125
723 PREM 15/986, 25.02.72
724 Ibid, 28.02.72
725 PREM 15/1600, 30.04.72
726 CAB 130/577 and 130/579
727 CAB 164/1139, 26.04.72
728 Ibid, 01.05.72
729 PREM 15/2015, 03.08.72
730 Ibid
731 PREM 15/977, 30.08.72
732 CAB 164/122613.12.72
733 Ibid, 24.05.73
734 PREM 15/976, 07.08.72
735 Hughes, op. cit, p. 148
736 PREM 15/1904 and 1905, April-May 1973, Jellicoe caught up in the scandal of Lord Lampton's association with prostitutes
737 PREM 15/976, 09.01.73, CAB 134/3653, 12.01.73
738 PREM 15/976, 20.12.72
739 CAB 163/186 01.09.72
740 CAB 134/3653 12.01.73 brief on paper IRP(73)2
741 CAB 165/974, 24.01.73, brief on papers IRP(72)23 and 24
742 Ibid, 23.02.73, brief on papers IRP(73) 8 and 9
743 BBC news website, 07.08.72
744 PREM 15/1259, 25.08.72
745 Ibid, 28.08.72
746 Ibid, 06.09.72
747 Ibid
748 PREM 15/1260, 08.09.72
749 PREM 15/1973, 12.12.72 brief on paper OPD(72)55

4 Iron Fist in Velvet Glove

Sir John Hunt
Cabinet Secretary
1973–79

Hunt sketch: John Hunt by John Stanton Ward

Source: Martin J. Hunt

At the start of John Hunt's six years as Cabinet Secretary the Conservative government led by Edward Heath was brought to its knees by the miners and the power workers. Towards the end of his tenure the Winter of Discontent wrecked the Labour government led by Jim Callaghan. During the intervening years one crisis followed another. After 30 years of net immigration into the UK, net emigration during the period 1961–1981 averaged 20,000 p.a.[1]. Britain was in retreat as an international power, the economy was faltering; there was no clear national strategy and for much of the time the government was divided. It took a combination of dedication to the public interest and sense of personal destiny for Hunt to hold the central machinery of collective government together.

At home the nation faced indeterminate elections, weak governments and labour militancy; abroad Britain struggled to live within its means. There were four Prime Ministers: two Conservatives provided the bookends of the period (Heath and Thatcher); two Labour politicians led during the middle years (Wilson and Callaghan). Some historians and contemporary commentators have described a Britain close to being ungovernable;[2] and towards the end of the 1970s the political consensus between the two principal political parties came to an end.[3] In January 1973 Britain joined the European Communities. Later that year the Yom Kippur war in the Middle East and a subsequent dramatic increase in oil prices were spectacular destabilising events. Government struggled to understand the behaviour of the foreign exchange markets, to respond to labour militancy and to control public expenditure, culminating in the United Kingdom's application for assistance from the International Monetary Fund (IMF) in 1976. A continuing Cabinet split over European policy threatened unity, as did the existence of a rival focus of power in the elected National Executive Committee of the Labour Party. Meanwhile, pressures grew for more open government and for reform of Section 2 of the Official Secrets Act, 1911. Hunt found himself in the eye of the storm around publication of the posthumous ministerial diaries of Richard Crossman.

In retirement Hunt described how the Cabinet Secretary's role tilted away from running the collective elements of government towards acting as a personal adviser to the Prime Minister.[4] He and the Head of the Policy Unit under Wilson and Callaghan (Bernard Donoughue) had jockeyed to have the last word with the Prime Minister. In 1978 he said, 'I have made it a practice in this job never to let people in other Departments see copies of minutes which I have sent to the Prime Minister but which have not been copied elsewhere: and whenever I have departed from this practice I have nearly always had cause to regret it.'[5] There are few specific criticisms of his advice. One is Professor Alex Kemp's Official History of North Sea Oil and Gas which claims that Hunt gave bad advice on the viability of a North Sea oil fund,[6] but these are rare – a more telling challenge is whether, on politically difficult issues, he pushed hard enough for a clear decision – putting the preservation of collective responsibility first. In matters of military confrontation he was a dove – challenging (without obvious success) why Britain was so keen to prosecute the Cod War when it was accepted that the government's long-term strategy for the fishing industry was to reduce the distant fishing fleet[7] and consistently supporting serious negotiation with Argentina. The impression is that for all the excellence of analysis the appetite for hard decisions was poor. Fudge rather than crunch. Few Ministers resigned despite deep splits over policy.

Some of Hunt's contemporaries drew an unfavourable comparison with Trend's intellectual calibre. At least one, who had known Hunt for many years, formed the view that he did not change significantly between the 1950s and the 1970s.[8] Practical rather than intellectual, his character was straightforward, tough, demanding, direct, determined. A strong believer in teamwork, he was a brilliant chairman who knew what outcome he wanted and set about achieving it as efficiently as possible, encouraging others to help on the way. He was a superb organiser able to handle a large array of issues simultaneously and he had a prodigious memory, seemingly able to recall at will the arguments and conclusions of meetings.[9] He was noticeably effective as the personal envoy of the Prime Minister in relations with Dr Kissinger in the USA and with the Federal Republic of Germany over the results of the 1974 Defence Review.

He showed powerful insight into industrial innovation in analysis of the opportunities that would flow from micro-processors; yet scant feel for commercial realities when discussing British Airways' preference for Boeing aircraft, commenting that British Aerospace, 'needed additional orders from BA for 1–11s which would do no more then reduce BA's potential profitability.'[10] Similarly when, in September 1973, Pierre Messmer (the French Prime Minister) appointed Ingénieur Général René Bloch to conduct an enquiry into Concorde from the standpoint of project management it was the potential for strategic and political disagreement with the French that concerned Hunt despite well-known concerns about time and cost overruns.[11]

Cabinet paid tribute to, 'a wise and skilful adviser and counsellor, and indeed friend, to members of successive Cabinets.'[12] Colleagues, however, sometimes felt that he overreached himself in promoting the centrality of the Cabinet Office.[13] His judgement revealed at the 1983 Permanent Secretaries' Conference, was that all four Prime Ministers that he had served found the Whitehall machine flabby and unresponsive; 'Seen from my perspective,' he reflected, 'the time and effort he or she has to expand to achieve quite simple results and the difficulty in exposing different options to him are ridiculous. Heath didn't do the political side [of the role]; both Wilson and Callaghan went as tired men.'[14] Why then was there not more success with institutional reform in Whitehall? Heath, Wilson and Callaghan all came to the conclusion that they wanted to split the Treasury between an Office of Manpower and Budget and a Finance Ministry, though all shrank from doing so.[15] Attempts to reform the Public Expenditure Survey, to give a lead on transparency in government, and key initiatives to improve the handling of cross-departmental issues such as the Joint Action on Social Policy came to little.

Part of the answer lies in the composition of the various Cabinets and the thin Parliamentary majorities they enjoyed. But the machinery of government problems lay deeper than simply reform of the Treasury: power had tilted towards Departments and away from the centre; as Hunt' put it: 'Certainly no Prime Minister can, or should be able to, override the Cabinet: but [a] greater sense of purpose, greater consistency and more efficiency at the centre could help. Throughout the six years I have been worried by insufficient communication downwards; inadequate information upwards; lack of alternative ideas and initiatives.'[16]

Planning for the succession to Trend began in March 1972. Sir William Armstrong[17] and Trend himself were the lead advisors but the appointment lay in the hands of the Prime Minister, then Edward Heath. Armstrong was widely thought by contemporary Permanent Secretaries to be devious, often acting behind the scenes without their knowledge.[18] However, he gave unequivocal support to Hunt: 'My assessment of Mr Hunt is that he is absolutely first class and outstanding among his contemporaries ... what marks him out ... are his personal qualities of drive, energy and leadership. He combines a strong and stable personality with the ability to get on with other people both inside the Service and in public life generally.'[19] By this time Heath and Trend were increasingly divergent in their outlook but likely to be saddled with each other until early 1974 when Trend would reach 60 (then the compulsory retirement age for civil servants) – Heath had grown increasingly impatient with Trend and keenly awaited his successor, John Hunt who, as Trend's deputy, had shown a good grasp of Heath's managerial style and would mitigate the Prime Minister's frustration that William Armstrong could not be designated Chief of Staff[20] and would maintain the parallel position of the Cabinet Secretary with the Head of the Home Civil Service.[21]

Foreshadowed by the praise from Armstrong, Hunt arrived in the Cabinet Office on 24 March 1972 for a third spell in the Department – on promotion with particular responsibility for the co-ordination of economic policy. His earlier tours in the Department had been as Private Secretary to Norman Brook (1956–58) and Secretary of the Joint Intelligence Committee (1960–62). His career had spanned five Departments with two overseas postings (Ceylon and Canada). He had not, however, served on the Prime Minister's staff. He could be reasonably confident that, barring accidents, he would take over as Cabinet Secretary.[22]

A widower since 1971, with two young children, he remarried in September 1973. His second wife was the widow of Sir John Charles, the former Chief Medical Officer, and the sister of Basil Hume, then Abbot of Ampleforth and later Cardinal Archbishop of Westminster. Trend offered advice that it would be nigh on impossible to fulfil the roll of Cabinet Secretary and bring up young children without a wife's support;[23] and on hearing of their engagement, Heath said: 'Tell them to get married quickly because they won't have time later.'[24] Two weeks later Trend left to become Rector of Lincoln College, Oxford. His retirement had been announced well in advance. His parting gift was characteristically modest. He chose *The Oxford English Dictionary* and asked that the Cabinet should sign it, which they duly did and presented it to him at his last appearance as Cabinet Secretary on 27 September. On his last working day a poignant entry in his appointment diary simply says, '4 pm – the Prime Minister will telephone.' Then at 5 pm Michael Moss (the Establishment Officer)[25] arrived to collect Trend's security passes and remind him of his obligations under the Official Secrets Act. *Sic transit Gloria mundi.*

Hunt carved out an enhanced role for the Cabinet Office. This he did partly through the development of a new style of Cabinet Office, traditionally concerned with steering and recording collective Ministerial and official discussions on issues brought forward by Departments, but now seeking to intervene early on behalf of the Prime Minister to align governmental actions. In appointing Hunt Heath had taken on board his credentials as pro-European and his talents as a potentially active co-ordinator of policy across Whitehall. The European Unit (EU) and the Civil Contingencies Unit (CCU) were central to the new style. Formally, both had been suggested by Trend (in May and August 1972 respectively) but Hunt had made them real. They marked a turning point in the role of the Cabinet Office; as one contemporary put it, 'he turned the Cabinet Office into a proper central department.'[26]

October to February 1973

If the start of 1973 had been a time of optimism and renewal, the year's close was one of upheaval. Hunt's first week included attending three Ministerial discussions on pay and prices and a group grappling with the moral and political issues over the Kenyan expulsion of Asians (GEN 139). Then on 6 October Egypt and Syria attacked Israel starting the Yom Kippur War. This was followed, in his second week, by the oil producers' consortium (OPEC) announcing a partial ban on oil supplies to countries supporting Israel (including the UK). A lesser person might have been forgiven for wondering whether promotion was worth the candle. But Hunt harboured no such thoughts. A strong Roman Catholic faith gave meaning to his life. He carried in an inner pocket an extract from Cardinal Newman's *Meditations on Christian Doctrine*:[27]

> 'God has created me to do Him some definite service; He has committed some work to me which He has not committed to another. I have my mission – I may never know it in this life, but I shall be told it in the next … If I am in sickness, my sickness may serve Him; in perplexity, my perplexity may serve Him; if I am in sorrow, my sorrow may serve Him. My sickness, or perplexity, or sorrow may be necessary causes of some great end, which is quite beyond us. He does nothing in vain; He may prolong my life, He may shorten it: He knows what He is about.'

This faith provided both grounding in parish life and an inner strength. As Roy Hattersley recalled, if provoked he did not hold back: over lunch at the French embassy, in the course of a conversation about how Popes are elected, Hattersley asked, 'What about divine guidance? Don't you believe in any of that sort of thing?' To which the reply came, 'I don't believe that God plays conjuring tricks. Neither does anybody with any sense.'[28] Though usually kind and thoughtful, many of his colleagues found him unapproachable – partly because his energies were focused where he felt he could add value and because he was not averse to stepping aside from other matters on the basis of, 'it's not my problem.' Nor, unlike Brook or Trend, did he forge a close bond with any of the Prime Ministers he served.

He inherited from Trend a stellar civil service team in the Cabinet Office Secretariat. By virtue of their reputation in Whitehall it was perceived as free from

Departmental bias.[29] Under Hunt's guidance servicing of Cabinet continued at an increased tempo. There had been 40 Cabinet Meetings in the first 38 weeks of the year; there were 23 during the next 14 weeks. In addition Hunt dealt with 19 Cabinet Committee or ad hoc ministerial meetings chaired by the Prime Minister, including five highly varied ministerial ad hoc committees: GEN 79 – precautions against a mass break-out at the Maze prison; GEN 139 – nationality law and immigration; GEN 142 – prices and pay; GEN 182 – the oil crisis; and GEN 186 – the Channel Tunnel.

There are no indications in Hunt's briefing that UK intelligence assessments indicated an October attack on Israel and the rapid build-up of the conflict pointed to gaps in the British defence planning scenarios. In December Hunt drew out the lessons for crisis management: the main current assumption was that the UK would pass by stages from peace to conflict. However, an American red alert of 25 October had shown that matters could escalate more quickly than was allowed for in the planning. British organisation had fallen short in the speed with which Ministers were briefed and in the establishment of links between the Cabinet Office and other operations rooms. Hunt's response was to introduce procedures for the Cabinet Secretary, the Heads of the Foreign & Commonwealth Office (FCO) and the Ministry of Defence (MOD), the Chairman of the Joint Intelligence Committee and Chief of its Assessments Staff to work more quickly, in concert, to brief Ministers and for the Cabinet Office and FCO secure communications systems to be activated at one to two hours notice.[30]

Domestically, Ministerial attention was focused on industrial relations. Following a 13% pay offer, on 12 November the National Union of Mineworkers (NUM), rejecting the advice of its General Secretary and announced an overtime ban. Coal production fell by 20–25% in its first 3 days. The government immediately proclaimed a state of emergency (the fifth since 1970). So when the train drivers' union, ASLEF, also announced an overtime ban Ministers worried that it would only require the dockers to do something similar to replicate the precursor to the 1926 General Strike. (In December 1972 the Department of Employment had blocked a proposal to examine precisely this threat.)[31] In addition, a Task Force on Oil Supplies concluded that there would be a serious threat to the United Kingdom if the Yom Kippur fighting were to last longer than 10 days.[32] Contingency plans were put in place to have an immediate public impact, including petrol rationing – though this offered little in the way of savings: about 3% of supplies when fully implemented.[33] The Ministerial Economic Strategy Committee met six times between 2 November and 11 December including discussing how to respond to the commercial behaviour of the oil companies in diverting supplies to their most profitable markets.[34] By mid December Ministers were discussing a need to frighten people to encourage support for union moderates. A three-day working week was announced to come into effect on 1 January 1974. Then, on 25 December, OPEC announced an increase in oil prices from $3 a barrel to $12, triggering a recession in the West. By late January Departments were being told to re-examine their whole approach to contingency planning;[35] and on 5 February Hunt briefed Permanent Secretaries on the decisions Cabinet might have to make in the next day or two. These included using helicopters to bypass picket lines for essential staff, the possible use of troops to maintain essential services, and the allocation of steel and chemical stocks to priority users. Permanent Secretaries were asked to ensure that all Cabinet Ministers were aware that it was not just the physical amount of fuel stocks that would limit the ability to hold out against the miners, but a shortage of basic materials and other economic factors.[36]

Arguably, what Heath most needed was help in formulating messages that would resonate in the country. The channel of advice to him was, however, narrow, dominated by the doom-laden William Armstrong[37] – other senior officials, including the PUS at HM Treasury, had difficulty in getting their messages through to the Prime Minister, often not knowing whether they had been passed on by Armstrong.[38] Nevertheless, on 17 December 1973 four senior officials (including Armstrong) minuted Heath seeking his support for the Chancellor of the Exchequer's impending economic package.[39] The minute was a signal both that the centre of Whitehall was united in support of the proposed measures and of the seriousness of the situation. But Heath already knew what might be needed. He had warned the Copenhagen Summit on 14–15 December that his government would have to deal with the worsening economic situation through expenditure cuts and higher taxes.[40]

At the same time, Heath was increasingly concerned that behind the industrial unrest there might lie political intent to bring down the government by extra-constitutional means. In a personal message of 15 January 1974 he asked the Lord Privy Seal (Lord Windlesham)[41] to assume responsibility for publicity based on six-monthly factual reports about subversion and industrial militancy, produced by the group on Subversion in Public Life (SPL).[42] That group was charged with developing methods to counter subversive activity, including some that were covert. Hunt had been inducted into the arrangements in October 1972. In December 'Burke electrified [the JIC Assessment Staff] by calling a meeting on Friday, 29 December at very short notice to discuss the handling of current intelligence by the Subversion in Public Life Group.'[43] The result was the creation of the Industrial Assessment Group (IAG) meeting weekly at 11.00 am on Wednesdays to produce an assessment of the current industrial relations position by the evening. Hunt put it to Heath: 'This is not a matter of establishing a mini-Ministry of Information or of involving Civil Servants in party political activity. But where there is open evidence that militants are trying to destroy the democratic system as we know it or to use industrial action rather than the ballot box to bring down the Government, it seems proper and desirable that officials should collate it so that Ministers may use it if they judge it wise.'[44] By July 1976, however, Hunt had become concerned at inactivity in the SPL group with the consequent risk that IAG output could produce a distorted picture unless fitted into periodic, balanced assessments. He gave the SPL new terms of reference to make clear the Group's assessment function, as well as its role in controlling the collection of information. Though the group would not be precluded from indicating directions in which action was needed it was not for them to initiate or recommend action. That would be the responsibility of a reactivated Home Security Committee (S(H)) chaired by the Cabinet Secretary. This group, in turn, would advise Ministers on appropriate measures to counteract subversion in the United Kingdom and would not be confined to industrial subversion: subversion in the public service, in education, and in the media was specifically mentioned. Thus assessment and policy formulation were separated in a similar manner to operation of the JIC. The SPL Committee was, in all but name, a JIC(C) and first met at the end of January 1977. Its assessments were reassuringly dull, indicating that although a number of extreme groups were seeking to subvert British life, few reached anywhere near critical mass in their numbers or influence – the most worrying being subversion in the media – especially, but not exclusively, in television which might provide the opportunity for extreme groups to 'chase the mike'.

From the outset Hunt also kept a weather eye on the European Unit. On 20 September Jean Monnet met the Prime Minister to advocate regular meetings of the heads of government of the Nine – which, to Heath's dismay, he wanted to call a provisional European Government.[45] Subsequently, Heath spoke at the autumn Conservative Party Conference in favour of EEC heads of government meeting regularly and later that his Principal Private Secretary warned Nairne that Heath now expected action, not the low profile follow-up favoured by the European Unit.[46] Whitehall was worried by Heath's impetuosity and Hunt joined Robert Armstrong to warn against lobbying in favour of summit meetings, as 'there is a difference between the UK and France on coverage.'[47] There was also a potential gap opening up between the government and the City of London over the need to co-ordinate activities bearing on the future of London as a financial centre.[48] The new Governor of the Bank of England (Sir Gordon Richardson) was distinctly cautious about reactivating the City Liaison Committee and the associated GEN 150 Whitehall group.[49]

EEC Heads of Government met at the end of 1973, in Copenhagen, and Hunt was a member of the Prime Minister's party. The meeting was not a success. In a British post-mortem Hunt declared that it had fallen between the stools of 'a fireside chat between Heads of Government' and a decision-making body. Too much time had been spent on a press communiqué and too little on the issues. He proposed that, in accordance with original suggestions from President Pompidou of France, twice-yearly Heads of Government meetings should concentrate on informal exchanges over a limited number of topics, prepared in advance but not tied down or with options closed. Attendance should be severely limited and there should be no communiqué. Perhaps in addition, every two years there should be a summit to chart a course for the Community covering a large number of issues and producing a package deal.[50] Heath agreed and planning for a meeting in June 1974 was moving along these lines when a General Election was called for February.[51]

The UK entry into the European Communities had the potential to alter Britain's position in the geo-political atlas. Henry Kissinger[52] complained to Lord Cromer[53] in November 1973, that 'the special relationship was collapsing'[54] –

Britain's entry into the Communities should have raised Europe to the level of Britain, it had in fact reduced Britain to the level of Europe.[55] An article in *The Washington Post* referred to Heath as, 'some kind of decadent Gaullist.'[56] At this time Hunt did not have Trend's closeness to Kissinger – it is unclear if he had ever met him in person before he became Cabinet Secretary. That soon changed; he met Kissinger six times during 1974, starting with a mission to Washington on 30 January 'to smoke out the American intentions about oil supplies and oil prices'[57] in preparation for an Energy Conference due to take place in Washington between 11–13 February. The UK had begun secret contingency thinking on how to react if the United States resorted to the use of force in the Middle East. The JIC Assessment Staff had concluded that if the Western European and Japanese economies looked like collapsing the most likely action would be for the US to seize control of the oil fields in Saudi Arabia, Kuwait and Abu Dhabi. Hunt sent Heath a five-page commentary on the implications for the UK and Europe.[58] With 30,000 British nationals in the Middle East it would not be possible to evacuate them all at short notice. In a chilling phrase he reported that, 'We might have to write off many of our people,'[59] and went on, '... the consequences of American intervention at the early stage would be disastrous for Europe's interests ...' Even US action at a late stage would be likely to split Europe, encourage the Russians to make threatening moves and might in itself be too much for the political stability of some of the European countries.[60]

Before Hunt left for Washington Sir Thomas Brimelow[61] gave him a copy of early thinking by the FCO planning staff about how foreign policy might change in response to the oil price rise.[62] Hunt commented at some length.[63] The UK needed to economise and to borrow to get it through the lean years until North Sea oil began to flow in earnest. The ability to borrow would depend on the progress in the domestic economy but also on the perceived value of the UK as a military or political ally, for which the British contribution to NATO was crucial. At all costs, he wrote, 'we must not antagonise at the same time both the United States and the Community ... With hindsight have we tended in the last year to see them too much as alternatives.' If the Conservatives got back in power would a more *communautaire* approach in our policies help bring the French along?

Hunt's intentions in travelling to Washington were to strengthen Kissinger's view of the UK as an ally through support for what was believed to be a conviction that there must be a Middle East settlement in which the Israelis would have to surrender some occupied land. In the event, the discussions revealed that the American emphasis had shifted from concern about supplies of oil to concern about its price in the light of OPEC actions. Kissinger was endeavouring to form a Western block of oil consumers for negotiations with the oil producers, but recognising that bilateral deals were inevitable, argued that what was important was to establish rules of behaviour. Knowing of French suspicions that the US motive was to corral the Nine behind US leadership, Hunt concentrated on teasing out the US view. He argued that the UK was already getting into problems over coal and that its first priority must be to ensure reasonable continuity of supply. However, the UK appreciated the dangers of beggar-my-neighbour policies and did not think that harm had been done by the recent bilateral deal with Iran – at about $7 a barrel the deal could not be construed as bidding up the price. Kissinger was unmoved, 'a situation in which 40 million backward people were able to dictate to 800 million others their style of life, their standards of living and even the relations between them was basically intolerable ... It would have to be made clear to the oil producing countries that the balance of payments consequences of recent price increases were not just intolerable, but made the whole world trading system unworkable. The oil producing countries simply did not need sufficient goods from the industrialised countries to close the payments gap.'[64] Later in the year Hunt pressed the case for the US administration to withdraw its objections at COCOM[65] to the proposed sale of Spey aircraft engines to China, and alerted the Americans that the British might approach them for a crash programme of coal sales if the domestic industrial relations situation worsened.[66]

The Mechanics of Government

By 1972 the initial reforming zeal of the Heath administration had run into the sands but there were still echoes in continued complaints about Cabinet Committees. Trend had taken criticisms of *his* Cabinet Committee system badly; seeking to preserve what he believed was the safeguard of collective responsibility and the strongest bulwark in protecting the Prime Minister's position.[67] By contrast, Heath informed Hunt that he had four months to read himself into the Cabinet Secretary position and asked for a report on the organisation of committee business by the end of September.[68] The bedrock of Hunt's enquiry was a questionnaire to Ministers in which he sought opinions on the time taken up in committee, the appropriateness of topics, a possible wider use of focused task forces, the use of mixed Ministerial and official membership and perceptions that issues were being blunted by the search for compromise before Ministers were involved. By early November Hunt was ready to give an optimistic interim report – the Cabinet Office was becoming more cohesive and more dynamic; a forward look at government business was planned for completion during each of the Parliamentary Recesses, starting in January 1974; the Secretariat would act to prevent more than one brief going to the Prime Minister from different parts of the Cabinet Office. Heath scribbled, 'Thank God!' in the margins.[69]

Finally, on 23 November, Hunt reported. 166 Cabinet Committees (46 Ministerial and 120 Official) should be reduced by a third. Significantly, no attempt was made to assess the saving in time this would make – during 1973, for example, of the 17 Committees (excluding Cabinet) involving the Cabinet Secretary in 51 meetings, no fewer than seven met only once, only four met six times or more. So the savings of Ministerial and official time would have been much less than one third. Heath commented waspishly, 'I thought 53 was only a beginning. Can we not abolish a lot more? It still leaves 113 Committees.'[70] All that Hunt could offer in return was that 53 had now risen to 55 of which 21 were Ministerial Committees.[71] One interpretation is that as these were early days

Hunt did not want to cause too much of a stir, or perhaps Ministers did not give him the evidence he needed to be more radical. But the creation of co-ordinating units in the Cabinet Office suggests a softly-softly tactic to avoid Ministerial revolt over centralisation of power. Hunt kept a tight control of Committee membership and agendas – denying many their wish to become members and consigning unwelcome requests for items to be included in the Cabinet agenda, in particular, into a void between him and the Prime Minister, with each referring anyone who protested to the other.

Robert Armstrong delivered Heath's decision to call an election to the Leader of the Opposition on 7 February 1974. For some time it had been clear that the result could be a Hung Parliament. The Civil Service Department had examined the constitutional precedents for a coalition.[72] But the major discussants were the Queen's Private Secretary, Sir Martin Charteris, Robert Armstrong Heath's Principal Private Secretary, and Hunt. Armstrong and Hunt had been giving independent thought to the actions that The Queen might then take. The approaches covered the circumstances around a request for a Dissolution from a 'minority' Prime Minister; that The Queen might, on occasion have to undertake informal consultations with political leaders if the result was not clear from the outset – along the lines followed by Continental Monarchs or Presidents; and considered a decision tree based on the various permutations of possible results. In the event the result was 301 Labour seats, 297 Conservative and 14 Liberal. Labour arrived as a minority government on 6 March after the collapse of Conservative-Liberal talks aimed at a coalition government. In this position the new Prime Minister, Harold Wilson, faced the possibility of defeat over the Debate on the Address (normally regarded as a vote of confidence) and at his request the government's constitutional adviser, Lord Crowther-Hunt,[73] and Armstrong secretly advised on the options were the vote to be lost: (a) try to put together a coalition; (b) tender your resignation and advise The Queen to send for the leader of the Conservatives; (c) request The Queen to dissolve Parliament and call another election. Crowther-Hunt thought that the Queen would be obliged to grant a Dissolution; but after consulting Hunt, Armstrong advised that she would not be obliged to do so and might consider that the country would be best served by one of the other options.

Wilson was unfamiliar to Hunt, who had been a Treasury official during the 1964 Labour government and there is no evidence he was party to the demarcation arguments between the Treasury and the Department of Economic Affairs. He was First Civil Service Commissioner from 1967 to 1971. Nor did the Labour front bench know Hunt, except by reputation. The general perception was that he was very capable, if also very mysterious.[74] Nevertheless, Wilson kept both Hunt and Armstrong in their positions. Hunt had only been Cabinet Secretary for five months and could claim to be untainted; Robert Armstrong, however, had been Principal Private Secretary since 1970 and was known to have been personally close to Heath. With great skill Armstrong moved seamlessly to offer all his accumulated knowledge, contacts and procedural artistry to bring the new Prime Minister an efficient central machine and the promise of enough collective Cabinet responsibility to keep Labour in power.

Hunt's opening briefing for Wilson identified five immediate decisions:[75] (1) how to bring about a return to normal after the state of emergency; (2) whether to choose a British or American upgrade to the strategic nuclear deterrent – a decision Wilson put with a small ad hoc Ministerial group outside the Cabinet Defence Committee;[76] (3) the role of the Cabinet Office Briefing Room (COBR), the existence of which was confidential, in handling terrorist actions in the UK; (4) the channels for intelligence reports; (5) the future of the CPRS. The briefs were partly factual and partly set out options. Hunt also submitted separate notes on two matters likely to be new and where, perhaps, the Cabinet Office was vulnerable – the day-to-day machinery for European Community matters and arrangements for the EEC renegotiation promised in the election manifesto.[77] After describing the reasons why the Heath Administration had decided not to have a Ministry of Europe he pointed to a parallel need for strong co-ordination of the renegotiation strategy, given the extent to which trade-offs were a feature of Community life. He suggested that Wilson should chair such a senior Ministerial committee. More routine work could be left to the Foreign and Commonwealth Secretary, supported by a junior colleague who could handle Parliamentary interest at a detailed level.

It was an open question where this junior minister might sit in the government. But then Hunt deftly brought in the idea of preserving the European Unit. This would both reassure departments and ensure that the Prime Minister was kept closely in touch with key issues. Then he struck a final blow: if the co-ordinating role were to be put with the FCO Hunt was '... quite sure we would find Treasury officials tending to put the shutters up. I think it is particularly important to ensure that there is strong central direction at official level to ensure that the task of renegotiation is undertaken energetically in the way that Ministers wish.'

The Cabinet Office Deputy Secretaries met Hunt, usually on Thursday afternoon, to plan Cabinet and committee business prior to his briefing the Prime Minister on Friday morning.[78] Wilson would have been familiar with this from the service provided by Trend. However, Hunt pointed up a distinction: 'With the appointment of Deputy Secretaries to each main area of the Secretariat, I have encouraged them to play a rather more active role in ensuring that the Committee system does not operate in a passive or reactive way. There is an increasing need to plan the forward decision taking process taking full account of political requirements and timescales. We also aim to let you have a 'forward look' towards the end of each Parliamentary Recess of work ahead against a timescale of when decisions will be needed.'[79]

Although the Cabinet Office grew from 598 staff in 1973 to 630 by 1979,[80] the burden on Hunt was by no means lightened. In a typical year he had to deal with 40–60 Cabinet meetings and at least as many Cabinet committee meetings or ad hoc groups chaired by the Prime Minister. After a short description of the background a brief would summarise the key issues for decision, leading into advice on how to organise the discussion – who to call to speak in what order and how to focus speakers on the key points – ending with possible conclusions from the meeting. No advice was proffered on timing; if time ran out the record would say that the committee had not been able to reach agreement and discussion would be resumed. It was not uncommon for discussion of later items on the agenda to be perfunctory.

Hunt's briefs often attempted to enlarge the Cabinet Office role by appeals to the inter-departmental neutrality of Cabinet Office chairmanship. In addition he codified procedures and precedents in a revised 'Guide to Minute Taking' of February 1974 and in a companion guide to chairmanship in 1977. The former had last been revised in 1969; the new version principally recognised entry into the European Communities but also a tendency for the record of meetings to take the chairman's formal summing up as the outcome of the discussions. 'It is right,' the guidance said, 'to make [the summing up] as firm as the consensus reached will allow; but this must be done with complete integrity and any temptation to ascribe more than is justified must be revisited.' The latter guide was a new departure following a request from Donald Maitland in October 1976, in anticipation of the first United Kingdom Presidency in the European Communities, for something that would help prepare officials for the task ahead. Hunt could see that it might be helpful to set down guidance for Deputy and Under-Secretaries with little experience of inter-departmental chairmanship. The result, *Dos and Don'ts of Chairmanship* encapsulated the skill of 'knowing where you want to get to – and getting there'.[81]

Attempts to use the CPRS as a collective briefing agent for Cabinet as a whole were mixed. Hunt thought that presentations on strategy for the Cabinet would improve discussion. But he had a number of major criticisms of the first CPRS paper and decided that it should not be circulated. Rothschild withdrew all copies, including those circulating within the CPRS, prompting *The Sunday Times* to speculate (erroneously) that, 'the Cabinet Secretary, Sir John Hunt, ordered all copies to be destroyed.'[82] He returned to the challenge in March 1974 telling Wilson that: 'I have long felt that the CPRS ought from time to time to give a presentation to introduce Ministers to a major topic which is going to preoccupy them over a period of months and on which decisions will be needed.' The medium-term economic assessment and social issues, such as the poverty trap, might be candidates for discussion.[83] Wilson approved the suggestions in early April but it was not until November that there was an experimental discussion at Chequers and Hunt left it until March 1975, to suggest more sessions, proposing meetings two or three times a year.[84] Wilson was lukewarm; immediate problems meant that it would not be possible to decide whether to go ahead before June.[85]

The Policy Unit

Immediately, Wilson introduced a major organisational change and strengthening of the Prime Minister's staff with the formation of the Downing Street Policy Unit, comprising six external appointments working under the direction of Bernard Donoughue, on leave of absence from the London School of Economics. Unlike some of his senior colleagues, Hunt's response to the potential threat to the civil service was to hold the new unit in a close embrace. He later explained that different perspectives and timescales meant that Ministers (from any political party) largely felt no identification with the civil service at large.[86] Hence, he recognised the legitimacy of an internal source of political advice. However, there could be confusion between the respective roles of the Policy Unit, the CPRS[87] and the Secretariat. All parties needed to know the appropriate demarcations and procedures for the discharge of business. Hunt took the initiative with Donoughue on 2 April to discuss the Policy Unit's work programme and suggested to Wilson that its relationship with the civil service should be codified.[88] After two discussions a workable draft concordat emerged and was subsequently agreed by all the parties. Hunt wrote to Permanent Secretaries on 9 May with a summary. Policy Unit staff were civil servants. Their special role was: 'advisers to the Prime Minister in his role as guardian of the Manifesto and of the direction of policy of the Parliamentary Labour Party'.[89] Subject to the agreement of the Departmental Minister concerned the Unit should be granted access to officials to inform themselves factually or about the development of official thinking on Departmental policies. This access should not, however, be a channel for conveying proposals, decisions or major comments on questions of policy, which would be handled between Ministers and Private Offices in the normal way.[90] Risks to the Cabinet Office's position would be mitigated by relating the Unit's work programme to the regular Cabinet Office forward look and by instructions that Cabinet Office briefs should not be sent to Donoughue, nor should his Unit be used as a channel of communication to the Prime Minister or his Private Office. Thus the separateness of the Policy Unit was established.

The Crossman Diaries

On 5 May 1974 the former Cabinet Minister Richard Crossman died,[91] bequeathing to his literary executors the task of seeing through to publication a three-volume diary intended to blow apart secrecy at the centre of government. Originally conceived as a quarry for a work of serious political commentary,[92] Crossman had kept a blow-by-blow account of all meetings he attended as a Minister supplemented by his candid observations on policies and people. Over the next 17 months, on behalf of Wilson, Hunt sought to prevent publication of detailed accounts of Ministerial meetings and official advice, culminating in a failed injunction against volume 1 of the diaries. Then, for a further 18 months, he was engaged in a battle of attrition as volumes 2 and 3 were crawled over to achieve compliance with the requirements of national security and foreign policy. It was the nadir of his career and left him exposed and bruised.

It was widely known that Crossman was keeping a detailed diary. In that knowledge Wilson had set up a committee under the Lord Chancellor (Lord Gardiner) to review the arrangements which allowed Ministers to publish memoirs in advance of the release of documents under the 30-year rule enacted in the Public Records Act 1967. The Committee's report was discussed, inconclusively, at

Cabinet on 21 September 1967 with Wilson offering to put forward proposals himself. But this was never done and in 1971 Wilson published memoirs that breached the conventions.[93] These reflected a principle that those who are accountable publicly for their actions should be allowed to explain and defend those actions; but they also acknowledged a wider obligation to protect the confidentiality of Ministers' exchanges in the interest of the collective responsibility of government.[94] Ministers seeking to publish memoirs had long been expected to submit their text to the Cabinet Secretary for vetting.[95] This practice had not been universal[96] but in April 1971 Crossman had agreed with Trend to comply with the requirements for protecting national security.[97] However, as early as July 1971 Trend reported that Crossman was unwilling to accept that he could not be accompanied by a research assistant when consulting departmental papers.[98] The Permanent Secretaries, led by Sir William Armstrong were keen to assert a strict doctrine that only former ministers themselves could have access.[99] However, Heath thought that the civil servants weren't behaving like adults;[100] and, in any case, Trend had declared himself uncertain about trying to apply the conventions because there was no means of enforcement.[101] He told Heath that, 'it is now almost unsustainable to maintain the convention of confidentiality' in Ministerial memoirs.[102] Heath offered Crossman a compromise – only he could have access to papers but Departments would try to help with checking facts – and Crossman accepted.[103] But when Crossman was diagnosed terminally ill he again made a request for Janet Morgan, his research assistant, to be allowed to accompany him and on compassionate grounds Hunt overruled civil service advice to allow this provided that she did not have independent access to the papers.[104] Less than a month later Crossman died.

After a decent interval, Hunt wrote to Janet Morgan to seek reassurance that the text would be cleared with him,[105] and Volume 1 was delivered ten days later. Initially Hunt thought that realistically there did not seem much scope to achieve substantial alterations,[106] but by the end of May 1974 he was increasingly troubled by the issues of principle the diaries raised.[107] But the author was dead, and although Crossman had appointed Literary Executors – which included Michael Foot, a political friend, but also Secretary of State for Employment – he had also bequeathed an obligation on them to resist pressures to cull the diaries.[108] So what powers did Hunt have and towards whom should they be deployed?

In the face of the uncertainties, Hunt put a submission to Wilson on 7 June to clear the lines of his approach to the Literary Executors – he would seek to prevent publication *tout court* to avoid bringing the whole system into disrepute.[109] Wilson gave his approval on 11 June, also authorising an informal approach to Foot to stress the likely effect of publication on Crossman's reputation, and a formal approach to the Attorney General to consider the legal aspects of the case.[110] By mid June the government seemed poised to move quickly towards an injunction should agreement not seem possible with the Literary Executors.[111] On 24 June Hunt made a formal request to the Literary Executors not to publish Volume 1. He briefed the Leader of the Opposition (Edward Heath) who agreed with the undesirability of publication.[112] The government position looked hopeful[113] and this may have coloured its reactions to a new development. At the beginning of July Lord Goodman came on the scene representing the Literary Executors. To the government officials he appeared conciliatory, suggesting that excisions could meet the requirements of confidentiality. The Literary Executors had agreed a contract with *The Sunday Times* for serialisation of the diaries which would comprise extracts from whatever form the book would take. Hunt would get 14 days' notice of the intention to publish the book.[114] On 10 July Hunt tabled four criteria which he would use to assess the acceptability of what it was proposed to publish: (a) no blow-by-blow accounts of Cabinet discussions or the revelation of differences between members of the Cabinet or detailed discussion of other Ministers' policies; (b) no breach of the confidentiality of the advice given by civil servants to Ministers; (c) preservation of the confidentiality surrounding senior civil service appointments; (d) no details of discussions between Ministers on policy matters which one of the parties must have regarded as private.[115]

Over the next six months negotiations continued. Hunt thought that the diaries were 'deplorable';[116] Michael Foot had told Hunt that although he felt obliged to respect Crossman's wishes to have the diaries published *in toto* he personally would regret publication;[117] and Lord Goodman told Wilson that Counsel's opinion had ruled against publication of the material relating to Cabinet discussions and of descriptions of confidential advice from civil servants to Ministers.[118] Goodman also offered a personal opinion that the comments on individual civil servants in the diaries should be excised.[119] Hunt was alive to the risk that *The Sunday Times* had not given an assurance of prior notice of publication of the extracts;[120] and by November he was becoming worried that *The Sunday Times* might start with innocuous extracts and then escalate the content to establish precedents of revelations[121] (which was precisely their strategy). He saw Goodman's suggestions as an ingenious way of furthering his clients' interests yet leaving an impression that the government had won the argument. He also knew that Wilson had asked that nothing should come out before a General Election and that Bernard Donoughue[122] had reliable information that *The Sunday Times* would comply with this request. In these circumstances an early resort to an injunction was impossible politically.[123] The fact that Goodman gave the appearance of not knowing of the undertaking given by the editor caused Robert Armstrong to record that it left him with 'a scintilla of doubt.'[124]

In answer to Tam Dalyell[125] in the House of Commons, Wilson sought to explain in detail why the conventions existed, why they mattered and why the Cabinet Secretary was acting under his authority.[126] Yet events started to slip away from Hunt's control. The *Sunday Times* refused to give a requested undertaking of prior notice of publication[127] and immediately afterwards announced the intention to publish an edited version of Crossman's introduction to the diaries (which contained the intention to blow away the secrecy of government). Counsel's opinion was that the legal basis for an injunction crucially depended on establishing a public interest case for banning the whole book[128] and that the Official Secrets Act would not bear the weight of the legal case.[129]

The initiative had passed to *The Sunday Times* and the Literary Executors with the former forcefully rejecting Hunt's criteria;[130] Goodman wrote tetchily that Hunt was seeking to act more strictly than in past cases of memoirs. *The Sunday Times* would no longer have to await agreement on Volume 1 before extracts could be published.[131] Hunt's hurt reply ('I have bent over backwards to help') was sent three days before the first extracts appeared without warning in the newspaper.[132] At first the Cabinet Office thought that the first two extracts had taken sufficient account of their points to obviate legal action. The Policy Unit was briefing against trying to stop publication and thought that Hunt would not wish to fight exposed battles with nobody else's head above the parapet.[133] Just before Hunt left with Wilson for Ottawa and Washington it was agreed with the Attorney General to defer any question of proceedings against *The Sunday Times.*[134] From Washington Hunt telegraphed, 'I am impressed by the skill with which the interests of all concerned have been taken into account and I am grateful for the extent to which our views have been met.'[135] Thereafter, however, the extracts gradually increased the frequency of blow-by-blow accounts of Cabinet and other Ministerial meetings to the extent that a month later Hunt reported to Wilson that the understanding had broken down.[136]

Still the politicians hesitated[137] and skilful work by *The Sunday Times* editors kept the newspaper just the right side of an injunction.[138] As the extracts came to an end the Cabinet Office view was that flagrant breaches of the criteria in the penultimate extract would normally have led to an injunction but they understood that the last extract would be inoffensive so that action could not be justified.[139] They were wrong; Hunt later told Wilson that the extract was a significant escalation and reinforced the need for an authoritative redefinition of the conventions through an examination by a committee of Privy Counsellors.[140] Wilson annotated his note with: 'We need an independent committee; in 1967 the Home Secretary and others stymied serious discussion.'

Hunt knew a trap had been sprung, that the cumulative precedent would be trouble.[141] He now faced two key questions. First, how to shore up the conventions – or were they 'almost unsustainable'? Second, how to deal with the breaches of confidentiality that would appear if Volume 1 of the diaries proper were published? On the first question the government moved swiftly to announce a Committee of Privy Counsellors, under Lord Radcliffe to review the rules governing Ministerial memoirs during the 30-year period.[142] On the second, Goodman took the initiative to claim that the increasingly revealing extracts had established a new situation so that the Literary Executors would go ahead with publication of Volume 1 as soon as possible. How the government responded would depend on whether the Attorney General, acting as a Law Officer independent of government, decided to go for an injunction. On 5 June the Treasury Solicitor gave notice of proceedings to seek an injunction.[143] Wilson was unenthusiastic. In a meeting with Hunt on 23 June he said that he would not have chosen to go for an injunction but it was now too late.[144] Later the same day he told the Attorney General that he was worried about creating an impression of a crusade against the press.[145] Was there scope for mediation and whom might the

Cabinet Secretary approach? Wilson ruled out Goodman and authorised Hunt to approach Michael Foot informally to explore the scope for a settlement. He did so the following day, subsequently reporting that Foot thought that whilst the actions of *The Sunday Times* were 'reprehensible' the instructions Crossman bequeathed to the Literary Executors left little scope for compromise.[146]

A hearing on the injunction opened on 15 July 1975 under Lord Justice Widgery, the Lord Chief Justice of England. Questions remain about Hunt's preparation for his appearance in court and about the negotiations that preceded it – mainly about the extent to which the government side fought to win rather than to compromise. Although Goodman appeared to hint early on that the Crossman estate was not rich and could not afford a court battle[147] its significance appears not to have been explored and once *The Sunday Times* came on the scene it was Goodman's masterstroke to put a contractual barrier between the Literary Executors and the executors of the Crossman estate. It is also significant that between May 1974 and July 1975 Hunt was involved extensively with Wilson on other matters, including significant overseas travel.

Hunt gave evidence on the first and second days of the hearing. *The Observer* described him as 'a man in a fog putting up a fence on marshy ground' and referred to a tenseness playing around his mouth.[148] Judgement was reserved until after the summer recess. The Attorney General was confident of victory to the extent that Hunt attended court to hear Lord Justice Widgery's ruling on 1 October. The crucial judgement came like a bolt from the blue[149] and went in favour of the defence. Although Lord Widgery accepted that the Court's power to protect confidentiality extended to the public sector he added that such protection could not last indefinitely and he did not think that the contents of Volume 1 of the diaries would damage Cabinet confidentiality or any of the other criteria after nine years. Benner recalls that if the case had been listed earlier, so that Lord Widgery would not have had time to do more than scan the Crossman diary cursorily, the decision could well have gone the other way.[150] Taking comfort from the ashes of the case, Hunt telegraphed Wilson in Canada, 'This judgement is disappointing and leaves no one clear where they stand on Volumes 2 and 3 of Crossman. However, ... acceptance of the principle of Cabinet confidentiality and the fact that it can be protected by law coupled with his view that such protection is not indefinite ... may establish some frame of reference for ... the Radcliffe Committee.'[151] Lord Widgery hinted that he expected the Attorney General to appeal. However, the government side had no appetite for this. Hunt thought an appeal might look like a witch hunt.[152] At the meeting on 7 October at which the Attorney General decided not to appeal he indicated he would draw the Radcliffe Committee's attention to the importance of augmenting the Lord Chief Justice's judgement with rules, preferably enforceable, possibly by statute.[153]

Radcliffe reported on 16 December 1975 and was published on 22 January 1976.[154] Its central argument was that the conventions were still valid and it went on to translate them into rules of behaviour: Ministers should be free to give an account of their own work subject to restrictions – not to contravene the requirements of national security at the time of publication; not to disclose things injurious to the UK's foreign relations; not to publish information destructive of the confidential relationships on which the UK system of government was based (notably, not to reveal the views of other Ministers) – nor to reveal advice given in confidence, nor to make public assessments of those who had served under them). The restrictions about confidential relationships could be regarded as lifted 15 years after the events, subject to the end of the service life of an adviser. The restrictions concerned with national security and international relations could not. Compliance should be left to the free acceptance by Ministers of an obligation of honour, the occasional breach of which, no matter how sensational, should not be interpreted as having shattered the fabric of a good system. Ministers should have their attention explicitly drawn to their obligations on taking office, including signing a declaration that this had been done. Manuscripts should continue to be sent to the Cabinet Secretary for vetting against these obligations. In the case of national security and international relations the author could appeal to the Prime Minister of the day, whose decision would be final. In regard to confidential relationships authors should listen to the Cabinet Secretary's advice but the final responsibility would rest on their own shoulders.

Foot and Benn wanted publication without a government response.[155] Hunt was dismissive, 'Public discussion would be unlikely to be informed or helpful'; and 'Mr Foot also claims that it is hypocritical to take steps on the lesser evil of memoirs while the greater evil of current leakages continues unchecked. This argument is quite illogical – in principle, the fact that one evil is continuing is no reason for not dealing with another.'[156] On publication day Wilson gave a Written Answer which said, 'The Government, having considered the Report, have decided to accept the Committee's recommendations in full. They trust that they will also command general acceptance and observance ... I shall be arranging for all present Ministers to be informed of the new arrangements and, as recommended in the Report, shall invite them to sign an appropriate declaration.'

Hunt was resigned to defeat when he briefed Wilson's successor, Callaghan, on Volume 3: 'There is no way therefore in which the text could be brought into conformity with Radcliffe by specific amendment; and I recommend that, on the volume as a whole, my advice to the literary executors should be, as it was for Volume 2, that publication should be deferred until 15 years after the events in question. This advice would be, as it were, for the record. I would not expect the Executors to take it and we would not seek to enforce it by an injunction.'[157] The most telling judgement came from Callaghan: 'Yes, this runs directly counter to the 15-year Convention – and may make it a dead letter before it even starts, e.g. Barbara Castle. Of course Crossman had neither sense of obligation nor honour and should never have been in the Cabinet. Clem Attlee told me once that he would never include him – and no more would I. Barbara has a greater sense of responsibility – I hope! If you wish you can tell Lord Goodman that in my view this breaches Radcliffe, and that the literary Executors should have regard to the new rule, even though it is post Crossman's death. But it won't do any good for they sniff scandal, character assassination and profit – an irresistible combination to the Executors.'[158]

40 years on what is the significance of the diaries? It is now clear that they are Crossman's public legacy. He is remembered in the public mind for little else. Similarly, Lord Widgery's judgement was a defining moment for Hunt; at the end of his life he still spoke with feeling of 'a mistaken judgement'.[159] Partly because they lacked reflection and objectivity, the diaries damaged understanding of the trade-offs that are a fundamental to national cohesion. Nor did they add significant insight into the dilemmas and choices facing the holder of a Ministerial office and the coolness of judgement required to respond to them. In Rodney Lowe's harsh but memorable phrase, Crossman's Diaries marked the death of Ministerial honour and in that sense, at least, Hunt was right to oppose publication to protect the integrity of governmental processes. A current of public opinion was beginning to set in which meant that in the long run it was inevitable that the old conventions about non-disclosure would largely be overthrown. But it was not apparent at the time that developments in technology would drive media frenzy for instant comment and greater openness. In Benner's judgement, 'Hunt was dealt an unpromising hand and played it sensibly.'[160]

The Death of the Post-war Consensus

If the public face of the Cabinet Secretary was in the courtroom, the reality of his focus was behind the doors of Whitehall. The difficulties with the economy and over miners' pay, which characterised the end of the Heath Administration, had not been solved by the change of government. If anything discussion of economic, energy and industrial issues within Whitehall intensified so that analysis of Hunt's appointment diaries suggests that between 1974 and the fall of the Callaghan government he spent about a quarter of his time servicing these discussions. In the early stages of the Wilson administration his contribution was to inject countervailing realism to any tendencies towards euphoria after agreement was reached between the National Coal Board and the miners early in March 1974. The government was committed to abolish the statutory Pay Board in favour of a voluntary policy. But the detail remained to be filled in and on the morning following the miners' settlement Hunt briefed Wilson drawing attention to a long list of employment groups expected to be knocking on the door for increased pay. He suggested avoiding a lengthy discussion of substance in Cabinet in favour of asking the Chancellor and the Secretary of State for Employment to work in an ad hoc Ministerial group to submit the main strategic options to a new Ministerial Committee on economic strategy (MES). Meanwhile, Ministers should avoid commitments on public sector pay that would tend to close options prematurely.[161]

Economic issues dominated; in particular energy policy as the producers found new muscle, cheap oil became a thing of the past, coal sought to emulate oil but failed despite aggressive industrial action and the UK government tried to reach a balanced view about nuclear energy. Pay and prices were a constant challenge in an economy with weak export performance and overhanging international debts. Attempts to restructure the industrial base were all too often diverted into mitigating the decline of uncompetitive industries, which had failed to invest wisely in productive capacity and suffered from poisoned industrial relations. Over the six year period he was Cabinet Secretary Hunt was the senior member of the secretariat at 74 Ministerial discussions on energy, 47 on pay and prices and 45 on industrial policy. In retrospect the 1970s saw the death throes of the post-war settlement as the country lost trust in macro-economic solutions and industrial relations fractured with, eventually, the most militant trades unions overreaching themselves.

A focus on risks rather than opportunities and on what should be done rather than how to do it characterised civil service advice, leaving the rest to political advice. At the end of 1974, for example, Hunt briefed for MES[162] that, 'The only issues on which the Committee need reach decisions at this meeting are: (i) whether and how to try to influence the size of the miners' claim before it is formulated; (ii) whether the National Coal Board should be told to consult closely with the government and make no offer without Ministerial agreement.'[163] In a separate brief Donoughue pointedly concluded that whilst the officials' paper correctly laid out the options it 'gives very little precise indication of how the claim is to be influenced, and no analysis whatsoever of the political make-up of the [National Union of Mineworkers] nor of the position of the moderates.' In one vivid sentence he captured the essence of the government's political case – 'After all one might recall that Allende was "killed" not by the right wing but by the copper miners – which was hardly in the copper miners' interest ...' Later in the year the coal pay negotiations were in trouble.[164] Hunt identified the main issue for MES as which options could produce a settlement that could be claimed to be within the pay guidelines and cost no more than £250 million; as much as possible should be achieved by restructuring differentials in favour of underground workers; a loosely drawn productivity scheme or a new Retail Price Index threshold would not be acceptable. Andrew Graham of the Policy Unit pointed to the Emperor's new clothes, 'In one sense the paper by officials might get the Government off the hook by its imaginative interpretation of the TUC guidelines, but in another sense this just shows the emptiness of the TUC guidelines – if the guidelines can be stretched to include pay increases of 30–40% then we are almost bound to lose control of inflation.'[165]

Defence and Intelligence

The 1974 Labour Party Manifesto said that the burden of the country's defence spending should be progressively reduced to bring costs in line with those of the UK's main European allies. Immediately on taking up office Wilson was briefed by Hunt there was a grave danger that defence policy would lack credibility if the UK went on trying to do all the things currently being done. He proposed a review of defence policy to allow Ministers to decide what changes they wanted to make to commitments and to the associated level of resources.[166] He would chair a steering committee comprising the PUSs of the FCO, Treasury, MOD and the Chief of the Defence Staff (CDS) because of the very different interests involved. It would 'review defence policies and priorities taking into consideration probable constraints upon public expenditure in the next ten years, identify options for changes in our capabilities and commitments, taking into account the implications for our defence and oversea interests, and make recommendations to the Defence and Overseas Policy Committee not later than July 1974.'[167]

The Steering Committee proposed analysis against four possible target reductions in the defence share of GNP (the most extreme being a reduction to 4%).[168] Savings would be over £1,000 million p.a. In April Hunt saw Henry Kissinger at the State Department to explain the background and to reassure Kissinger that major decisions would not be taken without consultation with the United States and other UK allies. The first substantive Ministerial discussion took place on 18 July. The argument turned on whether to assume continuation of the current NATO strategy. The Chancellor of the Exchequer pressed for a review because Soviet willingness to risk war in Europe had been greatly reduced by fear of China.[169] In contrast, the general view was that the risk of NATO unravelling was high so any suggestions of a change in NATO strategy would need to be handled cautiously. The Foreign Secretary was a lone voice in favour of out-of-area forces – they were relatively cheap and of value for British influence in the world. Others thought that decisions to reduce non-NATO forces could be taken quickly – though the savings would be small (£70-£80 million a year compared to the £1,000 million being looked for).

When the Committee met again on 1 August it had a Steering Committee recommendation for the retention of forces in Hong Kong, Cyprus and Gibraltar to meet non-NATO commitments with others being wound up as soon as practicable. Hunt pleaded for better Ministerial guidance on the minimum British contribution to NATO – known as the Critical Level. It would not be enough just to ask officials to find further savings without such guidance.[170] He pointed out that the Chancellor was still trying to announce cuts in non-NATO commitments before the review was completed and wanted to start consultations with allies. There were three counter arguments: (1) the position was far from clear cut with decisions outstanding on the Falkland Islands and Belize; (2) a two-tier announcement would lead to questions that the UK was in no position to answer; (3) the effect of announcing small savings could backfire – the big savings involved NATO commitments.

As the October election would mean delay of about six weeks Hunt pressed for Ministers to consider the Critical Level before the Dissolution. This would allow the military planners to press on and early decisions after the election. OPD met on 18 September; Hunt's brief argued that the Polaris improvement programme was both necessary for a credible deterrent and relatively cheap; he proposed a reduction in the British Army of the Rhine from 58,000 to 50,000; but noted that the Army had to be aware of the demands of Northern Ireland. The Navy should withdraw from the Mediterranean and the Far East but North Sea oil and seaborne supplies needed protection. Air defence was already thin but some economies were possible in transport aircraft; and the Mobile Force could abandon reinforcement capability for the Southern Flank and reduce it for the Northern and Central Regions.[171] Even so the Chancellor of the Exchequer reserved his position. Summing up, Wilson said that the general view was to agree the reduced non-NATO commitments and to ask officials to examine whether the Critical level could be reduced further.[172]

The further work by officials during the election period meant that OPD could consider a draft report to Cabinet on 23 October. The share of GNP devoted to defence should come down from 6% (in 1973/75) to 4½% by 1984 (a saving of £750 million). Hunt was at pains to do his utmost to ensure that it presented a united front at Cabinet despite the Chancellor's reservations – he suggested that Wilson should see the Chancellor immediately before Cabinet on 31 October to persuade him that the reductions were as far as could realistically be achieved. Attention should now switch to presentation of the results rather than on trying to unpick the conclusions of the review.[173] Wilson minuted to put an end to the Chancellor's persistence in asking for more reductions: 'I think it would be wrong to reopen at this stage the question of the defence figures for the next few years.' He also wrote to President Ford in emollient terms, 'I do not think that any of our allies could justifiably use our proposed reductions as an excuse for cutting their contributions ... We have to be true to our priorities ... I have noted very carefully what you say about Cyprus ... we are ready to agree to your proposal about Diego Garcia ... and we shall clear with [your people] the text of the passage [in our statement to Parliament] on Diego Garcia.'[174]

If the work of officials and the defence planning staffs had been relatively smooth, the implementation of Ministers' decisions was not. The Americans thought that the West should be increasing its defences and not reducing them; but the real shock was the plan to withdraw from Cyprus and the Eastern Mediterranean. On both issues the UK came under intense pressure to reconsider.[175] Kissinger argued that the present Soviet leadership was ageing and conservative. When they went there might be more aggressive Soviet behaviour and it was disquieting to think that the United States would be the only Western country capable of intervening. Hunt and the CDS then went to Bonn to consult the Federal Republic. The Germans were detailed in their questioning but more relaxed about developments than the Americans. The formal US State Department response was delivered on 18 November. It was full of doom and gloom: 'Our belief [is] that the proposed UK reductions will degrade alliance capabilities to reinforce, especially on its Southern flank; will risk further upsetting the political situation in the Eastern Mediterranean; will contribute to public and parliamentary pressures elsewhere in NATO – and particularly the US – to reduce defense forces and spending ... The British bases at Cyprus and Malta ... should not be closed.'[176]

Hunt had been quick to reassert his control over the Secret Vote and the activities of the agencies. In mid January 1974 he revived the Permanent Secretaries committee, first set up in 1952 following Brook's review of MI5 and MI6, which scrutinised the agencies' budgets (PSIS).[177] It had not met since July 1970 and there was a new situation after the emergencies of 1973. On the one hand, 'pulling the plant up by its roots ... at a time of detente and Watergate could well be counter-productive.'[178] What was clear, however, was that the UK must continue to demonstrate the ability to use intelligence well, to safeguard it and to make a valued contribution to its provision. Hunt told Wilson: 'Like my predecessor I provide the channel of advice to you on intelligence matters and act as Accounting Officer for the Secret Vote. I also chair a small Committee of senior Permanent Secretaries, which reviews the state of our intelligence, approves its broad objectives, and examines the future programmes …'.[179] The backbone of the Committee's work was a meeting in the summer to approve five-year forecasts of the intelligence programme on the basis of a submission by the Intelligence Co-ordinator (Joe Hooper). An assessment which was challenged in October 1974 by the MOD's Director General of Intelligence who was strongly resistant to the division of national intelligence requirements into areas of higher and lower priorities.[180] Each autumn, the detailed staff and budgetary estimates were scrutinised. The Committee also considered precautionary actions to anticipate future intelligence issues. Thus, in July 1974 the Intelligence Co-ordinator reported to the Committee on the implications for the United Kingdom if the Americans were once again to withhold intelligence for political reasons such as had occurred in August-September 1973.[181]

A preliminary discussion at JIC(A) of the likely implications of the Defence Review concluded that 'there is a potential conflict between what we need to do to meet our own national intelligence interests and what we need to do to maintain the value of our intelligence effort to the Americans, on whom we in turn depend for much of our high-priority intelligence requirements.'[182] When the results became clearer a PSIS discussion of February 1975 concluded that it was essential that there should be some external mechanism by which the size of, for example, MI5 could be agreed and Hunt agreed to discuss how this could be achieved with the Director General.[183] The Security Service presented a special challenge since the directive given to Sir Percy Sillitoe[184] by the then Home Secretary, Maxwell-Fyfe, in 1952 allowed for the Service to be self-tasking and, therefore, to some extent to settle its own resource requirements. From time to time, however, Cabinet Secretaries would be moved to put a ferret down that particular rabbit hole – Sir John Wilson of MOD in 1975 and a review of financial control by the Principal Finance Officer of the Home Office which gave the Service a clean bill of health and implied that control was a good deal better than in the Home Office.

Northern Ireland

In April 1974, following violent incidents inspired by the Ulster Workers' Council (UWC) in opposition to the 1973 Sunningdale agreement, Hunt urged the need for contingency planning against a possible collapse of government in Northern Ireland. On 19 May the government announced the deployment of extra troops, including to man petrol stations.[185] Officials, meanwhile, reported on the constitutional options: (a) a continued partnership between the United Kingdom Government and a regional Northern Ireland Government; (b) direct rule; (c) some degree of withdrawal by the Westminster Government.[186] Wilson made a Ministerial broadcast on the worsening situation on 25 May. Ministers met in the IRN Committee, for which Hunt suggested that although they had refused to discuss constitutional matters with the UWC it might be important to see if any of the demands were such that they offered the prospect of a dialogue. The discussions led to officials being instructed to update their work on possible longer-term options by early June. Hunt took control. Meanwhile, as the Province slid seemingly inexorably towards anarchy Wilson put thoughts on paper that would reappear as in a recurrent nightmare.[187] Only four copies were made. Contingency planning urgently needed revisiting, '... we are in the position of "responsibility without power" ... if we seek any action unacceptable to the UWC and their political associates, then as soon as their constituents have got over the effects of the recent strike, we are at their mercy again.'[188] The Army could not sensibly be expected to maintain essential services if a hundred thousand or more workers were on strike from those industries. Hence, the Doomsday scenario was withdrawal (in panic or in a controlled fashion) by the United Kingdom Government leaving the Province ultimately on their own as far as economic and social standards went. Officials should now proceed to plan for Dominion status for Northern Ireland.

Two weeks later, Hunt presented the report by officials, steering Ministers firmly away from the more radical options: integration with Great Britain or with the Republic or a sudden unilateral withdrawal by the Westminster Government were not viable policies; redrawing boundaries would raise great problems and not solve any. The most attractive option was a continuing slog towards a reconstituted power-sharing Executive devised by the Northern Irish themselves.[189] A month later he added that there was a real fear that the Official IRA and the Loyalists, fresh from a taste of power through the UWC, might exploit the lack of sophistication of the Northern Irish working classes ('waiting to be exposed to politics as we know them') to promote a Marxist basis for working-class co-operation. 'In virgin soil things can grow quickly.'[190]

At the same time, in the run-up to a Constitutional Convention Hunt advocated an approach to the BBC for help to get across twin messages: (a) Northern Ireland was materially dependent on the United Kingdom as a whole; (b) other countries with mixed communities managed the issues of political and economic power.[191] However, despite Wilson's worries it proved difficult to get Ministers to set aside time for reflective thinking about longer-term options. Anticipating the likelihood of the Constitutional Convention failing, Hunt asked for a rather longer and more searching discussion than was usually possible in a meeting of IRN.[192] Originally planned as a six-hour discussion at Chequers in late November the date was first pushed back to January 1975 and then faded away in the face of possible short-term actions to seize the initiative before the time bombs hidden in Gardiner the likely failure of the Convention could detonate. Longer-term thinking did not surface again until April 1975.[193]

New Initiatives

Wilson knew that he would have to go to the country long before the Parliamentary term expired and that to improve his electoral position he needed to project the idea of a reforming socially just party. Hunt's role was to keep track of the initiatives and to drive the most important through the collective machinery. Hunt launched the Joint Approach to Social Policy (JASP) experimentally in June 1974 to improve co-ordination across Departments in the development and execution of social policies.[194] There were two strands of work, both under the leadership of the CPRS:

a. 'Establishing experimentally an early warning system, which will enable us to identify major proposals likely to be coming forward in the social field during the next 12 months or so;
b. Organising inter-departmental work designed to seek to identify the areas where real difficulties are being caused by the failure to relate Departmental programmes to one another, and to see what would be involved in establishing agreed statements of objectives which would give practical guidance on priorities.'

The proposals were: (a) a strategic Ministerial forum on social policy to discuss broad objectives and priorities; (b) an improved information base (including a continued forward look on social policies); (c) studies on problem areas (financial aspects of poverty; working relationships between central and local government; social aspects of housing policy; women at work; the disabled of working age; the implications of a possible long-term decline in the birth rate and the distribution of the population).[195] Hunt thought the proposals were 'realistic' rather than revolutionary. They did not attempt to define social policy – which was in fact only the totality of social policies. Nevertheless, while expectations must be realistic, Ministers must realise that JASP was a move of major significance. The Prime Minister wanted to make an immediate public announcement; the Policy Unit thought that the report travelled a bland middle way and lacked a political dimension and teeth – future work on social monitoring would be too slow, the studies too narrow. Both agreed, however, that the oxygen of public discussion would be beneficial.

After Callaghan replaced Wilson he created the Ministerial Committee on Long Term Social Policy (LSM). A rerun of the CPRS presentation was fixed for 8 June. It was a disaster. Hunt subsequently reported that insufficient time had been allowed for questions, Ministers were suffering the effects of a 04.00 am all-night sitting, the CPRS team were off form, Callaghan already had an advance copy of the booklet the CPRS wished to end on, and a band was playing on Horse Guards. It was an inglorious end to JASP, which never recovered its appeal.[196]

A Second General Election

Wilson went to the country on 10 October 1974 and was returned with a wafer-thin majority of four seats. At the start of the election campaign the Lord President (Edward Short) proposed a senior Minister to oversee the machinery for collective decision-making. Not surprisingly this posed a potential threat to Hunt's primacy BOSS central team to handle forthcoming constitutional issues such as devolution; relations between Parliament and the EEC; Church and State; House of Lords reform and the State financing of political activity. But 'we ought to pause before setting up another central body – particularly if, as I believe, the Cabinet Secretariat and the CPRS can meet all the Lord President's aims if we are given sufficient encouragement.'[197] The suggestion came to nothing but after the election Wilson asked Hunt to consider integrating the Policy Unit more into the work of the Cabinet Office. This produced a strong rebuttal on the grounds of politicisation of the civil service and steps towards creating a Prime Minister's Department by the back door.[198]

EEC Renegotiation and the Referendum

The first election manifesto contained a commitment to renegotiate the terms of entry to the EEC and a promise to submit the results to the judgement of the British people through the ballot box. The manifesto presented a challenge of conscience for the senior pro-Community officials such as Hunt and Michael Palliser (then at UKREP)[199] until it became clear that the Prime Minister and the Foreign Secretary saw renegotiation as a way of Britain staying in the Community despite the widespread Labour opposition to membership.[200] The problem was to make the economic considerations fit the political objectives.[201] Over the next 11 months, until the Referendum of 5 June 1975, three intertwined issues dominated British EEC policies: the renegotiation, how to put the result of renegotiation to the British people, and how to avoid catastrophic resignations from the Cabinet. Wilson had agreed relatively easily to the continuation of the Cabinet Office European Unit. So whilst the Foreign Office bore the brunt of the renegotiation effort Nairne (the European Unit leader) was able to reflect on strategy and progress.[202] Without Nairne Hunt would have struggled to cover the ground. The division of labour between the two may have been informal but is a good example of actions taken at the level where information and familiarity with the issues are strongest. Nairne led on renegotiation and the practicalities of a referendum. Hunt focussed on the Prime Minister's domestic and international political requirements. At a Summit dinner planned for 14 September, for example, the Prime Minister was expected to launch renegotiation with a speech about British attitudes to the EEC and the British Government's essential requirements. Hunt rejected the Foreign Office draft as 'anodyne, negative and confusing;' and submitted a fully fledged short speech of his own which, whilst taking account of Wilson's known position, probably reflected Hunt's own views.[203] He included that if the British people opted to remain members of the

Community, 'we shall have removed the so-called European question once and for all from British politics.' But the UK contribution to the Community Budget (24% in 1980) would sit ill with the forecast UK share of the Community's GNP (14%); 'This does not correspond to the economic facts of life.' 'What surely matters in a Community is that we should have regard to each other's interests and try to act together on practical issues that matter ... [rather than] maintain its impetus by harmonising for harmonising's sake.' In the event, however, Wilson made his own (less visionary and rather dull) speaking notes during the dinner.[204]

Meanwhile, pro- and anti-marketeers mobilised. Nairne submitted first thoughts on a referendum in mid October 1974[205] and reported on its practical implications. In November three Cabinet Ministers who felt that, 'however great the improvement in the terms may be, the loss of sovereignty implicit in membership [of the EEC] would involve paying too high a price' sought approval to 'express their convictions publicly.'[206] The result was the 1975 'agreement to differ' that preserved the fig leaf of Cabinet collective responsibility. It was pure Wilson. Helmut Schmidt addressed the Labour Party Conference (postponed to 28 November 1974 because of the election) at Central Hall, Westminster, in a very tough way, passionately advocating continued UK Community membership and condemning opposition as short-sighted. The following weekend he was Wilson's private guest at Chequers, where he offered help in securing an acceptable result from renegotiation and said that he would speak to President Giscard d'Estaing to urge a Wilson-d'Estaing meeting before the Dublin Summit.[207] During that weekend Wilson shut himself away in the study for about two and a half hours, and made a telephone call to the Foreign Secretary, Jim Callaghan, to whom he expressed himself a good deal happier about the possibility of an acceptable outcome to the renegotiation that would be consistent with the 1974 Manifesto.[208] He emerged with a plan for a referendum, a campaign and the 'agreement to differ' compromise to keep the Labour party together – calculating that withdrawal from the EEC would have led to much worse trouble from the Jenkins wing than could be expected from the EEC dissidents.[209] Robert Armstrong assembled first thoughts on the sole precedent for an agreement to differ, warning that it was, 'an extremely rare, rather strange and potentially dangerous device'.[210] Furthermore, the argument was weak. Of the claimed 1932 precedent, concerning tariff duties as a solution to the then financial difficulties under the National Government, Ivor Jennings, the constitutional expert, had written, 'A Cabinet that is agreed upon fundamentals can compromise upon incidentals,' and 'An "agreement to differ" in order to maintain a coalition is an attempt to break down the party system and to substitute government by individuals for government by political principles. No harm was done by the precedent of 1932 provided that it is not regarded as a precedent.'[211] Armstrong went on to advise that a decision to agree to differ must be a collective Cabinet decision and could not be taken in advance of the outcome of renegotiation.[212]

Hunt was not formally copied into these early thoughts and started his own research into the 1932 precedent. He came to a more positive conclusion, recognising that in 1932 there had been a coalition government, which made the parallel inexact, but concluding that the 1932 specific limitation of the 'agreement to differ' to 'import duties and cognate matters' as a deliberate decision by Cabinet could be useful in the circumstances of 1975.[213] Cabinet should consider the proposed referendum arrangements on 21 January[214] and, assuming agreement, on 23 January announce the decision.[215] On the other hand, although there would undoubtedly be pressure to announce an agreement to differ at the same time, Hunt hoped that the Prime Minister would resist: (a) to keep the period of dispensation from collective responsibility as short as possible; (b) to honour the agreement in Cabinet on 12 December that the dispensation should apply when the results of renegotiation were clear; (c) to allow renegotiation to continue in good faith; (d) to avoid embarrassing those members of Cabinet who wanted to reserve their position pending the results of renegotiation or who might subsequently prefer to resign.

At an informal meeting on 20 December with Wilson, the Lord President, Foreign Secretary and Home Secretary (Roy Jenkins) Hunt advised delaying the Referendum Bill until after the renegotiation to avoid collateral damage to the earlier pledge that government would negotiate in good faith. He suggested that there would need to be some facility for public information to be supplied to the voters, 'most of whom did not feel they had sufficient understanding or information on which to cast a vote.'[216] In a postscript two days later, prompted by a discussion on devolution he raised the possibility of a scenario where the UK as a whole voted to stay in the Community but Scotland voted 'NO'. This he argued, contrary to Nairne's view, pointed to a central count and a central result in the referendum.[217] The political advantages of a central count (to mark the nationwide nature of the result and to minimise the risk of collateral damage to the devolution policy) were supported by some Ministers (mainly pro-European Community) but there were strongly opposed views (including some who wanted a constituency count so that MPs would be clear where there constituents stood). Also, there were practical risks in a central count, as it had never been tried. Was there a middle way of counting and declaring by county?[218] A central count was agreed at Cabinet on 6 February but the decision was reversed after representations from the electoral returning officers and a free vote in the House of Commons on 23 April.[219]

Keeping a lid on the tendencies for the government to split over the terms of renegotiation and the referendum was a constant task. Wilson issued a number of reminders about the requirement for Ministers to observe the rules of collective responsibility.[220] But by 30 December *The Times* had got wind of the timing issue over the Referendum Bill, publishing an article which reflected a fairly detailed knowledge of the informal discussion. A leak inquiry was launched early in the New Year, to no avail. Armstrong reported to the Prime Minister that, 'There has been a full inter-departmental leak inquiry, but it has, as usual, given no indication of the source of the leak.'[221] A second leak on 3 February 1975 referred to a Chequers discussion on 17 January and named Ministers who had wanted to proceed slowly with devolution; it also discussed the possible use of reserve powers that implied knowledge of specific papers discussed at Chequers. Again a leak enquiry was launched, the results implying that the journalist concerned may have duped a Chequers participant into confirming information from another source or guesses. Yet a further leak occurred in the *Evening News* on 18 March, about the sensitive issue of how many Ministers had given notice in Cabinet that they would invoke the right to differ. It was investigated with the same negative result.[222]

On 18 March 1975 Cabinet agreed to a positive government recommendation on the results of renegotiation. Seven Ministers dissented.[223] As to the question on the ballot paper, the debate was between asking if the United Kingdom should 'stay' in the European Community (technically the correct formulation) or if the UK should 'be' in the European Community – which presented the choice most neutrally?[224] (On 20 February Cabinet endorsed the 'stay' formulation.)[225] A decision on whether to have a government information programme was urgent but Hunt warned that there were difficulties over (a) how to present the cases for and against; should the government present both? (b) how the government might use its information machine in support of its own recommendation compatible with its responsibility for the fair conduct of the campaign;[226] (c) should there be restrictions on information activities of outside bodies similar to those in normal electoral circumstances?[227] (d) though a close result in the poll could be awkward against the background of the 'whole-hearted consent of the British people' it would not make things easier to attach special conditions to the size of the poll and/or the majority.[228]

After consultation with Douglas Allen, Pat Nairne and Robert Armstrong, Hunt drafted guidelines for the conduct of Ministers and officials during the referendum campaign. These advocated comradely debate in the country between members of the government whose views differed and proposed that in Parliament dissenting Ministers should speak from the back benches and should not handle ongoing Community business for the duration of the campaign either in Brussels or in Parliament.[229] Special Advisers would be required to resign if they wished to play a public role in the campaign but could otherwise support their Minister in the normal way, even if he or she was exercising their right to differ.

After discussion with the Wilson and Callaghan the ability for dissenting Ministers to speak against the government recommendation was further curtailed by being restricted to the campaign in the country, excluding any opposing speech in Parliament or abroad. This version was handed round Cabinet by the Prime Minister on 18 March and discussed two days later when it proved impossible to reach agreement.[230] Seven Cabinet Ministers and 20 Ministers outside the Cabinet registered their dissent from the recommendation to stay in the European Community.[231] Cabinet returned to the issue on 25 March and favoured softening the guidelines but to avoid publishing them.[232] The restrictions on appearing on a platform with members of different political parties was removed, as was the block on dissenting Ministers handling ongoing Community business. Dissenting Ministers should avoid the opportunity of government business to make points against the government recommendation. They would not be permitted to speak during the main debate. All instructions for officials for work in Brussels should be in line with government policy. Parliamentary Questions would be reallocated as necessary between Ministers.[233]

The gag on speaking in the House was particularly irksome to dissident Ministers. Eric Heffer complained that it put them at a disadvantage, 'I feel that we dissenting Ministers must have the right to speak in the debate (if the Speaker so decides to call us) and I feel it right to approach the Speaker accordingly.'[234] To which Wilson responded that this was Cabinet's decision (taken when he was absent in Belfast) and related solely to the exceptional circumstances of the referendum campaign in the country, 'It was never envisaged as a licence to Ministers to express views contrary to the policy of the Government in the House.'[235] Ministers would have to resign from the government if they wished to speak against it in Parliament. Just how divisive the issue was can be understood from a minute by the Chief Whip (Robert Mellish) which pressed for a free vote in the House, and reported that at least four Whips would be likely to vote against the government recommendation whatever the whipping arrangements.[236] On 8 April Cabinet upheld the ban on speaking against the government but agreed there should be a free vote.[237] (Eric Heffer, Minister of State, Department of Industry, could not accept the ban, however, and spoke opposing the government on 9 April, returning to the backbenches shortly thereafter.)

By 14 May, however, an unintended consequence of the arrangements to prevent un-comradely behaviour was apparent. Direct confrontation between Ministers was banned, but the anti-Marketeers had difficulty in fielding good speakers other than Ministers; with the result that Ministers who supported the government recommendation were being denied a good crack of the whip and in these confrontations the pro-Market case was largely in the hands of the Opposition. Hunt wrote, 'This seems to me very undesirable, and clearly the Government would not want the Opposition to be able to claim undue credit for getting an endorsement of the Government's recommendation.'[238] He proposed maintaining the ban on the cut and thrust of face-to-face debate but relaxing the ban on sequential appearances in the same programme (subject to BBC and IBA assurances that the editing of programmes would not fabricate such confrontations). The next day Cabinet relaxed the rules even further – the ban on direct confrontation would not apply during the last few days of the campaign (1–5 June); but after the poll closed on 5 June the 'agreement to differ' would expire and Ministers would have to reunite or resign.[239]

Jim Callaghan and Harold Wilson were determined that the government case should not go by default. It was fine for the leading Ministers to stress willingness to accept the verdict of the people because, for the most part, they were wholly committed to winning a 'YES' vote. The same officials whose main purpose was to support Ministers in securing that result had also to contemplate the unthinkable – the possibility of a 'NO' vote and the abrupt reversal of government policy that would have meant. Contingency work began seriously (in secret) on 16 April with a meeting of the European Unit at which several streams of work were set in hand to identify and prepare: immediate actions to steady national and international confidence; the modalities of withdrawal in as orderly a way as possible both practically and legally.[240] The work was reported to MISC 82 at its meeting on 23 April, shortly after which the Prime Minister and Hunt departed for the eight-day Commonwealth Heads of Government Meeting – CHOGM – in Kingston, Jamaica. (It was at this meeting that the Commonwealth leaders told Harold Wilson that it would serve the best interests of the Commonwealth for Britain to remain a member of the Community.)[241] On their return they were told that the most recent opinion polls predicted a 'YES' majority in every part of the United Kingdom; Brussels opinion more or less took it for granted that the referendum would be won; the anti-EEC voice, however, was getting a full share of coverage, mainly because of the newsworthiness of Tony Benn and there had been two leaks of information. Though there were rational grounds for optimism it was impossible not to feel uneasy. Voices in the corridors were comparing the situation to just before the 1970 election when everyone in Whitehall assumed that the Labour government was bound to win.[242] Two weeks later Stowe and Hunt discussed the immediate aftermath of the poll informally and submitted agreed advice.[243] The weekend of 7–8 June could require tight Ministerial discipline as the media would keep a running tally of the results declared in each county yet the official result might not be reported to the Home Secretary by Sir Philip Allen (Chief Counting Officer) until Sunday. As soon as the result was clear the Prime Minister should give a lead to other Ministers on what he proposed to say and when.[244] There should then be a Cabinet on the morning of 9 June to consider the Prime Minister's statement to the House that afternoon.

> On 9 June Sir Philip Allen submitted the official tally on a 64.5% turnout:[245]
> YES – 17,378,581;
> NO – 8,470,073;
> Spoilt papers – 54,540.

Harold Wilson's statement to the House of Commons that day referred to 'the high turn-out and the clear and unmistakeable nature of the decision, but also the consistent pattern of positive voting over almost every county and region of the United Kingdom.'[246] The referendum had been a success, no dissenting Cabinet Minister resigned and 'The Agreement to Differ of 1975 served its purpose with the least possible lasting damage to the unity of the Government.'

Sherpa

The 1970s saw a significant increase in economic and political Summits. Building on the role which Brook and Trend had played in the design and running of the biennial meetings of the Heads of Commonwealth Governments (CHOGM), Hunt and his successor, Armstrong, undertook most of the shuttle diplomacy involved in Summit meetings and also co-ordinated preparation for bilateral meetings between the Prime Minister and other Heads of Government. Shortly after taking office in March 1974 Harold Wilson expressed his wishes to visit Paris and Moscow as part of a strategy to put relations on a personal footing with, respectively, the French President and the Russian leaders. The latter visit was the first by a British Prime Minister since January 1968. For this Moscow visit preparations started in earnest in late December 1974. By the turn of the year the interdepartmental discussions had identified six main British objectives including to explain the British approach to détente and to agree a joint statement establishing guidelines for the future development of Anglo-Soviet relations. 35 departmental briefs were commissioned, almost all through the Foreign and Commonwealth Office.[247] When the visit did eventually take place (from 13–17 February) Wilson's increasing conviction that he was being bugged led to extreme precautions – including dragging Hunt into the middle of a rhododendron bush at a reception at the British embassy to ask about travel arrangements.[248]

Preparation for Summits was led by a small group of personal envoys with the diplomats and the Departmental specialists in a supporting role. The pattern was one pioneered by Sir Burke Trend for the Meetings of Commonwealth leaders. But by now meetings of the Heads of Government of the leading industrial economies were more important. Thus, on Sunday 14 September 1975 George Shultz arrived at Chequers to convey a message that President Ford favoured a suggestion from President Giscard d'Estaing for a G5 economic summit (USA, France, Germany, Japan, United Kingdom). There were a number of complications: no one wanted to raise great expectations and for the Summit to fall short; the discussions should be wide-ranging and should not take over the job of the Finance Ministers; the economic concerns of the five were different, ranging from exchange rates to interest rates, from inflation to unemployment. Non-participants would need to be reassured that the conference was worthwhile and, in particular, that it was not seeking to dictate a master plan to them. The aim, therefore, should be to understand not to decide; and that would mean careful and comprehensive preparation, going as far as a draft communiqué, before even a decision to hold a conference or not was taken and certainly before any hint of a possible Summit was public knowledge. Hence, the preparation should be through meetings attended by only one person from each country, who carried the confidence of the Heads of Government involved, so that internal differences were settled outside the preparatory meeting and secrecy could be ensured.[249]

For the United Kingdom Harold Wilson decided that person would be Hunt. A meeting of the personal envoys was arranged for 5/6 October in the penthouse of the Carlton Hotel in New York (from whence it took its name, henceforth the Carlton Group). By then the five intended participants had grown to six (with the addition of Italy) and a seventh was mooted (Canada, as the USA's largest trading partner).[250] The proposed delegations had also been widened, to include Finance and Foreign Ministers and, following leaks by the Japanese, the secrecy of the proposals was blown. Hunt cleared his lines with the Prime Minister on 3 October, the main thrust of which was that he would not reveal too much of the

United Kingdom's hand in advance by putting forward hard proposals at the preparatory meeting but, in the spirit of the Summit as, 'an opportunity for those taking part to concert their thinking,' he would aim for the sort of proposals which the United Kingdom wanted (such as American resistance to Congressional protectionist tendencies) to emerge in the Carlton group discussion and then to be developed by Wilson at the Summit itself.[251] His ploy was successful; he was able to report back four days later that the discussions in New York had gone well and would result in 'orientations' as a result of which Heads of Government would subsequently be able to concert their policies. A threatened American – French disagreement over the desirability of a return to fixed exchange rates looked as if it could be avoided. Hunt had also managed to defuse German and Japanese worries about pressures in the United Kingdom for import controls, without conceding that controls would never be used selectively and temporarily if circumstances so required. He had done so by acknowledging that, 'there were currently many voices on this subject at home. This was understandable because we were grappling with a very serious situation. But the voices to listen to were yours [the Prime Minister's] and those of the Ministers directly concerned,' which were anti-restrictionist and had consistently condemned 'beggar-my-neighbour' policies. A further Carlton Group meeting would be held in London (and therefore under Hunt's chairmanship) just before the Summit when the vexed issue of a communiqué would be returned to. The Group had agreed a suggested agenda to promote 'a demonstrated capacity on the part of leading democratic nations that together they can recognise key issues and deal with them in a spirit of conviction, of common understanding, and of forward motion. This is a time of great and testing issues. This meeting must help meet these tests and convince the watching world of that fact.'[252]

The follow up meeting took place on 11 and 12 November at Admiralty House in Whitehall, three days before the start of the Summit at Rambouillet as guests of President Giscard d'Estaing. In a brief report to Wilson Hunt said that Callaghan's suggestion to widen discussion beyond economics had been signalled to the Carlton Group as a marker that the United Kingdom might want to raise nuclear proliferation as an issue. Otherwise, the Americans (the Germans and the Japanese) had brought draft texts of a possible communiqué but had not carried the day on the form it might take, which would be left to the Heads of Government to decide in the light of the discussions. However, to avoid undue time being spent at the Summit on drafting some progress on the themes to be reported and the wording to be used had been possible. In the course of which Hunt had detected indications of a harder United States line; in particular, 'a disregard of the susceptibilities of others,' characterised by American pressure for announcement of follow-up action and infelicitous wording such as, 'the massive increase in oil prices … that are within our power to remove.'[253]

In the event, however, the short 15-paragraph communiqué (issued on 17 November) emphasised the fight against unemployment and the search for steady growth in the leading industrial countries and declared a willingness to work constructively with the rest of the world.[254] A second summit (now G7 with the addition of Canada) was held at the invitation of President Ford in Puerto Rico from 27–28 June 1976[255] thus establishing a regular pattern.

Harold Wilson's Resignation

Harold Wilson announced his retirement on 16 March 1976. He quoted Chamberlain: 'Once I leave, I leave. I am not going to speak to the man on the bridge, and I am not going to spit on the deck,' and he advised his successor to remember that the Party was the Party in the country – not the Palace of Westminster, not Party HQ.[256] Jim Callaghan was elected Leader and became Prime Minister on 5 April. Prior to the leadership election he had asked Hunt to let him have ideas about the theme of a Ministerial broadcast if he were to win. Hunt gave him a draft six days before the election. It suggested four objectives:

(1) strike a positive note; (2) make a rallying call to the Labour Party, the nation as a whole to bolster international confidence in the new government; (3) offer hope whilst not concealing that there would be hard times ahead; (4) scotch any notion that this was a caretaker administration or that there would be an early General Election.[257] Three days later Hunt submitted a second, three-page note on the challenges of forming an administration – chief among them a need to reinforce the prices and incomes policy by retaining Denis Healey and Michael Foot in post until the end of the summer and, therefore, the need to appoint a stop-gap Foreign Secretary pending the opportunity to move Healey.[258] And on the day Callaghan took over he submitted a further nine pages covering the issues likely to require collective decision in Callaghan's first few weeks. Two issues stand out.[259]

First the Treasury short-term economic forecast was dire – predicting heavy unemployment, inflation still over 10% per annum and a balance of payments deficit that it would be difficult to finance. But the forecast was based on computer models that assumed the future would be like the past and the world was emerging from an unprecedented boom and slump. So Ministers should not take precipitate radical action, though neither could they ignore action to hold down public sector and consumer demand to allow the financing of industrial modernisation and productivity improvement. Bringing the TUC along with the economic strategy would be crucial Hunt thought, failing to recognise that here too the world was changing and the ability of the TUC to deliver moderation was weakening.

The second issue is the prediction of Parliamentary problems over devolution – which Hunt believed Wilson had based on a cynical calculation that it was essential in order to win the 1974 election rather than because it was right in itself.[260] The White Paper on Scotland and Wales had promised a Bill at the start of the 1976–77 Parliamentary Session. Ministers would have to decide whether to press on more or less regardless, or whether the awkwardness of the Parliamentary position pointed to a referendum, to separate Bills for Scotland and

Wales and to an attempt to do a deal with the Conservatives. And what of England? The main problem, wrote Hunt, 'is a situation in which 71 Scottish MPs continue to vote on legislation for England, Wales and Northern Ireland but MPs would have no voice in legislation for Scotland.'

Uncertainties around the use of Special Advisers re-emerged when Callaghan wanted Donoughue, Tom McCaffrey and Tom McNally to sit in on Ministerial committees chaired by Shirley Williams. Hunt challenged this: 'When Mr Callaghan first became Prime Minister he was good enough to say that I should never hesitate to let him know if I felt a wrong decision was being taken.'[261] He continued, whilst a Prime Minister could, of course, have whomever he wished to support him in meetings at No 10, committees chaired by another Minister were of a different character and attendees might well see the presence of Policy Unit personnel as Prime Ministerial spies in their midst. Another sensitive issue was whether to follow custom and appoint the Lord President to the Defence and Oversea Policy Committee (DOP) in view of his pacifist and anti-nuclear background. On balance Hunt thought it better for the Lord President to have the opportunity to take part in detailed discussion on issues on which he felt strongly before they came to Cabinet. Callaghan agreed: 'He is a patriot,' he scribbled in the margin of Hunt's memo.[262] But Callaghan rejected Hunt's suggestion that Messrs Benn, Foot and Shore comprised too strong a representation of 'the general import control school' on the Economic Strategy Committee, commenting about Benn, 'I am going to give him a chance' – a not entirely successful generosity seen from the Prime Minister's point of view. Hunt also worried about balance in the European Community Strategy Committee between the pro and anti factions – Callaghan preferred to abolish the Committee altogether; a decision which appeared not to be implemented.

Openness

In mid April Hunt sought Callaghan's guidance on how hard to press for reform of the Official Secrets Act whilst discouraging any intention to reduce the 30-year rule as 'there is no evidence that the media or public opinion generally equate "open government" with a reduction in the 30-year Rule.'[263] GEN 29 (the successor to MISC 89, chaired initially by Callaghan) decided to abandon criminal sanctions for leaking Cabinet documents if they merely caused political embarrassment. Also that there should be no public right of access to information but perhaps the 30-year rule might be reduced to 25 years. Hunt was concerned that the consequences of abandoning criminal sanctions for the disclosure of Cabinet documents had not been sufficiently thought through. Prefaced with, 'I do not want to advise against this provisional conclusion,' he then listed areas where sanctions would not be possible, mainly in the home and economic policy areas. For example, someone who, 'handed the Press a copy of the record of this week's EY discussion [the Cabinet Committee on Economic Strategy] on an alternative economic strategy would no longer be committing a crime.'[264] GEN 29 was asked to reconsider the issue,[265] which it did on 8 November, confirming an exclusion of Cabinet documents from the relaxation of criminal sanctions. Callaghan then withdrew as chairman but by April of 1977 things had turned sour. Hunt reported that he doubted whether the Home Office was making much progress with the preparation of the Official Information Bill, through a combination of inertia and staff shortage.[266] This was, however, only part of the story. The government could not be sure of a majority in the House. The Lord Chancellor thought the drafting of the proposed Bill was too restrictive and likely to be controversial and divisive to the government's supporters.[267] In Hunt's words, 'Much therefore depends on whether the Secretaries of State for Foreign and Commonwealth Affairs and for Defence are ready to get back to the position that Ministers originally took and to stop the process of the departmental rats nibbling away at the relatively simple package which was in prospect.'[268] Subject to that the right course was to continue with the drafting of a Bill.

However, Cabinet decided on 11 October that there was no prospect of room for the Bill in the forthcoming Parliamentary Session, throwing the issue back to a holding White or Green Paper. When a draft White Paper was circulated at the end of January 1978 it revealed that GEN 29 was still floundering, the No 10 Private Secretary commenting to Callaghan that, 'Sir John Hunt is suggesting that if you don't get involved in this ... you may have a mess in Cabinet. On balance I think it would be time well (though not congenially!) spent,'[269] and by 17 February the long-running saga once again seemed to be mired. Hunt advised that if agreement could not be reached at the next meeting of GEN 29 the whole thing should be put in cold storage, he did not see any prospect of producing a more attractive package.[270] Events were taking over. By mid May political pressure was mounting in Parliament and through pressure group activity for a Freedom of Information Act. The Lord President (Michael Foot) thought that progress was so far short of the 1974 Manifesto commitment to reverse the burden of proof on access to government information that he preferred to postpone action until after the next election. Hunt advised against this, as he feared the government would be tempted to succumb to external pressures and would include in a new Manifesto a commitment that they would later regret.[271] Cabinet, however, deferred a decision until after the Home Secretary had consulted the National Executive Committee of the Labour Party.[272] He did so (and also the Parliamentary Labour Party) to hostile receptions, which left the government playing for time yet again.

In combination with Stowe (Callaghan's Principal Private Secretary) and Berrill, Hunt helped draft a Note for the Prime Minister identifying two crucial problems: the lack of clear-cut principles left the government continually on the defensive; and the absence of an appeal mechanism independent of Ministers meant that any proposals would be greeted with suspicion in the country. Openness, 'is surely an area of policy where a radical, constructive government ought to be able to look to an initiative,' they wrote. 'At the moment the Civil Service machine is playing for time in effect, not in my view out of a sense of obstruction, but simply because it does not see where the government wants to go.'[273] Throughout, much of the civil service leadership had been supportive of releasing more of the information that lay behind policy decisions. Ministers were split on the issue and Callaghan had been reluctant to take the lead. Thus, Sir Douglas Allen had issued a directive in July 1977 (later known as the Croham directive) encouraging Departments to make available as much as possible of the factual and analytical background used in major policy studies.[274] Also, Hunt had proposed releasing details of the 20 standing Cabinet Committees (excluding the 25 or so active ad hoc ministerial groups) possibly with the names of their chairmen but not their composition. Callaghan responded, 'I am a hard-liner on this. No official disclosure.'[275] To add further spice, Tony Benn was added to the membership of GEN 29.[276]

However, officials were also split in their opinions. Bancroft of the CSD led opposition to a right of access to government information. It would entail an irreversible shift of power away from Ministers and the costs were currently unknown.[277] The informal exchanges between the most senior officials over lunch in the Cabinet Office Mess cannot have been at full throttle because Hunt and Stowe were outraged. Stowe minuted Callaghan, 'It took a lot of pushing from Sir John Hunt and me to get this far and I think you will need to give firm directions to GEN 29 if the whole thing does not collapse.'[278] Once again the Prime Minister was keen to put limits on the movement to openness. 'Ministers ... are entitled to exchange views frankly and privately with each other; and they should not be required to make public all their discussions and exchanges ... It would change the very nature of Cabinet Government as we know it if Ministers were not able to conduct their affairs in this way: and the breaking of this mutual trust, whether it be by Minister or civil servant, has nothing whatever to do with open government.'[279] Hunt once again advised Callaghan to step in to chair the next meeting of GEN 29, which now faced the challenge of responding to Clement Freud's Private Member's Bill on the freedom of information. Under the chairmanship of the Home Secretary it had, 'so far shown little sign of being able to come to conclusions on the basic issues' and of giving a lead to officials on the line the government wanted to take.[280] GEN 29 was surrendering the initiative on the Committee stage of Clement Freud's Bill[281] and the extremists were taking over.[282] The Prime Minister was still reluctant to drive proposals, which remained the situation until Freud's Bill fell at the Dissolution of Parliament prior to the May 1979 General Election.

Four months later, the Prime Minister approved Hunt writing to Barbara Castle reminding her of the policy on Ministerial memoirs which the government adopted following the Radcliffe recommendations and which largely relied on Ministers' honour not to breach confidences.[283] (Hunt had been tipped off that her diaries were in the hands of the *Sunday Times* and were 'sensational'.) In his submission he noted that Mrs Castle was present when the Cabinet discussed the Radcliffe Report and had opposed accepting it (as had Michael Foot).[284] So Hunt did not expect her to take any notice of his letter; and nor did she, replying in formulaic terms. 'I have, of course, read the Radcliffe Report and will bear in mind what you say.'[285] It was an experience to be repeated again in 1978 when Mr Hugh Jenkins MP submitted a forthcoming memoir as Minister for the Arts which the Cabinet Secretary described to the Prime Minister as driving a complete coach-and-horses through the Radcliffe conventions about revealing the opinions or attitudes of other colleagues or identifying and criticising civil servants (who were in no position to reply). 'I am bound to add that the whole account of his Ministerial experiences is singularly tasteless ... A lot of the book is, I am afraid, badly written and very coarse. I do not think it will do anyone any good, least of all Mr Jenkins.'[286]

New Technology

The pattern of economic activity was starting to change. In September 1976 Ferranti announced a 16-bit electronic chip. The advent of microprocessors provoked alarm in a political discussion that usually associated new technology with job losses.[287] After television criticism of the government reaction to the prospect of very rapid technological change and growing public concern,[288] Callaghan tasked Hunt with advising on the best way of tackling the issues raised.[289] Concurrently, the Secretary of State for Industry (Eric Varley) proposed to authorise the National Enterprise Board (NEB) to inject £50 million into a start-up company, KMOS Semi-conductors Ltd (later known as INMOS) in return for 71% of the equity. There was no collective Ministerial strategy for microelectronics and the prospective very large rewards to the founders of KMOS, were it to succeed, were politically awkward. So the stage was set for inconclusive debate fuelled by traditional suspicions of entrepreneurial rewards and procrastination when faced with unfamiliar territory. Even so, Hunt sought to dissect the issues and to force Ministers to confront the questions, displaying an intuitive grasp of future business school debates on innovation. His first brief pointed out that the new technology was here to stay.[290] More important than a British capacity to make the chips was the extent of British ability to make good use of them. He pointed to a key question: '... is it really important to "invest in innovation" and copy the American experience of rapid growth by small new companies not locked into existing product lines like GEC and ITT?' On balance he recommended letting the NEB go ahead and warned that a decision deferred would be an opportunity closed. (Authorisation was later given to the NEB on 2 June after two split Cabinet discussions with about one third of Cabinet Ministers opposed.)[291] Hunt had noted that, 'at one extreme some economists think that the normal growth of output, income and hence demand will create new industries to take up the slack created by technological unemployment. Others believe that a whole new order of difficulty has been created. It is also the area where least work has been done.'[292] New Whitehall machinery focused on the CPRS was needed to reconcile the views of the technological forecasters with those of the economists and when the CPRS reported in November it was optimistic – provided that British industry did not fall behind competitively in the use of micro-electronics the fears for unemployment frequently did not take sufficient account of the employment creating potential. Case studies pointed to a more complex situation in industry than simple labour substitution, more closely aligned to better production methods, better quality and improved process control.

The IMF Crisis

At GEN 26 on 21 September 1976 the Chancellor had concluded that it would be necessary to go to the IMF again for a second loan. At this stage there was no talk of changing Labour's economic policies. The following month Hunt started to play a distinct role when he became central in the Prime Minister's strategic decision to play the crisis politically, away from the hands of the technicians. Callaghan became convinced of this after a three and a quarter-hour talk alone with Chancellor Schmidt of the Federal Republic of Germany, during which he pressed the case for a $10 billion safety net to guarantee the Sterling Balances and thereby reduce the risk of currency speculation against the pound. West Germany, he thought, would both take the initiative with the United States in support of a safety net (opposed at the time by the US Treasury) and would use its foreign currency reserves to maintain the pound – but only if the negotiations were kept out of the hands of the conservative bankers.[293] During these talks Schmidt vouchsafed that he was worried by 'aggressive and militaristic tendencies emerging in Germany' and emphasised that Germany needed Britain in the EEC to provide 'a safe haven for the German psychology'. He would speak to Herr Pöhl (State Secretary, Ministry of Finance) to explain what was needed. Callaghan then despatched Hunt secretly to see Pöhl in Bonn on 18 October (Douglas Wass, the Permanent Secretary of HM Treasury was briefed orally by Hunt on his return but was not given Hunt's note of the meeting pending Callaghan authorising release to the Healey.)[294] Pöhl reported that the Americans would 'fight to the last against weak conditions' by the IMF partly to discourage others (notably Italy and France) from thinking that recourse to the IMF second tranche was a soft option.

The question, argued Hunt, was whether the Labour government could succeed on its present course or whether it would be forced by events to choose an alternative strategy. (EY had discussed an alternative economic strategy at its 10th meeting of 1976 on 2 August and a scheme for import deposits as late as five days before Hunt's trip. It returned to a discussion of a possible siege economy on 20 October on the basis of a CPRS paper.)[295] Increased indirect taxation would feed directly into the RPI and public expenditure cuts would raise enormous political problems over social security and defence – thus putting the Germans on warning that cuts in the British Army of the Rhine would be hard to avoid. Also, the British would want to be sure that a safety net would be possible *before* agreeing to any IMF terms. The German position was, however, similar to but not as extreme as that of the Americans. A successful settlement with the IMF had to come before a safety net.

Douglas Wass has argued[296] that it is hard to avoid the thought that a combination of extreme secrecy, the closeness of Callaghan and Schmidt and British ignorance of the German financial structure[297] led to unrealistic expectations. To some extent this is borne out by Hunt couriering an explanatory document on the safety net to Pöhl on 28 October only to discover that Chancellor Schmidt's chef de cabinet had suppressed it as not worth troubling him.[298] On the other hand when the Prime Minister gave an interview to BBC Television's current affairs programme *Panorama* on 25 October he raised the political stakes. 'I would love to get rid of the reserve currency ... I would very much like to see us get into a situation where these liabilities of ours which we have as a reserve currency were taken over in some form or other ... I think that Germany and the United States, and perhaps Japan, have got some responsibility here. They have got vast reserves ...' And when asked if the object was to avoid being forced to pursue policies against 'our better judgement' the Prime Minister replied, 'Right! ... the IMF ... have got a great responsibility here ... unless the sterling balances are met in some other way [the IMF policies] could be very harmful to the whole politics and whole structure, not only of Britain but of the West.'[299]

Hunt reported on his discussions with Pöhl at an informal meeting called by the Prime Minister on 1 November, which excluded those members of EY who had argued for a siege economy (notably Anthony Wedgwood-Benn, Peter Shore, and Michael Foot). The Chancellor stressed that the key issue was market confidence – and the view of the market was essentially short-term. This meant an IMF settlement that would be convincing to currency men, buying time for the solution of the sterling balances problem to be pursued through a safety net or through a new multi-lateral loan.[300] Informal talks with the IMF had started in London but the serious negotiation was expected to begin the following week. However, the British were not in a good position; the Conservative Opposition were manoeuvring in Washington against the government[301] and, if anything, the split between Ministers was widening. At EY on 3 November there had been talk of the collapse of all the government's economic and social targets and the need for a bold but unspecified move that would mean that the country would accept a shift of priorities and sacrifices.[302] The Prime Minister had striven to maintain morale and now Hunt and Palliser did their bit to reassure him. Palliser wrote that he was confidant Schmidt would not swerve from his fundamental political judgement that it was right (and in German interests) to do all he could to help. Moreover, our partners knew that we were negotiating from weakness and this worried them very much. But they also knew that in a few years' time the UK would be strong as North Sea Oil began to flow. Provided the politicians kept the upper hand over the technicians, 'I believe that the Prime Minister can get what he wants.'[303] Hunt too encouraged the Prime Minister not to be disheartened by a further letter from Schmidt once again arguing that a settlement with the IMF was a prerequisite to a safety net.[304]

On 17 November EY gave the Chancellor a negotiating mandate to smoke out the IMF – the Prime Minister summing up as per the brief Hunt had submitted.[305] The Chancellor was to explore the possibility of settling the PSBR at various levels, none below £9 billion, and should not commit to a firm figure without reporting back. Nor should he be drawn into a division between public expenditure cuts and increased taxation. Import *deposits* were not ruled out though there was no encouragement for import *quotas*. Hunt was deputed to chair a group of Permanent Secretaries to work up the practicalities of a scheme.[306] The collective discussion then moved to Cabinet, which met nine times between 18 November and 14 December to discuss the negotiations – finally authorising the Chancellor to sign a letter of intent with the IMF on 15 December in return for Special Drawing Rights of £3,360 million. For three of these Cabinet meetings, unusually, manuscript notes passed between the Prime Minister and Cabinet Secretary are preserved.[307] The Chancellor was under pressure from his colleagues for much of the time up to 6 December and the notes show Hunt advising on how to prevent a premature breakdown in Cabinet. He thought that Cabinet would, in the end, support what the Prime Minister said and this was the best chance of maintaining unity. Hence the Prime Minister should adjourn the meeting on the basis that: 'We must have the IMF loan. The alternative strategy would need 12 months to bite and would need legislation; on the other hand the cuts asked for may be too great; you have already spoken to President Ford and to Chancellor Schmidt; you will now see the IMF team personally; you will then make a recommendation to Cabinet; they must decide on Thursday [25 November].' Which is precisely what the Prime Minister did – and in those terms.[308]

Then, in preparation for a two-day IMF Cabinet on 1 and 2 December, Hunt briefed forcefully that the Prime Minister should aim not for an agreed, or even a majority, view on the preferred option but to get to a point at which the siege economy alternatives were put to one side (at any rate provisionally). The choice would then be between a tough set of cuts and a 'soft' IMF package. The former might be politically difficult domestically; the latter might fail to convince the markets or fail to get the sterling safety net without which Cabinet would have to face the same, or worse, agonies again before long. Cabinet should neither look at the loan in isolation from the safety net nor be mesmerised by what to do if the IMF were to turn down the UK request (which he volunteered was unlikely). Cabinet should concentrate on what they thought would be right in terms of the British economy (which meant both sides of industry not just the Social Contract) and what was politically possible. A conclusion to aim for on 1 December would be that Cabinet still wanted to try to get the loan and the safety net. On 2 December it would be necessary to turn to the size and broad composition of the maximum price the Cabinet was prepared to pay.[309] These conclusions should then be rehearsed with the IMF, Germany and the United States.

At the second Cabinet the Chancellor and Prime Minister spoke at length introducing the discussion jointly with the Prime Minister concluding that if the Chancellor's proposal were rejected the effect on friendly governments and on the market would be such that there was no chance of the government surviving. They were opposed by the Lord President (Michael Foot) who argued that the price of a loan was a betrayal of the egalitarian basis of the Social Contract which would not get Parliamentary approval and it was more important that the Labour movement should hold together than that they should stay in government. As the debate flowed, Hunt slipped a note to the Prime Minister: 'the

Cabinet don't really know how hard you and the Chancellor have been fighting. They don't know about W's [Johannes Witteveen, Managing Director of the IMF 1973–1978] visit.[310] They don't know about your exchanges with Ford and Schmidt[311] other than what is in the press. They have the impression of a dialogue between Treasury officials and Whittome. While it will certainly be right to decide how far to go and then to tell the IMF that this [is the] most that can be done, I don't think the Cabinet realise that settling on a billion [off the PSBR] won't be all that easy. The Chancellor is on this point now: but what he is saying is very oblique.'

Though Hunt's public face to the Prime Minister was optimistic over an IMF deal his private preparations were precautionary. At the same time, at the request of Stowe, he submitted a three-page note prepared jointly with Sir Kenneth Berrill of the CPRS: '*What happens if we do not get the IMF loan?*'[312] The answer – an immediate sterling crisis, closure of the foreign exchange market for a few days, public threats to abandon the UK's defence commitments, winding up the Rhodesia conference and moving to a protectionist strategy that would cause maximum international ill will. There would be massive forestalling on imports. There would be irreversible damage to London as an international financial centre. If sterling began to slide when the markets reopened there were insufficient reserves to do other than to let it go. The only hope was to make all of this plain to the UK's friends as the result unless they were to help us. Only four copies of the note were made – HM Treasury was not a recipient though a precautionary check was made with Treasury officials that they had dusted off their contingency plans for closing the foreign exchange market. (Sir Douglas Wass of the Treasury was also preparing contingency plans, which the Chancellor submitted, to the Prime Minister on 5 December.)[313]

A particular difficulty for Cabinet was that the scale of public expenditure reductions (finally agreed at a p.m. Cabinet on 7 December – the third meeting in two days – as just over £1 billion for 1977/780) required a contribution from the Defence Budget which had already been subject to repeated slicing and which would run counter to the message given to President Ford and Chancellor Schmidt that unless the UK got the IMF loan 'we will have to cut Defence.' Hunt doubted the competence and knowledge of most Cabinet Members to debate defence matters – he was also personally sympathetic to the defence predicament. He had, therefore, a very private talk with the PUS at MOD (Sir Frank Cooper). He put the result in a note of 3 December to Stowe. Up to £50 million p.a. could come off the Defence Budget without serious damage. At £100 million, '… the view would probably be taken that we should scrap (or at any rate abandon the improvement of) the deterrent rather than reduce our NATO conventional commitments further.' At over £100 million a major review of defence commitments would be needed.[314] The figure agreed by Cabinet on 7 December was £100 million in 1977/78 and £200 million in 1978/79 causing the Chiefs of Staff to exercise their right to make representations to the Prime Minister three days later. Finally, seemingly tireless when most of the others concerned were showing distinct signs of fatigue, Hunt still had the energy and commitment to advise that the proposed statement to be made by the Chancellor about the Statement of Intent was too dull and flat, it should be made more of a selling document.[315] Throughout, the advice offered by Hunt to the Prime Minister focussed on managing the politics of the crisis. On more than one occasion a Minister voiced personal doubts about the reliability of the Treasury short-term National Income Forecasts – the Bank of England was described as more optimistic about the economic outlook than the Treasury.[316] However, Hunt appears not to have questioned the computer models, which, as later statistical revisions were to show, had shaky foundations. But nor did the currency markets which, although the NIF forecasts were not published, would have worked off similar models such as that of the Department of Economic Affairs at Cambridge (led by Wynne Godley the former Treasury forecaster-in-chief).

One result of the IMF deal was that Denis Healey's position at the Treasury became less secure. The need for further public expenditure reductions meant that Treasury Ministers found themselves relatively friendless in Cabinet. Callaghan had to keep in mind that if there were to be another crisis of confidence in the economy he might have to sacrifice the Chancellor. He warned David Owen of this orally when appointing him Foreign and Commonwealth Secretary in 1977[317] and he had earlier asked the Cabinet Secretary for his views on a potential successor to the Chancellor. Hunt's advice was to split the Treasury into a Ministry of Finance dealing with economic policy and taxation etc. and a Bureau of the Budget dealing with public expenditure and manpower. Historically Chancellors had been unwilling to contemplate this because of the importance of the public sector in the management of the economy and the 'Chancellor's prerogative' not to discuss macro-economic policy and taxation matters with their colleagues collectively. 'I believe that this objection has now been completely eroded,' wrote Hunt.[318] The erosion had begun with the increasingly close interaction of taxation and benefits uprating and had been accelerated by the need for collective discussion of macro-economic policy surrounding the IMF negotiations. 'The skies have not fallen in and I do not believe that any future Chancellor could set this particular clock back.' Too many arguments are settled behind closed doors in the Treasury that ought to be argued out between Ministers, he claimed. Furthermore, a fatal weakness of the Civil Service Department (CSD) – its isolation from the real dialogue on policy between the centre and departments – would be cured if it were turned into a Bureau of the Budget with manpower and financial control reunited, removing the softer personnel functions of the CSD to a Public Services Commission. Though this never happened, it is significant that in appointing Dr Owen, not only did Jim Callaghan speak of his contingency plan to move Denis Healey to the Foreign Office; he also said that the Treasury would then be split between Dr Owen and Peter Shore.[319]

Sherpa

The following year London was the venue both for the G7 nations and also a further Commonwealth Heads of Government meeting, which coincided with the British Presidency in the European Communities. Hunt supported an initiative by the Foreign and Commonwealth Secretary to divert attention away from uncomfortable topics at the Commonwealth meeting (notably industrial co-operation within the Commonwealth and the North/South dialogue) by developing a Commonwealth – European Community theme to be introduced late in the day as a diversionary tactic. For the G7 meeting President Carter, who had replaced President Ford in January, was keen to introduce political topics to the agenda: arms sales, nuclear proliferation and human rights. The French and Germans sought, initially at least, to restrict the issues to macroeconomics. The British stayed neutral although their preferred focus was on unemployment, inflation and co-ordination between the stronger and weaker economies – recognition, as John Hunt put it, 'that the laws of macro-economics had to be given a political dimension.'[320]

As the representative of the host nation Hunt acted as chairman. The sherpas from the stronger economies (United States, Germany and Japan) did not like the message that they should stimulate their economies further to help world recovery. At the end of the first day of discussions Hunt recorded, 'We retired to bed pretty depressed.' Rather than persist with the troublesome discussion he moved on to discuss draft texts on balance of payments financing, trade, energy and relations with developing countries, reaching agreement (*ad referendum* to the Heads of Government) after a hard day's slog. It was then possible to return to the discussions about economic stimulus at a strategic and political level rather than by looking at texts. 'I made good use of your recent remark,' he subsequently told Callaghan 'that last year we had the support of the people but not of the market: now we had external confidence but risked losing the support of the Unions etc.'[321] This was followed up by a personal message from Callaghan to Carter which stressed his personal fears that unemployment (particularly among the young) might lead to a growing disenchantment among our peoples that could put a risk open democratic society.[322] A theme he later developed in the opening statement at the Summit on 7 May and that underlay the communiqué's declaration that, 'Our most urgent task is to create more jobs while continuing to reduce inflation. Inflation does not reduce unemployment. On the contrary, it is one of its major causes. We are particularly concerned about the problem of unemployment among young people.'[323]

A follow-up meeting took place in Washington on 29/30 September to monitor the results of the Downing Street summit. The British were keen to see a special conference on youth unemployment, despite German opposition, partly under OECD and partly within the EEC.[324] Furthermore, Callaghan felt that the commitments for economic growth entered into at the Summit were not being met.[325] OECD in particular, but also smaller EEC members and the European Commission, were sensitive to a new monitoring arrangement that bypassed existing institutions – a valid 'non-duplication' point but one which would make it the more difficult to exclude these institutions from attendance at future Summits. And in the run-up to the monitoring meeting the Americans were initially resentful at the Prime Minister's reported comments about the failure of the Summit [to tackle unemployment] but President Carter later relented, commenting that he 'quite understood how such comments might have been made on the stump in a high unemployment area.'[326] In the event the British objective of getting 'an agreed analysis of the situation following which the strong economies [Germany and Japan] may feel that they can act in concert,' was more than achieved and, in Hunt's words: 'this report goes further in placing responsibility for action to reduce their deficits on the Japanese and Germans than any other collective statement.' But what did that amount to? The monitoring meetings were not negotiations (indeed the Japanese and Germans said that the Summit undertakings themselves were a factor, real but not decisive which had affected their domestic actions.)[327] Some decisions in the margins of Summits had great importance but probably the deepest importance lay in creating the mutual understanding whereby Heads of Government could readily pick up the telephone to each other on sensitive and urgent matters.

Intelligence

Callaghan was less intrigued by intelligence than Wilson. As Prime Minister he asked: 'Is the Foreign & Commonwealth Secretary formally responsible for MI6 and the Home Secretary for MI5 – or am I? When I was Home Secretary I thought the Prime Minister was responsible but as Foreign & Commonwealth Secretary I thought I was!'[328] This view is echoed by Lord Owen who has said that when he was Foreign & Commonwealth Secretary he sometimes felt that Hunt would have preferred it if the intelligence agencies had reported directly to the Prime Minister (through himself of course) in all aspects.[329] One reason behind this protectiveness was that the mutual exchange of intelligence material between the United States and the United Kingdom was at the heart of the special relationship. But early in June 1977 Lt. General Sir David Willison (DGI)[330] reported that a vital flow of raw photographic intelligence data from the United States to the United Kingdom had been postponed indefinitely. It was a body blow.[331] The Callaghan Government had planned an expensive expansion to the Joint Air Reconnaissance Intelligence Centre (JARIC) to process this material as a key contribution to NATO. It wasn't the first time intelligence co-operation had been suspended, though this time the hiatus lasted much longer and was a more serious threat to the perceived value of the United Kingdom contribution to the exchange of information with the USA. The suspension coincided with the arrival as Director of the CIA and Director of Central Intelligence of Admiral Stansfield Turner. His remit was to stir up and revitalise a stagnant command. In some ways Hunt and Admiral Turner were alike – both were Navy men, direct and powerful, intransigent.[332] (A British diplomat reported a comment from a career CIA officer that Turner's expectation, which was a tiresome factor, was that when he put forward a suggestion it should be followed by results. The British assessment included the view that there was no record of any occasion when Turner had not achieved his aim – right or wrong. He played games to win.)

Turner visited Hunt in September to describe how he planned to restructure the CIA and to hear how the British tasked and controlled their intelligence agencies. Hunt emphasised the duty on the British to ensure political control and clearances of intelligence operations because of the Westminster form of government, which had fewer formal checks and balances than the United States system. Turner expressed some admiration of the thoroughness of the controls in place in the United Kingdom but had also said that one of his aims was to retain the security of what should remain secret and here he was tightening up considerably. The United States was concerned to preserve the secrecy of its latest reconnaissance satellites (known as KH 11, or by the codenames 1010, Crystal and Kennan, and commonly as 'Key Hole').[333] First launched in December 1976 the satellite utilised electro-optical digital imaging to produce real-time images. Turner judged that the extent of the distribution list for KH 11 output was a security risk. Hunt was fearful that the progressive degradation of the British intelligence database was leading some members of the United States intelligence community to a view that, 'we were now contributing insufficient to the United States/United Kingdom intelligence relationship.' A British charm offensive was launched in March 1978 to show the value of its work to the CIA and to differentiate its contribution from that of the Australians, Canadians, New Zealanders, French and Germans. A deadline of the Bonn Summit, due in July, was set for Callaghan to tackle Carter if things had not sorted themselves out. The Prime Minister was prepared to be very robust, taking the line 'Either the United States trust us or not ... Turner cannot be allowed to play around with this.'[334] Hunt duly tackled Turner late in May and Callaghan wrote to Carter at the end of July: 'if our analysts do not have access to this special material, the accuracy of their work is bound to decline ... If you felt unable to trust us with this material, subject to whatever handling procedures your people and mine may agree, this is something which would concern me very greatly.' However, by the late summer of 1978 the system was already known to be compromised when a junior CIA employee[335] was charged and convicted of selling the Soviet Union a technical manual describing the design and operation of the satellites.[336] Supply to the United Kingdom was resumed shortly afterwards.

Machinery of Government

The 1975 referendum had removed membership of the Community temporarily from the political agenda but the UK's performance in Brussels still gave grounds for concern. In the eyes of the Foreign Office at least, the French seemed so much more consistent and organised, allowing them to dominate the Six. Hence, in late summer 1977 Michael Palliser suggested that Britain should emulate a strategic group under the economic adviser to the French President, which seemed to foster a common view of French interests and aspirations in the Community.[337] Against FCO advice he had proposed Cabinet Office chairmanship of the European Unit as it was perceived as neutral in Whitehall and this would not tie the hands of the Foreign Secretary in negotiation with his colleagues. Thus Hunt led on the new

PUS group and convened a first meeting for 18 November to discuss a paper from Palliser on Community enlargement.[338] It was attended by Neale (MAFF), Rampton (Energy), Carey (Industry), Pliatzky (Trade), Couzens (HMT), Franklin (European Unit) and Palliser (FCO) but not by Wass (PUS HMT). No formal record was made though Hunt subsequently set out the salient points in a letter to participants.[339] In Palliser's view the group provided valuable background for UKREP, particularly in COREPER.[340] But it struggled to find its feet. A second meeting, 3½ months later, concluded that the UK, 'had no overall concept of the way we wanted to use our membership ... [and] tended to react to events and developments promoted by others and to lose the initiative and the means of making our influence positively felt.'[341] Such conclusions as there were about British interests were narrow (e.g.: the UK was better served by the application of EEC competition policy than by the Brussels sectoral initiatives).[342] By June 1978 Hunt felt that none of the subjects he could think of filled him with enthusiasm but he was reluctant to let the group fall into disuse.[343] Palliser thought it would be worth waiting until September for a meeting on the enlargement of Community 'own resources'[344] and how this might be used to leverage CAP reform.

Both were wrong. By the time the group met for the third time there was a meaty topic – the European Monetary System – and this time Wass opened the discussion.[345] FCO participants were enthusiastic about the discussion;[346] but the Treasury was anxious to keep macroeconomic policy at a distance from interference by Hunt, possibly partly because of his known sympathy for splitting the department. So it was perhaps no surprise that, in November, Wass did not send Hunt or Palliser a copy of a letter to Dr Otto Schlecht, Staatssekretar Bundesministerium für Wirtschaft and chairman of the Communities Economic Co-ordinating Group,[347] which suggested enhancing its role to act as a steering group for the Finance Council. Having got wind of the suggestion, Hunt successfully asked for a copy and then plotted with Franklin of the European Unit to 'bounce' the Treasury (with FCO and UKREP support) at a meeting of the PUS group on 30 January 1979.[348] His subsequent informal record of the meeting said, '... we agreed that if the Co-ordinating Group developed into a Convergence Committee its ramifications would extend to a number of Whitehall Departments, and that the line we take there might call for co-ordination through the usual Cabinet Office machinery.'[349] But the Treasury would not lie down. Couzens replied, 'I had not understood ... that we were making such an agreement and I am not sure that it would be necessary or profitable to impose too much bureaucratic processing on Co-ordinating Group briefing, as distinct from ad hoc consultation when necessary.'[350] Which, in turn, prompted Maitland of UKREP to say that if he'd been consulted he would have advised against the timing of Wass's letter, coming close to the end of the German Presidency of the Communities and just before the French Presidency who were thought to be less than enthusiastic about the Co-ordinating Group.[351] In the event this Whitehall spat fizzled out as the Treasury became disenchanted with the possibility of joining the EMS and when the Conservative election victory of May 1979 put paid to any residual interest.[352]

The PUS group met three more times whilst Hunt was Cabinet Secretary. The first (30 January 1979) was preoccupied with the budgetary position, concluding that continued pressure across a wide front would need to be kept up. The second (20 July) focused on the run-up to the European Council on 29–30 November, identifying a need to agree a fisheries policy to prevent it obstructing the budget discussion. The third (10 October) intensified preparations for the Council, including the possibility of a nuclear sweetener to encourage French co-operation over the budget. It did not meet again until budget proposals had been agreed at the Foreign Affairs Council of 29–30 May 1980 by which time Robert Armstrong was Cabinet Secretary.[353] Its relaxed style suited Armstrong more than it suited Hunt. There are hints in the correspondence that Hunt was uncomfortable with discursive discussion and looked for a clear output from meetings. There was a sense of relish on the occasions when the outcome contributed to a Ministerial brief; and whilst Hunt and Palliser were on a wavelength over the Community, Palliser could seem most interested in longer-term aspirations for the Communities.

Underlying all these moves was a belief that the machinery of government ought to reflect not only the changing nature of the problems but also the administrative ideas and working methods of the Prime Minister of the day and their colleagues.[354] The possibility of splitting the Treasury was a case in point. Hunt developed this theme in the autumn of 1977 in the wake of an Expenditure Committee Report on the Civil Service:[355] '… we should not forget that other countries operate perfectly satisfactory models which are claimed by the Select Committee to be "irresponsible" or "indefensible".' In addition to repeating the arguments he had advocated at the end of 1976 he added that the CSD had become a Department <u>for</u> the civil service not a Department <u>of</u> the civil service. The concept of a Bureau of the Budget would have to rebut any thoughts that it would be 'soft' on public expenditure control. But nor was the Treasury without problems: the Chancellor was hopelessly overloaded ('Very few people have the physical and mental toughness of Mr Healey') and whilst internal Treasury discussion was open up to the point when the Chancellor made up his mind, the Cabinet expected – and rightly – to hear the arguments for itself.

Operation of the Public Expenditure Survey remained unsatisfactory; most notably because attention was focused on incremental changes despite numerous attempts to put some teeth into the annual discussion of priorities. Because the overall rate of growth in public expenditure was, at best, constrained this focus tended to freeze existing patterns of spending with major changes only occurring at a change of administration. At the time of a particularly confused 1978 public expenditure round[356] Bancroft, Berrill, Wass and Hunt discussed ways of improving the process of public expenditure control and Bancroft put in a report to Callaghan – to the annoyance of Hunt and Berrill who no doubt felt that their power had been usurped.[357] A few weeks later Joel Barnett (Chief Secretary to the Treasury) put forward suggestions for changing PES 1979 by introducing a small committee of senior Ministers to set priorities after discussion with spending Ministers.[358] The problem was that no one had a convincing strategy for forcing Ministers to look seriously for things to give up. Although Permanent Secretaries socialised with leaders of large private sector undertakings the idea that they could transfer or adapt processes of resource allocation used in complex companies was not considered. Nor did the idea of assumed productivity gains to be surrendered for reallocation seem to have been discussed.

Hunt doubted, 'whether in the present Cabinet a group of this kind would carry enough weight, simply as "wise men".'[359] 'Cabinet cannot allocate public expenditure sensibly if Ministers disregard the remits they are given.' He proposed instead that the new committee should be composed almost entirely of the Chairmen of the main standing committees of the Cabinet sitting under the chairmanship of the Chancellor – holding out the prospect of zero-based budgeting. However, Callaghan was sceptical of both the Chief Secretary's idea and of Hunt's.[360] Instead Callaghan asked Barnett to produce a mock-up of how extra health spending could be paid for by reductions in the education or housing programmes. A mock-up circulated on 28 December, supplemented by detailed programme information about housing and nationalised industries, was well received by Hunt and Berrill, mainly on the basis that it suggested that £400 million a year could be saved if the emphasis in the housing programme were switched from new construction to rehabilitation. They suggested an immediate launch of Hunt's idea for a committee composed of the Chairmen of the main standing policy committees for the 1979 PES exercise, which was somewhat grudgingly accepted by Callaghan, who was worried that it might be seen as a 'cuts committee.' It met as the PXP Committee in March 1979 to agree a programme of work to feed into the normal PES round in June.[361] But, as so often with ideas late in the Parliamentary cycle, work was halted by the General Election and PXP disappeared.

There was also talk of a Prime Minister's Department, which Hunt saw as likely: 'I personally believe that at some point in the future the need for a Prime Minister's Department will become imperative, but equally so I doubt very much whether it would be right or acceptable at the present time.'[362] The risks included potential isolation of the Prime Minister from colleagues, as discussion would be conducted between civil servants and not through the Prime Minister exercising a dominant influence in direct discussion with them. This would be alien to the whole political tradition in the United Kingdom. However, the doctrine of collective responsibility tended to be asserted rather than reasoned and, perhaps signifying some unease at this, Hunt discussed the position with Berrill at the time of a proposal from Stan Newens MP[363] that the Parliamentary Labour Party should elect 'the nucleus of the Cabinet.' Whilst this would not require a formal constitutional change it would be a departure from all precedent and would have undesirable consequences. A Cabinet elected by the Party would weaken the likelihood of the Prime Minister presiding over an efficient, harmonious and broadly representative body and would curtail the powers of patronage to the point where it would be almost impossible to maintain discipline and coherence. It would erode, not strengthen, the accountability of Ministers to Parliament and ultimately to the electorate, substituting accountability to the Party.[364]

Not all of the manoeuvrings to enhance the role of the Cabinet Office went well. Shortly before the March 1979 referenda on devolved powers to Scotland and Wales, John Garlick moved on from Head of the Constitution Unit leaving suggestions how Whitehall should organise for devolved power sharing.[365] It included a suggestion for a central secretariat in the Cabinet Office to support Ministers. Hunt seized on the recommendations, adding for good measure that issues around Community obligations, the role of the Crown and the consequences for reform of the Westminster Parliament would also need to be considered.[366] When it came to a discussion with interested Whitehall parties in May, however, Bancroft and Hywell Evans[367] disagreed so strongly that Hunt backtracked: 'There had been no intention,' he said with supreme irony, 'to imply any weakening of the position of the Departments of the Territorial Secretaries of State; secondly, that reference to monitoring in the paper had not been intended to imply either that devolution should not be a reality or any wish to backseat drive.'[368] However, he claimed support from Downing Street that there would be major political, constitutional and economic questions that would far outstrip the responsibilities of the Territorial Secretaries of State. A central unit would inevitably be required to deal with questions of *vires*, of override powers, of the devolution implications of proposed legislation and queries about the boundaries between devolved and retained powers. Clashes of authority were inevitable if there were administrations of different political complexions. The traditional position of the Cabinet Office as an honest broker pointed to a small but proactive unit (replacing the Constitution Unit and serving a strong (and secret) Ministerial Committee) to ensure consistency in approach to the devolved authorities thus avoiding being picked off by the Scots and Welsh.[369] The participants did seem to recognise, though, that it would be undesirable for any central unit to involve itself in functions which had been wholly devolved – understanding what the devolved administrations were doing on such matters would fall to the relevant Whitehall functional departments. But then in the referendum in Scotland the devolution proposals failed to receive sufficient support. As a crisis developed contingency preparations were activated for the possibility of a General Election. Hunt was optimistic about the government's chances, 'If I were a betting man I think I would put my money on the Government just winning Wednesday's Vote ...'[370] he wrote to Callaghan on the Monday before a 'no confidence' vote which the Government narrowly lost (by 311 to 310 votes).

Defence

The defence problem centred on what the United Kingdom could afford – could it meet the NATO target of 3% per annum growth in view of the slower-than-expected growth in GDP, which would mean that the defence share of GDP would rise – contradicting the 1974 Manifesto promise? DOP (the successor to OPD) discussed this inconclusively on 15 November 1977 and briefly on 21 November when it was agreed to plan growth of 3% in 1979/80 followed by 2% in 1980/81 and 3% again in 1981/82. Hunt briefed that those who regarded defence expenditure as a mistaken order of priorities would complain whether the growth was 2% or 3%, whereas those who wanted to comply with the NATO Alliance's target annual growth would be satisfied.[371] Similar concerns returned in the spring of 1978 as the UK prepared for a NATO Summit where a main focus would be progress with an American initiative to offset a growing imbalance in conventional forces between NATO and the Warsaw Pact (known as the NATO Long Term Defence Programme, LTDP). The US Secretary of Defense (Hal Brown) accepted that 3% growth in national defence spending in 1978/79 and 1979/80 was as much as could be expected but Hunt thought this might not be enough to satisfy President Carter who needed to demonstrate that his initiative had made a significant difference to NATO's defence effort.[372] As budgets were not going to increase markedly this meant better collective use of available resources. But it was essential, briefed Hunt, that this was not simply a cover for a hard sell for American equipment. Also, the UK Government would want to be seen to be playing a full part to improve defensive capabilities in the Alliance but would need to make it clear that this was not a way of increasing the defence budget by the back door – especially as the gap between the UK's share of the full LTDP and what could be afforded was some £250–£300 million a year. Rumbling away in the background there were concerns whether NATO was allocating enough resources to defence of the United Kingdom. A JIC assessment of the direct Soviet threat to the country[373] caused Callaghan to ask about the capability to meet the threat.[374] Despite acknowledging an uncomfortably thin capability to defend the country Hunt briefed against the Foreign Secretary who wanted to divert Tornado aircraft from the NATO Central Front to air defence of the United Kingdom. The best security, he argued, lay in collective deterrence under the NATO Alliance whose forward defence should not be weakened.[375]

Arms sales were a thorn in the flesh as the government was caught between conflicting pressures. Many British jobs depended on sales – in 1978–79 defence exports were estimated to account for 70–80,000 jobs and to be worth £900 million to the balance of payments.[376] But some of the customers were judged of poor quality – because the arms would be imported into areas of high volatility, or potentially might be used against British troops, or were destined for countries with bad human rights records, or because the purchaser had a poor payment record. Countries concerned included El Salvador (armoured vehicles), Libya (frigates and Hawk training aircraft), Egypt (Chieftain tanks), Israel (tanks), Portugal (frigates), India (corvettes), South Africa (spare parts), Chile (aero-engine repairs, submarines, Seacat missiles and naval ammunition), Kuwait and Algeria (Harriers), China (Harrier aircraft, marine propulsion units, army equipment). Hunt usually briefed in favour of sales, sometimes with strange results. On the El Salvador case, as a final decision whether to supply armoured vehicles drew near the Committee received a letter from Cardinal Hume (Hunt's brother-in-law) strongly urging a moral imperative not to go ahead. There is no suggestion that Hunt had put the Cardinal up to writing – he had briefed in favour of the sales against an assurance that in no circumstances would the vehicles be used against Belize – but he was visibly amused as Callaghan read out Cardinal

Hume's letter and as a decision not to permit the sales was clearly influenced by it.[377] He supported the sales to Libya (as not significant in disturbing the balance of arms in the Middle East); in favour of supplying 200 Chieftain tanks to Egypt since, 'we should not adopt a policy of unilateral self-denial which would let our competitors get ahead of us'; and in favour of sales to Portugal provided satisfactory financial arrangements could be achieved.

The Chilean case was complex. Chile had a poor payment record and by 1978 shop stewards in Scotland were threatening to block the despatch of repaired aero-engines because of human rights transgressions and general left-wing hostility to the regime. Ministers dithered, reflecting the political divisions in the Labour party and the absence of a clear test of the acceptability of sales. The repaired aero-engines already belonged to the Chilean air force, which left them no legal alternative but to honour the deal and Callaghan declared that he, 'disliked not fulfilling a legal obligation because of a few shop stewards'.[378] The government should seek to persuade Hawker Siddeley to surrender its repair contract with the Chilean air force and make sure that the trades unionists understood that the government could not act illegally to stop the return of the engines to their rightful owner. But how could the engines be got out of the factory without labour trouble? At DOP it was decided that export licences would be issued but then it was over to the Chileans to find a solution, if necessary allowing the legal process to grind slowly on.[379]

On top of these concerns at home there were also worries about the reactions of our allies and of the Soviet Union in regard to Chinese purchases. There was a formidable case against the sale of Harriers in the light of likely US opposition, COCOM Committee objections that it would be impossible to shift without US support, an expected sharp reaction from the Russians. Additionally the Lord President's forecast an adverse reaction from the backbenches. Hunt initially advised cautiously feeling a way towards a sale, weighing carefully Soviet and American reactions before making any commitment to the Chinese and he later supported the Foreign Secretary in advocating a slightly more positive response to the Chinese.[380] President Carter had indicated a more positive US line but, as the Secretary of State for Defence reported on 31 July, the State Department and the Pentagon were unforthcoming about their likely posture at COCOM. So, despite pressure from the Secretary of State for Trade and the advice of the UK ambassador in Beijing (Sir Percy Cradock) that now was the time to take advantage of the newly adopted Chinese policy of opening doors to Western experts and technology, Callaghan was unwilling to agree to a more positive line. His annotation reads: 'I am not anxious to be the first to offer to supply the Chinese with offensive equipment. Hasten slowly.'[381]

The Economy

These dilemmas were taking place against a fluctuating economic situation. By 1977 a fundamental question had arisen about the future of the Social Contract and the counter-inflation policy that depended upon it. Hunt's main preoccupation was whether the policy was still viable – a 12-month period between pay settlements and self-financing productivity deals, which were being opposed by the miners.[382] As the issues dragged on he went further in pointing out the risks of the government being thought to have caved in, but also of being seen as confrontational, though there was wide public support for pay policy and the TUC were not supporting the miners.[383] He pushed Jim Callaghan to intervene and floated a possible secret exercise to ascertain the up-to-datedness of contingency planning and coal endurance in case things turned for the worse.

By December, however, the economic situation looked better and the Economic Strategy Committee discussed the form of a new Letter of Intent to the IMF, which the Chancellor argued would not restrict the UK's freedom of action for 1978. Hunt reminded Callaghan that whilst IMF supervision was generally perceived as distasteful in the government, the standby enabled it to get cheap money and the Treasury to keep up the pressure on public expenditure. He steered the Prime Minister to fight for an extension of the IMF standby, making clear that the UK intended to terminate the agreement sometime in 1978. Inflation was coming down, the Chancellor's target of wage settlements less than double figures looked feasible. Callaghan suggested a 5% pay limit for 1979 in a television interview; it was confirmed as the pay norm at the second of two Cabinet meetings in July[384] but rejected at the Labour Party Conference in September.

In August at Callaghan's request, he submitted a secret and personal brief on the main policy decisions foreseen for the period October to April. He surmised that this would be a key input to the Prime Minister's decision about the date of the General Election and provided evidence against deferring going to the country. In particular, Hunt thought that the tightness of the PSBR forecast against the target in the IMF Letter of Intent would mean there was a good chance that deflationary measures would be needed – an interpretation stoutly rejected by the Treasury and the Policy Unit. Other difficulties ranged from pressures on sterling to pay strikes, from a long string of industrial firms holding out the begging bowl to the growing problem of an estimated 200,000 stray dogs. 'The main success of your Administration,' he wrote, 'has been in establishing itself as one which in its handling of the economic situation is ready to take difficult decisions, seek public acceptance for them and then not run away from the consequences. This is clearly a big electoral asset. But if you are considering a later rather than an earlier General Election ... The worst of all courses would be the impression of a weak Government holding on at all costs in the hope that something favourable would turn up ... A Government facing up to [difficult decisions] would probably get great credit.'[385]

Unexpectedly, Callaghan announced on 7 September that he would not be going for an early election and in an attempt to ginger up the troops after standing them down he called on Cabinet to suggest the main themes to which policy measures should relate over the next five years.[386] Their ideas were to be discussed in GEN 140 under the chairmanship of the Lord President (now Michael Foot).[387] Meetings of the Group were unstructured, causing confusion with some participants urging the Group to examine the government's record against the Manifesto in preparation for discussions with the National Executive Committee of the Labour Party on the drafting of the next Manifesto. There was general confusion over the appropriate time horizon to be considered. Just before the Blackpool Party Conference Hunt warned: 'I think the Prime Minister should know ... that the work of the Ministerial Group on the Forward Look (GEN 140) is not going very well: and that the Lord President hopes to discuss with the Prime Minister in Blackpool both the Group's remit and how its work might proceed.'[388] In fact, when Foot discussed the Group with Callaghan on 9 October he made it clear that GEN 140 could not make progress with Cabinet's remit and that his strong inclination was to give up the attempt. Callaghan proposed a note of his own on the broad political approach to the next 12 months and the Cabinet Office was charged with preparing the first draft.[389] Amongst the ideas floated, but not implemented, was a forerunner of the Blair Government's 'Grid' for ensuring that individual Departmental policy announcements were set in the context of the themes that informed the Government's policy as a whole.[390]

A tidal wave of wage demands hit the scene (Ford workers – a 30% claim; oil tanker drivers – 40%; road haulage drivers; British Leyland; water and sewage workers; BBC electricians; dock workers; and NUPE public sector workers); the associated industrial action becoming identified in the public mind as the Winter of Discontent when strikes by refuse collectors and municipal gravediggers provided vivid images for evening television broadcasts. EY discussed pay policy six times in the last quarter of the year. Hunt's concern was for the government to keep something of the initiative on pay in the face of the union challenges. A full-scale debate in Cabinet must be deferred until the Prime Minister's ad hoc Group[391] had a degree of consensus on what it wanted to do. By November Hunt was briefing in favour of a joint Government/TUC statement which agreed the objectives but not the means of pay policy from July 1979;[392] a statement rejected by the TUC on 14 November after a tied vote. For the most part the central machinery of government worked satisfactorily but officials felt that more positive collective leadership was needed from Ministers. Hunt submitted 50 briefs – and the frustration of officials occasionally showed through. On 13 December, in connection with a possible oil tanker drivers' strike in the New Year, Hunt advised that the Ministerial Committee on Pay (EY(P)) was too cautious in balancing the risk of a leak if contingency plans to use troops to distribute oil were activated with the chances of avoiding strike action by a lower key approach; and too accommodating in supporting a proposal from Benn that Ministers should, as an alternative to using troops, invite the Transport & General Workers' Union to maintain supplies and services essential to the life of the community (in effect accepting the union's view on what were essential services). The subtext of much of this briefing was that the government's policy was slipping away in the light of union militancy and the rapid spread of secondary picketing. Berrill minuted Hunt on 10 January: 'I feel that there is a general impression that incomes policy is slipping out of the Government's hands because there have, perhaps understandably in the Prime Minister's absence [he was at the Guadeloupe Summit] been comparatively few Ministerial speeches and what there have been have not faced up to what is implied if the 5 per cent [norm] is breaking up.'[393]

Guadeloupe

In October 1978, during the Labour Party Conference in Blackpool, Zbignieuw Brzenzski brought a suggestion from President Carter to Callaghan that there should be a quadripartite meeting (United States, France, Germany, and United Kingdom) on politico-security matters, especially the possible extension of the Strategic Arms Limitation Talks (SALT) to include Theatre Nuclear Weapons (TNF) or so-called grey area systems. The meeting would be informal discussions on political matters and international developments between the four Heads of Government with no other Ministers present and limited support staff. UK Ministers had decided on 3 April (against the advice of David Owen, the Foreign Secretary) that the balance of advantage lay in excluding the grey areas from the arms limitations talks – not least because reductions in American TNF could bring political uncertainty about commitment of the United States to the defence of Europe. France had adopted a similar position and was unwilling to have any of its nuclear arsenal included in the SALT talks. Germany, however, was deeply concerned about the threat from Russian SS20 missiles and the Backfire bomber, arguing that the Americans had made a grave error in excluding TNF from the talks as this would leave untouched the Soviet capability to deploy weapons of enormous destructive capacity in the European theatre. Chancellor Schmidt's aim was to prevent Soviet nuclear weapons being pointed at the Federal Republic. Thus, he was wholly opposed to the prospect of medium-range strategic weapons in German hands on German soil. However, American cruise missiles would undoubtedly be included in SALT III talks and the United States was keen to have a high-level political dialogue with those countries most affected before it started to firm up its SALT III negotiating position.[394] United Kingdom Ministers discussed grey area systems again in a restricted session on 17 November. Hunt advised, 'This may be a difficult meeting to handle because there are related issues on which your colleagues are not informed about recent developments.' His paper sought agreement, amongst other things: to explore the case for bringing grey area systems into SALT III with an open mind (a switch of emphasis from the previous stance). He suggested that the Prime Minister might emphasise in his summing up that:

> 'Over the years, it has proved extremely difficult to devise any satisfactory solution to the grey areas problem. It contains political and military ingredients that are vital for the future both of NATO's strategic posture and of political relations within the Alliance. The requirements of these two aspects are not always easy to reconcile.'[395]

The sherpas now took up the mantle, initially bilaterally as the first challenge was to persuade President Giscard d'Estaing to participate. To help persuade the

French President it was proposed that France should host the meeting in a suitably remote and secure location. In the event Giscard favoured the meeting without a great deal of persuasion and Martinique was chosen as the venue; but the location was switched during December to Guadeloupe because the island was less accessible to airlines (and therefore to journalists). The Germans were particularly keen not to budge from President Carter's original suggestion that the meeting should be attended only by Heads of Government accompanied by a very small number of advisers – probably because of Chancellor Schmidt's difficulties with his coalition partner (and Foreign Minister) Hans-Dietrich Genscher of the Free Democratic Party.[396] Hunt proposed that as this would not be a negotiating meeting the briefs should be primarily informative in character and should eschew the normal format of line to take, background and speaking note. With a prophetic note of flippancy Brian Cartledge (the foreign policy private secretary) annotated this suggestion: 'I imagine you will still want to have cards in your pocket, rather than a briefing folder at the edge of the pool!'[397]

Callaghan added a number of topics to the proposed list, including developments in the Middle East (mainly the developing crisis in Iran). Hunt and Cartledge along with Tom McNally, Head of the Prime Minister's Political Office, travelled with the Prime Minister to Guadeloupe. The British had a particular dilemma: whether to raise informally with Carter the question of a possible update for the ageing Polaris missiles of the British nuclear deterrent. The decision would be taken after the next General Election.[398] But should Callaghan ask the President, 'to authorise extremely restricted and discreet talks on an entirely non-committal basis about certain aspects of technology and cost on which we need further information before we can reach any decision ourselves?' Or, 'Do you put a more specific request to him as Dr Owen would like?'[399] Callaghan decided to adopt the tactic of seeking the President's advice on (i) the nature of the choice, (ii) a possible exchange of technological information and (iii) the prospect of purchasing a replacement from the United States.

At 9.30 am on the first morning in Guadeloupe the four sherpas sat down among the thatched beach accommodation, starting with a politico-strategic tour d'horizon which revealed significant differences of opinion. Brzezinski of the United States said that the international situation was more stable than at any time since World War II but Wahl of France relayed a sombre message: Soviet policy was to isolate China, paralyse the United States, neutralise Europe and dominate the Third World. Hunt, supported by Ruhfus of Germany, argued that the United States view could be optimistic, impending changes in the Soviet leadership might lead to rash actions vis-à-vis China. On SALT III he argued, in the face of a common assumption amongst the other sherpas that Europe would not have a seat at the negotiating table, that if that were to be the case there would have to be very special arrangements for consultation by the Americans that recognised European special interests. He was stung later in the morning when Brzezinski claimed that his relationships with the Elysée and with the Chancellery were closer than with the UK. However, his abiding memory of the Summit was of the Prime Minister going off down the beach to discuss Polaris replacement with President Carter and 'coming back with more than we'd asked for.'[400] The abiding memory of others about Hunt is seeing him striding through the sand in blue suit and black leather shoes alongside Brzezinski, head down, hands clasped behind his back, deep in conversation and oblivious to the charms of the half-naked Belgian working girls enjoying R&R at the neighbouring hotel.[401]

Callaghan reported to Cabinet on 11 January[402] – the Summit had concluded that whilst the West wanted to work with the Soviet Union and not against her, they could not allow relations with China to be dictated by the Soviets. Disappointingly, it had not been possible to arrive at an agreed European view on grey area systems though participants had been left in no doubt about the profound disquiet in Germany about the Soviet predominance in these systems. Neither at Cabinet nor in his statement to the House of Commons on 16 January did Callaghan report that follow-up action would include discussions at a technical and contractual level on the possibility of taking Trident C4 as the Polaris replacement – the most immediate tangible outcome of the Summit.

But in the folk memory it was Jim Callaghan's unwise impromptu airport comments at the height of the Winter of Discontent that stuck. His irritation with the line of questioning was perhaps forgivable given his opening comment that, '... the peace and security of the world has been strengthened and that every man and woman and child in our countries can feel that there is a better prospect of their security than there was before.'[403] But back in early November Ken Stowe had warned of the risks of being out of the country if there was industrial unrest to sort out.[404] And he was unwise to say, 'I don't think that other people in the world would share the view that there is mounting chaos.' The voters took a different view. Nor did the follow-up go as smoothly as would have been hoped. At the start of February, David Aaron of the US National Security Council toured the three European capitals. He appeared to weaken the link between TNF modernisation and the SALT III talks that had been agreed at Guadeloupe. Hunt was firm – it would be quite wrong for Europe to leave aside arms control only to find itself bounced by United States pressures later. It was clear that there would be a hard slog and that the full weight of Departmental expertise should be mobilised through the Cabinet Office Official Committee system (handled by the group on international aspects of nuclear defence policy, GEN 63). The sherpa had returned to base camp.

Three days before the General Election he gave Callaghan direct advice for an early reshuffle should Labour win, both on policy grounds and on Ministerial performance. In a frank assessment Hunt thought that Roy Mason's credibility in Northern Ireland was running out, the state of David Ennals's health was worrying, a more collaborative Secretary of State than Tony Benn was needed at Energy, the Prime Minister was having to keep a closer eye on foreign policy than was ideal; there were too many Ministers in Environment, too few in Trade, and in Defence Ministerial posts were poorly structured.[405]

After the Conservative election victory on 3 May 1979 the emphasis in Cabinet and its committees changed subtly – there was still an immediate requirement to discuss pay policy but the emphasis moved to public expenditure control. European Community business continued unabated; the frequency of Cabinet continued at roughly one meeting a week and Hunt's involvement with Cabinet Committees at roughly two a week.[406] Additionally Hunt worked hard to establish a trusting relationship with the new Prime Minister. The appointment diaries show that he saw Thatcher informally 24 times in the first three months of her administration, compared to 13 informal meetings with Jim Callaghan between January and the end of March. Thatcher described her initial briefing as, 'a masterly analysis' – particularly the summary of urgent economic issues and their timing – the most pressing was the shape of the Budget and the associated money supply targets, closely followed by the need for a strategy for public expenditure (though there was no mention of very recent attempts to identify the scope for transfers between programmes in the PXP committee).[407]

The first Cabinet briefs were submitted on 9 May for the opening Thatcher Cabinet the following day. The top priority was approval of the draft Queen's Speech for the State Opening of Parliament on 15 May. Here Hunt patiently reviewed each of the amendments the Prime Minister suggested, including a lengthy educative explanation of the intricacies of language in the negotiations with the Russians over a Comprehensive Test Ban Treaty. He gave her strong guidance that the standing Foreign Affairs and Community Affairs items on the Cabinet agenda were 'for information' but there was always a risk that some Minister would try to bounce through a decision on something that had not been properly discussed and for which there was no paper: 'I am sure you will want to resist any such tendency.'[408] Finally, the Prime Minister was urged to impress on her Cabinet the need for collective responsibility and mutual trust.[409]

It was not long before Thatcher started to put her own stamp on what was required for Cabinet. On 14 May, responding to a draft 'annotated agenda' on pay and cash limits she commented, 'Discussion on this paper in Cabinet would be futile – and on any other paper which raises such enormous questions and supplies so few answers. It would weaken our hand – not strengthen it!' Within two days Hunt demonstrated that he had taken the message to heart. In a brief, 'The Way Forward on Pay,' he discussed four major aspects of pay ranging from influencing the pay climate to the manifesto commitment that, 'in the great public corporations pay bargaining should be governed by what each can afford.' In each case he recommended specific actions pinning responsibilities to Ministers: 'the conclusions reached by Cabinet on these issues will be of considerable operational importance and you will need to record as clear a statement of the Cabinet's view on each as is possible in the light of discussion.' 'We have a dreadful inheritance ... but our economic strategy depends critically on making a significant start in the reduction of direct taxation in this Budget. The Chancellor will therefore require all the help he can get from his colleagues in making immediate cuts in public expenditure' 'You are more likely to get sensible offers [to cut expenditure] ... at this early stage of the life of the Government than you will later on when they have become more identified with their Department and clients.'

Committees

In other ways too the environment was different. The new Prime Minister was temperamentally opposed to co-ordinating machinery, preferring to nominate a lead department charged with consulting others as necessary. She did, however, go with the grain on Cabinet Committees. Hunt recommended nine main standing Committees.[410] Thatcher reduced this to seven, making European questions a sub-committee of OPD (Defence and Oversea Policy) with largely the same membership – which solved a problem as Lord Soames (a Foreign Office Minister) bid to be chairman and Hunt worried that to appoint him might erode the Cabinet Office European Unit. More generally, Mrs Thatcher commented that she wanted the number of committees kept down at the start, as she wanted to keep as tight a rein as possible on Ministerial Committees and upon the amount of time that Ministers devoted to them.[411] Initially she was also inclined to change the format of Cabinet Minutes, which she thought should be confined to recording decisions. Hunt convinced her, however, of the importance for Whitehall (and history) to know why decisions had been taken and, therefore, to retain the format developed over the years.

The Defence Budget resurfaced as an issue. Hunt advised Thatcher not to push the Secretary of State for Defence into a corner. His solution lay in avoiding direct contact between the Prime Minister and the Ministers concerned until intermediaries had cleared the way for an agreement: 'Your own position is too important to be compromised at the start,' he briefed, 'and I am sure it is best to operate at one remove, coming in yourself only when there is some prospect of an agreement.'[412] There were eight Public Expenditure Cabinets in the first four months. Some Ministers were already disposed to argue that the economic climate had changed (notably John Nott at Trade and Jim Prior at Employment) so he suggested that the Prime Minister might bring this to a head by asking the Chancellor to say what would happen if the savings fell £1 billion short. 'There really is no alternative to flogging through the whole list [of options for reduction]' and although the choice of cuts was illustrative 'If any Minister feels he can achieve the same total in a different way, ... it is important that his alternative should be a viable one' unlike the Secretary of State for the Environment (Michael Heseltine) who '... had £70 million up his sleeve at E(DL)[413] the other day, which the Committee were disposed to accept: on investigation, it proved illusory.'[414] 'The time to think of spending more money will arise when we have earned it.' 'The only possible answer to this seems to be that no-one should argue that the Government should abandon its priorities now. Equally, however, no decision now can be binding on discussions in future PESC years.'[415]

The transition to a new government philosophy fitted the textbook concept of civil service neutrality. Though probably personally unsympathetic to some of the new thrust of policy and certainly, from time to time, exasperated by Thatcher's style[416] the transition is hard to fault. A number of Ministerial discussions were 'Second Reading' sessions to hammer out a sense of direction. The Secretary of State for Employment was invited to bring forward proposals accordingly. His subsequent paper[417] (and a later paper in September on reform of trades union immunities) were criticised by Hunt for their caution, the proposals were 'gradual' and underplayed the importance of starting a process of changing attitudes. A discussion in early July of a paper entitled, 'Pay: Some Current Questions'[418] had him briefing: 'Does the Committee feel that the Government should mount a major educational effort, and if so how and when? What more should be done to influence employers – for example, to take full advantage of their existing and future legal rights vis-à-vis the employees?' Similarly, his brief on John Hoskyns' proposals for priorities was generally supportive (including the criteria that they should be 'beneficial in themselves and have some psychological shock effect,' building up gradually towards a cumulative effect which suddenly becomes apparent to the public. He did, however, fire a warning shot across Heseltine's bows, advising that to expect instant decisions on new ideas was impracticable.[419]

Efficiency

Efficiency in government was, almost throughout Hunt's period as Cabinet Secretary, a responsibility of the Civil Service Department. There were two principal mechanisms used by the CSD to investigate efficiency, staff inspection (largely seen in Departments as a mundane and hostile activity) and Management Review (a more strategic approach). Hunt fed in views to the latter based on Cabinet Office experience of Departmental performance in committee. With the advent of the Thatcher administration came proposals for improving efficiency and reducing waste associated with the initiatives led by Sir Derek Rayner. Hunt had not been responsible for a major executive department, his spell as First Civil Service Commissioner being the nearest he came. However, he recognised that, 'the ability to deliver the policies which Ministers – <u>any</u> Ministers – want is not the same as being 'one of us' in a political sense.'[420] The insight he brought to the initiative was how to engage Ministers on management matters, advising Rayner that Ministers would sometimes see management as humdrum stuff and that the way to their hearts was through policy – which would inevitably become a central question if the scrutinies, as they were known, made sure that a key early question was, 'Why do we undertake this activity at all?' He also reinforced Rayner on the importance of being seen to have the personal support of the Prime Minister, the avoidance of formal committee work (which had bogged down the PAR exercise) and a new emphasis on project teams directly responsible to a Minister. At some point it would be valuable to have a collective endorsement of the work to be done in the scrutinies and also to brief the press, but in both cases a discussion of procedure was likely to be sterile and would be best avoided in favour of clear target areas (for Ministers to discuss) and clear results (for presentation to the press).[421]

Finding a Successor

As retirement began to loom so speculation about a potential successor began to bloom. In February 1979 *The Observer* reviewed a field comprising Robert

Armstrong (described as the front runner), Michael Palliser (described as a friend of Callaghan and Frank Cooper, PUS MOD, (described as a Manchester radical).[422] Stowe told Hunt and Bancroft that the question of a successor had not been broached; and since a General Election had to be held in 1979 it would make sense for the new Cabinet Secretary to be chosen by the Prime Minister after the election.[423] Hunt responded that he hoped to be consulted over the succession as Cabinet Secretary both because he had views of the kind of job it would be over the next five years and because he would wish to put forward options wider than those the CSD would suggest.[424] Callaghan, meanwhile, replied to a letter from Mrs Thatcher, as Leader of the Opposition, confirming that he had not yet begun to form a view himself on the successor and reassuring her that he did not think it would be difficult to maintain the constitutional position that, 'the Secretary of the Cabinet is the loyal servant of any administration.'[425] Left-wing back benchers were not so sure about the political neutrality of a successor. Brian Sedgemore MP (a former civil servant himself) wrote to Callaghan on 5 March anxious lest the result would be, 'too many people who take too uncritical a view of the EEC occupying top jobs.' Callaghan slapped him down: 'You may be sure that I also know what factors to take into account when approving such appointments.'

In keeping with Hunt's personal modesty each Cabinet Minister subscribed £9.60 towards a typically middle-brow retirement gift – an engraved Waterford crystal vase and a signed *Times Atlas*. And at the farewell dinner given by Mrs Thatcher at 10 Downing Street in October 1979 he admitted that if asked in future how a Cabinet works he would be tempted to use a quotation from Eugenius about Emperor Justin's court of 520 AD: 'It is well known that when the Emperor calls the principal Senators together to ask their advice, the simplest and most obvious conclusion is rejected as being unworthy of such experts in wisdom as these hoary old men, and an obscure alternative is warmly debated and then rejected; finally a most far-fetched and marvellously improper conclusion is found and unanimously adopted' – because, 'clearly that could bear no resemblance to what happens today!'[426]

Notes

1 House of Commons Library briefing paper SN06077, 02.10.15
2 See Dominic Sandbrook, *State of Emergency: The Way We Were. Britain 1970–74*, Allen Lane, 2010; Richard Clutterbrook, *Britain in Agony: the Growth of Political Violence*, Penguin, 1980
3 Paul Addison, *The Road to 1945 – British Politics and the Second World War*, Cape, 1975
4 Speech to Wilton House Conference, December 1984, private information
5 Cabinet Office file 487/9 part 1, 26.09.78
6 Alex Kemp, Official History of North Sea Oil & Gas, Routledge (2008)
7 Brief on DOP(76)5, 14.05.76
8 Interview with Sir Michael Palliser, 06.08.08
9 Interview with John Wilkins, former editor of *The Tablet*, July 2008
10 PREM 16/1499, brief on GEN 130(78)11, 03.07.78

11 PREM 15/1563, 28.09.73
12 CC(79) 18th Conclusions, Minute 10
13 Both volumes of Lord Donoughue's diaries describe numerous irritations with the Cabinet Secretary and both Lord Croham (Head of the Civil Service) and Sir Douglas Wass (PUS, HMT) found him remote
14 Reflections to the autumn Permanent Secretaries' Conference, 1983
15 Ibid
16 Ibid
17 Head of the Home Civil Service 1968–74
18 Interview with Lord Croham (formerly Sir Douglas Allen), 09.09.08
19 Cabinet Office paper, 02.03.72
20 Interview with Lord Croham 09.09.08
21 *The Hugo Young Papers*, Allen Lane, 2008, p. 83
22 Brook and Trend had both been Deputy Cabinet Secretary immediately prior to their elevation. Contemporaries saw the appointment as Cabinet Secretary in waiting, interview with Sir Douglas Wass, formerly Permanent Secretary of the Treasury, 18.08.08
23 Private information; in a conversation with the author shortly before he retired Trend commented that he had seldom managed a full night's sleep during his almost 11 year tenure of office
24 Private information
25 Head of finance, personnel and corporate services
26 Interview with Sir Douglas Wass, 18.08.08
27 Information kindly provided by Martin Hunt (son) and Catherine Hickman (step-daughter)
28 Roy Hattersley, *Who Goes Home*, Little, Brown & Co (1995), p. 140
29 Interview with C J Brearley, private secretary to Hunt 1974–1976, 20.05.08
30 PREM 15/2035, 19.12.73
31 CAB 164/1226, 13.12.72
32 DBPO Series III Volume 1V NB 12/5, 09.10.73
33 PREM 15/1841, 15/1842 and 15/1843
34 Ibid
35 CAB 164/1307, 29.01.74
36 Ibid, 05.02.74
37 Interview with Baroness Williams, 02.07.09
38 Interview with Lord Croham, 09.09.08
39 PREM 15/1429, 17.12.73
40 Interview with Sir Douglas Wass, 08.08.08
41 Lord Privy Seal 1973–74
42 PREM 15/2130, 15.01.74
43 Cabinet Office paper, brief for Michael Herman, 05.01.73
44 PREM 15/2130, 18.12.73
45 PREM 15/152, 20.09.73
46 Ibid, 23.10.73
47 Ibid, 30.10.73
48 PREM 15/2074, 26.10.73
49 Ibid, 08.11.73
50 PREM 15/2078, 15 .01.74
51 Ibid, 13.02.74
52 US National Security Adviser 1969–74, US Secretary of State 1973–77
53 UK Ambassador in Washington 1971–74
54 In 1973 President Nixon was facing disgrace over the Watergate scandal
55 DBPO, iv, no 412
56 PREM 15/2034, 04.02.74

57 Cabinet Office paper, 21.01.74
58 DBPO Series III Vol iv document 490, 03.01.74
59 Ibid
60 Ibid
61 Head of the Diplomatic Service 1973–75
62 The paper was severely criticised within the FCO for raising unrealistic radical options and effectively abandoned. A revised document which sought to reconcile wider Western unity under American leadership with European integration and British control of its own affairs in key areas was circulated for discussion at the US/EEC Group of Permanent Secretaries on 28.02.74
63 FCO 49/503,13.02.74
64 CAB 164/1255, 30.01.74
65 The NATO committee controlling export of sensitive equipment to Communist and other non-NATO countries
66 Cabinet Office paper
67 PREM 15/940, 04.01.72
68 PREM 15/2014, 10.05.73
69 Ibid, 05.11.73
70 Ibid, 07.01.74
71 Ibid, 14.01.74
72 BA 6–54, 04.03.74
73 Constitutional adviser to the Labour Government March–October 1974
74 Interview with Baroness Williams of Crosby, 2.07.09
75 PREM 16/103, 04.03.74
76 OPD, the Ministerial Committee on Overseas Policy & Defence
77 CAB 193/49 and PREM 16/103, 04.03.74
78 This short-term forward look is not to be confused with the CPRS ill-fated early warning exercise to build a government risk register (abandoned in 1972 after three rounds); nor with the thrice yearly Forward Look Exercise launched in April 1974 which looked 6 months ahead at business which should come to Cabinet or its main committees, nor with the 1978 Forward Look Exercise undertaken by GEN 140 which sought to reinvigorate the incoming Callaghan government
79 BA 6/54, 27.02.74
80 *Civil Service Statistics 1981*, CSD, HMSO
81 Identified by Sir Michael Palliser at interview as a particular skill of Hunt, 06.08.08
82 *The Sunday Times*, 29.02.76
83 PREM 16/116, 26.03.74
84 CAB 184/297, 25.03.75
85 Ibid
86 Reflections at the autumn Permanent Secretaries' Conference 1983
87 Wilson's decision to continue the CPRS under Lord Rothschild was announced on 14.03.74
88 B Donoughue *Downing Street Diary*, Pimlico 2006 p. 85
89 BA17/992, 21.010.74, annex
90 BA 17/989, 09.05.74
91 Minister of Housing 1964–1966; Lord President of the Council 1966–1968; Secretary of State for Social Services 1968–1970
92 In an interview on 30.09.08 with Lady Balfour of Burleigh (formerly Janet Morgan, editor of the diaries) she said that the decision to abandon the ambitious political work and to publish the diaries was taken when Crossman was diagnosed as terminally ill
93 Harold Wilson, *The Labour Government 1964–1970*, Weidenfeldt, 1971
94 CAB 164/1292, 14.06.74
95 Report of the Committee of Privy Counsellors on Ministerial memoirs, January 1976 (Cmnd 6386) paragraph 7

96 Research by Michael Moss (Secretary of the Radcliffe Committee of Privy Counsellors on Ministerial Memoirs) in June 1975 listed 4 post-war cases where manuscripts had not been submitted in whole or in part; CAB 164/1291; an earlier relatively full history of Ministerial literary activities is on CAB 164/1287
97 Quoted in H Young, *The Crossman Affair*, 1976, page 13; also in Hunt to Child, 30 April 1974; CAB 164/1291
98 PREM 15/902, 05.07.71 and 03.08.71
99 Ibid, 22.10.71
100 Ibid, undated note from Robert Armstrong
101 Ibid, 27.10.71
102 Ibid, 05.07.71
103 Ibid, 16.03.72
104 CAB 164/1256, 11.03.74
105 Ibid, 06.05.74
106 Ibid, 16.05.74
107 Ibid, 04.06.74
108 Ibid, 25.06.74, reported to the Prime Minister after Hunt met Michael Foot
109 Ibid, 07.06.74, and Donoughue, *Downing Street Diaries Vol 1*, Pimlico 2006, page 135
110 Ibid
111 Ibid, 17.06.74
112 Ibid, 25.06.74
113 Although Donoughue told Graham Greene on 27 June that Ministers were not taking much interest in the diaries, Donoughue, p. 149
114 CAB 164/1256, 03.07.74
115 Ibid, 10.07.74
116 Ibid, 09.08.74
117 Ibid, 14.06.74
118 Ibid, 11.09.74
119 Ibid
120 Ibid, 22.07.74
121 CAB 164/1257, 04.11.74
122 A friend of Harold Evans, the editor of *The Sunday Times*
123 CAB 164/1257, 26.11.74, 'I don't feel therefore that it is in our interest to do anything which might seem to be seeking a confrontation with them' [the Literary Executors] even though legal loopholes remained
124 CAB 164/1256, 11.09.74
125 Labour member for West Lothian, later for Linlithgow, former Parliamentary Private Secretary to Richard Crossman
126 Hansard 15.11.74 cols 273–274
127 CAB 164/1257, 15.11.74
128 Ibid, 05.12.74
129 Ibid, background notes for Willie Hamilton's PQ on 05.12.74 which stated that the OSA could not be applied to Ministerial memoirs because its coverage was too wide to be enforceable – Ministers' whole official lives are concerned with the receipt of information formally covered by the Act
130 Ibid, 21.01.75
131 Ibid, 20.01.75
132 Ibid, 23.01.75
133 Donoughue, p. 295
134 CAB 164/1289, 28.01.75
135 CAB 164/1288, 31.01.75
136 CAB 164/1289, 14.01.75
137 CAB 164/1290, 17.02.75, and 24.02.75

138 Ibid, 21.02.75
139 Ibid, 27.02.75
140 PREM 16/466, 06.03.75
141 CAB 164/1290, 27.02.75
142 *Hansard* Vol 888 col 549
143 Ibid, 06.06.75
144 PREM 16/466, 23.06.75
145 Ibid, 23.06.75
146 Ibid, 24.06.75
147 CAB 164/1256, 01.07.74
148 *The Observer*, 24.07.74
149 Interview with Pat Benner, 14.04.09
150 Ibid
151 PREM 16/466, 01.10.75
152 Ibid
153 CAB 164/1293, 08.10.75
154 Cmnd 6386
155 PREM 16/904
156 Ibid, 20.01.76
157 Ibid, 04.04.77
158 Ibid, 14.06.76
159 Conversation with Lord Hunt, 9 April 2008
160 Ibid
161 CAB 16/135, 07.03.74
162 MES (74)29
163 CAB 16/135, 04.12.74
164 Ibid, MES (74) Papers 34, 37, 39
165 CAB 16/135, 19.12.74
166 PREM 16/27, 05.03.74
167 Ibid
168 OPD(74)7th meeting 04.04.74
169 OPD(74)11th meeting, 18.07.74
170 PREM 16/27, 30.07.74
171 PREM 16/28, 17.09.74
172 OPD(74)15th meeting
173 CAB 128/55/17, 21.10.74
174 PREM 16/29, 20.11.74; Parliamentary statement 03.12.74
175 CAB 148/72, 13.11.74
176 PREM 16/29, 18.11.74
177 CAB 163/228
178 Ibid
179 PREM 16/103, 04.03.74, brief 3
180 Ibid
181 CAB 163/228, 10.07.74
182 Ibid
183 Ibid
184 Director General of the Security Service 1946–1953
185 PREM 16/146, 17.05.74
186 PREM 16/467, 22.05.74
187 Wilson wrote a similar note in January 1976
188 Prime Minister to Armstrong, 30 May 1974, PREM 16/148
189 Brief on IRN(74) 15 and 16, 11 June 1974, PREM 16/149 subsequently promoted in the July White Paper
190 Brief on the political situation in Northern Ireland (IRN(74)19), 16 July 1974, Ibid

191 Brief on IRN(74)22, 23 October 1974, PREM 16/151
192 Hunt to Prime Minister, 5 November 1974, PREM 16/152
193 IRN(75)7th meeting, 24 April 1975
194 PREM 16/429, 04.07.74
195 MISC 78(75) 1 and MISC 78(75)2
196 Cabinet Office file C488C/2 part 2
197 Cabinet Office paper, 24.09.74
198 Ibid, 21.10.74
199 The UK Permanent Representative to the Community
200 Interview with Sir Michael Palliser, 06.08.08; confirmed in conversation with Sir Kenneth Stowe, 07.11.08
201 PREM 16/74, 19.07.74
202 Ibid, 13.08.74
203 Private information
204 PREM 16/78, 12.09.74
205 PREM 16/87), 11.10.74
206 PREM 16/558, letter to Wilson from Michael Foot, Tony Benn and Peter Shore, 27.11.74
207 The President of the Commission (Xavier Ortoli) brokered a deal at the Dublin meeting of Heads of Government 10–11 March 1975
208 Interview with Lord Armstrong, 16.07.08
209 PREM 16/84, 01.12.74
210 PREM 16/558, 29.11.74
211 Sir Ivor Jennings, *Cabinet Government* (3rd Ed. Cambridge, 1959) pp. 279–281
212 Ibid
213 CAB 193/123, 15.01.75
214 CC(75)4th Conclusions
215 CC(75)5th Conclusions and Hansard Volume 884, No 52, Cols 1745–1764
216 PREM 16/558, 17.12.74
217 Ibid, 26.11.74 and 19.12.74
218 PREM 16/404, 05.02.75
219 CC(75)7th and CC(75)23rd
220 See PREM 16/558, PREM 16/404, PREM 16/405; PREM 16/407 and CAB 193/12 for the various documents
221 PREM 16/656, 19.02.75
222 PREM 16/658, 11.04.75
223 CC(75)14th
224 PREM 16/658, 10.02.75
225 CC(75)9th
226 PREM 16/658, 10.02.75
227 Ibid
228 Ibid, 19.02.75
229 PREM 16/405, 07.03.75
230 C(75)41, CC(75)15th and 16th
231 N PREM 16/405; 20.03.75, PREM 16/844
232 CAB 193/123, 27.03.75
233 Hansard Volume 889, No 98, Col 351, 07.04.75
234 PREM 16/406, 04 and 07.04.75
235 Ibid, 08.04.75
236 Ibid
237 CC(75)18th Conclusions
238 PREM 16/407, 14.05.75
239 CC(75)24th Conclusions
240 PREM 16/407, 18.04.75

241 PREM 16/317, 06.05.75
242 PREM 16/407, 08.05.75
243 Ibid, 23.05.75
244 Ibid, 04.06.75
245 PREM 16/844
246 *Hansard* 1974–1975 No 893, fifth series, cols 29–3
247 PREM 16/282
248 Private information
249 PREM 16/356, 14.09.75
250 The Canadians were not included, largely because of French objections
251 PREM 16/357
252 Ibid
253 Hunt to Prime Minister, 13 November 1975, PREM 16/358
254 www.g8.fr/evian
255 Foreign and Commonwealth Office, *Declarations of Annual Economic Summits, 1975–1986*
256 Prime Minister's personal minute M34/76, 16.03.76
257 Cabinet Office paper, 30.03.76
258 Lord Owen confirmed in interview on 14.05.76.09 that when appointed Foreign Secretary in February 1977 he had been warned by Callaghan that it might be necessary to move Healey to the Foreign and Commonwealth Office later in the year
259 PREM 16/908, 05.04.76
260 Reflections at the autumn Permanent Secretaries' Conference, 1973
261 Cabinet Office file 487/8 part 3, 21.05.76
262 Ibid, 12.04.76
263 Ibid, 15.04.76
264 PREM 16/1856, 05.08.76
265 Ibid, 08.10.76
266 PREM 1856, 25.04.77
267 Ibid, 25.07.77
268 Ibid, 03.08.77
269 Ibid, 31.01.78
270 Ibid, 17.02.78
271 Ibid, 17.05.78
272 CAB 128/63/20, CM(78)20th Minute 6
273 PREM 1856, 25.09.78
274 PREM 16/1856, 06.07.77
275 PREM 16/1857, 0.02.78
276 Ibid, 26.10.78
277 Ibid, 27.10.78
278 Ibid, 30.10.78
279 Ibid, 08.11.78
280 CO file C1C/2 part 11, 17.01.79
281 Ibid, 19.01.79 and 23.02.79
282 Ibid, 05.03.79
283 CAB 16/920, 12.10.76
284 Ibid, 08.10.76
285 Ibid, 22.10.76
286 Ibid, 28.02.78; the memoir was eventually published as *The Culture Gap: An Experience of Government and the Arts*, 1979
287 For the flavour of the debate see the *New Scientist* 08.06.78 which contained a section on the likely employment and social effects of the new technology under the banner A-U-T-O-M-A-T-I-O-N
288 *Now the Chips are Down*, BBC2 *Horizon*, April 1978

289 PREM 16/1891, 09.05.78
290 Ibid, 17.05.78
291 PREM 16/1891, 18.05.78
292 Ibid, 25.05.78
293 PREM 16/799, 10 .10.76
294 Ibid, 19.10.76
295 EY(76)10th, EY(76)14th and EY(76)15th meetings
296 Douglas Wass, *Decline to Fall*, OUP 2008, pp. 244–250
297 Pöhl explained to Derek Mitchell (Head of Overseas Finance in HM Treasury) on 2 November that the German foreign exchange reserves belonged to the Bundesbank, not the Federal Government, so Chancellor Schmidt did not control their use
298 PREM 16/799, 03.11.76
299 BP 98/16/02
300 PREM 16/799, 01.11.76
301 Ibid, 02.11.76
302 EY(76)17th meeting, 03.11.76
303 Ibid, 04.11.76
304 Ibid
305 PREM 16/801, 17.11.76
306 Ibid, 18.11.76
307 PREM 16/808
308 CAB 128/60/11, CM(76)33rd
309 Hunt's Cabinet brief for the Prime Minister, 30 November 1976, PREM 16/804
310 The Prime Minister met the IMF team immediately before and then after Cabinet on 1 December, note for the record, NA Ibid
311 The Prime Minister spoke to President Ford after Cabinet on 1 December, and wrote to him after Cabinet on 2 December; he spoke again with Chancellor Schmidt at 5.30pm on 2 December, In both cases the Prime Minister said that whilst there had been majority support in Cabinet for the loan he was not sure that he could hold Cabinet together, NA Ibid
312 Hunt to Prime Minister, 1 December 1976, NA Ibid
313 Attached to Hunt to Prime Minister, 5 December 1976, PREM 16/805
314 Ibid, 03.12.76
315 Ibid, 13.12.76
316 Chancellor's opening statement at MES(76)16
317 Interview with Lord Owen, 14.05.09
318 Cabinet Office paper, 16 .12.76
319 Ibid
320 PREM 16/1222, 28.04.77
321 Ibid
322 Ibid
323 Foreign and Commonwealth Office, *Declarations of Annual Economic Summits, 1975–1986*
324 PREM 16/1222, 27.05.77
325 Ibid, 03.08.77
326 Ibid, 14.09.77
327 Ibid, 03.10.77
328 Ibid, 20.06.76
329 Interview with Lord Owen, 14.05.09
330 Head of the MOD Intelligence Service
331 Cabinet Office paper, 02.06.77
332 Interview with Sir Michael Palliser, 06.08.08
333 Quoted in Bill Yenne, *The Encyclopaedia of US Spacecraft*. Exeter Books, 1985, p. 82 and in John Pike, *KH 11 Crystal/Kennan*, Retrieved, 27 July 2007

334 Cabinet Office paper, 04.05.78
335 William Kampiles, convicted on 17.11.78 and sentenced to 40 years in gaol (later reduced to 19 years)
336 Patrick Radden Keefe, 'I Spy' in *Wired*, February 2006
337 Conversation with Sir Michael Palliser, 06.08.08
338 CO 35/41 part 1, 15.09.77
339 Ibid, 25.11.77
340 The most senior committee of officials supporting the Council of Ministers
341 CO 35/41 part 1, 16.03.78
342 Ibid
343 Ibid, 22.06.78, and 26.06.78
344 Under an agreement from 21.04.70, Member States' contributions were replaced by agricultural and customs duties, 0.5% was added to national VAT rates and a proportion of national income paid to the Community Budget
345 CO 35/41 part 1, 04.10.78
346 Ibid, 16.10.78
347 The origins of the group lay in the 1970 Werner Report on EMU and followed a suggestion by Raymond Barre, conversation with Sir Douglas Wass, 23.10.08
348 CO 35/41 part 1, 23.01.79
349 Ibid, 02.02.79
350 Ibid, 21.02.79
351 Ibid, 28.02.79
352 Interview with Sir Douglas Wass, 23.10.08
353 CO 35/41 parts 1 and 2, 24.06.80
354 Ibid, 28.09.77
355 Eleventh Report of the Expenditure Committee, *The Civil Service* (HC 585 1976–77)
356 PREM 16/2009, brief on CP(78)107, 108, 111, 25.10.78
357 PREM 16/1598, 31.07.78 and 01.08.78
358 Ibid, 20.09.78
359 Ibid, 26.09.78
360 Ibid
361 Ibid, membership comprised the Lord President, Foreign Secretary, Home Secretary, Secretary of State for Industry, Chief Secretary and Head of the CPRS under the chairmanship of the Chancellor of the Exchequer
362 Cabinet Office paper, 06.01.77
363 Labour member for Harlow 1974–83
364 Ibid, 16.02.79
365 CO 182/12, Sent initially only to Bancroft, 05.01.78, circulated more widely on 06.04.78
366 CSD:PSO G/R (5), 06.04.78
367 Head of the home Civil Service and PUS of the Welsh Office respectively
368 PREM 16/971, 09.05.78
369 CO 182/12, 06.06.78
370 Hunt to Prime Minister 26 March 1979, Ibid
371 Ibid, 18.11.77
372 Ibid, 28.04.78
373 JIC(77)10
374 DOP(78)9th Meeting, 12.09.78
375 Brief on DOP(78)12, 01.08.78
376 CO file C23C/2, 02.05.78
377 Interview with Lord Owen, 14.05.09
378 DOP(78)6th meeting 21 June 1978
379 DOP(78)7th meeting

380 PREM 16/1535, 19.06.78, and 01.08.78
381 Ibid
382 Ibid, 08.07.77
383 PREM 16/1386, 04.11.77
384 CM(78)27, 20.07.78
385 PREM 16/1610, 03.08.78
386 PREM 16/1667, 11.09.78
387 Comprising the Home Secretary, the Secretaries of State for Education & Science, Energy, Environment, Northern Ireland, Prices & Incomes, the Head of the CPRS and the Head of the Policy Unit
388 PREM 16/1667, 28.09.78
389 Ibid, 09.10.78
390 Ibid, 12.10.78
391 Ibid, Denis Healey, Albert Booth, Eric Varley, Roy Hattersley and Michael Foot
392 CO C333C/2 part 5, 10.11.78
393 Ibid, 10.01.79
394 PREM 16/1984, 18/19.10.78
395 Ibid, 16.10.78
396 Ibid, 21.11.78
397 PREM 16/2049, 07.12.78
398 Hansard HC [960/1497–1506, 16.01.79
399 PREM 16/2050, undated aide memoire with Callaghan's manuscript notes
400 Interview with Hunt, April 2008
401 Private information
402 CM(79)1st Conclusions, Minute 2
403 PREM 16/2050, 10.01.79
404 PREM 16/2049, 10.11.78
405 Hunt to Prime Minister, 1 May 1979
406 Hunt appointment diary 1979
407 Cabinet Office 273/9 part 5
408 Ibid
409 Ibid
410 Ibid, 06.05.79
411 Ibid, 08.05.79
412 Cabinet Office file 250/15 part 3, 19.10.79
413 E(DL) was the Ministerial Committee on The Disposal of Public Assets
414 Ibid, 11.07.79
415 Ibid, 11.09.79
416 Private information
417 Ibid, E(79)11
418 Ibid, E(79) 13 and 17
419 Ibid, 23.07.79
420 Quoted in Hunt's 1993 Thomas More Lecture at Oxford University.
421 Hunt to Rayner, 10 August 1979, CO 487/11
422 *The Observer*, 18 February 1979
423 Cabinet Office
424 Hunt to Stowe, 13 February 1979
425 Prime Minister to Margaret Thatcher, 21 February 1979, Ibid
426 Private information

5 The Ultimate Courtier

Sir Robert Armstrong Cabinet Secretary 1980–87

Armstrong and Lovelock: Irresistible force and immoveable colleague

Source: The National Archives

Armstrong arrived as Cabinet Secretary on 27 October 1979 with a CV embossed in gold leaf. He had a consummate record as the compleat civil servant and over the next eight years he was indispensable to Thatcher's success.'[1] Yet his public reputation was damaged by the government's struggle to prevent publication of Peter Wright's self-styled (and later partly discredited) exposé of

Armstrong ×4: Aspects of Robert Armstrong by Daphne Todd
Source: Photographed by Hugh Gilbert

Security Service and Secret Intelligence Service activities.[2] His triumphs were largely private, his failures visibly public. William Armstrong (no relation) judged him politically sensitive, with good judgement of people, and excelling at drafting.[3] An earlier assessment, from the Treasury mandarin Sir Alan Neale,[4] described him as a synthesiser, best in an established framework, better at managing upwards than downwards, not a natural delegator and someone who redrafted too much himself.[5] Four spells in Treasury Private Offices and five years as Principal Private Secretary to two temperamentally different Prime Ministers (Heath and Wilson) established his eminence as master of the interplay between the two most powerful Offices in government. His drafting skills had been honed as Secretary to four public enquiries (including the 1957 Radcliffe enquiry into the workings of the Monetary System). He had had a role in the negotiations culminating in the French agreement to the United Kingdom joining the European Communities. He had also been a channel for contact with Irish groups during the 1970s. He had been the lead Treasury official on monetary policy and, latterly, had spent four years in the Home Office. During his years as Cabinet Secretary (six of them also as Head of the Home Civil Service) the government held a comfortable Parliamentary majority and the domination of the Prime Minister over Cabinet colleagues grew.

In thanking Cabinet for their retirement gift Armstrong wrote of the privilege and the fun of playing a part: 'in keeping the engines of the ship of state in good working order for "full steam ahead".' He believed passionately in the Northcote-Trevelyan vision of an incorruptible civil service whose duty it was to support, advise and, where necessary, warn Ministers.'[6] It has been alleged that this dedication inadvertently fostered a permissive politicisation of the civil service, encapsulated in 'Is he one of us?' However, if one political party is in power for a long time there is likely to be some identification by higher civil servants with the policies of the incumbents and Ministers' ideas about the qualities to look for in new appointments will play out in senior appointments. The appointment from the private sector of Peter Levene as Chief of Defence Procurement and Monty Alfred as Head of the Property Services Agency pushed the rules of 'fair and open competition' to their limit, and in the former case almost led to the resignation of the First Civil Service Commissioner. But I can detect no willingness by Armstrong to support appointments because they would be politically in tune with the government (as he himself sometimes was not), or a willingness to turn a blind eye to the promotion of those who might otherwise not have qualified. It was, in the words of Geoffrey Howe that: '... officials in No 10 came to regard the Prime Minister's passion as entitled to prevail.'[7]

Nevertheless, by the end of 1987 the Cabinet Secretary's world had changed forever. Both Hunt and Armstrong were thrust unwillingly into the public gaze by the activities of investigative journalists. Armstrong hardly ever appeared publicly or in print. In 1981, in turning down a request for an interview, he wrote: 'I have made it a rule since I came to this office not to give interviews; I have stuck to the rule rigidly; and experience has confirmed me in the view that the rule is right for someone in my position.'[8] But times were changing. John Cassels, writing during his short spell as Head of the Management and Personnel Office (MPO), challenged that: '... in the long sweep rising standards of education are bound to lead to more searching interest in the way government business is handled and in the sort of people who do the handling. It is an inescapable part of modern democracy. If civil servants remain entirely faceless, they lose the game.'[9] Yes, replied Armstrong: 'I accept that there are going to be some of us at the top of the Service who cannot and should not remain entirely faceless ... But I think that the dangers must be evident to you ... Ministers must be convinced that we are not setting out to make ourselves media personalities in our own rights ... For myself, I am not discontented with my reputation for being cautious and enigmatic in my dealings with the press.'[10] By contrast, when Sir Gus O'Donnell was appointed Cabinet Secretary in September 2005 he could point to five years as a press secretary (first to the Chancellor of the Exchequer and then to the Prime Minister).

Speaking at Armstrong's retirement dinner, Margaret Thatcher said: 'At a time when customs and conventions have been eroded you have upheld them. When in some quarters the word duty has been derided, you have raised it to new levels of honour and service. When humanity has so often been interpreted more by what is said than by what is done you have shown thoughtfulness and daily acts of kindness which we shall forever remember.'[11] This was a sentiment recalled with fondness by those who worked closely with him. In Christopher Mallaby's words: 'Robert was the supreme mandarin – vastly dedicated, determined, patient, firm, ingenious and humorous. He was never the servant of the ideology of the government of the day or its manifestos, but advocated to Ministers what he saw as the right course in the national interest and within the scope of the government's overall attitude. He wrote with outstanding elegance, clarity and subtlety. His humanity was clear to his colleagues, in many of whom he inspired not only admiration and loyalty but also much affection.'[12] He treated as an equal those subordinates he trusted.[13] He was a master at papering over the cracks.[14] No Prime Minister could have asked for a more devoted or skilled bodyguard who would shield them and take the intellectual bullets intended for them. Yet he left a civil service with low self-esteem, wounded by the criticisms and indifference of Ministers. In retrospect he seems an outstanding Cabinet Secretary and a strong motivator at a personal level, but less able to reach out and touch the lives of the rank and file.

Cabinet and Committees

Hunt bequeathed a Cabinet Office more powerful than ever, able to act with initiative and less dependent on Departments over the timing of collective discussion. He had protected the traditional machinery of interdepartmental working during the first six months after the General Election. However, as Thatcher became more experienced there was a shift in the nature of Cabinet and the use of Cabinet committees. Regular stewardship of public expenditure, the defence estimates and other major issues continued to be discussed at full Cabinet. Difficult political disagreements were also brought from Cabinet Committee or ad hoc meetings. But, whereas initially there were large flagship policies to be agreed, in the later years it became usual for Cabinet to be a forum for bringing Ministers up to date on decisions taken elsewhere (especially regarding the European Communities); ratification of important decisions taken in subordinate groups; and broad-ranging strategic discussions during which no specific decisions were sought.[15] Ad hoc meetings chaired by the Prime Minister became more frequent, sometimes as preparation for Cabinet or its Committees, sometimes as the decision-taking body itself. One consequence was a change of emphasis in the role of Cabinet Secretary and his staff. The record of ad hoc meetings increasingly tended to be issued in the name of the Prime Minister's Private Office in the form of a letter to participants[16] – a subtle centralisation of business under officials who were agents of the Prime Minister, unlike the Cabinet Office staff who worked on behalf of the Cabinet as a whole and were still perceived as broadly neutral between competing Ministerial views.

This change is illustrated by Armstrong's unsuccessful attempt to bring implementation of the memorandum of understanding with the United States on research for the Strategic Defence Initiative into the Cabinet Office via MISC 117, which had co-ordinated the negotiations. Charles Powell (the foreign affairs Private Secretary) advised: 'I am very suspicious of this [Armstrong] minute. It tells us nothing that we do not know … I think its real purpose is to try to counter No 10's influence on matters concerned with the SDI … In short, it smells to me of bureaucratic gamesmanship.'[17] Thatcher agreed; she was entirely satisfied with existing arrangements. But it would be wrong to think that there was wholesale slaughter of formal committees. One year into the Administration John Nott (Secretary of State for Trade) queried the value of Cabinet Committees. Thatcher replied:

> '… we must make the system work for us and not let it take us over … But do not let us lose sight of what the system can do for us. Apart from the advantages you mention – the crystallisation of issues and the proper recording of decisions – it is one way of enabling senior Ministers to exercise political influence on decisions going beyond their departmental interests; and it helps us to know, and so to be able to defend, what each other is proposing and doing. The system provides a convenient framework for that, and for enabling us to deal with issues in an orderly way and at the right time.'[18]

However, reporting in February 1981 Armstrong calculated that the number of Ministerial meetings under the Cabinet Office umbrella was down 37% on 1978.[19] Faced with an increased workload as Head of the Home Civil Service, he began to leave Cabinet Committee briefing to the Cabinet Office machine. There were also spasmodic efforts to resist escalation of issues to Cabinet, as had been a long-standing complaint;[20] but Thatcher was pragmatic. Contemplating disagreement over the Protection of Official information Bill in October 1979 her response was to resist escalation to Cabinet, but when the newly appointed Secretary of State for Transport (David Howell) argued that he should be a member of the Economic Strategy Committee (E) she responded that if it were to be enlarged to accommodate all the Secretaries of State who thought that they should attend, there would then be little point in remitting things to Cabinet.[21] And after the 1983 election victory the Ministerial Committee on Economic Strategy (E) was pared down from 17 to half a dozen members under Thatcher's chairmanship to handle major issues inappropriate for specialist sub-committees or before they were opened to Cabinet.[22]

The weekly Thursday meeting of Cabinet Office Deputy Secretaries continued to manage Cabinet and Cabinet Committee business three weeks ahead and Armstrong saw the Prime Minister most Friday mornings to discuss future business. In the minutes of the former the emerging future work programme looks more cut and dried than was usually the case. But there are clues about the discussions. In the spring of 1982 the head of the OD Secretariat (Robert Wade-Gery) reported to his staff that Armstrong had insisted that Departments should provide full papers for the committee to discuss and not rely on correspondence between Ministers. A 1982 meeting of OD must discuss Northern Ireland before it turned to discuss economic measures against the Soviet Union. Around the beginning of April 1982 there should be a Cabinet discussion on Northern Ireland, but no one could yet tell how much time might be needed. As the Foreign Secretary would be out of London on 6 April, could the committee discuss the Falkland Islands in his absence; and so on.[23]

In 1986 David Jago of the OD Secretariat illustrated the principles governing where a given subject should be discussed: 'I have found that there is no strictly logical division of business between those matters, which are taken formally in OD and its supporting sub-committees, and by informal meetings of Ministers. A point often comes in consideration of a particular subject when security or other issues call for a small informal meeting, chaired by the Prime Minister, or where the need for wider Ministerial consultation produces the opposite effect.'[24] Nevertheless, there was a pattern. The OD Committee would discuss:

- Foreign policy of wide relevance (e.g. extension of United Kingdom territorial waters; the United Nations Law of the Sea Convention);
- Regional issues (e.g. the Falklands; South Africa);
- Defence policy (e.g. the annual Defence Estimates; United Kingdom participation in the Strategic Defence Initiative);
- Political aspects of defence equipment issues (e.g. the European Fighter Aircraft; arms sales).

But occasionally there were unusual circumstances such as when President Reagan sought agreement to use F1–11 aircraft from bases in Britain for military action against Libya in response to SIGINT information about the bombing of the *La Belle* discotheque in Berlin that had killed three people and injured over 200 (including 53 Americans). Cabinet was told that the government was considering what position to take on press reports that the United States was planning military action;[25] but also that a decision over the use of the US bases was so sensitive that it must involve only the ministers most directly involved in conformance with the manner in which such matters were usually handled.[26] (Thatcher wanted to exclude the Chancellor of the Exchequer. On the advice of Harold Macmillan she had excluded the Chancellor from the Falklands War Cabinet, reflecting a view that, in wartime, the natural financial prudence of the Treasury could inhibit decisive action.) When Armstrong suggested either a revision of the terms of reference and membership of the relevant Sub-Committee or a new Sub-Committee for international emergencies not involving British troops he was ignored. As Thatcher later put it: 'This sort of request or situation we have to deal with must be handled only by those who now deal with security or intelligence or who have dealt with it in the past ... We had better stick to ad hoc groups.'[27] [*Original underlining.*] Cabinet was advised of the decision retrospectively, shortly following the sorties from bases in Britain, during the night of 14/15 April.[28]

Aware of Thatcher's tendency to lead from the front, Armstrong kept a weather eye on the risks of unnecessarily using up political capital, as had Hunt, who had done so in respect of a 1979 discussion of the Defence Budget, cautioning that: 'Your own position in this is too important to be compromised at the start, and I am sure it is best to operate at one remove, coming in yourself only when there is some prospect of an agreement.'[29] Fifteen months later, when the Economic Strategy Committee (E) had one of its many discussions on the future of the ailing

British Leyland Motor Company Armstrong's brief offered a heartfelt piece of advice: 'I think it very important that you should not show your own hand in the discussion. I believe that serious consequences could ensue if ... it then came out (as I fear it might) that that decision had been taken against your advice ...'[30]

Occasionally, when especially sensitive items were at issue, the advice was positively devious, such as to tell Cabinet of an imminent British underground nuclear test but not to say that it was the first of a planned programme of five,[31] continuing the practice that issues concerning the British nuclear deterrent were reported to Cabinet only in the most sparse and general terms. Similarly, knowledge of operational military decisions or associated diplomatic initiatives were kept tight. After negotiations in New York over the Falklands dispute broke down on 19 May 19282 Armstrong advised that: 'The Cabinet have come a long way since their initial wish to be consulted before landing was authorised. Yesterday, I gather, most members seemed glad not to be in the full military picture. This suggests that you should not tell them tomorrow that the landing is expected tomorrow night or as soon thereafter as local conditions allow. To do so would burden them with too much secret knowledge.[32]

Overt policy advice was rare but from time to time Armstrong acted as a moral compass, repeatedly emphasising the need to be seen to treat the various public sector groups (including Ministers and Members of Parliament) fairly in respect of the internal consistency of the approach to public sector pay;[33] or in consideration of index-linked public sector pensions where he both reminded Ministers of their 1979 election promise not to abandon index-linked benefits and pointed to the electoral fact that 10 million voters would be affected by the decision.[34] He warned of potential pitfalls, for example from appeasing Parliament over MPs' pay, pensions and allowances during the civil service pay dispute of 1981,[35] or of the likely mass resignation of the Top Salaries Review Board if their recommendations continued to be flaunted.[36] From time to time he attempted to make discussion more strategic. After the Chancellor had expressed concern in 1982 about the longer-term prospects for public expenditure the CPRS was asked to prepare a paper 'thinking the unthinkable' about the scale and pattern of public expenditure.[37] When it came to discussion, over a full day of Cabinet in September, Armstrong argued that the Cabinet should look for the root causes that lay behind the tendency for public expenditure to increase irrespective of circumstances. Why did officials always take it for granted that improvements in medical care would mean more expenditure? Industry would probably think it as important to find ways of doing the same thing at less cost as to find ways of doing new things. 'The discussion should be not just on the size of public expenditure in relation to the gross domestic product but about the role of the Government and the public sector, particularly in the fields of education, health and the social services.' Furthermore, discussion should encompass not just ends but also the means of implementation. As to further work, nothing should be ruled out (not least so as to keep the array of spending Ministers in the tent); and perhaps should include the effects on incentives of the structure of taxation, benefits and public sector charges.

Armstrong continued the practice of normally copying his briefing for the Prime Minister to no one outside the Cabinet Office or No 10 Downing Street. It was widely understood and accepted across Whitehall that such was the case. Indeed, when Christopher Mallaby (head of the OD Secretariat) copied a 1987 brief on a tedious dispute between the Department of Education and Science (DES) and HM Treasury over which department should pay for replacing the British Antarctic Survey (BAS) ship *RRS John Biscoe* to other Ministers he was brought up short. Sir David Hancock, PUS at the DES: 'asked in emphatic terms for my note to be withdrawn on the grounds that it was a usurpation of Departmental rights for the Cabinet Office to proffer advice to Departmental Ministers.'[38] Hancock did not object to Mallaby offering advice to the Prime Minister; it was copying that advice to other Ministers that transgressed. The note had to be withdrawn.

Cabinet attendance was tightly controlled. Policy Unit members were sometimes allowed to observe the discussion of items of direct concern to them as a special privilege and under terms of strict confidentiality. Junior Ministers attended by invitation for relevant items if the Secretary of State was absent and the Prime Minister agreed. Collective responsibility was firmly policed. This was not such a problem as had dogged Wilson and Callaghan but there was a new dimension from the importance of European negotiations. It could be a tricky judgement how far positions agreed in Cabinet Committee had to be maintained during fraught negotiations at a Council of Ministers. In April 1981, for example, Armstrong queried how far the Minister of Agriculture's actions at an Agriculture Council had been compatible with the collective wish of Ministers expressed at the OD Committee three weeks earlier. Michael Franklin, then leading the European Unit and later to be PUS at the Ministry of Agriculture, Fisheries and Food reported that a lack of firm instructions from OD: '... allowed the Minister of Agriculture, by flexible interpretation of (and in one case turning a blind eye to) his instructions, to give priority to the interests of the farming industry and to pass up the chance of getting firmer commitments from the French on fish.'[39] Not a hanging offence per se but illustrative of a dilemma which ran wider than any single policy. Collective responsibility was further challenged later in 1981 when Cabinet had a divisive discussion on public expenditure. The following day *The Times* carried a report that gave an accurate account of what had happened – it could not have been written without access to someone or some people present at the meeting. To make matters worse, the leak had occurred despite a strong oral request by the Prime Minister at the end of the discussion for all Ministers to conform with the line they had agreed for dealing with Lobby correspondents. There was speculation about who could have leaked but no firm evidence; so Armstrong rehearsed the options:

- Do nothing – very difficult given the flagrant disregard of the request made by the Prime Minister;
- A political enquiry conducted by the Chief Whip and a senior Minister – almost certain to end without a definite conclusion and a debating gift to the Opposition;

- An official leak enquiry by questionnaire – on past form this approach would get nowhere;
- An enquiry by an investigating officer – disagreeable because private secretaries would be interviewed about their Minister's contacts and it would probably be inconclusive though it may have a deterrent effect;
- Read the riot act orally – not in terms of the challenge to the Prime Minister's authority but of the challenge to the coherence, authority and effectiveness of Cabinet. Anyone who was not prepared to accept a duty of confidentiality to their colleagues should resign – though that was risky unless the Prime Minister was surer than Armstrong thought she could be about who was responsible;
- Put the same message in writing – which would probably leak and might have less impact than a face-to-face message.

In the longer term, he added, coherence could be strengthened by a reshuffle of Cabinet to eliminate opponents, but it was doubtful if a smaller Cabinet was politically acceptable. An alternative was to keep the most controversial business out of full Cabinet. There were significant political implications with either course: 'All this points to the rather dismal conclusion that you may not be able to do very much in the longer term.'[40] In the event Thatcher used the notes provided by Armstrong as a speaking note at Cabinet on 29 October. Only very occasionally would Thatcher seek Armstrong's opinion on the performance of a Minister or the options for a reshuffle – usually orally and sometimes at inconvenient times. On a memorable journey back from a Summit meeting in Tokyo he was physically very tired after only a few hours of sleep over two days of working on the communiqué, and was somewhat dismayed when she called to him as he boarded the plane, 'Cabinet Secretary, we have two six hour flights ahead of us. I should like to talk to you about changes I am contemplating in Ministerial allocations.'[41]

Plenipotentiary

Brook and Trend had overseen the dismantling of Empire and experienced the disappointment that the Commonwealth was split over developments in Africa. Hunt had begun a relationship with the personal representatives of the Western leaders in the Summit preparations and had played a strong role in support of relations between Britain and the United States. Armstrong continued this but also had strong European credentials and sought to redefine the relationship with America to take account of the Franco-German axis and the declining emotional pull of Britain in the United States as memories of World War II faded. He did so against a background where the 1979 Conservative Manifesto identified three key initiatives for European policy: reform of the Common Agricultural Policy, budgetary control, and relating member states' payments into the Communities to their ability to pay.[42] These were handled in broadly three phases: getting the issue of a budgetary rebate for the United Kingdom on the European Council agenda (initially concluded with a short-term deal in May 1980); seeking a long-term solution to the United Kingdom's budgetary problem (from May 1980 to the agreement at Fontainebleau in June 1984); pressing for budgetary discipline and responding to calls for a longer-term vision about the future direction of Europe (still ongoing when Armstrong retired at the end of 1987).

The Cabinet Office Secretariats on Economic and European matters sought to corral Whitehall interests into a coherent negotiating strategy. Though both nominally reported through Armstrong, and were assiduous in keeping him informed, he played a cameo role, initially advising Thatcher on negotiating tactics, but after 1981 increasingly confining his effort to leveraging his personal connections with fellow "sherpas" – notably from France – on the budgetary question. The weekly brief for the Prime Minister covering the standing Cabinet item on Community Affairs rarely went beyond a descriptive summary of outcomes at the various Council meetings. The main outcome from these updates appears to have been to strengthen the resolve of Ministers not to succumb to calls for compromise and occasional bullying by partner states and the European Commission. As Stephen Wall put it, from personal experience, there was: 'the sense, when [Mrs Thatcher] walked into the room, of a measurable rise in the tension and the temperature.'[43] Some of that intransigence and determination was intended to rub off on other Ministers who might otherwise have been tempted to weaken in their resolve to protect perceived British interests.[44]

By the end of 1979 the first attempts to secure a budgetary rebate were faltering. The European Commission proposals were not enough to reduce the British net contribution to much below that of the richest country in Europe (Germany) and about twice as much as that of France. Armstrong provided a summary of the negotiations[45] and sought to cool down potentially fraying tempers:[46] 'officials have intensified their bilateral contacts with the French, the Germans and the [Italian] Presidency … the evidence from these various contacts confirms that the gap is still large [a proposed refund of 900 million European Units of Account versus a 1,500 million reduction sought from the 1980 UK budgetary contribution of 1,700 million]; but nevertheless there are several signs of a desire to settle.'[47] The OD Committee had reached no conclusion on possibly withholding part of the British contribution to the budget. Such a decision would have large consequences and ought certainly to require authorisation from Cabinet: 'If you are seeking authority to threaten withholding before June, and to do so before you can discuss that further with your colleagues, you should seek and obtain that authority from the Cabinet before you go to Brussels.'[48] However, temporary relief covering three years was agreed after a nineteen-hour Foreign Ministers' session on 29/30 May 1980. The European Commission was charged with finding a long-term solution but the problem was, of course, that for every reduction in the United Kingdom contribution someone else would have to pay more.

In August 1980, the Foreign Office circulated a bland planning paper that argued: 'no radical change in the pattern of our existing relationships is necessary or even feasible; but … we need to try at bit harder with the Americans, with the French and Germans and with the European Community,'[49] Armstrong begged to differ. He argued for a realistic reappraisal that recognised a strong Franco-German axis could greatly enhance the ability of the Europeans to get their way with the Americans. What Britain should do about this was one of the most important issues for the country in the eighties; and he made no bones about his own preference for: 'a relationship of parity and confidence, severally and together, with the partners in the Paris-Bonn axis.'[50] The alternative, he thought, was to end up bleating more or less ineffectively from the sidelines. Realistically, he added, no wise foreign policy could save the United Kingdom from international insignificance unless relative economic decline was checked. Armstrong repeated the arguments a couple of months later to the Foreign Secretary, Lord Carrington; with the added attraction that Jacques Wahl of the Elysée had confided that the President wanted to see France working as closely with Britain as with Germany and that Chancellor Schmidt wanted the same sort of relationship with Britain as he had with France.[51] What Armstrong had not allowed for sufficiently, however, was that the agreement limiting the United Kingdom's budgetary contributions was a temporary measure with hard negotiations to follow in pursuit of a lasting solution.

Initially Armstrong continued in an upbeat manner, including on the budget mechanism where the Commission appeared to have been convinced that some form of adjustment mechanism was necessary.[52] In the second half of 1981, however, the rotation of the Presidency of the Council came to the United Kingdom, which was a mixed blessing. On the one hand it enabled the UK to control to some extent the agenda for Council meetings. On the other it inhibited British delegates from arguing the UK case too strongly as one of the roles of the Presidency was to seek and represent the collective positions of the member states. Not that this stopped the Chancellor of the Exchequer suggesting to the OD Committee that the budget strategy should be stepped up a gear to seek to make the United Kingdom a net beneficiary from the budget based on the principle that resources should flow from the more prosperous to the less prosperous regions and not vice versa.[53] Armstrong briefed delicately: 'There must of course be a difference between the Government's publicly expressed aim and what might be acceptable at the end of the day ...' and steered Thatcher towards a conclusion that the United Kingdom: 'must continue to take a robust line on the need for lasting arrangements to ensure that our net contribution is reduced to a defensible level.' In her summing up she referred to a public line of seeking: 'a fair and lasting solution of the United Kingdom's net contribution problem' with a private fallback position of a nil net contribution.[54]

The natural allies in seeking to curb the Community budget ought to have been the German Government as by far the largest other contributor. But the German coalition was split with the Foreign Minister (Hans Dietrich Genscher)[55] disposed to play down the German budget position whilst Chancellor Schmidt and the Finance Minister Hans Matthoeffer would have liked a ceiling on the German net contribution.[56] The position was further complicated by the then German lack of assertiveness and unwillingness to upset the French Government. Internal debate in the British Government centred on whether to make a gesture towards the Germans. The Foreign Secretary told Cabinet, meanwhile, that they should hold their nerve as the Council rarely made decisions until the last minute or so.[57] But, in preparation for the November Council, Armstrong had to report that the indications were that the Germans thought that a reduction to even a small net contribution to the budget for the United Kingdom was an unattainable goal. He found himself here, as in many other areas, trying to get a peg in the ground to prevent the base position being swept away.[58] The Cabinet nerve held;[59] and Armstrong resumed a shuttle diplomacy with French interlocutors (on 23 November with the Elysée Secretary General Pierre Bérégovoy supported by Jacques Attali (Special Adviser to President Mitterrand) and his deputy Morel; Attali in February and May 1982, in June 1983 – this time at the suggestion of Jacques Delors the Minister of Economics and Finance, Attali once more in February, March and June 1984, the latter shortly before the Fontainebleau Council at which final agreement on the budget contribution was reached).

In preparation for his meeting with Attali in February 1982 Armstrong cleared some daunting objectives with the Prime Minister: to convince Attali of the merits of the UK budgetary case, to expose the unreasonableness of the French position and to establish in their minds a link between a budgetary settlement and progress on farm prices and further development in the Community. In so doing he would say that the British recognised the great importance of the CAP to France (especially specific support to small milk producers) and would be prepared to see something done that was helpful to France. But the British Government needed a fair and durable solution to the budget problem in order to defend at home a farm price settlement acceptable to France. Unless there was progress in all three areas the Community would face a major crisis that would endanger its ability to measure up to world problems.[60] A week later he reported back: President Mitterrand needed a budgetary settlement lower than the temporary settlement of 1980. The political requirement for the French President was determined by his attack on the 30 May agreement as a defeat for France (it had cost the French budget 4.6 billion French francs for 1980 and 1981). The French had proposed 'secret and direct talks' between the President's staff and those of Mrs Thatcher, which he supported. Armstrong had come away with the impression that a four-year deal could be had provided it was at a lower level than that of 1980 and provided it was degressive (but not down to nil).

Attali telephoned Armstrong on 2 March 1982 suggesting a first round of the 'secret and direct talks' ten days later. Armstrong then submitted to Thatcher a note of the line they might follow and the limits within which they might be instructed to work: using a formula based on the actual outcome for 1980 and 1981 (which had been much more favourable to the United Kingdom than had been foreseen) thereby allowing the French to claim that the new settlement was lower than before and the British to claim that it was higher than had been the intention in 1980.[61] A conversation in Bonn with Manfred Lahnstein (Finance Minister) had left Armstrong with the clear impression that the key to success lay in persuading the French to accept a settlement; the German Government would not, in the last resort, create great difficulties over money.[62]

At the same time Thatcher ran a parallel track through which the formal negotiations were controlled. She agreed the mandate for an Anglo-German Summit on 19 March, the Foreign Affairs Council on 22–23 March and the European Council on 29–10 March.[63] The British position was stubbornly reiterated with deliberate brinkmanship. At Cabinet on 18 March Thatcher reported a conversation with the Presidents of the Council of Ministers and of the Commission: 'They showed no comprehension of the true nature of the problem … unless other Governments moved towards the British position, there could be no agreement on agricultural prices … But there was no need to be too pessimistic, because the Community never summoned up the determination to solve a problem until it was right on the brink of disaster.'[64]

Two secret meetings took place in the space of a week – on 24 March the two sides circled each other with all the wariness of professional heavyweight boxers in the first round of a 15-round contest: concentrating on the figures for a rebate that might be politically acceptable. Both were in their element with jabs, feints and probing sallies. It was, as Armstrong later admitted, enjoyable in retrospect.[65] Armstrong maintained that the United Kingdom wanted 90% of its net imbalance with the Community refunded: 'I thought that I could detect an extremely indirect hint that if the British would help keep the cost to them below five billion French francs they might be able to go further than what was then on offer.' But President Mitterrand reacted badly to the secret talks and at the European Council in March blocked agreement. Contact with Attali was not reopened until May when Armstrong telephoned to ask Attali to receive David Hancock: 'to ensure that each side had a full and correct understanding of the other's position' before Thatcher and Mitterrand met on 17 May (he could not himself leave London because of the Falklands crisis). The British were worried that events might take over – officials had calculated that an 80% rebate would meet both British and French political requirements.[66] Attitudes were indeed hardening in the Community. By the time the OD Committee met on 21 May three decisions had gone against the United Kingdom: the Community had renewed trade sanctions on Argentina but only for one week; other member states had presented a take-it-or-leave-it offer on the budget that fell short of United Kingdom requirements; and the United Kingdom veto under the Luxembourg compromise (by which a member state had the right to ask that voting be deferred on a proposal if it considered that an important national interest was at stake) had been brushed aside on the agricultural settlement.[67]

Towards the end of May Armstrong's relationship with Attali was once again the route to try to persuade France to relax its conditions for a settlement – once again with limited signs of success.[68] It seems likely that the intervention influenced the French Government's position at the Foreign Affairs Council under way when the conversations took place. A further temporary agreement was brokered for 1982 which the Foreign Secretary judged to be not ideal but at least had avoided breaking off negotiations which, in turn, might very well have led to an even worse outcome.[69] At the same time contingency planning included the possibility of illegally withholding part or all of the United Kingdom contribution to the Community budget during the autumn negotiations, legislating retrospectively to deal with the legality of the action – or at least threatening to withhold[70]. Ministers were, however, anxious not to force the pace down a road which could lead to a position from which opponents of membership of the Community could benefit – at OD on 22 July 1982 the Prime Minister was moved to state that: 'it was the Government's firm intention to remain full members of the European Community and to resist any attempt that might be made to force Britain to accept second class status in any form. But the budget problem had to be solved.'[71] The first part of this statement was particularly important because the Community was starting to address wider issues that might be grouped under a 'Whither Europe?' banner. The abandonment of the Luxembourg compromise during the farm price negotiations in the first half of 1982 came as a complete shock to the United Kingdom. Cabinet saw the Luxembourg compromise as a fundamental part of the basis on which the United Kingdom had joined the Community. Reluctantly, however, it had to accept that that was a political agreement, not a legal one. During the agricultural price crisis the United Kingdom's partners had put a limit on that political agreement – it would no longer be possible to invoke the Luxembourg compromise in one Council to achieve an objective in another.[72]

It was not until 1983 that Armstrong resumed his diplomatic round. The President of the Commission (Gaston Thorn) invited him to informal talks in January. Armstrong expected neither a miraculous conversion to the United Kingdom case nor much in the way of decisive action from the Commission. It would not be sensible, he argued in his draft mandate for approval by Mrs Thatcher, to try to persuade Thorn to agree to a complete specification of a solution – that would cause him to retreat into clouds of protestation about the political difficulties of the Commission. Better to register a limited number of vital points and to look to Thorn for action to help the United Kingdom on the way to a successful negotiation following the German elections on 6 March. These points were: the need to pay the 1982 refund (which had fallen victim to the European Parliament's rejection of the 1982 Supplementary Community budget) before the end of March; British Ministers had not accepted there was a case for an increase in Community own resources; but they had accepted a need to reform the Community's financial system (the forthcoming Commission Green Paper on this should include a lasting solution to the budgetary imbalance); the United Kingdom would bring the budgetary imbalance issue back to the European Council if there had not been good progress towards a solution; and he would reveal by implication that British Ministers had scaled down the extent of the rebate expected to 66% as had been decided at an informal meeting on 20 October 1982).[73]

The discussions took place without note takers or any other participants. Armstrong had trained himself to listen acutely during such talks, without taking notes, and then immediately to dictate a record of the meeting.[74] In this case he reported back with mixed feelings. The talk had been at a level of generality that made it impossible to table figures. Thorn had forecast that with a European Parliamentary election due in 1984 MEPs would be ready to trim their sails over the budget crisis to ensure their prospects of re-election. For his part, Armstrong had pointed out that the British Government would also face a General Election within 15 months and it was particularly important politically to have agreement on the budget imbalance (and on fisheries) by the end of June 1983. Whilst neither thought a long-term solution was feasible by then, Thorn appeared to be saying that France was the key to the issue and that he envisaged some form (unspecified) of redistributive arrangements at the end of each budget year that would improve the position of Britain and of Italy. 'I found Monsieur Thorn's train of thought difficult to follow at this point,' he concluded. The message can hardly have been reassuring and, in any case, the British election was called for 9 June.

Armstrong's dealings with Attali built on their association as sherpas for the well-established annual cycle of Economic Summits begun at Rambouillet in 1975. All told he helped prepare and attended eight Summit meetings each, typically, preceded by three sherpa meetings:

- to identify the issues and commission papers;
- to discuss the papers and establish guidelines for a draft communiqué; and
- to discuss the draft communiqué, followed by a night-time meeting between the first and second days of the Summit itself to prepare the final version.

In this role he had the trust of the Prime Minister but was not in tune with her. Towards the end of his tenure the centre of gravity for the UK preparation of Summit meetings started to move towards the Prime Minister's private secretary for foreign affairs, as a putative political adviser, and away from the Cabinet Secretary as a mediator between the sometimes conflicting interests of United Kingdom Departments. On economic matters, especially, the paper prepared in advance by the sherpas was important in allowing the Heads of Government to use their time sparingly, but during the Summits themselves it was often Treasury officials who had the lead in supporting the Prime Minister. What had begun as an informal 'library discussion' between the leaders of five Western nations had increasingly turned into a media circus often with unrealistic public expectations of miracles to be worked by the Heads of Government. Despite repeated calls for a return to the original idea of informal strategic discussion, the burdens of preparation, agreement of a communiqué and press briefing loomed large. Senior Treasury officials thought of the Summits as largely public relations exercises.[75]

It is important, however, to distinguish between the discussions between Heads of Government and the preparation of those meetings. In the same way that it takes more effort to write a short document than a long one, so it takes intensive preparation for a successful meeting that is not to waste the scarce time of Heads of Government when they are only able to meet for two days at a time.

The leaders may feel that they are perfectly capable of having meaningful discussions without burdensome briefing, but to spend time most profitably they must concentrate on the issues that can only be resolved at their level – and then with a view to convergence rather than divergence. That required intensive preparation by their staffs. But throughout the period, Thatcher maintained pressure to simplify the preparations. For the 1980 Summit she reminded Armstrong 'that the arrangements for the Summit risk becoming excessively cumbersome ... the bureaucratic infrastructure [should] ... be kept to the absolute minimum.' Despite assuring her in 1980 that: 'I share the Prime Minister's concern ... . Her views ... will strengthen my hand in my continuing attempts to prevent the bureaucratic infrastructure ... getting out of hand,'[76] Armstrong struggled to translate these intentions into actions. Thus, although there were early indications that the Canadian hosts for the 1980 Ottawa Summit had taken note of a general wish to reduce the scale and heavy bureaucratic preparation, there was little sign of this on the ground.[77] At a preparatory meeting, a report from the Foreign and Commonwealth Office that reviewed previous summits was met with acclaim. It concluded that: 'on balance the time and effort ... have been justified by the results and by the impression made on public opinion, though ... the summits have tended to lose the spontaneity originally envisaged.' Armstrong was commissioned to prepare a paper on the future shape of meetings. The result was a distillation of the views of the sherpas themselves, with unremarkable recommendations: (1) Continuation of annual Summits to provide the opportunity for strategic and general discussion of international economic and financial issues not to reach specific decisions or commitments; (2) the bureaucratisation of preparation should be reversed; (3) political questions would inevitably be discussed but the function and character of the meetings should be for economic discussion.[78]

A combination of reasons made reform difficult: the intractability of familiar problems (notably inflation, recession, trade and aid) and the rise of new ones such as the price of oil; the intrusion of political issues; disagreements between participants; and the incessant media hype. 'Please see that Alan Waters[79] is engaged on this operation at every stage' Thatcher wrote in March 1982.[80] Three months later Walters complained that he was at first omitted from the invitees to a Summit briefing session at the end of May and then only received the paperwork literally five minutes before the meeting. Thatcher was growing increasingly impatient: 'After all the preliminary meetings, I doubt whether we shall need the actual Summit!' 'The whole Summit has become a circus.'[81] When Armstrong reported on the emerging sherpa ideas for discussion she responded: 'These plans are running away from us without any prior reference to myself or the Foreign Secretary and the Chancellor. We must discuss.'[82] Further, in March 1983 Armstrong effectively vetoed Walters attending sherpa meetings. (Which was something of a pity because he brought a new perspective on managerial as well as economic issues – arguing, for example, that Armstrong's brief for an OD discussion of policy towards Japan failed to recognise that the dominant reason for the superiority of Japanese industry lay in the quality of their management. Japanese-managed firms in Britain, he argued, using unionised labour, produced at least twice as much per head, with the same technology, as UK-managed firms and to far higher product quality standards.)[83]

It was always unrealistic that Heads of Government would refrain from discussing political matters even though both Presidents Giscard d'Estaing and Mitterrand were hostile to the idea. At the end of 1979 the Soviet invasion of Afghanistan switched attention to political co-operation between Western leaders and in February 1980 the American embassy in London floated the idea with Armstrong that: '... it would be neither possible nor desirable to exclude from the Summit discussion of the geo-political implications of the Soviet invasion of Afghanistan.'[84] Armstrong had attended a meeting with the Americans, French and Germans the preceding month arguing that whilst the invasion was principally defensive it would be important for the West to preserve the strength of the Islamic reaction to the Soviet action.[85] His subsequent report to Thatcher warned, however, that the sherpa group was not the right forum in which to prepare political issues for a Summit discussion – most of the participants (himself excluded) were not authorised to commit their principals on such matters. One way forward would be to establish a sherpa network for political issues, meeting regularly. There were increasing political exchanges between some of the sherpas. When Armstrong reported to Thatcher on the idea of a political sherpa network she reacted sharply. Why invent a new diplomatic network when a perfectly adequate one already existed? The emergence of such a group should be discouraged.

A third reason why sherpa meetings were somewhat elaborate was that there were often significant transatlantic differences. There were tensions with the Carter regime in 1980 over the American hostages held in Tehran and over the potential deployment of short-range missiles on the European mainland. During the preparations for the 1981 Ottawa meeting Armstrong reported that he detected signs that the Americans were about to do a deal with the Japanese on trade and, if so, would lose interest in discussions to protect the openness of the world trade system. He also reported his worry that the French and German speakers at the sherpa meeting had been overtly hostile to the American and British positions on aid and to the US on interest rate volatility – the French delegate spoke of 'killing our economies.' The British tended to agree with them but were constrained by Thatcher's unwillingness to criticise President Reagan. Also in 1982 Armstrong reported emerging disagreements between European countries: between France and the UK over industrial policy (dirigisme versus market forces), between Japan and the rest of the countries on restrictive practices in international trade and, especially fraught, between the United States and the Europeans over the basis on which credits were provided to the Soviet Union. The Americans argued that trade with the Soviet Union was different from other international trade – witness the likely French, German and Italian dependency on Siberian gas – and pressed for a doctrinal statement on East-west economic relations that was vigorously resisted by those countries.[86] A sherpa meeting in Williamsburg was characterised by, 'extreme mutual suspicion, amounting almost to hostility, between the United States and French delegations.'[87] As a result, the sherpas decided that the first draft of the declaration to be issued after Williamsburg should not be prepared by the Americans on their own. Who else was better suited to be the honest broker than Armstrong? In the United Kingdom a number of high-profile statements and actions on arms control, relations with the Soviet Union, extra-territoriality and anti-trust proceedings suggested that the Reagan Administration did not heed its allies.[88] Whilst Armstrong successfully calmed down those around the Prime Minister over a misleading report that President Mitterrand might be preparing a series of proposals for Williamsburg based on discussions between Socialist Heads of Government,[89] for a second time he reported that the United States delegation was incoherent and apparently unable to get its act together.[90]

The Americans attached great importance to the communiqué as an instrument for influencing public opinion on economic policy. The Europeans did not. However, massive sherpa effort went into drafting the 1980 communiqué, spread over three full meetings (Sardinia in April, Paris in May and June). An American-led group wanted the main theme to be about energy; the British and others favoured inflation/recession. Previous Summits had not said much about the North/South dialogue; the sherpas felt that perhaps there should be more. All felt that the draft communiqué was worthy but dull and, in Armstrong's eyes, American insistence on targets, yardsticks and commitment to action, particularly on energy, contributed to inordinate length. Continuing a precedent set by Hunt, Armstrong briefed the press immediately prior to the Summit[91], defending the sherpa role (they did not 'pre-cook' the discussions but helped focus them so as to use the limited time of the Heads of Government to best effect) and refuting suggestions of strain in the Western alliance. He conceded, though, that the political limelight in which Summits took place encouraged too great a sense of expectancy. By March 1983 Mrs Thatcher was even more irritated: '... a lot of this (United Kingdom] briefing is (in my view) facile and unsound ... We are in danger of becoming committed to something fundamentally unsound just for the sake of saying something in a communiqué.'[92] 'Anything you can do to reduce the number of media representatives at Williamsburg and the demands which their presence makes upon us will be appreciated,' she wrote to President Reagan. But in vain: for Williamsburg the Americans were expecting 6,000 journalists.[93]

Perhaps arising directly out of the personal relationships Armstrong forged with his fellow sherpas he was used by Thatcher to convey sensitive messages. When the United Kingdom successfully sought American agreement to replacing the Polaris deterrent with Trident it was Armstrong rather than a member of the diplomatic corps who travelled to Bonn and Paris to deliver, by hand, Thatcher's letters of forewarning to Chancellor Schmidt and President Giscard d'Estaing through Herr Bernd von Staden and M Jacques Wahl, respectively, of their offices. Schmidt asked to see Armstrong and in an hour-long conversation ranged widely over his impressions of the Soviet leadership from a recent visit to Moscow and over his worries about the world industrial economy. In the French case discussion traversed the UK budgetary arguments in the European Community through to French interest in British policies towards Namibia (the source of uranium for both countries). Of course these messages were intended to be reported to Thatcher – which they were – including Schmidt's comment that when in Moscow: 'he had spoken with a determination and stubbornness which could not have been surpassed by the Prime Minister herself.'[94]

The Nuclear Deterrent

The decision to acquire the Trident 1 (C4) missile was taken in December 1979 by the MISC 7 Committee,[95] building on the discussion Callaghan had had with President Carter at the Guadeloupe Summit. The deal was to be kept secret for fear of upsetting the Strategic Arms Limitations Talks (SALT II) and of NATO allies going slow on modernisation of conventional forces. Hence, it was not until July 1980 that Armstrong set about orchestrating the exchanges of letters and notification of allies that would be necessary. He drafted for Thatcher to write formally requesting the United States to supply the Trident delivery system; he also supplied draft wording for the President to grant the request;[96] and he checked the precedent of the 1963 Nassau Polaris agreement that had been negotiated with President Kennedy *ad referendum* to the Cabinet.[97] The plan was to follow a similar course, with Cabinet ratification on 17 July followed by announcement in the House of Commons. Unknown to the British, however, on the American side the plan was to smooth approval by Congress by a briefing from the White House to Congressional Leaders. This took place on 11 July. Three days later the White House warned Downing Street that a correspondent of *The New York Times* had the story and was planning to publish the following day. President Carter had therefore sent an immediate reply conveying the agreement of the United States and the British Secretary of State for Defence advanced the date of his statement to the House of Commons to 15 July. At Cabinet on 17 July the Prime Minister explained both the decision to select Trident and the enforced 48-hour acceleration of the announcement.[98] It was, Armstrong suggested, ironic that: 'this leak, at the eleventh hour, should have come on the American side, and apparently at a political level.'[99]

Just over a year later the American Government announced it would be upgrading its deterrent force from Trident C4 missiles to the D5 MIRV[100] system and that the C4 would be scrapped. Britain faced the question of whether to follow suit (with greater cost uncertainty). MISC 7 first discussed the issue in November with Armstrong's brief to Thatcher leaning towards supporting the Secretary of State for Defence in wishing to switch to D5, but he did not explicitly come out in its favour. MISC 7 decided that it needed more time and more information and at 10.00 am on Tuesday, 12 January 1982, around a dozen and a half men and one woman assembled in the Cabinet Office Briefing Room (COBR) for a 'teach-in' by an MOD team that included the Secretary of State for Defence (Nott), Chief of the Defence staff (Admiral Lewin), Chief Scientific Adviser (Sir Ronald Mason) and the PUS (Sir Frank Cooper).

An augmented MISC 7 met immediately after the 'teach-in'. Armstrong submitted a brief which reminded Thatcher of points made at the earlier MISC 7 meeting, including the fundamental question of whether an independent strategic nuclear deterrent was still realistic, and it recommended ratification of any decision in MISC 7 by Cabinet, followed by an immediate message to President Reagan – but no public announcement until the detailed technical and financial arrangements had been negotiated (so as not to weaken the British negotiating hand). These negotiations should be carried out by a Cabinet Office team and not, as Armstrong had got wind, under an MOD proposal to deal directly with the Pentagon: 'This is a decision not to be hurried, if it is not yet ready to be crystallised ... It is understandable, given the Pentagon's, and in particular Mr Weinberger's, support for our acquisition of Trident, that the Ministry of Defence hope that this would secure us the best terms. But it would run the risk of mixing us up in internal Administration politics and perhaps alienating the State Department, whose support we shall need as well as the Pentagon's.'[101] Armstrong got his way; after a first Cabinet discussion, a team led by Robert Wade-Gery[102] of the Cabinet Office had two rounds of negotiation with the Americans during February, concluding a deal which was ratified by Cabinet on 11 March[103] and which Mrs Thatcher described fulsomely: 'These terms are excellent – I think you have done a wonderful job.'[104]

The Remaining Defence Programme

Armstrong soon found himself nudging the parties closer together as the OD Committee queried the affordability of the remainder of the defence programme. He set up an official Committee (MISC 32), also under Robert Wade-Gery, to examine the case for out-of-area capabilities.[105] Similarly, in June 1980 OD commissioned an examination of the case for flexibility between the Defence and foreign affairs budgets, at the request of Lord Carrington (MISC 42).[106] The OD secretariat interpreted this as: 'the Foreign and Commonwealth Secretary, having been accustomed as Defence Secretary in the previous Conservative Administration to operate within the dimensions of the defence budget, finds his style very cramped within his present financial resources.'[107] But by November a crisis was looming. The gap between the Ministry of Defence and the Treasury over the 1981/82 budget was around £150 million[108] – not large in terms of a total Defence Budget of over £13 billion, but significant in terms of the Secretary of State's room for manoeuvre, which was largely limited to that part of the equipment spend which did not attract penalties for cancellation. Armstrong advised Thatcher to see the Chiefs of Staff to hear their protests, after which he judged that the Secretary of State would be willing to move a little further towards the Treasury position and a settlement would be possible at about the halfway mark – as indeed happened in mid January 1981. The immediate difficulties did not stop there, however, as there was potentially a knock-on effect on the sales prospectus for the planned flotation of British Aerospace. At a meeting of Ministers on 19 January it was agreed that in his statement on the Defence Estimates the Secretary of State would be more candid than was normal about the prospects for relevant weapons programmes.[109]

By March the short-term fix for 1981/82 was exposed as a sticking plaster on a festering sore. Nott told OD that: 'the need for a fundamental review to match defence commitments with the available resources still exists, and that he expects to reach conclusions in the summer.'[110] In fact, Nott gave Thatcher an explanation of his proposed re-balancing of the Defence Budget on 14 March. He would impose marginal reductions on the Army and the RAF but the surface fleet of the Royal Navy in the Atlantic would be severely cut in favour of the submarine-borne nuclear deterrent. 'This may be the best way of presenting it,' Armstrong argued; 'but the proposed reduction in naval manpower of nearly one-third by 1991, the closure of Gibraltar and Chatham dockyards and the sharp reduction in the size of the Portsmouth dockyard will all be very bitter pills to swallow ... What is more, the frigates and the destroyers of the surface fleet have probably been of greater operational value to us in the last ten years than the submarine fleet: if you were sending ships to the Gulf, for instance, frigates might be more to the point than submarines.' He then reminded Thatcher that in the original Trident agreement President Carter laid great stress on the importance of the United Kingdom continuing to improve its conventional forces.[111] In his judgement the Chief of the Naval Staff would not press his unhappiness with the proposals to the point of resignation, though the Navy Minister (Keith Speed) might. In this he was right.

Within a year the Falklands emergency would amply demonstrate the risks and impermanence of the decisions. But before then Armstrong was charged with leading an investigation into the validity of MOD claims that defence equipment prices rose faster than the inflation allowance proposed by the public expenditure 'Star Chamber'.[112] The investigation was rapid but inconclusive. A later, more thorough, investigation was undertaken by a joint Treasury-Defence working group under the leadership of Brian Unwin of the Economic Secretariat. After the Argentines occupied the Falkland Islands on 2 April 1982 the Statement on the Defence Estimates was postponed.[113] Future defence plans were adjusted to make good the losses of equipment and yet to avoid spending less on the perceived main threat to the United Kingdom which remained the Soviet Union and its Warsaw Pact allies. In these circumstances Cabinet concluded that it was doubtful whether it would be right to take on any new commitments outside the NATO area.[114] Faced with other demands for his attention, such as the War Cabinet, Anglo-Irish negotiations and the *Spycatcher* debacle, the work of briefing on the Statement on the Defence Estimates and other issues for discussion at OD fell increasingly to the OD Secretariat, led by David Goodall.

The Falklands Conflict

Though the invasion may have come as a surprise there had been many exchanges and discussions of the Falkland Islands from the outset of the Thatcher administration. A chronology of OD involvement lists 67 interdepartmental or Ministerial exchanges between September 1979 and April 1982; and talks with Argentina were authorised by the OD Committee at the end of January

1980. Armstrong's forward look on Cabinet business included many references to the need for Falkland Island discussions.[115] By the early part of 1982 there were signs that the Argentine junta were contemplating escalation of the dispute. On 26 March Armstrong made precautionary provision for an OD meeting – initially scheduled for 11.30 on 22 April. 'We do not know how matters will develop over the Falkland Islands in the next few weeks but it is prudent to include this in forthcoming business for OD, since the Foreign and Commonwealth Secretary may wish to seek his colleagues' approval for measures which could involve a call on the contingency reserve.' Treasury Ministers were opposed to call on the reserve. Meanwhile, the Joint Intelligence Committee reported that the worst case scenario was: 'a steady deterioration in relations … Argentina might be obliged to resort to force between the middle and the end of the year.'[116] On the day Argentina invaded Armstrong's appointments diary records an emergency Cabinet at 9.45 am followed by the routine Friday morning business meeting with the Prime Minister, after which he set off on a long-planned visit to the Security Service in their Curzon Street building for the rest of the morning. In the afternoon he attended a Treasury meeting of Permanent Secretaries on financial management, followed by another Cabinet in the early evening when decisions were taken to order a naval task force to sail on 5 April and also to freeze the $1.4 billion Argentine financial assets in London. His notes record the Lord Chancellor (Lord Hailsham) striking a defiant note: 'Take your courage in your hands and go all out. We may take a bloody nose, but if we don't destroy their fleet in being we can never hold up our heads again.'[117]

Over the weekend Armstrong met Frank Cooper and Antony Duff (then Intelligence Co-ordinator in the Cabinet Office) to discuss the central organisation that would be needed. As a result, a first meeting of the informal official group of PUSs that prepared the ground for Ministers (variously known as the Armstrong Group or the Mandarins Group) met at 15.30 on 5 April. It comprised a core membership of Armstrong, Acland (FCO), Cooper (MOD), Lewin (CDS), Palliser (No 10 Downing Street) and Wade-Gery (OD secretariat), others attending occasionally. By Cabinet on 6 April Thatcher was ready to announce that there would be an inner group of Ministers (OD(SA)) on duty the whole time to take day-to-day charge of the war, with major decisions being referred to OD and to Cabinet. Wade-Gery was the Secretary, thus ensuring a strong link into the Armstrong Group); it first met at 09.00 the following day.[118] In the 10 weeks to the Argentine surrender on 14 June Armstrong attended 42 OD(SA) meetings and chaired 24 meetings of the Armstrong Group. [119] The latter focused on the preparation of politico-military decisions to be taken at OD(SA) or reported to Cabinet. A prime concern was the rules of engagement for British forces, discussed intensively from 22 April to 11 May when an array of rules was rationalised. Other issues discussed included the arrangements for repatriating Argentine prisoners of war and ranged from the prospects for the United States mediation efforts, to the announcement of exclusion zones and to the political challenges of post-recovery government. Armstrong would later confide that the War Book, so painstakingly compiled and revised during the previous 70 years,[120] had little to say which was of use for a limited conflict. It addressed a scenario of World War III and was not relevant to a situation where almost all normal government had to proceed in parallel to the requirements for fighting a war.[121]

Thatcher was true to her reassurances to Cabinet about its involvement (less so in relation to the OD Committee). Operational decisions were particularly sensitive. The British landings were planned for the evening of 20/21 May and a decision to go ahead taken by OD(SA) at 10.00 on Thursday 20th. Cabinet met at 11.00. Armstrong advised that to give Cabinet the full picture would burden them with too much secret knowledge during a Parliamentary debate scheduled for later in the day. Wielding a magical pen he suggested: 'the Force Commander's instructions extend to a full-scale landing when the time is right. He now has OD(SA)'s authority to proceed as his military judgement and local conditions (including weather) dictate.' Two former Cabinet Secretaries sent messages of support which greatly bolstered Armstrong's morale: On 24 May Burke Trend wrote: 'I think of you, and my old office, a great deal at this moment; and I hope, very much, that all goes well. Just stick with it!' John Hunt wrote of Trooping the Colour on 12 June: 'But yesterday was special and moving for other reasons [than the precision of the manoeuvres]. The maps in your room and the one-minute silence seemed to bridge the distance between London and the South Atlantic: and underline in a dramatic way that it is not just a spectacle that one sees on Horse Guards Parade.'[122]

Armstrong briefed Thatcher on: 'an acutely difficult problem of political management when we have repossessed [the Falklands].'[123] Suggesting that she should raise the possibility of an Anglo-American trusteeship for the Falklands that would meet the British requirements for an affordable guarantee for the islanders and demonstrate a willingness to listen to our allies (notably the Americans and the French) that there should not be a simple return to the status quo as at 1 April 1982. The Argentine garrison surrendered on 14 June though it was still unclear at that stage whether the Argentines would continue hostilities from the mainland. On 15 June, at Cabinet, Thatcher congratulated the military forces on: 'a mission accomplished, a fantastic success,' adding 'let us remember those who died.' That same evening the BBC broadcast a programme with allegations about intelligence gathering during the conflict which caused Armstrong, with full Ministerial and senior official backing to complain to its Director General of 'shockingly irresponsible' behaviour. Whitehall anxiety about a perceived media tendency to consider the specifics of intelligence gathering as open house for comment and speculation meant that the outgoing Director General (Trethowan) and his successor (Milne) were left in no doubt by more than one mandarin that more attention was required to BBC managerial control over programme makers.

By August thoughts in Whitehall were turning to the lessons to be drawn from the episode. It was completed 11 weeks later[124] and recommended:

- A permanent Ministerial sub-committee of OD (provisionally designated OD(EM)) to provide a basis for managing political and military emergencies abroad and the handling of the media;

- A supporting official committee (ODO(EM)) at Deputy Secretary level;
- A small informal 'Mandarin Group' at PUS level to sort out sensitive politico-military issues with stronger record keeping than had been possible during the Falklands conflict; but which still avoided the traps of acting as a steering group for ODO(EM) or of usurping the role of Secretaries of State as the means by which papers or advice were submitted to the Prime Minister;
- Active management of the tension between strategic and operational secrecy and essential interdepartmental information flows;
- Augmentation of the War Book and WINTEX/HILEX military and counter-terrorism exercises to deal with the scenario of a local limited conflict.

The revamped four-strong Mandarin Group was launched on Christmas Eve 1982 'to identify and monitor those issues in the field of foreign affairs and defence policy which needed to be brought to the attention of the Prime Minister and her senior colleagues; to consider how best such issues should be presented to Ministers; and to commission any preparatory work that might be required.' During 1983 it met four times covering a wide range of issues: Anglo-French arms co-operation; arms control; withdrawal of the Belize garrison; the multi-national force in the Lebanon; Brunei defence arrangements; dual key control of cruise missiles;[125] the Falklands airport; the Falklands garrison; Falklands mine clearance; Greece/Turkey relations; Hong Kong; Iran/Iraq relations; military training for Zimbabwe.

Intelligence and Counter-Terrorism

The Committee of Permanent Secretaries on Intelligence Services (PSIS) continued to assess and approve the budgets and manpower of the Agencies and Armstrong remained Accounting Officer for the Secret Vote. In addition, PSIS discussed the periodic reviews of peacetime intelligence needs by the JIC to provide a two-year framework against which the Agencies could plan the deployment of resources. Unprecedentedly Thatcher attended a JIC meeting on 29 February 1980 having given notice that she wanted a wider discussion than usual that would cover the motivation and foreign policy intentions of the Soviet Government.[126] In the subsequent requirements framework, reported by Armstrong in August, intelligence about the Soviet threat was given a higher priority than hitherto. Subsequently Thatcher's Private Office offered further additional areas of interest such as intelligence-affecting dependencies (post-Falklands), nuclear and biological weapons proliferation, and specific targets drawn from current international concerns.

At home, in April 1980 the government published a White Paper on the interception of communications by the police and the intelligence agencies[127] containing a commitment to appoint a senior judicial figure to audit compliance with the underlying policy on such sensitive matters. Lord Diplock was appointed in early June:

> To review on a continuing basis the purposes, procedures, conditions and safeguards governing the interception of communications on behalf of the police, HM Customs and Excise and the Security Service as set out in Cmnd 7873; and to report to the Prime Minister.'[128]

His first report, in what was to become an annual cycle by the Interception Commissioner, was published on 3 March 1981. During the 1980 debate on the White Paper, the Home Secretary (Whitelaw) reaffirmed the assurances given by Harold Wilson in 1965 – that there was no tapping of telephones of Westminster MPs and that if developments required a change in this policy he would make a statement to the House when the security of the country permitted – the so-called Wilson doctrine. For the Cabinet Secretary, however, the main concern was a practical one – the effect that liberalisation of the telecommunications market would have on the government's ability to carry out interception. The first instinct of officials was to curtail the liberalisation proposals under the rubric of 'protecting the integrity of the network.' The Minister of State at the Department of Trade & Industry (DTI)[129] warned, however, that the argument was beginning to wear a bit thin and, in any case, technological and commercial development would be likely to bring licensing of whole networks in competition to BT.[130] This happened in mid-year when the proposal for a second national network by the Mercury consortium was published. Having pointed to the potential damage to operations against drug smuggling, money laundering, currency and commodity speculators, arms dealers and espionage targets, Armstrong had two suggestions: (a) defer the go-ahead for Mercury for about three months to allow further consideration of how to reconcile the conflicting requirements of two important government policies; (b) exhort the Agencies to move as a matter of urgency to address likely technological developments that would require adaptation of techniques. Thatcher responded: 'I feel that we shall have to develop new techniques [of interception] in any event because present ones will become increasingly vulnerable. I believe we should go ahead with Mercury and soon.'[131] Her instinct was buttressed by advice from the Central Policy Review Staff that technology was moving so fast that a new approach would soon be both necessary and feasible.[132]

Armstrong, meanwhile, reported that he could not advise that the commercial gain would justify the Anglo-American intelligence pain. This did not find favour with Thatcher who saw the heads of the Agencies on 28 July, concluding that whilst the announcement on Mercury could not be before the summer Parliamentary Recess, it should be as soon as possible. Meanwhile, the Cabinet Secretary should explore securing the co-operation of Cable & Wireless and should resolve any associated legal uncertainties. He reported early in August that there looked like being no technical or legal insuperable obstacles, though he judged that the basis for an agreement with Cable & Wireless would be fragile politically.[133] There remained one significant disagreement, whether to rest on a general condition that the licensee would be: 'required to provide in relation to the Crown all such facilities and assistance as the Crown would be entitled to if the activities of the licensee were being carried out by British Telecommunications' or whether to make an explicit reference to interception. Discrete and as tight-lipped as ever, Armstrong favoured the former course.

Proposals for further liberalisation continued. Officials were pessimistic. The combination of privatisation and liberalisation would damage counter-terrorism and intelligence gathering. The advent of cable (the subject of a study by the former Cabinet Secretary Lord Hunt) would further complicate things. The situation would, however, be different were interception to be put on a statutory basis, which might then make it easier politically to retain a BT/Mercury monopoly of voice telephony in the United Kingdom and of international telex links. Even so, Armstrong said: 'I would not suggest that security interests should be overriding, you ... will want to have them in your minds as you take decisions on the future regime for cable and telecommunications.'[134] This remained the position until November 1983 when, in anticipation of an adverse European Court of Human Rights ruling, preparation started for putting interception on a statutory basis.

There was another aspect to technological development that was less well understood. After allegations by Chapman Pincher that Roger Hollis, the former Director General of MI5, had been a Russian agent the efficacy of the government's security precautions at the most sensitive levels was called into question. Thatcher announced in March 1981 that she was asking the Security Commission: 'To review the security procedures and practices currently followed in the public service and to consider what, if any, changes are required.'[135] The statement had gone through 10 drafts before being presented to Cabinet and Parliament.[136] Furthermore, the chairman of the Security Commission[137] was persuaded to defer retirement until after the Commission had completed the task. By the end of the year Armstrong had sufficient knowledge of the likely recommendations to reconvene a working party under Antony Duff, to look again at the arguments for and against avowal of the existence of MI6 and GCHQ as intelligence agencies.[138] In a preliminary discussion on 4 December, the general view was strongly opposed to avowal; it would bring questions about Ministerial control and the Secret Vote and would lead to pressures for some form of Parliamentary scrutiny of the intelligence agencies. Some thought that it would damage MI6 relations with their agents. One member argued that the Commission should be told that if they were to make a strong recommendation in favour of avowal the government would not publish this part of their report.[139]

The Commission reported in mid December and strongly recommended the avowal of MI6. 'I see no need for the Prime Minister to make an immediate announcement,' advised Armstrong.[140] To publish the unexpurgated report would be impracticable because of overriding security objections, but Lord Diplock would not accept partial publication because, in his view, it would risk being misleading. With great subtlety Armstrong drew on a precedent from 1956[141] to suggest that the government publish a full written statement that would contain the substance of the Commission's findings (and be agreed with Lord Diplock) together with its response.[142] 'The Commission's report is generally reassuring … the security procedures in the public service as they have been applied since Radcliffe[143] have worked well.'[144] The question was would they continue to work well in the coming digital age? The Commission saw an exposure – the problems of computer security were highly technical and subject to rapid change, the staff were birds of passage with result that there was likely to be a flow of people to outside the public service who had intimate knowledge of government computing. It considered existing arrangements did not adequately reflect the risk of: 'what it considers may well present today and in the foreseeable future the greatest potential threat to classified information.'[145] The point was not lost on Thatcher: 'The computer section is very worrying. There is a problem but no recommendation.'[146] The Security Service responded seriously and Armstrong instructed his Private Office to pay attention to the risk without giving a hint as to how (he never had a computer terminal on his own desk). But he did not follow up with Departments and there is no immediate evidence that those involved with the SO committee followed up on the point; their concerns were more focussed on the issue of avowal.

The Economy

For the most part, on economic issues he gave tactical political advice and promoted improvements in Whitehall procedure. On industrial disputes this tended to be cautious, closer to the approach advocated by Jim Prior (Secretary of State for Employment) and away from a more hawkish stance. It is best described as helping Ministers come to terms with the realities of power. Thus, although reform of industrial relations law was a flagship policy from the 1979 election manifesto Armstrong argued that a search for perfection would risk the whole project and briefed in favour of pragmatism, especially on employee rights and trade union immunities.[147] 'All of us would ideally have liked … to ban secondary action altogether. But we have to have regard to what is possible [and the proposals] will broadly restore the law to the state we thought it was in last year.'[148] Hunt had taken a comparable line. Similarly, on reducing the access of strikers and their families to social security payments, noting that irreconcilable views were held among Cabinet members over whether the reductions should bear equally on union and non-union members, Armstrong did not try to find an agreed way forward. He suggested recording the majority view as the Cabinet's decision.[149] And again, in early 1983, he tried to steer Cabinet away from confrontational actions, indicating that postponement of a decision on union immunities in essential services until after the election would probably be the best course because of the difficulties that officials were having in finding a durable way forward. Rather than drift into a confrontation on union funding for political parties, he preferred a fudge under which the government said it would tolerate the onus being on the individual to contract out of the levy, provided that no unreasonable obstacles were put in their way.[150]

A dispute at British Steel (BSC) at the start of 1980 exemplifies this caution. Initially the strike had been handled by a small informal group of Ministers. It came to Cabinet after ten days of dispute. Armstrong speculated about what could be the catalyst to bring the parties together in meaningful negotiation; legislation on picketing could provoke a more widespread strike and the legal basis for requisitioning vehicles for use by troops did not cover the steel industry. Would external pressures by the industry's customers be sufficient or would the BSC try to bust the government's refusal to make any more money available to finance its borrowing requirement? Could government maintain a hands-off stance for another two weeks? This reluctance to move to a position that might draw in the government as an overt protagonist was consistent with the policy of distancing itself from specific private sector disputes, relying on reform of the law to create a more benign climate for the proper conduct of industrial relations. It was also evident in the briefing he offered during 1980 on disputes in British Leyland, the water industry, gas, the fire service, the Port of London Authority and scientific officers in medical laboratories.[151] In October, however, dealing with a prison officers' dispute the confidence of a former Permanent Secretary at the Home Office came through as he supported proposals for emergency action: '... you might guide the Cabinet to endorse the line taken by the Home Secretary,' he suggested, 'There are very high stakes at issue here: essentially whether the Prison Officers' Association are to be allowed a stranglehold over the prison system whenever they take some form of industrial action.'[152]

A further flagship economic policy was to demonstrate public expenditure was under control. By October 1979 Thatcher's Cabinet brief pointed to, 'the extent of the gap which still has to be bridged, even to avoid any increase in taxation ... Cabinet should not spend the increment [from the effects of the government's other policies] until it has been earned.' The Prime Minister must support the Treasury in the remaining battles with spending Ministers and may feel it better to get all the difficult decisions out of the way, and on the public record.[153] And before the end of the year Armstrong argued in relation to cash limits that Ministers had had no comprehensive account of the way the public expenditure negotiations fitted together.[154] However, whilst he was in office a regular pattern was established: first, a discussion of the economic outlook, then the balance to be sought between expenditure and taxation, followed by guidelines for the Public Expenditure Survey; bilateral negotiations between the Treasury Chief Secretary and Departmental Ministers; a small 'Star Chamber' of Ministers to adjudicate when the Chief Secretary and Departmental Ministers could not reach an accommodation (first tried in October 1981), and a final Cabinet to sign off the Public Expenditure White Paper.

The general discussion of economic prospects as background to decision making was a departure from the historic secrecy of the Chancellor of the Exchequer about Budget matters. He would still reserve his position not to put Budget decisions into commission, but the old tensions from the 1960s that Trend had struggled to overcome were of the past. In July 1980 there was a Cabinet discussion of the economic prospects for public expenditure[155] and in January 1981 Armstrong suggested extending the practice to a pre-Budget understanding.[156] His proposal (agreed with the Chancellor) was for discussions in January, May and October and to encourage general Ministerial discussion without the presence of the CPRS or Treasury officials.[157] The first took place over one and three quarter hours on 18 June 1981 with the aim of ensuring that Cabinet was satisfied that it had had a meaningful input to the Chancellor's thinking.[158] One potential innovation, which was not taken up, was when Michael Heseltine (Environment) suggested an interdepartmental group to investigate the state of the public capital stock. Armstrong briefed against – the proposed terms of reference were loaded with questions to which the only answer would be 'more money;' not only was some current expenditure as valuable economically as capital expenditure (education might be one example) but investment was of little value if it failed to earn a proper return and much nationalised industry investment had failed to do just that.[159]

Local government spending was a continuing threat to public expenditure control. The real work to link local spending more closely to local accountability started early in 1982 after the Green Paper *Alternative to Domestic Rates*.[160] The CPRS was charged with a study of the relationship between central and local government, the methods of raising revenue and the problems of local accountability versus central control. Many of the alternatives to be considered (local income tax, local sales tax, poll tax) would not be practicable for several years. The first two, Armstrong pointed out, were dependent on computerisation of Pay as you Earn and Value Added Tax respectively; the third was a regressive tax which would bring problems of social justice and whose method of collection would be dependent on co-operation by the local authorities.[161] An ad hoc Ministerial Committee on Local Government Organisation and Finance (MISC 79, chaired by the Home Secretary) was created in the summer. It recommended no further work on new sources of revenue in favour of concentrating on reforms to the rating system.[162] Amongst these was a proposal to offer rate relief to single occupancy property. In line with Treasury orthodoxy on the hypothecation of taxation Armstrong's brief put an impermeable membrane between taxation and expenditure. Rates were a tax on the occupancy of property not a surrogate charge for the consumption of services; if rates were to be paid in proportion to the call on local services where would the claims for relief stop? What about a young couple, never using public transport, with no children or with children educated privately? 'But the Cabinet will wish to bear in mind that MISC 79 have explored the issues thoroughly; and that proposed changes in local government organisation and finance inevitably involve both losers and gainers and tend to displease at least as many as they please,' he cautioned. Cabinet rejected the report of MISC 79 as an inadequate response.[163] MISC 79 was replaced by a Ministerial Sub-Committee on Local Government Finance chaired by the Prime Minister (E(LF)) which reported to Cabinet in May 1983 on a system of control by central government of the rates of individual local authorities but was split both on the constitutional propriety of central government control and on whether to replace the rates with an alternative tax. Armstrong put forward a powerful submission arguing that a Royal Commission on local government was needed. But when that fell on deaf ears, apart from interventions on smaller questions he focused on the practical issue of what to say in public.[164] Having briefed in 1983 against the poll tax by 1986 Armstrong's judgement was that the sub-committee (E(LF)) had constructed the proposals carefully so that the impact between areas and on different household types were judged politically acceptable.[165] The Secretary of State for Scotland, he advised, regarded it as a political imperative to introduce the new tax in Scotland in advance of England and Wales and added, '... although it is not without political and practical difficulties.'

Northern Ireland

Armstrong's involvement with Northern Ireland went back to the Conservative administration of Edward Heath and his attitude to the problems of the Province was less concerned with the Unionists than was Thatcher. As he took over from Hunt, the Conservatives were split over the approach to political progress. Humphrey Atkins[166] wanted a Consultative Assembly to be elected in 1981, initially at least without formal powers. The OD Committee judged this to be too little, too slow, and asked for options for a conference of the main Ulster political parties.[167] However, in his first brief on the prospects for a conference Armstrong struck an upbeat note: 'I believe that it is fair to say that [the Conference] has been as well received as could possibly have been hoped and that the difficulties which are at present being encountered should not by any means be regarded as insuperable.'[168] Whilst sceptical about Garda anti-terrorist activity, Armstrong advised Thatcher that in meetings with the Taoiseach (Charlie Haughey) she would need to 'pour cold water on some of his more far-reaching ideas [for a modification of the guarantee to the people of Northern Ireland] without rebuffing his desire to contribute to the resolution of the Northern Ireland problem' through support for improved security and political discussions.[169] By October 1980 Cabinet had concluded that the political talks had run out of steam and that the situation was too uncertain to say anything in the Queen's Speech more forthcoming than, '[My Government] will continue to seek a solution on which to base legislation to involve locally elected representatives in the administration of Northern Ireland.'[170] Thatcher had told Haughey, however, that she wanted to spend time over the summer looking at the history of the Northern Ireland problem. She believed that he genuinely wanted to improve relations between the United Kingdom and the Republic and, although she feared that he would eventually be disappointed by what could be achieved, she intended to look at the problem in the context of the prospects for developing this relationship in the long-term interests of both countries.[171] In the Cabinet Office Wade-Gery advised, 'I think we should at least be ready for the possibility that Mr Haughey may really intend, for whatever reasons, a major shift in southern Irish attitudes. This idea sounds very odd, if one is steeped in traditional southern Irish attitudes. But then so did the idea of President Sadat going to Jerusalem, if one was steeped in traditional Arab attitudes.'[172] Armstrong replied, 'I am very much of the same mind as you about the idea of a "Federal framework" linking the

United Kingdom and the Irish Republic.' He tentatively christened the idea of a federal framework, 'islands of the North Atlantic association' (IONA). Under conditions of extreme secrecy Thatcher agreed to further work by officials on the Anglo-Irish dimension. The outcome was that the Anglo-Irish summit in December 1980 commissioned joint studies on Northern Ireland. Despite ill feeling around the deaths of Republican hunger strikers in the Maze prison Anglo-Irish common ground on co-operation over Northern Ireland simply would not go away – Armstrong and his Irish counterpart (Dermot Nally)[173] spoke several times during June 1981 and met on 27 July to discuss the Maze crisis.[174] It was then perhaps no surprise when the joint studies recommended an Anglo-Irish Intergovernmental Council (AIIC) with a steering committee to be chaired by Armstrong and Nally.

Security and Secrecy

Throughout this period Armstrong was fighting a three-headed monster: (a) charges that the Security Service had been penetrated by the Russian Intelligence Service at the highest levels; (b) damage to morale in the intelligence agencies by alleged revelations about their activities; (c) the challenge of ensuring that those agencies were under viable (external) democratic control. Allegations (and some hard evidence) of the penetration of the highest reaches of government by Soviet intelligence persisted. Early in the Thatcher administration knowledge of espionage on behalf of the Soviet Union by Sir Anthony Blunt, Keeper of the Queen's pictures and former MI5 officer, was admitted in a Parliamentary statement.[175] Blunt had been identified as a likely spy as early as 1951 and had confessed in 1964 when offered immunity against prosecution. Contingency arrangements had been put in hand in 1972 for the possible revelation of Blunt's crimes when it was thought that a diagnosed cancer would be terminal, but they were not activated when this proved wrong. These arrangements were updated periodically, in 1977 prompting the then Prime Minister, Jim Callaghan, to put on record his disagreement with the kid glove treatment Blunt had had and the failure to expose him earlier.[176] But it was the likely 1979 publication of a book by Andrew Royle, which revealed the identity of Blunt as the Fourth Man in the Burgess-Maclean-Philby scandal that led to Mrs Thatcher breaking with the convention of silence in regard to intelligence matters. After Thatcher's statement to the House of Commons and just before a subsequent debate[177] Armstrong was advised by the Attorney General's office that he should seek to vet any public statements to be made by Blunt to ensure that national security was not affected.[178] He saw Blunt's solicitor (Michael Rubenstein) and reported on 19 November that the immediate statement Blunt proposed to make showed contrition but not regret. It was the first of a good number of meetings with Rubenstein that led to misunderstandings in the press that Armstrong was advising Blunt on what he could say about the Russians – *The Guardian* called it a stately minuet.[179] Armstrong told Bernard Ingham in the No 10 press office that the article was: 'an absolute travesty of the facts.'[180] Throughout an intensive series of exchanges into January 1980, in fact, Armstrong was at pains to tell Rubenstein that he was not vouching for the accuracy of what Blunt might say, only for its relevance to national security.

Just over a year later Armstrong warned the Prime Minister that a confidential source had given the Security Service the text of a forthcoming book by Chapman Pincher[181] that would reopen the allegation that Sir Roger Hollis[182] had been a Soviet spy.[183] Publication was due on 26 March 1981.[184] Its contents were generally sufficiently accurate to suggest that information had come from an insider – the most likely candidate being Peter Wright, a former senior officer who had been a member of the original team investigating Hollis (codename FLUENCY). Wright was known to hold a grudge about his pension and, furthermore, lived in Australia, beyond the reach of the Official Secrets Act (OSA). In a flurry of activity in the ten days before publication Armstrong contacted the publishers to request a copy of the text (without revealing that government already had one) thereby protecting the source of the illicit copy. He was also heavily involved in preparing a House of Commons statement for the Prime Minister which referred both to the majority of investigators' conclusion that Hollis had not been an agent of the Russian Intelligence Service and to the subsequent review in 1974–75 by Burke Trend of the conduct of that investigation in the light of dissenting voices in the team.

Attempts continued to identify, and secure sufficient evidence to prosecute, any insiders who had helped Chapman Pincher in contravention of the lifetime expectation of secrecy from officers of the intelligence agencies and possibly in contravention of the Official Secrets Act. At the time a link between Pincher and Wright was suspected but conclusive evidence was lacking, that would not come until July 1984 when Wright submitted a dossier of allegations to Sir Anthony Kershaw[185] and in September 1986 when the government learned conclusively that Wright had been put in touch with Pincher in 1980 after an abortive attempt to raise his concern about Hollis with Thatcher and Sir John Hunt. However, a second source of potentially damaging insider information (including the names of past and present members of the Security Service) came to light in connection with another proposed book, by Nigel West, covering MI5's activities 1945–72. Armstrong told Thatcher that, '... following the publication of Chapman Pincher's book, [the text] could make it look as if there was some sort of implied licence to former members of the Security Service and the SIS to be indiscreet.'[186]

Led by Armstrong, officials advised that the main objective should be to 'prevent or at least minimise the damage that would be caused by publication' and that would be best served by attempting to negotiate excisions from the text with the threat of possible later civil or criminal proceedings. To prevent immediate publication the Attorney General would, on instruction from Ministers, seek an ex-parte injunction (under which West would only become aware of the government's intentions after the injunction had been obtained). Negotiations would then continue either to a successful conclusion or to the point when the Attorney General took a decision on criminal prosecution of West or his source.

In the short term the strategy was successful: Armstrong reported that, 'The Treasury Solicitor has had greater success than many of us had expected,'[187] the agreed amendments would remove virtually all that had not previously become public, they would be embodied in a court order (punishable as contempt of court if breached) and would also apply to the text to be published in the United States. West also had books on SIS and the Metropolitan Police Special Branch in the pipeline. Former senior members of MI5 would be warned about the dangers of talking to him; Ministers would need to emphasise their disapproval (indeed Cecil Parkinson, the Chairman of the Conservative Party, was commissioned to suggest to West – the pen name of Rupert Allison – that his ambitions as a Conservative parliamentary candidate would be better served if he ceased publishing books of this kind).[188]

Meanwhile, Armstrong conducted an urgent study of recent United States legislation making it an offence to reveal individuals concerned with intelligence organisations. He reported in December 1983 that although the American legislation had never been tested in the courts and there would be difficulties of disclosure if it were, British legislation to protect intelligence identities was technically feasible.[189] In briefing for a subsequent Ministerial discussion some months later, however, he admitted that consultations with senior officials had led to the belief that whilst all those I have consulted would wish to protect intelligence identities, 'none of us would wish to argue that the gain would be worth the cost of winning it.'[190]

Head of the Home Civil Service

The Conservatives had defeated Labour in 1979 partly on a manifesto promise that: 'The reduction of waste, bureaucracy and over-government will also yield substantial savings.'[191] After the abolition of the Civil Service Department in 1981 Armstrong sought to ride the twin horses of Cabinet Secretary and Head of the Home Civil Service where he had to reconcile the interface with his political masters with professional leadership for the civil service. He had not sought to be the civil service leader and accepted the role more from a sense of duty than because he saw a need to change things. Later he estimated that the role took no more than 20% of his time – an estimate confirmed by analysis of his appointment diaries. In large measure his focus was on Whitehall and those whose regular dealings were with Ministers and Parliament, describing his main function as to advise on senior appointments.[192] To his Private Secretary he maintained that, 'I don't think that the present incumbent has been less able to 'speak up for the Civil Service' – or less forward in doing so – than his predecessors.'[193] It is likely that his strong support for the 'Next Steps' reforms sprang partly from a wish to put a *cordon sanitaire* between the delivery of services to the citizen (which would be the arena for decentralised departmental control and responsibility) and the service to Ministers (which would, in his view, be subject to civil service-wide standards from a golden age – the Northcote-Trevelyan paradigm). As a result there is little sign of a strategy for civil service management in the

1980s and beyond, rather a series of patches to close breaches in the culturally walled city of Whitehall and indecision stemming from Ministers' unfamiliarity with management issues.

As reality began to bite on the 1979 manifesto promises to reduce the size of the civil service and to reduce its concentration in London, Ministers came under pressure. On 1 May 1979 Cabinet agreed a target reduction in civil service numbers from 708,000 to 630,000 (11%) by 1 April 1984. But by November it was clear that achievement was falling behind expectations. In six months the numbers in post had come down by 2.7%; firm promises (before allowing for possible offsetting increases from demographic influences or new policies) brought the likely reduction to 8.1% and Departments had many a reason why it was a good idea to slim down in general but then to argue, 'not me, at least not yet'. The Treasury, for example, overturned a decision of the Callaghan Government to abolish Vehicle Excise Duty – putting fiscal flexibility ahead of administrative economy (the saving would have been 1,450 staff or £8 million p.a.).[194] Confronted with the policy to disperse jobs from London to areas of high unemployment Lord Carrington invited his colleagues to: '… imagine telling a diplomat on return from Phnom Penh that his next posting was to Bootle,'[195] bearing out Hunt's observation that 'everyone supports dispersal but no-one wants to be the one to go.' Armstrong warned that, whilst the Parliamentary position would not be too difficult and the National Staff Side would probably be privately relieved, there was still a risk of local industrial action where the cuts went very deep (e.g. in the Department of Employment).[196] He reminded the Prime Minister that whilst it was normal business practice to set target employee numbers, too rigid a policy had prevented some initiatives that would have been financially beneficial because they would have increased staff numbers.[197] But in general he stayed clear of the debate over numbers.

Ministerial frustration over reducing staff numbers threw a shadow over the Civil Service Department (CSD) and invited unfair comparison with Treasury prowess at controlling public expenditure. It was widely believed that after the initial flush of responding to the Fulton Report, and especially after the fall from grace of its first Permanent Secretary Sir William Armstrong, the Department had been a disappointment. As early as 22 November 1979 Lord Plowden gave Armstrong a note in which he argued that since 1973/74 the CSD had become increasingly peripheral and the means of reversing this decline were not present.[198] Departmental Permanent Secretaries resented what they perceived as interference in the running of their Departments. Following a visit to the Department by Thatcher on 11 January 1980 (one of a series to the various Whitehall Departments) she recalled that: 'I met able and conscientious people attempting to manage and monitor the activities of Civil Servants in departments of which they knew little, in policy areas of which they knew even less.'[199] By March, following Parliamentary criticism of CSD and advice from Sir Derek Rayner that central control of money and manpower should be under one authority (as it was departmentally under the Permanent Secretary) she instructed Bancroft (CSD), Armstrong, Wass (HMT) and Rayner to investigate the case for a merger of the CSD and Treasury.[200]

Shortly afterwards a reluctant Armstrong gave evidence to the Treasury and Civil Service Select Committee (TCSSC) on the future of the CSD: 'I favour putting the CSD manpower divisions into the Treasury' he told Clive Whitmore of Number 10.[201] This was a different view from Hunt who had favoured splitting public expenditure control from the Treasury to create an office of management and budget.[202] Bancroft disagreed and said so in uncompromising comments on Armstrong's draft speaking note: 'I don't think that it is unfair to say that your notes tend to convey three impressions. First, the CSD has failed to acquire the knowledge it needs and is inadequately coordinated with the Treasury. Second, all but the manpower and management and organisation functions of the CSD are pretty trivial. Third, only splitting the Treasury is more unattractive than the status quo.'[203] Armstrong retreated, assuring Bancroft that: 'I shall try not to disclose any bias, but I may not be able entirely to prevent my slip from showing ...'[204] but their relationship had been damaged.

Despite his isolation Bancroft was able to nullify the instruction from the Prime Minister, by ensuring that a merger would bring neither rationalisation of effort nor staff savings. As he put it in a covering note to the report: 'My own (as it happens, extensive) experience of machinery of government changes has taught me that the costs of re-organisation are usually under-estimated and that policies and personalities are more important than organisational theories. The penalties of disruption .... are immediate and substantial: the benefits come in the longer term and are inevitably speculative.'[205] This was not language likely to resonate with the Prime Minister and was reminiscent of the defensive posture Bancroft had struck at the legendary dinner she had given for Permanent Secretaries on 6 May 1980 which Thatcher described as: '... one of the most dismal occasions of my entire time in government ... such a menu of complaints and negative attitudes as was served up that evening was enough to dull any appetite I may have had for this kind of occasion in the future.'[206] The regular Wednesday morning meeting of Permanent Secretaries, with Bancroft in the chair, had briefly discussed the forthcoming dinner on 30 April when it was billed as, 'a frank exchange of views on Government policy towards the civil service and current management problems.' Armstrong was present but did not provided the Prime Minister with a brief for it. Her Principal Private Secretary, Clive Whitmore, counselled Thatcher to stay cool in the face of likely Permanent Secretary attitudes.[207] The Permanent Secretaries conducted a post mortem on the morning after the event. The main beneficiary was Sir Derek Rayner, Permanent Secretaries deciding that his association with their efforts to improve efficiency in their Departments would be 'a useful help in convincing Ministers that all avenues were being vigorously explored.'[208]

On 23 July Thatcher chaired a discussion of the report on the feasibility of a HMT/CSD merger[209] – '... there is so much dissatisfaction with the performance of the CSD that something has to be done,' Whitmore briefed. Yet she was indecisive: her instinct was close to Bancroft's view: it was more important to have the right Departmental Permanent Secretaries than to endure the dislocation of a merger. But she respected and trusted Derek Rayner and he was strongly of the view that Departmental officials would not display the required hunger for improving value for money at a detailed level until the macro-level organisation had unified control of all administrative costs. A preliminary decision in favour of merger was agreed subject to: 'aborting the whole merger if the detailed work suggested much greater costs and dislocation than were at present anticipated.'[210] And even that decision was rescinded 24 hours later in favour of a further study to be completed by the end of October.[211] Ian Bancroft had drawn a 'Get out of Gaol' card.

Meanwhile, as the draft report began to circulate for comment, Armstrong asked for a view from Robin Ibbs, the Head of the CPRS. The response was so far ahead of any thinking displayed by officials that it bears repetition in full. He advocated:

> 'That creative thought right down the line is concentrated on problems that are going to emerge rather than those that are past; that within Departments as well as overall, traditions that remain appropriate are preserved and others discarded; that accepted constraints are challenged and radical alternatives thoroughly and positively explored; that opportunities offered by new technologies are pursued vigorously rather than accepted belatedly; and that the overall shape of the organisation changes to fit new circumstances – the sort of change which individual decentralised Departments left to themselves seldom foster. 'Would a full merger produce these changes or perhaps this is a responsibility the Secretary of the Cabinet should shoulder?'[212]

The second study (known as the Hawtin-Moore report after its lead authors) was published on 10 November. Armstrong argued for the merger of public expenditure and manpower control down to desk officer level and pointed out that whilst the expected savings were not negligible (£500,000 per annum net) they were far from the whole story. Improved effectiveness of departments was the greater prize. And in response to Ibbs' advice he argued for recruitment and training to be the responsibility of the independent Civil Service Commission. He was doubtful whether it was necessary or advantageous to retain the title Head of the Home Civil Service – not least because, unlike say the Commissioner of the Metropolitan Police or the Chief of the General Staff, the incumbent could not go public on matters of disagreement with Ministers.[213] Bancroft, he reported, was exaggerating the support for retention of the CSD amongst Permanent Secretaries – 'a significant number are not party to the alleged consensus.' Nevertheless, for reasons of charity and recognition of past service he suggested that perhaps Bancroft should become First Civil Service Commissioner presiding over a strengthened independent organisation retaining the title Head of the Home Civil Service.[214] Once again Mrs Thatcher inclined against a merger;[215] and a month later the TCSSC also came out in favour of revitalising the CSD.[216]

Having decided against even the relocation of the CSD manpower divisions into the Treasury Thatcher was once again thrown back on her doubts about the

Department when Bancroft submitted the draft of a response to the Select Committee's report. In her eyes its complacency simply demonstrated what was wrong with the CSD. Rayner was also critical – the CSD is not doing its job and intends to carry on as now, he argued.[217] Action by CSD top management to revitalise itself was noticeably lacking. Rayner diagnosed that Bancroft was very tired and, in consequence, that it was very risky to keep him on what had plainly become a treadmill.[218] Departments smelled blood – Frank Cooper, PUS of MOD, wrote to Armstrong in early September: 'I simply do not believe that one can even strive for effective resource management without looking single-mindedly at all the resources likely to be consumed ... the CSD ... is in almost every area away from the main stream of policy discussion. It is not well informed about what is going on – or might be going on – within Government[219] Mrs Thatcher's inclination was to run it down by progressively distributing its responsibilities to other departments, including the Cabinet Office. Armstrong had to guard against the Cabinet Office looking like a putative Prime Minister's Department (which he and Rayner opposed but which was attractive to Thatcher).[220] The route devised by the two of them was for a Second Permanent Secretary working to Armstrong, as Head of the Home Civil Service, who would be in charge of a semi-independent Department into which the small Rayner Unit dealing with value for money initiatives would move, together with the rump of the CSD. As became abundantly clear over the next couple of years, it was not a good solution and did not last. However, that is to run ahead; first there is the question of Armstrong's role during the civil service strike of 1981 and then of how the Civil Service Department was finally killed off.

The Civil Service Strike

In October 1980 the government unilaterally abandoned the long-standing approach to civil service pay through comparability studies. The Civil Service Unions submitted a claim for a 15% rise in February, shortly after the Government announced a cash limit of 6% on civil service pay. The offer was increased to 7% later that month but the unions stated selective strikes on 9 March when 273,000 civil servants struck. Co-ordination of the management response to the strikes fell to Bancroft as professional head of the service and operationally to the Permanent Secretaries of the Departments affected – notably the Inland Revenue, the social security side of the Department of Health and Social Security and the Government Communications Head Quarters (GCHQ). Armstrong was no more than on the fringes, mainly through his briefing for Cabinet, which, in the early period of the dispute, encouraged firmness combined with recognising the position of moderate union leaders faced with increasing militancy at junior grades. Thatcher had asked Armstrong to consult Alan Lord (who had left a position as 2nd PUS in the Treasury in 1980 to become managing director of Dunlop Holdings plc.). He reported back that Lord's advice was to take a firm line and not to make any improvement to the 7% pay offer. It was a view that sat well with Treasury thinking. The Chancellor and his senior officials were well content to let Mrs Thatcher be a hawk on civil service pay.[221] But Armstrong's own view was less confrontational. He briefed that: 'There are no signs of weakening by the civil service unions. The dispute is ugly in the Inland Revenue ... Under the surface damage is being done ... in order to retain [widespread political] support, and to give the moderates some sign of hope and something to respond to, I believe that the government needs now to be seen to make a constructive move.'[222] He and Lord both felt that the main grievance was the removal of a previously agreed system of pay comparability without putting anything in its place. In addition he reported Alan Lord's view that: 'Ministers might find it easier to deal with the civil service, and to bring them to accept the realities of the situation in relation to pay, if they abused them (his word) less in public.'[223]

Armstrong maintained this stance throughout, focusing on the long-term issue and the financial weakness of the unions that made an all-out strike unlikely.[224] The longer the dispute continued the more union attitudes would harden; play the arbitration card for 1982 he urged in April.[225] And he tried ineffectively again in late May: 'There is now a "window" during which it may be possible to get some sort of discussion going. But the omens for an early settlement are not very propitious.'[226] Nor were Ministers in a mood to compromise; counter escalation was being studied – abandonment of the 1 April settlement date for 1981, imposition of a 7% award; legislation to allow civil servants not on strike but whose work was affected by the strikers to be laid off. Senior officials were appalled. Peter Le Cheminant, an experienced former private secretary in Downing Street, advised Armstrong that laying people off without pay would amount to expropriation of a valuable right without compensation, for which the government was unlikely to get Parliamentary approval.[227]

By early June Armstrong was posing a further direct challenge to the Prime Minister. There was another window of opportunity to settle since the union leaders were anxious to do so before they had to intensify the dispute. Did she want to show moderation or firmness of purpose? 'Ministers should be in no doubt about the effect the dispute has already had on the sense of loyalty to the government; that will become worse if the dispute is escalated. A growing number of relatively senior people are saddened and dispirited: "this is not the Service we joined." Escalation will strengthen the hands of the militants, will reduce willingness to co-operate in the implementation of policy changes (in such matters as overtime to implement tax changes, introduction of new technology), and increase the extent of 'politicisation' in the Service.'[228] He could not have been plainer short of spelling out that the national union leaders were an important instrument for controlling increasingly militant clerical staff and first-line managers. Nevertheless, the briefing was ambivalent as he also recognised that there were wider issues at play: 'The arguments for trying to settle are seductive: they always are. On the other hand the political case for standing firm and making no even marginal concessions is clear and strong.' He did not mention (as he might have) that the strike was costing the government large amounts in lost revenue and extra interest payments on loans – a secret post mortem on the lessons of the strike later put the financial costs at £870 million[229] compared to the direct extra costs of the additional 0.5% on top of the 7% offer which the Lord Privy Seal and the Government's chief negotiator believed would have settled the strike within a week. That cost was estimated by Armstrong to be £30 million a year (not allowing for any repercussive effects on other pay settlements).[230] In the end the unions settled at the end of July for an increase of 7.5% for 1981, no predetermined limit on the 1982 negotiations and an inquiry into the longer-term arrangements under Mr Justice Megaw. It was a mutual defeat and a catastrophe for the Civil Service Department.

The Coup de Grâce for the CSD

The strike ended on 31 July 1981 to be followed by the sound of nails being hammered into a coffin for the CSD. Thatcher met the Chancellor and told him: '... in the light of experience over the last few months, the time is ripe to abolish the CSD and to distribute its central functions to the Treasury and the Cabinet Office.'[231] It fell to Clive Whitmore rather than either of the Permanent Secretaries to whom the functions and staff of CSD would be transferred, to prepare Bancroft for what would be a potentially fraught interview with the Prime Minister. He did so on the afternoon of 22 September. Members of the Rayner Unit later spoke of seeing Whitmore stride across Horseguards' Parade from the rear of 10 Downing Street to the Golden Gate of the Old Admiralty Building where he was to deliver the death sentence on the head of his own profession (two ranks his senior in status and 12 years his senior in age). It was a dramatic and unenviable task. The decision to wind up the CSD, he reported, came as a complete surprise to Bancroft who was visibly shaken by the news yet showed every sign of being ready to co-operate in carrying through the Prime Minister's decision. 'It was a very big pill to swallow and digest' and Bancroft sought a clear day to order his mind on both the official and personal implications of the decision.[232] Hence, at 9.45 am on 24 September Mrs Thatcher confirmed the decision face to face with Bancroft in an unhappy meeting[233] and instructed him now to prepare, in conjunction with Armstrong, Wass and Rayner, the detail of his Department's demise. For the sake of security the staff work could not be entrusted to a serving CSD officer; Clive Priestley, Rayner's chief of staff who, ironically, was on loan from the CSD, undertook it. Announcement of the decision was planned for late October (it later slipped to 12 November); one risk was that Bancroft would 'go public' and denounce the decision, stirring up political opposition. Neither Armstrong nor Wass thought that was likely: 'He has accepted the decision ...' Armstrong reported;[234] and nor did he. Armstrong and Wass became joint heads of the Home Civil Service.

Bancroft left with his dignity intact. However, the feeling among Permanent Secretaries was that this was not their finest hour. Sir Brian Cubbon (then at the top of the Home Office) reflected: '... the demise of the CSD is infinitely depressing. No one, not even Armstrong or Middleton, understood the real issues. It was just as bad as a Ministerial squabble – everyone thinking of their own position, and not knowing what we are all there for.'[235] As one of the main beneficiaries from abolition of the CSD, Armstrong felt wretched about the fate of his friend and colleague of many years. It was hardly surprising, therefore, that when he received a supportive letter from Lord Trend it had a powerful positive effect on his morale. Trend wrote: 'The briefest note – simply to say that I'm delighted, both for you and for Whitehall as a whole, that at last the right decision seems to have been reached. I'm sorry for Ian [Bancroft] and will try to write to him. But in all other respects I'm immensely pleased – partly (and rather smugly?) because it is what I've always advocated but mainly because I'm sure that it's right and will make the machine much more efficient now that there should be an end to the tensions and frustrations which, with the best will in the world, have inevitably hampered the relationship for nearly twenty years.'[236]

With the retirement of Bancroft, Armstrong became joint Head of the Home Civil Service with Sir Douglas Wass, PUS of HM Treasury. They met informally each Monday morning to swap notes. But neither was a natural fit for the role; their management experience was principally of leading 'high-flying' policy advisers and, as the civil service strike had shown, there were serious challenges of motivation and willingness to change in the rank and file who were faced with simultaneous Ministerial calls for reductions in staffing and greater output. The civil service problem, wrote Ken Stowe (by now PUS at the Department of Health and Social Security) was that the process from analysis to action was all too slow.[237] Although ostensively Armstrong agreed with Stowe's view, progress was slow and the mould was not broken: 'I believe that we have in the last year or two greatly improved and sharpened the process of investigation, but we may all have tended to underestimate the problems of implementation ... [especially] the capacity and willingness of the machine at different levels of operation to cope with what amounts to a formidable programme of change. Central to this, I am sure, is the motivation of middle and junior management.'[238] A couple of ranks below him a new generation of emerging leaders recognised the problem and had ideas on the way to solve it. An autumn 1982 seminar for Under-Secretaries held at the Civil Service College under Stowe's chairmanship produced some surprising ideas, which in time would become mainstream thoughts, but at the time surprised the civil service leadership. Armstrong responded that 'It would require a new political initiative to promote greater delegation and devolution on the lines that the seminar evidently had in mind,' adding: 'It is clearly very much a matter for political decision how much further we should go than we already have [on openness], and how fast,' further adding – perhaps fearful of politicisation: 'I should not myself want to lose the notion of a career Civil Service, or of the Civil Service as a *carrière ouverte aux talents* – and *ouverte* right to the top.'[239]

Meanwhile, Douglas Wass reached retirement age in April 1983 to be succeeded at the Treasury by Peter Middleton, one of the new breed of mandarins. He was 49. To his great irritation Middleton was not, however, appointed joint Head of the Home Civil Service. Mrs Thatcher was heard to say that she did not want to continue with a 'Pinky and Perky solution'.[240] One of the last acts of Wass was to launch the Financial Management Initiative. Spurred on by findings in the Rayner programme that those who took the decisions that committed expenditure were too often divorced from financial accountability and responsibility for the results of the expenditure, HM Treasury responded with a programme to align financial and managerial responsibility. A crucial part of this was to delegate decisions to the lowest sensible point in the Departmental chain of command. Armstrong might have been expected to be at the centre of the reforms, but the FMI was seen by the Treasury as its preserve and he struggled to get recognition of the importance of wider general management[241] and he never quite understood the art of delegation. When, as late as 1985, a political row erupted over publication in a submission to the European Regional Development Fund of quantified forecasts of regional job shortages, Armstrong's response was wholly risk averse: 'Material which is to be published by a Department should be approved by a Minister before it is sent for publication.'[242] Nigel Wicks, who had replaced Whitmore as Principal Private Secretary, revised the draft speaking note for the Prime Minister at Cabinet: 'The important managerial point is that the responsible official (typically at Assistant Secretary level – grade 5) should be under a duty to decide whether the material is of such sensitivity for it to be referred up to a Minister ... The whole thrust of the Financial Management Initiative is to delegate responsibility down.'[243]

From the summer of 1982 over the next 12 months Thatcher came close to creating a Prime Minister's Department (PMD). Ferdinand Mount (head of the Policy Unit in No 10) recommended that the CPRS should report directly to her as a personal research department.[244] Under his proposals the Cabinet Office would have remained independent, responsible for Cabinet business and for management of the civil service, but reduced in size and its briefing for Cabinet and its committees would have been emaciated. The PMD: 'would hope to preserve ... the flexibility and the lack of 'rank-consciousness' which makes Number Ten ... an efficient and fast-moving place,' and would bring in a mixture of non-party talents. Armstrong naturally favoured strengthening the Cabinet Office, 'without major visible institutional change or upheaval' by greater use on the Prime Minister's account of the CPRS, the MPO and a unified defence and oversea policy secretariat and intelligence assessment staff. On 30 July 1982: 'The Prime Minister said that she felt very strongly the need to have a source of advice which was independent of Government departments ... Intelligence was a good example of the problem ... If she had her own source of advice in this area she would be better able to take initiatives and to follow up her reaction to intelligence assessments.'[245] This was a long way from the historical situation in which Armstrong's predecessors had made significant contributions on intelligence and it pointed to a weakness in succession planning for that role.

Armstrong was charged with developing the concept of a small new unit in 10 Downing Street to cover foreign affairs, defence and intelligence. His proposal was for a unit of three or four people in addition to the proposed special adviser, Sir Anthony Parsons, who had come to Mrs Thatcher's notice when UK Ambassador to the United Nations during the Falklands conflict. The unit would not have executive, operational or diplomatic functions and would be accompanied by reform of the Joint Intelligence Committee (JIC) to increase the element of judgement independent of the Foreign and Commonwealth Office and the Ministry of Defence. The JIC would also be charged with giving adequate warning of developing threats to British interests – with members of the assessments staff directly charged with a 'watch' responsibility in their own area.[246] The JIC terms of reference would be augmented, 'to give early warning of developing foreign threats to British interests, whether political, military or economic, and whether direct or indirect.' The chairmanship passed from the Foreign Office to the Cabinet Office in the shape of an Intelligence Co-ordinator (then Sir Anthony Duff). The changes raised questions about how well the PSIS committee reflected the needs of the customers for intelligence; and raised doubts about the interpretation of their role by successive chairmen of the JIC. But there are other interpretations of the amendment, ranging from a device to assuage the Prime Minister's irritation to an attempt to steal the thunder of the Franks report into the Falklands war. Thatcher was not fooled, commenting: 'This seems to me a change without much of a difference except the adverse one that it increases the already large number of people involved.'[247] The Foreign Secretary (Francis Pym) was, unsurprisingly, worried about his own position, pointing to, 'the dangers and disadvantages of having a National Security Council … with a Kissinger or Brzezinski-type figure …'[248] Thatcher and Pym had a fraught discussion on 15 October when she told him that she had in mind to appoint Sir Anthony on foreign affairs and someone else on defence and intelligence but, in a semantic retreat from the Armstrong suggestions, 'They would be special advisers, and could not be described as a "unit".'[249]

On 9 June 1983, Election Day, Armstrong travelled to Paris for further talks with Attali about the EEC budget issue. Attali told him that it was unlikely that a solution would be agreed at the European Council in Stuttgart later that month but that President Mitterand was anxious to reach an early settlement and would like to see the Stuttgart meeting agree a mandate indicating an agreed basis for a solution. The British now faced a choice of whether to go along with the proposals for an urgent study of the long-term solution, leaving the 1984 rebate to be discussed at a later stage in the budget process, or whether to threaten to withhold part or all of its contribution to the Community budget due at the end of June.[250] At a Ministerial meeting on 14 June Thatcher, freshly elected with an increased majority of 144 seats, concluded that Cabinet should be advised that if the Stuttgart Council did not show sufficient signs of serious intent to solve the budgetary imbalance the United Kingdom should withhold funds from the Community in July.[251] She hoped that it would not be necessary to carry out the threat but Armstrong should write to Attali immediately to put the United Kingdom's impatience on record.[252]

Armstrong did not do so – at least not on the record – but in March 1984 he again met Attali in Paris to take stock of the post-Stuttgart negotiations. He concluded that Mitterrand was looking at a deal in which the British could say they had secured a long-term arrangement that more clearly related payment to the ability to pay, with a specified duration for that understanding, and France would be prepared to be flexible on the amounts involved.[253] Meanwhile, Armstrong sought to calm tempers in Whitehall. David Williamson (Head of the Cabinet Office European Secretariat) submitted a brief for Cabinet on 22 March. He made clear that, whilst a current French and Italian block on payment of the refund due to the UK under the temporary rebate (worth around £450 million) was unjustifiable, withholding UK funds due for the Community Budget would be illegal in Community and English law and would precipitate the worst crisis since the French withdrawal from the negotiating table in 1965.[254] Again, no formal threat was made and at Cabinet on 10 May Thatcher was guardedly optimistic about a settlement before the end of June (when the French Presidency of the Community would end), referring to the possibility: '… that a further small move [on the amounts involved] could be contemplated, provided that it clinches the whole settlement.'[255] This Armstrong reported to Attali on 2 June, seemingly to the surprise of the French who had missed a hint Thatcher had sought to give to Mitterrand when they had last met.[256] Over lunch Attali, revealed that Mitterrand's sticking point was a rebate of 66⅔% of the net United Kingdom budgetary contribution[257] – Thatcher finally settled at 66% during the Fontainebleau Council of 25/26 June – an agreement that was not seriously challenged until 2004.

Translation of the Fontainebleau accord into detailed texts was laborious and not without scares but Armstrong's work was almost done, save for one contingency. The House of Commons debated the Fontainebleau agreement on 12 July and the government secured a majority of 165 (21 higher than its majority of seats despite 18 Conservative back benchers voting against the deal).[258] A week later Armstrong advised the Prime Minister that she would have to allow, at a minimum, seven to eight weeks between announcing and holding a referendum.[259] Nothing came of the possibility but it is intriguing to wonder what might have triggered even the possibility of a referendum given the large government majority in the House of Commons debate a week earlier.

Armstrong was not the lead negotiator, nor the prime influence on British Ministers, during the budgetary crisis. But in so far as the French were important to British success, Armstrong's relationship with Attali, in particular, was crucial in ensuring that the two sides understood each other's basic negotiating position. Not only did the French often take the initiative to involve Armstrong in secret diplomacy between the two countries but they appeared to value his patience and negotiating skills. In mid 1983, in a conversation between the Chancellor, Gerhard Stoltenberg (FRG) and Jacques Delors (France) Delors had spoken particularly warmly of Armstrong.[260] Armstrong himself confessed to admiring the silky sinuousness of the French: 'Jacques Attali and I always spoke together in English: he was virtually bi-lingual. I got on well with him, and there was a degree of mutual respect, trust, confidence and even friendship. Other British officials – and Ministers – distrusted him, but I never felt let down by him. Of course I knew that he would be speaking with the President's authority and as his master's voice, though I think that he was given a good deal of discretion. On this particular occasion [the lunch shortly before the Fontainebleau Council] we knew that President Mitterrand was very keen to have a successful outcome to the meeting ... I believe that [Mrs Thatcher's] object ... was to ensure that, when she had the crucial bilateral meeting with the President, she could reserve to herself the final concession to 66%, so that the President could feel that he personally had wrung the last drop out of her and there was no more to come.'[261]

Armstrong summarised the outcome as: for the United Kingdom a durable system with satisfactory budgetary relief; for the Germans some moderation of the extra amount they would have to pay and improved help for their farmers; for the French the ability to claim credit for the removal of a blockage at an affordable cost, for enabling further topics to be examined to benefit 'the citizens of Europe' and the implementation on 1 April 1985 of significant steps towards a single European market.[262] The British too were looking beyond the immediate budgetary issue to the future of the Community. Thatcher had told Chancellor Kohl of the Federal Republic of Germany at the end of February that the United Kingdom would produce a paper on the future of the Community – primarily its relationship with the outside world. The Foreign and Commonwealth Office were commissioned to prepare a draft covering the European contribution to NATO; links with democracies across the world; links with Eastern Europe; preserving and developing essential technologies; the trans-Atlantic relationship; the Community's strategic trade routes and sources of raw materials; a possible role for the Community in the Middle East. In addition, Thatcher instructed Armstrong to arrange for officials to look at the scope for British initiatives in two domestic areas: specific products or product areas in which the absence of common standards within the Community was a clear barrier to trade; obstacles to collaboration between enterprises in specific sectors of technological importance such as biotechnology and telecommunications.[263] Shortly before the Fontainebleau Council the paper promised to Chancellor Kohl, now entitled *Europe the Future*, was given to all the Community Heads of Government and circulated to the European subcommittee of OD in September.[264] Much more *communautaire* than anything previously circulated by the British Government, '... the most complete and coherent statement of European policy made by any British Government,' it signalled a commitment and a vision that, had it been given publicity in Britain itself, would have ignited informed debate and had the potential to lift the level of discussion above the mundane.[265]

Leaks Threaten Civil Service Political Neutrality

A particularly embarrassing number of leaks occurred during the 1983 General Election. In the circumstances of a General Election they were unlikely to have come from political sources and so could be assumed to come from officials. In Armstrong's view the leaks threatened the civil service's position and standing as a non-political public service: 'they represent serious disloyalty and a flagrant breach of trust and I should like, as Head of the Civil Service, to express to you my deep regrets and apologies. My sense of outrage and regret is fully shared by my fellow Permanent Secretaries ... and they would wish to be associated with what I have written.'[266] Regrets there were; but ideas for preventing a recurrence were thin on the ground. Armstrong proposed new instructions and procedures for handling the most sensitive Cabinet documents, technical developments to make individual copies of documents more traceable and an exhortatory letter to PUS colleagues drawing to their attention that it was their responsibility to counter, 'some sort of change of culture, as a result of which not only have leaks become more frequent but there has also grown up a greater readiness to overlook or condone them.' But the perpetrators of leaks continued to be elusive and difficult to prosecute. 'I am clear that we cannot allow this to go by default. It is a matter which requires positive action by all of us, each in his own way and at his own time; and it is a responsibility we cannot shirk.' Quite what happened as a result is unclear.

Privately (or so he thought) Armstrong was prompted to think aloud at an Oxford dinner table on 8 July 1983 about the mechanisms by which greater openness about the rationale for policy decisions could be achieved. A fellow guest was the journalist Hugo Young who subsequently wrote in the *Sunday Times* recounting the dinner conversation, albeit without naming Armstrong. Though he prompted Armstrong's ire,[267] Young might have been helpful in identifying a position short of a Freedom of Information Act and in publicising a constructive response to the mandarins' fear that the growth in instances of leaks was: 'spreading selective and over-excited titbits, to kill off rational discussion.'[268]

Enhanced Support for the Prime Minister

The Prime Minister replaced Francis Pym as Foreign Secretary with Geoffrey Howe, following the General Election and went ahead with personal advisers on foreign policy, defence and intelligence; her ambition to strengthen the support available in Downing Street was widely known. A leader in *The Times* on 8 June argued that: 'The test for the Prime Minister and her future chief-of-staff must be: will the remodelled office survive a change of government? Or will it be seen as an artefact of an over-mighty premier and suffer the fate of Lloyd George's "Garden Suburb" in 1922? If she returns to Downing Street on June 10, Mrs Thatcher has a chance to build something of value, not just for herself, but for the future holders of prime ministerial office.'[269] Yet four days after the election Thatcher decided that the CPRS did not have a future. It would be abolished and its Head, John Sparrow, would return prematurely to Morgan Grenfell. The Management and Personnel Office would be amalgamated with the Cabinet Office. The Rayner Unit would return to the fold – responsible to her under a successor to Derek Rayner who returned to head Marks & Spencer; Sir Robin Ibbs – ironically a former Head of the CPRS – was confirmed as his successor on 8 July.[270]

The boundary hastily drawn between the Treasury and the Cabinet Office (MPO) on the abolition of the CSD was not stable. Armstrong favoured a modest redistribution of the Treasury functions to the MPO (industrial relations, superannuation and staff inspection). Peter Middleton (PUS, HM Treasury) had more radical ideas, bidding for efficiency work (other than the Efficiency Unit itself) to be centred on his Department.[271] He raised objections to a draft White Paper about the Financial Management Initiative on the grounds that the text went beyond finance into general management.[272] Armstrong played for time citing the imminence of a Rayner scrutiny report on the government's central inspection, review and consulting capabilities (CIRC) and challenged Middleton that he was in danger of appearing to suggest that financial management was simply an instrument for limiting public expenditure.[273] Ibbs forcefully opposed the transfer of efficiency work to the Treasury on the grounds that this would inevitably lead to identification of efficiency with budget restraint. His intervention prompted an intemperate outburst from Middleton accusing Armstrong of having copied his letter to Ibbs when they had agreed to discuss things only between the two of them. But, as Armstrong explained in an apologetic response, Ibbs had been shown the letter by the Head of the Efficiency Unit not by anyone reporting directly to him.[274] Middleton then returned to the charge later in the month after the CIRC report: 'I have a minute in draft to the Prime Minister which explains that the arrangements [for efficiency work] are inefficient in themselves making value for money more difficult to achieve and certainly inhibiting the control of public expenditure as they operate at present! I have not yet got to the point of tearing this up. And pieces of work like Robin Ibbs' CIRC review which suggests that we need yet more central units to co-ordinate the Treasury and MPO don't make me feel any more inclined to do so.'[275] In the event, at a meeting chaired by Armstrong on 10 October, the Treasury argument was defeated, largely on the grounds identified by Ibbs.

Armstrong and Middleton compromised; improved co-operation between the two Departments should be sought by creating a small secretariat to support the Joint Management Board for the Civil Service covering financial and personnel management.[276] It was to be led by a high-flier from a large management Department (Valerie Strachan from HM Customs & Excise).[277] For his part, Ibbs took great care to keep Armstrong informed and on side, conscious that his independence and authority hung on that narrowest of threads, the goodwill of a Prime Minister. And in this Armstrong was a first class guide through the Whitehall jungle, warning when extension of the scrutiny technique to policy issues in central government and to the wider public sector of local government and the National Health Service was under consideration, that the Efficiency Unit would risk being over-extended and: 'It will not help if the impression is created that you want to recreate the CPRS under a different name!'[278] A careful redraft drew a clear distinction between the substance of policy and the value being delivered by its delivery. Thatcher commented: 'I am simply delighted with these proposals' reiterating that she looked to Ibbs to represent her interest in securing improvements in value for money and that he should report directly to her, seeking her personal involvement whenever he thought it necessary.[279] Avoid committing yourself to a numerical target which could become an albatross round the neck, Armstrong advised, and emphasise that value for money is to some extent a subjective criterion at least partly dependent upon a political judgement of what constitutes value.[280] When Thatcher suggested that the public sector could benefit from the prompt removal of those whose performance failed to come up to standard he sidestepped the issue of poor performance. 'What I am doing,' he reported, 'is to create space for the promotion of high-fliers through facilitating premature retirement of those who are no longer performing as well as they used to perform – which is different to the prompt removal of those whose performance fails to come up to standard, *for which considerable provision already exists.*'[281] The role of the Head of the Civil Service was, in his view, to design the engine not to drive it.

Until late 1986, Armstrong's comments on the government efficiency drive were supportive but were often akin to those of a referee, protector or a commentator rather than a participant. Reporting to Mrs Thatcher he was reassuring: 'In my view, the reforms introduced since 1979 and focusing on value for money in the public services are now solidly established in Departments ... there may now be a need to allow the new structures to settle down and produce results.'[282] But all changed when Ibbs told the Prime Minister that: 'it is time to find out what more we can do to accelerate the change in management style throughout the Service.'[283] He welcomed the suggestion of talking to Ministers and Permanent Secretaries about how to change attitudes and make sure that the changes in practices that had already been agreed were really carried through.[284] It was the conception of the *Next Steps* revolution and of what would be known a decade later as the Delivery Agenda. Executive operations of Departments would be established as 'agencies' at arm's length from Ministers and with a greater degree of managerial freedom than hitherto.[285] In January 1987, as the emerging findings became available in the Efficiency Unit, he held two meetings in quick succession with Ibbs and the iconoclastic Head of the Efficiency Unit, Kate Jenkins. At the first he listened without substantive comment as the scrutiny team spelled out their findings. At the second Ibbs spoke of: 'breaking down the monolith which inhibited managerial freedom.' Armstrong stressed the need to be practical in what was proposed and to have thought through its implications most thoroughly.[286] The emerging ideas were presented to Thatcher on the same day with much the same response. The record of the meeting says: 'The Prime Minister told you not to underestimate the enormity of what you were proposing.'[287]

Ibbs submitted the final report (which went by the bland title: *Improving Management in Government*) on 2 April.[288] Concurrently Armstrong received advice from Ken Stowe, who had been brought into the Cabinet Office shortly before retirement to conduct a review of the central management of government, which was unambiguous in its support for the Ibbs prescription. 'The great virtue of the Efficiency Unit review,' Stowe wrote: is that it recognises the constraints on the ability of civil servants to manage. 'Better policy determination should go side by side with better management of service delivery.'[289] *Next Steps* provided an opportunity to transform the relationship between the centre and the Departments without recrimination and fault-finding. His soundings of PUSs had universally resulted in the view that the Head of the Civil Service and the Cabinet Secretary should not be the same person.

'I agree with Sir Robin Ibbs that the [removal of Ministerial day-to-day oversight of executive operations] is a necessary condition, and a worthwhile price to pay, for the further improvements in management and efficiency which this [Next Steps] change will make possible,' Armstrong advised.[290] 'The Treasury are likely to be lukewarm about these recommendations, which they will see as weakening Treasury control of public expenditure: we shall have to allay those fears.' Over the next nine months three issues dominated a sometimes acrimonious debate: how Ministers would discharge their accountability to Parliament; what would be the effect on public expenditure control; and how single-mindedly the reforms should be pursued by a senior project manager visibly responsible for their implementation.[291]

Peter Middleton duly sounded a cautionary note on behalf of the Chancellor of the Exchequer who, 'would not be prepared to relax controls over the running costs element in public expenditure or pay until alternative systems were sufficiently robust,'[292] – a chicken-and-egg situation well known to Departments. HM Customs and Excise were quick off the mark to nominate the whole Department as an agency even before the Chancellor of the Exchequer had seen the report,[293] earning a sharp rebuke from Middleton: 'I therefore think that you would be unwise to take any further action on Angus Fraser's latest letter, until after the Election. And I am totally unwilling to allow anyone from the Treasury to get involved in discussing it in any form whatsoever.'[294] He had a point. Several Permanent Secretaries registered concerns about the haste with which Armstrong, egged on by Ibbs and the Efficiency Unit, was moving to get Ministerial approval.[295] On 19 June he had suggested the Prime Minister should put the recommendations straight to Cabinet. She refused. A 'small' group of Minsters (actually 14 strong) met on 9 July 1987.[296] Summing up, the Prime Minister said that before coming to decisions, Ministers needed to know how the proposals could be applied in particular instances and needed reassurance on key concerns.[297] She wanted to say as little as possible until decisions had been made.[298]

Interwoven with the debate around the creation of Executive Agencies was the continuing issue of how the centre of Whitehall should be organised. The turf squabbles between Armstrong and Middleton were signs of instability and, nearing retirement, it was natural for Armstrong to want to leave a stable legacy in this area. He invited Sir Kenneth Stowe of the Department of Health and Social Security into the Cabinet Office during the last few months of the latter's service, to review the functioning of the centre in relation to the heavy programme of efficiency work which lay ahead. Stowe's 21-page report concluded that organisation was not the issue. The missing link was a process at the centre for driving change through a slimmer and better-directed management effort. Ministerial collective responsibility was not mirrored by Departmental collective responsibility. There was too much of a mismatch between the management strategy of the centre and that of Departments. The solution was to have an advisory Management Board for the civil service which would put pressure on Departments continually to seek improvement in their management function but which would do so in sympathy with what they were striving to achieve for their Ministers. Armstrong put this forward in June 1987.[299] The Principal Private Secretary (Nigel Wicks) briefed in support of the Board (and recommended abolition of the MPO).[300] Ibbs was in favour provided that the Board had a clear role to bring pressure to bear for year-on-year improvements.[301] At a meeting on 28 July Mrs Thatcher pronounced herself not yet ready to decide finally on any of the three main issues (the future of the MPO, the proposed Advisory Board and the Next Steps project manager), instructing Armstrong to work up detailed proposals. This he did in a further submission during the first week of August.[302] However, at a further discussion with the Prime Minister on 6 August Armstrong was outgunned by the Treasury contingent: Nigel Lawson, Middleton and Butler – the meeting note makes only a passing reference to the benefits of an Advisory Board and the Prime Minister expressed herself not attracted to the concept. Neither Stowe nor Ibbs was present, nor were they sent copies of the meeting note.[303] The MPO was to be split between the Treasury and the Cabinet Office and an announcement made the following day. Its Permanent Secretary (by then Anne Mueller) would transfer to the Treasury to take charge of the civil service pay and industrial relations and the personnel functions being transferred in. A draft press notice circulated on 6 August for issue the following day was the first she knew of the changes. As to the Next Steps project manager, a decision was deferred until October – when it was finally agreed against strong Treasury opposition. The saga would continue, however, long after Armstrong had retired.

In the face of Peter Middleton's intransigence over the Next Steps initiative Armstrong found himself open to attack on all sides. Reporting to the Prime Minister in advance of a further Ministerial meeting he pointed to 12 'case studies' ranging from the Employment Service to the Queen Elizabeth II Conference Centre. Departments in general welcomed the Ibbs approach but were apprehensive (not without reason) that they would be given increased responsibilities without the means to discharge them: '... it is impossible to demonstrate that the Ibbs approach will work ... unless the Treasury is prepared to take some risks ... ' The key issue was to persuade the Treasury that Ministers would constrain their agencies to stay within the resource frameworks laid down by them.[304] He offered a 'step change' option or an evolutionary approach. Ibbs was insistent: 'merely to establish some agencies will not be enough ... If you are unable to proceed with the full approach it will be better to keep your powder dry until proper reform can be attempted at some later date,' he advised Thatcher.[305] On 22 October the majority of Ministers favoured the step change but the Chancellor resisted strongly, arguing that to do so would be imprudent and a signal to the markets that public expenditure control was being abandoned. The Prime Minister would not overrule her Chancellor, instructing Armstrong, in consultation with Departments, to produce worked-up proposals to meet his concerns.[306] The Efficiency Unit continued to press for a public announcement, their arguments falling on deaf ears. For the first time a real difference on tactics emerged between Ibbs and Armstrong. Ibbs told Armstrong that: '... the redrafting has moved so far from the position that emerged at the end of the last meeting that I should not be happy for the proposals as they now stand to be adopted ... if the "Next Steps" approach is not carried through whole-heartedly ... it would be far better not to touch it.'[307] The nub of the dispute concerned a leap into new waters or a gradual immersion, which would most likely leave existing central controls untouched and provide alibis for lukewarm commitment to delivering results. As Armstrong annotated in the margins of Ibbs' letter: 'The fact is that there is a policy difference between Robin Ibbs and the Treasury ... It remains my impression that Ministers don't want to tie themselves to a timetable or to publishing a timetable.'

And so it remained through the rest of 1987 with Ibbs continuing his vigorous advocacy: '... the decisions which are now to be taken will determine whether we achieve a breakthrough to a much better style of management in government or merely create a rather ineffective new variation within the present pattern.'[308] Official silence about the 'third-term' actions 'to enhance the ability to manage great blocks of men and money' gave the impression that the classic mandarin – 'part policy adviser, part courtier' – had prevailed over the reformers and 'HM Treasury had reproduced the status quo ante 1969.'[309] Due to retire at the end of the year, on 21 December Armstrong put to Middleton yet another version of a paper for further Ministerial discussion asking for acceptance of the proposals 'in the spirit of Christmas.' Sufficient agreement was reached at official level to enable one of Armstrong's final actions on New Year's Eve to be submission of a paper for Ministers, albeit with outstanding differences bequeathed to his successor, Sir Robin Butler – ironically coming to the post from HM Treasury where he had been in charge of public expenditure control. Ever gracious, he added a postscript to the letter to Middleton that enclosed a copy of the submission: 'My last missive to you on this letterhead! With best wishes for 1988, and with happy memories of, and much gratitude for, all we have done together.'[310]

The Anglo-Irish Agreement

During the Falklands Campaign the British Government felt that the position adopted by the Irish Government was an example of the old tensions epitomised by, 'England's difficulty is Ireland's opportunity.' Work on the Anglo-Irish Intergovernmental Council (AICC) was stopped barely a year on. But in the summer of 1983, after the November 1982 Irish General Election in which defeated Fianna Fáil and Garret Fitzgerald succeeded Charles Haughey as Taoiseach, the Irish suggested reactivating the Council and resuming work on the joint studies. Henceforth, from the British point of view, negotiation of what became the November 1985 Anglo-Irish Agreement fell into four phases: (1) surprise at the forwardness of the Irish; (2) courtship; (3) seeking parental approval; (4) day-to-day life together.

In December Thatcher told David Goodall,[311] in the margins of a discussion on the future of the Falklands, that if the Conservatives won the 1983 election she would want to do something about Northern Ireland.[312] Goodall travelled to Dublin the following September to explore how to reactivate the AIIC. It was during that first talk that his Irish opposite number (Michael Lillis)[313] proposed 'a walk by the canal' during which he put forward the Taoiseach's private thoughts (not at that stage endorsed by the Irish Government) that unification of Ireland was not realistic; it was vital to get the minority in the North to identify with the Province and this could best be achieved by granting the Republic 'joint authority' with the UK Government over law and order in the Province. In return for which articles 2 and 3 in the Irish Constitution of 1937, which referred to a unified Ireland, might be amended. (This became known in the British camp as the 'basic equation.' Though it was never expressly formulated the British team understood it to be: closer security co-operation and some form of Irish involvement in the North in return for Irish recognition of the Union – possibly including repeal of the two articles constituting the Republic's territorial claim on the North.). Lillis asked that the ideas be fed back to London.[314]

Lillis' approach and the apparent sharing of confidence by the Taoiseach took Goodall aback. British officials doubted if the Irish Government could deliver his ideas in a form that would meet British political requirements. However, Armstrong advised Thatcher not to reject the ideas out of hand, it would be better to probe the details in a non-committal manner. The process of exploration and negotiation, '... would be delicate and long drawn-out; but ... the Governments in London and Dublin can both look forward to a period of some years in office without national elections.'[315] Shortly before the November Anglo-Irish Summit Armstrong heard the Taoiseach's view, first hand, that he was seeking to use the New Ireland Forum of Irish political parties to re-educate the public about the opportunity for a new approach on Northern Ireland. What was needed was something upon which the confidence and the loyalty of the minority in the North could be focused – in the shape of law and order institutions such as special mixed courts dealing with cases of violation of human rights, criminality and subversion together with some measure of joint policing. How would Mrs Thatcher be likely to react to these ideas? Armstrong reported that he had said that the Prime Minister would not want to exclude from consideration anything that might hold out the possibility of reducing violence in the North but that with ideas as yet vague and unformed her reaction was bound to be cautious. 'Joint sovereignty' or anything that seemed likely to affect the constitutional status of Northern Ireland would not be acceptable.[316]

After the Summit, at the Prime Minister's request, he put forward a paper for discussion at a Chequers seminar early in the New Year. It included, for the sake of completeness, a number of possibilities that all the officials concerned thought politically unrealistic. In practice, he argued, the choice of a new initiative lay between three options, each with their own risks: (a) integration of Northern Ireland in the United Kingdom (described as 'j'y suis, j'y reste'); (b) a move to accommodate the concerns of the minority community in the North; (c) continuing with provisional direct rule until there was sufficient measure of agreement on the form of devolved government.[317] Ministers concluded that simply to continue direct rule with no modification would be difficult to justify in terms of the risk to the lives of British servicemen and decided to commission an illustrative package, without commitment, to put flesh on the bones of the options.[318]

The courtship phase of the negotiations lasted from the start of 1984 to March 1985 under the guidance of a sub-committee of the OD Committee. Thatcher oscillated between wanting an agreement of some kind – particularly to help with the security situation – and not wanting one at all because it would involve giving the Irish a say in the government of a part of the United Kingdom – and she hated any thought of rewarding terrorism. Those around her followed a strategy that it was better to do something than to do nothing. Armstrong's drafting skills were crucial as he mediated between Thatcher and the Taoiseach, seeking to present things in such a way that he did not get a direct rejection from either party. Goodall is full of praise: 'whenever we reached an impasse over wording, and it seemed that there was simply no form of words which would satisfy Irish requirements without going beyond what the Prime Minister would accept, Robert was able to come up with a formula which worked. His frequent written reports to the Prime Minister on the negotiations as they progressed were skilful in the same way, always truthful and yet usually managing to convey a positive flavour and avoiding turns of phrase calculated to provoke an anti-Irish explosion from Mrs Thatcher.'[319]

On 16 February 1984 Cabinet agreed to confidential talks with the Irish. Armstrong had advised that the essence of the approach was the 'basic equation' and that it would be made clear to the Irish from the outset that everything was dependent on the foundation stone of acknowledging the Union, at least for the foreseeable future.[320] There were seven Armstrong-Nally sessions during the year. Throughout, Armstrong was at pains to clear his negotiating lines with Thatcher in advance and assiduous in reporting back promptly. It was essentially a year when the British sought to manage down the expectations of the Irish over how much they might share in the running of the North. He reported that the Irish side had taken on board the importance of movement on their 'territorial claims' on Northern Ireland.[321] Meanwhile the report of the New Ireland Forum was expected in April. When the Taoiseach sent Thatcher an early copy of the report the British reactions were that it disappointed.[322] They recognised the political importance in the Republic of a report that had the support of all the Irish political parties and the SDLP in the North (who were kept closely informed by the Irish). But initial British reactions were that the general tenor was strongly nationalist and did not face up to the Unionist objection in principle to a United Ireland.[323] The Irish thought that the British position was too heavily focused on security. 'My judgement,' said Armstrong, 'is that some sort of Irish involvement at political (not just administrative or security) level is an indispensable condition for the Irish Government.'[324]

Despite the misgivings negotiations continued and Armstrong reported in mid July that: 'The Irish side took on board the fact that joint authority was not on offer and that they must concentrate their minds on possible consultative arrangements combined with the establishment of a devolved government in Northern Ireland ... We have moved the dialogue on to a more realistic basis.'[325] Mrs Thatcher was being coaxed along. Charles Powell wrote several times to Armstrong to slow matters down.[326] Comments ranged from, 'glad you stressed any Irish role will be consultative,' to 'the Prime Minister thinks the pace is being forced too quickly for the Unionists,' and 'your draft letter to the Taoiseach is too apologetic.' But in the wake of the IRA bomb attack on the Prime Minister in Brighton on 12 October and a visit to Dublin by the new Secretary of State for Northern Ireland (Douglas Hurd) during which he had been noticeably firm on the constitutional position of the Province, the Irish feared an imminent breakdown of the talks. Armstrong speculated that: (a) all parties looked to the British Government to pull the irons out of the fire – the Republic had less to lose than the British from being seen to have tried and failed; the Unionists were sitting pretty playing political games behind the absolute shelter of the guarantee [of no change in constitutional status without the consent of the majority population]; (b) Northern Ireland Office (NIO) officials (but not necessarily the Secretary of State) thought the talks precluded any advance on devolution. The Irish Government saw devolution as a counterpart that would reassure the Unionists; (c) it might be that the window of opportunity for a bolder approach was closing.[327]

For the Irish Government a proposed constitutional amendment would be an enormous political risk, against which mere consultation on the affairs of Northern Ireland would not be sufficient makeweight. To the British, looking at the issues with orange-rimmed spectacles, amendment of the Irish Constitution would be mere recognition of reality and it would then be an enormous step to admit the Irish Government to a formal role in decision making about Northern Ireland. Both were right – the trouble was both were looking in different directions.[328] At the next Anglo-Irish Summit in November 1984 (which the Tsaoiseach had agreed should be at Chequers instead of Dublin, out of consideration for Mrs Thatcher) the Prime Minister warned FitzGerald that none of the options in the New Ireland Forum Report (a unitary state, a federal/confederal state or a joint authority) were acceptable to the British; and at her press conference, when asked whether the British Government had ruled out the three models in the New Irish Forum Report she caused great offence to the Irish by the vehemence with which she publicly dismissed them: 'That's Out ... That's Out ... That's Out,' she said – dealing a profound political and personal setback to the Taoiseach which a subsequent emollient letter only partially countered. But as David Goodall later commented, this setback may inadvertently have saved the talks by forcing each side to realise the limits of what was politically feasible for the other.[329] Thus, 1984 ended with far greater clarity about the respective governmental positions but with the talks hanging by a thread.

Thatcher doubted whether the two governments would find a way forward.[330] Armstrong confided to Robert Andrew – by now Permanent Secretary at the Northern Ireland Office – that new thinking was needed, on which he would spend some time over the turn of the year. On 11 January he delivered a 24-page analysis and two options for future negotiations – one confined to limited consultation on security and legal co-operation (unlikely in his view to persuade the Irish to amend their constitution) and one based on a wider consultative approach with the Republic that it would be difficult to get the Unionists to accept. He favoured the second option; the Prime Minister the first. Nally and his team reacted with a mixture of relief and disappointment; relief that the British had put something authoritative on the table that would justify further negotiation; disappointment that it was too narrowly based to meet Irish requirements. There was no mention of an Irish quid pro quo. Both sides seemed to recognise that the discussions should now move from exploration to hard bargaining.

The intensity of work increased – Armstrong was involved in 53 meetings associated with the negotiations during 1985. He met Nally 17 times before the Agreement was signed on 15 November. The first British action was to create the machinery to achieve collective Ministerial endorsement of whatever texts might emerge from the Armstrong-Nally teams. A sub-committee of the OD Committee was set up, OD(I) under the Prime Minister's chairmanship: 'to keep under review the United Kingdom's relations with the Republic of Ireland, particularly in the context of Her Majesty's Government's policies in Northern Ireland.' This greatly increased the number of Ministers involved in the Irish negotiations.[331] The parameters for Armstrong's negotiations were reset: only cross-border (as distinct from internal) economic and social issues would be within the remit of the proposed joint body; that body must be clearly seen to be consultative and nothing more; in return for which the British would look to the Irish Government's recognition that the constitutional position of the North could not be changed without consent; and the SDLP must be ready to play a part in moves towards devolution in the Province.

Armstrong dug in to defend the negotiations – standing up to Thatcher – the very minimum required to keep the negotiations going was a text that was explicit about the seriousness with which the Irish Government's views would be taken and the British should avoid rubbing Irish noses in the fact that Her Majesty's Government retained the sole executive power in Northern Ireland. Otherwise the Irish would break off the talks, would blame the British for the rupture and accuse them of bad faith in going back on the earlier British proposals at the Anglo-Irish Summit.[332] On the plus side, the agreement would be formal and binding on the two sovereign governments, registered with the United Nations, and would be the first time that the Irish Government was formally committed to the principle of consent and to recognition that the majority in Northern Ireland wished to remain part of the United Kingdom. Further, Armstrong resisted instructions from OD(I) to draft clauses enabling the British to renege on the agreement without bringing down the Irish recognition of the constitutional position of Northern Ireland. He pointed out that to do so would be seen as a wrecking tactic and, in the event that suspension of the agreement was necessary, the lack of provision in the text would be the least of the worries.

The Whitehall machine was fired up, particularly the Attorney General's office on the possibility of joint courts. Clive Whitmore at the Ministry of Defence was asked to examine what could be done to make visible changes on the ground affecting the UDR.[333] By late June the chances of reaching an agreement were finely balanced.[334] Both governments were keen, however, to demonstrate that any agreement would be operative from day one, with the announcement of an early meeting of the new Intergovernmental Conference and an agenda for the discussion, including measures to build confidence in the agreement. Armstrong showed immense perseverance and stamina for redrafting and fine-tuning the language as well as for interpreting nuances in the presentation of British ideas to both his political masters and to the Irish negotiators. He was no doubt encouraged in this by his close dealings with Nally, both having immense personal capital invested in the talks and both of the view that, despite the outstanding thorny issues an agreement was within their grasp. [335] When the Irish observed, not unreasonably, that the reshuffle of British Ministers in early September, which had seen Douglas Hurd replaced by Tom King, gave them pause for thought he found just the right words to provide comfort to the Irish without antagonising the Prime Minister: 'I said that your personal commitment to securing a worthwhile Anglo-Irish agreement had not changed …'[336] Tom King minuted the Prime Minister on 27 September arguing that the whole process should be slowed down. Thatcher, meanwhile, saw an Irish decision to withdraw their commitment to accede to the European Convention on the Suppression of Terrorism as a seriously retrograde step[337] yet authorised the continuation of the Armstrong-Nally dialogue pending Ministerial discussion of the minute from Tom King. Armstrong chided officials in the NIO for creating an impression that if agreement were reached they would try to stop it working properly.[338]

In these final days, before the two governments had to decide whether to accept or reject the negotiated agreement as a whole, Armstrong's drafting skills enabled officials to navigate a course between the differences of view: for example, Irish Ministers wanted the scope of the agreement described as, 'concerned with relations between the two parts of Ireland;' British Ministers wanted, 'concerned with relations between the Republic of Ireland and Northern Ireland.' Armstrong and Nally settled on, 'concerned with relations between the two parts of *the island* of Ireland' [emphasis added] – thereby ensuring that the reference was geographical rather than political.[339] Armstrong also provided subtle words for the Prime Minister to answer likely Unionist probing over the extent to which the British were ceding influence in Northern Ireland to the Republic.[340] The British Cabinet meeting when a final decision would be taken whether to sign the agreement was fixed for 31 October with Armstrong stressing that in public presentation a joint Anglo-Irish press release would reduce the risk of the two governments diverging seriously but that it was also essential for the Prime Minister's personal authority to be invested in the Agreement from the start. The Irish Government took a final decision to go ahead on 12 November and the British Cabinet did so two days later and the Agreement was signed on 15

November followed by a joint press conference by Thatcher and FitzGerald at Hillsborough Castle.

There was widespread international praise and support but the domestic scene was less welcoming. Armstrong continued to be involved as the government responded uncompromisingly to Unionist grievances that the Agreement had been negotiated over their heads. He alerted Ministers to a possible need for rapid ad hoc meetings at short notice, 'to work hardly less quickly and flexibly than we did during the South Atlantic War.'[341] He attended a meeting of the Liaison Committee of Catholic Bishops to seek their support in encouraging church members to give the Agreement a chance to work. (And in an aside, when Edward Heath issued a statement that the Hillsborough accord was nothing new since the Sunningdale Agreement of 1973, though a close friend of Heath, he commented: 'Anything you can do I can do better; I can do anything better than you.')[342]

When he next met Dermot Nally, however, on 7 December – shortly before the first meeting of the Intergovernmental Conference was due to take place in Stormont Castle – there was a note of pessimism in his assessment of the Unionist reactions: 'The Unionist Parties were united and there was little sign of a voice of moderation.' The Cabinet Office also watched with some alarm as the NIO withdrew into a policy bunker, declining to share policy-making and information with other Departments.[343] And at a round-up meeting of senior officials at Christmas the signs were bad – Robert Andrew had been publicly denounced in Belfast as a traitor and judged that those principally involved in promoting the Agreement were at some personal risk; 49 out of 50 callers to the Secretary of State in a 'phone-in' had been hostile. 100,000 people had demonstrated outside Belfast City Hall against the Agreement; 90% of Harland & Wolff workers had walked out. Even SDLP support had not been forthcoming.

Senior Whitehall officials tended to think that the NIO needed a transfusion of senior policy talent[344] but, as Robert Andrew pointed out, all outsiders to Belfast were fast becoming seen as potential traitors. The obvious interpretation was of political hostility to the Agreement; what was less clear was how ordinary Belfast residents felt in the privacy of their own hearts and minds. In mid January 1986 Armstrong was sent a copy of an assessment by Dervla Murphy, the Irish travel writer, who had returned to Belfast for an intensive seven days to assess the mood: there was a growing divide between the politicians and non-politicians on both sides. 'Why can't the politicians shut up and stop messing and leave us to make the best of it the way it is? We were picking up the pieces ... The Loyalist working-class are the real victims, with no self-respect left ... I've never before been so conscious of the built-in compulsion to surrender to intimidation. There is a muddled embryonic feeling amongst both [Orange and Green] that they have been betrayed.'[345] The only strategy was to resist infection by the mood of doom and gloom and to play for the long term. As Armstrong reported from the annual conference of the British-Irish Association held in Oxford in January 1986: '... the Government must above all make it clear that the Agreement could not be moved or destroyed. The unionist politicians remember that they destroyed Sunningdale, but they are not convinced that they can succeed again this time.'[346]

Armstrong continued to meet Nally and the Taoiseach, reporting in June 1986 that the Irish felt they had delivered their side of the bargain but the British Government still had some way to go in delivering theirs.[347] In a conversation with the Taoiseach at the start of October Armstrong was advised that the Irish would proceed towards ratification of the European Convention on the Suppression of Terrorism (which would make extradition for alleged terrorist offences possible) but needed a quid pro quo on mixed courts from the British. The window of opportunity was narrowing.[348] In the event, the British felt unable to move on mixed courts [and the Irish ratification went ahead on an unconditional basis] but when the Irish General Election came in February 1987 Garret Fitzgerald and Fine Gael suffered a defeat (arguably on domestic economic policies rather than the Agreement).

The Agreement survived because it was an inter-governmental agreement and, thus, could only be broken if one of the governments walked away from it – which they never did. Historically it was a small but significant step which pointed to a willingness of Unionists and nationalists to cooperate in running the Province and, hence, towards later agreements – the Downing Street Declaration of 1993, the Good Friday Agreement of 1998 and eventually the St Andrews Agreement of 2006. It introduced for the first time an 'Irish dimension' into the government of Northern Ireland by giving the Irish Government a consultative role there; and from that developed the mutual confidence and understanding between the British and Irish Governments which made the subsequent agreements possible. Armstrong's commitment to securing a deal and his role in so doing cannot be overestimated. Thatcher's trust in him was vital. It had been built up over three years by the time of the Taoiseach's initiative – things might have been different if the timing had been earlier when Thatcher was cautious about Armstrong's enduring closeness to Edward Heath. Even the Harrods bomb just before Christmas in 1983 and the Brighton bomb in 1984 did not stop the talks continuing though they did cause Mrs Thatcher to pause over whether to continue.[349]

Why were both sides so committed to the negotiations? Partly this was because both feared the instability of a political vacuum; partly because of the relationship Armstrong and his team established with the Irish negotiators. Garrett Fitzgerald said of Armstrong: 'a man for whose ability, diplomatic skill and constructive approach to Anglo-Irish relations and to the Northern Ireland problem I came to have deep respect.'[350] He also said of David Goodall: 'David Goodall's interest in Ireland was not merely professional: he himself came from a Co. Wexford family, and one of his ancestors had been a member of the Irish Parliament who in the middle of the eighteenth century had been actively involved in one of the earliest challenges from within the Anglo-Irish community to the Dublin castle establishment. Despite marked differences of temperament, Michael Lillis and he struck up a warm friendship, which proved of major importance to the negotiation we were seeking to initiate.'[351] The routine of European Community meetings also contributed significantly to the process as the Prime Minister and the Taoiseach were often able to have informal exchanges in the margins of its meetings to close 'the factory of grievances.'[352] It is difficult to disentangle intellect and emotion in Armstrong's approach but he was wholly committed to the negotiation. In an unpublished doctoral thesis by Martin O'Brien on 'Margaret Thatcher and Northern Ireland', written in 1993, Armstrong is quoted as saying that he was: 'motivated by a desire to make amends for Britain's ill-treatment of Ireland down the centuries'.[353] His contemporaries on the Anglo-Irish negotiations saw a new Armstrong: 'his style in the talks showed that the negotiation was particularly close to his heart in a way that I never saw in his handling of any other subject ... Robert wanted to make a difference on an immensely complex subject which had brought terrorism and suffering to the United Kingdom. He coaxed a conservative Prime Minister to do something that seemed contrary to her instincts and those of much of her party. His care and tenacity in keeping the negotiations in being and helping both sides to adjust their expectations might have been beyond the skills of almost any other official in my time.'[354]

GCHQ – *Cause Célèbre*

During the 1981 Civil Service strike one of the targets selected for selective industrial action was the secret Government Communications Headquarters (GCHQ). On 9 March 1,971 GCHQ staff supported a one-day strike, followed by various forms of industrial action until 14 April.[355] It was a calamitous mistake. During the strike the union claims included 'our ultimate success depends upon the extent to which ... defence readiness is hampered ... by this and further action,' and, '48 hours of walkouts have severely hit secret monitoring stations ... The Government will be subjected to huge pressure from NATO allies.'[356] An informal approach by the Civil Service Department to national union officials, requesting that specific operations at GCHQ should not be disrupted, was refused.[357] Furthermore, GCHQ had a mixed industrial relations record – over 2,000 staff had struck in February 1979 and between then and April 1981 over 10,000 working days had been lost to industrial action, often in key areas of operation.[358]

Anglo-American intelligence relations had been threatened by the break in service due to industrial action – the more so because the electronic intelligence capabilities of the two countries were inextricably intertwined with the British contribution arguably the most valuable component received by the Americans from the special relationship. GCHQ management had recommended in 1982 that national trades unions should be banned:[359] 'The Director, GCHQ,[360] thinks that relations between management and staff at GCHQ would be improved, and the risks of GCHQ being caught up in industrial action by the Civil Service and thereby obliged to interrupt its service and default on its commitments to the United States intelligence agencies, would be much reduced, by the proposals for depriving GCHQ staff of the protection of the Employment Protection legislation and debarring them from membership of national unions.'[361] Not all members of PSIS had been convinced; Armstrong warned of likely strong union reaction and possible industrial action but advised that the Director judged the latter would be patchy and short-lived, defensible as the price of desirable change. However, Ministers had concluded: '... on balance that avowal of GCHQ as an intelligence agency and the use of such avowal to debar staff from trade union membership was not the course to take.'[362]

No further action was taken until after the avowal of GCHQ in May 1983, following the conviction of one of its staff, Geoffrey Prime, for espionage Prime. Thatcher asked for a re-examination of the possibility of banning national unions. In a long submission of September 1983, after discussion at PSIS, Armstrong rehearsed the arguments once more. He noted increased militancy in civil service unions that could exploit GCHQ vulnerability to selective industrial action. Moreover, the Employment Protection legislation gave employees access to industrial tribunals, where public interest immunity would need to be claimed to avoid disclosure of sensitive documents. He rejected a 'no disruption' agreement as potentially costly and providing no absolute guarantee (though later he would change his mind); he also advised that to withdraw negotiating rights from national unions in favour of a 'house union' would not remove the individual's ability to join a national union. The best way forward was a Ministerial certificate of exemption from the Employment Protection (Consolidation) Act, 1978.[363] This would remove the employees' rights to union membership and to challenge management decisions at industrial tribunal, together with immediate revised conditions of service. Amongst these could be the tighter security arrangements recommended by the Security Commission, which included a trial of the polygraph during vetting and was strongly opposed by all the Civil Service Unions. In a fateful comment he also relayed employment lawyers' advice that to avoid an employee resigning and claiming constructive dismissal it was important that a Ministerial directive should be issued before any announcement of the government's intentions either to Parliament or to GCHQ staff. Later, this counter-intuitive action was justified by reference to the attention that a prior announcement would have drawn to the vulnerability of GCHQ to those who had shown themselves ready to organise disruption.[364] The decision would prove to be inflammatory and would look high-handed.

Once again the judgement of management at GCHQ was that local disruption would soon ebb away – indeed they thought that many staff would welcome the respite from union pressure that a ban would bring – but that a one-off payment of £1,000 per head was needed to compensate employees for the loss of their rights. Armstrong concluded it was unlikely that prompt action would bring more than a limited and short-lived supportive revolt outside GCHQ. Delay would risk linking the union issue with the introduction of legislation to govern interception. His worries were focused on the transfer of GCHQ staff and operational funding to the Secret Vote, which would be more than doubled and would increase pressure for Parliamentary scrutiny. 'Despite the difficulties, the case for de-unionising GCHQ remains strong. The probability is that, unless it is achieved, the disruption experienced in recent years will be repeated.'[365]

The case for de-unionisation was further strengthened by legal advice that neither the polygraph pilot nor random exit searches of bags, as recommended by the Security Commission, could be effective without the individual's consent unless staff terms and conditions were amended – probably unilaterally – exposing management to allegations of constructive dismissal. By December 1983, opposition to the introduction of polygraph tests during vetting procedures had greatly worsened the prospect of securing de-unionisation without cash compensation; the key question was whether the judgement of GCHQ managers about staff attitudes was still valid. At a meeting on 22 December Ministers decided to go ahead immediately after the Christmas/New Year break with the exemption certificate, to notify GCHQ staff in mid to late January and to tell the General Secretary of the TUC and the leaders of the civil service unions an hour or so before the staff. The polygraph pilot would, however, be delayed so as to distance the two issues. Accordingly, the Foreign Secretary made a Parliamentary statement on 25 January announcing the changes at GCHQ; Armstrong saw the civil service unions at 3.00 pm the same day, reading over to them the statement to be made by the Foreign Secretary at 3.30 pm. 'The union representatives expressed outrage both at the substance of the proposals and at the manner of conveying them.'[366] A government argument that it was logical to put GCHQ on the same basis as the two other intelligence agencies (where staff were not allowed to belong to a national trades union) was rejected. GCHQ employees were civil servants whereas employees of MI5 and MI6 were Crown servants. The £1,000 compensation was roundly condemned as a bribe. Cabinet was not told formally until the following day.[367]

The civil service unions repeated their shock in a strongly worded letter to the Prime Minister, asking for an urgent meeting with her.[368] Within four days the unions were back with Armstrong. Armstrong reported that the Council of Civil Service Unions (CCSU): 'wished me to know, and to tell you before Wednesday's meeting, that the Civil Service unions were ready and willing to meet the Government on all these points ... ' – i.e. the removal of access to industrial tribunals, minimising the role of full-time union officials in GCHQ affairs, the need to ensure uninterrupted service in GCHQ '... for the trade unions, the crucial factor is the right to be a member of a trade union, and that the Civil Service unions would be prepared to agree to almost anything for which the Government might ask in pursuit of its objectives for GCHQ, provided that that right was preserved.'[369] Political sources on both sides of the House of Commons provided corroborating evidence that this judgement was correct.[370] Armstrong sought a compromise, advising Thatcher to tell the unions: 'But if you believe it is possible fully to meet [the Government's] objectives without withdrawing the right to membership of the national trade unions, we shall be ready to listen.' Robin Butler and the Press Secretary (Bernard Ingham) strongly advised against this – 2,000 staff had already signed up to the new conditions and any sign of weakening would stop the momentum; if she were to stand firm she would win. 'If you are not resolute about this, it will be taken as proof positive that you are not as resolute in your second Administration as you were in your first.'[371]

Armstrong met the unions two days after they had seen the Prime Minister. He left them with the thought that he could seek instructions only on the basis of detailed proposals from them.[372]

Meanwhile, the House of Commons Select Committee on Employment entered the fray. A draft speaking note for the Foreign Secretary to use at the Committee contained a potentially explosive sentence: 'This is not 'union bashing' for the sake of it,' prompting an anonymous member of Armstrong's private office to scribble in the margin, 'So it is union bashing. 3 cheers for the Trades Union Bill!!!' Many civil servants shared similar views. Armstrong reported widespread interpretation of the union ban as a threat to the long-standing principles of 'Whitleyism' that had been the bedrock of industrial relations in the civil service since 1919: '... a number of my Permanent Secretary colleagues have reported to me their surprise at the strength of reaction in their Departments.'[373] Several Departmental staff sides drew up petitions against the action, including in the Treasury that read: 'We are deeply concerned by the ban on trade unions at GCHQ. We do not accept that trade union membership is incompatible with proper concern for national security. We consider that the staff at GCHQ have been treated in an unsatisfactory and authoritarian manner.' The petition was signed by 70 senior people (including Gus O'Donnell, a future Cabinet Secretary, and two others who would later become Permanent Secretaries).

The CCSU submitted proposals to the Employment Select Committee, which Armstrong viewed cautiously, arguing that there was not enough detail to form a proper judgement. Nevertheless: 'The general tone of the note, and particularly of its last paragraph, confirms their extreme desire to preserve the right of national union membership for GCHQ, at almost any cost.'[374] There were reports of a split in the Cabinet; Thatcher was dismissive: 'We have more than enough to do without adding an extra discussion.'[375] But the public relations battle was fast being lost. *The Daily Mail* reported on 9 February that a survey had found that more than three quarters of the public thought that the government had mishandled the GCHQ union ban. *The Guardian* thought that resistance at GCHQ could force the government to rethink. *The Daily Telegraph* reported that Lord Bancroft criticised the ban as 'insensitive and ill-thought through.' It was certainly impeding other business. On 16 February Ministers were forced to concede that the experimental polygraph scheme: 'should not be extended to senior staff at GCHQ until there could be confidence that it would not distract them from dealing with the present problems over de-unionisation.'[376]

February 1984 was the decisive month. The Prime Minister held seven meetings on GCHQ during the month, including two with the CCSU. The unions tabled a draft Whitley Council agreement, which they claimed would achieve the substantive government objectives without a need to ban national unions: removal of the right of access to industrial tribunal; amendment of the conditions of service for GCHQ staff to require that there would be no interference in GCHQ's activities and operations by industrial disruption; negotiations on Departmental issues must be carried out by Departmental staff representatives answerable to the staff of GCHQ and no one else; the maintenance of GCHQ's service must not be put at risk by any conflict of loyalty of the staff.[377] Back-bench government supporters were reputed to favour an arrangement on the lines of the Army 'union card in the back pocket, 'which gave no recognition or negotiating rights but allowed soldiers to join a national union.' Armstrong's final assessment was delivered on 17 February, in a lengthy and balanced appraisal, which started with praise for what had already been achieved: 'It is clear that the unions are prepared to go ... certainly a great deal further than they would have gone if the Government had not acted as it did on 25 January.'[378] An offer of 'no disruption' to GCHQ activity was on the table but the fundamental sticking point remained the proposal that unions should be completely excluded from recognition and that staff representation should be entirely in the hands of a departmental staff association. 'They have some justice in claiming that their requirements are the cardinal principles of 'Whitleyism'' Armstrong advised. The union officials with whom he was dealing were relatively moderate men who heartedly wished that the attempt to cause disruption at GCHQ in 1981 had not happened. Maybe the only safe GCHQ would be one without unions, but there was a case for giving the unions a chance to prove themselves. The management's view at GCHQ remained that the great majority of staff would accept the offer – rejections might be up to 2% of staff, at 7% the effect would be serious but not disastrous.[379] But smaller losses in specialist areas would be especially difficult. Management was also of the view that any sign of weakening by the government would further undermine morale and make their role more difficult.

The final decision was taken on 21 February with the Prime Minister in the chair. The note of the meeting refers to general agreement that there was no basis for negotiation with the unions (which may indicate that the decision was not unanimous). The government position remained that GCHQ should be put on all fours with MI5 and MI6. It could not be right that staff in such important and sensitive areas of national security should be exposed to conflicts of loyalty. For them the maintenance of GCHQ's operations must come an unquestioned first. Geoffrey Howe would later claim that Thatcher showed an inability to accept the parallel legitimacy of someone else's loyalty. A citizen could not be allowed to carry more than one card in his pocket.[380]

By 1 March over 90% of staff had accepted the new terms[381] and by the middle of the month this had risen to 98 per cent. But the battle continued to be fought through judicial review (which found against the government on the lack of consultation but in favour of it on all other grounds), the Court of Appeal (unanimous in favour of the government on all counts), the House of Lords (unanimous in favour of the government, largely because of the 1981 behaviour of the unions),[382] the International Labour Organisation (which found the United Kingdom not to be in breach of Convention 87)[383] and the European Commission of Human Rights which ruled on 20 January 1987 that the union evidence was inadmissible.[384] The uncertainty undoubtedly damaged morale at GCHQ and delayed management action to deal with the hard core of at least 30 recusants. It also delayed setting up the GCHQ staff association, prevented the extension of the polygraph experiment to GCHQ and fed trades union outrage, leading to the repudiation by the annual Conferences of the two larger civil service unions of the CCSU proposal for 'no disruption' agreements. Peter Jones, General Secretary of the CCSU, wrote to Armstrong: 'We do not accept ... that the decision in the Lords disposes of the issue in any way ... '[385] Staff wastage at GCHQ in the first six months of 1984/85 was as high as in the whole of 1983/84 and recruitment was down by about 15%. Paradoxically, when the new Staff Regulations were promulgated they contained provision for staff to join a national trades union with the prior and continuing consent of management *in connection with any outside activity*. Thatcher demanded an explanation. It had to be explained that with so many staff it was inevitable that some would have spare-time activities that required a union card, such as musicians or teachers at evening classes. Meanwhile, Marychurch reported that management's task had been considerably eased by the changes: '... problems which had previously taken months to solve were now being dealt with in days ... The Staff Federation ... was now the largest single representative body in GCHQ history.'[386] (How much of this improvement was due to a reduction of demarcation disputes following unified grading – which the unions opposed – and how much was down to the advantages brought by site negotiation is not clear.)

But there was a price to pay in paralysis over the recommendations of the Security Commission. On 12 May 1983 the Prime Minister told Parliament that the government accepted the Commission's recommendations and would implement them as quickly as possible. Senior American intelligence officials, meanwhile, indicated that the government's resolve had been noted; the Prime case had left no ripples in their confidence in the United Kingdom intelligence agencies.[387] Some of the Commission's recommendations were judged to fall within the framework of existing security systems: a wider use of random searches of staff leaving government buildings where substantial quantities of highly classified material were handled; greater emphasis on the responsibility of line managers for security supervision; access, with the individual's consent, to medical records. Others were new: more rigorous Positive Vetting for staff in intelligence agencies; consideration of introducing psychological testing as part of the recruitment process; interviews during the vetting process with a wider group of witnesses than the nominated referees; a pilot scheme to test the feasibility of polygraph security screening in the agencies. Staff and the CCSU were particularly opposed to the polygraph experiment. As Armstrong reminded the Prime Minister, however: 'There is no doubt that [the United States officials] have come to believe in the efficiency of the polygraph as a tool of security vetting investigation.'[388] The polygraph trial started with 200 tests in the Security Service and a small number of volunteer senior staff at GCHQ. The intention was to extend the tests to less senior staff selected randomly at Cheltenham. Less than a month after the Foreign Secretary announced the de-unionisation policy Ministers decided that such an extension of the pilot scheme would be too distracting for GCHQ management.[389] The Employment Select Committee made clear its misgivings about the use of the polygraph generally but conceded possible overriding considerations of national security and Armstrong told Peter Jones that he could not advise abandoning the scheme.[390] Nevertheless, Ministers were not ready to move forward on it and decided on a further deferral in August 1985. By March 1986 the position had hardly changed but was needed for the training of testers at GCHQ if the option of starting the pilot there in January 1987 was to be kept open. Approval for training was forthcoming though the Foreign Secretary went on record that he did not see a case for proceeding with the experiment; Thatcher annotated the submission: 'I see little point in going ahead with this scheme. It seems more and more doubtful to see the polygraph having useful value.'[391] And later, she expressed doubts that Ministers would in the end sanction use of the polygraph so what was the point of the experiment. The trouble was that the experiment in the Security Service had generated a *prime facie* but temporary conclusion that the polygraph was of value in security screening. 'I share an instinctive aversion to the polygraph,' Armstrong told her, but '... the difficulty is to find arguments for abandoning the experimental scheme at this stage.'[392] In June it was agreed that staff would be told that preparations were being set in hand for the GCHQ pilot though no starting date had been decided. Further independent research into the validity of the technique in the form of a literature review was being commissioned from Dr Levey of the Medical Research Council. It took until May 1988 for this work to be completed when Armstrong's successor, Robin Butler, reported that on the basis of the findings senior officials from the intelligence agencies had reluctantly concluded that the GCHQ pilot was not worth pursuing. On the basis of this report the Thatcher finally killed off all prospects of implementing the Security Commission's recommendation.[393]

As to the recommendation about exit searches, GCHQ management's heart appeared not to be in it. Initially their proposals were so lacking in grip that an exasperated Armstrong exploded in response to Tovey's advice that the restricted number of exits and volume of staff leaving the complex would rule out effective random searching.[394] This response contrasted with the 'wily-ness' of Clive Whitmore who appeared willing to surmount obstacles in the way of the application of exit searches for military and civilian staff at the MOD. However, the practical problem at GCHQ was that there was only one exit for cars from the Oakley site, which at that time had no car searching area. Hence, to stop a car would create a massive hold-up. At the MOD, by contrast, what looked to be compliance with the recommendation did not translate into a noticeable change – one senior MOD official commenting: 'The MOD did not introduce random exit searches, or at least if they did they were quickly scaled down to the point of invisibility to this member of the MOD at the time!'[395] As late as June 1987 the Director GCHQ was complaining that the layout of the buildings bedevilled exit searches and a report by the Cabinet Office Head of Security (Rex Davie) pointed to further weaknesses. What had started out in 1983 as a measure against the removal of paper files had, by 1987, become outdated with the risk having shifted to the removal of computer disks. Seeking to reassure, GCHQ had originally proposed to advise staff that there would be no searches of items such as raincoat pockets and no body searches. Their revised proposals now said that car searches would include glove compartments etc. but that it was not proposed to include coat pockets.

The Miners' Strike

The government defeat of the year-long miners' strike in March 1985 was a defining moment. It had started in early March 1984 when the National Coal Board announced a pit closure programme and was challenged by the National Union of Mineworkers. Mindful of the 1974 Heath Government defeat by the miners and the earlier dispute when Thatcher had concluded that the government could not win a battle given the state of coal stockpiles at the power stations, this was an expected showdown. Though the Cabinet was kept informed, the real work on handling the dispute was run from MISC 101,[396] chaired by the Prime Minister and serviced by the Cabinet Office – notably Armstrong and Peter Gregson. Throughout, Armstrong sought to protect the freedom of action for MISC 101 by dampening down any thoughts of Cabinet taking control.[397] Nor was this a suitable case for the Contingencies Unit, which 'is concerned with situations threatening the "essentials of life", and is primarily an organisation for planning and co-ordinating responses on the ground.'[398] By May, however, the Cabinet sessions were clearly set up as opportunities for updating colleagues – partly because of the developing flux of events for which MISC 101 was more readily suited by the nature of its size and composition. But these were not cursory briefings; to illustrate: on 9 May Armstrong suggested structuring the oral updates as: Secretary of State for Energy – numbers working; likely developments after a NUM National Executive Committee scheduled for 10 May; Home Secretary – Law and order situation; financing the costs of policing; Secretary of State for Scotland – situation at Ravenscraig steel works; stopping Strathclyde pickets before they could assemble in large numbers; Scottish TUC day of action in support of the miners; Secretary of State for Trade & Industry – Ravenscraig; other problems for British Steel and the coal-burning industry; Secretary of State for Transport – coal movement; support by the railwaymen for the miners. By contrast, on 27 June he ruled out discussion at Cabinet of a possible civil action in the courts by British Steel, suggesting diverting Cabinet discussion on to how to improve communications in relation to getting the miners back to work and explaining to the public what was at stake and why it was necessary to stand firm.[399] It is possible that the briefing he gave Thatcher in July 1984 on the processes and timing required for a referendum was against the possibility of using it to bring public opinion to bear on the parties to the miners' strike without having to go to a General Election. However, finally, almost a year later a brief of 6 March 1985 starts: 'You will wish to record the Cabinet's congratulations to the Secretary of State for Energy on the conclusion of the dispute,' any emerging complications in connection with the ending of the strike would be swept up in a meeting of MISC 101 the following week.

Duty and Matters of Conscience

Armstrong had the misfortune to be Cabinet Secretary when established norms relating to officials' duty to protect the confidentiality of official information came under increasing pressure. Not immediately; shortly after the Provisional IRA murdered Earl Mountbatten in 1979 Armstrong was told that Mountbatten had left a memoir in the shape of six television programmes to be shown as soon as possible after his death.[400] The material had been shot in 1971 and belonged to the Broadlands Archives under an unusually privileged arrangement whereby Mountbatten had been permitted to retain official documents relevant to his war and peacetime roles. Under the terms of this agreement the Trustees of the Archive ceded power to the Cabinet Secretary to require amendments or omissions in the public interest before release of the documents. The Broadlands Trustees were understood to have contracted with the BBC for transmission. Accordingly, Lord Brabourne (Mountbatten's son-in-law) had sent the scripts to Armstrong who judged that the assertions and revelations in the programmes breached professional and private confidences. They were inaccurate and unfair to others involved: 'an abuse of Lord Mountbatten's special relationships which we should have put to Lord Mountbatten himself, had he been alive.'[401]

Armstrong's dilemma was that, after the 1976 Radcliffe recommendations on Ministerial memoirs, the Cabinet Secretary's writ was focused on the effects of proposed revelations on security and international relations. In matters of taste and confidence, though the Cabinet Secretary was to be listened to most seriously, the final judgement was left to the author. In this case, with the exception of a programme about the 1956 Suez invasion, neither security nor international relations was involved. Hence, in a detailed letter to Brabourne, whilst Armstrong formally queried the accuracy, or advised the deletion of over 20 references in four of the six programmes, it was only in relation to the programme about Suez that he was on sure ground in seeking deferral of transmission.[402] Nevertheless, he felt sufficiently strongly about the issues of accuracy and lack of generosity towards others to write a personal letter to Brabourne indicating that one Minister at the time had provided a detailed rebuttal of a number of Mountbatten's claims and had described the programme: 'this is not history but fiction.'[403] Armstrong also picked up on the Prime Minister's worries (though without praying her name in aid) that great offence would be given to The Countess of Avon, Harold Macmillan and Lord Hailsham, concluding with a quotation from Lord Hailsham: 'I have been trained to a profession which is taught that it is wrong to give other people away.'[404]

Armstrong explained: 'For me to seek to exercise a right of veto (if I have it) would not only go well beyond the duties laid upon me by the Radcliffe Committee; it would take the responsibility off the shoulders of Lord Brabourne, on whom it should rest.'[405] For his part, Lord Brabourne acquiesced; the changes requested would be made and the Suez programme would be dropped.[406] Knowledge of the exchanges was, however, leaked to Bernard Levin on *The Times*[407] with extracts from the script of the Suez programme (without Brabourne's knowledge). This led

Armstrong to write to the Countess of Avon in strong terms; 'I regret as much as you must do the breaches of confidence which the account contained, the disloyalty that he showed to those who were his friends as well as his colleagues, and the distress that the articles must have caused you.' He had won the television battle but the breach of confidence was a portent of trouble to come.

Three subsequent episodes stand out: first there was Clive Ponting's crisis of conscience over the sinking of the Argentine warship *GENERAL BELGRANO* during the Falklands conflict. The case raised questions of where an official's duty lay in matters of conscience – wholly to the government of the day or also to Parliament and the public interest. Second, the Westland affair, during which an official, acting on political instructions, leaked a crucial document from the Law Officers. Third, the government attempts to stop the publication of a memoir by a former member of the Security Service. These episodes severely tested Armstrong's leadership as principal adviser to the Prime Minister on both civil service matters and security and intelligence. Where he was on firm ground, such as following the recommendations of the Radcliffe Committee on ministerial memoirs, Armstrong was an adroit negotiator. But his evolutionary and intellectual approach to the lessons from these three episodes struggled to find fixed points around which Ministers, officials and the public could coalesce.

Clive Ponting was a 'fast-stream' MOD official who passed two classified documents to Tam Dalyell (Labour MP for Linlithgow) in July 1984 revealing that the Argentine ship GENERAL BELGRANO, sunk during the Falklands conflict had been sighted a day earlier than officially acknowledged and that she had been outside the British declared exclusion zone, steaming in away from the Royal Navy. Ponting owned up to being the source of the leaked documents within days of the start of a MOD police inquiry.[408] A decision to prosecute under Section 2 of the Official Secrets Act (1911) was taken by the Law Officers shortly afterwards.[409] He was initially suspended without pay – a decision reversed after Thatcher queried the harshness such a decision would impose on his family.[410] His defence was that the disclosure was in the public interest and was protected by Parliamentary privilege. Despite the trial judge directing that: 'the public interest is what the government of the day says it is' Ponting was acquitted by a jury verdict on 11 February 1985. Armstrong played no part in the proceedings but was left to ponder how, in the absence of a revised Official Secrets Act, to define and enforce the standards of confidentiality expected of civil servants. The Westland affair raised different challenges as a breakdown of Cabinet collective responsibility was triggered by the commercial difficulties of the Westland helicopter manufacturing company, with dramatic consequences for two senior Ministers and at least one senior official. The fate of Westland touched on several pressure points in the government strategy. The company was British, had a turnover of £300 million p.a., produced the Sea King and Wessex helicopters (both basically United States Sikorsky designs) and employed 12,000.[411] Its principal customer was the Ministry of Defence (MOD) and some share of the market for aircraft servicing the offshore oil and gas installations. A takeover bid from a British firm (Bristow) foundered in the second half of 1985 despite government agreement to write off £40 million of government launch aid for the design of a new medium-size helicopter.[412] Westland then wanted to accept a minority shareholding from the American United Technologies Company and Fiat (the Sikorsky solution); but Michael Heseltine[413] wanted a European-led solution and mobilised the National Armaments Directors (NAD) of France, Italy, the Federal Republic of Germany and Britain to declare that they would, in future, only buy helicopters from European manufacturers.

At the Economic Affairs Ministerial Committee (E(A)) on 9 December the Chairman of Westland (Sir John Cuckney) argued the case for the offer from Sikorsky: when Westland's results were declared shortly the company would be insolvent unless a deal was in place; a government declaration rejecting the NAD resolution was important for Sikorsky support. However, Ministers decided that the declaration should be held back until p.m. on 13 December, pending a European consortium bid acceptable to Westland.[414] Heseltine lobbied for a further Ministerial discussion as the European bid began to take shape. But there was confusion. The E(A) meeting on 9 December was described by one senior official as 'unpleasant' (which he put down to the lack of a calming influence usually provided by the Lord President, Lord Whitelaw, who was absent due to illness). When the sentiment of the discussion went in Heseltine's favour Thatcher had summed up that, as the Committee were not agreed, discussion would be adjourned for reflection. Discussion would have to resume on 13 December at the latest because of the deadline for issuing the declaration rejecting the NAD resolution. The Cabinet Office committee section were, therefore, instructed to ring round Ministerial offices to ask that Friday afternoon be kept for a meeting of E(A). A later phone call from one of the private secretaries in 10 Downing Street said that there would be no meeting and Ministerial diaries were then freed up.[415] When Cabinet met on 12 December, though it was not on the agenda, Heseltine tried to have Westland discussed. The Prime Minister ruled that there was nothing since 9 December to invalidate the conclusions of the E(A) committee and therefore a discussion was unnecessary – further, no notice had been given that he intended to raise the matter.[416] But, due to what Armstrong later called a misunderstanding with the economic secretariat, no record of the protest made by Heseltine during the tense discussion of 12 December was circulated until 19 December. On that same day Cabinet resumed discussion, when it was agreed that it was for Westland to decide what was best; consequently no Minister was entitled to lobby for one proposal rather than another.[417] Undaunted Heseltine wrote to Thatcher on 23 December arguing that further collective discussion was needed because of the loss of a British defence company to a US-led consortium, one of whose members (Fiat) was partly owned by the Libyan Government. One week later, the Prime Minister's office replied to the effect that the Cabinet decision of 19 December still stood.[418]

From then onwards Cabinet solidarity disintegrated fast. Leon Brittan[419] and Heseltine were at loggerheads over the bids and by the time Cabinet met for the first time in 1986 there had been a number of significant developments. Details of the European bid were available. Thatcher had sent a carefully worded reply to queries from Sir John Cuckney with assurances that, whilst the decision on financial restructuring was for the company, the government would continue to regard Westland as British as long as it carried on business in the UK. Government policy would remain procurement from the most cost-effective source and the government would resist moves to end Westland's part in European collaborative projects.[420] Meanwhile, a letter from Heseltine to Lloyds Merchant Bank, which gave his view of the consequences of a Sikorsky investment had been given to *The Times*.[421] The Solicitor General (Patrick Mayhew) warned him that on the evidence available there were material inaccuracies in the letter which he should correct, not least because in coming to their decision about which bid to accept (if any) Westland shareholders could be expected to rely on a Ministerial statement. (A judgement which Heseltine did not accept and he immediately wrote to Lloyds Merchant Bank to that effect.)[422] Meanwhile, on the same day extracts from the Solicitor General's advice were disclosed to the Press Association by the press secretary at the Department of Trade and Industry.

On 9 January at Cabinet the Prime Minister moved to steady the troops, citing the damage that was being done to the integrity of the government. She recapped on the discussion of 19 December with the decision that it was for Westland to decide its future (knowing that the Westland board would choose the American deal because the company had said so on 13 December). Information on government procurement intentions would be made available equally to both groups of bidders and no Minister was entitled to lobby in favour of one proposal or the other. She summarised what had happened since then, concluding that the government had been made to appear completely at odds with itself and had entered the new year in a way damaging to its esteem; and she concluded: 'We cannot go on like this. We must restore the Government's standing.' At this point it looked as if a compromise would be reached, but then the Prime Minister said that as the Westland shareholders would meet on 14 January to vote on the Board's recommendation in favour of the United Technologies-Fiat proposals, there was a risk of misrepresentation during a period of sensitive commercial negotiations and, thus, of further indications of Cabinet disunity. To avoid this all answers to questions should be cleared interdepartmentally through the Cabinet Office. Officials were dumbfounded, not knowing where the suggestion came from nor how it could be implemented.[423] Heseltine accepted the procedure for new statements but argued that the European consortium proposals rested in part on statements he had already made and that, if asked to confirm these earlier statements, the delay inherent in interdepartmental clearance would be damaging to the European consortium. He also argued that it could not be constitutionally right for a departmental Minister to be obliged to clear interdepartmentally through the Cabinet Office replies on matters that fell within his Ministerial responsibility. (Although it was well established that politically sensitive decisions on defence procurement were for collective discussion.) This time no one spoke in his support. As Thatcher had been warned shortly before Christmas,[424] Heseltine then said that as he could not accept the Prime Minister's summing up, 'I must leave this Cabinet,' and walked out.

Officials were once again unsighted, unclear whether he meant that he could no longer take part in the discussion or whether he meant resignation from the government. The confusion was, however, resolved when the policeman on duty at the door of 10 Downing Street came in to say that Heseltine had just announced to the press that he had resigned; but not before a moment of pure farce. Officials from the Secretariat attend Cabinet only for the items they are to minute. This means that there are usually officials waiting to dart into the Cabinet room as one discussion ends and another starts. Hearing the inner doors open, a waiting Cabinet Office member of the secretariat who was not particularly tall rushed to get through the outer doors and almost headbutted the tall Heseltine in the stomach as he rushed out.[425] After a 30-minute adjournment Cabinet moved seamlessly to close the hole left by the resignation.[426] The sheer speed of this action provokes a thought that maybe the provocation had been planned, or at least contingent plans laid against the possibility of Heseltine's resignation. On Sunday 5 January Thatcher had been joined at Chequers by Whitelaw (a political ally of Heseltine's successor, George Younger), the Chief Whip (Wakeham) and her Principal Private Secretary (Wicks) – the right people to plot an exit route from the disintegrating situation.[427]

The leak of the Attorney General's letter had undoubtedly pointed to disarray in the Cabinet. In addition, the DTI action had breached a convention enshrined in *Questions of Procedure for Ministers* and confirmed at Cabinet on 17 January 1980 that even the fact that the Law Officers had given an opinion (let alone the opinion itself) should never be revealed outside government. Returning from sick leave the Attorney General[428] insisted on an inquiry. He argued that because it was a prime facie breach of Section 2 of the Official Secrets Act 1911, he had to decide whether or not to institute police inquiries and without an internal inquiry to inform that decision the impartiality and independence of his Office could be thought to have been compromised. Under this pressure a reluctant Armstrong, who had earlier concluded that no useful purpose would be served by a formal investigation, now sought the Prime Minister's authority for an inquiry and floated the possibility of offering immunity from prosecution or disciplinary action to secure truthful and frank answers.[429] Thatcher approved an inquiry, to be undertaken by Armstrong himself, on 14 January; it was announced in a Parliamentary Answer two days later.[430]

The Prime Minister was told of Armstrong's conclusions on 22 January and made a statement on it to the House of Commons on 23 January.[431] The key finding was that the gist of the Solicitor General's letter had been given to the Press Association by the DTI press secretary (Colette Bowe) under instruction from the Secretary of State's office in the belief that the disclosure had been sanctioned by Downing Street. The Prime Minister, herself, the report concluded, had not known of the proposed action. Officials had, said the Prime Minister acted in good faith though, had she been consulted, she would have said that a different way of making the relevant facts known should have been found.[432] Colette Bowe, who had been granted immunity from prosecution, co-operated fully with the inquiry but never spoke publicly about the circumstances of the briefing and in 1987 left the civil service. The Attorney General concluded that, as the disclosure had been authorised by the Secretary of State, there was no case to answer under Section 2 of the Official Secrets Act. Leon Brittan resigned one day after the Prime Minister's statement.

The Opposition failed to make much headway in an adjournment debate on 27 January but then the House of Commons Defence Select Committee (DC) decided to take evidence on the government decision-making process and on the defence implications of Westland. Controversially, Armstrong put himself in the firing line as the person responsible for the inquiry. He had a number of reasons for doing this. Principally that he was the best person to prevent the Defence Committee from re-inquiring into the circumstances of the disclosure of the Attorney General's letter; but in addition, partly in an unsuccessful attempt to keep the names of officials confidential, partly to prevent officials in the Prime Minister's private office from having to give evidence[433] and partly to avoid the individuals concerned being subject to the 'double jeopardy' of investigation by both the internal inquiry and that of the Defence Select Committee. Armstrong gave evidence twice,[434] defending the actions of officials in carrying out Ministerial instructions and robustly refuting a charge that they had paid no penalty – on the contrary, they had paid a considerable penalty of anxiety and public exposure. He had to admit, though, that officials had failed to recognise the protection of confidentiality owed to a Law Officer's advice.[435] The media, meanwhile, revealed names with relish – Sir Brian Hayes,[436] for example, complained to Armstrong on 14 April that *The Listener* and *Breakfast Time* had unfairly criticised two of his officials, wrongly identifying them as originators of the idea to leak the Attorney's letter.[437] And in a nice irony, the Defence Select Committee's own deliberations were themselves leaked. Armstrong wanted the Lord Privy Seal to write in complaint but the Prime Minister scotched the idea.[438]

The leaks of the Committee's deliberations gave officials time to consider how government should respond to the likely criticisms, especially the immunity granted to Colette Bowe, the Select Committee's frustration at not having as witnesses officials from the Prime Minister's office and the DTI and the Committee's conclusion that Armstrong had a conflict of interest as both head of the Home Civil Service and the principal investigator in the internal inquiry.[439] On the first of these issues Armstrong argued that, when she asked what her position was, immunity had been granted to ensure that Miss Bowe would co-operate fully with his inquiry '... the question of refusal to give evidence never came up, since the answer to her question what her position was gave her the reassurance she sought. I do not know whether she would have refused ... but the fact that she asked the question suggests that the possibility of refusing could not have been absent from her mind.' Sir Brian Hayes was quick to come back: on the contrary, Armstrong had himself sought the immunity for Miss Bowe. 'As to what you suggest would be a truthful answer, it is of course truthful, but it is not the whole truth.'[440] Armstrong had himself suggested that Miss Bowe should ask about her position so that he could then make the offer of immunity he had already obtained from the Attorney General. Earlier, in evidence to the Defence

Committee on 5 February Armstrong had said, 'I think that anybody would [seek immunity] before making a statement which was liable to incriminate her.'[441]

Armstrong had the MPO Machinery of Government Division look into Ministers' responsibility for the actions of their officials. A submission of 1 August concluded that a Minister (including the Prime Minister) is accountable for the actions of their officials in the sense of being bound to explain to Parliament the part that their staff had played. '... it does not follow,' the submission added, 'that the Prime Minister should take blame or pay any penalty [for their actions],' – especially if the Minister did not know of them and would have disapproved of them.[442] (In the event this section was excluded from the government's reply to the Committee's recommendations as likely to provoke controversy rather than settle matters.) When the report and the response were debated on 29 October the Lord Privy Seal[443] replied to the debate with further details: a Select Committee's power to call for the attendance of individuals with regard to civil servants must be limited in practice so that the principles of Ministerial accountability are not undermined. Hence it is for Ministers to decide who should attend on their behalf.[444] He added, to the consternation of some members, that the government would instruct civil servants that they should not answer questions which are, or appear to be, directed to their conduct or that of other named civil servants.[445] Disciplinary hearings or the like were not for Parliament to hold. A Ministerial meeting chaired by the Prime Minister had concluded on 16 September 1983 that the chain of command should follow, '... the principles of natural justice in which discipline was left mainly to the Permanent Secretary in each Department, and which left room for both the answerability of the Ministerial Head of each Department for the conduct of his Department, and for the Prime Minister's general responsibility for the conduct of the Civil Service.'[446] In conversation with Terence Higgins MP[447] Armstrong drew a distinction between the actions of civil servants (which could appropriately be probed by a Select Committee) and the conduct of civil servants (which could not since discipline was a Departmental and Ministerial matter). Despite some Parliamentary concern that the Government proposals were an attempt to muzzle Committees in their investigatory role Cabinet agreed, at the end of January,[448] that these restrictions could be incorporated in guidelines for civil servants appearing at Select Committees (popularly known as the Osmotherley Rules).[449]

On the question of a possible conflict of interest, the Prime Minister was dismissive: 'I do not accept the Committee's comments on the role of the head of the home Civil Service. He continues to enjoy the Government's total confidence, and I am glad to express our confidence in his distinguished service.'[450] The Permanent Secretaries rallied round at their weekly Wednesday morning meeting of 30 July: 'we were deeply offended by the criticism of him [Armstrong], as Head of the Civil Service, in the Defence Committee's report on Westland; that the criticism was in our view wholly unwarranted; and that he enjoyed the full confidence of all his colleagues.' In reply Thatcher referred to Armstrong as: 'one of the finest public servants we have ever had. It is due to people like him that the highest traditions of the Civil Service are maintained'[451]

Some two years later Leon Brittan appeared to suggest that the Prime Minister's press and foreign affairs secretaries had not just been informed of his instruction to leak the gist of the Solicitor General's letter but had approved it. The Defence Select Committee considered reopening the case but put the issue on hold when Brittan wrote to confirm that it was not his intention to reveal anything new: the DTI thought that the Prime Minister's private office gave their approval, the latter thought they were simply being informed of a decision by the Secretary of State for Trade and Industry.[452] However, in his memoirs published in 1994 Lord Howe appeared to support the claim by Leon Brittan, writing that the failure to rotate Messrs Powell and Ingham in the conventional civil service manner after a tour of duty of three to four years damaged the provision of independent professional advice.[453]

Spycatcher

Eight months after the successful handling of Nigel West's book on MI5, Chapman Pincher's allegations that Hollis had been a Soviet agent reappeared (as they did repeatedly up to Pincher's death in 2014, notably after the publication of the authorised history of MI5).[454] On 16 July 1984 Granada Television's *World in Action* alleged that new evidence suggested there had been a mole at the summit of the Security Service. Armstrong was unable to get a preview tape but advised Thatcher that claims by the former MI5 Officer, Peter Wright, that her statement of 26 March 1981 at the time *Their Trade is Treachery* had been published was 'equivocal,' and 'a masterly piece of Whitehall deception,' were unfounded. It seemed highly likely that Wright had committed a clear breach of the Official Secrets Act (OSA): 'We are considering whether there is a case for abating or discontinuing his pension.'[455] However, such actions were quickly ruled out as this could only be done if Wright had been convicted of a criminal offence and the timing for a court case was not judged to be propitious.[456]

The first hint that Wright might be preparing to publish came at the end of July. Sir Anthony Kershaw MP[457] told Armstrong that he had received a dossier from Wright comprising 160 typescript pages, divided into chapters, like a book. He subsequently gave Armstrong a copy,[458] and an internal meeting on 6 September[459] came to a damning conclusion: the dossier contained nothing new of significance, was factually inaccurate, ignorant of some material facts, made weak or faulty inferences and was selective.[460] Armstrong then advised Thatcher that though the material was old hat it demonstrated clearly that Wright was Pincher's source for *Their Trade is Treachery.* The effect of the dossier, he argued, was to strengthen Lord Trend's conclusion that Hollis was not a Soviet spy. But Pincher was known to have another book on the stocks under the title *Too Secret Too Long*, for publication later in 1984. With the Prime Minister's agreement Armstrong (accompanied by the Director General of the Security Service and his deputy) saw Kershaw on 24 September prior to her writing formally, in advance of Pincher's book, to put the record straight.[461] Her letter revealed: '... we have special standing arrangements for reviewing all available information concerning threats of penetration ... they include an element of regular oversight from outside the services as well as the use of specialist analytical and investigative capacity within them.' Kershaw suggested that, in order to get the information into the public domain, he should speak during the Debate on the Address suggesting the need for a monitoring system and the replying Minister could then put on record in the House of Commons that such a system already existed. Armstrong had doubts about opening up an issue on which Parliament could run ahead of where the government wished to be, advising: 'I think we must reserve judgement on whether a speech by Sir Anthony Kershaw would be useful, and discuss that with him when we have read and digested [Pincher's] book as a whole.'[462] His doubts were justified; Kershaw told him on 30 October that he did not regard the arrangements as sufficient – he wanted something like a standing Security Commission – but if this idea would be rejected by the government then he would pursue matters outside Parliament and would not raise this matter in the Debate.[463] In January 1985 Kershaw returned to the charge. He had been informed that Lord Trend's 1974 investigation into the conduct of the Hollis investigation had not summoned all the FLUENCY team and could not, therefore, 'be as profound as necessary to clear up any doubt.'[464] Armstrong confirmed that Trend had not interviewed everyone who had interrogated Hollis, but added that he did not think any great significance could be read into that as Trend had interviewed the most senior officer who had led the sessions. Trend had also interviewed Peter Wright and others who shared the same view about Hollis. Hence, Armstrong's judgement of Trend's inquiry remained that, 'no one outside the Security Service – certainly not a judge – could have brought to his task a greater degree of knowledge, greater thoroughness or a more objective approach.'[465]

By the end of May 1985 newspapers in the UK and Australia were reporting plans for publication of a book by Wright.[466] He had been warned in July 1981 that he was under an obligation not to make a record of his time in the Security Service whether for publication or not, and Sir Antony Duff (by now Director General of MI5) pressed for early action 'to deter potential UK publishers.'[467] Henry Steel (Legal Secretary to the Attorney General) equivocated: a warning would imply legal proceedings if ignored. Could the government deliver on that given that Wright was outside UK jurisdiction? The Attorney General would be the plaintiff in any such proceedings and would have to answer for the result. Further, if Wright were to come within UK jurisdiction the Attorney General would want to prosecute him and that would be made the more difficult the more fuss was made now. On the other hand, it might be better to have tried and failed than to give the impression that the government did not care enough about conduct of this kind to do anything about it.[468]

Meeting under Armstrong's chairmanship on 17 and 25 June officials concluded that legal action should be taken both in the UK and in Australia provided that there was a reasonable chance of success. Any action would have to rest on the general principle of damage from disclosure by former intelligence officers, to avoid the need for detailed discussion of the content of the book, which was not known but, given the breadth of Wright's experience, was likely to be wide-ranging. (Subsequent analysis of the text between March and June 1986 confirmed that it revealed techniques, liaison arrangements with other security services and past targets for surveillance that could adversely affect relationships with other countries.) Counsel in the UK thought there was a good chance of victory provided that action was also initiated in Australia; counsel in Australia stressed that it would be necessary to establish a breach of duty on Wright's part. Despite Henry Steel's earlier opinion that it would be the Attorney General who would be the plaintiff, the legal team in the UK and Australia now took the fateful decision that it should be the Cabinet Secretary who should swear the affidavits. Ostensibly the reasons were that he: 'knows far more about the circumstances of Peter Wright as well as a great deal about the Security Service rather than Henry Steel who knows nothing of either matter.'[469] Other possible plaintiffs might have been Cubbon (PUS Home Office) or Duff. As Armstrong was Head of the Civil Service it was reasonable to expect that he knew more than the former about the duty of confidentiality; he certainly knew less about the operations of the Security Service than Duff but at that time the identity of the Director General was not avowed. Havers later claimed in a television interview: 'It seems to me that he [Armstrong] was the natural fall-guy – the one who knew the most, if I can say that.'[470] He accepted the advice that he should swear the affidavit on behalf of the Attorney General as, 'Cabinet Secretary and the Prime Minister's principal official adviser on matters of security and intelligence.' adding that, 'I hope that it may be possible for someone to [swear the affidavit] on my behalf in Sydney.'[471] Mistakenly, Armstrong was under the impression that he would not be required to attend the New South Wales Court in person and was shaken when his Private Secretary subsequently told him that it was likely that he would.[472] (The hope was probably always optimistic and was finally crushed in October when Australian Counsel advised that under the rules of the Court in New South Wales the plaintiff would be required to attend in person.)[473] It is not clear, however, to what extent Armstrong's lack of familiarity with courtroom behaviour and the entirely foreseeable emphasis on legal as opposed to substantive arguments were taken into account. Armstrong would be vulnerable to courtroom antics and to accusations that he was neither fish nor fowl, neither with legal expertise on the duty of confidentiality nor experience of how MI5 personnel policies worked in practice. Sir Robert would be entitled to disclaim direct knowledge of specific actions but in Australia, in particular, he would need to be given strong protection by the government's counsel and, hopefully, from the presiding judge. In the event he received neither.

The government case was to be based on the commercial law of confidentiality – notably Wright's alleged breach of contractual obligations and duty of confidence to the government. Junior Australian Counsel (William Caldwell) pointed to a potential weakness in the government case stemming from the earlier failure to act against Wright when *Their Trade is Treachery* was published. Hence, it might be necessary to establish that the particular content of the manuscript was specifically damaging to the UK or Australia or the United

States. (During preliminary proceedings in Sydney on 14 August 1986 counsel for the Crown said that 'for the purposes of these proceedings and not otherwise' the British government accepted that Wright's manuscript was accurate. A legal ploy to avoid discussion of the content of the manuscript that was widely misunderstood and led to *The Guardian* reporting, erroneously, that allegations of criminal malpractice by MI5 were soundly based.) Armstrong now proposed that an arranged Written Parliamentary Answer should say that new evidence from Russian defectors had decisively confirmed that Hollis had not been a spy, thereby damaging Wright's allegations, discouraging others from repeating the charges, reassuring the intelligence community and helping to redress a feeling of grave injustice among members of the Hollis family. But Thatcher judged that such action would inflame the debate rather than calm it and could lead to exposure on other security matters.[474] Heinemann, meanwhile, agreed to submit to the injunction but warned that they were not sure they could carry Wright with them in this course. He might go for publication in the United States (where the chances of a successful injunction would be less likely).[475] In Britain, injunctions preventing *The Observer* and *The Guardian* from publishing extracts from the book were upheld in the Court of Appeal. Armstrong now moved to enlist the support of the Australian Government on the grounds that, 'we think that we are fighting a battle whose outcome is important to others as well as ourselves.'[476]

In a surprising twist late in August, Jonathan Aitken MP reported to the Attorney General that the lead Australian defence lawyer (Malcolm Turnbull) had contacted him as a go-between to offer a deal to the British Government under which, 'in return for a few cuts (not too many) in areas where it could be agreed that the book prejudices UK national security the book would be published, the British Government's face would be saved and Sir Robert would avoid 'getting carved up into little pieces under cross examination.' The British Government's concern to prevent other would-be whistle-blowers could not be done either by a courtroom defeat or by a pyrrhic victory. 'Malcolm Turnbull simply cannot understand why no-one in the UK seems willing to make a political deal instead of continuing with a lawyer's kamikaze mission.'[477] Armstrong told Thatcher: 'it is suggested that we should do the same sort of deal with Mr Wright as we did with Nigel West on his history of MI5. The crucial difference is, of course, that Mr West was not and Mr Wright was a member of the Security Service.'[478] Emboldened by the decision of the Australian Government to file affidavits based on Wright's duty of confidentiality, the Attorney General rejected Turnbull's approach in forthright terms: 'There is no possibility of a settlement on the basis of Mr Turnbull's proposals.'[479]

A view started to crystallise in the minds of British officials that the deterrent effects of proceedings to prevent publication were more important than winning.[480] Armstrong told the Treasury Solicitor that he would not want to give evasive answers at the outset only to have things rung out of him in court.[481] Concerned that the allegations of criminal action in the Wright manuscript could be used to argue for publication in the public interest, he consulted the Attorney

General about a possible reference to the Director of Public Prosecutions (DPP) and later that month Thatcher asked the Law Officers to consider whether to refer the manuscript allegations of criminal activity to the DPP (which they sought to do but were prevented by the refusal of the Australian court to permit this.)[482]

Court proceedings proper began on 17 November 1986. Armstrong had flown out from London on 12 November and lodged with the British Consul General in Vaucluse. He did not return to the UK until 5 December. Unaccustomed to public attention, his departure had been marred by a minor scuffle with a photographer outside the VIP suite at Heathrow airport. There were protracted arguments in court about the defence lawyers' demands for disclosure as they sought to argue that the British Government was inconsistent in allowing other books but not that by Wright. The British case was that Wright's revelations were different because they carried the implied authenticity of a former Security Service officer. So strongly was this felt that, at a meeting of Ministers on 19 November, the Prime Minister said that if the discovery order went ahead there would be very good reasons for abandoning the main action.[483]

One week into the trial Turnbull again sought a settlement – this time speaking directly to Armstrong as they were walking away from the courtroom. In a long telegram analysing the options Armstrong saw advantage in a deal that would establish the precedent of publication by insiders only on agreed terms (a procedure followed by the CIA) but said that the British team had no enthusiasm for negotiation as it did not trust Turnbull's motives, which could be to test the resolve of the government.[484] After a discussion between key Ministers instructions were sent to Sydney that, 'the Government could not compromise its point of principle ... Removal of the offending passages was impracticable ... The makings of a deal were, therefore, not present.'[485]

Defence cross-examination of Armstrong sought to damage his credibility as an accurate witness, making much of an error in the written interrogatory evidence in which he had said (erroneously) that the Attorney General had taken the decision not to prosecute Chapman Pincher in 1981 over *Their Trade is Treachery* and of the letter to the publishers seeking a copy of the manuscript without telling them that the government already had one. The latter exchange included Armstrong's unhappy use of a quotation from Edmund Burke: 'an economy with the truth' which press reporting would ensure would stick with him for ever. However, the contest was far from one sided and many, including Armstrong himself, felt that the British press allowed itself to be manipulated by the defence.[486] At its close, the Australian Solicitor General (Gavan Griffith) who had sat through the trial wrote: 'to my observations you are the most effective witness I have seen in court ... I cannot recall a better witness ... a splendid job performed under adverse, and often very trying circumstances.'[487] The UK Cabinet recorded its thanks, 'for the admirable way in which he had given evidence ... '[488] The New South Wales Chief Justice said: 'I see not the slightest justification for casting aspersions on the credit of Sir Robert Armstrong; and I specifically reject the claim ... that Sir Robert Armstrong deliberately set out to mislead the court.'[489] Armstrong himself showed exemplary generosity of spirit in opposing action to require the forfeiture of Peter Wright's CBE, partly, it has to be said, because it would add to Wright's sense of injustice at the hands of the British Government and would increase the risk of further damaging disclosures.[490]

The Australian judgement came in the late hours of 12 March (UK time). Mr Justice Powell found wholly in favour of the defendant; Peter Wright had no contractual obligation of confidentiality except in respect of information which retained its quality of confidentiality and most of the material in *Spycatcher* had lost that quality because of its availability in publications that had been authorised or acquiesced in by the British Government. Armstrong would later joke: 'When I was in Sydney for Spycatcher the English were thrashing the Aussies in a Test series in Australia, and I think that Malcolm Turnbull and Mr. Justice Powell enjoyed taking their revenge on me in the Supreme Court of New South Wales.'[491] The Attorney General immediately proposed an appeal.[492] Advice from the Solicitor General of Australia to seek a new lead counsel[493] was, however, rejected.[494] The appeal was not heard until four months later (opening on 27 July 1987) and went against the government, which then appealed to the High Court of Australia. This court accepted that Mr Wright owed an obligation of confidence to the Crown, as contended by the government, but held that the Australian Courts did not have jurisdiction to enforce it.[495] A by-product of this experience was an instruction from the Prime Minister to press the Australians, the New Zealanders and possibly the Americans for provisions to be made for the bilateral recognition and enforcement of judgements.[496]

Even before the judgement in Australia Ministers started to consider the implications for future policy on unauthorised disclosure. They commissioned work under Armstrong, which included how to prevent the kind of disaffection and sense of grievance that had contributed to Wright and to a less-publicised but more dangerous case – that of Michael, who was an MI5 officer convicted in April 1984 of seeking to pass secrets to the Soviet Union. Though his approach to the Soviet residency in London had been unsuccessful the authorised history of MI5 describes the episode as: 'By far the most serious counter-espionage case for the Security Service in the final decade of the Cold War.'[497] Bettaney was sentenced to 23 years of imprisonment – the third longest sentence for espionage in modern times after George Blake (sentenced to 42 years in 1961) and Geoffrey Prime (sentenced to 35 years *plus* three further years for sexual offences in 1982). It was a heavy sentence given that the Russians had not followed up his approach; comparable to those passed on the most important of the spies at the Portland Underwater Detection Establishment – 25 years for Gordon Lonsdale, an illegal Russian intelligence officer, and 20 years each for Peter and Helen Kroger, his technical support team. Christopher Andrew records that Bettaney told the team of investigators that there was no simple motivation for his actions, it had been a cumulative process, including disillusion connected with a posting early in his career to Northern Ireland,[498] on the basis of which the subsequent Security Commission report recommended improved postings policies and the appointment of a staff counsellor.

Armstrong's proposals for handling policy included a Cabinet Committee under the Prime Minister, supported by an official committee, which he would chair himself (the official committee on security – SISC).[499] A draft statement was prepared in which the Prime Minister gave strong support to the armed forces, the police and the intelligence agencies.[500] Officials then had second thoughts because of the likelihood of a protracted appeals process in Australia and despite opposition from Duff the statement was watered down to avoid accusations of contempt of court.[501] A gulf opened up between those close to the operational front line and those who looked more towards possible Parliamentary reactions. Duff opposed 'a style which does not seek to raise the temperature of domestic controversy.'[502] 'I am not skilled in these matters. But my gut feeling is that if a statement is to be made ... the sort of impact we will be hoping for is more likely to be achieved by a colourful choice of words than by a carefully balanced statement in which every word is judged by reference to its precise bureaucratic meaning.'[503] Armstrong was known for those skills and submitted 'something brief but trenchant' attacking irresponsible investigative journalism and the Opposition MPs who aided and abetted it.[504] However, the former Prime Minister, Jim Callaghan, was pressing for an enquiry into the Wright allegations of a plot in MI5 against the Wilson administration and this seemed to signal a possible snowball of Parliamentary indignation. Duff accepted that, for the time being, the priority was to have available a convincing public rebuttal of Wright's allegations about Hollis and Wilson.[505] (Ministers now seemed likely to be hoist by the petard of their courtroom ploy to accept the truth of the Wright manuscript for the purposes of the court hearing only so as to avoid having to discuss its substance. Legal advice was expected to be that they could not now reverse that formal admission.) Armstrong, meanwhile, was despatched to persuade Callaghan not to persist in calling for an enquiry. Callaghan was not persuaded and would, therefore, seek a meeting with the Prime Minister to discuss the targeting, structure and oversight of the Security Service.[506]

This third strand of issues (improved governance and management of the Security Service, particularly in regard to domestic subversion) was now in the spotlight. Armstrong had submitted advice in early April 1987.[507] This included study of a possible statutory basis to underpin operations, but stopped short of recommending options for external oversight because of the difficulties about where 'the fence of confidentiality' would sit (in his personal opinion this was a matter of political judgement). MISC 132, an official group on enforcing the duty of confidentiality turned its attention to closing the loopholes in employment conditions that had been brought home during preparations for the Australian trial. The focus was on drawing attention to the absolute duty of confidence at recruitment, during service and on retirement, tightening up the OSA and enabling powers to withdraw pensions from offenders living abroad. Consideration was also given to lowering the hurdle for a successful injunction based on risk rather than probability of disclosure. With a note of sadness Armstrong admitted that recent difficulties in going to law to prevent disclosure had meant that, 'I am reluctantly driven to the conclusion that we have to consider seriously whether the most practicable sanction against another Peter Wright ... would be forfeiture of pension.'[508]

The Prime Minister had a preliminary meeting with the heads of the agencies on 18 June 1987 at which Duff argued that, in the absence of legislative cover, the ability and willingness of members of the Security Service to undertake activities that would otherwise be illegal were being inhibited.[509] At about the same time the Home Office Permanent Secretary (Brian Cubbon) was advising that proposed reform of the Official Secrets Act, with its continued protection for security information, would struggle in Parliament unless it was shown that the Service had legal validity.[510] Armstrong briefed defensively for Thatcher's meeting with Callaghan, pointing to the improvements in control made since he had left office (warrants for interception and a Commissioner reporting to the Prime Minister on interception, the imminent appointment of Sir Philip Woodfield[511] as Staff Counsellor for the three agencies to provide a safety valve for problems of conscience or propriety, improvements in vetting and personnel management in line with the Security Commission's recommendations following the Bettaney affair). Lord Trend had, following his inquiry into the conduct of the Hollis enquiry, held an unpublicised role in relation to all cases of suspected espionage involving members of MI5 or MI6 (a role which Armstrong himself would shortly assume on retirement).[512] He argued that provided the Service behaved with propriety and within its Directive there were advantages in Ministers not riding it on too close a rein. He opposed a new oversight mechanism (would a committee of Privy Counsellors still the voices of criticism?) and an enquiry into the alleged Wilson plot ('let the dust settle').[513]

Meanwhile Callaghan went public with his thoughts in a *Panorama* programme, 'State of Secrecy,' on 14 September. Initially Thatcher ruled that neither Armstrong nor the Security Service should co-operate with the programme makers;[514] but after intervention by the Attorney General Armstrong was given limited discretion to do so and met David Dimbleby and others off the record on 8 September for two and a quarter hours.[515] He subsequently reported that he had formed the conclusion that the compilers of the programme were genuinely addressing themselves to issues; and after the programme was broadcast he reported that it had been 'more balanced than I had expected: the problem was discussed surprisingly fairly.'[516] Later, in October 1988 when the Ditchley Foundation mounted a conference on the oversight and the limits on intelligence work in a democracy under the chairmanship of Lord Hunt Thatcher opposed attendance by any present or former UK officials.[517]

After May 1987 the government's attempt to ban the Wright book all but fell apart. Trevor Woolley (Armstrong's Private Secretary) summed up the situation: 'The question which needs to be answered is: Why is the Government continuing with legal action in this country and abroad when the contents of 'Spycatcher' are widely known and anybody who wishes to get hold of a copy of the book can do so relatively easily?' 'The fact that legal remedies may not be available in certain jurisdictions, or wholly effective in others, does not absolve the Government from its obligation to do its utmost to prevent the publication and distribution of Wright's book when and where such remedies are available.'[518] On his return from summer holiday Armstrong was told that the Attorney General was now more concerned to win the point of principle (which would allow an action for an account of profits) than either to prevent circulation of the book (which was in any case published in Australia in 1985) or to win the public relations battle.[519] A major disagreement had developed between the Security Service and the Whitehall lawyers. Duff remained concerned that the Government was still not projecting its message on Wright as forcefully and effectively as it should; Bailey and Saunders, on the other hand, argued that it would be unwise to launch a briefing campaign of any detail as the government case could not be made without going into details that could not be revealed.[520] At the end of the year Armstrong retired, leaving the unfinished business to Robin Butler. The issues continued for a further five years, into the premiership of John Major.

Further unfinished business concerned reform of the Official Secrets Act. After the first flurry of activity to reform Section 2 had failed in 1979 the government retreated into the status quo. This period lasted until spring 1987 when the Home Secretary (Douglas Hurd)[521] told Thatcher that it was inevitable that the unfinished business of reform would return to the Parliamentary agenda. Juries were confused by arguments that were really about the proper scope of the law – that should be made self-evident. The *Spycatcher* case had highlighted a gap in the measures intended to ensure the lifetime protection of confidentiality. Also, in the intervening period Parliamentary opinion had hardened around the notion that reform was merely a step on the path to Freedom of Information.[522] It would not be sufficient to re-present the 1979 Bill. Hurd proposed an interdepartmental committee of officials to make revised proposals, including an assessment of how recent cases would have fared under their proposals. Ministers would then consider how to construct a political majority in Parliament and the country for what might be put forward by way of legislation. Armstrong saw this as a possible plank on which to build a coalition government should the 1987 General Election produce a hung Parliament, writing to Cubbon to expedite work, 'so that we are ready to give informed advice at short notice immediately after [the General Election], if we are called upon to do so.'[523] They were not called upon to do so – the Conservatives had an overall majority of 102. Work on reform was still ongoing when Armstrong retired, another illustration that even when the term of office is eight years a Cabinet Secretary can inherit an issue as work in progress and yet pass that same issue on to his successor, still as work in progress.

Sherpa

When the United States invaded Grenada on 25 October 1983 the British Government was presented with a *fait accompli.* Armstrong observed that his relationship with the National Security Adviser had effectively ceased under President Reagan for reasons (he suspected) of internal American politics.[524] Two weeks after the invasion the newly appointed Robert 'Bud' McFarlane sent him a message of 'profound disappointment at the British Government's public reaction to their [United States] effort to restore democracy and order to Grenada.' Armstrong interpreted this as a feeler to test the British appetite for restoring the link between himself and the National Security Adviser. He wanted to respond in a conciliatory way. Thatcher would have none of it. Armstrong's draft response would let the Americans off the hook too cheaply. John Coles responded: 'Mrs Thatcher does not wish to give the impression that we were grateful for the advance notice of the Grenada operation (which she considers quite inadequate) nor that our views, private or public, would have been different if we had had more time or more knowledge.'[525]

London was the Summit venue for 1984. President Mitterrand had spoken about the 1983 Williamsburg meeting in terms that led some of the French press to conclude that he might not attend the 1984 Summit. That was wrong, Attali assured Armstrong: 'But the fact remained that ... the occasions presented him with some difficulty: he was the only man of the left at the table and (so long as that was the case) could not expect to get a great deal out of the meetings.' Hence, he wanted to scale down the public relations element and to increase the extent to which Heads of Government met alone.[526] Mitterrand had felt bounced into a statement on Defence and Disarmament at Williamsburg and felt strongly that political discussion should be restricted to mealtimes. Unless a pressing need was to develop in the meantime, there should be no political communiqué.[527] In this the French were opposed by the Germans, Japanese and Americans who were in favour of a declaration on a full range of political questions.[528] Thatcher wanted a declaration on combating state-sponsored international terrorism and led a move for the Heads of Government to reaffirm the political values of the West in the form of *The London Charter* as a counter to the propaganda assaults of Communist countries. Attali was adamant that only the sherpas should be responsible for the drafting of statements to be made at the close of the Summit and that these must be thoroughly prepared before the event. Even in this, however, French wishes were not entirely met; British Ministers were heavily involved in the drafting of both the London Charter and the thematic paper on Opinions that were far from convergent. Some of the Europeans found the British draft thematic paper too optimistic and wanted stronger criticism of interest rate levels and the American budget deficit. The Americans, on the other hand, found this too critical and pointed to European failures to create jobs. The French thought that references to aid were patronising and paternalistic. Small wonder, then, that Armstrong had a specially difficult task piloting the text through British Ministers – 'The Prime Minister was dissatisfied with the language of the thematic paper which contained too much economists' jargon ... Even though it would not be circulated under her name, she could not allow it to go out in this form.'[529] 'Do we really wish to hit the U.S. so hard? I should have thought we could be less specific,' she argued, shortly afterwards. It must have appeared to Armstrong that the trust so carefully built with his fellow sherpas was being stretched to the limit; in May he wrote: 'I hope that the Prime Minister will bear with us on the fact that the other countries concerned have already seen and commented on a first draft of the Thematic Paper, which was approved by the Prime Minister and discussed at the meeting of Personal representatives early in April.'[530] Then he was instructed that the speaking notes provided by UK Departments were too bureaucratic in style to meet the Prime Minister's wish to release them to the press in support of her argument in favour of deregulation.

Potential disarray carried over into 1985. The Germans were the hosts. To mark the 40th anniversary of the end of the Second World War Chancellor Helmut Kohl proposed a declaration that the participants had learnt the lessons of history and would make reference to the division of Europe and of Germany. Armstrong correctly anticipated that the latter would not be to Thatcher's taste and also judged that the language of the first draft, which included phrases such as 'victims of oppressive racism,' 'victims of expulsion' and reference to 'social justice' without the addition of 'obligations and rights' would cause problems for her. Exploiting his reputation amongst the sherpas as a draftsman, he therefore recast the declaration to shorten it, make it less lyrical and in the course of doing so to remove the offending words.[531] In general this was a successful move; however, he found himself a lone voice opposing German unification and knowing that the Prime Minister recognised the need to 'court the Germans'[532] he did not enter a formal reservation on it. A reference to, '... a state of peace in Europe in which the German people will regain their unity through free self-determination' appeared in the declaration.[533]

Though Armstrong judged the German draft thematic paper very thorough and well done, he reported spats between the French and the Americans.[534] An ill-tempered exchange between the American political director (Burt) and the Attali revealed that since France was not a party to the Geneva negotiations between the United States and the Soviet Union on arms control and disarmament, President Mitterrand insisted that in welcoming the negotiations it would be wrong to make any reference to the United States.[535] Thatcher thought this petty and instructed Armstrong to arrange for wording that: 'would be considerably more objectionable to the French Government, in the hope of being able to arrive at a more balanced final view.'[536] The French were also party to much of the disagreement in Tokyo in 1986 on terrorism where they professed to be reluctant to see the Summit usurp other organisations.[537] Within the French delegation tension between the socialist President Mitterrand and the Gaullist Prime Minister Chirac led to Armstrong reporting that Mitterrand: 'will not put his name to any published document at the Summit which might seem to imply his endorsement of his Government's domestic policies.'[538]

It seems clear, in retrospect, that the sherpas were pushing ahead with institutionalising the Summits when the preconditions of political unity did not exist. Thatcher put down a marker against what she saw as empire building. She instructed Armstrong to veto any proposal for a study group about the effects of industrial activity on the environment, which had begun to feature in German views.[539] Armstrong and Attali were agreed on this, concerned that, like the issue of new technology, the result would be more superstructure.[540] By contrast, the British were keen to introduce discussion of anti-terrorist co-operation – an area where Armstrong felt very much at home given his Home Office experience. By the end of March 1985 Armstrong could report with some satisfaction that pressure to simplify Summit arrangements was beginning to pay off – the general presumption amongst the sherpas was that the working group on Technology, Growth and Employment should cease to exist once a final report had been prepared. (It lasted until November.) Further, the environment technical study group had been instructed to report early in 1986 with the clear implication that it would then be wound up.

But he also had to report that there were few new ideas on the economic front; the focus would be on the liberalisation of world trade. Co-ordination of domestic economic policies had been taken back into the G5/G7 finance ministers' meetings. Hence, the main themes for the 1986 Tokyo Summit would be similar to those of the preceding two meetings: steady progress in the consolidation of sound non-inflationary growth. A Japanese suggestion that the economic exploitation of scientific and technological education merited discussion had been greeted with a lack of enthusiasm, not least because the national governments in Canada and Germany had very limited constitutional competence in the area. As Coles' successor (Charles Powell) observed, 'Tokyo seems a long way to go for the same agenda and no doubt the same discussion.'[541] Among the new topics were a suggestion from Armstrong that the agenda should include discussion of long-term trends in social expenditure, and American threats of retaliation for the enlargement of the European Community to include Spain and Portugal. The sherpas generally agreed there was an important issue on social expenditure but at first thought that it was politically too sensitive for discussion,[542] perhaps work should be put in hand for the meeting in two years[543] – showing just how far the arrangements had moved away from the original concept of private discussions between heads of government on subjects of importance. Armstrong's discussions in Washington pointed to an American desire to discuss over-capacity in agriculture which, he warned, might be code for the consequences of European Community enlargement, though he did not think so.[544] Nevertheless, at the sherpa meeting in April 1986 the United States representatives: 'were very clearly put on notice that the climate at the Summit would be seriously damaged if the United States Administration carried out its threat to institute on 1 May measures in reprisal for the alleged costs to the United States of the enlargement of the European Community.'[545]

Most of the new topics put forward for Tokyo were on the political agenda. These included reports on drugs, terrorism and sub-Saharan Africa commissioned at Bonn in 1985 and a declaration on 'the next forty years' (to parallel the Bonn declaration which had looked backwards for forty years). And once again the master craftsman offered the Japanese a redraft of their first draft thematic paper, which they could circulate without acknowledgement.[546] He headed off American intentions to raise the position in South Africa because he knew that the Prime Minister would want only an informal discussion with the President on the issue.[547] It also became clear that the Americans wanted to make international terrorism one of the major themes of the summit. But the French

Government would only do so 'in other international organisations which have a competence to deal with the problem.'[548] In Thatcher's view the draft statement agreed by the sherpas had no teeth and she asked for a British version that was fuller, firmer and more specific.[549] The resulting Foreign Office draft met her needs (it included six specific actions to which all attending the Summit could be asked to subscribe) and was passed directly to the Japanese Prime Minister, Nakasone, for him to draw upon in producing the final declaration.[550] What the sherpas finally agreed at 4 a.m. on 5 May, ad referendum to the Heads of Government, was an amalgam of the Rambouillet anti-hijacking statement and the British draft text. The British felt that it fell short of the commitment to vigorous concerted action that they would have wished and it was left to Thatcher to toughen up the text during the leaders' meeting the next morning. In the face of Japanese and French opposition to the principle of discussion rather than to substance, and the lack of drive from the United States team the British reported that it would have been impossible to reach full agreement on anything stronger.[551] Nor was it possible to reach agreement on the terms under which the security experts should undertake further work. Armstrong added that Attali had indicated that Mitterand would: 'readily pursue some of these matters further in private discussions with his colleagues.'

Nor was 1987 any easier. The Japanese were unwilling to accept references to opening their domestic market more effectively to imports, but failed to convince the other sherpas that their plans were satisfactory. The British Cabinet had discussed initiatives to open the Japanese market in early April when Armstrong had pressed for specifics such as using the powers of reciprocity in the Financial Services Act if there was no firm timetable for access to the Tokyo Stock Exchange, slowing down the administrative processing of authorisation for Japanese firms to trade in London and blocking Japanese access to the British telecommunications market if Cable & Wireless did not get a fair share in Japan.[552] But British attempts to mediate on debt relief for the poorest countries, particularly in sub-Saharan Africa also met with resistance and the Heads of Government were split on arms control coverage of tactical nuclear weapons.[553]

By 1987 Armstrong's influence on Thatcher in foreign affairs was significantly weakened. In the early years there was an unresolved disagreement between her and Armstrong on how they should work in preparation for the meetings. When Charles Powell replaced John Coles as the Foreign Office private secretary not only did the relationship between Thatcher and the foreign affairs private secretary became closer, but Powell judged that a more combative approach to international relations would reflect Thatcher's growing distaste for a diplomacy that involved finding compromises and fudging differences. British diplomats observed that she had begun to prefer making progress at other people's expense.[554] The language in which the Prime Minister's views were relayed to Armstrong became noticeably blunt, colourful and aggressive. In 1985 Powell wrote: 'You will wish to know that the Prime Minister does not like the formulation, "better integration of the developing countries in the world economy"'; stinging Armstrong into pointing out that he was using reported speech by, 'my

German colleague.'[555] Similarly, he prompted the Prime Minister to respond to Armstrong's report of a sherpa meeting in 1985: 'that you wish your Personal Representative to take a more robust line on GATT at the next meeting.' Once more provoking a robust reply: 'I can assure the Prime Minister that [my intervention] was in line with the briefing,' and hence with existing United Kingdom policy. On which Powell commented to Thatcher, 'Policy on a new GATT round is wrong and will need to be corrected.'[556] When the French Ambassador in London sounded out Armstrong on the British attitude to a co-ordinated European response to American requests for a declaration of support for the 1983 Strategic Defense Initiative (SDI) Powell commented that: 'RTA went a bit further than he should have on the need for a European response on SDI research.'[557] In 1986 he instructed the No 10 Diary Secretary to set up a meeting with the Prime Minister, Foreign Secretary, Chancellor of the Exchequer and himself to discuss the Tokyo Economic Summit – but perhaps by oversight did not put Armstrong on the invitation list.[558]

A strengthened foreign affairs capability in Downing Street inevitably tended to undermine the Cabinet Secretary's influence. Responding to Armstrong's report of the first sherpa session in February 1987 Powell pulled no punches: '[The Prime Minister] finds the failure to exert pressure on the Japanese representative inexplicable ... She does not recall yet having been consulted about the issues ... [she] wonders whether the nugatory results do not lead to the conclusion that we could manage with fewer meetings in this forum.' When Armstrong responded that the Japanese would have been left in no doubt about the views of other governments Powell wrote in the margin: 'Not what the first minute said!' – which was strictly correct.[559] On receiving Armstrong's minute seeking the Prime Minister's clearance for the line to be taken at the second sherpa meeting in preparation for the 1987 Summit he advised the Prime Minister: '... by the time the papers reach you, it is just a question of reacting to a paper which is already well advanced rather than planning some objectives of our own.'[560] Unlike previous years the steering brief for the Summit was prepared by Powell[561] and when Armstrong submitted the draft economic declaration just before the Summit meeting Powell responded that: 'The Prime Minister has not yet had an opportunity to read it. But I think she would take the view that it is too long and too wordy and that a text on these lines would risk ridicule.'[562]

Duties and Responsibilities (Again)

Early in 1985 Armstrong was helping pilot through a revision of the rules governing the take-up of business appointments by civil servants on retirement or resignation. In this area Parliament had long been attracted by notions of celibacy, whilst at the same time acknowledging that interchange between the public and private sectors was insufficient. The Treasury and Civil Service Select Committee had recommended some tightening of the business appointment rules in 1980 to require staff at Under-Secretary and above to submit proposals for external employment voluntarily to the Business Appointments Committee headed by

Lord Diamond. That committee could recommend a cooling off period of up to two years and there was an unwritten expectation that the individual would abide by their suggestion. At the time Armstrong had argued that: 'it would be very regrettable if men and women retiring from the public service for no better reason than that they were 60, with considerable personal qualities and much to contribute, came to be more or less debarred from making that contribution in areas of industry and commerce where they would do a useful and socially valuable job, just because of excessive precautions to ensure propriety.'[563] Now, prompted by an upturn in appointments to the private sector (notably by senior staff in Defence) the Committee conducted another enquiry into the 'rules' in 1984, this time advocating a fallow period of up to five years. Armstrong gave evidence on 8 August (refusing to give details of individual cases on grounds of privacy and commercial confidentiality) and subsequently led on the government response, which conceded some procedural tightening and greater openness, but rejected the proposed increase in the fallow period. Such an increase would inhibit movement undesirably; it would be unfair to individuals and was not justified on the evidence adduced by the Committee. In his judgement, 'The more restrictive we try to make it, the greater the danger that someone will flout it, or even seek to challenge it in the courts and subject it to judicial review.'[564] Legal advice was that the rules would not stand up to judicial review.[565] Few thought it worthwhile to seek legislative backing, so there had to be a delicate balance in which civil servants would acquiesce in restrictions in the interests of perceptions of propriety, provided the restrictions were fair to them.

Later that year, continuing in the tradition of Bridges' *Portrait of a Profession* lecture of 1950, Armstrong spoke to the annual conference of the Chartered Institute of Public Finance and Accountancy (CIPFA) in Brighton. In advance he submitted his text to the Prime Minister seeking approval, in particular, for what he would say about allegations of politicisation of appointments of Permanent Secretaries. Recognising his role of head of profession, Thatcher wrote on the top of the draft: 'Robert says whatever he wishes to say,' adding, 'I believe that some of this lecture will cause quite a stir.'[566] Prompted by the Ponting affair Armstrong had sought the Prime Minister's approval in February for a formal restatement of the duties of civil servants, which had not been promulgated for over 30 years. He did not envisage anything new in the provisions, nor a tightening of existing arrangements, simply a reminder that civil servants were servants of the Crown and that the Crown was, to all intents and purposes, synonymous with the government of the day. The statement went through four drafts in the space of 10 days (including two in one day) – the Permanent Secretaries consulted saw nothing controversial and no great gaps in the text. It was issued to civil servants on 26 February with a parallel announcement by a written Parliamentary Answer. Thatcher did not intervene in its drafting save to agree that the statement should be released with a message that she had both agreed to it being drafted and with its substance. There were, however, two significant omissions as the draft developed. First, a proposal to clear it with former Prime Ministers and with the Leader of the Opposition was dropped. Second, a proposal that: '...

it would greatly enhance the value of the operation if the Prime Minister felt able to go on and say something about the reciprocal responsibilities of Ministers in their relations with civil servants,' was watered down to omit wording that could have been seen as telling Ministers how to do their job. The text, 'Ministers have a responsibility to take due account of information and advice given to them by their civil servants in good faith, and not to find fault with an adviser for giving honest and impartial advice just because it happens not to coincide with their own views,' did not make it to the final version.[567]

Publication was not greeted with the acclaim Armstrong might have hoped for. Rather than a return to a 'gold standard' the general reaction was that it belonged to a bygone age – perhaps not helped by the inclusion of a sixteenth century quotation from Queen Elizabeth I. Within a month Austin Mitchell MP wrote directly to Armstrong – in itself a highly unusual step. He charged that the Crown functions in Parliament with a clear interest higher than that of the 'Government of the day' yet politicisation of the civil service had gone farther than ever before and as a result there would have to be drastic changes at the top of the Service if there were to be a change of government. Later in the year the Treasury and Civil Service Committee set up a sub-committee (chaired by Mitchell) to enquire into civil servants' duties and responsibilities with particular emphasis on the relationship with Ministers, seeking initially by means of a questionnaire to probe how the conventions worked in practice.[568] The government played a straight bat, confining itself to repetition of the earlier statement. Armstrong was then duly summoned to give oral evidence, which he did on 28 February 1986, by which time the Westland affair had blown up and the committee spent some time on the application of the duties to civil service press officers. The testimony is unremarkable for the most part. In two respects, however, Armstrong offered opinions that might have been controversial. He said that he had not encountered any conflict of interest between his twin roles of Cabinet Secretary and Head of the Home Civil Service, nor had they been particularly onerous in terms of workload; 'It is an illusion that the Head of the Civil Service is there to defend the Civil Service against Ministerial criticism,'[569] an unusual argument given the excisions that had been made to his draft statement of the obligation on Ministers to listen to their officials.

The MPs did not wholly believe him. They made ten main recommendations (the government response in brackets):[570]

1. Formulation of parallel guidelines to the Armstrong memorandum covering Ministers' duties to Parliament and responsibilities for the civil service (rejected);
2. Specific proposals on how accountability of civil servants to Ministers and Ministers to Parliament should be dealt with in future (rejected);
3. Revision and expansion of the Armstrong memorandum to become a code of ethics (not convinced but would explore);
4. No external right of appeal for civil servants but appeal to the Head of the Home Civil Service (agreed);

5. Ministers able to play an active role in the selection of their officials (already adequately provided for);
6. Regular infusions of talent into the higher civil service (qualified agreement);
7. Option for political appointments as press officers (rejected);
8. Expansion of Private Offices to include Ministerial Policy Units (not ruled out on a case-by-case basis but no central initiative);
9. A single Minister for the Civil Service with his/her own Department (rejected);
10. Separation of the Cabinet Secretary and the Head of the Home Civil Service (rejected).

As is evident, the government response was yet another restatement of the traditional relationship. In another respect the perceived fragility of Ministerial confidence in the civil service is illustrated by an earlier episode, shortly before the 1983 General Election. Sir Brian Cubbon at the Home Office raised a perennial worry of the senior civil service: 'I have long thought it a major defect of our system that there is virtually no policy contact between Permanent Secretaries and Opposition Leaders until they are thrown together upon a change of Government … It cannot be sensible, or even democratic, that the Conservative manifesto at the forthcoming Election will inevitably have the benefit of substantial civil service advice, whereas the other manifestos will not. Only senior civil servants can hope to solve the problem, and I believe that we have a duty to try to do so.' Armstrong had agreed that this was a shortcoming but confessed himself unable to see what could be done: 'It would be a lot to expect of the party in power to sanction, let alone approve, such contacts. I fear that Ministers, of whatever party, tend to suspect their senior civil servants of having some sort of allegiance to other parties.'[571] These suspicions tended to be nurtured by the press, which would report such contacts mischievously. Perhaps this was a subject for the Wednesday morning meeting of Permanent Secretaries; Armstrong would be well content if Cubbon were to raise it – though it appears that he did not do so.

The Combined Role: Cabinet Secretary and Head of the Home Civil Service

The government rejected the Treasury and Civil Service Select Committee's advice of May 1986 to separate the roles of Cabinet Secretary and Head of the Home Civil Service. Opinion inside the civil service was divided. Sir Kenneth Stowe reported in his 1987 valedictory analysis, *Better Management in Government*, that the consensus amongst Permanent Secretaries was to separate the two roles. Armstrong responded with a defence of the status quo. 'At the top of no other organisation, public or private sector, would one suggest that top level responsibility for management should be divorced from top level responsibility for the main stream of policy formulation and advice. I certainly have not felt inhibited in giving you advice on management issues, *when I thought it right to do so* [emphasis added].[572] ... By no stretch of imagination do those duties and responsibilities [of the head of the Civil Service] amount to a full-time job.'

The parallel with the private sector is not strong since the role of Ministers and the political survival of a government has no equivalent. But the mismatch between Armstrong and Stowe is striking. Armstrong looked top-down, taking it as read that the Head of the Home Civil Service should be a person close to the Prime Minister since she was also Minister for the Civil Service. Stowe was more concerned with the bulk of the civil service (i.e. in the large operational Departments) and less impressed by the implied influence of the joint position. Thatcher's seeming lack of understanding of the scope for professional leadership of the civil service and her belief that in the final analysis public servants should show the selflessness required to give way to the national need as perceived by the government (and, to be fair, as usually evidenced in public opinion) revealed the ultimate impotence of the position. Indeed, from time to time Armstrong showed his distaste for the title since it seemed to promise more than it could deliver.

There were, however, areas where the joint position was advantageous: (a) on organisation where Armstrong was a strong advocate of the *Next Steps* reforms, which was important given Thatcher's caution in unfamiliar territory where her principal allies (the Treasury and the Efficiency Unit) disagreed; (b) on a better link between reward and performance where Armstrong maintained strong support for the principle of performance pay despite the misgivings of the Permanent Secretaries who were concerned about the risk of divisiveness;[573] (c) on succession planning at the highest reaches: at a crucial moment in 1984 when the Prime Minister was questioning the wisdom of a proposed early retirement programme he argued persuasively that the £6 million costs to fund 100 early retirements would increase the number of planned retirements by 25% and buy 500–600 promotion outlets, creating much needed mobility in staffing.[574] Many of those taking early retirement would have been opponents of the government's reforms whereas some, at least, of those promoted would have been more open to the new ideas; (d) on personal development, where once again Armstrong stood up to the Prime Minister – over the introduction of both the Top Management Programme (mandatory for those entering Grade 3) and the Senior Management Development Programme – based on service-wide competencies for senior managers with the emphasis on individual initiative and self-development based on a personal 'training budget' of five days a year recorded in training logs.[575] For a man whose career had been built almost entirely on training and development 'on the job' it was an epiphany; (e) on ensuring that private secretaries understood their responsibilities to collective government as well as to their Minister: Sir David Omand[576] recalls a threatening telephone call from Armstrong when MOD Principal Private Secretary to the effect that civil servants who let their Ministers resign would not find that career enhancing – Armstrong suspected that the MOD PUS (Frank Cooper) and Omand were putting John Nott up to resigning over the 1982 Defence Review;[577] (f) on rare submissions about civil service morale. Armstrong had told the Treasury and Civil Service Select Committee that his job was not to defend the civil service against Ministers' attacks. Nevertheless, in June 1985 he sent the Prime Minister a long submission about the state of morale in the civil service. The thrust of the argument was that many were speaking of a crisis of morale deriving fundamentally from the low esteem in which Ministers held the civil service as an institution. There were many symptoms but the deeper cause – identified more clearly in the briefing from the Principal Private Secretary (Robin Butler) and the Policy Unit than by Armstrong himself, was loss of self-esteem by the Service. The evidence consisted of reports by Permanent Secretaries (two of which were sent anonymously to the Prime Minister), a drop in the quality of fast-stream applicants to join the Service, senior staff seeking to leave and junior staff increasingly militant. The conclusion was stark: 'I fear that the situation is coming towards a point where the damage to the effectiveness of the public service and to the qualities that have led successive Governments to claim that the British public service was second to none may become profound and difficult to reverse.'[578] Two things seem to be missing. First, there is only a weak sense of personal belief from the head of profession: in arguing that blue chip companies sought to offer job security to key white collar staff nowhere is it explained why; an assertion that better housekeeping implied past inefficiency was unchallenged; in discussion of merit pay the importance of team effort went unsung. Second, in a culture where civil servants made written submissions to Ministers but rarely spoke at Ministerial meetings the record of the Ministerial meeting the Prime Minister held in July on civil service morale (attended by Armstrong)[579] shows no evidence that he fought his corner and appears to bear out that Ministers (led by the Chancellor of the Exchequer) did not believe their advisers.

Armstrong's initiative failed. There are three plausible interpretations of why it was so unsuccessful. The first is that the Prime Minister did not understand the importance of her own attitude to the morale of civil servants; the second, that she was unconvinced by Armstrong's arguments; the third that she did not feel able (or want) to challenge the attitudes of her colleagues in this matter. Given the frequent evidence of her challenging arguments in other spheres the lack of challenge here rules out the second. That not all Ministers present would have been so dismissive as the Chancellor of the Exchequer points away from the third interpretation. We are left with the first; which is supported by the summing up: 'the Prime Minister said that a number of proposals had been identified and she invites Lord Gowrie and the Treasury to follow them up vigorously.'[580]

Retirement

Armstrong reached retirement age (60) on 30 March 1987. However, in a submission in the spring of 1986, perhaps mindful of the fate of Sir Thomas Padmore in 1951 who was designated Cabinet Secretary by Clement Attlee only to have the appointment rescinded before he took up office by the incoming Winston Churchill, Armstrong reported that with a General Election due in 1987 it could be awkward to make an appointment whose tenure might be short-lived if the Conservatives were defeated.[581] He offered to defer retirement until after a suitable bedding-in period for the newly elected government. The announcement of the extension 'until not later than September 1988' provoked some hostile press comment[582] but it was not without precedent. Sir Warren Fisher (Head of the Civil Service) and Sir Edward Bridges (Cabinet Secretary) both stayed on beyond age 60.

In the event, the General Election was held in June (with a Conservative overall majority of 102). Armstrong's retirement was fixed for the end of the year and on 25 June (after consultation with three senior Permanent Secretaries who were time-barred from being potential candidates) he put forward a short-list of five possible successors. His advice was to appoint Sir Clive Whitmore (PUS Ministry of Defence) and formerly one of Thatcher's Principal Private Secretaries. However, the mantle passed to Robin Butler of the Treasury. The grammar school girl opted for the Harrow and Oxford educated Butler over the Sutton Grammar School and Cambridge educated Whitmore – principally because she judged that Butler could reach people emotionally, and not just engage with them intellectually.[583] As Sir Kenneth Stowe had observed earlier in 1987, there had never been a specification of the role or the personal attributes for the Cabinet Secretary and few people understood either.[584] Thus, it was 17 December when Armstrong attended his last Cabinet meeting and was presented with a, by now traditional, gift – in this case a George III silver plate coffee pot for which Cabinet Ministers subscribed personally, contributing £12.60 each to cover the £280 cost.

Notes

1 Geoffrey Howe, *Conflict of Loyalty*, Macmillan 1994, p. 147
2 Peter Wright, *Spycatcher*, Stoddart, 1987
3 Note by Sir William Armstrong on Robert Armstrong's career file, 27.06.74
4 Then Deputy Secretary HM Treasury, later PUS Ministry of Agriculture Fisheries and Food
5 Appraisal on Robert Armstrong's career file, 09.12.69
6 Interview with Sir David Wright, Armstrong's Private Secretary 1980–82, 01.06.10
7 Howe, *Conflict of Loyalty*, p. 473
8 Cabinet Office file C1/2 part 14, 09.09.81
9 Ibid, 02.02.83
10 Ibid, 03.02.83
11 Quoted by Sir Robin Butler when taking up the Cabinet Secretary post, Cabinet Office paper
12 Ibid
13 Interview with Sir David Goodall
14 Correspondence with Sir Douglas Wass, 05.11.10
15 Cabinet Office file C1D/2, 12.12.79
16 Analysis of Cabinet Office file, C1D/2, 1979–87
17 Prime Minister's papers – US SDI, 02.04.87
18 Prime Minister's papers – Cabinet and Committees, 10.04.80
19 Cabinet Office file 26/25 part 1, 06.02 81
20 See, for example, Harold Wilson's restrictions on escalation of issues from a Cabinet

Committee to the full Cabinet without the Committee chairman's agreement and Edward Heath's complaints about the slowness and reductive influence of Cabinet decision making
21 Prime Minister's papers – Cabinet and Committees, 17.09.81
22 Ibid, 11.06.83
23 Cabinet Office file C23D/5 part 2, 19.03.82
24 Cabinet Office file C23D/5 part 4, 23.04.86
25 CC(86)14^{t,h},10.04.86
26 Prime Minister's papers – Cabinet and Committees, 22.04.86
27 Ibid, 17.04.86
28 CC(86)15th, 15.04.86
29 Cabinet Office file C23D/5, 19.10.79
30 Prime Minister's papers – The Future of British Leyland part 4, 21.01.81
31 Cabinet Office file C1D/2 part 3, 23.04.80
32 Cabinet Office file C1D/2 part 5,19.05.82
33 Cabinet Office file C1D/2 parts 3–7 1980–83
34 Cabinet Office file C1D/2 part 5, 09.12.81
35 Ibid, 06.05.81
36 Cabinet Office file C1D/2 part 7, 20.07.83
37 C(82)31, September 1982
38 Cabinet Office file C23D/5 part 8, 09.07.87
39 Cabinet Office file C23D/5 part 2, 07.04.81
40 Ibid, 23.10.81
41 Interview with Lord Armstrong, 11.02.10
42 *Manifesto for Victory*, launched on 11.04.79
43 Wall, *A Stranger in Europe*, Oxford (2008) p. 39
44 The briefs for the Cabinet Community Affairs item are filed on: Prime Minister's papers, European Communities Budget
45 Cabinet Office file 467/15, 18.03.80
46 Cabinet Office file C1D/2, C(80)23, discussed on 20.03.80
47 Ibid, 19.03.8
48 Ibid
49 PM/80/6404.08.80
50 Cabinet Office file 354/11 part 1, 14.08.80
51 Cabinet Office file 354/11 part 2, 23.10.80
52 Ibid, 11.06.81
53 Ibid, 04.08.81, and 07.08.81
54 OD(81)15th meeting, 09.09.81
55 Foreign Minister and Vice Chancellor of the Federal Republic of Germany 1974–82 and 1982–92
56 Cabinet Office file 354/11 part 2, 09.10.81
57 CC(81)34th, item 3; CC(81)35th, item 3
58 Cabinet Office file 354/11 part 2, 11.11.81
59 CC(81)36th 12.11.81, item 4, CC(81)37th 19.11.81, item 3 and OD(81)17th 12.11.81, item 1
60 Cabinet Office file 354/11 part 2, 25.02.82
61 Ibid, 05.03.82
62 Ibid, 11.03.82
63 Ibid, 26.02.82
64 CC(82)11th item 2
65 Interview with Lord Armstrong, 11.02.10
66 Cabinet Office file 354/11 part 2, 10.05.82
67 OD(82)8th, 21.05.82
68 Cabinet Office file 354/11 part 2, 24.05.82

69 CC(82)29th item 2, 25.05.82
70 Cabinet Office file 354/11 part 2, 13.07.82
71 OD(82) 16th item 2, 22.07.82
72 CC(82)11th, 17.06.82
73 Cabinet Office file 354/11 part 2, 17.01.83
74 Interview with Lord Armstrong, 11.02.10
75 Private information
76 Cabinet Office file 354/11 part 2, 01–03.04.80
77 Ibid, 11.09.80
78 Prime Minister's papers: Ottawa Economic Summit *The Future Shape of Economic Summits*, May 1981
79 Economic Adviser to the Prime Minister 1981–89
80 Cabinet Office file 354/11 part 2, 04.03.82
81 Ibid, 30.04.82 and 07.05.82
82 Ibid, 04.03.82
83 Cabinet Office file C23D/5 part 2, 02.05.82
84 Ibid, 04.02.80
85 Cabinet Office paper, 15.01.80
86 Ibid, 20.04.83
87 Ibid, 23.03.83
88 Ibid, 18.05.83
89 Ibid, 11.02.83
90 Ibid, 27.09.82 and 20.04.83
91 The briefing was on 20 June; the Summit was 22–23 June 1980.
92 Cabinet Office paper, 24.03.83
93 Ibid, 23.03.83
94 Prime Minister's papers, Update of the United Kingdom Nuclear Deterrent, 14.07.80
95 MISC 7 comprised the Prime Minister, Home Secretary (Whitelaw), Foreign & Commonwealth Secretary (Carrington), Chancellor of the Exchequer (Howe), Lord President of the Council & Leader of the House of Commons (Pym), Secretary of State for Defence (Nott)
96 Prime Minister's papers, Update of the United Kingdom Nuclear Deterrent, 07.07.80
97 Ibid, 16.07.80
98 CC(80)29th Conclusions, Minute 1
99 Prime Minister's papers, Update of the United Kingdom Nuclear Deterrent, 16.07.80
100 Multiple Independently targetable Re-entry Vehicle
101 Prime Minister's papers, Update of the United Kingdom Nuclear Deterrent, 11.01.82
102 Diplomat who was then Head of the OD Secretariat.
103 CC(82)10th, Conclusions, Minute 1
104 Prime Minister's papers, Update of the United Kingdom Nuclear Deterrent, 25.02.82
105 Cabinet Office file 154/24, 10.01.80
106 Prime Minister's papers, Defence Budget part 4, 05.06.80
107 Cabinet Office file C23D/5 part 2, 25.06.80
108 Prime Minister's papers, Defence Budget part 4, 17.11.80
109 Prime Minister's papers, Defence Budget part 419.01.81
110 OD(81)13
111 Prime Minister's papers, Defence Budget part 5, 15.05.81
112 Prime Minister's papers, Defence Budget part 7, 19.11.81
113 Publication was deferred to 22.06.82
114 CC(83)15th item 4
115 Cabinet Office file C23D/5 part 3
116 Freedman, *The Official History of the Falklands Campaign*, Routledge, 2005, Vol I pp. 158–167
117 Cabinet Secretary's notebook 02.04.82

118 OD(SA) comprised the Prime Minister, Home Secretary (Whitelaw), Foreign Secretary (Pym), Defence Secretary (Nott), Leader of the House of Lords (Lady Young) and Paymaster General (Parkinson)
119 Analysis of Armstrong appointment diaries, Cabinet Office papers
120 The War Book was started by Hankey in 1911, Hennessey, *Whitehall* p. 60
121 Interview with Lord Armstrong, 28.10.10
122 Cabinet Office paper
123 Ibid, 02.05.82
124 Ibid, 09.08.82 and 25.10.82
125 Interview with David Goodall, who went to Washington twice, in March 1983, to negotiate a secret agreement, 20.01.10
126 J25/8/1, 03.10.79
127 *The Interception of Communications in Great Britain*, Cmnd 7873, 01.04.80
128 *Hansard*, 05.06.80, Vol 985 col 780
129 Kenneth Baker MP, member for St Marylebone
130 Prime Minister's papers, Interception, 30.01.81
131 Ibid, 14.07.81
132 Ibid, 21–22.07.81
133 Ibid, 07.08.81
134 Ibid, 05.11.82
135 *Hansard*, 29.03.81, col 1081
136 CC(81)13th item 1
137 Lord Diplock
138 Cabinet Office paper, 02.12.81
139 Ibid, 04.12.81
140 Ibid, 21.12.81
141 *Statement on the Findings of the Conference of Privy Counsellors on Security*, 1956
142 The Prime Minister made a brief reference in a written answer on 19 May and the written statement was published as a White Paper *Statement on the Recommendations of the Security Commission* Cmnd 8540 on 20 May
143 HC deb 07.05.63, vol 677 cc 240–372, Radcliffe Report on Security procedures, 1962
144 Prime Minister's papers, Security Commission, 05.03.82
145 Ibid, 17.03.82
146 Ibid, 05.03.82
147 Cabinet Office file C1D/2 part 2, 17.10.79 and 21.11.79
148 Cabinet Office file C1D/2 part 3, 13.02.80
149 Ibid, 12.03.80
150 Cabinet Office file C1D/2 part 6, 09.05.83
151 Cabinet Office file C1D/2 parts 2–4
152 Cabinet Office file C1D/2 part 4, 22.10.80
153 Ibid, 16.10.79
154 Ibid, 12.12.79
155 Cabinet Office file C1D/2 part 3, 02.07.80
156 Cabinet Office file C1D/2 part 4, 06.04.81
157 Cabinet Office file C1D/5 part 2, 30.01.81
158 Cabinet Office file C1D/2 part 5, 16.06.81
159 Cabinet Office file C1D/2 part 8, 08.02.84
160 *Alternative to Domestic Rates*, Cmnd 8449, December 1981
161 Cabinet Office file C1D/2 part 5, 03.02.82
162 Cabinet Office file C1D/2 part 6, 17.01.83
163 CC(83)1st Conclusions, Minute 7, 20.01.83
164 Cabinet Office file C1D/2 part 6, 08.05.83
165 Cabinet Office file C1D/2 part 10, 08.01.86

166 Secretary of State for Northern Ireland 1979–81
167 PREM 19/82, 16.10.79
168 Cabinet Office file 110/20, 27.11.79
169 Ibid, 09.05.80
170 Ibid, 22.10.80
171 Ibid, 05.08.80
172 Ibid, 15.10.80
173 Secretary to the Irish Government, 1980–1992
174 Cabinet Office paper
175 *Hansard*, 15.11.79, cols 679–682
176 Cabinet Office papers, 18.06.77, and 21.06.77
177 *Hansard*, 21.11.79, cols 402–410
178 Cabinet Office paper 16.11.79
179 *Guardian*, 05.12.79
180 Cabinet Office paper 05.12.79
181 Harry Chapman Pincher, investigative journalist specialising in defence and intelligence, writing for the *Daily Express*
182 Director General of MI5 1956–65
183 Prime Minister's papers, Security of the Secret Services, 17.02.81
184 *Their Trade is Treachery*, Sidgwick & Jackson, (1981)
185 Chairman of the House of Commons Foreign Affairs Select Committee 1979–87
186 08.10.82
187 Ibid, 18.11.82
188 Prime Minister's papers, Security of the Secret Services, 20.06.83, Parkinson reported that West would abandon plans for a follow-up to the first volume history of SIS which had covered 1909–1945
189 Prime Minister's papers/Publication of *British Intelligence and Covert Action* by Jonathan Bloch and Patrick Fitzgerald, 19.12.83
190 Ibid, 20.07.84
191 *Manifesto for Victory*, Conservative Party 11.04.79
192 MPO 2nd Permanent Secretary's files, 18.12.86
193 Ibid
194 Ibid, 31.10.79
195 Cabinet Office file C1D/2 part 2, 03.10.79
196 Ibid, 21.11.79
197 Prime Minister's papers, Long-term management of the civil service part 12, 14.12.82
198 Cabinet Office paper, 22.11.79
199 Thatcher, *The Downing Street Years*, p. 48
200 Lowe, *The Official History of the British Civil Service. Reforming the Civil Service, volume 1: the Fulton Years, 1966–81* (Routledge, 2011) chapter 7.5 *The Demise of the Civil Service Department*
201 Cabinet Office file190/6 part 6, 21.05.80
202 Prime Minister's papers, Future of the Civil Service Department, 22.04.80
203 Ibid, 17.06.80
204 Ibid, 18.06.80; Armstrong's evidence is at TCSSC Session 1979–80, Wednesday 18 June 1980, HMSO 333-ix
205 Ibid, 30.06.80
206 Thatcher, *The Downing Street Years*, p. 48
207 Interview with Clive Whitmore, 22.02.10
208 Cabinet Office file 35/40 part 7, PS(80)17th and 18th Meetings, minutes i
209 Attended by the Chancellor of the Exchequer (Howe), Lord President (Soames), Rayner, Bancroft, Wass, Armstrong, Whitmore, Wolfson (Downing street staff, and Pattison (private secretary)

210 PREM 19/250, 23.07.80
211 Ibid, 24.07.80
212 PREM 19/250, 31.10.80
213 Ibid, 31.10.80
214 Ibid, 12,11.80
215 Ibid, 14.11.80
216 First Report from the Treasury and Civil Service Committee, Session 1980–81, 11.12.80, HMSO
217 Prime Minister's papers: Government Machinery part 3, 16.01.81 and 22.01.81
218 Cabinet Office paper, 19.06.81
219 Ibid, 07.09.81
220 Prime Minister's papers: future of the CSD, 08.09.81
221 Interview with Sir Douglas Wass, 05.11.10
222 Cabinet Office file C1D/2 part 4, 08.04.81
223 Ibid, 07.04 81
224 Ibid, 13.04.81, 13.05.81, and 20.05.81
225 Ibid, 29.04.81
226 Ibid, 20.05.81
227 Ibid, 20.05.81
228 Ibid, 03.06.81
229 Cabinet Office paper 11.02.82
230 Cabinet Office file C1D/2 part 5, 03.06.81
231 Prime Minister's papers: Government Machinery part 4 18.09.81
232 Ibid, 22.09.81
233 Prime Minister's papers: Future of the CSD, described in these terms by Thatcher to Armstrong and confirmed by Bancroft shortly after the session, 30.09.81
234 Ibid, 16.10.81
235 Interview with Sir Brian Cubbon, 30.09.10
236 Cabinet Office paper, 14.11.81
237 Tony Blair said much the same some 20 years later, *A Journey*, Hutchinson, 2010, p. 19
238 Cabinet Office file 487/11 part 11, 03.02.82 and 10.03,82
239 Ibid, 09.12.82
240 Private information
241 Cabinet Office file 487/19 part 2, 21.06.83 and 29.06.83
242 Prime Minister's papers, European Community Budget, 11.11.85
243 Ibid, 14.11.85
244 Prime Minister's papers – Government Machinery part 5, 15.07.82
245 Ibid, 30.07.82
246 Ibid, 06.08.82 and 09.08.82
247 Prime Minister's papers, Government Machinery part 5, 06 and 09.08.82
248 Ibid, 29.07.82
249 Ibid, 15.10.82
250 Cabinet Office file C1D/2 part 8, 10.06.83
251 Ibid, 14.06.83
252 CC(83)19th item 3, 16.06.83
253 Cabinet Office file C1D/2 part 8, 02.03.84
254 Ibid, 21.03.84
255 CC(84)18th item 3, 10.05.84
256 Cabinet Office file C1D/2 part 8, 04.06.84
257 Ibid, undated
258 HC deb 12.12.84 vol 69 cc 1050–52
259 Cabinet Office file C1D/2 part 8, 17.07.84
260 Ibid, 30.05.83
261 Interview with Lord Armstrong, 03.11.10

262 Cabinet Office file C1D/2 part 8, 27.06.84, and CC(84)24th item 3, 28.06.84
263 Ibid, 11.05.84
264 OD((E)(84)10, 06.09.84
265 Wall, *A Stranger in Europe*, OUP 2008, pp. 41–43
266 Prime Minister's papers – Security, 10.06.83
267 Cabinet Office archive, Armstrong wrote an anguished manuscript letter to his host pointing to the difficulty of people like himself taking part in discussion if anything they said might appear in the media
268 H Young, *Discipline by publicity*, *Sunday Times* 17.07.83
269 *The Times*, *Prima Inter Pares*, 08.06.82
270 Prime Minister's papers – Government Machinery part 6, 13.06.83
271 Ibid, 18.06.84
272 Cabinet Office file 487/19, 21.06.84
273 Ibid, 29.06.84
274 Cabinet Office file 487/11, 28.06.84 and 02.07.84
275 Ibid, 19.07.84
276 Ibid, 10.10.84
277 Mrs Strachan later became the Head of HM Customs & Excise 1993–2000
278 Cabinet Office file 487/11, 08.09.83
279 Ibid, 29.09.83 and 06.10.83
280 Ibid, 26.10.83
281 Ibid, 14.11.83
282 Cabinet Office file 487/11, 05.11.85
283 Ibid, 16.10.86
284 Ibid, 21.10.86
285 Ibid, 31.10.86
286 Ibid, 05.01.87 and 26.01.87
287 Ibid, 27.01.87
288 Cabinet Office file 487/24 part 1, 02.04.87
289 Ibid, 02.04.87
290 Ibid, 03.04.87
291 It is arguable that this single-mindedness led to a crude numerical target for the numbers of Civil Servants to be put into Executive Agencies that contributed to some of the later public failures such as the ill-fated creation of the Prisons Service as an Agency
292 Cabinet Office file 487/24 part 1, 05.05.87
293 Ibid, 20.05.87
294 Ibid, 21.05.87
295 Ibid, 24.06.87
296 In addition to the Prime Minister other attendees were the Lord President, the Chancellor of the Exchequer, the Secretaries of State for the Home Department, Environment, Employment, Social Services and Defence, the Lord Privy Seal, the Chief Secretary, the Minister of State Privy Council Office, Sir Robin Ibbs, the Head of the Policy Unit and Armstrong
297 Cabinet Office file 487/24 part 1, 09.07.87
298 Ibid, 21.07.87
299 Prime Minister's papers – Government Machinery part 7, 25.06.87
300 Ibid, 22.07.87
301 Ibid, 24.07.87
302 Ibid, 05.08.87
303 Ibid, 06.08.87
304 Cabinet Office file 487/24 part 3, 15.10.87
305 Ibid, 20.10.87
306 Ibid, 22.10.87

307 Cabinet Office file 487/24 part 4, 05.11.87
308 Ibid, 13.11.87
309 *The Times*, *When the Music Stops*
310 Cabinet Office file 487/24 part 4, 31.12.87
311 Goodall succeeded Robert Wade-Gery as head of the OD secretariat in May 1982. He became closely involved with Armstrong on the negotiating team with Ireland, continuing to play a key role after he returned to the Foreign Office in 1984
312 Interview with David Goodall, 20.01.10
313 Head of the Anglo-Irish Division in the Department of External Affairs
314 Goodall, *An Agreement Worth Remembering*, Dublin Review of Books, 2010
315 Cabinet Office file 110/20, 21.09.83
316 Ibid, 03.11.83
317 Ibid, 20.12.83
318 Cabinet Office archive 07.01.84
319 Interview with Sir David Goodall, 20.01.10
320 Cabinet Office archive, 07.03.84
321 Ibid, 05.03.84
322 New Ireland Forum report, 02.05.84, The Stationery Office, Dublin
323 Cabinet Office archive, 30.04.84
324 Ibid, 23.05.84
325 Ibid, 19.07.84
326 Ibid, 20.07.84, 06.08.84, 26.09.84, 20.10.84, 25.10.84, 01.11.84, 05.11.84, 28.11.84
327 Ibid, 28.10.84
328 Ibid, 16.11.84
329 Goodall, op. cit
330 Cabinet Office archive, 02.01.85
331 Other members were the Lord President of the Council, The Foreign Secretary, the Secretaries of State for Defence, for Trade and Industry, and for Northern Ireland, the Chief Secretary, HM Treasury, the Chancellor of the Duchy of Lancaster and the Attorney General
332 Cabinet Office archive, 07.05.85 and 13.05.85
333 Ibid, 14.06.85
334 Ibid, 02.07.85
335 Armstrong was significantly more optimistic about the outcome after his meeting with Nally on 30–31.07.85
336 Cabinet Office archive, 11.09.85
337 Ibid, 27.09.85, and 28.09.85
338 Ibid, 26.09.85
339 Ibid, 14.10.85
340 Ibid, 31.10.85
341 Ibid, 25.11.85
342 Ibid, 23.11.85
343 Ibid, 19.11.85
344 Ibid, 09.01.86
345 Ibid, 13.01.86
346 Ibid, 15.01.86
347 Ibid, 12.06.86
348 Ibid, 01.10.86
349 Ibid, 24.10.84
350 Garret FitzGerald, *All in a Life*, Macmillan, Dublin 1991 p. 381
351 Michael Lillis had been a very successful Irish information officer in the United States and was a key member of the Irish negotiating team
352 Quoted in P. Buckland, *The factory of Grievances: devolved government in Northern Ireland 1921–39*, Gill and Macmillan, Dublin 1979

353 O'Brien describes the source as 'unattributable interview'
354 Correspondence with Sir Christopher Mallaby, 13.10.10
355 *Hansard* 6th Series, Vol 53 No 87, 30.01.84
356 *Hansard* cols 28 and 77, 27.02.84
357 Armstrong affidavit, 13.04.84
358 Ibid
359 Prime Minister's papers, 11.02.82
360 At that time Sir Brian Tovey; Director 1978–1983; he was replaced by Sir Peter Marychurch
361 Prime Minister's papers: GCHQ, 11.02.82
362 Prime Minister's papers: Security Commission, 17.03.82
363 First introduced in the 1971 Industrial Relations Act under the Conservatives and confirmed in the Labour Employment Protection Act of 1978
364 Prime Minister's papers: GCHQ, 13.04.84
365 Ibid, 21.09.83
366 Ibid, 25.01.84
367 CC(84)3rd, item 2, 26.01.84
368 Prime Minister's papers: GCHQ, 25.01.84
369 Ibid, 30.01.84
370 Ibid, 31.01.84
371 Ibid, 31.01.84; at the Conservative Party Conference in Brighton on 10.10.80 Thatcher had defiantly said, 'The lady's not for turning'
372 Ibid, 06.02.84
373 Ibid, 17.02.84
374 Ibid, 08.02.84
375 Ibid, 08.02.84
376 Ibid, 16.02.84
377 Ibid, 23.02.84
378 Ibid, 17.02.84
379 Comments by the GCHQ Director, Sir Peter Marychurch, at the Prime Minister's meeting of 21.02.84
380 Howe, *Conflict of Duty*, pp. 347–8
381 CC(84)8th item 2.
382 Prime Minister's papers: GCHQ 21.11.84
383 Freedom of Association and Protection of the Right to Organise Convention, ILO, 1948
384 MPO PUS files, GCHQ 21.01.87
385 Ibid, 05,12.84
386 Ibid, 20.12.85
387 Prime Minister's papers, USA (misc), 20.10.83
388 Ibid, 20.10.83
389 Ibid, 16.02.84
390 Ibid, 04.04.85
391 Ibid, 21.03.86
392 Ibid, 24.03.86, and 21.04.86
393 Ibid, 27.05.88
394 Private information
395 Private information
396 MISC 101 comprised the Prime Minister, Home Secretary, Chancellor of the Exchequer, Lord President, Secretaries of State for Defence, Energy, Transport, Trade & Industry, Scotland, Chief Secretary to the Treasury, Attorney General. Minister without Portfolio. It met frequently and deputies at Minister of State or Parliamentary Under-Secretary level were allowed
397 Cabinet Office file C1D/2 part 8, 21.03.84

398 Prime Minister's papers, Government Machinery, reactivation of the Civil Contingencies Unit, 02.03.81
399 Cabinet Office file C1D/2 parts 8 & 9
400 Mountbatten was murdered in August 1979, Armstrong was told of the films in December
401 Cabinet Office file 199/48, 02.01.80
402 Ibid, 08.02.80
403 Ibid, Lord Hailsham's comments on the Suez script, 10.01.80; Hailsham was First Lord of the Admiralty in 1956
404 Hailsham, *Door Wherein I Went*, Collins, 1975
405 Cabinet Office file 199/48, 11.07.80
406 Ibid, 01.07.80 and 21.07.80
407 *The Times*, 11.11.80
408 Prime Minister's papers/ Leak at MOD and trial of C Ponting, 13.08.84
409 Ibid, 17.08.84
410 Ibid, 18.08.84
411 Prime Minister's papers/aerospace (1), brief on E(A)(85)72, 11.12.85
412 CC(86)1st Conclusion 2
413 Secretary of State for Defence 1983–86
414 E(A)(85)24th meeting, conclusion 1, conveyed to Westland by the Secretary of State for Trade & Industry on 12 December
415 Prime Minister's papers/aerospace; private information 16.12.85 and 10.01.86
416 CC(85)36th meeting conclusion 4
417 CC(85)37th meeting conclusion 1
418 Prime Minister's papers/aerospace; private information, 23.12.85 and 30.12.85
419 Secretary of State for Trade and Industry 1985–86
420 Prime Minister's papers/aerospace, 01.01.86
421 *The TIMES* 03.01.86
422 Prime Minister's papers/aerospace, 06.01.86
423 Private information
424 Ibid, on 23 December Michael Alison, her Parliamentary Private Secretary, had reported a conversation which had given that impression
425 Private information
426 CC(86)1st meeting, item 2
427 Cabinet Office archive, Prime Minister's appointment diary 1986
428 Michael Havers MP, Attorney General 1979–87
429 Prime Minister's papers/aerospace, 10.01.86
430 *Hansard*, 16.01.86, col 614
431 *Hansard*, 23.01.86 cols 449–460
432 *Hansard*, 23.01.86 col 450.
433 Prime Minister's papers/aerospace, 29.01.86, the argument was that private offices have no position other than as assistants to and channels of communication for their Ministers: they have no standing or responsibility in their own right. Armstrong Chief Whip
434 On 5 February (a hearing of about 3 hours) and 5 March
435 Fourth Report from the Defence Committee Session 1985–86, HC 519, question 1174
436 Permanent Under-Secretary, Department of Trade and Industry
437 Cabinet Office archive, 14.04.86
438 Ibid, 15.07.86
439 Ibid, 21.07.86
440 Ibid, 13.10.86 and 16.10.86, 22.07.86 and 14.10.86
441 Ibid, 05.02.86
442 Ibid, 01.08.86

443 John Biffen MP, Lord Privy Seal 1983–87
444 *Hansard*, 29.10.86 col 412
445 *Hansard*, 29.10.86 col 413
446 Cabinet Office archive, 16.09.83
447 Ibid, 07.11.86
448 CC(87) 3rd item 5, 29.01.87
449 Draft Guidelines attached to the Government response to the 1st report from the Treasury and Civil Service Committee (Session 1986/87, HC 62) and to the 1st report from the Liaison Committee (Session 1986/87, HC 100), circulated to the Permanent Heads of Departments on 28.04.87
450 *Hansard*, 24.07.86, Col 588
451 Prime Minister's papers/aerospace 01.08.86, and 04.08.86
452 Cabinet Office archive, 10.05.89
453 Howe: *Conflict of Duty* p. 474
454 Shortly after the publication of Christopher Andrew: *Defence of the Realm* (Allen & Lane 2009) Chapman Pincher wrote to *The Times* (27.10.09) challenging Andrew's conclusion that Hollis was never a spy for the Russian Intelligence Service
455 Prime Minister's papers, Security of the Secret Services, 16.07.84
456 Ibid, 03.08.84
457 Conservative Member for Stroud 1955–87 and Chairman of the House of Commons Select Committee on Foreign Affairs 1979–87
458 Prime Minister's papers, Security of the Secret Services, 31.07.84
459 Including Lord Trend, Sir Brian Cubbon (Home Office), Sir Antony Duff (Cabinet Office), Sir John Jones (Security Service)
460 Cabinet Office archive, 07.09.84
461 Prime Minister's papers, Security of the Secret Services, 08.10.84
462 Ibid, 24.10.84
463 Ibid, 06.11.84
464 Ibid, 18.01.85
465 Ibid, 11.02.85
466 *The Observer*, 31.03.85; *The Age*, 11.04.85
467 Cabinet Office archive, 31.05.85
468 Ibid, 04.06.85
469 Ibid, 31.07.85
470 *Newsnight*, 04.01.88, BBC Television
471 Prime Minister's papers, Security of the Secret Services, 07.08.85
472 Cabinet Office archive, 18.09.85
473 Ibid, 04.10.85
474 Ibid, 27.11.85
475 Ibid, 19.12.85
476 Ibid, 04.08.86
477 Ibid, 27.08.86
478 Prime Minister's papers, Security of the Secret Services, 05.09.86
479 Ibid, 07.10.86
480 Cabinet Office archive 29.09.86
481 Ibid, 19.09.86
482 Prime Minister's papers, Security of the Secret Services, 24 October 1986
483 Ibid, 19.11.86
484 Ibid, 24.11.86
485 Ibid, 25.11.86
486 Cabinet Office archive, 06.12.86
487 Prime Minister's papers, Security of the Secret Services, undated
488 CC(86)41st Item 2.
489 Prime Minister's papers, Security of the Secret Services, 24.09.87

490 Cabinet Office archive, 05.10.87
491 Interview with Lord Armstrong, 07.12.10
492 Prime Minister's papers, Security of the Secret Services, 13.03.87
493 Cabinet Office archive, 23.03.87
494 Prime Minister's papers, Security of the Secret Services, 30.03.87
495 Cabinet Office archive, 02.06.88
496 Prime Minister's papers, Security of the Secret Services, 31.10.88
497 Andrew, op. cit, p. 714
498 Andrew, op. cit, p. 720
499 Prime Minister's papers, Security of the Secret Services, 12.12.86 and 17.12.86
500 Ibid, 19.12.86, 19.01.87 and 03.02.87
501 Cabinet Office archive, 17.02.87
502 Ibid, 02.04.87
503 Ibid, 27.04.87
504 Prime Minister's papers, Security of the Secret Services, 28.04.87
505 Ibid, 30.04.87
506 Ibid, 05.05.87
507 Ibid, 03.04.87
508 Ibid, 15.07.87
509 Ibid, 03.07.87
510 *Defence of the Realm*, p. 766 and interview with Sir Brian Cubbon, 07.12.09
511 Retired PUS, Northern Ireland Office
512 Prime Minister's papers, Security of the Secret Services,, 26.10.87
513 Ibid, 26.10.87
514 Ibid, 02.09.87
515 Ibid, 09.09.87
516 Ibid, 15.08.87
517 Ibid, 08.06.88
518 Cabinet Office archive, 06.08.87
519 Ibid, 17.09.87
520 Ibid, 28.08.87
521 Douglas Hurd, Home Secretary, 1985–1989.
522 Prime Minister's papers, Reform of the OSA 07.04.87
523 Ibid, 14.05.87
524 Prime Minister's papers – UK:US relations part 2, 09.11.83
525 Ibid, 11.11 83
526 Ibid, 10.06.83
527 Ibid, 06.03.84 and 22.03.84
528 Ibid, 30.04.84
529 Ibid, 30.04.84
530 Ibid, 08.05.84
531 Ibid, 27.03.85
532 Ibid, 18.04.85
533 *Political Declaration on the 40th Anniversary of the End of the Second World War*, Bonn, 03.05.85
534 Prime Minister's papers – UK:US relations part 2, 22.01.85
535 Ibid, 22.04.85 and 29.04.85
536 Ibid, 01.05.85
537 An informal association of the security services in EU states, known as the Bern Group, had been created in 1971 to exchange information on terrorism and subversion
538 Prime Minister's papers – UK:US relations part 2, 23.04.86
539 Ibid, 25.02.85
540 Prime Minister's papers: Economic Summit, Bonn 09.01.85

541 Ibid, 04.12.85
542 Ibid, 07.01.86
543 Ibid, 26.03.86
544 Ibid, 07.04.86
545 Ibid, 23.04.86
546 Ibid, 07.01.86
547 Ibid, 07.04.86
548 Ibid, 21.04.86
549 Ibid, 27.04.86
550 Ibid, 30.04.86
551 Ibid, 05.05.86
552 Cabinet Office file C1D/2 part 11, 01.04.87
553 Ibid, 05.05.87, 13.05.87,18.05.87 and 03.06.87
554 Private information
555 Cabinet Office file C1D/2 part 11, 10.01.85
556 Ibid, 22.02.85 and 08.03.85
557 Ibid, 29.04.85
558 Ibid, undated
559 Ibid, 11.02.87, 13.02.87
560 Ibid, 28.04.87
561 Ibid, 04.06.87
562 Ibid, 05.06.87
563 Prime Minister's papers, Civil Service, business appointments, 07.08.81
564 Ibid, 08.02.85
565 Ibid, 16.07.85
566 Prime Minister's files, Speeches by the Head of the Civil Service 14.06.85
567 Prime Minister's files, long-term management of the civil service part 17
568 Prime Minister's papers: long-term management of the civil service part 18, 01.11.85
569 Ibid, note of evidence taken by Michael Stark, private secretary to the Cabinet Secretary
570 Treasury and Civil Service Committee, *Civil Servants and Ministers: Duties and Responsibilities*, HC 92, 22.05.86
571 Cabinet Office File C35/54, 22.03.83 to 08.04.83
572 Prime Minister's papers, the position of Head of the Civil Service, 25.06.87
573 Cabinet Office file C1D/2 part 8, 25.07.84
574 Prime Minister's papers: long term management of the Civil Service, 29.11.85
575 Ibid, 23.07.84
576 PUS Home Office 1998–2001 and Security and Intelligence Co-ordinator, Cabinet Office 2002–5
577 Correspondence with Sir David Omand, 17.10.10
578 Prime Minister's papers: long term management of the Civil Service, 07.06.85
579 Prime Minister's papers: long term management of the Civil Service, meeting on 23.07.85; other attendees were the Lord President, Chancellor of the Exchequer, Foreign Secretary, Chancellor of the Duchy of Lancaster, Minister of State Treasury
580 Ibid, 23.07.85
581 Cabinet Office archive 23.04.86
582 Notably in *The Guardian*, 27.06.86
583 Private information
584 Prime Minister's papers: Government Machinery, part 7, *Better Management in Government*, 25.06.87

6 Captain of the First XI

Sir Robin Butler
Cabinet Secretary
1987–97

Butler portrait: Robin Butler by Rosemarie Timmis

Source: Robin Butler

Robin Butler's appointment as Cabinet Secretary and Head of the Home Civil Service was announced on 8 July 1987. It came as no surprise to his fellow mandarins and was interpreted by Whitehall watchers in the media as potentially rejuvenating, bringing an open, and outgoing style.[1] In terms of the apostolic succession he lacked only one qualification – he had never been head of a department. (A proposal by Robert Armstrong to appoint him Deputy Head of the Inland Revenue in 1984 was blocked by Margaret Thatcher who thought Butler would be better deployed in the Treasury dealing with overseas finance.)[2]

In September 1961, straight from Oxford, with First Class Honours in Classics (Greats), he joined HM Treasury as an Assistant Principal and was allocated to the section concerned with control of the aid budget. He was soon earmarked for the top. By 1965 he had his first promotion (to Principal aged 27) and from 1965 to 1969 was secretary to the Budget Committee. A 1972 staff report said: 'Mr Butler should go to the top of the Service. If he does not, there is something wrong with the Service.'[3] Repeatedly he was praised for his enthusiasm, intelligence, speed, resilience under pressure and charm. Occasionally, there was mild criticism, such as 'a hint of ruthlessness' (Peter Carey) and, 'his drafting, which is very good but not yet of the highest elegance' (Robert Armstrong). But Armstrong also wrote: 'It seems unfair that nature should have endowed any one mortal so richly: with intelligence, humour, moderation, modesty, charm, vitality, physical prowess and good looks.' Together with his contemporaries Peter Jay[4] and David Walker,[5] the trio were known by contemporaries as *la jeunesse dorée.*

In common with Armstrong, Butler's milieu was that of the ministerial office, with substantial spells in Private Office serving Heath, Wilson and Thatcher and a foundation spell in the newly formed Central Policy Review Staff under Victor Rothschild in the early 1970s. He was the project manager for the design and build of the Treasury's Financial Information System following the public expenditure crises of the mid-1970s. Not known as a profound thinker, he did not philosophise, nor often go back to first principles. He was a doer – and a very good one.[6] Few expected him to be a radical reformer, though he was known to be concerned about the state of morale in the Service he inherited. His outgoing and positive approach where: 'He has no enemies and practically everyone in Whitehall claims him for a friend,'[7] were characteristics of his public persona throughout his career. To his own Private Office, however, he could sometimes be brusque – a strong, competitive instinct requiring speed, accuracy and judgement from his staff, superior to that in other Private Offices.

His career had seen little adversity. His personnel file records an unsuccessful attempt in March 1984 to be appointed Chief Executive of the Property Services Agency; and on other occasions, like the Inland Revenue opportunity and, for example, a possible tour with Lord Carver in Zimbabwe, postings had not come to fruition. The Treasury never let go of the umbilical elastic. So it was an important signal that one of his first actions in 1987 was to clear diary space for a greater involvement with the civil service outside Whitehall. Two weeks into the job he told the Prime Minister that he wished to be relieved of duties as 'sherpa' for the global Economic Summits.[8] In the first 12 months in office he made 22 visits to establishments, 20 outside London, establishing a pattern of approachability and interest in the bulk of the civil service. He estimated that the Headship of the Home Civil Service took about 50% of his time.[9]

Though he came from much the same background as Robert Armstrong – Harrow and University College Oxford versus Eton and Christ Church – a crucial distinction was that Armstrong had the Headship of the Home Civil Service thrust upon him when already in the role of Cabinet Secretary. For Butler it was always part of the deal and a part for which he was well suited. A second difference was that whilst Armstrong's pastimes were intellectual, for Butler it was relaxation through competitive sport – he was the first Cabinet Secretary to declare a supporter's allegiance to a football league team (Crystal Palace). His relaxation came from cricket, golf, swimming and squash. (Throughout his period as Cabinet Secretary he rarely missed a Wednesday morning game of squash with Sir Michael Quinlan of the MOD and he explicitly used sport as a means of encouraging a team spirit amongst those working in the civil service.) John Major described Butler as 'one of the most competitive men I have met.'[10] This competitiveness could emerge in an unlikely manner. Friends commented that walking on holiday became a time trial; one Private Secretary recalled a particularly bad day during which Butler emerged with 'Wall-walker' toys, bought for his grandchildren, that were thrown competitively against the corridor walls to flip-flop downwards in a race to the floor. After a few minutes he was sufficiently restored to pick up the traces as if nothing difficult had happened that day.[11]

From 1987 it is impossible to disentangle the roles of Cabinet Secretary and Head of the Home Civil Service. In 2011 when it was announced that the roles were once again to be split Butler argued that the one sustained the other, as he had done to Blair in 1997.[12] Other former Cabinet Secretaries who had combined the two roles argued similarly. However, there are contrary points to be made. The load is exceptionally heavy for one person and tends to favour process over substance. Accommodating that load led Butler to give up the sherpa role and later Cabinet Secretaries to weaken their hold over intelligence matters. It can be argued that these, in turn, tended to weaken their influence on the Prime Minister in the crucial areas of government cohesion. Butler described his approach to Cabinet Secretary as 'serving Ministers collectively in the conduct and process of Government business and to assist the co-ordination of policy.'[13] By contrast the *Guardian* argued that he saw being Head of the Home Civil Service as more important than Cabinet Secretary and that 'he does not see it as a part of his role to take political decisions to get Ministers out of a hole, whereas John Hunt saw it as very important to have a 'political nose ... '[there is] no coherence in decision making and when John Major does take decisions he is unpredictable.'[14] To lay the blame on Butler in this way underestimates the growth of Downing Street special advisers after 1979 that inevitably meant that the ubiquitous Cabinet Secretary became a thing of the past. To expect Butler to have promoted an image of policy cohesion where cohesion was essentially patchy is to set the bar too high. Especially as Major's political secretary, Judith Chaplin, put it: 'It is possible to understand [Major] if you recognise that every decision is taken on how it affects and promotes him.'[15] David Lipsey recalls Butler as a hands-off Cabinet Secretary content to keep the show on the road and not much interested in where the road was running.[16] It is one description of a politically neutral Civil Service but, as Lipsey also acknowledges, it was a highly appropriate response under Major when many of the Conservatives were trying to run the government off the road over Europe. Butler's advice to the incoming Major to find a loyal political confidante comparable to the role played by Willie Whitelaw for Margaret Thatcher[17] was as far as he felt able to go in bridging the gap where rational policy had to meet political reality. The ghost of William Armstrong still flitted between the filing cabinets lining the narrow corridor between the Cabinet Office and the Downing Street Private Secretaries' room and much of Butler's most sensitive advice was given in the intimacy of weekly bilateral meetings between Major and his Cabinet Secretary. Butler's Cabinet Office was not a machine feeding a personal confidante of the Prime Minister but one that set out to provide reliable and traditional briefing in tune with a return to a more consensual style of government after Thatcher.

There is widespread praise from Butler's senior contemporaries that his steadfastness in times of trouble, his ability to open Whitehall's most obdurate doors and his willingness to promote success through others marked him out as a procedural trouble-shooter *extraordinaire*. As the Permanent Secretary of the Department of Employment, Geoffrey Holland, put it when he left Whitehall to become Vice Chancellor of Exeter University: 'You have not reached your present eminence at the expense of other people or their feelings or, indeed, their own careers. Quite the contrary. You have been kind and generous throughout. You have always been there if I have been in difficulty and I know that everyone else finds exactly the same.' Nevertheless, there was a small minority who felt differently, claiming that his ease with junior staff was patrician and that he only really valued the opinions of the Oxbridge elite. (Holland had been at Oxford at the same time as Butler and had come second to Butler in the 1961 Civil Service exam.)

Where Butler did provide a vision for the wider civil service was about its future role and structure. At the outset of his tenure *The Times* had argued that the Cabinet Secretary and Head of the Home Civil Service was too rarely seen in the flesh.[18] He understood the difficulty of communicating with the bulk of civil servants, most of whom would never see him in the flesh. His press interviews, regular pastoral visits, occasional television and radio appearances and at least one major public speech a year sought to meet that challenge. They set a bright tone of optimism that sought to combat fears of job insecurity, pay deterioration and the lack of public regard that many, if not most, civil servants felt. Nevertheless, his response to influential criticisms of the civil service continued to be exercised behind closed doors, invisible to those he led. When a 1992 leader in *The Times* doubted whether the Next Steps initiative was producing real benefit, or when the Leader of the Opposition, John Smith, publicly criticised the civil service for declining public standards, Butler's response was to speak privatcly to the complainants. But the damage to civil service morale was done. Bridges might not have replied publicly himself but he would have engineered an authoritative public reply; asking Ministers to do so might no longer have been a possibility for Butler, but perhaps more might have been done to feed a support group of influencers who could seek to put better balance into the public debate.

Despite the substantial effort by officials and individual successes in management reform it proved impossible for the politically neutral civil service to straddle the roles of policy advisor and project implementer. The former CPRS secondee, William Plowden, noted in 1994: 'Ultimately the Cabinet Secretary is the servant of Ministers. He is the quintessential insider ... As champion of the Civil Service he is bound to find himself, at the very least, inhibited. His Cabinet Secretary's hat is bigger than his Head of the Home Civil Service hat and can easily hide it from view.'[19] Further, despite the efforts expended on management review for individual departments, until Gus O'Donnell introduced Departmental Capability Reviews in 2005 competency analysis was conducted at the level of the individual with little systematic attention on the capabilities required of Departments collectively. What had been a breath of fresh air in the late 1980s could look a bit stale by the late 1990s. Operational experience was more highly valued than before, but the method of selecting names to recommend for Grade 2 posts and above had not advanced much. The marriage of track record in improving service delivery in an Executive Agency with success in policy formulation and handling Ministers was still difficult and with a few exceptions the Senior Appointments Selection Committee struggled to rebut perceptions that: 'there was a charmed inner circle of those who had been in certain Departments or who had occupied certain central posts.'[20]

Overall, Butler probably married the requirements of the two roles as well as they could be in the political circumstances of the troubled Major Government. Yet his influence did not survive the transition to the Blair administration, where he was seen as a cross between the mandarins' shop steward and yesterday's man. Blair describes him as: '... professional, courteous and supportive ... He didn't like some of the innovations, but he did his level best to make them work ... But he was a traditionalist ... who did not recognise that the skill set for making the modern state work effectively is different from that needed in the mid-twentieth century.'[21] Jonathan Powell was less kind: '... an old-school Cabinet Secretary who was anxious to assert control over a new and inexperienced prime minister.'[22] New Labour wanted to govern in a new way; some senior officials queried whether those who would have to implement a decision were in the room often enough when the decision was taken and whether policy became synonymous with politics, accelerating a decline in the civil service ability to formulate imaginative and innovative ways of delivering Ministers' goals.

Cabinet and Committees

His time in Private Office had given Butler a familiarity with the importance of risk management. Some ten years earlier, preparing for the publication of the Public Expenditure White Paper, shortly after taking charge of the Treasury General Expenditure Policy Division, he had worked through the small hours to identify and mitigate risks from hostile questioning.[23] Now he asked for hand-over briefing to include:

- Fallout from the *Spycatcher* affair, including the policy on enforcing a life-long duty of confidentiality on employees of the Intelligence Agencies;
- Intelligence expenditure issues;
- Follow-up to the Anglo-Irish Agreement of 1985;
- The state of play on a review of the preparation of legislation commissioned by Cabinet in January 1987;
- Economic issues (including local government finance in the light of the plans to reform rating);
- The Civil Contingencies Unit;
- Science and technology issues;
- Impending senior staff moves;
- Civil Service reform – particularly the 'Next Steps' initiative

By now Thatcher's style of governing was well established, as was the pattern of Cabinet and its Committee meetings. There was little change over the next three years. From time to time there were experiments bringing Ministers into the Cabinet Office with special responsibilities for co-ordinating policy in which the Prime Minister took a personal interest. Urban policy was a case in point. In December 1987 it was announced that the Chancellor of the Duchy of Lancaster, Kenneth Clarke, would have responsibility for the co-ordination and presentation of urban policy. He was to be supported by a small co-ordinating unit but executive action was to remain with Departments. Inevitably, there were tensions between Clarke's ambition to make things happen and colleagues' protection of their empires. So when Clarke wanted to develop a role towards private enterprise that would avoid businesses being contacted on the same issue by different Departments, he ran into difficulty. A suggestion for a 'Freephone' manned from the Cabinet Office met with stiff Departmental opposition.[24] The Department of Trade and Industry (the sponsor department for industry), the Department of the Environment (sponsor department for local government) and Butler all confronted Clarke. Butler feared that the proposals would take the Cabinet Office well beyond its remit of servicing the Cabinet and Cabinet Committees and would leave the Prime Minister open to questions in Parliament about the activities of the Cabinet Office unit[25] – an argument that proved conclusive.[26]

Thatcher continued to be respectful of Cabinet as the final arbiter of policy but became increasingly intolerant of debate and bullied Ministers when a decision had to be made.[27] The frequency of Cabinet meetings hardly changed in the last part of her premiership, (between 37 and 40 meetings a year compared to an average of 42 meetings a year between 1980 and 1987). But she was suspicious of Cabinet committees, regarding them as too often delaying effective action and perhaps (as John Major later found) too numerous to control from Downing Street. Even so, nuclear defence was only mentioned at Cabinet in a low-key manner, if at all. Butler told Powell at the end of 1989 that he did not intend to record notification of a proposed nuclear test in the Cabinet minutes and subsequently advised Thatcher not to mention at Cabinet the postponement of the test due to bad weather.[28] The Ministerial committees on nuclear policy met only twice in the three years 1988–90 to consider a total of nine papers.

Cabinet & committee meetings 1988-90 (Nos)

	Chair	*Meetings*			*Papers*		
		1988	*1989*	*1990*	*11988*	*1989*	*1990*
Cabinet	PM	40	39	37	15	14	10
OD							
Sub cttees	PM	6	7	11	12	13	24
	Various	11	19	25	101	44	44
E(A)							
Sub cttees	PM	16	12	4	57	38	12
	Various	27	16	10	77	39	23
H							
Sub cttees	Lord President	5	8	6	8	11	15
	Various	5	1	2	20	3	13
Legislation	Lord President	10	17	23	51	53	52
MISC cttees	Various	22	28	24	65	92	107
Other	Various	8	11	6	45	42	37
TOTAL		150	158	148	451	349	337

E(A)= Economic affairs H = Home & Social

In February 1990 Thatcher expressed a wish to have more meetings of OD. In a neat reversal of attitude Butler confided to Charles Powell[29] that he did not wish to have meetings simply for the sake of having them, especially as the price to pay might be delay in processing government business. Nevertheless, their discussion generated an intriguing list of potential discussion topics, which Butler rehearsed with the head of the OD Secretariat, Len Appleyard of the Foreign Office:[30] German reunification; coherence in the UK negotiating position at the European Council, notably when concerned with German reunification, NATO, the CFE, COCOM and CSCE; Anglo-French co-operation. The number of OD meetings rose to eleven over the next nine months with two discussions on German reunification and two each covering the coherence of the UK negotiating position at COCOM and reform of the European Commission. But on 2 August 1990 Iraq invaded Kuwait and subsequent OD meetings focused on the British response to that act of aggression. There had been little warning; the Joint Intelligence Committee had last discussed the Iraqi build-up of troops on 26 July concluding that it was more likely to be an act of bullying than a presage of imminent invasion.[31] An ad hoc Ministerial co-ordinating Group (known as AHGG) operated between August 1990 and November when, with the fall of Thatcher it became the official group supporting a Ministerial Cabinet committee (badged as OPD(G)).[32] AHGG initially met daily but after mid September meetings were held on Monday, Wednesday and Friday. Cabinet Office support came through the OD Secretariat. There were no formal minutes; Butler recorded the discussion in letters sent to a long list of Departmental contacts (sometimes over 30 people from a dozen Departments). William Waldegrave (Minister of State FCO) took the chair for the first four meetings but by the middle of August the Foreign Secretary (Major) or the Defence Secretary (King) normally presided.

It was also to Butler as master of the committee system that Thatcher turned in October 1991 when Lord Rothschild suggested a 'characteristically brilliant'[33] scheme covertly to introduce a pest that would attack the Coca crop as part of the battle against crack cocaine. The Government Chief Scientist, John Fairclough, concluded that, combined with action to strengthen the United Nations fight against harmful drugs, the introduction of the moth Eloria to eradicate the Coca bush was sufficiently promising to warrant further consideration.[34] But, he added: the assistance of the host government would be essential if sufficient numbers of moths were to be raised and, as an article in *New Scientist* in February 1988 had rehearsed the possibility, this could not be described as an unknown threat. Nevertheless, he recommended that British scientists should be asked to investigate a synthetic diet to help the breeding of moths in sufficient numbers in the wild. Butler was charged with the administrative arrangements for a secret project, involving the microbiological research establishment at Porton Down.[35] Four months later, however, the *Daily Telegraph*[36] carried an American report of a similar secret project, and Downing Street told Rothschild that: 'Alas, what were once 'secret' tests are no longer. No doubt the race will be on in the producer camp to develop a counter.'[37] The UK ceased work on the project and transferred the initiative to the Americans. However, Butler persuaded Thatcher that the FCO was not taking the Ministerial Group on the Misuse of Drugs sufficiently seriously and she reluctantly agreed to his suggestion to recalibrate the Committee as a fully-fledged MISC Group under the chairmanship of the Home Secretary with, *inter alia*, the Minister of State, FCO as a member.[38] This Ministerial Group (MISC 146) met once during 1990 and considered 13 papers; its official shadow group (MISC 147) had three earlier meetings to consider the papers subsequently put to Ministers.

Butler's focus on procedure depended crucially on Departmental officials' success in analysing policy options and risks. So whilst the Downing Street Policy Unit often commented on policies within an individual Minister's remit, Butler would not intervene unless asked to do so by the Prime Minister. Thus, he was not substantively involved in the sensitive issue of immigration and asylum which surfaced in 1991, and when the autumn 1994 Sunningdale Permanent Secretaries' Conference decided to establish an interdepartmental working group on under-achievers in society he was content to let Andrew Turnbull (by then Permanent Secretary at the Department of the Environment and thus concerned with inner-city poverty) make the running. Nor is there evidence of Butler's involvement in the formulation of the failed Thatcher policy for a 'Community Charge' based on a modified poll tax. He played a straight bat and, as a result, never achieved true closeness to the Prime Minister, unlike, say, Charles Powell with Thatcher.[39] Powell showed extraordinary perceptiveness about foreign policy and strong skills in upward management. A submission to Thatcher in August 1987 was a tour de force. He was arguing for more money for the Foreign Office (not an easy task). His submission started by establishing rapport, moved to exploit one of Thatcher's instincts (concern for the families of those who serve the state), gave her a small number of highly practical actions and then closed with a rebuttal of likely counter-arguments from those who may have opposed the suggestions. All in two and a half sides of A4 paper!

Informal weekly meetings between the Prime Minister and Butler took place throughout his tenure: 214 over the ten-year period (53 with Thatcher, 141 with Major and 20 with Blair). Unusually the discussions were minuted (at least in part) and analysis of these records confirms that Thatcher took a stronger interest in senior appointments than either of her immediate successors; that Major's efforts towards greater openness were a frequent topic of conversation; that Major also used the Cabinet Secretary to pursue his strong desire to reform the Honours system; and that the constitutional implications of the marital break-up of the Prince and Princess of Wales, was a frequent topic. With Tony Blair's arrival the New Labour approach to collective discussion led to an unprecedented concentration on Cabinet management, media handling and machinery of government issues. Overall, however, the impression remains that, especially in the Major years, the exchanges were tactical and short-term with little sign of a strategic compass.

Intelligence and Security

Though he had no direct experience of intelligence and security Butler had observed the Cabinet Secretary's involvement in these matters from the vantage point of Private Office and as Second Permanent Secretary in charge of public expenditure control in the Treasury. In his handover briefing he was advised by his future Private Secretary (Trevor Woolley) that the arrangements for supporting him were untidy and potentially problematic.[40] In the Cabinet Office there was overlap between the Intelligence Co-ordinator, the Security Division and the Overseas and Defence Secretariat and yet some issues still fell between the cracks. Work leading to Thatcher's statement of 6 May 1987 clearing the Security Service of allegations that it had destabilised the 1974–76 Wilson Government had had to be undertaken by the Cabinet Secretary and his private office despite the other calls on their attention. Interdepartmentally, co-ordination had failed when the Home Office had neglected to circulate a draft submission on Security Service legislation before the Home Secretary wrote formally to the Prime Minister with a proposal.[41] Analysis of 17 intelligence issues ranging from Peter Wright and *Spycatcher* to investigations of suspected Soviet agents, pointed to a confusing picture, not least over just who should report operational activities of the Security Service to the Prime Minister.

The result was that over a 15-month period Butler painstakingly negotiated an agreed statement of his role with the Intelligence Agencies, the Home Office and the Foreign and Commonwealth Office. Even before that work was completed, however, he set out to stake his claim to the inheritance as the Prime Minister's adviser on intelligence. So when Thatcher was due to see Patrick Walker, the new Director General of the Security Service, on 28 January 1988, he argued that he should also attend: 'to hear the PM's pre-occupations about the Service. I will promise to say nothing!'[42] And perhaps mindful of the influence of Charles Powell in Downing Street he made clear that he should be sent copies of any notes of meetings the Prime Minister might have with the Agency heads.[43] When Powell replied evasively Butler's steely core came out: 'I shall be happy to fall in with whatever arrangement is easiest. The best may be that either I sit in on the meetings or whoever of you does so looks in afterwards to give me an oral rundown. I have asked my office to make sure that they know from you when these meetings are taking place.'[44] The agreed statement of the Cabinet Secretary's role in intelligence matters was promulgated in mid 1989:

> 'The role of the Cabinet Secretary in intelligence matters stems from the Prime Minister's overall responsibility for security and intelligence, and the Cabinet Secretary's role in supporting her in that capacity and his position as Accounting Officer for the secret Vote.'[45]

The Permanent Secretaries Committee (PSIS)

In 1974 when John Hunt revived the committee of Permanent Secretaries to scrutinise the budgets of the Intelligence Agencies the most significant threats to the UK were the Soviet Union, the IRA and domestic subversion by industrial action. By 1988 the risk of subversion by industrial action was minimal and soon afterwards the fall of the Berlin Wall heralded the collapse of the Soviet Empire with the associated calls for a 'peace dividend.' However, the agency budgets had grown under the protection of Thatcher and Treasury Ministers had begun to feel that PSIS advice came too late in the public expenditure round to be taken properly into account.[46] Moreover, following a 1988 review of the effectiveness and costs of personnel vetting, Departments were now required to take greater responsibility for preventative security. It remained government policy that: 'no one should be employed in connection with work the nature of which is vital to the security of the state who is, or has recently been, a member of any organisation which has advocated [subversive] activities.'[47] But the cost of centralised vetting had become untenable: involving over 600,000 individual checks by the

Security Service in 1987, occupying the equivalent of 64 full-time staff. Although this change and other changes such as a greater emphasis on personal finances in the vetting process,[48] allowed the Security Service to redeploy resources against the higher risk categories of terrorist activity, the financial demands were further exacerbated by a requirement for large investment to respond to technological advances in communications (notably at GCHQ). So it was no surprise when the Treasury Chief Secretary (John Major) raised the issue of alleged uncorrected overlaps between departmental and intelligence agency spending.[49] Spurred on by her foreign policy adviser, Percy Cradock, Thatcher took a strong line to protect funding of the Agencies as a central resource: 'We should resist firmly the position [that the Agencies' budgets should be subject to the hazard of the fate of individual departments' claims] so that there is no doubt. Silence could be quoted against us next year.'[50]

Nevertheless, the Treasury returned to the issue in September 1989. Despite access to the Agencies' records it had not been able to make specific proposals for savings. Butler reacted crossly. A minute to Turnbull at the Treasury accused the Chief Secretary of ignoring known efficiency savings made by the Agencies, pointing out that staff numbers had fallen 2.9% since 1979 and that despite unease at the security implications, the PSIS Committee had made some small reductions in budgets. The battle was largely symbolic – the gap between the parties was less than £50 million over three years. However, perhaps sensitive to the cost overruns on the new accommodation at Vauxhall Cross (MI6) and Thames House (MI5), and aware of the large investment projects in GCHQ, Butler floated a face-saver for the Chief Secretary: a further 0.5% reduction in budgets for unspecified efficiency savings.[51]

GCHQ and the Unions – Unfinished Business

By January 1988 it looked as if the tussle over union recognition at GCHQ was over, with victory for Ministers. The International Labour Organisation (ILO) had conspicuously failed to back the civil service unions in any meaningful way. Management had improved the flexibility of manpower deployment by reducing the number of staff classes from around 100 to 15 and all that now remained was to implement the management initiatives that had been on hold: introduction of the polygraph as part of security screening and of random searches as staff left GCHQ sites. However, following a negative assessment of the efficacy of the polygraph in May 1988 by Dr A B Levey from the Medical Research Council's Applied Psychology Unit at Cambridge,[52] it soon became clear that Ministers and officials had grave doubts about introducing such an invasive procedure. Within a week Thatcher had jettisoned the idea, leaving officials to square the American intelligence authorities.[53] Butler reported back in September that he had secured their reluctant agreement and also that of the Security Commission to abandoning the polygraph.[54] The decision was announced on 8 December.[55]

A further factor strengthening the Downing Street grip on intelligence was the continued combination of the posts of foreign policy adviser to the Prime

Minister and chairman of the Joint Intelligence Committee, much of the intelligence material sent to the Home Secretary being copied by the Agencies to Downing Street. Percy Cradock held both positions from 1985 to 1992 and Rodric Braithwaite followed him from 1992 to the end of 1993. The pattern was broken with the short-lived appointment of Pauline Neville Jones as JIC chairman in December 1993 in addition to being the head of the OD secretariat; that arrangement lasted until David Manning became Tony Blair's foreign policy adviser – Manning did not want to chair the JIC. Also, from 1989 onwards the volume of reporting on operational matters from the Director General of the Security Service to the Cabinet Secretary greatly increased, leaving Butler with the decision whether to pass on the information to the Prime Minister. Annual reports from all three Intelligence Agencies also became the norm.

Personal Envoy

Outside defence and intelligence Butler undertook sensitive foreign initiatives on behalf of Cabinet, none more exotic than the pursuit of a possible artistic coup when, in February 1988, Sir Peter Smithers[56] tipped off Thatcher that Baron Thyssen was searching for a permanent home for: 'the most important private collection of paintings in the world, valued last year at over one billion dollars.'[57] Thatcher was keen to capture the collection as part of the Millennium celebrations, noting that the United Kingdom had missed out on the Gulbenkian Collection:[58] 'because we did not act in time.'[59] In the belief that the Trustees of the Collection were expected to take a decision in June Butler set about assembling a British bid for presentation in May.[60] The two-month delay from first notification of the possibility would, however, prove fatal as the British never properly understood the competition for the collection from Spain. Messages from the Thyssen camp were ambiguous. Shortly before the British submission was ready to be approved by Ministers Thyssen wrote with news that on 7 April he had signed an understanding with the Spanish Government to enter into detailed negotiations for the loan of a significant proportion of his 1,375 paintings. Smithers' mistaken view was that this was a bluff, driven by Thyssen's Spanish wife to scare the British off from making a bid as the agreement with the Spanish had no validity, only the Trustees of the Collection had power to reach a decision.[61]

Thatcher did not think that the Trustees would go against the Baron's wishes but was nervous that news of a British bid would leak and would be politically controversial. Butler, meanwhile, was trying to ascertain with whom the British should be negotiating, the Baron or the Trustees, and opposed indirect negotiations via an intermediary (as the Baron appeared to favour). He presented Ministers with a balanced analysis of the prospects for success on 9 May, coming down marginally in favour of proceeding: '... if an offer from the British Government made a favourable impression on the [Thyssen] Foundation and the Trustees, there is a fair chance that the Baron would be persuaded by them.'[62] Cabinet agreed to the bid on 19 May and two days later Butler (accompanied by Hankes Drielsma, a friend of the Baron) conveyed the bid personally to the

Baron in Lugano, together with a manuscript letter from Thatcher which said: 'I have felt a growing sense of excitement and gratitude that you and your Trustees should be prepared to consider entrusting the core of this supreme and unique Collection to Britain.'[63] However, the personal endorsement from Thatcher was also accompanied by information that the bid would remain on the table only until the end of July.

Thyssen appeared receptive but discussions with his eldest son and current wife (known scurrilously in the British camp as the 'fifth edition')[64] confirmed the Spanish obstacle – a matter of family honour not to welsh on the agreement.[65] Butler advised that he should remind the Chairman of the Trustees, the Baron's lawyer Paul Coleridge, that the British offer would expire at the end of July, in the hope that Thyssen would prompt them to decide in favour of the British offer despite the Spanish memorandum of understanding.[66] He spoke in these terms to Coleridge on 8 July but at the same time persuaded Hankes Drielsma not to provoke Spain by drawing to the Trustees' attention the provision of Bermudan law (where the ownership of the paintings was vested) that they had a duty and responsibility to beneficiaries which must be discharged, even if this might appear dishonourable to third parties.[67]

The Trustees decided, however, not to proceed with the British offer while the prior negotiations with Spain were ongoing, but admitted that they had already indicated to Spain, before receipt of the British proposal, their intention to try to reach a preliminary accord. They had neglected to tell the British negotiators that this was the case.[68] After nine months of negotiation an agreement was reached between the trustees and a Spanish foundation guaranteed by the Spanish Government for a loan of 700 paintings (just over half of the total) for up to ten years. At this point the British lost interest; there is no evidence of consideration of a possible shared deal with Spain to cover all of the collection. So Butler's foray into European arts politics was unsuccessful and, with hindsight, it is evident that the delay between the initial alert in February and the presentation of a British case in May was fatal.

Domestic Policy

Handover briefings prepared for Butler's arrival included a description of the way the Civil Contingencies Unit operated. He had not hitherto been involved with the Unit, whose operations were shrouded in mystery at that time. (It was not until October 1991 that, on Butler's suggestion, John Major agreed to acknowledge the existence and role of the CCU publicly.)[69] Fresh in Butler's mind would have been memories of the fire of 18 November 1987 at King's Cross Underground station when 31 people had died. Typically, immediately on the threat or the occasion of an emergency there would be a rush to handle the immediate issues followed by a long-drawn-out tail of activity until the affair could be declared closed, often many years after those first involved had moved on. In the King's Cross case the report into the causes of the disaster and the response of the authorities by Desmond Fennell QC took 18 months to prepare.

Fennell referred to excessive fragmentation of effort and a relative isolation of emergency services, arguing that 'Consideration should be given to a national planning desk where the experience gained from disasters and their investigation and civil emergencies can be retained.'[70] However, Thatcher was not a centraliser and preferred to preserve the structure whereby response to particular disasters should remain at local levels with the relevant Whitehall department in the lead. Butler's interest was to preserve the co-ordinating role of the Cabinet Office, but he acknowledged that the CCU remit was narrow and hence that significant improvements to preparedness were possible through expanding liaison with local and voluntary bodies. This latter activity properly belonged with the Home Office (whose Minister usually chaired the CCU committee) but to reduce the risk of local authority pressure for more public expenditure he suggested that it would be better to focus action a little outside government provided that bureaucracy could be avoided.[71] A year later he recommended a small but significant refinement when the nominated list of lead government Departments for different categories of civil emergency was enlarged to cover natural or man-made disasters and industrial accidents.[72]

The Collapse of Barlow Clowes

Early in 1988 a misfortune of a different kind hit the government. How it was handled illustrates how Butler could remain calm at the centre of a storm. In mid January DTI investigators reported that the Barlow Clowes investment company was not 'fit and proper' to hold a licence to receive investor funds and on 1 March concluded that client money appeared to be missing; at which point the Department moved for a winding-up and Sir Godfray Le Quesne QC was appointed to carry out an inquiry.[73] Barlow Clowes had operated a Ponzi scheme since 1983[74] and had obtained millions of pounds from investors, inducing them to invest by misrepresentation that their monies would be securely invested in gilt-edged stock but would pay higher dividends than was normal at the time. The DTI had been ignorant of the true nature of the companies and had first given Clowes misleading advice in 1975/76 such that he thought he did not need to be licensed to operate in the United Kingdom. Then in October 1985, when a licence application from Clowes was considered, the Department had issued a licence in the belief that the firm had corrected concerns about the proper handling of client accounts.

As Le Quesne began his investigation Butler moved into risk mitigation: (1) which Ministers had been involved in the DTI authorisation and to what extent were they vulnerable to criticism? (2) Should the government pay compensation to the victims, irrespective of whether Sir Godfray found that it had a duty of care to investors? (3) Would DTI officials be found to have been negligent? (4) Despite all the precedents, would official advice to Ministers have to be published? Le Quesne reported in September 1988. 'Investors' moneys were stolen and used to buy houses, farms, yachts, cars, antique furniture, a vineyard and shares in public and private companies … A rate of return was declared each month and paid by money put in by other investors and not from any gains on buying and selling stocks.'[75] Even so, Butler and Sir Brian Hayes, the Permanent Secretary at DTI, judged that Ministers had done all that could be reasonably expected of them and that conclusion was never challenged. Butler thought it likely that court proceedings and the likely actions of the Parliamentary Commissioner for Administration (the Ombudsman) would have substantial implications relevant to all financial supervision. Thus, initially he steered Thatcher away from the idea of compensation. But Thatcher held a first meeting on 19 September at which it was decided that the only way to bring the Barlow Clowes controversy to an early end would be for the government to pay up. The Treasury and DTI were instructed to examine the potential repercussions of so doing.[76] Two weeks later there was a second meeting. This time in the face of determined opposition by the Chancellor of the Exchequer, Nigel Lawson, the presumption was reversed in favour of waiting to see if the Ombudsman intervened.[77]

The Ombudsman reported the following year. His findings were highly critical of the government, to the extent that the Secretary of State for Trade and Industry, Nicholas Ridley, supported by the new Chancellor of the Exchequer, John Major, argued that the findings advocated standards that went beyond what was reasonable and should be challenged.[78] A meeting between Thatcher, Ridley, Major and Mayhew the Attorney General was set for 30 November 1989 immediately after Cabinet. Butler took control on the Prime Minister's behalf through a masterful brief that argued there was a contradiction between challenging the report (and so denying maladministration), yet at the same time paying compensation. Payment would fly in the face of the principle championed by the government that individuals must expect to take responsibility for their actions and not always look to the government for protection. However, he acknowledged that in the final analysis the decision turned on a political judgement of whether the government could command a majority in the House of Commons if it rejected the report.[79] Ministers' judgement was that political necessity required the government to make *ex gratia* payments to the victims of the fraud, (amounting to 90% of their loss) whilst at the same time continuing to dispute the Ombudsman's findings.[80]

Hayes told Butler that up to three DTI officials could be liable to disciplinary proceedings. If so, would the Cabinet Office 1996 Civil Service Code, which did not permit external involvement, be good enough to command public confidence? Butler advised waiting before taking a decision.[81] He was vindicated when Hayes later wrote that Counsel's definitive opinion: '... criticises officials only in relation to the 'ambulatory pace' of action in 1983/84 and of the time it took in July/September 1987 to decide to recommend an investigation.' Hayes had interviewed the officials concerned and concluded that there were extenuating circumstances in both cases, with no grounds for disciplinary action.[82] Butler took the precaution of checking that Thatcher was content with this conclusion.[83]

On revealing the advice given to Ministers the government had to balance the risk of a groundswell of public indignation if they refused, possibly leading to a Tribunal of Inquiry, against the possible precedent revelation would set.[84] Butler penned a clever formulation: 'I have decided that in this exceptional case it is in the public interest to include the submissions to Ministers and other material that would not normally be published.'[85] A fifth issue came into play: should the government response refer to events in 1975/76 under the government of Harold Wilson, despite the convention that Ministers of one administration do not normally see the papers of a previous administration of a different political hue? Butler went back to first principles. The prohibition was intended to prevent exploitation of earlier papers to embarrass members of a former administration. But as Ministers had not been brought in to the picture in 1975/76 they could not be so embarrassed. 'I therefore see no difficulty in defending access by the current Ministers to the 1975/76 departmental papers on Barlow Clowes.'[86] On the other hand, as the present government had no intention of holding itself accountable for those events, it would be better not to make a reference to them in any written response.[87]

A statement was made to the two Houses of Parliament on the afternoon of 19 December at the same time as the Ombudsman's report and the government observations on it were published.[88] In all £189 million was paid out in compensation, the government later recovering £156 million from third parties over the next 21 years. The case eventually closed on 7 February 2010. An issue that had come out of the blue early in 1988 ran on until three Cabinet Secretaries later.

The Constitution

The IRA bomb of 12 October 1984 at the Grand Hotel, Brighton, which nearly succeeded in killing Margaret Thatcher, had led to speculation about what might happen if a terrorist incident were to kill the Prime Minister and other leading members of the Cabinet. (The last Prime Minister to die in office had been Lord Palmerston in 1865.) Robert Armstrong had briefed the media on the constitutional position[89] – but had refused to be drawn on contingency plans. These included that, whilst the election of a permanent leader for the governing party would be a matter for the politicians alone, the Cabinet Secretary would play an important temporary role in ensuring that government could carry on in the meantime. This would mean consultation with surviving senior Cabinet Ministers to recommend a caretaker Prime Minister to The Sovereign as quickly as possible (ideally someone who was unlikely to be a candidate as a new party leader). Speed would be of the essence; a formal meeting of surviving Cabinet members would not be necessary and the Cabinet Secretary would do all he could to avoid the need for new policy decisions until a caretaker Prime Minister had been appointed.

When the Conservatives revised their rules for the selection of the leader of the Party early in 1989, this was the spur for a new round of exchanges. Andrew Turnbull, newly appointed Principal Private Secretary in 10 Downing Street, wrote to Butler querying whether the new Conservative procedures would mean an unacceptably long hiatus before a new leader was confirmed in office.[90] It could take up to three weeks to regularise the position. Such a situation was not entirely without precedent. R.A. Butler had been de facto Prime Minister during Winston Churchill's recovery from a stroke in 1953 and again immediately after the Suez episode in 1956. He had also chaired Cabinet during Harold Macmillan's long absences on Commonwealth tours. However, the 1953 situation had been kept secret at the time and chairing Cabinet during a Prime Minister's absences abroad was not in the same league as being a caretaker Prime Minister pending the election of a new party leader.

Butler repeated the Armstrong doctrine. He argued that: 'It is, however, essential that in appointing a caretaker, The Queen is not subsequently regarded as having committed a political act by giving an advantage to one contender over others. I therefore think that it would be useful if there was an accepted procedure which could be followed in helping The Queen's Private Secretary to give advice to The Queen which would recommend drawing on someone with no political axe to grind.'[91] One consideration was whether, if there was someone designated as Deputy Prime Minister, The Queen ought to turn automatically to the holder of that title as the caretaker Prime Minister. Butler thought not as the appointment as Deputy Prime Minister would have been made by the Prime Minister and not by The Queen. Hence, The Sovereign would not be protected against charges of having acted politically were she to select the Deputy Prime Minister automatically without further soundings of political leaders. This advice that there would be no automaticity in choosing someone holding the title Deputy Prime Minister was confirmed under Operation CLUNY (the Continuity of Central Government Plan established in the aftermath of the 9/11 terrorist attacks in the United States in 2001).

Coincidentally, on the same day that the incumbent Deputy Prime Minister, Sir Geoffrey Howe, resigned on 1 November 1990 Butler told Turnbull that he proposed to set in hand work to be more specific about the scenarios that might surround a sudden loss of a Prime Minister. The result was a Cabinet Office note *Death of a Prime Minister in Office* circulated on 16 November which advised that: 'Once an acceptable caretaker had been identified, it would not be necessary, or in most circumstances desirable, to appoint him or her as Prime Minister. The Queen would no doubt wish to let it be known, either by granting an Audience or some other way, that the arrangement for the Minister concerned to take charge of the government during a leadership election period had Her Majesty's approval but there is no reason why the post of Prime Minister should not remain vacant for a short period.'[92] In parallel Butler suggested to the Chief Whip that the Conservative Party might consider introducing a *force majeure* clause into its leadership election procedures to deal with a situation of crisis such as might follow a terrorist incident.[93]

The Role of Local Government

In the latter months of Thatcher's Government, spurred on by the controversy over the Community Charge (or Poll Tax as it was popularly known), Ministers started to examine the role of local authorities and set up an inter-departmental exercise to examine their functions. The Cabinet Office was the natural home to manage such an exercise and Butler was involved in setting the scope and allocating the work. He pointed out that changes in central government policies were imposing additional responsibilities on local authorities (Community Care proposals being a good example).[94] Did the Prime Minister want an urgent look at controlling the additional burdens for local authorities or did she want a more fundamental look which would challenge the conventional allocation of responsibilities between central and local government for 'upper tier' services which were heavily influenced by national standards, compared to more genuinely local services such as street lighting or refuse collection?[95]

Two exercises were launched, one on the short-term implications of new legislation and the other to look at existing services.[96] This initial work concluded that increased control over local authority spending implied either centralisation of service provision or prescriptive actions to make local authorities the agents of central government working to expenditure limits it set.[97] Both ran counter to the underlying justification for the Community Charge that, as it was local people who received the services provided by local authorities, most local people should pay towards them. On education (the largest component of local authority spending), for example, Thatcher's response was that she preferred greater devolution downwards in the form of grant-maintained schools rather than centralisation upwards towards central government. No real progress had been made before Thatcher resigned but in the spring of 1991 the Local Government sub-group of the EA Committee considered a draft consultation document on the structure of local government in line with a steer from Cabinet on local government taxation and structure.[98] Butler restricted his advice to the handling of Cabinet, leaving it to the Secretariat to provide advice on handling the EA(LG) discussion and the Policy Unit to raise doubts about whether the proposals were yet ready to open up publicly and whether the linkage to finance was clear enough.

Transparency

Issues about greater openness in government and reform of the Official Secrets Act (OSA) had begun to emerge seriously under Harold Wilson in the 1970s with publication of the Crossman Diaries. The subsequent Radcliffe rules had sought to deal with the position on ministerial memoirs but there had been little change more generally after the Croham directive of 1977 that encouraged departments to reveal the analysis behind policies. Early attempts at reform of the OSA by the Thatcher Government had been scuppered by Andrew Boyle's outing of Anthony Blunt as a Russian spy.[99] But the Westland and *Spycatcher* affairs had once again pointed to the inadequacies of the position. Concern continued and the government published a White Paper on reform of the OSA in June 1988 in which it deployed the attractions of narrowing the scope of the law and introducing tests of the harm done by unauthorised disclosures.

Butler had let it be known right from his appointment as Cabinet Secretary that he intended to steer well clear of exposure such as had tarnished the reputations of

John Hunt and Robert Armstrong, but he could not avoid involvement with the clearance of a steady stream of memoirs. A slough of books on intelligence crossed his desk, including *Big Boys' Rules* by Mark Urban dealing with alleged covert action in Northern Ireland, for which the DA Notice procedure was used to get newspaper editors' agreement to the deletion of information on the grounds that it would harm national security. By the 1990s the prevailing official view was becoming generally more relaxed whilst still concerned to enforce the lifelong duty of confidentiality imposed on intelligence staff, but there were notable irritations. One was the news that Jonathan Cape planned to publish George Blake's[100] memoirs in September 1990.

Butler reported that the official committee that supported the Ministerial Committee charged with giving strategic direction on the handling of disclosures relating to defence, foreign policy or intelligence (OD(DIS)) had discussed the Blake book on 12 September and concluded that: '... while this is a distasteful and unwelcome development the book cannot be said to be damaging to national security.'[101] Nevertheless, suspecting (correctly) that Blake had received a sizeable advance he recommended that, as Blake was still under a lifelong duty of confidentiality, the Crown should reserve its right to hold the publishers to account for any profits accruing from the book. Thatcher agreed and the Treasury Solicitor warned Jonathan Cape Ltd. By mid 1991, however, the publisher was maintaining that the book had been a commercial failure and Butler recommended to John Major that proceedings against the publisher should be stopped, whereas those against Blake should continue. Much later, however, on 19 May 1996, the then Vice Chancellor of the High Court, Sir Richard Scott, ruled against granting the government an account of profits on the grounds that Blake had not been subject to an express contractual obligation and did not have a continuing duty towards the Crown beyond not disclosing secret or confidential information. Since many earlier employees of the intelligence agencies were in the same situation, (contractual undertakings were not introduced until after the *Spycatcher* affair), officials were fearful of a massive loophole. They advised Ministers to lodge an appeal,[102] and this was done on 20 May 1996. Eighteen months later, at the end of 1997, three Court of Appeal judges headed by Lord Woolf, the Master of the Rolls gave a verdict favourable to the government. No more money was to be sent to Blake by Jonathan Cape.[103] As it was, in the meantime, for a memoir Butler called: 'A wise and beautifully written book ... the most blatant breach of the Radcliffe principles by an official that we know,'[104] Sir Percy Cradock flagrantly refused to abide by the Radcliffe rules that confidential advice to Ministers should not be revealed until at least 15 years had elapsed.[105]

Back in 1988 Butler had convened officials to look for ways of closing loopholes left by the *Spycatcher* judgements to enforce the duty of confidentiality on Crown servants. In a complex report, which demonstrated that no simple solutions existed, one idea was to build on the Law Lords' suggestion in the *Spycatcher* appeal case that in a breach of confidentiality copyright of published material may vest in the Crown. An attempt at retrospective action was not advisable but in future a claim of copyright might be used as a second barrel to claims of breach of confidence.[106] A second idea was to secure forfeiture of pension if, as in the case of Peter Wright, former Crown servants moved outside the jurisdiction of the UK. Hitherto, pensions could only be forfeit if someone had been convicted of a serious offence – as Butler pointed out with some glee, Kim Philby the absconded Soviet spy was still entitled to claim a British pension![107] A third proposal was to seek international agreement amongst the most important English-speaking countries to prevent publications that breached UK confidentiality. Cradock pointed out, though, the United States was the most important market for such revelations, and the prospects there of success were remote.

OD(DIS) discussed the options on 28 November 1988 commissioning further work on pension forfeiture with the Prime Minister emphasising that penalties should not be automatic. She directed that the possibility to be examined was to proceed by judicial tribunal, with discretion over penalties and, characteristically, taking into account the implications for dependants. The Home Secretary was strongly of the view that the Official Secrets Bill should not be encumbered by legislation to close these loopholes as the Bill would be difficult enough to pilot through Parliament without substantive amendment, especially as attempts to attack pensions would involve a judicial tribunal – which could be challenged as trial *in absentia.*[108] After two days in Committee, MPs were still on the first clause, with 16 still to be considered. Most of the time had been taken up by the government's own supporters, thus weakening the Chief Whip's position in imposing a guillotine on discussion.[109] Almost a year later (and after the Official Secrets Act 1989 had been passed) officials offered four options for the possible forfeiture of pension, three of which would require legislation. Butler's submission, somewhat complacently and paradoxically, claimed (without citing evidence) that: 'The present arrangements [under which forfeiture is dependent on conviction for a serious crime] have worked well in the few cases that have arisen.'[110] The balance of Ministerial views was to do nothing unless the system of reciprocal agreements being negotiated with other English-speaking countries failed.

A curious by-product of the discussions was interdepartmental inability to agree on whether the government document classification system should be revised to take account of the narrower scope of official secrets and to improve its evidential value – perhaps by adding the prefix OSA to existing classification markings. Thatcher responded with clinical analysis, perhaps also with a touch of irritation: 'I think this is a man-made problem. The documents remain Confidential, Secret or whatever. That has not changed. It is only the mode of enforcement that has changed [and] … it is still dishonourable to give away sensitive information even though [sanctions are] not enforceable.' Turnbull added that whether the OSA protected a document was for the court to decide (not the originator of the document) and would depend on when it was revealed rather than on a classification at the time it originated. So the debate rumbled on until Butler advised in July 1988 that the only acceptable compromise was to leave things as they were, foregoing the evidential benefits and re-emphasising that the classification system was about the handling of documents within government not their protection under the OSA or other statutes.[111] The issue would not re-emerge until February 1992.

A further significant policy issue of the late 1980s and early 1990s concerned control of the intelligence agencies, including whether to put their activities on a statutory basis. Following the Master of the Rolls judgement in the Spycatcher case, which pointed to putting the Security Service on a firmer footing, and rulings from the European Court of Human Rights against Security Service information held on Harriet and Patricia Hewitt, Sir Anthony Duff persuaded first the Home Secretary, Douglas Hurd, then the Cabinet Secretary (Robert Armstrong) and finally Thatcher to put the Security Service on a statutory basis. Under the Security Service Act (1989) its remit was established as:

> To protect national security against threats from espionage, terrorism and sabotage, from the activities of agents of foreign powers, and from actions intended to overthrow or undermine Parliamentary democracy by political, industrial or violent means;
>
> to safeguard the economic well-being of the UK against threats posed by the actions or intentions of persons outside the British Isles; and
>
> to act in support of the activities of police forces and other law enforcement agencies in the prevention and detection of serious crime;
>
> and with the Director General responsible in law for ensuring that the Service does not act to further the interests of any political party.[112]

The existence of GCHQ had been publicly acknowledged in 1983 in connection with the case of the spy Geoffrey Prime but there was still confusion about its tasking and line of accountability. Its Director (Marychurch) favoured something on the lines of the Maxwell-Fyfe Directive of 1952 to the Director General of MI5. But whereas MI5 and MI6 were not part of the civil service, GCHQ was; and thus required a subtly different approach. That something was required was clear – the GCHQ statement of tasking authority dated back to a SIGINT Charter of 1972. So, in July 1989, PSIS considered a draft memorandum updating the position. The content was quickly agreed but there was controversy from the outset over whether to publish the memorandum. Whitmore of the Home Office and Quinlan at Defence inclined towards greater openness. Butler did not, favouring issue as a GCHQ domestic notice and low-key incorporation in the Civil Service Yearbook. Middleton at the Treasury pointed out that consideration should be given to making GCHQ a Next Steps Agency, which would offer the prospect of wrapping up the details in a Framework Document.[113]

Civil Service Leadership

Unlike Armstrong Butler was confident and comfortable as a public face of the civil service. By passing on the 'sherpa' role to the Principal Private Secretary he had made room for getting out to tour civil service establishments as a morale booster and visible leadership. During 1988, for example, he made visits to offices ranging from Darlington to Cardiff to Worthing. In September that year he persuaded a doubtful Thatcher to allow him to be interviewed by the BBC on civil service management matters. 'It would be a useful opportunity to talk about the direction in which management of the Civil Service is moving and ... [it] should be possible in this context to keep away from matters on which I would not be willing to answer questions,' he argued.[114] The latter were, of course, his duties as Cabinet Secretary for which Thatcher refused to countenance television access.[115] But she accepted the distinction in roles, as Butler put it: 'a strategy, with your advice, for occasional appearances on the national media ... in a modest way, I believe, to improve the morale of the Civil Service.'[116] The programme was transmitted on 20 December 1988, by BBC2, with the title, 'The Modern Mandarin.' In it Butler gave a half-hour interview in which he presented a positive image of a modernising civil service.

Despite this willingness to be seen and heard the Butler years were a period of upheaval for the civil service and the changes were only partially successful in modernising it for the turn of the century. This was not wholly down to a failure of professional leadership. From 1979, under media pressure, policymaking became an intensely party political matter in which those who were politically committed squeezed out the civil servants who became seen as executors of policies often determined before they became involved. Ministers became increasingly dissatisfied with the senior civil service, who raised difficulties over policies in whose formulation they had played no part. They espoused views that challenged the Northcote-Trevelyan and Warren Fisher legacy of a politically impartial civil service. Civil servants lost self-worth and public esteem in like measure.

The key milestones from 1988 to 1997 were the restructuring of service delivery along 'Next Steps' principles;[117] the introduction of the Citizens' Charter and kitemark for public service; competitive tendering for those services; the introduction of greater open competition for some (but not all) top posts; delegation to Departments of recruitment, pay and grading authority at junior and middle levels and de facto Permanent Secretary contracts with associated performance pay determined by an independent authority. Butler supported these developments in the context of wider attempts to improve the competitiveness of the UK economy but also to resist the spectre of a 'politicised' civil service. Whilst he was welcomed as 'a breath of fresh air' as he articulated both a confident personal vision of what the civil service should be and explained the limits to his powers as its Official Head. He was fond of arguing: 'It is a chimera that we can – as staff sometimes demand – publicly represent the interests of the Civil Service <u>against</u> the policy of the Government of the day'.[118]

The early speeches on visits to Departments described a civil service where morale was low: loss of public esteem associated with the promotion of enterprise and a devaluation of the social and caring services; rapidly reducing numbers and a consequent reduction of promotion opportunities; a restrictive attitude to public service pay; a need to adapt to greater career mobility; closer monitoring of officials' performance by the media and the judiciary and greater hostility towards officialdom from citizens; higher staff turnover (at 2% per annum or less at Grades 5–7 still very low by the standards of knowledge workers in privately owned businesses), recruitment difficulties and union militancy. After reminding his audience of the importance of public service and the extent to which those same politicians who demonised the civil service were dependent upon it to deliver their own successes, his list of aims for the next ten years was equally crisp: first-class recruits from a wider range of universities; improved careers marketing; greater willingness to take responsibility and carry accountability at junior levels; pay targeted at the main staffing requirements in terms of geography, skill and merit; a more mobile labour force, including removing obstacles to people returning to the civil service after working elsewhere; more identification by junior managers with senior management proposals; improved equal opportunities; refinement of training in response to the emphasis on service delivery proposed by the 'Next Steps' initiative; less defensiveness in the provision of facilities for staff.

This was a traditional Northcote-Trevelyan vision updated to late twentieth century social values, typified by Butler's open commitment to gender equality[119] and ethnic parity. It was a clear symbol of equality that all three Private Secretaries he appointed were female and that other members of his personal staff were more representative of the changing racial composition of the civil service than hitherto. Equally, his extensive Private Office experience had left its mark. In December 1996, interviewed for the Cabinet Office in-house journal on 'My Working Week' he recalled that: 'I always try to keep in mind the Private Secretary's adage: *What comes in in the day should go out in the day*,' which could pose an acute dilemma for the poor Private Secretary faced with the choice between a sub-standard submission and the delay inherent in sending it back for rework.

Next Steps Agencies

The early years of Butler's tenure saw the struggle continuing between those worried about loss of control of spending, notably Sir Peter Middleton and the Treasury, and the reformers led by Sir Robin Ibbs and the Efficiency Unit. The dispute arose over the structural reforms recommended by the Efficiency Unit's *Next Steps* report of 1987. Thatcher did not rush to embrace the proposals under which executive functions would be put at arm's length from the Departments responsible for policy. After the June 1987 General Election, at a meeting of Ministers on 22 October at which the majority of Ministers agreed that the Government should commit itself wholeheartedly to the Next Steps approach, she asked for more work to be done on the scope for privatising executive functions, on how to regain Ministerial control of quangos, on the risk/reward package for Agency chief executives and on the legislative implications of the proposed Executive Agencies. Butler responded on 14 January.[120] He set out a route map by which each case was to be considered. First, consider if the function is most appropriately carried out within government – which became known as a 'prior options review.' Then, in cases where the answer was yes, consider the options for Agency status with particular attention to rigorous control of costs and the scope for distancing day-to-day operations from Ministers using a policy and resource framework designed to improve performance. He continued: 'It might on occasion be appropriate to recruit a Chief Executive from outside the Civil Service, on a contract with a substantial performance-related element ... But in most cases a career civil servant will be the best choice ... ' For external appointments, Butler thought that there had been a watershed in that, provided the Civil Service Commission was involved in the original appointment to ensure fair and open competition, there would be no difficulty if an appointment were to be extended or made permanent.[121] But this ignored differences in salary between external recruits and serving civil servants, which would later become a festering sore in many departments.

Thatcher made an oral statement to the House of Commons on 18 February. The government accepted the four key recommendations of the Next Steps report: Executive functions should be carried out by clearly designated units within Departments (Agencies); there should be a programme for progressively attaining this objective; staff should be properly trained in the delivery of services; a project manager at senior level should ensure that the programme of change takes place. But the announcement came with a warning about unrealistic expectations over the extent to which the agency approach would be applied, because departments had significant fears that the Treasury might block or delay changes.[122] Ibbs, meanwhile, was determined that implementation should be led by a senior official on a full-time basis. Despite Treasury objections and Thatcher's initial doubts over the seniority of the appointment,[123] he won the day with Thatcher's acceptance, in February 1988, of the Senior Appointment Selection Committee (SASC) recommendation[124] to appoint the maverick Peter Kemp as Head of the Office of the Minister for the Civil Service and project manager for the Executive Agency programme at grade 1A (Permanent Secretary). Kemp was an untypical mandarin, qualified as an accountant and a late entrant to the civil service, responsible in HM Treasury for public sector pay policy and known for an energetic determination to make things happen. It was to prove a successful but controversial appointment.

The first Executive Agency (the Vehicle Inspectorate of the Department of Transport) was established on 1 August 1988. Initially about 71,000 civil service posts were planned to be covered by the programme (about one in eight) but by July Kemp could report that putative agencies employing 170,000 staff were already in the pipeline and at least 50,000 more staff were under consideration. Thatcher expressed herself delighted.[125] However, at the same time Butler found himself in a spat with Ibbs over Efficiency Unit involvement in the implementation programme. On the one hand Ibbs did not want the Unit absorbed into the Kemp camp; on the other hand Butler would not countenance the Unit interposing itself between himself and the Prime Minister. 'I would not wish to interfere in what you personally may wish to say to the Prime Minister at any time ... [But] the responsibility for implementing Next Steps has been placed on Peter Kemp, reporting through me to the Prime Minister, and I must make clear that I am not willing to have the discharge of my responsibilities to the Prime Minister as Head of the civil service monitored and reported on to the Prime Minister by junior civil servants in the Efficiency Unit.'[126]

Nevertheless, Butler gave enthusiastic support to the reforms.[127] He weighed in in favour of restructuring the Departments of Social Security, and of Agriculture, chivvied the Chancellor about his Revenue Departments and MOD about its slowness in responding to the opportunities presented.[128] The recommendations provided the opportunity to simplify management structures, he argued, provided that departmental tendencies to create shadow hierarchies were controlled.[129] Often, however, the problem – such as in the MOD – was that departments also had their own reform programmes and had limited capacity to respond to central initiatives that were not central to its own reforms. In the MOD case, for example, the strict application of direct accountability of agency chief executives to the Secretary of State would have resulted in over 30 such reporting lines without an integrating authority to meld their intermediate output (repair, supply, logistics etc.) into a cohesive defence capability.

Over the next four years Kemp successfully drove the conversion of service delivery by civil servants into operating divisions, mirroring similar re-organisations taking place in industrial organisations to a point where it covered about half the civil service.[130] By 1990 Butler could report good progress with structural improvement, 'Next Steps' Agencies, a firm grip on running costs, signs of improved recruitment, emerging recognition that pay should reflect the ability to recruit and retain staff. But still too much upward referral of detail, too many controls, restricted opportunities for people to make their mark, insufficient adaptation to continental methods of administration, limited imagination to recognise and act on the opportunities and challenges of emerging communications technology, including the enabling of greater geographical dispersal of back-office work.[131]

Two doubts about the reforms refused to go away. Externally there continued to be confusion over the discharge of Parliamentary accountability. Vernon Bogdanor, Reader in Government at Oxford, for example, argued that whilst private sector techniques could benefit the taxpayer and the customers for public services this would be at the price of reduced Parliamentary accountability.[132] His claim prompted a denial by the Minister for the Civil Service, Richard Luce, on the grounds that Next Steps would change no constitutional arrangements and Butler thought that Ministers' formal accountability to Parliament would be unaffected though there would be changes in the way in which it was discharged. Later cases where Agencies were set up where executive functions were hard to separate from political issues created significant problems in this area. A rumpus over the actions of Derek Lewis, the Chief Executive of the Prison Service, in 1995 and a 1999 case concerning the Passport Agency provide strong evidence of a tension between political accountability and allowing 'managers to manage' that was not at first recognised.[133] In the latter case the Home Secretary (Jack Straw) refused to accept the protestations of the Permanent Secretary (David Omand) that as an Executive Agency he had no authority over the Passport Office. 'If I go down over it, you come with me,' was his response.[134] In 2014 Theresa May (Home Secretary) stripped the Passport Office of its Agency status.

By early 1991 experience with the Defence Research Agency and the Chief of Defence Procurement had shown that 'pay for the job' was significantly higher than civil service pay. Whilst at that time serving civil servants who were successful in open competition for the Agency posts preferred to stay on civil service terms (in the belief that this would protect their job security) the recruiters had increasingly to turn to headhunters for advice on the appropriate rate to attract external good candidates. Later, as external appointment on the basis of scarce IT skills in particular became widespread, the assumption that candidates could later transfer to other more general roles risked increasing damage to general employee morale from distorted pay scales. Butler's determination to break the linkage with civil service grades for Agency Chief Executive posts started a swing to personal salaries, associated behaviours that weakened team spirit and fragmented the collegiality of the unified civil service.[135] Significantly, in July 1992 when Peter Kemp fell out with the then Minister for the Civil Service, William Waldegrave, over the Minister's wish that Kemp should spread his energies more widely than the 'Next Steps' programme, Butler was unable to find an alternative posting for him and Kemp had to retire early. Some of this difficulty in finding him a new post can be attributed to Treasury opinion and to Kemp's reputation as a maverick who was difficult to corral. Characteristically, Kemp refused to leave amicably, to Butler's chagrin, who thought that there would have been many private sector opportunities if he had presented the case as moving on in a spirit of interchange between sectors.[136] To a civil service that was not privy to the career discussions, the treatment of an energetic reformer who had challenged the established mandarins was not lost – calling to mind Douglas Wass' advice that political neutrality requires withholding the last ounce of enthusiasm for the policies of the Minister of the day.[137]

The Fall of Thatcher

On 22 November 1990, after a Party leadership challenge that she failed to defeat decisively enough on the first ballot, Thatcher was forced to resign by her Cabinet colleagues after 11½ years in office. John Major took over as leader of the Conservative Party on 28 November. International tributes to her leadership poured into Downing Street from a very wide range of people, some in quite emotional language – including Mikhail Gorbachev[138] addressing her as 'Dear Margaret' for the first time and Henry Kissinger saying that her loss was worse than a death in the family.[139] Butler prepared, meanwhile, lest there be a challenge that a change of Prime Minister should be ratified immediately by a General Election. In a note to the Prime Minister's Principal Private Secretary he pointed out that the electorate votes to choose a constituency MP not to elect a government, a Prime Minister or an individual Minister. The Sovereign had the duty of finding a Prime Minister who could form a government that commanded a majority in the House of Commons and if that condition were met there could be no question of an automatic General Election. Further, there had been many changes of Prime Minister without an immediate General Election, most recently the Wilson-Callaghan change in 1976.[140]

Immediately when Major was declared the victor of the leadership contest Butler sought to assure him that the inherited civil service staff would loyally switch their support. 'Congratulations and best wishes,' he wrote, 'All of us in the Civil Service will do our utmost to support you and your Government.'[141] He presented the new Prime Minister with an immediate shopping list of actions ranging from formation of his government to the allocation of Ministerial residences; from a growing crisis in the Gulf to the existing domestic crisis over the Community Charge; from physical personal security to the letters of 'last resort' for the nuclear deterrent. The emphasis was on continuity. Leave machinery of government changes until after the next General Election, he advised. Make minimal changes to the make-up of the 22 Ministerial Cabinet Committees and the 12 live ad hoc MISC groups to reflect the new cast of Ministers.[142]

The Gulf Crisis

As preparations accelerated for military action to expel the Iraqi invaders from Kuwait the ad hoc group AHGG was reconstituted as a formal sub-committee of the Cabinet Overseas and Defence Committee (OPD(G)). Butler and Major's press secretary Gus O'Donnell (later to be Cabinet Secretary 2005–2011) were relatively full participants – unusually for a Ministerial committee. Butler reported, for instance, on possible terrorist threats to the United Kingdom; O'Donnell advised on media handling. Formal Cabinet authority to commit British troops to enforce the United Nations resolutions calling for the withdrawal of Iraqi forces from Kuwait[143] was given on 10 January 1991.[144] An aerial bombardment started on 17 January, followed by a ground assault on 24 February – codename Operation DESERT STORM. Hostilities ceased on 28 February 1991 when Kuwait was liberated.

The bulk of the action arising from the OPD(G) discussions fell to the Foreign and Commonwealth Office and the Ministry of Defence; the Department of Transport also had a significant role. The Cabinet Office established a unit to handle enforcement of the United Nations trade sanctions on Iraq and played an important part in negotiations to obtain financial support from rich neutral countries, together with co-ordinating domestic arrangements for the support of returning refugees and the families of those detained as hostages.[145] At the outset of hostilities Butler instructed the OPD Secretariat to log the lessons of the conflict.[146] Its most senior official, Len Appleyard, presented a full assessment shortly after the end of the fighting.[147] The crisis had been different from the Falklands war in that it involved coalition forces led by the American generals Norman Schwarzkopf and Colin Powell, who had largely dictated the timetable and key decisions had been taken elsewhere than in the United Kingdom. On the positive side: (a) in the run-up to the conflict the AHGG had worked well, casting its net wider than the later official committee supporting OPD(G) which had focused on a narrower circle of departments involved in the running of the war; (b) overall, OPD(G) had operated well as a formal Cabinet sub-committee, with an agenda that was sufficiently flexible to handle urgent issues, papers for discussion, recorded decisions and an implementation schedule; (c) a set daily schedule of meetings had played a central role, focusing on clearing the way for the Ministerial War Cabinet and enabling the overnight briefing for the Prime Minister to be up to date. (A small PUS group OPD(G)(O) had an evening discussion of the agenda for the next day; there was a JIC meeting at 6.00 am to prepare an assessment for circulation between 7.30 and 8.00 am; the OPD(G) agenda was finalised at 8.30 am; Departments briefed their Ministers between 9.15 and 10.00 am; OPD(G) met at 10.00 am.) Much of the success of OPD(G)(O) came from PUS membership which ensured that its work could be prepared with the full authority of Departments and because, by and large, the same people attended each time; (d) OPD(G)(O) had also looked at the decisions that would be required in the weeks ahead enabling Ministers to stay ahead of the game (which was especially important in avoiding having to handle things at the last minute with the United States where inter-agency rivalries could slow things down). It had enabled UK thinking to be part of the American decision-making process; (e) Government stayed ahead of the media; (f) the Cabinet Office Embargo Surveillance Centre had been effective and the Assessments staff and JIC had worked well with OPD(G)(O).

But there had also been problems: (g) the distribution of AHGG minutes in letter form had been too wide; security had been compromised for speed – though this was over-corrected when OPD(G) took over, as the secrecy of less sensitive operational matters had sometimes been overdone so that Departments had not been fully aware of what decisions had been taken on the basis of what information; (h) OPD(G) had taken time to settle administratively and initially had not worked smoothly with the official structure.

Northern Ireland

There had been steady if unremarkable progress after the hostile Unionist reaction to the Anglo-Irish Agreement in 1985. When Major replaced Thatcher he put Northern Ireland in the top four priorities. (The others were counter inflation, public services and unemployment.)[148] Three sets of talks were put under way simultaneously (known as three 'strands'). One focused on the Unionist desire to re-establish a Northern Ireland Assembly and some self-government; a second considered relations between the North and the Republic; a third relations between the UK and the Republic. The Irish Government were involved in strands two and three, as was Butler who had inherited Armstrong's link with Nally. Nally told him that the Irish Government attached importance to the three strands moving 'in unison.'[149] Nevertheless, their preparation was long drawn out and by June 1991 Butler was pressing Nally for progress on procedural issues prior to Major and Haughey meeting for talks over dinner. The Downing Street brief to Major prepared by the foreign affairs private secretary, Stephen Wall, advised that Haughey would argue that the two leaders should give the 'three strand' talks strategic direction – which Wall interpreted as a plan for North-South relations based on Haughey's underlying objective of a united Ireland.[150] Wall went on to say that though relations between Haughey and Thatcher had become unnecessarily bad, there was no reason now not to have a friendly but wary relationship with the Taoiseach.

Butler did not attend the Major-Haughey dinner, which took place on 21 June, but later advised that part of Haughey's intent was to conduct talks on the model that had led to the Anglo-Irish Agreement. The exclusiveness of these talks had been a necessary but unpopular device on the British side; it seemed unlikely that they could repeat the process. A particular problem was that the Haughey proposals would leave the politically most difficult element (to bring along the Unionists) in the UK Government's court and would let the Irish Government off the hook of having to do some fresh thinking.[151] Butler then spoke to Nally at an Anglo-Irish meeting of officials on 26 July (known as the Anglo-Irish Diner) to encourage continued informal discussions over dinner (so that both sides could say that no new mechanism had been set up) and also to convey that Major would participate freely and privately; but 'unless the Irish Government is prepared to undertake a serious effort to build up the confidence of the Unionists we will never get anywhere.'[152]

The understanding built up between the two Cabinet Secretaries through the informal 'diners' paid off as Haughey ran into serious political trouble over his implication in financial scandals and ultimately led to his downfall. Butler argued that planned talks between Haughey and Major should go ahead, because to withdraw would be seen as an affront to the Republic whereas to go ahead would not be interpreted in Ireland as assistance to Haughey.[153] A meeting took place (in Dublin) on 4 December with Butler in the UK delegation. The main thrust of the agreement reached was that some form of joint declaration by the two countries had a fair chance of ending the violence in Northern Ireland. Haughey thought he had detected a sea change in the attitude of some leading PIRA members to violence; Major was sceptical but accepted that: 'we must look privately at whether any wording can be achieved to … (i) retain the confidence of the people of Northern Ireland, (ii) ensure that others believed that matters were being looked at equitably, (iii) come up with a declaration that would be persuasive enough to stop the violence. That was quite a three card trick.'[154] Butler and Nally were put in the lead to take things forward in the utmost secrecy. Their talks continued and as the deadline for a UK General Election approached (one had to be held before 11 June 1992) Butler judged that the

Irish proposals for a draft declaration: 'did not appear too bad, from our point of view.'[155] But he warned Nally that: the British would not risk anything that would, 'risk embarrassing Ministers or giving authenticity to Sinn Fein in the lead up to the General Election.'

Major was cautious. He had commissioned an exercise from the Chiefs of Staff that concluded the UK had no militarily strategic interest in Northern Ireland. His reaction to the Irish draft was that it would commit him to Irish unification (albeit in ambiguous wording) and he instructed Butler to 'kick this whole issue into the long grass.'[156] On 7 February, Butler told Nally that in view of the impending General Election and the imminent departure of Haughey, Major did not believe it possible to make further progress at this time. If the new Taoiseach were to return to the issue, the Prime Minister would 'listen with interest to what he had to say;' and he went on to make substantive points to Nally about the principle of a declaration, thereby keeping the dialogue open. As a golfer Butler recognised that the ball may have been in the long grass, but it was still in play.[157]

Citizens' Charter Initiative

A second priority from the outset of Major's administration was to improve public services. Here Butler found himself providing what amounted to a counselling service. Major launched the Citizens' Charter at a Conservative Party meeting in Southport on 23 March 1991. The initiative sought to improve public services by publicly defining what the public could expect; improving access; enhancing responsiveness by revealing how standards would be measured, with transparency over performance against the standards and redress when services fell below acceptable levels. Although the Financial Secretary to the Treasury was the Minister made responsible for the Charter, Butler secured for the Machinery of Government division in the Cabinet Office the task of supporting him. His argument ran that too close an association with the Treasury would be likely to divert attention from the performance of public services to cost minimisation. Also, as Sarah Hogg, the Head of Major's Policy Unit pointed out on more than one occasion, this was a policy closely identified in the public mind with Major personally and could not be left to departmental Treasury Ministers without some loss of that identity. Nevertheless, as by now Terry Burns had replaced Peter Middleton as PUS at the Treasury, Butler encouraged a close relationship between the two of them, often consulting Burns about the drafting of key documents to emanate from Downing Street.[158] The relationship with Middleton had been decidedly scratchy, partly because Thatcher had not wanted Middleton to lead the civil service and partly, no doubt, because Butler had been his junior in the Treasury but had leap-frogged him in the hierarchy.

The Charter occupied Major right up to his election defeat in 1997; it was discussed at Cabinet on three occasions[159] and was the subject of an annual seminar for Ministers as well as the spur for awards for the best performing public service offices. One of Butler's tasks was to chivvy Permanent Secretaries whose

Departments were slow to rise to the Charter challenge – in July 1991, for example, chasing the Lord Chancellor's Department about the courts, where the contribution submitted for the Citizens' Charter White Paper 'combines the complacent with the inadequate;'[160] and about the Patients' Charter, the Tenants' Charter, the Benefits Agency Charter and the Northern Ireland Charter, all of which were seeking to resile on commitments from the White Paper.[161] Butler also provided a trip wire to identify potential problems before they became too intense, warning that The Economic Secretary, Francis Maude, was pursuing enhanced standards for the Social Services Inspectorate that would meet fierce departmental objections and suggesting, unsuccessfully, that the proposals should be postponed until after the General Election.[162]

The General Election and its Immediate Organisational Aftermath

A General Election had to be held before 11 June 1992. With just under 18 months to put his stamp on government it was perhaps inevitable that Major would turn to how well the government was getting out its positive messages. (Thatcher had had a similar concern before the 1987 election, writing that, '... we are not functioning as well as we might as a Government and are not telling our story to our best advantage.')[163] Late in May 1991 he sought to tighten up on the timing of policy announcements, pointing out in specific detail to individual Ministers where opportunities for good publicity had been missed.[164] Imminent announcements were discussed at Cabinet on 23 May with the Policy Unit subsequently analysing the pluses and minuses of each and their timing.[165] Observing the proprieties over government versus party matters Butler stayed out of the debate. In another aspect, however, he took the initiative to tighten up on what had become lax Cabinet procedures. In August, under the guise of seeking Major's views on how collective government business was being handled, Butler sought to eradicate growing Departmental slackness over Cabinet discipline. A practice of circulating correspondence as the basis for Cabinet discussion, rather than submitting papers, had developed. Unless there are proper papers, Butler wrote, it is impossible for busy Ministers, who are not closely involved in the build-up to Cabinet discussion, to take in the subtleties and detail of the relevant considerations.[166] Furthermore, oral items to be raised under the standing items on the Cabinet agenda should be notified to the Cabinet Office each week. As a result, to some extent Major was able to re-establish Cabinet formality and to use Cabinet to agree negotiating briefs for the increasing involvement with European discussions.

By 1992 the Conservatives had been in power for 13 years. Political commentators were contemplating the possibility of change and, especially, the possibility of an indecisive election result where no one party had enough seats to provide a stable majority in the House of Commons. With Butler's approval (and clearance of his speaking notes) Robert Armstrong (by then Lord Armstrong of Ilminster) appeared on the BBC radio programme *Analysis* to rehearse the constitutional position.[167] This led to an invitation for Armstrong to join the BBC team on election night itself, which Butler blocked on the grounds that participation would inevitably develop into a 'ball by ball commentary.' 'What would the Queen be considering now?' was bound to arise and whatever answer Armstrong might give would itself become a factor in the post-election situation. The 'Three Golden Rules' first mooted when Edward Heath's government failed to secure a majority of seats at the 1974 election were resuscitated:[168] (1) The Prime Minister remains in office until he or she tenders their resignation and, whilst it was possible to have no Prime Minister for a brief period, that situation should be kept to a minimum. (Butler subsequently confirmed with Parliamentary Counsel that the Prime Minister is formally appointed to the office at the moment when he or she accepts the Sovereign's invitation to form a government.) (2) The Queen will refuse a further request by the Prime Minister for dissolution of Parliament (and therefore a second immediate election) only if there is a chance of an alternative administration commanding a majority in the House of Commons or ruling as a minority government; (3) except in extreme circumstances (such as the Prime Minister refusing to go after losing a vote of confidence) The Queen does not have to take any action until the Prime Minister resigns.

Preparations were set in hand for briefing a new Prime Minister; Andrew Turnbull listed the 39 briefs prepared for Mrs Thatcher in 1987. The Opposition were contacted. Paddy Ashdown (leader of the Liberal Democrats) was advised that civil service logistical support for possible coalition discussions could only be activated with the agreement of the Prime Minister.[169] Butler also had two spirited exchanges with Charles Clarke from the Leader of the Labour Party's office. Discussion centred on what constituted 'winning' an indeterminate election – Clarke argued that if Labour gained a substantial number of seats (but not a majority) the Conservatives would have lost their moral authority and that it would be odd, in those circumstances, if The Queen did not ask the leader of the Opposition to form an administration. Butler fell back on the basic principle that an incumbent Prime Minister remains in office until he or she resigns. That apart, his subsequent advice would give particular weight to the party with the largest number of seats.[170] Clarke subsequently wrote a piece in *The Sunday Times* arguing that the principles underlying the advice that would be given to the Sovereign should be made public.[171]

Also, in anticipation of a new government, Major launched a substantial project to consider machinery of government changes (abolition of the Department of Energy, splitting the Departments of Trade and Industry, and Employment, enhancing the Department of National Heritage, tidying up responsibilities ranging from the probation service to policy on science).[172] In the event Major was returned to power with a significantly reduced overall majority, down from 100 seats to 21 seats. His new administration battled on, with the Conservative Party increasingly split over European policy and with growing signs of exhaustion. Management as a concern of ministers had come to the fore with Thatcher's reforms of the civil service. Without her commanding authority over departmental ministers the risks to policy coherence and to delivery of the government's priorities were the greater and in February 1992 *The Economist* had run an article critical of Major for failing to deal with: 'the system with a hole in the middle' of government.

The immediate aftermath of the election, however, was taken up by urgent tactical issues – how to organise the portfolios of central ministers; whether to brigade all units concerned with civil service value for money under one Minister; whether to enlarge the remit of The Office of Arts and Libraries; whether to create a new Office and Minister for Science?[173] Thatcher had rejected the idea of a Minister for Science preferring to take an interest herself in science as a whole, leaving Departments to look after their own spheres of interest. Major too was reluctant to make ambitious changes since he believed the current arrangements had worked reasonably well and that the scientific community attached importance to his own general involvement. The problem was a dearth of Ministers in the House of Lords with an understanding and enthusiasm for science who could answer where most of the heavyweight scientific debate took place.[174] Major asked for further advice, which Butler provided in mid April, recommending consolidating policy for civil science around responsibility for the £1,050 million annual scientific research budget. Other science remits should remain where they lay. Major agreed and a new Office of Science and Technology was born with around 90 staff under the day-to-day leadership of Professor Sir William Stewart the Government Chief Scientific Adviser and under the political leadership of the Chancellor of the Duchy of Lancaster, William Waldegrave.[175] On the arts Major decided to enlarge the remit of the Office of Arts and Libraries to include broadcasting, sport, tourism, heritage, film, licensing of the export of antiques, royal parks and palaces. Butler hesitated, as he feared that the most powerful unifying force would be a common desire to extract money from government. Major countered that the existence of a National Lottery and a Millennium Fund would offset such tendencies and provide focus. But a decision on whether responsibility for press freedom and regulation would remain with the Home Office or move to the OAL with broadcasting was deferred.

The machinery of government, in the sense of the organisation of Departments, continued to be treated by officials as separate from the organisation of interdepartmental discussion. The one came with the role as Head of the Home Civil Service; the other was a historic preserve of the Cabinet Secretary. Politically this was a false separation. Ministerial appointments, the ambit of their powers and membership of Ministerial committees are linked to the political position of the Prime Minister in the governing Party. Managerial considerations take second place to realpolitik. Butler advised: wind down the Efficiency Unit or integrate it with other units operating in a similar space.[176] Major thought this politically unwise. But nor did the Prime Minister agree to Michael Heseltine's proposal for a separate central 'Efficiency Office' outside the Treasury staffed by officials on secondment from Departments.[177] Opposed by the Treasury, which did not want to lose its own leverage over Departments[178] Heseltine's idea was dismissed with surprising brusqueness: '[The Prime Minister] will give careful thought to the points made.'[179]

The Heads of the Cabinet Office Secretariats came forward with proposals for radical restructuring of committees. They diagnosed a need for greater cohesion in policy and suggested a single, small committee, chaired by the Prime Minister, for each major area of policy plus more specific committees to be chaired by non-Departmental Ministers. (Their experience indicated that when Ministers with a direct interest in the matters under discussion chaired committees too many issues were referred to the Prime Minister for arbitration.) One result was that the most important issues of economic policy were taken in a new committee (badged EDP), much smaller and more flexible than the old EA committee, which had amounted to virtually the whole Cabinet. Between 1992 and 1994 this new group met quarterly, but in 1995 it was, in turn, replaced by a Ministerial Committee on Competitiveness (EDC), which met more frequently, supported by a large official ad hoc group (GEN 30) tasked with preparing a White Paper on competitiveness.

Butler returned to the allegations of a hole at the centre of government in the autumn of 1993. He hosted a working dinner for Major, Sarah Hogg[180] and Alex Allan[181] on 7 September, at his home in Half Moon Lane. Mary Francis (the private secretary for domestic affairs) advised: 'I do not know exactly what the Prime Minister is looking for – and I suspect he is not entirely sure himself. It lies somewhere amongst getting more interdepartmental advice via the Cabinet Office; more/better longer term thinking; improved trouble-shooting; and having more opportunities to discuss informally what is on his mind.'[182] Rodric Lyne (the private secretary for overseas affairs) thought that important EC issues often arrived too late on the Prime Minister's desk and that the Cabinet Office should give a lead on a long-term approach to the European Community.[183] As preparation, Butler submitted a reflective note.[184] Britain enjoyed a great advantage from the flexibility of the central machinery of government. 'I do not think that you can turn the clock back entirely on the decline over a long period of the formal use of Cabinet and Cabinet Committees to make decisions,' (Cabinet meetings were down from a high of 108 in 1945 to 40 in 1992; Cabinet papers down from 468 to 22 in the same period). The change arose because of the increasing speed of political life, requiring more to be cleared by correspondence; and from disunity, which brought leakiness. He accepted that the Cabinet Office ought to do more in spotting things before they got into a mess (citing that, with hindsight, it was always likely that the Department for National Heritage and the Home Office would not be able to cope with the issues raised by the Calcutt report on privacy). The real Achilles heel of British Government, however, was lack of strategic thinking.

He suggested that Major should use the Cabinet Office more frequently to sort issues, using Cabinet Office Ministers as chairmen if necessary. Downing Street should also make more use of the Cabinet Office as a source of advice and commissioned work (operating with a renewed concordat with the Policy Unit about who did what). Three times a year (in September, January and at Easter) the Cabinet Secretary should, in conjunction with the Head of the Policy Unit, submit a list of 'hot' domestic issues likely to arise over the coming term. In addition, Major might use his weekly bilateral meetings with the Foreign Secretary and Chancellor of the Exchequer for more strategic discussion. Alex Allan subsequently recorded points of agreement over the dinner table, including: Ministers too often showed no flexibility in their Departmental positions with the result that the Prime Minister was dragged in to arbitrate. Arrangements should be made to give Ministers chairing interdepartmental meetings a steer on what the Prime Minister wanted from the discussion. (This was not new. In late April Butler had made a similar proposal to invite the Lord Privy Seal (chairman of the main domestic policy committees) to his weekly short-term business meeting with the Prime Minister so that Major could indicate his wishes.)[185] In addition, the Cabinet Secretary should try to induce some flexibility in Departmental positions that threatened to become entrenched. The amount of paper submitted to the Prime Minister for meetings should be reduced to one single brief wherever possible. A standard format should be adopted to give a clear summary at the beginning. Some means should be found of enabling longer-term presentational strategies on important issues to be planned. Butler should activate a four-monthly listing of 'hot' topics later in the month.[186]

Economic Competitiveness

The development of the Citizens' Charter continued. Closely linked to it were initiatives for reducing the burdens of compliance which regulations placed on the economy and for introducing competition into the provision of public services. The 1992 Conservative manifesto had said:

> 'The compliance costs of new UK and EC regulations must be assessed properly. Existing regulations that are outmoded and burdensome must be simplified or removed. We will give priority to the work of the DTI Deregulation Unit in these areas.'

But as Heseltine pointed out to Cabinet in July 1992, efforts had been flagging.[187] Over the next year or more a great deal of Ministerial energy was committed to delivering the manifesto promise. It was hard going. Taken individually, a good case could be made for most regulation – there were some oddities such as the EC proposal that all fishermen should wear hairnets,[188] and regulations to govern the froth on beer (designed to ensure that the drinker received a full measure of liquid).[189] But most regulations had been introduced in response to public pressure. Further, Departmental hearts did not seem to be in the reforms. Despite Heseltine's undoubted commitment and energy the DTI unit was criticised from time to time as obsessed with process over results.[190] Butler's involvement was marginal, confined to issues such as pointing out that a proposal from Peter Levene that Lord Sainsbury should provide a focal point for business complaints about specific regulations would (as Sainsbury was a DTI adviser) blow a hole in the concept of official anonymity. Sainsbury would not be able to let it be known that he had given advice that was unwelcome to Ministers.

This was not a totally convincing argument, however, since advisers were in a special category and it was well known that Derek Rayner, for one, had unsuccessfully advocated ploughing back savings from the scrutiny programme into civil service working conditions.

By June of the following year Ministers were looking to put the involvement of the private sector in the provision of public services into a wider context. Butler argued that a paper for the EDI Committee should cover privatisation, contracting out, market testing and the role of strategic outsourcing. It should stress continuity from the *Competing for Quality* White Paper,[191] especially as many civil servants, facing the prospect of transfer to an Executive Agency, were fearful that this would be the first step towards privatisation. Butler and Heseltine later came to blows on this very point over the Civil Service College which Heseltine wanted to privatise and which, amongst more serious arguments about control of crucial training for those who had to work with ministers, Butler said would mean that: '... a private purchaser would close it down and turn the Sunningdale site into flats.'[192] It was ironic that Major now championed privatisation; in 1990 he had concluded that privatisation of the Inland Revenue computer division was not feasible: '[The decision] is wildly disappointing but I am sure it is right. The potential future advantage does not merit the certain immediate row on privacy,' he had told Thatcher.[193] It is also the case that in retrospect Butler thought he ceded too much to those who wanted to contract out or privatise services, notably when the Civil Service Commission became the Recruitment and Assessment Services executive agency in 1991 and found itself unable to compete with faster-moving private sector organisations in the speedy handling of applicants.[194]

Openness

Public attitudes were changing fast. When *British Social Attitudes* polled citizens in 1991 to ask if government should be able to keep secret the facts about (a) minor radiation leaks, (b) weapons systems or (c) the reasons for a Cabinet resignation those in favour of secrecy were, respectively, (in round figures) 25%, 55% and 5%.[195] Thus, in January 1992 the Foreign Secretary (the former Home Secretary, Douglas Hurd) returned with radical proposals for developing the Open Government policy. 'I believe that we could benefit politically from a further initiative,' he claimed.[196] Dire predictions about prosecutions following the 1990 revision of the OSA had proved untrue. 'There are no editors in jail ... In my view we still hold too much back ... The aim of such an initiative would be to head off the pressure for a Freedom of Information Act which I would not regard as helpful or sensible, and refute the reputation which we undoubtedly acquired in the 1980s as a government which was unreasonably secretive and too quick to use its authority to conceal information ... I think it fits with your general concept of government to let in some more fresh air.'[197] Major was sympathetic: 'I am keen to do what we safely can as soon as possible.'[198] The trouble was that political safety shortly before a General Election, allied with Whitehall risk aversion, was too powerful. Butler exemplified the conservatism of the senior civil servants: uneasy about disclosing the existence of all ad hoc Cabinet Committees, against the immediate avowal of MI6 lest it be drawn into a fraught electoral arena, opposed to reducing the 30-year rule for the release of files to the Public Record Office, unconvinced that a package would be an effective alternative to a Freedom of Information Act (FOI) as the government would never satisfy the FOI campaigners and this would cause the package to be discounted.[199] Nevertheless, he did his best to assemble proposals should the Prime Minister wish to announce something before the election (including 16 categories of common criticisms about the failure to disclose information ranging from advice on the safety of British goods and services available from American public records to the paucity of consumer representatives on advisory bodies). However, Major decided that the package was not strong enough to publish until after the election, even details of the two most attractive items in the list (*Questions of Procedure for Ministers* and a list of Cabinet Committees).[200]

The 1992 Conservative Manifesto[201] duly contained a commitment to greater openness and the FOI campaigners also had a stroke of luck when Mark Fisher MP was successful in the ballot for Private Members' Bills and chose to present A Right to Know Bill. Butler submitted a draft Cabinet paper that successfully proposed 19 May 1992 as publication day for a list of Cabinet Committees together with the most recent edition of *Questions of Procedure for Ministers*.[202] But so as not to raise undue expectations, the answer to a June Parliamentary Question about the newly formed Ministerial sub-committee on London was used to say that Major did not intend to give details of the topics discussed, nor the timing of meetings, nor their proceedings.[203] Updating the list would be annual.

The Chancellor of the Duchy (William Waldegrave) took on the reforming baton from Douglas Hurd and in November came forward with comprehensive proposals to seize the initiative and, 'mark our determination to change the culture of anonymity and secrecy, with greater personal accountability to the users of services, more approachable and identifiable public servants, and a much greater determination to make Government information open to the public except where there are sound public interest reasons for confidentiality.' But, he warned: 'A sea-change in attitudes will not be achieved without clear leadership,' and '... we cannot afford the legal bureaucracy of FOI.' Furthermore: 'A commitment of this kind will not in my view be taken seriously unless it is subject to independent supervision by an Information Commissioner.'[204] Officials close to Major were divided. Butler favoured reissuing the Croham Directive of 1977 that encouraged Departments to make available the analytical basis for policies and supported the proposal for an Information Commissioner. But he opposed to relaxing the 30-year rule. Alex Allan was attracted to the relaxation of the 30-year rule as he thought that the Croham Directive had not worked well because there was no real distinction between analytical material and internal advice. He thought that an Information Commissioner with statutory powers would make things worse.[205] Others challenged Major's commitment to openness with the question, what would have been published about the background to recent events such as Black Wednesday? Gus O'Donnell thought the benefits unclear but the costs evident: '… there is a great danger in this initiative becoming a liability … I am not sure who gains from this kind of initiative and it is quite clear there will be significant costs, particularly in terms of officials' time. It would also establish a mood of extreme caution. The civil service is a very risk averse institution and greater moves to openness might exaggerate this tendency.'[206] The politicians also had worries; for example, whether access to safety information would merely prove to be fodder for lobbyists wanting more regulation – in contrast to the government's policy of deregulation.[207] Waldegrave was caught between the FOI enthusiasts and the die-hard attitudes of some of his colleagues: 'I am certain that I will not be able to persuade colleagues to accept proposals which mean anything without your clear backing.'

Major wobbled. Unhelpfully, the same Ministerial meeting that considered openness also covered the Calcutt Committee's report on regulation of the press. The latter contained a recommendation to move from self-regulation to a statutory basis and was likely to be highly inflammatory, influencing media reactions to any package on openness. Also, the judgement of the Party Business Managers was that Fisher's Right to Know Bill could not be defeated at Second Reading and would need to be 'talked out' at the Committee stage. Hence there was no rush to put out government proposals, some of which needed further careful thought.[208] The Policy Unit reminded Major that since the proposals would change the way in which government worked and have cost implications, they should be discussed at Cabinet or Cabinet Committee.[209] Butler also submitted a brief but in more neutral terms. He identified Cabinet on 18 February for the proposals to be adopted as government policy and looked to a White Paper to be published after the Second Reading of Fisher's Private Member's Bill.[210] Whilst Waldegrave was firmly driving progress it was the Policy Unit rather than the Cabinet Office that reviewed the text of a White Paper, rewriting the introduction to be more positive and pressing for a date for the application of the proposed Code of Practice on Openness which Ministers preferred over a statutory route.

Defence and intelligence were in a different category from other state activities. There was still support from the public at large for secrecy in these areas. Political pressure about the oversight of the intelligence agencies was less intense, but a number of factors now combined to prompt officials to recommend that the best form of defence was attack: (a) Despite the 1989 Security Service Act there was still a strong risk of a challenge to existing arrangements under the European Convention on Human Rights (which required a basis in public law for wire-tapping and bugging, independent oversight, including a channel for independent investigation of complaints of abuse of power and redress if proven); (b) MI5 and MI6 were due to move into two new large buildings – Thames House for the Security Service (project AWARD) and Vauxhall Cross for SIS (project FINALIST). Reasonable questions about which departments would occupy these buildings would be difficult to answer in the absence of avowal for SIS and questions about finance would reveal that not all agency expenditure was covered by the Secret Vote; (c) other Western intelligence services were already acknowledged by their governments; (d) with the collapse of the Soviet empire SIS staff began to see avowal as a government acknowledgement of the continuing need for their activities; (e) the 1989 Act had not led to the collapse of the Security Service and most of its staff liked the comfort that Parliament acknowledged the existence of their employer.

Inevitably in such a sensitive area, the outcome would be difficult to control. A particular risk was that Parliament would impose unwelcome oversight arrangements that would unduly hamper the agencies. It would come as a surprise to most backbenchers that SIS conducted operations in the UK (albeit against foreign targets), which would raise questions about the adequacy of Ministerial control. There were also more arcane Parliamentary considerations: announcement would have to be by Ministerial statement as using a Parliamentary Question to make the announcement would undo the convention that officials of the House do not accept questions touching on matters of intelligence and security. Nevertheless, the judgement of officials was that in the longer term the non-avowal of SIS was not a tenable position and that later avowal under pressure would be neither desirable nor reassuring.[211]

Although Major was disposed to offer greater openness in government business than his predecessors, his initial reaction was negative. He supported the principle of avowal as an important part of an open government initiative. But a statement so long in advance of when legislation could be ready was asking for trouble.[212] Further, as 1991 turned into 1992, the imminence of a General Election brought added delay because of the need to avoid making SIS part of the election agenda.[213] It was not until three weeks after the election that Butler came back to the issue of avowal adding a further handful of sand to tip the scales in favour of legislation; it had been discovered that for more than 40 years, unknowingly and unnoticed, some activities overseas had been potentially open to prosecution under the Criminal Justice Act 1948. He suggested that the new Ministerial Committee on the Intelligence Services (IS) should address the interlocking issues involved, including for the first time, declaring the full amount of intelligence spending through a single intelligence vote. At about the same time he also recommended extending the term of Sir Colin McColl as 'C' for two years beyond normal retirement because of the new public persona that avowal would entail.[214]

The Conservative Business Managers were unenthusiastic about the prospects of a Bill. With a reduced overall majority of 21 seats the Leader of the House of Commons, Tony Newton, could not give a clear-cut assurance that the Bill would pass intact. To the risks previously identified by Butler he added a possible call for the extension of warrant procedures to SIS activities abroad, a call for oversight of all intelligence agencies by a Committee of Privy Councillors, queries about the extent of NAO/PAC access to the Agencies' books and resurrection of questions about earlier *causes célèbres* such as Duncan Campbell's allegations about the Zircon satellite, the sinking of the BELGRANO, allegations of 'dirty tricks' in Northern Ireland, the Iraqi Supergun affair and, of course, union rights at GCHQ. But as Butler pointed out, legislation followed inevitably from avowal and avowal was rapidly becoming unavoidable.[215] A Bill would probably take six months from introduction to Royal Assent, hence a Bill introduced immediately after the Summer Recess would not be impossible.[216] Meanwhile, Butler had become more and more distracted by the Scott inquiry into the Matrix-Churchill affair.

Shortly after the 1992 election victory things turned bad for the new government. Within a year Major was embattled with a fractious Parliamentary party and accident-prone government. One Conservative MP wrote in his diary in September: 'The party is profoundly divided, our economic policy is discredited, we're on the brink of being dragged into a Balkan war, and the PM talked about the Citizens' Charter!'[217] The most damaging to the credibility of Major and his government was when sterling was forced to leave the European Exchange rate Mechanism on 16 September, Black Wednesday. This was Treasury and Bank of England territory and Butler was mainly a spectator, though he recalls standing horrified with Major and his Chancellor Norman Lamont in Admiralty House as the gold and foreign currency reserves haemorrhaged. At other times, however, the Cabinet Office was at the centre of things as government seemed to lose its head.

Matrix Churchill

The Opposition accused Conservative politicians of conflating the interests of the state and those of the Party.[218] The accusation stuck as the government was rocked by a series of ethical scandals. The first of these concerned arms exports to Iraq during the Iran-Iraq war of 1980–88. In November 1992 Major set up an inquiry under Lord Justice Scott to investigate allegations that the Thatcher government had, between 1984 and 1990, colluded in the sale of arms to Iraq in breach of its own guidelines.[219] Butler narrowly avoided significant public damage from the inquiry. Having given evidence to the Scott inquiry in 1994 he made handling the publication of the inquiry report his priority objective for 1995/6 and in his self-appraisal at the end of that year he recorded: 'I have not been in any personal trouble and came out of the Scott Report unscathed.'[220] But it was a near-run thing. During his evidence he asserted that it could sometimes be acceptable for a Minister to give half the picture, implying that it was not always necessary to speak the whole truth to Parliament. This was controversial, though Douglas Hurd made the same point to some effect by giving an example of sensitive negotiations between Egypt and Israel that could not be wholly revealed. Nevertheless, *The Observer* questioned Butler's behaviour under the headline: 'The most powerful man in Whitehall is emerging as a potential target for the Scott inquiry.'[221]

HMG had operated a policy not to supply lethal goods to either combatant in the Iran-Iraq war. In April 1990 British Customs seized a consignment of components destined for Iraq and believed to be for the construction of a large calibre armament.[222] However, the consequent prosecution of two employees of the British firm concerned, Walter Somers Ltd, was halted when Counsel decided there was insufficient compelling evidence that: 'they knew what was afoot and, knowing that, participated in the intention of evading export controls.'[223] Then in 1992 three former Directors of Matrix Churchill Ltd of Coventry were charged with falsifying documents to obtain export licences for high-technology lathes, about which the government had clandestine information suggesting that the lathes were to be used for the manufacture of munitions in Iraq. That case collapsed when oral evidence by the Minister for Trade, Alan Clark MP, concerning the advice he had given to the Machine Tools Trades Association (MTTA) in 1988 about how to frame export licence applications contradicted his witness statement to the Court.[224]

There were two stages to Butler's involvement: the events leading up to the collapse of the Matrix Churchill prosecutions and the firefighting that followed. Anthony Bevins of *The Observer* raised three serious charges against him. First, as the Prime Minister's principal adviser on intelligence matters Butler was somehow responsible for the failure to share knowledge across Whitehall; he should have known that arms-related equipment had been exported to Iraq and should have ensured that Customs officials knew of the DTI knowledge about the circumstances surrounding the exports when the Matrix Churchill prosecution was mooted. (Bevins was not to know that Customs investigators did have this knowledge.) Second, that in December 1990 Butler did not guard the newly appointed Prime Minister against falling victim to the ambiguities in Clark's stance. Third, that Butler was complicit in Major misleading the House of Commons by encouraging a distinction between arms per se and arms-making technology.[225]

Butler's knowledge of the events under investigation by Scott went back to 1990 shortly before the 'Supergun' arrests. On 20 April he received a briefing from Len Appleyard of the Cabinet Office Defence Secretariat about the evidence linking British companies to breaches of export controls.[226] Four days later Sir Hal Miller MP sought a meeting with him to explain approaches he had made in good faith to the government in 1988 on behalf of Walter Somers Ltd; and to record that he had raised the issue of export licensing with the DTI and the MOD. On 26 October, Butler received a copy of the record of Alan Clark's meeting of 20 January 1988 with the MTTA. With great perspicacity, Andrew Turnbull, Major's Principal Private Secretary, annotated the record in manuscript: 'The companies concerned may claim in court that [a phrase in the record] was a nod and a wink for them to describe the machines as civil even though they could have military application. In this they might prove more convincing than any interpretation Mr Clark offers.'[227] Butler may have been unaware of this comment, however, as it was between Downing Street officials.

DTI officials were in some difficulty because they had known of relevant intelligence that raised doubts about the peaceful purposes of machine tools exports to Iraq even before Clark's 1988 meeting with the MTTA. But they could not act on the information because of the need to protect the intelligence source and had not shared it with other departments. So Butler agreed to warn Brian Unwin, the head of Customs & Excise, that there was a potential public interest aspect of the decision whether to prosecute Matrix Churchill. Hence, Unwin should consult the DTI about this when he was ready to do so.[228] Unwin was aware of his legal responsibilities, however, and sensitive to anything that might be construed as seeking to influence his judgement in the case. As a result, neither side was satisfied. Unwin came away with the impression that Butler and Gregson[229] would prefer the case to be dropped, but felt an obligation to Customs staff who were convinced that the prosecution case was sound. He asked Butler to bring to Customs' attention any specific evidence in the proper way (i.e. formally) otherwise, as the Chairman of Customs, he could not be influenced by what was said.

Meanwhile, the *Sunday Times* Insight Team had the story of Clark's meeting with the MTTA and ran it on 2 December 1990 as the Iraqis consolidated their occupation of Kuwait.[230] Forewarned of the article, Butler advised Major's Private Office that Clark was confident his advice had been precisely phrased.[231] Even so, the Prime Minister decided that there should be something on the record quickly in support of Clark's advice to the MTTA.[232] He summoned Clark to explain that advice. Butler's record of the meeting said that Clark had argued that: 'He was in effect advising [machine tools manufacturers] to downgrade the specification of the machine tools they provided so that they would not be seen as suitable for military purposes.' It was totally false to suggest otherwise. He was totally unrepentant about his role in this. This was not, however, precisely what the official record of the MTTA meeting had said – yet Butler advised that Clark's explanation should stand as an aide memoire in case the issue arose at Prime Minister's Questions later in the week.

Unwin advised Butler on 18 February 1991 that he had discussed the sensitivities fully with the relevant Departments and that the prosecution of three former directors of Matrix Churchill would go ahead.[233] Gregson later recalled that Customs had known of the intelligence that exports may have been intended for warlike purposes before this decision and that all the information held by DTI, including that from sensitive sources, was examined by Customs investigators before decisions on whether to proceed with a prosecution.[234]

Shortly before committal proceedings Butler advised that, in a highly unusual step, two Ministers would be required to give evidence in court (Alan Clark and Lord Trefgarne) because the defence would be likely to argue that the government were aware that the exports in question were specifically designed to have a military application. Tom King, Secretary of State for Defence, thought that for Ministers to appear was a bad idea, as did Michael Quinlan, his Permanent Secretary. King because it would set a precedent;[235] Quinlan also because of the occasionally idiosyncratic behaviour of Clark.[236] Ministers believed that they had a duty to apply Public Interest Immunity Certificates and did so in the knowledge that at full trial (if matters went that far) it would be for the judge to balance the arguments between Public Interest Immunity and the interests of justice in disclosing the documents to the defence.[237]

The trial started in the late summer of 1992. An article in the *Sunday Telegraph* on 2 August included a passage, which said that Clark had tipped off manufacturers on how to frame their export applications to get round the guidelines for trade with Iraq. This contradicted his witness statement for the court and also the statement Customs officials had obtained from him, with great difficulty, by telephone. But the press allegation was confirmed when Clark gave evidence to the court on 4–5 November. Counsel, Alan Moses, then reported to Unwin that he could no longer sustain the prosecution and hence, on 9 November, Unwin conceded defeat with a decision to drop the prosecution.[238] Unwin was so concerned by the behaviour of Clark, however, that he formally asked the Director of Public Prosecutions whether, in changing his evidence, Clark had been guilty of perjury (or the equivalent). The DPP decided that they did not believe there was a sufficient case to press charges.[239]

Butler immediately summoned representatives of the DTI, Customs and the Law Officers' Department to discuss the likely consequential Parliamentary pressures. They recommended a prompt statement to the House of Commons, in which the Attorney General would propose 'a full and independent enquiry into these events.' At a hastily convened Ministerial meeting at 1 pm the following day[240] Major accepted this advice with instructions that the statement (to be made that same afternoon) would announce a wide-ranging enquiry by a single judge who would have access to all relevant evidence and witnesses. On the advice of the Lord Chancellor, Lord Mackay, and supported by the Master of the Rolls, Sir Thomas Bingham, Lord Justice Richard Scott was approached to take on the task. The Prime Minister was sure that the government would come out of an inquiry without blemish. Scott was known as independently minded, liberal in outlook and had previously refused the Thatcher Government's request to ban *Spycatcher*. He seemed a good choice to carry conviction with the liberal establishment and so head off further trouble. So much so that it was left to Scott to decide how the inquiry should be run and how much of the evidence should be heard in public.

After much discussion it was also agreed that press briefing should deny that the Cabinet had endorsed a secret policy to allow defence exports to Iraq.[241] There had been an ad hoc Ministerial meeting on 19 July 1990 under the chairmanship of the Foreign Secretary, Douglas Hurd, at which the general view was to replace strict 1985 guidelines with more limited and clearly defined controls, involving equal treatment for Iraq and Iran and a continued ban on the export of lethal equipment, but with no special constraints on machine tools, which were no longer caught by COCOM controls. Hurd put the proposed revision to Thatcher on 26 July advising that she should await developments in the tensions between Iraq and Kuwait before taking the proposal further. Iraq invaded Kuwait a week later.[242]

At the same time as Butler set the wheels in motion for handling the Parliamentary fallout from the decision not to continue with the Matrix Churchill prosecution Unwin wrote to him to ask the Cabinet Office to take a lead in sorting out inter-departmental difficulties brought to light by the case. In particular, how the policy departments (DTI, FCO, MOD) could formulate reliable and unambiguous guidance on export licensing policy that the enforcement authorities

(HMC&E) could rely upon.[243] Pauline Neville-Jones of the OD secretariat advised Butler of the inherent unenforceability of the policy in regard to machines that could have multiple uses.[244] She also alerted him to Michael Heseltine's worries that Ministers issuing PII certificates could be interpreted as concealing official incompetence, but dismissed them: 'though the judgements made may be questionable, they did not betray total incompetence, they were not arbitrary and they were certainly not corrupt.'[245]

Although the events in question had taken place under the preceding regime, Major's reputation was at severe risk and what may have seemed like a convenient way to buy time for controversy to die down carried a longer-term threat. This is where a second, and more serious, group of questions arises about Butler's response. Was he right not to challenge the setting up of a judicial inquiry was it the best way to proceed? Did he confront Scott sufficiently over the hostile treatment of civil servant witnesses at the Inquiry and did he put the nation's security into commission by allowing Scott to assert that he personally would decide for the report whether any official secrets disclosed during inquiry sessions 'would cause serious injury to the interests of the nation.'[246]

Attention switched to the inquiry and how witnesses should conduct themselves. A special unit was set up in the Cabinet Office under Philip Calcutt to co-ordinate matters and to keep a record of all submissions made to the inquiry. Butler reassured Scott that this did not stretch to central direction of government witnesses.[247] Although he acknowledged that the experience could be stressful for a few, Butler told departments that the Prime Minister had decided that all officials would be expected to give evidence if asked to do so and that if they wished to have independent legal representation they should seek the advice of their Departmental Legal Adviser who would decide whether it should be provided at the department's expense. 'I know you will do all in your power to ensure that [your officials] have both the moral as well as the material support which is their due,' Butler wrote to Permanent Secretary colleagues.[248]

But it did not seem that way to some of those giving evidence. Scott appointed Presiley Baxendale QC as counsel to the Inquiry and she did most of the questioning – in the words of one journalist attendee, regarding the press as her jury. Scott also ruled that though a legal adviser might accompany witnesses that person would not be allowed to address the Inquiry or to question witnesses. And Scott reserved to himself the ability to decide whether classified information (however high that classification) justified a closed hearing. On Butler's advice Major agreed that whilst very sensitive intelligence material would be provided to the inquiry in the form of relevant extracts from documents Scott would be permitted to inspect the complete documents in the Cabinet Office to satisfy himself that the extracts were not misleading.[249]

In a subsequent meeting with Scott it was agreed that witnesses would have advance notification of the areas to be covered by questioning and that Scott would invite comments from departments and witnesses about the extent to which hearings ought to be held in closed session, though the judge also made clear that hearings would normally be held in public.[250] Civil servants would be granted immunity from prosecution or disciplinary action in relation to admissions made during the Inquiry.[251]

There were early signs of conflict between the Inquiry and the government. The gloves came off in a heavyweight contest likely, in the words of Gus O'Donnell, then press secretary in 10 Downing Street, to become a media circus.[252] Butler objected to Scott releasing without prior agreement correspondence between himself and the judge about the criteria for closed sessions.[253] The Inquiry secretary, Christopher Muttukumaru, responded with an argument to be used more than once '... the Prime Minister has assured Lord Justice Scott that: '[He] will be entirely free to decide on the publication of his report and of the evidence he takes.'[254] (An interpretation of Major's guidance which Butler rejected[255] and which Neville-Jones characterised as an indication that Scott wanted to present himself as champion of the public interest.')[256]

Safeguarding the legal rights of witnesses proved a thorny issue. The government felt that those offered by the Inquiry were insufficient.[257] Scott stonewalled: 'Lord Justice Scott's overriding concern will be fairness to witnesses and the efficiency of the Inquiry. In deciding on procedures he will take full account of the points which you have made.'[258] (Interpreted by Neville-Jones as recognition that there was substance in what was said but an unwillingness to make explicit acknowledgement of it.)

By mid June 1993 there was concern in Whitehall about lines of questioning which invited witnesses to comment on the actions of others (including Ministers) from a time before the witness held the relevant post. Butler proposed that in these circumstances a witness would be entitled to decline to answer.[259] But the Attorney General thought it would not be right for Ministers to instruct potential witnesses that they should refuse to answer questions within the wide terms of reference given to Scott. So the problem was partly dumped back on the individual witnesses who were advised that they could reply to such questioning if they felt that they had sufficient knowledge to respond reliably. If not: 'you may reasonably consider that you should say so.'[260]

The Inquiry team, meanwhile, thought that its requests for intelligence material were not being dealt with constructively. Muttukumaru wrote in these terms to Gould (Cabinet Office) who replied that he didn't understand to what the complaint referred.[261] This prompted a flash of anger: 'The Judge is not satisfied with the Cabinet Office's explanation. The scope of the request was plain ... The progress of the Inquiry has already been hampered and the Judge considers that there is nothing now to be gained from prolonging this correspondence.' Referring to a warning by Gould about the possibility of inadvertent revelation of information which would put the safety of an individual at risk, Muttukumaru told him: '... your comment is irrelevant to the contents of my letters to you of 20 and 26 May.'[262] A week later Butler wrote to Scott that: 'I am satisfied that the Cabinet Office complied fully and helpfully with the Inquiry's requirements,' but he did no more than request forewarning if the Inquiry were minded to criticise the Cabinet Office on that score.[263]

And so it continued. Scott produced a discussion paper on export controls and licensing procedures. Butler commended an approach that indirectly sought to counter Scott's general proposition that the right to export property is a fundamental human right guaranteed by the European Convention on Human Rights. A more direct refutation would be likely to bring a protracted and ultimately unproductive debate.[264] By October 1993 Neville-Jones and Butler had worries that Ministers might have bullied officials into ignoring the ban on exports so as not to hamper British industry. Butler discussed the risk that revelation of this could add to the 'sleaze problem' at one of his weekly bilateral meetings with Major. Meanwhile, the head of the Scott Unit in the Cabinet Office catalogued complaints about the continuing conduct of the Inquiry: using the public hearings to lead witnesses to agree with a prejudged position; an abrasive style of correspondence by the Secretary towards Departments; counsel playing to the press presence as if it were a jury; lack of concern for distress caused to witnesses, unwillingness to recognise that some intelligence material was sensitive by virtue of the manner in which it was obtained regardless of content. 'The flavour of the Inquiry can therefore be bitter, and an impression of prejudice is sometimes conveyed.'[265]

At about the same time a number of senior diplomats complained to the Head of the Diplomatic Service about their hostile treatment as witnesses and he in turn raised it with Butler.[266] The concerns centred on five aspects: conduct of the Inquiry akin to a court room rather than an inquiry; leading witnesses to prejudged conclusions; insufficient time to refresh memories about events, some of which pre-dated their personal involvement; approaching the issues with the benefit of hindsight, notably about Iraq's invasion of Kuwait; lack of understanding that the paper records did not represent the whole of the picture. The result of these complaints was that when Butler gave evidence to the Inquiry on 9/10 February 1994, with the Prime Minister's agreement, he made a statement as the Head of the Civil Service.[267] The intention was 'to speak up for the Civil Service on the matters which have most concerned them, namely the burden of work involved and the unfair and prejudicial comment to which the Inquiry has exposed them; and to draw attention to some of the demonstrably wild allegations which have been made in the hope of making serious commentators more cautious generally about taking at face value media allegations ahead of the Inquiry's findings.'[268]

The language was typically that of a mandarin rather than characteristic of the type of exchanges Scott and Baxendale would have been used to in court: 'Whilst I make no criticism or complaint about the Inquiry's procedures, the absence of the restraints which would apply to speculation about the outcome of proceedings in progress in a court of law, combined with the public nature of the hearings, has permitted wild allegations and pre-judging of issues in media reports.' Which of course was meant to signal that Butler was critical of the Inquiry's procedures, particularly as the examples then quoted were pointed: 'One [example] is the constant references, which have become common currency, to 'arms sales to Iraq'. There were in fact no licences for the export of arms, that is lethal goods, issued by the British Government in this period. The second gross distortion is the references to Public Interest Immunity certificates as 'gagging orders'.'

Was all this too little too late? The initial draft provided by the Cabinet Office Inquiry Unit put the onus to ensure fair play on Scott himself but this was toned down by Butler in favour of: 'I register my concern, on behalf of the civil servants involved, that the Inquiry should in due course put the record straight and undo, so far as in its power, the damage which has been unfairly done to the reputation of the Civil Service and individuals.'[269] For a naturally competitive person this was mild indeed.

Ministers thought that the report was likely to be unfair, tendentious and sensationalist. After three and a half years of inquiry the government spokesman (the President of the Board of Trade) would have to respond on day one and what he would say would have to be collectively agreed. The government had acted honourably in not commenting on the matters under review during the Inquiry but must now get on the front foot rejecting unsupported smears and unjustified criticisms of individual Ministers. Individual officials criticised should, exceptionally, be allowed to make personal statements following publication and would be supported from the public purse in legal action if they had acted honestly and in good faith.[270] Major, meanwhile, enjoined that Ministers should consider legal proceedings against those who had spread falsehoods about them.[271] But this was later dropped after advice from Counsel (George Carman QC) that issuing libel writs would be 'utter folly', the case was 'not even borderline.'[272] Major himself was caught in double jeopardy, potentially pilloried for supporting Ministers criticised by Scott and facing muttering on the Conservative back benches for having set up the Inquiry in the first place. It was likely that the exoneration of Ministers from having lied and covered up in a conspiracy to send innocent men to gaol would be conveniently ignored.[273]

The inquiry had developed a momentum of its own and itself attracted criticism for profligacy. Simon Jenkins called the inquiry a costly farce whose lawyers, 'high on politics, publicity and paperwork seem determined to keep their show running for ever.'[274] Not knowing that the Prime Minister had ruled that officials had no choice but to appear, he expressed surprise at the supine behaviour of officials called as witnesses. The inquiry, he thought, traded heavily on hindsight whereas government was more immediate. Allan Massie, writing in *The Daily Telegraph* agreed: 'The truth is that different departments quite properly pursue different policies, because they have different, often conflicting, roles.'[275] Writing in *The Spectator* in late January 1996, shortly before Scott reported, Sir Geoffrey Howe described Scott as having: 'A disposition to challenge convention, to defy precedent, to present issues in black and white terms ... matched by tenacious enthusiasm for his own views.'[276] Howe rejected the expected criticisms of Ministers and officials in forthright terms: 'The Scott inquiry is not a tribunal upon whose judgement the reputation of anyone should be allowed to depend,' he argued.

Friction between Butler and Scott continued with the former reporting the outcome of a meeting of nearly two hours that, 'after a good deal of hard pounding ... I found myself dealing the whole time with an entirely unrealistic attitude on Scott's part to the extent to which Ministers would be subjected to questioning on the publication of the report and therefore the extent to which they would have to prepare themselves and get advice.'[277] Scott was not to be budged, however. Ministers and a small group of officials would get sight of the report one week in advance to trawl the 1806 pages for damaging quotes and to prepare counter proposals. On 8 May 1996 Scott startled the Commons Public Service Select Committee, with a thinly veiled claim that the Secretary to his Inquiry, Christopher Muttukumaru, on loan from the Government Legal Service, had been threatened that his career as civil servant, 'might suffer from the assistance he was giving me,' adding, 'Those who have dealt with him ... have come to understand that he cannot be intimidated.'[278]

It had been a three-year marathon: three volumes but no conclusion (and no examination of the Clark affair), 1806 pages and 130,000 documents scrutinised. At the press conference on the report the second question asked Scott if his conclusion was that there was no conspiracy and no cover-up. Scott's reply was 'Yes, though you must read the whole report.' The historian Peter Hennessy later lamented that the inquiry achieved so little – a House of Commons Resolution on Ministerial accountability and little else of great significance.[279] For Ministers the most important point was that Scott had rejected allegations of conspiracy. However, by not commenting during the Inquiry proceedings Ministers left the field to the government's opponents; and in the public mind the Inquiry hammered further nails into the coffin of honesty and fair dealings under the Major administration. The government won the battle but lost the war. There were several important lessons, including that once set up, a judicial inquiry develops its own momentum which overrides any prior instructions on timescale and that at the end of the process winning the public relations battle can be more important than winning the arguments. The latter was a lesson not lost on the Opposition as Major repeatedly complained to Blair about his inaction to rein in the 'gutter politics' from members of the Opposition front bench using allegations that Scott had shown to be untrue.[280]

Problems with Coal

The Cabinet Office Secretariats provided not just a solid foundation for building cohesion across government but also an intricate series of tripwires to warn of impending risks. When those tripwires failed a rapid descent into chaos could follow, as the 1992 furore over pit closures demonstrates. The facts are that in the summer of 1991, as a result of analysis of the viability of British deep-mining undertaken by Rothschilds for the Department of Energy and work carried out by British Coal, the President of the Board of Trade, Michael Heseltine, accepted that the long-term market for coal pointed to closure of more than 30 pits.[281] A sharp fall in demand for coal and high levels of coal stocks pointed to rapid closure, ideally before the end of 1992/93. However, the Conservative election manifesto of 1992 had said: 'We will privatise British Coal in a way that enables employees to enjoy a stake in the industry,' which sat awkwardly with Heseltine's conclusions.[282]

The Ministerial Committee on Economic and Domestic Policy (EDP) discussed the coal industry on 17 June 1992 in the context of a Bill to privatise British Coal. Subsequent correspondence during July confirmed the need for closures and discussed the redundancy terms to be offered. British Coal initially ignored government requests to supply Ministers with a list of planned closures and did not do so until Monday 12 October, probably mainly because they did not decide on the final list until shortly beforehand. But also because, earlier, when a government list of likely closures had been distributed widely to Ministers the National Union of Mineworkers had quickly obtained a copy, which it had leaked to the press. Hence, Heseltine announced 12 unspecified closures at a press conference on 13 October and British Coal issued a press notice with news that it planned the closures by the end of the month, including six immediately. Cabinet did not come into the picture until 15 October, triggering complaints that colleagues had not been consulted sufficiently and that British Coal had not complied with the statutory provisions requiring 90 days' notice of redundancies to the Department of Employment. Conservative backbench opinion, anticipating a public view that the announcements were brutal and uncaring, was hostile to what would be seen as government (and not British Coal) plans.

A further Cabinet discussion was scheduled for 19 October with a Parliamentary statement due to be made by Heseltine later that day. Cabinet was preceded by an informal Ministerial meeting during the evening of Sunday 18 October which decided on a partial backtracking involving a moratorium on closures beyond those already announced – believed at that time to be nine – and a further review to cover the remainder (the Coal review). It then transpired that due to British Coal's convoluted Colliery Review Procedure the list of planned closures was not a robust basis for announcement. So government attention switched to whether a pit was uneconomic, with British Coal telephoning through a list of 12 such pits shortly before Cabinet on 19 October, based on contract prices with the electricity supply industry for the following year. However, Cabinet preferred to use current prices rather than future prices and this reduced the number of uneconomic pits to ten, which were currently loss making and had no prospect of viability.

Heseltine announced a review of the remaining 21 pits on 26 October.[283] Meanwhile, the closure decisions were successfully challenged in the courts on the grounds of an alleged failure to direct the Coal Board appropriately with regard to consultation over closures. The High Court found conclusively that Heseltine and British Coal had acted illegally. The original announcement (of 31 closures) ignored the requirement for 90-day consultation under the Employment Protection Act and the statutory duty on British Coal to apply the Colliery Review Procedures set up under the 1946 Coal Act. (DTI officials had erroneously believed that these procedures were a voluntary matter.) The subsequent announcement that only ten pits would close immediately still ignored the Colliery Review Procedures and especially the provision that there had to be an element of independent review.[284]

It was a public relations disaster, which left the government looking, at best, shambolic and out of control. The basic flaw was a failure to manage the various interest groups. David Poole of the Policy Unit identified as many as ten distinctive groups: the miners, British Coal management, Conservative supporters, the media, industry pressure groups, voters, regulatory bodies, the European Commission, the environmental lobby, the nuclear lobby. He questioned whether Heseltine had a strategy for marketing his proposals to them.[285] In a harsh judgement he reported that DTI officials thought Heseltine lacked political sensitivity,[286] and he accused Heseltine in forthright terms of failing to become sufficiently involved: 'Rather than being about to take the credit for the next major, popular privatisation, he [Heseltine] discovered that he was to act as undertaker to the coal industry. At no point until the crisis broke did he properly engage himself in what was taking place.'[287]

Hardly anyone escaped Poole's withering judgements. Gregson, said Poole, had failed to step in when DTI officials had been unable to engage the attention of Heseltine and had not monitored the direction taken by officials. Butler may not have been convinced by the DTI attempt to pin the blame on British Coal – in November he had commented that: '… It seems to me a legitimate criticism that the Department should have realised that, if there were flak it would be directed at Government and should have insisted that, in these circumstances, the independence of British Coal could not be maintained … it explains why officials were short of essential knowledge on matters in which Ministers had to become involved once the row broke out,'[288] but, Poole asked, what was he going to do about it? Major repeated these criticisms orally with Butler at a bilateral meeting on 21 December. He said that he was appalled at the deception of British Coal and wondered whether officials should have done more to warn Ministers. There were also, Major believed, large questions over the performance of Rothschilds in carrying out adequate due diligence on British Coal's figures and on the advice they had given. Gregson had been insufficiently ready to take a hands-on approach.

It must have been uncomfortable for Butler to hear such pointed criticism about a senior colleague – especially as a clear Ministerial steer had not always been given to officials, including by Major himself.[289] He pointed to Gregson's sure handling of Heseltine during the Matrix Churchill affair and to public protests from the First Division Association that officials were being unfairly blamed. Nevertheless, he would speak to Gregson, '… and say that he should, in future, be especially conscious of the need, both in the coal review and elsewhere, to make sure that political traps were avoided and that the necessary factual backing for any decisions was fully taken into account by Ministers.'[290]

Even so, questions remain about why the political risks were not acted upon sooner. Had public opinion shifted unnoticed or were Ministers misled by the failure of the NUM leak of September to provoke an immediate outcry about closures? Why did Heseltine press on with his announcement on 13 October when there were significant uncertainties and why did Major not step in to see the public relations baton was gripped after his press secretary, Gus O'Donnell, had provided a forthright justification for the policy and a crushing rebuttal of the counter-arguments, variously described as erroneous and pathetic?[291] Should Butler's brief for Cabinet on 19 October have waved more of a red flag about the risks involved? Or had the informal exchanges between Permanent Secretaries based around the Wednesday morning meetings failed to alert him to these risks? Should Major have reacted more decisively when his staff reported that the strategic direction of the Coal Review was far from clear[292] and when they told him of British Coal's unwillingness to provide crucial information.[293] In reading the files it is impossible not to feel that most submissions were written from the point of view of a spectator rather than as analysis that would lead to action. Meanwhile, a DTI post mortem made clear that over the period 19–22 October relevant officials were wholly swamped by the need to provide extensive written (and verifiable) defensive briefing material for at least three different Ministers.

Disharmony over Europe

Movement towards closer union in Europe through the 1992 Maastricht Treaty – described by the BBC as ' another step towards political and economic union' – brought constitutional as well as political challenges, notably from the implications of its Social Chapter and the prospect of a single currency.[294] Ratification of the Treaty was initially defeated in a Danish referendum in June 1992 and only narrowly approved in September by a French referendum.[295] In Britain Major at first made it clear that there would be no similar opportunity for a popular vote. During a statement on the implications of the Danish rejection of the Treaty he told the House of Commons: 'I am not in favour of a referendum in a parliamentary democracy, and I do not propose to put one before the British people.'[296] But by March 1996, after Mrs Thatcher had undermined his position by calling for a referendum if there was any prospect of joining a monetary union, he had modified his position to: 'I believe that a referendum on joining a single currency could be a necessary step.'[297] The United Kingdom had negotiated an opt-out from the Maastricht Treaty's social provisions. The Labour and Liberal-Democrat Opposition opposed the opt-out and in the Conservative ranks the Euro-sceptics opposed the Treaty as a whole. As a result the number of potential rebels when it came to ratification by the House of Commons was greater than the government majority. Hence, Butler started to work up tactics for handling a Parliamentary debate scheduled for 22 July 1993.

In a section of briefing headed: 'Doomsday scenario – handling on the night,' he stressed that if the Opposition succeeded in amending the government motion a decision on what to do next would need the authority of Cabinet. But the problem was that a contingency could not be discussed in Cabinet until the day after the debate because of the risks of a leak that would strengthen opposition to the government position. Should the vote go against the government he recommended immediately introducing a Motion to reverse the Opposition-sponsored amendment and making this an issue of confidence. He argued that the United Kingdom had given its word to its European partners, so a defeat in the Commons could appropriately be regarded as an issue of confidence and he was worried by the prospect of uncertainty festering over the summer period. All other options (save that of defeating the Opposition amendment) would result in a constitutional or political crisis. To ignore the amendment (as some Ministers were inclined to suggest) would be deeply controversial, would shock many constitutionalists and, as Butler put it: 'I really don't think it is honourable.'[298] To accept the Social Chapter would be too many words to eat and would be difficult to get through Cabinet, probably leading to a split of the Conservative Party. To say that the government would not ratify the Treaty if the Opposition Motion were to be passed would play into the hands of the Euro-rebels and would probably also mean the Conservative party would split. Hence, the most viable option would be to seek to reverse the amendment as a matter of confidence. So tight was the Parliamentary situation, however, that there was a risk that if nine Euro-rebels would rather bring down the Government than accept the Maastricht Treaty, the Queen would be very unlikely to refuse a dissolution. The government would face a General Election that, according to the opinion polls, it would be likely lose. However, a saviour came from an unlikely source. Lord Rees-Mogg sought a judicial review of the proposal to ratify the Treaty, thereby putting the ratification ball into the long grass and putting more public pressure on the Euro-rebels to come to heel.[299]

On 4 November the House of Commons voted – the government secured 319 votes and the Opposition 316. This was not, however, the end of constitutional issues involving European policy. In late 1994 the government expected trouble over the European Community Finance Bill. Once again there was a question of whether defeat would lead to a General Election. In a letter to *The Daily Telegraph* Lord Blake thought that it would since the Queen would be highly unlikely to refuse a dissolution;[300] and once again Butler reminded Major that the crucial decision was whether to make the vote on the second reading of the Bill an issue of confidence.[301] Shortly afterwards papers were dusted off in preparation for a possible referendum on whether the United Kingdom should join the single European Currency. The Machinery of Government Division of the Cabinet Office analysed the 1975 referendum experience (including the Cabinet 'agreement to differ' and the House of Commons vote in which 38 Ministers, including 7 Cabinet Ministers, voted against the government). Early in December Butler put down a marker that: an 'agreement to differ' might be needed (though it should not apply to differences about whether to have a referendum at all). More importantly, it was essential that all Cabinet Ministers agreed to accept and support the outcome of a referendum, as had been the case in 1975. Moreover, if the government envisaged referendums on the outcome of the 1996 Inter-Governmental Council (IGC) and a single currency both should be announced before the IGC and before attempting legislation on either topic.[302] In the event, Cabinet agreed a compromise by which the Conservative Manifesto for the 1997 General Election would say that if a Conservative government felt it right that the United Kingdom should join the single currency in the next Parliament a referendum would be held to obtain confirmation of entry.[303]

Northern Ireland: the Downing Street Declaration

Things were not all bad; there were some encouraging signs. In Dublin Albert Reynolds became the Taoiseach on 10 February 1992 and soon took up the reins to push ahead with a joint government declaration with the British.[304] An Anglo-Irish summit followed in September; and on 6 June 1993 Reynolds gave Butler, for further transmission to Major, a draft text that he believed would be acceptable to Sinn Féin and to the IRA. This was discussed at a second Major/Reynolds led Anglo-Irish summit ten days later with Butler and Nally both present when further informal discussions between the two of them over dinner were agreed (the so-called 'diners').[305] Their meetings continued through to mid December when a joint government statement on the future of Northern Ireland (known as the Downing Street Declaration) was launched. However, the path from June to December was not smooth. Butler sought to play things long to give Major the confidence that he was not being rushed into an unsatisfactory deal and to bolster the government's political courage.[306] On 15 November, in his speech to The Lord Mayor's Banquet, Major took the brave step of announcing that Sinn Féin could have a future negotiating role if the violence in Northern Ireland stopped.[307] But the existence of the secret talks leaked, to be followed immediately by a joint statement from Gerry Adams of Sinn Féin and John Hume of the SDLP in Northern Ireland. Major thought these developments were the kiss of death for any text intended to secure acceptance on both sides of the Community in Northern Ireland but sent Butler as his emissary to see Reynolds.[308] On Friday 26 November an angry Reynolds told Butler that a great opportunity was being thrown away by the British hesitation – their excuses were thin.[309] The SDLP/Sinn Féin talks were a sideshow. Reynolds then repeated the same angry messages to Major by telephone on 29th November. At about this time Butler advised Major to update the next Cabinet meeting on progress with the Anglo-Irish talks (it happened to be a Budget Cabinet) prior to the planned Anglo-Irish summit for early December.[310]

The summit took place despite dire Irish warnings that it would be a waste of time unless the British position changed. It was a scratchy affair and once again Butler and Nally (this time accompanied by a number of other officials from both sides) followed up to smooth things out and to prepare for the next Major/Reynolds encounter that would take place in the margins of the European Council in Brussels. Butler concluded that amendments offered on both sides meant that officials had taken the negotiation as far as they could. 'It will be open to you then either to agree that the text is now close to being acceptable or to resolve any outstanding points of principle,' he told Major.[311] The two leaders reached a compromise at the European Council and settled the final differences by telephone on 14 December. Reynolds and Major then launched the declaration to widespread acclaim at a joint press conference the following day. The

Declaration built on the Anglo-Irish Agreement and was in turn built upon by the 1998 Good Friday Agreement. Major later claimed that 90% of the Good Friday Agreement on Northern Ireland was within the framework of the Downing Street declaration,[312] and Tony Blair acknowledges that Major had spotted the early green shoots of peace and had put together some of the elements that could make up an agreement.[313] Butler and Nally were at the centre of the negotiations in the former two cases but an important difference between the circumstances confronting Armstrong and Butler was the involvement of Major in driving the process of negotiation compared to that of Thatcher who was prepared to let it happen.

Collective Discussion

Formal Ministerial committees remained important. This was not just because government is complex and interrelated. Private business had begun to realise in the early 1980s that the extent to which executive directors spent working together as opposed to working with their Departmental staffs was important in building cohesion and innovation at the top. John Harvey Jones of Imperial Chemical Industries had restructured his Board in 1982 to reduce the influence of departmental silos and, 'to reduce the number of those who can say 'no' and increase the motivation of those who can say 'yes'.'[314] Cabinet met weekly for most of the year (around 40 meetings) and other interdepartmental Ministerial groups met between 100 and 200 times per annum in total.[315] Cabinet procedures had become cumbersome. Those drafting papers were pulled in opposite directions. On the one hand Major wanted short, clear, papers and minutes of meetings. On the other hand Departmental Ministers wanted to be sure that their concerns were recorded. Yet, over ten years on, the accretion of rules about the points to which Cabinet Committee papers should draw attention was formidable:[316]

Expenditure implications (adopted in 1920 – Coalition Government, McDonald)
Statistical tables (1942 – War Coalition, Churchill)
Manpower (1947 – Labour, Attlee)
Legal implications (1967 – Labour, Wilson)
Accommodation (1974 – Labour, Wilson)
European Community implications (1974 – Labour, Wilson)
Means of evaluation (1985 – Conservative, Thatcher)
Presentation (1985 – Conservative, Thatcher)
Business compliance (1988 – Conservative, Thatcher)
European Convention on Human Rights (1991 – Conservative, Major)

Butler kept a strict eye on procedure. Ministers had become accustomed to discussion in informal groups during the Thatcher years, with decisions ratified in formal committee, but these attempts to cut corners threatened collective responsibility. In March 1992, for example, Butler admonished Heiser[317] of DOE in imperious terms about discussions based on oral presentations without papers: 'I hope therefore that in future you will advise your Secretary of State to give Ministerial colleagues a written paper on which to take major decisions ... I shall in future advise Number 10 and the Economic Secretariat to resist proposals for dealing with issues without such papers.'[318] Powerful Deputy Secretaries heading the Cabinet Office Secretariats briefed the Prime Minister directly, continuing the practice started by Robert Armstrong. However, whereas briefs for Thatcher's Cabinets in the late 1980s were little more than a list of events that might be reported, under Major officials felt empowered to give a stronger steer to the discussions. This left Butler free to sit back and observe how well the system was working, submitting his own brief selectively (typically on around 17 topics a year).

For his part, Major discussed the short-term management of committee business in groups that other Ministers chaired with Butler on 76 occasions, covering 160 individual issues between the latter part of 1993 and 1996. The Home and Social Affairs Committee (EDH) is by far the most frequently mentioned in the record of these informal talks – as many times as the next four most popular committees combined, which raises the question why Major did not take over chairmanship of the group. Discussions went at a fast pace – by January 1996 their duration had come down to 15 minutes. Major let it be known what he wanted to be the outcome of discussions – from avoiding own goals such as privacy proposals focused exclusively on press intrusion, to the co-ordination of Departments' plans for SMART Cards offering the prospect of a national ID card by the back door. Butler's meetings were largely used for exchanges on sensitive matters such as open government, constitutional issues, intelligence and security.[319] The main forward planning for policies had, by this time, long since been captured by the Downing Street Policy Unit which serviced annual Chequers policy seminars where Major used to hear what Ministers of State and junior Ministers thought (and incidentally to talent-spot for future Cabinet members).

As early as December 1992 the press reported that Major had called 'a New Year meeting of Downing Street policymakers to relaunch the government's domestic agenda after the crisis management of the past few months.'[320] Butler did not attended nor feature on the distribution lists for notes of the meetings or comment on the performance assessment of participants prepared by Major's personal staff.[321] This may have been the correct constitutional judgement, but the price was a weakened role as policy adviser to the Prime Minister and ruffled feathers amongst Permanent Secretaries.[322] Meanwhile the Opposition under Tony Blair took note of the political damage inflicted on the Conservatives by their failure to manage media relations effectively and may also have been influenced by the burgeoning role played by the political appointees in the Policy Unit and the pivotal position of the Principal Private Secretary.

The records of the bilateral meetings between Major and Butler on short-term business illustrate a gradual run-down of new ideas as the Parliament progressed;

particularly given that some of the politically more difficult topics were discussed interminably: privacy and the media no fewer than 22 times; ID cards 14 times, and there was persistent concern over delayed decisions about the future of the Royal Navy Dockyards at Devonport and Rosyth. Also, towards the end of the Major Administration the topics often touched on Major's difficulties with Party management.

CABINET COMMITTEES – BUSINESS MEETINGS WITH JOHN MAJOR							
		1993*	1994	1995	1996	1997*	TOTAL
Nos meetings		16	30	20	10	2	78
Topic	Symbol						
HOME & SOCIAL AFFAIRS	EDH	38	72	36	21	1	168
INDUSTRY & CONSUMER	EDI	17	33	20	3	0	73
LEGISLATION	LG	4	19	10	3	1	37
ECONOMIC STRATEGY	EDP	4	19	7	6	0	36
ENVIRONMENT	EDE	9	9	9	3	0	30
PUBLIC EXPENDITURE	EDX	6	17	5	2	0	30
CABINET	C	4	3	17	1	0	25
DEFENCE & OVERSEAS	OPD	3	10	6	2	0	21
EUROPEAN UNION	OPD(E)	5	8	7	1	0	21
PUBLIC SECTOR PAY	EDI(P)	1	7	5	1	0	14
DEPENDENT TERRITORIES	OPDK	1	4	5	3	0	13
LOCAL GOVERNMENT	EDL	1	5	5	0	0	11
SCIENCE & TECHNOLOGY	EDS	0	4	6	0	0	10
CIVIL CONTINGENCIES	CCU	0	5	1	1	2	9
LONDON	EDL(L)	1	3	2	0	2	8
DRUGS	EDH(D)	1	3	2	0	0	6
HEALTH	EDH(H)	0	2	3	0	0	5
ECONOMIC DEVELOPMENT	EDC	0	1	2	0	0	3
REGENERATION	EDR	1	1	0	0	0	2

* = part year data

Leaks, Spin and Attempts at News Management

As victory turned sour one of Major's main problems was that a disunited Cabinet became bedevilled by leaks.[323] Analysis of leak enquiries under Butler's authority indicates a maximum of 13 a year between 1988 and 1990, between 16 and 20 a year from 1990 to 1993 and then a jump to between 35 and 40 a year between 1994 and 1996, largely due to preliminary investigations that were not taken further. There were 37 leaks in this latter period that can be classified as political (31% of the total) with no fewer than 23 enquiries abandoned after preliminary groundwork. In February 1993 Major had sought Butler's advice about why there were so many leaks and what could be done to tighten up on them. In a long litany of possible causes Butler pointed to political jockeying for position as a result of ministerial insecurity, rival camps created by the strain in government ranks over the Maastricht Bill and a widespread feeling that public opinion was not being sufficiently prepared in advance of government policies. In a list of possible counter measures it is clear that Butler underestimated the extent to which disunity, spin and news management fed off each other. 'We need to stop the agenda being set by the Press,' he argued, advocating putting the No 10 press office entirely 'on the record' with circulation of a daily summary of Lobby meetings to be sent to Cabinet Ministers. A reshuffle of Ministers would remove the source of insecurity and give the Prime Minister a chance to demonstrate that he would come down hard on those suspected of leaking. Media tactics should be controlled centrally. Free enterprise in media management would not be condoned whether by Ministers or those who believed they were acting in Ministers' interests.

After 1994 there were three overlapping groups concerned with information management: Committee 12 of the Conservative Party for short-term political reaction to the day's news; a group meeting daily under the Prime Minister or Deputy Prime Minister to review issues needing media action by the government; and a Cabinet Committee (EDCP) under the Chancellor of the Duchy of Lancaster (successively William Waldegrave and David Hunt) to advise on communications strategy and presentation. After a slow start the EDCP Committee was busy (eight meetings, 43 papers in 1995, 45 meetings, 70 papers in 1996). At various times, however, in the face of adverse political fortunes this Committee was found wanting,[324] culminating shortly before the 1997 General Election with suggestions that Gus O'Donnell, the Prime Minister's Press Secretary (a civil servant), should be given formal responsibility for all government press and media handling.[325]

The issues were difficult for Butler. They illustrated a tendency towards cacophony with conflicting messages from Secretaries of State more concerned with Departmental issues than with the collective impact. This was classic territory for him to step in. On the other hand the issues were close to the boundary between government and Party matters (which he was at pains not to cross). He took a conservative view and stayed out of the fray except on procedural issues. As a consequence, the main official input to co-ordination of government messages came from Alex Allan, the Principal Private Secretary, in whose view the main 'hole at the centre' arose from an emerging need for continuous political campaigning between elections.[326]

Sleaze and Scandals

Further damaging blows came from allegations about the behaviour of Jonathan Aitken, Minister for Defence Procurement, who had denied an accusation by *The Guardian* that he had accepted improper hospitality from sources close to Prince Mohammed bin Fahd of Saudi Arabia when staying at the Paris Ritz in September 1993. Major asked Butler to investigate. This was a controversial step as the Cabinet Secretary's role was limited in a way not readily understood by the public. In Butler's first month in office Thatcher had insisted that propriety was a matter for the Cabinet Secretary and that she looked to Butler, as she had to Armstrong, as the champion of Ministerial and official rectitude. But the Cabinet Secretary's role with regard to Ministerial behaviour could only be to establish the facts – and lacking an investigative capacity had to rely on a Minister's honour to elicit the truth unless there was contradictory evidence in Departmental files. Cabinet Secretaries have argued that it is for Ministers to justify their conduct and for the Prime Minister to decide whether that conduct is appropriate.

In early 1994 both the editor of *The Guardian* and Aitken sent Butler copies of their correspondence. As Aitken was a Minister, Butler stood ready to advise him 'on the circumstances he has outlined to me,' but Butler would not share that advice with *The Guardian's* editor, pointing out that: 'Contrary to some popular belief, I am an adviser not an arbiter on these matters.'[327] He advised Major that if the meeting in the Ritz had had no business connotations it did not fail the test of propriety as implied by *Questions of Procedure for Ministers*. Aitken sent Butler a copy of a letter from the Ritz that indicated an old family friend rather than a business associate had paid the bill (though the copy had been doctored to omit the fact that the payment did not cover the whole bill). *The Guardian* knew of this gap in the payments and was also able to show that Aitken's claim that his wife paid the residue could not have been true. Not realising this, Butler told Preston that he believed Aitken, using the phrase 'I believe this sucks this lemon dry.' As subsequent events discredited Aitken Butler was publicly criticised for this judgement. *The Economist* commented that 'he let himself be drawn into providing public cover for the prime minister in two highly political cases involving the alleged misconduct of ministers.'[328] The article went on to argue that a code of ethics for civil servants (which had been opposed by Butler in evidence to the Treasury and Civil Service Select Committee) would have offered Butler the prospect of demurring to be put in that position on a matter of party political controversy. Furthermore, it argued, the interest of the Cabinet Secretary as the Prime Minister's confidential adviser (as Butler had initially been at pains to point out) sat ill with the interest of the Head of Home Civil Service in protecting a non-partisan civil service.

Standards in Public Life

Meanwhile, in the autumn of 1994 the Major administration was wounded by further embarrassing revelations, this time about the behaviour of Conservative MPs. At the 1993 Party Conference Major had launched a 'Back to Basics' campaign that was widely interpreted as a call for the return to stricter moral values. Then, during 1994 the media reported a string of sexual scandals and *The Sunday Times* trapped two Conservative MPs (Graham Riddick and David Tredinnick) through a sting operation that led to allegations that they were prepared to ask Parliamentary Questions in return for money. Both were temporarily suspended from the House of Commons. In October *The Guardian* alleged that two Conservative junior Ministers had accepted cash in exchange for asking Parliamentary Questions. Tim Smith (Parliamentary Under-Secretary Northern Ireland Office) resigned from the government on 20 October 1994. The following day Major asked Butler for proposals to reassure the public about the maintenance of standards in public life. Butler rehearsed the options from a Royal Commission to a Tribunal of inquiry and recommended an advisory committee reporting to the Prime Minister, which was announced with wide terms of reference under Lord Nolan, a Lord Justice of Appeal, on 25 October.[329] In an accident of timing Neil

Hamilton (Parliamentary Under-Secretary DTI) resigned on the same day also as a result of the 'cash for questions' scandal.

The Nolan Committee's first report was released on 11 May 1995.[330] Civil servants had observed open sessions so the government had been aware of the direction of likely recommendations throughout. Two caused general concern: likely proposals covering ex-Ministers' employment, and what might be appropriate limits on Members of Parliament accepting payment for services. Butler was also keen to have his own role in pursing these matters clearly defined. An earlier Royal Commission on Standards of Conduct in Public Life under Lord Justice Salmon had reported in 1976. On the advice of the then (Labour) Government, it had excluded Ministers from restrictions on business appointments comparable to those imposed on civil servants. By 1994 the arguments had not changed but the politics had. Salmon had accepted that it would not be appropriate for Ministers of one persuasion to apply rules in respect of Ministers of a former government of a different complexion.[331] Now Nolan was minded to recommend Minsters' inclusion. Butler proposed a compromise. Ministers should agree, when they were appointed, to seek the advice of the Advisory Committee on Business Appointments if they wished to work within a specified period in an area related to their Ministerial responsibilities – on the assumption that they would be bound by the advice.[332]

Major was lukewarm. Alex Allan recorded that: 'The Prime Minister thought there was a respectable case for saying that Ministers should be subject to the same business appointment rules as civil servants.' But he feared that some Cabinet members would argue that this was a restraint of trade and might demand additional severance pay in compensation.[333] A leading opponent was the Chief Whip, Richard Ryder. Allan described him as, 'hugely hostile to any restrictions on business appointments,'[334] and 'apocalyptic' whose 'fears are wildly exaggerated.'[335] Allan asked Major if he wished to give a steer to colleagues, not least because they seemed to have no recognition of the damage being done to the government from the drip of sleaze stories and the need to be seen to take a lead in demonstrating that action was being taken.[336] Butler, meanwhile, was instructed to make clear to the Nolan committee that there were good reasons for excluding Ministers. He did so, but in a manner that suggested that he did not wish to be associated with the decision: 'I have done this in a factual way to avoid any criticism that I am pleading the case for Ministers,' he told David Hunt.[337]

As early as November 1994 Butler had argued that: 'it was essential to emphasise my advisory role in these matters … [and that] the Cabinet Secretary's duty is only to advise on the application of the rules, not to police or adjudicate on them (or investigate, unless specifically asked to do so).'[338] On 19 April 1995 Nolan sent him a draft relating to the role of the Cabinet Secretary in relation to Ministerial misconduct. This accepted that a clear distinction must be drawn between the report of an investigation, which it might be appropriate to publish, and the Cabinet Secretary's advice, which should never, or very rarely, be made public. In some circumstances (such as the allegations where it was difficult to check their accuracy with the source and there was scope for checking them against government papers) the preparation of advice might require investigation into the facts, but in general it was normally a case of advice rather than investigation. In his response Butler stressed that it was misleading to give the impression that the Cabinet Secretary was the only person inside government from whom the Prime Minister would seek advice 'The choice would depend on the circumstances but if the alleged misconduct is a breach of Questions of Procedure for Ministers, the Cabinet Secretary would normally be one of the people referred to, not least because he is aware of the precedents.'[339]

Members of the Downing Street Private Office were concerned by the possibility that internal Conservative opposition to Major would use Nolan as a stick to beat the Prime Minister. Allan said: 'What worries me is a whispering campaign against the Nolan recommendations, perhaps including criticism of you for having set up the Committee.'[340] Christopher Meyer (who had succeeded Gus O'Donnell as press secretary in 1994) wrote: 'When you announced the creation of the Nolan Committee, the Opposition charged you with making policy on the hoof and seeking a quick fix to extricate the Government from sleaze allegations ... To be seen to be trapped by your own creation would be humiliating ... the best presentational strategy will be to take the initiative, seize the high ground and give as positive a response as possible.'[341] Private Office advice was that as long as Major welcomed the thrust of the proposals addressed to the government he would be able to say that the proposals addressed to Parliament (about which there was a high level of uneasiness amongst Conservative MPs[342] and on which a debate was expected on 19 July)[343] were a matter for Parliament and not the government.[344] Cabinet, meanwhile, failed to get behind the recommendations. A draft government response was so difficult to craft that for Cabinet on 13 July Allan reported that colleagues who had discussed the draft could not agree, that colleagues who had not been involved would be ratty about not having the papers in time with a deadline at close of play that day. He summed up the confusion: '... you've got to chair OPD, answer [Prime Minister's] Questions and write and deliver two speeches. Hopeless.'[345]

Indeed it proved difficult to translate the 50 Nolan recommendations into actionable propositions. The House of Commons clerks found it impossible to draw up a working definition of 'lobbying' that could serve to implement the recommended ban on such activities or payment for 'Parliamentary services.' Even a proposition to ban the tabling of questions, motions or amendments by anyone who is a paid consultant to a relevant body ran into trouble – it might mean that a Member sponsored by a trades union would be barred from asking a question about a minimum wage![346] Guidelines on business appointments for Ministers were not lodged with Parliament until 30 October (just in time for a debate on Nolan scheduled for 2 November). And as a curious byproduct, Questions of Procedure for Ministers was found not to contain an explicit duty to comply with the law although the parallel Civil Service Code suggested that it did.[347]

'Back me or Sack me'

In an attempt to improve government discipline and assert his authority Major resigned as Conservative Party leader on 22 June 1995 and forced an early contest for the position,[348] defeating John Redwood by 218 votes to 89 on 4 July. Immediately prior to that Major discussed options with Butler for merging the Departments of Employment and Education and for deploying Michael Heseltine out in the country, prominent in the media, promoting and defending the government's policies as First Secretary of State.[349] Heseltine opted to move from the DTI to the Cabinet Office taking with him responsibility for competitiveness and deregulation. He was shown through to Butler's office by Alex Allan who reported that he was clearly very taken with it and started eyeing it up. Butler adroitly showed Heseltine round the Cabinet Office, including the large Conference Room B where it was reported that Heseltine shortly had a desk, a table and vast acres of carpets.[350] There were later clashes too. The role of Deputy Prime Minister was unclear, leaving Heseltine free to roam where his special interests took him. One such area was his undimmed energy for Whitehall reform. He encroached on Butler's patch as Head of the Home Civil Service when he advocated privatisation of the Civil Service College, which Butler blocked by consulting Permanent Secretaries but coaching them in how they should argue against privatisation proposals.[351] Heseltine also trod on his toes over Committee membership where, after receiving a message that the First Secretary and Dr Mawhinney[352] had agreed the latter should become a member of the EDX committee, Butler's private office had to point out that: 'membership of Cabinet Committees was not within the gift of the First Secretary,' that right belonged to the Prime Minister alone.[353]

GCHQ Again

The government interpreted ILO reluctance to intervene in the GCHQ dispute as dependent on Ministers being seen to be prepared to continue talks aimed at reaching an accommodation with the unions. Norman Willis (General Secretary of the Trades Union Congress) sought talks with Major six months after he became Prime Minister. This approach was rejected[354] in favour of Butler meeting the general secretaries of the civil service unions, which he did in February 1992 and again on 10 November 1993.[355] The compromise he proposed was that the GCHQ staff federation should be allowed to affiliate to the Council of Civil Service Unions. This was not attractive to the unions who demanded a meeting with the Prime Minister. Despite misgivings in the Private Office (Alex Allan wrote: 'I am not convinced we should care much about what the ILO may do') it was decided that the precedent set by Thatcher by seeing the union leaders could not be ignored.[356] Butler returned to the hard line he had previously taken. The words he sought to put into Major's mouth included: 'We appear to have reached an impasse.' And when the two sides met on 20 December 1993 in what the union side described as a civilised discussion, there was no progress. But the atmosphere was less strained than with Thatcher. Major was at pains to emphasise that he neither thought that the unions or staff of GCHQ could not be trusted, nor did he bear any hostility to the trade unions. But he could not agree to go back to a position that would recreate the pre-1984 anomaly of GCHQ among the intelligence agencies.[357]

The likelihood of ILO condemnation continued to haunt the Secretary of State for Employment who judged that it would be difficult to rally the support of the employers' delegations and that the Clinton administration might join those voting against the United Kingdom.[358] He thought that the ILO would suggest 'a wise man' to act as honest broker and was inclined to accept such a proposal. Butler weighed in fiercely, partly on the basis of an incautious remark by one of the leading unions about the issue coming to a head at the ILO before the next General Election. 'It would not be unreasonable,' he wrote, 'to ask the ILO on what authority it sees itself mediating in issues of national policy in this way … once the Government begins to treat with the ILO on this proposal we will find it more, rather than less, difficult to turn it down … my own preference would be, if and when the ILO make their proposal, to tell them in short order to mind their own business.'[359] The Prime Minister agreed, but more diplomatically.

When the sniff of a possible accommodation with the unions did occur, in May 1995, it centred on improving the chances that the staff federation could be granted a Certificate of Independence by cosmetically removing the powers of the GCHQ Director to approve its membership (rather than recognise it for the purpose of negotiation) and removing his power to veto staff from joining a union of which he did not approve. Butler argued that the government had enjoyed the benefits of the current arrangements for ten years and that the industrial relations climate at GCHQ was much improved. However, neither side was greatly attracted by what looked like a political fudge to get the issue off the agenda before the next General Election. Major commented: 'Frankly I prefer the status quo but … '[360] and in a number of exchanges made plain that the change must not be presented as a government climbdown. The idea limped on until the Party Conferences in the autumn when Tony Blair made an uncompromising speech in which he said that a future Labour government would restore the full rights of the national unions at GCHQ, thereby strengthening the hands of the hardliners. Following talks with the IPCS Butler reported that Ministers' hopes that the unions could be persuaded to ask for the removal of the Director's veto and the government be seen to be meeting their request was a non-starter.[361] Nevertheless, Ministers did go ahead with announcement of the withdrawal and with granting staff in all three intelligence agencies access to industrial tribunals,[362] only to find that the Department of Employment inspector refused to grant a certificate of independence to the GCHQ Staff Federation.[363] The election of the Labour government in May 1997 swept the decks clean. The new Director, David Omand, immediately put forward proposals for restoring union rights. Tony Blair agreed subject to union acceptance of a robust no strike agreement – characterised in *The Observer* as a betrayal of GCHQ by the Foreign Office.[364] Finally, agreement was reached and signed on 3 September 1997.

Intelligence Priorities and Requirements

Priorities were changing with the risks of nuclear proliferation increasing as the Soviet Union broke up. The intelligence agencies redeployed resources in response to the new environment. The Security Service produced a medium-term strategy paper, circulated to PSIS in April 1991,[365] pointing up Irish Republican terrorist groups as the most serious threat to national security and to the potential erosion of traditional methods of investigation and control of espionage as visa relaxation and an increase in joint ventures made it easier for hostile intelligence services to operate in the United Kingdom. The paper concluded that it would be necessary to place greater emphasis on protective security in counter espionage and counter terrorist work (especially on achieving a satisfactory balance between physical and personnel security).[366] GCHQ shifted resources away from the traditional concern with the military capability and intentions of the Soviets towards combatting terrorism, proliferation of nuclear weapons (including Russian supplies of weapons of mass destruction) and serious international crime.[367]

The Treasury, meanwhile, had been concerned for some time that the agencies had done well in budgetary terms and in 1988 had tried unsuccessfully to introduce a regime ending their central funding as a government-wide resource.[368] In 1992 Major found himself the recipient of further Treasury pressure for deeper probing of the Agencies' expenditure. The medium-term strategy, it pointed out, did not contain cost estimates. Major discussed the situation with Butler at an informal 'forward look' in November shortly before Butler patched up a deal with the then Chancellor (Norman Lamont). But a longer-term solution required a fundamental look at the whole process of requirements definition and their translation into budgets. When Kenneth Clarke replaced Lamont in 1993 he made such a review a condition of agreement to the 1994/95–1996/97 budgets, specifying that the aims should be (a) a system that ensures requirements are placed in a clear order of priority; (b) clarifying the relationship between the requirements process and the budgetary process; (c) building effective challenge into the system; and (d) streamlining the process and timetable.[369] He was supported from within No 10 by Rodric Braithwaite who advised that: 'The intelligence agencies are getting off lightly this year',[370] and also by Alex Allan. The Foreign Secretary (Douglas Hurd) weighed in, commenting that he was finding it increasingly difficult to judge whether the balance between overt and covert activities was right and that: 'I am not convinced that the untidy format of the [Chancellor's] 1 November meeting was best designed to [review the agencies' programmes].'[371]

Butler was charged with taking the review forward. A concurrent decision to bring intelligence spending together into a Single Intelligence Vote (SIV)[372] sat well with a movement towards Parliamentary oversight. Butler's proposal was a review to be conducted by Sir Michael Quinlan who had recently retired as Permanent Secretary of the Ministry of Defence.[373] It would cover SIS and GCHQ but exclude the Security Service (which had a very different role from either) and the Defence Intelligence Service (DIS), which would be reviewed as part of a Defence Costs Study. Quinlan's review would consider both the process for setting requirements, priorities and resources and the scale and breadth of intelligence effort taking into account the changing circumstances of the late 1990s and beyond, the costs of rapidly developing technology and the scope for greater efficiency.

Quinlan reported in late March 1994 with 14 recommendations about the priority and resourcing system ranging from a clearer distinction between the application of existing capability and investment in future capability, to a firm rejection of any notion that the Treasury should be a participant in the formulation of the SIV proposal for the Public Expenditure Survey (PES). He made no fundamental suggestions for changing the scale or balance of effort, which he assessed as 'national assets of high standard' that 'should be sustained broadly at present levels.'[374] Butler enthused that Quinlan had: 'succeeded in condensing complex and arcane issues into a lucid and readable report' which 'will not put an end to debate,' but will, 'inform this year's PES round and provide for the future valuable standard reference.'[375] Ken Clarke was not impressed: 'Some of Sir Michael's findings are both illuminating and compelling ... But several of Sir Michael's judgements do not go quite far enough.'[376] Despite successes in disrupting the supply of arms to the Provisional Irish Republican Army (PIRA) he pointed to the limitations of covert intelligence, arguing that the linkage of costs, activities and achievements should be given more attention and sought a full-blown Defence Costs Review of GCHQ involving the private sector and the Prime Minister's Efficiency Unit. Butler reported that the Chancellor was isolated,[377] which was not the whole truth: the Foreign Secretary's view was that: 'I am not sure that the Quinlan Review answers completely my lingering doubts as to whether all the activities of the agencies really are needed in order to maintain the level and quality of output we need.'[378]

Ministers were not agreed on how to take matters forward, which Butler exploited to contrast the lack of convincing evidence in the Chancellor's position and 'the reasoned approach recommended by Quinlan, disciplined by the normal rigour of the PES round,' with enhanced machinery for oversight. Major accepted Butler's view and replied to the Foreign Secretary without amending Butler's draft. It remitted the big questions on scale and breadth of effort to the 1994 PES bilaterals with the Treasury Chief Secretary in the hope that something would turn up. A few weeks later Major instructed Butler that he was wary of making a step change in the deployment of resources but that he supported the appointment of a non-executive Director at GCHQ who was experienced in the management of large technological concerns.

The arguments rumbled on through two meetings of the Ministerial Intelligence Committee (charged: 'To keep under review policy on the security and intelligence services') in December 1994 and May 1995. And the former Ministers were irritated that no genuine choices or competing arguments about future priorities were presented; the decisions had been pre-cooked in the JIC. For the second, Butler suggested presentations by the heads of the three agencies followed by general discussion of the relative priorities of intelligence about the former Soviet Union, proliferation of weapons of mass destruction, serious crime and terrorism. He suggested Ministers probe what hard choices had been confronted by the agencies but thought it doubtful that the Committee would wish to reach any formal conclusions. In fact the Committee endorsed the emphasis on counter terrorism, questioned the efficacy of some other activities and instructed the Cabinet Secretary to prepare a paper showing intelligence expenditure over the most recent years, adjusted for exceptional items such as the costs of the new buildings for SIS and MI5.[379] Butler had prevented a dramatic shift in the balance of power over intelligence matters from officials to Ministers, appropriately maintaining political control by Ministers and focusing the politicians on goals, strategy (including affordability) and political cover for operations whilst avoiding them second-guessing management. All in all there was little improvement in Ministerial oversight of the agencies, perhaps some incremental benefit because agency heads would know that they would be in the PES spotlight. But the real step change came in external oversight by the Intelligence and Security Committee (ISC).

Butler was well aware that the technical world was changing fast and that significant investment in GCHQ would be needed to maintain SIGINT and electronic security validation standards. Rodric Braithwaite argued that the time had come for a searching analysis of GCHQ costs.[380] A year later terms of reference and a suitable person to lead a review of management at GCHQ came to the fore. John Adye had succeeded Marychurch in 1989. He recommended a review led by Roger Hurn, the Chairman and Chief Executive of Smiths Industries. Butler was enthusiastic: 'From what I know of him, he is an excellent manager in a conglomerate, technology based business … he is successful, sensible and discreet.' Butler and Adye disagreed, however, over the scope of the review. The Director wanted a restricted remit. Butler said that unless Hurn was given a free rein the study would not carry conviction with the Treasury. He recommended that Hurn should be asked: 'to look at the organisation as if he had just been made Chief Executive of it with a remit to producing a better return on the stockholders' investment.'[381] At a meeting a couple of days later he further argued for Treasury inclusion on a steering group for the study but resisted Treasury calls for an indicative target for savings, going so far as to say that if the Treasury proposed to take the disagreement over a specific savings target to the Ministerial Committee on Public Expenditure he would wish to attend as GCHQ's representative. A compromise was reached on 2 November – the Foreign Secretary (Douglas Hurd) and Chief Secretary (Jonathan Aitken) would jointly chair the Steering Group and, whilst a specific target savings figure would be avoided, it would be known that the Chief Secretary expected at least 5% reduction to be feasible.

Hurn started work (unremunerated) in December 1994, with David Pepper of GCHQ (later to become its Director) leading a team in support. In March they presented the emerging findings to Butler. Hurn described GCHQ as massive, high-class, well-funded, superbly equipped, competent, with clear aims and severe challenges but monastic and insular, 'not disposed to breed managers with a wider view of the world.'[382] To a clearly sceptical Butler he outlined his most controversial thought: long-term rolling contracts with customers who would be charged for GCHQ output, underpinned by an Ombudsman figure who would rule on whether the national interest was in any particular instance threatened by a customer decision. Charging would start with a pilot exercise in the Communications-Electronics Security Group (CESG) whose managers were already keen on the idea. The next Director should be drawn from government but outside GCHQ to refresh the inward-looking body and a big-budget cull would be recommended (perhaps 10%). In fact the final report confirmed Roderic Braithwaite's earlier suspicions that tighter management was possible, with estimated savings of 17.5% over three years. David Omand (formerly of GCHQ but now of MOD) became the next Director, with a remit to push the Hurn reforms.

The Foreign Secretary accepted all but one of the recommendations.[383] The exception was the regime for charging, where he commissioned further work by a Cabinet Office-chaired group to consider whether the Hurn mechanism was the right one, whether the difficulties could be overcome and what were possible alternatives to charging, such as making the link between the JIC requirements and the Single Intelligence Vote more effective. The Cabinet Office chairman, Paul Lever, also the chairman of JIC, described it as: 'a thankless and fractious task' but unavoidable. Its report in May recommended deferment of a decision until GCHQ had the systems in place for Resource (i.e. commercial) accounting.

Meanwhile, to a sceptical audience Adye reported good general progress on implementation of Hurn's recommendations in January and June 1996. Tighter management, that linked individual performance targets to their contribution to an organisational strategic plan, promised better control of effort. But the dilemma still persisted that GCHQ was difficult for Ministers to penetrate. Much depended on the skill, rigour and determination of the Permanent Secretaries Committee to combat the tendency in defence and intelligence circles, described by John Chisholm as: 'In the public sector we believe that money grows on trees; and each Spring there is a new crop.'[384] Whilst, in principle, activity based costing that informed PSIS about inputs in relation to JIC requirements superficially offered a way forward Michael Quinlan, (a regular squash opponent of Butler), had demolished the arguments for activity costing on the grounds that fixed costs in intelligence work were high (supercomputers, overseas stations for MI6 etc.) whilst the marginal costs of switching priorities was low. Activity costing would not provide appropriate signals to enable prioritisation of requirements. Further, the new Chief Secretary (William Waldegrave) did not have the same attachment to a charging regime as his predecessor, arguing that, like basic research, much of intelligence was not suitable for the Rothschild customer-contractor principle.[385]

The Intelligence Services Act 1994

On 14 December 1994 the status and credibility of the intelligence agencies took a major step forward with the passing of the Intelligence Services Act, which put GCHQ and SIS on a statutory basis. An oversight Committee of Parliamentarians reporting to the Prime Minister (the ISC) was established the following day. The origins of the change were two years earlier when the Prime Minister's hand was forced by a story that began to circulate in Washington about the imminent avowal of SIS and was reported in *The Sunday Times* on 3 May.[386] Once again the government had been unable to get ahead of the curve and an announcement of a forthcoming Intelligence Bill in the next Parliamentary Session was made in the Queen's Speech of 6 May 1992. The following day Major had to apologise to Cabinet for not having been able to give them advance warning.

Work started in the Ministerial IS Committee on the likely consequences of legislation, predominantly the arrangements for oversight of the Agencies. A Cabinet Office paper argued that the introduction of legislation to place SIS and GCHQ on a statutory basis would almost certainly provide an opportunity for pressure to be put on government for some form of Parliamentary oversight. Unsurprisingly, the paper concluded that the key was whether Parliament could be satisfied without imposing undesirable constraints on the Agencies and it identified the best option from the government point of view as a Committee of Privy Counsellors reporting to the Prime Minister.[387] The following month, at a meeting on 25 June, the IS Committee concluded that an initiative on oversight would be necessary in order to secure passage of the Intelligence Bill and commissioned work to illustrate how that might work in practice.[388] This was discussed in July[389] and a decision taken that oversight proposals should be included in the legislation from the outset (i.e. not conceded later during the passage of the Bill). On the difficult question of how to specify operational information to which the Committee would not have access, drafting should look at both a general and a specific provision for further consideration in the autumn.

Butler was strongly opposed to Parliamentary oversight: 'I think that we shall be deluding ourselves if we believed that it will do any practical good, and it may do some considerable harm,' he wrote; adding: 'The real guarantee of the proper behaviour of the Intelligence Agencies is bound to be the independent Commissioner … Parliament exists for public discussion and, by the nature of things, this is not possible for the Intelligence Agencies.'[390] Nevertheless, the IS Committee decided in favour of oversight by a hybrid Parliamentary Committee of Privy Councillors. The Private Office brief drew attention to the sensitivity of clause 7 of the Bill, that: 'gives SIS what would be seen as a "licence to kill;" the Secretary of State has power to authorise "any act" overseas.' Major annotated the text with a single word: 'Hitler'[391] and during the Committee stage on the Bill the Foreign Office Minister Douglas Hogg assured members that '… the Secretary of State would not, in ordinary circumstances, issue a Clause 7 authorisation in respect of the use of force.'[392]

When the drafting of the options on non-disclosure to the Committee was available for consideration Ministers were attracted to arrangements under which the heads of intelligence agencies would be empowered to disclose information other than that in defined excluded categories. However, the agencies should have discretion not to disclose the fact that an operation had taken place (even without details) subject to the Committee being able to appeal to the relevant Secretary of State. This, in turn, would underline that it was Ministers who were directly accountable to Parliament, not Agency Heads.[393] On access to financial information Butler was charged with discussions with the Comptroller and Auditor General to secure agreement that would limit access to the Chairman and Deputy Chairman of the Public Accounts Committee. Concerns were expressed that proceeding with the Bill might prejudice the judicial inquiry into the Matrix-Churchill affair. Rodric Braithwaite was particularly forthright in rejecting that argument, – '... continuing evidence that the Government really is concerned to provide proper democratic accountability for the activities of the Intelligence Agencies goes with, rather than against, the grain of the Inquiry and the press and other comment which has surrounded it.'[394] By November one issue of substance remained – authorisation by the Secretary of State of actions overseas that would otherwise be unlawful under extra-territorial legislation. Butler's unequivocal advice was that the clause must be retained. And on Guy Fawkes Day 1993 Cabinet took the decision to proceed.

During the passage of the Bill through Parliament the government refused to be drawn on the detail of which information might be disclosed 'subject to and in accordance with arrangements approved by the Secretary of State' (as described in the Bill). Recognising the likelihood that the arrangements would have to be shared with the Committee at an early stage, however, Butler set out a relevant framework and mechanisms. If information were to be refused the Committee would be informed in writing by the Head of the Agency concerned, with a reason for the decision and confirming that the Secretary of State had been fully consulted and had had full opportunity to override the refusal if he considered it in the public interest to do so.[395]

The ISC usually met once a week on Cabinet Office premises to take formal oral or written evidence. Its first report was sent to the Prime Minister on 15 December 1995 and discussed with him on New Year's Eve. Initial relations with government were smooth. After two years' experience, Butler circulated guidance on the conduct of business with the Committee.[396] The most important outstanding areas of disagreement concerned the Committee's wish for access to JIC papers on a regular basis and its belief that the Prime Minister should be actively engaged on Agency issues. On the former, Butler feared exposure of the Agencies' sources and operations and pointed out that an important principle that advice to Ministers was not made available to Parliamentary Select Committees would be breached. As a compromise, he suggested that if the Committee sought a memorandum on specific subjects, the Cabinet Office would draw on JIC assessments excluding anything thought to be operationally sensitive.[397] On the latter Butler saw the proposal as an unnecessary addition to the normal political clearance for Agency operations by the Home Secretary and the Foreign and Commonwealth Secretary.[398] The discussion was to rumble on without a final accommodation during the Blair administration under a new Committee membership and with the rival Home Affairs Committee seeking in vain to extend its remit at the expense of the ISC.[399] Meanwhile, Butler gave evidence to the original Committee on 19 February 1997. He estimated that intelligence matters took up, on average, around 5% of his time, though the incidence was uneven. He found himself defending the balance between risk and reasonable employment practice against a committee and pressing for tougher personal security obligations on employees, much influenced by the damage done by the American CIA spy Aldrich Ames who had betrayed many agents.[400]

Counter Terrorism and Communications Interception

Butler's familiarity with Irish terrorism went back to his time as Principal Private Secretary to Thatcher. He is publicly thought to have saved her life when he asked her to look at a submission from Patrick Jenkin about the future of the Liverpool Garden Festival site in the early hours of the morning during the Conservative Party Conference and thereby miss the direct force of the IRA Brighton bomb of 12 October 1984.[401] The IRA threat, including on the mainland, claimed successes such as the Baltic Exchange bombing (April 1992) and that of the NatWest Tower in Bishopsgate (April 1993). As Joe Pilling of the Northern Ireland Office wrote shortly after the Baltic Exchange bomb: 'Only a combination of good intelligence, good policing and good luck prevented several more incidents on a similar scale.'[402] The government was aware of mainland vulnerability. In November 1991 Major commissioned work to explore the case for the Security Service extending its primacy in the intelligence effort beyond Northern Ireland to include Great Britain, which historically fell to the Metropolitan Police Special Branch.[403] The following February Butler warned that the timing of work ran an appreciable risk of falling foul of electoral purdah[404] should a General Election be called in early April (as indeed it was). On the other hand, implementation of a change would be dependent on buy-in from the Metropolitan Police in particular, so it was clearly right to strive for a report that would minimise the risk of friction and in-fighting after Ministers' decision. Unspoken, there was perhaps an expectation in his mind that the election result would not be clear-cut and so the opportunity for change would be lost. In the event, however, the decision to place the Security Service in prime position was announced on 8 May to take effect from October and to be reviewed after six months.

That review, conducted by Gerry Warner, the Intelligence Co-ordinator in the Cabinet Office, reported in January 1994 that the arrangements were working well largely due to the sensitivity of the Security Service under Stella Rimington and the determination and persistence of the Metropolitan Police Commissioner, Sir Paul Condon, to remove obstacles to success.[405] Three months later Warner reviewed the operation of the Director and Co-ordinator of Intelligence for

Northern Ireland, leading to a significant increase in the availability, quality and distribution of intelligence assessments. But on 9 February 1996, one hour after the IRA announced the end of a seventeen-month ceasefire, a huge bomb devastated the South Quays Docklands Light Railway station at Canary Wharf, putting more pressure on Butler to advise the Prime Minister on progress in securing improvements in intelligence coverage of PIRA.

Two aspects of the interception of communications and eavesdropping were integrally related to countering PIRA and other terrorism. The first was the possible use of intercept as evidence in court; the second the implications of the liberalisation of the telecoms market and the growing availability of encryption techniques. Late in 1994 Stella Rimington advised that the restrictions on the use of intercept material in the prosecution of alleged terrorists should be lifted and Butler told Alex Allen that he supported her in this.[406] Major agreed to further work on how best to make such a change and how to handle those agencies and services who opposed a change. Home Office officials reported in November 1995 with options for a blanket removal of restrictions or for a two-tier system of evidential and intelligence gathering interception. However, in the face of continuing opposition from most of the law enforcement agencies, and the opinion of Leading Counsel that the scheme would fail the human rights challenge, Major reluctantly agreed with Michael Howard not to take matters further forward for the time being.[407]

On the second issue, a Standing Committee on Interception (SCI) was established in January 1991: 'to ensure that provision is made to safeguard national security and related interests in telecommunications developments.'[408] It reported to PSIS through the Cabinet Secretary and in June 1994 started a review of the Interception of Communications Act 1985. Market fragmentation and new entrants using technologies unforeseen at the time had driven a coach and horses through the 1985 Act. By 1991 there were over 150 licensed telecommunications operators in the United Kingdom and, furthermore, their networks were largely digital, capable of providing services unimagined when in the analogue networks held sway. As a result there were increasing difficulties in protecting the security of the state and in combatting serious crime. The roll-out of intercept capability had been just too late to pre-empt the actions of the PIRA unit that carried out the Bishopsgate bomb of 1993.[409] At the same time the competitiveness of British firms was endangered by the absence of a system to licence commercial encryption services. Quite apart from technical issues, the closure of legal gaps and the licensing of encryption services would require primary legislation. The Prime Minister did not think this would be possible before 1997; and though it was known that the Americans were shortly to announce a temporary relaxation of export controls on some advanced encryption products, DTI officials did not think the benefits to UK competitiveness would be significant enough to put the licensing of the provision of encryption systems among its highest priorities. A consultation paper on the licensing of 'trusted third party' encryption services was announced on 19 March 1997. As PSIS was informed in July that year, however, the response had been disappointing with little support for mandatory licensing and virtually none for government access to the keys for decryption. Further work was commissioned, including: 'a revised presentation of the overall concept, to counter apparently widespread misunderstanding.'[410] By the time Butler handed over to Richard Wilson at the end of the year neither the gaps in legislation nor the licensing of encryption services had been resolved.

Constitutional Issues

In constitutional matters there was a long tradition of Cabinet Secretaries acting as a go-between for either the Prime Minister personally or the Cabinet as a whole. One reason for this was that by convention the Prime Minister did not appear before Select Committees and hence could only be questioned on the floor of the House of Commons, regularly during Prime Minister's Questions (PMQ) and also on the occasions of a Prime Ministerial statement. In 1995 the Procedure Committee suggested amending PMQ arrangements to have substantive questions on Tuesdays and to restrict open questions to Thursdays.[411] In preparation for considering the proposal Private Office looked at the time spent across Whitehall preparing for open questions to the Prime Minister on a typical occasion (23 March was chosen), estimating that a 15-minute session had required 233 man-hours of preparation (including almost 60 hours in Number 10 itself).[412] So seriously was this twice-weekly session taken that towards the end of 1992 Major had started to study video replays of his performance.[413] So when Butler submitted a response to the Procedure Committee report he reluctantly admitted he might have to attend the Committee himself to protect the convention that a Prime Minister did not appear.[414]

After five years in power the Major Government had transacted a substantial package of constitutional changes that the Prime Minister both wished to have widely recognised and to take further. The reforms achieved included the Northern Ireland Downing Street Declaration, response to the Nolan Committee recommendations on standards in public life, the Citizen's Charter, and greater openness about the conduct of government. At Major's request, Butler submitted a comprehensive list of changes achieved (over 50 individual items), changes in the pipeline (10 items) and more speculative ideas for further reform. The latter looked at the balance of power between the Executive and Parliament, at cheap, fair, quick and transparent judicial processes and at enhancing local democracy.[415] He pointed up that constitutional initiatives tended to be at the expense of the dominance and power of the centre and might sit uncomfortably with Ministers' ambitions to drive through radical change and could result in further divisions over European policy.

An intensive period of policy development followed, led politically by Lord Cranborne[416] and at official level by Bill Jeffrey and Andrew Whetnall in the Cabinet Office. Butler mainly held a watching brief, leading only on issues affecting Royalty in his role as part of the 'golden triangle' of Private Secretary to H.M. The Queen, Cabinet Secretary and Prime Minister's Principal Private Secretary. Discussions centred on the treatment of Roman Catholics marrying someone in line to the throne, parity for females in the line of succession, the requirement that The Queen should approve marriages of all direct descendants of George II and the representation of different faiths at State events. The officials concerned were clearly sympathetic to the cause of change but extremely cautious, even anxious, about its potentially divisive effects with the result that the first three of these issues were deemed to be too controversial to pursue at that time. However, in March 1996 Butler argued for a referendum if proposed reforms were to include the choice between Proportional Representation and 'first past the post' systems for General Elections.[417]

A Search for Coherence in Civil Service Reform

During the early Butler years there was a definite tension between the Treasury view of civil service issues (led by Peter Middleton) and that of the Cabinet Office or Office of Public Service and Science (OPSS) led by Butler and Peter Kemp. Kemp felt that the Treasury were trying to marginalise the Executive Agency concept whereas he and other OPSS officials saw a process of change leading to greater decentralisation of authority and fragmentation of the unified civil service.[418] The Permanent Secretaries supported the Agency idea, welcoming the relaxations it promised from central standards and bureaucracy and recognising that most officials had a loyalty to their local organisation rather than to a civil service they did not feel part of in their day-to-day work. Performance in delivering services improved and Ministers were said to be more appreciative of the contribution of the civil service.[419]

After Terry Burns succeeded Peter Middleton on the latter's retirement from the Treasury in 1991 relations with Butler's departmental *alma mater* improved considerably. Butler and Burns were to become close professional associates, reminiscent of the relationship between Trend and William Armstrong or Robert Armstrong and Wass. Even so, Butler was sometimes critical of the Treasury approach to reform, as too prescriptive and too negative, not giving enough credit for success.[420] He wrote to Terry Burns, in January 1994, for example: 'I fear that if you drive [the running costs negotiations] further, the instrument will break in the Government's hands.'[421] Nevertheless, harmony between the two was generally prevalent with both men in favour of delegated management authority matched by accountability for results. They saw it as absurd, for example, that the Treasury Defence Materiel division (DM) should think to second-guess the MOD on the equipment part of its £20 billion annual block budget.[422]

The Autumn Conference of Permanent Secretaries (held at the Sunningdale site of the Civil Service College) had become established as a forum for discussion of internal management questions.[423] The agenda during the Armstrong years had been essentially top-down covering topics he chose, including, for example, political and social attitudes to Government (1984); morale motivation and pay in the Civil Service (1985); inner cities (1986); and the Official Secrets Act and Open Government (1987). Butler introduce a more consultative and systematised approach, under which one of the three conference sessions was devoted to civil service developments; a second session covered an emerging policy area (such as the environment in 1989) and a third was focused on a European or wider international topic.

Internally, Treasury Ministers claimed that a presumption of greater delegated authority to agency chief executives was too often unmatched by a presumption of specific targeted benefits.[424] Butler feared a Treasury move to supervise the development of agencies too closely, quoting RTZ, P&O and GEC as examples where headquarters staff used very small numbers of people to control worldwide operations. A report by the Efficiency Unit had suggested that headquarters finance and personnel staff could be cut by 25%.[425] Turnbull sympathised with the Treasury: 'Trading greater freedoms only where better performance is promised gives [the Treasury] an important leverage,'[426] – perhaps feeling his way towards a surrogate for the market analysts who kept the pressure to improve on public companies. Later, whilst acknowledging a dilemma over allowing public sector bodies to compete with the private sector, Butler called a paper by the Chief Secretary (Mellor), 'a good example of the dead hand of the Treasury on the motivation of the Civil Service'; in intellectual terms the Treasury paper represented a fair balance, but emotionally the checklist of prior questions and the consultations required were stultifying: '... like Dr Johnson's remark about a dog walking on its hind legs – it may be done very well but one wonders why it is done at all.'[427]

However, concerns also began to surface over the unintended consequences of restructuring into Agencies. Most notably over the reduced career attractiveness of policy work and the difficulties of maintaining a unified service in which senior staff moved between Departments. By 1990 the Permanent Secretaries reported that the civil service was losing a valuable sense of unity that threatened its core values of integrity, political neutrality and willingness to compromise Departmental goals in the wider interests of collective success. Terry Burns (Middleton's successor) told the 1991 and 1992 Conferences that the Treasury was struggling to manage decentralisation and delegation without a loss of control over expenditure. Budgeting and audit should be strengthened to counterbalance delegated authority.[428] Butler argued that the Treasury would always need good information to enable it to advise on the allocation of resources. 'Subject to that, the principle should be that, provided the necessary system of controls and incentives is in place to ensure that managers comply with the Government's objectives, services are likely to be best run if decisions are taken as close as possible to the point of delivery.'[429] The best guarantee of good performance, he argued, was the spirit of altruistic public service at the heart of the civil service. New challenges were emerging such as living up to the claims of 'Next Steps' that the service would remain unified though not uniform: 'It will continue to be the case,' he assured the FDA, 'that once people have been recruited they can move anywhere within the Civil Service without the need for further formality – they are within the fence.' But, he added: 'We are challenging individuals to do more to shape their own careers.'[430]

Major's priorities were to improve the delivery of services to the public (the Citizens' Charter), to involve the private sector in the provision of those services (market testing) and to reduce compliance burdens on business (deregulation). Major's special adviser, Peter Levene, was particularly associated with market testing but did not have as close a relationship with him as had Rayner or Ibbs with Thatcher.[431] Nor was Major as interested as Thatcher in the scrutiny programme or the value for money seminars with Departmental Ministers managed by the Efficiency Unit as windows into departmental performance and stimulus for Ministers to keep up the pressure for improvements (they were cancelled after January 1992).[432]

One of the bedevilling complications in the drive for improved public services had been that Parliament (and the public) were concerned with all public services, not just those delivered directly by civil servants. The 1987 Stowe report on governance had pointed to this, referring to the activities of government as a whole, including the National Health Service and the politically independent local authorities. Butler was only Head of the Home Civil Service and had no direct responsibility for wider efficiency. For the civil service the strategy continued to be to reduce the size of departments at their centre, having central staff concentrate on policy advice and contract management using improved systems for planning and reporting, underpinned by commercial (accruals) accounting. In this vision, services would be largely provided on contract or by agencies, with delegated pay and grading authority and clear targets and objectives.[433] The civil service had been reduced from 730,000 in 1979 to 550,000 and was expected to shrink modestly to 500,000 by 1996; market testing was continuing to show savings of 25% or more, though it was proving difficult to maintain the momentum in the face of laggard departments. Tough controls on running costs (not just manpower) were central to the strategy – an important decision being whether to anticipate savings from laggard departments in setting running cost controls.

Pushed by Permanent Secretary pressure to give staff a sense of purpose and direction through a statement of the core attributes and framework of the modern civil service,[434] and by the interest of the TCSSC in managerial reforms, the government gave an assurance that it would provide a strategic description of its policies for the civil service. The initial idea was to link publication of a White Paper to a Deregulation Bill to be introduced in November 1993. This would have allowed government to keep the initiative in the face of Select Committee pressure for a code of ethics and an associated Ombudsman.[435] But when the Prime Minister reviewed progress in November 1993 his conclusion was that progress towards a smaller, less costly yet more effective civil service was not fast enough.

These concerns were important in leading to a remit for the Efficiency Unit under John Oughton[436] to examine career management policy for the most senior officials. At the suggestion of the Chancellor of the Duchy (Waldegrave) Butler notified Major of the intention at the end of June 1992 – noting that: 'I would not normally have bothered the Prime Minister with it, but ... the Press might try to link it with the Top Salaries Review Board (TSRB) …'[437] The study led to the creation of the Senior Civil Service (SCS), designed to replicate the former mobility across Departments at the top levels, and also to rolling employment contracts for SCS members. The Autumn Sunningdale Conference was then a key element in marshalling Permanent Secretaries' support for implementation of the report's recommendations including the creation of an independent senior remuneration committee analogous to those operating in the corporate sector. (Not least as the cold wind of redundancy touched even their own number.) Under the new pay system Permanent Secretaries were required to specify key personal targets for the year ahead. Butler was no exception and for 1995/96 he identified keeping the Permanent Secretaries on side as a priority in the light of the reduction in civil service numbers and the continued containment of running costs.

Oughton reported at a PUS seminar on 3 November 1993. He presented a challenging agenda designed to produce a mix of skills similar to that required in the private sector and yet to retain corporate knowledge and continuity. In his judgement there would be advantages in moving to new contract terms for senior officials rather than trying to use existing arrangements better. Butler spoke in support, adding his weight behind a proposal to require all posting to senior posts *to consider* whether it was necessary to look outside for a suitable candidate, (emphasis added.) He thought the case for a new employment contract for senior officials was persuasive – though personally favoured a period of notice to a rolling contract; and he subtly introduced the thorny topic of pay: increased reward for increased risk, expected to be covered in a report from the Senior Salaries Review Board (SSRB) at the end of January 1994. At a meeting with the Chancellor of the Exchequer in December he went further, arguing that 'on any objective basis,' the Senior Open Structure (Under-Secretary and above), 'were underpaid given their calibre, – (original emphasis).'[438] The pay system was becoming unworkable but performance pay offered a route out of the mess.

There were good grounds to be sceptical. Although Ministers had approved his and Terry Burns' recent evidence to the SSRB they had not sustained the position when pay decisions had to be taken. In the previous year, Major had voiced concerns that: 'with 60 per cent of the Civil Service likely to be in Next Steps agencies, and considerable [political] pressure to recruit private sector candidates as Chief Executives and to other posts, there would be increasing difficulties over salary levels.'[439] He threw in a suggestion that: 'There might, for example, be a move towards making senior civil servant posts subject to fixed short term contracts.' With Allan reporting that the original proposal for director of the prison service, then a Next Steps agency, was: 'for a salary package of over £200,000 as against the internal deputy secretary candidate who would have been paid £68,000'[440] the urgency of a coherent politically approved strategy for the management of the civil service was plain. A seminar scheduled for November was to point the way forward.

The seminar took place on 3 November[441] but whilst it was agreed that the public presentation of issues of ethics and accountability should be separated from those of management, there was no general agreement that a White Paper describing the strategy on civil service management was desirable – causing delay that meant the eventual White Paper, *Continuity and Change* did not appear until July 1994. And despite Oughton's plea that the civil service should 'grow its own timber' it fell to a private sector participant in the shape of Peter Levene to stress an appropriate balance between open competition and promotion from within for agency Chief Executives, similar to that exercised by private sector firms which: 'did not uproot their senior management all the time, and if they had an excellent in-house candidate they did not bother to look elsewhere.'[442]

The problem was agreeing what constituted an excellent candidate and how to arrive at a fair comparison of internal and external candidates. The President of the Board of Trade, Michael Heseltine, had one view; Butler had another. Heseltine had not been invited to the November seminar. That did not stop him writing to Major that whilst the objective of a flexible structure for the civil service was right, a more radical approach to achieving it was needed. The key principles of impartiality, incorruptibility and public service had to be applied within a framework that had changed out of all recognition since the traditional structure had been conceived. Skills and experience should determine who took on tasks rather than seniority or grade. A spell in the private sector could be a key source of new skills but: 'If it is not going to benefit a civil servant's promotion prospects then they are not likely to want to go out and work in the private sector. This has to change.' Further: 'Running an agency with a £bn spend and employing several thousand people is regarded as admirable but in the final analysis it is not quite thought to match what can be offered by a policy generalist. This also needs to change.' Unless the composition of SASC was changed: '… we would be entrusting the introduction of people with new skills and experience to a small group who appear … not only to lack such skills and experience themselves but to be the product of the very culture we wish to change.'[443]

Butler was incensed and defensive: 'I cannot let pass without protest some of your dismissive remarks about the Civil Service. The allegations about SASC were untrue and unfair to people who had led, over the last few years what was generally agreed to be the biggest change in Civil Service structure and culture for the last 150 years. The outward secondment programme belied Heseltine's worries about the attractiveness of a spell in the private sector.[444] The improvements in representation of women at higher levels of the Service, which he had reported to Thatcher in 1989, had been partly due to the loss of high-flying men to the lusher pastures of the City of London and this had opened up opportunities for women.[445] He might perhaps have added that work then in train to identify a formal competency framework for senior civil servants would potentially revolutionise the appraisal and selection processes. Heseltine too was unrepentant, but pulled his punches arguing that the comments objected to by Butler were 'statements of the obvious'.[446] As Lucy Neville-Rolfe of the Policy Unit subtly argued, leading change in others is not the same as demonstrating the flexibility to cope with change oneself.[447]

There were disagreements too over how to accelerate progress. Butler argued that new central initiatives were not necessary, sufficient policy instruments already existed.[448] Despite Treasury protestations of innocence he feared a return to manpower targets, preferring reliance on tough running cost controls. Mottram thought that the Treasury approach was unbalanced with too much emphasis on privatisation at the expense of the Competing for Quality initiative.[449] The result was a submission to the Chancellor of the Duchy that recommended sweating existing mechanisms more effectively. However, neither Butler nor Mottram quite trusted Ministerial instincts when it came to difficult decisions on pay and public expenditure. Butler emphasised to Waldegrave that the proposed package of changes would come as a shock to civil servants, altering the time-honoured Northcote-Trevelyan trade-off of tenure in return for objectivity and commitment. With the introduction of new employment contracts for the Senior Open Structure job security would be significantly reduced and pay would be performance-led.[450] The plan was for a tripling of enforced early retirements over a five-year period. (The actual numbers of early retirements reached a peak of 9,090 in 1995–96 compared to 4,920 in 1993–94 and fell away dramatically to 1,220 in 1998–99.)[451] But there was understandable (and partly justified) concern among officials that Ministers would not deliver on the reward side of the package. As chairman of SASC Butler saw increasing difficulty in the face of political pressures to open up more opportunities to external competition in securing planned management moves to prepare rising stars for senior office.[452]

Oughton also recommended replacing the 1000-strong Senior Open Structure with a wider, 4000-strong, Senior Civil Service from Grade 5 upwards. The main justification was to combat fragmentation of the service. Initially Butler opposed the change as it would be impracticable to manage such a large group centrally and he saw little point in trying to create a group with a single identity without that.[453] But Ministers were attracted by the possibility of increased delayering, which they felt a wider group would offer, and the two Chancellors (of the Exchequer and of the Duchy of Lancaster) agreed to advocate the wider interpretation of the Senior Civil Service to include Grade 5.[454] One problem was that it was all very well to talk about delayering, more pay for more performance and more acceptance of risk but the implementation of the associated initiatives could be incompatible. In January 1994 Butler noted that it was unlikely that many senior staff could be persuaded to go early on a voluntary basis if they believed there was a significant pay increase in the pipeline even if it was circumscribed in terms of performance and risk.[455] On the other hand, numbers in the Senior Open Structure were down 200 since 1979 with consequent reduced promotion prospects and increased importance of pay in retaining and motivating Grade 5 staff and below. The hard line being taken by the Treasury on pay and on Senior Open Structure numbers further complicated implementation. A cold wind was blowing through the upper corridors. The target reduction in senior posts meant getting rid of almost one in every two of the present incumbents over three to four years, doubling the rate of departure and halving the rate of promotion.[456] Butler thought that the Service had a good record on reform, but alterations to job security and career progression on that scale were frightening – at one point he hinted that a 20% reduction over three to four years with the introduction of outside appointments for 10% of the remainder would lead to mayhem.[457]

The most thoughtful analysis came from William Waldegrave; the most radical from Michael Heseltine. Ken Clarke spoke toughly on pay and running costs, his key officials, Burns and Mountfield together with Butler, sat somewhere in between on the most sensitive issues. Briefing for a second Prime Ministerial discussion Waldegrave spelled out that: 'The maintenance of the non-political, meritocratic, uncorrupt civil service is an important element of our unwritten constitution,' which should not be damaged.[458] Work to develop the reforms had proceeded on the basis that major efficiency gains were possible but recognised that not everything was suitable for the private sector and that the civil service contributed something special. Reductions in the policy advising hierarchy carried risks ('wise heads are not always a bad idea'); delegation must not become fragmentation; 'if the policy is wrong it is Ministers' fault,' was the British civil service really so bad? And if Ministers were not brave enough to face the odium of the media and the electorate on their own pay, could they be expected to do so with the civil service?

Heseltine was, by now, an active participant in the debate and attended the second seminar with Major on 10 May 1994. He had four clear demands – more ambition in reducing running costs; comprehensive management information to show how many people with what resources yielded what results; a massive increase in delegation to Departments; much greater interchange between the public and private sectors. He did not, however, favour publishing targets or illustrative numbers of the future size of the service and argued that: 'we should in future look more to Permanent Secretaries as the professional managers, rather than Secretaries of State, to be properly trained in management with practical knowledge of how things are organised in the private sector.'[459] Some central means of fixing the pay of Permanent Secretaries was necessary; otherwise there would be real problems of pay drift. Clarke introduced the discussion with a plea not to present the changes as hostile to the civil service and proposed six issues for discussion: (1) Whether to publish an indicative range for the future size of the civil service – Butler thought that publishing an indicative range would give people a sense of what the reforms might produce (and perhaps he also felt that announcing a potential loss of 100,000 jobs overall would put the Senior Open Structure reductions into context); (2) whether it was desirable to maintain a coherent civil service at its most senior levels and just how far down the structure should it go – Butler recognised the risk to collective government if the policy cadre were to fragment but was unconvinced that the Senior Open Structure should be extended down to Grade 5; (3) whether to delegate fully to Departments responsibility for pay and grading and whether (and how) to relate senior pay more closely to the market – Butler supported the case for greater delegation but also supported the Heseltine argument for some central controls over Permanent Secretaries' pay, which he argued could be used to provide a pay ceiling for the delegated powers. Whatever arrangements were made, however, should not obscure the fact of the ultimate accountability of Ministers and the Prime Minister for the pay of senior civil servants; (4) whether to introduce explicit written contracts for the Senior Civil Service – Butler agreed with the view that their introduction would be largely symbolic. They could not be forced on people but he did not think it would be necessary to purchase agreement to the new regime with an across-the-board pay rise; if they were made a condition of eligibility for a wider range of performance pay or on promotion that would be enough; (5) how to encourage Departments to shorten the hierarchy – Heseltine argued for review by an independent team from outside the Department concerned. Butler's silence on the point implied his agreement; (6) how to introduce these ideas into public consideration – Ministers instructed officials that the proposals should be for consultation, not presented as final decisions.

On most of the issues, and especially on the key issues around senior pay and delegation of authority to Departments Major preferred to leave decisions open pending further work on the practicalities of implementation and this set the agenda for an intensive two months of work. At the outset Butler prepared an anodyne note for wide circulation announcing the intention to publish a White paper on civil service management reform. It sought to dampen the likely trepidation in the service by suggesting that the focus would be on career management 'set in the context of [the Government] reforms of the Civil Service more generally … [and would] give a firm indication of the direction which the Government expects reform in the management of the Civil Service as a whole to take in the remainder of this Parliament.' By contrast, the government response to concerns about ethics being investigated by the civil service sub-committee of the TCSSC would have to wait until that committee had reported.

The next big set piece occasion was a further meeting with the Prime Minister scheduled for 16 June. Mountfield produced further ideas on Permanent Secretary pay involving a small central Remuneration Committee composed of Butler, Burns and Gillmore of the FCO but expressed pessimism about the viability of the reform package in the face of Ministerial reluctance to make a step change in the levels of pay to reflect reduced job security, increased risk and market rates of pay. 'We would be presenting major delayering and a significant increase in external appointments … reduced promotions but more unsupervised responsibility when younger; and little compensation in pay apart from a little rhetoric about the market, at odds with the systems we would be installing. This has led me to ponder whether we still have a viable proposition. I doubt if we have.'[460] In his brief to Major Butler built upon this warning and that of others, who pointed up internal incoherence in the proposals. He identified two key issues: (1) 'Is it right to give departments and agencies further freedom to manage according to their own particular circumstances, and that this is the strategic theme of the White Paper?' (2) 'If it is to be saleable to senior staff, the approach to careers and rewards needs to be a coherent one. Ministers saw difficulties about moving fully to a high risk, high reward, market-based approach; how then do they see the balance being drawn?'[461]

He touched on these points at an informal bilateral meeting with Major on 14 June 1994. The Prime Minister said he would accept greater delegation if the intention was serious and if the Treasury and the Efficiency Unit probed rigorous annual departmental efficiency plans. More generally, however, he wanted the radical proposals on organisation and risk/reward to be cast in consultative terms and a muted tone. The more threatening aspects of the proposals for senior careers (such as estimates of numbers of redundancies and reductions in senior ranks) were not to be included.[462] Butler then raised the issues at a Wednesday morning Permanent Secretaries' meeting the following day. There was no enthusiasm for the proposals but no outright opposition either. The main concerns were how to allow departments credit for efficiency plans already in train (previous good behaviour should not be penalised) and how to sell the ideas to staff (what was the single message of the proposed White Paper; did a civil service career still exist?). Meanwhile Heseltine weighed in once again on the ambition behind the proposals and on management information. His contention was that senior officials had no personal incentive to manage with fewer resources. Linking Open Structure pay to the delivery of improvements in efficiency was the single most promising move the government could take and would provide political cover for, 'allowing the excellence that undoubtedly exists across the top of the Service to receive its due reward.'[463]

The Meeting of 16 June reached agreement for a consultative White Paper advocating greater delegation of authority over pay grading and recruitment to Departments but with Treasury and Efficiency Unit scrutiny of annual efficiency plans. There would be no published benchmark for the scale of reductions in the overall size of the civil service or of its senior ranks. Ministers failed to agree, however, on the extent to which a Remuneration Committee for Permanent Secretaries should take account of performance or just of the management span and weight of the job. The majority felt that there would be great difficulties in explaining and justifying performance assessments for individuals, particularly in relation to the role of Ministers and the successes of what were government policies. (The Australian Cabinet Secretary, Michael Keating advised that his government had resiled from individual performance pay for Permanent Secretaries as the achievements of top officials and ministers were too closely intertwined to be disentangled for this purpose.)[464] By now Major was contemplating amending the Civil Service Order in Council to allow Ministers a greater say in the final selection of senior appointments but was dissuaded by a combination of Anne Bowtell, the First Civil Service Commissioner, and Richard Mottram who argued that it would be open to a charge of politicisation and would confirm the fears of serving civil servants that Ministers were being given too much authority to over-rule the Commissioners.[465]

Butler showed Permanent Secretaries a draft of the White Paper on a personal basis on 20 June and Major met them for one and a half hours nine days later. All pointed to a need for the government to offer clarity and stability about its intentions on the basis of a cross-party consensus. Reaffirmation of traditional values would be important as staff were worried about possible hidden agendas.

What was needed was to absorb the extra dimension of change without feeling that the essential character of the civil service was being undermined. The ending of tenure for those involved in policy advice to Ministers was unsettling and a focus for worries around politicisation. A potentially serious consequence of the proposals was a modular civil service and a reassertion of the primacy of a career civil service would be welcome. Major summed up in a low-key manner – there was no hidden agenda but the aim was stringency in running costs; the status quo was not an option. He made no commitment to meet the Permanent Secretaries' concerns on market rates of pay other than to recognise: 'that rates in some cases were well adrift from the market and [he] hoped this could now begin to be addressed, though there were not huge extra sums of money available',[466] nor did he pick up on the fears expressed about the possible fragmentation of the service. Chris France, PUS at the MOD sent him a minute of 1883 abut the creation of The Royal Corps of Naval Constructors with the words: 'I do not think we could get closer to the point of balance between saying "Yes" and intending "No".'

William Waldegrave's office, on the other hand, thought that whilst there was excellent material in the draft, it was damaged by a negative tone and a tendency to look backward – why, for instance, talk about preserving civil service values as if they belonged to the past instead of extolling them as relevant to the future? Butler prepared to undertake extensive briefing of the media alongside Waldegrave. Internal communications for the civil service included a summary of the White Paper, a briefing pack for senior staff with '20 questions answered' and open meetings. The White Paper text was circulated to Cabinet on 4 July with a 72-hour deadline for written comments. At this eleventh hour the Prime Minister asked for a number of drafting changes: (a) to make clear that those not performing satisfactorily would be asked to go, believing that such presentation would help reassure junior staff that the increased pay was not just a cosy deal; (b) to make the prospect of a civil service career sound more exciting and challenging; (c) to make some of the more radical ideas, such as on pay structures, more tentative. He authorised Butler to brief the leaders of the Opposition and the chairman of the TCSSC on his behalf shortly before the final document was published on 13 July.[467]

The White Paper, *Continuity and Change*,[468] sought to present the reforms as a coherent vision and programme linked to the earlier *Competing for Quality*[469] document. Meanwhile, Parliament and Ministers started to move to a more restrictive view of the civil service role and a weakening of its policy influence, casting forward the long shadow of a free market in policy advice, particularly from the politically committed, and increased emphasis on policy presentation. Early media coverage put the story low in the pecking order and concentrated on potential losses of jobs and job security. In that regard, the *Evening Standard* said: 'it goes far further towards shaking up the civil service than anything Lady Thatcher ever dared to propose.'[470] There was some hostile comment from the civil service unions and a sceptical appraisal from Peter Kemp who, by now was outside the Service. He argued that the government was trying to bring reform to

2,000 civil servants who had survived 150 years with no change – the proof would be how they would be hired, assessed and fired.

After reflection the more thoughtful commentators concentrated on the possibility that contracts for senior officials would reduce their propensity to 'speak truth unto power' for fear of discrimination and possible loss of job. The journalist Norman Macrae described it as: 'an interesting account of some recent half-reforms, and of the government's wish (under a lot of soft soap and flannel) to limp forward with them,' continuing with a lament for times past when: 'Mandarins used to meet journalists such as me over lunch and bubble forth ideas about what they would like to persuade the government next to do.'[471] Butler responded by stressing the importance of the independent role of the Civil Service Commissioners in recruitment as a safeguard against politicisation and by placing articles in staff and other journals where he described the intention as saving money whilst raising already high standards.[472]

There can be little doubt that a consequence of the energetic pursuance of Executive Agencies put stress on the cultural ties that had, hitherto, been the basis of what a civil servant was and should (or should not) do. As a sportsman Butler was well seized of the need for a successful team to forge an identity based on values and techniques. There was a long tradition of Departmental socialisation for newcomers at junior levels and a combination of 'learning by Nellie' and inter-departmental group bonding for the fast-streamers through induction and intensive common courses at the Civil Service College and its predecessor. But the focus had been on a fast stream recruited straight from university for a life-long career. Reappraisal was needed. One result was to encourage a public sector MBA programme with contracts initially for 40–60 students offered to Imperial College, London and a consortium led by Cranfield University.

Meanwhile, work continued on two fronts: employment contracts for the Senior Civil Service and arrangements to govern the pay of Permanent Secretaries. On the former a pressing question was how to handle those who refused to sign. The Treasury position was that staff would sign because of the clarity and certainty contracts would provide.[473] But the continuing Royal Prerogative (which allowed the Crown to dismiss at will) could be thought of as undermining the whole idea of a contract anyway.[474] Moreover, Departments judged that the draft contract was too detailed and asked how was its purpose and importance to be explained if, as was claimed, it did not change anything.[475] The lawyers agreed; there was already perfectly good evidence of the contractual relationships between the Crown and its staff. The Head of the Diplomatic Service thought that the effect would be to undermine the concept of a public service career.[476] Perhaps, mused Butler, the Crown should make an authoritative statement that the Royal Prerogative would not be used to undermine the employment contracts of senior civil servants.[477]

The employment contracts issue dragged on through 1995 and became more fraught. In May Butler learned that since the Prerogative gave the power to dismiss at will, compensation already paid in lieu of notice might be argued to have been *ultra vires*; and, to add further pain, that the Inland Revenue was gearing up to tax the payments in lieu of notice on the basis that there was no contractual liability and the payments could not, therefore, meet the key test for tax-free payments (compensation for damages).[478] The challenge put to the lawyers was to draft their way around the problem in such a way as to prevent the lack of proper powers in the past becoming apparent. As to the concerns of the FCO Board of Management, Butler could point to the popular belief that civil servants had a job for life as an illusion, since they could, in theory, be dismissed at will and, in practice, over the past seven years over 40% of those leaving the Senior Open Structure had done so before normal retirement age, often at the instigation of management. However, 'There was likely to be something wrong with any organisation which embarked on filling its top posts with an explicit belief that it was incapable of nurturing its own talent for the majority of its needs.' Hence the focus in the consultative documents sent to the Senior Open Structure was on training and development and succession planning.[479] Senior staff were formally invited to sign the employment contracts early in 1996.

On pay the focus was on the Permanent Secretaries. The White Paper had proposed an independent Remuneration Committee along the lines becoming commonplace in business, conforming to the recommendations of the Cadbury Report.[480] The plan was for David Nickson the chairman of the Senior Salaries Review Board also to chair the Remuneration Committee and for the committee to consider each year fully worked up salary proposals from the Heads of the Home Civil Service and Treasury prior to making recommendations to the government. It would be for the latter to accept or reject the recommendations but no system would be credible unless acceptance was virtually guaranteed.[481] The Permanent Secretaries themselves had two significant observations: the lack of a reference to their role in offering policy advice in the terms of reference for the Remuneration committee; and the extent to which a Minister's input to the assessment of their performance should be mandatory and substantive because of the risk of charges of politicisation.[482] Of Ministers, Michael Heseltine was characteristically forthright in arguing that whilst job weight might be appropriate for determining the starting position for a Permanent Secretary, it was performance that should determine pay progression.[483] Later, after discussion with Major, Butler wrote to Nickson with the final terms of reference for the Remuneration Committee.[484] In three respects Nickson's advice was not followed. The Committee should not take account of differences in terms and conditions between the public and private sectors at the level of the individual (that was a matter for the SSRB across the whole of the grade); there should not be a simultaneous listing of those in the Department earning more than the Permanent Secretary minimum (in practice some Agency Chief executives); and a requirement to have regard to the government policy on public sector pay should be retained. Major announced the new arrangements in early February[485] to an accusation from the trades unions: 'that the role of the trades unions is [now] entirely negligible in [establishing Senior Civil Service pay].'[486]

Implementation of the delegated pay scheme was a priority objective in Butler's own targets for 1995/6. He favoured a post-event audit of how Permanent Secretaries used their delegated powers on pay rather than prior approval. Rogue elephants, as he called them, would be open to public exposure after the audit; fear of that publicity should be enough to keep Permanent Secretaries in check.[487] A compromise was reached: the reporting year would end on 31 March, Departments would be asked to complete performance assessment by 30 April and to make performance pay proposals by mid May which the centre would moderate (only looking at awards in detail for those above grade 5) in June allowing awards to be settled and paid before the summer break.[488] Significantly, this early reference was a relatively isolated example of a personal target. During the first two years of the Permanent Secretaries' scheme Butler's recorded achievements were indistinguishable from those of the government as a whole and this state of affairs was quite general. But two years in, the chairman of the SSRB (Sir Michael Perry) reported to the Permanent Secretaries that their personal objectives needed to be tightened up by identifying two/three main areas on which the individual should be judged. Despite colleagues' reservations that this would distort behaviour, at a Wednesday morning meeting on 23 October 1996 Butler asked for more focused and measurable objectives.[489] He set his own objectives for 1997/98 as: To manage the transition to the new government; to give the Cabinet Office a more proactive role in formulating and progress-chasing Departmental contributions to the government's objectives; to reduce the number of leaks and increase Ministers' confidence in the loyalty and security of the system; to get his successor approved in good time, to achieve an effective transition and to leave the civil service in a healthy state.[490]

Four months after the publication of *Continuity and Change* the government had received around 50 responses to the invitation to comment on the proposals and the TCSSC had reported on the role of the civil service.[491] Major had a preliminary discussion of the Committee's main recommendations with the most relevant colleagues a week later: (1) A new Civil Service Code – accept with minor amendments as a basis for further consultation; (2) an independent line of appeal on matters of conscience to the Civil Service Commission – unlikely to do much damage, accept; (3) a Civil Service Act – think further about the proposal and consult on a draft Bill; (4) the Civil Service Commission to take over the internal filling of posts – reject but propose that the First Civil Service Commissioner – who should no longer be a serving civil servant – should join the Senior Appointments Selection Committee (SASC); (5) direct accountability of Agency Chief executives to Select Committees – reject because it would bypass Ministers' accountability to Parliament; (6) the Efficiency Unit to report on Ministers' work and their support – reject as inappropriate for a political task.

Permanent Secretaries discussed a draft Command Paper on 11 January 1995. Their principal concerns were on drafting changes since *Continuity and Change*. The new draft made no reference to the assumption that internal appointments to senior positions would dominate, it was not clear on the criteria for going for an internal or outside appointment, it did not reconcile open competition with career planning and the case for contracts was not made, nor why they were to be confined to the Senior Civil Service.[492] In anticipation of a House of Lords debate planned for 1 February, Butler sent copies of the Command Paper (*Taking Forward Continuity and Change*) to peers who were former civil servants. Eight such peers spoke in the debate, as did six ex-ministers and two former academics. The ex-civil servants welcomed the idea of a code and most also welcomed an independent route of appeal on matters of conscience.[493] However, they fired warning shots over the potential fragmentation of the service and of consequent damage to the public sector ethos and lines of accountability through the Minister to Parliament, together with the attempt to separate policy and operations. They generally thought that reform had gone sufficiently far for a period of consolidation to be needed. The ex-Ministers and academics were a little more positive about the government's proposals but, in addition to echoing many of the points made by the former civil servants, were concerned about the ability to continue to recruit people of the requisite quality into the service. Taken as a whole, the government was put on warning where peers would be watching developments with care, but no lasting damage was done to the proposals. On the other hand some felt that an important message was that the civil service was not immune from change and that such a message would be appropriate provided that an intelligible strategy for management reform could be spelled out. The upside was the prospect of better pay for good work, but unless that became more than mere words on a page the strategy would trigger a new round of cynicism. Equally, care was needed not to give the impression that senior staff were feathering their own nest.[494]

Promulgation of the Civil Service Code meant that the Armstrong memorandum of 1985 on the duties of civil servants was partially overtaken. But if it were simply withdrawn a number of constitutional clarifications about the status of the civil service would be lost. Butler decided to use the cover of waiting for the report of the Scott inquiry to permit drafting on these issues in slower time.[495] The aspect of the Armstrong memorandum most needing reassessment was the statement that: 'For all practical purposes the Crown [in the context of the duty of service to the Crown] means and is represented by the government of the day.' The FDA queried the completeness of Butler's interpretation that a civil servant had no direct duty to Parliament, arguing that there was also a duty to be as helpful as possible to Select Committees and that the Procedure Committee of the House of Commons had asserted that: 'the House itself has the power to enforce its rights to secure information from the Executive at a level below that of the Ministerial Head.'[496] The dilemma was not, however, resolved and still persists.

The use of political appointees as special advisers to Ministers (SPADS) continued to grow. Under Harold Wilson there had been 30 appointees in 15 Departments; under John Major this rose to 38 (a salary cost of £1.8 million p.a.);[497] by the autumn of 1998, under Tony Blair, there were 70 (at a salary cost of £2.7 million p.a.).[498] The justification for this dramatic rise was partly to strengthen policy formation and the capability to track progress centrally, partly to improve links between the Prime Minister and the Party and partly for media management. But signs were beginning to emerge that hidden costs in terms of senior official time devoted to managing the SPADS was significant. Butler and his successor Wilson were heavily involved with these issues. For Butler there were three main areas of concern: (1) Protecting the civil service against real or imagined acts of politicisation; especially in view of the foreseeable General Election after 16 years of rule by the Conservatives; (2) controlling the number and recruitment of SPADS; (3) enforcing compliance with their contracts;

Ministers recognised the force of argument in favour of political neutrality for the civil service but could still inadvertently put it at risk. Butler had to be vigilant in preventing action that might compromise neutrality, without jeopardising Ministerial trust in him. When Michael Heseltine was put in ministerial charge of the Civil Service he saw his role as hastening reform.[499] With an active reforming Minister there was plenty of scope for friction with the Head of the Civil Service. Some were straightforward disagreements of policy – such as Heseltine's wish to privatise the Civil Service College. Others involved circumstances that could be maliciously construed as a step towards politicisation. In 1996, for example, during a seminar chaired by Heseltine on improving standards in public services, participants urged that the government should organise panels of people associated with the public services who could be vigorous and attractive proponents of government policies.[500] Butler immediately responded that: 'In my view it would be more appropriate for [the support] to be organised on the political net, by Special Advisers … '.[501] Sadly, however, though Heseltine readily accepted Butler's argument, the original formulation leaked, once more putting the government on the back foot. The FDA trade union was suspected of the leak but strenuously and comprehensively denied the allegation; and the real source was never identified.[502] Again, when the government opposed proposals from the Scottish National Party that a devolved authority should have tax-raising powers, Michael Forsyth, the Secretary of State for Scotland, coined the term 'the tartan tax' to indicate that these taxes would be an extra burden for taxpayers in Scotland alone. Butler refused to countenance using a politically coined phrase in civil service material in public debate, taking the issue all the way to Major who reluctantly supported Butler's position against that of his Cabinet colleague.[503]

A particular threat to the status of the civil service was that the press sometimes alleged that many years of Conservative rule had, perforce, brought politicisation. In early March 1996 *The Observer* launched a survey into the attitudes of civil servants on a range of issues such as morale and job security. The civil service had no comparable information (Butler had ruled out the idea in 1995) and in that sense the results could have been instructive for Ministers and civil service leaders; but the survey went further by asking about attitudes to privatisation and political influence within the civil service. 10,000 questionnaires were distributed to a random selection of middle-ranking civil servants through their trades unions, achieving just under a 20% response by the end of the month. Butler did not hear of the survey until 13 March when he moved quickly to ask

Permanent Secretaries to remind all staff that they should not take part. This was not just being fussy. The Cabinet Office reported that *The Observer* had put a spin on some of the findings to suggest that 91% of respondents thought that privatisation had gone too far and that 77% would welcome a change of government. Similarly, in mid April 1996 *The Observer* and *The Times* ran stories that civil servants had been ordered to provide Ministers with political ammunition from costing Opposition parties' commitments and Derek Foster MP[504] wrote to Lord Nolan asking his committee to investigate. The long-standing position, however, was that since Departments provided factual answers to queries from MPs about the costs of identifiable changes to policy, there was no objection to doing the same for Ministers about specific Opposition proposals should they be asked to do so.

For much of his tenure Butler's advice on management matters was exercised in secret at Monday morning bilateral meetings with the Prime Minister. A general reticence to respond to criticism in public applied even when the Leader of the Opposition, John Smith, made a strong public attack on the civil service as tainted by declining standards of government, including claims of: 'a revolving door which increasingly sees senior civil servants pass directly from top jobs in Whitehall to top jobs in industries closely connected with their former departments' and accused the Service of partisanship: '... sometimes forgetting that they have a role and a duty above service of the government of the day, which is *service of the country*.'[505] Expressing himself 'dismayed' by the Smith attack, Butler nevertheless told Major that: 'I cannot cross swords with Mr Smith publicly, but if you or the Chancellor of the Duchy of Lancaster have no objection, I propose to write to him privately to express my concern ...'.[506] Major was then put up to make brief supportive comments in a speech at the Civil Service Club – 'not the occasion for anything which is too heavy or party political.' The result was hardly likely to be reported prominently and indicated a serious limitation to Butler's ability to defend his profession. By the latter part of his time, however, he began to be more assertive publicly such as the opportunity he seized to defend civil servants when giving evidence to the Scott inquiry and in the briefing of former officials who were members of the House of Lords in 1996 on the White Paper *Continuity and Change*.

Additionally, Butler sought to expose mandarin minds to a wider range of influences, not least concerning the management of complex organisations. Steps were taken in January 1989 to remove a ban on the reinstatement of those who had left the civil service to a grade higher than they held when they had left.[507] In 1991 he began a series of seminars involving Permanent Secretaries and leaders of large businesses. The civil servants were surprised by the commonality of challenge and approach between the two groups. Michael Partridge of the DSS, wrote to Butler after the first seminar drawing attention to the parallels between the Next Steps reforms in government and the restructuring of commercial businesses to identify separate operational units within a unified single organisation. Less comfortable was the private sector participants' prescription for the role of the chairman or CEO: 'to provide a clear lead and purpose for the organisation as a whole with emphases on the questions 'What are we here for?' and 'How can we do that better?' ... [taking] personal charge ... of the main processes or resource allocation, targets, monitoring and regular review, ensuring proper systems, rewards and penalties and ensuring effective necessary action.'[508]

Butler led an initiative with the Economic and Social Research Council to improve academic access to government for research into public administration and to encourage mutual secondments between government and academia, echoing the successes of the war years.[509] The former was decidedly more successful than the latter, as civil service careers could still be managed actively whereas academics were more akin to sole traders. The Spring Sunningdale Conferences were another opportunity for a select group of Permanent Secretaries (usually 15 of them) to meet a similar number of businessmen to discuss broad developments in society and in the competitiveness of British industry. Inevitably the businessmen came from 'blue chip' organisations. Topics ranged from inner cities to the implications of Perestroika (1987) from cost-effectiveness of social security to corporate governance (1997).

Preparation for a new Government

Butler had seen five General Elections at close hand before the New Labour victory of 1997. He was well aware of the suspicions new and inexperienced Ministers might hold about the loyalties of the civil service after many years in Opposition. There had been disturbing signs that Labour was suspicious of the higher reaches of the civil service. In 1989 Jack Cunningham MP had attacked Terry Heiser as too close to the Conservatives; Michael Meacher MP told *The Independent* in November the same year that Labour could make the civil service open to direct political appointments to ease the introduction of radical changes in policy; in 1990 Dr John Marek MP had said that the Next Steps project manager, Peter Kemp, would be moved on in the event of a Labour victory at the polls;[510] and shortly before the 1992 General Election Butler speculated that Duncan Nichol would not survive as Chief Executive of the NHS Management Executive under a Labour administration because he had made sceptical comments on its health policies in a published interview.[511]

Tony Blair was aware of the charge of hubris that had stuck to Neil Kinnock in 1992 when a political rally held in Sheffield immediately before the General Election had been seen as triumphalist and (as it turned out) premature. Nevertheless, Labour had to prepare for office, especially as Blair had no ministerial experience and no experience of running a large, complex organisation. Hence, in early 1997 some of the leading back room figures in New Labour, including Jonathan Powell, took part in private seminars with people who had that experience, including a session chaired by Lord Bancroft, the former Head of the Civil Service, and which included at least one leading member of the Major Downing Street team. Butler had also hosted a private dinner for Blair at his home in 1996.[512]

As expected, on 1 May 1997 Labour won a convincing victory at the polls with 43.2% of the votes delivering 419 seats in the House of Commons (63.6%). Butler and his senior colleagues recognised the limitations of the direct government experience of the new front bench (none of the Secretaries of State had been Ministers before) but they consoled themselves with the knowledge that Blair had good contacts with experienced politicians such as Roy Jenkins whom they saw as Blair's political mentor. In consequence they underestimated the extent to which New Labour's leaders saw themselves as a new generation of politicians who had rebelled against Labour's legacy and would now rebel against established governmental practice. They also underestimated the centralising intentions of Blair and his immediate team despite the new Prime Minister accompanying Butler to speak to the first Wednesday morning meeting of Permanent Secretaries after the election (on 15 May). If further proof was needed of both the impatience of the new team and its innocence of how government functions, it was at about this time that Blair told Butler he wanted the devolution arrangements (a policy largely inherited from John Smith's leadership) through the political processes by the Summer Recess.[513]

Alex Allan and Butler refreshed their memories on what had to happen when the political complexion of a government changed and Allan started to draft a pre-emptive job description for Chief of Staff to the Prime Minister.[514] But they found that Tony Blair did not recognise formality and had a poor feel for the significance of constitutional procedures.[515] What had worked well in Opposition did not bear the weight of government. The rushed announcement of Bank of England independence on 6 May, without Cabinet discussion despite Butler's protests, set the tone. Butler and Jonathan Powell received a tongue-lashing from Blair after the first Cabinet meeting on 8 May – he did not want issues raised in Cabinet unless he was briefed in advance.[516] But Blair was also averse to predetermined agendas set 48 hours in advance, as was the historical norm. As a result, the weekly ring-round by the Cabinet Office to ascertain what Ministers would raise became an empty ritual; 'common Private secretary responses to [the] weekly question are: 'Haven't the first idea what, if anything, he's likely to raise.'[517] Some Private Offices (notably that of the Deputy Prime Minister) construed the new approach as absolving them from divulging anything to the Cabinet Secretariat before Cabinet.[518] By the end of the year it could be embarrassing to keep Cabinet going for more than 30–45 minutes.[519] It became a meeting for agreeing what would be 'on message' and discussion became chaotic as Blair darted around without following the agenda.[520]

The problems of informality are well illustrated by a shambles surrounding the launch on 22 July 1997 of Blair's innovative move to create a special Cabinet Committee for consultation between the government and the Liberal Democrat opposition. Planning had been in hand since the beginning of the administration on the precedents for a Ministerial group including members of the Opposition.[521] Butler had been kept in the loop and was himself the senior secretary to the committee. When it came to announcement and activation of the committee, however, confusion reigned. There was no single person in charge of the launch and an immediate debriefing by Butler's Principal Private Secretary, Jan Polley, listed a catalogue of basic omissions. Her analysis included six examples of how the Opposition technique of giving lobby journalists the basic outline of an idea without taking decisions on the detail could not work in government. No one had questioned making the announcement to the press rather than to Parliament – and, coincidentally, the morning's press on that same day had described the Speaker's annoyance over the practice. The Minister deputed to handle the press (Ann Taylor) was not told until 15 minutes after the deadline for the announcement and knew nothing about it. There was no agreed title for the Committee, no terms of reference, no confirmed membership and no knowledge of what issues might be sensitive. Peter Mandelson was under the impression that he would be a member of the Committee but Butler's office knew nothing of this. And finally, when Jan Polley checked with the Downing Street Press Office, she discovered that no announcement had been made because no one had prepared a press announcement or Q&A briefing for use on the day.

Teething troubles were to be expected for a new and inexperienced administration. But the problem seems to have been that Ministers and officials did not know enough about their respective preferred ways of working to ask relevant questions. Ironically, in 1992 when the then Leader of the Opposition, John Smith, asked whether it would be possible to second occasional civil servants to work for the Opposition front bench, Butler had advised Major against the idea on the grounds that it would risk political labelling of individual civil servants. It was probably a failure to recognise that absence from office for 18 years had eroded knowledge of procedures that were second nature to officials that led to many of the hiccups. Yet it is puzzling why such basic infrastructure as assigning responsibility to a single point had been neglected.

For some time before 1997 academic commentators and former senior officials had been asking awkward questions. There was general agreement on the symptoms, summed up in the words of Sir Brian Cubbon in 1994: 'No one could claim, whatever their Party political position, that government decisions in the last 30 years have been of a high standard' and 'Britain now stands out amongst comparable European countries, and perhaps amongst liberal democracies as a whole, as a state unusually prone to making large-scale, avoidable policy mistakes ... '[522] But there was no agreement on the diagnosis let alone the prescription. Some saw it as a failure to speak truth unto power;[523] others as a failure in competence: '[Civil servants] under-rate their own deficiencies in tackling issues of strategy and policy.'[524] Preparing for the autumn 1996 Sunningdale Conference of Permanent Secretaries Butler invited reflections on policy-making capabilities from the Heads of the Cabinet Office Secretariats.[525] All noted a distinct shift away from 'blue skies' policy towards implementation management and media handling, attributing this in part to the longevity of Conservative rule and increased political control by experienced Ministers that had led to the demise of 'the stately process of policy formulation by Departmental Committees' – including the death of Departmental policies. (The European Secretariat commented, significantly, that 'on the biggest EU issue facing the Government,

EMU, ... strategic thinking at official level is off-limits.')[526] 'We are rewarded less for innovative ideas than for being a safe pair of hands for implanting Ministers' policies in a cost effective way.'[527] The optimists hoped that a new government would find that policy-making capability was simply in hibernation, but dangers lurked in 'a decline in the relationship of partnership between Ministers and civil servants' and in the 'roles which the likes of Peter Mandelson, Jonathan Powell and Alastair Campbell [would] play.'[528]

Blair decided against a formal strategy committee, in favour of pursuing an approach believed to be similar to that operating in New Zealand, whereby Departments would be asked to draw up their key strategic objectives in relation to a centrally promulgated set of government-wide objectives based on the ten vows Labour had made in the election campaign. This would be led top-down and would not be collectively agreed. Monitoring and control would be exercised through bilateral meetings involving Blair's close ally Peter Mandelson, who was appointed Minister without Portfolio in the Cabinet Office.[529] No role in the process was specified for the Treasury though it is highly likely that Butler alerted his PUS colleague Terry Burns in view of their close working relationship.

The Cabinet Office Secretariats started a process to design the necessary machinery; Nick Montagu (Head of the EDS Secretariat) identified key components: the 10 key government objectives must be backed up with tasks, outputs and measures, a balance must be struck between superficiality and drowning in detail, it would be advisable to 'top-slice' Departmental budgets to fund cross-departmental task forces and policies. This broad outline was agreed by Mandelson at a meeting on 12 May involving Butler, Allan, Powell, Miliband and Hyman of the Policy Unit and Montagu who was instructed to produce an operational note for the strategy, including timing of actions.[530] (At that meeting Butler argued against following the New Zealand model of contracts between Ministers related to the objectives, which would then be published.) Montagu's response, of 15 May, pointed obliquely to the risk of ignoring the Treasury as controller of the purse strings, by raising the question of co-ordination with the PX Committee's work to review public expenditure.

In a private note to Blair (copied to no one else) at the end of the first month of office Mandelson spelt out the dilemma. 'Whereas we used to rely on speedy, informal ways of working ... this is now more difficult. I do not yet feel I have fully developed habits and routines of working that support my role [of strategic implementation of our policy objectives]. My meetings with you and Gordon [Brown] are not as productive as they could be ... What has held us up is the formation of PX as I do not want to appear to be setting up rival systems ... My exclusion from PX has sent a damaging signal about my strategic role ... we [need] a new, permanent function in government called strategy and performance ... you can see how PX (paying for it) fits in to it. At the moment, PX is trying to substitute for it, with my efforts operating at the margin.'[531] What Mandelson appeared not to know was that PX was not the powerhouse he imagined, it met once in the first three months of the new government. If Butler had been brought into the loop it is conceivable that his close links with Burns could have bridged this gap.

At the end of July Blair and Butler met over dinner for a progress report on the work of government. Butler was armed with the views of Allan and the Heads of the Secretariats.[532] These assessments stressed that the traditional UK system of government did not encourage the Prime Minister to play a big role in domestic affairs and that, consequently, the Treasury had killed the scope for the Mandelson role in the Cabinet Office. Whilst it was evident that the purpose of Cabinet was now to tell people what was going on and to give political messages, too much was kept secret (especially on the economic and domestic agenda), points were overlooked, there was a declining sense of what the government stood for and too big a risk that Departments' own policies would be dangerous for its overall reputation. Meanwhile, Robin Young, Montagu's successor, wrote: 'the Chancellor shows no desire at all to hold EA or PX meetings ... [nor] that he wants, or will try, to be a neutral or consensus-building Committee Chairman.'

On the other hand, all the respondents recognised that the Cabinet framework was there to meet Ministers' needs rather than the other way round and so they did not openly criticise the prevalence of discussions in small informal groups of Ministers. Indeed, Ministers were showing a refreshing interest in substantive policy. There were two major problems: (1) the Prime Minister's authority was being spread thin whereas, they argued, it was prudent to use it sparingly, structuring Cabinet Committee discussions to secure desired outcomes and to bind people into the decision taken; (2) the Chancellor was not keeping the Prime Minister or colleagues informed about significant decisions that fell firmly in their territory. As the OD secretariat put it, 'The ship will run on smoothly enough so long as no reefs are struck, but when they are, it will come in handy if the crew is larger rather than smaller, and especially so if the crew in question is used to acting cohesively.' There was much praise for Mandelson's chairmanship – described by the Constitution Secretariat as 'a model of responsible, considerate and decisive chairmanship on a subject [the Referendum campaigns publicity] that comes close to the delicate boundary of propriety.'

Butler followed up the dinner conversation with a number of structural suggestions to enable Blair to keep on top of the domestic policy agenda, the most important of which were: use EDS to keep tabs on the policy activity of the most important home departments; meet the Heads of the Secretariats briefly on a weekly basis; have a note-taker at bilateral meetings with the Chancellor and have what has been agreed recorded in a private office letter to the Treasury; encourage the Chancellor to bring senior officials to meetings he has with you. Sensing that Blair and other senior Ministers were as yet unwilling to confront Brown, Butler stopped short of tackling the interpersonal issues, falling back on indirect structural suggestions. Nor did he press the case for an alternative tactic involving wider use of Mandelson as a committee chairman. It was a month before Blair got round to discussing the suggestions, agreeing to most of the structural changes, including a short, weekly meeting with the Heads of the

Secretariats. However, the note from Jonathan Powell recording the decisions merely said: 'The Prime Minister will reflect further on your suggestions on the Treasury.'[533]

The method Blair chose to drive co-ordination of policy was to promote a strong narrative in key areas of reform, summed up by Mandelson as: 'to govern is to choose. But to govern is also to communicate.'[534] Blair would himself, from time to time, draft strategy papers, which he shared with Downing Street staff and Butler.[535] By early 1998 these notes had become quite elaborate, running to 13 pages of A4, double spaced, covering: (a) the central theme/message of the government; (b) how that applied in each main policy area, with objectives and outcomes: (c) immediate priorities and problems.[536] Thus, when *The Financial Times* reported confusing plans to reform welfare[537] Butler recommended (supported by Mandelson) that whilst it was the case that there were seven separate reviews in train, the pressing need was for a better public explanation of how these exercises fitted together.[538]

The Chancellor of the Duchy, David Clark, responsible for civil service reform, speculated over the possibilities offered by either a formal Prime Minister's Department or a Ministerial Management Board for Government (i.e. supervising Ministers as had been tried under Churchill in the 1950s and was current in Canada). Both ideas were given short shrift by Butler. A Prime Minister's Department 'would be a major innovation and would undoubtedly arose (sic) strong views.' 'There is, however, another way forward … .to propose to the Prime Minister … a new Cabinet Committee to secure the degree of co-ordination and coherence necessary to deliver the Prime Minister's vision of a "modern, fair and strong" Government machine.' Once again defence of a hallowed committee system sat at the core of the official response to Ministerial disquiet, in spite of growing evidence that the new Ministers did not appreciate why officialdom set such store by them. The government had, as, Richard Wilson would later describe, 'a curious belief in its own inviolability.'

Continuing Emergencies

If the first Gulf War was different from the Falklands conflict then the Bosnian war of 1992–95 was different again. Not only were the underlying causes complex and steeped in centuries of enmity but the difficulty of assembling and operating a multi-national military force (UNPROFOR) for humanitarian purposes was acute and the British Cabinet were split on the wisdom of committing troops on the ground.[539] By the end of May 1995 the OPD Committee had had its confidence shaken.[540] Faced with the prospect of Ministerial disarray, Butler convened a small, informal senior group of officials to ensure that the main contingencies were properly examined and put to Ministers at an appropriate time.[541] The group operated between the end of July 1995 and the beginning of May 1997 and met weekly during the summer of 1995. It prepared and kept up to date contingency plans against the possibility that the military strand would eclipse the political strand in Western policy, and that this would lead to an air campaign that would entail the withdrawal from Bosnia of UNPROFOR. Butler urged on Major that the UK needed to think out its position in the light of threats to the clarity of the UNPROFOR mission – the warring parties had rejected an initiative for mutual recognition proposed by Carl Bildt (the European Union special envoy), the United States position was not wholly in line with that of the European allies and Croatian troops were making headway against the Serbs.[542] Major steered the group towards a course that would breathe life into the political track and encourage conditions on the ground that would allow UNPROFOR to stay.[543] Its task did not end, however, with the Dayton Peace Agreement of December 1995. Discussions continued on ensuring that the Dayton edifice did not crumble because the military and civilian aspects (notably policing) of peace implementation were out of step. A task made harder because the OPD Committee was determined to limit the UK non-military contribution;[544] and because of an assessment that underlying ethnic tensions and a lack of political will to create a lasting unified Bosnia might lead to renewed fighting. Once again an ongoing emergency had to be handed over from one Cabinet Secretary to another.

BSE

A second inheritance from the Major Government was an outbreak of BSE – a ticking time bomb. It had first been detected in West Sussex eleven years earlier, in 1986. On the basis of the then scientific evidence John Major had asserted in December 1995 that: 'There is currently no scientific evidence that BSE can be transmitted to humans or that eating beef causes CJD in humans. That issue is not in question.' But in the following March British scientists announced that they believed there was a link between BSE and Variant CJD. It was possible, they thought, for the disease to be transmitted between cattle and humans.

The initial concern government was not to overreact, but when a further ten people died of nvCJD, Stephen Dorrell (Secretary of State for Health) claimed that: 'The most likely explanation is that these cases are linked to BSE before the offal ban in 1989.' A ban on beef seemed extreme. Alex Allan asked: 'Why think of banning beef when you do not ban smoking which is far more dangerous?' Kenneth Clarke, the Chancellor, agreed. The government had a duty to set out and explain the scientific advice it receives, he thought, but should pause before accepting responsibility for what people should do on receipt of that advice.[545] On this basis Major made a reassuring statement to the House of Commons in May 1996.[546] However, it was recognised that the crisis would go on for some time and that there would be a need for inter-departmental co-ordination at official level in support of a Ministerial ad hoc group. At first the former was created under a Cabinet Office Deputy Secretary from the economic and domestic secretariat. MAFF fought to restrict its ambit to the presentation of policy rather than the co-ordination of policy towards the handling of the crisis itself. So that towards the end of May Butler was asked by the Downing Street Policy Unit to create an official group to service meetings chaired by the Major, leaving the Cabinet Office-led group to support a larger group of Ministers led by Roger Freeman (Chancellor of the Duchy) concerned with the eradication of BSE in the UK.[547] Butler told MAFF that he was prepared to let the meetings develop in whatever way seemed most useful and suggested as a start that there should be four headings: (a) progress on a framework for getting the European ban on beef exports, dating from March, lifted; (b) progress on the domestic eradication of BSE; (c) the extent of British non-cooperation to be exercised in the EU; (d) the presentation of policy.[548] In practice the Secretariat-led group under Kenneth MacKenzie continued to do most of the detailed interdepartmental work. Butler's group (sometimes chaired by Brian Bender of the European Secretariat) stuck to strategic issues such as questioning the PUS at MAFF, Richard Packer, about staff resources to deal with the crisis and reporting to Alex Allan that Packer had assured him that he was not aware of obstacles in obtaining the necessary resources.[549]

In the first week of the new government Gordon Brown expressed worries that the BSE outbreak could be a big drain on the public purse and Agriculture ministers complained about the performance of MAFF.[550] Later in the month, instinctively, Blair resisted pleas from Alex Allen, still the Principal Private Secretary, to drop BSE from his radar screen. By August, under pressure from solicitors acting on behalf of victims' families lobbying for a 'no fault' compensation scheme, the Minister for Agriculture, Jack Cunningham, tentatively concluded: 'I am inclined to the conclusion that an inquiry into the circumstances leading to the BSE epidemic and the subsequent incidence of nvCJD should now be held.'[551] The Policy Unit and Butler were opposed to the suggestion, on the grounds that an inquiry would be likely to delay lifting the European ban on beef.[552] But by mid September Blair was shifting his ground;[553] and on 10 October Jonathan Powell wrote to Cunningham that the Prime Minister had now agreed to an inquiry, but he did not favour a judicial tribunal which would be expensive, long drawn out, unnecessarily adversarial and would not avoid the risk of legal action by the victims' families. He preferred a quick, focused inquiry into what went wrong and what should be the lessons, to report within six months. Butler should put forward draft terms of reference and other details.

Butler's analysis was submitted on 14 November. He pointed out that if the inquiry was to investigate culpability of businesses and individuals it would be hard to resist full legal procedure and delay and that, in the judgement of the Ministers concerned, anything less would not satisfy the families.[554] But he also pointed out (again supported by the Policy Unit) that there was a perfectly defensible case for doing nothing. Blair compromised in favour of a 'weighty, essentially public ad hoc inquiry led by a judge'[555] and after an ad hoc Ministerial discussion[556] judge Sir Nicholas Phillips was appointed. He was set a deadline for reporting of 31 December 1998 with guidance that his focus should be on the adequacy of action under the preceding Conservative government.[557] The inquiry started work in late January 1998 but failed to meet the original deadline, eventually reporting in early October 2000 at a cost of £30 million. A selective cull of cattle most at risk from BSE was introduced in 1997 and at the end of the year a ban introduced on the sale of beef on the bone in the UK. In response to public concern public hearings into the handling of the crisis began in March 1998. Thus, a crisis that had begun in 1986 with the discovery of BSE in a West Sussex herd of cattle, that had intensified in 1996 with the discovery of a link between BSE and variant CJD, continued beyond the retirement of Butler at the end of 1987 and would go on to plague the early years of Richard Wilson's tenure. The direct government costs were around £2 billion. Over four and a half million cattle were slaughtered and 80 people died from definite or probable cases of CJD.

Special Advisers

The position on SPADS when Labour came back to power had been defined by Major in 1992: he had to authorise the employment of paid special advisers; only Cabinet Ministers could make such appointments; and they were restricted to one adviser of a political kind – but there were to be no limits on the number of expert advisers.[558] Ministers also had to seek his approval for unpaid advisers. The restrictions had been somewhat honoured in the breach, however, with many Ministers having two political advisers and some even more. Also, formal job evaluation for SPADS had foundered on the technical difficulties the varied role might present and, more importantly, on the political difficulties arising from the sensitivity of Ministers to what job weighting might imply about their own role.[559] Consolidated guidance to Departments was prepared early in 1997 (including the introduction of a Ministerial remuneration committee to decide annual pay increases for individual SPADs). Simultaneously with submission for Major's approval, Butler slipped a copy to Jonathan Powell in Blair's office as an indication of what he had in mind for special advisers after the General Election.[560]

Not long before the General Election Permanent Secretaries were alarmed by reports from Australia that John Howard's Liberal Party had replaced nine out of 18 Departmental Heads in an overt act of politicisation at the top of the civil service. However, Blair set a limit of two special advisers per Cabinet Minister and kept unpaid advisers within the requirement that the Prime Minister (advised by the Head of the Home Civil Service) should authorise all appointments.[561] New Labour Ministers were understandably suspicious of how much support they could expect from a civil service that had served governments of the same political colour for 18 years and some jibbed at the restriction on Special Adviser numbers – notably David Blunkett who, not having seen the Blair document, sought five (and achieved four). Butler tried to help, suggesting, for example, that Michael Barber be appointed as 'standards and effectiveness adviser' on the lines previously adopted for Peter Levene as adviser to John Major.

The model employment contract for SPADS was a contract between the Minister (acting on behalf of the Crown) and the adviser. In a number of cases Butler ruled that external involvements risked accusations of conflict of interest and SPADS were either rejected or refused permission to continue with their external activities. The Public Administration Select Committee pressed him about disciplinary issues when he appeared before them on 28 October 1997. The trigger arose from confusion over what press secretaries other than those in 10 Downing Street were authorised to do. The Committee were unclear who was responsible for ensuring that SPADS abided by the terms of their contracts; who would investigate any complaints; and by what means agreements between a Minister and a SPAD (especially over the authority of the latter) were reported to the Department.[562] Butler's response was a model of its kind: he had no role in individual cases; his role was confined to advising on the general parameters. Individual cases were a responsibility of the employing Department.[563]

It was also clear that Blair would rely heavily on Jonathan Powell (his chief of staff) and Alastair Campbell (his press secretary) not just for advice but to act in his name in directing Downing Street staff and Departments. Strictly, this was precluded by their status. The Civil Service Orders in Council of 1995 and 1997 said: 'Special Advisers are exempt from the general Civil Service requirement that appointments be made on merit on the basis of fair and open competition, so long as they are appointed 'for the purpose only of providing advice to any Minister.'[564] To regularise how Blair was going to operate Butler moved to give executive powers to Powell and Campbell (and potentially one other special adviser to be named later if necessary) through an Order in Council of 3 May 1997. This led to extensive press questioning and a flurry of commentator articles, mostly supportive of the change. The Civil Service Commissioners, however, who had not been consulted, fired a warning shot: 'It was essential, for the upholding of the fundamental principle of selection on merit on the basis of fair and open competition, that the new provision did not come to be extended more widely.'[565] Not wanting to seem obstructive, the Cabinet Office gave advice that the list of cases where Ministers had wanted to bring in staff using exceptional means was 'reassuringly short.'[566] But, in the same advice pointed out that it was imperative to control the dispensations given to the Downing Street staff. In a move open to many interpretations, an attempt was made to rein in press secretaries, such as Charlie Whelan in the Treasury, with instructions that they were not authorised to brief 'in the political context' but were restricted to explaining the views of their Minister if authorised by that Minister to do so.[567]

Rumours that Blair wanted Powell to succeed Allan as PPS pointed to a reversion to the days of Asquith's premiership (1908–16) when a political appointee had held the post of Principal Private Secretary and before the creation of the Cabinet Secretary post. Butler recalls that at a private supper at his home in 1996 Blair had said that he had no intention of appointing Powell as Principal Private Secretary but that at a meeting a week before the 1997 General Election, in Powell's presence, he reversed this point of view.[568] Butler argued that the modern-day position was not suited to a political appointee because of the sensitive tasks it handled.[569] (He had in mind relations with the Royal Household, dealings with the Leader of the Opposition, and intelligence matters.) His view prevailed with the appointment of the diplomat John Holmes to replace Allen.

Butler retired at the end of 1997, like those before him he immediately entered the House of Lords as a life peer. His final Cabinet meeting was on 18 December when Tony Blair paid tribute to his ten years in post, adding: 'Over that period, he had probably faced no more challenging task than to usher in the new government. Both Sir Robin personally and the civil service generally had responded magnificently to that challenge.'[570] In a break with tradition, however, Cabinet did not give a retirement present. In April 2003 he was appointed Knight of the Garter, a distinction shared only by Edward Bridges amongst the Cabinet Secretaries; and in 2004 when appointed to lead a review of intelligence on Iraq's weapons of mass destruction he became a Privy Counsellor.

Notes

1 *The Independent*, 09.07.87; *The Times*, 04.01.88
2 Butler's personal file, 25.10.84
3 Ibid, comment by Peter Carey, 17.07.72
4 Economic commentator and UK Ambassador, Washington 1977–79
5 Later an executive director at the Bank of England and chairman of Morgan Stanley International
6 Butler's personal file, comment by Douglas Wass, 14.08.81
7 Ibid, 10.08.82
8 Cabinet Office archive, 14.01.88
9 Evidence to TCSSC, 11.03.88
10 John Major: *My Autobiography* p. 101
11 Private information
12 Interview with Lord Butler 24.09.13
13 Job description on personal file, 04.04.91
14 *The Guardian*, 10.03.93
15 Diary 27.11.90 quoted in Seldon *Major A Political Life* Phoenix, 1997 p. 130
16 D Lipsey, *The Secret Treasury*, Viking, 2000, p. 57
17 Hogg & Hill *Too Close to Call*, Warner Books (1995) p. 10
18 *The Times*, 20.02.88
19 William Plowden, *Ministers and Mandarins*, Institute for Public Policy and Research, 1994, p. 110
20 Cabinet Office archive, SASC meeting, 06.05.92
21 Blair, *A Journey*, Hutchinson, 2010 pp. 17–19
22 Powell, *The New Machiavelli*, Bodley Head 2010 p. 18
23 Conversation with Butler, Spring 1977
24 Prime Minister's files: Regional Policy/ Inner Cities part 12 19.02.88
25 Prime Minister's files: Regional Policy/ Inner Cities part 12, 19.05.88
26 Ibid, 20.05.88
27 Interview with Lord Butler, 17.12.10
28 Prime Minister's files: Independent UK Nuclear systems 27.11.89 and 06.12.89
29 Influential foreign affairs private secretary 1983–90 who, after Willie Whitelaw's resignation from government following a stroke in December 1987, was sometimes referred to as the real Deputy Prime Minister
30 Prime Minister's files: Cabinet: Forward Look exercise part 3, 16.02.90
31 JIC(90)(IA)41 *Saddam Turns Up The Pressure* discussed at the 29th meeting on 26.07.90
32 Major was the chairman; other regular attendees were Hurd, Wakeham, Mayhew, King, Craig, Cradock, Butler and O'Donnell; the Chancellor (Lamont) was invited to two of its twenty-six meetings

33 Prime Minister's files: Drugs, 03.08.89
34 Ibid, 27.09.89
35 Ibid, 27.10.89
36 *Daily Telegraph*, 21.02.90 p. 9
37 Prime Minister's files: Drugs, 26.02.90
38 Ibid, 30.3.90 to 03.04.90,
39 Howe *Conflict of Loyalty* p. 537; Trewin *The Hugo Young Papers* p. 309
40 Cabinet Office archive, undated December 1987
41 Ibid, 14.04.88
42 Cabinet Office archive, Prime Minister's meetings and visits with the Security Service, SIS and GCHQ, 12.11.87
43 Prime Minister's files: Security, The Intelligence Agencies (MI5 & MI6) 26.05.89
44 Ibid
45 Ibid, 04.07.89
46 Prime Minister's files: Economic Policy: Secret Vote cash limits 25.04.88
47 Statement on vetting policy 24.07.90, *Hansard* col 160
48 In 1991 the vetting criteria were further amended to remove the automatic bar to security clearance for highly classified information arising from homosexuality. In 1994 the processes were once again re-engineered to reduce costs
49 Prime Minister's files: Economic Policy: Secret Vote cash limits 21.10.88
50 Ibid, 26.10.88
51 Ibid, 29.09.89
52 Dr A B Levey, *Polygraphy: An Evaluative Review*, July 1988
53 Prime Minister's files: Intelligence Agencies: GCHQ pt 6, 01.06.88
54 Ibid, 06.09.88
55 *Hansard* HC 08.12.88, cols 268–269
56 Sir Peter Smithers, Secretary General, Council of Europe, 1964–69
57 Prime Minister's files: Arts and Amenities, Thyssen Collection 27.02.88
58 6,000 fine art works which were secured for display in Lisbon on Gulbenkian's death
59 Prime Minister's files: Arts and Amenities, Thyssen Collection
60 Ibid, 27.04.88
61 Ibid, 08.05.88
62 Ibid, 09.05.88
63 Ibid, 20.05.88
64 Private information
65 Prime Minister's files: Arts and Amenities, Thyssen Collection, 23 05.88
66 Ibid, 06.07.88
67 Ibid, 08.07.88
68 Ibid, 15.07.88
69 Prime Minister's files: Government Machinery, Reactivation of the CCU in the Cabinet Office, 24.10.91
70 Prime Minister's files: Government Machinery, Civil emergencies, 07.04.89
71 Ibid
72 Ibid, 08.05.90
73 Prime Minister's files: Economic Policy, Barlow Clowes Group, pt 1
74 So-called after Charles Ponzi, a fraudster in the United States in the 1920s
75 Court of Appeal, R v Clowes and another, [1994] 2 All ER 316
76 Prime Minister's files: Economic Policy: Barlow Clowes Group, pt 1 19.09.88
77 Ibid, part 2, 03,10.88
78 Ibid, part 3, 23.11.89
79 Ibid, 29.11.89
80 Ibid, 30.11.89 and 06.12.89
81 Prime Minister's papers: Economic Policy: Barlow Clowes Group, pt 1, 06.07.88 and 05.08.88

82 Ibid, part 2, 18.10.88
83 Ibid, part 3, 19.10.88
84 Prime Minister's papers: Economic Policy: Barlow Clowes Group, pt 1, 19.09.88
85 Ibid, part 2, 11.10.88
86 Ibid, 10.10.88
87 Ibid, 17.10.88
88 *Hansard* 19.12.89 cols 202–206 and House of Lords *Hansard* cols 138–140
89 Cabinet Office archive, 06.03.85
90 Ibid, 31.01.89
91 Ibid, 06.02.89
92 Ibid, 16.11.90
93 Ibid, 05.12.90
94 Prime Minister's papers: Local Government: Relations between local and central government 02.05.90
95 Ibid
96 Ibid, 03.05.90
97 Ibid, 17.05.90
98 Ibid, Cabinet agreed the broad outlines of policy on 21.03.91 and paper EA(LG)(91)2 was discussed in the sub-group on 18.04.91
99 A Boyle *A Climate of Treason: Five Who Spied for Russia*
100 Blake was convicted of espionage in 1961 and sentenced to 42 years imprisonment. He escaped from Wormwood Scrubs in October 1966, helped by three former prisoners who had befriended him in gaol, and defected to Moscow via East Berlin.
101 Prime Minister's files: Security of the Secret Service part 14 13.09.90
102 OSIP(96)1, 08.05.96
103 *The Independent*, 17.12.97
104 Cabinet Office archive: Security: Publications, 20.12.96
105 *In Pursuit of British Interests*, John Murray, 1997
106 Prime Minister's files: Security: Reform of the Official Secrets Act, 08.11.88
107 Ibid, 07.11.88
108 OD(DIS)(88)2nd meeting
109 Prime Minister's files: Security: Reform of the Official Secrets Act, undated manuscript note
110 Ibid, 14.09.89
111 Ibid, 14.07.89
112 MI5 web site, https://www.mi5.gov.uk/home/about-us/how-mi5-is-governed/statutory-basis.html
113 Ibid, July/August 1989; GCHQ was established as an Agency with a framework document in April 1995
114 Prime Minister's files: Civil Service: BBC TV series on the Civil Service 09.09.88
115 Ibid, 17.08.79 and 11.02 80
116 Ibid, 27.04.89
117 Under the initiative service delivery would be at arm's length from the centre of Departments with enhanced freedom to manage and accountability for the results.
118 Extracted from 1988 talks to Departments
119 Prime Minister's files: Civil Service, Long-term management and manpower policy, 03.02.89
120 Prime Minister's files: Government Machinery, The Rayner Programme part 26, 14.01.88
121 Ibid, part 27, 04.03.88
122 Ibid, part 26, 28.01.88
123 Ibid, part 25, 11.01.88
124 Cabinet Office archive, SASC meeting on 19.01.88

125 Prime Minister's files: Government Machinery, The Rayner Programme part 27, 14.07.88
126 Cabinet Office archive, 01.03.88
127 Prime Minister's files: Government Machinery, The Rayner Programme part 29, 14.04.89 supporting agency proposals in the Department of Social Security typifies Butler's enthusiasm
128 Ibid, parts 30–33
129 Ibid, part 21, 27.05.88
130 Ibid, part 39, valedictory report by Kemp, 29.07.92
131 Redcliffe-Maud memorial lecture, 10.10.90 and FDA lecture on The Future of the Civil Service, 15.10.91
132 *Financial Times*, 08.03.90, 'The problem of making Whitehall accountable,'
133 The Borders Agency was created in 2008 out of the immigration service, a move having previously been rejected by Jack Straw when Home Secretary
134 Correspondence with Sir David Omand 13.12.13
135 Cabinet Office file A 2/19, 26.02.91
136 Interview with Lord Butler 24.09.13
137 D Wass, Reith Lectures 1983
138 Leader of the Soviet Union 1985–91
139 The letters of appreciation and Thatcher's individually tailored replies are on the Prime Minister's files: The Resignation of The Prime Minister, Margaret Thatcher November 1990
140 Ibid, 20.11.90
141 Prime Minister's files: Briefing for a new Prime Minister and spouse, 27.11.90
142 Prime Minister's files: Cabinet: Committee Structure and membership, 29.11.90
143 Resolution 660 of 02.08.90 and succeeding resolutions 661 and 678, www.un.org/en/sc/documents/resolutions/1990.shtml
144 CM(91)1st 10.01.91 conclusion
145 Prime Minister's files: Middle East, Conclusions of the Ad hoc Group on the Gulf (AHGG)
146 Cabinet Office archive, 16.08.90
147 Ibid, 05.03.91
148 *John Major the autobiography*, HarperCollins, 1999, p. 203
149 Prime Minister's files: Ireland: Meetings with the Taoiseach, pt 21, 13.06.90
150 Ibid, 20.06.91
151 Ibid, 18.07.91
152 Ibid
153 Ibid, part 22a, 04.11.91
154 Ibid, part 22b, 04.12.91
155 Ibid, 23.12.91
156 Ibid, part 23a, 04.02.92
157 Ibid, 07.02.92
158 The initial call to arms on the Citizens' Charter was agreed between Butler, Burns and Turnbull (Principal Private Secretary to Major) on 17.05.91, Prime Minister's files: Government Machinery, Citizens' Charter, part 1. The follow-up action after the White Paper was agreed on 18.07.91
159 Ibid, there were two discussions in 1991 in the run up the Citizens' Charter White Paper and another in 1993 as the vehicle for presenting the Government's public sector reforms as a coherent whole
160 Ibid, part 3, 03.07.91
161 Ibid, part 7, 13.11.91
162 Ibid, part 9, in which he reported that the Permanent Secretary of the Scottish Office had said that imposition of the requirements on Scotland would be 'disastrous'.

163 Prime Minister's files: Government Machinery, Presentation of Government Policies, November 1986
164 Ibid, Major wrote on 20.05.91 to Cabinet colleagues in general and to the Secretaries of State for Education & Science, the Environment and Health with specific charges
165 Ibid, 24.05.91
166 Ibid, 02.08.91
167 *Analysis*, 20.06.91
168 Prime Minister's files: Parliament: electoral process 21.01.92
169 Ibid, 28.02.92
170 Ibid, 06.03.92 and 12.03.92
171 *The Sunday Times*, 24.01.93
172 Prime Minister's files: Government Machinery Changes part 8
173 Ibid; discussed shortly before the election in correspondence between Butler and Turnbull, and at a meeting between Butler and Major on 10.04.92
174 Prime Minister's files: Government Machinery Changes part 9, 02.03.92
175 Ibid, 15.04.92
176 Ibid, part 37, July and October 1991 respectively
177 Ibid, 02.03.92
178 Ibid, part 9, 27.02.92
179 Ibid, 04.03.92
180 Head of the Policy Unit 1990–1995
181 Principal Private Secretary, Prime Minister 1992–97
182 Prime Minister's files: Government Machinery, Changes, part 9, 06.09.93
183 Ibid, 06.09.93
184 Ibid, 06.09.93
185 Prime Minister's files: Cabinet Business (part 25) and Cabinet: Cabinet Committee structure and membership (part 5), 30.04.93, 29.05.93 and 11.06.93
186 Ibid, part 26, 22.09.93
187 CM(92)23rd 22.07.92 conclusion 2
188 Prime Minister's files: Government Machinery, Rayner Programme, Promotion of Efficiency part 41, 29.01.93
189 Ibid
190 Ibid, part 47, 16.07.93
191 Cabinet Office file A 5/9, 17.06.93
192 Prime Minister's files: Government Machinery, Changes, part 10, 19.09,95
193 Prime Minister's files: Civil Service, Long-term management and manpower policy 08.02.90
194 Interview with Lord Butler, 24.09.13
195 *The Independent*, 21.11.91
196 Prime Minister's files: Home Affairs, Open Government, 06.01.92
197 Ibid
198 Ibid, 10.01.92
199 Ibid, 21.01.92 and 27.01.92
200 Ibid, 04.02.92 and 17.02.92
201 The Best Future for Britain, Conservative Party 1992
202 Prime Minister's files: Cabinet: Cabinet Committee structure and membership, pt 5, 12.05.92; HoC *Hansard*, 19.05.92 cols 110–118
203 *Hansard* 02.06.92, Written Answers col 394
204 Prime Minister's files: Cabinet: Cabinet Committee structure and membership, pt 5, 03.11.92
205 Ibid, 20.11.92
206 Ibid, 13.11.92
207 Ibid, 23.11.92
208 Ibid, 13.01.93

209 Ibid, 08.2.93 and 29.06.93
210 Ibid, 08.02.93
211 Prime Minister's files: Security of the Secret Service part 15, 03.10.91
212 Ibid, 07.10.91
213 Ibid, 03.02.92
214 Cabinet Office archive, 13.04.92
215 Ibid, 01.05.92
216 Ibid, 01.05.92
217 Gyles Brandreth, *Breaking the Code. Westminster Diaries*, entry for 28.09.92
218 Charles Clarke, *The Times*, 24.09.93
219 *Report of the Inquiry into the Export of Defence Equipment and Dual-Use Goods to Iraq and Related Prosecutions*, 1996
220 Cabinet Office archive, self-assessment for 1995/96 and objectives for 1996/97, 13.05.96
221 Anthony Bevins, 'Yes' men who threaten the Minister, *The Observer*, 17.10.93
222 *Hansard*, 18.04.90, cols 1427–1436
223 Prime Minister's files: Iraq, exports to Iraq (Scott inquiry) part 2, HM Customs and Excise press notice, 15.11.90
224 Ibid, part 3, 09.11.92
225 Anthony Bevins, *'Yes' men who threaten the Minister, The Observer*, 17.10.93
226 Prime Minister's files: Iraq, exports to Iraq (Scott inquiry) part 1, 20.04.90
227 Cabinet Office archive: 26.10.90
228 Ibid, 06.11.90
229 PUS at DTI, 1989–96
230 *The Sunday Times*: *How Minister helped British firms to arm Saddam's soldiers, 02.12.90*
231 Prime Minister's papers: Iraq, exports to Iraq (Scott inquiry) part 2, 29.11.90
232 Cabinet Office archive, 03.12.90
233 Ibid, 18.02.91
234 Ibid, 28.06.93, and Butler's notes for his evidence to the Scott Inquiry, question F. 1.5
235 Ibid, 15.11.91
236 Scott Inquiry evidence, (DTI 145.3.10674), 31.10.91
237 Prime Minister's files: Iraq, exports to Iraq (Scott inquiry) part 3, 13.11 92
238 Ibid, 09.11.92
239 Interview with Sir Brian Unwin, 23.02.12
240 Meeting on 10 .11.92 attended by, John Major, the Attorney General, the Home Secretary, the Lord Advocate, the Minister of State FCO, the Minister for Industry, the Minister of State for Defence Procurement, Unwin and Butler
241 Prime Minister's files: Iraq, exports to Iraq (Scott inquiry) part 3, 10.11.92
242 Ibid, minutes of ad hoc Meeting of Ministers, Cabinet Office Conference Room A, 2.45 pm 19.07.90
243 Cabinet Office archive, 09.11.92
244 Ibid, 16.11.92
245 Ibid, 20.22.92
246 Simon Jenkins, *Whitehall's costliest farce, The Times*, 11.12.93
247 Cabinet Office archive, 30.03.93
248 Prime Minister's files: Iraq, exports to Iraq (Scott inquiry) part 6, 02.12.92
249 Ibid, 02.02.93
250 Ibid, 12.02.93
251 Ibid, 17.03.93 and 02.04.93
252 Ibid, 20.04.93
253 Ibid, 30.03.93
254 *Hansard*, Written Answer of 16.11.92 from the Prime Minister

255 Prime Minister's files: Iraq, exports to Iraq (Scott inquiry) part 6, 01.04.93
256 Ibid, 30.03.93
257 Ibid, 30.03.93
258 Ibid, 30.03.93
259 Ibid, part 7, 16.06.93
260 Ibid, 17.06.93
261 Ibid, 10.06.93 and 15.06.93
262 Ibid, part 7, 17.06.93
263 Ibid, 24.06.93
264 Ibid, 23.07.93
265 Cabinet Office archive, 18.11.93
266 Ibid, 03.11.93
267 Prime Minister's files: Iraq, exports to Iraq (Scott inquiry) part 9, 07.02.94
268 Ibid, 04.02.94
269 Ibid, Butler annotations to draft statement
270 Ibid, part 15, 21.11.95, and 23.11.95
271 Ibid, 04.12.95
272 Ibid, part 16, 09.01.96,
273 Ibid, part 15, 22.11.95
274 Simon Jenkins, *Whitehall's costliest farce, The Times*, 11.12.93
275 Allan Massie, *Secrecy is here to stay, Daily Telegraph*, 06.12.93
276 Geoffrey Howe, *A Judge's Long Contest with Reality, The Spectator*, 27.01.96
277 Prime Minister's files: Iraq, exports to Iraq (Scott inquiry) part 15, 05.12.95
278 *Scott: My assistant was threatened, The Independent*, 09.05.96
279 Interview with Lord Hennessy, 14.12.11
280 Prime Minister's files: *Contacts with the Leader of the Opposition*
281 Prime Minister's files: Nationalised Industries: Coal Industry part 23, 24.11.92
282 Conservative Party *The Best Future for Britain*, April 1992
283 Prime Minister's files: Nationalised Industries: Coal Industry part 23
284 Ibid, part 25, 31.12.92
285 Ibid, 15.12.92
286 Ibid, 08.12.92
287 Ibid, 04.12.92
288 Ibid, part 23, 27.11.92
289 Ibid, 23.09.92
290 Ibid, 21.12.92
291 Ibid, 20.10.92
292 Ibid, 05.11.92
293 Ibid, undated manuscript note between 23 and 27 November 1992
294 Signed on 07.02.92 paving the way to the European Union and the single European currency
295 The Danish referendum result was narrow – a majority of less than 50,000 votes; a repeat referendum in Denmark in May 1993 overturned the first result. The French voted 51.05% in favour
296 *Hansard HC*, 03.06.92, col 830
297 Cabinet Office archive, 07,03,96
298 Ibid, 16.07.93
299 Ibid, 20.07.93
300 Letter to *The Daily Telegraph*, 24.11.94
301 Cabinet Office archive, 23.11.94
302 Ibid, 05.12.94
303 *John Major, the Autobiography*, Harper Collins 1999 p. 688
304 Prime Minister's files: Ireland, meetings with the Taoiseach, pt 23a, 26.02.92
305 Ibid, part 24

306 Interview with Lord Butler, 24.09.13
307 John Major the autobiography, p. 451
308 Prime Minister's files: Situation in Northern Ireland, pt 36, 25.11.93
309 Ibid, 26. 11.93
310 Ibid, 30.11.93
311 Ibid, part 37, 07.12.93
312 Talk at the London School of Economics, 24.04.07
313 Tony Blair, *A Journey*, Hutchinson 2020 p. 152
314 Interview with Sir Robin Ibbs 29.06.10
315 Analysis taken from Cabinet Office committee records
316 Prime Minister's papers: Cabinet: Quality of Cabinet papers, 14.11.89
317 Sir Terry Heiser, PUS at DOE, 1985–92
318 Prime Minister's files: Cabinet: drafting of Cabinet papers 05.03.92
319 Interview with Lord Butler, 17.12.10
320 Philip Stephens, Political editor *Financial Times*, 24.12.92
321 Prime Minister's files: Machinery of Government, Presentation of Government policies
322 Prime Minister's files: Government Machinery, Promotion of Efficiency part 40, 24.12.92
323 Conversation with Lord Butler, 17.12.10
324 Prime Minister's files: Machinery of Government, Presentation of Government policies, April 1995, January 1996 and April 1997
325 Ibid, 03.04.97
326 Ibid, 18.04.95
327 Prime Minister's files: Machinery of Government: Standards of conduct in public life, part 3, 18.02.94
328 *The Economist*, 26.11.94
329 *Hansard (HC)*, 25.10.94, col 758
330 HMSO CM 2850
331 Prime Minister's files: Government Machinery: Standards of Conduct in Public Life, 13.01.95
332 Ibid, 13.01.95
333 Ibid, 16.01.95
334 Ibid, 20.01.95
335 Ibid, 04.05.95
336 Ibid, 04.05.95
337 Ibid, 19.01.95
338 Ibid, 06.11.94
339 Ibid, 20.04.95
340 Ibid, 04.05.95
341 Ibid, 04.05.95
342 Ibid, 25.05.95
343 Ibid, 05.07.95
344 Ibid, 10.05.95
345 Ibid, 12.07.95
346 Ibid, 04.10.95
347 Ibid, 23.11.95
348 The Conservative Party held an annual re-election of the Party leader each November
349 By 1995 it was normal for the Private Office to sit in and record the Prime Minister's conversations with colleagues during a reshuffle of Ministers
350 Heseltine: *Life in the Jungle*, Hodder and Stoughton (2000) pp. 483–4
351 Ibid, *p.* 493
352 Brian Mawhinney MP Chairman of the Conservative Party 1995–97

353 Prime Minister's files: Cabinet: Cabinet Committee structure and membership, 07.07.95
354 Prime Minister's files: Intelligence Agencies: GCHQ pt 1, 25.06.91
355 Ibid, 18.02.92 and 11.11.93
356 Ibid, 11.11.93
357 Ibid, 20.12.93
358 Ibid, 22.02.94
359 Ibid, 25.02.94
360 Ibid, 12.05.95 to 02.06.95
361 Ibid, 16.11.95
362 *Hansard* HL, 20.12.95 cols 147–8 WA and 23.07.96, col 101 WA
363 Prime Minister's files: Intelligence Agencies: GCHQ pt 1, 07.11.96
364 *The Observer* 17.08.97
365 Cabinet Office archive, 19.04.91
366 Reviews of protective security were undertaken in 1991 and again in 1994
367 Prime Minister's files: Security: GCHQ's Annual Report for 1992–93
368 Prime Minister's files: Economic Policy: Secret Vote cash limits, Intelligence Agency Estimates 29.09.88 and 26.10.88
369 Prime Minister's files: Intelligence Agencies: Policy 08.11.93
370 Ibid, undated
371 Ibid, 10.11.93
372 HC *Hansard*, 24.11.93. col 52
373 Prime Minister's files: Intelligence Agencies: Policy, 23.12.93
374 Ibid, 01.07.94
375 Ibid
376 Ibid, 13.07.94
377 Ibid, 04.08.94
378 Ibid, 29.07.94
379 IS(95)1st meeting minutes, 01.05.95
380 Prime Minister's files: Intelligence Agencies: Policy, undated
381 Ibid, 03.10 94
382 Ibid, 09.03.95
383 Ibid, 07.06.95
384 Chisholm, by then chief executive of the Defence Research Establishment, made this comment at a private seminar in Washington on reform of defence management organised by Price Waterhouse in 1986 involving British, Australian, American and Canadian senior officials
385 Prime Minister's files: Intelligence Agencies: Policy, 04.06.96
386 *The Sunday Times*, 03.05.92
387 IS(92)3
388 IS(92)1st meeting minutes, 25.06.92
389 IS(92)2nd meeting, 22 .07.92, paper IS(92)5 and minutes
390 Prime Minister's files: Security of the Secret Service part 15, 23.06.92. It is ironic that 18 years later, as Lord Butler of Brockwell he was appointed to the Intelligence and Security Committee established by the Intelligence Services Act, 1994
391 Ibid, 14.10.92
392 Quoted in *The Guardian*, 14.02.12
393 IS(92)3rd meeting minutes, 14.10.92
394 Prime Minister's files: Intelligence Agencies: policy 22.10.93
395 Ibid, 20.07.94
396 Ibid, 13.12.96
397 Ibid, 25.02.97
398 Ibid, 18.12.96
399 See, for instance a Parliamentary Question on this issue from Chris Mullin, Chairman of the Home Affairs Committee, *Hansard* 04.06.98, col 506

400 Prime Minister's files: Intelligence Agencies: policy, 19.02.97
401 PREM 19/1615, 30.12.84
402 Quoted in Christopher Andrew, *Defence of the Realm* page 845
403 The Metropolitan Police Special Irish Branch was formed in March 1883 to combat the Irish Republican Brotherhood
404 By convention Ministers do not take or announce major policy initiatives once a General Election is called- The Draft Cabinet Manual paragraph 68, Cabinet Office, December 2010
405 Cabinet Office archive, 18.01.94
406 Prime Minister's files: Intelligence Agencies: Interception 19.04.94
407 Ibid, 15.11.95
408 Cabinet Office archive, SCI(94)4 Annex A
409 Cabinet Office archive, 03.06.96
410 Ibid, PSIS (97)6, 23.07.97
411 Prime Minister's files, Parliament, Prime Minister's Questions, 29.03.95
412 Ibid, 29.03.95
413 Ibid, 29.03.95
414 Ibid, 04.04.95
415 Prime Minister's files: the Constitution: Constitutional Reform, 15.12.95
416 Lord Privy Seal 1994–97
417 Prime Minister's files: the Constitution: Constitutional Reform, 15.03.96
418 Cabinet Office file A13/31, 27.05.88
419 Cabinet Office file A13/27, 13.10.89
420 Cabinet Office file A5/9, early 1994 undated
421 Ibid, 27.01.94
422 Interview with Lord Butler, 24.09.13
423 The Autumn Sunningdale was attended by most Permanent Secretaries. A Spring Sunningdale comprised 15 Permanent Secretaries and 15 captains of industry discussing broad issues involving Government/industry relations
424 Prime Minister's files: Government Machinery, the Rayner programme, part 36, 04.03.91
425 Ibid, *Making the Most of Next Steps*, Efficiency Unit, April 1991
426 Prime Minister's files: Government Machinery, the Rayner programme, part 37, 02.05.92
427 Ibid, 03.06.91
428 Cabinet Office file A13/32, report on session 1: Strategic control of public expenditure, 11.10.91
429 Ibid, manuscript speaking notes for Autumn 1991 Conference
430 Ibid, 11.10.91
431 Levene's scheduled meetings with Major were often postponed, Prime Minister's files: Government Machinery, Rayner programme for the promotion of efficiency part 39; Neville-Rolfe later reported Levene to be losing heart, ibid, 23.04.93, and Levene complained about Major's lack of interest, Cabinet Office file A20/7, May 1994
432 Prime Minister's files: Government Machinery, Rayner programme for the promotion of efficiency part 38, 17.01.92
433 Ibid, Richard Mottram (Head of OPSS) at the Prime Minister's seminar on civil service reform, 03.11.93
434 Discussed at the 1992 Autumn Sunningdale Conference
435 Cabinet Office file A5/9, 17.06.93
436 Head of the Efficiency Unit 1993–98.
437 Cabinet Office file A5/9, undated late June 1992
438 Ibid, 08.12.93
439 Prime Minister's files: Civil Service Pay and Pensions, 08.03.93

440 Ibid, undated
441 Ibid, in addition to Major participants were the Chancellor of the Exchequer (Kenneth Clarke), the Chancellor of the Duchy of Lancaster (William Waldegrave). David Davis MP, Butler, Sir Christopher France (MOD), Sir Terence Burns (HMT), Sir Peter Levene (Efficiency Adviser), Sir James Blyth (Businessman and Chairman of the Advisory Panel on the Citizens' Charter), Andrew Turnbull ((HMT), Richard Mottram (OPSS), John Chisholm (Chief Executive, Defence Research Agency), John Oughton (Efficiency Unit) Sarah Hogg and Lucy Neville-Rolfe (both Policy Unit)
442 Ibid, 09.11.93
443 Ibid, 17.01.94
444 Ibid, 21.01.94
445 Ibid, 03.02.89
446 Ibid, 07.02.94
447 Ibid, 09.02.94
448 Running cost controls, central help with redundancy costs, efficiency targets, Citizens' Charter pressure on quality, withdrawing from central oversight of privatisation, competitive tendering and market testing programmes, extended pay and grading delegation, better financial systems
449 Cabinet Office file A5/9, draft letter to Andrew Turnbull, 16.12.93, toned down at Butler's request
450 Cabinet Office file A5/9, 17.02.94
451 Cabinet Office, *Civil Service Statistics 1999*, table I, entrants and leavers, non-industrial staff
452 Interview with Lord Butler, 24.09.13
453 Cabinet office file A5/9, 14.01.94
454 Ibid, 07.03.94
455 Ibid, 14.01.94
456 Cabinet Office file A5/9, 27.01.94 and 10.05.94
457 Ibid, 27.01.94
458 Ibid, 04.05.94
459 Ibid, 03.05.94
460 Ibid, 18.05.94
461 Ibid, 10.06.94
462 Ibid, annotations on the draft agenda submitted with the brief of 10.06.94
463 Ibid, 15.05.94
464 Ibid, 17.06.94
465 Ibid, 08.06.94
466 Ibid, 29.06.94
467 HMSO, *The Civil Service, Continuity and Change*, HMSO, 13.07.94
468 Ibid, 13.07.94
469 HMSO, *Competing for Quality*, Cm 1730, November 1991
470 *Evening Standard*, 13.07.94
471 *The Sunday Times*, 17.07.94
472 Articles appeared in the MOD's *Focus*, the Treasury's *Chequerboard*, and in *Parliamentary Brief*
473 Cabinet Office file A5/9), 03.08.94
474 Ibid, 25.11.94
475 Ibid, 29.09.94
476 Ibid, 21.07.95
477 Ibid, 25.11.94
478 Ibid, 25.05.95
479 Ibid, 03.08.95
480 Sir Adrian Cadbury had chaired an influential inquiry into *Financial Aspects of Corporate Governance* which had reported in 1992

481 Cabinet Office file A5/9, 05.09.94
482 Ibid, note of a discussion at the Permanent Secretaries' Conference, Sunningdale, 14.10.95
483 Ibid, 28.10.94
484 Ibid, 09.01.95
485 *Hansard*, 09.02.95, cols 345–6
486 Cabinet Office file A5/9, 28.04.95
487 Ibid, 02.12.94
488 Ibid, 17.01.95
489 Cabinet Office archive
490 Ibid, 23.10.96
491 Fifth Report of the Treasury and Civil Service Committee of Session 1993–94, 24.11.94, HC 27
492 Cabinet Office file A5/9, 11.01.95
493 The Code was introduced in late November 1995 and incorporated the recommendation of the Nolan Committee that civil servants should be able to raise concerns confidentially with an individual outside line management
494 This feared reaction is in marked contrast to staff reactions in professional services firms who show little hostility to high pay for senior managers because they want to work and learn from successful people
495 Cabinet Office file A5/9, 09.10.95
496 Ibid, undated, late February 1995
497 Excluding 13–20 staff in the CPRS (1970–83)
498 Prime Minister's files: Special Advisers, 09.10.98
499 Heseltine, *Life in the Jungle* p. 491
500 Cabinet Office file C696/5, 03.09.96
501 Ibid, 03.09.96
502 Ibid, 11.11.96
503 Interview with Lord Butler 24.09.13
504 Labour Spokesman shadowing the Chancellor of the Duchy of Lancaster 1995–97
505 John Smith speech to the Labour Finance and Industry Group, 28.01.93
506 Prime Minister's files: Civil Service, Contacts with the Opposition, 01.02.93
507 Prime Minister's files, Civil Service Long term management and manpower policy 13.01.89
508 Cabinet Office file A13/35, 23.10.91
509 Frank Stacey memorial lecture, Annual Conference of the Public Administration Committee of the Joint Universities Council, 07.09.92
510 HC *Hansard*, 08.01.90 col 738
511 Cabinet Office file A17/3, 07.02.92
512 Interview with Lord Butler, 24.09.13
513 Ibid, 24.09.13
514 Prime Minister's files: Elections: election procedure, 21.04.97
515 Interview with Lord Butler, 17.12.10
516 Ibid, 17.12.10
517 Cabinet Office file A9/31, 03.10.97
518 Ibid, 03.10.97
519 Interview with Lord Butler, 17.12.10
520 Ibid, 17.12.10
521 Cabinet Office archive, 14.05.97 and 16.05.97
522 P Dunleavey *Policy Disasters: Explaining the UK's record*, Public Policy & Administration, Vol 10 No 2 (1995) pp. 52–70
523 Butler, Adonis & Travers *Failure in British Government. The politics of the Poll Tax*, OUP 1994, pp. 222–3
524 D Hague, *Transforming the Dinosaur: How Organisations Learn* 1993, pp. 20–1

525 Cabinet office file A5/10, *The Policy Making Capacity in Whitehall*, 02.10.96
526 Ibid, 10.10.96
527 Ibid, 10.10.96
528 Ibid, 10.10.96
529 Ibid, 08.05.97
530 Ibid, 13.05.97
531 Ibid, 31.05.97
532 The request and replies are on Cabinet Office file A/43A
533 Ibid, 02.09.97
534 Speech to Birmingham University Conference, *Modernising the Policy Process*, 16.09.97
535 See, for example, Prime Minister's files: Domestic Policy, 09.10.97
536 Ibid, 07.01.98
537 Nicholas Timmins *Plethora of panaceas*, Financial Times, 18.09.97
538 Cabinet Office file A9/31, 19.09.97
539 *John Major the Autobiography*, HarperCollins, 1999 p. 536
540 Ibid, p. 544
541 The initial membership comprised CDS, PUS FCO, PUS MOD, Political Director FCO, DUS (Policy) MOD
542 Cabinet Office archive, 07.08.95
543 Ibid, 11.08.95
544 Ibid, 24.02.96
545 Prime Minister's files: Agriculture policy pt 45, 18 & 19.03.96
546 *Hansard* HC 21.05.96, cols 99–113
547 Prime Minister's files: Agriculture policy pt 20, 22.05.96
548 Ibid, 22.05.96
549 Ibid, 22.05.96
550 Alistair Campbell, *Power and the People*, 08.05.97, p. 13
551 Prime Minister's files: Agriculture, BSE Inquiry, 22.08.97
552 Cabinet Office file A10/1, 29.08.97
553 Prime Minister's files: Agriculture, BSE Inquiry, 17.09.97
554 Ibid, 14.11.97
555 Ibid, 17.11.97
556 Held on 01.12.97 involving Blair, Cunningham (MAFF), Dobson (Health), Dewar (Scotland). Mowlam, (NI), Darling (CST), Mandelson with Butler and five other officials including Packer the PUS at MAFF
557 The full terms of reference were 'To establish and review the history of the emergence and identification of BSE and NV CJD in the United Kingdom, and of the action taken in response to it up to 20 March 1996; to reach conclusions on the adequacy of that response, taking account of the state of knowledge at the time; and to report on these matters by 31 December 1998 to the Minister of Agriculture, Fisheries and Food, the Secretary of State for Health and the Secretaries of State for Scotland, Wales and Northern Ireland.'
558 Prime Minister's files: Special Advisers, 14.04.92
559 Ibid, 04.04.97
560 Ibid, 14.02.07
561 Ibid, 16.05.97
562 Ibid, 04.11.97
563 Ibid, 21.11.97
564 Article 3(2) of the Civil Service Order in Council 1995 as amended by the Civil Service (Amendment) Order in Council 1997
565 Prime Minister's files: Special Advisers, Minutes of the Meeting of Civil Service Commissioners, 12.05.97
566 Ibid, 30.05.97

567 Ibid, 03.05.97
568 Interview with Lord Butler, 24.09.13
569 Ibid, 24.09.13
570 CC(97)25th minute 4

7 Mission Impossible

Sir Richard Wilson
Cabinet Secretary
1998–2002

Wilson reading: A relaxed Richard Wilson

Source: Photographed by Mark de Rond

Inkstand: Retirement gift from the Blair Cabinet

Source: Photographed by Ian Beesley

On 3 July 1997 Robin Butler reported to the Prime Minister the results of a consultation with selected Permanent Secretaries[1] over who should succeed him in the combined roles of Cabinet Secretary and Head of the Home Civil Service. There were three names on the paper, each annotated with Butler's judgement on suitability. His recommendation was for the then Permanent Secretary at the Home Office (HO), Sir Richard Wilson, who: 'made his reputation as Head of the Economic Secretariat in the Cabinet Office when the quality of his intellect, his persuasiveness and his skill in chairmanship enabled him to take the lead in calling in and resolving a succession of knotty issues over which Ministers and Departments were floundering.'[2]

Wilson was presented publicly as the next Cabinet Secretary on 1 August 1997, five months before the handover from Butler, as: 'a modernising force in preparing the Civil Service for the challenges of the 21st Century.'[3] 'Why me? You cannot be less like me,' he asked Butler; 'Perhaps because you are the opposite to me,' was Butler's reply. In a number of ways the appointment broke the mould. Trend, Hunt, Armstrong and Butler all had strong Treasury and central private office experience. None was closely associated with what Treasury officials disparagingly called 'spending departments' whereas Wilson had spent significant parts of his career in Trade and Industry (DTI) and in Energy

(DEn). It was true that from May 1990 to June 1992 he had been in the Treasury as a Deputy Secretary on industrial policy, but he had not felt that he contributed a great deal – his Treasury colleagues were so good that there was little to be added to their work.

His Final Selection Board (FSB) for entry into the fast stream of the civil service had been contradictory: the examiners were put off by his gangly figure, yet attracted by his enthusiastic energy, commenting: 'The more he is pressed, the more cheerful he becomes.' He came out joint second in the competition despite comments at the FSB that: 'He is a good, though not exceptional, candidate.'[4] However, this grudging recognition was soon disproved as, once in the thick of the action, Wilson was consistently seen as a high-flyer in the DTI and the DEn where the maverick ex-Treasury Permanent Secretary Sir Kenneth Couzens annotated Wilson's annual appraisal with: 'The Secretary of State (Mr Walker)[5] has entire confidence in him and like me, sees him as a future Permanent Secretary.' Early in his career he was a member of the Joint Intelligence Committee's Assessment Staff during the Heath administration, where he shone as an economic analyst. A paper in 1972 on the prospects for the rice harvest in Vietnam and its implications for the Viet Cong's military campaign had greatly impressed the then Cabinet Secretary, Burke Trend.[6]

Though his private office experience was not deep and he had never worked in 10 Downing Street, Wilson made his name as a senior official handling Margaret Thatcher (when head of the Economic Secretariat in the Cabinet Office 1986–90) and Michael Howard (when PUS at Environment (DOE) 1992–94 and at the Home Office 1994–98). In particular, under Robin Butler's hands-off approach he made a name as a Whitehall fixer, able to turn political ideas into practical policies. Earlier he had been private secretary to two Ministers of State and to a Parliamentary Secretary, but the Secretary of State, Tony Benn, had turned him down for private office in Energy on the grounds that, educated at Radley and Cambridge, he appeared to be too much an establishment figure. Benn preferred Bryan Emmett, a grammar school boy from Tadcaster who had started out as a clerical officer in the Ministry of Labour and National Service in 1959. Then, in 1976, the Department of Energy put Wilson forward as a candidate to succeed Nick Stuart, the Harrovian private secretary in Number 10 who dealt with Parliamentary business including preparing the Prime Minister for the twice-weekly Prime Minister's Questions. Wilson was not interviewed and heard nothing back until he learned that Jim Callaghan had selected another grammar school boy, Nigel Wicks, who served there until 1978 and became Principal Private Secretary to Thatcher from 1985–88.

Most people who worked with Wilson were impressed by his emotional intelligence, general openness and commitment to fairness in his dealings. A few found him less straightforward when Cabinet Secretary – Richard Packer, for instance, commented in this way in his memoir *The Politics of BSE*.[7] But part of this could be Packer's anger at his treatment over the 2001 Foot and Mouth epidemic and, as many have pointed out, high office sometimes demands sinuous behaviour and half-truths. He transferred as Permanent

Secretary from the DOE to the Home Office in June 1992 when Michael Howard became Home Secretary. Howard wanted Wilson's help in improving the relationship between Ministers and their officials; at that time the Home Office still had a reputation for pursuing departmental policies independent of Ministers. At the DOE Wilson had started a large programme of change to respond to environmental issues but had had to leave at the point of their implementation to follow Howard to the Home Office. There he acted swiftly and decisively to move a number of powerful departmental barons so as to improve responsiveness to Howard's policies.

Tony Blair saw Wilson as promising a fresh approach to reform, untainted by the inertia he judged to be the main problem with civil servants.[8] Wilson saw the challenge as bringing the civil service round to a new way of working with a new breed of politician, yet preserving the eternal verities of collective government. He was heir to a tradition where paper brought precision and was to be preferred over the informal discussion practised among members of the inner circle around Blair.[9] In his memoirs Blair commented that: '... to be fair [Wilson] got behind [Civil Service reform] thoroughly. But – and this is a criticism of me, not him or the Civil Service – they were like many other reforms: talking the right language but shying away from the really radical measures.'[10] What those radical measures were could be hard to fathom and judgements were often made on the basis of if it was not hurting enough then it could not be for real.[11] Blair and Wilson had first met on January 16 1996 at an informal dinner in Notting Hill hosted by Roy Jenkins[12] and attended by Butler's potential successors. He had sat next to Blair and had an extended conversation about modernisation of government. He was a proven moderniser. However, on that first (wet) Monday as Cabinet Secretary, January 5 1998, Wilson recalls being summoned to see Blair around lunch time when the Prime Minister had a list of half a dozen or so things to discuss. The main one was welfare reform where, unrealistically, Blair wanted to know by the end of January what would be the conclusions of the recently launched Welfare Review. Wilson also recalled that other topics included Ireland, the Euro, candidates for the Presidency of the European Commission and how to get across the government's economic message. He took away the clear impression that the Prime Minister wanted to receive early warning of decisions that the government would need to make but there was no mention of management or civil service reform.

Blair had not been a Minister before he became Prime Minister and the management of large and complex organisations was new to most of his colleagues. This brought certain strengths in not being beholden to the past but it carried significant risks – notably over the legal powers and finance Parliament gives to individual Secretaries of State, who are then accountable to it. The Prime Minister's power comes from patronage in appointing Ministers and political importance as the leader of a ruling Party. But Blair wanted a more hands-on role, with direction set from Downing Street to be followed by Secretaries of State. As some holders of the office before him he could be irked by the independence shown by political colleagues, though he disliked confronting them about this, particularly those associated with the Chancellor, Gordon Brown. Though the fall-out from the fractured relationship between the Prime Minister and the Chancellor deteriorated over time, this was a major complication for Wilson and his team even during the first term of government.[13] Downing Street looked to Wilson to compensate by holding the Permanent Secretaries to account through pay, deployment and bonuses. In this model the Secretaries of State looked after the politics (i.e. media and campaigning) within the confines of a communications grid plot controlled by Number 10 and helped in a policy-making process again controlled by Number 10. Delivering results from these policies was down to Wilson and the Permanent Secretaries driving the delivery agenda. It was a flawed model given the British constitution and the Cabinet Secretary's position. Further, Wilson's natural style was collaborative; his loyalty to the Prime Minister and belief in the general civil service omerta code meant that he refrained from mobilising his Permanent Secretary colleagues sufficiently. Few knew of the tough advice on the nature of power that he was giving to the Prime Minister.[14] Also, he could not rely on a favourable wind from Permanent Secretaries who had their own relationship with their Ministers to consider, especially as Ministers in the Brown camp could be particularly difficult to influence by a Cabinet Secretary whom they saw as a 'Blairite'.

'What Tony wants' was a rallying cry used by Special Advisers (SPADS) at many interdepartmental meetings. But could they be trusted to be really speaking for Blair? Ministers or SPADS might add their own gloss or slip in their own pet ideas. Jonathan Powell, Blair's chief of staff described Downing Street as: 'a court and not the HQ of a multinational corporation.'[15] How would a 'Brownite' Minister be likely to respond? Downing Street often referred to a desire for a tighter command and control system without sufficient regard to the personal dynamics at the top. From the Cabinet Office David Omand wrote to Geoff Mulgan, the Head of the Performance Improvement Unit in Downing Street, quoting Rupert Smith, the deputy Supreme Allied Commander Europe, who defined military command and control as: 'I as the Commander am responsible for both but I only do command. It is the function of the chief of staff and the headquarters to do my control for me … As a general rule, the further away you are from the point of execution in time and space, the less likely you are to know all the facts and figures, and therefore you can't give any kind of detailed orders.'[16] Omand added that if those responsible for execution did not feel really trusted and empowered then delivery would be hesitant not bold and vigorous. Those who must deliver needed to know that their own tribal leaders (whom they trusted to watch their backs) had been in the room when the decision was made. These conditions did not exist in the government, as the political memoirs of those at the centre of New Labour have shown. The experiment left a lasting policy question of whether the Treasury can ever be a domestic policy department led by a Chancellor who has his own social agenda.

Wilson, meanwhile, admired the Burke Trend years and had worked closely with Armstrong and Butler. He recognised that under Thatcher the Permanent Secretary had come to be seen as responsible for management of the Department and was expected to do more than delegate that responsibility beyond the fast stream to the heirs of the old Executive Class. Nevertheless, he saw the core of the Cabinet Secretary's role as: 'fundamentally to support good, strong, effective collective government.'[17] [Emphasis added]. He put a duty on himself to preserve the architecture of collective government for when it would once again be needed. He did not envisage a return to some past golden age; he envisaged that at the turn of the twenty-first century Cabinet would provide strategic leadership from close colleagues with a common vision, a common view and a degree of coherence – rather than as the supreme decision-taking body of yesterday when decisions could be taken at a more leisurely pace and the global economy had yet to emerge. Blair could of course seek to govern however he wished but Cabinet cohesion would again matter when the political position of a Prime Minister demanded it.

This was dangerous territory for any official. The leadership style of Downing Street under Blair was summed up by the columnist Hugo Young who recorded that Tony Blair 'thinks himself above politics and Party.'[18] Wilson suspected that Blair used him to propitiate people and for protection against their wrath – sometimes as a scapegoat. This use of Wilson to broker deals with Ministers is well illustrated by the unsuccessful attempts to find a role for Frank Field in the light of his inability to work with Harriet Harman at the Department of Social Security. There was little risk to Wilson as the Ministers concerned were not the government's 'Big Beasts' or closely linked to one; but as the collateral damage to Wilson from other attempts to impose the will of the Prime Minister over the proposal for a Working Age Agency and over the Robinson and Hinduja affairs demonstrates, in this environment self-sacrifice could be thrust upon the Cabinet Secretary.

Cabinet and its Committees

The initial pattern established between Butler and Blair (itself a continuation of the practice under Major) was for the Prime Minister to have an hour's session on current issues with the Cabinet Secretary and his top secretariat team on Monday morning. This arrangement stopped in 1998 after which Wilson saw Blair by himself to discuss a forward look based on a thorough weekly Cabinet Office meeting of Deputy Secretaries focusing on what was live in Whitehall.[19] Jonathan Powell told Wilson in late April 1998 that Blair found the note useful and hoped that it would continue to be updated.[20] The lists for that year typically comprised 16–18 items, never fewer than 12 and once as many as 25. The consequences of the devolution of powers to the Scottish and Welsh Assemblies appeared on the list throughout the year, as did welfare reform. Other frequent items in the year were House of Lords reform, United Nations resolutions permitting the export of Iraqi oil to meet the humanitarian needs,[21] sectarian violence in Northern Ireland, civil war in Kosovo and the Balkans, a first Comprehensive Spending Review to set public expenditure limits, continuing problems over beef exports following the late 1980s-early 1990s occurrence of

Bovine Spongiform Encephalopathy (BSE or 'mad cow disease'), consolidation in European defence industries, public sector pay and the future of the Post Office. These weekly notes were also supplemented at the end of each month by even fuller reports looking further ahead.[22]

In an Attlee Foundation Lecture,[23] fresh from the fray, Robin Butler described Cabinet in the 1990s as having reverted: 'to what it was in the late eighteenth and early nineteenth centuries – a meeting of political colleagues at which the issues of the moment were informally reported or discussed.' He contrasted the Attlee experience of an annual average of 87 Cabinet meetings and 340 circulated papers with the 1990s where there were no more than 40 meetings and usually fewer than 20 papers. Wilson found that Blair, typically, held around 35 Cabinet meetings a year – often short (rarely more than 45 minutes and in April 1999 down to 30 minutes). In 1998 there were 37 meetings but only eight papers. No formal agenda was circulated in advance though the Prime Minister would often receive contrasting lists of suggested topics (one from Wilson the other from Jonathan Powell). The meeting always covered Parliamentary business in both the Commons and the Lords and, after March 1999, discussed a grid used to plot the release of government announcements against a strategic communications plan and to provide the means by which to ensure that Ministers stayed 'on message'.

There were sometimes significant ministerial absences: on two occasions in 1999 five Ministers were absent from Cabinet and on one occasion eight were away. Secretariat members recall that the Blair-Brown split meant that Blair was reluctant to press for decisions on contested issues lest the sense of the meeting went against him, anticipating that such an event would be leaked.[24] Observers reported that Brown could be a largely silent brooding attendee, working on papers, not joining in the humour and disdainful of colleagues. They cited that for the 1999 Budget, Number 10 had such little notice of the contents that David Miliband, as head of the Policy Unit, asked the economic and domestic secretariat (EDS) to trawl the Chancellor's speeches and Treasury press notices to gain some idea of what might be coming. Though this was a one-off request, getting the Chancellor to be open with the Prime Minister about the Budget remained a problem throughout Blair's premiership. A Chancellor had always had a fair degree of freedom not to involve colleagues in the run-up to the Budget but this pushed those boundaries much further. When he did take his colleagues through the Budget at Cabinet on the morning of the announcement it was at such speed as to discourage questions or challenge. He launched a blizzard of numbers that were difficult to take in and quite significant changes in tax were often buried in the small print of the Budget Red Book and not mentioned to Cabinet. Budgets became an occasion to make numerous policy announcements and Departments often had little notice of what was coming. Recording such meetings was a challenge.[25]

Other set pieces included the traditional Cabinet blessing of the work of the Legislation Committee, which continued to have the difficult task of selecting and prioritising Bills to be presented for Parliamentary approval, and ratification of the most important White or Green Papers – which were expected to have been knocked into shape in Cabinet Committee. There were oral reports on European Union or foreign negotiations and on the situation in Northern Ireland. As with the Chancellor, the historical latitude accorded to the Foreign Secretary about how far to take the Cabinet into his confidence was much in evidence. Discussions were often about political issues – such as getting close to the Germans, not neglecting backbenchers or getting across the big picture. Blair fretted that government communications did not adequately reflect a consistent communications strategy through themed announcements.[26] During this first term of office it seemed that the Cabinet was in constant campaigning mode and Wilson was troubled by the way that discussion quite often drifted into party political ideas to 'dish' the Opposition or about organising election campaigning. He established a convention that he would put down his pen when he considered the discussion not to be government business and the secretaries at the end of the Cabinet table would follow his lead.[27]

It was a struggle to stop announcements being made before collective discussion and outside Parliament. David Blunkett[28] complained to Blair in May 2000 that: 'reports and pronouncements are starting to pre-empt decision making by Cabinet Ministers ... causing us considerable difficulty publicly;' and 'that there are a number of people ... who are working in parallel rather than together.'[29] Blair's Principal Private Secretary wrote to private offices in December drawing attention to a Green Paper on planning that had been circulated: '[with] no time fully to resolve some issues on which views differed and understandings between departments about how the proposals would operate were not set out in writing.'[30]

Why had Cabinet developed so? First, Labour had been out of office for 17 years so that the new Ministers mostly had experience only of Opposition, where articulation between portfolios is less important than when in government. As Andrew Turnbull told the Chilcot Inquiry into Iraq,[31] part of the clash between the politicians and the civil servants was that New Labour was used to agile small organisations whereas the Permanent Secretaries had grown up in large organisations – the speedboat versus the super tanker. Second, the rise of a professional political cadre in the UK meant that Ministers were mainly used to associating with like-minded souls and were reluctant to widen their interlocutors. Third, the political relationship between Blair and Brown dogged everything. The frequency of the same Blair doodle is intriguing, suggesting that he found formal sessions restricting:

Fourth, there was a shift of gravity towards EU and UN forums where policy had to be negotiated with willing and unwilling partners under the critical watching eyes of 24-hour TV news with network slots to fill. Ministers were impelled towards continuous political campaigning at home and abroad. They had, after all, been campaigning for a very long time when out of office. With the result that there was both awe and indulgence towards a leader who had ended years of political drought and who then went on to win a further two General Elections. At bottom the main reason Cabinet became emasculated, however, was because Ministers were content for it to be reduced in importance. That is not to say that

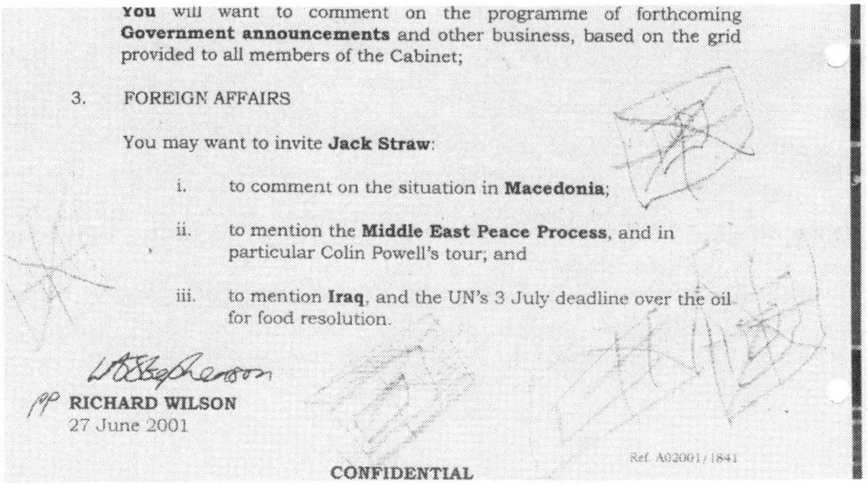

You will want to comment on the programme of forthcoming **Government announcements** and other business, based on the grid provided to all members of the Cabinet;

3. FOREIGN AFFAIRS

You may want to invite **Jack Straw**:

i. to comment on the situation in **Macedonia**;

ii. to mention the **Middle East Peace Process**, and in particular Colin Powell's tour; and

iii. to mention **Iraq**, and the UN's 3 July deadline over the oil for food resolution.

RICHARD WILSON
27 June 2001

Ref. A02001/1841

CONFIDENTIAL

Tony Blair's doodles.

Cabinet Committees and formal MISC ad hoc groups were also in disrepair. On the contrary, many continued to thrive:

Secretariat supported meetings

Number

	1998	*1999*	*2000*	*2001*	*2002*
Cabinet	37	35	36	33	38
Other	233	242	220	224	267

Source: Cabinet Office records

Blair had said shortly before the 1997 General Election: 'People have to know that we will run from the centre and govern from the centre.'[32] Butler had persuaded him that he should chair five standing Cabinet Committees even though he did not accept formal chairmanship was a good use of his time.[33] These were Defence and Overseas, Europe, Intelligence, Northern Ireland, and Welfare Reform. In a forward look at issues coming to decision shortly before the end of the Parliament there were mentions of 29 Cabinet Committees and sub-committees, six MISC groups and 18 other ad hoc groups.

Like Cabinet Secretaries before him, Wilson acted as the senior secretary for those committees and groups chaired by the Prime Minister and had overall responsibility for advising on all matters of committee business. He had been given an open pass by Blair to attend any committees or groups he chose but Secretariat members, nevertheless, felt that Blair often feigned surprise when he did.[34] But it was through the committees and formal MISC groups that Wilson kept the collective Ministerial process alive – on life support and vulnerable to neglect like an ancient relative needing transfusions, but alive nevertheless.

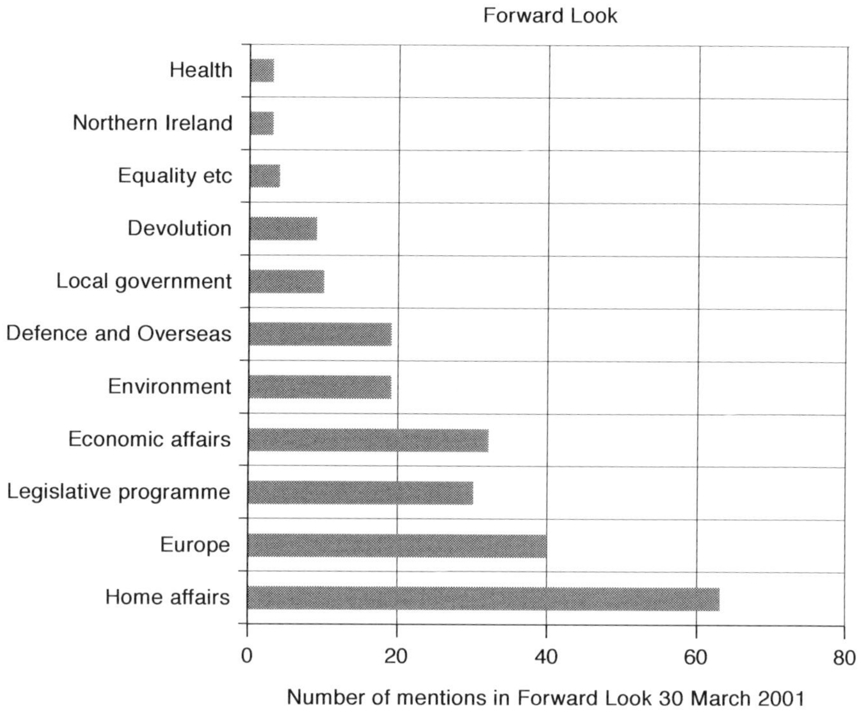

One source of new collective discussion was that as the devolution of powers to the Scottish and Welsh Assemblies was implemented it was necessary to agree concordats about policy. Blair chaired a plenary Joint Ministerial Committee with the devolved administrations, charged with oversight of the implementation of devolution. It was committed to meet at least once a year but was outside the UK Cabinet Committee system. (In addition in the first Parliamentary session Blair chaired a sub-committee on health, the Chancellor one on poverty and another on the knowledge economy, and the Foreign Secretary one on the European Union). These arrangements came out of claims by the putative First Ministers of the devolved assemblies that they should have a seat in deliberations on non-devolved matters that would affect their territories. They went as far as arguing to be both Secretary of State for Scotland/Wales in the UK Parliament and First Minister in the devolved Assembly. The Cabinet Office Secretariat that serviced the Devolution Policy Committee (DP) sometimes felt that as a Scot its chairman, Derry Irvine, might be conflicted and that constrained their willingness to offer decisive views. Wilson, however, successfully opposed the claims. He argued that, whilst the devolved Assemblies might currently be of the same political persuasion as the UK Government, this would not always be the case. Reserved powers meant exactly that.[35]

The Cabinet Committee regularly attended by Wilson was Defence and Overseas Policy. This was something of a paradox: membership was small and strategic, requests to be appointed to the committee (for example from Clare Short as Minister for Overseas Development) were habitually refused, but attendance was flexible and widespread; non-members tended to participate fully in the debate whereas the Chancellor, a full member, rarely attended. The various heads of the secretariats in the Cabinet Office organised other committees. Wilson's task of organising and recording collective discussions was made difficult by Blair's habit of having a running levee in his den or in the flat so that what might start with a meeting on one subject seamlessly became another as courtiers came and went and telephone calls were made. Restrictions on the size of the Cabinet Office did not help either. The Treasury kept a tight hold of the joint Number 10 and Cabinet Office budget, with the result that since the expenditure of Number 10 took precedence, when David Omand became Accounting Officer for the Cabinet Office he found that there was not enough money to buy the licence to upgrade to the latest Microsoft Windows software.[36] In March 1999 Willie Rickett (Head of the EDS Secretariat) complained that his committees were proving difficult to run because of poor discipline in circulating papers and informal working between Ministers.[37] This and a later report from the Performance and Innovation Unit (located in the Cabinet Office but working exclusively for 10 Downing Street): '*Wiring It Up; Whitehall's management of cross-cutting policies and services*' led to a further report in January 2001 focusing largely on the effectiveness of the Economic and Social Affairs Committee[38] which contained innovative ideas on how to foster Ministerial interest and a sense of collective ownership of policies by a wider involvement of outside experts at the early stages of discussion and more willingness from chairmen to encourage honesty about disagreements. These ideas formed the basis for Wilson's submission on Cabinet Committees after the 2001 election.

The submission was designed to keep the collective shop open as Blair moved to appoint executive units inside or close to Downing Street in a significant strengthening of central direction of policy.[39] Wilson explicitly linked committees to manifesto commitments in an effort to put the system back at the centre of Ministerial priorities. And in an attempt to bolster collective working he successfully proposed merging the Home and Social Affairs Committee (HS) and the Economic Affairs Committee (EA) under the chairmanship of the Deputy Prime Minister (John Prescott) who was known to be more traditional about Cabinet than the Prime Minister. However, his submission acknowledged opposition from the Chancellor who did not want to lose control of the main economic committee. The compromise he offered and accepted by Blair was to set up a new freestanding Economic Affairs, Productivity and Competitiveness Committee (EAPC) under the Chancellor. Private Office recorded that the Prime Minister had decided that the new committee: 'will handle all economic issues and issues bearing on the country's productivity and competitiveness,'[40] further underlining the power ceded to the Chancellor. In the past it had been usual – though not an inviolate rule – that the Prime Minister chaired the main economic committee. Those officials closest to Blair (notably the Cabinet Secretary and the Principal Private Secretary) had known about the destructive tension between Brown and Blair from the outset of the administration[41] but had maintained a discreet silence in the interests of presenting the government in as good a light as possible.

Further evidence of the Chancellor's hegemony of economic matters was that the Committee on Public Services and Public Expenditure (PSX), which he chaired, continued to be responsible for delivery of the planning agreements with Departments that lay behind the three-year Comprehensive Spending Reviews (CSR) even after Blair established a Delivery Unit (PMDU) inside 10 Downing Street under Michael Barber. Indeed, Wilson soon established that the targets to be set by the PMDU had to be consistent with the Public Service Agreements (PSA) in the CSR. That was crucial to good government if Departments were not to be pulled in different directions, but it was also recognition of Treasury power over the domestic agenda since neither the Prime Minister, his staff nor the EDS secretariat had been closely involved in the setting of PSAs, which were agreed and monitored in the PSX committee. But PSX did not discuss resource allocation: 'PSX was not the public expenditure "Star Chamber" of the 1980s; it was Gordon Brown's toy.'[42] In the first round of CSRs the Treasury imposed many of the targets on Departments who did not feel ownership of them and in some cases were not prepared to accept accountability.[43] In consequence Wilson's post-election submission of 2001 suggesting that Blair might chair PSX when PSAs of interest to him were discussed got nowhere – Jonathan Powell wrote in the margins of the submission: 'GB will cause real trouble if you do this formally.'

Wilson and other senior officials felt that Blair, unlike Thatcher, doubted the usefulness of committees, particularly those with a standing membership, as opposed to ad hoc groups put together for specific tasks. The latter were less susceptible to the state of the relationship between the Prime Minister and the Chancellor. In the early days of the government, for example, Wilson persuaded Blair to have a Cabinet Committee on welfare reform. The move failed, however, partly because despite the heavy calls of welfare spending on the public purse the Chancellor did not support it and partly because of uncontrolled in-fighting between departmental ministers. Blair was conflict-averse with his colleagues and often looked to officials to sort things out afterwards without giving a decisive ruling.[44]

In 2001 Blair was inclined not to have a committee on European Policy preferring to handle these issues informally, later rescinding his initial view but making the Foreign Secretary the chairman – against Wilson's recommendation that he should do this himself. A second recommendation – for a sub-committee of PSX to be responsible for improving performance in schools, the NHS, the police and local government – provoked: 'No. Why do we need such a committee?' But one committee to which Blair did attach importance was the Joint Consultative Committee with the Liberal Democrats (JCC) – which was a Cabinet Committee – as he tried to re-engineer the Centre-Left of British politics. At first it was ruled to be too political to be serviced by civil servants.[45] But this decision was later reversed and, as the Prime Minister was in the chair, Wilson became the senior secretary. The Secretariat noted that Blair was alone in championing the Committee; his colleagues were a reluctant and sometimes hostile presence. When Wilson queried whether the committee had outlived its usefulness in August 1999, Blair instructed that: 'It must continue.'[46]

Organisations as complex as government cannot function without co-ordinating mechanisms; that had been the distinctive genius of Hankey. Yet if the Prime Minister put committee work low down in his priorities and the government collective instinct was weak it was not surprising that Secretaries of State sometimes did not bother to attend committees, even when they had previously agreed so to do. Indiscipline had become so bad by March 2002 that the Deputy Prime Minister, John Prescott, had to remind Ministers that according to the Ministerial Code Cabinet Committee meetings should take precedence over all other business save the Privy Council (and Parliament) adding that it is important that: 'having confirmed their attendance at a particular meeting, colleagues do indeed attend ... '

Ministerial Appointments and Machinery of Government Dispositions

Though neither Wilson nor Blair had first-hand experience of organising widespread ministerial changes, at the first reshuffle on 27 July 1998 Blair asked him to sit in on meetings with incoming and outgoing Ministers as a general calming presence during the interviews. Blair's Principal Private Secretary took over the role in July the following year.[47] This position of trust stems in part from a relationship which poses no threat to the Prime Minister and in part because a Cabinet Secretary or Principal Private Secretary has more direct knowledge than a Prime Minister of how individual Ministers are perceived in their departments. In addition, the corporate memory of the Cabinet Office Secretariat and the Number 10 Private Office can be called on in the shape of a checklist of things to have in mind during the planning stage of a reshuffle.[48] Thus the advice covers the legal limits on the number of Ministers and more prosaic but very important guidance on physical arrangements, including: the advice Butler left behind: 'Experience suggests that the most important rule is: do not offer someone a post until it is vacant.'

After the first reshuffle and until the General Election of 2001 Wilson tended to recommend continuity in tenure pending big decisions about machinery of government changes. In July 1999, following the discussion of possible minor shifts in Ministerial dispositions after devolution, which raised the unwelcome spectre of a Whitsun reshuffle,[49] Wilson told Blair that the room for a major Cabinet reshuffle was very limited: 'The image of a confident Cabinet performing well with interesting new faces lining up behind them for the future could be the best outcome this Summer.'[50] And in October he again advised that the room for manoeuvre was pretty limited – offering scope only for perhaps two new faces at the Cabinet table.[51] The same message came in July 2000, recommending maximum continuity at Parliamentary Secretary level since the new departments to be launched by machinery of government changes after the General Election would mean big changes in the responsibilities of the Secretaries of State.[52]

Wilson and Blair grappled with a complex set of structural changes to government that posed severe political and organisational challenges. In July 1999 Wilson pulled the threads together from discussions with Blair of possible big changes in the structure of departments. He declared a general aversion to such changes, citing the short-term disruption they caused and the need for clarity about how the assumed benefits would be made to flow. Nevertheless, he admitted to a sense of strong pressures building up under the surface. 'Do you want some form of department for the UK? Do you need a Minister for the Cabinet Office? Do you think that MAFF has a future? Where do you see the long-term future of the Department of Social Security (DSS)? What about the Home Office?'[53] Jeremy Heywood joined in, offering a view that the Home Office/Lord Chancellor's Department split made no real sense; MAFF would be weakened by the creation of the Food Standards Agency and didn't work well anyway; the Department of the Environment, Transport and the Regions (DETR) was too unwieldy; the DSS combined 'bad' benefits (i.e. those paid to people who should be in work) and 'good' benefits paid to provide security for those who could not work. Bold solutions were needed.[54]

The most urgent change politically was to reorganise those parts of the system involved in the fight against crime. Wilson favoured the radical creation of a completely new department (justice) focused on reducing crime and built out of parts of the Home Office and the Lord Chancellor's Department. The former would be much reduced, but still busy and the latter would be 'a rather curious rump.'[55] Though difficult enough in themselves, these and other proposals were intertwined – bound with the sinews of Ministerial ambition, external vested interests and Whitehall infighting. They were coterminus because of the intricacies of Ministerial reshuffles and required delicate skills to massage egos. A second major change arose from Gordon Brown's crusade to eliminate child poverty through a switch from payment of benefits to credits against tax liabilities, with lead responsibility transferring to the Inland Revenue. In two confidential submissions Wilson came down firmly in support of Brown's vision: 'I think that Gordon Brown's long term strategy for distributing the work of the DSS between the Inland Revenue, DfEE [the Department for Education and Employment] and the Department of Health is attractive and makes a lot of sense ... and the work that we have done so far suggests that Gordon Brown is moving very much in the right direction ... [but] it is a hugely ambitious project: probably the biggest and most complex restructuring within Government ever.'[56] Yet by June there were also half a dozen or more other proposals ranging from the merger and subsequent demerger of the Inland Revenue and Customs and Excise to splitting the DETR. This was an ambitious and far-sighted attempt to reshape government wholesale, moving from a producer structure to one based on client needs.

The Working Age Agency

The most difficult change was the dismembering and reassembly of Departments to create a Working Age Agency (WAA). Wilson recognised that sensitive handling that would be required to deal with Alistair Darling (Secretary of State for Social Services and a 'Brownite') and his PUS, Rachel Lomax, to reassure them that the reorganisation would be seen as a personal success not a defeat. Its temporary shelving at the end of the year was a contributory factor in Blair's conclusion, around the time of the 2001 General Election, that the Wilson reforms were not enough to reform the civil service as fully or as quickly as he wanted.[57] Blair's vision for the WAA was one government front office dealing with adults capable of work, operating with a robust approach to moving those capable of work off benefits and into employment. The residue of the DSS (augmented by elements such as responsibility for disability policy) would form a focus for adults who were not capable of working. The Inland Revenue would take on responsibility for child welfare – based around Gordon Brown's policy for an Integrated Child Credit but also including the struggling Child Support Agency. The DfEE would retain the full range of education policies.

Ministers gave the go ahead to the WAA in late January 2000, following pilot projects.[58] An early announcement was desirable both politically and managerially but the two main Departments concerned (DSS and DfEE) could not agree on a proposed vesting date. DfEE argued for April 2001; DSS for shadow working from that date and a full launch in April 2002. Both Departments were bidding to be in the lead and differed over structure and status for the new body. It was Wilson's challenge to reconcile the two. However, Wilson had not been able to get agreement between the two Permanent Secretaries, Rachel Lomax of DSS and Michael Bichard of DfEE. He told Blair that he favoured making the WAA accountable to DfEE, and not the joint responsibility proposed in the paper from Lomax and Bichard, with a low-key early announcement before the 2000 Budget: 'that the Government's intention was to establish the new agency during 2001'. He added that it was very important that those at the top of the DfEE (Blunkett the Secretary of State and Bichard) accepted that this was the opportunity to create a completely new and innovative organisation with a new approach to client service. To that end he recommended that political leadership would be needed to drive the project given the differences between the 'Brownite'-led DSS and the 'Blairite'-led DfEE. For this task he proposed the Chief Secretary (Andrew Smith) and that: 'I personally think it is important that the Chief Executive of the new organisation should come from outside, without any presumption that the post will go to the existing chief executive of the Employment Service (Leigh Lewis), very good though he is.'[59]

In view of the intense political interest in the operation of the benefits system DSS wanted the new organisation to have a Board chaired by Ministers and in a pre-emptive move Lomax announced a 'Focus on Delivery' initiative on 29 February 2000; a plan to focus the DSS more on client groups and to bring benefits design back to the centre leaving the Benefits Agency to implement them. She told Wilson that she and Alistair Darling would be upset if single accountability under DfEE was what was decided. Both expected the creation of a new department. For its part, the DfEE argued that a Board with Ministerial membership would return to the bad old days of micromanagement, and was inconsistent with the modernising government agenda.[60] Establishment of viable business-critical systems was vital and lack of clarity made for vulnerability: 1998 a new National Insurance Recording System (NIRS) – touted at the time as the largest and most complex IT contract in Europe – had suffered a massive breakdown, erasing personal records potentially affecting up to 80,0000 benefit applications.

Political status was at the heart of the dispute. Darling wanted either an announcement of joint accountability of the Agency between himself and Blunkett (whilst recognising that this would probably be reversed later in the year) or a separate new department. Blunkett wanted only a joint responsibility for developing the new Agency to be followed by announcement of DfEE assuming responsibility.[61] Wilson favoured the latter but accepted that a temporary, but risky, face-saving fudge was needed for Darling.[62] However, when at Wilson's suggestion, Blair spoke to Darling there was no indication from either party of when the temporary joint responsibility would end.[63] Downing Street told Sebastian Wood of Wilson's private office that: '[Wilson] has succeeded in the difficult job of achieving a fair degree of consensus despite often obstructive behaviour by departments;' but also suggested that 'The biggest danger we face now is that the process becomes mired in bureaucratic infighting, ending up with a fudge. The next phase should be about designing a new agency, focused on the labour market, clear on outcomes, using personal advisers, new technologies &c rather than a negotiated merger between two existing agencies ... [with] much sharper performance monitoring ... more clearly independent [of DfEE] than they envisaged.'[64]

Blair announced 'a brand new modern agency ... with a clear focus on work ... [with] the technology to provide the most up-to-date service to more than ten million customers each year' in a Written Parliamentary Answer on 16 March, 2000.[65] No firm date was set for the launch beyond 'as soon as possible in 2001–02.' A businessman, Richard Lapthorne from British Aerospace, was appointed to design the Agency – working to a Ministerial Steering Group under Andrew Smith. Lapthorne excluded both Lomax and Bichard from his thinking about oversight of the new body[66] and operated without a shadow group of officials. Blair again saw Darling on 3 October when Darling (backed by Brown) refused to accept that the new WAA would be accountable to the DfEE. The Prime Minister's position was revealed as weakening. Wilson's role as honest broker ended and he accepted his own exclusion from Smith's Steering Group with a grace bordering on relief.[67] In the event, the matter was overtaken by wider concerns. Lapthorne summed up the deteriorating position in a letter to Wilson of 30 October. Whilst 'there is no acceptable reason why the Prime

Minister's business wishes for the agency cannot be implemented safely and professionally for the summer of 2001' it was evident that the DSS were continuing to undermine decisions taken by the Ministerial group and through the 'Focus on Delivery' initiative were attempting to implement processes to by-pass the WAA project. '... the stark truth is that there is a very high risk of failure if the key leaders in DSS continue not to accept the fundamental goal towards which we are working.' And Lapthorne went on to suggest that unless these senior figures were moved and replaced the project should be closed down at least in its current form.[68]

Shortly before the 2001 General Election Wilson told the Civil Service Senior Appointments Selection Committee (SASC) that the work to create a WAA had reached an impasse and, as a result, he had advised that the project (including their suggestion that Lewis be made CEO) should be put on ice.[69] Hence, when the announcement of machinery of government changes came, one month after the General Election of 2001, it simply recorded the creation of the Department for Work and Pensions comprising the DSS and the Employment responsibilities of the DfEE, plus disability rights. In the eyes of officials Blair had signally failed to impose a solution on Alistair Darling whom they felt thought that an early announcement would leave him looking like a lame duck.[70]

It seems likely that the problems with implementing the WAA project damaged Wilson in Blair's eyes – he saw it perhaps as an example of the civil service, 'talking the right language but shying away from the really radical measures.'[71] But unlike other fierce disagreements between departments the WAA changes involved the Blair/Brown split. It is also the case that Blair had already recognised that, in total, the machinery of government changes planned in 2000 made for a hefty morsel to bite off. Nevertheless, at a Chequers meeting with Wilson and others in early June he decided that: 'Unless we move now we never will.' Meanwhile, the HO/LCD changes were thought likely to be bitterly resisted by the judiciary, and the civil liberties lobby and the police would fight to prevent their law enforcement activities being corralled with those of the Inland Revenue and HM Customs and Excise. So whilst Wilson and those close to Blair wanted to make the changes, they continued to be worried by the spectre of planning blight, a steep fall in staff morale and possible industrial action. Wilson in particular was faced with putting forward options and trying to broker a way forward without the means to settle arguments. When machinery of government options were debated they were hampered by the lack of agreed criteria on which to judge the best way forward.[72]

The General Election (on 7 June 2001) provided the key to releasing the machinery of government logjam. It gave Blair 412 seats in the House of Commons (a very comfortable overall majority of 165). On election eve Wilson signed off a large briefing document for major machinery of government changes in anticipation of the expected Labour victory. It started with 'Welcome back!' and continued, 'You will be in as strong a position to do what you want as any Prime Minister has ever been.'[73] The document included 11 separate briefs ranging from European issues to 16 different speaking notes for Blair to use in appointing Cabinet Ministers. These speaking notes explained the reasons behind the extensive departmental structural changes, then went on to describe in detail the specific appointment, domestic arrangements, any Cabinet committees to be chaired, the structure and role of the Department(s) involved including junior Ministerial appointments (and in the case of Gordon Brown, how the new Delivery and Strategy Units in 10 Downing Street would work with the Treasury), together with a few key policy priorities.

The old DETR was broken up between a new Department for the Environment, Food and Rural Affairs (DEFRA) and a Department for Transport, Local Government and the Regions DTLR). Blair was very concerned to ensure that DEFRA was a genuinely new department and not just MAFF in a new name. Such had been the legacy from the BSE crisis that he personally scrutinised appointments to the DEFRA top team to satisfy himself that there was new blood and new personnel throughout with enhanced crisis management and delivery skills.[74]

The Lord Chancellor's Department acquired the Home Office Constitutional responsibilities (including Freedom of Information, Data Protection and Human Rights) but the mooted Ministry of Justice was not carved out until May 2007 and the first stage of the IR/HMCE merger had to wait until April 2005. The planned subsequent demerger of its law enforcement sections never happened though the new Department (HMRC) subsequently lost its powers of prosecution to the Crown Prosecution Service in January 2011.[75]

Civil Service Reform

Arguably Richard Wilson was the first Head of the Home Civil Service who understood the delivery agenda. New Labour had new needs – though it accepted most of the Thatcher reforms to improve economic efficiency it had concluded that the Conservatives under Thatcher had neglected public services and that Major had had little success in moving the government on from that legacy. Hence, New Labour would bring a new emphasis on the delivery of public services and the resulting outcomes. As Wilson had found on his first day as Cabinet Secretary, however, the Prime Minister's interest in the detail of how the bulk of services were specified and delivered was limited. He was to find over the next five years that those in Downing Street who spoke for Blair quite often did have firm views on what modernisation should entail but little experience of altering the direction of travel in a large organisation. In Wilson's words, 'They were not reformers, they had staged a political coup in the Labour Party and their approach was that of a coup against the Civil Service establishment.'[76]

At the outset Blair tasked Wilson with looking at the role of the Cabinet Office and its satellites in modernising departments.[77] His report was presented in December 1998. It proposed a Performance and Innovation Unit in the Cabinet Office to evaluate the effectiveness of policies across government on specific issues, including improvements in delivery. The report also proposed a Centre for Management and Policy Studies (including the Civil Service College at Sunningdale) to be a focus for excellence in training, research and the spread of good practice. Corporate management of the Service would be strengthened by integrating the management side of the Cabinet Office into the main department so as to work in close co-operation with departments.[78] Meanwhile, in July 1998 Wilson found out that Gordon Brown was contemplating a Modernisation of Government Fund with a budget of £150 million to 'promote innovative and more efficient ways of delivering public services through inter-Agency working', far larger than the sums being sought for the Cabinet Office.[79] Mindful of potential media stories about turf wars, and supported by the civil servants in Downing Street and by James Purnell of the Policy Unit Wilson argued that the Prime Minister's approval should be required for all projects the Modernisation Fund would finance.[80]

One important challenge was whether the government could articulate a simple, clear vision for the civil service that could be used to show the end game – 'the last 10 minutes of the film'. At Wilson's suggestion an early opportunity was created 'to give a representative group of senior civil servants from all Departments the opportunity to hear at first hand the Prime Minister and other key players talk about the Civil Service and what they want from it.'[81] Wilson organised for Blair, supported by Brown, Cunningham (Cabinet Office Minister for Civil Service reform) Miliband (Head of the Policy Unit) and Campbell (Press Secretary), to give the keynote speech at an innovative Islington Senior Civil Service Conference on 13 October 1998 on the theme of 'Modernising Central Government' under Wilson's chairmanship. Based on a draft text from Wilson, Blair put forward key objectives for the reform: (a) there should be one unified civil service for the whole of Great Britain after Devolution; (b) British officials should have close relations with their counterparts in European Union partner countries; (c) policy development, its implementation and its evaluation should be a seamless process; (d) officials should be more innovative in policy formulation; (e) new ways of working across structural boundaries must be found; (f) these ideas should be captured in a new vision for how the civil service would work in the twenty-first century; (g) senior officials should be thinking about the future and the policies that would be needed as a result.

The audience was wowed by the New Labour rhetoric. Rachel Lomax, who was no sycophant, wrote to Wilson to say that her staff judged the conference to have been a 'smash hit.' Jonathan Powell thought that it had gone exceptionally well; Blair had enjoyed his participation. David Miliband and Alastair Campbell also reported positively on the event. It was now down to Wilson to build on the momentum created. But an agreed plan was not yet in place and Permanent Secretaries were not wholly on board, wary of central direction and aware of the Blair/Brown problem. The Civil Service Management Committee set up by Wilson had met for the first time at the beginning of October and was still finding its feet. Five working groups were set up, each under a Permanent Secretary, to cover the vision and values for the future civil service, improving diversity and the opportunities for the disabled in the Service, the development of talent, performance management and business planning. Whilst Wilson had promised the Prime Minister a 'road map' to reform by Christmas 1998, by the second meeting of the Committee on 8 February 1999 there were signs that Departments were resistant to new ideas if they conflicted with existing Departmental policies.[82] They and their Ministers understandably had local priorities to follow. Wilson was not alone in experiencing this hesitancy. Powell submitted a personal note to Blair at about the same time arguing for a more directive approach:

> 'You complain, correctly, that the government machine is too unresponsive to your directions. The reason is that the system of government in this country is essentially feudal. Each of the Departments is a huge barony with its own armies, its own interests and its own priorities. They pay homage to the court at the centre, but they basically get on with their own thing. If you want it to be more responsive we need to transform it into a Napoleonic system in which there is a pyramid, with instructions flowing from a strong centre to departments, and a new incentive system which makes the departments respond. That would be a major change of our existing system. It will not be achieved easily.'[83]

Similarly, Blair's Principal Private Secretary Ivan Rogers advised the Prime Minister that: 'You need to give Richard a clear message that he needs to up the tempo on this. The Civil Service Management Committee is an unsatisfactory beast with 18 Permanent Secretary members. No outsiders. No new blood. It is four months since your Islington speech and only now, finally, are some subgroups being set up to take forward key issues.'[84]

Over the next two years a great deal of energy went into reform. Wilson faced occasional blocking from the Treasury (such as funding for better performance pay and a refusal to provide funds for redundancy, which meant that it was difficult to shift people who tried to block the changes). He felt that he was trying to move forward in the face of a headwind of indifference from the Prime Minister and his immediate staff. However, in hindsight the indications are that what Blair wanted (and what he eventually created for himself with the Delivery Unit, the associated bilateral meetings with Ministers and with the appointment of officials to champion 41 key projects) was a civil service with flexibility and focus on his priority policies such as education and crime prevention. Unsurprisingly, he was not interested in management per se, or in the day-to-day operation of Departments. What the civil service reform programme offered was a sheep-dip aimed at all of the civil service – a corporate change programme with new collective corporate governance. Though much was made of the need to focus on outcomes, inevitably the change programme itself focused on enabling actions.

Drafting the *Modernising Government* White Paper[85] was a troubled process and in Ministers' eyes allowed to drift until Brian Bender of the Cabinet Office made 'a heroic effort' to turn it around for publication.[86] Progress had to be by way of negotiation between the Permanent Secretaries led by Wilson as Head of

Profession but without the power to instruct. Fearful of perceived politicisation of the Service Blair wisely insisted that the modernisation programme had to be civil service-led. Ministers' hostility to elitism (focused on recruitment) and Departments' sensitivity to any hint of a reversal of recently delegated powers over staff did not help. The historic Parliamentary approach to control and accountability through inputs and shadowing of Departments also contributed to the difficulty of achieving what became known as 'joined up government.' In private Blair fumed at the lack of progress. Ministers needed to give more weight to ensuring that the government as a whole was successful; the Policy Unit showed daily that you did not have to be over 40 to be effective yet there were no 35–40 year old Permanent Secretaries; the legal advisers were too risk averse, gold plating the implementation of EU Directives at huge cost to small businesses.[87] When David Miliband eulogised over a 'surprisingly avant-garde New Labour position' at the Department for International Development where the focus had switched from aid to development, Blair commented: 'Are we sure they aren't crippling our trade effort by being too politically correct?'[88] But his dissatisfaction was not harnessed effectively. James Purnell[89] warned that too few people had heard the message and believed that Blair and Wilson really meant it. A root cause was the behaviour of Ministers, who, to the centre, were addicted to 'departmentalitis' and did not challenge their departments enough to wind down non-priority work. A further significant problem was that officials who opposed change could not easily be shunted out of the way.[90] Training for Ministers was introduced (only to be cancelled by Blair because of the risk of adverse publicity) and there were two full-morning seminars for Cabinet Ministers and their Permanent Secretaries to discuss how they could work better together. Blair and Wilson were joint chairmen. From the Departments' viewpoint, however, things could look different. They worried about how far they had to abandon their own modernisation initiatives, announced with fanfare and in which they had invested much personal credibility with staff and Ministers in order to adopt a sheep dip that might be less potent because more general. 'We genuinely felt our reforming ambitions for our departments about which we cared deeply were being undermined by the centre's amateurish approach.'[91]

Blair sought changes to the remuneration of the PUSs based on centrally agreed personal objectives with rewards for significant achievement as a first step to increased central influence.[92] He told Wilson that: 'It would be well worth paying a bonus of, say, £500,000 to the civil servant that sorted out the [Home Office Immigration Department] computer project. This would send a massive signal into the system.'[93] But in the first round of objectives many PUSs failed to address the key issues for modernisation or key government policy objectives, with the result that with Blair's agreement Wilson made significant changes to nine of the submissions on policy targets and gave all PUSs additional corporate targets on diversity, the Millennium Bug threat to IT systems,[94] Investors in People accreditation, meeting Public Service Agreement targets and effective arrangements for rebutting inaccurate media stories.[95] Moreover, the Chancellor opposed the idea of significant bonuses for outstanding performance[96] and by the time that Wilson submitted pay scheme proposals for Blair's approval the bonus element had been watered down.[97] Beneath all this friction lay a deeper dilemma that was not satisfactorily resolved until Michael Barber in the Delivery Unit switched the emphasis from the delivery of outcomes in society, given that these were often inevitably at the mercy of external events that the civil service could not control nor sometimes influence, to a focus on delivering agreed programmes of action, even though intermediate product.

By the end of July 1999 it was clear that despite the constancy of message and all the efforts there was still much to do to bring a step change in 'delivery' – which unhelpfully had become shorthand for the civil service modernisation objectives. Blair pronounced that he was encouraged: 'I believe the British Civil Service is the best in the world and we are already achieving miracles of change. It's just that the challenge is so great.'[98] But sympathetic media commentators were beginning to express doubts. Peter Riddell reported that the modernisation agenda was being interpreted as a move to increase Downing Street's control over the government and that Wilson's attempts to knit the Blair style with the traditional civil service could be criticised by both groups.[99]

The 1999 autumn PUS Conference, which focused on reform, got off to a depressing, if traditional, start with a shot across the bows from Treasury Ministers about avoiding decisions that would require additional expenditure.[100] Despite some overt resistance and inertia, PUSs agreed with Wilson's proposal that 'a new phase' of civil service modernisation was necessary to include: (1) stronger leadership; (2) improved business planning; (3) a step change in performance management; (4) a dramatic improvement on equal opportunities; (5) more people brought in from outside the civil service and 35% of senior jobs to be advertised openly; (6) improved development of internal talent. But there was not enough to convince Gordon Brown to invest more money in Blair's initiatives.[101] His PUS (Andrew Turnbull) had previously told Wilson that Brown, unlike Blair, did not accept the case for higher performance pay.[102] Though in December Brown did agree to an investment of £100 million for the Civil Service Modernisation Fund (which was controlled by the Treasury) over 2000/01 and 2001/02.[103]

Wilson, meanwhile, reported that by April 2000 Blair would see the beginning of a big change with targeted early retirement covering up to 80 senior people, diversity targets in each department, 100 inward secondments to the civil service, and that by 2005 65% of the Senior Civil Service (SCS) would have outside experience. There would be an electronic marketplace promoting mobility between departments, the introduction of team (in addition to personal) bonuses, and steps to ensure that future members of the SCS would have experience both of frontline operations and of working in another culture.[104] Private Office blew hot and cold, pointing out to Blair that Wilson was personally very committed to the recommendations in his note of 28 October and had stuck his neck out to go further than the package agreed at Sunningdale; but also critical of most of the proposals as too timid and failing to follow up on Wilson's own identification that the civil service no longer had the same pulling power for the nation's finest talents.[105] Blair's response was to agree that the keys to reform were: (1) attracting real talent and giving people high rewards (and honours) for real achievement; (2) exchanges with the private sector; (3) a big departure from the traditional civil service by focusing on delivery. 'Having said all that we should encourage [Richard Wilson] – it's good work – and we need to see how he presents it.'[106]

Wilson's July report showed solid progress – five important changes at PUS level; a doubling of the number of senior vacancies put to open competition from 1998/99 and two thirds filled from outside, amounting to just over 100 appointments (which represented one in three entrants to the SCS but was still consistent with the Prime Minister's Islington message that: 'a clear majority of the future leadership will be grown within the Service').[107] 180 posts had been identified for inward secondment and 1000 organisations contacted for nominees; the internal job market website was up and running; as was succession planning and 360-degree reporting for the top 150 posts; there was progress on diversity targets; a sharper focus on leadership qualities in candidates for top posts; peer review of business planning and wide acceptance that delivery mattered. But the improvements in delivery had yet to come through and central monitoring would be needed. Heywood thought that: 'frankly, it does not feel as though much has changed' pointing to large bonuses for achievement as distant as ever, PUSs as grey and old as ever and spending too little time on policy or delivery, little sign of any outbreak of joined-up thinking.[108] He wanted to redefine the role of the Minister for the Cabinet Office to become a 'delivery czar.'[109]

Autumn Sunningdale 2000 took place against a backdrop of Wilson reporting to Blair that despite the symbolic act of (literally) signing-up to the modernisation programme a year earlier the PUSs were not seen to own the modernisation programme sufficiently.[110] The meeting devoted one third of the discussions to delivery covering health, transport, crime and education, followed by new proposals for SCS pay which held out the prospect of 50% bonuses for turning round a failing organisation and more discrimination between the best performers and the rest. Distressingly, however, a report sponsored by the CMPS and the Institute for Personnel Development into how 500 employees viewed their employers indicated that those in central government had lower levels of trust in their organisations than those in local government, health or the private sector.[111] Some PUSs reported contrary evidence. In the Home Office, for example, staff surveys were reporting much improved staff confidence in management, largely because the Department was tackling racism in services like prisons and immigration/nationality. These were key priorities for the Home Secretary (Jack Straw) and his PUS (David Omand) for which they felt they were never given proper credit by Downing Street.[112]

Meanwhile, Ed Richards of the Policy Unit had been working with a 'ginger group' of Cabinet Office secretariat staff including Martin Donnelly, Jonathan Tross and David Bostock for a more radical shake-up to be implemented on day one if Labour won the anticipated General Election. Wilson had been tacitly supportive, allowing the Cabinet Office staff their head and was described the

Richards' work as 'far more radical than most of his colleagues' having 'shown a willingness to exercise leadership and is certainly up for another wave of change.'[113] The essence of what the 'ginger group' proposed was a seven-point 'manifesto': (1) Reshaping of the Home Office, LCD, DETR and DSS; (2) the CSMB to be replaced by a smaller group of 10 people with 3–4 non-executive members meeting weekly; all SCS members to be employed by the Cabinet Office and deployed across the Service to meet priority needs; (3) a Chief Secretary to the Cabinet acting as 'delivery czar' supported by a Delivery Unit in the Cabinet Office; (4) a strong central input into performance appraisal for Ministerial teams and cross-cutting units; (5) restructuring the PUS role to strengthen delivery performance and to receive external policy audits; (6) Ministers for the Government Regions who could report on delivery issues in the relevant areas and run with cross-cutting tasks regionally; (7) possibly allowing the take over of part of the work of less successful departments by the better-performing departments.

Formally Wilson was not yet involved but his thinking was being influenced. After Blair's historic electoral victory of 7 June with a net loss of only six seats and the subsequent Ministerial reshuffle Wilson drafted a letter on 'the agenda for change' for the Prime Minister to send to his Ministers.[114] It followed a discussion between the two on 12 June and proposed a Delivery Unit 'to ensure that each [priority] objective is pursued single-mindedly and relentlessly through the next few years.'[115] He proceeded to flesh out the details of a *modus operandi* for the unit to be part of the Cabinet Office.[116] However, unknown to him an internal discussion in Number 10 had come to a different view on the location of the Unit[117] so that in a rear-guard action Wilson submitted another list of actions under way to tackle civil service reform[118] and belatedly agreed that: 'My honest view is that we do not have all the people we need, with the right skills and experience, at the top. This is going to mean some tough decisions, particularly on shedding people, and on bringing in some excellent people from outside … [But] if we are serious about this we are going to have to be prepared to pay far higher salaries than we have hitherto been prepared to pay.'[119]

What David Miliband called 'TB's style of "chaos management", in [which] no one really believes they get fully managed, but they all know if they screw up they will get clobbered'[120] now blossomed more fully. The Delivery Unit (PMDU) and Office of Public Sector Reform (OPSR) were created, a Ministerial Reform Network (MRN) created at Minister of State level from five 'delivery departments' together with the Chief Secretary under the chairmanship of the Minister for the Cabinet Office. Events were now moving against Wilson. He had had no foreknowledge of the setting up of the OPSR and was left with enabling actions in support of reform rather than a place on the delivery spotlight. One of these was to encourage leading public sector figures, including the Government Chief Scientific Adviser Professor David King to stimulate better horizon scanning and risk assessment through the interdepartmental Chief Scientists Advisory Committee.[121] It was an initiative that illustrated Wilson's interest in civil science – the first Cabinet Secretary since Burke Trend to do so – amply illustrated by seminars he started at Sidney Sussex College Cambridge to bring together leading scientists, Ministers and officials to talk about current scientific advances and their implications for government policy. On the other hand Wilson strongly opposed a suggestion from Lord Sainsbury that the Chief Scientific Adviser should be able to go public with advice if he had serious concerns about the way a department was managing research or handling scientific advice. Such a new power might be important in demonstrating publicly how issues were being taken forward and thus strengthen public confidence. But it would break the normal chain of Ministerial accountability and breach the confidentiality of advice given to a Minister.

At the suggestion of Alice Perkins, the head of civil service corporate development who was located in the Cabinet Office, he launched successive programmes under the banner 'Make it Different' involving 500 SCS members each time, starting in the summer of 2002 and intended to challenge participants to think, act and lead innovation.[122] Whole-day road shows were taken to cities around the UK in a huge and groundbreaking project to roll out the reform agenda and to give individual officials a sense of involvement and personal responsibility for doing things differently. At the close of each programme Wilson would draw the threads of the table discussions together after presentation by rapporteurs to a plenary session – recognised by the PUS colleagues as an intellectual tour de force. He formed a group to determine the future strategy for reform and he successfully blocked proposals that would cut across the thrust of reform, including a recommendation from the Senior Salaries Review Body to increase target pay rates over a 22-year timespan which cut across the more urgent emphasis on pay progression implied by the reform agenda.[123] Similarly, a decision in the Domestic Affairs (Older People) Committee (DA(OP)) that would have required departments to raise the retirement age to 65 for all staff was contrary to steps being taken to bring young talent to the fore (including an informal rule that Permanent Secretaries should not stay in the same job for more than five to seven years). In combination with the Chancellor's refusal to fund early retirement packages, Wilson argued that to delay 'normal' retirement would be taken as an indication that the centre of government was half-hearted about reform.[124]

Similarly, on pay incentives for key priorities Wilson battled against a strong Departmental headwind. The Cabinet Office proposed a voluntary scheme. Wilson's attempts to put in place a radical bonus scheme to reward the 17 civil servants charged with achieving Blair's delivery priorities was: 'met with a wall of hostility from departments.' Downing Street described the Cabinet Office compromise as 'a real cop-out'. The PUSs feared micromanagement by the centre and struggled to accept a distinction between their personal objectives and the objectives of their Department as a whole. Andrew Turnbull captured the spirit of this unease in late July 2001 when he wrote to challenge the distinction between Departmental and personal objectives in the case of a permanent secretary.[125] Alice Perkins later reported that despite extensive explanation Turnbull was still unpersuaded and 'cutting up rough.'[126] Despite all the frustration at the speed of change the Blair camp did recognise Wilson's personal commitment to change, nowhere more so than in his championing of equality and diversity. When he took over as Cabinet Secretary the proportion of women in the SCS was 17.8%, that of ethnic minorities 1.6% and that of disabled people 1.5%. By the end of 2001 these had risen to 25.3%, 2.3% and 2.0% respectively. Targets had been agreed for 2004 of 35%, 3.2% and 3.0% and enabling actions set in hand. Here too Blair and his advisers were impatient with progress but the gains were not won without significant effort. Jointly with the civil service unions a charter for action to redress the under-representation of ethnic minorities in the SCS was launched in February 1999 and Permanent Secretaries asked to sign up personally to its implementation. By May Wilson was able to report action and further proposals. Nicholas Montagu from the Inland Revenue was leading a group to improve equality and diversity, including the employment of disabled people. Three departments (Home Office, Inland Revenue, Customs) had become pilot sites for establishing best practice in promoting diversity. Research had been received from Schneider Ross into barriers to entry and progress within the SCS. There were proposals for an ethnic minority recruitment fair, a mentoring scheme for ethnic minorities and inward/outward secondment schemes. A senior ethnic minority adviser was appointed. But Wilson acknowledged to Rachel Lomax that: 'We appear to have a particular challenge to meet the 35% target for women in the SCS,' when she complained that his first report to the Prime Minister on diversity had not mentioned the DSS even though 30% of its SCS and 80% of its SASC filled posts were filled by women.[127]

At the start of the second Blair term of office the foundations for a major change programme were coming together but progress was agonisingly slow. Lord Simon, formerly chairman of BP, told Blair that the programme was in good shape:

> 'The Civil Service reform programme is working. I have no doubt of it. People won't praise it because they don't realise the yardstick against which you are measuring yourselves. This is bigger than most things in the private sector. You need to have confidence in what you have achieved and in the continuing programme.'[128]

But the rate of progress was not good enough for the Prime Minister as he contemplated the limits on what had been achieved in his first term and his political weakness in the face of the Chancellor's use of the CSR and PSA to further his own domestic agenda and in the face of the constitutional independence of Secretaries of State. As he returned to Downing Street after the election, Wilson told Blair that he would never be more powerful than at the moment he won a second consecutive term of office. The Prime Minister wondered whether now was the time to consolidate the energies of the centre by merging Downing Street and the Cabinet Office. The prospect had long been debated. It would be a Prime Minister's Department in all but name.

The Centre

Shortly before Wilson took over from Butler Peter Mandelson, then Minister without Portfolio in the Cabinet Office, put three options to Blair for the Cabinet Office:

1. To reorientate the Cabinet Secretariat to a more proactive strategic role under your direction;
2. To streamline and revamp the Office of Public Service [part of the Cabinet Office] as the arm of central government focusing on questions of organisation and structure across Whitehall, while the Cabinet Secretariat and Policy Unit help you to develop the strategy;
3. To go for the radical option of a Department of the Prime Minister.[129]

Wilson's diagnosis did not differ from that of Blair: a government that was weak at linking policy formulation and execution, poor at handling cross departmental issues, where short-term decisions were taken in isolation from long-term strategy, where there was little evaluation of policy outcomes against original objectives and where there was a yawning gap where there should be a corporate headquarters for the Home Civil Service.[130] But the prescriptions diverged. Blair's preference was closest to the last of the three options – which was also Mandelson's recommendation – Napoleonic 'Command and Control' direct from 10 Downing Street into Departments. But this cut across the constitutional grain in a way that the Prime Minister found hard to understand. Butler and Wilson favoured the second option, fearful of the first because of the potential damage to the perceived interdepartmental neutrality which they saw as key to the Cabinet Office's influence with semi-autonomous departments responsible to Secretaries of State who had constitutional responsibilities to Parliament in their own right. It was a fault line that marked an unbridgeable gap.

By February 1999 the Permanent Secretaries were reporting at their Wednesday morning get-together with Wilson that, in a more testing policy environment with resourcing difficulties, collective mechanisms were failing and Downing Street was more controlling than empowering.[131] Blair's voice had become fragmented through widespread use by Special Advisers of the mantra: 'What Tony wants.' All of which reinforced Wilson's determination to preserve in the background the skills needed for a return to classic Cabinet collective government whilst supporting Blair's immediate instincts. In April 1998 he had started a weekly listing of the state of play on the most important current issues – an initiative warmly welcomed with Blair annotating the first submission: 'This is just what I need.' But a week after the Wednesday morning meeting of PUSs of 26 February 1999, Wilson fired a broadside: 'I sense a lack of intuition for political danger in the Government, a curious belief in its own inviolability and a dangerous view that conventions are for wimps'[132] and he submitted three powerful analyses: '*Getting the Best out of the Government*,' '*Getting Departments to Respond*' and '*Improving Rebuttal*'.[133] The proposals included appointing a

Minister to chair meetings on Blair's behalf, aimed at improving feelings of collective involvement by ensuring that everyone had their say and then taking decisions so departments knew exactly what they had to do. Blair commented: 'We need to discuss this, because I don't understand how our system differs from other Governments.'[134] As Hugo Young would comment, government under Blair lived in a Parliamentary system whilst harbouring a presidential impulse.

Other proposals from Wilson were better use of Blair's personal political power to bring forward a sequence of thought-through big, new policy ideas at careful intervals; action to demonstrate that Blair was the senior partner in the relationship with Brown; personal objectives for Permanent Secretaries that were directly related to delivering the government's desired outcomes and linked to their pay (together with a presumption that senior officials would not stay in one post for more than five to seven years); 24-hour Departmental monitoring of the media with a rebuttal capability against hostile news.

A fourth heartfelt submission '*The Nature of Power*' was so sensitive that Wilson handed a copy to Blair personally rather than allow it to go through normal channels where the Private Office and perhaps others in 10 Downing Street would see it. The document contained some of the most powerful examples of truth unto power on record: 'You have the levers to hand. You choose not to pull them. (1) Do not try to use the Policy Unit to run the Government; (2) do not attempt to divorce Permanent Secretaries from their Cabinet Ministers; (3) do not be tempted by Napoleonic models, shifting resources such as the PIU from the Cabinet Office to No 10; (4) above all do not spend too much time on foreign affairs. It is of course fun, and much easier than domestic policy. But the FCO is only one of 20 departments and wins you the fewest votes.'[135] Wilson's Permanent Secretary colleagues had no idea at the time that he was giving such tough advice and did not realise quite how hard it was behind the scenes.[136]

Blair was assailed by often contradictory ideas and it is likely that he did not read Wilson's four submissions. Nor was he ready to act – he believed that the problem was with departmental officials rather than politicians.[137] So much so that Powell told him: 'you need to decide what you want to do;'[138] and the action plan for a project to 'create a better structure to get collective agreement to policy' could only register: 'You are considering this.'[139] Heywood argued that 'we need to change departments' incentives and priorities so they do what we want voluntarily.'[140] Powell argued that: 'we need to bind Richard Wilson in more, the Economic and Domestic Secretariat is the problem in the Cabinet Office.'[141] However, Blair's working habits included a running levee in his den or in the flat so that what started as an informal meeting on one subject would migrate to other subjects seamlessly as courtiers came and went and telephone calls were made, making it very difficult for Wilson and the Cabinet Office Secretariat members to keep up with the hunt and maintain adequate records.[142] Also, the Treasury tactic was to keep money tight for 10 Downing Street and the Cabinet Office with the result that, as Downing Street took precedence, the Cabinet Office was further squeezed (even to the extent of not being able to afford licences to upgrade its Microsoft software).[143] Whilst Downing Street felt that the Secretariats were too even-handed, they felt undermined and disempowered by the behaviour of those closest to Blair.[144] Willie Rickett (the Head of the EDS Secretariat) argued: 'we must get Departments to deliver, not just strengthen No 10,' and made proposals for building a corporate culture in the Cabinet Office.[145] John Sawers (Foreign Affairs Private Secretary) argued that No 10 needed strengthening on foreign policy issues; its role needed better definition, but also that Cabinet Ministers needed more involvement in collective policy making and should shape policy at an earlier stage, looking further ahead, quoting policy towards Russia as an example.[146] David Miliband identified that Downing Street resources needed to be better mobilised: too often issues were raised but not dealt with and the Cabinet Office Secretariats stood to one side.[147]

A year after Wilson's mammoth submissions on how to run government the position had not improved. Powell expostulated that the centre was dysfunctional – the Treasury had become over dominant; the status quo was unrealistic and the process of government 'in disarray'; Blair had neither managed nor been managed in a large organisation – and it showed – he did not mind getting multiple advice on a topic because then he could choose the one he liked best.[148] Argument continued throughout 2000. What the Prime Minster was edging towards was a merger of Downing Street and the Cabinet Office. He continued to talk the issues through with Wilson who, for his part, looked for ways of meeting the Prime Minister's wishes whilst protecting the constitutional position. It was clear to all in Downing Street and in the Cabinet Office that should Labour be returned for a second term there would be changes at the centre. On 7 February 2001 Wilson advised: 'My own view is that you should draw a line under your first term and do the second term differently. This does not mean that you got your first term wrong but that it is the beginning of a new phase.'[149] He speculated about the advantages of moving the office accommodation from Downing Street to Old Admiralty Building: 'My perception is that you have never really been comfortable with the working patterns which the layout of Number 10 dictate[s] ... A change in accommodation would be a dramatic way of signalling change,'[150] and went on to provide detailed internal reorganisation proposals and advice on further regularising the use of political advisers to distinguish non-political experts, those would work partly for the Labour Party and party for the government, and those who would be employed as temporary civil servant key advisers to Ministers.

24 hours later things were back in the melting pot. Blair offered Wilson the official leadership of a merged Downing Street/Cabinet Office. But acutely aware both of the constitutional position and the political furore that was likely to follow such a move Wilson demurred: 'I am a bit worried from our conversation that I am not understanding clearly what it is you want,' he wrote. 'From our telephone conversation just now I think I may be barking up the wrong tree, and that what concerns you is the organisation of work under the people whom you deal with directly in Number 10.'[151] Conversation continued, with Wilson registering concern about emerging proposals for all the work of Number 10 to

be grouped under three political appointees: Alastair Campbell on communications; Anji Hunter on political management and Jonathan Powell on government and strategy.[152] A further message to Blair was hard-hitting, delivered through a note to the Principal Private Secretary, not directly. In it Wilson accepted that there was a case for strengthening and rationalisation in three areas: day-to-day operations, delivery, and forward strategy. He went on, however, to spell out that by law the Prime Minister had virtually no executive powers, finance flowed from Parliament to Secretaries of State via the Treasury, the more the Prime Minister moved towards an executive role the more vulnerable he would be to attacks in Parliament, and although political colleagues might be quiescent for the present they could never be taken for granted. Quoting Blair's words back at him Wilson added: 'These constraints are hard facts, not surreal pieces of theology ... I am very strongly opposed to merging the Cabinet Office and Number 10 ... [and] I believe strongly that a system in which power is distributed reasonably evenly and operated by collective agreement is vastly preferable to one in which it is concentrated in one Office.'[153] Few Permanent Secretaries knew the precise way in which the poisoned chalice of a Prime Minister's Department had been offered to Wilson but most knew of, and supported, his stand.

Finally, on 16 March Heywood was able to record broad agreement to brigade Number 10 staff as: (1) domestic operations (headed by Heywood and formed out of Private Office and the Policy Unit); (2) EU issues; (3) Foreign policy and defence; (4) Delivery – a new element that would negotiate and monitor outcome targets in areas of key priority to the government (initially health, education, transport, law and order); and (5) Strategy. Jonathan Powell would remain Chief of Staff; there would be no merger with the Cabinet Office. The Order-in-Council that allowed Powell and Campbell to manage civil servants directly would not be renewed provided that it was understood that they could ask officials to carry out tasks (whilst respecting their political neutrality). The scope and plans of the new Delivery Unit were settled amicably and relatively quickly after an initial flurry with Gordon Brown over possible conflict with the Public Service Agreements. The Unit was announced under a banner of Agenda for Change late in June. It is clear from the text of that announcement (and from a warning note to Blair of 1 June about Wilson not being in the know) that a further innovation, a freestanding Office of Public Service Reform (OPSR), was to be created without consultation with Wilson on the principle or the practicalities. He had no hand in its concept, or in the choice of its head (Wendy Thompson, formerly of the Audit Commission). The first he knew of the proposal was on 13 June at the conclusion of a 6 pm meeting with Blair about setting up the Delivery Unit, when Blair and he had ten minutes alone on civil service reform. Wilson recalls that Blair 'treated me like a grenade with the pin pulled out.'

On 20 June Wilson and Heywood saw Thompson and she saw the Prime Minister at 8.45 am the following day. Wilson was present and, characteristically, Blair asked him to describe the nature of the new unit, thereby binding him into the new structure. There were eight Wilson/Thompson meetings over the course of 2001 and a further four in the first five months of 2002 all aimed at shaping a role for the Office. The appointment (styled by Thompson as the Prime Minister's chief adviser on public service reform) was a public humiliation for Wilson, visible to PUS colleagues and weakening his clout in holding them to account for delivering against the Prime Minister's priorities. Increasingly after 14 February 2001 when Wilson had revealed to PUS colleagues the full story of the second Mandelson sacking and his advice against that course of action, the Permanent Secretaries sensed that Wilson had become less able to protect their backs than before.[154] Corridor talk began to reflect a view that the relationship with Blair had broken down and, mistakenly, that Wilson now seldom saw Blair, whereas the Monday tête-a-tête and his involvement in crisis management continued unabated.

John Major had struggled to control the allegations of sleaze that dogged his government. Press scrutiny of the Blair administration followed on. On 5 November 1997 a story broke that Max Moseley (president of the Fédération Internationale de l'Automobile) and Bernie Ecclestone (CEO of Formula 1 racing (F1) and a significant Labour Party donor) had successfully lobbied for exemption of F1 from a proposed ban on tobacco advertising. In July 1998 *The Observer* ran a story about claims of influence on Ministers from former Labour political advisers. Alastair Campbell recorded that: 'we were kidding ourselves if we didn't realise there were people who used to work for us who were now in companies pushing on government the whole time, and abusing the circumstances,'[155] and, 'I felt that though the detail may be wrong, there was enough in the general point for us to be worried about.'[156] Blair responded in writing marked as strictly personal – 'get Wilson to enforce a new culture in all departments and ensure all colleagues [i.e. Ministers] review their arrangements to make sure they are squeaky clean [and] Tell our own folks they have, from now on, to be very careful indeed. We are all too talkative and indiscreet.'[157] The choice of words is important. Wilson was to ensure that *Ministers reviewed their arrangements* – there was nothing to suggest that the Cabinet Secretary had a role in investigating those arrangements or allegations of misbehaviour. Ministers were responsible for policing and accounting for their own compliance with the Ministerial Code.

The Geoffrey Robinson Affair

On 23 December 1998 Peter Mandelson (Secretary of State for Trade and Industry) and Geoffrey Robinson (the Paymaster General based in the Treasury) resigned over a private loan of £300,000 from Robinson to Mandelson that looked as if it could have compromised Mandelson's position as Secretary of State for Trade. Robinson revealed that on 27 July 1998 Wilson had brought him a message that the Prime Minister wanted him to resign.[158] Wilson was criticised by the media for carrying a resignation message to a Minister. On the face of it, to have done so sits oddly with Wilson's repeated call that it was for Ministers to judge their own behaviour against the Ministerial Code and for the Prime Minister in the last resort to take a view whether they had transgressed sufficiently to merit dismissal.

However, Wilson describes the situation somewhat differently. He says that he went to see Robinson on the Prime Minister's behalf because Blair and his entourage were reluctant to do so (Gordon Brown, a close ally of Robinson, had cancelled a meeting between Blair and Robinson and had given instructions that no calls from Number 10 were to be put through). In essence Wilson's task in seeing Robinson was to ask him to go and see Blair and to remind Robinson that he had said that his job was at the Prime Minister's disposal if Blair ever wanted to sack him. He accepted the task because he felt it was important to demonstrate that this was Blair's Administration and that Blair was the senior partner in it.[159] His action was at first greeted with acclaim by Downing Street when he returned from the talk with Robinson but he was then undermined the following morning by Blair who saw Robinson and subsequently wrote: 'As you had indicated to me and I agreed, it would be better to leave any change until September when there would be a good personal reason for it and when you could leave your job as a Minister but continue in the government as Chair of a [Public-Private Partnership] Task Force based in the Cabinet Office.'[160]

There were a number of allegations and inquiries into Robinson's business affairs. He was twice cleared of charges that he breached the rules of the House of Commons, but criticised for the state of financial accounts in Hollis Industries plc of which he was chairman.[161] Shortly afterwards it emerged that Hollis shares had been sold to Robert Maxwell unbeknown to Robinson,[162] fuelling further doubts whether it was appropriate for him to remain a Minister.[163] Powell described Robinson's explanations, 'as usual, about as clear as mud.'[164] Robinson resigned on 23 December. His letter of resignation said: 'There comes a time when, after more than twelve months of a highly charged political campaign, the point has been reached when I feel it is no longer right that you or your Government should be affected by or have to contend with these attacks.'[165] The Conservative MP Peter Lilley wrote to Wilson about his role in assessing Robinson's suitability as a Minister and in Parliament Geoffrey Clifton-Brown MP, speaking of the Robinson affair, said; 'I know that this matter should be investigated by the Permanent Secretary of the Department concerned, and ultimately by the Cabinet Secretary ... '[166] In both cases Wilson sought to put the record straight by re-emphasising that: 'Ministers are themselves responsible for ensuring their own compliance with the Ministerial Code and for justifying their conduct to Parliament, as the Code makes clear. It is not, and never has been, the job of the Civil Service to enforce compliance with the Code or to be the arbiter of the propriety of Ministers' financial arrangements although Permanent Secretaries are of course available to give advice in confidence where their Ministers seek it.'[167]

Subsequently, in November 1999 Robinson suggested to Blair that Wilson had instructed the DTI to conduct a fact-finding investigation under Section 447 of the Companies Act 1985 into Hollis Industries plc.[168] Wilson submitted a draft letter for Blair to send to Robinson refuting the allegation and then provided a detailed account of the origins of the DTI inquiry, which spelled out: 'Just to repeat, for the record, Michael Scholar [PUS at DTI] never asked me for a view on whether or not DTI should investigate Geoffrey Robinson and I never gave him one … Michael Scholar did tell me what decision he had taken after he had taken it, because Geoffrey Robinson was a government Minister, which I passed on to you. He also did discuss with me briefly, after he had taken the decision, the arrangements for keeping Peter Mandelson away from the investigation.'[169] Blair commented; 'This destroys his [Robinson's] belief that Ministers or you [Wilson] were involved in [this] nonsense. I'd like to tell him so.'[170] In the event DTI officials concluded that there was insufficient evidence of possible criminal offences to merit further investigation.[171] Meanwhile the letter with a detailed rebuttal of the allegations that Number 10 and/or the Cabinet Secretary instigated the investigation for political motives was sent to Robinson by the DTI PUS Michael Scholar and validated by a shorter note from Blair to Robinson – sent by a curious coincidence on the first anniversary to the day of Robinson's resignation.[172]

The Hinduja Passport Affair

Shortly after Wilson's role in the resignation of Geoffrey Robinson had been put to bed publicly Blair asked him to ascertain the facts behind an emerging allegation that Peter Mandelson (now reinstated in the government as Secretary of State for Northern Ireland) had lobbied the Home Office in 1998 when Secretary of State for Trade to grant a British passport to one of three Hinduja brothers in return for the Hinduja Foundation donation to the Faith Zone of the Millennium Dome.[173] After consulting the Home Office and seeking Mandelson's account via the PUS of the Northern Ireland Office (NIO) Wilson reported that:

> 'My best guess is that this case falls into the slippery area where a Minister, having official dealings with someone, coincidentally and separately … passes on a question about an application for a passport from that person to the Home Office … Home Office Ministers and Mr Mandelson have made clear their view that he did nothing improper … no one has produced a shred of evidence that anything improper took place.'[174]

Mandelson was not a copy addressee of Wilson's submission to Blair and the following day, despite Wilson's exoneration, Blair accepted Mandelson's resignation because of the damage continuing speculation would be likely to do to the government's reputation. (Two of the Hinduja brothers had written regularly to the Prime Minister, who had attended a number of events in which they had been involved.) To Blair's irritation Private Office records and the memories of the Ministers concerned had proved to be inconsistent over an alleged conversation between Mandelson and the Home Office junior Minister (Mike O'Brien) who handled naturalisation requests at the relevant time. The air needed to be cleared. So, on 24 January Blair asked Sir Anthony Hammond QC a former Treasury Solicitor to review the full circumstances surrounding the approaches to the Home Office about the possibility of granting British passports to the Hinduja brothers. There was some speculation around this time that Wilson had recommended that Mandelson should be asked to go. Mandelson contacted Wilson on

28 February reporting that the columnist Hugo Young had asked directly about how Wilson had been involved. 'I think the record will be redressed as far as you are concerned and that is only just,' Mandelson wrote.[175] In fact, after his report of 23 January, Wilson's involvement had been procedural, including attendance at a meeting with Blair at which possible candidates to lead the inquiry were discussed.

Hammond reported on 9 March 2001,[176] concluding that the applications for naturalisation had been handled properly and within established criteria; no improper pressure had been brought to bear by any Minister though there had been lapses in record keeping by the Private Offices concerned. But the story was not to end there. A complaint about Ministerial behaviour was made to the Parliamentary Ombudsman (PCA) who was granted access to the papers concerning the naturalisation applications. Two difficulties then arose. Additional documents surfaced from Mandelson's private papers in the form of an exchange of notes with his Private Office about contacts with the Home Office that Mandelson believed provided further evidence of his innocence[177] (though neither Downing Street officials nor Wilson thought they cleared him in the way he suggested).[178] Then later in the month the PCA complained that he had not had full access to Home Office papers.[179] Blair was horrified: 'We cannot have a PCA report in these terms,' he wrote, urging John Gieve at the Home Office to ensure personally that the Home Office co-operated fully with the PCA.[180] Wilson decided to ask Hammond to reopen his inquiry to review the new material provided by Mandelson and this Hammond agreed to do in private.[181] Meanwhile Mandelson also voiced reservations: 'There is a fundamental injustice which resulted in my ejection from office – a 'muddle' as the Prime Minister puts it – and I have to recognise that the possibility of this being remedied by anything Sir Anthony says is remote … Reluctantly, I must ask you not to pursue the matter further.'[182] Only to be told that the Prime Minister had taken the view that in the interests of good government Hammond should be asked to review his earlier conclusions in the light of the new evidence.[183] When Hammond reported for the second time on 25 February 2002 he was at pains to say that the question of whether Mandelson had spoken to O'Brien was 'intrinsically insignificant,' what mattered was whether the application for naturalisation had been handled properly and the newly discovered papers did not affect his original conclusion that that was the case.[184] Mandelson welcomed the clearance of his name in connection with 'my forced resignation.'[185]

The Committee on Standards in Public Life

John Major set up the Committee in October 1994 in the aftermath of the 'cash for questions' scandal that had cost Neil Hamilton and Tim Smith their political careers. It was charged with examining current concerns about standards of conduct across a broad swathe of the public sector and with recommending changes to ensure the highest standards in public life. What was ambiguous, however, was whether the Committee could undertake investigations in its own right or whether it could only act on referrals by government. A linked ambiguity was whether the Committee was in continuous session or whether it should only meet when undertaking a specific inquiry. The original chairman, Lord Nolan, stood down in late 1997, to be replaced by Sir Patrick Neill QC. Over the next five years Sir Patrick battled determinedly for the Committee to have a degree of independence from the Executive in the choice of subjects to investigate. This intention surfaced at Wilson's first meeting with Neill on 25 June 1998 when, reporting progress on the government's proposals of summer 1997 for an inquiry into the funding of political parties, Neill said he was considering the possibility of an inquiry into the police, causing Wilson to swallow hard and emphasise the number or people who would have to be brought on side for an inquiry to succeed.[186] They met again on 6 October. Neill ran through the Committee's recommendations on Party funding – described by Downing Street as a 'surprisingly radical' step change in transparency.[187] Neill admitted that the Committee had not yet been able to give much thought to its future work programme but again spoke of a possible inquiry into the police, once again receiving a lukewarm reaction from Wilson.

Neill was starting to prove a handful for the government. Blair's internal response to the report on Party funding, was: 'Clearly we should welcome the report while not committing ourselves to implement every single detailed proposal that it makes.'[188] The government would not include a Bill in the 1998–99 legislative programme but promised to publish a draft Bill before the Summer Recess of 1999. Amongst other things, the report contained 11 recommendations on the conduct of referendums including a strongly worded requirement that:

> 'The government of the day in future referendums should, as a government, remain neutral and should not distribute at public expense literature, even purportedly 'factual' literature, setting out or otherwise promoting its case.'

The contrast with the conduct of the 1975 Referendum on the renegotiated terms of Britain's membership of the Common Market was marked. Wilson recorded a personal view that it was perfectly proper for the government to state its views on the subject matter of a forthcoming referendum and to use government resources to do so provided this did not happen during or so close to the vote that it was accused of attempting to steamroller the outcome.[189]

Meanwhile the Neill Committee took the initiative in announcing that it intended to consider the implementation of recommendations in its first report on civil servants and their relationship with Ministers and referred to itself as a Standing Committee, promising more details of its planned programme of work for later in the year.[190] Wilson submitted a carefully worded recommendation to Blair that the Committee should be asked to concentrate on House of Lords arrangements for dealing with conflicts of interest and on propriety relating to British Members of the European Parliament. Thereafter, he thought, its remit and way of working could be changed. As Jonathan Powell interpreted it, when Neill had tentatively suggested that the Cabinet Secretary should not get involved in issues of Ministerial behaviour Wilson had 'told him to get lost;' and on the future work programme had told Neill that: 'we decide the subjects for investigation not them.' Downing Street was for putting the committee on a care and maintenance basis as soon as possible.[191] Blair scrawled: '... there is a point of principle. Who runs this committee?' and instructed Wilson to see Neill to clear the air.[192]

The fifth anniversary of the Committee fell in October 1999 and, in common with other Non-Departmental Public Bodies, a Quinquennial Review of its performance and rationale was due.[193] Faced with advice that, despite the general view of those outside government who valued the independence of the Committee, the Downing Street view was hardening in favour of winding it up. Wilson insisted that a review should go ahead without a prior decision on the outcome.[194] He asked Philip Colcutt (a Cabinet Office official appointed reviewer) to consider replacing the Committee with a body comprising the heads of the various ethics bodies (the Business Appointments Committee, the Commissioner for Public Appointments, The First Civil Service Commissioner, the Political Honours Scrutiny Committee and the Appointments Commission). The benefits of such an approach would be that a reformulation could be used to spread best practice and would be seen as a constructive gesture towards a committee that was already looking for a compromise over tasking.[195] Hence, by January 2000 Wilson was able to suggest a six-point approach: a relatively innocuous topic to see out the present membership of the Committee (all bar one of whom would come to the end of their term by the end of the year); appoint a new chairman (Sir Nigel Wicks was appointed as Lord Neill's successor on 29 January 2001 following a public competition); bring on board new members acceptable to the government; reach an understanding with the Committee that subjects would proceed only on the basis of mutual agreement (accepted by Wicks on 5 September 2001); reach an understanding that the Committee does not have to be in constant session; confirm that it is not part of the remit to investigate or comment on individual cases.[196]

The 'innocuous topic' turned out to cause more of a stir than had been imagined. A minor constitutional storm blew up when Neill announced a review to consider arrangements governing the conduct of members of the House of Lords (in particular avoiding conflicts of interest). Viscount Cranborne, supported by a lengthy column from William Rees-Mogg in *The Times*, argued that this was: 'a matter which seems to me to reflect directly on the right of the House to regulate its own affairs.' Neill pointed out that in 1994 Cranborne himself had said that the House of Lords was within the scope of the Committee; provoking a revealing admission from Cranborne that when presenting the Conservative government's proposals in October 1994 he had loyally omitted that privately he thought it was outrageous that either House of Parliament should meekly accept that it should be investigated by a committee set up under the Royal Prerogative.[197] Wilson told Neill that he sympathised with his predicament – the current row was scarcely credible – and he would ask the Prime Minister to underline the Committee's independence.[198] Neill agreed to press on, adopting the position that the Committee was just doing its job and it would carry on doing it. (In private Labour accused Tory peers of running scared of greater scrutiny.)[199]

The results of Colcutt's Quinquennial Review were released in January 2001. They included a conclusion that: 'the Committee should continue in its present form for the time being. [The Review] notes that there may not always be a need for the Committee to be continuously involved in a full-time enquiry but that in the future less active periods of monitoring may be called for.'[200] With one exception that marked the end of government squabbling with the Committee over its remit and procedures. In July 2002 when the Committee wanted to summon Downing Street staff as witnesses for its inquiry into the structure of the Executive Wilson proposed a response that said the government would prefer the staff to decline to appear as managerial responsibility appropriately rested with Ministers, Permanent Secretaries and the Cabinet Secretary who should be the people to give evidence.[201] The Committee had not been tamed, however. Two ongoing inquiries continued to cause difficulties for the government – who should investigate and who should be the judge of alleged Ministerial breaches of the Ministerial Code and how to control the behaviour of Ministers' Special Advisers (SPADS).

Neill believed that Ministers should be subject to external invigilation in cases of alleged scandal;[202] which left Wilson in a difficult position. He was not willing to see outside incursion into one of the areas where the Cabinet Secretary traditionally played a role as confidante to a Prime Minister; equally, however, he did not want to be set up in judgement of Ministerial behaviour.[203] Twice he had persuaded Neill not to include the handling of allegations of Ministerial or SPAD misconduct. But the resignations of Geoffrey Robinson and Peter Mandelson caused Neill to want to reopen the issues as he thought it would look very odd if the Committee were not to address them. Wilson did not think it wise to go back a third time to try to persuade Neill to drop these topics and added: 'Apart from anything else, the David Hencke article of 23 December [in *The Guardian*] to which [Neill] refers was critical of me personally for my role in the Mandelson affair (on a misunderstanding of what I actually did). I do not want it to be thought that I am trying to protect myself from proper scrutiny.'[204] Rather better would be to let the Committee do what they thought right but encourage Neill to conduct both aspects in as general and low key a way as possible, keeping in close touch with the government given the sensitivities and the Prime Minister's personal responsibility for the conduct of Ministers.[205] Blair agreed to speak to Neill on these lines.[206] Nevertheless, on 29 January Neill put on record to the Prime Minister the Committee's determination to press ahead.[207] Six weeks later the Committee published an issues and questions paper.

It was important to preserve the position whereby Ministers were responsible and accountable for their own conduct. Hence, in answering Parliamentary Questions the Prime Minister must not say that he had asked the Cabinet Secretary to investigate or make enquiries in relation to Peter Mandelson at the DTI or any such investigations more generally, as this would be untrue and would amount to misleading the House.[208] Wilson re-emphasised the point to Permanent

Secretaries at the end of July[209] and to the Neill Committee on 12 January 2000.[210] Nor would it be wise for the Prime Minister to refer to an examination by the Parliamentary Commissioner of Standards of an allegation that the Deputy Prime Minister had failed to register an interest in a flat in his declaration of interests as this could be taken to imply that she was an arbiter on the Ministerial Code.[211] As the Committee's deliberations proceeded Neill rehearsed with Wilson that they were minded to repeat a recommendation from the First Report of the Nolan Committee that whilst it was for Ministers to judge how best to act in order to uphold the highest standards it was for the Prime Minister to determine whether or not they had done so in any particular circumstance. The then Labour government had rejected the idea on the grounds that it suggested the Prime Minister's relationship with Ministerial colleagues was that of 'invigilator and judge'[212] and this proved to be a long-running sore. In July 2000 Wilson warned that 'We are heading for awkward territory with [the response to] the Neill committee [6th Report] – in particular with regard to the Prime Minister's role in relation to other Ministers, the Committee's call for a Civil Service Act and its call for a Code of behaviour for SPADS including a legal cap on numbers.[213]

There were signs of fracturing in Ministerial ranks; Prescott thought that the Prime Minister should be the judge of Ministerial behaviour but Blunkett suggested a committee of Privy Counsellors to rule on alleged breaches of the Ministerial Code.[214] Both were rejected. In addition, the Public Administration Select Committee favoured an independent watchdog for the Code.[215] However, after some to-ing and fro-ing with Neill Blair acknowledged that he did get involved in major cases where his confidence in a colleague might be called into question.[216] Neill wanted to make Blair's acknowledgement public[217] but later settled for the Ministerial Code making the Prime Minister's involvement in the most serious cases clear.[218] On SPAD numbers Blair was minded to accept the recommendation for a limit but not to say what it was.[219] Initially he favoured accepting a distinction between political advisers and expert advisers but reversed his position after a powerful intervention by Gordon Brown who argued that political advisers were often experts too.[220]

When Nigel Wicks replaced Lord Neill he gave Wilson a first taste of the likely future focus of the Committee. Two key areas would be MPs relationship with Parliament, where a high-powered Standards and Privileges Committee with a commanding chairman not drawn from the government's supporters was needed, and revision of the Ministerial Code to make clear that the Prime Minister was the final arbiter in cases of alleged serious Ministerial misconduct. Additionally, the Committee were interested in having a rolling benchmark showing the perception of British citizens of ethical standards in public life.[221] Meanwhile, after a strong note from Powell about public suspicions of politicians involvement with sleaze[222] Blair asked Wilson to undertake work for announcements shortly after the 2001 Election on a revised Ministerial Code, clear guidance and advice on ethical issues for Ministers on taking office, and a new code for SPADS to include coverage of relationships with lobbyists.

However, at this stage Blair rejected an idea first put up by Wilson and Wicks (in an earlier incarnation) in December 1997 and resurrected in March 2001 for an independent commissioner on ethics.[223] A watered-down proposal for a commissioner with only an advisory remit was finally accepted in September 2003. The Wicks Committee started an inquiry into SPADS in March 2002 issuing a consultation paper.[224] Wilson submitted a draft government response in May; Blair and his advisers found it too focused on SPADS, wishing to widen the response to take in civil service reform and international comparisons of the support available to heads of government.

Whistle-Blowers and Memoirs

Amongst the unfinished business left by Butler was the handling of allegations made by David Shayler about his former employer MI5 and by Richard Tomlinson, formerly of the Secret Intelligence Service (SIS or MI6). Their claims were at least as explosive as those made by the discredited Peter Wright, which had been so troublesome to Robert Armstrong. Butler had been determined not to become mired in a similar situation to that suffered by Armstrong, but towards the end of his ten-year tenure, on 24 August 1997, *The Mail on Sunday* published allegations by Shayler about Security Service files on prominent politicians and others. Then at the end of August 1998 Richard Tomlinson absconded after serving five months of a 12-month sentence imposed in 1997 under the Official Secrets Act (OSA) for giving the synopsis of a proposed book describing his career in SIS to an Australian publisher. Aware of the trouble that had befallen Armstrong in trying to pursue the hard line sanctioned by Thatcher, Butler advised a positive but cautious response to an approach from Shayler's solicitor to explore the scope for a deal.[225] The overriding objective was to find a way of preventing Shayler from further publication and to avoid encouraging any other disaffected members of the intelligence agencies from making disclosures. Although Shayler had fled the country, Blair felt 'very robust about the basic principle' and that 'we don't want to give any solace to [Shayler].' This was the lie of the land when Wilson took over.

The lawyers' talks came to nothing. During the first week of August 1998 Tomlinson and Shayler were both detained temporarily but separately, by the French police. At the suggestion of the Home Office the Cabinet Office took over the interdepartmental lead in coordinating the handling of their cases in Whitehall. Above all, government wanted to stop the damage from the vehemence and, as government saw it, untrustworthiness of both men but repeatedly found that the law did not quite provide the means of doing so. In the case of Shayler, Wilson was asked to adjudicate between prosecution and negotiation. He concluded that negotiation was the least bad option and suggested that the Attorney General should review other current cases, in the expectation that it would show government to be in a weaker position than anyone would like.[226] At first Blair reluctantly agreed to proceed by negotiation: 'we should nonetheless protest vigorously at this appalling man.' but then switched to being pro-prosecution. Arguments continued to seesaw between negotiation and prosecution ending with the arrest of Shayler on 21 August 2000 on his return to the UK. Blair became frustrated at government's failure to rebut 'press nonsense' on Shayler and to put across the positive need for the agencies to require absolute confidentiality from their employees.[227] As Wilson pointed out, however, the silence of government spokesmen was the direct result of the Attorney General's advice to avoid saying something that might prejudice Shayler's trial, also pointing out that an Intelligence and Security Commission (ISC) investigator had concluded that Shayler's allegations about the Security Service's use of IT could be discounted as unjustified. The Attorney General, meanwhile, had unsuccessfully advised the Home Secretary to drop the case against Shayler,[228] which came to trial in the latter part of April 2001 and resulted in a conviction and sentence of six months in prison. Two and a half positives can be associated with these sagas: the ISC took up the case for Agency employees to have access to employment tribunals; the Home Secretary asked The Advisory Council on Public records to examine the criteria used by the Security Service for deciding whether to retain or destroy files on individuals; and the description of when the Security Service would provide advice on the suitability of potential Ministers on security grounds was recast as: 'No representations are made to [the Prime Minister] by the Service about proposed Ministerial appointments. Advice is available to [the Prime Minister] when relevant.'

Hurricane Stella

It may have looked as if government was at last getting on top of the breaches of trust if officials sought to publish memoirs. Former Ministers, including John Major, Michael Heseltine and Norman Lamont, were abiding by the Radcliffe Rules. But in February 2000 Hurricane Stella struck. Stella Rimington had been Director General of the Security Service from 1992 to 1996. Her tenure had been notable for adopting a successful public relations strategy for the Service, which had increased public understanding of its activities, including publication of *The Security Service*, the first official release of the duties, activities and a description of the operations of MI5.[229] In late February 2000 her successor, Stephen Lander, notified Wilson with dismay that Mrs Rimington had sought permission to publish a 350-page memoir, three quarters of it dealing with her time in MI5 under the working title *A Life of Surprises*.[230] The Treasury Solicitor described a legal position that was complex and uncertain: publication should be resisted but the stakes were high.[231] An appeal not to publish, on the grounds of double standards (her memoir stressed the importance of trust in the work of MI5), might be more effective than legal threats.[232] Wilson was personally shocked. He accepted that circumstances change and that earlier assurances that Rimington would not publish a memoir could have become redundant. He also acknowledged that the manuscript was a very good read '... streets ahead of most memoirs by politicians and public servants ... She writes ... in the way that people write about traumas, and much of it comes across with that immediacy and power.' But he also said, 'What I think I object to most is the sense of betrayal which I feel about her writing the book ... She is proposing to sell confidences which are not hers to sell.'[233] And of course, though recognising that the comparison would not have been fair, he knew that a provocative media could make mischief over one law for Stella Rimington and another for, say, David Shayler.

'Knowing her,' he told the Home Secretary [Jack Straw], 'I guess that she may well be very keen on publication and hard to persuade out of it. She may well relish the thought of a battle ... '[234] With Ministers' blessing he met Rimington on 18 April to appeal in person to her protective instincts towards the Security Service. However, she showed 'energetic determination to publish and a conviction that she was entitled to do so' but agreed to meet Lander to discuss possible modifications to the text, without commitment on either side. Sawers in Number 10, meanwhile, indicated that opinion was divided, commenting that he was struck by how many former Directors of the CIA were able to write memoirs without lasting damage to that Agency and adding that 'We risk being old-Labour and old-Tory on this. The key is that Stella abides by the rules, not that she has taken a vow of silence.'

A second meeting took place on 5 May, this time with the participation of Lander. Rimington declared her determination to publish but also her willingness to compromise on specific references thought to be offensive or dangerous. However, her text must not be seen as a whitewash – there were some subjects which people would expect her to address, including the perception amongst some that she was personally responsible for the destruction of the National Union of Mineworkers during the Thatcher years.[235] The stress of a potential courtroom battle with the government had taken its toll – she had been suffering from shingles and when Wilson encouraged her to get well soon her reply was telling: 'I will now' and said how pleased she was that they were 'doing something collaborative.' She made wide-ranging changes to the original text and Wilson concluded in May 2001 that, though he still found the book deeply unwelcome, the legal uncertainties and the political opprobrium that a court case would be likely to bring did not merit action against a text which revealed no secrets and which many informed commentators would find anodyne. Accordingly, government should grant clearance to publish the revised text but make clear publicly its disapproval of what Stella Rimington was doing.[236] Jack Straw proposed a fiercer form of words deploring publication but reluctantly agreed to Wilson's proposal and in July so did Blair: 'There is nothing we can do except accept this.'[237] He was worried by an allegation of sexist bullying that appeared in the preface;[238] nevertheless, Rimington was given formal authorisation to publish on 6 July 2001 and the book, now with the title *Open Secret*, was published in September to a generally underwhelming reception. But difficulty with memoirs did not end there. Wilson's successor, Andrew Turnbull, faced renewed problems over Robin Cook's *The Point of Departure* in 2003; and nor did Wilson's involvement cease – highly unusually, a former Permanent Secretary at MAFF (Richard Packer) published a scathing attack on him in 2005 over the handling of European negotiations about the BSE scare. The Public Administration Select Committee took oral evidence from Wilson in November 2005 about desirable revisions to the conventions governing memoirs. The following year Sir Christopher Meyer released a controversial memoir of his time as UK Ambassador in Washington.[239] The upshot was an announcement in March 2007 by Wilson's successor but one (Gus O'Donnell) that the rules were being tightened for officials.

The Eternal Verities of the Civil Service

On 26 March 2002 Wilson spoke to an invited audience of academics, journalists and civil servants in the Banqueting House Whitehall to lay out his case for a Civil Service Bill. The title of the speech, 'Portrait of a Profession Revisited' echoed the 1950 description by Sir Edward Bridges of a self-confident post-war service in his Rede Lecture.[240] But the tone was very different and the Prime Minister advised against Wilson giving the talk, asking how do you want to be remembered?[241] The Bill was intended to be the keystone of Wilson's legacy – a civil service responsive to the demands of modern government yet upholding the eternal verities of integrity, honesty, impartiality and objectivity. Throughout his four and half years as Cabinet Secretary he had been on a constant alert to protect the boundary between government and Party matters in an environment where pressures of policy presentation and increased numbers of political appointees provided a recurring challenge. However, it was not until 2010, under the guidance of Gus O'Donnell, that the Constitutional Reform and Governance Act was enacted with protection for these eternal values.

Almost from the outset Wilson had been concerned about political messages intruding into official publications. In preparing the first Annual Report by the Blair Government a question arose over to what extent it was appropriate for Departments to include 'the problems left behind by the previous Government, as well as any strengths that could be built upon.' Wilson asked the Number 10 Private Office to take care to avoid anything of this nature, 'perhaps phrasing contributions in terms of the challenges facing this Government,' adding that he seemed 'to be getting quite a lot of letters challenging Government publications for being too political.'[242] Later in 1998 the Prime Minister's Press Secretary, Alastair Campbell, requested guidance on what he could and could not do at the Labour Party Conference. Wilson advised: '... you have to stay within your role as a government spokesman and not operate as a spokesman for the Labour Party or for the Prime Minister in his capacity as leader of that party.' But as he pointed out, that still left open a wide field of operation including help in drafting the Prime Minister's speech (since it would concentrate very largely on the government's future programme), and explaining the actions and policies of the government in a party political context. But in general Campbell should avoid playing a high-profile public role at the Conference.[243]

The practical application of civil service impartiality in government communications had always been something of a maze. Kenneth Clarke[244] had worried that the rules hampered him in his proposed Health Service reforms. Bernard Ingham's role as a Civil Servant Press Secretary to Margaret Thatcher had been controversial. Now Mike Granatt, the Head of the Government Information Service, had concerns over possible charges of politicisation over the creation of Departmental Media Monitoring Units since they would inevitably touch on government rebuttal of press comments.[245] Alun Evans, a civil servant who was the first Head of the Downing Street Strategic Communications Unit, was warned not to stray into Party matters when he attended a Cabinet 'away-day' in September.[246] Alastair Campbell was given another warning in February 2000 about putting Party material on the Number 10 website.[247] Material from the burgeoning Whitehall Knowledge Network should only be given to MPs on a cross-party basis.[248] And so it continued, with frequent allegations from Conservative and Lib Dem Members of Parliament that civil servants were being used improperly.

Wilson saw the putative Civil Service Bill as a bulwark of protection. The political appointees in 10 Downing Street thought that Wilson's consultation document opened up a flank through which to attack SPADS and did not discuss the civil service enough.[249] Wilson told Baroness Prashar, the Civil Service First Commissioner, that he hoped to go public with the proposals in January 2002 and to secure cross-party support.[250] One Downing Street adviser summed up the position: 'Richard Wilson is keen to go out to consultation on a Civil Service Bill; we aren't.'[251] Permanent Secretaries were divided in their opinion; those who were retired were particularly hostile to the idea, fearing that the safeguards would be muted and so would weaken the independence of the civil service.

Staff appointments were another sensitive area. Given the close working of civil service and SPAD staff in 10 Downing Street, pragmatically SPADS wanted to sit on selection panels for the appointment of civil servants to the Prime Minister's office.[252] Wilson was opposed to this and also, when Gordon Brown wished to appoint Ed Balls, his special adviser, as Chief Economic Adviser in the Treasury, he was moved to protest.[253] Judicious semantics came to the rescue. He reassured Powell, who had said that many people were irritated by the appointment, that Balls might hold the title, Chief Economic Adviser, but did not hold the post.[254] In October 1999 Dame Rennie Fritchie, the Commissioner for Public Appointments (not to be confused with the First Civil Service Commissioner) told Chris Kelly of the Department of Health and Michael Bichard of DfEE that it was not always necessary to appoint the best person, as other considerations could come into play.[255] By contrast, in 2000 Baroness Prashar, the First Civil Service Commissioner, declared that the Commissioners were unwilling to give Ministers flexibility of choice for appointments to permanent posts.[256] (SPADS were temporary civil servants.) She repeated this position in November 2001, later indulging in her own semantic massage to draw a distinction between Ministerial choice and Ministerial involvement in appointments. Controversy continued with Richard Mottram, PUS at DTR, having to defend his Secretary of State (Stephen Byers) in public from charges of improper interference in the appointment of the Department's Head of News. The difficulties were not entirely resolved by the 2010 Act, with the Conservative/Lib Dem Coalition in 2013 once again resurrecting proposals to increase Ministerial influence on senior appointments.[257] However, to Wilson the importance of the 2010 Act was that it entrenched the position of the Civil Service Commission in law so that a government could not simply change appointment procedures and standards without legislation.

A third area of friction concerned the authority of SPADS to instruct and to manage civil servants. The 1997 Order-in-Council that permitted up to three SPADS in 10 Downing Street to do so – though only two (Powell and Campbell) were nominated – was not renewed after the 2001 General Election in the face of charges of incipient politicisation. However, in May 2001 as Blair's first term was coming to an end Wilson explained in the context of a draft code of conduct for SPADS that they could 'advise and co-ordinate' on behalf of their Minister and hence issue de facto instructions provided that they were on behalf of their principal and not on their own account.[258] (A ruling that was later challenged by the First Division Association as a step towards politicisation.)[259]

Domestic Affairs

E-commerce

The prospect and promise of e-commerce came to the fore around the end of the twentieth century. According to the market intelligence company IDC (International Data Corporation) web usage increased over fourfold between 1995 and 1998 and doubled again during 1998 to 147 million users worldwide. Initially the concern in the UK was the threat to law enforcement, security and the risks of cyberattack but later attention switched to the opportunities for economic growth and serving the citizen.

Commercial software developers had started to market encryption programs in the early 1990s and in late 1997 Wilson (then still PUS at the Home Office but Cabinet Secretary elect) alerted Robin Butler to the difficulties that widespread adoption of these products could bring.[260] The fear was that if the market for public key cryptography services was allowed to grow without regard to the needs of the law enforcement and intelligence agencies the consequences could be severe and irremediable. Other allied governments were grappling with the same issue and discussions were multilateral. In the UK legislation would be necessary to protect the interests of the state and should be given a high priority.[261] But Wilson faced a tricky interdepartmental situation. Though the Secretaries of State from the Home Office, the Foreign Office and Defence were convinced of the need for early legislation, the Department that would carry the Bill (the Board of Trade) did not see it as a high priority and agreed only reluctantly to proceed provided that this was not at the expense of any of its high priority legislative bids.

Further, after government had issued a consultation document in March 1997[262] many argued that the lead proposal was flawed. The procedure was known as 'key escrow' and required users of encryption software who wanted their electronic signature to be legally recognised to lodge with a certification authority the keys that allowed them to decrypt messages. Doubters argued that legitimate users would face extra costs but illegitimate users such as criminals or terrorists would simply ignore the requirement. Businesses would be likely to locate outside the UK to avoid these extra costs.[263] Ministers and senior officials faced a steep technological learning curve (as indeed did much of senior British business leadership) but led by Blair the government signalled the importance it attached both to secure electronic transactions as the bedrock for e-commerce and to legitimate state monitoring of electronic communications under appropriate legal warrants. A tug of war between the requirements of e-commerce and those of law enforcement continued throughout 1998. Companies giving evidence to the Trade and Industry Select Committee warned of the impracticability and damaging effects key escrow would have; none supported its introduction and by early February 1999 over half of the bodies submitting evidence to the government consultation had opposed the approach.[264] The Home Secretary, however, stoutly defended the law enforcement needs, arguing that the debate had all the hallmarks of a dialogue of the deaf. Those outside the 'ring of secrecy' tended to dismiss those within it as latter-day James Bonds and displayed a blasé attitude to the Intelligence Agencies' ability 'to find a way.'[265] What was at stake was how to prevent an otherwise benign market development undermining law enforcement and the fight against serious crime.[266]

Faced with opposition from business, leading industrialised countries signalled their intention to abandon key escrow. Wilson withdrew his support. He told Blair that the moment had passed for presenting the policy in a straightforward manner at a sufficiently senior level to secure the co-operation of industry. The key escrow option had required a sophisticated approach and skilful presentation, which it had not got. He urged the Prime Minister to make it clear to all concerned that if an answer existed it must be found. The political stakes were very high not just for the government but for industry too. If the government were thought to have carelessly brushed aside a licensing regime that could have prevented secure communications for terrorists, other extremists and paedophiles the political fallout would be even more damaging. Blair agreed.[267] Politically the next question was what to do about the draft Secure Electronic Commerce Bill pending a satisfactory solution to the encryption problem. Initially Wilson favoured putting the question of legislation to one side since the government did not know what it wanted to do. He argued that once an agreed approach with the e-commerce champions, the law enforcement agencies and senior industrialists was reached drafting of a consultation document and a Bill could be quick.[268] After Blair had discussed the issues in an ad hoc meeting with senior Ministers, however, a parallel engineering approach was adopted.[269] All agreed that a workable solution to the requirements of the law enforcement agencies was required and a task force under David Hendon of the Performance and Innovation Unit in the Cabinet Office was charged with engaging with industry and officials to produce a framework for a solution by the end of March (i.e. in roughly six weeks). In addition, because of the need to press forward with a framework for encouraging e-commerce a DTI consultation document (which did not contain a reference to key escrow) should be issued as soon as possible and the Prime Minister would invite key industrialists to 10 Downing Street to urge industry help find a solution.

The PIU report was submitted to Blair on time on 1 April.[270] It concluded that the government's initial thoughts were now obsolete. The team had come to the uncomfortable conclusion that law enforcement would inevitably suffer as a result of the rise of encryption technologies. Nevertheless, the risks could be mitigated to some extent by creating a new government-industry forum and establishing a Decryption Centre within the Home Office to work on interception authorised by warrant. With the support of the Home Secretary the Prime Minister accepted the recommendations *faut de mieux*[271] and launched the prospects with industry at a second breakfast session on 26 May. But the way forward was still not entirely straightforward. The Chief Secretary refused to allow funding for the Decryption Centre as a charge on the public expenditure Contingency Reserve and immediately after the launch of the report, to the horror of the Home Secretary, the Secretary of State for Trade and Industry proposed a further retreat in the shape of a self-regulatory approval scheme for encryption with a statutory scheme only in reserve in case industry did not deliver.[272] By November 1999 the Home Secretary felt further embattled as he reported to the Prime Minister that lobbyists within the e-commerce industry swallowed every concession and then sought more. They wanted no legislative framework whatever and their behaviour threatened the delicate balance the government had to make between enthusiastic support for the potential of e-commerce and other interests including law enforcement.[273] The Prime Minister was also required to rule on a disagreement between the Home Office and the DTI over whether to rule out key escrow explicitly on the face of the E-commerce Bill. Blair decided to do so to avoid the Bill being attacked because it would give the government the power to introduce mandatory key escrow as a condition of obtaining a licence to sell encryption software.[274] But whilst IT industry leaders welcomed the revised government approach[275] Blair was warned by Lord Falconer of a sense among the wider business community that the government had lost its strategic direction. Delays in the publication of the Bill and in the appointment of a central E-envoy (who, after a false start late in 1998, was not expected to take up office until January 2000) had added to the sense of procrastination.[276]

Further, the potential of e-commerce was not understood widely enough by business leaders; a survey by the Institute of Directors (mainly covering small to medium size enterprises) put 25% of businesses adopting a 'wait and see' approach and only 2% of UK Board Directors thinking that e-commerce would have a significant impact on their business. A similar report commissioned by large IT companies reinforced the picture: over half of UK directors had never had a technology briefing.[277] For his part Blair stressed the importance of signalling the government's commitment to the development of e-commerce through the appointment of an e-Envoy and through a determined push towards electronic procurement and service delivery.[278] Wilson was tasked with the daunting requirement to ensure that departmental procurement units were staffed with people who had the professional expertise to handle IT projects and were fully up to date with current internet and e-commerce developments, if necessary paying market-related salaries.[279] His response was protective of the civil service, sounding caution over the sometimes exaggerated claims from suppliers in competitive tenders and arguing that: 'We also need to share our knowledge of suppliers across departments;' and 'We are taking these issues forward through the Modernising Government and Civil Service reform programmes.'[280] The reply lacked hard evidence and did not convince Downing Street critics. Heywood queried whether the actions in hand went far enough to fill the gap of people with the skills or imagination required to identify and establish possible internet start-ups.[281] Progress was slow in getting services delivered online. 'It would be straightforward,' the economic private secretary advised Blair, 'to deliver, say, Passports or Driving Licences over the internet, but a combination of caution and lack of vision in the Civil Service means it isn't happening.' 'Then let us make it happen,' Blair replied testily.[282] Neither understood that the then technology could have left business wide open to fraud and criminality. There was a real risk that in such an unknown technological area a rush to compete could be as moths to the flame. Wilson proposed asking PUS colleagues to look for innovative partnerships with the private sector, for ways of being more imaginative over rewards and to put more energy behind CMPS efforts directed towards internet awareness and literacy. At Ministerial level a group chaired by the Chief Secretary was set up to drive Electronic Government (MISC 14), initially targeted on services to business such as Company start-up and expansion, taxation and business regulation.[283] But by July it was still clear that the Gateway scrutiny of major projects showed 70% still suffered critical weaknesses.[284]

With the arrival of Alex Allan as E-envoy in January 2000 and under his successor Andrew Pinder Wilson was content to leave the central drive towards e-government safely in the hands of others. However, he retained his involvement as Accounting Officer for the Single Intelligence Vote supporting, for instance, a report in December 2001 by Sir Edmund Burton on initiatives (and new expenditure) needed on information assurance. In the same month Blair declared: 'We are now beginning to see transactions [between government and the citizen] coming online.' But, as he also noted, none of this would count unless those services were used and he appealed to his colleagues to demonstrate their personal commitment: 'I look to your leadership, and to each member of Cabinet, to ensure that we seize this opportunity to transform service delivery.'[285] By the end of 2003 Wilson's successor, Andrew Turnbull, could report that two thirds of government services were available online.[286]

Privacy

In economic policy Wilson was largely hands-off, given the Blair/Brown acrimony, leaving the running of the secretariat to others; in social policy he appears as a liberally minded influence concerned to protect freedoms and to encourage those who were disadvantaged because of gender or ethnicity. In the aftermath of the death of Diana Princess of Wales on 31 August 1997 there was an intense debate over the possible limitation of press freedom to intrude on the lives of celebrities and others who found themselves in the public limelight. Shortly before the tragedy Chris Smith, Secretary of State for Culture, Media and Sport, had declared himself satisfied that self-restraint by the newspapers, and self-regulation under the Press Complaints Commission (PCC) was fairly effective.[287] On 2 September, however, he reported that the PCC was now undertaking an urgent review with editors across the newspaper industry on what action they proposed to take to tackle the problem of aggressive paparazzi photographers and wider media intrusion into personal privacy.[288] Both the outgoing Major Government and now the Blair administration favoured self-regulation. But Smith had to admit that many of the proposals in the July 1995 government rejection of the Calcutt enquiry's call for a statutory tribunal and a privacy tort had not been satisfactorily applied.[289]

The government was already committed to adopting the European Convention on Human Rights (ECHR), Article 8 which guaranteed that: 'everyone has the right to respect for his private and family life, his home and his correspondence.' But the ECHR balanced this right with a right to freedom of expression. The death of Princess Diana closed down any faint hope there might have been in the media for exemption from Article 8; but there were further options for a tougher regime in support of the right to privacy.[290] Furthermore, as the Lord Chancellor indicated, in interpreting the ECHR judges were likely to develop the common law of privacy.[291] Officials were reluctant to go further down the track of regulation. Butler had fed three suggestions into Downing Street by the time Wilson came on the scene. These were: (1) the PCC needed to show it was independent minded; (2) if the press refused to disclose their sources in confidence to the PCC they should expect to face a higher hurdle of substantiation to show that their story was justified; (3) corrections should be given greater prominence in the newspapers. Wilson brought no great change of emphasis but offered a more complete proposal[292] – he tied his colours firmly to the mast of self-regulation and opposed media exemption from Article 8 of the ECHR even if it was unclear whether the Human Rights Bill, which only created rights in relation to public authorities, would capture media behaviour. (Government lawyers had identified that the courts might allow cases to be brought using 'the court as [a] public authority').[293] The government should concentrate on the remedies available to an aggrieved individual. In a prescient move he also opposed prior restraint injunctions if the media were willing to defend the lawfulness of publication – if the media lost, however, they should pay damages to those with a legitimate grievance. Nor should the government be drawn into approving a code of conduct, which would be a clear and unwelcome step towards government control.

The argument was proving difficult to corral so Wilson advised allowing the Home Secretary to explore with the editors an alignment of the Human Rights

Bill with the Data Protection Bill which would require the courts to have particular regard to the importance of freedom of expression – a British adaptation of the First Amendment of the United States Constitution which *inter alia* guaranteed the freedom of the press. But many editors saw through the manoeuvre and voiced fears of a privacy law developing through common law and/or of the PCC becoming more under the control of the courts. Wilson saw that the Human Rights Act (HRA) would have as big an impact on Whitehall as the 'Judge over Your Shoulder' of Judicial Review. He pushed Departments into thinking ahead about the challenges that the HRA would bring. Reassurances from Downing Street that if the courts were to undermine press freedom of expression the government would consider legislation to correct the situation were hastily assembled. Some ten years later the editor of the *Daily Mail* (Paul Dacre) reignited the debate in colourful terms by claiming just that – the ECHR had moved English law closer to a common law right to privacy: 'It is the others I care about – the crooks, the liars, the cheats, the rich and the corrupt sheltering behind a law of privacy being created by an unaccountable judge.'[294] The government response by Lord Falconer (the Lord Chancellor) simply said that the judge concerned had acted in accordance with a law democratically passed by Parliament.

Freedom of Information

As late as February 2001 the practical implementation of the (by then) Data Protection Act (DPA) was far from settled. Heywood warned Wilson that: '... there is not even an agreed process on how departments should register their [information] systems.' Seen from Downing Street there were two main issues – coherent government-wide procedures and greater clarity about the law. These needed senior Cabinet Office-led consideration at a policy (as opposed to administrative) level, including the question of whether to charge for information provided under the DPA since it was proving to be extremely labour intensive.[295] These issues were being considered inter-departmentally under Constitution Unit leadership[296] but it was not clear that Ministers and Permanent Secretaries had hoisted on board the full import of what lay ahead. In particular, the interaction between the DPA and Freedom of Information (FOI) became potentially toxic.

The 1997 election manifesto of New Labour had said: 'Unnecessary secrecy in government leads to arrogance in government and defective policy decisions ... We are pledged to a Freedom of Information Act, leading to more open government.'[297] The subsequent proposals in 'Your Right to Know'[298] were greeted with widespread surprise and some incredulity: 'This White Paper offers a very generous FOI regime – probably the most generous yet seen amongst countries that have introduced Freedom of Information. It is almost too good to be true. That is the central concern: that this is an unreal White Paper which has been brought out without full understanding or wholehearted commitment on the part of Departments or their Ministers, or proper consultation of the other public bodies which will be affected,' wrote the former Home Office official Robert Hazell, now at the Constitution Unit, University College London.[299] His shrewd judgement was that the document was aspirational rather than realistic. Resource implications were not mentioned and without adequate resourcing the FOI risked becoming a hollow shell. Similarly, it appeared not to take into account that in Australia and Canada FOI conditions included a category exemption for Cabinet papers and a general exemption for policy advice.[300] Officials charged with turning the White Paper into reality agreed. Andrew Adonis of the Policy Unit told Blair that the thinking underlying the treatment of policy advice to Ministers was muddled. The White Paper had said: 'there would be no disclosure if any harm would thereby be caused to the public interest ... It was intended by everyone involved ... that this would exclude Whitehall policy documentation entirely.' But the Information Commissioner was likely to argue that if this had been the intention why was policy documentation within the ambit of FOI at all?[301] Ministerial responsibility rested with David Clarke in the Cabinet Office, who was a strong advocate of FOI, supported by the Lord Chancellor, Derry Irvine. Before the July 1998 reshuffle of Ministers there was no restraint in the system; no counterweight to their enthusiasm as neither Blair nor the Policy Unit gave it much attention.[302]

Blair discussed the application of FOI to 10 Downing Street with Lord Falconer and officials, including Wilson, on 16 December 1998 and again on 12 January 1999 with the Home Secretary and the Lord Chancellor when he expressed concerns about the treatment of policy advice. Jack Straw subsequently proposed an exemption based on the reasonable opinion of a Minister of the Crown.[303] Wilson's response was to return to basics and list eight options ranging from abandoning the FOI Bill to total exclusion from the Bill for policy advice, pointing out that the world was about to change – enactment of the European Convention on Human Rights (ECHR) would influence judicial culture and might change the use of Judicial Review.[304] Abandoning the Bill was by no means ruled out. Adonis argued that further significant exclusions would mean there was little point in continuing with the Bill.[305] Blair favoured a simple, clean exclusion of policy advice from FOI but left open the possibility of allowing the factual material on which policy was based within the FOI ambit. In broad terms campaigners wanted a return to the generous proposals in Cm 3818 and the Home Secretary sought colleagues' support to limited the concessions: 'After careful consideration, we concluded that the White Paper proposals would have significantly disrupted the effective conduct of Government. I do not think we can return to them.'[306] Blair took an even harder line, annotating Adonis' advice on detailed possible concessions: 'Yes, but let me add a word of real caution. You probably think the FOI stuff is v[ery] heavy and difficult for us. I think it barely registers on the radar screen. So don't do any of this unless it leaves intact effective government.'[307] Nevertheless, in a move reminiscent of the Croham Directive of 1977[308] work proceeded on a possible distinction between advice and the factual basis on which the advice rested and Blair sought Wilson's advice.[309] The answer was: 'I recommend that you should agree to this relaxation [a public right of access to factual and background information] on the basis that it will only be introduced from a future date.'[310] Shortly thereafter Wilson followed up with a note to the Minister of State, Cabinet Office, acknowledging that FOI legislation was inevitably going to be a thorn in the side of government but nothing could be done about that short of abandoning the whole idea, which was unacceptable. However, factual information meant just that; it did not imply access to documents and even factual material could be withheld if it would be likely to inhibit the free and frank provision of advice or otherwise prejudice the effective conduct of public affairs.[311] The effect, it was decided, would be to put the existing Code, which derived from the Croham Directive, on a statutory but not obligatory basis, subject to a test of harm.[312]

The advisers were divided. Some, including Wilson, favoured further work on possible concessions to the FOI lobby;[313] but others, notably Lord Falconer, took the view that: 'The public aren't interested. We will survive in Parliament because the Lords will not regard this as an issue on which to take on the Commons.'[314] Reluctantly, Blair was swayed by the arguments in favour of concessions. Adonis said: 'In my view we are merely conceding in law what we will inevitably concede in practice anyway, and it is nonsensical to go to all the effort of passing FOI legislation only to end in a reputation for being no better than the Tories;'[315] and after the euphoria of the White Paper the more limited proposals came in for a rough time at Select Committee hearings and in the media. The government came under pressure at the Committee Stage of the Bill to be more liberal, as a result of which Jack Straw proposed three amended concessions: (1) a statutory duty to disclose information which was exempt from FOI (such as policy advice) if the public interest outweighed that of withholding; (2) the Information Commissioner could request such disclosure and only an accountable person (i.e. a Minister) could defy such a request; (3) factual and background information should cease to be exempt from the FOI and should be subject to a simple harm test.[316] Wilson suggested allowing Straw to put the first two points to colleagues for agreement but thought that the third went too far and countered by proposing that this information be subject to a 'reasonable opinion' test which would leave the final say to Ministers.[317] During passage of the Act, however, the Bill was amended to allow people to appeal against a Ministerial decision not to disclose information and to permit the Information Commissioner to direct disclosure subject to a final Certificate of Exemption signed by a Secretary of State. Expectations had been heightened.

But this political pressure was tame in comparison to the problems caused by interaction between the Data Protection Act (DPA) and FOI, which threatened serious damage to government policy. Whilst policy advice continued to be exempt under the FOI Act (2000), requests by an individual for information held about them in information systems under the Data Protection Act (1998) did not give such an exemption. 'We have two acts on information management that contradict one another,' Heywood reported.[318] Counsel had advised that the DPA was badly drafted and did not offer the prospect of exemption on the grounds of disproportionate effort: 'I had to read 3,000 pieces of paper for one of the requests,' admitted one of Blair's team.[319] Heywood feared that the government had: '... in effect introduced a freedom of information act via the back door without realising it.'[320] Amongst the worries were that the result threatened negotiations over Northern Ireland and the handling of David Shayler under the Official Secrets Act (1989). The view of the SPADS in Downing Street was that the civil service had mishandled the DPA.[321] To an extent Wilson agreed: 'My own view is that the legislation is flawed, not least because we have not taken full advantage of the exemptions allowed under the [1995] EU directive [on the protection of personal data].'[322] The Danes, for example, had introduced in their legislation enacting the Directive an exemption to protect 'vital public interests'. But in the same submission he also pointed out that the Lord Chancellor seemed more optimistic about the government's ability to be robust over what it released than experience with the DPA suggested and '... accepts rather lightly the extra work which [DPA] cases involve for Number 10 and the Cabinet Office.' He listed the items that, despite a robust approach, lawyers had advised had to be disclosed in an intelligence case and asked Haydn Phillips, PUS at the Lord Chancellor's Department, to look urgently at the extent to which further legislation could offer extra exemptions under the DPA.[323]

As this History is being drafted the issue of a 'safe space' for the consideration of policy advice continues to rumble. Back in the 1970s President Richard Nixon of the United States had said: 'Unless a President can protect the privacy of the advice he gets, he cannot get the advice he needs.' In a House of Lords short debate on 17 January 2012 several speakers were still echoing this thought as they discussed deficiencies in the Freedom of Information Act (2000).

Controlling Costs

Wilson continued with the significant role in intelligence and security inherited from his predecessors both as Accounting Officer, personally responsible to Parliament for the Single Intelligence Vote and as the Prime Minister's most senior adviser on intelligence and security. Though both roles were traditional his period cannot be understood without recognition of the seismic shift caused by the Al Qaeda terrorist attacks on the United States on 11 September 2001. Before 9/11 four managerial themes underpinned Wilson's approach: (1) tauter budgetary restraint; (2) improving the usefulness of JIC reports; (3) responding to increasingly strong demands from Parliamentarians for access to and oversight of intelligence (4) reconciling government encouragement of secure electronic commerce with the Intelligence Agencies' capacity to penetrate electronic communications (ELINT). Intelligence-led action against serious crime was becoming an important element in the Agencies' tasking. After 9/11 priorities shifted radically towards counter-terrorism strategy and inter-agency co-operation. Despite military successes against the Al Qaeda network the emergence of 'home grown' terrorism in the West created a new situation. The National Security Strategy of 2010 added a wider range of strategic intelligence goals, notably how to deal with a growing cyber threat from state-sponsored agencies and common criminals and the risks the scope of electronic technology offered to disaffected staff with access to secret material.[324]

The incoming Labour government of 1997 promulgated draft terms of reference for a review of the Single Intelligence Vote, to be led by the Intelligence Coordinator John Alpass: 'To determine how best the security and intelligence agencies may contribute to the achievement of the Government's objectives for this Parliament.' Key questions included whether it was possible to put a cash value on any of the Agencies' output, how the non-cash value to the UK could sensibly be assigned and whether requirements for intelligence might be linked more closely to departmental objectives, which under resource accounting would be costed and monitored? The Treasury was seeking to reshape the objectives of the Vote and the allocation of financial provision over sub-objectives split between the Agencies. The Chief Secretary (Alistair Darling) reopened the debate about charging Departments for the agencies' services, arguing that the risk of distortion of priorities was high when a free good was on offer and he raised the prospect of departmental payment for non-security work (e.g. on serious crime).[325] Michael Quinlan's review *Intelligence Requirements and Resources* from June 1994 had comprehensively demolished the idea because of the high fixed costs of such activities but tactically Wilson conceded the possibility of repayment for a limited area – protective security work covering critical national infrastructure.[326] However, the idea of repayment by Departments was not mentioned in the final report, which gave the SIV a clean bill of health and endorsed the Agencies' valuable contribution to security, defence and foreign policy. The savings promised were a modest 6% in real terms by 2001–02 and in the Autumn of 1998 a PSIS review of priorities at a detailed level produced only minor readjustments. 'The Agencies deserve strong support and I agree with these conclusions,' Wilson told Blair.[327]

This comment, together with the post-9/11 support Wilson gave to increased budgetary bids from the Agencies, might suggest he acted as a shop steward for the intelligence community. This was not the case. As Accounting Officer he was tough in probing the Agencies' bids for funds and only robust in defending the bids towards the Treasury when he had been satisfied on their reasonableness – often in the face of Downing Street indifference prior to the attacks of 9/11. In June 2000 he rejected a draft submission to the Treasury on Agency resources as not sufficiently geared towards persuading Blair to confront Brown in support of the Vote, following up the revised submission with a plea to the Prime Minister to intervene as the bid would only bring the Vote total to 1999/2000 levels in real terms.[328] There is evidence that before 9/11 he had concerns about the rigour of the scrutiny of the SIV and the manner in which resource bids were presented. His Private Secretary Sebastian Wood recorded in a note to Cabinet Office intelligence staff Wilson's musings that the PSIS scrutiny of resource bids was not rigorous enough, did too little to encourage customers to be selective and should 'present customers with tough choices rather than an unlimited menu.'[329] Following a highly critical report issued on 20 April 2000 by the Intelligence and Security Committee on MI5's handling of suspected Soviet spies revealed in the Mitrokhin Archive,[330] Lander proposed improvements in tasking[331] and Wilson advised that oversight would be improved if the JIC took responsibility for vetting Security Service priorities and performance, bringing the Service into line with SIS and GCHQ.[332] The arrangement lasted until spring 2002 when, partly reflecting the Prime Minister's increased attention to intelligence after 9/11 and partly Wilson's successor's need to create even more space for attention to civil service reform, Sir David Omand was appointed as the PUS-level Cabinet Office Security and Intelligence Co-ordinator. In further steps to tighten financial management in MI5 Wilson supported the appointment of an efficiency adviser and contemplated creating an audit committee.[333] Thereafter there was relative silence until Wilson finally killed off the notion of charging for intelligence[334] accepting instead an instruction from the Chief Secretary to improve JIC prioritisation.[335]

The attacks of 9/11 on the Twin Towers changed the landscape. Less than a week later Wilson submitted bids for extra funding for the Agencies to allow a step change in counter-terrorist capabilities. Blair supported the bids in principle, urging the Andrew Smith to reach an early agreement on 2001/2 funding but, on Jeremy Heywood's suggestion, asked the Chief Secretary to scrutinise the bids for the two succeeding years to eliminate any tendency to 'gold plating.' When the Treasury did so, Wilson told Heywood that the proposed settlement was at the bottom of what was acceptable, allowing no scope for new counterterrorist capabilities and he wrote to Paul Boateng (who had replaced Andrew Smith) to express personal reservations about the assumptions behind a settlement which was below what the intelligence agencies had sought for 2003/04 to 2005/06.[336]

A Changing Security Environment

The old threats to national security were much weaker and public attitudes to privacy stronger. By June 1998, almost 50 years after the Attlee Government had started the enhanced security vetting of civil servants (known as Positive Vetting),[337] the Security Service could report that the threat to national security from subversion was negligible. It proposed withdrawing routine notification to departments of an individual's past involvement in subversive activities unless circumstances made an individual record relevant to national security. The key phrase was 'relevant to national security.' MI5 pointed out that involvement in extra-parliamentary organisations (such as single-issue pressure groups) might still raise doubts about an individual's trustworthiness for certain types of employment even if national security was not involved. But it was for departments to consider these issues as part of employment decisions.[338] Wilson worried that departments might not grasp the significance of what was being said.[339] At the end of the year the Home Secretary took the initiative for a seminar to examine long-standing questions about Section 9 of the Interception of Communications Act 1985 in the light of the Human Rights Act 1998 and the Criminal Procedure and Investigations Act 1996. This review eventually led to the Regulation of Investigatory Powers Act 2000, which widened the scope of the Chief Surveillance Commissioner to satisfy himself that the Agencies were compliant with the law. And following a visit by the Intelligence and Security

Committee to the Security Service in December 2001 the Committee asked the Director General to put on record the current policy on interception of communications made to or by MPs. As this was a policy matter rather than one of operational practice the Home Secretary replied, confirming that there had been no change in policy since Harold Wilson had set it out in 1966 – no tapping of phones of MPs and that if there were developments which caused a change of policy he would, at such moment as seemed compatible with the security of the country, on his own initiative, make a statement in the House of Commons.[340]

But there were new serious threats, including from cyber attack (then known as information warfare). Though individual departments might be aware of the threat there was no clearing house through which experience could be shared. Wilson's first instinct was to float the idea of a Cabinet Office Committee for this purpose; however, he acknowledged that all the parties involved had strong territorial imperatives that might impede the sharing of information unless carefully handled.[341] The issue would be best handled obliquely. Hence, on 3 June the Security Policy Division in the Cabinet Office proposed an interim report to Ministers on Defensive Information Warfare which would assess the range of UK government activity, look at what the private sector was doing in this area and also the activities of close allies before making proposals for Ministerial responsibilities. A discussion was slated for the Official Security Committee (SO) for 10 June (though postponed to 8 July). Meanwhile, *The Sunday Times* ran a story on 6 June that there would be a secret 'information warfare' exercise in London at the end of the month in which officials from Britain and America would test the defences against cyber attack on airports, transport systems, power supplies, hospitals and banks etc. The Clinton administration was reported to have set up monitoring against the threat to this 'critical national infrastructure.' It was the first time that the work by government in this area had been publicised and consequently relevant Ministers urgently needed to be briefed.[342] In doing so the intelligence co-ordinator, John Alpass, drew a neat parallel with the emerging threat of German espionage before the First World War when: 'It suddenly dawned that espionage was both a significant threat against which we needed to defend ourselves and a useful tool if practised by us. The initial solution was to set up one agency – the Secret Service Bureau – to do both tasks. But it was not long before it split into the two separate agencies MI5 and MI6.'[343]

SO met under Wilson's chairmanship on 8 July and again on 4 November. The Committee endorsed the policy framework, which sought to identify vulnerabilities irrespective of the source of the threat (state-sponsored attack, terrorism or individual hackers). It covered the financial sector and other economic key points outside government and discussed how to respond to attacks in real time. Telecommunications and energy were identified as the top priorities with the relevant Departments responsible for their protection. Additionally, Departments would be required to have in place by the end of 2000 plans for achieving an auditable standard of their own information security using BS 7799 (a recognised world-leading standard) as a starting point.[344] A single Ministerial lead for public presentation and liaison with the owners of economic key points proved difficult. The Home Secretary and the Secretary of State for Trade and Industry had direct but clashing interests – the one concerned with security, the other with secure transactions to underpin electronic commerce. A compromise was crafted with the Home Secretary in the lead, assisted by the Secretary of State for Trade and Industry, drawing on a Ministerial contact group for advice.[345] Ministers endorsed the SO proposals in November 1998. They were announced in January and by July Wilson was able to report good progress, including awareness raising in government and the private sector. An Electronic Attack Response Group involving government and the police would react rapidly to serious attack.[346]

The 1998 initiative had been precautionary, officials seeking to stay ahead of potential trouble. Wilson's note to the Prime Minister on 31 July had said: 'There is little evidence of threat from Information Warfare, yet.' Two years later, however, a progress report showed how the e-environment had progressed. It assessed the number of electronic viruses appearing each day at between 20 and 30 and pointed out that whilst few posed a threat to national security the political risk was high. Public opinion would be likely to hold Ministers to account for what they had done (or not done) to prevent a serious incident and that there was an attendant risk that Ministers would be drawn into accepting responsibilities that implied a greater degree of control than they could have in the real world. What had started as concern with protection for a relatively small number of economic key points (albeit with 30 papers discussed in the Information Systems Sub Committee of SO in 1998) had broadened with the growth of e-commerce into a major awareness-raising requirement.[347] In April 2000 Wilson noted that by the end of the year it might be sensible to consider widening the protection plans to cover not only 'the six areas key to ensuring that the country continues to function; but also, as the US do, the wider infrastructure, not critical as such but whose collapse or serious damage would carry significant political consequences.'[348] The SO Committee took up the challenge at a meeting on 18 March 2000 when it discussed how to encourage awareness and alert systems owners and users.[349] It was steady, if unspectacular, progress.

As can happen, however, steady progress was shown to be insufficient. On 4 May 2000 the 'I-Love-You' computer virus, originating in the Philippines, severely affected government networks and those of many private sector organisations worldwide. As a precautionary measure many mail systems were closed down. The BBC reported that up to 10% of UK businesses had been hit by the bug, mainly affecting administrative processes. Wilson annotated one of the Cabinet Office reports of damage with, 'It ducks the point that we were slow to pick up the threat,'[350] and Edna Chivers, (Head of the Cabinet Office Security Policy Division) pointed out both that cross-governmental co-ordination was weak and that the existing Critical National Infrastructure Protection policy could not prevent major political embarrassment. On the other hand, she added, there were real and hoax virus threats every week and Ministers would not thank officials for overreacting. The 'I-Love-You' virus ought to bring a realisation that the business community should take security seriously as integral to the e-commerce message.[351] More urgency was needed.

The Joint Intelligence Committee (JIC)

In a memorable introduction to a report on JIC activity in 1998 Michael Pakenham, the Chairman, said that annual reports: 'should be like a smart dress: long enough to cover the subject but short enough to be interesting.'[352] Having secured the reader's attention he went on to pose challenging questions about the role of JIC and Ministerial awareness of its output. One result was an (unsuccessful) experiment in 1999 to give the Prime Minister daily extracts from single source intelligence material prepared by the Chief of the JIC Assessments staff Richard Gozney, on secondment from the FCO.[353] The Agencies, MOD and FCO were all unhappy about the idea of daily assessments/judgements going to the Prime Minister unless they had cleared them (which would inevitably have delayed submission and defeated the objective of a rapid digest of overnight news).[354] GCHQ and SIS suggested appointing an intelligence attaché to the JIC – opposed by Lander, Director General of the Security Service, which did not want someone potentially from another organisation to come between it and the Prime Minister. At about the same time Wilson met the Agency Heads (without Pakenham's presence) to discuss another investigation, by Francis Richards Director of GCHQ, into possible reform of the JIC.[355] Richards had confirmed the JIC position as the single interdepartmental authority was a fundamental strength but Wilson queried whether the current size of the Assessments Staff could be justified and was minded to commission a short, sharp, six-week study of the role and resourcing of the Joint Intelligence Organisation (JIO) and Coordinator's offices to be carried out by Ivan Wilson (no relation), a retired Treasury official.'[356] Wilson told Kevin Tebbit of the MOD that the JIC product needed to be modernised – it had scarcely changed for 30 years – and that he was under pressure from Downing Street to strengthen the Cabinet Office role in the fight against serious crime.[357] The issue was not about operational units – the field was already well populated. His concern was more to reform the JIC/Co-ordinator/OD interface.

JIC had a preliminary discussion of possible restructuring at the end of March 2000 with Pakenham in the chair.[358] Some JIC members suspected that he was pushing his own agenda but things began to clear when, on 18 April, Wilson circulated a proposed job description for a successor (Pakenham was due to leave in the summer). This described the main areas of responsibility as:

a. To chair the Joint Intelligence Committee and give direction to its work.
b. To supervise the operations of the Joint Intelligence Organisation.
c. To manage the Single Intelligence Vote Spending Review process.
d. To coordinate and review intelligence community issues as required.
e. To supervise the [Cabinet Office] Security Division.
f. To coordinate Government policy on information warfare.[359]

Kerr (PUS at the FCO) claimed that the JIC chairmanship was in the gift of the Foreign and Commonwealth Secretary, only to be trumped by Wilson's counterclaim that it was a Prime Ministerial appointment.[360] In the event the person chosen (Peter Ricketts) came from the FCO though he held the post for only a year. Responsibilities for the OD secretariat and the JIO were split. This proved unsatisfactory; Ricketts expressed his frustration over limited access to the Prime Minister. Wilson proposed that the JIC should be chaired by the Prime Minister's foreign policy adviser (Sir David Manning) but Manning made it clear that he did not want to take on that task. This refusal left a simple choice between a producer of intelligence from one of the Agencies or MOD or a user of intelligence, predominantly from the FCO. The FCO and the Security Service favoured a chairman from a customer department, not a producer agency. As a later Security and Intelligence Co-ordinator, Richard Mottram, expressed it: 'a customer [is] used to assessment of intelligence material and perhaps more aware of the difficulties of telling policy-makers what they need to know, not what they want to hear [in] assessments [that] can often make uncomfortable reading.'[361] Yet when Ricketts moved on, a selection board under Wilson's leadership interviewed two candidates, recommending the appointment of John Scarlett of SIS. In a report of May 2002 when the Cabinet Secretary designate (Andrew Turnbull) posed the possibility of delegating the traditional intelligence and security responsibilities of his future role he asked David Omand – who was likely to take on this mantle – to examine the options. Omand reported concern not about the provenance of the JIC chairman but that a number of senior officials: 'have emphasised to me that there must not be ambiguity over who is representing the view of the intelligence community when it comes to a debate over the meaning of the intelligence.'[362]

Omand's appointment in June 2002 as Cabinet Office Security and Intelligence Coordinator was not without controversy.[363] His credentials were strong – he had been Director of GCHQ, DUS(Policy) at MOD, PUS of the HO and runner-up to Andrew Turnbull as Wilson's successor. Nevertheless, the FCO objected to the use of 'Intelligence' in his title and sought safeguards about the independence of the JIC. Its chairman, Scarlett, raised the issue of his own reporting line. Turnbull ruled that Scarlett would be accountable to Omand who would not interfere in the operations of the Assessments staff.[364] Omand would report to Turnbull as Cabinet Secretary and be responsible as:

- Accounting Officer for the SIV. (A responsibility that reverted to the Cabinet Secretary under proposals from Gus O'Donnell to Gordon Brown on 17 July 2007 'to set in train a process to make sure that intelligence assessment is kept 'independent of the political process'.)
- Chair of PSIS, i.e. responsible for negotiating resources with HMT and resolving the final allocation [of the SIV] to the Agencies.
- Co-ordinator of common interests of the intelligence community: e.g. relations with oversight bodies, legislation, and other legal issues affecting the agencies.
- Promoter of joint working between Agencies and other Departments.
- Chair of the Official Committee on protective security policy.

- Overseer of the Civil Contingencies Secretariat and supporting the Home Secretary in his role as chair of the Civil Contingencies Committee.

Fears that the post would be underemployed led to an additional responsibility as Accounting Officer for the Cabinet Office/Number 10 Vote. But in the detail of implementing the UK domestic response to the 9/11 attacks (including the CONTEST counter-terrorism strategy) Omand was obliged to focus on the Security and Intelligence duties which became a full-time PUS post.[365]

Parliamentary Oversight on Security and Intelligence

Throughout the period relations between the government and Parliament on security and intelligence continued to require nurturing. Since its inception in 1994 under Tom King MP the Intelligence and Security Committee of Privy Counsellors (ISC) had progressively enhanced its independent influence and effectiveness in holding government to account for its actions. The Committee was, however, the creature of the Prime Minister and reported to him, not to Parliament. The boundary between democratic accountability and legitimate secrecy around some of the actions of the Intelligence Agencies had not been defined to the satisfaction of all the parties. The ISC itself faced pressure from the House of Commons Select Committees to cede territory, notably to the Home Affairs and the Defence Committees. The Prime Minister did not want any suggestion that he might be open to agreeing to an expansion of the remit of the Home Affairs Committee to cover the Agencies.[366] Hence, it was in the interests of the government to strengthen the perceived effectiveness of the ISC in Parliamentary eyes; but in practice this was difficult to do, particularly when the Committee sought additional information. Thus, whilst the Agencies had, from the outset, co-operated with the ISC (Stella Rimington first gave evidence in 1994) they were particularly concerned to avoid compromising their covert capabilities. And though the instincts of the Blair administration were to recognise a legitimate Parliamentary interest in oversight there was a general worry that release of, for example, JIC assessments to the ISC (as the Committee wanted) would open up a crack in the blanket refusal to make available to Select Committees the advice that a Minister received from officials. Wilson was very familiar with this ground. At Michael Howard's request, when PUS at the Home Office, he had prepared Stella Rimington for her 1994 appearance and was consulted by Butler in November 1997 prior to Butler advising Blair that the ISC should be allowed to see sample JIC assessments and, as before, summaries of the JIC contribution relevant to particular inquiries – but should not be given regular access to JIC output.[367]

Towards the end of his first year as Prime Minister Blair promised the Parliamentary Labour Party an annual House of Commons debate on the Agencies.[368] Wilson was already worried by widespread access to JIC material – thought to amount to maybe 10,000 officials in the United States.[369] As late as October 2001 the Secretary of State for Health was refused general access to JIC assessments and in March 2002 the JIC Secretary Eddie Alleyn had to make a special case for the Attorney General to have access to sensitive JIC papers on Iraq and Weapons of Mass destruction.[370] Blair, meanwhile, viewed the ISC intention to investigate the involvement of the Intelligence Agencies with Sandline International[371] in Sierra Leone potentially as headline chasing and a move towards political rather than all-party behaviour.[372] He instructed Wilson to meet Tom King to discourage the Committee from this course. There were two meetings in June, a visit by the Committee to the JIC and a working dinner for Committee members to meet the Heads of the Intelligence Agencies. During these discussions it was clear that Tom King felt that the ISC needed to demonstrate that it was doing a worthwhile job. Access to JIC papers and recognition that the Committee's remit covered all of the intelligence community (i.e. including the JIC and the Defence Intelligence Service) were important elements in this self belief. The Agency Heads offered the Committee quarterly oral reports on their activities and the results of a full customer satisfaction survey done as part of the recent Comprehensive Spending Review, but Wilson dug in over access to JIC material, arguing that at a general level it was not a good indicator of Agency performance as it drew on a wider range of material. However, he conceded that access to JIC material relating to specific Committee inquiries could be forthcoming. This continued to be the position throughout Wilson's tenure, including the ISC questions, based on their sight of JIC papers during their work on the 9/11 terrorist attack, (a) whether JIC reports were sufficiently sharp to provide Ministers with warnings of threats and (b) about the relationship between analysis and policy advice.

As the time for the first annual Parliamentary debate on the Agencies drew near Wilson saw the Prime Minister as the natural choice to open the debate;[373] but he was rebuffed. The Home Secretary proposed tasking officials with reviewing the scope for modifying the terms of reference of the ISC with a view to making its scrutiny more open and more directly accountable to Parliament without damaging the Intelligence Agencies' operations. There were two additional concerns in Wilson's mind: (1) How to shore up the position of the ISC in the light of the Home Affairs and Defence Select Committee incursions? The Home Secretary did not rule out Select Committee status for the ISC in the medium term. (2) Whether to agree to a proposal from the Committee that it should have its own investigative resource? Blair was opposed to even hinting that the ISC might become a Select Committee and against modest steps in that direction such as involving the Commons Committee on Selection in nominations for ISC membership. But he was prepared to consider a small addition to Committee resources at a junior research level. He told the Committee as much at a friendly, hour-long meeting on 14 October 1998 – a meeting described by Wilson's office as 'Tom King out to extract as much as he could from the Prime Minister,' notably on the proposed senior investigative capability. The discussion was ambiguous leaving it unclear whether the ISC would go ahead anyway or would defer to the Prime Minister after both sides had reflected further. In the event, after Wilson had sought to mediate, King told the Prime Minister that the Committee was 'minded to appoint' as its investigator John Morrison, a former Secretary of JIC and DIS official.[374] In the interests of getting something moving the ISC agreed to government ground rules concerning the Investigator's operations, the most important of which required him to consult the Heads of the three Intelligence Agencies before starting work on a particular topic and to seek to agree factual matters with the Agencies before the Committee drew on them. Access by the investigator to the DIS was not ruled out but was not automatic, requiring an approach to the Secretary of State for Defence on a case-by-case basis.

The ISC also wanted information about the SIV analysed by Agency[375] but government was nervous that this would be a step too far because of likely sensitivities over the Northern Ireland Intelligence Vote.[376] After some confusing to-ing and fro-ing with officials Ministers decided to maintain the status quo as this was thought to make it easier to defend the ISC boundaries against Select Committee incursion. Thus, Wilson opposed requests by the Commons Defence and the Foreign Affairs Committees to examine JIC conclusions on Kosovo, arguing that it was better to stick to examination by the ISC.[377] By the end of February 1998 the ISC had been sent memos on The Millennium Bug; Montenegro; Iran/UAE; Milosevic; Chechnya and the departure of Boris Yeltsin from the Presidency of the Russian Federation. When Wilson gave evidence to the Committee on 12 April 2000 he agreed that the government posture should be to provide the maximum of information possible.

The later Wilson years were defined by the Whitehall response to civil and terrorist-induced emergencies. The emergency arrangements were characterised by running hard to stand still – applying the lessons of earlier crises but moving ahead of a giant wave of potential destruction. More than any other post-war Cabinet Secretary Wilson faced acute real time threats to perceptions of the Government's ability to stay in control of events and safeguard its citizens. Brook and Trend had been much concerned with civil defence and Cold War precautions. During the Cuba crisis of 1962 these had not been activated and remained untested. Civil contingencies during the time of Hunt and Armstrong had largely been concerned with the potential disruption from industrial action in the docks, mines and railways which were co-ordinated by the Civil Contingencies Committee (CCC) with help from ad hoc situation arrangements. The miners' strikes during the Thatcher years were handled ad hoc.

The Cabinet Office Briefing Room (COBR) was reserved for military or terrorist threats. After years of retrenchment the government's residual civil defence plans were underpinned by emergency planners in local authorities, funded by a reduced civil defence grant. The Home Office had no cross-departmental responsibilities outside those associated with civil defence and could not require other departments to undertake work against possible civil emergencies. Each emergency was handled ad hoc under the concept of 'lead departments' for different crises using the relevant Secretary of State as chairman.[378] Although the CCC was chaired by the Home Secretary and unusually comprised both ministers and officials (who usually sat on related but different committees with officials often shadowing and preparing discussion for their ministers), it had no policy responsibilities and met only in a crisis. The Home Office Emergency Planning Division, which led on these issues, had faced more pressing issues and, as the fuel crisis of 2000 would show, the civil defence dedicated communications were not suitable for a civil contingency; questions about mobilisation had largely dropped off Ministers' radar screens. COBR had to build its own database of contacts.[379]

1998 and 1999 saw the development of a strategy to protect 'critical national infrastructure' from the threat of terrorist attack and the revamping of systems thought vulnerable to the so-called millennium bug (aka Y2K).[380] In September 2000 emergency planning arrangements were blown apart by protests against rural fuel prices. In October 2000 the long-running Phillips inquiry into the handling of the 1986 outbreak of Bovine Spongiform Encephalopathy (BSE) reported, with accusations that the government had not communicated the possibility of a risk to humans to the public or to those whose job it was to implement and enforce precautions. In September 2001 Al Qaeda (AQ) attacked and destroyed the Twin Towers of the World Trade Center in New York, triggering a crisis of confidence in Western security. In the same year there was also a serious outbreak of Foot and Mouth disease, which revealed that the relevant precautionary measures were 'fighting last year's war.'

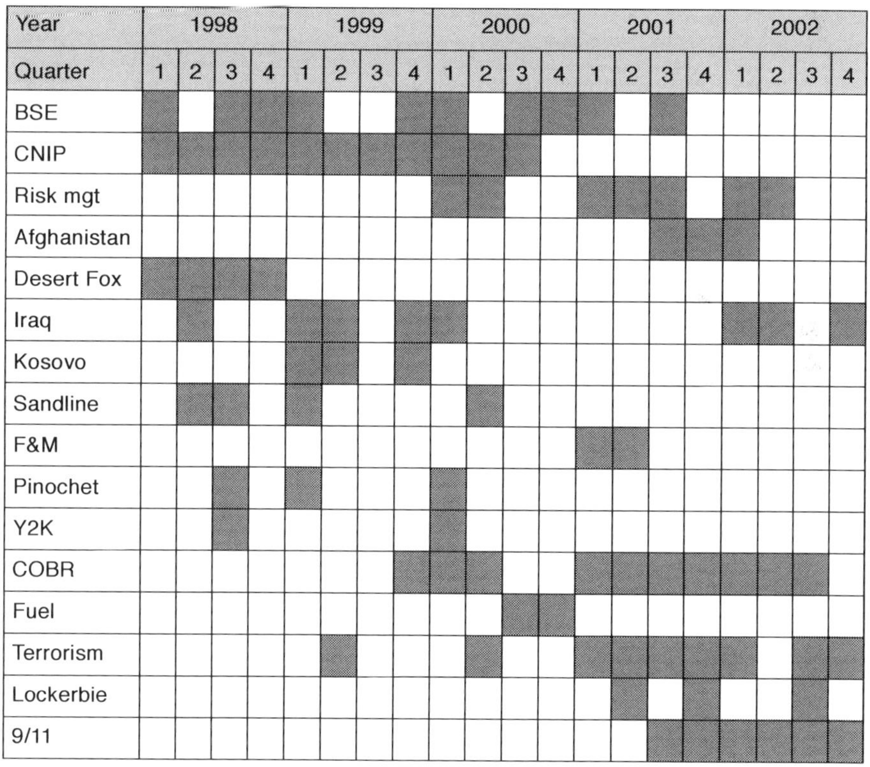

Wilson and risk management.

Robin Butler bequeathed to Wilson the main arrangements for a projected short inquiry into the handling of the BSE crisis, expected to report by the end of

1998.[381] He recapitulated the conventions governing access to (and possible publication of) documents. In essence, the consent of former Ministers to releasing papers from their period of office should be followed, and once launched an inquiry's work should be treated as if it were *sub-judice* with current Ministers avoiding any comment until after it had reported. In harmony with the long-established convention, current or former Ministers would have no access to the papers of a previous administration of a different political colour.[382] There remained the question of whether, in the interests of getting to the bottom of what happened, witnesses should be granted immunity from disciplinary proceedings. At first Wilson sought to distinguish between self-incrimination (for which there would be immunity) and incrimination by other witnesses (for which there would not). Blair, however, judged that the focus should be on getting at the truth and that this was best served by a full grant of immunity irrespective of whose evidence was involved.[383]

An important aspect of the Inquiry, repeated many times since, was that once commissioned the government lost control, not the least of timing. Far from completing its work by the end of 1998, by March it was already clear that what Lord Justice Phillips described as the 'mammoth task' of preparing evidence meant that the inquiry would miss its deadline – even when assisted by lawyers who, Phillips argued, 'are experienced in gathering documentary evidence and have the skills essential to ensure that witness statements cover the relevant ground, without becoming unnecessarily prolix.'[384] The report was eventually submitted on 2 October 2000. It made no suggestion of negligence or flagrant disregard of the risks of BSE/CJD. MAFF had acted throughout in good faith with the protection of the public always paramount. In moderate language it concluded that mistakes included delay in giving information to the public because of trying to avoid possible panic, inadequate contingency planning and a collective failure to keep key scientific assumptions under review. Officials discussed the report on 5 October and it then fell to MAFF to take matters forward in preparing a government response. David North of the Policy Unit was scathing. After almost three years, £30 million of the taxpayers' money and 17 weighty A4 volumes of report he pondered why the inquiry had not made more of the five year delay before MAFF officials addressed the unenforceability and widespread disregard of controls on slaughterhouses and rendering plants that had been issued in 1990.[385] North's note was not copied outside Number 10 and was not seen by Wilson who might otherwise have looked for incisive management action from Brian Bender (who had replaced Richard Packer as PUS at MAFF in early 2000).[386]

Fuel, Foot and Mouth and a Change of Emphasis

During the latter part of 1999 the Civil Contingencies Committee had met eight times and considered 45 papers and the Ministerial MISC 4 Group had met nine times (41 papers) to deal with the Y2K threat. The renewed focus here and in discussions about protecting critical national infrastructure revealed arrangements that were wanting – as Jim Gallagher of the Constitution Secretariat put it, whilst the UK emergency services were operationally extremely competent at handling the aftermath of a disaster, 'the hole is at the centre of the mint' and was not being filled successfully by the Emergency Planning Division.[387] Part of the explanation was that responsibilities under the 'lead department' doctrine were fragmented with no one to pull the various strands of activity together.[388] Wilson raised this issue with Omand at the Home Office, suggesting that central co-ordination of the preparation of contingency plans and lead in exercising the central and departmental emergency machinery should be ramped up. [389] Omand set in hand a scoping study to review the existing coverage of critical national infrastructure and the threats to the established processes, to be followed by a full study of possible reshaping of responsibilities, reporting by the end of March 2001.[390] But events intervened.

On 8 September the Stanlow Oil Refinery in Cheshire was blockaded by farmers in protest at the price of fuel, over 80% of which was due to tax.[391] The protests spread rapidly. Road hauliers joined the farmers and panic buying of petrol was widespread. For the first time the opinion polls put the standing of the Prime Minister below that of William Hague, Leader of the Opposition. Wilson told Omand that they both stood to lose their jobs if they could not show Blair that the situation was being gripped.[392] By 12 September 3,000 petrol stations were reported to be closed for lack of supplies.[393] COBR was transformed into a situation suite with an adjacent room staffed by senior executives of oil companies, each in turn with laptop connectivity to those who ran the refinery network globally. In the view of senior officials activation of the COBR machinery bought a few critical days of grace during which the Treasury could formulate a deal on fuel tax. Wilson brought Blair, Powell and Campbell to see COBR in operation. Blair had previously never attended; he had been told of its existence in early 1998[394] but it seems that in the absence of a substantive crisis this had not registered. Straw told him that this was the first time the COBR process had been used in a national civil emergency;[395] the Prime Minister became an instant convert.[396]

The government took emergency powers under the Energy Act, 1976, ostensively to protect fuel deliveries to essential services such as the National Health Service, which faced severe disruption. But there were doubts in officials' minds whether the powers could be effective short of a nuclear attack.[397] At the same time the government started to get out an effective public message of damage to essential services, aimed at the protesters' resolve, since they were not thought to be seeking to hurt their fellow citizens. Public support for the protest quickly started to fall from a high of 78% on 12 September to 36% (but 75% of those polled thought that the government had handled the crisis badly).[398] By 16 September fuel supplies started to return to normal. However, an Ipsos/Mori poll published after the ending of the protest still put approval of Blair at 23% compared with 32% for Hague.[399]

The protest was short-lived but it had been a near-run thing for the government and the Prime Minister had been badly shaken by the sudden drop in his personal standing with the public. He initiated contingency planning against a repeat protest[400] and despatched junior ministers to visit UK refineries to bolster the morale of fuel tanker drivers.[401] Wilson, Omand and supporting staff met in 70 Whitehall at 4.30 pm on 8 December to review the challenges the protest had posed. Omand put forward four propositions:[402] (1) ensuring the continuity of essential services should be seen as a core task of central government; (2) CCC and CCC(O) should become more proactive in assessing the potential for disruption in a modern economy; (3) escalation procedures from local agency activity to the full engagement of CCC should be clearer; (4) the Home Office should continue to be the lead Whitehall Department for responding to civil emergencies. Wilson argued for a shift in emphasis away from consideration of potential causes of disruption to managing its consequences and maintaining public confidence. Downing Street stressed that the fuel crisis had shown that there was a need for adequately assessed intelligence about what was happening on the ground and a better mechanism for the government to influence events.[403] What was clear to all was that the fuel dispute had revealed the inadequacy of the CCC mechanism and the extent to which modern 'just-in-time' society was vulnerable to trouble at logistical pinch points. It provoked a rethink from first principles.

At the start of 2001 Omand stood down because of health issues and was replaced after an interval by John Gieve. However, events once again both encouraged and disrupted progress towards improved handling of the aftermath of emergencies. On 19 February 2001 a first case of Foot and Mouth disease since 1967 was detected at an Essex abattoir in an animal from Northumberland. During the preceding 34 years the structure of agriculture and butchery had changed with much more movement of livestock around the country, so that whereas the 1967 outbreak had been confined to a relatively small area, in 2001 the epidemic spread quickly, to Devon within three days and to North Wales within a week. Government policy, based on the lessons from the 1967 outbreak, was to cull infected animals and their immediate neighbours. But the implementation of these measures to control the outbreak was slow and likely to be left behind by the rapid spread of the disease. An agricultural response that had not kept up with changes in the industry, combined with a narrow departmental view that gave insufficient attention to the impact on tourism, left the government exposed and in late March the Prime Minister asked Wilson to take control and get a grip on the developing situation.

Wilson made two crucial calls. He realised that the country faced a national epidemic and asked the government chief scientist, Dave King, to contact leading academic epidemiologists. Professor Roy Anderson of Imperial College modelled the likely development of the disease, his work pointing to the enormity of the cull that would be needed. As a result the Army was mobilised to manage the logistics of the government response. At its peak there were 80,000–90,000 animals slaughtered a week and by the time of the final case, reported in September, over 10 million sheep and cattle had been killed and the tourist industry had been severely damaged by the accompanying restrictions on access to the countryside, including the cancellation of horse race meetings.

Blair later described Wilson's initiative in tapping into the academic scientific advice as a masterstroke.[404]

Amidst the crisis and the accompanying slaughter of animals Wilson found time to think of David Omand and to give him a flavour of how Whitehall was coping as Omand underwent a stem cell transplant. He wrote:

> 'The biggest show in town of course is Foot and Mouth disease. We have COBR every morning at 8.30 with me or Geoff Hoon [Secretary of State for Defence] in the chair, and the Prime Minister occasionally wandering in like Hamlet, and the whole thing is an endless grind through detail and information of a kind which we would much rather not have to know about. The sheer scale of the logistics is extraordinary and not generally appreciated. According to our excellent Brigadier (who seems to be running MAFF rather like a glove puppet) the number of transport movements is so far several times greater than they had to make in the Gulf war. Brian Bender [PUS at MAFF] is bearing up but looks as if he has had several years of Permanent Secretary experience crammed into a couple of months. The jobs which we do really are very difficult indeed. It is something which worries me not a little.'[405]

On 25 April in the margins of the Wednesday morning meeting of Permanent Secretaries Wilson's private office told Kevin Tebbit (PUS at MOD) that, prompted by Blair's dissatisfaction, 'the Cabinet Secretary had it in mind ... to bring back to the Cabinet Office the responsibility for civil crisis management arrangements.'[406] The Home Office got wind of this and on 3 May Gieve wrote to defend the Department's responsibility for emergency planning. He pointed to the risks of duplication should the Cabinet Office take over since the Home Office would remain responsible for public order and for dealing with terrorist incidents.[407] A meeting was fixed for 14 May at which proposals for a transfer of the Emergency Planning Division to the Cabinet Office were discussed on the basis of a note from Lindsay Bell and Mike Granatt describing how the unit (to be renamed the Civil Contingencies Secretariat) might work and floating the idea of reviving a domestic equivalent of the JIC to assess the findings of an open horizon scanning team under the Secretariat.

At the interdepartmental meeting the broad shape of a unit in the Cabinet Office which would subsume the Home Office Emergency Planning Division was agreed and the change promulgated internally on 20 June.[408] There would be three capabilities: a new section for horizon scanning for threats to the critical national infrastructure; civil contingency planning; and expertise in response to a crisis. Location in the Cabinet Office would make it easier to trigger bringing the central apparatus (working through a refurbished COBR) routinely into play without loss of face for other departments. The Home Secretary would continue to chair the Ministerial Civil Contingencies Committee and there would be no change to arrangements concerning public order, civil defence, terrorist actions or overseas and defence-related crises. Ministerial championing and a reporting line to the Head of the Home Civil Service would be key in maintaining visibility – a particular challenge because, hopefully, the unit would often be planning for things which did not happen.[409] Mike Granatt, the new head of the Secretariat, was also at pains to distinguish between emergencies (which in his view crucially required plans and structures through which the excellent UK operational services could be deployed) and crises (defined as an overwhelming rush of problems, failure of conventional solutions and undetected changes in the paradigm such that the organisation usually did not know it was facing crisis until catastrophe loomed).[410] The doctrine later evolved into a distinction between sudden cataclysmic events and emergencies such as Foot and Mouth, which came up like a rising tide. Within two months the AQ attack on the Twin Towers in New York delivered a sudden cataclysmic shock to Western confidence.

The Attack on the Twin Towers and its Aftermath

Blair was in Brighton preparing to speak to the TUC annual Conference when news of the New York atrocities hit the lunchtime television screens. He watched in horror as the first of the twin towers collapsed. A plane had been flown into the World Trade Center. Then a second plane hit the second tower. A third plane had been flown into the Pentagon in Washington and a fourth attack thwarted when passengers stormed the cabin of United Airlines flight 93, possibly preventing an attack on the White House.[411] There had been no specific indications of the attack and such information as there was is notoriously difficult to pin down. Blair heard of the first attack about 40 minutes before he was due to address Conference. As the news worsened it became clear that to go ahead with his planned speech would be inappropriate; so after a brief few words of explanation to delegates Blair left for London, travelling on the 13.49 train.[412]

Wilson was in a car returning to 70 Whitehall after a lunch appointment in Wilton Road, behind Victoria Station, when news came in of the second plane hitting the Twin Towers. As his driver negotiated Parliament Square he received a call from Heywood in 10 Downing Street asking if the building should be evacuated. Downing Street was fearful of an imminent attack in London and, in view of the nature of the attacks in New York, it was thought that its current evacuation plan could have been an evacuation into danger. With no alternative plan of where they should go, Wilson told them to sit tight.

After seeking reassurance that assessment of the risk to the UK was in hand one of Blair's early concerns was how the United States would react. Wilson's focus was to deal with any possible threat to the UK (and particularly London) and to trigger the COBR mechanism for the Prime Minister's return. Both were easier said than done. In the summer months whilst Parliament is in recess officials are able to move outside London with greater frequency and on 11 September key personnel were away from the city. The newly created Civil Contingencies Secretariat was in Yorkshire on a team-building exercise at the Home Office Emergency Planning College; the Overseas and Defence Secretariat was en route, also for a team event, to Hereford; Sir David Manning, the Prime Minister's adviser on foreign policy was caught in New York by the immediate ban on flights.

Wilson called a meeting of official COBR for 4.30 pm and Blair decided on a Ministerial COBR to be chaired by himself at 5.30 pm. The 4.30 pm meeting was crowded and as Wilson chaired the discussion a summons came to attend Blair who would be back from Brighton imminently. Gieve of the Home Office took over the chairmanship as Wilson, accompanied by Lander (MI5) and Scarlett (MI6), went to brief the Prime Minister. Blair then decided that he should go down to COBR immediately and before the 5.30 pm summons. When he and Wilson arrived everyone seemed to have disappeared, gone to brief their Ministers. Undeterred the Prime Minister began the meeting with those who were there and one by one Hoon, Straw, Milburn, Blunkett, Byers and Brown and Balls turned up. When the meeting finished a small group including Straw, Hoon and Wilson went back with Blair to the study in Number 10 where it was agreed that Blair would speak to the press at 6.45 pm and the group jointly drafted a statement. After that everyone stood around watching the television while Scarlett assembled extensive briefing.

The following day (12 September) Ministerial COBR met twice. At an 8.00 am session an updated estimate of fatalities was tabled: 10,000 or more civilians in the Twin Towers, 266 passengers in four hijacked aircraft, 300–400 emergency service personnel, 800 Pentagon staff. Over 1,000 police had been deployed on the streets in London and at airports; six RAF aircraft were at 15 minutes' notice for air defence with a Ministerial authorisation mechanism in place. Wilson then chaired the Wednesday morning Permanent Secretary meeting at 10.00 am and a Civil Service Management Board at 11.00 am yet still had time to organise an impromptu presentation in the Cabinet Room on Bin Laden and the Taliban for the Prime Minister at 2 pm followed by an official COBR at 4 pm and a Ministerial COBR at 6 pm.

In addition to further updates on diplomatic activity, financial markets and intelligence the Ministerial COBR discussed air traffic and airport security and called for augmented emergency planning to encompass multiple or unconventional attacks on the UK. Wilson was particularly concerned about a possible challenge to the closure of London City airport, which was privately owned. It was agreed that the airport should remain closed for another day, with a presumption that it would reopen on Friday 14th. The no-fly zone over central London should continue but restrictions could be lifted elsewhere. The JIC Assessments Staff should assess the implications of the attacks in the US for the type of terrorist activity that might take place in the UK and this should inform the further work of the Civil Contingencies Secretariat. Meanwhile the public should be prepared for announcements of significant British casualties.[413]

The head of the OD Secretariat advised Wilson that the legal basis for any military response to the attack must be either a United Nations Security Council Resolution or self-defence (which in turn would be subject to a test that it was a proportionate response to an imminent threat with no other means to avert that threat).[414] Blair, meantime, sent a letter to President Bush identifying three goals: to bring to justice those responsible; to construct an agenda for action against international terrorism; to co-opt the world's leading countries in support of action.[415] Wilson asked Lander to make an urgent assessment of its powers and resources in the light of the attacks in the United States and Granatt to look at Departments' resilience to various types of threat and attack.

Thirty six hours after the first emergency Whitehall co-ordination had established a rhythm – a restricted pol/mil group chaired by Sir David Manning (the Ad Hoc Group on International Terror – AHGIT) would oversee the UK's political and military response; COBR would meet daily (shadowed by an official group under McKane) and COBRA would be manned on a 24-hour basis by the Cabinet Office. Departments, meanwhile, should remain at one hour's notice to attend COBR meetings, in accordance with existing terrorist alert procedures.[416] Within a further 24 hours business continuity plans had been updated for Downing Street and the Cabinet Office in the event of a terrorist attack.[417] By the end of the first full week after the attacks further steps had been taken: Lander had provided the Prime Minister's staff with an assessment of how existing UK law hindered the fight against international terrorism;[418] Whitehall remained on AMBER alert[419]; a planned Whitehall weekend Open Day should, at a minimum, exclude the Cabinet Office, FCO and MOD; a seven-man UK military team was deployed to Islamabad to undertake contingency planning for evacuation of UK citizens; the Cabinet Office circulated a draft strategy to combat terrorism.[420] Building on Lander's work, Wilson submitted a proposal to Blair for an additional 5% to be added to the budgets of the Intelligence Agencies: 'Last Tuesday's events changed our view of the threat from international terrorism,' he wrote 'I think we need to move now to show the Americans that we are stepping up our intelligence effort.'[421]

Heywood reported four important strands of Whitehall work:

a. Proposals from David Blunkett (the new Home Secretary) to strengthen the UK regime for deporting suspected terrorists; changing asylum rules to exclude claims by suspected terrorists, better information-sharing between and within governments and a move to compulsory ID cards.
b. Treasury and Bank of England measures to follow the money trail and to cut off terrorist financing.
c. Proposals to strengthen EU rules, particularly in countries with no anti-terrorism legislation.
d. A proposed new UN Security Council Resolution and enhanced pressure on all countries to ratify the existing UN convention on terrorism.[422]

Blair was bullish. 'The measures on asylum and immigration must be tougher; in particular dealing with manifestly unfounded claims; we must be able to get rid of terrorists operating in the UK … The only risk is not going far enough [on changes in the law]. The key to getting it through is cross-party agreement.'[423]

The Second Week After 9/11

The second full week saw Wilson seeking to engage a fuller range of Whitehall co-ordination in a less frenetic atmosphere. He wrote to the Permanent Secretaries of the FCO, HMT, MOD, HO, DTLR and DCMS and also to Manning and Heywood to explain the various committees: AHGIT (meeting twice a week) would develop strategy for the international response to the attacks in the US and to that end would be augmented by HMT and DfID; the Civil Contingencies Secretariat would handle consequence management including the repatriation of bodies from New York and would review Departmental business continuity plans in the light of possible mass terrorism. COBR would no longer meet daily but the situation room would continue to be manned on a 24-hour basis. The Official Committee on Domestic and International Terrorism (TIDO) would resume day-to-day responsibility for protective security and counter-terrorist measures (including airline security).[424] It met 12 times in 2001 and considered 30 papers. Wilson passed chairmanship of the Official Committee on Security (SO) to Omand who had returned from treatment for cancer. The Economic and Domestic Secretariat (EDS) would handle legislation; the Defence and Overseas Secretariat would consider urgently how to progress the Weapons of Mass destruction clauses in export controls. Blair later commented that: 'I was glad of the steady hand of Richard Wilson and his senior Civil Service colleagues.'[425]

On 20 and 24 September Wilson held small interdepartmental meetings to consider further measures to combat terrorism that could either be taken in the UK or by the UK on the international scene. These included, but were not confined to: special courts for terrorist offences; a protocol to amend the European Convention on Human Rights (ECHR); the use of intercept evidence in court and cutting off terrorist funds. Wilson also raised the possibility of a Marshall Plan for Afghanistan (modelled on experience in Kosovo) and at home the possibility of a special emergency power to enable the government to take action to prevent terrorist attacks in circumstances where it did not currently have the necessary powers.[426] When Heywood showed Blair Wilson's proposal the Prime Minister commented, 'This is an excellent idea. We could have the exercise subject to ex-post facto scrutiny as a check.' But the government lawyers poured cold water on the prospect, raising many difficulties over scope, definition and independent prior oversight of proposals to override the ECHR.[427] The suggestion was still on the table at an ad hoc Ministerial meeting on 24 September at which key officials were also present but appears not to have been progressed after a further meeting on 27 September when Wilson reported that a way had been found to enable the deportation of terrorists otherwise protected under Article 3 of the ECHR. This involved a Secretary of State being given power to certify that he/she was satisfied that an individual could be deported on the basis of a commitment from the receiving country that the person would not be subject to torture. The Special Immigration Appeals Commission (SIAC) would consider individual cases and if deportation was not upheld a derogation from Article 5 of the ECHR would allow indefinite detention of the individual.[428] (The derogation was subsequently struck down by a Law Lords judgement of December 2004 that detaining only foreign terrorist suspects without trial pending deportation was discriminatory. Either the government would have to take general powers for detention or find another way – the latter course eventually resulted in Control Orders.)[429]

Meanwhile attention moved to the challenge of educating public opinion. Manning reported on 23 September that: 'I have been struck in the past 24 hours by the degree of popular nervousness here over impending military action. Friends and contacts whom I would have expected to be more level-headed are asking some pretty daft questions about the nature of 'the war' we are about to wage, when will we introduce conscription etc. Perhaps I am over-endowed with daft friends. But if this anecdotal evidence is anything to go by, I think there is a case for the Prime Minister making a real effort very soon to steady people's nerves and put military action into an overall political context.'[430] Wilson annotated his copy with: 'I agree with this comment. A very senior ex-colleague rang me over the weekend to ask whether the PM really intended a declaration of war.' The JIC Chairman, John Scarlett, prepared a paper on evidence about the attack that could be quoted in public, including about the culpability of Usama Bin Laden (UBL).[431] Blair was becoming exasperated by the lawyers' caution: '... they cannot be serious about the Taleban ... how on earth do we satisfy [the imminence test]? We can't be sure, but we shouldn't take the risk!'[432] He asked the Security Service for examples that could be made public of where the government had been stymied in attempts to get terrorists deported or otherwise deal with them by legislation, tribunals or human rights legislation.[433] Lander was unenthusiastic as he foresaw 'real difficulty in using this material publicly' partly because some cases were still before the Courts and partly because, unless used under Parliamentary privilege, it could bring libel actions down on the government's head. A six-page unclassified draft under the title *Usama Bin Laden: Complicity in the US Atrocities* was ready by 26 September.[434] Wilson congratulated Scarlett for a first-rate piece of work and it was forwarded to the Americans who were understood to be preparing their own White Paper on culpability.[435] The response was not encouraging. Brent Scowcroft, the President's National Security Adviser, thought the evidence too circumstantial to publish.[436]

The end of a Frenetic Month

By the end of September preparations for a military input to bring UBL to justice were advanced. They included proposals for the daily Whitehall rhythm when the military phase started.[437] Wilson proposed building on the experience of Kosovo: at its centre would be a daily Ministerial meeting chaired by the Prime Minister at 8.30am involving the Secretaries of State for Defence, Foreign Affairs, and International Development with the Chief of the Defence staff (CDS), the intelligence agency heads and the JIC chairman. The Home Secretary and other Ministers would attend as necessary. Diplomatically, Wilson said: 'You will want to consider whether the Chancellor should be a member;' – Harold Macmillan's advice to Margaret Thatcher in 1982 had been not to include the Chancellor in a War Cabinet. As Blair was often at Chequers on Fridays he decided on four meetings a week, at least two of which should involve the Chancellor.[438] There would be an MOD press conference at 11.30am as required (i.e. not daily as had been the case during the Kosovo campaign). The full proposals were:

0600	Current Intelligence Group to provide an assessment update (key intelligence staff working through the night)
0745	One page situation report provided to 10 Downing Street
0830	Prime Minister's Ministerial meeting. Wilson objected to the shorthand of calling this a 'War Cabinet' as 'We are not at war'[439]
0900	No 10 media co-ordination meeting chaired by Alastair Campbell
1100	Lobby briefing
1130	MOD press conference (as required)
1230	Whitehall co-ordination meeting chaired by David Manning
1400	Humanitarian Group chaired by John Vereker of DfID
1600	Lobby briefing
pm (unspecified)	Chief of Staffs meeting

October – December

Four groups of issues continued to demand much of Wilson's time and energy throughout the remainder of 2001. The first was continued reappraisal of the state of readiness in government; a second centred on the legality of proposed government actions; a third, for which there were precedents, was about controlling military action; and a fourth was handling public opinion in a potentially charged environment previously largely unknown in the UK. At the heart of Whitehall lay the effectiveness of COBR and the Civil Contingencies Secretariat (CCS) not just in operational emergencies but also in prevention and in consequence management. COBR was run by the Defence and Overseas Policy Secretariat not the CCS and had never been intended to cover prevention. From the time of the BSE epidemic of 1986 through to 9/11 the story had been applying the lessons from the last emergency to civil contingency planning but never quite quickly enough to be ready for the next.[440]

On the evening of 3 October the Civil Contingencies Committee met under the chairmanship of the Home Secretary and agreed to set up three sub-committees dealing with, respectively, UK resilience to mass terrorist attack, London resilience to a similar threat, and the aftermath of possible chemical, biological or nuclear attacks by terrorists.[441] In mid month Wilson told Blunkett – possibly intended to get back to Blair – that after having been knocked sideways by events since 11 September the Civil Contingencies Secretariat was getting its act together.[442] The evidence is, however, that in general Wilson was not quite so confident. In a chilling progress report on 25 October the Defence Secretariat briefed on the nuclear threat, including intelligence that nuclear material may have fallen into terrorist hands; TIDO was pressing for new protective measures at ports of entry to the UK.

In mid October the National Audit Office announced 'out of the blue' an intention to audit the Civil Contingencies Secretariat. The Cabinet Office worried about two aspects of this. First that it set a precedent about the scrutiny of its Secretariats which hitherto had never been subject to NAO investigation; and also that: 'we are in the middle of a very significant crisis and do not want to direct effort away from this national priority.'[443] Meanwhile, Wilson continued to emphasise that Whitehall arrangements needed to be kept at high alert. At the end of October he once again wrote to Permanent Secretaries reprising Whitehall responsibilities and machinery for counter terrorism. The CCC asked all Departments to review their contingency plans.[444] Downing Street dismissed a report by the Civil Contingencies Secretariat on the preparedness of the UK for dealing with mass terrorism as complacent and unconvincing.[445] A report in December indicated how far departmental contingency planning had fallen into disrepair, identifying problems with the robustness of planning as well as with emerging vulnerabilities such as the storage of toxic chemicals, the risk of a dramatic loss of public confidence in the safety of London, and a rise in community tensions.[446]

There were also new demands. One was to establish procedures for authorising the RAF to fire on rogue aircraft balancing the risks of commission and omission (known as operation ADANA). Wilson first raised the issue at COBR immediately after the 9/11 atrocities. Manning, a frequent interlocutor of Condoleezza Rice the President's National Security Adviser, returned to it on 1 October seeking guidance from the MOD but volunteering that he did not favour the US protocol of having a serving military officer take the decision should it be impossible to contact the President.[447] Nor did Wilson, who favoured the Defence Secretary as deputy to the Prime Minister in this decision. Blair approved these arrangements (including the Secretary of State for Defence as his deputy) at the end of the month.[448]

At the start of October Wilson reviewed contingency planning for the evacuation of Downing Street and Cabinet Office staff, expressing concern that planning was at too high a level of generality. He commissioned urgent work to firm up operational instructions by which staff would move to the MOD bunker (PINDAR) and then to work up other options not using PINDAR, including how to maintain the chain of command.[449] By 5 October he could tell the Prime Minister that: 'It is essential that we have a clear, simple plan for evacuating Number 10 (and 70 Whitehall) quickly if we have to. A week ago we had no such plan ... we now have such a plan which covers the safety of you and your family as well as all staff.'[450] Which was as well for Condoleezza Rice alerted Manning on 13 October to 'real concern about the safety of the Prime Minister' who, in the second week after the attacks on the US, had embarked on a series of flying visits to rally world political leaders behind the US-led response. The warning followed an Al Qaeda broadcast on Qatari Al-Jazeera satellite television by Sulayman Abu Ghayth, an official spokesman for UBL, in which Blair was among a small group of people threatened with unspecified punishment.[451] At sessions on 18th and again on 23rd to review safety in the Downing Street/ Cabinet Office complex further measures were considered, including moving staff out of the 3rd floor of 10 Downing Street and the possibility of creating new offices for the Prime Minister away from Downing Street, using that complex solely for the staging of events.[452]

The legal position continued to be problematic. Wilson wrote to Gieve at the Home Office: 'I would like to return to ... the taking of emergency power. Let me explain why. Some of the situations which we might now face, and which we are having to address, in the world after 11 September could be very threatening to the orderly running of society. This is a factual observation. If they were to materialise we might have no warning of them before they occurred. But it is just possible that we might have some clue that something was up or that certain individuals – 'clean skins' in the phrase of your letter [of 3 October] – might be up to something without having the sort of evidence that would prove it. The legal position ... has baffled – I am tempted to say defeated – us all for years ... what does the Home Secretary do in practical terms if ... he is driven into an emergency situation for whatever reason where he urgently needs to detain people as a matter of public safety without having time to rush through legislation but with the possibility that his legal powers are inadequate? Could officials give the Prime Minister the assurance he wanted?'[453] Blair thought not. Heywood conveyed to the Home Office on 15 October that Blair was not clear why the earlier idea of a certification scheme for deportation had been dropped and that the Prime Minister was also keen that the Home Secretary should work up proposals that could be introduced at very short notice to allow the emergency detention of UK citizens who were a threat to national security.[454]

The immediate and long-term objectives for political and military action were circulated to the Deputy Prime Minister, Home Secretary, Attorney General and to members of DOP on 3 October and to Cabinet on 10th.[455] The air offensive (Operation VERITAS) started on 7 October with attacks on 32 military targets in Afghanistan. This opening phase of operations was expected to last 3–5 days. A day later a Ministerial Committee on International Terrorism was set up (DOP(IT)T) following precedents from the Falklands and Gulf conflicts. This represented a formalisation of arrangements compared to the ad hoc arrangements favoured by Blair during the Kosovo crisis with a remit: 'To keep under review the Government's policy on international terrorism, in particular the political, military and humanitarian responses to the attacks in the United States on 11 September and preventive security measures in the United Kingdom and overseas.' Its members were the Prime Minister, Deputy Prime Minister, Chancellor of the Exchequer, President of the Council, Foreign Secretary, Home Secretary, and the Secretaries of State for International Development and Defence. The Attorney General and CDS, together with Heads of the Intelligence Agencies would attend when necessary. A first meeting was scheduled for 8 October. Meanwhile Blair was urging caution over the effectiveness of a campaign without ground troops and the consequences if the conflict were widened to Iraq.[456]

Blair raised *inter alia* the question of 'Who keeps order in Afghanistan once we win?' and stressed the importance of UK co-ordination by co-location of staff.[457] On 7 November Wilson replied with advice on how to strengthen operational arrangements at the Whitehall centre.[458]

Structure of emergency control

- **CABINET**
  DOP(IT) – Weekly policy discussion
  DOP(IT) EXECUTIVE – Daily operations
  COBR – INFORMATION ROOM – Daily rolling brief by DOP(IT) Secretarit
  GOVERNMENT DEPARTMENTS AND AGENCIES

A strengthened COBR, open indefinitely on a round-the-clock basis, sat at the centre of the web. It would produce two situation reports. By 7.30 am each working day (10.00 am at weekends) it would issue a one page report covering the main international or military developments overnight; and by 7.00 pm a considered executive report covering:

a. Special operations
b. Future of Afghanistan
c. Humanitarian situation
d. Pakistan
e. Military campaign (including building the coalition)
f. Wider campaign against terrorism
g. Middle East Peace Process
h. Threat to UK interests
i. UK internal security

After the discouraging comments from Scowcroft about the document intended to show UBL's complicity in the 9/11 attacks, Wilson wondered whether the reaction was as much from not wanting to be upstaged as from concern about the evidential nature of the content. He floated the idea of a joint UK-US paper. Meanwhile Manning spoke to Condoleezza Rice and gained the impression that opposition to publication of the UK document might not be as strong as had been inferred. A joint paper, on the other hand, would signal that the response to 9/11 was an Anglo-American effort whilst the intention was to form a broader coalition.[459] Manning subsequently told Rice that Blair would release the UK document by putting it in the House of Commons Library on 4 October.[460] Some press reaction bore out the initial American reservations. *The Daily Telegraph*, for instance, carried the headline 'Legal proof 'is weak' based on comments from Matrix Chambers.[461]

Evidence about the public mood was presented to Granatt on 2 October based on media comment and work by the Police National Public Order Intelligence

Unit. It suggested that whilst the 'War on Terrorism' was losing its position as a lead story, there was support for controlled, targeted and proportionate military action. However, it also reported widespread xenophobic attacks against Islamic targets and that British military casualties or a perception that military action was an attack on Islam could bring public disorder on a national scale.[462] Three days later the Chief Medical Officer circulated a note on biochemical terrorism and its possible effects. Blair came down firmly against publicity for the preventative measures it described: 'Of course we must plan on every eventuality; but there is a fine line between preparation and panic.'[463] By December there were concerns that the impetus for improved protective security and public safety awareness could be flagging. In a discussion with Lander, Gieve, Heywood and others on 6 December Wilson suggested that colleagues (by which he primarily meant Permanent Secretaries) – needed to show that this was not so. He proposed major public action on security in, for example, the transport sector, as a clear signal that security was being tightened and thereby act as a deterrent.[464] Additionally, during 2002 there were three exercises to test the government's response to CBRN terrorism, including one on testing the actual response to a chemical release.[465]

January – October 2002

COBR continued to operate throughout 2002, moving to PINDAR for six months to allow a deep refurbishment and updating of the room and its equipment. What had started as a situation room became a suite for managing emergencies with three conference rooms and surrounding offices each equipped with communications to Departments, Agencies, police etc. A planned final session on international terrorism (11 January) was followed by revival on the face of likely attacks on the UK (1 May), assessment of the Bali bombing that had killed over 185 people including 26 UK nationals (17 October) and immediate authorisation of increased security at Heathrow airport (18 October).

In May Omand was asked to take a short, sharp look at the working of the Civil Contingencies Secretariat. The aftermath of 9/11 had understandably put the main focus on London as a possible terrorist target with a side order of protection for Critical National Infrastructure (CNI), including the nuclear sites.[466] Groups had mushroomed and demarcations were unclear. Omand delicately put it that all felt the timing was right to regroup in order to move quickly to the next stage of work – a switch from central direction of operational activity to ensuring delivery of the key capability improvements.[467] He described the situation as: 'One of the biggest muddles you have ever seen ... I have found widespread agreement that we could get the business done faster if we simplified responsibilities and working methods ... The single most cost-effective extra measure is to create a regional capability for emergency response ... taking advantage of the regional structures being set up for public health and military support.'[468] This should draw in local government Chief Executives to get a step change in commitment and performance across the country. The old loyalty to Civil

Defence was by now out of date and discredited: 'We must expect most overseas crises to have domestic security implications' and the Whitehall committee structures should be revised accordingly. The distinction between prevention of terrorism and managing its consequences meant that work streams that were closely related came together only with the Home Secretary as chairman of CCC and of DOP(IT)T. He proposed simplifying and consolidating structures under the Home Secretary:

Omand CCS proposals

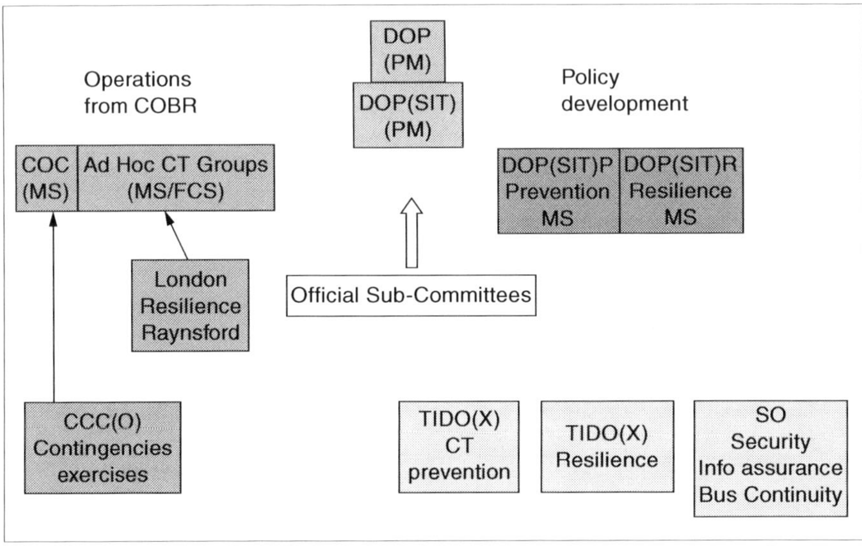

Wilson used the phrase 'In the end all crises are local' to good effect in support of Omand's proposals and by the autumn the arrangements had been further developed by elaborate flow diagrams describing the steps to be taken to ensure business continuity in the first 48 hours after a serious disruption to the operation of government.[469]

In March the Home Office had tentatively broached an idea to review the intelligence agencies' performance in the context of 11 September.[470] The Home Secretary's intention was for a small team led by a former Permanent Secretary to carry out the work over two to three months in the autumn concentrating on lessons learned rather than seeking to apportion blame. However, when Manning and Scarlett discussed the proposition with Wilson on 2 May he was sceptical both of the ability to avoid an exercise in bayoneting the wounded and in imposing a significant extra burden on the main players. Further, there had been no public or parliamentary demands for a review and no state of affairs to justify it. An informal exercise might be possible but he was reluctant to propose any formal machinery of inquiry.[471] He reported the initiative to the Prime Minister on 14 May excluding the possibility of an external formal review in favour of a secret internal study led by a JIC member and focussing on the intelligence community's assessment of the threat, the priority accorded to operational action to counter it, and co-ordination with law enforcement and policy makers. Blair was unenthusiastic: 'Fine. But I see no actual need for one and I certainly don't want the Service feeling under pressure; i.e. let us learn any internal lessons but no fuss and no publicity.'[472]

At the same time as he was helping Blair develop better emergency planning, Wilson's influence with the Prime Minister was being severely tested over the selection of his successor. Wilson would reach 60 on 11 October 2002 and planned to retire at the end of August so that his successor could have a clear run at the job before Parliament returned and the pace of business accelerated. In keeping with the improved transparency in appointments then widely expected and a wish to bolster the traditional political neutrality of the civil service, he proposed a formal process involving the identification of a short list by a panel which would include the First Civil Service Commissioner. The final choice would then lie with Blair from a list of two or three submitted by the panel with their recommendation for appointment. He argued for maintaining the joint role of Cabinet Secretary and Head of the Home Civil Service on the grounds that a split would weaken both positions and thereby Blair's own power and effectiveness.[473] By contrast, the internal advice from Downing Street staff and some Permanent Secretaries was to split the roles, appointing a Chief Executive for the Civil Service and a Cabinet Secretary subservient to that post for the traditional secretariat and other tasks, possibly merging the Cabinet Secretary and Principal Private Secretary posts.[474] Montagu, Chairman of the Inland Revenue, for example, argued that combining the roles: '... is a paradigm based on assumptions which do not fit the working methods of the present Government.'[475]

In the first of two personal notes, Blair concluded in December 2001 that the same result could be achieved without the likely constitutional row that would follow from a formal division of the posts. He could appoint a different type of Cabinet Secretary and delegate the traditional role, now of secondary importance, to a deputy, adding: 'The second issue is outsiders and the manner of appointment. The problem is [that] to have an outsider with no experience of the civil service is a bit like appointing a person to a big Cabinet job with no experience of politics. It might work but it might be disastrous and the precedents, frankly, aren't great. Plainly the optimum is someone who has done both. I have a real fear that if we just go for a [Civil Service] appointment, then radical change – real thinking outside the box will not happen ... But remember: it is substance, not poking our finger in the [Civil Service] eye that matters.' However, Jonathan Powell returned to the charge early in the new year with a strong message: '... we should not lose sight of our key aim: to appoint a reforming chief executive of the civil service and get them to spend 100% of their time on gripping the management of the civil service, civil service reform and delivery. Everything else is secondary.' Further, Powell introduced a new and damaging accusation that: 'There is a reason that Richard [Wilson] and his predecessors have spent *only one day a week* on the civil service'[476] [emphasis added]. It was a false charge. Butler had told the Public Administration Select

Committee that he had spent 50% of his time on civil service matters. Wilson, as evidenced by his appointment diaries, had clearly done more than Powell alleged.

Blair set up a brainstorming session with No 10 staff (Heywood, Powell, Thomson and Birt) excluding Wilson.[477] The result was to move the thinking towards either radical action to put an outsider at the top with the risk that the civil service would reject the transplant, or to appoint an insider who was sympathetic to reform with an outsider as the deputy, focused on management. But would any insider be strong enough to back the outsider if the Permanent Secretaries opposed proposed reforms? The next stage, recorded Powell, was to persuade Wilson to agree to a private search by an outside company for suitable outsiders for either option.[478] In addition, the opinions of a number of sympathetic senior businessmen were also canvassed. The message was consistent. A true outsider would have no chance of success; someone with experience of both worlds might pull it off.

In a second think piece from January 2002 Blair argued for delegating some existing Cabinet Secretary tasks such as propriety, ethics, honours, constitutional matters and increasing the scope of the No 10 Principal Private Secretary post to oversee the Cabinet secretariats etc. He felt sure that the constitutional implications of appearing to merge No 10 and Cabinet Office functions could be circumvented but the key thing was that: 'We can't have a No 1 who is non-reforming and a No 2 who reforms. It won't work. So we should start to seek out now the right person. I believe it could be Bichard.[479] But it could be someone from outside.'[480]

Not being party to these thoughts, Wilson reassured Permanent Secretary colleagues that the appointment would be internal, encouraging those he thought to be credible candidates. He believed that he had an agreement with Blair that an outsider would not be appointed as it was too big a risk and would further alienate civil servants.[481] Powell nevertheless told Blair that Wilson would go along with an approach to outside executive search as a political necessity.[482] Wilson did not know, however, that help from three executive search firms was sought.[483] He told Blair there were two serious risks in the latest proposals: (a) something that the Cabinet Secretary would normally have spotted and stopped would go wrong because he or she was concentrating on delivery – events would drag everyone back to the present arrangements; and (b) close identification of Blair with a Cabinet Secretary almost exclusively targeted on reform would leave the Prime Minister exposed when a Department hit trouble.[484]

Nevertheless, Wilson's draft announcement about the arrangements for selecting his successor contained the information that: 'The Prime Minister has made it clear, however, that he wants whoever is selected to concentrate primarily on the delivery of improved public services and reform in the Civil Service and other parts of the public sector, to reflect the government's top priorities.' 'If there is any chance of this being leaked,' wrote Blair, 'then this [sentence] should be removed.'[485] He went ahead with the arrangements he believed that he had agreed with the Prime Minister and had promulgated. A short list of possible successors would be selected by a panel of independent people including the First Civil Service Commissioner and Lord Simon. But the arrangements were not as settled as Wilson thought. Powell advised that Wilson was likely to try to bounce Blair into agreeing a successor in his own mould.[486] And when on 7 March Wilson learned that Bichard was still in the frame, despite widespread advice that he was too unpopular to be able to carry people with him, Wilson was outraged at what he saw as going back on a process previously agreed with the Prime Minister. He confronted Blair in the Downing Street study in strong terms.[487]

On returning to the Cabinet Office Wilson confided in Mavis McDonald that he thought he might have to resign. In the event, however, the Principal Private Secretary came to the Cabinet Secretary's panelled room at the rear of 70 Whitehall with an olive branch. Blair would stick by the formerly agreed process. Wilson had won the immediate battle but at a price – he was frozen out in his last few months from discussions on Iraq, by the team around Blair.[488] The Prime Minister now took the unprecedented step of inviting four leading candidates (not including Bichard) to submit personal statements in support of their candidatures. He interviewed each during late March and April, choosing Andrew Turnbull of the Treasury, whose personal statement to Blair included an intention, 'to lead a debate on the reform of the Civil Service which is performance led and not, as at present, nostalgic and ethics dominated.' Blair consoled at least one disappointed candidate that Turnbull had the edge because he would be better able to deal with Gordon Brown (a not entirely convincing argument since it would be the staff of Downing Street, and not those in the Cabinet Office, who would have the main task of linking with Brown politically). Powell, meanwhile, argued that Blair should see Turnbull again before announcing the appointment, 'to pin him down on certain key points before you offer him the job,' and 'to reassure [Turnbull] that he will be brought properly within the inner circle in a way that Richard Wilson never was,[489] which was not entirely the case beyond delivery and reform issues.[490]

The announcement of Turnbull's appointment as Secretary of the Cabinet and Head of the Home Civil Service was made on 19 April. He revealed plans for Cabinet Office restructuring taking in the 'young Turks' of No 10 but surrendering security and intelligence to David Omand. Wilson confided to Michael Jay of the FCO that he feared Turnbull was heading for overload and a focus on issues about which Tony Blair cared least. He told Alice Perkins that in his view it was a mistake to give up the intelligence work because it carried a unique authority with any Prime Minister.

The frustration of the New Labour leadership with the pace of change in delivering public services coloured the immediate aftermath of the Blair years as this irritation was vented in political memoirs. But their successors in Labour post-2007 and in the Conservative-led coalition of 2010 also felt frustrated in this regard. The later Blair years are indelibly associated with the decision to invade Iraq, but Wilson's time was also one of abnormally intense military activity with which he was deeply engaged – Operation Desert Fox, Kosovo, Sierre

Leone, Afghanistan – and which took up a great deal of time. In evidence to the Chilcot inquiry Wilson said of his involvement with the Afghanistan air strikes that in the 18 weeks between 11 September 2001 and 17 January 2002 he attended and took the record of 46 Ministerial discussions of which 13 were in Cabinet, 12 were in Cabinet Committee and 21 were ad hoc.

There were undoubtedly problems with emergencies, notably the fuel crisis of 2000 and the Foot and Mouth outbreak of 2001. But Wilson's actions were crucial to finding solutions and in creating the conditions that allowed the central machinery to cope well with the aftermath of the 9/11 attacks. His supervision of the Intelligence Agencies through their need to adjust to a new threat was successful. Some progress was made in improving the co-ordination of policy formulation across departmental boundaries but the weak link of delivery of services to the citizen remained. The Blair/Brown split ensured that Wilson could not command the wholehearted active support of all the Permanent Secretaries. Asked what he would like to be remembered for Wilson chose three areas: (1) to have served the Blair Government well whilst preserving the constitutional principles and form of Cabinet collective government for future governments; (2) to have led a major programme of change in the civil service which accelerated the pace of adjustment to the requirements of the twenty-first century yet preserved the strengths of the Northcote-Trevelyan tradition; (3) to have made a significant difference to the openness and fairness of the civil service, especially for those who have a disability or who felt discriminated against. To this list must be added the attempts he made to bridge the gap between the constitutional position of the office of Prime Minister and the manner in which Blair wanted to lead. Remarkably, Blair and Wilson acted as co-hosts and chairmen for the seminars involving Ministers and their PUSs aimed at a better working relationship between the two. Alastair Campbell records that Wilson had worries about Blair's isolation in government[491] and Wilson's submissions of March 1998 on getting the best out of government both show steeliness on the grand scale. In addition Wilson made many submissions on possible machinery of government changes and gave more localised feedback on departmental performance. Much of this confidential advice continued to be given during the weekly Monday morning tête-à-tête meetings he had with Blair. But it was one thing to carry messages to Ministers on behalf of the Prime Minister, and another to judge their behaviour. Wilson was clear that he should not go further than to get at the facts when things went wrong ministerially – it was up to the Prime Minister himself to manage his team.

Despite many examples of Wilson carrying the message of modernisation to PUS colleagues they were slow to recognise New Labour was a different government that wanted different things from its civil service and they underestimated the effect of Blair/Brown tensions. At the Wednesday morning PUS update meetings the corrosive effect on collective government business was mentioned anecdotally but not teed up for serious discussion – more akin to the visitation of a plague than a problem to be solved – though others, notably Heywood and Ed Balls, worked behind the scenes to mitigate the risks involved.[492] Omand has explained that almost all the Permanent Secretaries were engaged vigorously in their own Departmental modernisations involving lots of risk, but were slow to recognise that that they had not explained what they were about well enough and that key figures around Blair believed that it was necessary to destroy the old in order to create a new model for which they had not sought a public mandate. Perhaps Wilson protected his colleagues too much, and at a personal cost. Like Butler before him, he did offer PUS colleagues strong guidance about how they were seen by Ministers – Agriculture in August 1998; the Home Office in September and December 1999; DfEE in May 2000; the DSS in February 2001; DTI in July 2001); and the FCO in September 2001. He also acted to protect and guide his colleagues in the face of unfair attacks and the development of anonymous press briefing against named civil servants. There are examples involving Terry Burns of HM Treasury (January 1998), John Kerr of the FCO (1998), Kevin Tebbit of MOD (September 1999), Jon Shortridge of the Welsh Office (February 2000), Chris Kelly of the Department of Health (June 2000) and Richard Mottram of the Department of Transport (January 2002).

In retrospect the mismatch between New Labour's ambitions for the public sector and its inexperience of large-scale management made Wilson's job impossible. A few former senior colleagues think that he positioned himself too often on the boundary of personal disagreements, seeking fairness to all sides. Others saw his collegiate approach to PUSs using empathy and emotional intelligence to motivate. But his successor Andrew Turnbull could not wholly deliver either – he was described in March 2004 by Ivan Rogers, the Principal Private Secretary in 10 Downing Street, as: 'feeling fairly beleaguered, caught between reforming zeal from [10 Downing Street] and conservatism on the part of some Perm Sec colleagues.' Perhaps no one could have driven civil service reform far and fast enough for Blair without tearing up the constitution. As it is, one of Wilson's most lasting achievements was to preserve the Cabinet system of government for when a return to the more traditional approach would be sought – which was not long after he retired. In August 2003 Blair himself declared that he was 'keen to chair more Cabinet Committees and to make more use of the Cabinet as a forum for discussing domestic policy,'[493] and this came once again to the fore when Gordon Brown took over as Prime Minister in 2007.

A fundamental difficulty lay in the impatience of the Blair court with constitutional niceties and a mismatch of generations. Jonathan Powell, Blair's chief of staff who was less charitable about the Home Civil Service than others close to the Prime Minister, recalled that 'successive Cabinet Secretaries kept slipping back into policymaking and crisis management ...'[494] – policy making was not what the new generation of politicians wanted from the civil servants. Further, whilst Blair and his closest political colleagues were children of the 1950s, with the exception of Jeremy Heywood (born in 1961) Wilson and many of his colleagues were children of the 1940s; so although the frequency of exchanges between Blair and Wilson point to a degree of trust, Wilson did not have the closeness to Blair of Brook to Churchill, Trend to Wilson or Armstrong/Butler to Thatcher. The political closeness at the top of New Labour (and its tensions) together with the stronger presence of Special Advisers than before probably precluded such intimacy. He was never quite able to persuade Blair to accept a vision in which a streamlined and revamped Office of Public Service was the arm of central government focusing on questions of organisation and structure across Whitehall, while the Cabinet Secretariat and Policy Unit helped develop the strategy. Arguably no one could have been wholly successful in the Cabinet Secretary role during these years but it is intriguing to speculate whether Wilson's influence would have grown if he had gone along with Blair's wish to merge key elements of the Cabinet Office and the Downing Street staff with Wilson at its head and, conversely, whether his rejection of the plan marked the turning point of his relationship with Blair.

Notes

1 The convention was to exclude those who could conceive of themselves as candidates
2 Cabinet Office archive, 03.07.97
3 Blair, Cabinet Office press notice, 01.08.97
4 Cabinet Office archive, Civil Service Selection Board report, 19.04.66
5 Sir Peter Walker, Secretary of State for Energy, 1983–87
6 Interview with Lord Wilson, 12.02.13
7 RJ Packer *The Politics of BSE*, Palgrave Macmillan 2006 pp. 224–7
8 Blair, *A Journey*, Hutchinson 2010 p. 19; Campbell *Power and the People*, Hutchinson, 2011 p. 108
9 Hennessy, *The Prime Minister*, Allen Lane Penguin, 2000 pp. 497–500 assesses that Wilson never did better than reach the third rank of closeness to Blair and slipped to the fourth rank in 2000
10 Blair, op. cit, p. 206
11 Correspondence with Sir David Omand, Permanent Secretary and Security and Intelligence Coordinator, Cabinet Office 2002–05
12 Former reforming Home Secretary and a political mentor to Blair
13 Correspondence with Sir Paul Britton, Deputy Cabinet Secretary 2001–09
14 Correspondence with Sir David Omand
15 Op. cit, p. 81
16 Cabinet Office file A10/1, 12.05.01
17 These views are taken from an interview Wilson gave to Anthony Seldon on 02.11.12 for the history section of the 10 Downing Street website, available in full on the Mile End Group website www.cabinetsecretaries.com
18 *The Hugo Young Papers*, Ed by Ion Trewin, Allen Lane, 2008, p. 661
19 Correspondence with Sir David Omand. When the head of the Overseas Secretariat became also Foreign Policy Adviser to the Prime Minister attendance at the Cabinet Secretary's meeting was usually by the second in command
20 PREM: Cabinet Business, 28.04.98
21 UN Security Council Resolutions 1153 and 1175 in February and June respectively concerning the Oil-for-food programme
22 David Miliband, Head of the Policy Unit doubted if the fuller note was of use to the Prime Minister, Cabinet Office file A13/49, 23.04.98
23 Delivered on 18.03.98
24 Interview with Sir Paul Britton, 27.06.12
25 Ibid, 27.06.12

26 Cabinet Office file A9/32, annotation on the Strategic Communications Unit's proposed messages for Christmas/New Year 1998/99
27 Interview with Lord Wilson, 18.02.13
28 Secretary of State for Education and Employment 1997–2001
29 Cabinet Office file A13/50A, 03.05.00
30 Ibid, 18.12.00
31 The Inquiry was set up in 2009 to examine the United Kingdom's involvement in the invasion of Iraq, including the way decisions were made and actions taken, to establish what happened, and to identify lessons to be learned.
32 Address to the Newspaper Society, 10.03.97, Labour Party Media Office
33 Interview with Lord Wilson; Lord Turnbull evidence to the Iraq Inquiry 25.01.11
34 Interview with Sir Paul Britton, 27.06.12
35 PREM, Cabinet Committees 09.02.98, 24.02.98, 20.03.98
36 Correspondence with Sir David Omand
37 PREM, Cabinet Committees, 22.03.99
38 Ibid, *The Effectiveness of Cabinet Committees*, 24.01.01
39 The new units were the Delivery Unit, the Future Strategy Unit replacing the Cabinet Office Performance and Innovation Unit and the Office of Public Services Reform
40 PREM: Cabinet Committees
41 Interview with Sir Alex Allen, 09.09.11
42 Interview with Sir Paul Britton, 27.06.12
43 Ibid
44 Correspondence with Sir David Omand
45 Ibid, 26.08.97 and 18.12.98
46 Ibid, Wilson's post-election submission of 15.06.01
47 Cabinet Office file A16/7, 28.07.99
48 PREM: Ministers: Reshuffles, 23.07.98
49 Ibid, 01.04.99
50 Ibid, 21.07.99
51 Ibid, 04.10.99
52 Ibid, 06.07.00
53 Ibid, 01.07.99
54 Ibid, 02.07.99
55 Cabinet Office file A9/5. 25.02.00
56 Ibid, 17.02.00
57 Private information
58 Cabinet Office file A9/33, minutes of ad hoc meeting 'One', 27.01.00
59 Ibid, 25.02.00; later in the year a selection panel chaired by the First Civil Service Commissioner, Baroness Prashar, chose Lewis as the putative Chief Executive
60 Ibid, 22.02.00
61 Ibid, 10.03.00
62 Ibid, 02.03.00
63 Ibid, 06.03.00
64 Ibid, 28.02.00
65 House of Commons *Hansard*, WA, 16.03.00, cols 257–8
66 Cabinet Office file A9/33, 09.05.00
67 Ibid, 17.05.00
68 Ibid, 30.10.00
69 Cabinet Office file, A13/50A, 21.12.00
70 Correspondence with Sir Paul Britton
71 Blair op. cit, p. 206
72 Cabinet Office file A13/50A, 24.01.01 and 30.01.01
73 PREM: Ministers: reshuffles, 06.06.01
74 Ibid, 05–06.08.01

75 HMRC, NMWM16500 – Disclosure of information: Revenue & Customs Prosecution Office (RCPO), HMRC.gov.uk
76 Interview with Lord Wilson, 23.09.13
77 PREM Civil Service: Policy, 02.02.98, the report (submitted in December 1998) was later published by the Cabinet Office as CAB I99–5195/9912/D42
78 Extract from *Modernising Central Government, A Message from Sir Richard Wilson*, October 1998
79 PREM Civil Service: Policy, 01.07.98
80 Ibid, 03.07.98
81 *Modernising Central Government, A Message from Sir Richard Wilson*
82 Cabinet Office file A13/50, 08.02.99
83 PREM: Civil Service: policy, 12.02.02.99
84 Ibid, 13.02.99
85 CM 4310 published 30.03.99
86 PREM: Civil Service: policy, 26.02.99
87 Ibid, undated Blair annotation: 'I agree with all this … Is JC [Jack Cunningham] supposed to be the Minister driving this?'
88 Ibid, 29.03.99
89 A special adviser to Blair
90 PREM: Civil Service: policy 07.06.99
91 Correspondence with Sir David Omand, then PUS at the Home Office
92 PREM: Civil Service: policy, 30.03.99
93 Ibid, 14.06.99
94 There was a widespread worldwide fear that the turn of the century would cause computer systems to fail because they used only two numbers to identify a year in the date (e.g. 99 for 1999) and would not interpret 00 as a proxy for 2000
95 PREM: Civil Service: policy, 01.07.99
96 Ibid, 14.06.99
97 Ibid, 26.03.01
98 Ibid, 30.07.99
99 *The Times*, 24.08.99 and 30.08.99
100 PREM: Civil Service: policy, 28.09.99
101 Ibid, 04.10.99
102 Cabinet Office file A13/23, 04.10.99
103 PREM: Civil Service: Policy, 11.12.99
104 Ibid, 28.10.99
105 Ibid, 29.10.99
106 Ibid
107 Ibid, 31.07.00
108 Ibid
109 Ibid, 01.08.00
110 Cabinet Office file A13/50A, 25.09.00
111 D Guest (KCL) and N Conway (Birkbeck College) *The Psychological Contract in the Public Sector*, CIPD, 26.10.00
112 Correspondence with Sir David Omand
113 PREM: Civil Service: Policy, 16.10.00
114 Blair was first Labour Prime Minister to serve two consecutive full terms
115 PREM: Civil Service: Policy, 13.06.01
116 Ibid, 18.06.01
117 Ibid, 13.06.01
118 Ibid, 26.07.01
119 Ibid, 27.07.01
120 Ibid, 26.10.99
121 PREM, Agriculture policy 17.01.01

122 Cabinet Office file A13/23, 29.10.01
123 PREM: Civil Service: Policy, 13.12.01
124 Ibid, 12.04.02
125 Cabinet Office archive, 23.07.01
126 Ibid, 16 and 18.10.01
127 PREM: Civil Service: policy, 13.06.00 and 27.06.00
128 Ibid, 07.03.02
129 PREM: Government Machinery: Policy Presentation, 23.09.97
130 PREM: Civil Service: Policy, 09.04.98
131 Cabinet Office file A13/47, 26.02.99
132 Cabinet Office file A9/31, 05.03.99
133 Ibid, 05.03.99
134 Ibid, 05.03.99
135 Ibid, 05.03.99
136 Correspondence with Sir David Omand and Sir Paul Britton
137 Cabinet Office file A9/31, 08.03.99
138 Ibid, 09.03.99
139 Ibid, 01.04.99
140 PREM: Civil Service: Policy, 03.03.99
141 Ibid, 18.02.99
142 Correspondence with Sir David Omand
143 PREM: Civil Service: Policy, 18.02.99
144 Correspondence with Sir Paul Britton
145 PREM: Government Machinery: Policy Presentation, 04.03.99 and 08.03.99. Hugo Young later recorded: 'Unlike MHT TB cannot delegate, does not know how to get people to feel policies are theirs not his. Thinks brilliant analysis and policy is all that is needed.' *Hugo Young Papers*, Allen & Lane 2008, p. 799, entry for 15.11.02
146 PREM: Government Machinery: Policy Presentation, 10.03.99
147 PREM: Civil Service: Policy, 12.04.99
148 Cabinet Office file A13/47, 15.03.00
149 Cabinet Office file A13/50A, 07.02.01
150 Ibid, 07.02.01
151 Ibid, 08.02.01
152 Ibid, 04.03.01
153 Ibid, 04.03.01
154 Interviews with Permanent Secretaries
155 *The Alastair Campbell Diaries*, 07.07 98
156 Ibid, entry for 09.07.98
157 PREM: Ministers: Conduct, 09.07.98
158 Geoffrey Robinson, *The Unconventional Minister: my life inside New Labour*, Michael Joseph 2000
159 Interview with Lord Wilson, 22.05.12
160 PREM Ministers: Geoffrey Robinson, 28.07.98
161 House of Commons Select Committee on Standards and Privileges, 20.01.98 (HC 488) and 15.07.98 (HC 975)
162 PREM: Ministers: Geoffrey Robinson, 02.12.98
163 Ibid, 05.12.98
164 Ibid
165 Ibid, 23.12.98
166 HC *Hansard*, 11.01.99, col 57
167 PREM Ministers: Geoffrey Robinson, 05.01.99, and 13.01.99
168 Ibid, 12.01.99
169 Ibid, 05.11.99 and 11.11.99
170 Ibid, 11.11.99

171 Ibid, 10.12.99
172 Ibid, 23.12.99
173 Ibid, 22.01.01
174 Ibid, 23.01.01 subsequently reproduced as Annex P to the Hammond Inquiry Report
175 PREM: Ministers: Hinduja, 28.02.01
176 *Review of the Circumstances Surrounding an Application for Naturalisation by Mr S P Hinduja in 1998*, 09.03.01, HC 287
177 PREM: Ministers: Hinduja, 08.11.01
178 Ibid, 05.12.01 and 12.11.01
179 Ibid, 30.11.01
180 Ibid, 06.12.01
181 Ibid, 11.12.01 and 17.12.01
182 Ibid, 17.12.01
183 Ibid, 21.12.01
184 *Further Review of the Circumstances Surrounding an Application for Naturalisation by Mr S P Hinduja in 1998*, 25.02.02
185 Ibid, Mandelson statement, 01.03.02
186 Cabinet Office file A2/24, 25.06.98
187 Ibid, 09.10.98 and 12.10.98
188 Ibid, 12.10.98
189 PREM: Ministers: Conduct, 06.11.98
190 Committee on Standards in Public Life, Press Notice 29.10.98
191 Cabinet Office files A13/47 and A2/24, 17.11.98 and 20.11.98
192 Cabinet Office file A2/24, 09.12.98
193 *Non-Departmental Public Bodies: a Guide for Departments*, Cabinet Office and HM Treasury
194 Cabinet Office file A2/24, 23.03.99
195 PREM: Ministers: Conduct 05.11.99, and 15.11.99
196 Cabinet Office file A13/47, 26.01.00
197 Column and correspondence in *The Times*, 10–14.04.99
198 Cabinet Office file A2/24, 13.04.00
199 Rosemary Bennett, *Financial Times*, 14.03.00
200 Cabinet Office file A2/24, 08.12.00
201 PREM: Ministers: Conduct, 02.07.02
202 Cabinet Office file R5/6, 12.11.98
203 *The Alistair Campbell Diaries*, entry for 19.12.98
204 PREM: Ministers: Conduct, 11.01.99
205 Ibid
206 Ibid, 14.01.99
207 Ibid, 29.01.99
208 Ibid, 12.01.99
209 Cabinet Office file A13/23, 29.07.99
210 Committee on Standards in Public Life, 6th Report, 12.01.00, p. 52
211 PREM: Ministers: Conduct, 03.05.00
212 Cabinet Office file A2/24, 16.12.99
213 PREM: Ministers: Conduct, 07.07.00
214 The successor to *Questions of Procedure for Ministers*, published in 1997
215 Gavin Cordon, *PA News*, 14.02.01
216 Cabinet Office file A2/24, 13.09.00
217 PREM: Ministers: Conduct, 17.01.01
218 Cabinet Office file A2/24, 22.02.01
219 Ibid, 19.07.00
220 Ibid, 25.07.00
221 Ibid, 02.04.01

222 PREM: Ministers: Conduct, 06.04.01
223 Ibid, 08.03.01
224 *Defining the boundaries within the Executive: Ministers, Special Advisers and permanent civil servants*
225 Cabinet Office archive, 10.10.97
226 Cabinet Office archive, 04.05.00
227 Ibid, 30.10.00
228 Ibid, 15.11.00
229 First published on 16.07.93
230 Cabinet Office file A13/23, 22.02.00
231 Cabinet Office archive 28.02.00
232 Ibid, 28.02.00
233 PREM: Memoirs: Policy pt 1, 08.03.00
234 Cabinet Office archive, 07.04.00
235 Ibid, 05,05.00
236 Ibid, 04.05.01
237 PREM: Memoirs: Policy pt 3, 27.06.00
238 Stella Rimington, *Open Secret*, Hutchinson, 2001, pp xii-xiii
239 Christopher Meyer, *DC Confidential*, Weidenfeldt & Nicolson, 2006
240 Sir Edward Bridges, Rede Lecture 1950, Cambridge University Press
241 The speech is available on www.civilservant.org.uk/srwspeech0302.pdf;
242 PREM: Civil Service: Policy, 20.05.98
243 Ibid, 24.09.98
244 Clarke was Secretary of State for Health 1988–90
245 Cabinet Office file A13/47, 24.06.99
246 Ibid, 24.06.99
247 Ibid, 09.02.00
248 Ibid, 10.02.00
249 Ibid, and PREM: Civil Service:Policy, 28.11.01 and 05.12.01
250 Cabinet Office file A13/23, 14.11.01
251 PREM: Civil Service: Policy, 18.01.02
252 Cabinet Office files A13/47 and A2/5,11.10.99, and 03.11.99
253 Cabinet Office file A13/23, 26.10.99
254 Cabinet Office file A13/47, 03.11.99
255 Cabinet Office file A13/23, 26.10.99
256 Cabinet Office file A2/24, 26.06.00
257 *Civil Service Reform Plan*, 26.06.12, www.civilservice.gov.uk/reform
258 Cabinet Office file A13/47, 23.05.01
259 *The Financial Times*, 24.10.03
260 Cabinet Office archive, 02.10.97
261 Ibid, 02.10.97, and 22.12.97
262 *Hansard*, WA 19.03.97, col 634
263 PREM: Government Machinery: IT, 19.02.98
264 PREM: Home Affairs: Data Protection and Open Government, 04.02.99
265 Ibid, 08.02.99
266 Ibid, 12.02.99
267 Ibid, 12.02.99
268 Ibid, 12.02.99
269 Ibid, 16.02.99
270 Ibid, 01.04.99
271 Ibid, 10.04.99 and 12.04.99
272 Ibid, 27.05.99 and 11.06.99
273 Ibid, 05.11.99
274 Ibid, 08.11.99

275 Published on 22.07.99 to plaudits from industry leaders
276 On 22.07.99 the *Financial Times* carried a leader accusing the Government of insufficient action to live up to its rhetoric to make Britain the best location in the world for e-commerce
277 PREM: Home Affairs: Data Protection and Open Government, 22.07.99, and 29.09.99
278 Ibid, 29.09.99
279 Ibid, 13.12.99
280 Ibid, 17.02.00
281 Ibid, 21.02.00
282 Ibid, 28.02.00
283 PREM: Government Machinery: IT, 12.03.01
284 Ibid, 29.06.01
285 Ibid, 05.12.01
286 UK On-line Annual Report 2003
287 PREM, Home Affairs, Privacy, 22.07.97
288 Ibid, 02.09.97
289 *Privacy and Media Intrusion*, June 1990 HMSO Cm 1102
290 PREM, Home Affairs, Privacy, 02.09.97
291 Ibid, 25.11.97
292 Ibid, 28.01.98
293 Ibid, 09.02.98
294 Paul Dacre at the Society of Editors, reported on 10.01.08, *BBC News*
295 PREM, Home Affairs, Data Protection and Open Government, 09.02.01
296 Ibid, 12.03.01
297 'New Labour, New Britain,' Labour Party
298 Cm 3818, December 1997
299 *Commentary on the Freedom of Information White Paper*, The Constitution Unit, UCL, January 1998
300 Ibid, January 1998
301 PREM Home Affairs, Data Protection and Open Government, 13.10.98
302 Correspondence with Sir Paul Britton
303 PREM Home Affairs, Data Protection and Open Government, 25.01.99
304 Ibid, 29.01.99
305 Ibid, 01.02.99
306 Ibid, 12.07.99
307 Ibid, 16.07.99
308 The Directive from Croham, the Head of the Home Civil Service, promised increased openness through release of background evidence used in decision-making
309 PREM Home Affairs, Data Protection and Open Government, 16.09.99
310 Ibid, 23.09.99
311 Ibid, 06.10.99
312 Ibid, 11.10.99
313 Ibid, 05.01.00
314 Ibid, 05.01.00
315 Ibid, 07.03.00
316 Ibid, 09.02.00
317 Ibid, 21.02.00
318 Ibid, 06.04.01
319 Ibid, 06.04.01
320 Ibid, 06.04.01
321 Ibid, undated
322 Ibid, 16.06.01
323 Ibid, 16.07.01

324 *The National Security Strategy*, Cm 7953, October 2010, *The National Security Strategy and Strategic Defence and Security Review 2015*, Cm 9161, November 2015
325 Cabinet Office archive, 21.01.98
326 Defined as telecommunications, energy, transport, financial services, water and sewage, Government
327 Cabinet Office archive, 27.03.98
328 Ibid, 08.06.00, 09.06.00 and 14.06.00
329 Ibid, 18.04.00
330 The archive arose from information brought to SIS by a KGB colonel in November 1992 and revealed details of Soviet espionage against a wide range of countries including the UK and the USA. It was published by Allen Lane as a Penguin imprint on 20 September 1999
331 Cabinet Office archive 03.05.00
332 Ibid, 13.10.00 and 16.10.00, – previously supervision had been the responsibility of a sub-committee of the Official Committee on Security (Sub-committee on Security Service Priorities and Performance – SO(SSPP))
333 Ibid, 04.12.00; the efficiency adviser was Sandy Russell, a retired official who had been involved in the Rayner processes in the 1980s and had later been a Commissioner at HM Customs & Excise
334 Ibid, 10.01.01
335 Ibid, 23.04.01
336 Cabinet Office archive, 05.07.02 and, 23.07.02
337 A decision taken at GEN 183 on 13.11.50, under the chairmanship of Clement Attlee, to enhance the precautions taken to exclude Communist and Fascist sympathisers and others thought to be security risks from sensitive posts
338 Cabinet Office archive, paper for the Official Committee on Security, SO(98)5, 01.06.98
339 Ibid, 29.05.98
340 Ibid, 04.02.02
341 Ibid, 30.03.98
342 Ibid, 09.06.98
343 Ibid, 18.06.98
344 Ibid, 16.11.98
345 Ibid, 16.11.98
346 Ibid, 29.07.99
347 Ibid, SO(200 0)3, 13.07.00
348 Ibid, 10.04.00
349 Ibid, SO(2000)2nd meeting on 18.03.00 discussed the Government's responsibilities for protecting the e-environment (paper SO(2000)3) and the funding of 'common good' information security R&D (paper SO(2000)4)
350 BBC News, 04.05.00; Cabinet Office archive, 05.05.00 and 09.05.00
351 Cabinet Office archive, 11.05.00
352 Ibid, 08.01.99
353 Ibid, exchanges between 01.10.99 and 09.11.99
354 Ibid, 16.03.00
355 Cabinet Office file A13/23, 14.02.00
356 Prime Minister's file: Civil Service Policy, 29.02.00
357 Cabinet Office file A13/23, 22.02.00
358 A special JIC meeting was held on 23.03.00
359 Cabinet Office archive, 18.04.00
360 Cabinet Office file A13/23, 15.03.00
361 Cabinet Office archive, 28.06.07
362 Ibid, 06.05.02

363 Ibid, the appointment was announced on 19.06.02
364 Ibid, 19.06.02
365 Correspondence with Sir David Omand
366 Cabinet Office archive 05.01.00
367 Ibid, 10.11.97
368 PLP meeting on 11.03.98
369 Cabinet Office archive, 01.05.98
370 Ibid
371 'A private company supplying military support to governments in places of widespread brutality and genocidal behaviour,' Sandline commercial manager interviewed on BBC news 15.03.04
372 Cabinet Office archive, 28.05.98
373 Ibid, 18.09.98
374 Ibid, 11.02.99, Mr Morrison was removed from the post in 2004 after he appeared on the television programme *Panorama* maintaining that Saddam Hussein, President of Iraq, was not a threat to the United Kingdom
375 ISC Annual Report 1998–99
376 Cabinet Office archive, 20.07.00
377 Wilson note of 03.03.00, cabinet Office paper
378 A doctrine that survived all the changes introduced by Wilson
379 Correspondence with Sir David Omand
380 There was widespread fear that older IT systems which identified years by their last two numbers (e.g. 98 for 1998) would fail when faced with 00 for 2000, with potentially catastrophic consequences
381 Prime Minister's files: Agriculture, BSE Inquiry, 01.12.97
382 The convention had last been set out in a Written Answer by Mrs Thatcher on 24.01.80, HoC *Hansard*, cols 305–7
383 Prime Minister's files: Agriculture, BSE Inquiry part 2, 26.01.98
384 Ibid, 26.01.98
385 Ibid, 06.10.00
386 Packer later published a memoir, *The Politics of BSE*, in which he was highly critical of the over-optimistic attitude of Blair's staff and of Wilson's role in the crisis
387 Cabinet Office archive, 17.12.99
388 Ibid, 25.01.01
389 Ibid, 17.02.00
390 Cabinet Office archive, 08.05.00
391 BBC News 08.09.00
392 Interview with Sir David Omand: 18.06.13
393 BBC News 12.09.00
394 Prime Minister's files: Civil Service: Policy, 26.02.98
395 Cabinet Office archive, 02.11.00
396 Interview with Sir David Omand, 18.06.13
397 Ibid, 18.06.13
398 BBC News 13.09.00
399 *The Mail on Sunday*, 24.09.00
400 Prime Minister's files: Fuel, 09.10.00
401 Ibid, 11.10.00
402 Cabinet Office archive, 06.12.00
403 Ibid, 08.12.00
404 Blair, *A Journey*, p. 312
405 Private information: quoted with the permission of author and recipient
406 Cabinet Office archive, 25.04.01
407 Ibid, 03.05.01
408 Prime Minister's files: Government Machinery: Civil Contingencies, 20.06.01

409 Ibid, 15.05.01
410 Cabinet Office archive, *Building resilience: a new approach to crisis*, July 2001, paras 41–50
411 Blair, *A Journey*, pp. 341–2
412 Ibid, p. 351
413 Prime Minister's files: Foreign Policy, War on International Terrorism part 1, 12.09.01
414 Cabinet Office archive, 12.09.01
415 Prime Minister's files: Foreign Policy, War on International Terrorism part 1, 12.09 01
416 Ibid, 13.09.01
417 Cabinet Office archive, 14.09.01
418 Ibid, 15.09.01
419 An AMBER alert meant that specific information had been received and there was a substantial threat to government targets
420 Prime Minister's files: Foreign Policy: War on International Terrorism part 2, 17.09.01
421 Cabinet Office archive, 17.09.01
422 Prime Minister's files: Foreign Policy: War on International Terrorism part 3, 18.09.01
423 Ibid, undated, probably 18.09.01
424 Prime Minister's files: Foreign Policy: War on International Terrorism part 8, 20.09.01 and 26.09.01
425 Blair, *A Journey*, p. 351
426 Cabinet Office archive, 20.09.01
427 Prime Minister's files: Foreign Policy: War on International Terror part 5, 21.09.01
428 Cabinet Office archive 27.09.01
429 House of Lords judgement 56, 16.12.04
430 Prime Minister's files: Foreign Policy: War on International Terror part 6, 23.09.01
431 Cabinet Office archive, 20.09.01
432 Prime Minister's files: Foreign Policy: War on International Terror part 6, 22.09.01
433 Cabinet Office archive, 24.09.01
434 Prime Minister's files: Foreign Policy: War on International Terror part 8, 26.09.01
435 Prime Minister's files: Foreign Policy: War on International Terror part 7, 24.09.01
436 Prime Minister's files: Foreign Policy: War on International Terror part 9, 27.09.01
437 Ibid, 27.09.01
438 Ibid, 28.09.01
439 Cabinet Office archive, 29.10.01
440 Cabinet Office archive, 13.12.01
441 Prime Minister's files: Foreign Policy: War on International Terror part 11, 03.09.01
442 Cabinet Office archive 18.10.01
443 Ibid, 25.10.01
444 Ibid, 30.10.01, and Cabinet Office file A13/23
445 Prime Minister's files: Foreign Policy: War on International Terror part 12, 12.10.01
446 Cabinet Office archive, 20.12.01
447 Prime Minister's files: Foreign Policy: War on International Terror part 10, 01.10.01
448 Cabinet Office archive, 27.11.01
449 Ibid, 26.09.01
450 Ibid, 05.10.01
451 Recorded statement broadcast on 13.10.01, date and place not given
452 Cabinet Office archive, 18.10.01 and 22.10.01
453 Ibid, 09.10.01
454 Prime Minister's files: Foreign Policy: War on International Terror part 12, 15.10.01
455 Prime Minister's files: Foreign Policy: War on International Terror part 10, 03.10.01

456 Prime Minister's files: Foreign Policy: War on International Terror part 12, 11.10.01
457 Prime Minister's files: Foreign Policy: War on International Terror part 14, 29.10.01
458 Prime Minister's files: Foreign Policy: War on International Terror part 15, 07.11.01
459 Cabinet Office archive, 01.10.01
460 Prime Minister's files: Foreign Policy: War on International Terror part 10, 03.10.01
461 *Daily Telegraph* 05.10.01 page 6
462 Cabinet Office archive, 02.10.01
463 Prime Minister's files: Foreign Policy: War on International Terror part 11, 05.10.01
464 Ibid, 06.12.01
465 Cabinet Office archive, 29.07.02
466 Prime Minister's files: Foreign Policy: War on International Terror part 7, 24.09.01
467 Prime Minister's files: Government Machinery: Civil Contingencies, 18.07.02
468 Ibid, 18.07.02
469 Cabinet Office archive, 10.09.02
470 Ibid, 19.03.02, and 18.04.02
471 Ibid, 02.05.02
472 Ibid, 14.05.02
473 Prime Minister's files: Civil Service Policy, 16.12.01
474 Ibid, 21.12.01
475 Ibid, undated
476 Ibid, 07.01.02
477 Ibid, 14.01.02
478 Ibid, 25.01.02
479 Bichard had been a local authority chief executive and PUS at DfEE until 2001, when he left after the debacle of the Working Age Agency; he was unpopular with Permanent Secretary colleagues who saw him as non-cooperative and disloyal
480 Prime Minister's files: Civil Service Policy, 27.01.02
481 Ibid, 06.02.02
482 Ibid, 31.01.02
483 Interview with Lord Wilson, 22.05.12
484 Prime Minister's files: Civil Service Policy, 01.02.02
485 Ibid, 11.02.02
486 Ibid, 21.02.02
487 Interview with Lord Wilson, 22.05.12
488 Wilson told the Chilcot inquiry that he attended all the meetings on Afghanistan in late 2001 and early 2002 but attended very few on Iraq later in 2002
489 Prime Minister's files: Civil Service Policy, 15.04.02
490 Correspondence with Sir David Omand
491 Campbell, diary entry for 05.01.99
492 Private information
493 Prime Minister's files: Civil Service Policy 27.08.03
494 Powell, *The New Machiavelli*, p. 76

Appendix: Office Holders

Year	Monarch	Prime Minister	Cabinet Secretary	Head of Home Civil Service
1916	George V	David Lloyd George	Maurice Hankey	
1919				Warren Fisher
1922		Andrew Bonar Law		
1923		Stanley Baldwin		
1929		Ramsay MacDonald		
1935		Stanley Baldwin		
1936	Edward VIII			
1936	George VI			
1937		Neville Chamberlain		
1938			Edward Bridges	
1939				Horace Wilson
1940		Winston Churchill		
1942				Richard Hopkins
1945		Clement Attlee		Edward Bridges
1947			Norman Brook	
1951		Winston Churchill		
1952	Elizabeth II			
1955		Anthony Eden		
1956				Norman Brook
1957		Harold Macmillan		
1963		Alec Douglas-Home	Burke Trend	Lawrence Helsby
1964		Harold Wilson		
1968				William Armstrong
1970		Edward Heath		
1973			John Hunt	
1974		Harold Wilson		Douglas Allen
1976		Jim Callaghan		
1978				Ian Bancroft
1979		Margaret Thatcher	Robert Armstrong	
1982				Robert Armstrong & Douglas Wass
1983				Robert Armstrong
1988			Robin Butler	
1990		John Major		
1997		Tony Blair		
1998			Richard Wilson	
2002			Andrew Turnbull	
2005			Gus O'Donnell	
2007		Gordon Brown		
2010		David Cameron		
2012			Jeremy Heywood	Robert Kerslake
2014			Jeremy Heywood	

Index

Printed in Great Britain
by Amazon

44187217R00418